NAUVOO

A PLACE OF PEACE, A PEOPLE OF PROMISE

*This is the loveliest place and
the best people under the heavens;
little do they know the trials
that await them.*

JOSEPH SMITH, JUNE 24, 1844

NAUVOO

A PLACE OF PEACE, A PEOPLE OF PROMISE

G LEN M . L EONARD

DESERET BOOK COMPANY
SALT LAKE CITY, UTAH
AND
BRIGHAM YOUNG UNIVERSITY PRESS
PROVO, UTAH

Library of Congress Cataloging-in-Publication Data

Leonard, Glen M.
  Nauvoo : a place of peace, a people of promise / Glen M. Leonard.
    p.   cm.
  Includes bibliographical references and index.
  ISBN 1–57008–746–6 (alk. paper)
    1. Church of Jesus Christ of Latter-day Saints—Illinois—Nauvoo—History—
19th century.   2. Nauvoo (Ill.)—Church history—19th century.   I. Title.
BX8615.I3 L37   2002
289.3'77343—dc21   2002002065

Printed in the United States of America   18961-30006
R. R. Donnelley and Sons, Crawfordsville, IN

10   9   8   7   6   5   4   3   2

For
T. Edgar Lyon
Hermana Lyon
and the
Old Nauvooers

Contents

List of Maps ix

List of Illustrations xi

Preface xvii

PART I. ESTABLISHING NAUVOO: A PLACE OF PEACE

1. Joseph Smith's Plan for Zion 3

2. Finding a Place of Peace 19

3. A Beautiful Place of Rest 41

4. Gathering the Saints 62

5. Nauvoo's Magna Charta 91

PART II. LIFE IN NAUVOO: A PEOPLE OF PROMISE

6. The Promise of Prosperity 123

7. Economic Expectations 141

8. Neighbors in Nauvoo 173

9. A People of Faith and Destiny 200

10. The House of the Lord 233

Contents

Part III. Challenges to the City Beautiful:
Failed Promises of Peace

11. Patriots and Prophets   269

12. A Renewed Search for Refuge   301

13. Foes Within: The Church of the Seceders   341

14. "Joseph and Hyrum Are Dead"   380

15. "Who Shall Lead the Church?"   418

Part IV. Removal: New Places and New Peoples

16. The Peaceful Interlude   463

17. A Solution to the Mormon Question   508

18. Leaving Nauvoo   551

19. Transition and Expulsion   587

20. "The New Order of Things"   622

21. Remembering Nauvoo   652

List of Abbreviations   665

Notes   667

Sources   767

Credits for Maps and Illustrations   787

Index   799

Maps

A Map of Nauvoo, 1846   xxiv

Plat of the City of Zion   7

Upper Missouri Settlements   24

In Search of Refuge, 1838–39   32

At the Head of the Rapids   49

Homesteaders and Speculators on the Peninsula   50

Church Purchases and Original Plat of Nauvoo   56

Stakes in Iowa and Illinois   69

Routes to Nauvoo   84

Towns and Cities in Nauvoo History   100

Surveyed Plats to 1842   102

Landowners and Developers   134

Latter-day Saint Settlements and Farmland   138

Commercial Districts of Nauvoo   146

Hancock County   162

Occupied Lots, 1842 Census   176

The "English Countryside" near Nauvoo   185

Public Places in Nauvoo   203

Patterns of Conflict, 1843–46   290

"A Place of Our Own": Options for Relocation   322

MAPS

Carthage (1859)   385

A Map of the Great Dam   494

A Refuge in the Rockies   512

Carthage Convention   526

Negotiating Peace: Sheriff Jacob Backenstos   530

A City for Sale   560

Proposed Territory of Deseret   584

Nauvoo Town Limits, 1845–48   626

Dispersion: Northeast and Midwest   640

Illustrations

Corporation Seal of City of Nauvoo	1
The Kirtland Temple	13
Oliver Cowdery and Joseph Smith	15
Vigilantes at Independence, Missouri	23
Surrender of Far West, Missouri	29
Liberty Jail	37
Quincy, Illinois, and Ferry	45
James White's Stone House	51
Half Breed Land Company Stock Certificate	60
Joseph Smith	65
Portraits of British Immigrants	75
Farewell at Liverpool Harbor	79
Stake Presidents in Nauvoo and Zarahemla:	
William Marks and John Smith	93
The Nauvoo Legion	106
Metal Ballot Box	109
Leaders of the Nauvoo Legion: Joseph Smith and John C. Bennett	114
Flag of the Nauvoo Brass Band	117
Nauvoo from the River	120
The Nauvoo Temple	121

Homestead near Montrose, Iowa 126

"Widow's Row," Kimball Street, Nauvoo 129

A Nauvoo Neighborhood 140

Nauvoo House Association Stock Certificate 144

Maid of Iowa 150

Waterfront Businesses 157

Nauvoo City Scrip 163

Nauvoo Shops 167

Joseph Smith and His Friends 181

Joseph Smith and Hyrum Smith 189

Pizarro, or the Death of Rolla, Masonic Hall, Nauvoo 191

Nauvoo Music Association Stock Certificate 193

Ellen S. Pratt's Report Card 195

Lucy Mack Smith 198

Joseph Smith Preaching the Gospel 207

Joseph Smith's Office Sign 211

Teachers of the Restored Gospel 215

Latter-day Saints Millennial Star, July 1840 217

Emma Hale Smith, 1842 223

Manuscript of History of the Church 229

Early Designs of the Nauvoo Temple 236

Revised Designs of the Nauvoo Temple 239

Pulpits in the Kirtland Temple 243

Penny Collection Box 247

Nauvoo Temple with Font 250

Design for Angel Weather Vane 253

Joseph Smith's Store 259

Sun Stone Capital 263

Lieutenant General Joseph Smith and the Nauvoo Legion 266

Times and Seasons 267

Lieutenant General Joseph Smith and Red Wax Seal 273

Joseph Smith Preaching to the Indians 278

Lieutenant General Joseph Smith on Horseback 283

Caricatures of Leading Spokesmen Joseph Smith and
    Thomas Sharp 293

Thomas Sharp and Governor Thomas Ford 306

Details of Nauvoo Legion Musket 310

Warsaw, Illinois 317

Masonic Hall, Nauvoo 319

Joseph Smith Addressing Conference 332

Lieutenant General Joseph Smith 337

"Joe Smith of Nauvoo" and Eliza Partridge Smith 346

Mulholland Street Businesses 359

Prospectus of the *Nauvoo Expositor* 363

Nauvoo Expositor Building 365

Lieutenant General Joseph Smith Addressing the Nauvoo Legion 371

The Hamilton Hotel at Carthage 382

The Martyrs Joseph Smith and Hyrum Smith 390

A Memorable and Unjustifiable Assassination 393

Inside Carthage Jail 395

Death Masks of Joseph Smith and Hyrum Smith 402

Martyrs of the Latter-day Saints 411

Pistols held by Joseph Smith and Hyrum Smith 411

Courthouse at Carthage 416

Joseph Smith Jr. and Hyrum Smith 425

Sidney Rigdon and William Smith 432

Presidential Succession: Joseph Smith and Brigham Young 439

Brigham Young 443

Seal of the Quorum of the Twelve Apostles 447

Emma Smith and David Hyrum Smith 451

Joseph Smith III and James J. Strang	455
Defense of Nauvoo (detail)	460
Notice of Property for Sale	461
Brigham Young and Hosea Stout	470
Nauvoo Legion Arsenal Stock Certificate	472
The Temple at Nauvoo	476
The Nauvoo House	477
Seventies Hall Certificate of Shares	478
Marketing Advertisements	485
Tradesmen's Advertisements	489
Home Manufacturers' Advertisements	490
Brigham Young's Letter Opener	502
Hancock County Opponents: Brigham Young and a Mobber	522
Attack on Hancock Homestead	529
Model of the City of Nauvoo	540
View of Nauvoo	546
Lucy Mack Smith	554
The City of Nauvoo	564
Phebe Woodruff and Joseph Woodruff	572
The Ship *Brooklyn*	578
Crossing the Mississippi	583
The Nauvoo Temple	590
Temples for Sale	592
Fine Buildings for Sale	598
Notices: Report of the Troops, F. Hall and Co.	603
Powder Magazine	608
Defence of Nauvoo in September 1846	610
Expulsion from Nauvoo	614
Icarians at Nauvoo	628
Joseph Rheinberger's Home	631

Lewis C. Bidamon and the Smith Sons   646

Two Youthful Josephs: Joseph Smith III and Joseph F. Smith   648

Nauvoo, 1846   656

Missionaries and Their Friends at the Mansion House, 1907   658

Preface

Is it possible to understand Nauvoo . . . without grasping the spiritual power Joseph [Smith] exercised and still exercises? Every Mormon knows that the Church is held together by individual testimonies—that is, the connection the members have found with God through the Prophet's doctrine and the Church which he established. The power of Mormon leaders depends almost entirely on these individual spiritual convictions. . . . Through Joseph [his followers] found God, and it was the measure of divinity in him and his teachings that held them. Nauvoo would never have risen or fallen without that spiritual life. Belief powered the entire enterprise.

—RICHARD BUSHMAN

The religious community of the Latter-day Saints has crossed three major historical watersheds since the Prophet Joseph Smith's first vision in the spring of 1820. Each of them has marked a transition from one way of expressing basic beliefs and behaviors to another. The first happened during the 1840s when The Church of Jesus Christ of Latter-day Saints was headquartered in Nauvoo. The Prophet's revelations on the temple and its ordinances were at the center of this adjustment. Wilford Woodruff's revelation that led to the Manifesto of 1890 stopping the practice of plural marriage signifies the second and, according to some, the most dramatic transformation. Small schismatic groups resisted both the first and second transitions and formed separate churches. The most recent emphasis, a more gradual one, acknowledges an increasingly worldwide church. One measure of that reality is the revelation through Spencer W. Kimball in 1978 that broadened participation in the lay priesthood to include all worthy males. Another indicator is the recent underscoring of core beliefs in Jesus Christ and the central place of the eternal family unit.

It is the unfolding of temple doctrines to a gathered people during the seven-year Nauvoo period of church history that attracts our attention in this study. In 1858 Sidney Rigdon commented on the effect of the Nauvoo experience on the overall sequence of events up to that time. He told a friend, "From 1830 to 1840 those developments created an unbroken chain of history. In 1840 it culminated and its history tended in a different direction and found its level in the order of things which now exist in Utah."[1]

Some rejected the new revelations received by Joseph Smith between 1838 and 1844, but the majority did not. For Latter-day Saints who followed Brigham Young and the Quorum of the Twelve Apostles to Utah, the unfolding of the gospel during the last years of the Prophet's life set the patterns of their lives for a half century. The guiding principles behind those applications continue to affect millions of adherents to the faith. Those who, with Rigdon, held to the pre-Nauvoo formulation of Mormonism founded schismatic groups to lock in an earlier pattern. The principal heir of that reactionary response was the Reorganized Church of Jesus Christ of Latter Day Saints, headquartered at Independence, Missouri, and recently renamed the Community of Christ.

Because the enduring legacy of Mormon Nauvoo for those who care the most about its history is religious, it makes sense to tell the story from the perspective of revelations and doctrine. That is what we have chosen to do. Earlier studies of the Nauvoo years and of the people and issues of the pre-Utah period of Latter-day Saint history have laid the groundwork for such an endeavor.[2] As Richard Bushman concluded after an assessment of the historical literature in 1970, "The whole story has not yet been told. At their best Mormons appear [in Nauvoo histories] as enterprising, ingenious, and strong, but the spiritual dimensions of their faith are left unrecorded."[3] The story of spiritual yearnings necessarily plays out on a stage where political strains, economic realities, and social strivings in everyday life interact with the Latter-day Saint world view. The fresh perspectives and new information that we offer build upon a base of familiar narratives while enhancing the realization that the real story of the Church in Nauvoo is essentially one of a people of faith.[4]

In 1972, when T. Edgar Lyon accepted Leonard J. Arrington's invitation to write a history of the Nauvoo years, and when I joined the effort six years later, the book was intended as part of a larger project—a multivolume history of The Church of Jesus Christ of Latter-day Saints. After Ed's untimely death in September 1978, I was left with the task. Then, three years later, plans were changed. It took another invitation, this time from Nauvoo Restoration Incorporated, through its president, then Elder Loren C. Dunn, to revive a serious research and writing schedule. The intent at that time was to encourage the history as an independent effort for the Nauvoo sesquicentennial observance of 1989–96. Even with some arranged leave time, the task was bigger than expected. I completed a manuscript at the end of the seven-year anniversary period and then set it aside to tackle another more pressing book project. With the encouragement of Deseret Book, the final cutting and shaping began two years ago, resulting in the present volume.

Because of the complex nature of reminiscences, this history draws mostly from documentary evidence from the Nauvoo period. Hundreds of letters, diaries, minutes, and newspaper reports exist to be read, digested, and understood. Ed Lyon left numerous extracts from 1840s Illinois newspapers and notes on hundreds of topics. His marginal comments on historical articles and books drew attention to new information and often challenged an author's statements. The decisions about what to do with those helpful warnings were left to my own discernment. So, too, were many important judgments on interpretive focus and emphasis. While encouraged and helped along the way by many friends and colleagues, I accept full responsibility for the book, both its content and its message.

The resulting product is necessarily different from what it would have been had Ed Lyon written Nauvoo's history. For that reason, and because of the passage of time since he first outlined his book thirty years ago, T. Edgar Lyon's name does not appear as coauthor. His family endorsed that decision. Nonetheless, his influence on the manuscript is everywhere evident. I adapted some material from two preliminary drafts of chapters on pre-Mormon Nauvoo, considered two of Ed's published articles on doctrinal developments and the Quorum of the Twelve in Nauvoo, and retained much of the original outline of the book. His newspaper files, subject files, and biographical notes provided much useful information, but inevitably, much of what this beloved teacher of Church history and doctrine knew about Nauvoo was carried in his amazing memory, and he took it with him.[5]

Most of Dr. Lyon's research notes on Nauvoo were assembled while he served as historian for Nauvoo Restoration Incorporated. The steady research of long-time NRI employee Rowena Miller is also part of Ed's accumulation; much of what the Lyon family made available for my use is duplicated in the agency's collection. The focus of NRI was the physical city and the biographical profiles of its people rather than broader themes of religious history.

Here and there in Ed Lyon's extensive files I discovered notes he had written to himself; they confirmed that I was creating a story consistent with his own desires. He wanted to set Nauvoo in the context of religious as well as political history. In three conversations, all that Ed's health allowed, we agreed on the central place of the temple in Nauvoo's history, on the need to correct misremembered stories, and on the meanings of a few specific happenings.[6] Gradually, as I did my own extensive reading in diaries, letters, and other sources that he had not examined, I discovered new ways to tell the story of Nauvoo.

The completed book offers a narrative based on key religious themes from the Nauvoo years. The common thread is the Saints' search for places of refuge where they could unite in a quest for inner spiritual peace. In Nauvoo, they found the peace they were seeking when they entered the House of the Lord. There they received long-promised blessings for themselves. Through proxy baptisms, they offered opportunities for salvation to deceased ancestors. Despite the sacrifices, trials, and challenges of the Nauvoo years, their gathering place was a place of peace.

Moreover, the Saints defined themselves as a religious people who received God's promised covenant. The "restoration of all things" made the Mormons both latter-day Christians and modern Israelites. They became a set-apart people. Their diaries and histories became testaments of God's dealings with his children in a new "dispensation of the fulness of times." In short, they lived in places designated for sacred purposes, and their history was evidence of their belief in living prophets, new revelation, promised lands, and a chosen people. Throughout the book, I have allowed the Saints themselves to speak, to share their feelings about the meaning of the unfolding drama that defined the Nauvoo years.

To capture the religious feelings of the 1840s, the chapters in the first two parts of the book examine various aspects of the establishment of a place of refuge and the defining of a people of faith during the years 1839–43. These overlapping chapters reach backward in time to connect Nauvoo with foundational precedents in doctrine and events of the New York, Ohio, and Missouri years. This excursion beyond Nauvoo's chronological boundaries demonstrates that continuity and precedent are as important to an understanding of Mormon Nauvoo as is change. Parts 3 and 4 examine related themes in the context of the challenges of 1844 and 1845 that led to the abandonment of the region in 1846. A community of Saints socially and spiritually matured by their experiences in Nauvoo moved west. Schismatic groups who remained behind continued their quest for salvation in various places and with self-serving aberrations that changed or rejected core doctrines.

Sidney Rigdon boasted in 1858 concerning the history of the early church: "Perhaps I would not speak unadvisedly should I say that I am the only one now living who could write that history. Others may attempt it but they will fail."[7] In my own generation, it was generally agreed that T. Edgar Lyon was the person to write Nauvoo's history. I appreciate his family's confidence in my abilities to do justice to what was to have been their father's historical magnum opus. Until her passing in 1980, Hermana Lyon took an active interest in my work. She reminded me of her husband's desire for an honest assessment of the period and of his trust in my ability to complete his project. As a spokesman for the six sons of Ed and Hermana Lyon, Thomas Edgar Lyon Jr. (and, more recently, Joseph Lynn Lyon) maintained an understanding and patient encouragement.

It is with gratitude for the family's support and to acknowledge their father's influence on this book that I dedicate it to their parents—and to the Old Nauvooers, the old-timers who shared their fond recollections of Joseph Smith in the Salt Lake Twentieth Ward testimony meetings that Ed Lyon attended as a boy. My own great-grandfather was one of those who went about recalling his experiences with the Prophet Joseph Smith, his work on the Nauvoo Temple, and the final battle to defend Nauvoo. It was through these veterans and our other Nauvoo ancestors that Ed and I gained an early interest in the place and times and spiritual experiences of Old Nauvoo and the Old Nauvooers.[8]

Others who have made this volume possible include Steven R. Sorensen and the reference personnel of the Church Archives and Church History Library of what is now called the Family and Church History Department of The Church of Jesus Christ of Latter-day Saints. Equally helpful were David J. Whittaker and his associates in the Archives of the Mormon Experience and the Special Collections Department of the Brigham Young University library. The staffs of the libraries of the University of Utah and the Utah State Historical Society, the custodians of the vast collection of Nauvoo Restoration Incorporated, and the archivists and librarians of other repositories named in notes and visited by either me or Dr. Lyon graciously granted access to their collections.

Without the wise counsel of individuals who share my interest in Nauvoo, the manuscript would have retained many flaws of fact and message. James L. Kimball Jr. turned his intimate knowledge of Nauvoo and his familiarity with the NRI collection to my advantage by offering ready help in tracking countless errant facts. He read and critiqued the entire manuscript, as did Samuel Brown, Richard L. Jensen, Ronald W. Esplin, and Elder Loren C. Dunn. The observations of these and other friends have been invaluable. Commenting on specific chapters were Larry C. Porter, Dean C. Jessee, Kenneth W. Godfrey, and Lowell C. Bennion. Donald L. Enders and Stanley B. Kimball shared insights and information. Jan Shipps directed me toward helpful works in religious studies. Orson D. West, Michael D. Christensen, Christy Best, Ronald Read, and Bill Slaughter offered special assistance with bibliographies, facts, and illustrations. These and many other colleagues patiently listened to my musings on the meaning of Nauvoo as I sought to clarify my thinking.

At Deseret Book Company, Wm. James Mortimer, Lowell M. Durham Jr., and Sheri Dew were early and enthusiastic champions of this book. Overseeing publication under the guidance of Cory Maxwell were senior editor and project manager Suzanne Brady and art director Richard Erickson. They were assisted by Amy Felix, Shauna Gibby, Tonya-Rae Facemyer, and Kent Minson. Jack Welch, publications editor for the Joseph Fielding Smith Institute for Latter-day Saint History at Brigham Young University, suggested copublication with Brigham Young University Press. He offered the help of Robert Spencer, who expertly created the maps from the accumulated research of years. Under the direction of Anastasia Sutherland, Erick Carlson and others checked all quotations for accuracy.

Most important, my supportive wife, Karen, our sons, Cory, Kyle, and Keith, our daughters-in-law, Michelle and Shawnie, and our four grandchildren have allowed me to indulge my historical hobby without complaint. I appreciate their willingness to give me many evenings, weekends, and vacation days in "Nauvoo."

Barbara Tuchman has observed that a good historian should not subscribe "to the theory that all facts are of equal value." She advised, "If [the historian] cannot exercise judgment, he should not be in the business. A portraitist does not achieve a likeness by giving sleeve buttons and shoelaces equal value to mouth and eyes."[9] The depiction of Joseph Smith's Nauvoo offered here includes splashes of insight gleaned from other writers. It benefits as well from the reflections of Mormon historians who have grappled with the challenges of writing religious history. This weighty volume is not the only possible portrait. As Edmund Gaustad, a veteran in the writing of religious histories, put it: "We believe that there is meaning in history: this makes the quest worthwhile. We know that our perceptions are partial: this makes the quest fallible. . . . Even as we revise the work of an earlier generation, so verily, verily, shall we be revised!"[10]

It is hoped that this latest, but not last, look at Nauvoo will prove beneficial in some way to each one who views it. With the analytical tools of the historian, the literary devices of the writer, and the religious orientation of a Latter-day Saint, I accepted the challenge of discovering the meaning of a place and a time called Nauvoo.[11] If this retelling of the Nauvoo story realizes even a part of Richard Bushman's encouragement to give voice to the spiritual essence in the history of those years, we will have moved closer to recovering the real Nauvoo.[12] Nevertheless, I agree with Pliny the Elder, who concluded, "Even if we do not achieve our goal there is something beautiful and grand in having made the attempt."[13] The reward has been in the journey.

PART I

ESTABLISHING NAUVOO: A PLACE OF PEACE

We are comfortably, not splendidly situated. . . . Our place is rich and beautiful; half prairie, and is susceptible, by proper management, of supporting stock to almost an unlimited extent. But what is of infinitely more importance is that we reside within two miles of the City of Nauvoo, a place founded by the church of Latter-day Saints with whom we became acquainted, and after an impartial and thorough investigation of their principles have united ourselves in Christian fellowship. . . . If you ever heard anything, be assured it was either a gross misrepresentation or perhaps an utter falsehood. They have, to be sure, been driven from the state of Missouri, two years ago, by the force of arms, but certainly not for any criminal act, . . . but because there is a prophet at their head and because the church places implicit confidence in what he teaches. Equally with the primitive Christians, this church professes to have the same priesthood, together with the same power and gifts. . . . The organization of the church, according to the apostolic pattern, is a prelude to the Millennium, which is not very far distant.

—FROM A LETTER BY JOHN S. FULLMER, FEBRUARY 15, 1841

CHAPTER 1

Joseph Smith's Plan for Zion

Wherefore I, the Lord, have said, . . . go ye forth into the western countries, . . . and . . . build up churches unto me. And with one heart and with one mind, gather up your riches that ye may purchase an inheritance which shall hereafter be appointed unto you. And it shall be called the New Jerusalem, a land of peace, a city of refuge, a place of safety for the saints of the Most High God; and the glory of the Lord shall be there, . . . and it shall be called Zion.

—REVELATION TO JOSEPH SMITH, MARCH 7, 1831

For early members of The Church of Jesus Christ of Latter-day Saints, western Missouri was their Zion, a holy gathering place of peace. By revelation, Joseph Smith designated the region around Independence, Missouri, as the "center place of Zion," the site of a future millennial capital. Those who relocated to the City of Zion at the center place or to other designated gathering places were expected to live at a high spiritual plane in these cities of righteousness.[1] Dwelling in "a land of peace, a city of refuge, a place of safety for the saints" implied as well a heightened sense of community. The goal of a Zion society was to create unity and cooperation for the good of the whole.

Associated with these concepts of community was a religious view of how the church would accomplish its mission to gather a people and prepare them for the Second Coming. Joseph Smith, Parley P. Pratt, John Taylor, and other leaders defined the essential elements of what constituted

3

the church and kingdom of God on the earth. Pratt's *Voice of Warning*, first printed in 1837, offered a succinct summary of these factors. He wrote:

> Four things are required in order to constitute any kingdom, in Heaven or on earth: viz: first, a king [Jesus Christ]; second, commissioned officers duly qualified to execute his ordinances and laws; thirdly, a code of laws, by which the citizens are governed; and fourthly, subjects who are governed. Now, where these exist in their proper order and regular authority, there is a kingdom: . . . wherever we find officers duly commissioned and qualified by the Lord Jesus, together with his ordinances and laws existing in purity, unmixed with any precepts or commandments of men, there the kingdom of God exists, and there his power is manifest, and his blessings enjoyed as in days of old.[2]

In their forced departure from Missouri in 1838–39, the Latter-day Saints carried with them these principles for governing sacred gathering places. The ideas of a Zion place, a Zion people, and an ecclesiastical government that would be transformed into a millennial kingdom at some future time guided the creation of new gathering places at Nauvoo, Illinois, and elsewhere.

The interplay of ideal and reality, holiness and imperfection was another theme carried over to Nauvoo from the Ohio-Missouri period. Embedded into the Mormons' consciousness at an early day was the perception that they were victims of religious persecution.[3] During the winter of relocation, 1838–39, the Prophet reflected on how he and other Latter-day Saints should respond to those who challenged their Zion society. His counsel, given for circumstances surrounding the expulsion from Missouri, was equally good advice later on. Missouri's challenges were but prelude to the troubles of the Nauvoo years.

To understand the Nauvoo period, we turn first to the notion of Zion as a place and as a people. Then we review efforts to establish gathered communities and examine their failures. Finally, we summarize Joseph Smith's advice to his followers on how to view the tensions and conflicts that affected the course of Mormon history.

ZION: A PLACE AND A PEOPLE

The concept of Zion taught by Joseph Smith is central to an understanding of the events between 1839 and 1846, the years Nauvoo served as an administrative center for the church. For Latter-day Saints, Zion was a name used interchangeably for both a place and a people—a place where one could find inner peace by living a life devoted to God. These ideas were modified and amplified during the last years of Joseph Smith's life, creating cultural and religious landmarks that identify the significant elements of the Nauvoo story.

It is the religious world view behind the attempt to establish a Zion place and a Zion society that offers the most useful window for understanding the Nauvoo period. The spiritual perspective that defined the Latter-day Saints as a people affected not only their inner spiritual life but also how they lived from day to day. It influenced how they interacted with others, and how their neighbors who did not share their world view reacted toward them. And the experiences of life molded and reinforced their overall understanding of life's purpose and meaning.[4]

The founding generation of Latter-day Saints was significantly motivated by the geographical aspect of salvation. For that first group of converts, the most certain way to heaven included physically removing themselves from the evils found in worldly cities to a designated place of gathering. Figuratively and literally, they left Babylon for Zion, a city upon a hill. Zion's biblical name was reminiscent of David's royal city built around the temple knoll called Mount Zion. The July 1831 revelation that identified Independence, in Jackson County, Missouri, as the center place, called western Missouri "the land of promise, and the place for the city of Zion." Joseph Smith defined a city intended as a pattern for other gathering places. He called the secondary locations "stakes" to the "tent of Zion": "For Zion must increase in beauty, and in holiness; her borders must be enlarged; her stakes must be strengthened."[5]

The people who gathered to Zion and her stakes for refuge from the destruction of the last days saw themselves as a people of destiny. Their sense of being a special people gave the Latter-day Saints an identity that fostered the unity seen by their neighbors as a clannish self-righteousness. Latter-day Saints achieved their identity as a people of divine favor through ordinances that involved making covenants with God. The process began with baptism and eventually included other priesthood covenants and ordinances received in temples.

In biblical language, Zion was Jerusalem (literally, "a city of peace")— "the city of righteousness," seat of the "King of peace."[6] In Puritan discourse, which early Latter-day Saints knew well, Zion was celebrated as a City on a Hill, a pattern for their own communities and a light to the world. Like the New Testament Saints, who were the model for the Puritans, the children of the latter-day kingdom were supposed to be righteous examples to others, to "shine forth as the sun," to radiate the gospel in their lives and "shine as lights in the world."[7]

For the Latter-day Saints, the new American Jerusalem meant a real place, whose residents were distinguished by the way they lived. Geographically, Zion was the Holy City. Socially, Zion was a divine society, an organized community that would enjoy the promise of redemption in this life and a life of glory in the next. In the world to come, heaven would be right here on an earth brightened with its own celestial glory. For the Latter-day Saints in the 1830s, Missouri was both the literal site of the biblical Eden and the sacred place for the Saints of the last days as well as the place of eternal promise, a heaven on earth now and forever.

SEEKING TO ESTABLISH ZION

Building a new city—even planning it beforehand to fit some preconceived notion of an ideal physical or social pattern—was common in the America of the 1830s and 40s. In fact, right from colonial times, city planning occupied a central role in the process of defining the social and religious life of early settlers. In the new republic, Thomas Jefferson was an eloquent spokesman for those who saw four-square cities as an ideal pattern for an expanding nation. His influence in the western territories gave rise to many cities laid out geographically to symbolize the American dream.[8] To counter the image of European cities of sin and degradation, citizens of Jacksonian America sought to establish dwelling places imbued with the virtues of rural, agricultural, and small-town life. In implementing this dream, Americans developed two kinds of cities: first, the covenant communities of the New England world in which religion infused everyday life; and second, the collected communities organized under the rationalism of an Enlightenment world view requiring separation of church and state.[9]

Although they lived at a time dominated by collected communities, the Latter-day Saints and some other religious groups adopted the covenant community pattern. It spoke to their needs to create a community united not just geographically and socially but bound by a deeper

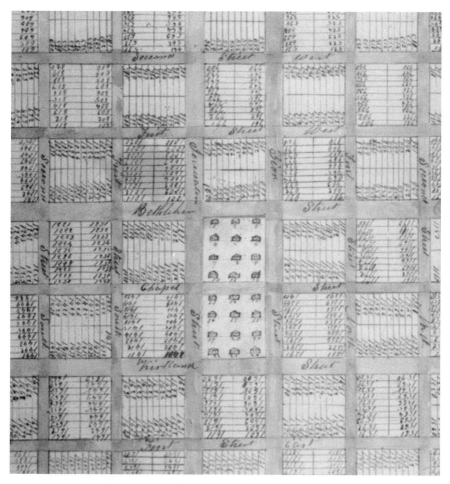

Plat of the City of Zion (detail). The major streets surrounding the temple blocks are named after cities sacred to Latter-day Saints: Jerusalem, Bethlehem, Zion, and Kirtland. No other plat for a Mormon city in Missouri carries named streets.

spiritual purpose. Even before they arrived in Missouri, the Saints developed a tradition of planning the places they wanted to live in, a tradition that persisted for a generation. In upstate New York and in Ohio, they lived in established towns but overlaid their own concept of sacred space—a separation from Babylon—and the need to congregate together. This adaptation was applied first in Ohio, where many converts from the Campbellite and related religious groups brought with them the experience of life in covenanted religious communities.[10]

During the 1830s, the Latter-day Saints exerted a concerted effort to realize the dream of an ideal City of Zion.[11] At Independence, Missouri, in June 1833, Joseph Smith overlaid on the existing town a City of Zion pattern. The plot for Zion was one mile square, made up mostly of ten-acre blocks, each one containing twenty half-acre lots.[12] Its streets stretched generously to widths of 132 feet and were squared with the compass. The Prophet limited the city's size to prevent urban crowding. (If each lot averaged five persons, the population would approach five thousand, but the planners inexplicably projected fifteen thousand or more for the city).[13] Public squares were planned for the center. Barns and stables to serve the city were to be clustered just outside the south boundary, while farms operated by the urban-based farmers would reach out north and south of the city.

All of this might be expected for any new western town; but Zion was not a secular American city. Zion was an overlay that not only echoed the American style but spiritualized it. Populated through the work of a far-flung missionary force, Latter-day Saint cities focused on religious worship with an educational emphasis and a Christian caring for the poor. These purposes were expressed architecturally in the public spaces, where the Prophet eliminated the traditional grand courthouse or city hall and substituted the House of the Lord, headquarters for the millennial King whose rule would preempt civil government in that long-anticipated Christian era of global peace. For the intended future world capital at Zion, not just one religious structure appeared on the plat but a complex of twenty-four temples situated on two sixteen-acre blocks. Plans of these projected meetinghouse-office buildings resembled the first Mormon temple at Kirtland. Joseph Smith intended them as administrative centers for presiding quorums and councils as well as halls for worship, religious observance, and schools. A third central block adjacent to the temple squares was reserved for storehouses for the goods donated as tithes and offerings. From this block, the bishop was to dispense needed resources to the poor and provide for general church needs.[14]

Anticipating other Mormon cities as stakes to support the tent of Zion, the Prophet instructed, "When this square is thus laid off and supplied, lay off another in the same way, and so fill up the world in these last days; and let every man live in the city, for this is the city of Zion."[15]

After the Saints were expelled from Jackson County in 1833, and while awaiting an opportunity to redeem or reclaim the center place, they laid out other temple-centered gathering places in fulfillment of the master plan. In the new county of Caldwell, created just for them, Far West and Adam-ondi-Ahman continued this ideal Zion city pattern, even though details differed. Each of these city-stakes of Zion anticipated a single temple situated in the central square to give the city its religious focus. Like Zion, the new cities were platted to lie four-square with the compass. In Far West, the four-acre blocks held four lots of one-acre each. In the two-mile-square Diahman, lots were one acre each, and blocks included six lots. Because it was to be the new (but temporary) capital of the church, Far West burgeoned on its hilltop site overlooking the rolling prairies. During the last days of the 1838 expulsion from Missouri, seven apostles and eighteen supporters slipped back into Far West to lay a symbolic cornerstone at the temple site and then depart on a mission to the British Isles. They offered their prayer in the dark of postmidnight to fulfill a prophecy that antagonists had threatened to frustrate.[16]

Implicit in the plan for the city of Zion were the values encouraged by the ideal covenant community. Living together as a community rather than in isolated farmhouses allowed Latter-day Saints to implement the social aspects of a shared destiny. "The cause of God is one common cause in which all the Saints are alike interested," Joseph Smith declared at Nauvoo in May 1842,

> we are all members of the one common body, and all partake of the same spirit, and are baptized into one baptism, and possess alike the same glorious hope. The advancement of the cause of God and the building up of Zion is as much one man's business as another. The only difference is that one is called to fulfil one duty and another another duty; . . . party feelings, separate interests, exclusive designs should be lost sight [of] in the one common cause, in the interest of the whole.[17]

Central to that "one common cause" was the "cause of God." Souls needed saving, and that meant the elimination of sin in all its forms, whether sins of passion or greed, of violence or pride. Replacing human failings with Christian values of love, charity, benevolence, patience, and humility ensured a Zion community. Residents of Zion and her stakes were expected to live lives of purity, unity, friendship, and Christian love.

Joseph Smith's revelations reaffirmed all of the obligations of the Ten Commandments and the teachings of Christ's ministry.

The "one common cause" invited the Saints to give of their means to build temples, to sustain the poor, and to support full-time church leaders. Implicit also was the obligation to assist others in gathering to Nauvoo and other stakes.[18] Through fulfillment of these obligations, Latter-day Saints expected to qualify as the Lord's people—the meek in spirit spoken of in the Sermon on the Mount who would inherit the earth in its glorified state. By revelation in 1833, the residents of Zion places were themselves called "Zion—THE PURE IN HEART," a reference to Enoch's ancient "people Zion . . . [who] were of one heart and one mind, and dwelt in righteousness; and there was no poor among them."[19]

Political unity—a sticking point in a pluralistic society—meant for the Latter-day Saints a commitment to elect "good men" so that governments would not trample on the individual rights guaranteed by the Constitution of the United States. Latter-day Saints pledged to obey and defend the law and the rights of all citizens. With those commitments in mind and to keep their opponents from enjoying political power over them, they voted for friends and against those whose interests ran contrary to their own. These practices built a wall around the Mormon community. Neighbors felt threatened. In response, they attempted to absorb or eliminate the threat.[20]

Whatever its external implications, Mormon city-founding grew from a deeply held belief in the necessity of a cooperative effort. "By a concentration of action, and a unity of effort, we can only accomplish the great work of the last days, which we could not do in our remote and scattered condition," the First Presidency declared in 1841. "The great profusion of temporal and spiritual blessings, which always flow from faithfulness and concerted effort, never attend individual exertion or enterprize. The history of all past ages abundantly attests this fact."[21]

Challenges to Zion

As with many ideals, achievement often falls short, and the Mormon experience during the early 1830s suffered from some shortfalls. Challenges both from within the clustered gathering places in Ohio and Missouri and from outside them severely tested Joseph Smith's program for a bonded community. Within months of the expulsion from Jackson

County, he organized Zion's Camp, an army of Mormon volunteers from Ohio and the Great Lakes region, and marched them toward Missouri to reclaim abandoned Jackson County property. He anticipated support from Missouri's governor in reclaiming the land but did not get it. Just short of the army's destination, a declaration known as the "Fishing River" revelation postponed the establishment of an ideal Zion society and the redemption of Zion's promised land. In northwestern Missouri and, later, in Nauvoo, this postponement allowed a transition to religious obligations easier for the Saints to live but still close to their overall objectives.[22]

The revelation at Fishing River laid responsibility for the failure of the expedition directly on the imperfections of the Saints. Armies could not redeem Zion. Nor was it the Missourians who had caused the lack of success in establishing Zion. It was an unrighteous people. The Latter-day Saints involved had not yet become separated from the world:

> But behold, they have not learned to be obedient to the things which I [the Lord] required at their hands, but are full of all manner of evil, and do not impart of their substance, as becometh saints, to the poor and afflicted among them; and are not united according to the union required by the law of the celestial kingdom.[23]

The testimony of this disobedience was evident in Zion. At Independence, a few outspoken church leaders and members had expressed concern about ecclesiastical management of their property under the economic program of consecration. At Far West, the Prophet began the shift away from Zion's economic plan. In this city of three thousand people, no one was asked to consecrate property to the church. Most of the land was privately owned and operated. Joseph Smith encouraged some cooperative farming enterprises. In response, the Saints set up huge farms managed under a neighborhood organization as a supplement to private—unconsecrated—land.

But this change in practice did not resolve every question over economic policy. In April 1838, the high council in Far West finally aired issues that had lingered for years. They did so during a trial of fellowship involving Oliver Cowdery, an early associate of the Prophet. At the core of Cowdery's disagreement, according to witnesses, was his refusal to "be governed by any ecclesiastical authority or revelations whatever, in his temporal affairs." Furthermore, he had sold his property in

Jackson County after the Prophet explicitly counseled against it. Cowdery admitted to his actions and criticized what he called "a kind of petty government, controlled and dictated by ecclesiastical influence, in the midst of this national and state government." Cowdery argued for his constitutional right to exercise personal judgment in matters of property.[24]

Other dissenters were less articulate in their opposition to a religiously motivated plan to share with the poor, but their unwillingness to live the religious order was apparent. These new Saints were not prepared, either by political upbringing or religious maturity, to live it. In their concerns over theocratic government, they appealed to the traditions of their political fathers. They preferred the safe haven of republican society and the secular, collected community.[25]

Even though Cowdery's opposition and other problems meant his excommunication, his argument helped to show why church members were not ready for such an undertaking. Within months of Cowdery's hearing, Joseph Smith offered a modified course for creating a more easily realized Zion society. The law of tithing, which the Lord introduced in a revelation on July 8, 1838, allowed the Saints to witness their dedication to the principles of a more equal economic society in a new way.[26] First, they made an initial offering to the church of their surplus property. "And after that," the revelation directed, "those who have thus been tithed shall pay one tenth of all their interest annually."[27] With the produce and cash thus collected into the bishop's storehouse, the poor would be supported, the debts of the church paid, and the families of the presidency sustained. Even though the ideal economic plan for Zion was on hold, a modified program for a stake of Zion could be accomplished.[28] Consecration, after all, was but one of many principles that defined the people of God, and the new law of tithing met most of its objectives.

The principal use of the tithing would be for constructing a temple. The House of the Lord dedicated in Kirtland in 1836 had been intended as a place where converts would worship, learn the word of God, and be endowed with spiritual power to ready them for the new age of peace and prosperity. The Prophet hoped this preparation would yield religious and doctrinal unity. But internal apostasy fed by external conditions cut short the dream of a temple-centered Zion at Kirtland. Plans for temples at Independence, Far West, and Adam-ondi-Ahman were abandoned

The first House of the Lord in Kirtland set the pattern for early Latter-day Saint temples with its rooms for worship and instruction, sacred ordinances, and administration.

because of external opposition to the gathered community and internal challenges to the economic order taught by Joseph Smith. As of 1838, Joseph's dream of a temple on America's western borders where the Saints could participate fully in the blessings that God had promised was yet future. During the Nauvoo years, building a House of the Lord and creating a covenant people through temple ordinances would replace the effort to fashion a more broadly consecrated society.

REFLECTIONS FROM LIBERTY

Many Latter-day Saints marked the transition between the Ohio-Missouri and the Nauvoo periods by moving out of Missouri. Joseph Smith spent those months in a county jail.[29] Incarcerated at Liberty, Missouri, only a dozen miles from the abandoned City of Zion in Jackson County, he reflected on many of the issues that had plagued the Latter-day Saints during their Missouri sojourn. For weeks at a time, as he sat on the cold stone floor, bounded by a four-foot-thick wall of limestone, loose rock, and oak timbers, he had time to meditate on the conflict between neighbors in Missouri and about the lack of unity within the church over economic policies both in Missouri and Ohio.[30]

The Prophet and other Latter-day Saints defined the two forms of opposition they had experienced in Missouri as persecution and apostasy. Opposition from outside the church had driven the Saints from several gathering places in Missouri. The vigilantes who drove them justified their actions as a political or social necessity. Church members perceived the expulsions as religious persecution and a denial of constitutionally guaranteed rights to property.[31] Disagreements within the church had challenged the standards for demonstrating faithfulness in the Lord's kingdom. Religious dissenters claimed they were trying to purify the church, but others saw them as enemies of faith. The external and internal challenges faced in Missouri would continue after the Saints established their new place of peace. Therefore, what Joseph Smith said at Liberty Jail about these Missouri experiences would have meaning later in Nauvoo.

"Brother Joseph," as the Saints sometimes called their prophet, shared his musings at Liberty in letters to family and friends. One such missive was written to church members still in Caldwell County, Missouri, in mid-December 1838, a few days before his thirty-third birthday. It offered consolation, commented on the Missouri persecutions and apostasies, and established a policy for responding to Missouri's old settlers. Joseph Smith reached into the New Testament to define the Missouri difficulties in religious terms. "It is for the testimony of Jesus that we are in bonds and in prison," he explained. "We glory in our tribulation. . . . We do not care for them that can kill the body; they cannot harm our souls."[32] The Prophet named directly those within the church who had turned against him and defected. Some of these early defenders of the faith later returned to the fold. In addition, Joseph Smith mentioned outsiders who had offended his rights—lawyers, judges, religious ministers, and officers of the militia, as well as the dregs of society—people in high station and low.[33]

The Prophet wished to heal wounds in the congregation of believers. He affirmed his own innocence and pronounced the charges laid against him as falsehoods. As he would do again in Nauvoo, he reassured those who had been influenced by his detractors that "the keys of the kingdom [have] not been taken from us."[34] In response to charges of murder laid against the Mormon militia and its leaders, he said, "We stood in our own defense, and we believe that no man of us acted only in a just, a lawful, and a righteous retaliation against such marauders." Rumors that the

Oliver Cowdery   *Joseph Smith*

Joseph Smith responded to Oliver Cowdery and other challengers of his leadership in Missouri with patience, forgiveness, and mercy.

elders shared "a community of wives" he challenged as a charge spread by dissenters "seeking to gain the friendship of the world." The distortion, he said, perverted a practice in which not only property but entire families—a man and his wife and children—were dedicated to the Lord's work. These covenanted families promised to care for the sick and the poor, and they consecrated their hearts to a life of virtue, honor, and charity.[35]

One more charge he wished to answer. Rumors had circulated linking the military assistance groups, the Danites, to illegal activities. Actually, according to Albert Rockwood, the Danite organization had two goals: to work cooperatively in meeting temporal needs and to defend the Saints against attack. At Liberty, Joseph Smith learned that Sampson Avard had organized one Danite group offensively, as a marauding band to steal from Missourians in retribution for wrongs against Mormon settlers. Avard had sworn his band to secrecy but informed them that like other Danite units, they were operating under the sanction of the First Presidency. Joseph Smith disclaimed any knowledge of Avard's group and denounced its activities. Even though the military attacks soon ceased, the rumors persisted.[36]

The Prophet claimed no ill feeling towards those who had wronged him or the church. Rather, he adopted the advice of the Book of Mormon prophet Amulek, who had told his similarly beleaguered people "to have patience, and . . . bear with all manner of afflictions; that ye do not revile against those who do cast you out."[37] The incarcerated prophet reminded the Latter-day Saints who were about to leave Missouri that judgment was the Lord's.[38]

Along with comments on the errors of detractors, Joseph Smith's letter to the Caldwell County Saints critiqued the faults of the imperfect faithful. He counseled against drunkenness, swearing, profane language "and from everything which is unrighteous or unholy; also from enmity, and hatred, and covetousness, and from every unholy desire." He encouraged honesty and charity and condemned greediness. Despite the weaknesses of his followers, the imprisoned prophet would not relinquish his confidence in the spiritual perfectibility of the struggling Saints nor the ultimate realization of his religious hopes. He reaffirmed: "Zion shall yet live, though she seemeth to be dead."[39]

Another letter has lingered in even greater prominence in the Mormon memory of the painful Missouri years. Because of the letter's spiritual power, Latter-day Saint historian B. H. Roberts called the county jail where it was written a prison-temple, a place of prayer and meditation.[40] The letter was written in late March 1839. Intended for a wide audience, this communication was published the following year at Nauvoo in the *Times and Seasons,* and extracts were later canonized by the church as scripture.[41]

Parts of the letter are written in the language of revelation, with the voice of the Lord offering advice to Joseph Smith in response to his deep introspection. The counsel expands on ideas explored sensitively in the Kirtland Temple prayer of dedication in 1836, where the Prophet sought to resolve the competing demands of justice and mercy toward those who caused the Saints' expulsion from Missouri's Zion.[42] The guidelines outlined in the letter (now sections 121, 122, and 123 of the Doctrine and Covenants) would have a future application in the gathering place that would be called Nauvoo.

The issue foremost in every mind was the recent persecution. "Avenge us of our wrongs," the Prophet appealed to God for himself and the suffering Saints. The Lord's response offered several observations. First, it postponed justice and placed it in an eternal perspective: "My son, peace be unto thy soul; thine adversity and thine afflictions shall be but a small moment; and then, if thou endure it well, God shall exalt thee on high; thou shalt triumph over all thy foes."[43] Second, as Joseph Smith's earlier letter had done, the revelation denounced Sampson Avard's avenging Danites and counseled all Saints to exercise godly patience and forbearance. The third message was a prophecy that even though the fools of the world would hold Joseph Smith in derision, there would be others—the pure, wise, and noble—who would honor his prophetic authority and seek blessings from him. The Prophet was reassured that he would retain his role as revelator to the church. Fourth, the Lord counseled, if there should be further persecution—false accusations, incarceration, fraud, conspiracy, or even death threats—"know thou, my son, that all these things shall give thee experience, and shall be for thy good." Finally, there follows a promise that Latter-day Saints in Nauvoo would recall five years later: "Thy days are known," the Lord reassured Joseph, "and thy years shall not be numbered less; therefore, fear not what man can do, for God shall be with you forever and ever."[44]

Writing in his own voice, Joseph Smith gave the Latter-day Saints a specific duty with regard to their persecutors. Everyone should become a historian, he said. All should compile the names of their Missouri oppressors and a list of losses, both in property and in personal injuries. A church committee would direct the effort, assemble all printed material relating to their grievances, and publish the findings. The effort, Smith said, would help to correct a tarnished public image created in the popular press. It would fuel appeals to governments and help future investigators sort out the evidence.[45]

The second message of the March 1839 letter from Liberty Jail addressed the consequences of dissension and apostasy. Among Latter-day Saint men of the time, priesthood was virtually universal. Those ordained to one of two lay priesthoods, the Aaronic and the Melchizedek, were given various assignments. They could administer the ordinances of baptism and confirmation, confer the priesthood on others, give blessings of healing or comfort, bless and serve the emblems of the Lord's Supper, serve as missionaries abroad, or minister to members at home. Without the authority of the priesthood, a Latter-day Saint man could not fulfill his responsibilities within the church.

The Prophet's Liberty Jail letter recognized both the rights and obligations of bearing the priesthood and identified a consequence for strident internal opposition. Those who turned against the church and its leaders, he said, would lose their right to the priesthood through excommunication.[46]

The inspired guidelines set forth by Joseph Smith for priesthood holders at Liberty Jail defined the ecclesiastical organization of the church as noncoercive. The revelation cautioned that "the rights of the priesthood . . . cannot be controlled nor handled only upon the principles of righteousness." Men who acted hypocritically or for self-aggrandizement or who attempted "to exercise control or dominion or compulsion upon the souls of the children of men" would find themselves stripped of their priesthood authority. Failure to use that authority properly, the Prophet warned, would lead to apostasy. The insights and prescriptions of this part of the letter both reflected conditions that had existed among disaffected leaders in Missouri and predicted challenges in church administration and secular authority yet ahead. The letter concluded with counsel that Joseph Smith would apply in his religious interactions throughout the Nauvoo years and that he would encourage other leaders to follow:

> We have learned by sad experience that it is the nature and disposition of almost all men, as soon as they get a little authority, as they suppose, they will immediately begin to exercise unrighteous dominion.
>
> Hence many are called, but few are chosen.
>
> No power or influence can or ought to be maintained by virtue of the priesthood, only by persuasion, by long-suffering, by gentleness and meekness, and by love unfeigned;
>
> By kindness, and pure knowledge, . . .
>
> Reproving betimes with sharpness, when moved upon by the Holy Ghost; and then showing forth afterwards an increase of love toward him whom thou hast reproved, lest he esteem thee to be his enemy. . . .
>
> Let thy bowels also be full of charity towards all men, and to the household of faith, and let virtue garnish thy thoughts unceasingly; then shall thy confidence wax strong in the presence of God; and the doctrine of the priesthood shall distil upon thy soul as the dews from heaven.[47]

CHAPTER 2

Finding a Place of Peace

Many of you have been driven from your homes, robbed of your posses-sions, and deprived of the liberty of conscience; you have been stripped of your clothing, plunder[ed] of your furniture, robbed of your horses, your cattle, your sheep, your hogs, and refused the protection of law. . . . Dear brethren, . . . although you have had indignities, insults and injuries heaped upon you, . . . we would say, be patient, dear brethren, for as saith the apostle, "ye have need of patience, that after being tried you may inherit the promise.". . . Do not breathe vengeance upon your oppressors, but leave the case in the hands of God, "for vengeance is mine, saith the Lord, and I will repay."

—BRIGHAM YOUNG, HEBER C. KIMBALL, JOHN E. PAGE, WILFORD
WOODRUFF, JOHN TAYLOR, AND GEORGE A. SMITH, JULY 1839

Troubles in Missouri in the fall of 1838 precipitated an exodus that launched the Nauvoo period of Latter-day Saint history. Joseph Smith spent much of that winter in a county jail at Liberty, Missouri, where he pondered the experiences of the previous seven years. The Latter-day Saints had tried in several locations and, because of opposition, had failed to establish sacred gathering places. In these places of refuge, they had hoped to create a people striving to prepare themselves for the second coming of Jesus Christ. While this dream of Zion was the overall objective for the church, the Prophet's immediate thoughts at Liberty Jail dwelt on the expulsion of thousands of Saints from Missouri. His counsel to the forced exiles was to find a place safe from the threats of state militias and informal regulators. Leave judgment to God, he said, and focus on the spiritual goals of building a religious society in whatever place the Lord had prepared.[1]

Even though the Saints were leaving Missouri behind as a dwelling place, the experiences of those years influenced what happened next. The events of the Nauvoo period were deeply rooted in Missouri and built upon ideas from the beginning years of the church in New York and Ohio. For example, the central goals of preaching the gospel, gathering the righteous out of a wicked world, establishing congregations in places of refuge, and building temples continued during the Nauvoo years.

Almost from the beginnings of the church in upstate New York in 1830, Joseph Smith had directed the Saints to look westward to find safety from the wicked and to nurture peace in their own lives. The earliest revelations to address the idea of migration invited the congregations in the Northeast to move to the state of Ohio. Here, the Lord wished to gather a righteous people, tutor them in His law, and endow them with heavenly powers.[2] But soon, another place was given priority status, even though its purposes were similar.[3] That place was in Independence, Missouri, at the western reaches of the United States,[4] a site designated by revelation as a future millennial capital:

> And it shall be called the New Jerusalem, a land of peace, a city of refuge, a place of safety for the saints of the Most High God;
> And the glory of the Lord shall be there, and the terror of the Lord also shall be there, insomuch that the wicked will not come unto it, and it shall be called Zion.[5]

As Joseph Smith revealed more about Zion, Missouri quickly became for Latter-day Saints the place to be. It was seen as a promised land for the pure in heart. The anticipated City of Zion was to develop after the order of the ancient City of Holiness established by Enoch and taken into heaven by the Lord.[6] In the latter-day Zion, temples were to be erected to welcome the returning King of kings for His millennial reign. If faithful, the Saints in Zion were promised "peace in this world, and eternal life in the world to come," a reward for all Latter-day Saints attainable especially by those living consecrated lives in Zion.[7]

Even before the designation in July 1831 of a center place, Kirtland,

Ohio, had been positioned as a staging ground for the gathering to the City of Zion.[8] In the temporary headquarters city of Kirtland, in northern Ohio's Western Reserve, the church dedicated its first temple in 1836, began a printing operation, and established a storehouse under a form of the law of consecration.[9] It was the Lord's will, Joseph Smith revealed in 1831, "to retain a strong hold in the land of Kirtland, for the space of five years. . . . And after that day, I, the Lord, will not hold any guilty that shall go with an open heart up to the land of Zion."[10]

The need to define relationships among various gathering places triggered a steady trickle of revelations and instructions over the remaining years of Joseph Smith's life. Consistently, the message was that both Zion and her stakes were sanctioned. All church members shared the responsibility to cry repentance to the world and to nurture the gathered Saints. In fact, the long-range expectation was that once the New Jerusalem had reached a fixed maximum size, the Saints would establish numerous other cities patterned after this central place of peace.[11]

Among the continuing threads of organizational history during the 1840s were the questions of when a stake should be organized, or disorganized, and when the Saints should gather in large cities, like Zion or Nauvoo, or when they should remain in other gathering places. The question was not new. In August 1831, an immediate surge of migration to Missouri was discouraged. Only those approved by local church leaders as ready to claim their inheritance in Zion could go.[12] Kirtland was not just a staging ground for the gathering to Zion but a gathering place itself, the first of many large congregations known as branches, or cities, or stakes of Zion. Kirtland became the pattern for other, yet future stakes. The revelations guiding the development of the "City or Stake of Zion at Kirtland, [known as] Shinehah," became an example applied in other places during the Nauvoo years, and beyond.[13]

TENSIONS IN ZION

Many of those who remained in Kirtland did eventually join in the movement westward, but not until Jackson County—the land of Zion—had been abandoned for an alternate gathering place in upper Missouri. The Saints had spent a short two years of rapid growth at Independence. One of the revelations had anticipated trouble in "the land of Missouri, which is the land of your inheritance, which is now the land of your enemies."[14] The "enemies" were earlier settlers, mostly from the upper South. In 1833, the old settlers expelled the Saints from Jackson County, fearful of losing political control to the culturally different Yankee Mormons. The Saints found refuge fifteen miles to the north at Liberty, across the Missouri River in Clay County, where they lived in relative harmony for another two years.

Clay County was an acceptable substitute for the designated center place. For the Latter-day Saints, the economic prosperity available to them in their western gathering places was an important aspect of their religion. As it had been with God's covenant people of the Old Testament and the Book of Mormon, those of the new covenant were promised prosperity as a blessing for their righteousness. The worthy poor would become self-reliant through the surpluses consecrated by the wealthy. And the promised land would itself yield ample harvests. "I feel well satisfied with this country," the Prophet's aunt Almira Mack Covey wrote from Liberty in 1835, in a down-to-earth reflection of the practical application of the promise:

> It is pleasant, and it is a good place to get a living. There is plenty of grain of all kinds; plenty of meat, milk, [and] butter; and we have plenty of hackberries, blackberries, strawberries, gooseberries, mulberries, blue grapes, little wine grapes, and grost grapes; hickory nuts, walnuts, chinkipins, pickeas, and some apples and sweet potatoes.[15]

The Latter-day Saints were not alone in recognizing the potential of America's frontier. From the day Daniel Boone followed an Indian trail through the Cumberland Gap to discover a "terrestrial paradise" in Kentucky, the yearning for richer farmlands impelled generations of Americans to go west in search of a more prosperous life. Missouri attracted slave-holding migrants from the South, and in 1820 the Missouri Compromise allowed the admission of Missouri to the Union as a slave state. In contrast, the Latter-day Saint newcomers hailed mostly from the North Atlantic states. "I must say that the society of the Missourians is not so agreeable as I have seen," Almira Covey noted.

> When I speak of the Missourians, I mean the old inhabitants, which are mostly southern people, and their living is mostly bacon and dodgers, . . . a sort of Johnny cake made of corn meal. This they eat in preference to wheat, which makes it much better for our eastern people who like wheat best. . . . The church in this land live in peace at this time.[16]

In July 1833, vigilantes in Independence challenged Latter-day Saint political and economic activities in Jackson County by ransacking the church printing shop (left) and the store of Oliver Granger and N. K. Whitney (center).

A preference for corn dodgers over wheat cakes was but one indicator of deeper differences between old and new settlers in upper Missouri. In a public meeting in late June 1836 at the Liberty courthouse, Clay County citizens identified what made them uncomfortable living as neighbors to the Latter-day Saints:

> They are Eastern men, whose manners, habits, customs, and even dialect, are essentially different from our own; they are non-slave holders, and opposed to slavery, which . . . is well calculated to excite deep and abiding prejudices in any community where slavery is tolerated and practiced. In addition to all this, they are charged . . . with keeping up a constant communication with the Indian tribes on our frontier, [and] with declaring, even from the pulpit, that the Indians are a part of God's chosen people and are destined, by heaven, to inherit this land, in common with themselves. We do not vouch for the correctness of these statements; but whether they are true or false, their effect has been the same in exciting our community.[17]

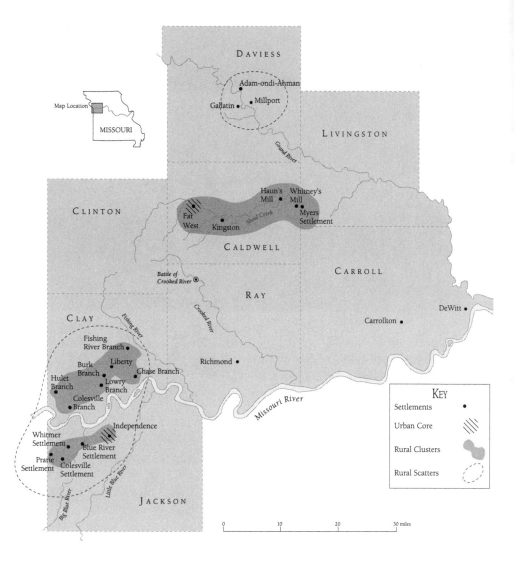

Map Location

MISSOURI

DAVIESS

Adam-ondi-Ahman

Gallatin • Millport

LIVINGSTON

Grand River

CLINTON

Haun's
Mill • Whitney's
Mill

Far
West • Kingston • Shoal Creek • Myers
Settlement

CALDWELL

CARROLL

Battle of
Crooked River

RAY

Crooked River

DeWitt

CLAY

Fishing River

Carrollton

Fishing
River Branch

Burk
Branch • Liberty

Hulet
Branch • Lowry
Branch • Chase Branch

Colesville
Branch

Richmond

Missouri River

Whitmer
Settlement

Independence

Prarie
Settlement • Blue River
Settlement

Colesville
Settlement

Big Blue River

Little Blue River

JACKSON

KEY

Settlements •

Urban Core

Rural Clusters

Rural Scatters

0   10   20   30 miles

Upper Missouri Settlements

Once again, social and political differences between two culturally dissimilar peoples led to a pressured relocation of the Mormon settlers. The citizens committee "advise[d] them to seek a home where they may obtain large and separate blocks of land and have a community of their own." The Saints moved in 1836 from Clay County to a site farther north created by state legislators as an exclusive Mormon gathering place. In Caldwell and Daviess Counties, the Latter-day Saints established settlements, the principal one being Far West.[18]

Around four thousand Missouri Mormons relocated onto the grassy prairies of the Far West region.[19] Here, in a land of deep loam and big promises, they sought to realize the American dream of rediscovering a new Eden and the revealed mandate to establish Zion. To Levi Hancock, raised in New York and Ohio, his dreams of a peaceable kingdom for his young family seemed in hand. On a sixty-acre farm plot, the thirty-four-year-old furniture maker

> built a house sixteen feet square of logs, . . . hired rails made and fenced four acres and planted it to corn, built a brush fence around my pasture, bought and paid for ten acres in the city of Far West, and partly paid for a city lot next to the temple block. . . . I had cows, hogs, and one good mare, sheep, and hens a plenty, and was in a good way to live with a plenty to eat.

Hancock captured the spirit of the search for a verdant place of peace in a song he had written, "My Peaceful Home, 1837," preserved in his memoirs. "When I got weary," he wrote, "I would take my babe and my little boy and sing these verses":

> *Here, far in the realm of Missouri,*
> *I'll sit and sing and tell thee a story;*
> *How many trials I have passed over*
> *Before I found this dwelling in peace.*
>
> *O here, here, beside of the fire,*
> *I have my sweet babe and little Mosiah;*
> *And here is Mother, I'll seat me down by her*
> *And sing, "I've found a dwelling in peace."*
>
> . . . .
>
> *Here in my field all things are a growing,*
> *And on the prairie I have men mowing*

That I may have feed to keep my stock;
While here at home I live and have peace.

. . . .

May we love [God] forever and ever
For peace bestowed upon the believer;
And turn from him, O never, O never,
But always love the spirit of peace.[20]

Levi Hancock's idyllic song captured the spirit of Latter-day Saint hopes in 1837. At last, they believed, they had found respite from earlier disagreements with Missouri's old settlers. Safe from physical violence, they could savor spiritual uplift and enjoy the harvest of their farms with their families. George W. Averett was another who celebrated the new-found refuge. "This land seemed to be a choice land, . . . a heaven in every deed. . . . I rejoiced exceedingly in this land of Zion."[21]

When the thirty-two-year-old Joseph Smith left Kirtland in the spring of 1838, he settled in Far West, which became the movement's new head-quarters. It was also the place of relocation for many Jackson County exiles. Anticipating rapid growth, the initial square-mile survey was enlarged to two square miles. The Prophet created a new city for Kirtland emigrants called Adam-ondi-Ahman (so named by revelation as the place where Adam last blessed his posterity). About a thousand people settled there. The Prophet designated both gathering places as stakes of Zion and chose temple sites. Other Latter-day Saints clustered in smaller settlements in the two counties, such as Gallatin, Millport, and Haun's Mill, or estab-lished homes at DeWitt in neighboring Carroll County.[22]

Despite the best of intentions on both sides in northwestern Missouri, tensions between old and new settlers increased. Two public statements in the summer of 1838 by Sidney Rigdon, the Prophet's counselor in the First Presidency and designated spokesman, fueled a growing discontent. His unsettling "Salt Sermon" in June targeted dissenters from within the church, and an Independence Day speech two weeks later sparked reac-tions from the non-Mormon settlers.

The first of these orations unloaded the frustration of the First Presidency with dissident members and led to extralegal actions against them. The critics were challenging church leaders and suing to reclaim Kirtland loans. Rigdon declared that these Saints, the "salt of the earth," had lost their savour (had apostatized) and were "good for nothing; but to be cast out, and to be trodden under foot of men." A few days later, in a signed petition, eighty-three Latter-day Saints challenged Oliver Cowdery, David Whitmer, John Whitmer, William W. Phelps, and Lyman E. Johnson, the most prominent of the dissenters, to get out of town—and they did.[23]

On July 4, the Saints met in Far West to place the cornerstones for a temple. Levi W. Hancock composed a new "Song of Freedom" for the event. A large procession of church members, some of them acting in their capacity as militiamen, encircled the excavation. In ringing tones that gave voice to the deep feelings of his audience, Rigdon declared the church's deep support for religious freedom. He reviewed the injustices endured with patience. But the time had come, he said, for the Saints to defend themselves. Referring to "The Political Motto of the Church" that Joseph Smith and eight others had signed a few months earlier, Rigdon issued what the Prophet later called a "Declaration of Independence." "Our rights shall no more be trampled on with impunity," said Rigdon. "We will never be the aggressors, we will infringe on the rights of no people, but shall stand for our own until death." Physical and verbal threats from Missouri antagonists must end, Rigdon proclaimed. If attacked, "we will follow them until the last drop of their blood is spilled; or else they will have to exterminate us."[24]

Rigdon's prepared speech had been approved by church leaders and was published in Liberty, the county seat of Clay County. In the *Elders' Journal,* Joseph Smith endorsed the talk's central message: "We are absolutely determined no longer to bear [mobbing] come life or come death for to be mobbed any more without taking vengeance, we will not." Attacks on DeWitt would soon turn the Saints to a defensive posture that would lead to expulsion.[25]

Within weeks, confrontations appeared in the northern counties. Voters scuffled at the August state election at Gallatin. As rumors magnified the problem, both the old settlers and the Mormons armed for defense against feared uprisings. Sporadic raids ensued. Both sides burned buildings and hauled off booty. Major General David R. Atchison's indecisive state militia monitored the anxious peace. Early in October, fighting broke out at DeWitt. "Far West is headquarters of the Mormon War," Albert P. Rockwood informed his parents. "The Armies of Israel that were established by revelation from God are seen from my door every day with their captains of 10s, 50s, and 100s." In addition to their daily drills, he said, the citizen soldiers helped with basic survival needs. They provided wood, meat, and other provisions, built cabins, stood watch or spied out the enemy, gathered scattered Mormon families, and cared for the sick. "The companies are called Dan," Rockwood explained, "because Prophet Daniel has said the Saints shall take the Kingdom and possess it forever." Rigdon sent off an armed Mormon militia, "the horsemen of Israel," to disperse the anti-Mormon regulators. "The fear of God rests down upon them and they flee when no man persueth," Rockwood reported. "The brethren are fast returning from the northern campaign with hearts full of gratitude. Not a drop of blood has been spilt. The mob disperse by hundreds on the approach of the Danites."[26]

Bloodless dispersions soon ended. On October 25, a battle at Crooked River, twenty miles west of Far West, left one Missouri regulator and three Mormon militiamen dead, including Elder David W. Patten of the Council of the Twelve Apostles. First reports of the clash exaggerated the number of deaths in Captain Samuel Bogart's Ray County camp. Two days later, Governor Lilburn Boggs was informed that the Mormons had risen up in an insurrection. He issued a declaration to the state militia: "The Mormons must be treated as enemies and must be exterminated or driven from the state, if necessary for the public good." Violence next erupted at Haun's Mill, where on October 30, Colonel William O. Jennings led more than two hundred Missourians from Livingston County in an unprovoked attack. Casualties at the small Mormon settlement included seventeen men and boys killed and as many wounded.[27]

At Far West, Major General Samuel D. Lucas and his Missouri militia, some of them dressed and painted like Indian warriors, met a barricaded Mormon town ready for self-defense. The Mormons assembled a militia of about five hundred men, a fifth as many soldiers as Lucas commanded. The Kentucky-born commander of the Mormon militia, Colonel George M. Hinkle, recognized the disadvantage. Disillusioned with the Danite retaliatory raids on the old settlers, Hinkle quietly negotiated a truce with Lucas. The terms: disarm the Latter-day Saints and turn over their leaders to the Missourians. Unaware of the treacherous surrender arrangement, Joseph Smith and his companions thought they were convening to negotiate terms. On October 31, 1838, Joseph Smith, his

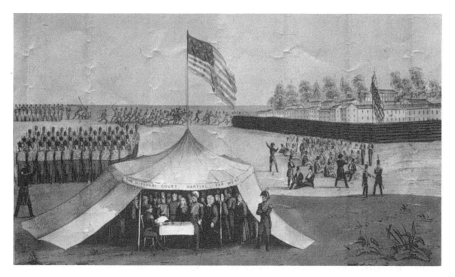

Times and Seasons *editor John Taylor criticized Sam Brannan's 1845 lithograph of the surrender of Far West for its inaccuracies: Missouri militiamen in full uniform, Mormon defenders fleeing, and a Far West city too compact and surrounded by a stockade. The temple, planned but never built, stands within the timber wall.*

counselor Sidney Rigdon, apostles Lyman Wight and Parley P. Pratt, and Rigdon's son-in-law George W. Robinson were arrested. The Missouri troops, Pratt recalled, surrounded the conference tent and let out "a constant yell, like so many bloodhounds let loose upon their prey." Some of the Mormon soldiers grumbled among themselves over the surrender of their arms. They would have preferred a fight to the death in the defense of their liberties. "I ask not to live one moment but to get revenge," Vinson Knight confided to a friend. "Indeed I go the whole hog for liberty or I die."[28]

The Prophet escaped summary execution under a military court martial decree because of Alexander W. Doniphan. A general in the militia, Doniphan had previously served as attorney for the church in Missouri. When ordered to have his men shoot Joseph Smith, Doniphan's sense of justice prevailed: He denounced the decision as cold-blooded murder and refused to carry out the order. Taken first to Independence, Joseph Smith pondered his future in a letter to his wife, Emma, on November 4: "God has spared some of us thus far; perhaps he will extend mercy in some degree toward us yet." The Prophet shared a bittersweet rumor: the people of Independence "would allow some of the Mormons [to] settle in this county as other men do." That is, by abandoning the idea of a gathered community, the Saints would be welcome in their Zion.[29]

The arrested leaders and forty-eight others indicted in the case were then moved to Richmond. After a two-week hearing, Judge Austin A. King released most of them. Parley P. Pratt and four others were held at Richmond Jail for trial. Joseph and Hyrum Smith, Rigdon, Wight, Caleb Baldwin, and Alexander McRae were loaded into a heavy wagon and moved to Liberty on December 1, escorted by an armed guard. Rigdon was released after three months because of ill health. The others spent four and a half winter months locked in the cellar dungeon or restrained on the main floor of the limestone county jail. While these leaders were imprisoned on charges of treason, arson, murder, burglary, larceny, and theft—based on actions taken in efforts at self-defense—their people fled from Missouri seeking new places of refuge.[30]

The Exodus from Missouri

The passing of October 1838 marked the end of the Latter-day Saint hope for a peaceful home in Missouri. Just as expulsion from Jackson County in 1833 ended the dream of establishing a Zion society in the designated center place, difficulties in Missouri's northwestern counties frustrated Joseph Smith's plan for new stakes of Zion. The governor's order to expel or exterminate the Saints turned the tables on Sidney Rigdon's imprudent indignation speech and made necessary a mass removal. The Latter-day Saints had no option but to accept the spring deadline mandated by General Samuel D. Lucas. After the initial flight of a few settlers even as troops approached Far West, the Saints responded with a slow but steady exodus. Removal started in earnest in early February 1839 and continued at a rapid pace through May. As counseled by their prophet, the Latter-day Saints leaving Missouri chose their own new places of refuge.

Many departed from Missouri in fear; all left filled with frustration. The first to go were several Mormon men who saw the Missouri militia as an immediate threat to their personal freedom. About thirty of David W. Patten's men stood accused of murder and arson for their part in a raid to free hostages claimed by Captain Bogart's state militia during the attack on Crooked River.[31] Fearing execution without a fair trial, these men first arranged for others to transport their families to the ferry crossing of the Mississippi at Quincy, Illinois. Then, as the Missouri militia approached

Far West, they fled northward to the Iowa border and headed east to safety. One group made their way to Warsaw, Illinois. Another party crossed the mile-wide river to Commerce, Illinois. They became the first Latter-day Saints to set foot on what would replace Far West as the site of the headquarters stake.[32]

The hasty departure from Far West of these few was followed gradually by an estimated three thousand or more settlers from Far West and surrounding Caldwell County. Perhaps another two thousand or more left Daviess, Carroll, Clinton, Livingston, and other counties. Besides these "settled" Mormons, another three thousand Saints from the Kirtland area had arrived in northwestern Missouri during the summer and early fall of 1838. In all, at least eight thousand people left their newly adopted western homeland and turned eastward. For Heber C. Kimball, the expulsion was a time of sifting: "The number that had gathered in to this state," he wrote to a friend, "is about ten thousand members. By the first of May there will not be one member left in the state that has any faith."[33]

In the spirit of the terms agreed to at the surrender of Far West, the Saints who could do so made their own plans and left during the winter on schedules that varied depending upon ability and opportunity. Those few families that struck out in mid-January for the two hundred mile trek to the Quincy ferry hit constant snow and rain; they walked from two to eight miles a day through mud and water.[34] More than a hundred families in Far West left during February and March to escape increased harassment by marauders; a few delayed departure until weather improved as the deadline approached. "When spring came, the Mormons left the state as soon as they could," one refugee remembered.

> We were on the road as soon as the snow disappeared. Teams were poor and often two or three families would be loaded into one wagon, but corn and meal were cheap and sometimes the teams were fed too much. The roads were muddy and our progress seemed slow while traveling through the enemy's country.[35]

For many of the Missouri Saints, neither the route to follow nor the ultimate destination was known in advance. To assist the exiles, a church committee of removal dispatched Reuben Hedlock and Levi Richards to Richmond, Missouri, where they helped ship families and their belongings down the Missouri River to the St. Louis area. Some of the Saints

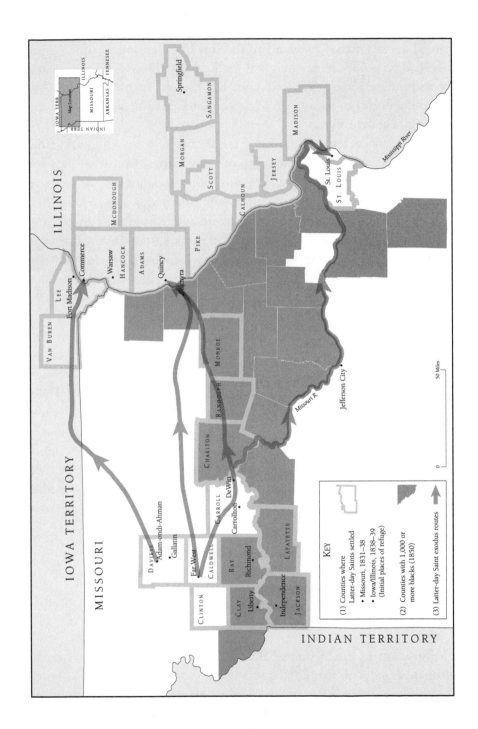

In Search of Refuge, 1838–39

cruised northward to Quincy, Illinois, a major port and one of the finest towns on the upper Mississippi. Ferries there had served many Latter-day Saints heading west from Kirtland in 1838; now the emigrant flow was reversed. An eleven-member refugee committee organized by Mormons at Quincy sought out arriving families at the river's edge and directed them from wintry refugee camps to the comfort of local homes and inns.[36]

The evacuation from Missouri was reported at the time and remembered later by participants as an arduous and exhausting experience. First, they had to fit up and get across the state with household furnishings, food supplies, and the implements of a farm or trade. Then, just as many of the Latter-day Saints reached the Mississippi River landing across from Quincy, river ice began breaking up. Some exiles walked over the frozen portions of the river. Others used skiffs, canoes, or other small boats to navigate the open waters because regular ferries had ceased operation for the season. More than once, Quincy citizens helped rescue Mormon groups stranded on the Missouri side of the river in snow storms without provisions or warm clothing. The citizens "donated liberally, the merchants vying with each other as to which could be the most liberal," a Mormon already living in Quincy said of one rescue effort. "They soon had their contributions together, which filled a very large canoe with flour, pork, coffee, sugar, boots, shoes, and clothing—everything these poor outcasts so much needed." A Latter-day Saint who admitted he couldn't swim volunteered to row the precious cargo across the ice-clogged river and "after much hard labor landed the canoe safely near the camp."[37]

Once they reached Illinois, every fleeing family faced two challenges. They needed a place to settle, even if temporarily, and work to earn a living. The Quincy area offered immediate haven for many, if only a rented room and odd jobs.[38] Jesse W. Johnstun remembered, "Everything was overrun, hundreds of men out of employ, wages very low." His mother rented an empty shell of a room for them at four dollars a month. Johnstun, a responsible thirteen-year-old, found Quincy shops fully staffed but worked a couple of days at a saw mill and then as a mail contractor for six dollars a month.[39] Not all were so lucky. Some exiles became so discouraged with the overcrowding along the Mississippi that they left the region entirely. After six weeks in Quincy, Jesse Haven, single and twenty-five, set off on foot for the East. He reached the home of relatives in Richmond, Massachusetts, in late June after a three-month journey.[40]

In a number of instances, fleeing Mormons found refuge with fellow church members. Wandle Mace, an 1836 convert of Parley P. Pratt in Illinois, had been stopped by bad weather at Quincy while headed west to Missouri in 1838. Mace's rented house served as commissary and meeting place for the Mormon refugee committee at Quincy and for church gatherings. As a makeshift inn, it became a shelter from the cold and storms. Mace later recalled, "Many nights the floors both up stairs and downstairs were so closely covered with beds, it was impossible to set a foot anywhere, without stepping upon someone's bed." The families of Joseph Young and John Taylor lived there all winter. Taylor used Mace's lathe to turn butter prints (used for imprinting patterns into fresh butter), bench screws, and other items to make a living. Israel Barlow boarded there and married the nurse who cared for Mace's wife during a February birthing. When the Maces left Quincy later that year, they moved to the old fort at Montrose, Iowa.[41]

Inland from Quincy, on the road toward Jacksonville and Springfield, were additional opportunities. The migrants found farms and houses to rent throughout Adams County and beyond. Other Latter-day Saints scattered into the northeastern quadrant of the county between Carthage and La Harpe, at such places as Ramus and Fountain Green.[42] Some of the refugees found an oasis of tolerance in St. Louis, where sympathetic newspapers were encouraging fund-raising for the Mormon exiles. Others found temporary refuge even farther south in Missouri. The Zodak Judd family spent two years farming at Bloomfield, in southeastern Missouri, and then a year just outside Springfield, Illinois, before joining his brother's family south of Warsaw in 1842.[43]

Although most of the Saints succeeded in getting themselves out of northwestern Missouri and settled in a safe haven, some lacked the means to do so. Under normal circumstances, the bishop of the church would have managed relief for the poor. Missouri's bishop, Edward Partridge, one of those tried and released at Richmond in November, was himself destitute and in failing health. He moved to Quincy and by February was helping with relocation there.[44]

Remaining in Missouri were the two senior members of the Twelve, Brigham Young and Heber C. Kimball, and the newly ordained apostle John Taylor. Joined by the Prophet's uncle John Smith, brother Don Carlos Smith, and others, they called for a mass meeting in Far West to organize for the task ahead. In a demonstration of their fulfilling their religious obligations to the poor, the Saints in Caldwell County agreed to share their resources. Groups were formed in late January 1839 to accomplish specific tasks to aid those financially unable to leave Missouri. Chairman John Taylor's committee of the remaining apostles and others agreed to petition upper Missouri residents for help. William Huntington headed an eleven-member body that assumed the "arduous task" of getting the poor safely out of harm's way.[45]

To encourage a united removal effort, Brigham Young proposed that the Saints sign a covenant making their surplus property available for the committee's use. Sensitive to the issue of control that had alienated some church members in Jackson County, Huntington's group made two allowances. First, they preserved agency: the Saints could give priority to their own needs and could volunteer help independent of the committee if they wished. Second, the committee promised to keep careful records and to refund surplus property. Young secured eighty subscribers immediately, plus another three hundred the next day.[46] The solicitation of resources continued for weeks—in Far West among those with known wealth, at a conference in Quincy, and via a traveling delegate to church members in the eastern United States.[47]

Another financial resource needing attention was the abandoned property owned by the church and its members in Missouri. Earlier revelation had prohibited its sale, but Joseph Smith now counseled property owners to move ahead. Committeeman Alanson Ripley secured the power of attorney from private Mormon landowners as far afield as Quincy. With the Prophet's blessing, the committee assigned Charles Bird and David W. Rogers to sell church holdings in Missouri. These two set off for Independence in mid-March and returned a month later claiming to have sold all the lands in Zion. Elias Smith sold his holdings at one-fourth their value.[48]

The committee of removal turned its attention to the needs of destitute families. An initial survey in Caldwell County located thirty-nine families without wagons, a number that later increased to nearly one hundred. The committee arranged for as many as possible of these families to sail with their goods from Richmond on riverboats down the Missouri River to Quincy, Illinois, an option recommended by a church relocation committee in Quincy. Others went overland to the ferries operating at several crossing places along the mile-wide Mississippi. The committee contracted ferriage for departing families and placed caches of corn along the road between Far West and the ferry landings.[49]

Committee members first looked after the families of the First Presidency and other Latter-day Saint prisoners. On February 6, Stephen Markham and an unnamed family started on the nine-day trip to the Mississippi with Emma Smith and her children in a carriage sent from Quincy. The Prophet's family found refuge for themselves four miles east of Quincy with Judge John and Sarah Cleveland. A week later, Joseph Sr. and Lucy Mack Smith left Far West in their wagon pulled by an ox team. The Prophet's father agreed to leave the appointed gathering place for Quincy only after a revelation from his imprisoned son satisfied him that it was the Lord's will.[50]

On April 6, a Saturday, the Missourians in Daviess County delivered a petition to Far West demanding that all remaining Latter-day Saints leave Caldwell County within a week. The committee on removal scoured the countryside for teams to transport people the twenty-five miles to Tenney's Grove. At that way station, crews chopped firewood, furnished cornmeal ground at the committee's horse mill at Far West, and slaughtered livestock for meat. By April 15, three days beyond the deadline, the last of the destitute families was out of Far West. Shortly afterward, the Saints at Tenney's Grove were on their way to Illinois.[51]

The removal of the Saints from Far West did not satisfy the Missouri enforcers. They entered the settlement and smashed tables, windows, clocks, and other property of the committee and a few other remaining residents. The church committee gathered up what they could but left behind several thousand dollars' worth of property that had been contributed to help the poor. The loss of many of the committee's financial records in the hasty retreat made their promised accounting infeasible. Nonetheless, the Latter-day Saint commitment to remove the poor had been met. It was an experience that would prove useful for the future. With its job completed, the committee on removal disbanded and fled.[52]

During all this time, Joseph Smith and his companions remained incarcerated at Liberty, and Parley P. Pratt and others languished in Richmond. The prisoners at neither place accepted their fate quietly. Both groups worked vigorously through legal appeals and grassroots petitions to win release from their Missouri captors. Sidney Rigdon won his

After nearly six months as prisoners in Liberty, Missouri, Joseph Smith and four others were allowed to escape in April 1839 while being moved from their Daviess County cell to Boone County.

freedom on a plea of habeas corpus in January 1839 before Judge Joel Turnham of Clay County. His jailers helped Rigdon sneak out of town during the night. Similar writs submitted by the others failed. So did two attempts to break free.[53]

In the long run, it was the incessant petitioning for legal relief that brought release. These appeals took place on two fronts and over a long period of time, first through the courts and then in appeals to government officials. To aid in their defense against the first Missouri indictments in September 1838, Joseph Smith and Sydney Rigdon had even begun the study of law with their attorneys, David R. Atchison and Alexander W. Doniphan, whom they considered the finest counsel available in upper Missouri. Because of Judge Austin A. King's anti-Mormon bias, the prisoners avoided appeals to the Fifth Circuit Court.[54] Instead, they turned to other local courts and twice sought help from the Missouri Supreme Court. Each unsuccessful petition recited the facts of the illegal hearings, recounted false testimony, and pointed out failed justice.

The more effective approach reached beyond the local courts to state lawmakers and officials. Even though state officers lacked the power under

Missouri's strong county government system to interfere locally, they could exercise leverage in the crisis. During the winter of 1838–39, the Missouri legislature considered material on the "Mormon War" submitted to it for study by Governor Lilburn Boggs. With legal action still pending and to avoid jeopardizing a fair trial, legislators twice recommended against further consideration of the governor's message. By July, the pressure to resolve the matter had quieted; the issue remained unresolved.[55] When a new legislative session began in December 1840, debates over the governor's missive once again divided delegates. Those embarrassed by the unchecked vigilante action against the Saints and the resulting condemnation by the national press encouraged an unbiased examination to clear the state's name. In the end, however, lawmakers opposed to Mormon expansion and others seeking to hide their own participation in the vigilante action prevailed. The House took no action.[56] The same fate met Latter-day Saint appeals for redress for lost property and requests for an impartial trial for Joseph Smith.[57]

In a final effort, Heber C. Kimball and Theodore Turley personally carried entreaties to state officials on behalf of the prisoners. After failing to find Governor Boggs in Jefferson City, they rode hundreds of miles only to learn that state supreme court justices would not issue writs of habeas corpus because of flaws in the legal documents. Nevertheless, the secretary of state, though lacking the authority to intervene, chastised Judge King in writing for holding the prisoners on such flimsy evidence.[58]

With national opinion strongly opposing the state's insensitivity to the civil rights of the Mormons,[59] with the legislature stalled, and with the need to prove or relinquish the claims against the prisoners ever present, it was time to act. On their way back to Far West in early April 1839, Kimball and Turley informed Judge King of their visit to Jefferson City. Angered that state officials had been informed of the case, the judge ordered all visitors barred from the county jail. Kimball and Turley nevertheless reported their trip to the prisoners through the iron bars of the dungeon. Then they headed to Far West. Two days later, on April 6, 1839, Joseph Smith and his fellow prisoners at Liberty were loaded into wagons. The drivers headed toward Daviess County for a hearing before Judge King at Gallatin. According to the prisoners, it was a drunken judge and grand jury that heard the case on April 11. The jury indicted the Prophet and his brother Hyrum, Lyman Wight, Alexander McRae, and Caleb Baldwin for murder, treason, burglary, arson, larceny, theft, and stealing.[60]

Because the legislature had granted the prisoners the right to seek a change of venue upon their own affidavit, they selected Boone County. On April 15, they set off for Columbia under a heavy guard commanded by Daviess County sheriff William Morgan and assisted by former sheriff William Bowman and three other men. According to Hyrum Smith, after traveling twenty miles, the prisoners "bought a jug of whiskey, with which we treated the company." Morgan showed his prisoners an undated, unsigned order and told them that the issuing justice had instructed him "never to carry us to Boon[e] county, and never to show the mittimus." The sheriff then said, "I shall take a good drink of grog and go to bed; and you may do as you have a mind to." Three other guards followed this example, drank freely of whisky that had been sweetened with honey, and were soon asleep in bed. The sole remaining guard helped the men saddle the horses. For their "negligence" of duty, Morgan and Bowman were roughed up by angered citizens of Gallatin. On April 22, Joseph Smith and his companions rejoined friends and family in Quincy. Their assisted escape granted them freedom, but the unresolved legal charges would yet again become a hindrance for the Prophet and his people.[61]

Release of the prisoners at Liberty left several others still under guard in Richmond. Two of them were dismissed on April 24 after a grand jury heard their case. Those remaining were granted an appeal to Judge King for a change of venue. In late May, they were moved to Columbia, in Boone County. While awaiting a trial, they planned and executed an Independence Day escape.[62]

Americans and the editors of the popular press responded to the "Mormon War" in Missouri with differing perspectives. Some saw the Mormons as law-abiding citizens whose constitutional rights had been violated by Missouri's citizens. In this view, the Missouri vigilante groups acted outside the law when they resolved tensions by robbing, raping, pillaging, and expelling the Mormons. The Latter-day Saints and their friends applauded this interpretation. In contrast, other editors characterized the Latter-day Saints as a rebellious, lawless group of religious zealots undeserving of the same rights as other Americans. This was the anti-Mormon viewpoint in Missouri. It applied the stereotype of other disfranchised people to the Saints and saw them as murderers, robbers, bandits, thieves, and counterfeiters. The two perspectives, though over-simplified in this summary, shared a common feeling that a lawless element had denied good citizens their rights.[63] Another view, held by people from many backgrounds, concluded that the Latter-day Saints were a distinctive people, defined by a religion that outlined a complete way of life. They created political strength by forming close bonds within a community or region. Their differences as a people simply made it impractical to live among others not part of their community.[64]

The lawless actions of their Missouri neighbors left deep, negative feelings with the Latter-day Saints. The refugees sometimes wondered if the answer to it all might not be another Zion's Camp—an armed invasion to recover their lost inheritances. Six members of the Twelve, preparing for a missionary journey to the British Isles, tempered these feelings in an epistle written in July 1839. Be patient in affliction was the message, echoing the Prophet's own counsel from Liberty Jail: Leave judgment to God.[65]

The friendly welcome in Illinois would soften the effects of the expulsion. Even though the Saints wanted to redeem their Missouri lands, they would set aside military options. For a half dozen years ahead, they would instead seek to redress the inequities committed against them by using legal supplications, public pleas, and presidential entreaties. They would exercise patience, but they would not soon forget the wrongs of Missouri.[66]

CHAPTER 3

A Beautiful Place of Rest

*I would suggest . . . that our brethren scattered abroad who understand
the spirit of the gathering . . . fall into the places of refuge and safety that
God shall open unto them between Kirtland and Far West . . . in the
most safe and quiet places they can find . . . until God shall open a more
effectual door for us.*

—JOSEPH SMITH, LIBERTY JAIL, MARCH 20, 1839

In early March 1839, Joseph Smith received at Liberty Jail a packet of letters from Bishop Edward Partridge and his associates in Quincy. The
refugees shared rumors of Smith's pending release and reported on the
growing number of displaced Saints congregating in and around Quincy.
Included were letters from Isaac Galland of Commerce, Illinois, to David
W. Rogers and Israel Barlow. Galland, who owned land in both
Commerce and across the river in Iowa, offered to help find rental homes
and farms for the Saints in both places. He claimed that territorial governor Robert Lucas had promised the Saints a safe refuge in Iowa.[1]

After reviewing the letters, Joseph Smith dictated a long response to
Bishop Partridge and the church. Among other things, the Prophet offered
observations on the pressing question of relocating the Saints. His sug-
gestions would set a course for settlement and lead to the creation of a
new headquarters city in western Illinois.

Joseph Smith moved cautiously on the issue of a concentrated relocation. For years, the Saints had longed to realize the Lord's counsel in a

December 1833 revelation to "gather together and stand in holy places."² Earlier in March, Joseph had authorized the Saints to sell their property in Missouri or to trade for available land elsewhere. "Concerning the places for the location of the Saints," he wrote, "we cannot counsel you as we could if we were present with you. And as to the things that were written heretofore we did not consider them any thing very binding," he told Partridge. Weighing present circumstances, the Prophet advised that those who understood the spirit of the gathering should seek a place of refuge and safety somewhere between Kirtland and Far West "in the most safe and quiet places they can find" until the Lord opened other doors.³

Perhaps that open door was the offered land in Commerce and Iowa. Willing to accept aid from helpful friends, the Prophet said that he was impressed to encourage church agents to secure a contract for Galland's land. He felt it wise to cultivate a friendship with the seller as long as "he shall prove himself to be a man of honor and a friend to humanity."⁴ Not wishing to mandate either of these solutions, Smith advised Partridge to counsel with available authorities and together find their own answer to the questions. He agreed to review minutes of their meetings and correct the leaders, "by the word of the Lord," if necessary.⁵

Joseph Smith soon would be personally involved in the question of defining a new Mormon community and in selecting Commerce, in Hancock County, Illinois, and Lee County, Iowa, as two sites among many for gathering places. Smith informed Galland that when he was freed he would personally sign a contract purchasing Galland's land if no one else had done so.⁶

Even though Joseph Smith left open to individual members the entire West between Ohio and Missouri as a field in which to find religious refuge, his acceptance of Galland's offer meant that the next attempt at defining a headquarters community would take place on lands in two counties on opposite sides of the Mississippi River. On the east side, at a wide bend in the river would rise a city of peace echoing the pattern of the New Jerusalem. Across the river, in the Half Breed Tract recently vacated by Native Americans, the Prophet would soon envision a New Zarahemla, a city of hope.⁷

THE WELCOME IN ILLINOIS

When Joseph Smith crossed into Illinois, he found a large number of exiled church members at Quincy, the region's principal town, with a population exceeding fifteen hundred.[8] Many other Saints had scattered beyond Adams County, wherever homes and farms could be found to rent or buy. The people of Illinois who offered much-needed help reacted with genuine reprehension against Missouri's extermination order, which they labeled illegal and cruel. For various reasons, the old citizens of Illinois and neighboring Iowa welcomed the exiles without much initial prejudice against this "peculiar people."

The kindly interaction of the Quincy Democratic Association with Latter-day Saint leaders and agents exemplified this friendly response with an outpouring of philanthropic sympathy. On February 25, 1839, Quincy Democrats appointed merchant J. W. Whitney to head an investigative committee. Whitney invited Mormon spokesmen to identify needs. A church committee led by Elias Higbee found only two dozen destitute widows and poor families but cataloged the consequences of the expulsion and prioritized needs: "We have been robbed of our corn, wheat, horses, cattle, cows, hogs, wearing apparel, houses and homes, and, indeed, of all that renders life tolerable," Higbee wrote. "We think that to give us employment, rent us farms, and allow us the protection and privileges of other citizens, would raise us from a state of dependence."[9]

In an effort to offer genuine help and to minimize local prejudices, Whitney's committee denounced the Missourians for their injustice and pledged that Illinois citizens would be "guided and directed by that charity which never faileth." The committee encouraged association members to lead out in finding jobs for the immigrants and reassured local workers that the job-hungry newcomers would not depress wages. The exiles, Whitney said, sought only "to procure something to save them from starving." They should not be viewed as a despised religious minority but as American citizens "entitled to our sympathy and kindest regard." The association solicited donations of cash, clothing, and provisions from its own members, from the Quincy Grays (the local militia), and from citizens at large. They raised one hundred dollars locally and signed endorsements for Latter-day Saint fund-raisers to use in St. Louis and New York City.[10]

Behind the warmth of the humanitarian welcome in Illinois lay other motivations as well. Located midway between St. Louis, Missouri, and Rock Island, Illinois, the Adams County seat acted as a river port for agricultural exporting and commerce. It served twelve thousand county residents and influenced others as the region's largest town. At the time, the state was suffering under a severe national economic depression, the Panic of 1837. Hundreds of destitute Latter-day Saints would be a welcome stimulus to the sluggish economy of Adams County as they purchased necessities or rented houses and farms. Sensing an economic benefit to themselves, Whitney and his associates—public-spirited merchants, lawyers, editors, doctors, and government officials—welcomed the Latter-day Saints.

They recognized as well political opportunities resulting from an infusion of new people. The local Democratic party was a key player in Quincy's public life, and its influence extended outward into rural northwestern Illinois. The community and county had been named in 1822 for John Quincy Adams, an independent-minded member of the national Democratic-Republican party, who was Secretary of State at the time. Adams's defeat of Andrew Jackson in the 1825 presidential election created a schism within their party and the subsequent creation of the Whigs. The citizens of Quincy in the 1830s and 1840s vacillated between the policies of the Jacksonian Democrats and those of the Whigs. With existing support almost equally divided between the two parties, both Whigs and Democrats began to contend for Mormon sympathy. The *Quincy Whig* denounced Democratic persecution in Missouri as immoral and Democratic charitable efforts in Illinois as an attempt to win votes. The Democratic *Quincy Argus* implemented the resolutions of the party's public meeting by condemning Missouri and her radical politicians as well as the local Whigs for their vote seeking.[11]

Latter-day Saint activist Lyman Wight, a forty-three-year-old New Yorker who had recently served in the Adam-ondi-Ahman stake presidency, joined in politicizing Quincy's humanitarian efforts. Despite cautions from local church members, Wight published three letters in the *Quincy Whig* criticizing Missouri Democrats for instigating the anti-Mormon mob actions. His comments offended Illinois Democrats, including some in state office. It was a delicate situation for Joseph Smith. Remembering the Missouri apostasies and interpersonal controversies, he

The businesses of Quincy served residents of Adams County and, by ferry connection, those across the Mississippi in Missouri.

wished neither to interfere with Wight's political opinions nor to alienate the charitable Quincy Democrats. Officially, he wanted to maintain political neutrality. A First Presidency letter published in the *Whig* thanked Quincy citizens for their support and defended Wight's freedom to speak out. The leaders added, "We disclaim any intention of making a political question of our difficulties with Missouri."[12]

Joseph Smith did not wish to offend Wight, "an old fellow prisoner" at Liberty Jail. The Missouri difficulties had helped the Prophet realize the importance of tolerance toward his trusted associates despite the difficulties they had caused. He would apply that principle in Nauvoo, sometimes with undesirable results. In a personal note to Wight, whom he would ordain an apostle two years later, he expressed confidence in Wight's good intentions but counseled him to avoid "making the Church appear as either supporting or opposing you in your politics."[13] The question of Latter-day Saint influence in politics would survive the move to western Illinois and grow with Nauvoo's burgeoning population.

THE WESTERN ILLINOIS FRONTIER

The eventual replacement for the abandoned headquarters settlement in Missouri was fifty miles upriver from Quincy on a peninsula-like piece of land jutting out into the Mississippi River. This place at the head of the Des Moines Rapids would soon be renamed Nauvoo. It had been identified by many visitors as one of the most beautiful sites along the river for many miles. A large, level floodplain with wooded bluffs beyond, it measured about two miles north to south and a mile east to west. The flatland rose gently toward the east, nestling against bluffs that rose seventy feet above the river. Small streams of water from the prairie to the east cut through the bluffs toward the river in ravines, nurturing groves of native oak, black walnut, butternut, birch, elm, locust, and sugar maple trees. In its general contours, the bluff at the bend in the river was not unlike a similar peninsular site along Missouri's Grand River that just a year earlier Joseph Smith had named Adam-ondi-Ahman.

Nearly forty years before the arrival of the Latter-day Saints, Native Americans abandoned the last of a series of agricultural villages on this Illinois site. They were led by a minor chieftain, Quashquema, who oversaw perhaps fifty Algonquin Indians of the confederated Sauk and Fox tribe. Migrants to Illinois from the Lake Michigan area, they later abandoned their bark lodges and moved west of the Mississippi.[14] William Ewing, a government Indian agent, lived among them for a time, as did Denis Julien, a St. Louis trader, who later became a western fur trapper. Major Zebulon Pike visited the site in 1805 during his expedition seeking out sites for military posts and the source of the Mississippi and Missouri rivers. Not long before they moved from the peninsula, the Indians helped Pike's exploring party get around the Des Moines Rapids.[15]

American military policy significantly influenced settlement patterns and the availability of land in the upper Mississippi River Valley. In response to Pike's report, the United States government established several army posts. Those affecting Mormon settlement were Fort Des Moines, south of present Montrose, Iowa, established after the Indian Removal Act of 1830, and Fort Edwards, founded in 1814 at the junction of the Des Moines River with the Mississippi. Barracks at Fort Des Moines provided a temporary refuge for the Saints fleeing from Missouri in 1839. By the time Fort Edwards was abandoned in 1824, a civilian population had assembled to form the beginnings of the town of Warsaw. In the 1840s Warsaw became a major competitor with Nauvoo for river trade and for political dominance in Hancock County.[16]

Military policy also helped veterans of the War of 1812 get farmland in the West. In Illinois, most of the region south of Rock Island between the Illinois and Mississippi Rivers was set aside as the Illinois Military Tract. Even though some veterans homesteaded their 160-acre claims as permanent settlers, many gave up after a short stay. Others sold their rights to land speculators at prices ranging from fifty cents to $1.50 an acre. It was from such speculators that Joseph Smith purchased some of the parcels of land that became Nauvoo.[17]

As the prairies opened up, publicity brought in a wave of settlers from the British Isles and later another one from northern Europe. These immigrants opposed slavery and prided themselves on becoming freeholders through their own hard work. Many of them found homes on the northern and central Illinois plains. In the twenty years following statehood in 1818, population density in the military tract tripled from two people per square mile to six. Density in other regions reached eighteen persons per square mile.[18]

To make way for this energetic influx, Native Americans along the upper Mississippi were pressured to relinquish their farms in treaties signed at St. Louis in 1804 and at Chicago in 1816. Not all of the Indians left willingly, however. Black Hawk led a thousand supporters in a resistance movement in 1832 that ended in the slaughter of 90 percent of those who followed him back to their former lands in Illinois. Afterward, a fifty-mile strip in Iowa called the Black Hawk Purchase was removed from Native American control and opened to white farmers.[19] To protect a new boundary between white expansion and the Sauk and Fox territory, in 1834 the army established Fort Des Moines, with Lieutenant Colonel Stephen W. Kearny in charge. When the army abandoned the post in 1837, a few white families in nearby Cut Nose Village renamed their community Montrose.[20] With Native American claims resolved, the Iowa region was prime for expanded white settlement. The fertile military tract across the river in western Illinois already was attracting large numbers of settlers and speculative investors.

SETTLEMENT AND SPECULATION

The formation of towns and governments on the riverside parcels that later became Nauvoo began with the arrival of white settlers in the 1820s. The growth of a settlement there paralleled the development of Warsaw downstream at Fort Edwards. The two emerging communities quickly became competitors for political influence in the region. Hints of the rivalry appeared first when residents at the site of Quashquema's Indian village at the head of the rapids petitioned Illinois legislators to create Hancock County to localize services for the people of what then was northern Adams County.

Among these petitioners was Captain James White. He had moved to the peninsula to tend to a flourishing keelboating business he had started while homesteading in the Half Breed Tract near Montrose, Iowa. With him came an extended family: his two sons, Alexander and Hugh, a son-in-law, Isaac Campbell, and their wives and children. The men unloaded the deep-river steamers, moved the cargo through the rapids, and loaded cargoes onto the smaller steamers navigating the upper Mississippi. The Whites may have lived in the log house reportedly built by Denis Julien half a mile downstream from the wharf at the head of the rapids. In 1824, according to family tradition, White paid the Indians two hundred sacks of corn to secure title to his quarter section.[21] Five years later, he built a handsome limestone dwelling using local stone and lumber. The two-and-a-half-story structure soon became a center for the social and political life of the emerging village.[22]

Active in Adams County politics, James White functioned as one of its three county commissioners. He served with his neighbors George Y. Cutler and Luther Whitney as judges of the fall election at Fort Edwards in 1829 that picked officers for the newly created Hancock County. Citizens elected the experienced White along with Cutler and Henry Nichols as the new county's first commissioners. These officers held quarterly commission meetings and all court sessions at White's new stone house.[23]

White's extended family and other settlers purchased land both on the flats and above on the bluffs extending eastward toward the prairie. Before long, homesteaders had built at least twenty homes within a mile radius of James White's limestone dwelling. As yet, these citizens had no town organization or formal name for the settlement beyond its identification as the place "at the head of the rapids." On March 13, 1830, in response to a petition from county commissioners, the United States Postmaster General named George Y. Cutler postmaster of a new post office to be known as Venus.[24]

At that time, Hancock County had only five hundred scattered residents. As the quarterly commissioners court and probate and circuit courts moved from place to place to meet the needs of citizens, the

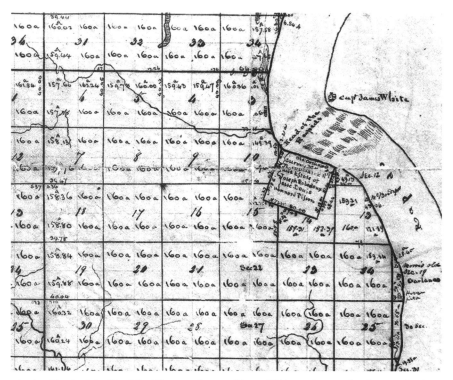

At the Head of the Rapids. *The stone house of James White and an orchard across the river on the estate of Joseph Robedeaux are features documented in this 1833 map of the region later settled by Latter-day Saint exiles.*

question arose of establishing a permanent county seat. Promoters at Fort Edwards (later Warsaw) most actively sought the honor. By then the largest town in the county, Fort Edwards was a thriving center of keelboat traffic and an export center for grain and livestock to St. Louis and other markets. Ignoring the plea from Fort Edwards, a county study committee followed an emerging Illinois pattern. They placed the seat of government at Carthage, a new settlement of scattered residents near the county's geographical center. For the residents of Venus, Carthage was an eighteen-mile trip southeastward along the Carthage Road. Carthage citizens applied for a post office immediately, and the state permitted the town to incorporate in 1837. Meanwhile, county commissioners hired a local builder to erect a courthouse of round logs in the summer of 1833. Six years later, they replaced it with a new building closer to the center of town. Another county necessity was a jail, completed in 1841 next to the

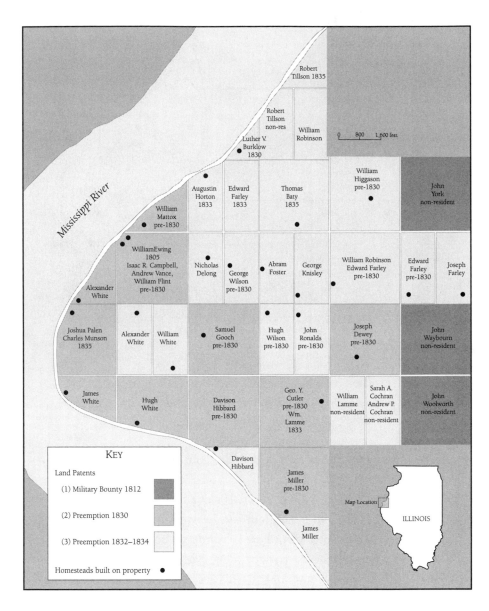

Homesteaders and Speculators on the Peninsula

The stone house built by James White (center) served as a meeting place for the first Hancock County commissioners. Sidney Rigdon later operated a post office there for Commerce and early Nauvoo.

original courthouse at a cost of $4,105. It was a two-story red sandstone building, providing space for the jailer's family and, upstairs, an extra bedroom and a small, secure iron cage for prisoners.[25]

While Carthage was establishing the structures of governance, citizens served by the Venus post office recognized in their cluster of settlers the potential for an important town.[26] Local landowners Alexander White and Joseph Teas surveyed a townsite and recorded it in county records as Venus. They sold a dozen or so lots, but their expectations of a growing city did not materialize.[27] By 1834, prospects for growth looked better, so White and Teas expanded their plat for Venus along the river northward and renamed it Commerce, a moniker reflecting hope for economic growth. Twenty-four of the town's 144 lots fronted the river, an appropriate location for keelboating and warehousing enterprises. Further expansion was possible, because the proprietors owned much of the adjoining land. The county approved the surveyor's plat in May.[28] The name Venus gradually dropped out of use after Commerce became the sole mailing address for the peninsula.

By 1835, changing times had replaced Quashquema's abandoned Indian village and its bark lodges with a small town and a few log and frame homes. In the speculators' dreams for quick fortunes for themselves, the flats along the river bore promise of becoming a thriving commercial center. These expectations were part of the general optimism found throughout western America in the mid-1830s. The United States government had a multi-million-dollar cash surplus and a reliable currency backed through the Second United States Bank with gold or silver. New factories, their products protected by high tariffs, were foreshadowing a great industrial revolution. Cities were springing up all along the large rivers of the country. Especially was this noticeable in the Mississippi Valley. At St. Louis, people arrived faster than houses could be built. Unemployment was unheard of in the city, and laborers were in demand by burgeoning industries. St. Louis land speculators were reporting profits of as much as 1,000 percent in two years as farmland was divided into city lots. Upstream and down, on both sides of the Mississippi, promoters surveyed scores of townsites, recorded them at county seats, and spread their advertising brochures proclaiming the coming greatness of their cities. Each sponsor envisioned for his own proposal a second St. Louis.

Feeding the growth was an increasing foreign migration, particularly from the British Isles and the Germanic states of northern Europe. America's constitutional self-government appealed to people living under monarchies in lands surrounded by constant threats of war. Just as alluring to many was the chance to buy land inexpensively, almost an impossibility in Europe. Immigrants flocking to buy cheap land found it easily in the Great Lakes area and in the Midwest.

In the expansionist spirit of the age, Commerce, Illinois, was but one of many towns awaiting buyers for its platted lots and available farms. By the time the first Mormons visited Commerce, the early promoters of the area were gone, victims of the devastating national Panic of 1837. The Latter-day Saints would meet and deal with others who had replaced the White family and who would have an influence extending throughout and beyond the Mormon era.

One of those who befriended the Saints was Hiram Kimball, who arrived at Commerce from Vermont in 1835. Soon afterward, he set up his mercantile business and became a land agent for absentee family members. The Kimballs purchased hundreds of acres in the Commerce area when land values dropped during the economic slump.[29]

Another friend to the Saints was Kimball's neighbor Daniel H. Wells, an emigrant from New York in 1834. Among his landholdings was an eighty-acre parcel of land strategically situated on the bluff overlooking Commerce.[30]

A third important settler on the peninsula was Amos Davis, a Vermont native, who arrived at Commerce in the fall of 1836. Not quite twenty-two at the time, Davis married Elvira Hibbard, daughter of Davison Hibbard, one of the original land patentees. The couple purchased two lots from Hiram Kimball in Commerce. Amos may have worked in Kimball's store, but by 1838 he owned his own mercantile business, operated a tavern, and held the franchise for the Commerce-to-Montrose ferry. A surviving store ledger for May 1839 lists ninety-five active credit accounts, many of them farmers homesteading parcels on the peninsula and to the east. The Panic of 1837 may have dampened land business in Commerce, but Davis served a growing regional clientele and carried on a brisk trade with steamer captains, to whom he sold cordwood, grain, and local meat and dairy products.[31]

The original land purchases by the Latter-day Saints were negotiated with Isaac Galland and with an Eastern land syndicate. Galland was a developer of Keokuk, Iowa, and agent for thousands of acres in Iowa's Half Breed Tract. At Commerce, where he lived and served as postmaster, he owned the 47.17 acres of James White's tract, including the stone house, as well as the Alexander White home and adjacent lots.[32]

A second speculative town had been created in April 1837 north and west of Commerce. It was carved out of a five-hundred-acre parcel purchased over the previous two years by absentee landlords Horace R. Hotchkiss, John Gillet, and Smith Tuttle.[33] The new townsite contained 376 lots of about 8,000 square feet each, with sixteen lots in each block. In contrast, the older Commerce plat had eight lots per block, each with 11,925 square feet. Hotchkiss and his associates promoted Commerce City with advertising handbills promising public parks and gardens, a town hall, hotel, and commercial warehouses, even though the official plat designated no land for public facilities. Lots were offered at a minimum price of $250. At an auction in May 1837, half a dozen bids were entered. Nobody actually built anything in Commerce City. Like so many speculators on the Illinois-Iowa frontier, the Hotchkiss syndicate owned only a "city on paper."[34] The venture was ill-timed. The initial sale failed just as news reached Hancock County that major United States banks had suspended specie payments for currency. The great Panic of 1837, brooding since March, unleashed its gloomy portents upon the nation. Local banks failed everywhere (including the Mormon bank at Kirtland). Inflated prices for land quickly deflated as the bottom fell out of the real estate market.

A RESTING PLACE FOR THE SAINTS

It was this buyers' market that the fleeing Latter-day Saints discovered in the upper Mississippi Valley. Mormon militiaman Israel Barlow, making his way across Iowa and into the Keokuk area, encountered Isaac Galland. Learning that Galland wished to help the Saints find shelter at Commerce and farms near Fort Des Moines, Barlow hurried on to Quincy. There he convinced a meeting of Latter-day Saints chaired by John P. Greene that the offer should be investigated.[35] Departing around February 1, Barlow and David W. Rogers traveled to Commerce, where they claimed to find as many as forty empty dwellings in the area. After making tentative arrangements to rent them, the agents crossed the Mississippi River to examine the military barracks built at Fort Des Moines during the Black Hawk War. These they estimated would house upwards of fifty families.[36]

The two men reported their findings in Quincy ten days later at a meeting chaired by William Marks, a former Kirtland high councilor. The explorers had set off to find winter housing and had done so. Beyond that, they had returned with information that raised a larger question. Only two high-level church authorities were available in Quincy, the former Campbellite colleagues Sidney Rigdon, a counselor in the First Presidency since 1832, and Edward Partridge, the guileless hatmaker who had been named the first bishop in 1831. The two had been released from Missouri jails and expelled from the state. One other high councilor besides Marks was in town, Elias Higbee, who had served in Missouri. Partridge, Marks, and Higbee all attended the meeting; Rigdon is not mentioned in the minutes. John P. Greene, spokesman for the agents, explained "that a liberal offer had been made by a gentleman [Galland], of about twenty thousand acres, lying between the Mississippi and Des Moines rivers, at two dollars per acre, to be paid in twenty annual installments, without interest." Rogers and Barlow encouraged purchase of the property. Marks tentatively supported the idea but wondered whether "we should again gather together."[37]

The question of gathering was on everyone's mind that winter. When Albert P. Rockwood arrived in Quincy near the end of January after a miserable twelve-day trek from Far West, the word circulating was "that the Prophet's advice for the brethren [was] to scatter, hold no meetings in this place, and be wise servants that the wrath of the enemy be not kindled against us." Rockwood wrote to his father, "It is thought by some we shall not gather again in large bodies at present, still we do not know. Our leader is gone. We have none to tell us what to do by direct revelation."[38] Marks wondered aloud if the consolidated settlements in Caldwell and Daviess Counties had not been a significant factor in the Saints' expulsion from Missouri. Even so, he was willing to support the purchase of a new Iowa gathering place, "providing that it was the will of the Lord that we should again gather together." He proposed an open discussion, convinced that, even in the absence of the Prophet, if "the brethren would speak their minds, the Lord would undoubtedly manifest His will by His Spirit." Barlow offered another theory of the persecutions—that the Saints had brought it upon themselves through their failure in "building according to the pattern." His explanation echoed the Fishing River revelation of 1834, which blamed the loss of Jackson County on the unwillingness of the Saints to live the law of consecration.[39]

After Mace encouraged "an immediate gathering," Bishop Partridge turned the thinking in the other direction. He "thought it was not expedient under the present circumstances to collect together, but thought it was better to scatter into different parts and provide for the poor, which would be acceptable to God." The bishop's comments convinced Higbee to abandon his strong support for the purchase. After hearing several other speakers, those at the meeting voted unanimously "that it would not be deemed advisable to locate on the lands for the present." Rogers so informed Galland in a letter written February 11. Even with this decision, which Sidney Rigdon supported, Partridge, Rigdon, and Higbee traveled to Commerce sometime between February 17 and 23 in company with Barlow as their guide. Hoping to meet Galland, they stopped at the old stone house, but the land dealer was away.[40]

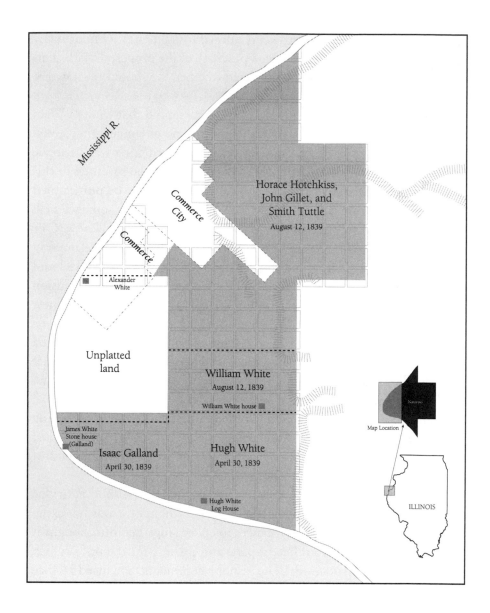

Church Purchases and Original Plat of Nauvoo

Meanwhile, like Isaac Galland, the Hotchkiss syndicate welcomed inquiries from Mormon agents. Since first advertising Commerce City lots for sale in May 1837, the Hotchkiss partners had sold only one lot and still lacked clear title to all of their land. The Latter-day Saints were without funds but had much in their favor as potential buyers. First, they owned thousands of acres of improved farmland in Missouri. They could not return to their lands, but they could sell or trade. Second, they had a reputation as hard-working people of integrity with a strong sense of community cooperation. Even during the economic depression caused by the Panic of 1837, they had built up Far West, Missouri, and had commenced other cities.

With these factors in their favor, the Saints were able to buy property in the Commerce area. Joseph Smith had urged acceptance of Galland's offer in his March 20, 1839, letter from Liberty advising Mormon agents "to lay hold of every door that shall seem to be opened unto them to obtain foothold on the Earth."[41] Galland was especially anxious to be helpful. In late February, the former minister informed one of the Mormon agents that although a stranger to the Saints and uninformed of "the doctrine, order or practice of the church," he saw himself as a friend, "both towards you collectively, as a people, and individually as sufferers." Joseph Smith responded with a long letter reviewing Mormon sufferings and outlining church beliefs. In a postscript, he accepted Galland's offer.[42]

In late April, the Prophet led a party north from Quincy to examine available lands on both sides of the Mississippi. On May 1, at Commerce, the men purchased the farms of Hugh White and Isaac Galland near the south end of the peninsula. For White's farm of 123.4 acres, the Prophet, his brother Hyrum, and Sidney Rigdon signed notes for five thousand dollars. For Galland's smaller 47.17-acre plot, plus other nearby land, the trio committed to pay nine thousand dollars. White turned over his small log house to Joseph Smith, while Galland gave up his two-story stone residence to Sidney Rigdon.[43]

The Prophet moved Emma and their four children into the log house on May 10, "hoping that I and my friends may here find a resting place for a little season at least." This did not end his traveling back and forth to Quincy, at least for a time. Compared with the trauma of the Missouri exodus, it was a leisurely season. While advising others on relocating at Commerce and conducting other church business, the Prophet found time on June 11 to sit down with his clerk, James Mulholland. On that day, Joseph Smith began a regular process of dictating his personal history, beginning with his youthful search for salvation in upstate New York.[44]

Other land purchases soon followed these first investments. On June 24, church agent Vinson Knight, soon to become bishop of Nauvoo's Lower Ward, acquired Galland's 13,000-acre parcel in the Half Breed Tract, together with the town of Nashville, Iowa, for more than $39,000. In mid-August, back in Commerce, church leaders made a large purchase from the Hotchkiss partnership with no down payment and nothing due on the principal for five years. In this acquisition, the church committed to pay $50,000 plus interest and fees for upwards of 500 acres on the Commerce peninsula. Located north of the first Mormon acquisitions, the parcel included the speculators' Commerce City and part of Commerce, both towns including valuable riverfront property where steamboat captains stopped to buy supplies and firewood from Amos Davis. The agreement, with interest and fees, payable in installments over twenty years, obligated the buyers for $114,500.[45]

On August 18, the church purchased William White's eighty-acre plot lying directly south of the Hotchkiss purchase; this bridged the gap between the Hotchkiss parcel and the land purchased in May from Hugh White. Apparently Hotchkiss shared an interest in this property with William White, because Hotchkiss received a $2,500 bond for the land and White a promise of $1,000 from Joseph Smith and Sidney Rigdon. Hotchkiss also later added to this sale a ten-acre strip reaching west from the William White property to the river.[46]

These purchases created the original property upon which the new Mormon gathering place was platted. Joseph Smith called the new community Nauvoo. The name is the English phonetic spelling (nah-VOO) of a Hebrew verb meaning "beautiful." A similar word appears in the grammar book assigned to the Prophet by his Hebrew teacher, Joshua Seixas, in Kirtland.[47] The verb is rendered "are beautiful" in Isaiah 52:7:

> How beautiful upon the mountains are the feet of him that bringeth good tidings, that publisheth peace; that bringeth good tidings of good, that publisheth salvation; that saith unto Zion, Thy God reigneth!

In a proclamation to the Saints, the First Presidency explained, "The name of our city (Nauvoo) is of Hebrew origin, and signifies a beautiful situation, or place, carrying with it, also, the idea of *rest;* and is truly descriptive of this most delightful situation."[48]

These understandings made Nauvoo an appropriate name for a city situated on the pleasant peninsula at the head of the rapids. More important for the Latter-day Saints who would live there, the implications of its religious meanings could be expanded. Nauvoo would become a city of refuge, where the Saints could rest from their troubles, as well as a place where they could unite in their search for an inner, spiritual peace.[49]

The name Nauvoo at first applied only to the newly platted area. Both the occupied town of Commerce and the speculative plat of Commerce City continued to exist on county records. Nauvoo merely included previously unplatted land on the peninsula. Commerce continued as an address for everyone, because its post office served the entire area. At first, Commerce was the name used in church publications, minutes, and other official records as well as in private correspondence. Before long, however, the minutes of meetings held within the new town adopted Nauvoo as the official place name, but most correspondence used Commerce until the Nauvoo post office commenced operation under its first postmaster, George W. Robinson, who was appointed April 21, 1840. Robinson operated the post office in James White's stone house, and it remained there after Robinson's father-in-law, Sidney Rigdon (who lived in the house), received the appointment on February 24, 1841. After the federal government recognized Nauvoo as a mailing address, Commerce as a place of reference quickly faded out of local use. As Nauvoo's population grew, the few residents of Commerce adopted that name and her government as their own. The city's promoters eventually vacated the old plats.[50]

Nauvoo would be the last name given to a place that had previously been known informally to the Indians as Quashquema, to the traders as the "head of the rapids," and to the early settlers as Venus and then Commerce. The change of name from Commerce to Nauvoo symbolized a shift in the central purpose of the community. Even so, both purposes would compete for dominance—the secular ventures of building the area as a center of industry and commerce and the religious program of promoting the good tidings of salvation. Both activities also would create tension between new settlers and old-timers in Hancock County.

Church land agent Vinson Knight acquired property in 1839 in anticipation of immigrants settling in Lee County and the towns of Keokuk, Nashville, and Montrose, Iowa. With that land and other holdings in the new town of Nauvoo, Alanson Ripley concluded, "There is no fear existing that the gathering will be too extensive."

Nauvoo was planned to support a rural lifestyle in an urban setting. To allow space for orchards, gardens, and quarters for livestock, the blocks contained about four acres of land divided into four lots. (Many of these one-acre parcels were soon subdivided to serve a rapidly growing population.) Like most American towns of that era, no provision was made for commercial sections. Business in Nauvoo was truly a home industry, existing to sustain a people whose purposes were to find salvation for themselves and to thresh the nations seeking converts. On their residential lots, craftsmen set up shop and merchants set aside a room or erected a separate building for a store. Whether farmer, housewife, public servant, churchman, craftsman, seamstress, or laborer, the men and women of Nauvoo sought a substantial part of the basic foodstuffs needed to sustain life by cultivating a garden and orchard on their town lot. Religious, social, and cultural groups built halls without attention to anything resembling a master plan. The Prophet did not immediately designate a temple site within the city, but one was soon found in an 1840 addition to Nauvoo, the Daniel Wells property on the bluff, at the geographical center of an expanded Nauvoo and with a commanding view of the river.

Besides grazing and some farming on undeveloped areas within the city limits, there were large agricultural plots beyond Nauvoo, reminiscent of those planned for Adam-ondi-Ahman. For convenience, farmers often lived on their farms, a departure from the original Zion concept. But even for these people, Nauvoo was a place of special interest. Those in the surrounding countryside and other nearby towns made regular visits to the City Beautiful to participate in its commercial, social, and religious life.

The initial plat of Nauvoo, filed with the county recorder on August 30, 1839, contained about 80 percent of the 671 acres of the original four purchases. Excluded were that part of the town of Commerce not in the Hotchkiss purchase and most of Commerce City. The original Nauvoo also wrapped around the riverside land of an absentee investor named Munson. As a reference point, surveyors planted a stone pyramid in the ground at the northeast corner of what became Block 155, the site of Joseph Smith's log homestead. On paper, the town stretched two miles from the White and Galland purchases on the south to the Hotchkiss purchase on the north, a strip about half a mile wide for most of its length. The original plat contained more than five hundred potential building lots. As Nauvoo's population grew, city leaders opened up new areas in the Commerce City area, and other landowners annexed property along Nauvoo's eastern boundary. By 1843, Nauvoo had more than fourteen hundred potential building lots available (plus those further subdivided) in an area nearly three times the size of the original Nauvoo plat.[51]

The city grew because church members in small Latter-day Saint branches in the United States and in the British Isles responded to an invitation to find refuge in this place of peace. Missionaries were already at work gathering modern Israel, and Nauvoo had a clear role to play in that proselytizing effort. As the new Mormon resting place, the city would become the central focus of a renewed effort at gathering Latter-day Saints into compact religious communities. The idea had not died with the expulsion order in Missouri. The benevolence of Illinois proffered another chance, according to the First Presidency: "From the . . . necessity of the gathering of the Saints of the Most High, we would say, let the brethren who love the prosperity of Zion, who are anxious that her stakes should be strengthened, and her cords lengthened, . . . come, and cast in their lots with us, and cheerfully engage in a work so glorious and sublime, and say with Nehemiah, 'we his servants will arise and build.'"[52]

CHAPTER 4

Gathering the Saints

Go ye forth unto the land of Zion. . . . Go ye out from among the nations, even from Babylon, from the midst of wickedness, which is spiritual Babylon. . . . Prepare ye the way of the Lord, and make his paths straight, for the hour of his coming is nigh.

—REVELATION TO JOSEPH SMITH, NOVEMBER 3, 1831

Where the fountain is, the Saints wish to be, and there is their asylum, and this of necessity requires a gathering together. Like cleaves to like, intelligence to intelligence, and Saint to Saint. Consequently the Brethren naturally desire to be together. Every effort has been made all the while to accomplish this grand object, but never did Providence seem to favor our wishes so much as at the present time.

—NEWEL K. WHITNEY TO GEORGE MILLER, FEBRUARY 15, 1845

A most important concept for understanding the history of the Latter-day Saints in the nineteenth century, including the Nauvoo years, is that of the gathering. Fully half of Joseph Smith's revelations received during the six-month period beginning in the fall of 1830 emphasized the need to prepare a people to receive the returning Christ. Two additional revelations in November 1831 reaffirmed the role of missionaries in sounding the warning voice and helping the righteous to flee from wicked Babylon to places of spiritual refuge to await the imminent Millennium.[1] Early church publications reaffirmed and made widely available these basic teachings of a righteous people living together in harmony and love awaiting the Millennium.[2] Preaching and gathering, to "declare both by word and by flight that desolation shall come upon the wicked," were clearly defined components in Joseph Smith's revelations and teachings about the church's mission for the last days.[3]

When Joseph Smith and his generation spoke of "the world," they meant the "wicked people" of the earth and their wicked deeds.[4] To gather out of the world meant literally to isolate oneself from these wicked others, to establish a saving sanctuary apart from society's evils and evildoers.[5] "God has told us to flee, not dallying, or we shall be scattered, one here, and another there," the Prophet said in 1839. "The time is soon coming," he added, "when no man will have any peace but in Zion and her stakes."[6] "It is emigration," the Twelve declared in 1841, "that is the only effectual remedy for the evils which now afflict the over-peopled countries of Europe."[7] The Saints on that side of the Atlantic sought refuge in an American Zion, a New World of purity and promise. Those who already lived within the promised land found peace in congregations near their homes or headed west to the major gathering places, in Zion and her stakes.

The revelatory background to the doctrine of the gathering began with Joseph Smith's tutoring during successive visits by the angel Moroni, who quoted entire chapters from the Old Testament. During the translation of the Book of Mormon, the young prophet must have been impressed by the regularity of the Lord's promises to set his hand a second time to recover the remnant of his people. Then, he translated the book of Moses, which contained an outline of Enoch's original City of Zion, with a promise of its restoration in the last days.[8]

The terms the Prophet used to describe the gathering to others echoed the familiar images of peoplehood in the Bible and Book of Mormon— the chosen family of God, a sacred society sharing a common interest in salvation.[9] His own translations and revelations emphasized that there would be a coming together of all things from every period of Judeo-Christian history and the faithful remnant would be gathered. Conversion and baptism created *saints* in a New Testament sense; migration and temple covenants echoed Old Testament concepts to make modern *Israelites*.[10]

Many of those who gathered out of Babylon spiritually, by accepting the call to repent and be baptized, participated in a second, physical gathering as a further demonstration of their faith in the revealed word. In their letters and reminiscences, Latter-day Saints who gathered to Nauvoo in the 1840s saw their conversion and their migration as a seamless process. For them, to gather with the Saints meant two things: a condition of righteous living and residence in places of refuge. These converts saw themselves as both a Zion people (the pure in heart) and citizens of a designated Zion place (a new American Jerusalem, or its supporting branches and stakes).[11] In the places of safety from a troubled world, the nascent saints were promised they would learn more about God's reward for choosing righteousness, "even peace in this world, and eternal life in the world to come."[12]

The doctrinal basis of the gathering defined the need to identify a righteous people and bring them together in religious congregations or communities. The church did not neglect those who, for whatever reason, did not migrate to the centers of the gathering. An ecclesiastical organization cared for the spiritual needs of members everywhere. Presiding elders were responsible to nourish the flock, to care for their spiritual and temporal needs, wherever they lived. Both of these aspects of the church's mission to bring souls to Christ—by gathering them out of Babylon spiritually and physically and by teaching them the good word of God in congregations large and small, in stakes and branches in Nauvoo and beyond—shaped the lives of Latter-day Saints.

THE GEOGRAPHY OF THE GATHERING

To accomplish the goal of building a vast Zion society, from time to time church leaders adjusted specific geographical expectations of the gathering to meet immediate needs. That was true both before and after Nauvoo became the headquarters of the church. Always, the strategy included the idea of a central city to serve as a headquarters and other places for outlying congregations. When building up a headquarters stake, leaders generally encouraged the Saints to assemble in or near that central gathering place. A focused gathering helped build up that city in anticipation of an ultimate presence in dozens of other major cities. The policy during the initial and final years of the Nauvoo period, however, permitted the Saints to cluster more broadly in the United States.

Implementation of a physical gathering began in 1831 with the Lord's command to gather to Ohio to join converts previously affiliated with

*Joseph Smith's prophetic role
centered on the concept of
gathering a covenant people
and preparing them through
teachings and ordinances to
receive the millennial Christ.*

Alexander Campbell. Near the same time, Latter-day Saints began moving
to western Missouri to establish the center place of Zion in Jackson
County. Joseph Smith taught that the central City of Zion (and, later, the
cornerstone stake at Nauvoo) would give rise to other stakes. Instructions
penned on the Plat of the City of Zion anticipated that the Saints would
fill up the promised land with satellite gathering places for the righteous
after the center place reached its capacity.[13]

The revelations anticipated that the plan for the City of Zion would
not immediately succeed. The Lord's commission was to "lay the foundation for Zion." The designated gathering place would not be replaced or
relocated geographically. Rather, the revelations anticipated "other places
which . . . shall be called stakes, for the curtains or the strength of Zion."[14]

Expulsion from the designated center place in 1833 was followed by
the creation of several new stakes of Zion in northwestern Missouri. After
three years in Clay County, the church moved northward. Far West
became the headquarters city-stake until 1838, with nearby communities

as supporting stakes. This pattern was followed in western Illinois after a two-year period without a designated central temple city. With the rise of Nauvoo, the imperative to reclaim the center place in Jackson County, Missouri, was deferred.[15] So were directives to build up other major gathering places.

During the period between the expulsion from the Far West area and the focus on the region around Nauvoo, church leaders allowed members to choose their own gathering places over a broad area in the safest and quietest places they could find, somewhere between Far West and Kirtland.[16] "There will be here and there a Stake [of Zion] for the gathering of the Saints," Joseph Smith said in 1839. He authorized new Latter-day Saint settlements during the next two years and proposed other stakes for existing American cities.[17]

Then, to serve pressing spiritual and practical needs, the First Presidency in April 1841 called for a concentrated gathering to Nauvoo and nearby stakes. The Illinois legislature had approved a charter for Nauvoo. That document authorized a city government, a university, and a militia. Construction had begun on a temple and a hotel, and missionaries were steadily baptizing converts. It seemed to church leaders that a time of peace and prosperity lay ahead. "In the language of one of our own poets," an official statement noted, "we would say,

> *In Illinois we've found a safe retreat,*
> *A home, a shelter from oppressions dire;*
> *Where we can worship God as we think right,*
> *And mobbers come not to disturb our peace;*
> *Where we can live and hope for better days,*
> *Enjoy again our liberty, our rights:*
> *That social intercourse which freedom grants,*
> *And charity requires of man to man.*
> *And long may charity pervade each breast,*
> *And long may Illinois remain the scene*
> *Of rich prosperity by peace secured!*

With a place of peace secured, the focus on building up the Nauvoo region continued for three years. Church leaders encouraged a united effort to populate a city and erect its public buildings. They did not neglect the far-flung branches during this time. Nauvoo's priesthood holders had been newly organized into quorums. The First Presidency encouraged similar structuring of the priesthood holders "in every stake and branch of the church, for the Almighty is a lover of order and good government."[18]

In April 1844, Nauvoo was thriving. Construction of the temple was moving forward. Once again, the Prophet brought to the forefront the master plan and sanctified it with "a great, grand, and glorious revelation" that defined Zion to include both North and South America. After receiving their ordinances in the temple, he said, selected priesthood leaders could set up new stakes in major cities of the United States and beyond. The Prophet's vision of filling the New World with gathering places remained his ultimate goal.[19]

Geographically, the focus for a headquarters city in the 1830s and 40s was at the far western boundary of the United States. The City of Zion was near displaced Indian tribes. Latter-day Saints believed these people would play a major role in building a millennial capital and its great temple. Both this theocratic seat of government, at Missouri's western limit, and Nauvoo, on the Illinois frontier, qualified as border towns. Although located at the very edge of the United States, Zion was for Latter-day Saints the center place. When early Mormon writers mentioned the American continent, they meant both North and South America. The millennial New Jerusalem was to be at its center.[20]

In a discussion of this idea, William W. Phelps described the Indian preserve between the Mississippi and the Rockies as the land of Joseph, a reference to Book of Mormon peoples, descendants of the biblical Joseph. This land, said Phelps, lay midway between the Gulf of St. Lawrence and the Gulf of California and between Baffin's Bay in the Arctic and Cape Horn near the Antarctic. Parley P. Pratt anticipated that converted Gentiles would establish their gathering places in the region eastward from the millennial capital. In the wilderness to the west and extending through South America, he said, the continent's Indians would claim their inheritance. Pratt added: "Both the remnant of Joseph from the west, and the Gentiles from the east, [will] resort to the house of God, the Zion of the Holy One of Israel, to learn wisdom and to pay their devotions."[21]

NURTURING THE SAINTS

Latter-day Saints who had been expelled from Missouri found their own places of peace, sought out nearby members, and formed local churches where they could focus on spiritual growth. Numerous new groups came into being, adding to the hundreds of congregations of varying sizes already existing from a decade of missionary labor. Throughout the Nauvoo period, numerous Latter-day Saints continued their affiliation with these bodies away from Nauvoo, in many parts of the United States and in the British Isles.

The organizational structure to serve these clustered Saints consisted of branches and stakes. The branch could serve the smallest of groups, as few as four or five people, under the jurisdiction of a presiding elder or priest. Sometimes the leading officer served with two counselors. Men who had been ordained elders, priests, teachers, or deacons in the branch were registered as "official members," that is, persons who held priesthood office. Unordained men and all women and children were enrolled as "regular members." A clerk in each branch kept a record of the members, with dates of arrival or baptism, ordination, and departure or death.

Sometimes a decade's work by missionaries had developed larger branches. These were entitled to a more complex organization, a dual set of leaders. A presidency of three high priests (a president and his counselors) looked after the spiritual affairs of the branch, while a bishop (sometimes with two counselors) managed the temporal affairs. Though it lacked a high council, a large branch was sometimes called a stake. The two terms were often used interchangeably in these congregations. The few larger groups that did have a high council had the most ideal stake government.

On a regular schedule, usually quarterly, delegates from each branch or stake attended an administrative assembly known as a conference. The geographical sector within which these branches were located was also called a conference. (In later years, the geographical term was *district*.) The presiding officer of the assembly took care of administrative needs, instructed the delegates, and received statistical reports on the number of members in various categories. In their capacity as a traveling high council, members of the Quorum of the Twelve Apostles regulated the business of the branches through the conference meetings, which they often attended. In Great Britain and the eastern United States, one of the Twelve often resided in the locality and exercised jurisdiction over all of the conferences as a president over that area.

Even as the exiles from Missouri were settling into dozens of gathering

Stakes in Iowa and Illinois

places of their own choosing, one of those locations emerged as a head-quarters for the church. When Joseph Smith and his friends found refuge at the head of the rapids, Commerce became that place. For a short time, the Prophet encouraged everyone gathering nearby to congregate in what soon became Nauvoo. Church leaders had land to sell and loan repayments to make. But the church had purchased lands across the Mississippi as well. In April 1840, after Nauvoo had been sufficiently established, the Prophet relaxed his restriction and once again allowed the Saints to move onto the purchased lands in Iowa, "or wherever the spirit might lead them."[22]

The twin-cities area of Commerce and Montrose became part of greater Nauvoo. Because of a concentration of members resulting from an active promotion of building lots, both areas soon qualified for stake organizations.[23] But with the presence of the First Presidency at Nauvoo, and, after 1840, the designation of the headquarters city itself as a temple site, Nauvoo's rise eclipsed in importance that of the Iowa stake and other new Latter-day Saint communities. Nauvoo became the hub of a clustering of settlements that reached out radially into nearby areas on both sides of the Mississippi River.

On the western shoreline of the Mississippi, the abandoned Fort Des Moines and other opportunities in nearby Montrose, Iowa, attracted dozens of fleeing Latter-day Saints. Purchase of a vast tract from land speculator Isaac Galland in the late spring of 1839 opened the land to sanctioned settlement. Hundreds responded to the opportunity to begin again on cheap land. By October, the Iowa Saints, like those at Commerce, had their own stake. With Montrose as its center, the Iowa stake reached out as far as forty miles north and west to include several small congregations scattered over three counties. The Iowa stake (soon renamed Zarahemla) claimed a significant Latter-day Saint presence. At a conference in August 1841, officials reported 750 members residing in nine branches. Among its members were many of Joseph Smith's relatives from his parents' families.[24]

At first, it appeared that stakes similar to those named Nauvoo and Zarahemla would flourish wherever sufficient numbers of Latter-day Saints justified an organization. Joseph Smith's April 1840 directive allowed the Saints living in and around Hancock and Adams County, Illinois, and Lee County, Iowa Territory, to remain where they had settled. Several communities soon requested stake organizations. The first of these, the Ramus stake, was created later that year to serve the Saints in the Crooked Creek settlement, twenty-two miles southeast of Nauvoo. After the October 1840 general conference, four new stakes were organized in Adams County and three elsewhere in Illinois.

With gathering sanctioned elsewhere in the United States, other congregations soon requested and were granted permission to follow the example of the Saints in the upper Mississippi Basin. The October 1840 conference allowed the Kirtland Saints to reconstitute a stake in Ohio. The following April, the Saints in Philadelphia and New York City received authorization for stake organizations. For these congregations, perfection of their local organizations meant the appointment of a presiding elder and two counselors as a branch presidency "to preside over the spiritual affairs of the church in this place" and a bishop and two counselors as a bishopric "to take charge of the financial affairs."[25] Unlike the Saints living in Nauvoo, members in these urban stakes had no need to establish their own municipal governments. The Saints went about their way, a mere religious curiosity in the larger flow of society.

In Hancock County, the potential was different. The Latter-day Saints who moved into sparsely settled areas created both ecclesiastical congregations and the possibility of secular municipalities. The situation in eastern Hancock County exemplified the potential for replicating Nauvoo's boomtown growth in the nearby rural areas of Illinois and Iowa. The Latter-day Saints at Crooked Creek were delighted when Joseph Smith and Hyrum Smith approved their July 1840 request for a stake. Joel H. Johnson became president and William Wightman bishop of the new stake. The local leaders took seriously their opportunities. "A stake has been organized," Johnson reported in November, "lands purchased, a town laid out, lots sold, and already quite a number of buildings, mechanical shops, etc., have been erected, and many more in progress." When the county surveyor platted the new Mormon town, he named it Ramus, a word with Latin roots meaning "branch," because the town was to be a branch of the church at Nauvoo.[26]

Some believed Ramus was better situated than Nauvoo because of the beauty of its prairie setting away from the river lowlands. Johnson touted its healthful location twenty miles inland from Nauvoo "in the midst of a beautiful and fertile country, surrounded by a variety of prairie and timber land, the soil rich and productive." Besides plenty of available town lots, in both the original town plat and a first addition, Ramus was surrounded by cultivated farms and mills, plus convenient creeks for more mills.[27] The enthusiasm for building a city bode well for this new Mormon town (which, before long, was being called by a Greek name, Macedonia). The county had potential sites elsewhere as well.

Smaller branches outside the upper Mississippi headquarters region faced an uncertain tenure. Many of these scattered assemblies had existed for years; some sprouted in consequence of the Missouri exodus; others were raised up during the Nauvoo years through the efforts of missionaries. Because of new baptisms, apostasies, and migration, the branches constantly fluctuated in size. Sometimes they combined to form what was often termed a union branch. Taken together, the branches formed a widely scattered support network for the cornerstone stake at Nauvoo. Most of them sent funds to sustain construction projects in the headquarters city, enlisted subscribers for the church newspaper, and lost migrants to Nauvoo. Because of local kinship and friendship networks, the hometown branches often competed with Nauvoo for allegiance, but a number of them eventually dissolved when Latter-day Saints from their numbers gathered to greater Nauvoo.

In the first stage of the dispersion from Missouri, the paths of exile did not lead a large number to the Commerce area. Those for whom peace beckoned elsewhere often moved several times before settling in on their own farms. Many enjoyed the gracious hospitality of the people of Quincy, Illinois, but only a few stayed there for long. A good number found an enduring refuge elsewhere along the Mississippi River basin in the first tier of Illinois counties. When church leaders collected affidavits certifying losses in Missouri in the months and years following the expulsion, they found exiled Saints in ten counties in western Illinois and two in Iowa. To link these people with the church, by February 1840 the *Times and Seasons* had subscription agents serving in eight western Illinois counties outside Hancock County.[28]

A favored path from upper Missouri took many fleeing Saints along the Missouri River directly toward St. Louis. Had that booming river town not been in the state of Missouri, it might have attracted an even larger number. Missionary work in the mid-1830s had established a small Latter-day Saint branch there. St. Louis public opinion in 1838 opposed the Mormon expulsion from Missouri. Influential citizens condemned Governor Lilburn Boggs and through the winter welcomed refugees to a labor-hungry market. Local citizens even organized a Quincy-like fundraising effort to help the exiles. The Saints who accepted refuge in St. Louis kept a low profile to avoid raising the expulsion issue, and some crossed the river to settle in the east-side shadow of the busy port. Even after Nauvoo emerged as the designated gathering place, St. Louis attracted and retained Latter-day Saints. British immigrants traveling upriver from New Orleans stopped at St. Louis to change boats; some stayed for months and even years. In addition, the scarcity of jobs in Nauvoo fueled a constant flow of laborers downriver, seeking temporary and long-term employment. By mid-1844, Heber C. Kimball reported as many as seven hundred members in the greater St. Louis area. The St. Louis branch itself, formally organized by local priesthood officers that spring, reported four hundred members at its peak in early 1845. Not all Latter-day Saints in the city remained faithful. According to Joseph

Fielding, the area attracted those who "had been to Nauvoo but had not faith enough to live there." In nearby Belleville, Illinois, a handful of Saints organized a tiny branch.[29]

Another magnet for the Saints was the familiar territory of northern Ohio. The old Western Reserve had once been a favored gathering place, with more than two dozen branches functioning by 1838. The temple at Kirtland remained a physical reminder of the golden days of the early 1830s, and a sizable number of Latter-day Saints chose to remain (or return) there. Joseph Smith's directive from Liberty Jail named Kirtland as the eastern limit of the acceptable havens, and the old stronghold soon contended with Nauvoo for prominence. Branches also existed in southern Michigan.

In New England and the Atlantic States, Latter-day Saints who had not joined the migration to Missouri waited for direction, and some who had made the trek west returned to familiar scenes in their home states. The northeast attracted mostly those who had relatives willing to offer refuge. Throughout that area were kinfolk who had refused the message of the Restoration but who retained a willingness to nurture an errant son or daughter, brother or sister. In urban areas, concentrations of Latter-day Saints eventually resulted in relatively large branches, subject always to the diminishing effects of Nauvoo's primacy. The Philadelphia branch, organized in 1839, quickly grew to more than two hundred members. An active branch in Baltimore launched a short-lived newspaper, the *Mormon Expositor,* in 1842. A year later, the Boston area reported fourteen branches and hundreds of members. That same year the Peterborough, New Hampshire, branch had 115 members.

Some of the Saints hailed from the Southern United States, particularly from Kentucky and Tennessee. Many of these were converted as migrants in southern and central Illinois. They visited their ancestral homelands as missionaries during the 1840s but seldom went there to live. Except for Kentucky, Virginia, and North Carolina, not more than a few branches prospered in any of the Southern states.

In all of these North American areas, the nurturing of the Saints during the Nauvoo years continued as before. Branch leaders looked after the local Saints and welcomed returning members seeking safety from the Missouri extermination order. Those who had been gathered in this way met together to receive spiritual nourishment from local and traveling elders. They learned what they could of the Prophet's teachings at Nauvoo, but the church newspaper and word-of-mouth transmission sometimes left scattered members without a full understanding of key developments in doctrine.

In Great Britain, where missionary efforts harvested a vast number of converts, the organization for nurturing these new Latter-day Saints followed the same pattern previously established in North America. As in America, the reports at quarterly conferences that were passed along to the church paper reflected an active system of branches and conferences. In England, the first conference was established by Heber C. Kimball in Preston in 1837. During Nauvoo's founding years, the second wave of apostles expanded church organization to many other parts of the British Isles.[30] As the Twelve prepared to return to Nauvoo, Joseph Smith counseled them to "be diligent, organize the churches and let every one stand in his proper place, so that those who cannot come with you in the spring may not be left as sheep without shepherds."[31]

Relocating to Headquarters

Nurturing the branches of Great Britain carried with it an implication somewhat different from the same process in America. Whereas the elders in America were always free to explain the gathering to Zion at Independence and, later, to her northern Missouri stakes, across the Atlantic the message was kept quiet. At first, the Twelve emphasized the need for the British Saints to remain at home. They told the men that every able elder was needed for the work of threshing the Old World for converts. They were not to teach the millennial revelations of the Doctrine and Covenants. Joseph Smith had advised the missionaries to focus on first principles. "Remain silent concerning the gathering," he counseled, until the church was firmly established.[32]

Even with this restriction, new members heard in the voice of warning sounded by the elders an urgency to withdraw not just from spiritual Babylon but from its temporal host as well. The call to repentance was nested in an apocalyptic pessimism about existing social and political conditions in the Old World. Public discourse and private correspondence convinced British converts that dire consequences faced their ancient nation. Some in England speculated that serious rioting between Whigs and Tories would lead to revolution and social upheaval.[33] In addition,

These British immigrants to Nauvoo sat for portraits by unknown artists before leaving their homeland. The woman at left wears laces fashionable at the time. The woman at right is painted by a more skilled artist.

British cultural expectations ran parallel to Mormon concepts that cast America in the role of a promised land. Increasingly, missionaries and emigrant friends admonished the Saints to flee to the peaceful trans-Atlantic refuge.

By the end of 1840, migration was part of the gospel message in Great Britain. Besides, a yearning to meet the living prophet and listen personally to his counsel, a desire to live among the veteran Saints, and the promise of the temple added attractive reasons for breaking with the past. Commenting on the fervor of the English Saints to emigrate, Brigham Young said, "The Saints have got a start for to gather to America and go they will, and nothing can stop them. . . . They have so much of the spirit of gathering that they would go if they knew they would die as soon as they got there or if they knew that the mob would be upon and drive them as soon as they got there."[34]

Those who went first invited others to join them in the land of Zion. William Clayton, newly arrived in Nauvoo in 1840, advised his friend Edward Martin in England, "You must come or suffer the vengeance of heaven."[35] But it was not just the millennial judgments expected upon the wicked and their cities that motivated converts to escape to Nauvoo. For the poor of England, the United States offered economic opportunity unavailable to many in Europe. The same inducements that attracted Americans from the Atlantic coast pulled the British westward. Land was cheap and fertile. A man could be his own boss and enjoy prosperity unheard of in the homeland. Emigration agencies active in England promoted America and published attractive guides to the land of opportunity. The *Millennial Star* praised the New World as a place of abundant land where life was less difficult. "Living [in America] is about one-eighth of what it costs in this country," the periodical advised. "Millions on millions of acres of land lie before them unoccupied, with a soil as rich as Eden, and a surface as smooth, clear, and ready for the plough as the park scenery of England." Then, to disabuse the would-be emigrant of a popular misconception of America as untamed wilderness: "Instead of a lonely swamp or dense forest filled with savages, wild beasts, and serpents, large cities and villages are springing up in their midst, with schools, colleges, and temples . . . , there being abundant room for more than a hundred millions of inhabitants."[36]

For Latter-day Saints, the American refuge offered physical safety along with inspired preaching and temple blessings.[37] "The western continent is the place appointed of the Lord for the assembling of his people," the *Millennial Star* reminded the British Saints, "that they may learn his will, receive blessings at his hands, and escape the consequences of the fury that shall be poured out upon the nations."[38]

Nauvoo offered a special opportunity to be taught. Migrants from both sides of the Atlantic gathered there with eagerness to hear and see for themselves the man they accepted as God's living spokesman. "This day for the first time in my life did my eyes behold a Prophet of God," Millen Attwood wrote in his diary upon arrival from Connecticut. "I washt my body, bowd before the lord in thankfulness for the preservation of my life and the sight I beheld." These words mirrored an oft-repeated sentiment among those who gathered to Nauvoo in faith. "One Lecture from [his] mouth well repaid me for all my troubles and journeyings to this land, which were not a few," Alfred Cordon remembered. Newcomers to Nauvoo delighted in meeting this affable young man. "He was easy, free and sociable with all," Attwood discovered.[39]

The *Millennial Star*'s reminder of a place of learning and refuge cited numerous scriptural arguments for the gathering but did not neglect the practical needs of life. It concluded with a reflection of America as an agricultural Eden:

> *Then away to the west, the glorious west,*
> *The land which the Lord hath greatly blest;*
> *Where the soil hath rested for ages past,*
> *To make a rich home for the Saints at last.*[40]

Away to the west the Saints of the British Isles headed, beginning in 1840 and continuing through the Nauvoo years. The Twelve opened the doors to the British migration quietly in mid-April 1840 in response to an inquiry from Francis Moon. Spokesman Parley P. Pratt told Saints who lingered in Preston after a conference that the Twelve wanted to prevent a hasty, mass migration. Those desiring to leave, he said, should do so with as little public notice as possible. The policy echoed a pattern established in Kirtland and magnified in Missouri's exodus: Emigrants should use their resources to help others who were financially unable to gather.[41]

John Moon headed up the first British emigrant party, forty-one Saints who left from Liverpool on June 6, 1840. The voyage was rough, and many of the emigrants were seasick. But after they reached New York, Moon wrote back to friends in England, convinced of his decision. "You must expect great tribulation in the way to Zion," he said, adding, "I can say with truth that if things had been 10 times worse than they was I would just have gone right ahead through all." He found prices fair and commodities available and of good quality.[42]

The optimistic reports of the first British immigrants to Nauvoo and similar letters from later boatloads bolstered the desire among the British Saints to make the arduous trip. These encouraging words added a personal touch to the doctrine of the gathering. English immigrant John Greenhow published for his friends his discoveries of the stark contrasts between the old and new worlds. In vivid words, he compared the poverty and starvation among the English working classes with the comparative plenty and economic independence of the new migrants. "If peace and happiness is to be found in the world," he advised, "it is at Nauvoo."[43] The clear message to the English Saints was that Nauvoo delivered an improved life in this world besides its promise of a better one in the next.

Not all who made the trip to Nauvoo stayed there. Some left feeling unhappy with conditions in the undeveloped city and found other places to live in the United States. A few returned to England. Those most disgruntled published their unhappiness, but Latter-day Saint elders in England quickly countered.[44]

Not surprisingly, opposition papers in Illinois picked up on the murmurings of dissatisfied immigrants, who often criticized frontier living conditions of the new city. The negative message that reached England depicted Nauvoo as a wretched place of log and mud cabins and knee-deep muddy streets, where people lived in poverty and starvation under "the awful delusion of Mormonism" and the "villainy and roguery" of its inhabitants. Church spokesmen responded that dissatisfaction was limited mostly to those with unrealistic expectations. "Those who have come expecting to find gold in our streets, and all the luxuries of an old country, will find themselves disappointed," they said, "but those who have maturely considered the advantages and disadvantages, are perfectly satisfied and contented." One such satisfied immigrant, William Rowley, expressed surprise at how far the negative reports had missed the mark. Discovering a boomtown under construction in late 1843, he found "a most cheering picture of the enterprise and industry of its inhabitants." In contrast with many other and older western towns seen along his trip up the Mississippi, Nauvoo looked very good.[45]

A few discomforts and a few malcontents did not halt the gathering. The first expedition under John Moon had sailed on a commercial route to New York City, America's busiest port. In August, comfortable that they had the support of the Prophet, the Twelve launched an official church-sponsored emigration program, complete with chartered ships.[46] The second company of 1840 numbered 201 emigrants under the direction of Theodore Turley and William Clayton. When fifty of the Saints from Herefordshire could not come up with the fare, John and Jane Benbow paid for forty of them. Even with that subsidy, the party lacked the funds to complete the trip from New York. A number of these stranded Saints stopped off at Kirtland. Thereafter, church agents decided to route the British Saints through New Orleans, the world's fourth-busiest port. They also reinforced the need for a cooperative effort in the migration.[47]

Once the British floodgate to Zion was open, Brigham Young and his associates assisted in the enterprise and offered practical advice for getting to Zion. Ever mindful of the underprivileged, Young urged wealthy entrepreneurs to go first and build factories to employ the migrating poor.

Saints leaving home aboard church-chartered ships for Nauvoo were escorted out of Liverpool harbor by a tugboat and were sometimes followed a short distance in a small craft by friends bidding a final farewell.

He warned against fraudulent emigration agents and urged the Saints to travel under church auspices. "A word of caution to the wise is sufficient," he said. By chartering a ship and purchasing provisions wholesale, a company could guarantee cheaper passage. It helped that Mormon voyagers usually took the poorest accommodations, in steerage. In addition, a chartered company steamboat at New Orleans would save half on the upriver passage. Traveling together would ensure good company en route and the advantage of experienced men as leaders. Hard coin such as sovereigns rather than American bank notes was the preferred money for emigrants, the Twelve advised; and the heat of summer was absolutely the wrong time to travel through New Orleans. Finally, to prevent fraud upon the Saints at Nauvoo, departing members were encouraged to take along letters of recommendation from the local elders to identify themselves as trustworthy Saints.[48]

Late in 1841, Parley P. Pratt reorganized the Mormon emigration agency. Without diminishing comforts, he halved traveling costs. "The entire expense of a passenger from Liverpool to Illinois (1500 miles inland), including provisions, will not exceed 25 dollars," he noted;

"heretofore, it would cost them fifty at least." Pratt said that the economical plan astonished commercial agents in Liverpool.[49]

Between the first English boatload in 1840 and the last to Nauvoo in 1846, an estimated forty-eight hundred Latter-day Saints made the voyage from Liverpool. More than half the six-year total emigrated during 1841 and 1842 in seventeen voyages. England contributed significantly to Nauvoo's growth. Stranded in St. Louis with 250 British Saints, Parley P. Pratt observed in April 1843, "They are flocking as doves to their windows, from all parts of England and the States. . . . I think that thousands will land in Nauvoo in the course of the spring. Yes, as soon as the ice is out they will throng Nauvoo in swarms."[50]

The journey from Liverpool to New Orleans by sailing vessel averaged nearly eight weeks and often took twice as long as a trip to New York. From New Orleans, the steamship ride on a shallow-draft sidewheeler to St. Louis and then, often in a second boat, to Nauvoo, could add another two weeks to the trip. In low water, the river crafts sometimes ran aground on sandbars. The trip up the Mississippi on a noisy sidewheeler had its personal risks as well. Accidents of various kinds killed and injured hundreds of travelers each year. Disease claimed other victims, and rowdies sometimes assaulted passengers or stole their belongings. The Saints were not immune to these problems.[51]

For British converts, leaving home meant selling not only homes and land but most of their household goods as well. Shipboard passengers could take little more than the necessities and a few small personal treasures. Migrant Robert Crookston remembered, "Our Scots neighbors thought we were crazy, and as they knew we could not take much of our possessions with us, we had to sell everything at a great sacrifice."[52] But with the dream of Zion firmly implanted within, Latter-day Saints left for their new homes with hope for the future. One company of 207 Mormon passengers leaving Liverpool in September 1841 looked down on hundreds of well-wishers and burst into song as the boat moved slowly out into the Mersey River, singing:

> *Lovely native land, farewell!*
> *Glad I leave thee, glad I leave thee,*
> *Far in distant lands to dwell.*

As the American sailing ship lifted anchor the next morning and moved away "under the flag of liberty—the American stars and stripes, with a majesty seldom surpassed," the Saints on the deck sang "How Firm a Foundation," a familiar hymn that would become a Mormon favorite. Its verses noted the trials of discipleship and reflected the emigrants' own dependence upon their newfound faith in Jesus Christ:

> *In ev'ry condition—in sickness, in health,*
> *In poverty's vale or abounding in wealth,*
> *At home or abroad, on the land or the sea—*
> *As thy days may demand, so thy succor shall be.*[53]

THE CALL TO GATHER AMERICAN SAINTS

Even as the first British Saints were landing in Nauvoo, a number of factors made their arrival timely. Nauvoo was taking on an aura of permanence and centrality among gathering places with a new city charter and the launching of a major church construction program centered on the temple and the Nauvoo House, an inn for world visitors. With these significant projects underway, the First Presidency was ready now to invite scattered Saints from every location to relocate in Nauvoo. It would take "the concentration of the Saints, to accomplish [this and other] works of such magnitude and grandeur," they said. For those interested in assisting in "the work of the gathering . . . , we say let them come to this place."[54]

Three months later, in a January 1841 revelation, the Lord commanded the Prophet to proclaim the virtues of the Nauvoo stake. Nauvoo had been "planted to be a cornerstone of Zion," the revelation said. Only in Nauvoo would the Saints be able to receive temple ordinances. These ordinances, Joseph Smith taught, would allow the elders to preach the gospel in power and build up and govern additional gathering places.[55] Temples had been an important feature in every central gathering place before Nauvoo, and Nauvoo was both a temple city and the headquarters stake. Even though it was only one of several stakes of Zion designated "as a place of safety and gathering for the last days," it held a superior ranking in the years following the First Presidency's October 1840 proclamation and the Prophet's January 1841 temple revelation.[56]

Responding to the revelations, church leaders launched an active promotion of the new city. In a January proclamation to the church, the First Presidency applauded the virtues of Nauvoo as a healthy, rapidly growing city and endorsed the doctrine of the gathering as "a subject of paramount importance." Anticipating some opposition to this new emphasis, the presidency conceded that "the idea of a general gathering has heretofore been associated with most cruel and oppressing scenes." This time, because of "the liberal policy of our State government," they optimistically anticipated in Illinois "a scene of peace and prosperity."[57]

The Saints heard regular invitations thereafter to leave their homes elsewhere and move to western Illinois to help build the temple. In May 1841, the First Presidency decided to eliminate all stakes outside Hancock County, Illinois, and Lee County, Iowa. This meant the official end of the five gathering places in Adams County, although Lima, just outside the Hancock County border, remained an active branch. A directive from the First Presidency enjoined everyone living outside the two counties to move quickly to Nauvoo and help ensure "the prosperity of this the corner stone of Zion." The construction of a temple, university, and other edifices, they said, "can only be done by a concentration of energy, and enterprise."[58] To accomplish these purposes, the physical gathering would, for a time, be centered on a single region, reflecting the pattern of northwestern Missouri. A clustering of communities was once again the designated place of peace.

To help manage this concentrated gathering, the Prophet expanded the responsibilities of the Twelve at the headquarters stake. Previously, the apostles had traveled about on foreign missions or regulated those American branches without a high council. Among their new assignments was the task of helping immigrants get settled in designated refuges—Nauvoo, Ramus, and Warren in Hancock County, Illinois, and Zarahemla and Nashville in Lee County, Iowa. Warren, near the foot of the rapids on the Mississippi, one mile below Warsaw, was a new Latter-day Saint town endorsed by the Twelve and given their special attention. It had the advantage, they said, of proximity to the steam flour mill and lumber mill at Warsaw, a town of about five hundred residents. As an authorized place for settlement, it fulfilled the Saints' obligation to "stand in holy places" as the end of time approached.[59]

The newly formed Ramus stake at Macedonia in eastern Hancock County had been exempted from the consolidation during the summer of 1841. But in December, Hyrum Smith presided over its dissolution, accompanied on the assignment by Brigham Young, Heber C. Kimball,

Willard Richards, and John Taylor of the Twelve. Relieved of his responsibilities in managing the business side of the stake, Bishop William Wightman transferred to church trustee Joseph Smith the deed to all remaining unsold lots, notes from buyers, bonds on expansion property, and other resources. Besides the original plat and first addition, the bishop had anticipated future expansion by bonding for the property of John F. Charles and that of Ute and William J. Perkins, some newly converted old-timers. The church accepted all of these obligations along with ownership of the unsold property.[60]

The refining of the policy of the gathering in 1841 soon created a major Mormon core area in and around the Nauvoo stake and two minor clusters of settlements nearby. One of these clusters reached out twenty-five miles to the eastern border of Hancock County and another stretched an equal distance south to its boundary with Adams County. The old citizens at Warsaw and Carthage understood very well the potential effect of these settlement patterns. The old settlers in Nauvoo's commercial rival at Warsaw and her political nemesis at the county seat in Carthage were being surrounded by citizens they neither understood nor trusted. The *Warsaw Signal* promised to protect Latter-day Saint religious rights, but, its editor asserted in a prescient warning in May 1841, "Whenever they, as a people, step beyond the proper sphere of a religious denomination, and become a political body, as many of our citizens are beginning to apprehend will be the case, then this press stands pledged to take a stand against them."[61] Established residents could see their control of local politics shifting into the hands of a new majority, influenced, they suspected, by the leadership of a few. As the Latter-day Saints increased in numbers, Hancock County became increasingly and controversially Mormon country. The success of the gathering merely intensified the exchange between Nauvoo, the place of peace, and Warsaw, a center of opposition.[62] Two societies—one a covenant community seeking to unite all aspects of life, the other organized under a civic contract of individual effort—moved toward certain conflict.

The increase of population in the Nauvoo-Montrose area came about because the Saints responded positively to the call of religious gathering, although evidence is difficult to find concerning departures from nearby settlement clusters. From farther afield, reports document a small but steady departure of Latter-day Saints from branches throughout the

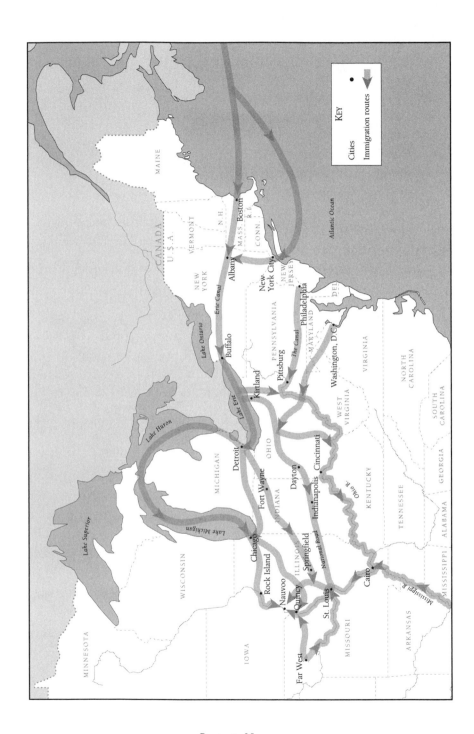

Routes to Nauvoo

Northeast and the upper South. A missionary passing through New York City en route to England reported in late 1840 that there were four hundred members living in western New York State and that another one hundred had emigrated westward. At almost every conference of members, tallies of membership in the branches were amended by the numbers who had departed for Nauvoo. When Isaac C. Haight resigned his presidency of the branch at Moravia, New York, in 1842 to move to Nauvoo, he was followed by Saints in nine other wagons who, on July 24, joined "God's people in Zion." In the six-month period ending in May 1843, the New York City branch lost a quarter of its 160 members— thirteen to excommunication and twenty-five to Nauvoo. The New York conference voted to excommunicate "any Elder who taught doctrine contrary to the spirit of gathering" if he did not repent. That singlemindedness in doctrine supported the call to Nauvoo, and church agents made the decision easier by offering to trade the land of departing Saints for property in Nauvoo.[63]

To get to the cornerstone stake in Illinois, emigrants in the East took established routes along rivers and rail and canal lines. The trip from New York along the Allegheny Portage Road crossed the mountains by railroad. The cars reached an elevation of nearly twenty-four hundred feet, assisted on the steep inclines by cable and stationary engines. From Pittsburgh to Cincinnati, travelers followed the "canal," a term used to refer, in part, to the Ohio River.[64] Converts from Kentucky joined the migration at steamboat ports in Cincinnati and Louisville, or they followed established roads from Louisville across southern Indiana through Vandalia to the Mississippi and from there along the river road to Quincy and Nauvoo. The Kirtland Saints joined the Ohio River route at Cincinnati or took a northern course along the Erie Canal from the Hudson River above Albany, New York, to Lake Erie. Passengers continued by lake steamer to Detroit and then went overland across northern Indiana and Illinois to their destination at Nauvoo.[65]

Many of the Saints chose commercial transportation for this most important trip of their lives. They crated their goods and shipped them west. Others loaded wagons and managed their own freighting to Nauvoo. To help those yet to make the trip, American travelers, like their English cousins, shared the experience in letters home to friends and family, with details of the trip—its costs and comforts—and descriptions of the new City Beautiful.[66]

Perhaps church leaders feared that their glowing praises of the new Eden at Nauvoo would disappoint some emigrants. As an occasional British emigrant had done, a few Americans went home after realizing that Nauvoo was not all that they had expected. For many United States returnees, the disillusionment lay not in the promises buried under the prairie sod but in the paucity of sainthood in Nauvoo's people. Apparently, they had expected the gospel net to be more selective in its harvest. Even though all Latter-day Saints were expected to live a minimum standard—especially those who gathered to the places of righteousness—some did not.[67] As the *Times and Seasons* editorialized in 1842, "Nauvoo, at present is, figuratively, the great fish market of the earth, where all kinds, both good and bad, are gathered—where the good are preserved, and the bad cast away—for until the savior comes, there will be wise virgins and foolish;—blessed are they that continue to the end *faithful*."[68]

The First Presidency had warned against such disappointments as early as January 1841. Those arriving in Nauvoo "must not expect to find perfection, or that all will be harmony, peace and love," the presidency cautioned. The city included people from many states and several nations. Despite their common religious conversions, they said, individuals "have their prejudices of education, and . . . there are many that creep in unawares, and endeavor to sow discord, strife and animosity." Church leaders encouraged migrants to tend to their own personal righteousness and to exercise patience "until 'the floor be thoroughly purged' and 'the chaff be burnt up.'" Subsequent statements cautioned those "who may feel disappointed in not finding the saints *angels*, to first cast the beam out of their own eye."[69]

From this counsel on interpersonal relationships in Zion and her stakes came an attitude and a commonsense aphorism popular in Missouri and often repeated in Nauvoo: "Mind your own business." As Amasa Lyman explained it, "Never be troubled about others' concerns but trouble yourselves just enough about your own, and not too much."[70] In short, the gathered Saints were counseled to be tolerant of imperfect people and leave them alone. The better effort would be to demonstrate through their own faith and actions what it meant to be a covenant people.

The traveling elders carried the message of the gathering everywhere, but some Saints simply stayed put. The reasons for remaining outside the stream of Saints gathering to Nauvoo varied with each individual— including matters of faith, funding, or family pressures. Some were short on zeal; others lacked financial resources. Unbelieving friends and families discouraged some, or even drew them into apostasy. Snug homes and adequate incomes held still others back. For many who were living comfortably away from the designated cornerstone stake of Zion and its satellite communities, small Latter-day Saint congregations elsewhere satisfied their spiritual needs.

Convincing lingering Saints in the Kirtland area to abandon their established homes and farms and the church's first temple proved an especially formidable challenge. Ironically, in the early 1830s, they had wanted to move west to Jackson County, but a revelation counseled them to retain a stronghold in Ohio for five years.[71] That barrier expired in September 1836, opening the way for the removal of more than sixteen hundred Saints to northern Missouri over the next two years. (Most of these people eventually resettled in the Nauvoo area.) Remaining behind in Kirtland in the 1840s were nearly 30 percent of the membership, or around six hundred people. Most of them remained loyal to Joseph Smith.[72] Some entrenched leaders left Kirtland for Far West in 1838 only because the Prophet chastised them in the name of the Lord and offered them new opportunities in Missouri. That is how William Marks became president of the Far West stake, Newel K. Whitney a bishop "not in name but in deed" in Adam-ondi-Ahman, and Oliver Granger the proprietor of a proposed church mercantile store.[73] Among the leaders remaining in Kirtland were dissidents whose actions gave the city an ill-earned reputation as a center of apostasy.[74]

As Nauvoo began attracting settlers, the Kirtland Saints who had been displaced from Missouri wondered if they should anchor themselves in Hancock and Lee counties or exercise the option of the Liberty Jail advisory and return to Kirtland. The First Presidency and Nauvoo high council in December 1839 acknowledged the agency God had given individuals to decide for themselves but urged the Kirtland Saints to remain in the Nauvoo area and accept that advice without murmuring.[75]

The following October, Kirtland gained short-lived recognition as a gathering place for the Saints from the East when the general conference held in Nauvoo accepted Joseph Smith's proposal to authorize a new Kirtland stake. Seven months later, the First Presidency disbanded all stakes except those in Lee and Hancock counties, thus returning Kirtland to its peripheral status.[76] Nonetheless, a council there quickly found in the revelations a justification for multiple gathering places. With this support, the former stake president, Almon Babbitt, advocated a continuing role for Kirtland as an administrative center and publishing hub. Ignoring a January 1841 reprimand for failing to follow counsel, he led an October conference that revived programs to help the poor, designated elders to serve as missionaries, and authorized a new religious periodical, *The Olive Leaf.* These actions heightened tension and placed Kirtland in direct competition with Nauvoo in a challenge to centralized authority.[77]

While the Kirtland Saints were approving these actions, a conference in Nauvoo disfellowshipped Babbitt for his intransigence and for encouraging British immigrants and others to settle in Kirtland. Nauvoo's *Times and Seasons* published an itemized rebuke of the errors of the church in Kirtland. Written by Hyrum Smith, the article called upon the Kirtland Saints in the name of the Lord to move to Nauvoo to help build the temple and enjoy its blessings. The letter declared that a formal branch in Kirtland was "not according to the spirit and will of God" nor were plans for setting up a printing press, the ordaining of elders, and the sending out of a committee "to beg for the poor." Surplus funds, the directive said, were needed for the Nauvoo Temple. The Lord's will was to develop Nauvoo first and then enlarge Kirtland as part of the premillennial master plan to fill up North and South America. The strategy in 1841 was to work toward that end one step at a time.[78]

Babbitt's counselors and the Kirtland bishopric next appealed the decision in a letter to Joseph Smith. Convinced of their loyalty, in December 1841 the Prophet granted their request for a temporary continuation of the stake as long as its leaders did not persuade westering immigrants to stop short of Nauvoo. Acknowledging their efforts and the desire of those wanting to stay, the Prophet said, "You may as well continue operations according to your designs . . . but do not suffer yourselves to harbor the Idea that Kirtland will rise on the ruins of Nauvoo."[79]

Despite this uneasy truce, a number of the Ohio Saints left. One of them told Lyman Wight that he was anxious to raise his children among a community of the faithful. "His oldest daughter," Wight reported, "said that she had always wanted to go to Nauvoo ever since she had heard there was a Nauvoo."[80] Overall, the effort to bring the Saints out of Kirtland during the mid-1840s was reasonably successful. Even so, that comfortable location remained an important, though tenuously sanctioned gathering place for some Latter-day Saints.

Farther to the east, in the Northeastern states and eastern Canada, lay the homelands of many of the church's first members and prominent early leaders. Those who answered the call to gather first to Ohio and Missouri and then to Illinois left behind family, friends, and farms. Many traced a proud heritage to America's Anglo-American colonists and the patriots of the American Revolution. These important economic and kinship ties had kept some converts from leaving. They remained as gathered Saints in dozens of small hometown church branches, each supervised by a presiding elder. The number of branches and their members changed constantly as new converts joined the church and others migrated. During the 1840s in New York State, for example, presiding elders reported members in sixty-eight different branches ranging in size from fewer than ten members in many of the smaller village branches to more than two hundred in New York City.[81] Members lived in small clusters in every other northeastern and Atlantic seaboard state as well. During the Nauvoo years, besides those in New York State, at least 109 branches operated at one time or another in this region.[82]

Across the border in eastern Canada, energetic missionary work in the late 1830s had generated at least thirty-eight branches serving about two thousand members. Most were English-speaking residents of upper Canada in the Great Lakes area. A few English-speaking Latter-day Saints could be found in Protestant townships south of the predominantly Catholic, French-speaking areas of lower Canada. Converts were made as well in the Maritime Provinces. Most Latter-day Saints in British North America moved to Missouri in the 1830s. Many of the remainder joined the migration to Nauvoo. Thus, during the late Nauvoo years, few Latter-day Saints remained in Canada. Missionary contacts were infrequent and relatively unfruitful.[83]

Nor were many Latter-day Saints living in the Southern United States at the beginning of the Nauvoo period. Sustained missionary work in that area was yet future. Preaching would increase in the 1840s as the elders of Israel expanded their work of warning the world.

For all who heard and accepted the message of the gathering, the invitation to repent and prepare for the Savior's return to earth changed their lives. Through the ordinances of baptism and conferral of the gift of the Holy Ghost, they launched a spiritual withdrawal from the world and accepted membership in a society seeking to protect itself from worldliness. Many of these converts left family, friends, and livelihoods as they relocated from local branches to central gathering places. Those who crossed the Atlantic or moved west from hometowns in North America during the years of Nauvoo's preeminence, 1841–45, found themselves in a place of growing civil and religious influence as the booming city of Nauvoo became a spiritual beacon (and a political lightning rod) in the wilderness of western Illinois.

CHAPTER 5

Nauvoo's Magna Charta

The legislators of this state, . . . without respect to parties, without reluctance, freely, openly, boldly, and nobly, have come forth to our assistance, owned us as citizens and friends, and took us by the hand, and extended to us all the blessings of civil, political, and religious liberty, by granting us, under date of December 16, 1840, one of the most liberal charters, with the most plenary powers ever conferred by a legislative assembly on free citizens, "The City of Nauvoo," the "Nauvoo Legion," and the "University of the City of Nauvoo."

—FIRST PRESIDENCY, JANUARY 15, 1841

Latter-day Saints of the Nauvoo period wanted the communities where they lived to provide a moral haven for their families. As a religious people, they strived for holiness by withdrawing from worldly attractions and temptations. To support this objective, they endorsed laws and lifestyles in their neighborhoods consistent with their own ideals. In addition, they wanted to live free from religious harassment. They wanted protection for the constitutional rights denied them in Missouri. To achieve this goal, they sought to elect public officials who would protect their civil and religious rights.

Because of this active citizen involvement in the public arena and because of the religious views of government held by Nauvoo's Latter-day Saints, the lines between church and state sometimes blurred. In Nauvoo (and, later, in Salt Lake City), local civil government began with a religious forum resembling a town meeting. Eventually, these central gathering sites not only were places to live apart from the world but became municipalities as well. As civil governments, the cities functioned under established legal principles alongside a separate but interested ecclesiastical organization.

In western Illinois, as in northwestern Missouri, citizens took seriously the operation of local government. County officials held the most significant authority and were the most politically important public servants. Following a pattern most strongly established in Southern states, the county provided such basic services as roads, business licenses, a judicial system, and law enforcement through the sheriff and the county jail. The county served residents in unincorporated areas known as townships and offered some benefits to citizens within organized towns and cities.

Town government in Illinois was available under an 1831 law to any cluster of 150 or more settlers. After registering with the county a plat no larger than one square mile, citizens sought incorporation through the state legislature. Commerce, Carthage, Warsaw, and most other Illinois communities functioned as towns. An elected five-member board of trustees appointed a justice of the peace and such other officers as policemen, assessors, and tax collectors. The town board could enact local ordinances; issue licenses; provide for streets, sidewalks, and fire protection; and levy taxes on real estate.[1] Larger communities could seek incorporation as a city by requesting a legislative charter. This created a relatively independent, self-governing community with expanded legislative and judicial powers. These options were available to the Missouri exiles seeking refuge in Illinois.

Government before Incorporation

When Nauvoo was first platted, the few residents used the traditional services of Hancock County and the justice of the peace and post office of the town of Commerce. Instead of organizing as a town under Illinois law, they adopted an ecclesiastical approach. For sixteen months, until a municipal government was set up, a religious body known as the high council functioned in a dual role as a town board and in its traditional ecclesiastical capacity. For a religious group whose millennial worldview defined all aspects of life as ultimately spiritual, this was not an unusual mingling of civic and religious governance.[2]

William Marks   *John Smith*

Leaders of the first stakes in the new, upper Mississippi gathering place were trusted men with previous leadership experience. President Marks, who served in Nauvoo, was a close friend of Joseph and Emma Smith. John Smith, president of the Iowa stake, was the Prophet's uncle.

High councils of twelve men appointed by church leaders and headed by a president, with or without two counselors, had been an important administrative-judicial body since 1834 in larger Mormon congregations, or stakes.[3] These bodies had functioned in Kirtland, Ohio, and in Jackson County, Missouri, essentially for ecclesiastical purposes. In its judicial role, the council heard grievances between and against individuals. As a church governing council, the group approved appointments and ordinations. In Far West, Missouri, the high council managed the sale of building lots on church-owned property, a quasipublic function.[4]

This precedent set the stage for an expanded role for a high council in the unincorporated Nauvoo area. A church conference authorized the council in October 1839 when it approved Joseph Smith's proposal that Commerce be "appointed a stake and a place of gathering for the Saints." The stake included the newly platted Nauvoo, the incorporated town of Commerce, and the region extending into the farmland to the east. William Marks was named stake president, with no counselors. He had served as the presiding elder in Commerce since early May and was a former high councilor in Kirtland. Of the twelve men named to the high council in Nauvoo, half had served elsewhere in the calling.[5]

From the time of their appointment until the transition to a city government was completed, the high council kept one eye on ecclesiastical needs and another on the process of getting a community up and running. At its weekly Sunday evening gatherings in the homes of council members, the group deliberated and issued resolutions to meet the day-to-day needs of residents as church members and as citizens. Council regulations were published in the *Times and Seasons* for all to see.[6] After Joseph Smith became a regular attender at the high council meetings in the spring of 1840, the body met on Saturday afternoons in his log home office and began to conduct certain business for the entire church.[7] This pattern had been set when Kirtland was the seat of church government. It exemplified the foundational principle of making important decisions in conferences and in leadership councils.[8]

The Nauvoo high council had precedents to follow in both town and ecclesiastical governance. The obvious civic model was that of the New England town, whose business included "land distribution, appointment of town officers, economic regulations and taxes, church affairs, farming, personal quarrels in the community, relations with neighboring towns, relations with Indians, and relations with the [state] government."[9] The guide for religious responsibilities was easily found in the revelations that defined the first high council in Kirtland and in additional instructions from Joseph Smith.[10]

That the high council operated in both arenas can be seen in a synopsis of typical actions. Among its first civic decisions were resolutions regulating ferries and stray animals.[11] The council devoted considerable attention to the sale of town lots from parcels owned by the church.[12] It regulated the construction of business buildings—a boarding house in upper Commerce and a water-powered mill adjoining Nauvoo. The council helped launch a public school system by appointing trustees, an architect, and a building committee for a stone schoolhouse. It appointed a committee to petition the legislature for changes in the boundaries between Nauvoo and Commerce, which had been subsumed into Nauvoo. Finally, it organized a committee that included representatives from the Iowa high council to gather affidavits itemizing grievances against Missouri and appointed delegates to seek redress in Washington for these losses of personal property.[13]

The other side of the high council's enlarged role was the regulation of ecclesiastical affairs of a general nature under the oversight of the First Presidency. As an ad hoc board of publications, it authorized a hymnbook, launched a religious newspaper, and sponsored a new edition of the Book of Mormon.[14] Certain economic matters that Nauvoo bishops could not resolve were handed to the council. It agreed to complete an office for the church president, provide financial support for the families of full-time church leaders, and arrange housing for the worthy poor.[15] As requested by Joseph Smith, the council authorized agents to conduct church business in the East. It advised against plans by certain Latter-day Saints to move back to Kirtland.[16] To resolve another lingering question, it released Missouri exiles from their written pledges to fund the Far West Temple. At times, the council regulated priesthood quorums but not without challenges from those somewhat self-reliant groups.[17] Along with these administrative duties, the council exercised its basic judicial function in the stake by resolving disagreements between members and by deciding issues of individuals' standing in the church.[18]

With no legal status under state law, the council's only recourse against individuals who acted contrary to its regulations was disfellowshipment from the church. Thus, the council threatened to withdraw fellowship from anyone who operated a Commerce-Montrose ferry in competition with the one they had sanctioned or who allowed stray livestock to destroy crops. Similar sanctions were applied against those who blatantly ignored its spiritual counsel or whose personal behavior flouted church standards.[19] This was a powerful tool, for in a religious society to be excluded from fellowship effectively curbed a person's opportunities—political, economic, social, and religious.

The high council began the shift to an exclusively religious role during 1841. The process began in February, after a city government took over temporal affairs and a special religious meeting appointed Joseph Smith as sole trustee over church finances.[20] Even with a civil court system in place, the council encouraged Latter-day Saints to bring to it all but the most serious issues. The body also continued to help the First Presidency with certain temporal matters until the Twelve returned from England that fall. Transferred to the apostles at that time were responsibilities for "the settling of emigrants and the business of the Church at the stakes," such as managing "all debts and temporal business."[21]

By February 1842, after a year in transition, members of the Nauvoo high council were ready to formally reemphasize their normal role "as watchmen upon the walls of Zion." Accepting an exclusively religious focus, the body became Nauvoo's conscience and schoolmaster. An open letter to local residents promoted social union and counseled against gossip, trivial lawsuits, immorality, drunkenness, theft, and other un-Christian conduct.[22]

Local governments for the Latter-day Saints who were assembling on church lands in the Montrose area of Lee County, Iowa, followed the Nauvoo pattern. So did some later branches in western Illinois. When questions of general policy surfaced, or when matters involved people from different stakes, Joseph Smith and his counselors in the First Presidency formed the bridge to encourage uniformity of action or to resolve issues.[23]

The same conference that established the stake at Commerce set up a stake for "the west side of the river, in Iowa Territory," with John Smith, the Prophet's uncle, as president. He was assisted by two counselors, a high council, and two bishops. The Iowa stake presidency and council met infrequently, as needed, on various days of the week and in rotating meeting places, but often they met at Montrose in the home of Elijah Fordham, one of Smith's counselors. Within two years, the stake was serving 750 members in nine branches over a three-county area, with the greatest concentration in the Montrose area.[24]

One of those branches was named Zarahemla, organized to serve a townsite chosen by Joseph Smith in 1839. The community did not attract many settlers, nor did it expand as anticipated to envelop the adjacent village of Montrose. A revelation in March 1841 designated Zarahemla and Nashville, three miles south of Montrose, as Iowa's central gathering places. Zarahemla grew to thirty homes that summer. At an August conference, the Zarahemla branch, which included the Saints living in Montrose, reported 326 members, the largest congregation in Iowa. The Ambrosia branch, two miles farther west, served another 109 scattered members. Nashville had 90. In August, under the direction of two members of the Twelve, the Iowa stake was renamed the Zarahemla stake. This name had meaning for the exiled Missouri Saints in Iowa. Zarahemla was an ancient American land of refuge for a Book of Mormon people who fled Babylonia's conquest of Jerusalem in 587 to 586 B.C. Later on in the Book of Mormon narrative, the city of Zarahemla became the center of political, military, and religious life for the Nephite people.[25]

Under John Smith's direction, the Saints in Iowa strived to build an ideal Zion society, but their efforts were not without challenges. In its efforts to address social and civic needs, the Iowa high council faced a number of issues carried over from Missouri. In the civic arena, for example, the council recognized the impracticality of requiring impoverished exiles to pay what they owed others. So, personal debts that Latter-day Saints had incurred in Missouri among themselves, including debts consecrated to Missouri's bishop, were invalidated. Related civil suits between members were forbidden, upon penalty of disfellowshipment. In other civic actions, the council implemented the Nauvoo high council's request to collect affidavits on property lost in Missouri. And it threatened to disfellowship Montrose branch members who persisted in keeping tippling shops.[26]

In its strictly religious rulings, the Iowa high council struggled with questions about the system of religious consecration that had been implemented unsuccessfully in Missouri. Conscientious exiles wanted to honor their Missouri consecrations. How else, they wondered, could they achieve the desired unity and equality of a Zion people? The council reminded them that the plan in Missouri for sharing surplus wealth to help the poor had been supplanted by the law of tithing. A Nauvoo sermon by Hyrum Smith supported this perspective. Until the Saints were restored to their confiscated Missouri property or compensated for their losses, he said, it was folly to try to keep that law of the Lord. Even after hearing his nephew's sermon, stake president John Smith struggled with the Iowa council's decision. The council revisited the question and reinstated the law of consecration after President John Smith convinced them that the revelations in the Doctrine and Covenants were still binding. It took a visit by Joseph and Hyrum Smith in March 1840 to finally resolve the issue. Supporting Hyrum Smith's perspective, the Prophet told the council that it was the Lord's will to suspend all efforts to apply the consecration law at that time and place.[27]

ACQUIRING THE CHARTER

Nauvoo's founders did not intend the new settlement to continue indefinitely without a civil government. By practice, by revelation, and by proclamation, the Saints had subjected themselves to secular rule under a Christian tenet that defined compatible allegiances to both God and Caesar.[28] When their spiritual expectations were misunderstood in Kirtland, Latter-day Saints had adopted a declaration on governments that defined separate roles for civil and religious powers. That August 1835 statement bound the Saints "to sustain and uphold the respective governments in which they reside, while protected in their inherent and inalienable rights by the laws of such governments." While faithful American Latter-day Saints looked forward to the ultimate reign of the millennial Christ, they lived under a federal constitution that preserved the autonomy of religion. They celebrated and emulated this American inheritance in Nauvoo because it guaranteed a neutral secular state that protected all religions without favoring any one.[29]

Before initiating a request for incorporation, the leaders of Nauvoo's covenant community presented the idea to a religious gathering, the October 1840 general conference. This gathering followed the pattern of the area's high councils. Echoing the role of a New England-style town meeting, the conference considered matters both temporal and ecclesiastical—ordinations and appointments, thieves and debtors, new stakes and a house of worship, the debt on Nauvoo's land, publications, persecutions, and a civil government for Nauvoo.[30]

Leading the way on incorporation, under Joseph Smith's direction, was Nauvoo newcomer Dr. John C. Bennett. The thirty-six-year-old physician had moved to Nauvoo from Fairfield, in neighboring Wayne County, just a few weeks earlier. Prior to his relocation, in letters to Joseph Smith and Sidney Rigdon, Bennett had used his typical flattery to declare his intent to accept "an immediate immersion into the true faith of your beloved people." "I hope that time will soon come," he wrote, "when your people will become my people, and your God my God."[31]

Bennett had first met Joseph Smith and Sidney Rigdon when introduced to them by William McClellin in Kirtland in 1832, a meeting Smith seems to have forgotten in the intervening years. That brief encounter failed to convince Bennett to sever his loyalty to Alexander

Campbell's version of restored Christianity. Bennett's renewed interest in Mormonism in 1840 was meshed within a larger pursuit. In July, he had been appointed Illinois Quartermaster General. For a year before that, he had served as brigadier general of the Invincible Dragoons, a multicounty private militia combining the men of three southeastern counties (White, Edward, and Wabash). Over the previous fifteen years, in Ohio and other states, Bennett had been a medical practitioner and teacher, a college administrator, an itinerant minister, and a promoter of agricultural and social causes. This impressive resumé helped him win the trust and friendship of influential people in the blossoming City of the Saints. He offered his talents, expecting to fulfill his ambitions for personal political power.[32]

Dr. Bennett fit nicely into Joseph Smith's strategy for neutralizing any future opposition to Mormon settlements in Illinois. During the Nauvoo years, the Prophet would accept the help of a number of influential men outside the faith to further his religious objectives. Smith had embraced Isaac Galland's offer to sell land, he would welcome Bennett as a confidant and adviser, and he would befriend other men of ability and position. Bennett's skills as a lobbyist had convinced legislators in Ohio, Virginia, and Indiana to support his ideas, and that was the present need in Nauvoo.

In one of his letters, Bennett had advised church leaders to concentrate their energies in a single gathering place "with Commerce for its commercial emporium." Smith's response acknowledged the region's potential for commercial and agricultural growth and applauded the state charter just issued for a Warsaw-to-Nauvoo railroad. If realized, that link would overcome the deficit of the Nauvoo rapids that hindered commerce by stopping the large riverboats. Smith encouraged Bennett "to come as early as possible. . . . You will be of great service to us."[33]

Bennett did come, and for thirty-nine weeks boarded in the Smith home. The next session of the state legislature was set to convene in late November at Springfield, the place designated in 1839 to replace Vandalia as the state capital. During the Sunday morning session of the October conference, church president Joseph Smith, his clerk Robert B. Thompson, and Dr. John C. Bennett accepted the assignment to draft legislation "for the incorporating of the town of Nauvoo, and other purposes." Following a one-hour adjournment, Bennett presented to the reconvened conference an outline of a proposed bill to authorize a city

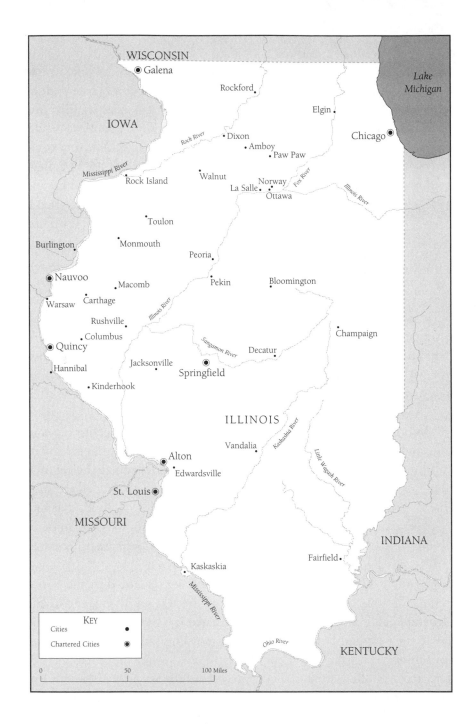

Towns and Cities in Nauvoo History

charter. No doubt considerable discussion of its contents and perhaps an entire draft of the bill had been underway prior to the weekend gathering. The conference assigned Bennett to guide a charter request through the legislature. Nauvoo leaders recognized that Bennett's knowledge of governmental affairs and acquaintance with state officials might help win approval.[34]

During the previous two years, the Illinois legislature had granted city charters to the lead-mining city of Galena on the northern border of Illinois, to the new state capital at Springfield, and to Quincy, Nauvoo's charitable Adams County neighbor. Prior to that, only Chicago and Alton had been issued city charters, both in 1837.[35] Each of the charters in that succession had built upon its predecessors, creating a pattern of familiarity for Illinois legislators. Quincy's planning committee had referenced the charters issued to Chicago and Alton and one in St. Louis, Missouri. Nauvoo's proposal patched together provisions imitating those already approved in the three more recent franchises—Galena, Quincy, and Springfield. A lengthy treatise on the Nauvoo city council's legislative authority was copied verbatim from the Springfield charter—a common and legitimate practice.[36]

Nauvoo's charter for municipal government provided for a city council, city officers, justices of the peace, and a municipal court. The council consisted of a mayor, four aldermen (one from each municipal ward), and nine councilors, all to serve two-year terms. Additional aldermen and councilors were permitted as the city grew and new wards became necessary. By December 1841, Nauvoo's mayor served with eight aldermen and sixteen councilors, equally divided among the four wards. To have both aldermen and councilors was a departure from the Illinois pattern. Commonly appointed officers were a recorder, treasurer, assessor, marshal, and streets supervisor.[37]

The charter defined a specific geographical area as the "City of Nauvoo" but allowed an unlimited expansion of city boundaries. Adjoining land would become part of the city by laying it out into town lots and recording the plat at the county courthouse. Quincy and Springfield enjoyed the same authority.[38]

Like the city councils in Galena, Quincy, and Springfield, Nauvoo's municipal council held legislative authority within its own jurisdiction like that of the state general assembly for the entire state. In effect, these

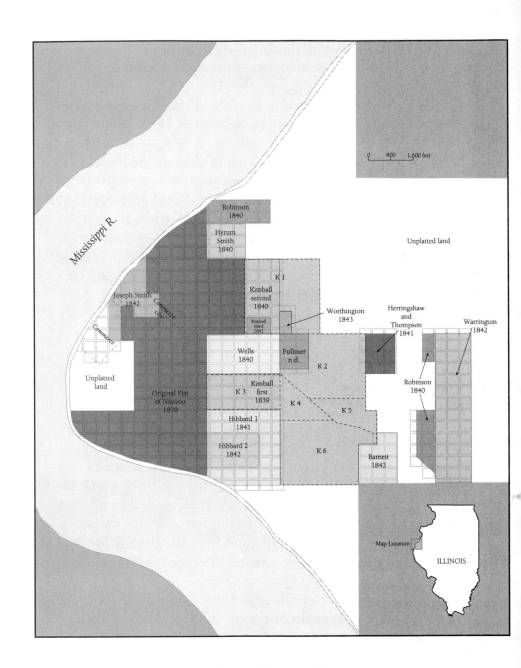

Surveyed Plats to 1842

city councils could pass ordinances that contradicted state law, as long as those ordinances did not conflict with the state or national constitution. Quincy lost that power in 1840.[39]

A provision in the charter that granted judicial functions to the Nauvoo city council was not unusual in American municipal government. It differed only slightly from other Illinois cities. Like Chicago and Alton, the City of Nauvoo had two juristic levels, justices of the peace and a municipal court. The Nauvoo charter named the elected mayor and aldermen justices of the peace. They received commissions from the governor. The mayor held exclusive jurisdiction over all judicial matters concerning city laws. He was joined by the aldermen when considering civil or criminal cases grounded in state laws. Decisions of the justices of the peace could be appealed to Nauvoo's municipal court, consisting of the mayor as chief justice and the aldermen as associate justices—in other words, all of the city's justices of the peace sitting together. Appeals could also be heard before the chief justice by a twelve-member jury. Decisions of the municipal court could be appealed to the Circuit Court of Hancock County.[40]

These provisions differed only slightly from other chartered cities in Illinois. In all Illinois cities, the mayor served as a justice of the peace. In Chicago and Alton, the only other cities with a municipal court, the municipal judge was not automatically the mayor, as in Nauvoo, but someone appointed by the governor with approval of the general assembly. Unlike in Nauvoo, this judge sat without associate justices. The courts in Chicago and Alton exercised concurrent jurisdiction with a circuit court, whereas Nauvoo cases had to go first to the Hancock Circuit Court before an appeal could be sent to the state supreme court.[41]

Another judicial provision granted to Nauvoo's municipal court "power to grant writs of habeas corpus in all cases arising under the ordinances of the City Council." The Alton charter had been amended in mid-1839 to give it this power, a precedent for the Nauvoo document.[42]

In all of these municipal arrangements, it was in their use rather than in their definition that Nauvoo city officials offended their neighbors. A number of Nauvoo's municipal leaders served at the same time in religious positions. So, when they used the charter to defend Joseph Smith and his colleagues against legal attacks and vigilante threats, opponents accused them of melding church and state authority to protect religious interests. In one sense, Latter-day Saints agreed. They believed that beneficent legislators had empowered them to protect their own civil and religious rights and to defend themselves against opponents. Nauvoo's charter may not have been as unique as it appeared to the First Presidency, who described it in 1841 as "one of the most liberal charters, with the most plenary powers, ever conferred by a legislative assembly on free citizens." But in a local context, Nauvoo's independent authority stood in stark contrast to the small town governments elsewhere in Hancock County. Ultimately, because of its large population, Nauvoo's influence at the polls in county and legislative elections were perceived as the greater threat to minority rights in the region.[43]

The Nauvoo city charter differed most significantly from others in granting power to the city council to organize "a body of independent military men" and "an institution of learning." In essence, the legislature wrapped three state charters into one—a city, a militia, and a university. Once they were set in motion by city council action, the University of the City of Nauvoo and the Nauvoo Legion became self-governing entities. Although no other city university existed in Illinois at the time, the legislature had created other colleges and named their boards in the authorizing charters. In Nauvoo, city officials named the board of trustees for the university, including the chancellor and regents. Similarly, the militia elected its own officers from among those commissioned by the state. The militia could be called into action by the mayor to defend city laws or by the governor. The board of trustees for the university and the court martial for the militia created and enforced their own laws. The only restriction was one applied to the city council as well: they could contradict existing state laws but not the state or national constitutions.[44]

With its base in a single city, Nauvoo's militia differed on paper from most other volunteer military groups in the state. The typical militia served an entire county or group of counties. The Nauvoo militia would soon take on that characteristic, like the multicounty Invincible Dragoons in southeastern Illinois that John C. Bennett had helped create. Bennett's previous experience with that military company and his role in creating the Fairfield Institute at Fairfield, Illinois, suggest that he played a key role in defining the university and militia in the Nauvoo charter. Similarities between the provisions for the Fairfield and Nauvoo schools and between charters for the two militias support that probability.[45]

The city charter proposed for Nauvoo seemed appropriately familiar to legislators at Springfield when introduced on Friday, November 27, 1840. More than 80 percent of its provisions closely followed franchises authorized for other Illinois cities. No one saw the need for extended debate. This was but one of many requests for political recognition in a rapidly growing state. Seven other requests for city charters were approved by the Twelfth General Assembly. More city charters would follow, until 1870, when a constitutional revision ended the practice.[46]

Whatever encouragement was needed to ensure passage came from John C. Bennett, who lobbied key political leaders, both Whig and Democratic. State supreme court justice (and later governor) Thomas Ford remembered, "Bennett managed affairs well for his constituents. He flattered both sides with the hope of Mormon favor; and both sides expected to receive their votes." The vivacious Bennett had hinted of such political promises when the October conference approved the charter proposal. It was a duty placed upon the Saints, he had said, to support with their votes those who had helped them as suffering exiles. The conference clerk described these as "very appropriate remarks," but they were later dropped from the historical record.[47]

The Nauvoo bill was the second of the session presented to the forty senators meeting in the new capitol building. Senator Sidney H. Little, a Whig who represented McDonough and Hancock Counties, was its chief sponsor. His brief introduction drew attention only to what he termed an "extraordinary militia clause" that he considered harmless. Little would be honored in Nauvoo as "a patriot, statesman, and lawyer" in a special day of fasting eight months later when he was killed jumping from a runaway wagon.[48] Following two readings of the bill by title, delegates referred the bill to the Senate's judiciary committee. Eight days later, the eloquent Adam W. Snyder of St. Clair County—the committee's chairman and Democratic nominee for governor in 1842—reported it back favorably with one amendment to adjust the city boundary. After a third reading, the Senate approved the bill on December 9 by voice vote.[49]

The following day, the ninety members of the House of Representatives, gathered in the Methodist Church, considered the bill on the motion of A. R. Dodge. Suspending the rules, the House read the bill the first and the second time by its title and sent it to the House judiciary committee. Reported unchanged to the full House after two days, it was read under suspended rules a third time by title and passed by voice vote

Illinois legislators asked few questions about the provision to create a city militia for Nauvoo. The state routinely authorized local military units to provide convenient opportunity for all able-bodied males to complete their required military service.

with only a few nay votes. The governor affixed his signature on December 16, and the bill was issued two days later. It became effective on the first Monday of February 1841, the day set for Nauvoo elections.[50]

Immediately, in a report to Nauvoo published in the *Times and Seasons,* John C. Bennett hailed the package as "very broad and liberal. . . . Every power we asked has been granted, every request gratified, every desire fulfilled." He specifically thanked Senator Little (for his "untiring diligence") and Representative John F. Charles ("an *acting* and not a *talking* man") and their colleagues for ensuring a unanimous approval in the Senate and little dissent in the House. "Illinois has acquitted herself with honor," he beamed, "and her State Legislature shall never be forgotten."[51]

Bennett paid tribute to Whig Representative Abraham Lincoln. Nauvoo's political leaders had removed Lincoln's name from November's legislative ballot ("not, however, on account of any dislike to him as a man, but simply because his was the last name on the ticket, and we desired to show our friendship to the Democratic party by substituting the name of Ralston for some one of the Whigs"). After the House vote, Lincoln personally and cordially congratulated Bennett on the charter's approval.[52]

Bennett's objective as Nauvoo's chief lobbyist, he said, had been to eliminate "unjust prejudice and unreasonable opposition." He called for a similar response from the Latter-day Saints: "I have said that we are *a law abiding people,* and we must now *show* it. . . . Justice, *equal justice,* should be our fixed object and purpose." Bennett encouraged the residents of Nauvoo to seek unity in basic principles, both religious and political, while allowing individuals the freedom to express their feelings in nonessentials. An accompanying editorial comment by Don Carlos Smith praised the charter for its permissive provisions, an idea repeated often in later commentaries.[53]

In a follow-up proclamation and taking their cue from Bennett's effusive report, the First Presidency published its own thanks to the legislature for setting aside partisan differences to grant a liberal and powerful charter and for granting these rights in "perpetual succession." Significantly for the future, church leaders interpreted this phrase to mean the conferral "in all time to come, irrevocably" of civil, political, and religious liberty. These rights had been denied the Saints in Missouri, church leaders noted; they belonged to all citizens—"'tis all we ever claimed." The presidency thanked Illinois for guaranteeing constitutional rights and "the protection of law—the security of life, liberty, and the peaceable pursuit of happiness." It was, they declared, "our *magna charta*." Church leaders promised to extend equal privileges and friendship to Nauvoo citizens of every religious persuasion.[54]

In a later personal reflection, Lucy Mack Smith, the Prophet's mother, saw the charter as a shield against Missouri's attempts to arrest the exiled Mormon leaders. Protections offered by the city government, she understood, would allow her fugitive son to "remain at home in peace."[55]

Passage of the charter drew an immediate response from the Whig press. At Warsaw, Thomas Sharp picked up on the Mormon delight in the charter's character. Ignoring the similar handling of other city charters, the twenty-two-year-old editor of the *Warsaw Signal* criticized the legislature's apparent nonchalance in authorizing the franchise. The editor of Springfield's *Sangamo Journal* reprimanded the Illinois senate and house for failing to record votes by name. If citizens objected to the provisions of Nauvoo's charter, he wrote, who among the elected delegates should they hold responsible?[56]

The Latter-day Saints were not interested in counting votes. In their minds, the Illinois legislature had acted above partisanship to secure their constitutional rights. Under the city charter, they could create any law not repugnant to the constitution of the state of Illinois or of the United States. The common political theory of the day, exemplified in other Illinois city charters as well, ensured the home rule of the common man through his own local representatives.

In an effort to reassure the old residents, church leaders publicly proclaimed that the Saints would exercise "implicit obedience to the laws." The new city would enact ordinances to serve the common good. By fulfilling their military obligations apart from other local groups, the First Presidency declared, the Saints would avoid conflict and demonstrate their loyalty to constituted government.[57]

NAUVOO'S CITY GOVERNMENT AT WORK

With the charter in place, the Saints turned their attention to the task of governing Nauvoo. From the beginning, Nauvoo's leaders attempted to assure Hancock County's doubters that the city would operate under civil rather than ecclesiastical rules. As a replacement for the high council, the city council reflected the secular pattern of other cities. In its day-to-day operations and passage of ordinances judged "necessary for the peace, benefit, good order, regulation, convenience, and cleanliness, of [the] city; for the protection of property . . . and for the health and happiness" of residents, Nauvoo differed little from other communities.[58]

John C. Bennett was still basking in the gratitude of the people of Nauvoo for his help in securing their city charter when he organized a series of public nominating meetings. The first convened at the store of brothers William and Wilson Law on January 2, 1841. Bennett encouraged a diverse slate of candidates. Seven men stood for the four aldermen slots; twenty-one for nine positions on the council. Only Bennett himself, seeking the office of mayor, was unopposed.[59]

At the February 1 election, majorities ranging from 330 to 337 votes elected the city's first officers. All of them reflected the electorate's preference for men of public stature and ability. Another possible influence on Latter-day Saint voters was an 1833 revelatory reflection on Missouri's troubles: "When the wicked rule the people mourn. Wherefore, honest men and wise men should be sought for diligently, and good men and wise men ye should observe to uphold." All but two of Nauvoo's first elected officers were Latter-day Saints. Considering the overwhelming Mormon character of the growing city of five thousand residents, that was a generous inclusion of old-timers among the good and wise men elected to office.[60]

Skeptics read the election as evidence not only that Latter-day Saints dominated public office but also that church leaders controlled civic affairs in Nauvoo. Among the winners were the entire First Presidency, the stake

In the 1840s, voters typically stated their preferences vocally to an election clerk, but this metal ballot box apparently was used in Nauvoo's Third Municipal Ward during the Mormon period.

president, and one member of the high council. Within a year, this question became an issue that enticed Ebenezer Robinson and Gustavus Hills, editors of the *Times and Seasons,* to offer a defense: "A large number of the officers of the *Nauvoo Legion;* several members of the *City Council,* both *Aldermen* and *Councillors;* and a large portion of the *Regents of the University;* are not members of any church—many of them are old citizens who resided here long before we were driven from Missouri." The civic councils of Nauvoo, they claimed, made room for "men of sterling worth and integrity," even though "they do not believe in our religion." The bottom line, they said, remained the equal protection for all citizens under the supremacy of the Constitution and the laws of the land.[61]

The reality in Nauvoo was that the various governing councils did indeed involve men of affairs regardless of their religious orientation, although nearly all were Latter-day Saints. During the four years through 1844, the city council always included two or three non-Mormons. Hiram Kimball, Daniel H. Wells, John T. Barnett, Hugh McFall, and Benjamin Warrington were those who served. But church leaders played an increasingly dominant role. After the first election, the council of nine always included five to seven members of the Quorum of the Twelve among its numbers. Joseph Smith became mayor in 1842 and played an active role in suggesting new laws. By 1844, only one apostle, John E. Page, had not served on the council (he spent most of his time as the presiding church officer in Pittsburgh). High council representation was more limited—three high councilors served as elected city officials; others accepted appointive positions.[62]

The university's twenty-three regents counted three who were not Latter-day Saints—Daniel H. Wells, John T. Barnett, and Zenos M. Knight. Two other old-timers on the board, Isaac Galland and Davison Hibbard, had been baptized. As with other civic bodies in Nauvoo, the university claimed in its highest councils its share of prominent Latter-day Saints, including all of the First Presidency and five other church leaders.[63]

Operationally, the municipal government of Nauvoo passed ordinances and functioned for the most part just as did any other government of a city of its size in the 1840s. Section 13 of the Nauvoo charter incorporated an exact copy of Springfield's list of legislative powers. Ordinances based on most of these topics became part of Nauvoo's corpus of laws during 1842. Echoing the pattern of the times, the city granted the franchise to white adult male citizens of good moral character who had lived in the state for six months.[64] In administrative matters, Nauvoo's city council opened and named streets and appointed a coroner, auctioneer, pound keeper, city attorney, and other officers.[65] Because of the press of legal work created by a booming town, the city appointed its own notary public. The council regulated the morals of the community by restricting entertainments, prohibiting brothels, and strictly controlling the dispensing of liquor.[66] It involved itself in economic life by licensing businesses and by regularizing weights and measures, brick sizes, and specie. The city owned two hay scales used by farmers to weigh their crops. In response to complaints, it issued edicts to control loose livestock and the removal of dead animals.[67]

One of Nauvoo's most perplexing problems was that of crime prevention. City officers contended with the vices of a few of Nauvoo's own population as well as those of undesirable visitors. As a river town, Nauvoo attracted the usual drifters—including thieves, counterfeiters, and renegades. Even though such ne'er-do-wells visited other Mississippi Valley towns as well, opponents of Nauvoo unfairly blamed all such crimes on the Latter-day Saints, when, in fact, lawbreakers were found among both residents and transients.[68]

The responsibility for maintaining peace and order within city limits fell upon the justices of the peace, a municipal court, and the marshals.

Although the marshals appointed in each municipal ward acted as policemen in the city, general law enforcement in western Illinois fell to the county sheriff, a system common in the Southern United States, where (unlike New England) county government played a primary role. But Nauvoo's residents knew another system, the English tradition of citizen responsibility employed in New England, in which men over sixteen took turns standing watch. That approach to peace keeping, operating in tandem with the court system, became the pattern for addressing Nauvoo's urban needs.

Like the municipal government, the police system of Nauvoo evolved over the years from a volunteer force to paid watchmen and back again. Sponsors included an unusual mix of religious, military, and municipal officials. The Quorum of the Twelve Apostles first proposed establishing a police force after some Latter-day Saints were expelled from the church and from the Nauvoo Legion for stealing property in Ramus in November 1841. Nothing came of that proposal.[69] Six months later, Mayor Joseph Smith, concerned by an alleged attempt on his life during a sham battle of the Nauvoo Legion, directed militia officers to organize a city watch. The Legion appointed sixteen men, headed by city marshal Dimick Huntington, to protect the city against theft and other mischief. The watchmen spent much of their time enforcing Nauvoo's laws against disorderly conduct and the sale of liquor by the drink.[70]

In January 1843, the city council exercised its legislative right "to establish, support and regulate night watches." The council appointed Jonathan Dunham as captain of police. Presumably, he took control of the municipal patrol named the previous spring by the Nauvoo Legion. In December, the city council increased the number of police to forty and defined their duties. They were to maintain the peace, enforce city ordinances, ferret out thieves, and act as watchmen day and night. They paid particular attention to the safety of Joseph Smith.[71]

Despite a promise to pay the men, the city lacked sufficient funds and soon owed its watchmen considerable back pay. Offers from several city councilors to forego their own salaries did not provide sufficient funds, so the police were dismissed. In November 1844, a council of religious and civic leaders met at the Masonic Hall. To satisfy the discharged police, the church agreed to pay their back salaries. Then the council authorized a corps of several hundred part-time volunteers. In just over two months, five hundred new policemen had been identified and oriented to their duties. These men assumed their duties just as the Nauvoo charter was being rescinded. Known thereafter as the "old police" and under church oversight, the volunteers continued service as personal bodyguards for the Twelve and nightwatchmen at the temple.[72]

THE NAUVOO LEGION

Another means for protecting life and property in Nauvoo was the municipal militia. Acting under the authority given it in the Nauvoo charter, the city council empowered the Nauvoo Legion on February 3, 1841. Formal organization took place the next day, with Joseph Smith at the head and John C. Bennett next in command. During the next four years, the military group played a visible role with impressive public appearances on Independence Day and for other ceremonial occasions. As an independent element of the state militia, the Legion or its subgroups drilled regularly to prepare the volunteer army to defend the city and her people.

Nauvoo's Latter-day Saints lauded their military organization as a means to protect their rights against threats by organized opponents. They defended the militia's motives in prose and poetry. "In the time of peace," wrote the editors of the *Times and Seasons,* "it is necessary to prepare for war." Then, quoting George Washington on defensive preparations, the editors added, "*If we desire to avoid insult we must be ready to repel it.*" Poetess Eliza R. Snow reaffirmed the Legion's role as the opponent of oppression, the defender of law, "a strong bulwark of Freedom—of pure Liberty."[73]

It was not the rights of the Saints that concerned citizens elsewhere in Hancock and nearby counties, however. As the old citizens watched the Mormon population and its militia grow in numbers, they came to believe that the Nauvoo Legion would be misused in offensive action against their own freedoms. When Nauvoo's militia first came under verbal attack in 1842, John C. Bennett defended the basis of its authority. Claiming authorship of the charters for both the Legion and the Invincible Dragoons, Bennett touted them as the two best militias in the state. If anyone had anything against Nauvoo's militia, he said, they should criticize the Dragoons as well.[74]

Nauvoo's militia followed an organizational system based on Roman legions. It consisted of two cohorts (or brigades), each commanded by a brigadier general and his staff. The first cohort was a mounted cavalry; the other, foot soldiers. By late 1841, the Legion had increased from six companies to fourteen in Illinois and two in Iowa, eleven of them infantry units. A few months later, a report listed twenty-six companies in the Legion.[75] Regulations adopted by the court martial allowed these companies to range in size from thirty-two to sixty-four privates. None of the companies was filled completely, nor was a full complement needed to function.[76]

Under Illinois law, the state militia was made up of the sum of all local military companies. Each elected its own officers, who were required to have a commission from the governor. Through his quartermaster general, the governor furnished the soldiers with arms. He could call up local units in times of need, or he might authorize Illinois mayors to activate a local militia to enforce laws or suppress riots. Most local groups were organized as county militias. They held general inspections at the county seat. As needed, detachments within the county were formed at the precinct level for convenience in drills. The state could also authorize multicounty units, such as the Invincible Dragoons, or independent city militias, such as those at Quincy, Carthage, and Nauvoo. The Nauvoo Legion's independent status meant that it was not subject to Hancock County's brigadier general. Like the county militias, the Nauvoo Legion and other independent groups reported directly to the governor.[77]

The Nauvoo Legion's most unusual organizational feature was its chief officer, who held the rank of lieutenant general. Not since George Washington had the United States known a lieutenant general; and during the war with Mexico in the late 1840s, Congress would refuse to grant the title to the head of the United States Army. Joseph Smith secured the unusual rank without contest from Illinois governor Thomas Carlin in March 1841, even though Smith's previous military experience was limited. He had led Zion's Camp, a group of willing volunteers, from Ohio to Missouri in 1834. In Missouri, the lasting effects of an early operation on his leg and his status as a full-time minister of the gospel had exempted him from official military service. Yet he did lead an armed force in one of the retaliatory raids.[78]

Lieutenant General Joseph Smith   *Major General John C. Bennett*

Leaders of the Nauvoo Legion. The leaders of Nauvoo's city militia also served together in city and church government. Joseph Smith nurtured his new ally's friendship, hoping that Bennett's talents and experience would help the Saints avoid conflict with their neighbors.

In practice, Lieutenant General Smith played only a ceremonial role in the Nauvoo militia. He left the details to his subordinates. Even so, he had a personal staff of fifteen men, including two colonels of cavalry and a third who oversaw a personal bodyguard of twelve captains of infantry.

As second in command, John C. Bennett took effective day-to-day control of the Legion through his appointment as major general.[79] Bennett's staff planned regular training for the Legion and organized its appearances in public engagements. His assistants included the operational officers and appropriate assistants. The major general's staff also served the brigadier generals, Wilson Law and Charles C. Rich, who headed the two cohorts. Bennett relished his military authority, as he had his previous experience as an officer in the Invincible Dragoons.

While in Nauvoo, Bennett continued to serve as state quartermaster general. It was in this role that he outfitted the Nauvoo Legion from the federal armory in Springfield. As was typical for state militia units, Nauvoo Legion troops received outdated weapons from an annual federal allotment to the states. Because they competed with other units for the meager supplies, some Illinois residents believed that Bennett favored the

Nauvoo Legion in his 1841 distribution.[80] A report the following year in the Alton *Telegraph* claimed that the Legion had received 5 six-pounder cannons, 500 muskets, 460 pistols, 85 rifles, 113 yeagers (a rifled musket), and 123 swords from the state armory. That summary prompted a short-lived effort in the state legislature to have the arms returned to the state and reallocated to militias that felt shorted.[81]

While the state copies of the legally mandated annual reports cannot be found in order to verify Bennett's dispersals, a year-end report completed in Nauvoo in 1843 does account for arms held by the Legion's second cohort, the infantry. That official register lists 63 muskets, 133 rifles, 98 swords, 4 pistols, and 3 cannons.[82] Major General Wilson Law stated in mid-1844 that the Legion's entire inventory included three cannons and "about two hundred fifty stands [complete sets] of arms and their accoutrements." If Law is correct, then the Legion's cavalry brigade, or first cohort, must have received around fifty long guns from the state. Officers typically provided their own swords.[83] Thomas Sharp disagreed with Law. "The fact is," he argued, "the Mormons had eight or nine hundred stand of state arms." But Sharp may have been remembering the Alton *Telegraph*'s controversial 1842 report.[84]

There are good reasons to accept the Legion's 1843 inventory as an accurate accounting of the arms held by the infantry brigade. If the cavalry were equally equipped (an unlikely situation), the Nauvoo Legion would have had around six hundred pieces, plus whatever individuals secured for themselves. In most American militias, the soldiers provided for themselves more often than they had arms furnished to them. That would have increased their defensive capability and, perhaps, explained the discrepancy in numbers.

Because Illinois did not provide uniforms for the militia, the soldiers depended upon their own resources for their dress. Most of them probably used whatever they could reasonably get but with some attention to consistency. Nauvoo's leading officers quickly outfitted themselves with a full and costly uniform consisting of coat and pantaloons, epaulets, sash, hat with feathers, gloves, spurs, sword, and belt—costing $208. Another $185 bought the necessary "horse equipments." John Bills, a Nauvoo tailor, made the military coats for at least the five top officers of the Legion. He used patterns secured from Philadelphia by Hyrum Smith.[85] By April 1841, more than a dozen of Joseph Smith's personal staff sported what were described as "splendid uniforms," and several entire companies had simpler but consistent attire. A year later, a large proportion of the soldiers wore some kind of uniform.[86]

One controversial issue in the first months of the Legion's existence was that of membership. All eligible Illinois males between the ages of eighteen and forty-five years were expected to enlist in a local militia and train a certain number of days each year. Nauvoo Legion officers secured a specific legislative act confirming that their militia could accept as a volunteer any eligible male in Hancock County. In addition, the Legion's legislative body, the court martial, banned city residents from enlisting elsewhere. The result was a countywide militia made up mostly of Latter-day Saints. Outsiders perceived the expanding Nauvoo Legion as a private Mormon army controlled by church leaders to serve their own interests.[87] Nauvoo militia leaders insisted that their forces played a traditional role:

> The Legion is not, as has been falsely represented by its enemies, exclusively a Mormon military association, but a body of citizen-soldiers organized (without regard to political preferences or religious sentiments) for the public defence, the general good, and the preservation of law and order . . . against misrule, anarchy, and mob violence.

In this same document, Joseph Smith and John C. Bennett encouraged existing militia companies in Hancock County as well as unaffiliated citizens to join the Nauvoo Legion. They promised "correct military instruction under the teachings of experienced officers, according to the drill and discipline of the United States Army."[88]

In response to this solicitation, Latter-day Saints soon formed detachments of the Nauvoo Legion at Ramus and Seven-mile Mound. (Interestingly, two other affiliated companies were formed in the Mormon settlements across the Mississippi in Iowa.) The officers in certain precinct units of the Hancock County militia challenged this clustering of their Latter-day Saint neighbors by levying fines when Mormons failed to register with local units. But an 1833 Illinois law that permitted such fines to discourage the formation of independent companies had been repealed in 1837. State supreme court justice Stephen A. Douglas confirmed the illegality of these fines. Furthermore, Douglas sustained the Nauvoo charter's provision exempting Legion soldiers, wherever they lived, "from all

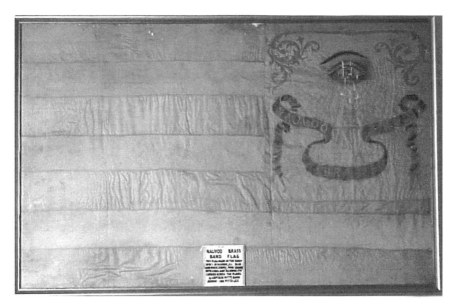

The Nauvoo Legion and its band, headed by Edward P. Duzett, each had its own flag. Captain William Pitt led another group, the Nauvoo Brass Band, whose flag of blue and white stripes is decorated with a name scroll and all-seeing eye sewn on a pink field.

other military duty." The Mormons in Hancock County could join the militia of choice, and they chose the Nauvoo Legion.[89]

Some men neglected their duty and ignored the state requirement to enlist. Legion commandants did what they could to "enroll every man residing within the bounds of their respective commands, and not attached to any other company of the Legion." An 1842 Legion ordinance authorized officers residing outside the city to withdraw if they proved enrollment within their own precincts. This minor exception did not silence critics who challenged efforts to enlist in the Nauvoo Legion every Latter-day Saint in the region.[90]

Like the population of Nauvoo itself, the actual number enlisted in the Legion was sometimes exaggerated. Presumed reliable is the annual report to the state adjutant general in September 1841, which lists 1,490 soldiers. An accounting two years later listed 1,751 men in the Legion's infantry brigade. No report has survived for the cavalry, which had only one-third as many companies as the infantry.[91] A St. Louis newspaper put the total number at two thousand in June 1844. The editor had heard Joseph Smith claim twice that many fighting men just a few weeks earlier.

Some reports had the Legion as high as five thousand men in 1845. If all eligible Latter-day Saint men in Hancock County were enrolled, along with some in Iowa, that number of men might have responded if needed for an emergency. Actual regular involvement probably fell short of the ideal.[92]

State military regulations required regular drills and reviews of the local companies, and the Legion marched at various places set aside for public use. Its first drills were near the site later used for the Masonic Hall. In June 1844, the Legion paraded at the Masonic Hall field one day, met at the Arsenal ground west of the temple the next day, then moved for drilling to "the ground near Spencer's northeast of the Temple." On June 27 they assembled again at "the parade ground North East of the Temple."[93] Companies living outside the Nauvoo precinct were excused from attending all but the July parade and the Legion's business meetings (the semiannual court martial) but were required to hold their own regular exercises.[94]

Besides its scheduled drills, the Legion participated in regular public appearances. Perhaps the best attended by the public was one in April 1841 when the troops assembled for their first full dress review behind the Masonic Hall on the flat before participating in the cornerstone-laying ceremonies at the temple site on the bluff. Every May and September thereafter, the Legion paraded to meet its military obligations and for the enjoyment of the citizens. The Legion also played a major role in the annual Independence Day patriotic programs. Although the general parades were always held in Nauvoo, musters of battalions and companies took place within the precinct defined as that group's boundaries.[95]

The general parades were spectacles of military pomp that attracted onlookers from Nauvoo and beyond. At times, thousands arrived by riverboat, wagons, and carriages for the event. In some officers' drills, on the two days preceding a general parade, the wife of an officer would ride alongside her husband. An 1843 report described "six ladies on horses, with white feathers or plumes waving over black velvet, riding up and down in front of the regiment."[96]

Observers were impressed by the precision of the military exercises and with the lack of intoxication. "This Legion will surpass anything for splendor and martial spirit in the State or perhaps all the States," John S. Fullmer boasted in March 1841. "It is determined that the scenes acted out in Missouri shall not be acted over again in any State with impunity, or at least without an honourable defence."[97]

But at least to a few, the military pomp portended an uncertain future for the City of Peace. Commenting on the physically short but ambitiously towering John C. Bennett's move to Nauvoo, Vilate Kimball informed her missionary husband, Heber, in England: "He is a big man and I hope a good one. He is a great warrior. Many of our brethren have got the same spirit. I expect it is all right."[98]

PART II

LIFE IN NAUVOO:
A PEOPLE OF PROMISE

The Lord called his people ZION, because they were of one heart and one mind, and dwelt in righteousness; and there was no poor among them. And Enoch continued his preaching in righteousness unto the people of God. And . . . he built a city that was called the City of Holiness, even ZION. And . . . Enoch . . . said unto the Lord: Surely Zion shall dwell in safety forever.

—FROM A REVELATION TO JOSEPH SMITH, DECEMBER 1830

As to the church at large, at home and abroad, if they will now repent of all these evils, and come together as the heart of one man; and be governed by counsel, and seek to employ themselves and each other, and to support and build up in perfect union, according to the plan of heaven; they shall be saved; and no power shall scatter or destroy them; but if not, behold your house is left unto you desolate, and the kingdom of God shall come with power for the deliverance of those who will do these things.

—FROM A LETTER BY PARLEY P. PRATT, SEPTEMBER 1844

CHAPTER 6

The Promise of Prosperity

The whole time and attention of the Saints in this place since their beginning have been, in consequence of persecution and banishment from Missouri, devoted to opening new farms, building habitations, and to supplying themselves with food.

—ORSON HYDE, FEBRUARY 1843

There is little hope for worldly prosperity in Nauvoo. The city is neither a commercial mart in itself, nor does it supply the markets of others. It is to a certain extent quite isolated, and has absolutely no principle of aggregation—if we except that of accumulating population.

—HENRY LEWIS, 1845

Every immigrant arriving in Nauvoo after 1840 and every visitor, too, it seems, noticed the same thing about Nauvoo. The city was growing, and growing rapidly. Wherever they looked, newcomers found the sights and sounds of buildings under construction. "The sound of the ax, the hammer, and the saw, greet your ear in every direction," Don Carlos Smith wrote in an article celebrating the arrival of spring in 1841. "Habitations are reared for miles in every direction, and others are springing up." He applauded the effort necessary to provide housing for arriving immigrants. "Hundreds of houses, shops, mills, &c., are expected to go up in the course of the summer, when," he noted, "our city will present a

123

scene of industry, beauty, and comfort, hardly equaled in any place in our country."[1]

Missionaries returning after extended service abroad reacted similarly. Heber C. Kimball arrived from England in July 1841. "When we got in sight of Nauvoo," he wrote back to Parley P. Pratt, "we were surprised to see what improvements had been made since we left home. You know there were not more than thirty buildings in the city when we left about two years ago, but at this time there are twelve hundred, and hundreds of others in progress, which will be finished soon."[2] Many of these new buildings were temporary log structures, created to offer immediate shelter and then abandoned when better was available.

Benjamin Winchester, who left Commerce just as Mormon settlement was beginning in the spring of 1839, was "completely astonished" at the progress he found two and one-half years later. From the vantage point of the temple, he observed the residential patterns that would define Mormon Nauvoo:

> On the left, south, as you front the river the lots are mostly taken, and a great share of the improvements seem to be bestowed upon this part of the city. . . . On the north of the Temple there has also been a great improvement, and a large portion of that part of [the] corporation is quite densely populated. East of the Temple lot some ten miles, which you are aware is more or less timbered land, it is completely spotted with dwellings. The large prairie east of the city presents a very pleasing prospect: several buildings are completed and others in progress. Some are engaged fencing, others plowing, and preparing their land for the ensuing season.[3]

Winchester's overview summarized the economic realities of Nauvoo. Nestled against a gentle bend in the Mississippi, Nauvoo was, first, a boomtown expanding to house a people and, second, a hinterland of outlying farms flourishing to feed them. The first need in the new city was to house a burgeoning population. Beyond that, the economy seemed devoted to sustaining the gathered people with foodstuffs. Little time remained for other tasks. Some wondered if Nauvoo's effort had been so singlehandedly focused on opening farms and erecting houses that other needs, particularly the creation of factories to provide goods and jobs, had been neglected.[4]

Despite the expectation of some that Nauvoo should join the industrial revolution to realize its urban potential, that dream would not be realized during the city's short life as a Mormon gathering place. Construction and crops would be the keywords in Nauvoo's economy. Commerce and crafts supported the task of providing basic human needs in an economy based on an agrarian credit system. Whatever their hope for societal change, the people of Nauvoo would maintain the agrarian lifestyle of traditional society.

As with other activities for the Latter-day Saints, the very task of housing and feeding a family in Nauvoo acquired a religious meaning. The Saints saw themselves as God's people of the covenant, eligible for the biblical promise of life's necessities if they lived righteously.[5] According to an apostolic proclamation from Nauvoo, "The saints have found a resting place, where, freed from tyran[n]y and mobs, they are beginning to realize the fulfilment of the ancient prophets, 'they shall build houses and inhabit them, plant vineyards and eat the fruit thereof, having none to molest or make afraid.'"[6]

With their American and scriptural ancestors, the Saints in Nauvoo believed that righteousness and hard work would bring economic as well as spiritual rewards. Not that they expected great wealth; on the contrary, the Book of Mormon contained regular warnings against those who were tempted "to seek for power, and authority, and riches, and the vain things of the world."[7] A tithe of everyone's income for the temple and occasional contributions for the poor would bring to all a comfortable sustenance and meet the needs of the church. Most Latter-day Saints sought not for riches but for the kingdom of heaven. In the meantime, the city's rapid growth focused much energy into building the city and feeding a growing population.

HOUSING THE GATHERED SAINTS

Right from the start, finding a place to live in this sacred refuge challenged the ingenuity of many Latter-day Saints. They sought out existing facilities to buy or rent. And when those filled up, they moved in with friends—and strangers. Their leaders and agents had scouted out Commerce, Illinois, and Fort Madison, Iowa, to identify housing for a people in exile. Isaac Galland claimed to own facilities for fifty families in the barracks at old Fort Des Moines and had "about 10 or 15 houses or

For many Latter-day Saints who gathered to western Illinois and eastern Iowa in the 1840s, a log building was the only home they ever knew. This detail from an 1848 painting shows a typical homestead in Iowa just across the river from Nauvoo.

cabins . . . and several farms" for sale in the Commerce area. Others also may have owned places abandoned during the exodus of old settlers caused by the Panic of 1837 and the resulting business stagnation.[8] Wandle Mace remembered only six unoccupied places available right in Commerce. But a year later, in June 1840, the *Times and Seasons* established the common view of the base from which Nauvoo was built: "We behold . . . the saints comfortably situated, with already about 250 houses put up by their own hands; whereas, only 12 months since, 10 or 12 houses were all that could be numbered in this place." That dozen or so cannot be identified with certainty; however, not all of them would have been for sale, since Davison Hibbard, Hiram Kimball, Amos Davis, Daniel H. Wells, and others stayed on after the Mormons arrived.[9] (See map, page 32.) Whoever the owners and whatever the numbers, the few ready rentals and quick buys did not last. The first Mormons to arrive rented or bought them. Thus, Sidney Rigdon acquired the James White stone house on the river bank, and Joseph Smith moved into Hugh White's two-story log home a quarter mile downriver on land purchased for the church. Other incoming Saints claimed what remained and then had to begin doubling up while building new structures.

Heber C. Kimball looked in vain for accommodations in Commerce around the end of May 1839. "I pulled down an old stable and laid up the logs at the back end of the Bozier house," he recalled, "putting a few shakes on to cover it; but it had no floor nor chinking; and in this condition I moved my family into it; whenever it rained, the water stood near ankle deep on the ground."[10]

Visitors and residents alike noticed how these ramshackle buildings gave the city the appearance of being a temporary camp during its early years. Charlotte Haven, a visitor who stayed more than a year, gave a frank interpretation of what she saw as late as January 1843: "Such a collection of miserable houses and hovels I could not have believed existed in one place," she wrote to her family in the East. "Oh, I thought, how much real poverty must dwell here." While Haven emphasized the scarcity of permanent homes, the Rev. Samuel A. Prior, a Methodist minister visiting from Carthage later that spring, recognized the potential manifest in Nauvoo's humble beginnings. He was surprised to see more than "a few miserable log cabins and mud hovels." He said, "The buildings, though many of them were small and of wood, yet bore the marks of neatness which I have not seen equalled in this country." Prior saw a few "tall majestic brick house[s]," which he took as representative of the true "genius and untiring labor of the inhabitants."[11] He correctly discerned the residents' interest in building a better Nauvoo than necessity had imposed at first.

In the same spirit, the church newspaper in Liverpool cautioned the British Saints not to see Nauvoo in 1842 as the way it would remain. "The buildings are mostly temporary cabins, built of wood, and are very small, unfinished, and inconvenient," an editorial noted, "but they are such as are generally erected in the beginning of new settlements in every part of the country, and will soon give place to those of brick and stone. Indeed, several brick buildings are already erected, and hundreds of others are in process of erection."[12] As soon as lumber or bricks could be found, and a way to pay for them, all of Nauvoo's families looked forward to a more comfortable abode.

While the church looked to the needs of the poor, able Nauvoo settlers left their temporary shanties and shared rooms in order to occupy homes of their own. Most of the more than two hundred houses built the first year were block houses. These log homes were typical of those found anywhere on the American frontier and could be quickly built. To dress them up, many Nauvoo residents whitewashed both the exterior and the interior of the cabin each spring.[13] In the late spring of 1839, after he had planted his corn and potatoes, Theodore Turley built what is credited with being the first new home in Nauvoo, on Hyde Street just northeast of Joseph Smith's homestead. Set on a simple stone foundation, the log house provided Turley's family a place to live when he left three months later for a mission with the Twelve in England.[14] Heber C. Kimball and Parley P. Pratt of the Twelve followed the process typical of all new immigrants. Anxious to get their families out of temporary shelters, in mid-July 1839 they purchased adjoining five-acre tracts from Hiram Kimball in a wooded area about a mile from the river. The nearest neighbor at the time was half a mile away. They went right to work, cut some logs and invited old citizens and new to join in a house raising.[15]

Some British immigrants to Nauvoo had their own version of a basic home—the wattle. Built of posts set into the ground, with willows woven between the posts and then plastered with mud, it formed a small but tight protection from the weather. The English Saints built a number of these homes in Nauvoo and in a self-appointed British gathering place about five miles east of Nauvoo.[16] Yankee converts seeking "permanent" housing preferred a New England-style frame or brick house. Lumber was less easily obtained and more difficult to fashion into a traditional frame home than were locally harvested logs or willows used for wattles and similar shelters. "There has been however several commodious framed houses built; and several more now in lively operation," the *Times and Seasons* reported in June 1840.[17]

Even as tiny frame homes began to appear in Nauvoo, the first brick structures were built. They, too, were small. According to John Taylor, "vast numbers of brick houses" were built during the summer and fall of 1843. That construction continued on during the succeeding two years, as Nauvoo reached its peak in population and gained its distinctive mix of log, frame, and brick dwelling places.[18]

For a full six years, the immigrants to Joseph Smith's Nauvoo kept tradesmen and laborers busy building houses. In the spring of 1844 John Taylor concluded optimistically, "In every direction may be heard the

As Nauvoo grew, frame and brick buildings became more common. This privately financed "Brick Row" on Kimball Street, between Main and Hyde Streets, offered apartments for widows. The complex became known as "Widow's Row."

sound of the mason's trowel, the carpenter's hammer, the teamster's voice; or in other words, the hum of industry." The industrial sounds Taylor heard were the sounds of the construction industry. Tradesmen commanded high prices for their labor, up to $1.50 a day in 1842, when common laborers received half to two-thirds that amount.[19] The few who specialized as building contractors could not meet the demand for housing nor was that necessary. Many would-be homeowners did some of their own building (especially on log homes). They often worked together as friends and neighbors, sharing skills and combining talents to raise a house or barn. For finer homes, they contracted directly with men of the building trades. Supporting these tradesmen were lime burners, sawmill operators, brickmakers, and hardware merchants. By 1843, Nauvoo booster John Taylor found the city well supplied with employment opportunities for brickmakers, carpenters, bricklayers, masons, plasterers, blacksmiths and other such tradesmen.[20]

Yet, not everyone shared immediately in the American dream. Some required help from the community to achieve that goal. In nineteenth-century America, that usually meant help from the church. Ever concerned about the poor and the fatherless, the Latter-day Saints in the Commerce area paid special attention to the needs of widows and missionaries' wives. The church offered free lots to the widows of men killed at Haun's Mill and to other widowed women.[21] A private developer built and rented ten or eleven one-room apartments, each with its own fireplace. This apartment unit was called "widow's row," a long brick home on the corner of Main and Kimball streets.[22] To look after the wives of the members of the Quorum of the Twelve Apostles during their mission to Great Britain, the high council appointed a committee to contract for the plowing and fencing of certain city lots for the women and for the building of houses on those lots.[23]

Although single-family housing was the ideal, it was often not a reality in Nauvoo. As the city grew, the demand for temporary housing did too. The old places, and new ones as they were ready for occupation, became immediate inns for the homeless. Of necessity, a house often served several families. Widows rented out rooms and did cooking and laundry for boarders to earn a living. Families made room for friends and relatives who arrived with nowhere else to go. Some individuals and families shared housing throughout their years in Nauvoo. When George and Ellen Douglas arrived in early April 1842, they felt lucky to rent a house with a wood lot and half-acre garden. "Our house is not such a fine one," Ellen informed her parents in England, "but there are many that are much worse, and I prayed that we might have one to ourselves for there is 3 or 4 families in one room, and many have to pitch their tents in the woods, or anywhere where they can, for it is impossible for all to get houses when they come in for they are coming in daily. Scores of houses have been built since we have come here and they still continue building."[24]

It was a speculator's dream fulfilled, but the promoters of Commerce and Commerce City had not realized it. It took a religiously motivated people intent on gathering to sacred places to turn the steamboat landing at the head of the rapids into a real town. By 1843, Nauvoo was beginning to look like an expansive city. The view discovered in February of that year by Parley P. Pratt was that "hills had been leveled, [and] blocks, streets, houses, shops, gardens and enclosures were now extending in every direction." When the boom ended—and that wasn't until the exodus from Nauvoo began in February 1846—newcomers had created around two thousand houses in the city and another five hundred nearby. Irving Richman counted the dwellings from the top of the temple: "One half of these were mere shanties built of logs and some poles; others were framed.

Of the remainder about twelve hundred were tolerably fit dwellings; six hundred of them at least were good brick or frame structures. The number of buildings made wholly of brick was about five hundred, a goodly portion of them large and handsome."[25]

As the inventories of 1845–46 suggest, the appearance of Nauvoo in these later years of the city's growth included houses built of every available building material—the earlier log, wattle, and frame homes, with the later frame and brick buildings. Even at the end of the period, Nauvoo was still a young city, anxious to gain respectability as a city of promise but not yet mature enough to overcome its log cabin beginnings.

THE AGRARIAN IDEAL AND ZION'S CITY

For all of the effort expended in building up a city, it was country life, not urban, that the Latter-day Saints sought. As with other nineteenth-century Americans, being a farmer and living on the land held meaning for the Saints beyond that of the practical needs of feeding the family. They felt at home with the views of such classic agrarians as Thomas Jefferson, who believed that human perfection was possible only through a rural and idyllic life. Being close to the soil was being close to God. "Those who labor in the earth," Jefferson wrote in his *Notes on Virginia,* "are the chosen people of God, if He ever had a chosen people, whose breasts He has made His peculiar deposit for substantial and genuine virtue." Yeoman farmers sought prosperity as independent, self-made entrepreneurs on new frontiers. Self-sufficient and distrusting of the privileged aristocracy, they feared city life, which represented Babylon, everything that was evil. As examples, they referenced the ugly cities of Europe, crowded with poor peasants and defamed by debauchery and sickness. The dream of the new world—for Europeans and Americans—was a country of landed gentlemen and private entrepreneurs, each the owner of his own healthful estate; however, this was beyond the dream of Levi Hancock in his peaceful dwelling place in Missouri and of Latter-day Saints gathered later on at the upper Mississippi. They wished to rise above poverty but shunned wealth. They sought the spiritual safety of the middle road, the prosperity of adequacy described in Proverbs: "Give me neither poverty nor riches; feed me with food convenient for me: Lest I be full, and deny thee . . . or lest I be poor . . . and take the name of my God in vain."[26]

In other ways as well, agrarian views dovetailed nicely with Latter-day Saint religious expectations. Agrarianism satisfied doctrines of the Millennium and the gathering among converts on both sides of the Atlantic. Latter-day Saint missionaries who visited European cities found evidence to support their pessimistic assessments of urban life. British converts from the industrial urban centers fled to America's agrarian Zion. English agrarians found new opportunities to till God's earth in the prairies near Nauvoo. The agrarian dream of American Saints likewise seemed attainable at Nauvoo. For all the Saints so attuned, agrarianism and millennialism were parallel dreams, yet, when pressed, they would give precedence to their religious dream of a special people and place. Nauvoo was first of all a religious sanctuary from a world doomed to destruction and only secondarily an agrarian Eden, although the Latter-day Saints typically failed to distinguish between the two in their predilection for subsuming the secular into the sacred. They spoke almost exclusively of their religious goals, but an undercurrent of the Jacksonian dream also moved them.[27]

In the City of God, Latter-day Saint agrarians had the possibility of realizing the best of both worlds. Of the thousands who lived in their small city, many traveled out to the surrounding countryside to work as farmers. The urban environment they built lacked crowding and held at bay many illnesses, and with their religiously motivated desire to work and live Christian lives, they eliminated much of the poverty and wickedness they identified with the old cities. Abundant land and hard work, they believed, would put an end to poverty. As William Mosely explained in 1844 to his father in England after he contracted for a fifty-acre farm near Nauvoo: "We are in a land of freedom where every industrious man may be his own landlord and pay his taxes to God. . . . I assure you a working industrious man will do well here. He will get him some land, a house, and things of his own, but an idle man will come to poverty and nobody wil[l] give him bread; we have not seen so much as one beggar since we landed."[28]

The city of Nauvoo blended gradually into the woodlands and then into the farmlands to the east, and the residents brought the country into the city in other ways. When the summer corn grew ten and twelve feet high on large city lots, it dominated the landscape. The city looked like a garden. More importantly, the Saints imported the values of agrarian life into the city. In this way, they found their rural Eden in a city purified from the sins of Babylon because it was a holy place. The Latter-day Saints sought for the best of both the agrarian and the urban worlds—the virtues of being close to God's natural world and the companionship of the community of the Saints in the Lord's holy city.

To a certain extent, every migrant to Nauvoo was a farmer. For some that meant a garden in the backyard. But for many, acreage outside the city demanded attention and qualified them as true agriculturists. "Extensive farms are beginning to spread themselves for miles in every direction from our city, on the bosom of the great prairie, as far as the eye can reach; fencing, ploughing and building, seems to be the order of the day," John Taylor reported in January 1844 in a report that made homesteading into a prophecy fulfilled: "'The wilderness is' indeed being 'made glad, and the desert blossoms as the rose.'"[29]

Those who did not own farmland often hired out as laborers during the labor-intensive seasons of plowing, planting, and harvest. Newly arrived young immigrants or part-time craftsmen were among those most anxious for work to help support their families. Harvest wages for adults ranged from $1.00 to $1.50 for a day's work, half that for young men. Those who owned oxen rented them out for the work and often hired themselves out along with the cattle to help in the redemptive effort of subduing the earth and of feeding Nauvoo's families.[30]

Latter-day Saints purchased or rented farms and farmland on both sides of the Mississippi, in the central counties of Lee and Hancock and in surrounding areas. The Pre-Emption Act of 1841 made land more affordable by reducing the minimum purchase required of homesteaders from 320 acres to 160 acres. This so-called Log Cabin Bill allowed settlers to stake out a claim and pay for it later at $1.25 per acre.[31] It was this provision that defined the 160-acre tract that Joseph Smith purchased in 1844 from the original patentee. Many first purchasers subdivided their land, making twenty-, forty-, or eighty-acre parcels available to others. Thus, one British immigrant purchased eighty acres of fenced and cultivated land, with a house, for £160 ($800) and found uncultivated land selling for from eight to twenty shillings ($2 to $5) per acre. Another English convert purchased a twenty-acre parcel "in its wild state at eight dollars per acre, with a tax title."[32] Land closer to Nauvoo sold at a premium of as much as twenty times the amount a similar parcel might bring farther

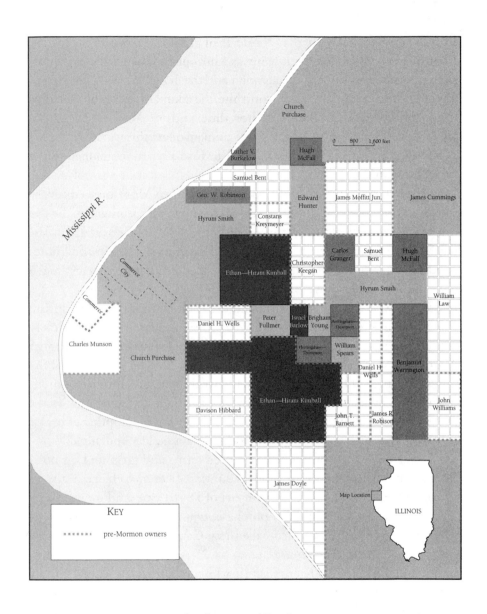

Landowners and Developers

away. The open prairie with its three feet of black loam topsoil caught the immediate fancy of the British Saints, accustomed to the rolling hill country of their native land. "The land which I have bought," William Mosely wrote home to his father in Staffordshire, "is a kind of common called in this country Prairie, which contains thousands of Acres uncultivated which could settle all England. . . . We cannot see anything at all but land, not a tree nor a hedge, but the land is as level as a board, not a bank nor a valley in all the plain."[33]

A huge community farm east of Nauvoo helped Mormon farmers get started. Surrounded by a single ditch-and-bank fence running three miles in one direction and two miles in another, the 3,840-acre "Big Field" contained parcels to meet every need: ten, twenty, thirty, forty, and sixty acres. A similar community farm had been established near Far West. Those accustomed to scratching an existence out of New England's rocky soils prospered when they applied themselves to the fertile plains along the Mississippi River Valley. Thriftiness learned the hard way paid great dividends in the New West. "It is a perfect garden as respects soil," George Alley noted in 1843.[34]

Unless the owner of small, individual farms hired extra help, which many of them did, a farmer and his older sons could open the larger farms to cultivation only gradually. The process of turning the fertile but heavy clay soil of the prairie was slow, because neither the old wooden plows nor the newer ones made of cast iron would scour—the moist muck would cling to the plows. It took at least three yoke of oxen or three teams of horses to break through the tough roots of prairie grass. One immigrant found that he could hire the work done at two dollars per acre; once broken up and given time to rot, the soil could be worked easily with one light horse.[35]

Fencing for protection from livestock was a necessary imposition on farmers. Livestock ran free, so crops were protected with fences built with scarce prairie timber or from plentiful sod. Many of the farm fences were the common worm fence, built by stacking rails in a zig-zag pattern. A man could enclose thirty acres this way with a week's hard work. The ditch and sod fence took more labor but cost less for materials. Some even surrounded fields with rough picket slab fences.[36]

Many farmers lived on the land they cultivated rather than in the city as Joseph Smith's City of Zion plan suggested. This scattering eventually put nearly three thousand Latter-day Saints into the wide rural area in the Nauvoo hinterland. Those closest to the city considered themselves adjunct members of the urban community because they had no towns of their own. Those farther afield, such as at Ramus (or Macedonia), became members of other church branches and clustered together for civic purposes in villages or, more often, simply resided as scattered farmers within a township. They found a sense of community despite their scattered condition with the members of the branch with whom they worshiped.[37]

For the resident farmer, a small plot within the farm became the family's residential lot. On it were the house and other outbuildings typical of any city plot, plus barns for livestock and their foodstuff and the storage of crops used for home consumption, for market, and for next year's seed. The barns in Mormon Illinois and Iowa were most likely simple log or frame structures of the rustic pattern common on emerging frontiers.[38] As was true of the structures in the new city of Nauvoo, agricultural buildings had yet to reach their potential.

For most Latter-day Saint farmers, it was the rich prairie soil rather than its lush grasses favored by grazing livestock that offered a living. Some farmers mixed grazing and cultivation, but in many instances, the only livestock kept were those needed by the farm family for their own sustenance. Every farmer needed a few oxen or workhorses to pull the plows and the wagons used for hauling crops to barns, mills, and markets. To sustain the family, every farmer and many city residents kept a cow for milk, butter, and cheese; hogs and sheep for meat; and chickens and other fowl for eggs and meat. If families needed to supplement their home production, they could find meat at reasonable prices in local markets for purchase from producers, butchers, or merchants. Prices were higher than in the East but were comparable to markets in other western towns.[39] In addition, many city-dwelling residents had not yet insulated themselves from the rural hunting life as a means of supplementing the diet. They stalked the nearby woods and prairies for game birds and waterfowl. Rivers and streams offered a variety of fish.

Agricultural mainstays throughout the region were corn and wheat. Farmers also produced hemp, oats, buckwheat, and potatoes.[40] Each year saw an increase in the acreage under cultivation. With few exceptions, the quality and quantity of the harvest increased. In 1843, for example, Latter-day Saint farmers had a bad year, but after a mild winter, they planted early in 1844 and enjoyed a good harvest. By 1840, Illinois ranked seventh of all twenty-six states in production of Indian corn; the Latter-day Saints grew their share for local consumption.[41]

Corn, long a Southern staple, soon rivaled wheat—the favorite of the Yankees and British—for the kitchen table. Corn meal could be baked into a bread, fried as corn pones, boiled as mush, and used in other ways. The wheat-flour Saints who were not accustomed to cooking with corn-meal soon adapted, for it was the most prevalent grain for household use in western Illinois. "Our family had not had any corn meal during the two years we were in England," Mary Ann Stearns Winters remembered, "and we were just feasting on it in any way it might be cooked, but the poor English Saints, who had never been used to eating it, fared badly with it; they did not relish it."[42]

Although summer meals included other fresh garden produce and winter suppers featured stored root crops (including potatoes) and dried fruit and vegetables, it was corn that fed Nauvoo, summer and winter. Corn stored on the cob or shelled into a sack or bagged as meal provided the source of flour for a variety of dishes. Wheat and other grains added variety to the diet, as did such mainstays as potatoes, beans, and cheese. It was corn that made Nauvoo most visibly a country town. With corn used in every diet and with every spare lot planted, the sprawling community appeared in summer as a scattering of buildings set into a corn-field. "The corn is so high we can [look] out upon the city and [only] see the tops of the houses," Irene Pomeroy wrote in July 1845. She measured selected stalks at nearly twelve feet high and observed, "We have had green corn here several days; green peas, shell beans, new potatoes, etc."[43]

Nauvoo, like small-town America everywhere, functioned economically in an agrarian model that celebrated the household as the unit of production for many needs. Each family sought self-sufficiency. Any land not developed for housing within Nauvoo's city boundaries and suitable for crops was turned to residential agriculture, if the owner was willing. Some craftsmen traded their wares for the foodstuffs needed by their families, but even these families kept a backyard garden, usually tended by the wife, and many of them kept small farms. One shoemaker, for example, harvested four acres of corn and a one-acre garden in 1843 and increased his farm to double the corn plus ten acres of wheat the following year. With that acreage under cultivation in his forty-acre plot in the Big Field,

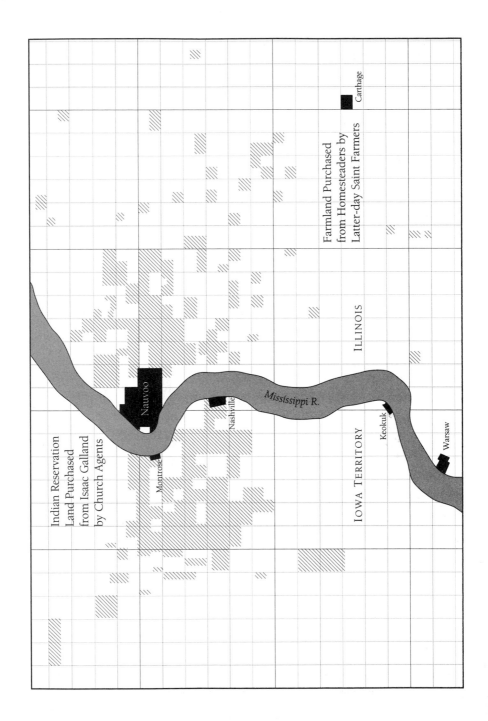

Latter-day Saint Settlements and Farmland

he expected "bread stuff enough for myself and to spare. . . . I find no reason to regret having come into the garden of the West," he informed an unbelieving relative.[44]

The backyard garden offered tasty produce throughout the harvest season. During winter months, fruit and vegetables that had been dried or stored in cool cellars, and fresh, dried, and smoked meat gave variety to the cornmeal diet. Wild honey, jams, and jellies added welcome flavor. "We have got our garden plowed and planted," Ellen Douglas reported to her parents in England two months after the family's early April arrival in Nauvoo, "and all our seeds have come up and looks very well. We have planted corn, potatoes, beans, peas, onions, pumpkins, melons, cucumbers and a many other things too numerous to mention, and we have all so got a pig . . . [and] a flock of chickens, . . . and I think we are far better here than in old England."[45]

Few Americans had learned to enjoy tomatoes, in part because of fear that they were poisonous. One of John C. Bennett's contributions to Nauvoo was his active promotion of tomatoes as a healthy food. During the winter of 1840–41, he published extracts from various horticultural publications on how to grow tomatoes and information on their history, botanical nature, and chemical properties.[46]

Trees for planting were gradually brought into Nauvoo by nurserymen to supply the demand met by an expanding city. By 1844, residents could select from thousands of fruit trees and berry plants in virtually every variety desired. Additional kinds were available from St. Louis.[47] Domestic fruits and berries supplemented berries gathered from wild plants on the prairie. A barrel of honey was another typical staple. In every garden, a large sampling of herbs provided seasoning for cooking and main ingredients for warm drinks. From ginger, for example, the Saints could make a mild tea or a hardtack candy.[48]

Perhaps mostly because of the gardens behind Nauvoo's houses, it was necessary to erect fences to protect the growing plants from wandering cattle, horses, and pigs. Nauvoo's governing high council threatened to disfellowship anyone who knowingly allowed his animals to destroy a neighbor's crops. Later on, the city council required hogs to be penned, levying a fine of five dollars against the owners of pigs allowed to run loose in the city. This regulation was enacted during a time when some people in Illinois were lobbying for state laws requiring hogs to be penned. In

This detail from a recent pencil drawing captures an accurate view of Nauvoo's urban land-scape in the spring of 1846. Seen are a typical mixture of log, frame, and brick homes between Hyde and Durphy Streets near Parley Street.

Nauvoo, several petitions circulated in the summer of 1843 seeking repeal of the local hog law, but the council let its progressive law stand.[49] To help manage loose livestock and for more effective feeding, herders gathered many of the milk cows each morning and took them out of the city to the pastures during the day, returning them for milking each evening.[50]

Many homes were surrounded by picket fences, often of split oak or maple. Others used rail and pole fences, a common fencing for the unde-veloped lots used for urban farming.[51] The Mansion House had such a rail fence around it in 1844, and Brigham Young hired Samuel Eggleston to build one around his house the following spring.[52]

In other ways, too, Nauvoo's citizens dreamed of improving their city. Housing and feeding their families were essential tasks for the men and women of Nauvoo. But the building trades, farming operations, and household tasks did not provide employment for everyone, especially not for British immigrants from factory towns. If Nauvoo was to achieve her full economic potential, the city needed manufacturing, and that required capital. Very early in the city's history, industrialization became a central theme for the most ardent champions of Nauvoo.

CHAPTER 7

Economic Expectations

Our affairs in Nauvoo are prosperous. . . . Great numbers of merchants have settled among us. . . . Vigorous efforts are being made to improve our wharves, and facilitate the landing of steamboats on our shores. . . . Many branches of mechanism are going on; . . . and many other branches of business have found abundance of employ. There is however one thing which we would respectfully call the attention of our brethren to; that is, the business of manufacturing. There is perhaps no place in the western country, where cotton, woolen, silk, iron and earthen-ware could be manufactured to better advantage than they could in Nauvoo.

—John Taylor, January 1, 1844

In earlier gathering places, Latter-day Saints had aspired to do away with poverty. This desire was an essential part of their spiritual goal to realize an equitable balance in material things. The ideal "to be one in all things" included religious and social activities as well. In church gatherings, the Saints acted in a spirit of common consent and sought unity in doctrine. In personal interactions, they tried to eliminate contention and strife. The revealed economic plan invited them to consecrate all their property to the church, with the bishop returning to each man an adequate means of livelihood, "as much as is sufficient for himself and family."[1] Retained surpluses were earmarked for ecclesiastical needs, construction of temples, and support of the poor.[2]

Expectations for living the law of consecration changed following the period of apostasy in Ohio and Missouri. After 1834, participants were invited to contribute only their surpluses. Then, at Far West and in Nauvoo, the tithing revelation of 1838 formalized this approach. The tithing law asked new converts to make an initial offering of their surpluses. This met the requirement for a consecration of property. Afterward, participating members contributed a tenth of their income. Once a year, they settled their accounts with the bishop.[3]

During the Nauvoo years, the Saints did not expect to attain the level of compliance reported among early disciples of Jesus Christ.[4] Instead, the revealed law of tithing set a preparatory standard grounded in the teachings of the Old Testament prophets. Nevertheless, it preserved much of the language and spirit of the law of consecration. Economic objectives remained unchanged: fund temple building, support administrative needs, and sustain the poor.

The move away from the economic ideal of Zion elicited a variety of responses. Most comfortable with the change were those who had opposed the original law of consecration as an inappropriate intrusion into personal finances. Least supportive were those who had been staunch adherents of consecration in Kirtland or Missouri. Some from both of these positions stayed away from Nauvoo. Others in various locations outside Nauvoo continued with the old plan or pooled their resources in the spirit of equity. These included ardent Saints in the Iowa stake; Mormon lumber workers in camps on the Black River in Wisconsin known as the Pineries; and a colony founded by James Emmett among Native Americans on the western frontier. Most converts had not been invited to participate in the ideal economic law (required especially for the Saints in Missouri's Zion). These inexperienced people adjusted comfortably to the law of tithing, with its simpler way to contribute their time and means for the Lord's work.[5]

In public pronouncements in Nauvoo, the Prophet made clear his support of the enduring economic principle of individual ownership. The issue was raised in September 1843, when a traveling English socialist, John Finch, preached from the stand in the grove. Smith responded by denouncing Finch's socialism. At the same time, he also discounted a communitarian system that Sidney Rigdon had endorsed in Kirtland before converting to Mormonism.[6] Kirtland's common stock "Family" effort had failed, Smith said, "the big fish there eating up all the little fish." In a second sermon ten days later, with Acts 2 as his text, the Prophet preached for an hour, "designing to show the folly of common stock. In Nauvoo," he said, "every one is steward over his own." Always the prevailing economic pattern within the church had given to the head of each family the individual responsibility to provide for his own.[7]

The Prophet had concluded that the leveling effect of the New Testament ideal could not be realized in the world of ordinary men. His coworkers agreed. John Taylor, an ardent opponent of common stock systems, had rebutted Finch in his own lengthy discourse. Taylor supported the law of tithing. The apostle also advocated a cooperative attitude among tradesmen in manufacturing and marketing their goods. While a missionary in England, Heber C. Kimball had concluded that the world would see an end to economic oppression by the rich and the achievement of universal peace and plenty only "when the Lord Jesus shall descend in the clouds of heaven."[8]

MERCHANDISING AND COMMERCE IN A ZION CITY

The law of tithing applied only to individuals. Yet Nauvoo merchants were not entirely free to operate under the American dream of unfettered competition. Not stated in the revelation of tithing but preached from pulpits in Nauvoo and discussed in private councils was an additional obligation expected of Latter-day Saint businessmen—that they be benevolent entrepreneurs. In the absence of total consecration, they were expected to exercise a sacred watch-care over their personal secular concerns. Church leaders encouraged prosperous businessmen to invest their surplus capital in business ventures that would both curb the export of dollars and create jobs for the poor. Expected also was, first, that businessmen would honor religious values in the community and, second, would donate generously to church building projects, namely, the temple and a hotel known as the Nauvoo House.

Whenever successful businessmen departed from these religious objectives, Joseph Smith and others reminded them that Nauvoo was a gathering place, a religious community created to save souls, not a commercial center where entrepreneurs could amass personal fortunes. For instance, two days after passage of Nauvoo's first commercial licensing ordinance in April 1842, the Prophet preached "concerning the building of the temple,

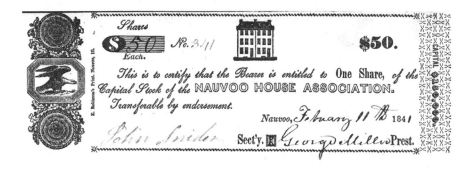

Competing for scarce resources was a church hotel called the Nauvoo House. An organization to support it was incorporated under state laws with stock certificates sold at fifty dollars each to fund construction.

and pronounced a curse on the Merchants and the rich, who would not assist in building it."[9] Regularly over the next two years, merchants heard admonitions to embrace community prosperity over personal wealth. Some businessmen struggled with these competing values. They had to choose between speculation and benevolent philanthropy, pursue the so-called American dream or strive to fulfill the hope of Zion.

Most of Nauvoo's merchants operated in one of two commercial zones in the city—on the flat at the south end of town or on the bluff near the temple. These areas in the new city of Nauvoo augmented the original riverfront business district in Commerce. A few tradesmen clustered near the merchants. Most, however, plied their trade in shops wherever they could obtain a lot and build a home.

The business sector on the flat centered in the original tract that Joseph Smith purchased from Hugh White. About half a dozen merchants sold goods in stores scattered over six blocks along and near Water and Main streets. Among the most enterprising of the lowlands merchants were the Irish-born Canadians William and Wilson Law. Immediately after these prosperous general merchants arrived in Nauvoo in November 1840, they saw opportunities for personal economic betterment. The brothers established a store on Water Street a short distance from the

Mississippi. They built steam-powered grist and lumber mills at the river's edge. Wilson and his wife, Jane, were especially generous with their substantial resources. Not only did they invest in businesses that provided much needed goods and services in Nauvoo, but for several years they supported the church with loans, gifts, and personal service. For a time, at least, they were exemplary stewards.[10]

The Laws had only one significant mercantile competitor on the flats. Beginning in January 1842, Joseph Smith tried his hand at merchandising, as his father had done for a time in Vermont. To house his venture, the Prophet built an impressive two-story red brick store just west of his log home on Water Street and directly opposite the Law brothers' store. The interior of the main floor interior was large and handsomely decorated "for a backwoods establishment" with imitation oak, mahogany, and marble finishes.[11] When Smith opened for business, he offered goods that Edward Hunter had shipped from the East as payment on a land purchase, plus an additional thirteen wagonloads of merchandise from St. Louis. The shipments included clothing, textiles, sugar, salt, glass, nails, and other goods not produced in Nauvoo.[12] This plentiful offering attracted a steady but modest flow of customers; a typical day averaged two dozen transactions.[13]

The Prophet tended store himself at first, but after a few months he hired others to manage it for him. In the spring of 1844, he got out of the mercantile business entirely, disappointed with its lack of success. Nauvoo had too many merchants, he noted. The unpaid bills kept his profits slim at best and contributed to the store's demise. His well-stocked store had attracted a broad clientele, including other church leaders and close friends. Smith's growing extended family of plural wives and their relatives were among those drawing upon the store's goods. In his merchandising, as in his land sales and other business dealings, the Prophet was a generous steward, anxious to lift those in need.[14]

From a financial perspective, a more successful buyer and seller of goods was Nauvoo's first merchant. The youthful Vermonter, Amos Davis, was in business near the upper landing for two years before the Saints arrived, and he kept selling for a decade after the Saints left the city. His account books reveal a prosperous business. The twenty-three-year-old merchant became an immediate friend to the Saints; he and his wife joined the church at the April 1840 conference. As his businesses grew,

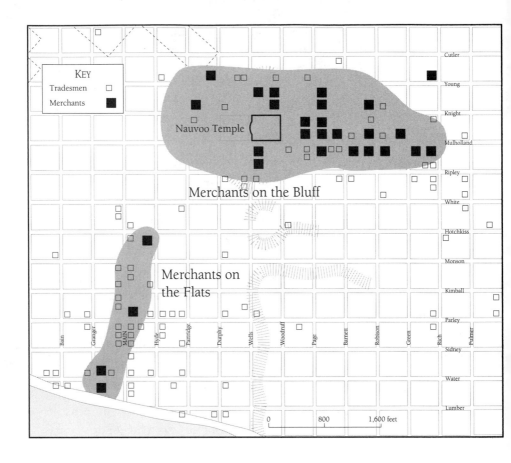

Commercial Districts of Nauvoo

Davis moved from his riverfront store in Commerce to a new brick building on Mulholland Street a block east of the temple. He completed an even larger, three-story store and warehouse immediately south of the temple early in 1846. Davis was a trusted citizen, active in Nauvoo's civic life. In that way, at least, he magnified the expectation of community betterment. Along with other merchants, he squabbled over Nauvoo's restrictive liquor laws.[15]

Other entrepreneurs besides Davis opened stores in Nauvoo's business district on the bluff. The dozen or so operating along and near Mulholland Street were all within the area opened in April 1840 by Daniel H. Wells. Wells owned the eighty-acre section before the Latter-day Saints arrived. Like Davis, he was a friend to his new neighbors and was supported by them as a justice of the peace and civic leader. In part because of his wife's resistance, he did not join the church until after the Nauvoo years. Several other merchants on the bluffs were likewise not Latter-day Saints. Some of these men sympathized with Joseph Smith's detractors or caused problems for city officials by ignoring laws regulating the sale of liquor.

At the west end of this secular business district, excavation for the temple began in the fall of 1840. This prominent site, with its adjacent outdoor preaching grounds, was located at the geographical center of Nauvoo and became the religious center as well. With the temple walls rising at the brow of the hill on Mulholland Street, the Wells Addition became an even more favorable location for businesses. New shops appeared there during a period of expansion between 1841 and 1843.

The number of mercantile establishments grew especially in 1843 to meet the needs of an exploding population.[16] That was the year Amos Davis moved onto the bluff. It was also the year the Prophet began to ease out of business. After Joseph Smith closed his store, the large room on the main floor attracted other merchants; the last of the renters left in 1846 with the exodus of the Saints.[17] Indeed, the roster of Nauvoo merchants changed constantly due to the economic hazards of such ventures, the difficulty of marshaling resources to capitalize a store, and the shifting interests and migrations of men involved in trade. These same conditions created many partnerships. It helped to have a junior partner to tend the store while the principal owner was off on a buying trip. Partnerships often lasted only a short time. (One agreement ended after the pair earned profits enough to pay for new houses and provide support for their families while they responded to mission calls.) Nauvoo's market even attracted the attention of some St. Louis merchants who advertised directly in Nauvoo's secular newspaper, the *Wasp*. These entrepreneurs, too, recognized in Nauvoo a people hungry for life's amenities.[18]

Competition in the marketplace benefited the buyer while reflecting the reality of an import economy. By the end of 1843, Nauvoo's most vocal supporter, editor John Taylor, could report that "the amount of merchandise which has been imported, has placed goods within the reach of the citizens of Nauvoo, at as reasonable a rate as they can be purchased at any of our western cities."[19] Even though prices were higher than the city's residents had been accustomed to paying in the East, rates reflected typical markups for goods imported to the upper Mississippi Valley. Imported goods sold briskly, and thus merchandising attracted much speculative investment. While other people in Nauvoo struggled to get established, the merchants fared well.

As Nauvoo's commercial activity burgeoned, the city council protected community interests with laws to license and regulate commerce. Beginning in April 1842, the city required merchants and grocers to take out licenses.[20] To ensure honesty in the sale of produce, the city appointed a sealer of weights and measures whose duty it was to check all scale-beams, weights, and measures—including steelyards and hay scales—at least twice a year. The inspector confiscated and adjusted any such devices found not to comply. Stiff fines punished violators. The sealer's mark ("W") ensured customers at Nauvoo's stores, shops, and markets of a fair measure for their money.[21]

Of particular concern to civic leaders in a community pledged to temperance out of religious principle was the matter of social drinking. Almost immediately after its organization, the city council took action on the issue. Mayor John C. Bennett named councilor Joseph Smith to head a temperance committee to draft a bill prohibiting the sale of liquor by the drink. The only legal exception—liquor for medicinal use—required a recommendation from a physician accredited by the chancellor and regents of the city university.[22]

To protect the community's moral values, the city monitored keepers of taverns (inns) or ordinaries (eating places). A half dozen hotels operated in the city, most of them near the river, where steamboat travelers sought board and room. To obtain a license, proprietors needed the written endorsement of six neighbors and the city inspector's verification that the tavern did indeed offer appropriate accommodations and a suitable stable. All of this helped to ensure that the tavern was used as a hotel, not as a bar. Stiff fines, including revocation of license for a second violation, were levied against those who sold liquor.[23]

Merchants in the new city imported goods from brokers in St. Louis and New Orleans and from sources in such places as Cincinnati, New York, and Boston. The Ohio and Mississippi rivers funneled a steady flow of goods to Nauvoo. Merchandise arrived on steamboats that kept regular schedules on the upper Mississippi above St. Louis. The ships and their captains became well-known in Nauvoo; others equally familiar docked ten miles downriver in the main channel port at Keokuk.[24]

Nauvoo was a river town, and the active movement of goods and passengers led church leaders to partnership with others in two steamboats operating on the Mississippi, the *Nauvoo* and the *Maid of Iowa*. Besides some expectation of profit, the shipowners, had they succeeded, would have helped keep scarce dollars from fleeing the specie-poor city, an economic objective increasingly supported by the First Presidency and the Twelve. Even so, church involvement brought mixed results in meeting these objectives.

The first of the Mormon steamboats was a surplus army riverboat built in Pittsburgh in 1838. Peter Haws, a Canadian convert, purchased the 93-ton *Des Moines* and two keelboats at public auction in September 1840 and renamed the steamboat the *Nauvoo*. The 120-foot vessel had been used by the Army Corps of Engineers to survey and clear the St. Louis harbor and Des Moines rapids. Four men cosigned as sureties on an eight-month note for just under five thousand dollars. The partnership included Joseph Smith and Hyrum Smith with two prosperous farmers from nearby counties, Henry W. Miller and George Miller (not related), providing the financial guarantee.[25]

The remodeled and renamed *Nauvoo* had every reason to succeed as an investment. It hauled freight in the active trade from Galena to St. Louis under the supervision of pilots Benjamin and William Holladay, who were hired because of their claim to experience on the river. But within three months, the pilots wrecked the *Nauvoo* by running it aground on rocks and sandbanks outside the deep steamer channel. The

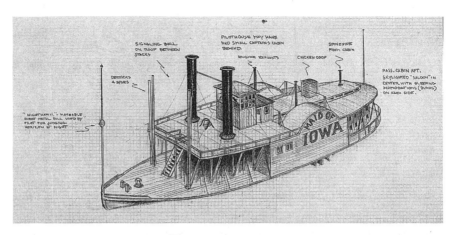

This recent drawing, based on historical information, offers a likely image of the Maid of Iowa, *a sixty-ton, 115-foot-long, Mississippi River passenger steamboat, and probably a side-wheeler.*

owners sued the Holladays, who posted bond and left the state (they later won fame as western stagecoach owners). The boat was raised and salvaged for use as a barge, but the owners were left with debts that were not settled for years.[26]

The second Mormon steamboat, a smaller and newer vessel than the *Nauvoo,* enjoyed a longer usefulness and fewer legal problems. The sixty-ton *Maid of Iowa* served as a ferry, excursion boat, and immigrant vessel as well as carrier of trade goods. Two non-Mormon entrepreneurs, Dan Jones, an 1840 Welsh immigrant, and his partner, Levi Moffit, built the side-wheeler in 1842, in Augusta, Iowa, upriver from Nauvoo.[27] The owners included the rapidly growing Nauvoo among their stops on the rivers of the upper Mississippi Valley. When they delivered a load of British immigrants to Nauvoo in mid-April 1843, Joseph Smith took an immediate liking to "this little man," Dan Jones. The Prophet's brother William Smith announced, "It is proposed to have this small but good ship make regular runs from Nauvoo to New Orleans and return."[28]

Jones soon converted to Mormonism and dedicated his energies to furthering church purposes. In May 1843, the church became his partner by purchasing Moffit's half interest in the steamer. Within a year, the church held full title. The steamboat's operators purchased dinnerware, bedding, and other supplies from Joseph Smith's new red brick store. They launched a festive maiden voyage to Quincy and back with invited guests and a brass band. The boat transported Latter-day Saint immigrants from New Orleans or St. Louis to Nauvoo, hauled corn and wheat to feed temple builders, served for pleasure excursions, and at times became a police patrol boat to protect Joseph Smith from arrest. Unlike the *Nauvoo,* whose fate was a common one for boats on the upper Mississippi, the *Maid of Iowa* fulfilled its owners' intentions and contributed toward the realization of Nauvoo's economic and religious goals.[29]

Church leaders assumed one other responsibility relating to use of the river for transportation. Through the first high council, they regulated commercial ferries between Nauvoo and Montrose. The first cross-river commercial operation authorized under church authority was Daniel C. Davis's horse ferry, the *Iowa Twins.* An Indiana immigrant family described it as "a primitive flatboat propelled by two horses, one on each side, working a treadmill. They [the horses] furnished the power to turn the wheels and propel the boat."[30] Officially recognized by the high council at Commerce in October 1839, Davis held a monopoly on the route and operated on rates set by Nauvoo's lawmakers for the mutual benefit of the owner and local citizens. In 1840, the high council gave control of the ferry to the First Presidency, but after city government began functioning, regulations were handled through the municipal rather than the ecclesiastical body.[31] Davis regularly advertised his ferry in an attempt to attract Iowa-bound immigrants, especially those who crossed the Illinois River east of Quincy and then sought a nearby Mississippi service. Davis's *Iowa Twins* met its fate in a river accident: it was lost in an ice jam off the Dundey's Island landing in 1846.[32]

In 1843, the city council gave Joseph Smith exclusive rights to land passengers along Nauvoo's Mississippi shoreline. Under this license, Dan Jones launched a steam ferry service between Nauvoo and Montrose using the *Maid of Iowa.* Despite the supposed monopoly given Smith, his friend Davis continued to offer his slower horse-powered service at the same time. To keep that business competitive with the horse ferry at Warsaw, the council posted new rates that imitated those set two years earlier in Warsaw. Nauvoo travelers could avoid paying the established fees only by crossing the shallow river on their own skiffs or rowboats, and many did just that. Under the law, individuals could transport only their own families or neighbors, the latter free of charge.[33]

Goods arriving in Nauvoo by steamboat were unloaded at one of two landings and then either warehoused temporarily or moved by haulers to the buyer's store. Some freighters used the ferry landing near the unfinished Nauvoo House on Main Street. More of them chose Kimball's landing, the main steamboat wharf near the upper stone house in old Commerce. As traffic increased, the wharves were improved to facilitate the landing of steamboats. Those dreaming of Nauvoo's potential as a commercial emporium expected that a project launched in 1843 to partially dam the Mississippi at Nauvoo would create "one of the best harbors on the Mississippi river, making the whole of our shore accessible at all times to the largest class of boats."[34]

That venture was not realized, nor were other proposed transportation schemes. Resources to accomplish ambitious improvements were not available before time ran out on the push to build up Nauvoo economically. A canal and a railroad were the dominant projects. The Saints had inherited a long-standing interest in improving access to river transport to support both commerce and travel. In the initial survey, planners projected a waterway down a wider-than-usual Main Street that sloped naturally from north to south. Workmen began digging the canal at the north but soon found themselves blocked by a substantial limestone deposit. Enterprising construction workers soon transformed that blockage into a bonanza—a quarry of stone for the temple. But the canal proposal was never realized.[35]

Another unfulfilled transportation goal was for a railroad connection between Nauvoo and Warsaw, a project intended to solve the problem of getting around the rapids. The Illinois general assembly chartered a company to build the railway in February 1839, with Isaac Galland as one of its directors. The firm graded about twelve miles of roadbed before running out of money. It was one of many such Illinois improvement projects of the era that were never realized.[36]

INDUSTRY, TRADES, AND PROFESSIONS

Because of its booming population, Nauvoo did not see itself as a small town. Its demographic dynamism notwithstanding, however, it shared the economic orientation of small-town Jacksonian America. In a nation in transition from traditional cottage industries to a factory system, the small towns necessarily lagged behind. This fact did not discourage Nauvoo's local entrepreneurs. They wanted new industries and manufacturing plants to correct local shortfalls. Nauvoo needed processing industries—grist mills to turn grain into meal and flour, and sawmills to transform trees into lumber. The city would further benefit from manufacturing plants to create such products as pottery and textiles. Joseph Smith urged the Saints to "surround the rapids" with factories to limit the import of products and outflow of cash. Promoters imagined locally produced wool and flax feeding the textile mills. These mills and potteries would provide much-needed jobs for experienced English immigrants who searched in vain for such work in Hancock County.[37]

The lack of certain basic industries struck Orson Hyde as Nauvoo's greatest need. "We have lands, we have houses, and an abundance of provisions" but produce no textiles, he said. Hyde encouraged immigrants from nearby states to bring in herds of sheep, Southerners to bring raw silk and flax seed, women in Nauvoo to teach their daughters how to spin and to weave, and immigrants everywhere to "bring with them all the wool . . . all the domestic flannel; and all the full cloth; common cassimers and satinetts, which they can procure."[38]

Others of the Twelve who had seen the operations of factories in Europe and in larger American cities envisioned the potential for Nauvoo, and Joseph Smith led the way in the call for industrial development. The Prophet's experience as a merchant in Nauvoo convinced him that the city's economy could be built up not through merchandising but only through manufacturing. John Taylor echoed his leader's enthusiasm for home manufacture at every opportunity. "Our calculation," Taylor said, "is to have the saints manufacture every thing we need in Nauvoo, and all kinds of useful articles to send abroad through the States and bring money here."[39]

As the Twelve prepared to leave England in April 1841, they summarized the church's plan for building Zion's cornerstone stake through benevolent entrepreneurship:

It will be necessary, in the first place for [British] men of capital to go on first and make large purchases of land, and erect mills, machinery, manufactories, &c., so that the poor who go from this country can find employment. Therefore it is not wisdom for the poor to flock to that place extensively, until the necessary preparations are made. . . . In all the settlements there must be capital and labour united in order to flourish. The brethren will recollect that they are not going to enter upon cities already built up, but are going to "*build* cities and inhabit them." Building cities cannot be done without means and labour.[40]

It was an appropriate sequence, except that the missionaries in Great Britain seldom gathered wealthy factory owners into the gospel net. The poor in heart—and in means—gathered first, despite counsel otherwise.

Community leaders in Nauvoo accurately reflected the need to create employment opportunities for immigrants. Not everyone could farm. From the perspective of those living in Nauvoo and her environs, except for construction, other jobs were scarce. For new immigrants and the unemployed, keeping food on the table was, at times, a real struggle. In their letters from Nauvoo and in later reminiscences, these people described themselves and their neighbors as poor when measured by their earthly possessions. Real prosperity for most of them remained an objective yet to be attained. A few examples will illustrate.

Alfred Cordon and his family arrived in April 1843 aboard the *Maid of Iowa* with one dollar. The Cordons took shelter in a log cabin with a leaky roof, spent seventy-five cents for a load of wood, and "commenced to barter away our things for something to eat." Cordon worked at ditching and brickmaking, "but the work being very hard and the wages small, I left there." In subsequent jobs, he took his pay in provisions or goods that could be bartered. The family shared a rented room in a brick house with another family for a time and then purchased a half-acre lot and built their own house, buying materials with bartered goods.

The experience of Curtis and Rebecca Bolton was similar. They arrived from New York in the spring of 1845 with fifty dollars, half of which they paid as tithing. The Boltons moved from place to place as renters, finally settling into a plastered room over the old Amos Davis store near the temple. Curtis worked for the church as a temple carpenter, bookkeeper, and clerk. "It was a time of great suffering for me," Bolton said of the summer of 1845, "as I had nothing for my meals but corn bread." Another immigrant, George W. Taggart, confessed in a letter home to his brothers, "I like the place very much, but there is many inconveniences which we will have to undergo in consequence of not having money; but those that have money can live here just as easy as they please. . . . The most of the people are industrious and honest but poor."[41]

These experiences were common among Nauvoo's residents. The lack of cash was not unusual in the barter economy of the Illinois frontier. The economic downturns of 1837 and 1839 exacerbated difficult conditions for all Americans. Nauvoo's men worked at one job and then another, usually receiving their pay in provisions, sometimes in bricks, store scrip, or not at all. Irene Pomeroy said of her husband, Francis, "He can earn one bushel of wheat or six bushels of corn in a day and we can sell them at the store and buy what we wish." Those most destitute depended upon the bishop or neighbors to provide basic needs or supplemental potatoes, bread, and meat. At times, families survived for months with nothing more than the basic foods of the time: parched corn and pickled pork, bacon, or ham. Men and young men sought work wherever they could find it, often away from Nauvoo. Men scoured the countryside in Hancock and surrounding counties and traveled downriver to St. Louis or upstream as far as Galena. George Taggart informed his family in 1843, "I could raise 5 dollars in the east . . . from my work easier than I can raise 45 cents here."[42]

The anecdotal evidence of meager living standards does not mean that Nauvoo lacked prosperous residents. A broad cross-section of men succeeded at housing and feeding their families in moderate comfort.[43] A few prospered. The resources of thriving merchants, farmers, artisans, and professionals supported local government through taxes on land and buildings. Church leaders tapped these same resources for support of ecclesiastical projects. The revelation calling on the Saints to build a temple invited seven men with means to buy stock in a hotel, the Nauvoo House, envisioned as a place to host visiting dignitaries from around the world.[44] Others contributed to Nauvoo's economic stability by sharing their talents and financial resources for the community's betterment. When two church leaders in Adams County asked Joseph Smith for the Lord's counsel in their affairs in early 1841, the Prophet advised them by revelation to "devote all their properties" to the Nauvoo House project so that "the poor of my people may have employment."[45]

Nauvoo's temple and hotel construction projects did keep many workers busy. But local businessmen envisioned other opportunities for creating jobs and for bringing profits to investors. Part of the attempt to industrialize the city included a joint-stock organization to raise money and manage appropriate business ventures. On February 27, 1841,

Governor Thomas Carlin signed into law an act incorporating the Nauvoo Agricultural and Manufacturing Association (NA&MA) in Hancock County, capitalized at $100,000, with stock set at $50 per share. Its thirty-four members included leading business and church leaders of Nauvoo. They had petitioned the state for the action, intending the association to promote all branches of agriculture, husbandry, and manufacturing. Twenty trustees managed the association affairs. Joseph Smith, Sidney Rigdon, and William Law (the church's First Presidency) were named commissioners.[46]

The association's founders hoped to develop flour mills and a lumber industry to help feed and house the people of Nauvoo. At that time, to get corn or wheat ground into meal or flour, and for most lumber, residents were taking their business out of town. Old-timer Davison Hibbard's small horse-powered mill two miles below Nauvoo had been torched by a supposed arsonist the previous May.[47] The *Times and Seasons* lamented in December 1841 that one steam mill in Warsaw alone boasted a daily business of fifty dollars just from Nauvoo residents. "It is bad policy to depend upon our neighbors for our home consumptions," the editor said.[48]

To correct that outflow of cash, early in 1842, association president Joseph Smith wrote to Edward Hunter, a wealthy farmer and mill owner in Pennsylvania, encouraging him to bring a steam engine to Nauvoo and start a flour mill. Hunter agreed to do so. When local entrepreneurs William and Wilson Law heard of this outward reach, they announced plans to build their own steam flour mill and to contract for the production of bricks in Nauvoo. They convinced Hunter to alter his plans and sell them the steam engine he was shipping west. Still anxious to support the association's campaign for home industry, Hunter set up a tool factory instead. The Law brothers invested an estimated fifteen thousand dollars to construct and outfit a large frame building near the foot of Water Street.[49] In this complex, they operated both a steam flour mill and a sawmill. In addition to the Hunter and Law enterprises, by the end of 1842 Nauvoo boasted a second steam sawmill, plus Newel Knight's small water-powered grist mill, and Hiram Kimball's and George W. Robinson's iron foundry.[50]

The first private industrial efforts in Nauvoo complemented an active agricultural economy and construction business. But this was not enough to halt the trade imbalance. Merchants were importing goods and

Waterfront Businesses. *The Law brothers built the large steam-powered grist and timber mill (center) next to an earlier stone building (left) that housed a water-powered grain mill. Ropes were manufactured in the long log building (right).*

exporting money. Even as he prepared to open his own mercantile store, Joseph Smith encouraged more local manufacturing. "The *fewer foreign goods* that are consumed among the saints," he wrote, "the better it will be for home manufactories,—and the nearer we shall come to the word of the Lord. . . : 'Let all thy garments be plain, and their beauty the beauty of the work of thine own hands.'"[51]

Nauvoo had the human resources in its British immigrants to make manufacturing work, the city's economic promoters insisted. "Here are men skilled in all the departments of cotton, wool, and silk manufacture, of cutlery, of morocco dressing, glove making, of queens ware and porcelain, of silver and gold ware, lapidaries, sculptors, engravers, &c., &c., &c." Why should raw materials be sent off to be processed and then returned for sale in Nauvoo, they asked. Why were there not processing industries employing the skills of immigrant factory workers, the British converts echoed.[52] To support their families, experienced factory workers were finding jobs as farmers or laborers, hiring on as construction workers on the temple, or leaving Nauvoo seeking jobs elsewhere.[53] The answer to both questions was the lack of willing investors. Nauvoo's wealthiest residents chose not to sponsor industries yielding exportable surpluses. For them it made good economic sense instead to fund brickmaking, lumber sawing and selling, milling, and merchandising. These businesses met urgent local needs—housing and feeding the rapidly expanding population.

As with other plans for moving the city beyond subsistence level, the Nauvoo Agricultural and Manufacturing Association accomplished little towards its goals. After more than a year, officers were still talking about launching their first project, a pottery factory to supply local needs and employ skilled British immigrants. Church leaders stepped forward to encourage action. In a series of public meetings in late June 1842, Joseph Smith and members of the Twelve chastised merchants for failing to "open their hearts and contribute to the poor" by creating industrial jobs for them. The merchants had the surplus cash to do so.[54] Brigham Young called for united action and invoked the spirit of consecration to build the temple and support the poor. Acting under the charter's authority to solicit funds and under the religious expectations of the church, Joseph Smith approached a number of men of means in small gatherings. The first to respond were Edward Hunter, Edwin D. Woolley, and Lewis Robbins, who not only agreed to consecrate their mercantile goods to a general fund but delivered goods and money to the Prophet's office. For at least some of the merchants, Smith's invitation might have been a test of loyalty—the Prophet returned Woolley's goods.[55]

That summer the manufacturing association raised to a height of one story the walls of a stone building for a pottery. But legislative talk about repealing Nauvoo's charter dampened investors' interest. In May 1843, with work stalled, the association's president, Sidney Rigdon, defended the enterprise against published criticism. Means, material, and workmen were available, Rigdon said, if only the legislature would quit playing politics with the city's future.[56] The legislature saw it otherwise, however, and the pottery building remained unfinished.

While awaiting industrial development that would not become reality, a traditional home industry flourished in Nauvoo in the ages-old shop system. Nearly every craft and profession needed for a city of its size could be found in the maturing city. The trades that supported agriculture and household needs had the greatest basis of support, but the city's economy enjoyed a great variety of talents and products.[57]

In the spring of 1844, Ellen Douglas estimated the number of shops in Nauvoo at one hundred to two hundred, compared with a mere two or three shops when she arrived from England two years earlier. The only product she couldn't find in the shops were dolls for her daughters.[58] Nauvoo had a wide variety of independent artisans skilled in fashioning wood, metal, and textiles into useful products. For example, to clothe a family, residents could buy locally produced hats, gloves, shoes, dresses, coats, and suits. But virtually all cloth and many other clothing items were imported. So were stoves, tools, pots and pans, tubs, and other manufactured iron items. In the preindustrial economy of Nauvoo, a thousand miles from the Atlantic seaboard, immigrants not surprisingly found both textile and iron products more expensive and harder to find than in the eastern United States or in England.[59]

Although most craftsmen in Nauvoo worked alone as independent entrepreneurs, some banded together for support and mutual benefit. The city's potters were a prime example. When Horace Roberts, an Illinois convert and experienced potter, moved to the city in 1841, Joseph Smith encouraged him to establish a pottery. He did so on his town lot, four blocks east of the temple, but his welcome output could not fully meet a pressing need for supplanting imports with locally produced goods. When the Nauvoo Agriculture and Manufacturing Association failed to complete the large pottery for which it laid the foundation during the summer of 1842, independent shops proliferated, and some potters organized for cooperative efforts.[60] The home pottery industry reached its stride during the summer of 1845, when the eight members of the Nauvoo Potters' Association, many of them English immigrants, advertised English-style wares for sale from a pottery a few yards east of the temple on Knight Street.[61] Those who preferred Old Connecticut pottery or more common earthenware could visit other potteries in town. Outside Nauvoo, Hancock County boasted of only one pottery in 1840, a one-man operation, so the growth of the industry in Nauvoo contributed significantly to the availability of local wares in the region. By 1845, the Illinois census reported twenty-three potteries employing fifty-six persons in Hancock County.[62]

The potters and numerous other specialists contributed to Nauvoo's attempts to develop a home industry. Craftsmen kept at least some wealth within the community while employing men and women and helping to provide for the temporal needs of the gathered people. For example, German immigrant George Riser sold his shoe business in Ohio after his conversion and established a shop on Nauvoo's Main Street in 1842. A year later, the twenty-five-year-old entrepreneur expanded his business by hiring four assistants: his brother, John, a shoemaker working in Quincy, and three other experienced shoemakers newly arrived in Nauvoo, two from Pittsburgh and one from England.[63]

Besides the craftsmen at work in Nauvoo, the city had numerous workers whose skills provided services needed by the residents or visitors from outlying areas. Services included those offered by doctors, midwives, dentists, lawyers, teachers, barbers, and undertakers. Eventually, Nauvoo also had its own part-time artists and a daguerreotypist.

As a booming river town, Nauvoo was outpacing economically its similarly motivated neighbors on the Mississippi. The Mormon city's preindustrial economy was similar to that of nearby Warsaw (a much smaller town than Nauvoo) and Quincy, the commercial center of Adams County. In addition to the direct threat in politics, tension existed because of the aggressiveness of Nauvoo businessmen and the city's as yet unrealized potential for becoming an economic power base. Intense competition existed among operators of mills and ferries in the riverfront settlements of the two counties. As early as 1842, farmers from as far away as one hundred miles relied upon Nauvoo's three grist mills.[64] The city's chartered ferry competed with the Warsaw ferry for regional traffic. In addition, merchants in Nauvoo and Warsaw vied for rural customers well beyond city boundaries. Although craftsmen served few customers outside Nauvoo's growing sphere of influence, talk of textile mills, potteries, and other industrial enterprises created an image of a rising regional manufacturing and trading center. Not surprisingly, economic dominance may have been feared by the opponents of Nauvoo's growing political influence, but by the mid-1840s the city's agrarian subsistence economy had not yet become the industrial emporium its promoters envisioned.

From a broader perspective, beyond the concerns of the prospering merchants and millers, ordinary Nauvoo citizens had material interests focused on personal needs—food, clothing, and housing. Additionally, most individual Latter-day Saints were investing their meager surplus earnings in building the temple, sustaining the poor, and supporting church leaders. At least a tithe of time and income went toward building the kingdom of God and thus laying up treasures in heaven. It was an expectation of a gathered people, the faithful Latter-day Saints concluded, to endure the temporal challenges of this time and place and await the spiritual prosperity of another. The daughter of a widowed mother of six, immigrants from England in 1841, remembered, "We were very poor and had very little to eat, corn meal being our main food. . . . We did not complain. We were too thankful to be at Nauvoo."[65]

BANKING, CREDIT, AND NAUVOO'S POTENTIAL

One service missing from Nauvoo and other emerging towns was banking. Nauvoo was founded during a time when banking was volatile nationwide, and no banks operated in the city from which to secure loans.[66] Without banks to support business ventures, city entrepreneurs turned for their larger investments to private wealth. Similarly, to meet church financial obligations, including shortfalls on land payments, Joseph Smith often borrowed funds from prosperous Latter-day Saint businessmen or others who had surplus cash.[67] Businessmen formed partnerships to accumulate the necessary funds to start a business. From family sources, businessmen obtained loans, investments, and inheritances. Another resource was the sale of property left behind when converts migrated to Nauvoo.

Individuals often depended upon family and personal sources for funds to buy land and build homes. Even without banks, the people of Nauvoo could secure loans, obtain credit, and handle transactions with an informal checking system using personal notes. Merchants provided some banking services by the way they bought and sold on credit. The church tithing office near the temple issued and redeemed notes that served as paychecks for temple construction workers. Sometimes the office made loans.[68] If borrowers turned to friends for loans, they usually secured the note with property. For example, a physician and his wife, Samuel and Selina Bennett, borrowed $382.37 from Daniel H. Wells in 1844 by putting up as collateral Samuel's five-hundred-volume collection of medical books, his surgical instruments, and his stock of medicines, along with the couple's most valuable furniture, plus part of their city lot, one thousand feet of pine lumber, and four thousand bricks.[69]

Obligations to the government, however, were payable only in specie or negotiable scrip. Local tax collectors, including those in Hancock County, often insisted that citizens pay their property taxes in coin. "Husband your bits [pieces of eight, or coins worth 12½ cents]," the agent at Carthage advertised as the due date approached in 1842.[70]

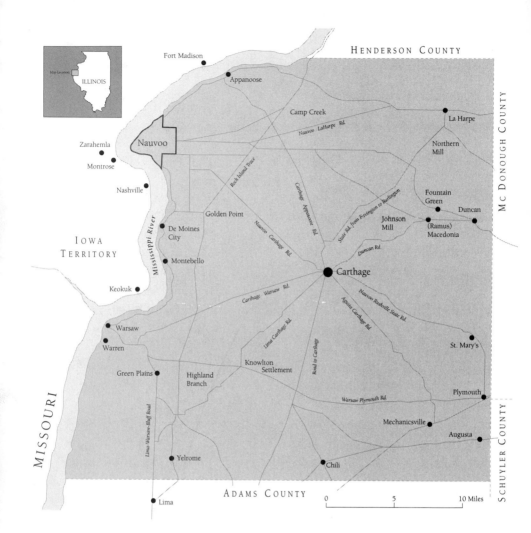

Fort Madison

Appanoose

Camp Creek

La Harpe

Nauvoo LaHarpe Rd.

Northern
Mill

Nauvoo

Zarahemla

Montrose

Rock Island Trace

Carthage Appanoose Rd.

State Rd. from Farmington to Burlington

Fountain
Green

Duncan

Nashville

Johnson
Mill

(Ramus)
Macedonia

Golden Point

De Moines
City

Nauvoo Carthage Rd.

Duncan Rd.

Mississippi River

Montebello

Carthage

IOWA
TERRITORY

Keokuk

Nauvoo Rushville State Rd.

Carthage Warsaw Rd.

Augusta Carthage Rd.

St. Mary's

Warsaw

Warren

Lima Carthage Rd.

Road to Carthage

Green Plains

Highland
Branch

Knowlton
Settlement

Plymouth

MISSOURI

Warsaw Plymouth Rd.

Mechanicsville

Augusta

Lima Warsaw Bluff Road

Yelrome

Chili

Lima

0   5   10 Miles

Map Location

ILLINOIS

Hancock County

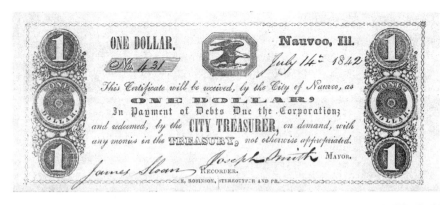

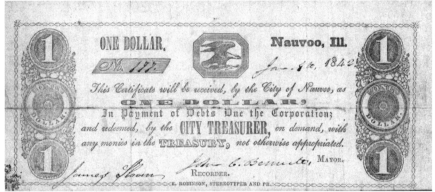

The Nauvoo city council issued one-dollar notes as a means of exchange in a mostly barter economy. Questions about the scrip's financial reliability forced its recall after only a short time.

Because money was scarce, the commercial marketplace allowed buying through credit or by exchanging commodities. Sellers could not conduct business strictly for cash if they wished a steady clientele. Merchants and craftsmen in Nauvoo found collecting on some debts took a constant effort. Most buyers attempted to clear their obligations with regular installment payments in cash or marketable goods.[71] Often, the debts were passed on from one person to another in the form of promissory notes, which functioned as a private form of money. Like a check, a note could be cashed only when the issuer accumulated the resources necessary to make good on his promise.

Merchants who found themselves short of cash for their own buying sometimes encouraged "cash only" transactions. For instance, because of a large number of unpaid accounts at his drugstore and general store, C. W.

Lyon offered a new shipment of dry goods, groceries, crockery, glass, hardware, medicines, and paints "for ready pay *only*."[72]

That "ready pay" requested by Lyon might include specie (gold or silver) or paper money issued by trusted banks. The United States government issued no paper money until 1861. Gold and silver coins were the official means of exchange. The same panic that had swept the Kirtland Safety Society into insolvency had seriously disabled the Illinois State Bank. In 1842, St. Louis merchants were discounting its currency at 55 percent below specie and 40 percent below currency exchanges. Few other banks in Illinois could be trusted.[73] "We cannot tell you what bank would be safe a month hence," Joseph Smith advised Edward Hunter. "I would say that gold and silver is the only safe money a man can keep these times; you can sell specie here for more premium than you have to give. . . . The bank you deposit in might fail before you had time to draw out again."[74]

The fragile condition of the banks in Illinois reflected the state government's own poor credit. Early in 1842, Illinois sold nearly a million dollars worth of bonds in Pennsylvania for fifteen to seventeen cents on the dollar. Two years later, with a debt of fifteen million dollars, the state was negotiating with Eastern and European bond holders for prices of forty-five cents. Two years later still, in December 1846, Governor Thomas Ford could tell the general assembly that the treasury had a positive balance (nine thousand dollars), that state warrants were selling at par, and that gold and silver coins were in good supply in Illinois.[75]

In financial transactions in an economy based on barter, the medium of exchange consisted of whatever tradeable item, including a worker's services, the two parties could agree on. When Hiram Kimball wanted someone to break up seventy acres of prairie land in 1843, he offered to pay for the job with city or country property. He also offered land for a pair of mules, a set of blacksmith's tools, or a first-rate two-horse wagon. Kimball offered to accept state bank paper money for property or debts due him at fifty cents on the dollar; and he offered to pay cash for untanned calfskins. A Mormon tanner in Zarahemla, Iowa, offered to trade flour for hides and skins needed for his business or to tan hides on shares. Blacksmith Alfred Lambson accepted as pay for his work such items as boots, books, clothing, orders on Hiram Kimball's store, flour, loads of wood, a bedstead, and cash. Lambson paid his rent as a boarder in various homes in 1844 and 1845 with clothing, fish, cucumbers, and wagon repairs and other blacksmithing work.[76]

During the difficult financial crisis still pinching Americans in 1842, a Nauvoo editor observed, "Our good city continues to go ahead notwithstanding the scarcity of money." And a St. Louis metals jobber, making the best of hard times, caught the eye of potential buyers with a business card reading, "All kinds of Produce taken in exchange,/From a pound of Rags to a Steamboat-load of Buffaloes."[77] A willingness to buy and sell through the exchange of goods and services was a way of life in the pre-industrial economy of Nauvoo and in cities around the country.

Church leaders had incurred significant debts when they purchased the land upon which the Saints settled in Nauvoo and Iowa. These investments allowed Missouri exiles to begin again while awaiting a compensation for their losses that never came. In the financially difficult 1840s, the obligations to pay off the land acquisitions created no end of trouble for those who had signed their names in an effort to secure a place of refuge for the Saints.

From Isaac Galland, the church had purchased one large parcel and two smaller ones totaling slightly more than fifty-nine acres in the Commerce area for eighteen thousand dollars. On the Iowa side, the purchase of nearly eighteen thousand acres from Galland obligated the church for just under fifty thousand dollars. The terms of the sale allowed small annual payments of cash over twenty years. After concluding the sales, Galland accepted baptism and moved his family back to his native Ohio. Ever the promoter, Galland put his name on an immigrant guide and issued a map of Iowa Territory—which extended at that time all the way to the Canadian border. With these publications, he hoped to encourage settlement on other lands he owned in Iowa. After about a year, to hasten the payoff on the church sale, Galland agreed to a land exchange. One by one, settlers on the lands purchased from Galland signed over their Missouri property to him. Through this arrangement, the full obligation of the church was met. Church leaders praised Galland as a benefactor, appointed him to the board of regents of the University of Nauvoo, and invited him to assist the church further as a sales agent and investor in the Nauvoo House.[78]

An exchange of lands was allowed as well for Latter-day Saints in the East as a means of meeting obligations owing on land at the north end of the Nauvoo peninsula purchased from Horace Hotchkiss, Smith Tuttle, and John Gillet, who formed a New Haven, Connecticut, land syndicate. With that purchase, the church had obligated itself to a fifty-thousand-dollar debt, plus fees and interest. After two years, six thousand dollars in interest was due. Attempts in 1841 to pay this through land exchanges with members in the East who were preparing to move to Nauvoo met with limited success. Isaac Galland was the designated agent for the church in the few transactions that did take place.[79]

That fall, Joseph Smith learned that Galland had not paid off the notes owing Hotchkiss as intended and had possibly diverted church funds to his own use. Church newspapers went public with the problem. To resolve the matter, the October conference in Nauvoo authorized the Prophet to negotiate a settlement.[80] Meanwhile, Galland had settled at Keokuk, where he was promoting his own interests in that city. When the Prophet's entreaties for an accounting brought only polite postponements, the church leader revoked Galland's agency. In February 1842, the two men finally conferred in Nauvoo and apparently reached an understanding. An undated note among Smith's papers records an $8,778 debt owed to the church by Galland. The two remained friends. Even though Galland distanced himself spiritually from the church, he consistently deflected the public scorn against the people whose search for a place of refuge he had assisted.[81]

In 1841, the Prophet had delegated to the Twelve the business of settling the Saints in the new gathering place. Now, he asked them to handle the land exchanges. This was one solution to the overdue payments owed Horace R. Hotchkiss and his partners for the land in northern Nauvoo. In a general epistle to the Saints living away from Nauvoo, the Twelve urged contributions towards the debt directly or by swapping land. Ignoring the interest that had accrued, they acknowledged as the church's obligation a debt of $53,500.[82]

Even with this delegation of duty, Joseph Smith, as the church's chief financial officer, was not far removed from the land business. From time to time, he offered explanations to justify church activities. In one such public comment in 1843, he said that when immigrants bought from private landowners, they denied church leaders needed resources. Yes, Smith admitted, he was speculating on church land—selling at a profit—but the process supported church purposes. Widows received building lots at no

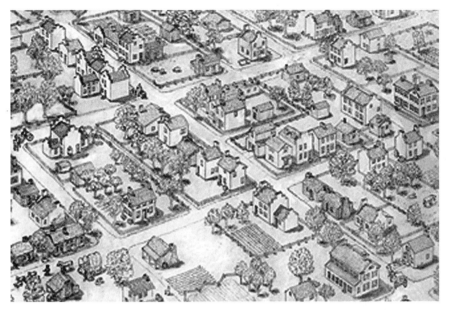

Nauvoo's economy thrived on agriculture, construction, and trades. A typical tradesman worked in a shop on his home lot. Scattered through this late twentieth-century drawing of Nauvoo in 1846 are examples of a typical nineteenth-century integration of residential and business buildings.

cost. Income from sales helped meet loan payments on the tracts. "We have claim on your good feelings for your money, to help the poor," he said, "and the church debts also have their demands to save the credit of the church. . . . Those who purchase church lands and pay for it, this shall be their sacrifice. . . . We have the highest prices, [the] best lands, and do the most good with the money we get."[83]

Even with this appeal, the obligations were greater than available resources. The Saints building on the Hotchkiss syndicate's land filed their deeds with the county, but, in fact, the syndicate still held title to the land. Because he did not want to foreclose, Hotchkiss offered to resolve the dilemma by charging these buyers a monthly rent. Joseph Smith left the matter with the Twelve. Financially strapped, in a depressed national economy, the optimistic hopes of paying the debt fell far short. The investors in the Hotchkiss syndicate trusted their buyers but failed to realize the anticipated profit on their initial investment.[84]

At times, personal debts went unpaid or uncollected. For individual debtors, the consequence was a loss of trust in the community. Claimants had several options. A hearing before the bishop's court or the high council was one. An appeal to the civil courts was possible, but attorney's fees made all but the most grievous complaints unworthy of the expense. Debtors prison was not an option; in its first constitution in 1818, Illinois had been among the first in the nation to abolish imprisonment for debt.[85]

In February 1842, a new federal law for unloading debt became available. In April, Quincy attorney Calvin A. Warren, of the firm of Ralston, Warren, and Wheat, advertised his services as a bankruptcy lawyer. On a visit to Nauvoo, he attracted the interest of a number of community leaders, among them Joseph Smith.[86] The Prophet's financial problems with the steamboat *Nauvoo* precipitated his decision to clear his debts. He and Hyrum were listed with their partners in a default judgment for more than five thousand dollars. Years of losses brought on by constant moves and harassment complicated the Prophet's financial life. In all, he owed $73,066.38, and his assets included less than twenty thousand dollars in notes receivable. Smith declared bankruptcy on April 18, 1842, filing with the assistance of Warren's firm in the district court at Carthage. That firm handled more than a dozen other Mormon bankruptcy cases.[87] The matter would have been considered routine had not John C. Bennett charged Joseph Smith with defrauding his creditors. An investigation led to proposals for settlements still unresolved at Joseph Smith's death. Finally, in 1853, the government sold land formerly owned by the church and Smith to satisfy its claim.[88]

Latter-day Saints were not convinced by Bennett's claim that the bankruptcy issue exposed Joseph Smith as an imposter. For years, they had dismissed newspaper reports insinuating that converts were being duped in a religious scam. "Now father," Helen Soby wrote in 1841, "if you want to know about us or Joe Smith read the Book of Mormon . . . instead of newspapers' statements. All the money that he has had of us is 100 dollars that I lent him, and that has been proffered to me three times and I would not receive it." The bankruptcy law was created to benefit the oppressed, Mary Ann Fullmer informed an unbelieving relative; Joseph Smith's action in seeking relief could not be held against him. Mary Ann's husband had also taken out bankruptcy. John Fullmer said merely, "A bird in *hand* is worth two in a bush."[89]

Joseph Smith defended his decision as the only way he could settle uncollectible debts he owed. "I was forced into the measure by having been robbed, mobbed, plundered, and wasted of all my property, time after time, in various places," he explained.[90] Some observers could not imagine that Smith lacked means, since as trustee-in-trust for the church he controlled vast assets in land and buildings. But these were not his own. When the Twelve took over management of Nauvoo property sales in 1841, the Prophet prepared an inventory. His personal belongings, said the Twelve, included "his old Charley horse, given him in Kirtland; two pet deer; two old turkeys, and four young ones; the old cow given him by a brother in Missouri, his old Major, dog; his wife, children, and a little household furniture." The Prophet kept his own real estate separate from land registered in his name as trustee-in-trust for the church by filing it in Emma Smith's name. Concerning a debt owed his loyal friend Edward Hunter, Joseph Smith said in November, "If I could pay you . . . I should do it with pleasure, but . . . true wealth is little to be found."[91]

In the final analysis, declarations of bankruptcy had little positive effect on Nauvoo's overall economy. Clearing away the debts of a few in the community did little to make capital available for new enterprises. At best, it freed financial risk-takers to take risks again.

Nauvoo's failure to prosper caused some to evaluate why the city had not realized its economic potential. One of those was Parley P. Pratt. In a direct plea to church members in September 1844, the energetic apostle laid the city's failure to become a major industrial and agricultural center at the feet of the Saints. The former Campbellite preacher blamed rich and poor alike for their unwillingness to accept the principle of the gathering. His argument was a summary of the expectations under the new economic emphasis in the years after Missouri, yet his reprimand echoed arguments that had explained the failure of the original Zion.

If properly understood, Pratt said, the gathering required an economic commitment. The rich must establish businesses in Nauvoo to employ the poor, and the poor must stay in Nauvoo to work. Some of the well-to-do, he observed, were unwilling to give up their prosperous businesses to buy farms or build workshops in the new gathering place. Even when they emigrated to Nauvoo, they too often divided their wealth among their unbelieving children who remained behind; or, they invested in St. Louis, Chicago, Peoria, or Burlington for better returns on their money. "The poor go unemployed, and are scattered to and fro over the earth, to seek to earn a morsel of bread; while the city of Nauvoo languishes in poverty, the

Temple is not built, business is at a stand, and the saints of the Most High are few in number, have but little means, and are persecuted, robbed, killed and destroyed all the day long."

Pratt also blamed those who were without material means for Nauvoo's economic weakness. "Many of the poor," he said,

> either stop on the road, or come here and go away again, as they say through poverty or necessity. But if they are not prospered abroad, they excuse themselves because they have no means to settle here; and if they are prospered, then they are doing so well that they think that they had better stay where they can do the best;—and they are led on by worldly schemes, and by drunkenness and whoredom, till they care nothing for the Lord, or his saints.

Pratt was equally frustrated by those without means who located in Nauvoo "with a view of being helped to a living, while they pray, and sing, and tattle, and hear and tell news" instead of working. The opportunities for prospering, then, are left to "merchants, lawyers, doctors, mechanics, and others who are not of our faith, and only here in our midst for speculation."

The apostle said that he held this uncomfortable mirror up to the Saints to awaken them to the truth. "Our city is impoverished, and many go hungry and destitute," he lamented. "Our people are scattered and not prepared to defend their freedom and their rights . . . and we are in danger of being scattered and driven." He pleaded with the scattered members to gather, to "be governed by counsel, and seek to employ themselves and each other, and to support and build up in perfect union, according to the plan of heaven." Pratt had high expectations for the City of the Saints. Had the Saints done their duty, he argued, "Nauvoo would now have contained a hundred and fifty thousand souls; with industrious work shops of every description, manufacturing every article for home use and comfort, and supplying the whole western states with every thing useful . . . from a cambrick needle or a pin, up to a steam engine." He imagined another one hundred fifty thousand residents in Hancock and nearby counties working as farmers, stock raisers and wool growers; a state legislature "filled with our wise men, to make just laws; and the executive chair with a man who would have administered them in equity and justice for the benefit and protection of all. Every foot of vacant land would have been cultivated like Eden," he projected.[92]

But Nauvoo would not become the flourishing economic Eden envisioned by her leaders. As Pratt correctly surmised, the city lacked both the population base and financial resources needed to gain economic dominance in the region. It would take greater resources and more years to accomplish the dream of prosperity, but neither sufficient money nor time would be available. The Nauvoo everyone knew continued to expand because of its need to house a growing population. That need kept many workmen employed. Agriculture remained the mainstay of Nauvoo's economy. Tradesmen and professionals provided some economic stability as they offered their goods and services. Nauvoo's Saints made the best of their situation and rejoiced in their lives as common working people.

"Labor is the manufacturer of wealth," John Taylor declared. "It was ordained of God, as the medium to be used by man to obtain his living." Like Pratt, Taylor was critical of those with means who lorded it over workers and failed to make others happy. "The merchants and great men of the earth must prepare to mourn," he said. When the ways of the worldly Babylon fail, "the kingdom of God [will] rise in holy splendor, upon her ashes, and the people serve God in a perpetual union! . . . Let the world traffic, we must make men better by wisdom, virtue, and industry."[93]

Ultimately, as Taylor understood, it was the religious values underlying Nauvoo's economy that were important for most of her gathered people. Similarly, despite the privations of subsistence living, and like many of his neighbors, a destitute Newel K. Whitney held to a religious perspective on the question of unrealized personal prosperity. Deeply in debt, he preferred to remain in Nauvoo rather than return to Ohio, even if moving offered the prospect of a faster repayment of his debts. "I say *liberty and poverty* is preferable to *imprisonment and riches* or bondage and wealth," he said of the option of leaving his Zion for Babylon.[94]

The treasures of heaven were a sufficient prosperity for most who gathered to Nauvoo. To a friend in Boston, Orson Spencer wrote of the Saints' dream of a Zion people:

> There is not a more contented and cheerful people to be found. . . .
> You must not marvel if we do not all at once become rich, and build

large houses, and enclose productive farms.—If riches were our object, we might readily gratify the most ambitious grasp. We possess every facility for being rich; but we long to behold the beauty of the Lord, and enquire in his holy Temple. . . . Our people . . . are prepared to endure all things with the assurance that their reward is great in heaven.[95]

CHAPTER 8

Neighbors in Nauvoo

*I find as the Saints advance step by step in the principles of righteousness
it tends more and more to unite and bring the Saints to act as one man.
The Lord has got a great work to do in the earth and that through
human instrumentality and this unity being brought about and the
temple completed. . . . Please remember us to our old neighbours and
acquaintances, uncles, aunts, and cousins. . . . I am anxious for you and
all the rest of our family to be here. . . . My desire is that you and I with
our families and connections may stand on Mount Zion where there
shall be peace and safety.*

—JOHN BENNION TO HIS PARENTS, FEBRUARY 16, 1844

In important ways, Nauvoo resembled the original City of Zion in
Missouri. Those similarities went beyond the obvious use of streets laid
off in lines straight with the compass. That pattern echoed a penchant in
postrevolutionary America for creating boundaries and laying out cities
using the orderliness of straight lines. For Latter-day Saints, the method-
ical arrangements of the urban landscape meant something more. In Zion
and her stakes, the Saints sought to achieve oneness, harmony, and order.
To eliminate confusion and to shape themselves as a Zion people, they
sought to be of one heart and one mind. It was a quest launched early in
the Restoration and founded in a full range of scriptural sources and
prophetic teachings. The foursquare cities of holiness in which they lived

represented the personal order and harmony the Saints sought for in their spiritual lives as a people.[1]

Beyond their desire for a unity in faith, they wanted to become a Zion people in their relationships with one another, within families, and among neighbors. Yet Nauvoo, as a newly founded city of "one heart and one mind," contained some hearts and minds distracted from the ideal of Zion. The Prophet acknowledged that Nauvoo's gathered people were not yet a clear light to the world. He warned potential immigrants in 1841

> to understand that, when they come here they must not expect to find perfection, or that all will be harmony, peace and love; . . . for here there are persons, not only from different States, but from different nations, who, although they feel a great attachment to the cause of truth, have their prejudices of education, and consequently it requires some time before these things can be overcome.[2]

The assortment of people in Nauvoo's imperfect spiritual community meant rough edges yet to be smoothed.

The social world of the city reveals other differences among the population within the church and between the Latter-day Saints and the people of nearby settlements. Nauvoo was not one large centrally orchestrated community but rather housed various self-defined clusters of families and friends, neighbors and fellow citizens. These networks crisscrossed greater Nauvoo to weave a social fabric of many differing threads. In short, within the rhetoric of unity, the Latter-day Saints shared many common objectives in their New Jerusalem. At the same time, they related to one another in selective social groupings, each with its own subset of interests, each interacting in its own way on the urban landscape.

THE URBAN LANDSCAPE

In its physical dimensions, Nauvoo was big enough for all of its intersecting, internal human communities. As surveyed, the original plat before its many additions contained about the same acreage as Missouri's City of Zion. But unlike its Jackson County model, whose 640-acre parcel fit nicely into one square mile, the original shape of Nauvoo reflected both the curve of the river and the boundaries of the four parcels acquired for development. Within the plat, surveyors oriented the streets according to the Jeffersonian foursquare ideal. "The city of Nauvoo is laid out the most beautiful," an English immigrant reported to his father in Staffordshire; "its streets go exactly North and South and East and West, which divides it into squares of 4 Acres which they call city Lots."[3] Because the streets were taken out of the adjacent blocks, the four lots in each block actually measured just under an acre in size.

The more than five hundred lots in the newly platted Nauvoo could be reasonably expected to hold over twenty-five hundred people. But only a month after surveyors filed the original plat, the new city expanded. Ethan Kimball, an Eastern investor, designated more than three hundred acres of his family's holdings as Nauvoo's first addition. Within that annexation, Kimball immediately surveyed and opened for settlement an eighteen-block area divided into seventy-two lots. The remaining land was separated into large numbered lots, some of them later subdivided. In subsequent years, other developers purchased and platted sections within the first Kimball addition or annexed their own subdivisions. The greatest increase came in 1842, when developers opened 412 lots to meet the rapid influx of immigrants. By the close of 1843, the number of platted lots in Nauvoo had grown to 1,430.[4] A city of that size could comfortably house more than seven thousand people, yet that would not end Nauvoo's expansion.

A prospective homeowner in Nauvoo could obtain a lot in one of several ways. If arriving immigrants asked Joseph Smith's advice, he encouraged them to buy church land from authorized agents. Such purchases in the original plat helped meet payments on the debt to the Hotchkiss syndicate. The Prophet adjusted the asking price according to a buyer's resources and sometimes gave away lots to widows. Church leaders did not object when individual lot owners resold or subdivided their own lots, a common practice. They did oppose competing real estate developers. Targeted were private Latter-day Saint land agents on the bluff who undercut church prices and pocketed the profits. Their error was in ignoring Joseph Smith's plan for a Zion where the rich gave generously to lift up the poor.

A public reprimand of such developers came during a special conference in August 1841. At that meeting, the First Presidency authorized the Twelve to act as church land agents. Their area of supervision included Nauvoo, Zarahemla (in Iowa), and the proposed settlement of Warren, near Warsaw. Church leaders warned private land dealers that active

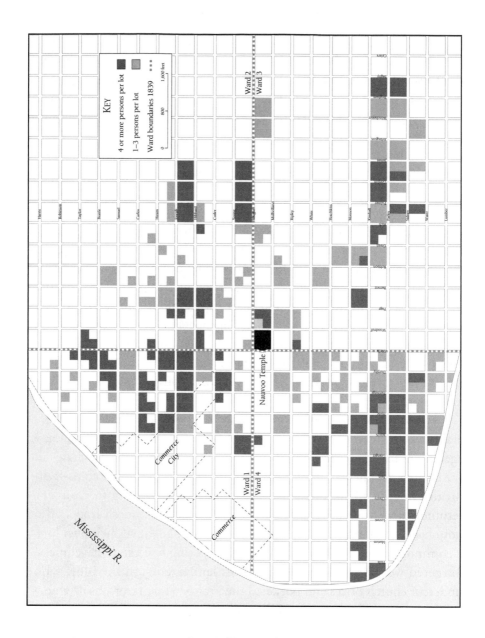

Occupied Lots, 1842 Census

competition with church agents might lead to a loss of fellowship for any-one rejecting counsel. As the church's new supervising land agent, Brigham Young endorsed the policy as a protection for immigrants against unprincipled speculators. The advice applied specifically to Wilson Law and other opportunistic Latter-day Saints who bought and resold land, mostly on the bluffs, for personal enrichment. The challenge directed at Law created tension in the competitive land market and strained relations between Joseph Smith and the brother of his first counselor.[5]

While the competition in the market created barriers between land merchants in new and old Nauvoo, other dividing lines did little to upset the people's striving for unity. In March 1841, the first Nauvoo city council created four municipal wards with boundaries almost exactly quartering the city's population. The lines intersected at the northwest corner of the temple block, the geographical and religious center of the city.[6] The four wards defined voting districts for the selection of alder-men and councilors in municipal elections. Even though these officers ostensibly represented their constituents in the city council, issues rarely divided the council geographically.[7] In their selection of county, state, and national candidates, Nauvoo's populace usually voted overwhelmingly together. That fact reinforced citywide unity but created tensions between Nauvoo and her neighbors in the region.

Similarly, the creation of administrative units for ecclesiastical pur-poses did not divide Nauvoo socially in any meaningful way. Nauvoo's single stake organization included the entire city and attracted the loyalty of other nearby Latter-day Saints. Nor did administrative subdivisions within the stake challenge this cohesion. At Nauvoo, the church for the first time divided a stake into districts named wards after their municipal counterparts.[8] Initially, the wards existed to help the bishops more conve-niently identify and meet the needs of the poor. The first conference held in Commerce in October 1839 recognized three ecclesiastical wards: the lower ward along the river, the middle ward, and the upper (bluffs) ward.[9] Then, in the spring of 1841, the lines were adjusted to follow the new municipal ward boundaries, and a fourth bishop was appointed.[10] The growing population led to a final reconfiguration of ecclesiastical bound-aries in December 1842. Again influenced by existing boundaries, the high council adopted lines created in February 1841 by the temple com-mittee. A chairman was already functioning within each of the ten city tithing wards and three adjacent rural tithing wards. It was his duty to organize work parties of men offering their temporal tenth to build the temple. It made sense for the bishops to care for the poor using the same boundaries. Mulholland Street became the axis for the new wards. The wards south of that street were narrow segments running north and south; the northern wards were even narrower strips extending east and west. Additional bishops were appointed by the high council to serve the new ecclesiastical units.[11]

Even though the bishops generally focused on the temporal needs of their own wards, at times they worked together. For example, in March 1841, Nauvoo's four bishops jointly organized the Aaronic Priesthood as stake quorums of deacons, teachers, and priests. That fall, two of the bishops discussed the needs of Nauvoo's poor before a special conference and then took a collection for their benefit.[12] The bishops rarely organized worship meetings, a function handled citywide by general authorities or by the invitation of the owners of large homes.

From the perspective of Nauvoo's residents, the divisions of the city into administrative units for collecting tithing and caring for the poor had little divisive impact on their lives. The boundaries were silent, almost unnoticed organizational conveniences—financial districts for important programs of the kingdom of God. Aside from the opportunities it gave members to meet together in a neighbor's home for occasional bad-weather Sabbath meetings and thus to renew and build friendships, the bishop's ward had little effect in defining neighborhoods.

INDIVIDUAL LANDSCAPES

The citizens of other communities in Hancock County and beyond saw Nauvoo as a tight-knit domain, largely because of the perception that the Saints spoke with a single voice in political and spiritual matters.[13] Yet, even as the Saints adhered to the community's common religious goals and supported shared political objectives, they held firmly to other loyalties as well. Within Nauvoo, life's affiliations were diverse. Out of practical considerations, the people of the city related to one another as neighbors in groups smaller than the whole. These social linkings were defined by place of origin, family relationships, friendships, informal social interactions, and formal institutional efforts designed to build a cohesive community.

The politicians of Hancock County worried about the voting strength of Nauvoo. The city had fewer voting males per capita than other towns, but Nauvoo was a rapidly growing hub with a steadily increasing number of votes. In a fall 1840 census, the town of Nauvoo listed 2,450 residents, making it the region's largest urban area. Until that time, Quincy City, with a population 2,296, had seen itself as the leading political and economic light of the Hancock-Adams Counties region. That same year, Lee County, Iowa, had 3,295 residents and Chicago reported 4,470. Seventeen months later, in February 1842, a church census of members conducted by the teachers quorum counted 3,564 Latter-day Saints (211 of whom lived outside the city limits). The number was almost evenly distributed among Nauvoo's four wards.[14] Springfield, the capital city of Illinois, had about the same population.[15] In sheer numbers, greater Nauvoo represented a political potential that concerned her neighbors.

In 1840 and again in 1850, after the Saints had left, Adams County was the most populous of the eighteen counties carved out of the western Illinois military tract. In 1840, Adams County reported more than fourteen thousand residents. In a state census five years later, Hancock County outranked every other county in the state, exceeding Chicago's rapidly growing Cook County by almost nine hundred. Not only was Hancock the most populated county, with 22,559 residents, but Nauvoo accounted for nearly half of that population. With the addition of the rural Latter-day Saints, that proportion made the Saints a huge majority in the county. The presence of an estimated fifteen thousand members in the region—more than two-thirds of them in Nauvoo—gave the Latter-day Saints a feeling of strength and security and a sense of unity in their majority position. The opposite feeling prevailed among the outnumbered residents of Hancock County. They felt weak, insecure, and threatened in their minority status. The same 1845 census that counted 11,057 Nauvoo residents found only 402 people living in Warsaw and 380 in Carthage. Chicago that year had 12,088 residents, only 1,031 more than Nauvoo.[16]

These figures demonstrate that the Latter-day Saints were not unreasonable in their expectations that the gathering to Nauvoo might create a major American city. Cities exceeding three thousand were rare in the American West in 1840. The growth of Nauvoo through 1845 placed it behind only Chicago and St. Louis in the region.[17] Church leaders and other Nauvoo boosters imagined the unimaginable for their place of refuge. When Parley P. Pratt returned in early 1843 after an absence of three and a half years, he was amazed at the city's growth. Pratt shared the popular hopes for the future. If the Saints continued to gather in earnest, he anticipated, "Nauvoo, in one year would be the largest city in the west—in ten years the largest in America, and in fifteen years the largest in the world."[18] Visiting journalists shared in the optimistic expectation. Their forecasts did nothing to calm the concerns of Nauvoo's neighbors in western Illinois.

Besides its challenging numbers, Nauvoo differed from its neighbors in the proportion and size of families. In most areas of Illinois, Missouri, and Ohio, and in Iowa Territory in 1840, young men in their twenties outnumbered young women of the same age-group by 20 to 60 percent. For obvious reasons, these regions were attracting young men seeking their fortunes in the New West. In St. Louis, this age-group claimed two men for every woman. In Hancock County, the census takers in 1840 found the young adult populations more nearly equal, with 115 men for every 100 women. Nauvoo itself had an equal number of males and females in almost every age group.[19] Similarly, a church census in 1842 counted 102 men for each 100 women. This ratio reflected the proportions in the older, settled counties of the Eastern states more than it resembled Nauvoo's neighboring communities on the frontier. The gathering had transplanted many entire families to the city, where children under five were twice as numerous as in other frontier regions.[20] Families, including children, were at the heart of Nauvoo's purposes.

These differences in family makeup seem not to have affected the political discourse that led to tension between Nauvoo and her neighbors. The settled people of western Illinois believed in families and in constitutional guarantees for the free exercise of religion. Except for their criticisms of rumored plural marriage, opponents of Nauvoo's political clout were willing to allow the gathered Saints to pursue their religious objectives as long as theocratic power did not interfere with political and economic life.[21]

When immigrants to Nauvoo moved from old cities and farms to new ones, they left behind their homelands but did not necessarily come away alone. Many of them traveled with friends and relatives. At Nauvoo, they transplanted old acquaintanceships into new neighborhoods. The larger the community grew with the influx of immigrants, the greater became the potential for internal networking. The small-town unity of the original

This 1845 painting portrays Joseph Smith with seven close associates: his brother Hyrum (at left), and apostles Willard Richards, Orson Pratt, Parley P. Pratt, Orson Hyde, Heber C. Kimball, and Brigham Young. All were Northeasterners: the Smith brothers, Kimball, and Young from Vermont; Richards from Massachusetts; the Pratt brothers from New York; and Hyde from Connecticut.

Nauvoo was gradually overwhelmed by increasing numbers of new immigrants. Even though they were Saints, the newcomers were strangers to the Mormon old-timers. They found friends among other immigrants from their home regions and renewed acquaintances with missionaries who had returned to Nauvoo. Through this process, the gathering of a diverse immigrant population preserved old friendships as subgroups within the larger community.

Latter-day Saints who had gathered from the tier of the Northern United States consistently made up Nauvoo's majority and provided a good share of the city's and the church's leaders. Apparently Joseph Smith felt a special kinship with people from the region of his nativity. "He was easy, free, and sociable with all," a newcomer from Connecticut reported upon arrival. "He said that he rejoiced to see us, being Yankees, for, said he, I was born in the state of Vermont."[22] From its start in New England

and the Mid-Atlantic states, the church had attracted additional converts in the upper Midwest among recently transplanted Easterners. Together many of this founding core group had shared the troubled years in Ohio and Missouri before heading into Illinois. Converts born in New York and the other Mid-Atlantic states accounted for at least a quarter of the adult population of Nauvoo. Native New Englanders added another 15 to 20 percent and British Canadians perhaps 5 percent. Except for some Ohio natives, few adults claimed birthplaces in the Midwest. Taken together, immigrants from states in the Northeast and the Midwest and from eastern Canada accounted for around half of Nauvoo's adults.[23]

The experiences of the Ohio-Missouri years reinforced a group cohesiveness founded in shared regional origins. Heber C. Kimball, who had built a log cabin on a five-acre wooded parcel bought from Hiram Kimball in July 1839, with "not a house within half a mile," returned from his mission two years later to find that "the place, wild as it was at that time, is converted into a thickly populated village." He informed Parley Pratt, "Our old friends, who were driven from Missouri, are my neighbours: for instance, the Allreds, Charles Hubbard, Charles Rich, and hundreds of others that I could mention that you know."[24] Similar friendship ties based on prior geographical linkages existed in almost every group arriving at Nauvoo. Just as the Kirtland Camp transported almost intact a congregation of Saints from Ohio to Missouri, so immigrant companies from Pennsylvania, Kentucky, and elsewhere preserved established friendship networks by settling together in their new homeland in Nauvoo.

The Saints of Chester County, Pennsylvania, exemplify a regional group that retained old associations in Nauvoo. For some time, they had lived as neighbors. They had cemented their relationships through business arrangements and some intermarriage. The restored gospel brought these neighbors together in the Brandywine branch and sent them off to Nauvoo in two or three companies in 1841 and 1842. Several of Edward Hunter's workmen on his prosperous 550-acre estate at West Nantmeal preceded him as settlers in Nauvoo and built him a house there. The Brandywine Saints retained their friendships, even though many of them found it necessary to spread out over the greater Nauvoo area.[25] A group from neighboring Lancaster County, Pennsylvania, bought farms within a mile or so of each other on the prairie east of Nauvoo.[26]

Less numerous than Northerners in Nauvoo were the Southerners, but they likewise remained aware of their regional origins. They accounted for perhaps 10 to 15 percent of the adult population in the area. Half of these Southerners were natives of Kentucky and Tennessee, with most of the rest from the South Atlantic states.[27] A few from the upper South who had migrated to Missouri returned there as missionaries. Their efforts increased the Southern contingent in greater Nauvoo, though it was still a largely invisible minority. Some Southerners who had joined a general regional migration into southern Illinois likewise became Latter-day Saint converts. Some of them remained where they were when they converted, in small clusters around Nauvoo. For example, the Ute Perkins family had moved to Illinois from North Carolina in 1826 before they joined the church. In 1840, their family settlement, known as Perkinsville, was incorporated as Ramus (later Macedonia); the Ramus stake served a broad sweep of the countryside, as far north as La Harpe. Among those absorbed into the Ramus stake were a few dropouts of the Kirtland Camp of 1838 who had stopped first at Springfield and then moved into the area east of Carthage in 1839 as mill operators and farmers along Crooked River. The leader of the Kirtland sick detachment, Joel Hills Johnson, presided over the Crooked Creek branch and the short-lived Ramus stake. Almon W. Babbitt, another Kirtland exile, presided for a season in 1843 in the Macedonia branch. Ramus thus included both a small, preexisting Southern kinship group and a friendship group from Kirtland.[28]

Southern immigrants built or retained friendship networks to support commonalities based on place of origin in part because they may have found some discrimination against them among the Yankee population in Nauvoo. John H. Henderson's situation reveals one instance of unfortunate bias. Orphaned at thirteen and left to fend for himself, he found sporadic work with farmers outside Nauvoo until someone placed him with a sixty-year-old New England veteran of the War of 1812, who promised to educate the youth. "I soon found that our ways of thinking and talking were quite different," Henderson remembered. "Mine were all of the Southern stamp, while his were of New England. This difference caused him to be continually making fun of my speech and ways." The prejudice extended into the classroom, where some of the students likewise mimicked Henderson's accent. Anxious to make the most of his first chance at an education, Henderson applied himself to his studies. He concluded that he was learning as fast as the others.[29]

Given the attitudes of the time, the few black residents of Nauvoo likely interacted with one another in a network of their common interests in addition to those shared with other church members. Several black Latter-day Saints lived in the city, and others resided in branches elsewhere. Perhaps the best-known black member was Elijah Abel, who had been ordained an elder and later a seventy during the Kirtland years. A missionary in the late 1830s and again in 1843, Abel worked as a carpenter and undertaker in Nauvoo for three years before relocating to Cincinnati, where he remained active in church affairs. Other black Saints in Nauvoo included Isaac and Jane Manning James, who married in the new city of the Saints, and other members of the Manning family, 1843 immigrants from Connecticut.[30]

Citizens of Nauvoo shared with most other Americans some attitudes toward blacks and rejected others. Typical was Joseph Smith's disapproval of marriage between the races. As a municipal judge in 1844, he fined two black men "for attempting to marry white women"; however, the Prophet did not hold to the common opinion of the day that blacks were congenitally inferior.[31]

The British were at least as numerous as the Southerners in Nauvoo. Not all of the forty-eight hundred converts who sailed from Liverpool before 1846 reached Nauvoo or remained there. Perhaps as few as one-fourth of them remained with the church in western Illinois to the end of the Nauvoo period. Some stopped in such way stations as St. Louis, while others left Nauvoo for work or settlement opportunities elsewhere. Even so, Great Britain contributed at least 10 percent of the adults in the Nauvoo area and may have accounted for double that number.[32]

The British in greater Nauvoo represented two economic groups. The first, represented by a few Englishmen from Herefordshire, were farmers. Because of their occupation, they resembled the typical non-Mormon immigrant to the upper Mississippi Valley who sought land in the fertile prairies of central Illinois. The second and much larger group was made up of Latter-day Saints from such industrial towns as Manchester, Liverpool, and Birmingham, or the Staffordshire Potteries. Drawn from England's poor laboring classes and industrial areas, they wanted jobs in factories, and church leaders tried unsuccessfully to provide such opportunities for them. Some left for work downriver. Others changed occupations.[33]

The British traveled together to Nauvoo in church-chartered ships

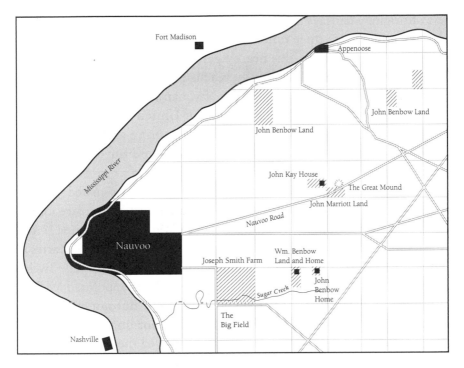

The "English Countryside" near Nauvoo

and often settled near their own countrymen for mutual comfort. In Hancock County, they kept track of one another and nurtured old friendships. For instance, when John Jones lost his wife, his daughters cared for him in the home of an English friend, John Kay. Later on, Jones married the widow of a former neighbor at Froomes Hill in England.[34] Jones found America's classless society a welcome change from his native England. He liked the quest for equality among the Saints and the lack of pomp and ceremony in American customs. "The rich here do not look down with a frown upon those that are poorer than themselves," he wrote home to a married son, "but treat them with familiarity and kindness. Indeed I find myself already at home at America."[35]

Nauvoo's transplanted farmers from England (and those from southeastern Pennsylvania) opened farms around an area known as the Mound, six miles east of Nauvoo. The families of John and William Benbow, William Kay, and others converted in Staffordshire and Herefordshire by Wilford Woodruff considered themselves neighbors linked by a common tie of origin. The Kays and Benbows often visited one another in their homes, which were three miles apart.[36] English immigrants arriving in Nauvoo soon learned of this nearby gathering place in the rural back-country. George and Mary Bundy reached Nauvoo in May 1843 and spent the summer and winter with the Newmans, whom they had known in the Mosley branch, made up largely of United Brethren converts. When they purchased a small farm the next spring and built a wattle house on it, the Bundys chose a site five miles east of Nauvoo among converts from Gloucestershire and Worcestershire.[37]

In July 1841, Joseph Smith and John C. Bennett designated Warren, a platted town just south of Warsaw, as a separate settlement place for the arriving British immigrants. Businessmen in Warsaw had invited settlement on the land as early as the fall of 1839. (Another option, 340 acres at Chili, near Hancock County's southern border, was rejected).[38] The Twelve soon were assigned to superintend the project. They appointed Willard Richards to live in Warsaw as resident sales agent. But not everyone in Warsaw agreed that having "a Mormon City on our immediate borders" was a good thing. The anti-Mormon press ridiculed the proposal by calling the town "Money-Diggersville" and by raising the old Missouri charge that the Saints were thieves.[39]

The first boatload of British immigrants to be directed toward Warren arrived in November. Under instructions from the First Presidency, they rented rooms in Warsaw. Almost immediately, the economic effects of the pending settlement of two hundred Latter-day Saints created a standoff. A local miller doubled the price of flour, and when the Saints gathered firewood from the Warren town plot, market prices for dry wood at Warsaw's dock fell twenty-five cents a cord. As winter settled in, tensions escalated. Richards sought counsel from headquarters and then invited the British Saints to move upriver and abandon plans for the ethnic gathering place. Some left immediately by sleigh; others waited for spring.[40]

In contrast to the difficult reception at Warsaw, the British found their American brothers and sisters in the Nauvoo area willing to welcome and accept them. The desire of the English farmers to withdraw to the countryside beyond Nauvoo created some geographical and social distance from other Saints, but distance did not eliminate all British-American social interaction. British factory workers mixed quickly into Nauvoo society because of the need for jobs wherever they could be found. Nauvoo's

Northeastern United States majority were not that far removed from their own British ancestors. Their Yankee patriotism for the new America had turned them against the British government, but it did not exclude from fellowship their converted cousins from the ancient homeland. British immigrant William Clayton was not alone among his countrymen when he considered his arrival in America as coming home.[41]

FAMILY AND FRIENDS

Other residential networks in Nauvoo and nearby Latter-day Saint settlements were defined by extended kinship ties. Relatives often shared common geographical backgrounds as well, but it was the marriages and descendancies that kept these people united as neighbors in Nauvoo. Their decision to join in the gathering meant for many of these families a unity of faith. This created a shared sense of belonging not just to a family but to a larger religious community. Extended families who shared their belief in the new religion helped to strengthen the overall unity of the church.

The family of Joseph Smith Sr. followed the Prophet to Commerce and became permanent settlers in southern Nauvoo. As might be expected of a family that had shared many experiences together, they shared resources, including housing, as necessary. The Prophet's parents and his brothers, except for William, lived as near neighbors in Nauvoo.[42] Other Smith relatives clustered in Lee County, Iowa, where the Prophet's uncle John Smith served as stake president and John's nephew Elias Smith was bishop. More distant kin settled in Wisconsin. Emma Smith had relatives in northern Illinois.

Many other family clusterings existed in Nauvoo and in nearby Latter-day Saint settlements. It was not unusual for parents and married children, siblings, in-laws, or even more extended kinship networks to work cooperatively in finding homes and looking after one another when they gathered out of Babylon.[43] Even when a woman's husband did not convert, both sometimes moved west. Economic opportunity was a sufficient incentive for him. Other Latter-day Saints left unconverted family members behind and sought new supportive relationships in Nauvoo.

People in Nauvoo maintained ties with their distant family members, if only through correspondence. Though infrequent, the letters were newsy and mostly concerned with family matters.[44] Very often missives from Nauvoo to relatives who were not Latter-day Saints contained an invitation to investigate the church and to do so in Nauvoo.[45] This anxiousness for the spiritual welfare of parents or siblings reveals a religious longing for a united family.

The pleadings extended as well in reverse. Those who had not joined the Saints tried to convince their gathered relatives to change their minds and return home.[46] Such earnest challenges from nonmember kin created a constant but friendly sparring. It pulled against Latter-day Saint unity and succeeded in drawing some members away from their commitment to the gathering.

Meanwhile, in designated gathering places, Latter-day Saints bound together through a shared place of origin or family relationship maintained old ties and established new friendship networks. The term *friend*—at its root a word for "loved ones"—was used in nineteenth-century conversation to refer both to cherished relatives and favored colleagues. Friendship among trusted allies strengthened shared values. When these values supported broad community interests, friendships built unity in Nauvoo. When friends shared minority opinions, their influence worked against homogeneity. This, for instance, was the case among the dissenters from Nauvoo's changing theology who set up a reformed church and challenged Joseph Smith's prophetic role.

Friendship played an especially important role in the relationships Joseph Smith enjoyed with others. The Prophet rewarded with enduring friendship those who demonstrated true loyalty. He recorded the names of such friends in his Book of the Law of the Lord, a private diary that also listed financial contributions to the church.[47]

Within the Prophet's friendship network were family members, private confidants, political compatriots, and benefactors. His closest ties were to those who shared his religious goals. "These love the God that I serve," he wrote; "they love the truths that I promulge; they love those virtuous, and those holy doctrines that I cherish. . . . I love friendship and truth; I love virtue and Law; I love the God of Abraham and of Isaac and of Jacob, and they are my brethren." Problems in Missouri had stripped him of such early supporters as Oliver Cowdery and the Whitmers. He retained the backing of Newel K. Whitney, the family of Joseph Knight Sr., Porter Rockwell, his own family, and others.[48]

At Nauvoo, Joseph Smith elevated to greater positions of trust his

John Taylor wrote of the friendship and spiritual synergy of the brothers Joseph and Hyrum Smith: "In life they were not divided, and in death they were not separated!" (D&C 135:3).

reliable brother Hyrum. "What a faithful heart you have got," he said of Hyrum. Gradually, he increased reliance on Brigham Young and Heber C. Kimball, senior members of the Twelve, and through them certain other apostles.[49] Within church circles but more distant spiritually were Sidney Rigdon and a few less reliable members of the Twelve, including Joseph's brother William Smith and John E. Page. It was through Rigdon that John C. Bennett, Rigdon's political ally and friend, was introduced into church leadership circles.[50] William Marks, a trusted friend of Emma Smith, did not enjoy the same confidence from Joseph but did serve as Nauvoo's stake president.

In secular life, Joseph Smith nurtured friendships in an attempt to influence public opinion, always a fickle and skeptical adversary. Among American journalists enlisted as friends and political supporters were James Gordon Bennett, of the influential *New York Herald*, and John Wentworth, a Democratic legislator and Chicago publisher. Another prominent New Yorker, attorney and educator James Arlington Bennet, lent his support as well. Nauvoo men of influence befriended by the Prophet included non-Mormon merchants and landowners Amos Davis, Isaac Galland, Hiram Kimball, and Daniel H. Wells. All of these men sooner or later accepted baptism, but their secular accomplishments gave them a prestige in the wider world that was important as an anchor. Smith included them and others like them in civic and educational positions in Nauvoo, where their participation helped legitimize those aspects of the religious community. Some Hancock County politicians likewise joined Joseph Smith's expanding network of friends; Sheriff Jacob Backenstos played the most active role. Certain legislators befriended the Prophet, while Representative (later Senator) Stephen A. Douglas received special attention during the early attempts to win congressional support for redress. Even though the Prophet worked through the established Illinois delegations in Washington, D.C., he had his own emissaries. Chief among them was Elias Higbee, tried and proven true in Missouri, and eulogized by Smith as "a just and good man—a great and mighty man."[51]

Joseph Smith did not forget those who helped him in troubled times. Such personal friends and associates as businessman William Law, clerk William Clayton, constable Dimick B. Huntington, and bishop and militia leader George Miller found a place in the Book of the Law of the Lord for their help when he was in hiding in August 1842.[52] Law and Miller were among those whose loyalty waned with time.

NAUVOO'S CULTURAL COMMUNITY

Individuals and families in Nauvoo enjoyed personal, recreational, and social interaction within the family and with friends. Such involvements supported existing kinship and friendship networks and created new ones. Likewise, dancing, drama, and music contributed to a sense of community in the city by helping to reinforce religious boundaries while offering recreational opportunities.

Dining and dancing were favorite pastimes for Nauvoo's citizens at social events. In intimate social settings, these cultural activities helped to create and bond friendships. Dancing and games were often the final activity in the popular dinner evening for adults or young adults. The Mansion House was a favorite place for dinner parties, but others convened in the Masonic Hall, aboard the *Maid of Iowa,* and in larger private houses, including Sidney Rigdon's.[53] Unlike some religious people of the time, Joseph Smith had no objection to dancing, as long as participants avoided bad company and kept proper hours. At Nauvoo, dancing was more liberally approved than among the Saints in their earlier gathering places.[54]

The Nauvoo Theater operated on the main floor room of the Masonic Hall.[55] Amateur dramatists in Nauvoo offered popular entertainment there, as did an occasional visiting theatrical company. Even before the hall was finished in April 1844, theater was offered in a tent and, in 1843, in the

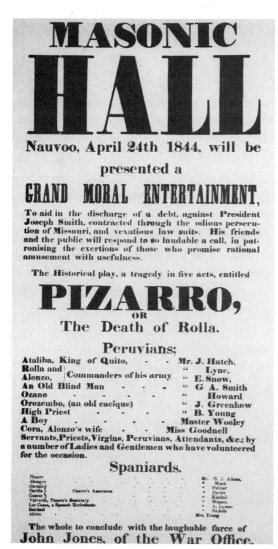

MASONIC HALL

Nauvoo, April 24th 1844, will be presented a

GRAND MORAL ENTERTAINMENT,

To aid in the discharge of a debt, against President Joseph Smith, contracted through the odious persecution of Missouri, and vexatious law suits. His friends and the public will respond to so laudable a call, in patronising the exertions of those who promise rational amusement with usefulness.

The Historical play, a tragedy in five acts, entitled

PIZARRO,
OR
The Death of Rolla.

Peruvians;

Ataliba, King of Quito,	- -	Mr. J. Hatch,
Rolla and	Commanders of his army	" Lyne,
Alonzo,		" E. Snow,
An Old Blind Man	- - -	" G. A. Smith
Ozano	- - -	" Howard
Orozembo, (an old cacique)	-	" J. Greenhow
High Priest	- - -	" B. Young
A Boy	- - -	Master Wooley
Cora, Alonzo's wife	- -	Miss Goodnell

Servants, Priests, Virgins, Peruvians, Attendants, &c.; by a number of Ladies and Gentlemen who have volunteered for the occasion.

Spaniards.

Pizarro		Mr. G. J. Adams,
Almagro		" Ward
Garzaio		" Fulmer
Davila	Pizarro's Associates	" Porter
Gomez		" Kimball
Valverde, Pizarro's Secretary		" Wasson
Las Casas, a Spanish Ecclesiastic		" A. Lyman
Sentinel		" Nichols
Alvira		Mrs. Young

The whole to conclude with the laughable farce of
John Jones, of the War Office.

Actor Thomas A. Lyne staged the historical play Pizarro *in Nauvoo's Masonic Hall to raise funds for Joseph Smith's legal expenses. Taking the stage in this "rational amusement with usefulness" were the Prophet's friends Eliza R. Snow, George A. Smith, and Brigham Young.*

"store chamber" above Joseph Smith's store. Dedication of the Masonic Hall was followed by a series of plays organized by Thomas A. Lyne, a New York actor, and his brother-in-law George J. Adams. Lyne and his wife took many of the leading roles in such plays as *Pizarro, or the Death of Rolla,* in which Brigham Young played the part of the high priest. Typically, an evening program began with excerpts from Shakespeare, followed by one serious play and a second lighter offering. The Twelve approved of theater only if the actors avoided "corrupt and immodest theatrical exhibitions."

They opposed entertainment that brought Saints and sinners together with offerings that demeaned efforts to live a religious life.[56]

Uplifting theatrical performances and dances supported Nauvoo's moral values and reinforced the city's wholeness as a gathering of covenant people. Not clearly as supportive were the common traveling entertainments offered by phrenologists, hypnotists, and other purveyors of curiosities. Following the pattern of many other cities, municipal law in Nauvoo licensed all shows and exhibitions in an attempt to prevent and to punish infractions of the city's moral harmony.[57]

Aside from hymn singing and parlor piano playing, Nauvoo residents enjoyed music as spectators. At least three bands functioned: William Pitt's brass band played for public and private gatherings; a dance band with stringed instruments accompanied the quadrille parties; and the Nauvoo Legion Band participated in military events. Most notable of the band performances were those associated with the cornerstone ceremonies at the temple and at Independence Day celebrations.[58] If weather hampered outside concerts, they were held in the largest available halls; after January 1845 that was the Music Hall, also called the Concert Hall.[59] These performances entertained and, more importantly, rallied citizens to common causes, whether patriotic or religious.

Vocal groups served like purposes. Choirs sang for citywide religious services, while individuals performed in concerts offered regularly in public halls and for social gatherings in homes. Music professor Gustavus Hills applauded the progress of a choral group in late 1841 for its progress in smoothing a choir with varied musical and cultural backgrounds into an orderly whole. These strivings were not unlike the broader challenge of blending disparate peoples into a Zion society. To solve the problem of financial support, musical groups charged entrance fees, and the Nauvoo Music Association offered shares at $2.50 each in its initial capitalization of $1,000 in January 1845.[60]

COMMUNITY EDUCATION

An opportunity to reinforce common bonds between the Saints and their neighbors existed in the educational system. Residents of Nauvoo shared with other Americans a need to teach the next generation basic skills and to prepare teachers. Yet this commonality was largely ignored in public discussions. In the predominant political discourse of the day, the

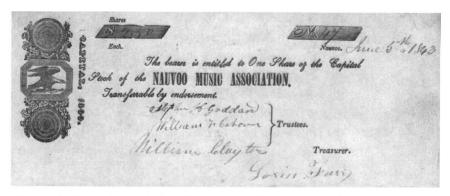

Concerts by Nauvoo bands, choir, and vocalists were frequent enough that the city's musicians raised funds through the sale of stock to build a concert hall.

differences received more attention among neighboring communities than the shared interests of educating the younger generation.

Latter-day Saints brought with them into the church varied experiences with formal education. Some, like Brigham Young and Heber Kimball, had spent very little time in a schoolroom and relied upon their own native intellect and gradual grasp of the skills of literacy. Others, like Sidney Rigdon and Orson Spencer, had enjoyed the luxury of college training. Those with advanced schooling became the teachers and administrators in Nauvoo's formal educational system, besides using their training in the cause of the church.

Whatever their backgrounds in book learning, the Saints accepted the Prophet Joseph Smith's teaching that gaining knowledge, both secular and sacred, was good. They willingly opened their minds to all branches of literary and scientific knowledge.[61] And, as encouraged by the published revelations, they applied their learning to church purposes, primarily to the work of proselytizing. Some felt that having a revelator at the head of the church equipped the Saints especially well to discover new scientific truths. The Latter-day Saint philosophy of education encompassed the idea of diligent effort through both secular and spiritual avenues.[62]

In one of its first legislative acts, the city council created the University of the City of Nauvoo, effective on February 9, 1841, to provide formal educational opportunities for adults. The law named Mayor John C. Bennett as the university chancellor and appointed city councilor William Law as registrar. Twenty-three regents guided policy, among them all four city aldermen and seven members of the city council.[63] The council gave the regents responsibility for all education, including the community's common schools, an arrangement rare in America. At the time of its founding, the Nauvoo university was only the fifth institution of higher learning in Illinois; the other four all operated as colleges.[64]

In the 1840s, American colleges and universities trained doctors, ministers, and teachers. Nauvoo had no use for a trained ministry, and many of the Saints favored self-taught botanic doctors. It is not surprising then that the proposed curriculum reflected a liberal arts offering of most use to prospective teachers. The city council appointed Nauvoo's best-educated men to the university's staff: specialists in mathematics, English literature, languages, church history, and music.[65] The school's founders had high ambitions. "We hope to make this institution one of the great lights of the world," Joseph Smith said, "and by and through it, to diffuse that kind of knowledge which will be of practical utility, and for the public good, and also for private and individual happiness."[66]

Unlike other Illinois colleges, the University of Nauvoo operated without its own buildings. In August 1845, a planning committee announced intentions to begin construction the next season, but vigilante actions weeks later thwarted the effort.[67] Not much evidence exists about the university or its class offerings. The regents met from time to time to conduct necessary business. Some students were matriculated and met for classes in existing public buildings or in homes. One professor published a list of textbooks approved for those wishing to train as music teachers.[68] An important institution in embryo, Nauvoo's university was outdistanced in effort and commitment by building projects more closely associated with the central mission of the church. Ultimately, higher education among the Saints waited for a more favorable place and situation.

Getting a basic education in Jacksonian America meant for most people gaining a simple mastery of the fundamentals of reading, writing, and arithmetic. To obtain at least that much training for their children, parents chose between public and private schools. Public schools, open to everyone and therefore known as common schools, were funded through local property taxes. With private (subscription) schools the families of the students paid the entire tuition. Private schools dominated early Illinois, and many citizens resisted tax-supported education.[69] Both kinds functioned in Nauvoo, but civic leaders reflected a Latter-day Saint

Ellen Sophronia Pratt, oldest of four daughters of Addison and Louisa Barnes Pratt, was twelve years old when her mother issued this handwritten report card. Louisa, an avid reader of literature and nature and an essayist and poet, taught school in Nauvoo while Addison served a South Seas mission.

preference that all children receive an equally good education. To accomplish this goal, they proposed to bring all schools under the watchful care of a single governing board.

As authorized under the Nauvoo charter, the city council established a common school system. It differed from that of most other area communities in that all boards and wardens (supervisors) were appointed instead of elected. The city council appointed the university board of regents to manage the system. The regents certified teachers, established an approved list of textbooks, and appointed three wardens in each of the four municipal wards of Nauvoo (in three of the wards, the ecclesiastical bishop was one of the wardens). The wardens chose teachers from among those certified, monitored their work, and arranged for schoolrooms (often a rented room in a home, public hall, or commercial building). The teachers collected tuition through a haphazard mixture of county and city funding, subsidized by parents. Pay was meager for teachers, and since most of them taught only a few months out of the year, other jobs supplied part of their income.[70]

The common schools sponsored under these laws flourished; twenty-seven teachers tapped into the county tax funds available to subsidize their services. Others functioned without tax support. As a non-Mormon in Nauvoo observed in 1843, "There are many Common Schools in Nauvoo, where the *germs* of greatness are planted," which, if nourished, could reap an abundant harvest "of the good things of intellect."[71]

Many Nauvoo teachers offered services privately; some taught under both systems in a combination of public and subscription offerings. Private schools depended upon the reputations of the teachers. For instance, James M. Monroe advertised classes in the basics plus "higher mathematics, philosophy, chemistry, Latin, French, Spanish, etc., etc.," and claimed that he had the "concurrence of the Twelve" in opening a school at Brigham Young's home in 1845. Monroe was already teaching the children of Emma Smith and some others at the Mansion House, where he boarded. It was possibly tension between the Youngs and the Smiths that made it necessary for Monroe to start a second school for the children of Brigham Young and others of his quorum. Independent teachers made their own arrangements for rooms, including public schoolrooms and the Music Hall.[72]

The mixture of common and subscription schools may have complicated the regents' desire for uniformity in the curriculum. In establishing Nauvoo's common schools, they had adopted an exclusive list of texts recommended by chancellor John C. Bennett. They even gave regent Ebenezer Robinson—a local editor, bookseller, and stationer—exclusive rights to sell the authorized books, obtained from the American Common School Society in New York. In return, Robinson agreed to stop selling the popular Eclectic series of graded texts, books steeped in Calvinistic moralism.[73] But other booksellers in Nauvoo soon offered alternate titles, presumably to meet the preferences of private school teachers. In matters of education, Nauvoo's educational community differed within itself on details. Those who favored a greater "concert of action" in classroom texts called the teachers together in September 1843 to rally support for uniformity.[74] To what extent they succeeded is not known.

To continue their education and keep abreast of current events, citizens of Nauvoo attended public lectures or read newspapers and books.

To develop speaking abilities needed for missionary preaching, men participated in small, informal debate groups. These meetings, or lyceums, began as early as January 1840. Speakers would address three or four topics, religious and secular, each evening, with a limit of thirty minutes for each presentation. Joseph Smith participated regularly as a speaker on religious subjects—such as the Godhead, vengeance, the Millennium, and equality—or as an umpire to reconcile doctrinal differences. "It was surprising how much good was accomplished in attending a Lyceum one winter," Wandle Mace remembered.[75]

In 1843, the city's young men formally organized the Nauvoo Lyceum, a local version of a nationwide movement. Some lyceums featured skilled lecturers on popular and educational topics. Others allowed local debaters to discuss such current political, social, and legal issues as capital punishment, education for women, physical evidences of the existence of God, and manners. The gospel-centered missionary lyceums continued as well. Both young men and young women attended the educational lecture schools on topics such as astronomy and history. Participants paid a fee to attend and took exams to measure their educational attainment.[76]

Like many other American communities, Nauvoo citizens formed lending libraries to support adult education. The libraries filled their shelves by recruiting members and charging fees. The Nauvoo Library and Literary Institute, organized in January 1844, may not have been the first such local effort, but it had the best start, with Benjamin Winchester as head. Funded through an offering of two thousand shares of stock, valued at five dollars each, the institute managed an active circulating library and sponsored regular lectures in space rented from James Ivins on Main Street. Sponsors launched their library with one hundred donated books. They lent them to nonmembers for a small fee. The disruptive events of mid-1844 brought an end to the Nauvoo Library and Literary Institute when several of its key trustees joined in the efforts to discredit Joseph Smith. The apostasies caused the community to distrust the institute. It apparently disbanded that fall.[77]

Toward the end of the year, a city ordinance authorized a new library, a task entrusted to Nauvoo's fourteen quorums of the seventy. The Seventies Library and Institute Association opened in the newly finished quorum hall. Like the earlier effort, the Seventies' library accepted cash or

Nauvoo's first "curator" was Lucy Mack Smith, custodian of the Egyptian papyrus associated with the book of Abraham. An image of Facsimile No. 1 hangs on the wall. Lucy, who holds a copy of the Book of Mormon, often testified of its divine origins.

"books at market value" from stockholders. Nearly one hundred donors immediately contributed books to the church-managed, municipally sanctioned effort.[78] A later list of 675 donated books reveals a special interest in religion, history, travel accounts, biography, and schoolbooks.[79]

Another beginning in Nauvoo that sponsors intended to be both global and grand in scope was that of a museum. During his years in Ohio, Joseph Smith had hosted numerous visitors anxious to see the Egyptian mummies and papyrus. For a time, he authorized an Elder Coe to set up a museum at John Johnson's inn in Kirtland to show the items during certain hours. The Prophet granted his mother, Lucy Mack Smith, that privilege in Quincy, Illinois, in 1839, and she continued to show the Egyptian curiosities in Nauvoo.[80]

When Addison Pratt left Nauvoo for a mission to the South Seas in the spring of 1843, he delivered to the president's office several specimens of natural history that he had collected years earlier as a whaler. Pratt's treasured "tooth of a whale, coral, bones of an Albatross' wing and skin of a foot, jaw-bone of a porpoise, and tooth of a South Sea seal" became the first, and perhaps only, offerings for the proposed Nauvoo museum. Eighteen months later, the city council gave the librarian of the Seventies Library curatorial authority to collect not just books and maps but sculptures, paintings, and antiquities.[81] This expanded role made the Seventy's Institute both a library and a museum. Ever the promoter of Nauvoo's development, John Taylor, editor of the *Times and Seasons,* encouraged "the Lord's 'Regular Soldiers'" in their missionary service abroad to "gather all the curious things, both natural and artificial, with all the knowledge, inventions, and wonderful specimens of genius that have been gracing the world for almost six thousand years . . . for the best library in the world!"[82] Under a municipal mandate, this priesthood brotherhood was prepared to enhance learning by study in a community of faith.

In their efforts to establish a library and museum, as in their educational and cultural activities, citizens of Nauvoo wished to enjoy in their Zion community the praiseworthy things of the society whose general wickedness they deplored. They desired secular learning in addition to religion, but they managed learning under spiritual standards that sifted from the world those facts consistent with faith.

Educational and cultural activities in the city strengthened the sense of community for all residents. Political and ethnic differences mellowed under the influence of a good laugh at the theater or the conviviality of a dinner party. Learning encouraged tolerance and expanded understanding. These endeavors enhanced unity in Nauvoo, as did the neighborhoods defined by geography, blood lines, and place of origin.

Ultimately, bonds of friendship, kinship, and shared experience did not matter as much as covenants of faith. An inner religious conviction of the primacy of prophetic leadership defined the most important community in Nauvoo. Some Latter-day Saints did not unite under the banner of continuing revelation. They remained behind or dropped out along the way when the community of faith moved on with an enlarged understanding of the doctrinal and geographical meaning of Mormonism. For those who rejected this expanded vision, ties to friends, relatives, and a static definition of their newfound faith took precedence over a religious commitment to sacrifice all for the kingdom of God.

CHAPTER 9

A People of Faith and Destiny

Well, here we are in the famous City of Nauvoo, and under the influence of the cheerful countenance of the Prophet, and the edification of his words of wisdom, which are truly such, notwithstanding what the world say; be assured by one who would by no means wish to misrepresent, but would give the truth in its naked simplicity, this is truth. . . . The power and wisdom of [Joseph Smith] in expounding the scriptures was a feast indeed of fat things.

—GEORGE ALLEY, APRIL 13, 1843

It is one of the few comforts of the saints in this world, to be settled in peace, and witness the rap[i]d growth of their infant city, as a place of safety and gathering for the last days. For three or four miles upon the river and about the same distance back in the country, Nauvoo presents a city of gardens, ornamented with the dwellings of those who have made a covenant by sacrifice, and are guided by revelation, an exception to all other societies upon the earth.

—JOSEPH SMITH, OCTOBER 1, 1842

Nauvoo existed for religious purposes. The city, its houses, its farms and shops, its families and neighborhoods all presumed a greater purpose. It was religion that bound the city's Latter-day Saint residents into a united community. Joseph Smith, in his capacity as a religious teacher of doctrine and conveyor of ordinances, played the central role in the religious experience of the Nauvoo years. Through worship and service, Latter-day Saints sought to bring God into their lives and to bless the lives of others. The sense of religious community was fostered by the presence of general church leaders and by the regular Sunday preaching meetings held in the public groves.

These gatherings, held during good weather, united the Saints through fellowship and instruction and attracted people from beyond Nauvoo. A master teacher, Joseph Smith infused new life into old sacred stories. He taught mostly with reference to the Bible, but he did so by selecting and explaining its messages for his own people and times. The Book of Mormon, another witness of God's dealing with his people in ancient times, likewise offered direct messages for religious seekers of the last days. Of special significance in the creation of a new people of faith was the story of fresh revelation and a living prophet for the latter days.

This story had been unfolding for twenty years. Parts of it had been preserved in print. At Nauvoo, Joseph Smith launched his final retelling of the story of the Restoration for all to read. This effort gave official status to the Saints' awareness of their own role in religious history and of the Prophet's life as a sacred story in its own right. During the Nauvoo years, the Latter-day Saints reaffirmed their belief that individually and as a people they were creating a new sacred history.[1]

The City of the Prophet

Nauvoo's greatest distinction among the cities of America was its claim to a resident prophet. Church members moved to Nauvoo at his request, upheld him as a religious leader, and trusted his counsel in practical matters. After attending one of the preaching meetings in front of the temple, a visiting journalist from the Chicago area claimed to discover the key to Smith's success as a leader. The Saints followed the Prophet, he wrote, "because, as we say in Illinois, 'they believe in him,' and in his honesty."[2] The devotion of members was, indeed, based in large part on their confidence in Joseph Smith and in the message he delivered to them.

Samuel A. Prior, a Methodist minister, traveled by foot sixty miles to learn for himself the key to this following. Hearing Joseph Smith preach at Macedonia melted away the prejudices of numerous written and oral reports and changed the minister's opinion: "Instead of the heads and horns of the beast, and false prophet, I beheld only the appearance of a

common man, of tolerable large proportions. . . . He commenced preaching, not from the Book of Mormon, however, but from the Bible." Prior
had expected a discourse challenging other sects; instead, the Prophet
wanted only to explain his scriptural text.[3]

Invited to preach that evening to a large and attentive audience at
Macedonia, Prior was surprised at the openness of the congregation.
Despite their claims to be the "only true church," he reported, the Latter-
day Saints denied no one the right to proclaim or live his own beliefs. A
Boston convert discovered that the Latter-day Saint view of heaven
included "mansions" of various sizes for believers of all kinds:

> They believe that every honest man, who acts up to the principle of
> reflection, and obeys those dictates of conscience that show him
> wrong from right, will be saved, no matter what his belief—whether
> Turk, Jew or Heathen. . . . The Mormons . . . do not want to ram
> Joe Smith or revelation down people's throats, without their knowing
> for themselves: all they want is to obey the words of Christ for the
> remission of sin. They want to terrify no man into belief.[4]

Many of Nauvoo's neighbors failed to investigate and thus never learned of
the tolerance of members of the city's religious community toward outsiders. What they did understand was the influence of Joseph Smith in
Nauvoo. Following his visit, the Reverend Prior deliberately designated
Nauvoo "the city of the prophet."[5]

CONFERENCES AND COMMUNITY

Particularly effective in strengthening common bonds among the
Latter-day Saints and in helping to unite them as a religious people in the
1840s was the conference. A general conference of members was convened
regularly at Nauvoo. Regional gatherings met at other designated places
in the United States and British Isles. Members often gathered from considerable distances to attend these annual or semiannual meetings.
Participation helped converts to feel part of a church larger than their own
family or small congregation. Because a conference offered an open forum
for discussion and polling, it built consensus on issues and support for
leaders. Much regular business, including the appointment and reaffirmation of officers, the calling of missionaries, and the airing of grievances
against members took place in these gatherings. Delegates from each

KEY

1. Cutler's Grove
2. Music Hall 1845
3. Arsenal 1845
4. Stand Near the Temple, Parade Ground, Militia Camp 1845
5. Meeting Ground/ Grove/Stand
6. Nauvoo Temple
7. Wells Block 16
8. Nauvoo Legion Parade Ground
9. Masonic Hall 1844
10. Old Burying Ground
11. Seventies Hall

Public Places in Nauvoo

branch or group of branches reported on the number of members and priesthood holders living in each locality. The business was followed by preaching from local and general church leaders. Sermons often lasted an hour or two. Typically, conferences convened for morning and afternoon sessions, with a mealtime break between. Some continued over two or three days.

An important role of the conferences was to confirm that members supported their leaders, who served only by common consent. When the name of each officer was presented, members with grievances against the officer's conduct of his office could step forward with information for consideration. Thus, at the April 1843 conference in Nauvoo, Joseph Smith told the congregation assembled on the floor of the incomplete temple,

> If . . . I have done any thing that ought to injure my character, reputation, or standing; or have dishonored our religion by any means . . . , I am sorry for it, and if you will forgive me, I will endeavor to

do so no more. *I do not know that I have done any thing of the kind; but if I have, come forward and tell me of it.* If any one has any objection to me, I want you to come boldly and frankly, and tell of it; and if not, ever after hold your peace.

A motion to continue President Joseph Smith in his office received a quick second, and with "one vast sea of hands . . . the motion was carried *unanimously.*" Similar reviews were held for the counselors in the First Presidency and members of the Twelve.[6]

Most voting at conferences was unanimous, or nearly so. Participants called this process an election, because it resembled the nominating and voting process used in civil elections.[7] Members by their vote and through the recommendations of leaders considered the cases of unworthy leaders; when appropriate, such men were dropped from office.[8] In this way, the sustaining process in quorums and conferences helped curb disharmony and build unity.

JOSEPH SMITH AS PROPHET-TEACHER

Until the temple was available for use, Nauvoo had no meetinghouse. The Saints met for a time beginning in October 1842 on a temporary floor on the temple's main level assembly room,[9] and three years later in an enclosed temple. But most large gatherings in Nauvoo assembled during good weather out-of-doors and in bad weather not at all. Preaching took place at designated meeting places in the oak grove on the brow of the hill just west of the temple or, later, at a nearby stand a quarter mile east and a bit north of the unfinished structure.

To supplement the general meetings, small groups congregated in the larger homes for occasional worship services, where singing, prayers, and a sharing of feelings about their newfound faith reaffirmed a common experience for gathered converts. Elders and church leaders often joined in these intimate gatherings to preach. Sometimes a home owner issued the invitation. A ward bishop called other meetings, even though his regular duties at that time did not include presiding over a congregation. The Saints in scattered branches followed a similar pattern of gathering in homes and halls and of taking turns preaching.[10]

Wherever they lived, preaching meetings contributed to the building of community for Latter-day Saints. Sermons played a central role in unifying them. The message of salvation explained from Nauvoo's makeshift outdoor stand or in sitting rooms and public halls throughout the church reinforced religious values for the Saints and strengthened a shared commitment.[11]

The highlight of any general gathering in Nauvoo was a discourse by Joseph Smith. The Prophet had begun his religious ministry in 1829 by preaching in the communities near Manchester, New York.[12] Although as president of the church he was necessarily involved some in administrative duties, he enjoyed most the role of prophet, seer, and revelator. The Lord had bidden him to speak and write but added, "in temporal labors thou shalt not have strength, for this is not thy calling."[13] The Prophet loved to share his religious insights, whether it was with an individual or a crowd. Throughout his life, and especially in Nauvoo, he became well known for his scriptural expositions. He gave priority to the value of revealed truths over scientific learning, celebrated the role of the kingdom of God in bringing souls to Christ, and encouraged his listeners to strive toward a society of peace and love.[14]

Most listeners were impressed by the clarity of his message. They felt that the Prophet's words rolled forth unlike those of the ministers of other religions.[15] "He . . . is ready to talk upon any subject that any one wishes," George W. Taggart wrote to a relative, "and, I assure you, it would make you wonder to hear him talk and see the information which comes out of his mouth, and it is not in big words either, but that which anyone can understand." His teaching won the hearts of his people. People discovered in his words a familiar biblical message enhanced and enlightened by insights they judged straight from God. It was, as George Alley put it, "a feast indeed of fat things."[16]

His listeners did not credit Smith personally with this understanding; instead, they ascribed his unusual insights to direct revelation. The Latter-day Saints rejected the notion of a trained clergy.[17] "If there is any true and correct source of intelligence," said John Taylor, himself once a Methodist lay preacher, "it must be that which proceeds from the Almighty" to the prophets of all ages. For the Latter-day Saints, a living prophet was an essential element of the true church, and Joseph Smith was that prophet.[18] "If they have not the oracles of God," Joseph Smith declared, "they are not the people of God."[19] Smith warned the Saints against the "danger of philosophizing upon religion." Worldly learning was not the path to religious knowledge, he declared. "The world by wisdom know not God. . . . Without the spirit you cannot *know the living God.*"[20]

The need to separate sacred wisdom from practical commentary was important to the Saints. The key to identifying spiritual truths was their own witness of the Spirit. Of the Prophet's source of truth, Orson Spencer told an inquiring friend,

> In doctrine Mr. Smith is eminently scriptural. I have never known him to deny or depreciate a single truth of the Old and New Testaments. . . . Certainly he does claim to be inspired. He often speaks in the name of the Lord . . . as [he is] moved by the Holy Ghost.[21]

The Latter-day Saints saw religious truth as a continuing unfolding of knowledge, dependent upon the listener's readiness to hear and God's willingness to teach. "If we improve upon the small things, greater will be given unto us," Brigham Young advised the Saints in 1845 as he made reference to his own right to revealed knowledge to lead the church.[22]

Most Latter-day Saints were as willing to listen to Brigham Young after 1844 as they had been to Joseph Smith before his death. They had received previous instructions from the Twelve and had been impressed by their doctrines. Said E. H. Davis after a meeting in New York,

> 'Twould have made the hair stand straight in your heads to have heard Bros Young & Kimball talk and preach on the necessity of gathering to Zion, & building the Temple and Nauvoo house, and being faithful and humble in all things.[23]

The Saints accepted the idea that the Spirit of God could work through any believer within the faith. Joseph Smith had instructed the elders that "whatsoever they shall speak when moved upon by the Holy Ghost shall be scripture, . . . the word of the Lord." All members expected that if they were diligent and faithful, they would gain spiritual knowledge for their own guidance in life and for others within the circle of their spiritual responsibility. Their individual experiences with the gifts of the Spirit helped foster a sense of participation in the spiritual life of the church.[24]

Despite this universal receptivity to the Spirit, only the church president could speak for the Lord to the whole church. As Joseph Smith

This 1853 image captures the essence of Joseph Smith's interest in teaching American Indians along with other peoples. The artist creates a fanciful, wilderness camp meeting setting.

taught in 1833, "The fundamental principles, government, and doctrine of the Church are vested in the keys of the kingdom."[25] His counselors and the Twelve played a supportive role in teaching the church. This hierarchical ranking of messages and message givers prepared the Twelve and their listeners for the transition to new leadership after 1844.

Believers outside Nauvoo, unable to hear their prophet's teachings in person, received the gist of his messages through personal correspondence or by word of mouth from the traveling elders. The *Times and Seasons* reported Nauvoo conference proceedings—and the *Millennial Star* copied them—but neither paper attempted to publish a consistent report of regular Sunday worship services. Some individuals kept private notes of the Prophet's talks, valuable mostly as historical records. Wilford Woodruff, William Clayton, and Willard Richards were especially diligent in recording the spoken word.[26]

The desire for direct instruction from Joseph Smith became another incentive for the physical gathering as Nauvoo became a center of gospel learning. The Twelve reminded the Saints and prospective missionaries in

1841 that they could know little "of the revelations of heaven, and the order of the kingdom . . . while they are scattered to the four winds."[27] The gathered Saints heard firsthand the deeper meaning of the scriptures that Joseph Smith offered in Nauvoo. This gave them an advantage in spiritual convictions over many scattered and less well-informed members.

A solid belief in contemporary revelation convinced the Latter-day Saints of the need for an open canon. They declared that God continually shared new knowledge through his prophet and with spiritually sensitized members. In his own calling as teacher and revelator, the Prophet searched prayerfully for spiritual insight.[28] He encouraged all to similarly "seek learning, even by study and also by faith." Ever open to inquiry, he allowed his reading and discussions to raise questions from every source, but for answers, he claimed only one basis: "If we have or can receive a portion of knowledge from God by immediate revelation, by the same source we can receive all knowledge." It was a foundational premise for the Latter-day Saints that God's children became more like their Heavenly Father as they gained spiritual knowledge and lived by that knowledge in righteousness. "The glory of God is intelligence, or, in other words, light and truth," the Prophet had explained in a revelation received in Kirtland.[29]

Joseph Smith learned from his youth to appreciate the Bible as a conduit for receiving God's word. His mother recalled that her son was not inclined to reading, but when it came to religion, he preferred solitary Bible study to church attendance. It was his search for a correct interpretation of holy writ that led him in 1820 to test James's prescription for those without the truth: "If any of you lack wisdom, let him ask of God." Joseph's earnest prayers in the family woodlot in rural Manchester Township, New York, opened the heavens and launched his spiritual ministry. After a period of personal preparation, which, he said, included extensive tutoring by heavenly visions and visitors, the Prophet began a life of explaining to others what God had taught him—and was still teaching him.[30]

Throughout his life, Joseph Smith sought to harmonize the truths he understood through revelation with the printed word in the King James Version of the Bible. Soon after organizing the church in 1830, the Lord directed the young church leader to translate the Bible, "and in it all things shall be made known . . . that you may be prepared for things to come." During the next three years, the Prophet was tutored through this process and given understanding in doctrines and things yet ahead. Sidney Rigdon served as principal scribe. Some new insights were noted as emendations to the Bible. Others, most notably the prophecies and visions of Enoch, restored entirely new scriptural messages to the scanty record in Genesis. An understanding of Enoch's Zion, which gave the Prophet an image of the latter-day Zion, was but one product of this steady learning process.[31]

In Nauvoo, President Smith set about to share more of what he had learned about the original doctrines of Christ in the Bible. Only Matthew 24 and a few excerpts, mostly from Genesis, had been published. In 1840, he sought relief from mundane duties and invited others to provide financial support necessary for him to make final changes to the Bible so that his new translation could be published. As before, interruptions constantly delayed the effort. Although he went through the entire Bible, he published only extracts from the book of Moses at Nauvoo, in January 1843. His death cut short the effort. The Prophet's work on the Bible would await publication in another time. In 1979, the more than six hundred significant changes made in the text became part of the Latter-day Saint edition of the King James Version of the Bible.[32]

Joseph Smith's earliest work of scripture also remains a keystone of the church that he launched. The record in the Book of Mormon of the visit of the resurrected Christ to a people in ancient America gave it stature as a second witness of Christ's ministry on earth. Furthermore, in its clarifying message about such timely issues as the nature of God, the fall and redemption of man, the baptism of children, Christ's atonement, the general resurrection, and punishment, the Book of Mormon served as a purveyor of a clearer and more understandable gospel. It helped many readers resolve pressing religious issues of their own day and decide which Christian church to follow.[33]

Those unable to obtain a copy of the 1830 printing of five thousand copies of the Book of Mormon in Palmyra, or the Kirtland edition of 1837, eagerly welcomed the 1840 edition of two thousand copies printed in Cincinnati, Ohio, from stereotype plates prepared by Shepard and Stearns.[34] The publishers, Ebenezer Robinson and Don Carlos Smith, offered discounts for prepublication orders and placed the delivered books on sale at their Nauvoo print shop in November for $1.25 each.[35] That edition, according to the title page, offered a text "carefully revised by the translator." Minor for the most part, these editorial corrections caught transcribing errors between the original and the printer's manuscripts. The Prophet later reprinted the stereotype edition in Nauvoo and offered it for sale in August 1842.[36]

Meanwhile, in Great Britain, the April 1840 conference in Preston authorized publication of a reprint of the Kirtland edition of 1837, with British spellings. Brigham Young sought bids from every printer in Manchester and Liverpool before selecting John Tompkins of Liverpool to print and bind five thousand copies (the printer actually delivered 4,050 books). Printing was already underway when Young learned of the Nauvoo edition of 1840. Of necessity, editorial changes in the Nauvoo printing were ignored. The Liverpool printing was advertised in placards and mailed to subscribers in February 1841.[37]

In the book of scripture entitled Doctrine and Covenants of the Church of the Latter Day Saints, members of the Nauvoo period had access to more than a hundred of the revelations of Joseph Smith the seer. This collection was assembled in Missouri in 1833 as the Book of Commandments, but publication was thwarted when vigilantes destroyed the print shop. An expanded edition appeared in Kirtland in 1835 under the new title. The Doctrine and Covenants demonstrated the Prophet's continuing influence on Mormon thought. Contained within it were inspired responses to immediate needs, answers to problems and questions, revealed as the Prophet turned to heaven for direction. Along with administrative directives, the 1835 edition included information about the law of consecration, marriage, government, temples, missionary work, the Millennium, personal worthiness, and many other topics.[38]

A new printing in 1844 with eight new sections again made this volume widely available. Among the new entries were the revelation about the temple in Nauvoo and two epistles on baptism for the dead. John Taylor issued the expanded edition from the Nauvoo *Times and Seasons* office under church sanction. Brisk sales soon required two more printings, in 1845 and 1846. Meanwhile, Wilford Woodruff issued the first European edition in Liverpool in late 1845.[39]

Another important scriptural contribution that Joseph Smith received by revelation reached completion in Nauvoo. The book of Abraham had its beginnings in Kirtland, when Michael H. Chandler, a traveling

The Prophet moved his office from the log homestead to a room in the upper level of his general store in January 1842. This painted tin sign reads: JOSEPH SMITH'S OFFICE. President of the church of JESUS CHRIST of LATTER day Saints.

entrepreneur, displayed a collection of mummies recovered from Egyptian tombs. With these four mummified bodies were papyrus scrolls containing hieroglyphic inscriptions. American scholars of the day likely could not read the hieroglyphics, and even though he had studied Greek and Hebrew in Kirtland with Joshua Seixas, Joseph Smith's biblical studies relied more upon supernatural knowledge than earthbound book learning. He said of his work on the reformed Egyptian text of the Book of Mormon, "I translated the record by the gift, and power of God." He did not define the process that yielded an English text of the book of Abraham; however, while first examining some of the characters, he noted, "Truly we can say, the Lord is beginning to reveal the abundance of peace and truth."[40] In the words of a twentieth-century student of the book of Abraham, "Since it is not known just how Joseph Smith translated, it is reasonable to postulate that, when studying the Egyptian papyrus purchased from Michael Chandler, Joseph Smith sought revelation from the Lord concerning them and received in that process the book of Abraham."[41] The product was a much more complete story of Abraham, his visions, and his interactions at the Egyptian court than was available in the Bible.

This new revelation appeared in the *Times and Seasons* in the spring of 1842, and Eastern newspapers copied parts of it. The book of Abraham expanded the biblical text found in Genesis.[42] In it, Joseph Smith revealed a prophet Abraham who understood astronomy, history, premortal life, and the creation story in new ways. Abraham's interaction with his hosts in Egypt took on theological import. His priesthood calling gave Latter-day Saints a new appreciation for their own inheritance from the high priest Melchizedek, from whom Abraham had gained his own authority to act in God's name. The Prophet had spoken earlier of a record of Joseph in Egypt on the papyrus in his possession, but political problems in Nauvoo apparently prevented the restoration of more ancient scripture.[43]

The messages triggered by the Egyptian sources that Joseph Smith had purchased in Kirtland prompted him to seek a deeper understanding of the meaning of the cosmos and its origins. Some of those insights emerged in other ways, including teachings and ceremonies shared privately in the red brick store and within the enclosure of the temple at Nauvoo.[44]

Some who doubted supernatural origins for scripture offered Joseph Smith a set of small metal plates in April 1843 to translate. The six brass-like tablets contained what appeared to be hieroglyphic inscriptions. Burial mounds created by Native Americans and their ancestors over generations abounded in the region from the Ohio Valley through western Illinois. It was from one of these ancient sites, near Kinderhook, about seventy miles south of Nauvoo, that the Kinderhook discoverers had, they said, removed this latest ancient record. Their discovery stirred an immediate interest. The *Quincy Whig* and the *Times and Seasons* reported the find, and the *Nauvoo Neighbor* reproduced the plates first in a broadside and then in the newspaper.[45]

While these strange metallic plates were in Nauvoo for a few days, various residents compared the writing with the Egyptian scrolls in the Prophet's office and wondered if the hieroglyphics resembled the reformed Egyptian on the Book of Mormon plates. Some understood that the writing told of a Jaredite descendant of Noah; others, that the man descended through Ham and an Egyptian Pharaoh.[46] The *Times and Seasons* reported: "Mr. Smith has had those plates; what his opinion concerning them is, we have not yet ascertained. The gentleman who owned them has taken them away." It was rumored in Nauvoo that the Prophet "thought that by the help of revelation he would be able to translate them." He made no translation, however. A man who confessed that he and two others had staged the "discovery" as a joke, said that Joseph Smith "would not agree to translate them until they were sent to the Antiquarian society at Philadelphia, France, and England."[47]

This request for authentication may have been what prompted the owners to offer them for sale. If the lenders had intended to trick Joseph Smith with their hoax, they failed. According to a later report, the inscriptions were examined by an expert and found not to match any known language. Doubts about the authenticity of the Kinderhook plates surfaced from time to time over the years. Some defended them; others pronounced them fraudulent.[48] A plate matching a published image of the 1840s was donated to the Chicago Historical Society in 1920. Physical tests identified this piece as a nineteenth-century bronze alloy engraved with acid. The ancients of this region would have etched their messages on brass. Perhaps the Prophet knew that these interesting but faked antiquities had nothing to offer the church.[49]

Joseph Smith's contribution to scripture during the Nauvoo years would remain with what became known as the standard works—his revisions of the Bible, minor corrections to the Book of Mormon, additions to the Doctrine and Covenants, and the issuance of major components of the Pearl of Great Price.[50]

Defining and Disseminating Latter-day Saint Belief

Because of their strong dependence upon the scriptures and the words of a living prophet, Latter-day Saints shied away from endorsing a fixed doctrinal statement or creed, as defined in traditional theology. "We have said so much about the creeds and theories of men," one Nauvoo writer observed, "that it may be a query in the minds of some, whether the church of Latter Day Saints, have a creed or not. To satisfy such queries, we would say that we have a creed but not of man. Our only creed is the Bible."[51] Although the Bible anchored Latter-day Saint belief, the Book of Mormon and the revelations in the Doctrine and Covenants expanded on this base with truths lost by apostasy or previously unrevealed.[52] The book of Abraham and parts of the book of Moses added to that doctrinal core.

One reason given by the First Presidency for publishing the Doctrine and Covenants was the need to encourage doctrinal consistency within the church and to correct misunderstandings without. Beyond that, Latter-day Saint leaders allowed theological issues to remain open for discussion, as informed by revelation. Early writers honored anticreedal sentiments in the church by limiting their summaries of church beliefs to basic principles.[53]

The Doctrine and Covenants represented the church's first effort at standardizing belief and behavior. The volume originally consisted of two parts: a first segment on "Theology," made up of seven doctrinal lectures on faith and on the nature of the Godhead, and a second part, headed "Covenants and Commandments," composed of church regulations and policies as set forth in Joseph Smith's revelations and writings. The church "Articles and Covenants" (D&C 20) and revelations on priesthood (D&C 84 and 107) were given primacy in the second part.[54]

Under inspiration, Joseph Smith and Oliver Cowdery may have prepared section 20 before April 1830; it was the earliest attempt at a systematic definition of basic beliefs and the duties of officers and members. A conference in June 1830 canonized the document.[55] Oliver Cowdery summarized these foundational principles in the first issue of a new church newspaper in Kirtland in October 1834. He began most of the nine points with the declaration, "We believe . . ."[56]

Soon afterwards, other members of the First Presidency prepared the series of seven doctrinal discourses known as the Lectures on Faith for delivery to prospective missionaries in Kirtland. A collaborative effort by Joseph Smith, Sidney Rigdon, and others, the lectures set forth basic doctrinal beliefs on the Godhead and first principles, especially the role of faith in gaining knowledge of God and in gaining salvation and perfection. One of the purposes of these and other components of the Doctrine and Covenants was to prepare men for the ministry and encourage a unity of faith among the Saints.[57]

These publications for internal use were followed in 1836 by a statement of the church's "principal articles of faith" prepared by John Young. He drew from the Doctrine and Covenants and Cowdery's list to prepare five statements for a book of religious creeds published in Boston. Similar succinct statements were included in tracts published by others.[58] Most notably, Parley P. Pratt's writings brought to Latter-day Saint theology a standardization previously unavailable. In 1840, his *Late Persecutions* gave American readers a list of eighteen "principles and doctrines" of the church. That same year in Scotland, Orson Pratt published for the first time an account of Joseph Smith's first vision, giving this seminal event a place in the story of the church. His tract, *An Interesting Account of Several Remarkable Visions,* offered the most complete history of the Latter-day Saints available in Great Britain and a careful "sketch of the faith and doctrine" of the church. Other writers used this publication as a model for their own tracts.[59]

The publication of materials for members and investigators became

The three seated apostles, Orson Pratt, Parley P. Pratt, and Orson Hyde, helped communicate Joseph Smith's revelations, translations, and teachings to a wide audience through sermons, missionary pamphlets, and periodicals.

an especially focused effort during the second mission of the Twelve in Great Britain. Besides publishing sixty thousand copies of missionary tracts, the Twelve established a church printing operation in Liverpool that supplied books, newspapers, and tracts throughout the British Isles and beyond.[60]

Some privately published works offered helps to members of the church during the 1840s, especially the doctrinal treatises and concordances prepared by missionary preachers. Parley P. Pratt's *A Voice of Warning*, published in New York in 1837, offered the church its first book-length explication of doctrine. Members made the volume a bestseller. Benjamin Winchester's pocket-sized scripture concordance in 1842 won the endorsement of Hyrum Smith for its scriptural extracts and summaries "on the most prominent articles of the faith of the Latter Day Saints."[61]

The effort to codify the gospel for members and explain Mormonism to nonbelievers sparked a growing public interest. The Latter-day Saints became well known in newspapers of the 1830s and early 1840s. Religious publications as well as secular newspapers attempted to explain Joseph

Smith and his followers to their readers. In 1842, John Wentworth, editor of the *Chicago Democrat,* invited the Mormon prophet himself to write a history and an explanation of beliefs for a history of New Hampshire being prepared by Wentworth's friend George Barstow. Smith completed the assignment and published his response in the newspaper he edited, Nauvoo's *Times and Seasons,* but the state history was published without the submitted information.[62] The short historical survey concluded with a concise statement of belief and practice. Later entitled the Articles of Faith, these thirteen statements of faith echo themes elaborated in earlier lists, especially section 20 of the Doctrine and Covenants and Orson Pratt's nineteen paragraphs in his Edinburgh sketch. Joseph Smith's concise statements were widely published. Though later writers annotated the list for their own tracts, the Prophet's version survived to become an official declaration canonized in 1880 as part of Latter-day Saint scripture.[63]

The Articles of Faith (and most of the other lists) reflected what Latter-day Saints believed when they arrived in Nauvoo. Except for Orson Hyde's mention of baptism for the dead in his German tract, these statements of faith focused on core principles. Most of them predated the introduction of some of the church's most distinctive doctrines and practices. "The Latter-day Saints have no creed," Joseph Smith said in 1843, "but [they] are ready to believe all true principles that exist, as they are made manifest from time to time."[64] By the time the Saints dispersed from the City of Peace, new revelation—enunciating a theology that gave meaning to the temple—had expanded the doctrinal basis of their religion.[65]

Other clues to the religious mind of the Latter-day Saints of Nauvoo can be found in hymns. Carefully selected to represent shared beliefs, the official hymnals serve as an index to central doctrines. Emma Smith and others who selected, adapted, and wrote hymns for the church's *Collection of Sacred Hymns* in its various editions accomplished the Latter-day Saint desire to sing messages "adapted to their faith and belief in the gospel." Ideally, the singing of hymns by congregations enhances a feeling of mutuality within the community and reinforces the ideal of doctrinal harmony.[66]

The Kirtland edition of the hymnal, assembled by Emma Smith and William W. Phelps, emphasized the doctrines of the Restoration. As many as forty of the ninety texts were original compositions by Latter-day

THE

LATTER-DAY SAINTS

MILLENNIAL STAR,

EDITED BY PARLEY P. PRATT.

No. 3. Vol. 1.   JULY, 1840.   Price 6d.

SKETCH OF TRAVELS IN AMERICA,

AND

VOYAGE TO ENGLAND.

COMMERCE is a small town on the east bank of the Mississippi River, in the state of Illinois. It is mostly owned and settled by the Latter-Day Saints; being one of the principal places where they took refuge, when driven from Missouri in the late persecution.

In this town, myself and a number of the elders resided, until we entered upon our late Mission to England.

From this place I started on a mission, on the 29th of August last, accompanied by my wife, three children, and Elders Orson Pratt, and Hyram Clark. We journeyed in our own private carriage, drawn by two horses. Our route lay through the wild and but partially inhabited Countries of Illinois, Indiana, and Michigan, for about 580 miles to Detroit, the capital of the state of Michigan, situated at the head of Lake Erie.

The first day we rode 17 miles through a beautiful plain, or prairie as the French would say, which

H

signifies meadow. Our route was a most delightful one. On all sides we turned our eyes, we beheld a boundless field of grass and flowers, with here and there a small grove of timber: the landscape was level, or gently rolling; the surface smooth as a garden; the soil extremely rich; and although there was no road worked by art, yet our carriage rolled as smooth and easy as if it had been on a railway. Most of this delightful prairie was without inhabitants, and could probably be purchased for less than £1 per acre. It is well calculated for the purposes of agriculture, producing in richest effusion, when cultivated, almost every kind of corn and grass, and every vegetable suited to the climate. After 17 miles through this delightful scenery, we arrived at Carthage, a flourishing village; stopped for the night with a member of our society, who received us kindly; and at evening preached in a large Court Room to an attentive audience.

Next day we rode some 25 miles through a similar country, and at eve, arrived at a fine village called Macomb. Here we were kindly enter-

Parley P. Pratt launched The Latter-day Saints Millennial Star *in Manchester, England, in May 1840 to share doctrine, history, conference reports, missionary letters, and other information with the Saints. The publication office moved to Liverpool in 1842.*

Saints, mostly Phelps. Many of the hymns sanctified the land as a dwelling place for the Saints and celebrated the building up of Zion.[67] The high priests quorum in Nauvoo offered to fund a new volume in 1839. Emma invited poets and others to submit to her "all *choice,* newly composed, or *revised* hymns." When it finally appeared in 1841, the Nauvoo edition of Emma Smith's hymnal expanded the content to 304 selections. The additions to this authorized hymnbook indicate a retrenchment from the celebration of restorationist and communal religion among the Latter-day Saints. Emma dropped two of William W. Phelps's corrected Protestant hymns and substituted the originals. She added other grace-oriented hymns that accentuated personal communion with a dying Jesus on the cross. Her revivalist, confessional texts placed less emphasis on the Saints' desire to rejoice in the establishment of Zion.[68]

Well-worn copies of the Kirtland hymnal and the expanded Nauvoo edition served the needs of the Saints until the exodus. Increasingly seen in Nauvoo was a British hymnal carried across the Atlantic by a flood of immigrants. Published by a committee of the Twelve in July 1840, it was reprinted three times through 1844. The Manchester hymnal added 193 texts to Emma Smith's Kirtland volume, including 44 by Parley P. Pratt. The new hymns stressed the Millennium, the restoration of priesthood authority, and the gathering of Israel from Babylon—ideas central to missionary work. In many ways, the British hymnal reflected more current Latter-day Saint teachings than the Protestant themes favored by Emma in her Nauvoo compilation. When new hymnals were published after the exodus, they built on the British edition. That volume reflected the zeal of the early years and events in Nauvoo that defined the doctrinal basis of Latter-day Saint hymnology for the founding generation.[69]

Everywhere the Latter-day Saints gathered in the nineteenth century, they made use of the printing press to share religious information with members. Of the several church periodicals issued during the Nauvoo years, two played a significant role in defining the meaning of religious community among the Saints. The *Times and Seasons* in Nauvoo and the *Latter-day Saints Millennial Star* in Manchester, England, served their respective geographic areas and were publications of record. Both papers regularly included such official information as the minutes of conferences, reports of membership statistics, letters from missionaries, and church histories. Accounts of the Missouri persecutions and Joseph Smith's official church history first appeared in print in these publications.

The Manchester periodical was a house organ for the British church, authorized by a conference and operated by the Twelve and other mission leaders.[70] The *Times and Seasons* functioned a bit more independently. It succeeded the *Elders' Journal,* a short-lived newspaper first issued in Kirtland and then cut short after two final issues at Far West. The *Journal's* Missouri proprietors, Ebenezer Robinson and Don Carlos Smith, lost no time in launching their successor paper in Commerce, Illinois, with promises to print doctrinal discussions, historical information, and a full account of the Missouri expulsion. The *Times and Seasons* appeared in a first, tentative issue in June 1839. Immediate problems delayed further publication until November, when the editors reissued a slightly altered first number and then continued with monthly issues during the next year. After that, the periodical appeared on a twice-monthly schedule but with occasional missed or late issues because of such problems as bad weather, which contributed to paper shortages.[71]

The print shop functioned for much of its tenure in the damp basement of a building at the corner of Water and Bain streets. It moved to better quarters on Main Street in May 1845. Operated first as a self-sustaining, private business venture, the *Times and Seasons* was purchased by the church in January 1842. Brigham Young supervised the purchase of the press, type, fixtures, stereotype equipment, and book bindery.[72] For the next nine months, Joseph Smith served as editor, with John Taylor assisting. From that point on, the *Times and Seasons* became, like its English cousin, an official voice for the church.

As reflected in their titles and as reinforced by their content, both journals reflected a continuing Latter-day Saint interest in news of earthquakes, wars, plagues, and other signs of the times—a steady reminder of the church's millennialist orientation.[73] Doctrinal articles educated the Saints in spiritual matters. Through historical articles generated in Nauvoo and reprinted abroad, the papers reinforced a self-definition of the Latter-day Saints as a biblical people, a community of believers persecuted for their religion. Like earlier church periodicals, both papers published revelations and prophetic writings and translations—the Nauvoo Temple revelation, epistles of the First Presidency and the Twelve, the book of Abraham, and reprints from earlier periodicals. The papers offered continuity for church members and a sense of belonging. In short, through their content, they helped define the Nauvoo-era Saints as a people of faith and destiny.[74]

Nauvoo readers also had access to a general newspaper, initially called the *Wasp* but later renamed the *Nauvoo Neighbor*. The named changed to shift the focus from a biting political voice to a friendly outreach to neighbors near and far. These secular newspapers reported news of the day, carried timely features, and subsisted through subscriptions and commercial advertisements. A major objective was to present the Latter-day Saint perspective on local political issues. William Smith edited the weekly *Wasp* for a year beginning in April 1842. John Taylor managed both the *Times and Seasons* and the *Neighbor* after that, with the help of Wilford Woodruff. All of these papers were printed in the same print shop, which also carried on a commercial business printing books, pamphlets, and stationery items.

RELIGION AND THE FAMILY

Religious consensus fostered by the church periodicals developed as well through the efforts of priesthood quorums for men and new organizations created in Nauvoo for women, young single adults, and children. These organizations supplemented and directly affected the family, where religious activity for Latter-day Saints found its most important center.

Latter-day Saints brought with them into their newfound religion certain traditional views of the family's central role in religious education and worship. Like their ancestors, the Saints saw the world through a religious frame of reference. They believed in God, sought his mercy, trained their children in righteousness, and lived in expectation of a final judgment and the ultimate triumph of good. The Americans and British who made up most of the membership of the church in the Nauvoo era understood family prayer and Bible study and family-centered Christian living. It was in the traditional family that personal religious duties such as these were taught and practiced.

A prominent example was the Prophet's own New England family. Every morning, Joseph Sr. and Lucy Mack Smith held family religious services that included reading from the Bible, singing, and praying. For private prayers, they had a designated place apart from the house in nearby woods where members of the family could retire when they wished to petition God alone.[75] Many other Latter-day Saint families followed similar patterns of personal and family worship born of long experience. Near Payson, Illinois, in 1843, a young sawmill worker experienced personal religion firsthand at the home of his future father-in-law:

> The first prayer I ever made before any person was at Father Myers, when I was called upon by Mother Myers to offer up the family prayer. It was a terrible hard task and perhaps what made it worse my future wife was present. When I went to boarding there I had to take my turn in reading a chapter and singing and praying morning and evening. Father Myers is very strict in his family worship.[76]

In nineteenth-century America, the husband and father presided in the home. This long-standing pattern in western civilization placed upon him certain obligations to support and lead his family. His responsibilities had legal standing and were recognized by the churches, including the Latter-day Saints. In the world's ordering of society, men owned property, voted, governed in the home, and conducted business for the good of the family. In addition, the Latter-day Saint male head of household was expected to preside in love in the family, to join with his wife in teaching religious principles to their children, to conduct family worship, and to represent the family in paying tithes and offerings. When the sick in the family desired a blessing of healing, or children were ready for baptism and confirmation, it came under the hands of the elders, sometimes including ordained fathers.

The official connecting link between the Latter-day Saint family unit and the institutional church was through the father. His first affiliation outside the family was his priesthood quorum. In Joseph Smith's lifetime, all men judged worthy of fellowship in the church could receive a priesthood office. This all-encompassing lay priesthood involved every willing man and gave him a sense of ownership in the church's destiny. Whatever the office conferred upon him, the priesthood holder joined a churchwide body of priests. He shared the ecclesiastical charge to spread the good word and nourish God's gathered children. "There are no big men or little men in the Kingdom of our God," Heber C. Kimball was fond of saying. All were laborers in the vineyard, with differing assignments but one reward for the faithful.[77] With broad geographical boundaries and tight collegial ties, priesthood quorums strengthened male unity and patriarchal roles and built support for institutional values and leaders.

Aside from their ecclesiastical roles, the Melchizedek Priesthood quorums contributed significantly toward a united Nauvoo. It was the duty of the presidency of each of the quorums of high priests, seventies, and elders to train, involve, discipline, and assign the members of their quorum in the work of that particular office. Training took place in quorum meetings, held as often as weekly. In them, leaders outlined duties, and leaders and members shared their religious feelings and took turns speaking on gospel topics. To maintain a oneness in faith and fellowship, each quorum attested to the worthiness of its members, heard grievances of one member against another, and excluded from fellowship any whose unworthiness disqualified him. The entire quorum membership usually participated in the disciplinary councils called by the quorum presidency.

Because their purpose was to restore members to full fellowship, they tended to leniency if a member confessed his wrongdoing and pledged future loyalty to shared principles. When members transferred from one place to another, they took a letter of introduction to certify their standing in the church and ordination to a specific office in the priesthood.[78] This kept unscrupulous intruders out of quorums and ensured an orderly process within a dynamic church.

Fathers of families received help in their domestic duties from the three quorums of the Aaronic Priesthood. In Nauvoo, the priests, teachers, and deacons—all adults—were organized into citywide quorums by the four bishops during a Sunday meeting on March 21, 1841.[79] As set forth by revelation in the "Articles and Covenants" of the church in April 1830, members holding this priesthood made regular visits to the homes to encourage fathers in their family duties. The visiting brethren were also to root out iniquity, including lying, backbiting, and evil speaking among members. They would call upon families, listen to them pray, and teach them their religious responsibilities.[80] In their efforts to strengthen families spiritually, the visiting lesser priesthood helped build religious commitment within the church.

Though everyone knew of this specific assignment of the lesser priesthood, the church did not always achieve its objectives consistently. A group of high priests in the Fifth Ward of Nauvoo in December 1844 groused over problems with the youth of certain families in their ward and wondered aloud if the Twelve should perhaps speak publicly to the subject. Some members recognized that it was the duty of the Aaronic Priesthood "to seek out and investigate such cases . . . and not lay the burden on the Twelve." Perhaps, they concluded, Nauvoo's stake president should instruct the priests and teachers to perform their duties.[81]

Until the spring of 1842, women of the church served others outside the formal church organization. While their husbands functioned in administrative and missionary callings, the women created informal visiting networks among friends. They shared the gospel through personal efforts. For their institutional tie with the church, they relied upon their husbands and fathers.[82] Joseph Smith expanded that connection when he organized the Female Relief Society of Nauvoo.[83]

Women meeting together as friends to sew shirts for temple construction workers had decided to organize and to include other friends in

Designated "an elect lady" by revelation in 1830, Emma Hale Smith was called to write for her husband, expound scriptures, and compile a hymnal published in 1835 and expanded in 1841. As president of The Female Relief Society of Nauvoo, she taught the women and oversaw efforts to help the poor.

the effort. A group assembled in March at the home of Sarah Granger Kimball (Hiram's wife) to formally create a benevolent society like those existing elsewhere in the United States. Eliza R. Snow drafted a constitution to guide the ladies' society in its objectives. Then Joseph Smith intervened to give the benevolent group a religious structure and purpose. The Prophet advised twenty women assembled on March 17 in the council room above his store to discard their written constitution. They should govern themselves after a pattern used by the priesthood, under a council form of government, he said, with a "living constitution." By this he apparently meant that decisions would be made without reference to a set of rules but through deliberations guided by the Holy Spirit. As a self-governing church organization, the women would function under general priesthood direction to avoid inconsistencies within the church. Their own officers would direct and teach them.[84]

The organizers accepted the Prophet's counsel on structure and method. They elected his wife, Emma Hale Smith, as their president. She chose as counselors Sarah M. Cleveland and Elizabeth Ann Whitney and as secretary Eliza Roxcy Snow. The word *benevolent* had earned a bad reputation among them because of publicized extravagances in certain Eastern organizations using that title, so they chose the name The Female Relief Society of Nauvoo. The Relief Society assembled an ever-growing membership weekly during the spring of 1842 and then adjourned until fall, when it resumed meetings. By June 1, membership numbered nearly nine hundred women.[85] It peaked two years later at more than thirteen hundred. To accommodate this growth, the women of each of Nauvoo's four wards were assigned a certain week each month to meet with the presidency.

By whatever name they called the new organization, one of its central purposes remained benevolence, or charity, or relief of the needs of the poor. The society's first obligation, the Prophet said, was to "provoke the brethren to good works in looking to the wants of the poor—searching after objects of charity, and in administering to their wants." The sisters were asked to coordinate their relief work with the bishops to avoid inefficient duplication. Another role for the Relief Society, Joseph Smith counseled, was public teaching. It was the society president's obligation "to expound the scriptures to all; and to teach the female part of the community." A related assignment was "to assist by correcting the morals and strengthening the virtues of the community, and save the Elders the trouble of rebuking." An English convert, not yet precise in her use of religious terminology, summarized what she heard at the Thursday afternoon meetings. "We receive instructions both temporary and spiritually," she said. To dispense goods to the poor was the Relief Society's temporal responsibility; to practice virtue and preach truth, its spiritual obligations.[86]

With humanitarian service as its primary objective, the society quickly developed a process for identifying and meeting the needs of the poor. At each group meeting, the assembled sisters reported needs and then volunteered resources to help. Through casual conversation and through organized committees assigned to visit the homes in each neighborhood, the women discovered widows without food, orphans with insufficient clothing, widowers needing bedding, unemployed persons lacking basic amenities, and so on, week after week. To meet these needs, the officers accepted cash and anything else that could be used. The treasurer kept an accounting of donations and expenditures.

While extending help, the sisters paid attention to the feelings as well as the physical needs of individuals. When the widowed Ellen W. Douglas became sick, she was unable to provide clothing for her family, which included sons old enough to hire themselves out to dig fencing ditches on the prairie and work in a saw pit. At first she resisted a suggestion that she apply to the Relief Society for help, but an acquaintance finally persuaded her to allow the sisters to assess her needs. "In a few days," she said, "they brought the wagon and fetched me such a present as I never received before from no place in the world. I suppose the things they sent were worth as much as 30 shillings." The widow also qualified to receive a free one-acre lot in Nauvoo, but she chose instead to rent a house.[87]

The counselors in the presidency kept close watch over charitable efforts, while the president herself took the greatest interest in a second objective. Emma had been called as a teacher. This special assignment formalized a calling promised in an 1830 revelation to the Prophet that identified her as "an elect lady" called "to expound scriptures, and to exhort the church, according as it shall be given thee by my Spirit."[88] Emma Smith's Relief Society position gave this elect lady her own role as a leader in spiritual things.

In an April meeting, the Prophet explained the opportunity he had given women by establishing an organization officially connected to the church. He had opened to them, he said, a way to receive knowledge, intelligence, and power from God. That endowment of wisdom and authority would come as women were set apart to preside and teach and as they received temple ordinances. Using the metaphor of opening a door to allow women to move from darkness into light as full participants in church affairs, he said:

> This Society is to get instruction through the order which God has established—thro' the medium of those appointed to lead—and I now turn the key to you in the name of God and this Society shall rejoice and knowledge and intelligence shall flow down from this time—this is the beginning of better days to this Society.[89]

Joseph Smith instructed the women to defend Nauvoo rigorously against actions that would destroy the virtue of the women and of the society. That very year, scandals perpetrated by John C. Bennett had rocked the city. Bennett had published articles and a book charging Joseph Smith and others with introducing a "spiritual wife system" that sanctioned promiscuous sexual relationships. Bennett and a few others had themselves behaved immorally and been excommunicated. Interestingly, just two days before Bennett resigned as mayor of Nauvoo, the city council enacted a strict ordinance against brothels, adultery, and fornication, with fines ranging from five hundred dollars to fifty thousand dollars and up to six months in prison.[90]

Emma Smith spoke out boldly in several Relief Society gatherings in defense of virtue. To the public, it would seem she was denouncing all relationships outside monogamous marriages, even though she knew of and at times supported her husband's plural marriages. Realistically, however, her public message probably was intended to denounce even the church-sanctioned marriage system with its biblical precedents. Emma vacillated in her support of the revelation. Her assignment to preach virtue, intended by Joseph to unify Nauvoo, instead increased tension between those tentative toward the new teaching and those converted to it. In the spring of 1844, the Relief Society ceased meeting. After Joseph Smith's death, Emma distanced herself from Brigham Young's leadership. The women's organization would be revived, with the Prophet's plural wife Eliza Snow as its leader, long after most Latter-day Saints had established themselves in a new gathering place in the Rocky Mountains.

The notion of community service to those in need spread beyond the women of Nauvoo to other interested groups. In early 1843, efforts were made to organize a Young Gentlemen and Ladies Relief Society of Nauvoo. This benevolent society for single young men and women under age thirty began in late January when Heber C. Kimball offered to address an assemblage of young people concerned about "the loose style of their morals—the frivolous manner in which they spent their time—and their too frequent attendance at balls, parties, &tc." In subsequent weekly gatherings of what they called the Young People's Meetings, held in larger and larger rooms—finally in the room over Joseph Smith's store (that, too, filled to overflowing)—Kimball and others counseled and taught the attentive youth. Moral instruction turned to community service when the Prophet complimented the youth for their interest in bettering themselves and "advised them to organize themselves into a society for the relief of the poor." On March 21, the assembled youth adopted a constitution and elected officers to one-year terms. As its first project, the society accepted Smith's challenge to collect funds to build a house for Sutcliffe Maudsley, an artist and a crippled immigrant from England. They agreed to seek out other persons needing assistance.[91] Like the women's Relief Society, this instructional and service organization apparently did not survive the Prophet's death. It was likewise reestablished in a slightly different form a quarter century later.

Some Nauvoo Saints later remembered the beginnings of a Sunday School as well. In early June 1844, according to these reminiscences, Joseph Smith suggested the creation of Sabbath classes for children. He designated Stephen Goddard to supervise teachers and invited the children to bring their testaments and hymnbooks for a meeting in the east grove. After two meetings, the disrupting events at Carthage ended the fledgling movement, but it may have been revived for a time the following year for both children and youth.[92]

The Nauvoo Sunday School was a new initiative for the Latter-day Saints, falling in with the Protestant Sunday School movement launched in Great Britain in 1780. A similar effort in the United States was formalized with the creation of the American Sunday School Union in 1824. For the most part, Latter-day Saint leaders had been comfortable leaving to parents the responsibility for the religious education of their children. An 1831 revelation had specifically charged parents with this duty.[93] That emphasis colored John Taylor's comments on the situation in Nauvoo that suggested the need for instructional organizations for youth and children:

> To see children break the Sabbath by running about and playing on Sunday; to see them saucy too to persons of riper years; to see them filling up the streets to play upon week days, and to hear them swear and use vulgar language, is a disgrace to their parents; a stigma upon the neighborhood; and a slow poison to themselves, that will eventually corrupt and ruin their reputations, unless cured by virtue and reason.

Thirty years later, Taylor would oversee creation of a Primary Mutual Improvement Association in Utah for the institutional training of children in just such matters. In Nauvoo, he was pleased to report the recent commencement of meetings "of the children and youth, to worship God, and to practice holiness by a recitation of scripture, by singing and by prayer. Such a course," he said, "is praise-worthy." For the continuance of the work, there needed to be a harmony of faith not just among those who first entered the church but between that group of adults and succeeding generations.[94]

THE DEFINING INFLUENCE OF CHURCH HISTORY

The past as well as the future concerned the people of Nauvoo. A sense of history had pervaded the Latter-day Saint organization right from the day of its formal creation as the Church of Christ on April 6, 1830. On that day, a revelation instructed the church, "Behold, there shall be a record kept among you." A succession of church historians and recorders, beginning with Oliver Cowdery, had kept some records, and clerks had preserved minutes of key meetings. But Joseph Smith desired a history encompassing the spiritual essence of the Restoration.

Not long after his arrival from Missouri, the Prophet revived an effort launched fourteen months earlier in Far West. On June 10, 1839, he engaged his clerk James Mulholland as scribe and set out to dictate his own history. Mulholland's death in November, after writing only fifty-nine pages, left the work to other clerks. Of greatest import was the work of Willard Richards. Before the Prophet's death, Richards completed the record to August 1838 and compiled most of the documents needed to finish the history of the Nauvoo years, which was accomplished by 1856.[95]

The text begun by Mulholland drew upon an 1838 manuscript prepared by the Prophet and Sidney Rigdon. It set a pattern of compiling the history from existing diaries, letters, minutes, and published sources. Documents of the early years were inserted to help carry the story forward. Those who completed the Prophet's history after his death relied almost exclusively upon the documentary evidence. Under the direction of the First Presidency, they drew from existing diaries as well to create a linking narrative, giving it a first-person voice, a customary practice in nineteenth-century historical writing.[96]

Essentially, "The History of Joseph Smith" was an eyewitness account following the pattern in scripture of the records of God's dealings with his people. It responded as well to the influences of inquiring outsiders and reflected the millennial worldview of Latter-day Saints. From the details of the events recounted in the history emerged several themes: the story

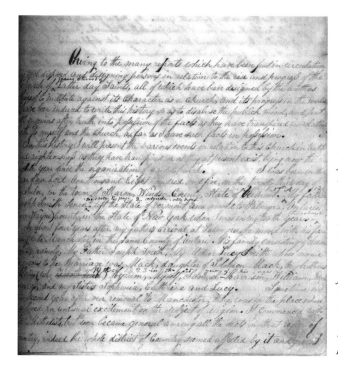

In June 1839, with James Mulholland as scribe, Joseph Smith resumed dictating the history of the Restoration. He intended to "put all enquirers after truth into possession of the facts as they have transpired in relation both to myself and the Church as far as I have such facts in possession."

of the Restoration, the history of persecutions, the signs of the times, and evidences of the true church of Jesus Christ.

First, Joseph Smith wished to give an accurate explanation of the personal experiences that had marked the beginning of the Restoration. As a newspaper editor in Nauvoo remarked,

> The coming forth of the Book of Mormon, the rise of the church, and the restoration of the Priesthood—these three subjects excite more curiosity, create more enquiry, and cause more labor to answer, than any others of our faith.[97]

The Prophet's firsthand recounting of church beginnings occupied a central role in the early pages of the history. This part of the history was eventually canonized as an official sacred account.

A second element of the history was an account of the tensions between the Latter-day Saints and their neighbors. The Prophet introduced this subject early in his record. As soon as he began sharing the story of his first vision in upstate New York, he said, "a great deal of prejudice" excited "the public mind against me, and create[d] a bitter persecution." The Missouri troubles, the last section prepared before Smith's death, filled numerous pages of the history. Latter-day Saints viewed their mistreatment by others as evidence of being followers of God. Like the persecuted in New Testament time, such suffering helped identify and define God's people.[98]

A third trademark of the Prophet's history was the inclusion of reports of the signs of the times, both natural occurrences and the commotions among people of the earth. This thread reflected Smith's own literal rendering of the scriptures as well as his upbringing in a rural America steeped in traditional beliefs and Bible learning. John Taylor believed it his duty as editor of the *Times and Seasons* to chronicle and interpret such events so that his paper would "contain a faithful history of the last days. The poet said, 'Coming events cast their shadow before,' and a discerning man has only to look, *to behold!*" It might have been this sense of historical mission that influenced Joseph Smith and his associates to flavor his history with foreshadowing evidences.[99]

Latter-day Saints found another important witness of the last days in the spiritual signs of their restored Christianity. They believed that the history being written about their prophetic movement would become another sacred record—scripture for another generation. It was important, therefore, that the record include an account of such spiritual experiences as dreams and visions, healings, prophecies, speaking in tongues, and other spiritual gifts. The pentecostal experience of the early apostles and the prophetic promise of Joel concerning dreams and visions were part of the scriptural record of the past. For Latter-day Saints, their own similar experiences belonged in the historical record of the last days as evidences of the true church.[100]

In the minds of the Saints, the people of the new covenant echoed the pattern of earlier sacred eras. Time began anew on April 6, 1830, and the years of the new dispensation were counted from that base mark forward.[101] "We are the favored people that God has made choice of to bring about the Latter Day glory," Joseph Smith wrote in 1842:

> It is left for us to see, participate in, and help to roll forward the Latter Day glory; 'the dispensation of the fulness of times, when God will gather together all things that are in heaven, and all things that are upon the earth,' . . . will be in one, even in Christ. . . . and our name will be handed down to future ages; our children will rise up

and call us blessed; and generations yet unborn will dwell with peculiar delight upon the scenes that we have passed through, the privations that we have endured; the untiring zeal that we have manifested; the insurmountable difficulties that we have overcome in laying the foundation of . . . a work that is destined to bring about the destruction of the powers of darkness, the renovation of the earth, the glory of God, and the salvation of the human family.[102]

This sense of mission helps explain why the Prophet put so much emphasis on keeping a record. Preparing the history of the new dispensation held a high priority in his life.[103]

While Joseph Smith and the historical clerks of Nauvoo worked at compiling the Prophet's history of the church, a few others prepared and published their own histories. For years, Lucy Mack Smith had been retelling privately and before congregations her family's experiences with persecution because of Joseph's teachings. In 1844 and 1845, with the help of two schoolteachers in Nauvoo, she preserved her memories of her son's life, in the context of family history. Orson Pratt published it in 1853 in England.[104] A prominent example of a history written by someone outside the church is the Reverend Henry Caswall's travel account, *The City of the Mormons,* published in London in 1842.[105]

Many Latter-day Saints kept personal histories in the form of daily summaries or retrospective life histories, or a combination of both. The hundreds of journals and autobiographies commenced or continued during the Nauvoo years attest to the interest in this effort. All participants in the Mormon religious movement, not just its leaders, saw themselves as important cogs in the Lord's machinery of winding down history toward the final end. Many diarists recorded their stories in the language of scripture. All of them recorded events deemed important as witnesses of God's workings in their lives. The effort clearly helped to solidify the Latter-day Saint sense of community.[106]

Encouragement to keep personal histories appeared directly through admonition and indirectly through the power of example. The editor of the *Millennial Star* invited "the Elders and officers in the church of Christ in these Last Days, to . . . write a history of their travels and labors . . . and the work of God in our day" like that found in the gospels and acts of the apostles. The church papers regularly published historical narratives. With these histories as exemplary models, readers sensed the importance of keeping records. Scriptural admonitions in the Doctrine and Covenants reinforced the interest.[107]

Latter-day Saint diarists adopted a pattern that varied little from one writer to another. Typically, after a brief summary of prior events, they began their accounts with the story of their conversion. This spiritual turning point received extensive elaboration in most accounts. The writers defined themselves as seekers after truth, noted their frustrations at being disappointed by other faiths, and rejoiced in finding the message of the restored gospel. In most narratives, conversion meant rejection by family and friends, but the move to Nauvoo or other designated gathering places solved this problem. The story of the migration and of the hardships endured occupied a part of most autobiographies, followed by a simple recital of day-to-day events. The badgering of Joseph Smith by Missouri authorities became part of many personal histories, and the assassinations of the Smith brothers almost always stood out as a significant turning point. Their reactions to these events, which the diarists had not witnessed, added poignancy to their accounts. The Nauvoo portion of their histories ended with the decision once again to move west.

The tone and content of the personal diaries and autobiographies reflected the convictions of these Latter-day Saints writers that they were witnessing the unfolding of a "marvelous work and a wonder" in the last days. Sometimes diarists recorded signs of the times. Often they testified of God's mercy to them or the church at times of sickness, persecution, or challenge. They reflected on the messages of their prophet-teacher. Like the official church historians whose works they echoed, the record-keeping Saints of the latter-days attested to their faith in their religion and their destiny as a people.

CHAPTER 10

The House of the Lord

There is another curiosity, the temple, under which is a baptismal font which stands on twelve oxen as natural as life in which we can be baptised for our dead and become saviors on mount Zion, in which, my dear mother, I have been baptised for . . . my dead friends.

—PHEBE CHASE, APRIL 5, 1844

There has been a glorious principle taught that has been revealed from the Lord to the Prophet, of being sealed for eternity to those that have lost their partners, and without this sealing power, no one can claim their bosom friends in another world. . . . Whether it can be done before the Temple of the Lord is finished I cannot tell as yet, but I assure you I am very anxious about it. . . . I know that it is the will of the Lord that every honest-hearted person must be to come here, for there is no other place of salvation for the human family.

—JAMES JONES, JUNE 10, 1844

To those gathered within a large square formed by the militia of Nauvoo on the brow of the hill overlooking Nauvoo, the religious service about to begin was, as Sidney Rigdon described it, "of no ordinary character, but of peculiar and indescribable interest."[1] Very early on April 6, 1841, fourteen companies of the Nauvoo Legion and two adjunct units of the Legion from Iowa Territory assembled for review. As was customary for that time, the participation of a local militia signaled to the public that this was a significant community event. At half-hour intervals through the morning, the discharge of cannon announced the arrival of officers to review the lines of soldiers, beginning with the brigadier generals and working up to Lieutenant General Joseph Smith in full military dress with his guard, staff, and field officers.

All of this was merely prelude to the important event of the day. After the military review, the Legion proceeded to a site at Mulholland and Wells Streets. Short trenches had been excavated at four corners of the intended building to the level of the basement floor, the stone foundation laid, and rough basement walls of unfinished stone raised five feet. A speaker's stand waited at the southeast corner of the site. The militia formed itself into a large square three men deep. Inside this human wall were militia officers, the Legion's band and choir, and horses of the officers and special guests. A curious crowd milled around outside the lines. When all were in readiness, the First Presidency, the architects of the building, and guests made their way to the stand, where the militia displayed a silk American flag presented earlier that morning to the Legion by the women of Nauvoo.

Though the assembled citizens faced an impressive marshaling of soldiers, this was no military proceeding. The Latter-day Saints were about to commence construction of a temple. Twice before, at Kirtland and at Far West, Rigdon had witnessed the laying of cornerstones for a House of the Lord. In his sermon at Far West, he had emphasized the need for the Saints to defend their rights against vigilantes. Now, he celebrated peace, centered his message on the church's religious mission, and proclaimed a muted determination to protect the Saints' constitutional liberties, including the right to the free exercise of religion. The Latter-day Saints, he said, desired "to honor, not the world, but him that is alive and reigns . . . [who] the Saints boast of [as] their King." After inviting another hymn, Rigdon closed with prayer, and the ceremony of placing the cornerstones commenced.[2]

The architects and crew lowered the southeast cornerstone into place on the foundation wall. Joseph Smith pronounced a benediction upon it, and his counselor offered a comment. After an hour's adjournment, the same procedure was followed at the other three corners, with stake and ward leaders officiating. "We never witnessed a more imposing spectacle . . . , such [a] multitude of people, moving in harmony, in friendship, in dignity, . . . a people of intelligence and virtue, and order," the Prophet's brother Don Carlos observed of the long day's activities.[3]

Construction of a building for religious assembly, instruction, and ordinances could now formally begin. The commanding limestone structure underway at the physical center of Nauvoo would symbolize as well the city's spiritual focus. In preparing his people to receive the ordinances of the House of the Lord, the Prophet would give new meaning to temples, unfold new doctrines relating to the eternal worlds, and forever change what it meant to be a Latter-day Saint. The temple—its doctrinal moorings and covenantal superstructure—would further separate the Latter-day Saints from other Christians and make of them a truly distinctive people.

EXPANDING THE MEANING OF THE TEMPLE

Nearly from the beginning of settlement in what was then called Commerce, the Latter-day Saints recognized the need for a House of the Lord to serve purposes that in later decades would be divided between a meetinghouse or tabernacle and a temple. They could worship in any setting, but the Saints wanted a formal gathering place for instruction, for partaking of the sacrament, for learning from the Lord's living prophet, and for special sacred priesthood ordinances. They had completed just such a place in Kirtland, and the Prophet had planned others in Independence, Far West, and Adam-ondi-Ahman. Nauvoo's dwelling place for the Lord would follow the revealed pattern and expand upon its uses to set a new model for the future.[4]

In the fall of 1840, the First Presidency paid eleven hundred dollars to Daniel H. Wells for a four-acre site that would command the attention of residents and travelers from all approaches. The October 1840 conference approved Joseph Smith's proposal to build a House of the Lord by appropriating the labor of all willing men every tenth day. The conference appointed a three-member building committee, and within a week a team of stonemasons had opened a temple quarry at the north end of Main Street.[5]

The much-anticipated structure took on additional meaning when a revelation on January 19, 1841 (D&C 124), gave the temple and a hotel known as the Nauvoo House the Lord's explicit sanction. This revelation was the Prophet's most significant recorded in nearly three years; it expanded the Saints' expectations for the temple, encouraged a renewal of commitment, and made the project of first importance among all church efforts. Digging of the basement began in earnest in mid-February.

The first design for the Nauvoo Temple by William Weeks (left) appeared as a border illustration on the city plat prepared by Gustavus Hills in 1842. James McCord prepared a modified elevation drawing that September.

Foundation stones were laid during March to be ready for the April 6 placement of the cornerstones.[6]

The revelation contained a special message to those who had been expelled from Missouri. Because of persecution, the Lord lifted from the Saints the commandment to build a temple in Jackson County. This drew their attention away from the "redemption of Zion" and turned it toward the work of building a temple in a place designated in the revelation as "the cornerstone of Zion."[7] In addition, it validated a long-standing priority established by revelation in 1834 and reaffirmed that same year as the Prophet urged completion of the Kirtland Temple. Joseph Smith had told the church in Kirtland:

> The Lord has commanded us to build a house, in which to receive an endowment, previous to the redemption of Zion; and that Zion could not be redeemed until this takes place. . . . We remind you of these things in the name of the Lord, . . . and ask, did we not instruct you to remember first the house, secondly the cause of Zion, and then the publishing of the word to the nations?[8]

The Nauvoo revelation fostered a sense of participation among all members of the church by inviting the Saints everywhere to contribute liberally of their means. But when the revelation invited every man to tithe his time—one day in ten—as a volunteer laborer, the gathering to Nauvoo became an imperative.[9] As a further inducement, the revelation restricted baptisms for the dead to the temple, except "in the days of your poverty," when the Saints lacked the resources for a temple. The revelation did allow the redemptive work to continue for a time while the temple was under construction, but only in the temple would the general population of the Saints receive their endowments.[10]

From a spiritual perspective, the revelation explained with greater clarity and added a new layer of meaning to what it meant to be a Latter-day Saint. Published in 1841 by the *Times and Seasons* in its June 1 number, and added to the Doctrine and Covenants in the 1844 edition, the revelation promised both a restoration of things lost and the deliverance of things not known at any previous time among God's people. It defined the temple as a place where God could "restore . . . the fulness of the priesthood," to reveal ordinances "kept hid from before the foundation of the world, things that pertain to the dispensation of the fulness of times." Also identified were other purposes that echoed some of those understood in Kirtland. The House of the Lord in Nauvoo would be a place for

> your anointings, and your washings, and your baptisms for the dead, and your solemn assemblies, and your memorials for your sacrifices by the sons of Levi, and for your oracles [revelations] in your most holy places wherein you receive conversations, and your statutes and judgments, for the beginning of the revelations and foundation of Zion, and for the glory, honor, and endowment of all her municipals.[11]

Joseph Smith had dedicated the Kirtland Temple in March 1836 as a place of learning and of solemn assemblies, a place where a pentecostal endowment of power could be experienced. It was to be "a house of prayer, a house of fasting, a house of faith, a house of glory and of God."[12] Years earlier, in 1829, Joseph Smith and Oliver Cowdery had received an angelic visitor who conferred authority to fulfill Ezekiel's requirement of a Levitical sacrificial offering to the Lord.[13] At Kirtland in 1836, some of the elders participated in preparatory ordinances in what was termed an endowment of power.[14] In Nauvoo, the Prophet brought together temple-related practices hinted at in both Old and New Testaments but expanded through new revelation.[15]

The most immediate and widely taught new doctrine authorized the practice of proxy baptisms for persons who had died without baptism by proper priesthood authority. The doctrine unfolded gradually. In 1838, Joseph Smith taught that those who had died without such saving ordinances must hear the gospel in the hereafter before they could be finally judged.[16] Two years later, he introduced the idea that an earthly ordinance was required for those who had accepted the doctrine of repentance in the world of departed spirits. He spoke of proxy baptism for the dead first on August 15, 1840, at the funeral of Seymour Brunson, a high councilor,[17] and again at the October conference. The following April all three members of the First Presidency discussed the subject. Thereafter, the Prophet elaborated on the idea in sermons and writings two or three times each year, often in response to inquiries.[18] While in hiding to avoid arrest, he wrote to the Saints on the topic.[19] In his letters and sermons on baptism for the dead, Joseph Smith pointed out that the objective of the doctrine was to offer salvation to all of humankind. This one great union of all of God's righteous children was not just between generations but from one gospel dispensation to another and between this life and the next.[20]

In the rite of baptism and in the use of the temple font, Joseph Smith described a religious symbolism that further united the living and the dead. The baptismal font, he explained, was placed below ground to remind the Saints of the grave. In both baptism and the resurrection, the corrupt body rises to a new spiritual life.[21] The Nauvoo Temple font consisted of a basin supported on the backs of twelve life-sized oxen, a reference to a similar basin, or "molten sea," in Solomon's temple.[22] For the Latter-day Saints, the oxen represented Israel's twelve tribes, whose physical and spiritual gathering was being accomplished through missionary preaching and the rite of baptism.[23]

The records kept of the ordinances were also an important element of this saving power. When Joseph Smith discovered, in the fall of 1842, an inconsistent pattern in the records of proxy baptisms, he explained the recording requirement in scriptural terms and taught that the record itself had legal standing in the next life.[24] A recorder should be present, he explained, as a witness who could testify that the event had truly happened. Clerks in each Nauvoo ward and in the outlying branches should submit certified records to the general church recorder. Multiple witnesses must be identified in the minutes, he said, "that in the mouth of two or

These front elevations of the Nauvoo Temple by William Weeks show an interim design (left) that adds sun stones and moon stones to the pilasters and the "final" rendering (right) with a full attic story replacing the pediment. In 1845, the attic windows were squared and an inscribed plaque filled the central opening.

three witnesses every word may be established."[25] Joseph Smith taught that the performance of a religious ordinance by proper authority and with a worthy recipient, if properly recorded and witnessed, created "a law on earth and in heaven, and could not be annulled, according to the decrees of the great Jehovah" as set forth in the conferral of apostolic keys to Peter.[26]

A related meaning devolved from John the Revelator's declaration that in the final accounting the dead would be judged out of the books. Two sets of books were implied here, the Prophet explained: the "books . . . of their works" kept on earth by a temple recorder, and a companion "book of life" kept in heaven by angels. As an indication of the sacredness of the earthly record, it would be deposited in the archives of the temple as a remembrance to the deceased.[27]

To prevent irregularities in the performance of the new proxy ordinance, the Prophet tried to limit the practice to Nauvoo.[28] As questions arose, he issued various regulations. One of these allowed proxies to be immersed only on behalf of relatives whom they had known personally and believed to have been of a mind to accept the restored gospel. For a time, only the church president could grant exceptions to this regulation.[29] He soon lifted the restriction and allowed members to give all of their ancestors an opportunity to accept earthly ordinances in the spirit world.[30] In 1845, Brigham Young added one other regulation to ensure greater orderliness—that men should be baptized for their male ancestors and women for women.[31]

Those who had found salvation in the restored gospel rejoiced in the prospects of becoming saviors on Mount Zion through proxy baptism for their ancestors. Converts had given up the association of unbelieving living relatives but could look forward to an eternal friendship with honorable deceased ancestors. "Is not this a glorious doctrine?" Vilate Kimball exulted in a letter to her missionary husband. "Surely the Gentiles will mock but we will rejoice in it." By extending the hope of salvation beyond the grave and by affirming a universal requirement for all times and places, Joseph Smith expanded the traditional understanding of Christ's relationship to the people of the world. This concept of universal salvation was a first major step in expanding church doctrine at Nauvoo. It demonstrated that new revelation existed and that essential priesthood authority had been restored—both identifiers of the Latter-day Saints as a distinctive religious people.[32]

In another doctrinal expansion, Joseph Smith unfolded a plan for the progression of God's children beyond this life and into the eternities. Drawing on what he had learned by revelation, he explicated texts from the Bible but relied also upon modern scriptures, including the book of Abraham. One of the Prophet's most comprehensive doctrinal speeches came in a commemorative funeral sermon for an elder in the church named King Follett. Delivered at a church conference in April 1844, the discourse became a touchstone in Latter-day Saint belief.[33]

In this comprehensive presentation, Joseph Smith summarized revealed doctrines on the origin and destiny of man, the character of God, the nature of creation, and the salvation of deceased ancestors. The discourse envisioned a universe peopled with human beings in various stages of development. Persons on the earth, he taught, had lived in a spirit world as the children of a loving Father and Mother in heaven who provided for them an earth life as a step toward godhood for themselves. That eternal plan was merely a replication of similar experiences on other worlds at other times. Individuals proven by their obedience would be blessed with eternal lives as rulers in the kingdoms of Christ and his Father.[34]

In Nauvoo, the Prophet expanded upon his vision a decade earlier of our Heavenly Father, the resurrected Christ, and the three degrees of glory. He began more openly teaching of the Godhead in ways different from that commonly understood by other Christians. In an interview in the fall of 1842 with an Illinois minister, Smith said, "We believe in three Gods. There are three personages in Heaven—all equal in power and glory, but they are not one God." In a footnote to a reprint of the interview, the Prophet added, "The Father, and the Son are persons of Tabernacle; and the Holy Ghost a spirit."[35] Joseph Smith reaffirmed this notion of corporeal gods with glorified bodies in discussions with the Saints at Ramus in 1843. Lucy Mack Smith remembered that the doctrine was known as early as 1829.[36] It was discussed in one of the "Lectures on Faith" published in 1835, in which the Father is described as a glorified being with a spiritual body, that is, a resurrected body of flesh and bones, in comparison to the natural bodies of humankind.[37] After the King Follett discourse, believing Saints had no doubt that if the veil were rent and they saw God, he would appear "in all the person, image, and very form as a man." And, with this understanding, they felt closer to the Eternal being in whose image they had been created.[38]

Joseph Smith taught that as eternal beings, men and women have the potential to partake of the divine. Through a gradual perfecting process, he explained, they may move "from grace to grace, from exaltation to exaltation . . . until [they] arrive at the station of a God." John Taylor added a careful scriptural argument to this explanation in 1845, adding, "Jesus Christ had a father and mother of his Spirit, and a father and mother of his flesh; and so have all of his brethren and sisters [people of the earth]: and that is one reason why he said, 'ye are Gods.'"[39]

Taken together, the doctrines summarized in the King Follett sermon gave new meanings to the temple. It made clear that the unity so much desired by the Saints for themselves extended across time and through the eternities. Through the promised blessings of the temple, the Saints could be one with relatives, with other righteous people, and with God.[40] In one of his last requests for a renewed effort on the temple project, on a blustery late January day in 1844, Joseph Smith said that the Saints could become saviors on Mount Zion and bring the desired unity of a Zion society by building their temples, erecting their baptismal fonts, and going forth and receiving all the ordinances, baptisms, confirmations, washings, anointings, ordinations and sealing powers upon their heads, in behalf of all their progenitors who are dead, and redeem them that they may come forth in the first resurrection and be exalted to thrones of glory with them; and herein is the chain that binds the hearts of the fathers to the children, and the children to the fathers, which fulfills the mission of Elijah. And I would to God that this temple was now done, that we might go into it, and go to work.

The effort of gathering the Saints and building the temple was falling short of Joseph Smith's expectations. Too many Latter-day Saints failed to take seriously the necessity of temple ordinances. Anguished by this lack of dedication, the Prophet said, "The Saints are slow to understand. . . . How many will be able to abide a celestial law, and go through and receive their exaltation, I am unable to say, as many are called, but few are chosen."[41]

Building the Temple

With all the rigors and distractions of everyday life, it took the Saints of Nauvoo more than five years to erect the House of the Lord on the bluff overlooking the city. From the time of the first announcement in October 1840 until the final dedication in May 1846, they poured countless hours and thousands of dollars in resources into building this imposing religious edifice.

At the outset, Joseph Smith invited several builders, carpenters, and architects to submit proposed designs. He liked none of them except that of William Weeks, a man in his late twenties trained as a builder by his father in New England and apprenticed as an architect and draftsman to his brother in the South.[42] Weeks adapted his design before achieving an acceptable rendering of the building. "I have seen in vision the splendid appearance of that building illuminated," the Prophet explained, "and will have it built according to the pattern shown me."[43] An early rendering appeared as an illustration on Gustavus Hills's *Map of the City of Nauvoo.* Weeks soon softened the squareness of the stone tower by redesigning it as an octagon and specifying wood construction. At the same time, he changed the traditional gabled front end to add an expanded attic space.

The general pattern of the Nauvoo Temple resembled that of its smaller predecessor in Kirtland. Both had two main floors rendered as

The priesthood pulpits in the Kirtland Temple, shown here, served as a model for those placed at both ends of the main assembly room in the Nauvoo Temple.

meeting halls with multitiered seating for presiding officers at both ends. Both provided small meeting rooms for quorum leaders. Kirtland had no baptismal font, a feature added in the below-ground level of the Nauvoo Temple. The temple in Nauvoo was to be 128 feet long and 88 feet wide, rising 65 feet above ground with a tower topping off at 165 feet. With nearly fifty thousand square feet of interior space (just over eleven thousand on the main floor), it was three times the size of Kirtland's House of the Lord. Illinois travelers inspecting the finished Nauvoo Temple would have found it about equal in size to the cathedral, the courthouse, or the theater in St. Louis. The footprint of the Illinois Statehouse, completed in 1853 in Springfield, was slightly smaller.[44]

Latter-day Saint temples reflected the basic architectural styles of existing meetinghouses in England and the United States. Using the visual language of public and religious architecture of the times, the design of the temple communicated to all viewers that its walls defined and enclosed sacred space. In some respects, the outlines of Nauvoo's temple hinted of the ancient House of the Lord in Jerusalem.[45] But Latter-day Saint temples incorporated some distinctive features as well. A single pulpit in most churches of the times lifted the minister above his congregation to symbolize his role as God's representative. Joseph Smith lowered the pulpit and added pews to place the emphasis on priesthood quorums. Behind the single pulpit at each end of the main floor hall were four rising pews. He placed the officers of the higher, or Melchizedek Priesthood at the east end, with the First Presidency seated at the top pew, inscribed with the letters P.H.P (Presidency of the High Priesthood). The presidency of the local stake of Zion sat one tier down, in a pew labeled P.S.Z., and the presidencies of the high priests (P.H.Q.) and the elders (P.E.Q.) sat on the two lower tiers. The Aaronic Priesthood officers had seats behind a pulpit at the hall's west end, from the bishop and his counselors at the top (P.A.P., or Presidency of the Aaronic Priesthood), to the presidencies of the priests (P.P.Q.), teachers (P.T.Q.), and deacons quorums (P.D.Q.) below them.[46]

In Nauvoo, exterior architectural symbolism played an even greater distinguishing role. From a distance, Nauvoo's most important building impressed all who saw it. Closer by, a finely detailed architectural message confronted the viewer. Each of thirty pilasters had decorations that resembled no traditional Greek design. At the base, as directed by the Prophet, Weeks had placed a moon in quarter phase facing downward, with the image of a face carved into the curved edge. Capping each pilaster was a stone carved to resemble the face of a rising sun, with a second stone above it portraying a pair of hands holding trumpets. Above that, around the frieze, five-pointed stars appeared as a final decorative element.

The Prophet and his architect left no explanation for these symbols nor their meaning, but possible religious meanings are suggested by the scriptures and in explanations given for similar decorations used on the Salt Lake Temple. In a revelation in the book of Abraham, published in Nauvoo as the temple iconography was being worked out, God notes that just as the moon is above the earth and the sun above the moon in the heavens, so are the stars above the sun. This describes exactly the vertical placement of these heavenly symbols on the Nauvoo and the Salt Lake Temples. Likewise, the revelation continues, just as one person has a greater degree of glory and light than another, so God is above them all in these eternal qualities. If the symbols represent a religious people's search for truth beyond the horizon of present knowledge, this explanation turns a seeker's attention upward toward God and is tied to the temple's purpose as a house of learning and a house of glory.[47]

A millennial message can be found in the stones as well. The heavenly spheres remind the observer that God set these bodies in their orbits as guides to the times and seasons. The rising sun with trumpets above it represents God's final judgment at the sounding of the last trump, which will come at the dawning of the millennial day. The star at the top thus symbolizes Christ, who comes forth in judgment as "the bright and morning star."[48]

A restorationist interpretation is also possible for the sun stone, given that the weather vane of the temple depicted an angel carrying both a trumpet to sound the warning and a book of scripture to declare God's word. Similarly, the sun stone, with "the sun rising just above the clouds," above which appears another stone representing "two hands each holding a trumpet," would then suggest the concept of restoration after a long apostasy.[49] This theme is expressed in a popular Latter-day Saint hymn written in 1840:

> The morning breaks, the shadows flee;
> Lo, Zion's standard is unfurled!
> The dawning of a brighter day
> Majestic rises on the world.[50]

Whatever their intended meaning or meanings, the astronomical symbols on the Nauvoo Temple certainly were intended to point Latter-day Saints toward the sacred purposes of the House of the Lord and its role in offering salvation to a religious people in the last days.

To superintend Nauvoo's most important building project, church leaders appointed a trusted three-member committee. Reynolds Cahoon, Alpheus Cutler, and Elias Higbee accepted the onerous responsibility of managing men, materials, and money. Cahoon and Cutler, builders by trade who had worked on the Kirtland Temple, supervised construction. Higbee, a church recorder, kept books full time until a temple recorder in the office of the trustee replaced him. After Higbee's death from cholera in June 1843, Hyrum Smith became general overseer.

Securing materials was the committee's first task. Limestone existed in abundance not far north of the temple site. Similar stone had been used for other buildings in Commerce and Nauvoo, so it was an easy decision to open a quarry for the temple. Timber was another matter. Supplies to meet Nauvoo's ravenous appetite for lumber were being purchased at premium prices from as far away as twenty miles. The committee needed large quantities and found them at a reasonable cost in pine forests four hundred miles away in the Black River region of Wisconsin. Men recruited for timber missions in the north country harvested trees and cut them into logs for rafting down the river to Nauvoo. On site, Wandle Mace oversaw all framing inside the stone walls. He built simple cranes of shaped timbers to hoist the stones and timbers into place.[51]

George Miller headed the committee charged with getting lumber from Wisconsin, assisted by Lyman Wight, Alpheus Cutler, and Peter Haws. Over four winter seasons, 1841–45, forest crews harvested something like 1.5 million board feet of milled lumber and 200,000 shingles, plus hewed timbers, barn boards, and loose logs. One shipment of lumber included 170,000 board feet of sawed lumber (including shingles) which Miller said had been sawed in just two weeks. More than one hundred fifty men, many of them experienced in lumbering, worked in the pineries at various times to produce lumber for the temple and Nauvoo House. They were paid with provisions from a company store and given tithing and temple credit and Nauvoo House stock. The initial party got into production quickly by purchasing an existing Wisconsin operation from Jacob Spaulding, an Adams County, Illinois, mill builder.[52] One workman boasted that two saws in the small sawmill could cut ten thousand feet of lumber in twenty-four hours and that plans were to erect two more mills. The committee ultimately operated four sawmills and maintained six logging camps along a forty-mile section of the Black River. They succeeded in harvesting much-needed lumber at a substantial savings to the church.[53]

In the uncertainty following Joseph Smith's death, many Latter-day Saint workers left the pineries; the following spring, Miller sold the mills back to Spaulding. After that, Miller bought lumber for the temple and Nauvoo House from agents rafting timber down the river past Nauvoo. The temple committee spent nearly four thousand dollars for lumber during the spring of 1845 alone. Samuel Russell, a Latter-day Saint, became a major supplier for the flooring.[54]

Funding for the temple came from the tithes of members in all parts of the church. The Twelve defined this tithe as "one tenth of all anyone possessed at the commencement of the building, and one-tenth part of all his increase from that time until the completion" of the temple. Members paid with cash, groceries, personal belongings, pledges, land, and labor.[55]

Mary Fielding Smith used this small wooden box for the pennies donated by women of Nauvoo's Relief Society to buy nails and glass for the temple.

Cash tithing helped buy building materials and pay part of the salaries of employees. In-kind tithing likewise could be traded for supplies or labor in Nauvoo's barter economy.

In Kirtland, a few sisters had sewn clothes to help temple construction workers; a similar interest surfaced in Nauvoo.[56] In addition, women of the church created a special penny fund to buy glass and nails. When unnamed critics challenged this effort, Hyrum Smith defended the organizers, namely, his wife, Mary Fielding Smith, and her sister, Mercy Fielding Thompson. Hyrum promised contributors a first choice of seats in the finished temple's assembly hall. The attempt to encourage each sister to donate a penny every week yielded a thousand participants in Nauvoo, and they sought another thousand in Great Britain. The goal allowed even the poor to contribute toward the objective of fifty cents per person for the year, or a thousand dollars in all.[57]

Because members understood that their tithing was needed for the temple, many of them contributed directly to the temple committee. Committeeman Elias Higbee kept the records of tithing and donations and workers' time sheets. In December 1841, the First Presidency and the Twelve directed all tithing and additional consecrations to the church trustees, who then allocated needed resources to the temple committee. Joseph Smith served as trustee during his life and was replaced by presiding bishops Newel K. Whitney and George Miller. The tithes were recorded in the Book of the Law of the Lord, a journal kept for the Prophet by Willard Richards, who was temple recorder, and his assistant, William Clayton. After Clayton became the chief recorder in September 1842, he moved the office from Joseph Smith's store to the committee house near the temple and later into his own new brick office.[58]

Because of problems with the collection of tithing away from Nauvoo, church leaders certified authorized tithing collection agents. Members had been giving donations for the temple and the Nauvoo House to any missionary who came through, and some of the funds were apparently used for missionary support. The Twelve had been serving as the authorized agents since 1841, but others continued to serve informally as couriers. In April 1843, at Joseph Smith's request, the Twelve were bonded in this assignment, and all other persons specifically excluded.[59] This proved not to be a practical measure. After the martyrdom, trustees Whitney and Miller certified and bonded forty-three agents in other parts of the United States.[60] Using a similar rationale, one conference in England appointed a treasurer in each branch to receive temple contributions and a general treasurer for the entire conference.[61]

Tithing paid in goods included not just foodstuffs but livestock, clothing of all kinds, quilts, tablecloths, jewelry, firearms, watches, and other items.[62] To support themselves and their families, the hired workmen drew from this stock of goods or received credit slips redeemable at local stores or for books or subscriptions at the church printing office.[63] Shift supervisors certified the work completed to credit workers for their labor.[64] Merchants who accepted the temple scrip could redeem it for cash or goods or, more commonly, for credit on their own tithing at the temple recorder's office.

At times, provisions were scarce at the temple storeroom. On one occasion, the temple committee sent the stonecutters into nearby branches to preach on tithing; the people responded with wagonloads of goods for the temple. Another time, when the temple recorder ran short of needed meal, flour, and other provisions, he placed an advertisement in the Nauvoo newspaper appealing to members "to consecrate such [items] on their tithing." The recorder complained in 1843 that some local citizens were intercepting goods intended for the temple by offering to labor on the temple in exchange for the provisions.[65] Of less direct use to the temple committee were the donations in land and jewelry. It was necessary for the committee to convert these to cash or trade them for usable resources. One cumulative list of donations to the temple included deeds to thirty-five lots in Nauvoo; another showed city lots and farmland in Far West, Missouri.[66]

The donated time counted as a regular tithing in lieu of cash or goods. The temple committee created this system on February 22, 1841, to meet Joseph Smith's April 6 deadline for the cornerstone ceremony. By the following February, donated time was providing much of the needed labor. The men worked one day in ten as assigned through the special tithing wards created by the committee. The committee appointed an agent in each of the ten city and three country wards to track participation and report the hours worked.[67] When a man could not meet his assignment, he would sometimes write out a note for the labor, with a promise to work the tithed day later.[68] Latter-day Saint women met in sewing circles to make mittens, socks, and clothing for the workmen. Families boarded single laborers, sometimes by assignment of the temple committee but often voluntarily. Men living away from Nauvoo lent their teams for hauling or sent hay, grain, meat and provisions.[69] In one way or another, everyone could help build the temple.

This vast construction project depended mostly upon two sets of trades: first, the stonecutters and stonemasons responsible for the limestone walls, and second, the sawyers, woodworkers, and carpenters who built the interior framework and did the finish work. Contributing as well were other tradesmen, including plasterers, painters, glaziers, and tinsmiths. After quarrymen blasted the limestone out of the quarry and shaped it on site, the masons and their tenders laid up finely finished exterior courses and somewhat rougher interior stones. Similarly, the lumbermen shaped massive framing timbers and the boards needed for the interior wooden shell of the temple, after which the plasterers and fine craftsmen began their decorative work. Occasionally, hundreds of workmen at a time could be found employed on the project. Over the time of construction, the temple committee employed more than fifty men as stonecutters at the quarry, two dozen men to operate the cranes and set the stone walls, and three dozen carpenters. In addition to these employees, at least four men

Twelve wooden oxen, later replaced with stone, supported the font built in the basement of the temple. This 1849 woodcut approximates the shape of the font. The artist foreshortens the building's height but renders the windows and tower accurately.

were involved in painting the interiors. Others worked as contract tinsmiths and glaziers. Hundreds more contributed work as tithing laborers.[70]

From the groundbreaking in the fall of 1840 to the final public dedication on May 1, 1846, progress in constructing the temple did not follow a constant upward path.[71] Of most pressing need after the cornerstone laying was to complete the excavation, build the foundation walls, and install a temporary font for proxy baptisms for the dead. During the first summer, as the hewed portion of the basement walls rose, carpenters completed a font of pine tongue-and-groove staves near the east end of the basement level. The basin stood seven feet high and measured twelve feet by sixteen feet. Workers enclosed it in a temporary clapboard building low enough for the timbers of the first story to fit above it. They sunk a well at the east end of the temple thirty feet deep to supply water. Ornamental moldings made by Iowa high councilor Elijah Fordham decorated the font's cap and base. Fordham also carved twelve oxen out of pine plank glued together to project from the paneling around the base. Two weeks after Brigham Young dedicated it on November 8, 1841, the font was opened for use.[72]

Work on the walls of the first level began late in the spring of 1842. The inexperienced masons sorely needed a skilled master. He appeared in June in the person of English immigrant William N. Player. Under Player's supervision, crews worked steadily with one crane and consistently kept ahead of the stonecutters. By fall, they had the stones up four to twelve feet, sills installed in a few windows, and one course of stones on the base of the columns.[73] Construction work lagged during 1842 because of distractions caused by the Bennett excommunication, the Boggs shooting, and attempts to arrest Joseph Smith. On October 30, the Saints crowded onto a temporary plank floor laid through a communitywide effort especially for an open-air Sabbath meeting, the first held in the building. A conference met on the same floor the following April.[74]

During 1843, construction moved steadily but slowly after the crews fixed runways for the crane. Before winter set in, the stonemasons had arched over the first-floor windows. Brigham Young urged greater effort on the project. As an essential part of the work of the church, he said, "We must build a house, and get an endowment, preach the gospel, warn the people, gather the Saints, build up Zion, finish our work, and be prepared for the coming of Christ." A Nauvoo conference in October pledged to renew exertions in the spring by supplying teams, provisions, iron, steel, blasting powder, and clothing requested by the temple committee.[75]

At the beginning of 1844, an observer reported, "The Temple has made great progress; and strenuous efforts are now being made in quarrying, hauling, and hewing stone, to place it in a situation that the walls can go up and the building be enclosed by next fall." The Nauvoo House, designed by architect Lucien Woodworth, had not enjoyed such progress during 1843, but foundation stone and brick for the hotel had been prepared and stockpiled. Besides, two sawmills acquired in the Wisconsin pineries were now poised to furnish both buildings with the necessary lumber. A second construction crane erected in March promised a doubling of effort by stonemasons on the temple. The sisters in the La Harpe and Macedonia branches collected funds for a third crane in July. Shortly before the murders of Joseph and Hyrum Smith, masons set the blocks for the circular windows on the upper portion of the first story. After a three-week interruption, work resumed on July 8, even though "the committee had not so much as a bushel of meal nor a pound of flour, nor a pound of meat to feed the hands with."[76]

With new leaders confirmed in August, the Saints united behind the Twelve on the temple project. By late September, the stonemasons had finished raising the second-story stones and placed the first capital stones. Two months later, all thirty of the sun stones and all but twelve of the trumpet stones were in place. Two accidents with the cranes slowed the work temporarily: In one, a crane toppled while raising a sun stone. The committee dealt with another concern in the fall of 1844. Because of rumors of threats against the project, the committee posted policemen as guards for the lumber and the temple.[77]

The arrival of two large rafts of Wisconsin lumber early in July, totaling nearly 156,000 board feet, anticipated the work of carpenters inside the temple. To facilitate this work, the committee enclosed a shop in the main floor hall of the temple in December, hired fifteen steady carpenters to prepare the timber for use when the stonework was finished, and added three workers at the temple sawmill.[78]

After a winter recess, work resumed with energy. Upwards of two hundred masons and carpenters were at work on the temple, pushing it toward completion and beginning a wall around the site. In March, the project recorded its only fatality, a man killed by a falling stone while rocks were being blasted. Later that month, workmen edged the last trumpet stone into place. By the end of April, carpenters had completed framing the second level and were well underway installing floor joists. On Saturday, May 24, 1845, Brigham Young tapped the final piece of stone—the capstone—into place in a ceremony at the southeast corner. The event featured special band music composed for the occasion. It being the seventh day of the week, Brigham Young dismissed the crews in a symbolic day of rest. In July, one observer noted, "The steeple of the temple is some distance above the roof. . . . We hear the laborers sing and shout as they raise the timbers." When workers added the tinned dome to the top of the tower in August, they celebrated with a watermelon feast on the roof and hoisted a flag.[79]

As construction neared completion, the building committee sent a special delegate to Chicago to buy glass for the temple. It was only after significant delays that George P. Dykes was able to secure the order at the Michigan Glass Works in Ann Arbor and ship the panes by lake steamer

for Temple

An angel weather vane with gold leaf on the trumpet and perhaps on other elements was installed in January 1846. This design by William Weeks guided the work of the tinsmiths.

to Chicago and then in wagons overland to Nauvoo. Three yoke of oxen donated as tithing for the temple pulled the precious load.[80]

With the temple entirely enclosed and the windows in place, Brigham Young held a conference in the first-story hall in October 1845, using temporary floors, pulpits, and seats. At this meeting, he dedicated the building, "thus far completed, as a monument of the saints' liberality, fidelity, and faith."[81] The attic floor was already receiving priority. Initially designed for a dozen offices surrounding a large council chamber, the upper level was chosen by Brigham Young in January 1845 for the endowment ceremony. Logistically, this worked better than the original plan of doing the washings and anointings in rooms adjacent to the baptismal font and administering the endowment in the rooms in the half-story above the main floor hall.[82] As soon as the roof was on the temple in September, the interior rooms were finished.[83] Young dedicated the attic rooms on November 30 so that endowments could begin. Meanwhile, framers hastened their work in the main halls. Beginning in November, they tore up and replaced the temporary floor on the first story, and in late January 1846, they laid the floor in the second-story hall.[84] The fine moldings and other finish work on the second level were not completed because of the exodus from Nauvoo.

Rising above the temple to a height of 165 feet above ground was an octagonal wooden tower that added a finishing visual touch to the building. It also afforded visitors who climbed the stairway to the top a commanding view of the city. The architectural design called for a bell in the tower and four clocks. Wilford Woodruff raised money in England for the bell and one of the timepieces. Topping the dome was a prone-angel weathervane. The Nauvoo Tinners' Association invested twenty-four man days making the vane and another nine days on the balls and ornament for the spire. The angel was set in place on the morning of January 30, 1846. Perrigrine Sessions described the wind vane as "an angel in his priestly robes with a Book of Mormon in one hand and a trumpet in the other which is over laid with gold leaf."[85]

Assembling the furnishings for the temple, especially for the top story, involved the church community in ways that made the building their own. The assembly rooms needed no special furnishings beyond seating and the fabric-covered pulpits. Not so with the priesthood quorum offices and endowment rooms fitted out in the attic level. The quorums were assigned to collect donations for the carpets in their own offices and in the long central hall, or council chamber. They also collected donations to buy olive oil for the anointing ceremony, candles for light, food for temple workers, and paper for the recorder. The men and their wives gathered up mirrors and rugs. Other items were offered but not always accepted because of the generous offering of decorative items.[86]

The attic chamber was divided with canvas partitions for the various "sacred departments" of the endowment ceremony. Adjacent offices served as dressing rooms and for initiatory ordinances.[87] Brigham Young performed eternal marriages, or sealings, in his office in the southeast corner. Little adornment was required in the small creation, telestial, and terrestrial "rooms." The garden room featured a path winding among thirty potted shrubs and flowers and small boxed evergreen trees furnished by local members. The terrestrial room included a veil patterned after the one Joseph Smith had used for the initial endowment in the upper room of his store. The celestial room, the largest of the ordinance spaces at nearly twenty-nine feet square, was decorated like a sitting room, with two large central tables, four sofas, and several chairs. On the walls hung paintings, mirrors, a marble clock, maps of the United States and the world, and nearly two dozen portraits, including depictions of Hyrum Smith, Brigham Young, and other leaders and their wives. Members lent the wall hangings, including their portraits; Joseph Smith's oil portrait, retained by Emma, was noticeably absent. Two large world globes sat on a table in front of the arched east window, which spanned more than twenty feet.[88] The celestial room thus served both its initial purpose as a council chamber and as a special part of the House of the Lord. Those who decorated the temple made it as pleasant and peaceful a setting as possible for the concluding stage of a long-awaited learning experience for participants.

ORDINANCES IN THE LORD'S HOUSE

As each portion of the temple reached completion, the Saints put it to use. Baptism for the dead was the first of the temple ordinances introduced in Nauvoo. Space for proxy baptisms was the first to be dedicated in the temple, and thus attention of the local members focused initially on that ordinance. They listed the dead known to them, scanned family Bibles, and searched out family members with information. Many Saints in Nauvoo wrote to relatives seeking such data. Some explained the intended use, giving scriptural references; others did not.[89]

With the names of loved ones in hand, anxious members sought out the elders and underwent the ordinance. The first proxy baptisms took place in the Mississippi River in September 1840. "Some have already been baptised a number of times over," Vilate Kimball noted on October 11, one week after the general conference announcement inviting participation in the practice. "Since this order has been preached here," she informed her husband, Heber C. Kimball, a missionary in England, "the waters have been continually troubled. During conference there were sometimes from eight to ten Elders in the river at a time baptising." Vilate Kimball announced her intent to proceed immediately to be baptized for her mother.[90] Like other families who had lost family members, the Prophet's parents rejoiced in a doctrine and practice that gave hope for their son Alvin, who had died in 1823. The Prophet's ailing father encouraged him to be baptized for Alvin immediately.[91]

For more than a year, the Saints continued to be immersed in the river on behalf of dead relatives. On October 3, 1841, Joseph Smith halted proxy baptisms conducted outside the temple and declared that thereafter the only proper place for this heavenly ordinance on earth was in the subterranean font of the Lord's House.[92] Postponing the practice of baptisms for the dead shifted attention to the need to complete the temple. The delay was short. Six weeks later, a temporary wooden font was finished, and baptisms resumed. The privilege of using the font was granted only to those who had helped support temple construction by paying their tithing in full.[93] Tithe-paying later became one of the requirements for receiving the endowment.[94]

Although proxy baptisms represented temple-centered activities between 1840 and 1845, the Saints did not forget the promise that they would receive something for themselves in the House of the Lord—their endowments. The Prophet had taught them that the temple existed to bless the living as well as the dead. The 1841 revelation on the temple promised "to restore again that which was lost" (which is followed by a description of baptism for the dead and a mention of anointings and washings, among other things) and "to reveal unto my church things which have been kept hid from before the foundation of the world" pertinent to the last days.[95] Until the Nauvoo years, most ritual in the church followed general Christian practice. The sacrament with its symbolism of bread and wine existed commonly among Christian churches, as did baptism by water in various forms. Ordinations and confirmations by the laying on of hands as a symbol of conferral of blessings or authority existed in a few other churches.[96]

In the House of the Lord at Kirtland, the elders preparing for missionary service had received a ritual cleansing and anointing called an endowment. Certain preparations were expected of them: to be morally clean and faithful, to strive for unison and harmony, and to avoid criticizing others. If worthy, they were promised an outpouring of wisdom and knowledge and the ability to overcome weaknesses, heal the faithful, seal up the law, and gather the Saints.[97] The minutes of one quorum notes: "Met to proceed with the anointing of the elders of the Most High. . . . The first presidency came and sealed our anointing by prayer and shout of Hosanna."[98] A member of the Kirtland High Council reported participating with this council and in a later anointing and endowment in the temple.[99]

But the endowment meant more than this to those involved. During the Kirtland Temple dedication, a number of participants experienced a feeling like that of a rushing of wind reminiscent of the New Testament report of the Day of Pentecost. As part of this religious euphoria, some of the Saints had spiritual experiences such as speaking in tongues or seeing heavenly beings.[100] It was during the week of dedication that Joseph Smith and Oliver Cowdery witnessed appearances of Jesus, Moses, Elias, and Elijah above the pulpits of the temple and received special priesthood authority from them. These visits, recorded in Doctrine and Covenants 110, had profound influence on the development of Nauvoo's temple theology. Joseph Smith told nine members of the Twelve, "It is calculated to unite our hearts, that we may be one in feeling and sentiment and that our faith may be strong, so that Satan cannot over throw us, nor have any power over us." To prepare for this endowment, he advised,

> Be faithful in all things . . . and we must be clean every whit. . . . Do not watch for iniquity in each other. If you do you will not get an endowment, for God will not bestow it on such. . . . You need an endowment brethren in order that you may be prepared and able to overcome all things. . . . The Saints will be gathered out from among them [the nations] and stand in holy places ready to meet the bride groom when he comes.[101]

From these teachings and his dedicatory prayer upon the completed temple in Kirtland, it was clear that Latter-day Saint temples would be places of sacred ordinances, worship, manifestations, and learning.[102]

Between the completion of the Kirtland Temple in March 1836 and his death at Nauvoo in June eight years later, the Prophet expanded the meaning of the endowment. He did not explain entirely his own revelatory learning process. Nor did he say what happened or even when it happened to expand his understanding of the "ancient things" and the "hidden things" that the last dispensation would receive. By May 1842, he began to introduce to others that which had been revealed to him—an endowment beyond the one shared in the House of the Lord in Ohio.

A published suggestion that a transformation of meaning was underway appeared in the March and May 1842 issues of the *Times and Seasons* after Joseph Smith took over as editor. In these issues of the church paper, he published the text of the book of Abraham, an autobiographical account of Abraham's experiences in Egypt, together with three facsimiles from Egyptian papyri acquired in Kirtland in 1835. In his explanation to Facsimile No. 2, Joseph Smith said of one cluster of symbols: "[It] contains writing that cannot be revealed unto the world; but is to be had in the Holy Temple of God." As he sought revelation to understand the religious meaning of the Egyptian papyri, it is possible that the Prophet received a revelatory understanding also of the teachings presented as the endowment.[103] According to one scholar,

> studies of Egyptian temple ritual since the time of Joseph Smith have revealed parallels with Latter-day Saint temple celebrations and doctrine, including a portrayal of the creation and fall of mankind, washings and anointings, and the ultimate return of individuals to God's presence. Moreover, husband, wife, and children are sealed together for eternity, genealogy is taken seriously; people will be judged according to their deeds in this life, and the reward for a just life is to live in the presence of God forever with one's family. It seems unreasonable to suggest that all such parallels occurred by mere chance.[104]

This explanation satisfies Joseph Smith's revelatory promise of a linking of both "ancient things" and "things which have been kept hid from before the foundation of the world."[105]

Joseph Smith first shared these sacred things with others in early May 1842, just as the *Times and Seasons* completed its publication of the book of Abraham. The Prophet invited to the upper room of his store a small group of friends and there introduced to them a ceremonial washing and anointing broader in its symbolic references than the ordinance used in Kirtland. Beginning in December 1845, scores of worthy Saints in Nauvoo received the endowment. It consisted of the ordinances of washing and anointing, followed by instructions and covenants setting forth a pattern or figurative model for life. The teachings began with a recital of the creation of the earth and its preparation to host life. The story carried the familiar ring of the Genesis account, echoed as well in Joseph Smith's revealed book of Moses and book of Abraham. The disobedience and expulsion of Adam and Eve from the Garden of Eden set the stage for an explanation of Christ's atonement for that original transgression and for the sins of the entire human family. Also included was a recital of

The first endowments were given in the upper room of Joseph Smith's store in 1842. In that same room, the Relief Society was organized and church and municipal councils met. A small room at the back served as President Smith's office and translation room.

mankind's tendency to stray from the truth through apostasy and the need for apostolic authority to administer authoritative ordinances and teach true gospel principles. Participants were reminded that in addition to the Savior's redemptive gift they must be obedient to God's commandments to obtain a celestial glory. Within the context of these gospel instructions, the initiates made covenants of personal virtue and benevolence and of commitment to the church. They agreed to devote their talents and means to spread the gospel, to strengthen the church, and to prepare the earth for the return of Jesus Christ.[106] Through personal promises to their Heavenly Father made in the Nauvoo Temple, the Saints expanded the meaning of being a covenant people.

Those first endowed on Wednesday and Thursday, May 4–5, 1842, included Joseph Smith and nine other church leaders.[107] In a day-long series of instructions "in the principles and order of the priesthood," Joseph and Hyrum Smith administered "washings, anointings, endowments and the communication of keys pertaining to the Aaronic Priesthood, and so on to the highest order of the Melchisedek Priesthood," outlining what the candidates must do to "come up and abide in the presence of the Eloheim in the eternal worlds." "In this council," Joseph Smith's history notes, "was instituted the ancient order of things for the first time in these last days." On the following day, the group met and administered the same sacred ordinances to Joseph and Hyrum Smith.[108]

Most of this same group and a few others met again in the upper room of President Smith's store more than a year later, on Friday, May 26, 1843. The report of that council says the Prophet gave them "instructions on the Priesthood, the new and everlasting covenant, &c. &c." Specifically, the men were informed about the covenant of celestial marriage.[109] In two subsequent meetings, on Sunday and Monday, May 28–29, a reduced group met again with the Prophet to attend to ordinances and to receive instructions "concerning the things of God." On these dates, several couples received the marriage sealing ordinance, among them, on the 28th, Joseph and Emma Smith.[110]

Those receiving these ordinances remembered the Prophet's concerns. First, he wanted others to receive the ordinances even before the temple was finished. More importantly, he was anxious to authorize the Twelve to administer the blessings to others should his own life be cut short before the temple was ready. During the winter of 1843–44, Joseph Smith conversed with the Twelve regularly about the temple and priesthood ordinances. In late March 1844, after conferring the keys of the sealing ordinances on their quorum president, the Prophet told the Twelve, "I roll the burthen and responsibility of leading this Church off from my shoulders on to yours . . . for the Lord is going to let me rest a while." This and other similar comments convinced the Twelve that they were the proper administrators of the kingdom after the Prophet's death. They held the office next in succession and, when activated by his death, the priesthood authority necessary to administer all the ordinances of exaltation.[111]

At least twenty couples, including the nine members of the Twelve who had served faithfully together in England, received another temple blessing prior to the Prophet's death. All of the recipients had already received the ordinances of the endowment and marriage for time and eternity, or what Joseph Smith called Abraham's patriarchal priesthood. The keys to this priesthood had been conferred upon Joseph Smith and Oliver Cowdery in the Kirtland Temple in 1836. They would now receive the crowning ordinance of the fulness of the Melchizedek Priesthood.[112] "For any person to have the fullness of that priesthood, he must be a king and priest," Brigham Young told an audience in Philadelphia on August 6. "A person may be anointed king and priest long before he receives his kingdom." In a public sermon in Nauvoo three weeks later, Joseph Smith explained this sacred ordinance that he was about to bestow on a select few before completion of the temple. It was, he said, a promise of kingly powers and of endless lives. It was the confirmation of promises that worthy men could become kings and priests and that women could become queens and priestesses in the eternal worlds. In its administrative aspects, he said, this leadership calling was "a perfect law of Theocracy holding keys of power and blessings . . . to give laws to the people."[113]

The administration of the endowment to the general adult membership began soon after the completion and dedication of a fully furnished space in the attic council chamber of the Nauvoo Temple. Completion of the temple was a step anxiously anticipated by the Latter-day Saints. "It is a matter here that engages the most of our attention," a resident of nearby Montebello wrote to relatives in New York. "And it will be a great privilege to be at or near Nauvoo."[114] The ordinance work began on December 10, 1845, and continued just short of two months, ceasing early on February 7, three days after the exodus began. One by one, groups known as companies entered the temple for the ceremony. By the end of December, one thousand had been endowed. In all, more than five thousand individuals experienced this new sacred rite, clothed in their "white temple robes symbolizing purity and the equality of all persons before God."[115] Designated church authorities and their wives, together with others, guided the recipients through the ritual, using a variety of teaching techniques—lectures, representations, and symbols. Brigham Young and other members of the Twelve directed the work and personally participated in the various sessions, with the wives of church leaders overseeing the initiatory ordinances for women.[116]

Invited next into the temple, to fulfill a promise of priority by Joseph Smith, were full-time construction workers. Most of the other endowment companies during December were organized by priesthood quorums and quorum members' wives, certified as worthy by their quorum presidencies. All who entered the temple were expected to be physically, morally, and spiritually clean. The same standards taught in Kirtland were used in Nauvoo. Candidates for the ordinances were expected to bathe before entering the temple and to arrive in a spirit of fasting and prayer.[117] Unlike the proxy baptisms for the dead performed in the temple, the endowments administered in Nauvoo pertained only to the living recipient. Not until 1877, in the temple at St. George, Utah, were members permitted to participate as proxies in endowing deceased ancestors.[118]

Another ordinance introduced to members in the Nauvoo Temple was that of sealing of couples in a marriage lasting beyond the grave and into the eternities. As with the endowment, Joseph Smith introduced this ordinance to a few people in May 1843, performed the marriages, and conveyed the sealing authority to the Twelve. In the Nauvoo Temple, couples previously wed "until death" received this covenant of eternal marriage at an altar in Brigham Young's office adjacent to the celestial room. The marriage altar featured a simple padded ledge of scarlet damask cloth on each side for kneeling and a central riser covered on its sides with white linen. Across the top of the altar, finished with scarlet cloth, the couple faced and joined hands in a token of unity with one another and with God.[119]

Brigham Young performed the first marriage in the temple on January 1, 1846, uniting in matrimony a temple stonemason's helper, Truman Leonard, and his fiancée, Ortentia White. Between January 7 and February 5, 1846, a few others were newly married, and dozens more expanded their original vows to an eternal commitment. During that same period, authorities performed a few proxy sealings of couples and some sealings of children to parents, both of the living and the dead. The sealing ordinance between parents and children created an eternal family unit linking one generation to another. It was yet another aspect of the Latter-day Saint view of the eternity of the family.[120]

The sealing ordinances rested upon a doctrinal understanding taught in a limited way by Joseph Smith from the earliest days of the church. At Kirtland, he and other elders performed marriages as would any ordained minister of religion. They used a ceremony prescribed in a statement on marriage adopted by an August 1835 general conference and included in the Doctrine and Covenants published that fall. The statement accepted as valid all existing marriages performed under civil law. In keeping with traditional patterns, the ceremony offered only a "covenant to be each others companions through life."[121]

At least from the mid-1830s, some Latter-day Saints privately speculated that a marriage under priesthood authority might extend beyond the grave. They understood marriage as a sacramental covenant first instituted

A carved stone featuring trumpets and the rising sun topped each of the thirty pilasters. This combination was the most prominent of the symbolic images on the Nauvoo Temple.

in the garden of Eden. Therefore, when their own marriage was "solemnized by the authority of the everlasting priesthood" it was sanctified "after the order of heaven." Joseph Smith concluded one ceremony with the bestowal of "the blessings of Abraham Isaac and Jacob and such other blessings as the Lord put into my heart."[122] Despite some limited talk of a marriage union for eternity, the church before settlement in Nauvoo did not administer that promise.

The doctrinal foundations of this religious view of marriage had its foundation in the Prophet's revision of the Bible at Kirtland. A revelation given in February 1831 commanded, "Thou shalt ask, and my scriptures shall be given as I have appointed."[123] Within weeks, Joseph Smith began an intensive study of the Bible. Very quickly that effort became a tutorial experience, for as he pondered the scriptures and asked the Lord, new understandings were revealed. It was then that he began to teach the idea of a priesthood-centered marriage covenant, its precedent being the marriage of Adam and Eve performed by God himself.[124]

In the newly dedicated Kirtland Temple in April 1836, Joseph Smith and Oliver Cowdery received a bestowal of keys from heavenly beings, among them the ancient prophets Elias and Elijah. The authority restored by these messengers opened the door to the saving ordinance of baptism and the exalting ordinance of eternal marriage, both received through priesthood authority.[125] In Nauvoo, Joseph Smith began to share with the Saints those things he had learned through revelation concerning God's covenant with Abraham and his seed and of Elijah's turning of the hearts of generations. Under the new and everlasting covenant of marriage, both marriage and procreation would continue without end for those worthy of a celestial glory.[126]

The essence of these teachings was embodied in a revelation that had been unfolding for more than a decade. Components of the revelation were committed to writing on July 12, 1843. The central focus was the principle of eternal marriage. Later published as Doctrine and Covenants 132, the revelation explained that Elijah's key was the same binding power given by Christ to Peter. Among other uses, this authority solemnized marriages with an eternal potential and bound generations together in a perpetual chain of families.[127]

Of this sealing power, the revelation said: "For I have conferred upon you the keys and power of the priesthood, wherein I restore all things . . . that whatsoever you seal on earth shall be sealed in heaven; and whatso- ever you bind on earth, in my name and by my word, saith the Lord, it shall be eternally bound in the heavens." The keys—that is, the authority to regulate the use of the sealing power—resided with the president of the church. (Joseph Smith conferred these keys on Brigham Young and the other members of the Twelve in late March 1844. Young's latent authority to sanction marriages would become active as the senior member and president of the Twelve only after Joseph Smith's death.)[128]

The sealing power had other implications beyond that of joining a man and a woman in eternal matrimony and of sealing their children to them. For a time in the 1840s (and again in the 1880s), adult men whose living parents were not members could be sealed to a substitute father under the law of adoption. Three-fourths of the Nauvoo adoptions involved sons who chose an apostle as a substitute parent in order to ensure a worthy lineage for him and his family. Occasionally, a woman was adopted by her husband's adopted father. A revelation to Wilford Woodruff in 1894 ended these sporadic adoptive sealings. Thereafter, nat- ural genealogical lines became the ideal sealing line for all Latter-day Saints. Woodruff and his associates reassured members that most of their ancestors would accept the gospel in the spirit world, and if they did not, adjustments in the sealing line could be resolved in the hereafter.[129]

As the flood of emigrants ferried their loaded wagons westward across the Mississippi in early February 1846, Brigham Young attempted to bring the administration of ordinances to a halt. Anxious to leave, he announced a cessation of the endowments and sealings. "I walked some distance from the Temple supposing the crowd would disperse," his history records on February 3, "but on returning I found the house filled to overflowing." The work continued for a few days so that hundreds more could receive the promised blessings. On Sunday, the eighth, after the work ended, Young met with the Twelve in the southeast corner room in the upper level. "We knelt around the altar," he explained, "and dedicated the building to the Most High. We asked his blessing upon our intended move to the west; also asked him to enable us some day to finish the Temple, and dedicate it to him, and we would leave it in his hands to do as he pleased; and to preserve the building as a monument to Joseph Smith. We asked the Lord to accept the labours of his servants in this land. We then left the Temple."[130]

This benediction upon an unfinished temple in Brigham Young's office did not end the effort to complete it. Even as the migration picked up speed, workmen heightened their efforts to perfect their monument to the founding prophet. With a few present on the evening of April 30, Joseph Young pronounced an official dedicatory prayer. The following day, residents paid one dollar to attend a public dedication. Funds thus collected paid the hands employed in the finishing work. Elder Orson Hyde pronounced the prayer.[131] In a spirit of jubilant celebration, the Saints concluded the sacred assembly with a ceremonial shout of praise to God, "Hosannah, Hosannah, Hosannah, To God and the Lamb," spoken three times and concluded with a triple "Amen." Based upon the plea "Hosanna," translated "Save now" in Psalm 118, it echoed for the Latter-day Saints the psalmist's praise for the Messiah's gift of salvation.[132]

Their conversion to the church had given the Latter-day Saints a hope of salvation through Christ. The ordinances of the Nauvoo Temple unmistakably confirmed that hope. The Saints believed that if they endured in righteousness, they now had an assurance that they would enter into the presence of God and enjoy the same relationships with spouses and children that had brought them joy in earth life. Through the ordinances of the restored gospel, they had emphatically defined themselves as a covenant people, a sacred family of families.

TIMES AND SEASONS.

CITY OF NAUVOO,

SATURDAY, JUNE 1, 1844

FOR PRESIDENT,

GEN. JOSEPH SMITH,

NAUVOO, ILLINOIS.

FOR VICE PRESIDENT,

Sidney Rigdon, Esq:

OF PENNSYLVANIA.

PART III

CHALLENGES TO THE CITY BEAUTIFUL: FAILED PROMISES OF PEACE

The reason why we do not live in peace is because we are not prepared for it. We are tempted and tried, driven, mobbed, and robbed; apostates are in our midst, which causes trouble and vexation of spirit, and it is all to keep down our pride and learn us to honor the God of Jacob in all things and to make us appear what we really are. The gospel turns us inside out and makes manifest every good and every evil way. . . . It is necessary that we should be tried and kicked, and cuffed, and twisted round, that we may learn obedience by the things we suffer. . . . I am glad to see people in trouble when I know that it is for their salvation. . . . I pray that I may . . . act all the time with reference to eternity. . . . Persecution is for our good, and if we have hard things to endure let us round up our shoulders and bear them in the name of the Lord, and not murmur.

—FROM AN ADDRESS BY JOHN TAYLOR, JULY 6, 1845

CHAPTER 11

Patriots and Prophets

The patriots of this country . . . stood up in defence of their rights, liberty, and freedom; but where are now those principles of freedom? . . . What say ye, ye saints, ye who are exiles in the land of LIBERTY. How came you here? Can you in this land of equal rights return in safety to your possessions in Missouri? No!—You are exiles from thence, and there is no power, no voice, no arm to redress your grievances.

—JOHN TAYLOR, APRIL 5, 1844

Latter-day Saints during the Nauvoo years held beliefs about government and politics defined by their own Anglo-American orientation and in even more significant ways by their religious worldview. As American citizens, they resonated with the issues of the day. They joined with others in the 1830s and 40s in a heady zealousness for grassroots participation in government. The old political parties of colonial days had faded with independence, and a new generation of patriots rushed to reorder loyalties. Following the election of 1828, the Democratic Party of Andrew Jackson emerged; an opposition party, the Whigs, took shape about 1832. These loose coalitions embodied no clear consensus in political questions. Rather, they represented an emerging redefinition of purposes for a young nation. Voters during these years were divided nearly evenly in national elections. Locally, many of the parties advocated regional issues different from those of the national leaders. In every election, candidates sought earnestly to attract a volatile electorate.[1]

This was true in western Illinois, where the rapid influx of Latter-day Saints added an urgency to the democratic process of republican representation. Whigs and Democrats alike courted the Latter-day Saint vote. Because of their numbers, the Saints soon exercised a decisive influence in Hancock County. The use of that political influence was one factor creating tension and eventual conflict. Ultimately, circumstances led to the forcibly negotiated removal of the Latter-day Saints from their chosen place of refuge.

Another factor in this tension during the Nauvoo years was the multi-faceted relationship of the Latter-day Saints with the United States government and its leaders. Their religious beliefs clearly supported constitutional government and encouraged support for constituted leaders. At the same time, their millennial orientation anticipated a future theocratic government following the Second Coming, and their experiences had taught them to distrust many elected and appointed officials. In attempting to resolve these tensions in their loyalties to God and country, the Latter-day Saints coalesced around their religious priorities. Their opponents saw this as a clear denunciation of the American way and justification for a strident opposition.[2]

AMERICAN GOVERNMENT AND THE MILLENNIAL KINGDOM

Latter-day Saint patriotism was based on certain fundamental premises about government and those who governed. In both discourse and written revelation, Joseph Smith frequently endorsed the Constitution of the United States. His position emerged during the difficult self-assessment after the expulsion from Jackson County. The Prophet declared by revelation in 1833 that the Lord had "established the Constitution of this land, by the hands of wise men" in order to ensure the moral agency and rights of the people.[3] He counseled the Saints to be patient in affliction and to support "the constitutional law of the land." At the same time, the Lord condemned bad law and bad leaders and set forth a precept that became a cardinal principle in Latter-day Saint attitudes toward government:

> I, the Lord God, make you free, therefore ye are free indeed; and the law also maketh you free. Nevertheless, when the wicked rule the people mourn. Wherefore, honest men and wise men should be

sought for diligently, and good men and wise men ye should observe to uphold; otherwise whatsoever is less than these cometh of evil.[4]

It was their attempts to identify "good men and wise men" for office that created problems for the Saints. Inevitably, the candidates who qualified under that rule were Latter-day Saints themselves or citizens so friendly to the church that antagonists classified them as Mormon sympathizers, or in popular parlance, Jack-Mormons.[5]

The Book of Mormon laid the groundwork for Latter-day Saint beliefs that rulers should be righteous and willing to sustain the right to religious freedom. Joseph Smith's statement of faith in 1838 summarized the Saints' willingness to render unto Caesar all that was due him and to be supportive subjects of kings, presidents, rulers, or magistrates.[6] But through their experiences in Missouri and Illinois, many Saints lost faith in government officials at all levels. At the same time, their neighbors questioned the possibility that Mormons could be loyal to both constitutional principles and to an influential religious leader.

Church leaders during the Ohio-Missouri years had tried to define for their neighbors a clear position on political questions. The "Declaration of Belief" canonized by the general conference of August 1835 reaffirmed the common American belief that government is instituted of God to protect citizens' rights. Additionally, the proviso called for the equitable administration of laws by government officers and required the Saints to sustain and uphold the law or suffer legal consequences. It claimed the right for citizens to seek redress for wrongs but only under the provisions of law. One other point remained pertinent during the 1840s. The declaration noted, "We do not believe it just to mingle religious influence with civil government, whereby one religious society is fostered and another proscribed in its spiritual privileges."[7]

Overall, the 1835 statement seemed to place the Latter-day Saints squarely in line with contemporary American feelings. It agreed with Missourians in part on one controversial issue by promising that missionaries would not interfere with slaves. But during the Nauvoo years a broader issue worried American observers of the new Latter-day Saint faith. The Saints believed in an ultimate end to all governments and religious systems. This they expected when Jesus Christ returned in glory to rule as King of kings. Many Latter-day Saints found evidence of the imminent end of secular governments when federal officials refused to help them redeem their properties in Missouri. They found it as well in the failure of U.S. policy to help Native Americans achieve their full human potential.[8] Nations were in turmoil and peoples were at war. The great nations of world history, John Taylor wrote, "had in themselves the seeds of destruction, and were destined to decay. We are laying the foundation of a kingdom that shall last forever—that shall bloom in time and blossom in eternity."[9]

These views reflected a common belief in the church that the blooming of Christ's millennial reign would require all earthly organizations to observe His principles of civil peace. According to William W. Phelps, Christ's kingdom would be "the great leveling machine of creeds, constitutions, kingdoms, countries, divisions, notions, notorieties and novelties." Latter-day Saints found the seeds of that leveling in the church established by God through his prophet, Joseph Smith. As Eliza R. Snow wrote in an 1839 letter, "The Lord has commenc'd a work that is destin'd to try the *sincerity* and the *strength,* yes, and the *legality* too, of every Creed and Profession, both political and religious, upon the face of the whole earth."[10]

For those listening to but not believing in this millennial forecast, these claims created concern. When the Latter-day Saints began to proclaim themselves as the rightful heirs of the paradisiacal earth and their unrepentant neighbors as the wicked who were threatened in scripture with destruction, the "wicked" living nearby saw Latter-day Saint religious claims as a threat to their own rights to life, liberty, and property. Some whom the Saints designated as "gentiles" believed that Joseph Smith had set forth a treasonous plan to overthrow civil government by one means or another and to assume control.

Latter-day Saints believed they should prepare for the Millennium by warning the nations and gathering out the righteous. The revelation to Joseph Smith about the Nauvoo Temple in January 1841 enjoined the church to proclaim the gospel not just to ordinary citizens but also to the monarchs and elected rulers of the world and then to invite them to Zion, to be hosted in comfort at the Nauvoo House. In the spirit of this admonition, Parley P. Pratt drafted and published later that year *A Letter to the Queen of England, Touching the Signs of the Times, and the Political Destiny of the World.* Declaring "that the world in which we live is on the eve of a

Military titles were commonly used by public figures in the 1840s. The detail (left) is from a full-figure watercolor created for use on the Map of the City of Nauvoo. The red wax seal was used on a letter to the Prophet from New York friend James Arlington Bennet.

revolution . . . on which the fate of all nations is suspended," Pratt interpreted Nebuchadnezzer's dream of the great image (representing the worldly governments) as a prophecy of the destruction of modern nations. "The government of England is one of the toes of this image," he wrote. When a stone "cut out of the mountain without hands" rolls forth to smash the image, he continued, quoting Daniel, "'The Saints of the Most High shall take the kingdom, and possess the kingdom forever.'" Pratt concluded that this new kingdom would be established over the whole earth only with the personal advent of the Messiah, who would come "with power and great glory." Pratt invited Queen Victoria to hearken to the message and enjoy the blessings of the Lord's new kingdom. If she did not, she would "be overthrown with the wicked, and perish from the earth."[11]

No record survives of the British monarch's reaction to this religious tract, nor even whether she saw a copy. Some of those who read one of the six thousand copies published in Manchester (or others issued soon afterward in New York) accepted the arguments. Others ignored the proclamation as another radical religious tract or found in it evidence of Mormon political disloyalty. However intended, declarations such as this defined the Mormons in some minds as revolutionaries. Latter-day Saints, however, distinguished between this enduring millennial loyalty and their patriotism and support for constituted government. Yet even though they were not out to destroy governments, their religious message clearly had political implications. As Sidney Rigdon explained it in April 1844,

> When God sets up a system of salvation, he sets up a system of government; when I speak of a government I mean what I say; I mean a government that shall rule over temporal and spiritual affairs. . . . The law of God is far more righteous than the laws of the land. . . . The kingdom of God does not interfere with the laws of the land, but keeps itself by its own laws.[12]

Revelations and millennial beliefs such as this encouraged political isolationism. These ideas fostered both a sincere reverence for the American Constitution and a skepticism toward government and its leaders. Eliza R. Snow celebrated the patriotism and revealed the tension of estrangement in a poem that begins in an expression typical of Latter-day Saint statements about their political heritage:

> *I love the land with banner spread*
> *And waving gloriously—*
> *The country where our fathers bled*
> *To purchase Liberty.*

Then, after ranging around the world through eleven verses exploring the superstitions and bigotry, the imperialism and mysterious cultures of other peoples, the poet returns, via "Europe's prouder standards," to America:

> *But O I find no country yet,*
> *Like our Columbia dear;*
> *And often times, ALMOST, forget*
> *I LIVE AN EXILE HERE.*[13]

This last sentiment, a pointed contradiction to the national pride outlined throughout the poem, reverberated through much of the political discourse among Latter-day Saints during the Nauvoo years. A sense of alienation appeared especially whenever the question of "redeeming Zion" surfaced. The Saints could not easily forget their treasured millennial gathering place in Missouri. As one of them put it in 1842:

> *Many a time we there did meet;*
> *Many a friend we there did greet.*
> *Now our friends are scattered from*
> *The sacred place they called their home.*
> *Still on Zion's flowery plain*
> *We all hope to meet again.*[14]

THE MISSOURI QUESTION

Demonstrating their support of legally constituted government, the Latter-day Saints in Missouri had consistently appealed through legal channels. They had done so to redress their loss of property in Zion, to secure release from county jails, and to hold their oppressors responsible for the wrongs committed. The process continued for five years after their removal to Illinois, with sporadic efforts after that.[15] Following Sidney Rigdon's lead and encouraged by Joseph Smith, the Saints compiled nearly eight hundred affidavits enumerating their claims. These, together with petitions to Congress in 1843 and 1844, consumed an enormous amount of time and money during Nauvoo's first years.[16] This effort demonstrated the intensity of their feeling, both for the principles of government under which they lived, and their feelings of frustration at being denied their promised land in Missouri.[17] Justice for themselves and for all others was an important theme in Nauvoo; within a year of its creation, the city had adopted a seal featuring the scales of justice. It was a fitting symbol for Latter-day Saint efforts to redress the wrongs incurred in Missouri and to govern justly in Illinois.[18]

The initial affidavits sought compensation for the loss of life, health, houses and farms, personal belongings, foodstuffs, and crops destroyed or abandoned in the forced moves in Missouri between 1833 and 1838. Submitted to Congress in 1839–40, this request included bills from 481 individuals against Missouri and a twenty-eight-page memorial signed by Joseph Smith, Sidney Rigdon, and Elias Higbee. In late October, these men and Orrin P. Rockwell left in a two-horse carriage for Washington, where the Prophet and Higbee met with President Martin Van Buren, Senator John C. Calhoun, and others. Even though President Van Buren sympathized with Mormon sufferings, his desire not to offend the Missouri electorate disappointed the exiled Saints. Joseph Smith reported Van Buren's words: "What can I do? I can do nothing for you! If I do anything, I shall come in contact with the whole state of Missouri."[19] The Senate Judiciary Committee considered and rejected the redress petition in March 1840.

Joseph Smith was himself willing to try only once for compensation at the seat of government.[20] In 1842, a second delegation went to Washington without him to appeal before the House of Representatives. This party carried a fresh copy of the lengthy 1840 memorial, signed this time by Elias Higbee, John Taylor, and Elias Smith, and dated January 10, 1842. Petitions, letters, and affidavits chronicling the abuses and depredations suffered by at least 229 individuals accompanied the memorial.[21] Also submitted for review were three published reports. Two were pamphlets by Latter-day Saint writers explaining the expulsion; the other was one issued by the Missouri General Assembly in 1841.[22] Missionaries had flooded the country with these pamphlets and newspaper articles in an attempt to influence public opinion.[23] As before, the delegates found congressional committees unwilling to endorse the redress bill.

A final effort in the spring of 1844 consisted of a three-page memorial presented in Washington by Orson Pratt, John E. Page, and Orson Hyde. The delegates offered to accept land outside United States boundaries in Texas, Iowa, or elsewhere if Congress declined to restore the abandoned Missouri property.[24] The signatures of 3,419 Nauvoo residents, not all of them Missouri exiles, extended this mass solicitation to a fifty-foot petition. Even this appeal to numbers and the support of such western congressmen as Stephen A. Douglas and John Wentworth failed to convince federal officials that they should, or could, act. In all, the financial claims against Missouri amounted to nearly $2.4 million in more than eight hundred petitions from nearly seven hundred individuals.[25]

In the individual claims, the petitioners tallied their losses or described their sufferings. For example, in a typical bill of damages, Andrew Moore's September 1839 claim asks for $2,933, itemized to include losses of town lots and farmland, crops, livestock, firearms, and travel expenses. Moore claimed twenty dollars for loss of time in being held under guard unlawfully for six days. Along with many others, he filed for a thousand dollars in damages for being expelled from Missouri "without any just cause or provocation." The petitioners frequently reminded Congress that their claims, though large, fell short of compensating them for their suffering. Lewis Abbot wrote, "I think the State had ought to pay me for my loss $1,500 at least, and for my damage a great sum, as money would not hire me to pass through the same scenes again."[26]

Though friendly to the Constitution of the United States and its laws, many Latter-day Saints felt rejected by the free nation established through the courage and blood of their ancestors. Patriots had defended their rights, John Taylor told a Nauvoo congregation, but liberty and freedom were denied the Saints in the expulsion from Missouri. They had become "exiles in the land of LIBERTY."[27]

Ultimately, when the appeals to judges, Congress, the country's president, and the American people yielded unsatisfying responses, the Latter-day Saints left the matter in the hands of God. The report of the Washington delegation to a general conference in April 1840 led the Saints to encourage further legal efforts, but, even then, a resolution anticipated failure. "If all hopes of obtaining satisfaction (for the injuries done us) be entirely blasted," the resolution read, the delegates should "appeal our case to the court of Heaven" for eventual resolution.[28]

Although they saw themselves as friends of the law, the exiled Latter-day Saints were wary of the way elected officials applied the law. Church members manifested no greater outrage during the Nauvoo years than against those who made four attempts to arrest Joseph Smith in his place of legal refuge in Illinois so they could extradite him to Missouri.[29]

The first attempts in 1840 and 1841 stemmed from the Prophet's original arrest for treason, murder, and robbery and his incarceration at Liberty Jail in 1838. Missouri's new Democratic governor, Thomas Reynolds, who succeeded Governor Lilburn Boggs in 1840, signed the first extradition order in September of that year. Church officials may have unwittingly invited the action. In their redress appeal to Congress a few months earlier, they had argued that Missouri's failure to seek extradition proved the falsity of the 1838 charges. Illinois governor Thomas Carlin, also a Democrat, invited the Hancock County sheriff to arrest Joseph Smith and five others under the Reynolds order as fugitives from justice.

Joseph Smith preaching to the Indians. Some Missouri residents feared that the Latter-day Saints were interested not just in preaching to the Indians but in enlisting them in a militia attack on the old settlers. This image reflects visits to Nauvoo by Sauk and Fox Indians from Iowa.

The men were away from Nauvoo at the time, so the sheriff returned the papers to Carlin.[30]

The following June, Joseph Smith visited Carlin at his home in Quincy. When the Prophet headed home, the governor dispatched Adams County lawmen and a Missouri officer to follow him; they arrested him on June 5 at Bear Creek, twenty-eight miles south of Nauvoo. Smith returned with his escorts to Quincy, obtained a writ of habeas corpus, and agreed to a hearing on the governor's order before circuit court judge Stephen A. Douglas in his regular court at Monmouth three days later. Six attorneys defended the Prophet. They argued that the Missouri indictment had been obtained by fraud, bribery, and duress. Attorney O. H. Browning brought the courtroom to tears in recitals of the sufferings of women and children leaving "their bloody footmarks in the snow" as they fled under the Missouri expulsion order. Douglas declared that the arrest warrant had become invalid when it was returned to Carlin the previous September.[31]

A third attempt to transport Joseph Smith into Missouri followed an unsuccessful assassination attempt against Missouri's fifty-year-old former governor, Lilburn Boggs. About nine o'clock on the rainy evening of May 6, 1842, as Boggs sat reading the newspaper in his home in Independence, a blast of buckshot from the window hit him in the back of the head. He survived the attack. Citizens initially conjectured that one of his political enemies had instigated the attack. Boggs, a merchant in Independence, had completed a single term as governor in 1840. At the time of the shooting, he was fighting a bitter campaign for a seat in the state senate. Two weeks after the shooting, the *Quincy Whig* reported an unsubstantiated rumor that in 1841 Joseph Smith had prophesied that Boggs would die a violent death within a year. Certainly the Latter-day Saints held no good feelings for the man they blamed for their Missouri troubles.[32] One of them had lamented "that a baser knave, a greater traitor, and a more whole-sale butcher or murder[er] of mankind never went untried, unpunished, and unhung."[33]

When rumors of the supposed prophecy appeared in public print in Quincy, Joseph Smith published a denial. He joined in the conjecture that Boggs had fallen "by the hand of a political opponent." Carlin nonetheless cautioned Smith that the public accepted the conspiracy theory because of "the repeated statements of a portion of your followers, that the manner of his [Boggs's] death had been revealed to you, and their exultation that it must needs be fulfilled." The governor did not expect any immediate threat of arrest or mob action against the Prophet. If he was pursued, Carlin advised, Smith's only recourse would be to "resort to the first Law of Nature, namely, to defend your own rights."[34]

Attention turned instead to Porter Rockwell, who had been visiting and working in Jackson County at the time of the Boggs shooting. Rockwell had taken his wife, Luana, to Independence in February to be with her parents until the birth of their fourth child. He worked as a stablehand under an assumed name to protect himself against the persisting hatred against his people. The baby was born in March. Immediately after the May 6 shooting, Rockwell left his wife to follow later and took a boat to St. Louis and from there to Nauvoo, arriving on Saturday, May 14. The following morning, a congregation gathered at the stand and heard Joseph Smith announce the rumored shooting. A writer in the *Nauvoo Wasp* calling himself "Vortex" responded to the news: "Boggs is undoubtedly killed according to report, but who did the noble deed remains to be found out."[35]

Shortly after the shooting, John C. Bennett had sounded out Governor Carlin in a brief note to see what his reaction might be to a rumored conspiracy to kidnap Joseph Smith and mob Nauvoo. The governor responded to a similar inquiry from the Prophet with a promise of protection for Nauvoo's citizens.[36] Bennett's note said that he was inquiring on behalf of Smith; he may have been testing the waters for his own purposes. Recently removed from his church and civic offices in Nauvoo, Bennett had been discredited in the eyes of the Saints. In letters published in Springfield's *Sangamo Journal,* he was already busy implicating Rockwell in the shooting. Bennett claimed that Joseph Smith had given Rockwell fifty dollars and a new carriage for the deed. Actually, Rockwell was using a new wagon in a service he had set up to carry steamboat passengers around Nauvoo. The discredited Bennett also shared his inferences with Boggs. If Joseph Smith had not ordered the attack, Bennett believed, Rockwell might have pulled the trigger of his own accord. That prospect, kept alive ever since by the testimony of former church members and controversial writers, remains a question of conjecture.[37] If Rockwell was innocent, as the best evidence suggests, his efforts to care for the needs of his pregnant wife had put him in the wrong place at the wrong time.

In July, Bennett turned up in St. Louis, where he again encouraged speculation that Joseph Smith had sponsored the shooting. He asked Governor Reynolds for a new warrant for the Prophet's arrest and promised, "Joe shall be delivered up."[38] Prosecutors, meantime, turned their attention toward Nauvoo and Rockwell.

With rumors circulating of a new attempt to kidnap Joseph Smith, the Nauvoo city council responded on July 5 with the first of several ordinances written specifically to protect Smith, who had replaced Bennett as mayor. The new law required the Nauvoo municipal court to review all such cases. Furthermore, the council expanded the authority of the municipal court in connection with writs of habeas corpus to allow it to examine all outside arrest warrants.[39] At the urging of Emma Smith and others, Governor Carlin reviewed the ordinance about habeas corpus and, in September, offered his opinion that it exceeded the scope of what was originally intended in Nauvoo's charter. Joseph Smith was entitled to a hearing in circuit court, Carlin informed Emma, "but to claim the right of a hearing before the municipal court of the city of Nauvoo is a burlesque upon the charter itself." Although Carlin's interpretation would ultimately prevail, not everyone agreed with this reading of the charter; many, including the city's own legal counsel, sustained the ordinance passed by the city council as proper.[40]

In July, Boggs filed an affidavit charging Rockwell with the shooting. Missouri governor Thomas Reynolds approved a request for extradition, and Illinois governor Thomas Carlin acquiesced. The deputy sheriff of Adams County and two assistants arrested Rockwell on August 8 and took Joseph Smith into custody as an accessory before the fact. The prisoners won freedom with a writ of habeas corpus issued by the municipal court of Nauvoo under the new city ordinance. With Hyrum Smith, as vice-mayor, presiding, the city council that afternoon passed another new ordinance. This one authorized the municipal court to discharge arrest warrants that it judged illegal or ill-founded—including those issued "through private pique, malicious intent, or religious or other persecution, falsehood or misrepresentation"—and to examine those deemed legal, including those issued by other states.[41] This law exceeded the powers of the council and the very writ of habeas corpus. Taking no chances with any promised legal protection, Smith went into temporary hiding in Iowa. Rockwell headed east for refuge in Philadelphia. "He is an innocent and a noble boy," the Prophet wrote of his friend and longtime protector, "a fellow-wanderer with myself, an exile from his home. . . . May God Almighty deliver him from the hands of his pursuers."[42]

The question of the Prophet's guilt dragged on through the fall elections. In consultation with friends, he decided to remain in seclusion in private homes upriver until after the elections. During his exile of two months, Smith kept in touch with church and militia leaders through visitors and letters and even sat for an oil portrait by visiting New York artist David Rogers. Several times Emma visited her husband in company with trusted friends, and Joseph made quiet visits home. At one time, the Prophet seriously contemplated George Miller's invitation to seek refuge for six months at the Wisconsin pineries. He agreed to leave only if he could take Emma and the children. A dream and vision during the night of August 15, he told Emma, had warned him against going without her. "My safety is with you," he confided.[43]

After Thomas Ford took the oath of office as governor in December 1842, he sought an early solution for the Missouri extradition orders. Ford was a lawyer who had given up his seat on the state supreme court to enter politics. Not surprisingly, he recommended that the extradition order against Joseph Smith and Orrin Rockwell be tested in the state courts in Springfield. Justin Butterfield, United States attorney for Illinois and counsel for the Prophet, had written in October that the writ against Joseph Smith was illegal, because Smith was not in Missouri at the time of the attempted killing and hence could not have fled from Missouri. Butterfield believed that the court in Nauvoo could legally examine the warrant. This opinion convinced Joseph Smith to come out of hiding. It also raised doubts in Ford's mind about the legality of the Missouri request. At a January hearing, Judge Nathaniel Pope threw out the extradition order because of its vagueness and legal inadequacy.[44]

To celebrate Pope's declaration, the Prophet hosted a dinner party at the Mansion House for twenty-five couples, plus his mother and two boarders, Eliza Snow and Hannah Ells. The Twelve proclaimed a general "day of humiliation, fasting, praise, prayer, and thanksgiving." The bishops in Nauvoo organized assemblies in every ward for the Saints to hear firsthand about the proceedings at Springfield. At the dinner on January 18 (coincidentally, the fifteenth wedding anniversary for Joseph and Emma), the assemblage sang a "Jubilee Song" by Eliza Snow and one of similar title composed by Wilson Law and Willard Richards to pledge Mormon loyalty to a supportive Illinois.[45]

Even as the friends of the Prophet celebrated the justice of the law and the blessings of God, Joseph Smith shared knowledge of new plans afoot to extradite him to Missouri. The information was contained in a letter written by John C. Bennett to Sidney Rigdon and Orson Pratt. Though he himself had been estranged from the church during the previous year, Pratt wanted nothing to do with Bennett's plan to resurrect the original Missouri charges. He handed the letter to the Prophet. Joseph immediately informed his attorney, J. J. Butterfield, in Springfield, of the plans. The Prophet hoped Governor Ford would not cooperate in the new extradition effort. As it turned out, the arrest did not immediately transpire.[46]

In mid-June 1843, Joseph left Nauvoo with Emma and the children to visit her sister and her family near Dixon, in Lee County, Illinois. While there, two men masquerading as Latter-day Saint missionaries approached Smith. The men, Joseph H. Reynolds, sheriff of Jackson County, Missouri, and Harmon T. Wilson, a constable from Carthage, arrested Smith without presenting the warrant they carried. Their

Mormon militarism was an issue in Missouri and again in Illinois. Opponents of the church distrusted Lieutenant General Joseph Smith's reassurances that the Nauvoo Legion existed only for defensive purposes.

strategy was to whisk him into Missouri before he could secure legal help. In the scuffle, they severely bruised the Prophet's sides with the butts of their pistols. After the pair threatened Stephen Markham, Markham had the Lee County sheriff arrest Reynolds and Wilson on charges of threatening harm and for falsely imprisoning the Prophet under a void writ.[47]

Meanwhile, Joseph Smith hired several attorneys, including Cyrus Walker, a candidate for Congress, who agreed to represent him in return for the Prophet's vote in the fall election. The attorneys secured a writ of habeas corpus returnable before Judge John D. Caton at the ninth judicial circuit court at Ottawa, Illinois. On June 24, the party headed north. At Pawpaw Grove, they learned that the judge was away, so they secured a new writ in Dixon valid in the court of Judge Stephen A. Douglas, some 260 miles distant in Quincy. Before heading by stage toward Quincy, the

Prophet sent Markham to Nauvoo to dispatch part of the Nauvoo Legion to meet him at Monmouth. As the Prophet's party moved south toward Quincy, Reynolds and Wilson tried to convince them to take a steamboat at Rock River. Friends of Smith had already learned that a group of Missourians were waiting there to spirit him across the river. The two lawmen now feared for their own lives. "We will never go by Nauvoo alive," Reynolds and Wilson complained. As the party neared Nauvoo, sixty men met them, the first of two groups of mounted horsemen from the Nauvoo Legion. A third Mormon posse, aboard the *Maid of Iowa,* was heading up the Illinois River toward Ottawa, but after getting word of the change in plans, they headed back towards Quincy.[48]

Joseph Smith now convinced his counsel that Nauvoo was the closest place to hear the writs, and the Prophet's group headed for the Mormon city. As the party proceeded westward, it grew to a hundred men. Just before noon on June 30, with their bridles decorated with wildflowers from the prairie at Big Mound, they met a welcome party a mile east of the temple. Following a tearful reunion with Emma and Hyrum, Joseph mounted his favorite horse, "Old Charley," and as the band played "Hail Columbia," rode into town, with Emma riding at his side and a string of carriages following. Citizens lining the streets shouted a welcome. Legionnaires sounded guns and cannon. Joseph invited Reynolds and Wilson to join a party of fifty friends for dinner at the Mansion House. Afterwards, the two lawmen fled to Carthage, where they petitioned Governor Ford for help in retaking Smith. The municipal court in Nauvoo heard various witnesses and, as anticipated, released the Prophet from his captors. The governor launched a private investigation and then denied Wilson's and Reynolds's request for a posse.[49]

The success in obtaining Joseph Smith's release reinforced attitudes in Nauvoo against those behind the extradition attempts. On June 30, feeling the strength of his position as a freed man once again, the Prophet stood before a congregation of thousands at the meeting place near the temple to declare his intent. "Before I will be dragged again away among my enemies for trial," he said, "I will spill the last drop of blood in my veins; and I will see all my enemies in hell. To bear it any longer would be a sin, and I will not bear it any longer."[50]

Speaking as mayor on behalf of the city, Smith denounced anyone who believed that the Nauvoo charter lacked the same authority held by other governments—city, state, and national. "I wish you to know and publish that we have all power," he declared.[51]

> The United States gave unto Illinois her constitution and charter, and Illinois gave unto Nauvoo her charters, which have ceded unto us our vested rights and [she] has no right or power to take them from us. All the power there was in Illinois she gave to Nauvoo; and any man that says to the contrary is a fool.[52]

> The municipal court has all the power to issue and determine writs of habeas corpus within the limits of this city that the legislature can confer. This city has all the power that the state courts have, and was given by the same authority—the legislature.[53]

This argument of a hierarchical granting of authority ignored the limitations placed upon Nauvoo's municipal government and courts by the state legislature. Nevertheless, the claim rang true in a pre-Civil War environment. Law was fluid and precedent not yet well established in the new nation. At issue was the right of the Nauvoo court to intervene in cases initiated by authority beyond its own. In campaign statements, the two candidates for Congress, Cyrus Walker and Joseph P. Hoge, agreed that the city court had the power to hear a state case. The judicial-minded Thomas Ford rebuked them for this interpretation and for politicizing the issue in an attempt to win Mormon votes. Yet legal precedent supported the Latter-day Saint view. A number of courts had ruled that municipal courts could issue a writ of habeas corpus in such instances. It was not until 1859 that the U.S. Supreme Court shifted the balance toward federal jurisdiction and limited the power of habeas corpus in federal cases to federal courts.[54]

John Wentworth's *Chicago Democrat* offered another perspective on the harassment of General Smith. This action, the paper said, "has made him many friends and created almost universal sympathy. Persecution or oppression always helps the cause of the persecuted or oppressed, whether their cause is right or wrong." The *Nauvoo Neighbor* reported simply, "Joseph Smith is at Nauvoo in peace, quietly pursuing his own business."[55]

Part of that business was to secure additional defensive city ordinances as protections against future extradition attempts. Joseph Smith distrusted professors of jurisprudence, as he did professors of religion, but he used the law to serve the ends of the Eternal. Most controversial of the new edicts was the "Extra Ordinance for the Extra Case of Joseph Smith and Others" enacted on December 8, 1843. It authorized the municipal court to try anyone attempting to serve on Smith any writ related to the Missouri problems and imposed a stiff penalty. This ordinance revealed the frustration felt by many in Nauvoo with the seemingly endless legal challenges thrown against their leader. It reflected as well a confidence in the city court's authority that was not shared by Joseph Smith's opponents. Section 17 of the Nauvoo charter, opponents argued, gave the court limited authority, or as it stated, "power to grant writs of habeas corpus in all cases arising under the ordinances of the City Council."[56]

A second ordinance passed on December 21 specifically allowed the municipal court to intervene when someone attempted to search or seize property or persons in Nauvoo using legal papers executed outside the jurisdiction of the municipal court of Nauvoo. This law expanded the court's geographical reach beyond the authority given it under the July 5, 1842, habeas corpus ordinance.[57] Because of the fuss created by the laws, on February 12, 1844, city officials repealed both of them.[58] Even so, the justices in Nauvoo were not deterred from intervening when they deemed it appropriate.[59]

In response to the legal maneuvering in Nauvoo, a citizens' meeting in Hancock County in September 1843 complained to Governor Ford about the apparent ease with which Smith had won release from extradition charges. He was freed, they noted, by appearing before a court in the city where he served as mayor and chief justice as well as the dominant religious leader. The convention asked Ford to amend or repeal the Nauvoo charter, disarm the Nauvoo Legion, activate a state militia to arrest Joseph Smith, and repeal offending Nauvoo ordinances. The Carthage gathering set up a central corresponding committee with agents in eleven other towns. They urged creation of an independent defense force and pledged to support Missouri's governor in returning Joseph Smith for trial. Governor Ford informed Governor Reynolds that the courts had ended the matter and that he planned no further action.[60]

When the Hancock County committee persisted, the governor replied on January 29, 1844, that he had no power to intervene in the ways they had requested. He added with irony that intelligent students of the law should know better. "If there is any thing wrong in the Nauvoo charters, or in the mode of administering them," he chided, "you will see that nothing short of legislative or judicial power is capable of enforcing a remedy." Ford had raised the question of repeal with the most recent legislature, but neither political party had been willing to act. It was politics as usual, the governor concluded. Warning against extremism on either side, he cautioned, "my interference will be against those who shall be the first transgressors."[61]

Both the *Warsaw Signal* and the *Times and Seasons* published Ford's reply to the resolutions of the citizens' meeting. Thomas Sharp, speaking for the critics, intimated that Ford had sided with the Mormons. John Taylor, editor of the Nauvoo paper, praised the governor's reply and urged both sides to respond with Christian benevolence. "Wise men ought to have understanding enough to conquer men with kindness," he editorialized. "The Governor has told you what to do: *now do it.*" Taylor concluded that if the unhappy Hancock County citizens would let "reason, liberty, law, light, and philanthropy" guide their actions, the region would enjoy "peace, prosperity, and happiness," and "future generations as well as the present one, will call Governor Ford A PEACE MAKER. . . . Our motto then, is, *peace with all.*"[62]

While the Prophet had been extricating himself from his difficulties, his friend Porter Rockwell faced his own legal challenges. Wearied by his unsuccessful attempts to find employment in the East, Rockwell had returned to St. Louis in March 1843 only to face immediate arrest. Shackled and in leg irons, he was transported by stage to Independence and held for trial. Rockwell succeeded in one short-lived jailbreak in May and then waited for an August hearing, chained in a basement dungeon. The grand jury refused to indict him on the Boggs shooting. Instead, it returned charges of escaping from the jail. With attorney Alexander Doniphan's help, Rockwell's trial before Judge Austin A. King in October won for him a welcome release in December, after nine months in jail. Rockwell paid the attorney fees with a hundred dollars that Joseph Smith had collected from temple construction workers and sent to Independence with Rockwell's mother.

The long confinement left Rockwell gaunt and bearded. After an arduous trek mostly on foot across Missouri, he reached Nauvoo. It was Christmas day. Guards refused him entrance to the Mansion House, where fifty couples were dining and dancing at the invitation of a fully uniformed Lieutenant General Joseph Smith. The general, surprised to learn the intruder's identity, turned the holiday festivities into a celebration of Rockwell's freedom. It was at this reunion, according to some reports, that Joseph supposedly promised his trusted friend safety from all future enemies if he would never again cut his shoulder-length hair.[63]

A different kind of petition to solve the problems between the Saints and their Missouri detractors surfaced about this time. On December 21, 1843, the city council, aldermen, and mayor joined in an appeal to the United States Congress. Like the earlier petitions for redress, this document reviewed the successive expulsions from various lands in Missouri and proposed a solution to the Latter-day Saint appeal for redress and protection. "If Missouri goes unpunished, others will be greatly encouraged to follow her murderous examples." To prevent such occurrences, the council's memorial proposed enactment of a new ordinance granting to Nauvoo City certain powers similar to those of territories. This authority would be in addition to those held by Nauvoo under the Illinois charter and would remain in effect until Missouri restored the vacated property and paid for damages for all losses. The single apparent purpose for the territorial designation was to extend Nauvoo's ability to protect itself against physical threats—"to repel the invasion of mobs, keep the public peace, and protect the innocent from the unhallowed ravages of lawless banditti that escape justice on the western frontier." Under the proposal, the mayor of Nauvoo would be empowered to call upon United States forces to join with the Nauvoo Legion in defending the Saints. The unusual ordinance made it mandatory for the United States Army to comply with such an order. It authorized federal pay for the Nauvoo Legion when it was involved in quelling mobs. It anticipated the possibility that other local militias might turn against the Latter-day Saint community or that vigilantes might masquerade as a militia. It was yet another action by Saints desperate to protect their rights and those of the Prophet Joseph Smith.[64]

This singular request did not directly propose separation of the city from the state of Illinois nor the creation of a territorial form of government. Its intent was to bring Nauvoo under federal protection by nationalizing its city militia and enhancing its corporate powers. Nauvoo would remain an incorporated city with a municipal form of government. The request argued, in an expansion of standard legal conceptions, that Congress could grant an enhanced authority under its constitutional powers to regulate federal territory and to protect the states against invasion and insurrection. The memorial reasoned that because the Saints in Missouri had lost land purchased from the United States government, Congress had the duty to protect them in their property rights. To accomplish this, the memorial proposed granting to Nauvoo "all the rights, powers, privileges, and immunities belonging to Territories," in addition to the powers of the city charter.[65]

A similar request drafted for the city council circulated elsewhere in Hancock County. Its proponents reasoned that if Congress could be convinced of widespread local support, perhaps the measure would be adopted. The attempt backfired. Its novel solution to the old Missouri problem merely reinforced perceptions of Nauvoo as an armed camp. It fed the political rhetoric that wrongly defined such militarism not as self-defense but as a threat to the peace of other residents. The anti-Mormon correspondence committees in eight communities met again and elected twenty-nine delegates to a convention in Carthage. These men became the active planners in the events that unfolded in succeeding weeks.[66]

CHURCH-STATE ISSUES AND ILLINOIS ELECTIONS

During the decade when Nauvoo served as the world headquarters of the Latter-day Saints, the American Midwest was home to a population eager for involvement in politics. The region experienced rapid economic and population growth, with people converging on this cultural crossroads from all corners of the nation and from Europe. As Illinois Democrats consolidated various factions, they gradually came to dominate politics in the Prairie State, with strongholds around Chicago and the southern counties. The less-disciplined and minority Whigs held a narrow belt in central Illinois. The state was a proving ground for national issues, and many local candidates—Abraham Lincoln and Stephen A. Douglas among them—launched national careers from their politicized home state.[67]

Preoccupation over the control of patronage and appeals to the immigrant vote dominated political campaigns of the decade. Before the Latter-day Saints arrived in great numbers in Illinois, the state had put Democrat Thomas Carlin into the governor's seat with support from 90 percent of the immigrant vote. Whigs challenged the right of implied citizenship for the alien voters and won their case in the lower courts, but Carlin pushed

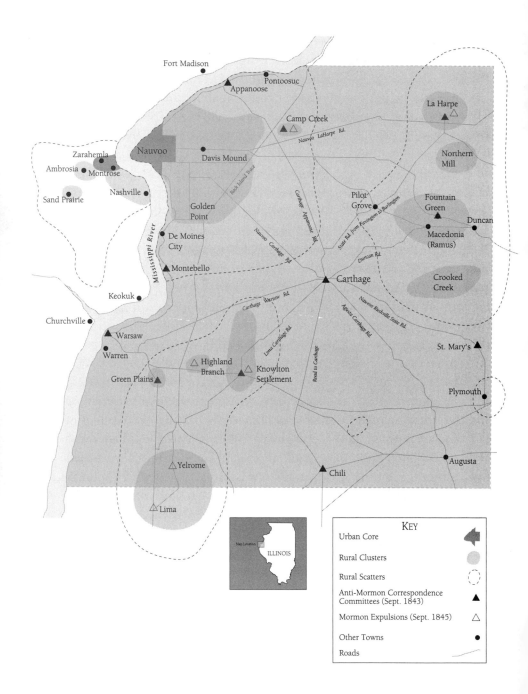

Fort Madison

Pontoosuc

Appanoose

Camp Creek

Nauvoo LaHarpe Rd.

La Harpe

Northern
Mill

Nauvoo

Davis Mound

Zarahemla

Ambrosia

Montrose

Rock Island Tract

Sand Prairie

Nashville

Carthage Appanoose Rd.

Pilot
Grove

Fountain
Green

Duncan

Golden
Point

Nauvoo Carthage Rd.

State Rd. from Farmington to Burlington

Macedonia
(Ramus)

De Moines
City

Duncan Rd.

Montebello

Keokuk

Carthage

Nauvoo Rushville State Rd.

Crooked
Creek

Churchville

Carthage Warsaw Rd.

Augusta Carthage Rd.

St. Mary's

Warsaw

Lima Carthage Rd.

Road to Carthage

Warren

Highland
Branch

Knowlton
Settlement

Plymouth

Green Plains

Yelrome

Augusta

Chili

Lima

ILLINOIS

Map Location

KEY

Urban Core

Rural Clusters

Rural Scatters

Anti-Mormon Correspondence
Committees (Sept. 1843)

Mormon Expulsions (Sept. 1845)

Other Towns

Roads

Mississippi River

Patterns of Conflict, 1843–46

through new laws in the 1840–41 legislature that gave all adult males the franchise after six months' residence. He added five justices to the state supreme court and appointed Democrats (among them Thomas Ford and Stephen Douglas) to all five new positions. This action ensured support for the new law. The church, initially all American-born but gradually becoming nearly one-fourth British immigrants, benefited from Democratic policy with this development. The Whigs of western Illinois were not pleased.[68]

In Hancock County, local and state actions quickly redirected party allegiances among the new arrivals. As an Illinois historian later observed, "From first to last the party rivalries of Whigs and Democrats had complicated the problem of the Mormon disorders."[69] When the Saints arrived in Illinois, the two parties claimed nearly equal support in Hancock and Adams Counties. In this situation, neither party could win election without claiming at least half the Latter-day Saint votes. Nor could they risk losing traditional support.

Consistent with the 1835 "Declaration of Belief regarding Governments and Laws," church leaders in Illinois retained a party-neutral stance. They swung their support to candidates in one party and then another depending upon who was judged to be a friend of the church in defending its constitutional rights. In Ohio and Missouri, the Saints had supported Democrats. When that party was blamed for the expulsion, it appeared that Whigs offered relief. Quincy Democrats welcomed the exiles, but in the first elections, local Whigs won favor from Latter-day Saint settlers. Adams County Whigs generally retained Mormon support, but in Hancock County, church members gradually reoriented their loyalties to Democratic candidates. This move helped to recast Hancock County politics.

The Whigs sought Latter-day Saint support by playing on the newcomers' memory of their treatment by Democratic elected officials in Missouri. At the same time, they sought the non-Mormon vote by promising to seek repeal of Nauvoo's charter and thus end Joseph Smith's political power. To help weaken their political opposition, Whig candidates defined Illinois Democrats as Jack-Mormons whose friendliness with the Saints worked against the broader good. The Whigs hoped that this position would garner support from anti-Mormons who generally voted the Democratic ticket. The Democrats responded to this anti-Mormon rhetoric with a similar balancing act. Like the Whigs, they courted Mormon votes, counting in their favor the friendly reception the Quincy Democratic Association had given the Saints during the winter exodus from Missouri. At the same time, they tried to win the anti-Mormon vote in both parties with promises to repeal Nauvoo's corporate charter. No wonder Nauvoo voters increasingly ignored party labels and looked within the contending parties for individuals friendly to the Latter-day Saint desire for religious and civil freedom unhampered by harassment.

Joseph Smith's problems with extradition were part of local political debates. Extradition was both an effort from across the state border to settle old legal issues and a partisan attempt in Illinois to sway Hancock County voters in favor of the Whigs. An important force in the Whig use of the extradition issue was the excommunicated John C. Bennett. Whig newspapers helped create a negative image of Latter-day Saint leaders by publishing Bennett's religious exposé in their columns. Whig anti-Mormons hoped to define the church as an ominous threat to civil freedoms. Whig candidates promised that if elected they would solve this "problem" by repealing Nauvoo's charter.

Another argument used to incite anti-Mormon political sentiment accused the Latter-day Saints of fusing church and state. The Saints and their opponents agreed with the constitutional mandate that government should not support one religion over another. The Kirtland declaration agreed precisely with the American practice of voluntary membership and funding for churches. Nauvoo's city fathers showed their tolerance and support for American religious pluralism by legislating equal protection to persons of all religious persuasions.[70] British converts in Nauvoo also supported American voluntarism. They had belonged to British reform churches that had rejected the common European pattern of a single, state-supported religion. Beyond the prohibition of an established religion, there persisted in Jacksonian America a feeling that religious bodies should not unduly interfere with the electoral or governing process. Men of the cloth could serve in public office, but when they used their religious influence among their followers to influence civil policy or the selection of officers, it became a matter of concern and raised fears that personal freedoms were being eroded.

The church-state issue emerged at Nauvoo in a number of ways. Most of them centered on the Nauvoo laws protecting Joseph Smith and the

These caricatures portray two leading spokesmen in the political debates in Hancock County: Joseph Smith, who defended the right of Latter-day Saints to unite in electing friends to office, and Thomas Sharp, who helped organize the opposition Anti-Mormon Party.

supposed ability of the Prophet to sway Latter-day Saint voters toward one candidate or another. If the church leader could put his own men into office, his opponents feared, what would stop him from influencing policy to the disadvantage of the minority? "If the Mormons wish to live in peace they must . . . cease from dictating who shall be our county officers," Thomas Sharp declared. The editor challenged Joseph Smith: "When you shall have ceased to control your people in temporal matters, and confine yourself exclusively to spiritual affairs, then you may talk of peace, but not till then."[71] The divisive issues of ecclesiastic influence, real and imagined, surfaced in the Illinois state and local election campaigns of the early 1840s in ways similar to the questions raised about the operation of Nauvoo's municipal government. In both instances, the debate revolved around Joseph Smith's political influence as a religious leader.

In the Illinois elections beginning in 1840, candidates from both parties courted voters in Nauvoo and her satellite communities. With Latter-day Saint voters a majority in Hancock County, the "Mormon question" preempted partisan issues. Political divisions began to fall along the lines of religious affiliation. The Latter-day Saint desire for social unity sustained this realignment. "Political views and party distinctions, never should disturb the harmony of society," John Taylor said in 1844, "and when the whole truth comes before a virtuous people, we are willing to abide the issue." Not only did the Saints vote for the man rather than the party but they disliked partisanship itself because of its "spirit of division and contention."[72] Had the Saints divided along individual party preferences, the question might have been resolved. But because they voted together for what they termed the good of the church, local politics in western Illinois was troubled by the presence of a misunderstood but influential religious community.[73]

The disruption of the old political order began immediately upon the arrival of the exiled Saints from Missouri. In 1839, Joseph Smith reprimanded Lyman Wight for denouncing Democratic anti-Mormonism in Missouri. Wight's criticism seemed to commit the Saints to Whig politics. The Prophet announced a position of political neutrality at the April 1840 conference, saying that "he did not wish to have any political influence, but wished the Saints to use their political franchise to the best of their knowledge." A majority of Latter-day Saints initially favored local Whig candidates. It had been the Whigs in the Illinois congressional delegation who had sponsored their petitions for redress in the Congress and a Democratic president who had declared his inability to help them. On the other hand, Democratic governor Carlin of Illinois had lent the Saints support. Whig state senator Sidney Little guided the Nauvoo charter through to enactment, with the support of Democrat Stephen Douglas, whose majority party ensured the measure's success. The Saints added nearly eight hundred votes to the Illinois electorate in the 1840 and 1841 elections over the 1838 balloting and gave two-thirds of those to the Whigs. The successful Whig congressional candidate John T. Stuart drew 481 of his 1,201 votes in Hancock County from the Nauvoo precinct. He received 70 percent of the county's vote, compared with a near-even split in surrounding counties. "We were distracted by the question of Mormon and Antimormon," a Carthage Whig observed, "or he would probably [have] got more." According to published rumors, Joseph Smith's disgust with Van Buren had turned him toward William Henry Harrison in the 1840 presidential election. In that contest, Latter-day Saint voters dropped one of Harrison's electors—Abraham Lincoln—because only one could go and Lincoln's name was last on the ballot.[74]

With the Mormon vote making the difference in Hancock County and with the Saints apparently firmly in the Whig camp, a number of the "old citizens" began worrying about their own political influence. Democrats especially exhibited jealousy over the new Latter-day Saint influence. One of them, William H. Roosevelt, urged his friends to line up behind an anti-Mormon ticket. They did so in a June 1841 citizens' meeting at Warsaw, where delegates were chosen to attend a countywide anti-Mormon convention. Organizers argued that when a religious denomination became a political body, citizens were bound to oppose such a concentration of political power. Not everyone agreed to abandon national party affiliations. As mentioned above, the Whig congressional third district nominee John T. Stuart won his seat in the state legislature with the support of church members. But Whigs opposed the immigrant vote, and many in Nauvoo continued to vote Democratic in the national ticket, particularly after Van Buren's departure from office.[75]

One Illinois politician most active in courting the Latter-day Saint vote was Democrat Stephen A. Douglas, a twenty-eight-year-old state supreme court justice who sought and won a seat in Congress in 1843. When Douglas visited Nauvoo in the spring of 1841 with Cyrus Walker, a Whig jurist from Macomb, Joseph Smith used the occasion to reinforce his nonpartisanship in politics. In a public gathering, the two visitors praised the citizens of Nauvoo for their industry in building the city. In turn, Smith commended the men in writing for their willingness to determine firsthand the character of the Saints rather than relying on biased gossip. He offered to support as friends those of any party who respected his religious rights and his use of habeas corpus. Douglas had discharged the Prophet in the Monmouth hearing in June 1841, a favor not soon forgotten. Orville H. Browning, soon to be the Whig candidate for the new fifth congressional district, ably represented Smith as an attorney in the case.[76]

In December, the Prophet spoke out, using his civic voice as Lieutenant General Smith. His published statement reflected the attitude prevalent in Nauvoo:

> In the next canvass we shall be influenced by no *party* consideration
> . . . ; so the partizans in this county who expect to divide the friends

of humanity and equal rights will find themselves mistaken—we care not a fig for *Whig* or *Democrat:* they are both alike to us; but we shall go for our *friends,* our TRIED FRIENDS, and the cause of *human liberty,* which is the cause of God.

The Democrats had nominated Adam W. Snyder for governor in the 1842 campaign and John Moore for lieutenant governor. John C. Bennett claimed close friendship with Moore, as with Douglas, during his years in politics in Springfield. Bennett had applauded them all for supporting enactment of the Nauvoo charter. As chairman of the Senate Judiciary Committee that year, Snyder had played a key role. "DOUGLASS is a *Master Spirit,* and *his friends are our friends,*" General Smith continued. "SNYDER, and MOORE, are *his* friends—they are *ours.* . . . We will never be justly charged with the sin of ingratitude—they *have* served us, and we *will* serve them." General Smith explained his vote for Harrison in the previous election similarly as one of friendship. But Harrison, he said, was now dead (he served only a month before dying of pneumonia), and there was no reason to be always governed by his Whig friends.[77]

The Whig newspaper read this endorsement of the Democratic candidates with chagrin. They pointed out that Joseph Smith's effort to speak as a citizen rather than as a prophet by using his military title could not hide his claim to be a theodemocrat—that is, both a believer in the divine rule of God in His church and kingdom and a supporter of democracy in civic life—with his all-encompassing prophetic role primary.[78] One Whig organ declared, "This is probably the first time that a public manifesto of this sort has been issued by a religious leader of this country. . . . We trust that all parties will see its dangerous tendency, and at once rebuke it." The *Quincy Whig* echoed the concern, arguing that "Mormons have a right to vote for Snyder and Moore, if they choose," but not "at the dictation of one man" who holds religious authority over them.[79]

The Whigs, divided by regional factions, had nominated former governor Joseph Duncan, a man previously uncommitted on the Mormon question. Yet, with Whig papers filled with John C. Bennett's lurid attacks on the church, Duncan avoided secular issues and made anti-Mormonism and the repeal of the Nauvoo charter the central issues of his campaign. The Saints, he reasoned, had already declared for his opponent, so he had nothing to lose among that "unimportant" segment of the electorate.[80]

Democratic gubernatorial candidate Adam Snyder died suddenly in May, and his party found a safe replacement candidate in the person of state supreme court justice Thomas Ford, who, like Duncan, was previously uncommitted on the Mormon question. The forty-two-year-old Ford had distinguished himself as a lawyer and as a court justice. Reared by a twice-widowed schoolteacher in St. Louis and then in Monroe County, Illinois, Ford had been imbued with the values of education and of public service; his eldest half-brother had served as Illinois attorney general.[81] The nonpolitical Ford supported repeal or revision of the Nauvoo charter and advocated retirement of the state's heavy public debt. These positions offended Latter-day Saints and party leaders alike, yet he won the election and carried Hancock County 1,174 to 711. Whigs thought that this evidence of a solid Latter-day Saint vote for Ford proved the existence of a secret bargain between Democrats and Mormons, but no evidence exists to question Ford's sincerity in his anti-Mormon campaign. Latter-day Saint Democrats preferred the honest, moderate Democrat and heir to their friend Snyder over his single-issue opponent. The Mormon vote was inconsequential in the statewide election. Ford took office on December 2, 1842.[82]

While the state at large worried about a new governor, local politicians fought for power in county offices. In Nauvoo, Latter-day Saint candidates seemed at first to sanction the religious polarity emerging in local politics. Editor William Smith began in earnest in the spring of 1842 to spar with anti-Mormon spokesman Thomas Sharp, who had called for an independent candidate to unify county citizens against the Mormon vote. In reaction, a group of Latter-day Saints met on June 1, 1842, and selected a "union" slate. The convention nominated Dr. John F. Charles for state senate and Mark Aldrich of Warsaw and Orson Pratt for the house. For county offices, the candidates were Jacob B. Backenstos for sheriff, Sidney Rigdon for school commissioner, Hiram Kimball for county commissioner, and Daniel H. Wells for coroner. Only Pratt and Rigdon were Latter-day Saints at the time, but the others were friends of the church (Aldrich later joined the Anti-Mormon party).[83]

Rigdon, an active participant in the union ticket convention, soon withdrew from its sponsorship and stood as an independent candidate for state senate.[84] He understood the political language needed to appeal to a mixed audience and to disabuse fears of religious influence. In a region where sovereignty was a state motto, he promised if elected to "bow with true loyalty to the will of the sovereign people." A public servant, he noted, cannot be "the representative of a large district and the servant of a faction in that district at the same time. . . . No man can serve two masters." His statement and that of John Harper, a non-Mormon state legislative candidate from outside Nauvoo, appeared together in the *Wasp,* where Harper deplored the deterioration of politics to a question of religious qualification. Harper was a farmer campaigning against the higher taxes needed for increased internal improvements. He said that he had happened in on the Carthage anti-Mormon convention and was appalled at the effort to recruit Whigs and Democrats alike under an anti-Mormon banner. He explained, "I believe we are a body politic, and that we should know no man as a religious man; but endeavor to know them as honest and capable men whose interest is with the people." The Mormon position exactly![85] In the end, these nonpartisan efforts failed. William Smith of Nauvoo was elected as a state representative on the Democratic ticket, and Thomas H. Owen, a non-Mormon from Carthage, got the second seat from the district.[86]

In 1843, the state held special congressional elections to fill offices in four new districts created by redistricting under the 1840 census. Hancock County joined the new sixth district, while Adams County went with the fifth. Because this boundary divided the Whig stronghold in west central Illinois, the Latter-day Saint vote became an issue in both regions. Whigs, who had pledged in 1842 to repeal the Nauvoo charter, debated the repeal issue in the 1842–43 session of the state assembly. Church leaders were astonished at the seriousness of the efforts. Proponents of a move to divide Hancock County approached Joseph Smith over that issue as well, and in January 1843, he announced his intention to withdraw from active involvement in politics. "I think it would be well for politicians to regulate their own affairs," he wrote. "I wish to be let alone, that I may attend strictly to the spiritual welfare of the Church."[87]

Later that summer, the Prophet's arrest at Dixon on the old Missouri charges brought him back into politics. Reassured by political friends that Governor Ford would not cooperate in a reported extradition effort, Joseph Smith had relaxed his vigil. The arrest under Ford's order came as a surprise. Smith had engaged as counsel Cyrus Walker, the Whig candidate for the sixth congressional district, who happened to be campaigning nearby. In exchange for his legal services, Joseph promised Walker his vote. The Whigs softened their anti-Mormon rhetoric. Was it just because one of their party members had the Prophet's vote? Or did they assume the entire Latter-day Saint vote was theirs? Democratic newspapers saw more to it. They speculated that John C. Bennett had planted Walker near Dixon and arranged the arrest as a ploy to win over the Mormon vote for the Whigs.

As the elections neared, both Walker and his Democratic opponent, Joseph P. Hoge, wooed voters in Nauvoo. Joseph Smith told an Independence Day crowd that his support of Walker was a personal commitment not binding upon them. He explained that the Saints had voted against Duncan because of his virulent anti-Mormon threats and in favor of Ford because of his friendliness. But Ford's recent support of the extradition attempts had caused Smith much trouble and expense, he said. His personal decision to support a Whig candidate was not sufficient reason for church members at large to flee from Ford's party. "With regard to elections," the Prophet explained, "some say we all vote together and vote as I say. But I never tell any man how to vote or who to vote for."[88]

As the election neared, John Taylor editorialized in the *Nauvoo Neighbor* (the successor to the *Wasp*) in favor of Democrat Hoge. The masthead of his paper, Nauvoo's secular voice to the outside world, heralded the motto "The Saints' Singularity is Union, Liberty, Charity." While claiming no right to dictate politics beyond the Mormon community, those within it understood that *union* meant not just doctrinal consistency among a gathered people but concord in political precepts as well.[89] On August 5, two days before the vote, Hyrum Smith endorsed Hoge in the name of the Lord. The Prophet once again found it necessary to explain his own position. Repeating his stand of noninterference in personal decisions, he said again that his support for Walker was an individual commitment:

> I have not come to tell you to vote this way, that way, or the other. ... The Lord has not given me Revelation concerning politics. I have not asked the Lord for it. I am a third party [and] stand independent and alone. ...
>
> Brother Hiram tells me this morning that he has had a testimony that it will be better for this people to vote for [H]oge; and I never knew Hiram say he ever had a revelation and it failed. ... (Let God speak and all men hold their peace).

The Prophet reaffirmed his friendship for Governor Ford, despite an error "of the head and not of the heart" in granting the writ.[90] This clear endorsement of ecclesiastical insight had its impact. On election day, the Saints in Nauvoo voted the Democratic ticket as a united community, guided by revelation. Their vote helped send Hoge to Congress.

These and subsequent elections solidified support among Latter-day Saints for the Democratic Party in Illinois. Looking back upon this development, which meant the effective end of Whig power in Mormon country, Thomas Ford reflected, "From this time forth, the Whigs generally, and a part of the Democrats, determined upon driving the Mormons out of the state; and everything connected with the Mormons became political. To this circumstance in part, is to be attributed the extreme difficulty ever afterwards of doing anything effectually in relation to the Mormon and anti-Mormon parties, by the executive government."[91]

The Latter-day Saint effort to protect their rights through block voting for their political friends so alienated the opposition that the division created the very problem the Saints had hoped to prevent. The citizens of western Illinois reacted against what they saw as untenable political and religious threats. In a religion that merged earthly and heavenly kingdoms, all attempts to publicly separate them failed, and the Saints themselves shared in both the causes and the consequences of that failure.[92]

CHAPTER 12

A Renewed Search for Refuge

It is the best policy, both of Missouri and Illinois, to let them alone; for if they are drove farther west, they may set up an independent government, under which they can worship the Almighty as may suit their taste. Indeed, I would recommend to the Prophet to pull up stakes and take possession of the Oregon territory in his own right, and establish an independent empire. In one hundred years from this time, no nation on earth could conquer such a people.

—James Arlington Bennet, October 16, 1841

As to politics I care but little about the Presidential chair. I would not give half as much for the office as I would for the one I now hold. But as the world have used power of government to oppress and persecute us it is right for us to use it for the protection of our rights. . . . If I should be [elected] I would not say that your cause is just and I could not do any thing for you.

—Joseph Smith, March 7, 1844

A central objective of the Latter-day Saints during the Nauvoo years was to establish a refuge in western Illinois and eastern Iowa against the storm of controversy that had surrounded them in northwestern Missouri. Expelled from the lands they had intended to possess as an inheritance, they found a new place of peace along the Mississippi. For a short season, they left behind the issues that had emerged from religious and

301

political misunderstanding and the resulting wall of alienation between competing societies. Then, as the spirit of benevolence toward the refugees wore off, similar tensions resurfaced in western Illinois. Political opponents struggling to maintain influence colored public opinion against the Nauvoo community through the partisan press. Businessmen watched with apprehension as the city's economic influence spread. Even attempts to share common values across political and religious boundaries through the fraternal brotherhood of Freemasonry led to misunderstandings and distrust.

Many of the misgivings between the Saints and their detractors centered in divergent attitudes toward Joseph Smith. Those outside the church misunderstood his prophetic calling. From their own secular perspective, they saw him only as a man of influence in the militia, city government, and economy of Nauvoo. In contrast, the Saints looked at him as a religious leader—a wise counselor, an inspired teacher, a prophet of God. Such trust led a recent convert to pledge in 1842 "that she would go to the Rocky Mountains if Joseph said so."[1] It happened that the Prophet was at that very time considering options for additional gathering places besides Nauvoo, including a refuge in the Rockies. Although Joseph Smith anticipated a geographical broadening of activities for the church, he was still trying through legal channels to recover abandoned property in Missouri. Close to his heart was the desire to do all he could to protect the God-given rights of all of his Heavenly Father's children.

By 1843, the Prophet had given a good deal of personal attention to the matter of righting wrongs against the Latter-day Saints. He had returned from a visit with President Martin Van Buren in 1840 discouraged that any public official in the United States, from the president on down, really had the will to defend a persecuted people's constitutional rights. As appeals for redress of the Missouri outrages failed, one after another, Joseph Smith concluded that only a righteous people acting in unison could achieve that goal of preserving constitutional guarantees. "We are republicans," he told an assembly in Nauvoo, "and we wish to have the people rule; but they must rule in righteousness. . . . I will have the voice of the people which is republican and as likely to be the voice of God."[2] On another occasion in the early 1840s, he spoke prophetically of things yet in the future:

Our cry from the first has been for peace and we will continue pleading like the widow at the feet of the unjust judge, but we may plead at the feet of magistrates and at the feet of judges, at the feet of governors and at the feet of senators, and at the feet of Presidents for eight years [and] it will be of no avail. We shall find no favor in any of the courts of this government. . . .

We shall build the Zion of the Lord in peace until the servants of that Lord shall begin to lay the foundation of a watch tower[3] and then . . . the enemy shall come as a thief in the night and scatter the servants abroad. . . . They will wake up the nations of the whole earth. Even this nation will be on the very verge of crumbling to pieces and tumbling to the ground, and when the constitution is upon the brink of ruin this people will be the staff up[on] which the nation shall lean and they shall bear the constitution away from the very verge of destruction.

These comments, reported by Martha Jane Knowlton Coray, go on to predict apostasy within the church with increased hatred directed toward the Prophet himself: "There are those now before me who will more furiously pursue me . . . and be more blood thirsty upon my track than ever were the Missouri mobbers."[4]

Until the end of his life, Joseph Smith continued to seek refuge for his people in whatever ways seemed likely to achieve his objective of softening attitudes toward the Latter-day Saints and resolving their grievances. He would encourage friendship among strangers within the Masonic fraternity, continue to plan for alternate gathering places, and even allow his name to be placed in contention as a candidate for the presidency of the United States.

Public Opposition and Misunderstandings

The concentration of Latter-day Saints and their devotion to Joseph Smith defined for outside observers the central issues of what came to be known as the Mormon question. Politicians in Hancock County feared Joseph Smith's political influence. The old settlers lived in a society of individuals who represented diverse backgrounds, religions, and political leanings. In contrast, the Latter-day Saints believed in divine guidance through a prophet. They accepted his counsel in all aspects of their lives. From a perspective outside the church, the cohesive Latter-day Saint community seemed closed and clannish, dominated by a charismatic leader who used his religious position to influence elections. Nauvoo's growth made the old settlers the new minority in Hancock County. They saw only one way to reverse the trend: challenge Joseph Smith's dominant political influence as a threat to American individualism and democracy.

The inability of the religious and secular communities of Hancock County to find a compatible middle ground led eventually to a repeat of the Missouri experience. Neither side intended that consequence at first. A St. Louis editor explained the dilemma:

> It has always been and always will be the case that when a set of people come into a country and undertake to array themselves as a peculiar people, that very course of conduct arrayed the community against them. We do not desire to see any further outbreaks with the Mormons, and greatly prefer that they and the citizens who are their neighbors might live in peace.[5]

Much of the public opposition to the Latter-day Saints in western Illinois grew out of the rhetoric created by politicians and the political press. In attempting to shape voting patterns and realign loyalties, partisan opponents created a negative image of the Saints. The Anti-Mormon Party hoped that by defining the Saints as an undesirable group under the control of a religious despot, they could win votes from persons of all political persuasions. They attempted to isolate the Saints politically and even proposed geographical separation. Ultimately, the anti-Mormon campaign revolved around the question of whether a gathered people could live among others not of their faith who needed to interact with them in a common arena.

The leading anti-Mormon spokesperson was Thomas Sharp, editor of the *Warsaw Signal* from November 1840 to December 1842 and again beginning in February 1844.[6] The Pennsylvania-born lawyer, age twenty-two when he arrived in Warsaw, proclaimed for his newspaper a non-partisan stance—but with Whig leanings. On the Mormon question, he pledged neutrality in doctrinal matters but promised "to oppose the concentration of political power in a religious body, or in the hands of a few individuals."[7] Despite his pledge to avoid religious issues, Sharp soon began ridiculing Joseph Smith's translating ability and characterizing the Saints as fanatics or dupes. He further demeaned the Prophet's religious intentions by charging him with blasphemy, hypocrisy, and militarism in the name of religion.[8] By echoing the charges of John C. Bennett and other excommunicated Mormons, the Warsaw newspaper became, in effect, a voice for opponents both outside and inside the church. Its editor echoed the parallel objectives of the two opposition groups—those working to eliminate Joseph Smith's political influence and those challenging his ecclesiastical leadership.

In their political rhetoric, the anti-Mormons challenged Joseph Smith's so-called authoritarian rule in Nauvoo. They vowed to abolish it and targeted repeal of the city charter as the means to do so. American citizens remembered with deep feeling the still-recent war of independence. Their parents and grandparents had fought to end the abuse of political authority. The anti-Mormon press echoed these anti-authoritarian arguments in their attack on the Latter-day Saints.[9]

Thomas Sharp launched his campaign in January 1841 after he read a First Presidency proclamation encouraging all of the Saints to move to the Nauvoo area. The Mormon gathering, Sharp contended, was a political threat to Hancock County: "What may be the result it is impossible to divine, . . . but now that their members are concentrating they begin to assume, at least in this state, a political and moral importance possessed by no other denomination." The editor argued that through the call to gather, church leaders were using moral power for political ends.[10]

With this introduction, the campaign against Latter-day Saint political dominance revived at each annual election and continued as an undercurrent in between. It reached a climax in the early months of 1844, when Sharp repeatedly claimed that Joseph Smith was misusing political power, both as mayor and as a justice in Nauvoo.[11] Sharp contended that the authority of Nauvoo's charter was being applied in ways not found in other chartered Illinois cities. He echoed the old Missouri charges of lawlessness among the Latter-day Saints, including acts of theft and counterfeiting. Additionally, he attempted to create an image of the Saints as gullible religionists misled by scheming leaders. "The Mormons have control of our elections," he wrote, "and while they see proper to obey the dictates of one man in political matters, what necessity is there for old citizens going to the polls? . . . Is it possible that [with] this state of things . . . there can be peace?"[12] His aggressiveness in these journalistic challenges to Nauvoo's political legitimacy and dominance reflected the

Editor Thomas Sharp   *Governor Thomas Ford*

In public discussions of how to solve the Mormon question, Warsaw Signal *editor Thomas Sharp (seen here later in life) ultimately advocated the assassination of Joseph Smith. As a law-and-order governor, Thomas Ford urged both sides to settle differences peaceably or in the courts.*

frustration of a minority political party unable to win any county elections after 1841.[13]

The Anti-Mormon Party had a term to describe Hancock County residents friendly to the Latter-day Saints. According to Sharp, who often used the term, they "are called Jack Mormons, because like the Jackass in the fable, although covered with the skin of a lion, the length of their *ears* discloses their real character."[14] These allies of the Mormon attempt to ensure liberty and rights for all preferred to call themselves "law-and-order" citizens.

Because of the way newspapers borrowed from one another's reports, Sharp's influence extended beyond Hancock County.[15] Other nearby Whig papers echoed the *Signal*'s political arguments. Reports copied verbatim in St. Louis newspapers spread across the United States and into Great Britain. One unnamed Englishman, confused by competing arguments, sailed to Nauvoo to find the truth for himself. He concluded that the Latter-day Saints were a sincere, religious people who had been wronged in Missouri. "Let the Mormons alone," he advised Illinois citizens:

> Let them be protected; let their rights and privileges be preserved unto them sacred, and they will soon become a great and a mighty people, and the governor who received them from the lawless Missourians will be held in everlasting remembrance.[16]

Illinois elected a new governor just as discussions over Nauvoo's city charter intensified. Anti-Mormons had seen to it that their proposal to repeal the charter received frequent serious attention. They were able to galvanize support for repeal from both gubernatorial candidates because of widespread dissatisfaction with governments in chartered Illinois cities. In a lengthy December 1842 inaugural address, Governor Thomas Ford briefly mentioned these efforts and promised to support amendments to make chartered cities closer in authority to incorporated towns.[17]

The governor's comments set off a reaction centered on Nauvoo. One representative proposed the outright repeal of the Nauvoo charter; others argued for the undoing of charters in all Illinois cities. Representative William Smith, the Prophet's brother, turned this last approach to the Saints' favor, noting that the Nauvoo charter granted no greater powers than did the charters of five other cities. After many delays, a House vote was called. A majority of the Whigs sided with Democrats in a 6 to 43 tally to defeat repeal. The state Senate voted 22 to 13 to table a similar repeal measure. Springfield's *State Register* commended Smith and his colleagues for their success but urged amendments to the controversial charter. Legislators were not in the mood to ignore the question. Wading through knee-deep mud to get to the capitol building helped them understand why Springfield residents wanted to repeal their own city's charter on grounds that it allowed officials to mismanage local affairs. The House took the *Register*'s suggestion and repealed portions of the Nauvoo charter on a 58 to 33 vote. Democrats in the Senate wanted to save the Mormon vote for the upcoming United States congressional race. By a single vote, they preserved the charter intact. Nauvoo's political voice, William Smith's *Nauvoo Wasp*, exulted that the legislature lacked the authority to repeal the city's charter, claiming that it had been granted "in perpetual succession."

This phrase from the charter remained at the heart of later Latter-day Saint defenses of their protective self-government.[18]

The same legislative session considered another approach to easing political tensions in western Illinois. Opponents of the Mormon majority wanted to carve out a new county from southern Hancock and northern Adams Counties. That would leave Latter-day Saints free to dominate northern Hancock County. The plan required the Saints south of Warsaw—in the Lima, Morley's Settlement, Green Plains, and Bear Creek areas—to sell their farms. Advocates argued that separate counties would allow the secular community of the old settlers and the religious community of the Latter-day Saints to govern themselves in isolation. On February 3, the House Committee on Counties approved the creation of Marquette County. The House had the partisan votes to pass the measure; the Senate did not, and the measure failed.[19]

The repeal attempt surfaced again in 1844. This time Sharp shifted the issue to the misuse of municipal powers. The Nauvoo city council had just repealed two controversial laws—one to protect Joseph Smith from arrest and seizure and another limiting the search and seizure of property and persons in Nauvoo.[20] This action did not silence critics, but it did weaken their support. Efforts to dissolve Nauvoo's government would be revived again after Joseph Smith's death.

To win public backing for their attempt to cancel Nauvoo's charter, opponents attempted to discredit Latter-day Saints as a lawless people. Many in Hancock County believed these claims. The Warsaw newspaper encouraged old settlers in the countryside to report trends in support of its claim that theft had increased steadily since the Mormons arrived. A resident at St. Mary's described the people of Nauvoo as "nothing but a pack of robbers and murderers, thieves, liars, and counterfeiters. . . . We gentiles are almost afraid to go any ways near that way for fear of our lives. . . . This is a fine country if it was not for these latter-day brethren."[21]

Order was difficult to maintain in the new frontiers of settlement. Illinois in this period attracted thousands of hardworking homesteaders. Farmers, merchants, tradesmen, and various other honest workers contributed to the state's growth, but the fluidity of the frontier encouraged fly-by-night hustlers as well. The constant river traffic pushed a transient traveling public in and out of river ports and with them an underclass working outside the law. Nauvoo's weekly paper joined other Illinois newspapers in denouncing these lawbreakers, among them professional gamblers known as blacklegs. In his memoirs, Thomas Ford remembered that in some regions, dishonest residents packed juries and presented perjured witnesses to avoid conviction for their crimes. In all parts of northern Illinois, he said, there were "organized bands of rogues, engaged in murders, robberies, horse-stealing, and in making and passing counterfeit money."[22]

Ford was convinced that charges of lawlessness against the Latter-day Saints were exaggerated or fabricated. But Nauvoo was not without its problems, and the city's leaders acknowledged that transient outsiders weren't the only ones guilty of crime in the city. Law officers in Nauvoo dealt regularly with petty theft and instances of juvenile pranks. More serious were charges carried over from Missouri days that accused the church of sanctioning theft as a religious principle—"one of the mysteries which the initiated only are acquainted with." The Missourians had misunderstood Mormon longings for a millennial world in which they would "inherit the earth." When the branch at Ramus excommunicated three men for larceny in December 1841, the Twelve issued a formal denouncement of thievery. Joseph Smith and Hyrum Smith published similar statements denying reports of secretly sanctioned bands of robbers sent out to take property from Gentiles. To set the record straight, the Twelve recited church regulations from the Doctrine and Covenants against stealing. Because the Saints themselves had lost horses, cattle, and other property to gangs of roving robbers, the Twelve announced the creation of a city police force to protect property and enforce the law. Guilty Latter-day Saints, they added, "will be cut off from the church and handed over to the law of the land."[23]

Seventeen months after these firm denouncements, Hyrum Smith warned that some church members had become involved in groups reminiscent of the Gadianton robbers of the Book of Mormon. When Joseph Smith pleaded in the *Wasp* for help in exposing such activities, one man confessed his involvement to the Prophet's brother. "He revealed to me," Hyrum said

> that there is a band of men . . . who are bound together by secret oaths, obligations, and penalties to keep the secret; and they hold that it is right to steal from any one who does not belong to the church, provided they consecrate two-thirds of it to the building of the Temple. They are also making bogus money. . . . I wish to warn you all not to be duped by such men, for they are the Gadianters of the last days.[24]

Members of the Nauvoo Legion received firearms from the federal armory in Springfield, Illinois, as did other militias in the state. This United States model 1816 Harper's Ferry flintlock musket was surrendered in 1844 and reissued elsewhere within Hancock County.

Those who thus confessed to such crimes faced justice through the civil courts.

The city fathers in Nauvoo established laws typical of the times to discourage abuses, and they set up police and a court system to handle problems. The statutes covered broad principles and specific problems to ensure the orderly society desired in all stable American communities. Some of the first ordinances passed by the city council supported the constitutional rights of religious freedom, peaceable assembly, and free discussion. The council issued business licenses to legitimize commerce and eliminate scams. Of particular concern in Nauvoo's competitive commercial environment was the regulation of wharfs and ferries. Laws governed the handling of vagrants and public nuisances. The city council frowned upon drunkenness, banned the sale of liquor-by-the-drink, and carefully regulated the social and medicinal use of spirituous liquors. Lawmakers outlawed brothels and licensed rooming houses. They regulated hawkers, peddlers, public shows, and exhibitions. Citizens could be fined for letting unruly dogs harass residents or livestock, but harmless dogs could roam at will, as could cows, calves, sheep, and goats. (Residents generally fenced in their gardens and crops against wandering livestock.) The city established minimum ages for marrying—boys at seventeen and girls at fourteen, with their parents' consent (thresholds typical for the times).[25]

With these and other efforts to ensure domestic tranquility, it could not be said of Nauvoo that it was lawless or that it tolerated lawlessness. Opponents of Nauvoo's political strength sought to influence public opinion by dwelling upon exceptions to the general rule of law and order in the City of Peace.

Less was said in the anti-Mormon press about fears of the growing economic influence of Latter-day Saint businessmen, who competed with their neighbors for local markets. Nauvoo's potential for becoming a regional economic center especially challenged the Warsaw economy. Both towns served the river trade, and both offered shippers and travelers such services as firewood for steam engines and board and room for overnight guests. It was difficult in a nation built on economic competition to politicize this process; perhaps for that reason little was said openly of Nauvoo's emerging economy and its potential for overshadowing Warsaw. The most public issue was the confrontation over the proposed Latter-day Saint town of Warren, but merchants and millers in Warsaw noticed the effects when rural farmers shifted their trade toward Nauvoo.

One economic issue that did feed political debates was currency. Opponents of Joseph Smith's influence highlighted reports of counterfeiting in Nauvoo and charged the prophet-mayor with full responsibility. In addition, they criticized the issuance of legitimate paper money. As mayor, Smith shared accountability with the city council for issuing city scrip. City fathers had hoped to protect immigrants from worthless paper money and to stimulate business. Chicago also issued city scrip to help in depressed times. Because some citizens could not spot counterfeit paper money, and because many merchants refused city money, in March 1843 the city quit issuing new scrip and set stiff fines for counterfeiting. Existing notes remained valid for private debts, but the city accepted only gold and silver. These actions did not end the controversy, so in February 1844, the city dropped its hard currency requirement and invalidated all city scrip. To demonstrate his compliance, Joseph Smith burned eighty-one dollars' worth of his own paper money.[26]

More common than paper money, coins of various denominations and origins circulated freely in American society, including among the Saints in Illinois. The diversity of accepted coinage in circulation made counterfeiting easier. Counterfeiters stamped out coins from cheap metal and then coated them with a thin layer of silver or gold. Thomas Sharp wrongly accused Joseph Smith of being responsible for all bogus coins circulating in Hancock County.[27] Sharp argued that the same Nauvoo ordinances that had protected Smith from outside legal harassment protected lawlessness. "The Nauvoo Bogus factories are in full blast, judging from the quantity of base and counterfeit coin in the city," Sharp charged. "Since the Mormons have learned they are safe as regards punishment by our laws, they seem bold in talking about their bogus operations."[28]

The actual counterfeiters sometimes claimed church sanction for their efforts, and some of them were Latter-day Saints. Sharp ferreted out examples in Warsaw in 1842 and in St. Louis two years later. In another instance, Hyrum Smith publicly denounced two boarders at his house for stealing and for making bogus money. The two tried to justify themselves by saying they had targeted only non-Mormons and were contributing generously to the church. Following their discovery, the men left Nauvoo for St. Louis. Nauvoo's March 1843 currency law set stiff penalties for bogus makers: dollar-for-dollar fines for the counterfeit money offered or passed, plus imprisonment at hard labor for up to fourteen years.[29]

With all the public discussion of the Mormon question, it is no wonder that individuals without independent knowledge of life in Nauvoo formed negative opinions of the community. The national press, reflecting the reports of hostile local editors, created a negative image of the Latter-day Saints believed by many readers. Offsetting this pattern were a few favorable critiques. One businessman visiting Nauvoo in May 1844 challenged the image created in the public press:

> I came here expecting to see an idle, indolent, brawling, intemperate and licentious people:—I found them on the contrary, industrious, enterprizing, orderly, temperate and chaste. I expected to see them

superstitious, bigoted, fanatical and blind followers of a blinded prophet:—I found them free from superstition, liberal, enthusiastic only in their desires to ameliorate the condition of mankind and convert them to the truth, and venerating their prophet to be sure, but no more than intelligent men should do, who [were] acquainted with his enlightened views, comprehensive knowledge and extended benevolence.

The businessman, who signed himself "Hospes," found a city of a few expensive homes dotting a landscape of well-kept cottages. "It is indeed a beautiful place," he wrote, "and viewed from the river makes a most splendid appearance." Hospes found no grogshops, no loafers or beggars, no drunkenness, and no evidence of the immorality alleged by John C. Bennett. He could not decide whether he was more impressed by the residents' "untiring zeal in the cause of their religion, or their determined perseverance in making the 'wilderness a fruitful field,' and building up a 'resting place where none can molest them and none can make them afraid.'"[30] This report, while exaggerated in its absoluteness and suspect for its anonymity, was a welcome respite for a community seeking to be accepted and left alone to pursue their religious quest.

The Political Fallout of Freemasonry

Besides the problems created by hostile newspapers, Nauvoo's people had other social difficulties with political consequences. One of these was their involvement in Freemasonry. Accepted as an opportunity for expanding friendship networks, participation in Masonic activities led to unfortunate difficulties with other Illinois Masons. The fraternity's acceptance in America had undergone a challenge during the 1830s fueled by William Morgan's 1826 exposé of Masonic rituals in New York. His book polarized American attitudes and nurtured an anti-Masonic political movement. A decade later, when the Latter-day Saints moved out of Missouri, the furor had quieted. Masonic lodges in Illinois were rebuilding themselves, with lodges at Quincy and Springfield leading out.[31]

Among the Latter-day Saints in Nauvoo and across the river in Lee County, Iowa, opinion on the anti-Masonic issue varied. Some had earlier affiliated with lodges and remained supporters of Freemasonry. Most prominent of these was Hyrum Smith, who had joined the Mount

Moriah Lodge at Palmyra, New York. Others with Masonic experience included John C. Bennett, John Smith (the Prophet's uncle), Heber C. Kimball, Newel K. Whitney, George Miller, and Lucius N. Scovil.[32]

A few Latter-day Saints had actively contested the movement, including William W. Phelps, who had published opposition newspapers in New York and helped form the state's anti-Masonic political party. Martin Harris, who did not join the Saints in Nauvoo, had been a member of an anti-Masonic vigilance committee in Palmyra. Other opponents were George W. Harris, expelled from the Batavia Lodge in New York for renouncing the fraternity, and Ebenezer Robinson, who became editor and publisher of the *Times and Seasons*.[33]

Two Illinois leaders during the period of Masonic rejuvenation in the 1840s played a central role in expanding Latter-day Saint involvement in Masonry. One of these was James Adams, probate judge in Sangamon County and a Latter-day Saint convert.[34] The other was Abraham Jonas, a Kentucky transplant who headed the Columbus Lodge. Joseph Smith befriended Adams during a stopover in Springfield while en route to Washington, D.C.[35] This friend of the church helped secure the Nauvoo charter, served as a trustee of the University of Nauvoo,[36] and became half-owner of the *Maid of Iowa*.[37] Appointed probate judge in Hancock County, Adams died of cholera in August 1843 just before a planned move to Nauvoo.[38]

With the encouragement of James Adams, in June 1841 Lucius N. Scovil and other Freemasons in Nauvoo submitted a request for a lodge. Proponents sought a required endorsement from the Bodley Lodge at Quincy, Illinois, the state's oldest group and the closest to Nauvoo. When Bodley's members declined,[39] Abraham Jonas and his Columbus Lodge brethren stepped forward as sponsors.[40]

Joseph Smith was not directly involved in these requests but was well acquainted with the organization. He had grown up with Freemasons in his family and community and had lived through the anti-Masonic fury in New York. Through his Masonic friends, he would have understood that Freemasonry held values cherished by religious persons of every faith.[41] Through ethical and moral obligations, Freemasonry aspired toward a universal brotherhood, justice, learning, and character development. Abraham Jonas, a Jew who spoke out against all religious persecution, emphasized Freemasonry's role "as a universal and social platform, upon which all good men . . . may meet on a ground of *equality* and *brother-hood,* irrespective of diversity and peculiarity of religious and political opinions."[42]

Some Latter-day Saints in Nauvoo who embraced Freemasonry and also participated in the temple endowment wondered about the relationship between the two ceremonies. An understanding of Masonic beginnings was one approach; however, historians of Freemasonry disagree about the origins of the Masonic order and its ritual. Organized Freemasonry likely began in medieval England, where craftsmen in the building trades organized guilds (later called lodges) to further their economic aims. By 1717, the order was essentially an educational self-improvement and benevolent association for men. The guilds used symbolism from their work as stonemasons. Over time, they adapted rituals and other ideas from Christianity and esoteric fraternities. Illinois Masons in the 1840s were among those who traced Freemasonry's past this way. Some adherents used this amalgam of ideas to claim a mythical origin with Solomon's temple, or even as far back as Adam.[43]

Latter-day Saints accepted the temple ceremony as a revelation from God to the Prophet Joseph Smith, who held the keys to the last gospel dispensation. The Lord had promised a restoration of "things which have been kept hid from before the foundation of the world, things that pertain to the dispensation of the fulness of times." In addition, the Prophet taught in 1840 that all of the sacred ordinances and priesthood duties of past dispensations would again be present on the earth, "bringing to pass the restoration spoken of by the mouth of all the Holy Prophets."[44]

The Prophet told Benjamin F. Johnson that "freemasonry, as at present, is the apostate endowment, as sectarian religion is the apostate religion." Latter-day Saints came to believe that ancient priesthood rituals first revealed to Adam and to successive Old Testament prophets had been dispersed widely, with portions imperfectly preserved among ancient Egyptians, Coptic Christians, Freemasons, and Israelites, and in the liturgies of Christian churches. Participants in these groups often wore special clothing and used symbolic gestures and dramatizations along with specific instructions and covenants dealing with creation and stages of life.[45]

The nineteenth-century makeup, teachings, and objectives of Freemasonry differed substantially from the Latter-day Saint endowment. Beyond a few actions and words, which the two groups interpreted differently, resemblances were few. Imperfectly preserved in Freemasonry were an emphasis on morality, service, sacrifice, and consecration. As a fraternal society, Freemasonry looked to earthbound personal improvements through mutual pledges to others and promotions to ranks determined by grading and voting by fellow Masons. The endowment is distinctive in its emphasis on God-given priesthood authority, covenants tied to eternal blessings through Jesus Christ, and acknowledgment of the battle between good and evil. Only in the endowment are women full participants. Because of its focus on the eternities, the endowment is family oriented and offers opportunity for proxy ordinances for the dead. The Lord restored the ancient endowment in its purity for use in Latter-day Saint temples for its intended religious purposes of preparing God's children for eternal life.[46]

John C. Bennett first raised the question of parallels in his ill-informed exposé, but concern over the issue in the two quite different ceremonies was not a pressing issue in Nauvoo. For Heber C. Kimball and others, historical dispersion explained occasional resemblances between Freemasonry and "the real thing." Said Kimball, "There is a similarity of Priesthood in Masonry. Brother Joseph says Masonry was taken from Priesthood, but has become degenerated." Joseph Fielding agreed with this explanation. For him, it was beneficial to participate in Masonry because it fostered a brotherhood that could be perfected through the priesthood endowment. Latter-day Saints who listened to the Prophet's doctrinal expositions, studied the Bible for themselves, and absorbed the teachings contained in the Book of Mormon, Doctrine and Covenants, and book of Abraham found much more to enhance their appreciation of the endowment in these religious sources than in Freemasonry.[47]

Whatever the social opportunities in Freemasonry for the Saints in Nauvoo, it was the politician Abraham Jonas, not Joseph Smith, who had the better reasons to want a lodge there. The Prophet might have hoped for increased tolerance in the broader community because certification as a Mason vouched for a person's general moral character. Yet even with the need for influential friends outside the church, the Prophet could achieve his religious objectives without Freemasonry. Jonas, on the other hand, needed an expanded network of friends to accomplish his personal political objectives.[48]

One of those ambitions was a movement in 1840 to relocate the

Warsaw began as Fort Edwards, a military post located atop a prominence near the foot of the rapids. Beginning in the mid-1820s, a thriving river town developed along the banks of the Mississippi, with mills, inns, and numerous shops and services. Nauvoo's dominance of Hancock County's public life in the 1840s directly challenged Warsaw as well as Quincy, an even larger river town in Adams County.

Adams County seat from Quincy to the more centrally located Columbus. Voters liked the idea, and Jonas launched his own newspaper, the *Columbus Advocate,* to strengthen support. In August 1841, citizens of Adams County approved the relocation proposal. A supportive voter in Columbus reported, "There was a great many people out, but the election was carried on very civilly."[49] Despite the electorate's approval, the county commission took no action.[50] Instead, they asked the legislature to create a new Marquette County in the eastern third of Adams County, with Columbus as its seat. The new county appeared on some Illinois maps, but because lawmakers had passed no enabling decree, it could not be organized.[51]

Defeated in his attempt to direct political opportunities home to Columbus, Jonas next reached out to a growing Latter-day Saint population to win friends in his bid for a seat in the state legislature. The request for a lodge in Nauvoo was already under consideration. Among its opponents were members of the Bodley Lodge at Quincy, whose members had opposed relocation of the county seat. Not only did this lodge oppose Jonas but it sought to embarrass him in his efforts to encourage

Freemasonry in Nauvoo. In their own ways, and contrary to Masonic policy, Jonas and Masons in Quincy politicized Freemasonry by taking opposite positions on the Mormon question.[52]

Abraham Jonas ignored the application from Nauvoo at the annual meeting of the Grand Lodge. Instead, he exercised his right to act unilaterally, and on October 15, 1841, created a temporary lodge of Ancient York Masons and appointed its leaders. The lodge's initial membership of thirty-three was about the same number as in the lodges at Quincy and Springfield but larger than the state's other three active lodges in Jacksonville, Columbus, and Decatur. Eighteen master Masons met on December 29 to begin the work of the Nauvoo Lodge, U.D. (Under Dispensation—a temporary status without charter). The new lodge accepted for consideration membership petitions from forty-one applicants, including Joseph Smith and Sidney Rigdon of the First Presidency and five members of the Twelve.[53]

Grand Master Abraham Jonas installed the Nauvoo Lodge at a meeting held in Hyrum Smith's office in Nauvoo on March 15, 1842. He authorized the new officers to move Joseph Smith and Sidney Rigdon through the three steps of the Blue Lodge ceremony "as speedily as the case will admit," without the usual twenty-eight-day waiting period for each step. This was an unusual but allowable procedure that made them master Masons.[54] Upon his return to Columbus, Jonas published a report written to demonstrate his friendship toward his new colleagues. He denounced those who would persecute the Latter-day Saints. He praised the residents of Nauvoo as "a peaceable and law-abiding people." Jonas signed the piece only as "An Observer," but Mormon readers understood. They rewarded his friendly words with their votes and helped elect him in August to a single term in the state legislature.[55] Joseph Smith encouraged his friend in his various public endeavors. "Success to freedom and peace," he wrote.[56]

Meanwhile, the Nauvoo Lodge met regularly to accept and move forward new members. By October 1842, the lodge counted 253 members. Both the pace of elevation and the number of candidates being accepted worried neighboring Masons. Even with the addition of six new Illinois lodges during 1842, the total of Masonic members in all lodges outside Nauvoo numbered only 227.[57] Two additional units were formed in Nauvoo in 1843. They were named for Jonas's fraternal and political

The Masonic Hall on Nauvoo's Main Street served three lodges and numerous public uses, including lectures, traveling entertainments, local theatricals, and art displays. Architect William Weeks created this rendering in 1842 or early 1843.

associates, Jonathan Nye, a past grand master of Vermont, and Dr. Meredith Helm, of Springfield, who succeeded Jonas as grand master of Illinois. Western Illinois Freemasons had reason to believe that Latter-day Saint men, who already dominated Hancock County elections, would soon control the fraternal association as well.[58]

Across the river in Iowa, a territory without a Grand Lodge, James Adams organized the Rising Sun Lodge at Montrose in August 1842. Within two months, the lodge had built a new blockhouse hall and won a charter from the Illinois Grand Lodge. Grand Master Meredith Helm authorized a second group at Keokuk, the Mormon-dominated Eagle Lodge. It was created in January 1843 by past Grand Master Jonathan Nye. With a total membership in the two states that eventually reached about fourteen hundred, Latter-day Saints soon controlled five Masonic lodges and were in a position to influence elections in the governing Illinois Grand Lodge.[59]

In a spirit of fraternal brotherhood, the Freemasons in Nauvoo invited colleagues at Quincy and Columbus to join in celebrating a Masonic holiday, St. John's Day, on June 27 and to participate in cornerstone ceremonies for a Masonic Hall planned for the three Nauvoo lodges. A building committee headed by Lucius N. Scovil had purchased a church-owned lot next to Scovil's bakery at a cost of twelve hundred dollars. More than one hundred members of the Nauvoo Lodge were joined by forty-three visiting Masons for the ceremonies. Hyrum Smith, worshipful master of the lodge, laid the cornerstone and hosted a dinner.[60]

The Bodley Lodge declined the invitation, citing lack of travel funds and complaining that Masonry in Nauvoo had been politicized and mixed with religion. Lodge members charged that Joseph Smith and Sidney Rigdon had been raised to master Mason improperly and for popular appeal and that Nauvoo's lodge membership increased faster than Masonic procedures allowed.[61]

These charges came forward during tense times for the church. It was during May 1843 that the wounding of former Missouri governor Lilburn Boggs led the Quincy newspaper to implicate Joseph Smith. That same month John C. Bennett resigned as Nauvoo's mayor and stood before Nauvoo's Masonic leaders in a tearful plea for forgiveness for his adulterous activities. Bennett denied hearsay that he had been expelled from the Pickaway Lodge in Ohio. Evidence in the Ohio lodge records later proved him correct.[62] Bennett left Nauvoo and retaliated with charges against the Nauvoo Lodge.[63]

An Illinois Grand Lodge meeting in October 1842 determined that the infractions listed by Bennett and the Bodely Lodge were minor technicalities and that the records of the lodge were the best kept in the state. As newly elected Grand Master Meredith Helm put it, the problems in Nauvoo were "matters of the head not the heart" caused by inexperience in managing Masonic business.[64]

But Illinois Masons who saw themselves being quickly outnumbered listened to proposals from members of the Bodley Lodge who wanted to disband the five Mormon-dominated units. Helm posed the critical question before the annual meeting of the Illinois Masons in October 1843. Did they want to yield control to Latter-day Saints?[65] They did not. With Nauvoo's supporters no longer in high places—and through a complex web of interpersonal ambitions and conflicting goals—the state organization suspended the charter of the Rising Sun Lodge and revoked the temporary dispensations given to the Nauvoo, Helm, Nye, and Keokuk (Eagle) lodges.[66]

The rejected units continued their activities informally for a time. In April 1844, more than 328 lodge members and 51 visitors attended dedication ceremonies for the elaborately furnished Nauvoo Masonic Hall. Six months later, the Illinois Grand Lodge permanently withdrew fellowship from all Latter-day Saint Masons as individuals. At the same time, these leaders condemned the assassination of Joseph Smith and Hyrum Smith as a "source of shame to the commonwealth." On April 10, 1845, Brigham Young urged Lucius Scovil to suspend all Masonic activities in Nauvoo. Only a few more meetings were held prior to the western exodus.[67]

The broadened involvement of Latter-day Saints in Freemasonry had failed to yield either a spirit of unity within the brotherhood or lasting political advantage to any of its supporters. The anti-Mormon feeling in western Illinois and the politicization of its ranks by the organization's own members, rather than wrongdoing by the Nauvoo lodges, was the real cause of the simmering conflict within the fraternity.

IDENTIFYING A NEW PLACE OF REFUGE

For several years, Joseph Smith and his associates had been quietly exploring geographical solutions to the political tensions fueled by Nauvoo's growing population. They redoubled their efforts during 1842 and 1843. New pressures to relocate were prompted by Joseph Smith's arrest on the Missouri extradition writ, the expelled John C. Bennett's public disclosures about plural marriage, and growing political unrest.[68]

Any discussion of a gathering place necessarily included consideration of the status of Missouri's Zion. Millennial expectations led some Saints to consider Nauvoo a temporary way station en route to a soon-to-be redeemed Zion in Jackson County. Joseph Smith's authorizing the sale of Missouri lands in 1839 and seeking compensation for losses should have signaled an end to hopes for an immediate redemption of the Center Place. New revelations confirmed that in the long view Nauvoo did not replace Zion; instead, it operated as a cornerstone to Zion, a stake. Members were increasingly reminded that the Lord expected many stakes—in every corner of America—with Nauvoo just the first of many supplements to the original Missouri gathering place.[69]

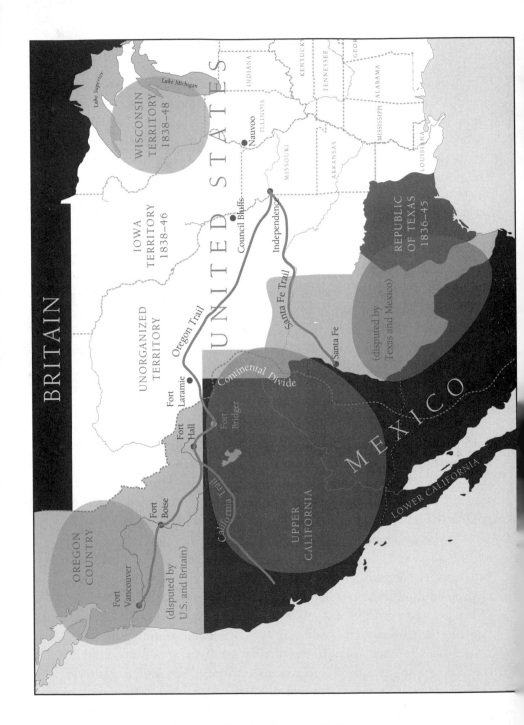

"A Place of Our Own": Options for Relocation

For many years, the Prophet had anticipated the removal of at least some Latter-day Saints to a place of refuge in the American Far West. These plans grew out of missions among Native Americans, people the Latter-day Saints called "Lamanites," "the sons of Lemuel," or "the remnants of Jacob." From the early 1830s, the Saints had talked of establishing Zion among the remnants of Book of Mormon peoples between the Mississippi and the Rocky Mountains. This western territory was the "wilderness," where they believed the Indians expelled by the United States government from their lands in the East would blossom as a rose under the influence of the restored gospel.[70]

Because of misunderstandings in Missouri over the Indian mission, planning for a place of refuge among the Indians continued under the careful protection of confidentiality. In the early 1840s, Joseph Smith sent out several unannounced Indian proselytizing missionaries to prepare the way for a refuge in the West.[71] During the last two years of his life, with the dual objective of converting Indians and protecting Latter-day Saints from persecution, the Prophet emphasized what came to be known as the Great Western Measure. He first dismantled all stakes outside the Nauvoo region in 1843 to concentrate energies on completing the temple. In April 1844, he promised that as soon as the temple was finished, the Saints could begin the long-range goal of filling up North and South America with Zion communities. Nauvoo would be the centrally located temple city to serve all those gathering places. Quietly during these years, Smith discussed confidential plans with trusted associates for exploring sites outside the United States as gathering places for the Saints and the remnants of Jacob.

Interest in the New West filled American newspapers in the 1840s and overlapped into public print and discourse in Nauvoo. American expansionists coveted the Mexican regions of Texas, New Mexico, and upper California and the contested British territory of Oregon. The press in Nauvoo followed with interest the tangled Oregon treaty negotiations between the United States and Great Britain from 1842 through 1846.[72] As early as 1842, the *Wasp* published an article about California and the route leading to it. Even the religiously oriented *Times and Seasons* was not without news about the American West.[73]

The frontiers beyond the borders of the twenty-six states piqued the interest of all Americans in an age of migration and expansion. Supporters argued that the United States was destined to occupy the West to enlarge the horizons of democracy. Latter-day Saints also saw the West as a place of freedom—especially as refuge from their own lost constitutional rights. As they fled from persecution and formed a righteous union with displaced Native Americans, the Saints would leave behind a country seen by many of them as ripe for God's judgment.

Joseph Smith's first step was to gather information about the West and to continue efforts to establish a base of friendship among Native Americans, in part through missionary visits. In May 1840, Jonathan Dunham set out for the Missouri River to meet with Indian chiefs near Fort Leavenworth, just upriver from Independence. Dunham, who identified himself as a Lamanite, had preached among Eastern Indians in the late 1830s. His missions aimed to help fulfill a Book of Mormon promise that its message would be shared with the descendants of pre-Columbian peoples of the Americas. After a few weeks in the western Indian Territory, Dunham returned to Nauvoo on his way east. At Kirtland, he stirred up concern among the Saints with talk of pending divine judgments upon the wicked in the United States. The Saints would find a place of safety, he said, "away towards the Rocky mountains."[74]

During the summer of 1842, plans for a Rocky Mountain refuge became known by some outside the leadership circles. In their intended place of refuge, one outsider noted, the Saints would "become a powerful people" in a society built upon harmony and faith. This contemporary written report reinforces the reminiscent accounts of other residents of Nauvoo who attested to similar knowledge of a plan at this early date for a colony in Mexican upper California.[75]

The following summer Dunham made another excursion into Indian country. This time, a six-week journey took him to the Missouri River settlements of the Pottawatomies near modern Omaha. The Indians sent a delegation back to Nauvoo with Dunham to seek a protective alliance. Lacking the authority of an Indian agent and recognizing the illegality of such a venture, the Prophet declined.[76]

Further discussions of the Great Western Measure resumed on February 20, 1844. In conversations with seven available members of the Twelve and a growing group of consultants over the next several days,[77] Joseph Smith invited his friends to select a company to "investigate the locations of California and Oregon and find a good location where we can remove after the Temple is completed and build a city in a day—and have a government of our own." The Prophet hoped this government in the West would protect the Saints against threats to life and religious practice.[78]

In a concluding discussion of the Oregon and California Exploring Expedition on the twenty-third of February, the council considered a route to encircle the Far West. From Independence, the explorers would follow the Santa Fe and Old Spanish Trails to the Pacific seaboard, travel up the coast to Fort Vancouver at the head of the Willamette Valley, and head eastward along the Oregon Trail. "Send twenty-five men. Let them preach the Gospel wherever they go," Joseph said.

> Let that man go that can raise $500, a good horse and mule, a double barrel gun, one-barrel rifle, and the other smooth bore, a saddle and bridle, a pair of revolving pistols, bowie-knife, and a good sabre. . . . I want every man that goes to be a king and a priest [i.e., endowed]. When he gets on the mountains he may want to talk with his God.

Within days, the Prophet had twenty volunteers ready to search out a new home for the Saints. Among the first to volunteer was Jonathan Dunham. As reported by Wilford Woodruff, Joseph Smith prophesied "that within five years we should be rid of our old enemies whether they were Apostates or of the world and wished us to record it that when it comes to pass we need not say we had forgotten the saying."[79]

On March 10, Joseph Smith met with a few church leaders to consider written proposals from Lyman Wight, George Miller, and others in the Wisconsin lumber camps delivered to Nauvoo by Miller. The lumbermen wanted to accompany several bands of friendly Indians at Black River Falls in a migration to the west Texas plains. Wight believed that these and other displaced tribes all the way from Green Bay to the Mexican Gulf were ready for conversion. Smith and his associates talked all afternoon and into the evening and then invited others to join a special committee or council the next morning. The twenty-three invitees accepted three related responsibilities. First, they would consider the Texas settlement proposal. Second, they would revisit attempts to gain compensation for Missouri property losses and prevent future harm. Finally, they would "secure a resting place in the mountains, or some uninhabited region, where we can enjoy the liberty of conscience guaranteed to us by the Constitution."[80]

The council formally organized on March 11 soon grew to a select body of about fifty trusted church and community leaders. Their combined practical experience was used to advise church leaders in temporal affairs. Known generally as the Council of Fifty, the group had other names used by its members, including the Special Council, the General Council, the Grand Council, the Kingdom of God, the Council of the Kingdom, and the Living Constitution. To protect itself against a misreading of its confidential discussions, this hand-picked body selected by church leaders operated out of public view.[81]

The creation of the Council of Fifty in 1844 as an advisory committee under the jurisdiction of the First Presidency and Twelve left Joseph Smith in his ecclesiastical role as president and prophet of the church. The spiritual focus of the church was on making ordinances of salvation available to all. Involvement in civil affairs thereafter sometimes involved the council, which was organized under a monarchical pattern with Joseph Smith as standing chairman over a cabinet of ministers. The council's civic role included interactions with states and nations to achieve the church's political and social objectives. The council looked forward to the time when a perfect government would exist on the earth, with the Lord reigning as king. In a simple way, the earthly political council symbolized that future, heaven-directed civil Kingdom of God on earth.[82]

In an 1842 editorial, not long after he received a revelation on the council's name and purpose, Joseph Smith explained both current and projected expectations of this advisory body. Moses, he said, had received God's word and shared it with Aaron,

> who taught the people in both civil and ecclesiastical affairs; they were both one; there was no distinction; so will it be when the purposes of God shall be accomplished; when 'the Lord shall be king over the whole earth' and 'Jerusalem his throne.' . . . As God governed Abraham, Isaac and Jacob, as families, and the children of Israel as a nation, so we, as a church, must be under his guidance if we are prospered, preserved, and sustained . . . and he alone must be our protector and safeguard, spiritually and temporally, or we fall.[83]

326

Two unresolved issues were the first assignments given to the Council of Fifty—the failure to gain compensation for property losses in Missouri and the growing tensions over the gathering to Nauvoo. Answers for both were gravitating toward one solution: to disperse many of the Saints living in western Illinois to gathering places in Texas, Oregon, upper California, Wisconsin, or elsewhere—perhaps to several locations.[84] Many politicians and newspaper editors throughout the region were suggesting this same resolution. The *Louisville Journal* suggested somewhat sarcastically early in 1844 that to find peace the Saints must go beyond the Rockies, to the Oregon Territory, where they could help secure the territory for the United States by defeating the British trappers and subduing the Indians. Soon after organizing the Council of Fifty, the Prophet confidentially informed Governor Ford that he intended to defuse political tensions in Hancock County by relocating a large number of the Saints to a new place of refuge.[85]

The first question for consideration was the Wisconsin plan for establishing a Mormon-Indian settlement in the tablelands of the independent Republic of Texas. Acting quickly, the Council of the Kingdom sent Lucien Woodworth to negotiate with the republic's president, Sam Houston, for a major Latter-day Saint gathering place. Woodworth reported back in May with a preliminary agreement; it needed only the approval of the republic's congress. Texas had land available and was seeking colonists to reinforce its borders. The Saints would occupy a large, uninhabited region between the Nueces River and the Rio Grande. Even as the Latter-day Saint body reviewed Woodworth's report, a letter from Orson Hyde, the Council's delegate to Washington, was on its way to Nauvoo, warning of the risks against becoming a buffer state between a quarrelling Texas and Mexico. The colonizing proposal died with the Prophet's murder in June, and Brigham Young refused pleas from Woodworth and Miller to revive it.[86]

Redress and the 1844 Presidential Campaign

The Council of Fifty had been organized in part "for the purpose of consulting on the best manner of obtaining redress of grievances from our enemies." Already the petitions of 1839–40 and 1842 had failed to win federal compensation for the financial losses of the expulsion from Missouri. Joseph Smith's response to his futile visit with President Van

Buren in 1840 had been to proclaim the government fallen and in need of redemption. It cannot "stand as it now is," Orson Pratt heard him say, "but will come so near desolation as to stand as it were by a single hair." The government's survival would require missionaries to gather a righteous army of Saints to America's promised land. "And this is the redemption of Zion—when the saints shall have redeemed the government and reinstated it in all its purity and glory."[87]

Others continued the effort that Joseph Smith had personally set aside as futile. Four months before the Council of Fifty received the assignment, a flurry of political appeals brought similarly discouraging results. A public meeting in Nauvoo in November 1843 considered a memorial giving Congress two options: "Either redress our grievances or shield us from harm in our efforts to regain our lost property, which we fairly purchased from the General Government." The march of Zion's Camp to Missouri in 1834 had anticipated state government protection or assistance. This new proposal sought federal military escorts to shield a return to Zion if political options failed.[88]

Nauvoo's best minds set about pushing for a legislative solution first. Recognizing the need for broad public support, Joseph Smith set the example with an appeal to the "Green Mountain Boys" of his native Vermont, asking that they "by all honorable means help to bring Missouri to the bar of justice." When William W. Phelps read the eloquent appeal aloud to a November 29 meeting in Nauvoo, it elicited an impassioned response and was ordered printed for broader circulation. Several Missouri exiles vowed never again to restrain the Saints under such conditions but to allow them to fight back. Joseph Smith had expressed similar sentiments five months earlier. Now, frustrated by the states' rights argument used by federal officials, the Prophet encouraged others to implore their home states for support.[89] The resulting written appeals typically asked friends to lobby with congressional delegates for passage of the Mormon reparation bill. One correspondent declared:

> We believe that government has the power, amply and adequately to redress us. We expect it. We have the most inalienable right to expect it. . . . We intend to test the efficacy of the government to the core. . . . We can never forget the injuries done us in Missouri. They are ever present to our minds.[90]

Replies from the appeals were few and unsupportive. Not many people in the era of Jacksonian democracy expected the national government to involve itself in local matters; it was created to tend to the general welfare. Vermont's spokesmen answered in February 1844 with an attack on Joseph Smith's patriotism and his sincerity as a religious leader. They advised expulsion of the Saints and execution of their leader.[91]

The Prophet had endured the latest Missouri extradition challenges in June 1843, and then in early December, Missouri agents kidnapped two other Latter-day Saints, Daniel Avery and his son, Philander.[92] A public meeting on December 7 petitioned Governor Ford for help. "Grant us peace," the citizens implored, "for we will have it." Without waiting for an answer, the city council passed its own law to protect Joseph Smith from further arrest.[93] With the events of recent months fresh in mind, the municipal body suggested another way to protect against mob attack. It was in this context that on December 21, the city council sought territorial powers for the city and authority for Nauvoo's mayor to command United States Army troops.[94] Like the others, this appeal to Congress failed. So did the spring 1844 submission of five thousand signatures on a fifty-foot scroll reiterating a plea for Washington's legislative support.

The frustration behind the winter talk by a few exiled Missouri Saints anxious to redeem their land by any means necessary soon subsided. New hope surfaced as the ice broke on the Mississippi and the river began rising in a sure sign of spring's arrival. In early March, Joseph Smith addressed "A Friendly Hint to Missouri," not to the state's officials, whom he had written off as corrupt, but to her people. He called for a grassroots effort "to petition your legislature to pay the damage the Saints have sustained in your State . . . or to restore them to their rights." Additionally, he invited Missourians to revise or repeal laws abhorrent to republican principles.[95] Despite the Prophet's hope that an enlightened populace would speak up for citizens' rights, this entreaty also failed to bring action favorable to the Latter-day Saints.

Church leaders next enlisted the help of their special council for public affairs to plan proposals for protecting the Saints against extralegal action while they sought a new place of refuge. On March 31, 1844, Joseph Smith signed a memorial to Congress (and a similar request to President John Tyler) drafted by Willard Richards on behalf of the Council of Fifty. Like the city council's December 1843 appeal for

329

expanded military authority, the emphasis in this memorial was upon military protection. This time, however, the mayor wanted congressional sanction to raise an independent army of one hundred thousand men. Its declared purpose: to protect American emigrants heading for Oregon and Texas and to support American territorial expansion. Texas had declared its independence from Mexico in 1836 and was seeking annexation to the United States; New Mexico and upper California remained under Mexican dominion. Oregon pioneers had organized a provisional government in 1843, even as the first large overland migration began. The Saints were offering their support for America's westward expansion.

Under the proposed legislation, Joseph Smith would be a commissioned officer in the United States Army, yet his troops would be totally unaffiliated with any government. The memorial explicitly forbade the army from entering land governed by other nations and from violating treaties with other nations. If followed, this would mean limiting the army to Oregon Territory and the Oregon Trail through unorganized Indian Territory.

The "Ordinance for the Protection of the Citizens of the United States Emigrating to the Territories, and for the Extension of the Principles of Universal Liberty" sought to prevent foreign control of the contested territories—to open Oregon, upper California, New Mexico, and Texas to American settlers. The memorial promised as well new exploration and business. It supported the arts and sciences by proposing the collection of antiquities. In this last point, the memorial echoed the purposes of such government explorers as John C. Frémont, whose report of his first exploring expedition had been excerpted in the *Nauvoo Neighbor* in 1843.[96]

Orson Hyde carried the memorials to Washington, D.C., where he and Orson Pratt met with the Illinois delegation in late April. The congressmen were all "Oregon men" but feared that sending American troops there would upset the joint occupancy treaty with England, which Congress had refused to vacate. Hyde's insistence that the troops would all be volunteers and the army independent did not reassure them. Senator James Semple worried that the Nauvoo plan might imply an exclusive right for the Latter-day Saints to emigrate to Oregon. Hyde explained that the Saints only wished to shield themselves against armed clashes with Missourians along the way. "When we get into Oregon," said Hyde, we will protect ourselves and all others who wish our protection. And after subduing a new country . . . we believe that the generosity of our government . . . will allow us a grant or territory of land, which will be both honorable to them and satisfactory to us.[97]

The Illinois lawmakers reaffirmed the Latter-day Saint right to emigrate to Oregon but told Hyde that a new law "would not prevent wicked men from shooting you down as they did in Missouri." In a private consultation with the two Latter-day Saints the following day, Senator Stephen A. Douglas encouraged them to move ahead without authorization. Within five years, he predicted, they would have their own independent Oregon commonwealth or a territorial government. He displayed a new map of Oregon and a report of Frémont's explorations along the Platte River as far as the Wind River Mountains and offered to mail a copy of the report to the Prophet.[98]

The deliberations left Hyde pessimistic. He judged Congress unwilling to act on principle, willing only to protect their own reelection. That evening he spent a cordial hour with President Tyler, a man Hyde described as "a very plain, homespun, familiar, farmer-like man."[99] Tyler said nothing to change Hyde's assessment. "Congress," Hyde wrote home,

will pass no act in relation to Texas or Oregon at present. She is afraid of England, afraid of Mexico, afraid the Presidential election will be twisted by it. The members all appear like unskillful players at checkers—afraid to move, for they see not which way to move advantageously.

He advised the Prophet to move quickly to claim desired land for settlement. "The most of the settlers in Oregon and Texas are our old enemies, the mobocrats of Missouri," he said. "If the Saints possess the kingdom I think they will have to take it; and the sooner it is done the more easily it is accomplished. Your superior wisdom must determine whether to go to Oregon, to Texas, or to remain within these United States" and send out missionaries to build up churches. He cautioned against expecting any government assistance. "Oregon is becoming a popular question: the fever of emigration begins to rage. If the Mormons become the early majority, others will not come; if the Mormons do not become the early majority, the others will not allow us to come."[100] Hyde outlined a proposed seventeen-hundred-mile route from Nauvoo to Oregon's Umpqua

In the midst of his campaign for the presidency of the United States, Joseph Smith prepared the Council of the Twelve to succeed him as spiritual leaders and in April 1844 taught the Saints that Zion included all of North and South America. This rare lithograph celebrates that significant sermon at the preaching ground northeast of the temple. Seated on the stand with the Prophet are other church leaders and chiefs of local Indian tribes.

and Klamath Valleys. Except for the trail beyond South Pass, it became the route followed by those who would leave Nauvoo in 1846.[101]

Democrat John Wentworth of Chicago attempted on May 25, 1844, to read the revised military ordinance before the House of Representatives. He was interrupted as soon as congressmen realized the memorial dealt with the Oregon question. Efforts by Wentworth to suspend the rules to move the bill directly to a committee of the whole failed on a 79 to 86 vote, and Joseph Smith's patriotic military memorial received no further attention in the nation's capital.[102]

Those who considered the failed military strategy understood it was more than just an offer to protect American interests and westward-marching American emigrants. The Army of the West was especially a plan to protect Latter-day Saint emigrants from their old antagonists. The request was evidence of plans to expand the gathering to new places of refuge in the disputed territories of Texas or Oregon or in Mexican upper California, identified vaguely in the proposal as "other lands contiguous to this nation."[103] The possibility of a sanctuary in Texas was one of the issues that had led to the creation of the advisory Council of Fifty in March 1844.

While awaiting news about western expansion from Washington, the Prophet disclosed a new direction for Latter-day Saint gathering places. In a revelation announced at the April 1844 conference, he provided answers to Hyde's questions of western settlement options even before Hyde had written them. For all who wondered, the Prophet clarified the definition of the geographical Zion. Even if the Saints could not yet redeem their Center Place in Missouri, they would expand their settlement options on the promised land. That land included the whole of the western hemisphere, the entire continent of North and South America:

> I have . . . a great, grand, and glorious revelation. . . . I will give you the first principles. . . . The whole of America is Zion itself from north to south, and is described by the Prophets, who declare that it is the Zion where the mountain of the Lord should be, and that it should be in the center of the land. . . .
>
> I have received instructions from the Lord that from henceforth wherever the Elders of Israel shall build up churches and branches unto the Lord throughout the States, there shall be a stake of Zion. In the great cities, as Boston, New York, &c., there shall be stakes.[104]

The Prophet set a condition for the development of these new gathering places. The elders must first receive the temple ordinances as preparation for creating new stakes. The Nauvoo Temple ("the mountain of the Lord . . . in the center of the land") would remain the place for proxy ordinance work for the dead, he said. Members could either move to Nauvoo or visit the temple from other stakes when they wanted to do that work for themselves or their dead.[105]

Brigham Young and Hyrum Smith applauded the Prophet's public announcement with enthusiasm. For Young, the proclamation solved two pressing issues—the anti-Mormon opposition to a regional gathering place and the desire of some Latter-day Saints to stay put in their own home states. "It was a perfect sweepstakes," Young declared. "It is a perfect knock-down to the devil's kingdom." Hyrum Smith, who had recently dismantled existing stakes, emphasized the need to complete the temple before authorizing new units. Even with the Saints in the United States remaining at home, he noted, the overseas gathering would continue. "North and South America are the symbols of the wings. The gathering from the old countries will always be to headquarters. . . . We will try and convert the nations into one solid union." The Prophet had said that his revelation dealt with "economy in the church." He was using the word in its theological sense, referring to the ecclesiastical administration of the world during a particular dispensation. Now, he had proclaimed, the church's divine destiny was to fill up North and South America with stakes.[106] This settled an ongoing discussion, he said, "in relation to Zion—where it is, and where the gathering of the dispensation is."[107]

To accomplish this far-reaching mission, Zion's people would need to live in a spirit of unity. The Council of Fifty had already announced its plans for accomplishing that objective. As a follow-up to the unsuccessful petitions for redress, the council had decided on a new political initiative to save the United States Constitution from the corrupt men who had failed to protect the Saints in their rights. Even as friendly appeals were going to Missouri and requests for a western army were headed east, the council launched a far-reaching effort to resolve the Mormon question and prepare a nation for its divine destiny as an incubator for an expanded Zion.

Once again, the strategy anticipated a grassroots appeal to American citizens. This time, rather than requesting legislative relief, Nauvoo's political advisors sought executive action. "Who shall be our next President?" the church paper had asked in October 1843, in a commentary on the forthcoming presidential election. The answer came four months later: Lieutenant General Joseph Smith. "If I ever get into the presidential chair," the Prophet responded to the small group that first nominated him, "I will protect the people in their rights and liberties."[108] Hyrum echoed that objective in his conference talk the following April:

> We engage in the election the same as in any other principle: you are to vote for good men. . . . Choose the good and refuse the evil. Men of false principles have preyed upon us like wolves upon helpless lambs. . . . Let every man use his liberties according to the Constitution. . . . We want a President of the U.S., not a party President, but a President of the whole people; for a party President disfranchises the opposite party. Have a President who will maintain every man in his rights.[109]

The Saints offered their own unity candidate to lead the nation only after dismissing as unacceptable the candidates of the two major parties.

To learn how those men might deal with the Missouri redress issue, in November 1843 Joseph Smith wrote to John C. Calhoun, a no-party man, and Henry Clay, a Whig. Also receiving letters were Democrats Martin Van Buren; Van Buren's vice-president, Richard M. Johnson; and Lewis Cass. Only Calhoun and Clay replied. Calhoun, a states' rights sectionalist from South Carolina, pledged a nonpartisan stance but restated his earlier conclusion that the limited powers of the federal government gave it no jurisdiction in the Missouri case.[110] The Whigs had already rejected John Tyler, the sitting president and a half-hearted Whig. They were encouraging former senator Henry Clay of Kentucky to make a third run for the presidency. Clay offered sympathy to the Saints for their "sufferings under injustice" and agreed that they "ought to enjoy the security and protection of the Constitution and the laws." But, he wrote in November 1843, "should I be a candidate, I can enter into no engagements, make no promises, give no pledge to any particular portion of the people of the United States."[111] On another occasion, Clay had suggested removal to Oregon as the way to set things right.[112] Martin Van Buren expected to become the standard-bearer for the Democrats after a term out of office (the convention later chose the little-known James K. Polk). The former president presented an easy decision for Nauvoo's leaders. They believed that it was morally untenable to vote for a man who had rejected their appeal for help in resolving the Missouri difficulties.

After examining the options, political strategists in Nauvoo had concluded that prospective candidates were ignoring the central issue. Where was a candidate who was willing to protect constitutional guarantees?[113] This expectation was part of the church's 1835 "Declaration of Belief regarding Governments and Laws in General."[114] The Saints had now exhausted the avenues of legal appeal prescribed by revelation.[115] To regain and secure their civil rights, planners accepted the only remaining option short of leaving the matter to God: they would attempt to install in the White House a man "who has both the disposition and moral fortitude to administer justice."[116] The elders of the church promised to step forward and help Lieutenant General Smith rescue the Constitution, whose very survival was threatened by elected officials unwilling to enforce it. At issue was the constitutional guarantee of federal protection against "domestic violence" and the "temporal salvation of the union."[117]

To accomplish this objective, organizers of the National Union Party needed broad national support. William W. Phelps, a frequent writer and political consultant for Joseph Smith, helped the independent candidate draft a consolidated position paper. Its purpose was to bring together various opinions and their proponents from all American political parties and to appeal to citizens at large. As a platform, *General Smith's Views of the Powers and Policy of the Government of the United States* addressed most of the issues that had captivated the nation since Andrew Jackson's party marched into Washington in 1828: increased political democracy, government corruption, economic problems, prison reform, care of the mentally ill, temperance, and education. From Jackson's inaugural speech, the document proudly quoted his patriotic endorsement of a government "administered for the good of the people, and . . . regulated by their will" to protect "the rights of person and property, liberty of conscience, and of the press."[118] These were principles that motivated Joseph Smith in his decision to stand as a candidate.

Most important for Smith, his union platform championed intervention by the president of the United States when local governments failed to protect citizens in their civil rights. This was a direct challenge to the states' rights argument of Van Buren and many others (an issue resolved finally through the Fourteenth Amendment after the Civil War). In economic questions, *General Smith's Views* followed Whig conservatism by proposing reduced taxes and a downsized Congress. The economic plank echoed Henry Clay's "American System," a conservative plan to expand the economy through a tax-generating tariff and a self-sustaining, government-owned national bank. The *Views* supported prison reforms that would incarcerate only those guilty of capital crimes. Other felons would work off their sentences on highways or public works projects. In foreign affairs, General Smith supported the Democratic call for the annexation of Texas, Oregon, and any other region whose people petitioned for inclusion in the union.[119]

On the controversial question of slavery, the Prophet's platform sided with the Liberty Party's denunciation of slaveholding but added provisions for a fair compensation of slave owners. For many years, church leaders had justified slavery as a constitutionally protected property right. Along with most other Christians in America, they found New Testament support for the practice. The Saints had condemned both the inhumane mistreatment of slaves and the proposals of strident abolitionists for infringing

This impressive portrait by Sutcliffe Maudsley in 1842 captures Lieutenant General Joseph Smith in full dress uniform. Besides his largely ceremonial role with the Nauvoo Legion, the Prophet served after May 1842 as mayor.

on property rights.[120] But beginning in 1842, the more open antislavery views of such advisors as Willard Richards and (for a time) John C. Bennett influenced public statements by church leaders toward a definite antislavery position. That stance came out clearly in candidate Smith's *Views,* which proposed a six-year plan to eliminate slavery through federal compensation.[121]

Initially, according to his backers, Joseph Smith declined to place his name in the ring as a presidential candidate. Willard Richards, who claimed the honor of being "the first to urge his nomination," said that Smith "very reluctantly acquiesced, . . . [and then] only to support a favorite maxim—'*the people must govern.*'" This sense of trust in the voice of the people was rooted in Mormon experience and scripture.[122] The Prophet had expressed his willingness as early as February 1843 to lend his personal influence in political affairs: "From henceforth," he told temple construction crews, "I will maintain all the influence I can get. In relation to politics, I will speak as a man; but in relation to religion I will speak in authority."[123] Rather than a religious crusade, he said, his candidacy was the action of a private citizen to contribute to the national welfare. That contribution, he said, would be to guarantee religious and civil rights to all American citizens by "maintaining the laws and Constitution of the United States."[124]

Willard Richards, John M. Bernhisel, Brigham Young, William W. Phelps, and other supporters insisted they had every confidence in their candidate's political potential for shoring up a weakened Constitution. While admitting that prejudice against him existed and would need correcting, they proclaimed, in Willard Richards's words, "General Smith is the greatest statesman of the 19th century. Then why should not the nation secure to themselves his superior talents?" They had a plan founded on principles of religious and civic freedom to get him elected by bringing about "a union of all honest men."[125] After the April conference in Nauvoo, Richards noted, "our Elders will go forth by hundreds or thousands and search the land, preaching religion and politics; and if God goes with them, who can withstand their influence?" The sweep of campaign rhetoric, he believed, would move "with the rush of a whirlwind, so peaceful, so gentle, that it will not be felt by the nation till the battle is won."[126]

Many newspapers in western Illinois responded to news of Joseph Smith's candidacy with cautious optimism. The *Springfield Register* praised General Smith for his forthright endorsement of Whig planks supporting a United States bank and a protective tariff. Smith "ought to be regarded as the real Whig candidate for President," the paper said, "until Mr. Clay can so far recover from his shuffling and dodging as to declare his sentiments like a man." The *Iowa Democrat* reprinted a *Times and Seasons* article praising Smith's candidacy and the quality of his aides. The *Democrat* tentatively concluded that the team had a favorable chance at getting their candidate elected. The *Quincy Herald* chided the *Quincy Whig*, the *New York Tribune*, and other papers for publishing articles critical of the Saints. The *Times and Seasons* actively solicited favorable letters from supporters outside the church to endorse Smith's qualifications as a unity candidate, "a 'Western man with American principles'" whose election would make him "the President, not over a clique or a party, but the President over the whole people of the United States."[127]

After agreeing to run, General Smith joined in the wave of optimism about his chances for winning the election. "The Whigs are striving for a king under the garb of Democracy," he said of Clay's candidacy. "There is oratory enough in the Church to carry me into the Presidential chair the first slide." The campaign–missionary force would carry a two-headed message of religion and politics into every state. The delegates would, Smith said, "electioneer and make stump speeches, advocate the 'Mormon' religion, [the] purity of elections, and call upon the people to stand by the law and put down mobocracy."[128]

In April, the conference recruited 244 volunteer campaign missionaries; another ninety-four joined the campaign later. Organized into groups of two to forty-seven, they were assigned to twenty-six states and Wisconsin Territory and to contact free blacks. Two weeks later, the Twelve designated two-day general conferences to extend from May through mid-September, beginning in Quincy, Illinois, and to conclude with a nine-day event at Washington, D.C. The missionaries were instructed to preach the gospel, print and share *General Smith's Views* with all who would listen, and recruit electors willing to support their candidate. In a public meeting on April 23, campaign managers speculated that they could attract as many as five hundred thousand voters. Both major candidates in the 1840 election had received more than a million votes each, but the field of six prospects in mid-1844 had not yet been thinned to Polk and Clay.[129]

Those who went forth as campaigners probably did as much to strengthen the existing church as they did to garner votes for their candidates. The regional conferences included a good deal of preaching and some sharing of political tenets from *General Smith's Views*. Not all attempts to deliver their messages to the general populace went well for the campaigners, however. They found very few people interested in the restored gospel, but they reported many listeners receiving the political views favorably. In some locations, they were denied permission to rent halls and were pelted with old tobacco chews and other filth. In Chicago, Jacob Terry presented Joseph Smith's platform to workmen gathered at a lakeside wharf. "I commenced reading," he said. "They tore the document to pieces. I called for the marshall of the city but only received more abuse."[130]

In Nauvoo on May 17, the nascent organization now calling itself the National Reform Party held its first state convention. Delegates nominated their candidate and selected Sidney Rigdon, listed as a resident of Pennsylvania, as vice-presidential candidate. Rigdon had agreed to serve after James Arlington Bennet of New York was found ineligible because of his Irish birth and Solomon Copeland of Tennessee declined. The short-lived campaign to save the Constitution from corrupt politicians was underway.[131]

With the Prophet's encouragement, the Twelve joined in the campaign. If refuge could not be found in one state or another, perhaps a place of peace could be created encompassing an entire nation. On his campaign visit to the nation's capital, Heber C. Kimball was surprised that the city seemed so small, a place of only thirty thousand residents. Yet one feature attracted his attention. "The President's house is as large as the Temple or larger," he wrote, "built of hued stone that is surrounded with a large park decorated with trees of all kinds and flowers. I want to see our Prophet here in the chair of states, then we will come and see him. It looks like a paradise."[132]

At the same time, as Kimball realized, the Twelve were planning for an escape route beyond the United States. Characteristically, in these efforts the Latter-day Saint religious world view with its millennial overtones brought the spiritual and temporal into one. "The government belongs to God," Brigham Young told the April 1844 conference.

> No man can draw the dividing line between the government of God and the government of the children of men. You can't touch the Gospel without infringing upon the common avocations of men. They may have helps and governments in the Church, but it is all one at last.[133]

A month later, Joseph Smith lamented the injustices wreaked by imperfect politicians and deficient governments. His immediate hope was to ensure constitutional rights for everyone. Long term, he awaited the ultimate refuge, the reign of justice of the Prince of Peace. The Prophet wrote, "I pray God, who hath given our fathers a promise of a perfect government in the last days, to purify the hearts of the people and hasten the welcome day."[134]

CHAPTER 13

Foes Within: The Church of the Seceders

We would wish the Saints to understand that, when they come here they must not expect to find perfection, or that all will be harmony, peace, and love; . . . for here there are persons . . . who, although they feel a great attachment to the cause of truth, have their prejudices of education, and consequently it requires some time before these things can be overcome. Again, there are many that creep in unawares, and endeavor to sow discord, strife, and animosity in our midst, and by so doing, bring evil upon the Saints. These things we have to bear with.

—JOSEPH SMITH, SIDNEY RIGDON, AND HYRUM SMITH, JANUARY 15, 1841

The Latter-day Saints in the Nauvoo era sought for a harmonious community. They wanted to replace partisanship and factionalism by agreeing on political candidates who would serve their common needs. At the same time, they sought unity on social and religious issues—a shared wisdom on how best to live and thus win God's favor. In all of these realms, they sought a oneness of heart among themselves, much like the early Christians of the New Testament and the righteous peoples of the Book of Mormon.[1]

Within the church could be found members along a wide spectrum of belief, behavior, and commitment. The creation of a people of promise took personal effort and time by those striving to follow in Christ's way and by those called to teach and guide the religious society. In Nauvoo, the First Presidency counseled patience in the perfection of the human soul and advised, "Let those who come up to this place be determined to keep the commandments of God, and not be discouraged" by the weaknesses of others.[2]

One way to eliminate spiritual disunity was to withdraw fellowship from unrepentant sinners. On the other hand, to those who confessed and pledged to live a new life, church councils and leaders offered another chance through the healing power of the Savior. Parallel actions were available to deal with political, economic, and social disharmony. Withdrawing support was the ultimate judgment when cooperation and consultation failed. Following the apostasy and persecution in Kirtland and Missouri, the Prophet Joseph Smith's inspired writings from Liberty Jail had enjoined members to use long-suffering, gentleness, and charity towards both friends and foes. His counsel encouraged Latter-day Saints during the Nauvoo years to exercise patience, to forgive the repentant sinner until seven times seventy, and to strive for consonance in all aspects of life.[3]

During the difficult years between 1842 and 1844, several Nauvoo residents struck such a strident tone of dissonance in their private and public behavior that decision makers could no longer tolerate the threat to harmony and righteousness in the gathered community. The temporal and spiritual unity of the Saints and the purity of the church was ensured in these instances only when the offending branch was cut off.[4] Of Nauvoo's prominent citizens, John C. Bennett fell first, followed by others who challenged Joseph Smith's leadership. Among those who became the Prophet's foes within the church were William and Wilson Law, Chauncey L. and Francis M. Higbee, Robert D. Foster, and Charles Ivins. Though given every opportunity to leave the church privately and quietly, the dissidents turned instead against their ecclesiastical judges. They rejected the Prophet's teachings and held to ideas taught in Kirtland and canonized there in an early edition of the Doctrine and Covenants.

Many became public antagonists after their excommunications. Bennett fed the political effort; others organized an opposition newspaper and a reformed church. The hostility of these dissidents dismantled efforts by exiled Latter-day Saints to resolve property issues with old antagonists in Missouri. The apostates disrupted a sense of community in Illinois and challenged the oneness felt by most Latter-day Saints in their religious convictions. Ultimately, the open resistance of these few led to the legal crisis that ended in the murders of Joseph Smith and Hyrum Smith.

Within and without, the actions of the apostates challenged for a time the church's quest for sacred and secular unity.[5]

Reactions to Plural Marriage

At the heart of the internal challenge were a few dissidents who rejected the Prophet's teachings on the nature of the Godhead and of mankind's eternal potential. They saw an opportunity to challenge Joseph Smith's power in the church and community by disclosing the privately authorized doctrine and practice of plural marriage, one aspect of the revelation on eternal marriage. These apostates knew of the Lord's strict requirements of virtue as a qualification for eternal marriage. Those same obligations of establishing a committed relationship between husband and wife existed for plural marriages. Many of these individuals had been denied the sealing blessings because of immoral behavior. Having disqualified themselves through sin, they turned against the Lord's spokesman and His church.

Latter-day Saints were grounded in the traditional pattern—a couple committed to each other after the example given by the Lord for Adam and Eve. The standard of one man and one wife was reinforced in the Book of Mormon when some men began straying into sin. Through pride and selfishness brought on when they began to seek worldly wealth, they began "to excuse themselves in committing whoredoms, because of the things which were written concerning David, and Solomon his son." Through His prophet, the Lord reminded them that only under His direction and for His purposes would plural marriage be sanctioned. "For if I will, saith the Lord of Hosts, raise up seed unto me, I will command my people; otherwise they shall hearken unto these things."[6]

Joseph Smith's puzzlement over biblical references prompted him to seek understanding from the Lord. While working on what has become known as the Joseph Smith Translation of the Bible (JST), he pondered the meaning of the Old Testament marriage practices described in Genesis. He also sought to better understand the Savior's comments to Sadducees that marriages contracted in this life without proper authority ended at death. Early in 1831, the Prophet asked the Lord for knowledge and was told how the marriage relationship could become eternal through sacred covenants made in this life.[7] The revelation defined as well the exceptional conditions under which the Lord might direct a man to marry and care for an additional living wife. Joseph Smith was told that Abraham, Isaac, and Jacob had married additional wives in righteousness under the Lord's law of eternal increase, and so had David, Solomon, Moses, and many others. They were married by "prophets who had the keys of this power." David lost his exaltation, the Lord explained, "in the case of Uriah and his wife."[8]

After receiving his first clear understanding of these divine principles in 1831, the Prophet shared them with only a few in Ohio and Missouri. He told some in Kirtland that the marriage relationship could continue beyond the grave. The key was authority. Religious marriage ceremonies performed under divine sanction, he said, were more authentic and enduring than secular marriages. In Missouri during July 1831, the Prophet first explained what he had learned about plural marriage to a few associates. At some future time, he said, the Lord might direct marriages similar to those practiced in righteousness by the ancient patriarchs.[9] One of those told of the teaching was Orson Pratt, who would be called in 1835 to the Quorum of the Twelve. "In the fore part of the year 1832," Pratt said, "Joseph told individuals, then in the church, that he had inquired of the Lord concerning the principle of plurality of wives, and he received for [an] answer that the principle of taking more wives than one is a true principle, but the time had not yet come for it to be practised."[10]

Although plural marriages were not approved initially for others, evidence suggests that before his incarceration at Liberty, Missouri, the Prophet accepted the Lord's direction and took his own first hesitant step as a signal of his obedience. His first plural wife was Fannie Alger. Her uncle Levi Hancock, an Ohio builder and furniture maker, performed the marriage, probably in 1835 when Fannie was nineteen, by repeating back words spoken by the Prophet.[11] Reports of the Prophet taking a second plural wife while living in Far West in 1838 cannot be proved by the limited surviving evidence. It seems more likely that Joseph Smith did not take additional plural wives until the Lord commanded it in Nauvoo.[12]

Even the Prophet's hints of future possibilities created such tension that he shared little more with associates in Ohio and Missouri. In Kirtland, Oliver Cowdery knew of the revelation on marriage but was denied permission to take a plural wife. He proceeded anyway and engaged in an illicit relationship. As Joseph F. Smith later explained it, the Second Elder "abused the confidence imposed in him, and brought reproach upon himself, and thereby upon the church by 'running before he was sent,' and 'taking liberties without license,' so to speak."[13] About this time, Oliver Cowdery helped counter speculation in Kirtland about plural marriage. In August 1835, he encouraged a general assembly there to adopt William W. Phelps's "Article on Marriage," which declared monogamy the only authorized Latter-day Saint marriage practice. This document, included in early editions of the Doctrine and Covenants, also defended the right of Latter-day Saint priesthood holders to perform marriages under the authority of civil law at a time when Ohio officials were denying them that right.[14]

According to a number of recollections, Joseph Smith postponed his own first involvement in plural marriage until commanded to do so by an angel. In a conversation with Lorenzo Snow in 1843, the Prophet spoke openly of the trial he had faced "in overcoming the repugnance of his feelings. . . . He knew the voice of God—he knew the commandment of the Almighty to him was to go forward—to set the example, and establish Celestial plural marriage." Joseph told Mary Lightner that "the angel came to me three times between the year of '34 and '42 and said I was to obey that principle or he would slay me." Joseph Smith's marriage to Fanny Alger in 1835 may have been a response to that first visit.[15] It was probably on the third visit that the angel brandished a sword. Threatened with the loss of his priesthood and death if he failed to act, he then expanded his own involvement and, as commanded, established the practice among others in the church.[16]

Joseph's second plural marriage took place under an elm tree in Nauvoo on the evening of April 5, 1841. Joseph Bates Noble performed the marriage of his wife's sister, Louisa Beaman, to the Prophet. The twenty-six-year-old bride was the first of twenty-eight women married to Joseph Smith at Nauvoo, some as connubial wives, others sealed to him only for eternity. Most of these marriages took place in 1842 and 1843. After his death, other women were sealed to the Prophet at their request, a practice later prohibited.[17] From the marriages consummated, family traditions identify three to five children born to Joseph Smith's plural wives. Because the Prophet's paternity was not openly acknowledged at the time, proof of the relationship for most of them is unclear.[18]

Soon after the Quorum of the Twelve returned from Great Britain in 1841, the apostles heard the new doctrine directly from the Prophet.

"Joe Smith of Nauvoo"   *Eliza Partridge Smith*

A visitor to Nauvoo in July 1842 drew this sketch of Joseph Smith not long after he married Eliza Roxcy Snow as his fourteenth plural wife. Eliza Maria Partridge (and her sister Emily Dow Partridge) were sealed to the Prophet the following March.

Brigham Young remembered his reaction to the law of Abraham. "It was the first time in my life that I had desired the grave, and I could hardly get over it for a long time," he recalled. Young was the first of the Twelve to take a plural wife, in June 1842, followed soon afterward by Heber C. Kimball and Willard Richards.[19] Others joined the limited marriage group one by one as invited to do so. Between January 1842, when Theodore Turley became the second polygamist in Nauvoo, and June 1844, more than two dozen of Joseph's confidants received sealing blessings with their first wives and then married additional wives.[20] The doctrine and practice of plural marriage were not publicly announced until 1852 in Utah, when, at Brigham Young's request, Orson Pratt preached the first public sermon on the subject. Plural marriage was prohibited by revelation in 1890. The First Presidency reminded the Saints a number of years later that plural marriage was not a condition for receiving celestial glory.[21]

All who eventually accepted the part of the revelation concerning plurality of wives did so only after intense personal struggles. Most resolved their concerns through a spiritual witness. They accepted participation as a religious duty that included the obligation of caring for a family under the strict covenants of the doctrine revealed by God.[22] Joseph Smith understood the difficulty with which others reconciled their feelings. He shared his newfound knowledge with those he felt were prepared to understand it. Wilford Woodruff heard the Prophet tell the Saints in Yelrome in May 1843, "It is not wisdom that we should have all knowledge at once presented before us but that we should have a little, then we can comprehend it." When they were ready, he would teach the Saints as he had been taught, "line upon line, precept upon precept."[23]

In Nauvoo, the Prophet first explained the blessings of eternal marriage. If the Latter-day Saint elders were to be heirs of Abraham, he said, they must gather out righteous Israel from the nations and they should raise up an honorable posterity for the Lord. The assurance of an eternal increase was a blessing reserved ultimately for couples sealed by God's power and otherwise worthy of the highest degree of the highest heaven.[24] For Joseph Smith and his followers, the celestial order of marriage erased the line between time and eternity and created a bit of heaven on earth. The potential of an eternal partnership was taught in various settings, both public and private, and the Saints anticipated the opportunity to participate in the temple sealing ceremony.[25]

As Joseph Smith spoke of the Lord's covenant with Abraham to close associates, he introduced the secondary concept of the divinely sanctioned practices of Isaac, Jacob, Moses, and Solomon, who "did none other things than that which they were commanded." In July 1843, he dictated the revelation on marriage to make it available in written form. Hyrum Smith was present. William Clayton recorded the words and made a copy for security. The document included the answers Joseph Smith received in the 1830s concerning his questions about the ancient patriarchs, plus guidance on more recent inquiries concerning adultery. Joseph had more to share, but this first, long installment included the Lord's guidance for Emma, and that was the immediate need.[26]

With Joseph present, Emma's mild-mannered brother-in-law Hyrum read the answers to her. According to Clayton, Emma "said she did not believe a word of it and appeared very rebellious." Emma saw to it that the paper was destroyed.[27] She already knew of some of Joseph's marriages to other women; the Lord encouraged her to "receive all those that have been given unto my servant Joseph, and who are virtuous and pure before me." The revelation reasoned that if a man had "ten virgins given unto him by this law, he cannot commit adultery, for they belong to him, and they are given unto him [of the Lord]; therefore is he justified." If Emma did not remain with Joseph, accept the law, and grant Joseph additional wives, it said, "she then becomes the transgressor."[28]

Over the years, Emma was at times supportive of her husband's plural marriage relationships; often she was not. She had rejected the principle in the 1830s. With others in Nauvoo, she challenged his public allusions to the doctrine in sermons.[29] Like all who learned of the revelation, Emma remained hesitant because of its challenge to her traditional upbringing. In the spring of 1843, she sanctioned Joseph's marriage to the orphaned teenagers Emily and Eliza Partridge but withdrew her support when the girls moved into the Mansion House. The 1843 revelation answered Joseph's question about his own moral standing before the Lord and offered Emma the same relief from guilt, if she would accept it.[30]

Because Sidney Rigdon and William Law rejected plural marriage as inconsistent with previously revealed doctrine, these counselors in the First Presidency did not receive the covenants of eternal marriage. Nor did John C. Bennett, an assistant president, who distorted his limited knowledge of the doctrine to justify immoral behavior. He was excommunicated for his promiscuity. Initially hesitant, Hyrum Smith, serving as both an assistant president and church patriarch, accepted the doctrine through his own prayerful searching and after talking with Brigham Young.[31] Those in church leadership councils who remained nonparticipants did so for various reasons, including opposition to the doctrine, absence from Nauvoo, Joseph Smith's judgment of them as unworthy, and general disaffection.

Some opponents of the church later claimed that because plural marriage was not publicly acknowledged until 1852, the doctrine had originated with Brigham Young. Historical evidence clearly demonstrates that Joseph Smith authorized plural marriages during the Nauvoo period. Among the thirty men who received plural wives before June 1844 were eight members of the Quorum of the Twelve, whose witness confirmed the early origin of the doctrine and practice. After the martyrdom, two other apostles married plural wives. Only John E. Page and Lyman Wight did not participate. In the Nauvoo Temple early in 1846, Brigham Young and Heber C. Kimball each married twenty-one wives, a number of them not connubial. At this time, Brigham Young was married to nine of Joseph Smith's widows, and Heber Kimball took responsibility for eight others. According to one tentative calculation, during the Prophet's lifetime, 114 women were sealed to 30 men. For the entire Nauvoo period, 153 men received 587 plural wives. Most of those men took only one or two additional wives. The typical plural family included three wives, but the range was from two to eleven. Notable exceptions were Joseph Smith with twenty-nine marriages and Heber C. Kimball with thirty-eight. Brigham Young left Nauvoo with seventeen wives (another two dozen or so had been sealed to him for eternity but were never part of his earthly household).[32]

A few of those introduced to plural marriage endured a more severe test of their faith. For example, Joseph Smith approached Heber C. Kimball and asked him for Vilate as an eternal companion. After much soul-searching, fasting, and prayer, Heber finally agreed. He was then told that the request was an Abrahamic test of his willingness to submit his will to the Lord's and that the sacrifice of his wife would not be required. The Prophet then sealed Vilate to her husband. John Taylor similarly passed this test when the Prophet inquired about securing Leonora as his own celestial wife. In some instances, the invitation moved beyond a theoretical proposal. In these few cases, about which little is known, the woman's husband was not a church member or was a Latter-day Saint who agreed to allow his wife to be sealed for eternity to Joseph Smith. This ordinance ensured the woman a marriage that would be valid in the resurrection no matter what became of her temporary, civil agreement. For some, it may have seemed the only way to gain that sacred promise.[33]

As the circle of knowledge about plural marriage expanded, word of its practice circulated in Nauvoo and beyond. The wives of the Twelve spoke of it to one another, and plural wives often shared the teaching with their families. Plural marriage was illegal under Illinois antibigamy laws adopted in 1833 and reaffirmed later.[34] Nor was it a doctrine or practice lawful for the church as a whole. Whispered rumors among neighbors caused no immediate problems, but when stories appeared in print or plural marriage was preached by indiscreet elders, church leaders faced a difficult challenge because of the need to protect the confidentiality of the practice and yet avoid misunderstanding, misuse, and criticism.[35]

The most difficult of the disclosures to manage began after the excommunication of John C. Bennett for adultery on May 11, 1842. Bennett had filled major roles of public trust in Nauvoo. Within a few weeks, he lost all of them. He resigned as mayor and was released as assistant president to the First Presidency, discharged in disgrace by the Nauvoo Legion, expelled from the Masonic Lodge, and dropped as chancellor of the city university.[36]

After his fall from grace, Bennett saw an opportunity to serve his own interests and took it. Rumors about plural marriage, counterfeiting, militarism, theft, and murder had been circulating against the Saints. As a former insider, he believed he could convince the public that he spoke with knowledge on these issues. In fact, he had created a counterfeit of the true coin; his debauchery had lost him his membership in the church. Bennett told his own skewed version of his life in letters published first in Springfield and copied in newspapers elsewhere. Then, he promoted his ideas in a fourteen-stop speaking tour reaching from St. Louis to New York and Boston, then to Chicago and back to St. Louis. Immediately afterward, his book *History of the Saints* appeared, weaving a tale of sexual promiscuity in Nauvoo through what he called "spiritual wifery." This term had been used by some communitarian groups in the 1830s to mean Christian plural marriages. A few Latter-day Saint women called themselves spiritual wives. But for Bennett's application it meant adultery—an illicit sexual relationship only.[37] What he said in his exposé attracted attention nationally because it seemed to confirm the worst of the anti-Mormon charges. Locally, it fed the political opposition. As did other Latter-day Saints, Parley Pratt found Bennett's exposé "beneath contempt. . . . His object was vengeance on those who exposed his iniquity." Pratt predicted it would have no lasting effect on the church.[38]

To counteract this influence, in June 1842 the Prophet published his own explanation of Bennett's fall from favor and sent out missionaries to explain the church's position. For nearly two years, Joseph Smith had kept confidential information labeling Bennett as "an imposter and base adulterer." Soon after arriving alone in Nauvoo in 1840, Bennett had begun courting a young woman. About this time, a letter from Springfield cautioned Nauvoo leaders that Bennett had abandoned a wife and children in Ohio. When confronted, he dropped his new fiancée but took a new approach. "He went to some of the females in the city, who knew nothing of him but as an honorable man, and began to teach them that promiscuous intercourse between the sexes, was a doctrine believed in by the Latter-Day Saints, and that there was no harm in it." Bennett persuaded the women that the Prophet and others sanctioned and practiced his doctrine of "spiritual wifery."[39]

In mid-1841, church investigators in Pittsburgh and Ohio confirmed that Bennett was still married and that his reputation was one of disrepute in many of the twenty or more places he had lived. When presented with evidence, Bennett acknowledged its veracity, but embarrassed by the disclosure, he soon attempted suicide with a dose of poison. His adulterous affairs continued until he was confronted with witnesses the following spring. After a private hearing, he signed a statement certifying that the Prophet had taught nothing contrary to gospel principles and had not sanctioned "illegal illicit intercourse with females." This admission separated Bennett's fraudulent and immoral actions from the authentic marriage practice.[40]

In an interview before the city council, Bennett reaffirmed his loyalty to the church, vouched for the Prophet's character, and asked to be restored to full fellowship. Councilmen feared that Bennett's excommunication might make of him another Sampson Avard—an open opponent of church leaders. Indeed, Bennett left Nauvoo and immediately published his self-serving exposé. Joseph Smith informed Governor Thomas Ford of Bennett's past and encouraged Nauvoo citizens to defend the church against the twisted claims.[41] Reports circulated that Bennett was plotting with Missourians for Joseph Smith's destruction. The Prophet posted a regular city night watch from the Nauvoo Legion as protection. One Nauvoo observer noted, "Joseph knew his enemies, and appreciated his friends."[42]

For too long and despite early cautions, Joseph Smith had counted the talented John C. Bennett as a friend. In March 1841, in a letter from Ohio, George Miller said of Bennett:

> He has the vanity to believe he is the smartest man in the nation; and if he cannot at once be placed at the head of the heap, he soon seeks a situation; he is always ready to fall in with whatever is popular; by the use of his recommendations he has been able to push himself into places and situations entirely beyond his abilities.

"In fine," Miller concluded, "he is an imposter, and unworthy of the confidence of all good men."

Bennett's baptism the previous August at the hands of Joseph Smith was likely taken as evidence of Bennett's complete rejection of past sins. A revelation soon afterward cautioned him to accept counsel and continue in good works—both admonitions he later violated. For more than a year, he accomplished many good things for the cause at Nauvoo, but, as Miller predicted, the little general had again sought out a situation that placed him "at the head of the heap" where he found himself in "places and situations entirely beyond his abilities." The appearance of greatness eventually proved hollow.[43] Bennett set out to discredit the church and to encourage the arrest of Joseph Smith on charges of sponsoring the attempted murder of former Missouri governor Lilburn Boggs. "If Joe is innocent," Bennett wrote in July 1842, "let him be acquitted; but if he is guilty, let his life atone for it."[44]

Bennett was involved as well in the difficulties that Sarah and Orson Pratt had with plural marriage. Bennett approached Sarah while her husband served his apostolic mission in England and explained his perverted doctrine of spiritual wives. If no one knew of the illicit liaison, it was right, he told her. Sarah's response was one of confusion, and she withdrew from involvement with the church. When Orson Pratt returned to Nauvoo and heard from her of Bennett's overtures, he, too, raised questions about Joseph Smith and the church. When a mass meeting of about a thousand Nauvoo men in July 1842 sustained a resolution commending the Prophet as "a good, moral, virtuous, peaceable and patriotic man," Pratt cast one of half a dozen negative votes. He explained his reservations to the meeting; Joseph Smith spoke in response; and then Pratt spoke again at length. A month later, a committee of the Twelve excommunicated Pratt. This action convinced John C. Bennett that Pratt was on his side. Friends feared that because of the disappointment he felt, the distraught Pratt would take his own life. Only when Pratt heard privately the Prophet's own explanation of the divine origins of plural marriage did Orson begin to sort things out. After much prayerful contemplation, he accepted the teaching. Ten years later, he offered the first public defense of plural marriage at a conference in Salt Lake City. Sarah, on the other hand, never seemed able to reconcile herself to the doctrine.[45]

After Bennett published his account of life in Nauvoo, he went on the lecture circuit in the Eastern states. In some locations, the elders paid the twenty-five-cent admission fee to confront Bennett, hoping to correct his distortions and to influence local newspaper reports. Bennett made extravagant claims for church doctrine and called for the total extermination of the Saints.[46] At a lecture in the Second Congressional Church in New York City in August, Robert D. Foster spoke out against Bennett's claims of Mormon thievery, seduction, murder, blasphemy, and theocratic rule.[47] In Baltimore, Benjamin Winchester's public denunciation convinced the local editor of the falsity of Bennett's claims. "We do not think that the Mormons should be made objects either of ridicule or persecution," the Maryland editor concluded. Freeman Nickerson, a church member in Boston, described Bennett as "godfather to all the lies that ever has be[e]n written that he could collect since the Church arose with all that he could invent." Nickerson had yet to hear of anyone in Boston paying the price of eighty-seven and a half cents for the book; he said that Bennett's preaching had put only a temporary damper on the faith of members and investigators.[48]

Taking no chances, editors in Nauvoo published some of the Eastern reports and responded to Bennett's charges. From the fall of 1842 through the following spring, the *Times and Seasons* published four comments on Latter-day Saint beliefs concerning marriage. As editor, Joseph Smith first published an extract from the 1835 statement on marriage from the Doctrine and Covenants. It acknowledged the validity of all marriages contracted before baptism into the church and declared "that one man should have one wife; and one woman, but one husband, except in case of death, when either is at liberty to marry again."[49]

During this time, Udney Hay Jacob published two chapters from a proposed book, *The Peace Maker; or, The Doctrines of the Millennium.* The excerpts defended plural marriage and divorce as biblically sanctioned. Even though Jacob was not yet a Latter-day Saint (he was baptized in 1843), he understood much about the sealing power and its relationship to the teachings on eternal marriage. This pamphlet offered an early glimpse at explanations that nineteenth-century church leaders would share in Utah. The author later claimed that he intended the essay as a defense of the Saints against public misunderstandings.[50]

With all of the confusion created by Bennett's claims and Jacob's pamphlet, many in Nauvoo sought clarification about the supposed practice that rumor would not let die. At a high council meeting on August 12, 1843, Dunbar Wilson wanted to know what was behind talk of a plurality of wives. Members of the Twelve were already party to the confidential knowledge. The high council was next in ecclesiastical priority in Nauvoo. Hyrum Smith responded with candor. He retrieved his copy of the July revelation from his home across the street and read it to the assemblage. Joseph was at home ill. After learning that an authentic revelation on plural marriage existed, the high council became divided in its loyalty. Thomas Grover and some councilors accepted it at face value. Others did not. William Law, the Prophet's second counselor, had believed Bennett's exaggerated claims of immoral behavior and was already a staunch opponent of anything resembling the teaching about spiritual wives. Siding with him were William Marks, the fifty-one-year-old Nauvoo stake president, and high council members Austin A. Cowles and Leonard Soby.[51]

In the succeeding months, others learned of the revelation. Ebenezer and Angeline Robinson heard about it from Hyrum Smith, who taught it to them and expected they would comply, but the Robinsons resisted.[52] Many problems surfaced because of misunderstandings and misappropriation of the principle. After the high council cleared one man of charges of seduction in November 1843, Joseph Smith told those present

> that the Church had not received any permission from me to commit fornication, adultery, or any corrupt action; but my every word and action has been to the contrary. If a man commit adultery, he cannot receive the celestial kingdom of God.

The Prophet counseled that the John C. Bennett case should have been "sufficient to show the fallacy of such a course of conduct."[53]

Many members of the church found it necessary to sort out for themselves the conflicting claims about whether plural marriage did or did not exist within the church. Mostly, they accepted the church's explanations, supported by the statement on marriage, that the practice was not authorized within the church (which it was not for the general membership). They concluded rightly that the so-called spiritual wife system was a fabrication by the adulterous Bennett. "He is a polished scoundrel," one Nauvoo church member wrote.[54] After investigating Bennett's accusations, a convert challenged readers of the *Boston Bee* to learn something of Mormon beliefs before they condemned them: "No sect have a greater reverence for the laws of matrimony, . . . and we do what others do not, practice what we preach."[55] Those few trusted Saints who were taught by the Prophet and who embraced the revealed truth accepted the sacred obligation to keep the practice of plural marriage confidential. They understood that that which was being condemned from the pulpit was adultery and that which had been sanctioned privately by revelation was a virtuous practice exercised under priesthood authority.[56]

The early months of 1844 saw an increase in public discussion of the doctrine of spiritual wives. Among the claims stirring gossip in Nauvoo was the *Warsaw Signal's* publication of a thirteen-stanza poem that bitingly satirized the private practice of plural marriage.[57] Missionaries and presiding elders away from Nauvoo weren't certain what or whom to believe. Some of them concluded that plural marriage was one of the mysteries of the kingdom and began to expound upon it from the scriptures. In Michigan, one local elder found himself out of the church for doing so. In China Creek, Hancock County, in March 1844, others were claiming "that a man *having a certain priesthood,* may have as many wives as he pleases, and that [that] doctrine is taught" in Nauvoo. The claim contained enough specific departures from the truth to make a public denial plausible. "There is no such doctrine taught here; neither is there any such thing practised here," Hyrum Smith responded, adding that anyone teaching such doctrine would be subject to a high council hearing. He advised the elders to keep to first principles. "Let the matter of the grand councils of heaven, and the making of gods, worlds, and devils *entirely alone,*" he urged. Those subjects were to be broached only "when God commands men to teach such principles." Hyrum acknowledged a hierarchy of privilege in knowing such things. "The mysteries of God are not given to all men," he said,

> and unto those to whom they are given they are placed under restrictions to impart only such as God will command them; and the residue is to be kept in a faithful breast, otherwise he will be brought under condemnation. By this God will prove his faithful servants, who will be called and numbered *with the chosen.*

Such restricted doctrine, he assured the Saints, was not necessary for a celestial reward; obedience to the principles of faith, repentance and baptism, and the laying on of hands for the gift of the Holy Ghost would do. To enjoy the additional blessings of eternal increase, those worthy of the celestial kingdom must enter into "the new and everlasting covenant of marriage."[58]

This message was repeated a month later in an unsigned editorial in the *Times and Seasons*. Its author, probably editor John Taylor, warned members abroad against Bennett's spiritual wife system and cautioned them not to believe reports that immoral conduct was sanctioned by the church. Unfortunately, he said, some men had received ordinations unworthily. In their high-mindedness and pride, they had preached degenerate principles, preying upon the credulity of the humble and meek. "There are other men who are corrupt and sensual, and who teach corrupt principles for the sake of gratifying their sensual appetites, at the expense and ruin of virtue and innocence. Such men ought to be avoided as pests to society." Anyone teaching contrary to scripture, he said, should be set down as an imposter and excommunicated.[59]

The circulating rumors stirred little concern among those practicing the true form of plural marriage with the approval of Joseph Smith, for their personal spiritual convictions gave them inner peace. The women who had been converted to the doctrine quietly shared with one another their faith in the divine origin of the principle and its positive influence in their lives. Looking back at her Nauvoo searchings, Elizabeth Ann Smith Whitney remembered that when she and her husband, Newel K. Whitney, first heard of the teachings of plural marriage, they "pondered upon them continually, and our prayers were unceasing that the Lord would grant us some special manifestation concerning this new and strange doctrine." They received an answer, she wrote, "and were convinced in our own minds that God heard and approved our prayers and intercedings before Him. Our hearts were comforted."[60]

ACTIONS OF THE APOSTATES

As questions about plural marriage surfaced publicly here and there, the issue became part of a larger set of challenges that began to polarize those in the church who knew about the private teachings. During the year after Hyrum Smith shared the new revelation with the high council, its members and others who were brought into the inner circle took their stand on the issue. Some remained loyal to Joseph Smith. Others rejected his revelations on temple doctrines, including celestial marriage and plurality of wives. Some of those disillusioned ones joined an active religious opposition movement that was reinforced by existing personal and economic tensions in Nauvoo. Others, including stake president William Marks, remained in the shadows for a time.

Centrifugal movements were not unknown to Joseph Smith. Disagreements over doctrine, policy, or administrative roles in Kirtland and Far West had spun prominent associates out of the church.[61] Typically, they had sought to "purify the church" by rejecting Joseph Smith and certain new doctrines or practices while holding fast to established ones. In Kirtland, disaffected members met under the "Old Standard" to preserve a "pure" Church of Christ, and some of them plotted to kill the Prophet. Apostasy similarly affected church leaders in Missouri. By mid-1838, Frederick G. Williams of the First Presidency, the Three Witnesses to the Book of Mormon, four members of the Twelve, and some of the First Quorum of the Seventy had left the church. Brigham Young defined the claims of the small band of Nauvoo reformers as "the same old story over again—'The doctrine is right, but Joseph is a fallen prophet.'" Joseph Fielding agreed with this sentiment and reflected, "I feel grieved that at this time of the greatest light and the greatest glory and honor, men of so much knowledge and understanding should cut themselves off."[62]

One of the most prominent leaders in the Nauvoo secessionist movement was William Law, second counselor in the First Presidency. The Irish-born entrepreneur became increasingly upset with Joseph Smith over economic as well as religious matters. At a personal level, Law took offense when the Prophet openly promoted church building lots on the flats in preference to Law's privately offered lots on the bluff. Institutionally, the counselor disliked his leader's impressive political and financial influence. Law preferred a more democratic and individual approach to public and economic affairs. Of greatest import to his faith, he disagreed with the emerging temple theology, including the eternal potential of human beings and the doctrine of plural marriage.[63]

During the Bennett scandal, Law had defended the Prophet against accusations of plural marriage. After the disclosure in the high council meeting, Law and his wife, Jane, read together Hyrum Smith's copy of the marriage revelation. They then confronted the Prophet, who defended its divine origin. William Law labeled the new revelation of the devil and pleaded with the Prophet to abandon the teaching. Joseph Smith responded that he could not withdraw the new commandment without bringing God's condemnation upon himself and the church. Emma Smith was a close friend of the Laws and of William and Rosannah Marks. This group of friends concurred in their opposition. Because the Prophet was convinced that Law had committed adultery, he refused to seal William and Jane when they requested it. In January 1844, he dropped his counselor from the First Presidency. The Laws were excommunicated in mid-April. Ten days later, William Law joined with others to form a short-lived separatist church.[64]

Excommunicated along with Law in April and among his supporters in the opposition movement were Robert D. Foster, Wilson Law, and Howard Smith (of Scott County, Illinois). All were cut off "for unchristianlike conduct."[65] A land developer like Law, Foster had his own real estate problems. He was charged with selling lots behind the temple that he had purchased on contract from Daniel H. Wells but not paid for.[66] Wilson Law was a partner with his brother in the milling business, a brigadier general in the Nauvoo Legion, and a former city councilor.[67] In May, the high council cut off James Blakesley, Francis M. Higbee, Charles Ivins, and Austin Cowles for apostasy.[68] The secessionists attracted both sincere opponents of plural marriage and opportunists. Among this last group was newcomer Joseph H. Jackson, who had been spurned in his attempts to marry Hyrum Smith's oldest daughter, Lovina. Jackson had then sworn to murder the entire Smith family.[69] Jackson claimed after the fact that he had attempted to infiltrate Nauvoo society in order to expose its inner workings. He had won the sympathy of the Prophet in 1842 by claiming to be destitute, thus gaining a job as a real estate clerk in Joseph Smith's office.[70]

The desperate men most opposed to Joseph Smith met regularly in secret meetings to plot a strategy. Among those invited to assist in the effort were some who disliked what they heard. These uncomfortable recruits reported to church leaders about Jackson's murderous plan and who the conspirators were. The informants heard many charges of activities supposedly sanctioned by Joseph Smith, most of them familiar from the Missouri days. One said that the conspirators signed an oath to do all in their power to destroy Joseph Smith and his faithful followers.[71]

The sparring with Robert D. Foster was an ongoing problem. In

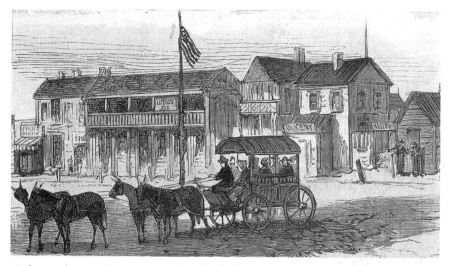

A thriving business district developed on Mulholland Street eastward from the temple. Among the merchants and tradesmen here were some who turned against Joseph Smith.

April, the Prophet told a congregation from the stand near the temple that conspirators were present. Foster complained that he was being harassed but refused to reveal his true feelings about Smith.[72] Two weeks later at the mayor's office, Foster's brother, Charles A., drew a pistol and threatened to kill the Prophet. Robert Foster falsely accused Smith of sharing in the spoils of a gang of supposed Nauvoo Danites and of attempting to recruit him to kill former governor Lilburn Boggs. This accusation prompted Brigham Young to denounce Foster from the stand at the Sunday morning service on April 28. As with other dissenters, Foster was soon excommunicated from the church, dishonorably discharged from his post in the Nauvoo Legion, and dropped from other civic posts.[73]

On the afternoon of April 28, the excommunicants met at Wilson Law's home near the sawmill to organize what one report called the "Reformed Mormon Church." The group appointed William Law as their leader. Refusing to be termed a prophet, he accepted the title of president. He appointed his brother Wilson (who was soon replaced by James Blakesley) and Austin A. Cowles as counselors, Robert D. Foster and Francis M. Higbee as apostles, and Keokuk hotel owner Charles Ivins as bishop, with a Dr. Green and John Scott Sr. as counselors. Eight of the organizers volunteered to canvass families in the city for additional members.[74]

The new church defined positions on both temporal and spiritual "Mormonism." The political stance of the reformers appealed to anti-Mormons seeking to weaken Joseph Smith's influence. They repudiated the mingling of church influence in civic life and pledged support for the repeal of the Nauvoo charter. To reinforce this notion, they spread reports that Joseph Smith and his followers were being made kings and queens in secret ceremonies. The mention of royalty reinforced the fears of citizens who were proud of having cast off rule by English kings.[75]

Law and his followers centered their religious challenge on two doctrines—the gathering and plural marriage. They claimed that the doctrine of what they called "gathering in haste, and by sacrifice" was contrary to the will of God. In 1841, the First Presidency had invited the Saints to "make a sacrifice of their time, their talents, and their property, for the prosperity of the kingdom, . . . bid adieu to their homes . . . and unite with us . . . and share in the tribulation, that they may ultimately share in the glory and triumph."[76] The dissidents challenged this invitation as well as Joseph Smith's 1843 designation of Greater Nauvoo as the sole gathering place in order to complete the temple more quickly. Instead, they wanted to allow scattered stakes. (Their challenge ignored the Prophet's April 1844 announcement of an eventual continental expansion.)

The more volatile issue was Joseph Smith's private sanctioning of plural marriage and his public discourses on doctrines related to the temple. The little group of dissenters denounced Smith as a fallen prophet and pledged themselves to accept what they termed the religion of the Latter-day Saints as originally taught by Joseph Smith from the Bible, the Book of Mormon, and the Book of Commandments. This was their way of rejecting the newly revealed temple theology with its ordinances and practices as well as the controversial practice of plural marriage. In response, Joseph Smith labeled his opponents false prophets.[77]

The two sides had reached a standoff. The protesters, Robert Foster said, had forever severed their bond of loyalty with the Prophet. "We are united in virtue and truth," he wrote, "and we set hell at defiance and all her agents." The *Times and Seasons* expressed a lack of concern: "One or two disaffected individuals have made an attempt to spread dissension," the editor wrote, "but it is like a tale that is nearly told, and will soon be forgotten. . . . By their fruits ye shall know them."[78]

The founders of the secessionist church soon offered public preaching sessions at William Law's home. On Sunday, May 12, a large crowd listened to sermons by Law and Blakesley. Some of the organizers wrote confidential letters to friends in the East slandering Joseph Smith in an attempt to win support for their movement.[79] Word of the claims of the dissenters spread locally as well. An observer in La Harpe informed his Latter-day Saint neighbors that because of the enmity manifested between the two parties, "Nauvoo would be too hot for them both but they would not believe it."[80]

Hoping to further discredit the Prophet and to force his resignation as church president, the reformers charged him publicly with immoral conduct. On May 6, Francis M. Higbee filed a plea in the circuit court at Carthage claiming that in 1842 Joseph Smith had seduced or attempted to seduce Nancy Rigdon. Higbee said that Smith's actions interfered with his own courtship of Sidney Rigdon's daughter. The Nauvoo Municipal Court took jurisdiction and dismissed the petition after nine witnesses convinced the justices that Higbee was a disreputable and immoral character intent only on a malicious prosecution.[81]

A second charge, filed by William Law, claimed that the Prophet had committed adultery with Maria Lawrence (one of Joseph's plural wives). Sidney Rigdon talked with Law on behalf of the Prophet, but the disaffected former counselor would not be reconciled. Law set forth his terms: "If they wanted peace," he wrote in his journal on May 13,

> they could have it on the following conditions, That Joseph Smith would acknowledge publicly that he had taught and practiced the doctrine of the plurality of wives, that he brought a revelation supporting the doctrine, and that he should own the whole system (revelation and all) to be from Hell.

In effect, Law was asking Smith to admit failure in his prophetic calling. Instead, the Prophet charged Law with perjury and slander.[82]

Also during May, on the advice of several friends, Joseph Smith decided to resolve indictments against him of perjury and polygamy. They had been issued by a Carthage grand jury on the witness of Joseph H. Jackson, Robert D. Foster, and William Law. On the morning of May 27, the Prophet mounted his horse "Joe Duncan"—named as a rebuke of a political nemesis—and, with a dozen supporters, rode up past the temple and on to Carthage. Several of his accusers saw him leave. Taking another route, they reached the county seat ahead of him. The judge in the case postponed the hearing so that the prosecution could call witnesses. Meanwhile, the Foster brothers confided to Joseph Smith and other members of his party that the litigation was merely a ruse to get Joseph and Hyrum out of Nauvoo so they could be killed. Joseph H. Jackson was seen loading his pistols and overheard swearing he would carry out the threat. The Prophet's party hurried back to Nauvoo, arriving after an absence of thirteen hours. They would return to Carthage within the month for another, final, court appearance.[83]

The Nauvoo Expositor Case

That second trip was precipitated by charges of riot and treason filed in response to a challenge over freedom of the press.[84] On May 7, 1844, the Nauvoo seceders established a printing shop on the north side of Mulholland Street in the block just east of the temple. Three days later, on a surplus press purchased in Adams County from Abraham Jonas, they issued a prospectus for a weekly newspaper, the *Nauvoo Expositor*. The new owners wasted little time. On Friday, June 7, they published one thousand copies of the first and only issue of the *Nauvoo Expositor*. They delivered half the issues to the post office for mailing to subscribers and newspaper editors.[85]

Geographically as well as philosophically, the *Expositor* represented a view from the bluff. The newspaper's writers claimed that Joseph Smith was deceiving the Saints by regulating prices and limiting competition when he encouraged immigrants to buy building lots only from the trustee-in-trust. Ostensibly a political paper advocating a Whig platform, the sheet supported repeal of the Nauvoo city charter and opposed "all political revelations and unconstitutional ordinances." Given this agenda, the *Warsaw Signal* predicted, the *Expositor* would lead to "the 'Decline and Fall of Mormonism.'"[86]

But more inflammatory were the *Expositor*'s religious arguments. The seceders hoped to convince Latter-day Saint readers that Joseph Smith had perverted the restored gospel and fallen from grace by introducing heretical doctrines. The paper's editors knew that the plural marriage doctrine had been taught privately; they had an advantage over most readers. William and Jane Law and Austin Cowles testified that they had heard

With this flyer, the seven publishers of the Nauvoo Expositor recruited subscribers and announced their intention to challenge alleged abuses under the city charter, the mixing of church and state, and "facts, as they really exist in the City of Nauvoo," a hint that they would talk about plural marriage.

William Smith read the revelation. "We intend to tell the whole tale," the newspaper exulted.[87]

Many in Nauvoo had heard the King Follett funeral discourse on mankind's eternal potential at the April conference. When the seceders challenged the doctrine, Joseph Smith preached at length on the subject again in mid-June to defend its consistency with scripture. In contrast, for two years members had heard condemnation of the counterfeit spiritual wifery. Not knowing of the true practice of plural marriage, many Latter-day Saints concluded that the *Expositor*'s claims were yet another ill-founded exposé like that of the disgraced John C. Bennett. One reader scanned the first issue and concluded, "They printed all the lies that the Devil could think of and some that he could not think of."[88]

Because the *Expositor*'s sponsors had lost their church membership, they were beyond further reprimand from priesthood councils. The only recourse open to those offended by the sheet lay with civil government. With alderman George W. Harris presiding, the city council heard evidence and considered options in lengthy sessions on Saturday, June 8, and again the following Monday. The hearing mixed doctrinal discussions with denunciations of personal character and reviews of civil law and political mischief. Ultimately, the council acted as a legislative body to create law and as a judicial court to review constitutional principles and precedent and to pronounce judgment. In effect, the deliberations resembled a New England–style town meeting convened to protect the community from heresy. The publishers were censured for preaching false doctrine, breaking God's commandments, and libeling church and civic leaders. They were condemned as conspirators against all that mattered most in Nauvoo's gathered community.[89]

On the question of the marriage revelation read to the high council, Hyrum Smith castigated Austin Cowles's published explanation. The Prophet added that William Law's explanation had transformed "the truth of God . . . into a lie." Without divulging its contents, Hyrum suggested that the "revelation was in answer to a question concerning things which transpired in former days." Similarly, Joseph Smith reminded the council that his public sermon was only "showing the order in ancient days." On that part of the revelation dealing with the eternal marriage covenant, he spoke at length. That information, he said, had come in answer to a prayer about marriage in the resurrection: "'Man in this life must marry in view of eternity, otherwise they must remain as angels, or be single in heaven,' which was the doctrine of the revelation." The Prophet defended the right of "a man to have a wife on the earth while he has one in heaven, according to the keys of the Holy Priesthood."[90]

The council quickly moved on. It spent much of Friday hearing testimony against the character and activities of *Expositor* publishers Wilson Law and Robert D. Foster and conspirator Joseph H. Jackson but did not neglect the other seceders. Witnesses and council members persuasively accused these men of oppressing the poor (through high land prices), of being involved in counterfeiting, theft, seduction, and adultery, and of conspiring to kidnap, seduce, and murder.[91]

Convinced of the publishers' crimes and sins, councilmen then soundly castigated the newspaper itself as a public nuisance. They cited the respected English legal authority Blackstone who held "'that a libellous print or paper, affecting a private individual, may be destroyed.'" Because the city had no ordinance on libel, on June 10 the council passed

The first and only issue of the Nauvoo Expositor *was printed in this brick building on Mulholland Street on June 7, 1844. The press was disabled and the type pied under orders of the city council three days later.*

one on the authority of the charter's provision "to declare what shall be a nuisance, and to prevent and remove the same." Then, after concluding that the *Expositor* was, in fact, a public nuisance and guilty of publishing libel, the council ordered it "removed without delay." Councilman Benjamin Warrington cast the only dissenting vote. An old settler "who did not belong to any church or any party," he favored a substantial fine. A nuisance declaration, he felt, should come as a last resort. After the vote, Joseph Smith, as mayor, directed the city marshal to destroy the printing press, scatter the type in the street, and burn all remaining copies of the newspaper and its advertising handbills. The decision, he said, was necessary to protect both civil and religious institutions in the city. With a force from the Nauvoo Legion standing by as a backup, Marshal John P. Greene and members of the city police completed the task of interdiction before six that evening.[92]

It was not the first time a printing press had been destroyed in America by someone offended by an editor, nor would it be the last. Under common law in the United States, public officials could remove or destroy ("abate") a nuisance if lesser means failed. Obviously, in such instances it was a local matter to decide what behavior was considered injurious to public welfare.[93] The Saints had seen one of their own presses destroyed in July 1833 in Jackson County, Missouri. A citizens committee there had appealed to "the law of nature" and "the law of self-preservation" to rid themselves of what they termed an unwanted intrusion. In a similar challenge to unwanted ideas at Alton, Illinois, in 1837, extralegal regulators stormed a warehouse where abolitionist Elijah Lovejoy was storing a press and fatally wounded the Presbyterian minister. Lovejoy's death stirred a national firestorm of protest. Illinois citizens did not want such an incident repeated.[94] Although it was based on the actions of a legally constituted municipal government, the *Expositor* incident touched off a similar reaction in Nauvoo and the surrounding region.

After assessing the damage wreaked by Greene's posse, the publishers dispatched Charles A. Foster to Warsaw. Consistent with its policy, the *Signal* published a report sympathetic to the seceders' viewpoint. To support a claim that the posse had committed riot, it emphasized images of violence. Foster reported that he and Francis M. Higbee had tried to prevent the marshal's party of more than two hundred armed men from entering their property. "They paid no regard to our commands, but marched up the [outside] stairs, broke open the door, entered the office, and demolished the Press." The men, he said, arrived

> armed and equipped with muskets, swords, pistols, bowie-knives, sledge-hammers, etc. . . . They tumbled the press and materials into the street and *set fire to them, and demolished the machinery with a sledge-hammer, and injured the building very materially.* We made no resistance; but looked on and felt revenge, but leave it to the public, to avenge this climax of insult and injury.

Sidney Rigdon's report to Governor Ford offered a much less inflammatory description: "The city marshal, in obedience to [the city council's] order, went and removed the press and destroyed it. This was done without tumult or disorder."[95]

The owners sought reparation for the damage in a series of legal actions. First, Francis M. Higbee filed a warrant in district court at Carthage charging city officials with inciting a riot (a reference to the posse) in destroying the press. On June 12, an officer arrested Joseph Smith and other city officials and attempted to convey them to Carthage for trial. The indicted men appealed to Nauvoo's municipal court, which released them. On June 17, the councilors faced a second riot charge, filed by W. G. Ware. This time, the defendants argued that the orderly execution of a municipal order could not be considered a riot. Justice Daniel H. Wells heard this case and discharged the city officials. In a third legal effort, William and Wilson Law failed in their attempt to get an indictment in Springfield against the municipal court for its part in trying the *habeas corpus* petitions. "They have sworn revenge," Vilate Kimball wrote of the dissenters, "and no doubt they will have it."[96]

The *Warsaw Signal* published the owners' explanation of the *Expositor* case and the *Nauvoo Neighbor*'s defense of the city council's actions. Rumors circulated of threatened retribution against the two Nauvoo newspapers and their editors. Editors across the state and in major cities nationally picked up the story. Many expressed concern over the controversy created by the destruction of the *Expositor*.[97]

In a special issue, the *Nauvoo Neighbor* jumped to the defense of the city council. It reinforced the evidence used against the censured publishers and supported the council's decision. At the same time, it responded to political and doctrinal charges raised by the *Expositor*.[98] The *Neighbor* ridiculed the schismatic leaders (two Fosters, two Higbees, two Laws, and Ivins) as the "seven sons of Sceva"—ineffectual exorcists in Acts 19:11–16 who met an almost laughable end. It charged them with counterfeiting and other crimes. The paper cited chapter and verse to prove that the centralized gathering of the Saints was scriptural and that the present was, in fact, "a day of sacrifice." The *Neighbor* paid particular attention to what it termed the publishers' "libels and slanderous articles upon the citizens and city council." To defend the city council's actions, the paper cited Nauvoo's charter and reviewed the legal opinions of Blackstone. Incorporated cities, the article said, held "reserved rights" like those granted states by the Constitution. Adding precedent to law, the writer claimed that "it is a common occurrence for city corporations to remove scurrilous prints." In Nauvoo, said the author, such actions would prevent Missouri-style mobbings. A patriotic conclusion echoed similar calls for redress of the Missouri wrongs:

> In the name of freemen, and in the name of God, we beseech all men,
> who have the spirit of honor in them, to cease from persecuting

us collectively or individually. Let us enjoy our religion, rights, and peace, like the rest of mankind: why start pressure to destroy rights and privileges, and bring upon us mobs to plunder and murder? We ask no more than what belongs to us—The *rights of Americans*.[99]

THE CALL TO ARMS

Reactions in area newspapers were only part of a broader discussion of the *Expositor* case. In speeches throughout western Illinois, the *Expositor*'s publishers denounced the Prophet and his influence.[100] At Warsaw and Carthage on June 11, indignation meetings convened to oppose Nauvoo's interference with the constitutional guarantee of a free press. The next day concerned citizens met again at Warsaw and at Green Plains. People resolved to exterminate the Latter-day Saints or to expel them by armed force.[101] When a Latter-day Saint living in Warsaw refused to take up arms against his own people, several men threatened to cut his throat and then expelled him at bayonet point. From Adams County, a non-Mormon wrote to his mother of an unusual excitement:

> Nothing else is talked of or thought at the present—men marching to and from head quarters—and what is to be the consequence God only knows. One thing is certain—that if the Mormons do not behave themselves better they will be driven out of the country as the people are determined not to bear with them much longer.[102]

The destruction of the *Expositor* and reports that a similar fate awaited his own newspaper caused Warsaw's critical editor Thomas Sharp to declare: "It is sufficient! War and extermination is inevitable! Citizens arise ONE and ALL!!! . . . We have no time for comment: every man will make his own. LET IT BE MADE WITH POWDER AND BALL!!!!" On the thirteenth, a countywide mass meeting at Carthage adopted the Warsaw proposal to drive the Saints from outlying settlements into Nauvoo. The old citizens resolved to exterminate the entire Latter-day Saint population if they did not surrender the prophet-mayor and his associates. A woman visiting in Carthage wrote to her husband in Warsaw, "You have no idea what is passing here now, to see men preparing for battle to fight with blood hounds; but I hope there will be so large an Army as to intimidate that 'bandit horde' [in Nauvoo] so there will be no blood shed." In Nauvoo, Mayor

Joseph Smith urged citizens to help him maintain "the public peace and common quiet" of the city to eliminate any justification for an invasion.[103]

Because of the hotly debated *Expositor* question and talk of vigilante action, Governor Thomas Ford feared the outbreak of a civil war in Hancock County. A confidential letter from Sidney Rigdon on June 14 asked for his help in dispersing "a great assemblage at Carthage threatening violence" against Nauvoo's citizens. Two days later, Joseph Smith urged thousands of assembled brethren "to keep cool, and prepare their arms for defense of the city." A general meeting that evening appointed delegates to visit all parts of the county to calm the citizens by explaining the city council's actions. The Prophet urged Ford to hear the council's reasoning personally in Nauvoo. In his capacity as lieutenant general of the Nauvoo Legion, Joseph Smith ordered militia units in outlying settlements to prepare to defend their communities or Nauvoo.[104] Several men at Ramus offered immediate aid. They headed off across the water-logged prairie, many without shoes or boots. During the all-night march to Nauvoo, they were challenged by unidentified troops flying two red flags. The weary volunteers reached Nauvoo safely and were boarded in a large unfinished brick house.[105]

The frantic reactions raised concerns. H. H. Bliss, a friendly non-Mormon at La Harpe observed:

> We never expected to see . . . our old neighbours shouldering their guns to go in defense of Smith, thereby showing a disposition to kill any or all of us if Smith gave them orders. . . . By this time Smith had collected his followers at Nauvoo to the amount of some thousands ready as some of them said *"to wade in blood up to their shoulder"* in defense of their Prophet.

Actually, in his position as lieutenant general, Smith assigned the militia to support the city marshal in maintaining the peace. On the eighteenth, he declared martial law. "By this time," Bliss explained, "we Gentiles here had formed ourselves into a Military Company for the protection of our place."[106]

To be certain that he had the support of Nauvoo's citizens in a climate of increasing divisiveness, the Prophet secured pledges of loyalty from the city council and the Nauvoo Legion.[107] On June 18, he assembled the militia in the street outside the Mansion House, and then, in full uniform,

Lieutenant General Smith climbed atop the nearby frame of a barbershop and inn being built for Porter Rockwell. William W. Phelps read the Warsaw convention's call for the extermination of church leaders and the expulsion of the Saints.[108] General Smith encouraged the men to arm themselves to defend their constitutional rights and their families. He directed them to take only defensive action and asked, "Will you all stand by me to the death, and sustain at the peril of our lives, the laws of our country?" He repeated the question three times. Each time, the soldiers shouted "Aye!" Smith then raised his sword skyward:

> I call God and angels to witness that I have unsheathed my sword with a firm and unalterable determination that this people shall have their legal rights, and be protected from mob violence, or my blood shall be spilt upon the ground like water. . . .
>
> . . . You are a good people; therefore I love you with all my heart. . . . You have stood by me in the hour of trouble, and I am willing to sacrifice my life for your preservation.[109]

Martial law restricted movements in Nauvoo. Pickets guarded all roads leading out of the city, all streets and alleys in the city, and key points along the river. A St. Louis newspaper imagined that the action was forcing the seceders to flee for their lives: "Several hundred Mormons, most of them hostile to the Prophet, have left Nauvoo with their property. Jo[seph Smith] had laid an interdict on further emigration." The same paper later editorialized, "At Nauvoo, a bayonet bristles at every assailable point! Boats are not permitted to tarry, nor strangers permitted to land. The Mormon force under arms is estimated at between 2000 and 3000 men."[110] Another St. Louis paper reported that *Expositor* publisher Francis M. Higbee had fled Nauvoo on June 11 in disguise to avoid reprisal. The *Nauvoo Neighbor* countered that the departing schismatics had left Nauvoo "as a matter of their own choice. 'The wicked flee when no man pursueth.'"[111] Robert D. Foster informed Joseph Smith that the dissenters would leave freely, but only after they had sold their property. Many of them were, in fact, rapidly selling out.[112]

Fearing an armed confrontation, and with mail service interrupted by bad roads, high water, and mob threats, the Prophet planned to send an express rider overland to the Illinois River or down the Mississippi to St. Louis with letters to each of the Twelve. On Thursday, June 20, he wrote

On June 18, 1844, Lieutenant General Joseph Smith rallied the Nauvoo Legion to defend the city and their rights against possible attacks by vigilantes. This 1845 drawing of the event near the Mansion House includes other Legion officers along with Nauvoo policemen and opponents of the Prophet's civic and religious leadership.

the letters, urging the apostles and missionaries to return quietly but immediately to Nauvoo. After further consideration, and with prospects bright for a negotiated settlement, Joseph decided on Saturday not to send any of the letters.[113]

That same day, Mayor/General Smith halted the inspection of travelers but advised the pickets to maintain vigilance. The Nauvoo Legion continued its parade ground reviews. Officers dug entrenchments and set up encampments. Scouts explored the back country east of the city, plotted a defense, and considered how to feed a city under siege. An unusually wet spring had washed out many bridges and left roads nearly impassable. Willard Richards wrote to James Arlington Bennet in New York, inviting him to gather volunteers for Nauvoo's defense. The Saints were ready to fight for their liberties, said Richards. If necessary, they would bring about "the second birth of our nation's freedom" by establishing a "'separate and independent empire'"—"that glorious 'vision in the west'" that Bennet had been encouraging as a solution to the Mormon question. To the militia, General Smith "gave orders that a standard be prepared for the nations."[114]

With both sides arming themselves and recruiting new militia volunteers,[115] Ford traveled to the county seat to seek a peaceful solution. An assembly of Carthage citizens pledged to support his effort to resolve the *Expositor* issue in the courts.[116] On Friday, June 21, the governor wrote to Nauvoo, asking city officials to explain their actions. Joseph Smith immediately sent political advisors John M. Bernhisel and John Taylor with documents and another plea for a personal investigation by the governor in Nauvoo.[117] "Our troubles are invariably brought upon us by falsehoods and mis-representations by designing men," the Prophet wrote. "We have ever held ourselves amenable to the law; and, for myself, sir, I am ever ready to conform to and support the laws and Constitution, even at the expense of my life."[118]

Several of the Prophet's opponents were on hand in Carthage when Taylor and Bernhisel presented their explanation of the *Expositor* affair. Ford listened to both sides and carefully studied the Prophet's letter and the accompanying affidavits. In a lengthy written response, the governor drew from his own experience on the state supreme court as he evaluated the concerns of the seceders. Ford denounced the destruction of the *Expositor* as an outrage on the laws and a restriction upon the liberties of free citizens. He cited technical errors in the conduct of the hearing and added that the existence of libel in a newspaper was no reason to destroy it. The city council had committed four separate violations of law, he argued. First, the council had breached the constitutional protection of a free press, and they had conducted unreasonable searches and seizures of the publishers' property. They should have allowed due process of law through a jury trial. Second, although the council had operated within its legislative powers in defining a public nuisance, they should have left to the courts a determination of guilt. "The Constitution abhors and will not tolerate the union of legislative and judicial power," Ford said. Third, under its charter, he said, Nauvoo's municipal court could deal only with city laws. It could not discharge the warrants filed against the city council in a district court at Carthage. Finally, the governor said, the city council failed to prove that "a newspaper charged to be scurrilous and libelous may be legally abated or removed as a nuisance." Ford said the accused men must allow a court to decide the issue. Any posse organized from the militia in Hancock County to enforce compliance, Ford warned, might quickly become a mob and destroy the fragile peace.[119] Vilate Kimball reflected concern in Nauvoo that Ford had sided with Law and Foster; she considered the governor's response "a saucy letter."[120]

Nauvoo's delegates left Carthage at five that afternoon with a state escort. Joseph Smith was already planning how best to defend Nauvoo against an attack. He told associates that the city would be safe if he and Hyrum fled. Rather than appear in Carthage for trial, the brothers and Willard Richards would seek refuge in the West. If the people of Nauvoo went about their business as normal, he said, they would be protected. According to Reynolds Cahoon, it was around nine when Hyrum came out of the Mansion House and declared, "A company of men are seeking to kill my brother Joseph, and the Lord has warned him to flee to the Rocky Mountains to save his life." The Prophet invited Porter Rockwell to accompany the refugees "on a short journey" and asked two others to escort his and Hyrum's families on the *Maid of Iowa* to Portsmouth, Ohio, to await further word. The Smiths and Richards headed for the riverbank to meet Rockwell.[121]

When Taylor and Bernhisel reached Nauvoo, they searched for Joseph Smith. Even though the hour was late, Smith wanted to consider and respond to Governor Ford's letter. He sent Rockwell home and returned himself to the Mansion, where Willard Richards, Hyrum Smith, William W. Phelps, William Marks, and others assembled with the delegates in an upper council room. Earlier in the year, the church newspaper had endorsed Ford's plea for a reasoned resolution of political differences in the county. An editorial in February had declared,

> Should reason, liberty, law, light, and philanthropy now guide the destinies of Hancock county, . . . there can be no doubt that peace, prosperity, and happiness will prevail, and that future generations as well as the present one, will call Governor Ford A PEACE MAKER. . . . Our motto then, is, *peace with all.*[122]

But those who reviewed Ford's response to the immediate emergency were not pleased with the governor's judgment. According to John Taylor, "It became a serious question as to the course we should pursue. Various projects were discussed, but nothing definitely decided upon for some time." Wearied from his arduous travels, Taylor left the meeting after two "legal and high-minded gentlemen," newly arrived on the evening steamship, requested an interview with the Prophet. One of them was a son of John C. Calhoun. These men advised the Prophet to appeal to Washington for help.[123]

After further lengthy deliberations, Joseph Smith formally rejected the governor's invitation to appear in Carthage. The Prophet had faced unfair judges in Missouri, had been fleeing from vexatious lawsuits for years, and feared for his life. In a letter written at midnight by one of his clerks, he agreed to face another magistrate but not in Carthage. As for the legality of the city council's action, he repeated the legal arguments behind the decision. He had declared martial law for self-protection, he added, and not to injure anyone. Joseph Smith said that the city council would correct any demonstrated wrongs and would welcome a review by the state supreme court. Acting upon their own best judgment, the council believed that their search and seizure had been reasonable, and that they had not mixed legislative and judicial power. The mayor cited several instances in which police in New York, Boston, and in Ohio had destroyed scurrilous publications. The destruction of "a little property," he said of the *Expositor,* was preferable to the "loss of character by libel and the loss of life by mobocratic prints."[124]

An appearance before a Carthage judge, the Prophet said, would only repeat the sham trial in Richmond, Missouri, where witnesses were jailed or not allowed to testify. "We dare not come," he said.

> Writs, we are assured, are issued against us in various parts of the country. For what? To drag us from place to place, from court to court, across the creeks and prairies, till some bloodthirsty villain could find his opportunity to shoot us. . . . Sir, we dare not come, for our lives would be in danger, and we are guilty of no crime.[125]

The Prophet concluded his letter with a plan of action. Upon the advice of certain "legal and high-minded gentlemen from abroad" who had arrived that night, delegates from Nauvoo would appeal once again to Washington. Why? The case involved an act of treason by one state against another (Missouri against Illinois) and by Missouri against Joseph Smith. "We shall leave the city forthwith to lay the facts before the General Government." The Nauvoo Legion had been disbanded as requested by the governor, Joseph Smith reported, and now Ford should act "to cause our helpless women and children to be protected from mob violence. . . . Disperse the mob, and secure to us our constitutional privileges, that our lives may not be endangered when on trial."[126]

The two Smith brothers and Richards picked up Porter Rockwell at his lodgings. The four men walked to the riverbank to find a boat, but the Prophet had unresolved concerns. Despite what he had told Ford, he wondered for a time about the value of another personal visit to Washington. He sent for W. W. Phelps and asked him to leave on Sunday's second steamboat for Cincinnati, there to prepare petitions to President Tyler and the Congress.[127] Smith instructed Phelps to invite Emma and Mary Smith and the children of the two families to accompany him. Leery of Governor Ford's plea to appear in Carthage for trial, Joseph and Hyrum Smith would go into hiding for their own safety. To protect the church from further misunderstandings, the Prophet also summoned William Clayton. Protect the records of the Council of Fifty, he advised. Clayton decided to preserve the confidential minutes by burying them.[128] It was two o'clock, Sunday morning, June 23, before Joseph and his three companions pushed off toward Montrose. The borrowed boat leaked profusely. Rockwell rowed while the others used their boots and shoes to bail water and keep themselves afloat.[129]

The refugees reached the Iowa shore at daybreak. Finding no one home at their intended destination, they located another Latter-day Saint in the Montrose area willing to board them. Meanwhile, Rockwell returned to Nauvoo for horses. He carried with him a letter for Emma, written from Joseph's secret hiding place, simply called "Safety." Joseph counseled Emma on how to find the means during his absence to support their family. The letter reflected the Prophet's concern: "Do not despair," he wrote. "If God ever opens a door that is possible for me I will see you again. I do not know where I shall go, or what I shall do, but shall if possible endeavor to get to the city of Washington."[130]

Rockwell found Joseph's family and friends uncertain about his decision to flee. Some in Nauvoo felt Joseph's absence would jeopardize their safety; others agreed that his departure would be a protection both for him and the city. A posse had arrived in Nauvoo early that morning to arrest Mayor Smith. Word spread that Governor Ford had vowed to bring the mayor to trial even if he had to dispatch troops to hunt him down like a fugitive. Ford's messengers repeated the governor's guarantee of a trial safe from vigilantes. Hiram Kimball, Reynolds Cahoon, and Emma's nephew,

Lorenzo D. Wasson, left for the Iowa hideout. They delivered the message from the posse and discussed the concerns over Joseph's decision: Nauvoo's opponents had threatened to destroy the city if he did not submit to a trial. The Saints feared a repeat of the Missouri mobbings. "Some were tried almost to death to think Joseph should leave them in the hour of danger," Vilate Kimball noted a few days later. "Hundreds have left the city since the fuss commenced. Most of the merchants on the hill have left. I have not felt frightened." Like Vilate, Hyrum remained confident in the legal process and in the governor's pledge. In contrast, the Prophet doubted the governor's ability to fulfill his promise. Hyrum's counsel eventually prevailed.[131]

At his home in Nauvoo, John Taylor awoke to news that the Smiths had crossed the river. He packed up the stereotype plates for the Book of Mormon and Doctrine and Covenants at the printing office and crossed to Montrose, headed for upper Canada. When he found the Smiths and learned of their decision to return to Nauvoo, he reluctantly altered his own plans and returned to his home. At two o'clock that afternoon on the Iowa riverbank, Joseph and Hyrum cosigned another letter to Ford. Encouraged by the governor's assurance of protection but still concerned, the Prophet told Ford that he had hesitated to stand trial for one reason— "on account of assassins, and the reason I have to fear deathly consequences from their hands." Because the governor had reportedly subdued antagonists in Carthage, Nauvoo's mayor would comply with the governor's request: "I now offer to come to you at Carthage on the morrow," Joseph wrote, "as early as shall be convenient for your *posse* to escort us into headquarters, provided we can have a fair trial, not be abused nor have my witnesses abused, and have all things done in due form of law." At half past five, the party crossed the river and dispersed to their homes.[132] At Nauvoo, they found other members of the city council packing their belongings for a possible hasty departure.[133]

The letter penned on the riverbank reached the governor by courier about nine that night. At first, Ford seemed willing to comply with Joseph's request for an escort. The governor's attitude changed when Wilson Law, Joseph H. Jackson, and their attorney argued against his plans. They convinced Ford that an escort would grant to Smith honors not accorded other citizens. The governor sent word to Nauvoo requiring those charged to appear at ten the next morning. It was the only way, he repeated, to prevent mobs from sacking Nauvoo. Joseph Smith received this request about four on Monday morning, June 24. He invited the city council and witnesses to prepare for the trip to Carthage. By half past six, the entourage had assembled on the flats.[134]

The company that headed for Carthage that morning included all eighteen under indictment, their attorney James W. Woods of Burlington, and perhaps a dozen others, including the Prophet's clerk, Willard Richards, and supporters Dan Jones and Henry G. Sherwood.[135] The party paused at the unfinished temple. From the edge of the bluffs, astride his pacer, Joseph looked admiringly at Nauvoo. He pondered what he had attempted to accomplish for his followers in this city of refuge. "This is the loveliest place and the best people under the heavens," he said. "Little do they know the trials that await them."[136]

It was half a day's travel on horseback to Carthage. Just before ten o'clock and four miles short of their destination, the party met a company of about sixty mounted militia from McDonough County under Captain James Dunn. The soldiers carried orders from Ford to collect the state arms from the Nauvoo Legion to calm fears in Carthage. Ford hoped to quiet both sides and avoid civil war. Those plotting Joseph's murder had encouraged the order. They hoped to prevent an expected spontaneous act of revenge. Acting in his military office, Joseph Smith immediately countersigned the governor's order. Then he and a dozen of his party returned to Nauvoo to ensure compliance. The state-appointed McDonough County militia agreed to accompany them. By this turn of events, Joseph Smith would enter the county seat that night under military escort.[137]

By sundown, the arms issued to the Nauvoo Legion in 1841 had been deposited in the Masonic Hall. The men responded reluctantly, fearing that the loss of their rifles would only encourage an attack. Surrendered were three cannons and about two hundred forty small arms. Anti-Mormons would claim that the Latter-day Saints controlled thirty state cannon and between five hundred and six hundred small arms. Captain Dunn and his quartermaster told the assembled Nauvoo officers that their compliance would ensure peace, and they pledged protection.[138] The militia had retained and hidden away their personal arms.[139]

The mood in Nauvoo was somber. For Henry Sherwood, the frank admission of the Prophet's fears rang in his ears: "I am going like a lamb to the slaughter," Joseph had confided en route to Carthage, but I am calm as a summer's morning. I have a conscience void of offense toward God and toward all men. If they take my life I shall die an innocent man, and my blood shall cry from the ground for vengeance, and it shall be said of me, "He was murdered in cold blood!"

Back in Nauvoo, Joseph repeated this sentiment to several others. Within days, they would recall it with a new understanding. Twice Joseph returned to his family at the Mansion House for another farewell. Mary Fielding Smith's brother found Hyrum "in better spirits by far than when he left. He told me," said Joseph Fielding, "that all things would go well."[140]

From the Smith home, the company rode up Main Street on horseback and in wagons. They waved goodbye to the state militia and local guard at the Masonic Hall and headed once more along the road to Carthage. At his farm, the Prophet turned his head for several last looks at the prosperous layout. To those who commented on the attention he was giving the place, Joseph said, "If some of you had got such a farm and knew you would not see it any more, you would want to take a good look at it for the last time." Just beyond the farm, the entourage met A. C. Hodge, returning from Carthage. His message, delivered privately to Hyrum, included Hodge's own summarizing advice: "Do not go another foot, for they say they will kill you, if you go to Carthage." A minister's reading of the mood of the community, Hodge reported, was certain death for Joseph and Hyrum. The proprietor of the Hamilton Hotel had pointed out the source of potential trouble. "Hodge," he had said, pointing to the Carthage Greys, "there are the boys that will settle you Mormons." Farther along, the Prophet and his traveling companions stopped to eat, and the governor's detachment caught up with them, hauling the state arms. With this escort, the company rode the final four miles to Carthage. It was well into the night when they passed the public square, where some of the Carthage Greys and a few other troops from the area had camped. Here, the citizen solders shouted obscenities and threatened "to shoot the damned Mormons." The raucous welcome aroused Governor Ford, now settled at the inn. He leaned out the window of his quarters and promised that he would cause Joseph Smith to pass before the troops the next morning if they would quietly return to their quarters. The troops responded, "Hurrah for Tom Ford," and obeyed his order.[141]

The Nauvoo party also put up for the night at the Hamilton Hotel. It was midnight. Inside the hotel, some of the defendants discovered that several apostates, too, were staying at Carthage's best inn. John A. Hicks confessed freely to Cyrus Wheelock that he and others, including William and Wilson Law, Chauncey and Francis M. Higbee, Robert D. and Charles A. Foster, and Joseph H. Jackson, had one intent. Whatever the outcome of the trial, they would shed Joseph's blood. Jackson spoke openly of the plan. Wheelock sought out Ford and shared this threatening talk with him. While acknowledging "that a great deal of hatred existed against" the prisoners, the governor treated the threats with indifference. "They were no more than the bluster which might have been expected," he wrote in a later reflection. Ford would not give up his hope that the *Expositor* case would be settled through legal process. Jackson's boast remained with Wheelock. The apostate had said, "You will find me a true prophet in this respect."[142]

CHAPTER 14

"Joseph and Hyrum Are Dead"

Now Zion mourns—she mourns an earthly head:
The Prophet and the Patriarch are dead!
The blackest deed that men or devils know
Since Calv'ry's scene, has laid the brothers low!
One in their life, and one in death—they prov'd
How strong their friendship—how they truly lov'd;
True to their mission, until death, they stood,
Then seal'd their testimony with their blood.

. . . .

Ye Saints! be still, and know that God is just—
With steadfast purpose in his promise trust;
Girded with sackcloth, own his mighty hand,
And wait his judgments on this guilty land!

—ELIZA R. SNOW, JULY 1, 1844

The events at Carthage, Illinois, during the last week of June 1844 would have a profound effect on the history of Nauvoo's gathered people from that time forward. The murders of Joseph Smith and his brother Hyrum by a mob with painted faces has forever etched itself in the memory of the Latter-day Saints. The deaths of the Prophet and Patriarch ended one era in the church's history and opened another. Within the church, the deaths of the two revered and respected leaders created a vacuum difficult to fill. Questions over succession to the prophetic office created divisions that have not yet healed. As Eliza Snow, one of the Prophet's plural wives, so tellingly wrote, Zion mourned both the loss of its earthly head and its faith in justice under civil law. To some Saints, it bolstered their questions of America's position toward the church and increased their skepticism about access to the freedoms their ancestors had defended. The disappointments suffered in seeking redress for the losses suffered in Missouri were born afresh when the musket balls of boastful assassins cut short the due process of law promised in a court chamber in Hancock County.

Deliberations at Carthage

Both sides in the *Expositor* case had committed themselves to pursue the issue through the courts, even though neither side expected satisfactory results. The mayor and city council of Nauvoo distrusted certain men who wore the robes of justice at Carthage. They expected to see witnesses detained and juries packed—such was their memory of similar trials in Missouri and their perception of the purposes of their accusers. The mayor, at least, feared for his own life—that justice would be cut short through assassination. The owners of the destroyed newspaper sought payment for their losses and more. For the Anti-Mormon Party, court hearings offered a pretext to remove two men from their place of safety in Nauvoo to a place where a lynch mob could mete out popular justice.

Those plotting Joseph Smith's death anticipated his release on the riot charge in the appearance before a court at Carthage on Tuesday, June 25, 1844. In their view, dismissal of the charge would release them from their promise to support Ford's efforts to resolve grievances through the courts and would free them to enact vigilante justice. Eight hours before Nauvoo city officials presented themselves for the hearing on the charge of riot, Constable David Bettisworth served warrants against Joseph and Hyrum Smith on charges of treason. These warrants stemmed from the activation of the Nauvoo Legion on the nineteenth.[1] The plotters bragged privately that if the treason charges did not succeed, they had eighteen others ready. An informant, just before the four o'clock hearing, reported having heard that the Laws, the Higbees, and Foster "had said *that there was nothing against these men; the law could not reach them but powder and ball would, and they should not go out of Carthage alive.*" As events of the next three days at Carthage would illustrate, the Prophet's enemies had designed a careful legal ruse to hide their widely rumored murderous intentions.[2]

Joseph Smith's party and some of his enemies stayed overnight in Carthage at the Hamilton Hotel (also called the Inn), a block east of the courthouse and five blocks from the county jail.

The charge of treason did not cause much immediate concern when it was delivered around eight o'clock on the morning of the original hearing. Two hours later, Joseph and Hyrum joined Governor Ford for a carefully organized appearance before the McDonough and Carthage troops. With Brigadier General Miner R. Deming between them, the two church leaders walked within a protective square formed by a company of the Greys. Others in the party followed behind the three or mixed among the crowd watching for trouble. The appearance met Monday night's promise to the McDonough troops. Having never met Joseph Smith, they did not know what he looked like. But certain Carthage soldiers took offense when Ford used military titles to introduce the Smiths. Witnesses remembered that "some of the officers threw up their hats, drew their swords, and said they would introduce themselves to the damned Mormons in a different style." The governor calmed the soldiers with a mild reprimand and hurried the church leaders safely back to their hotel room. Deming posted a guard to maintain quiet among the Greys.[3]

Rumors circulating during the day echoed the unsettled mood in western Illinois. One report said that troops from Warsaw were gathering uninvited at Carthage. Another claimed that the apostates had organized a party to plunder Nauvoo. The governor wished to prevent disruptions of the legal process. With the Prophet's endorsement, Governor Ford ordered Captain Singleton of Brown County to march a company of sixty men from McDonough County to Nauvoo to help the city police should disorder break out. Ford authorized Singleton to mobilize the privately armed Nauvoo Legion, if necessary, to protect the city from outside incursion.[4]

The encounter with the Carthage Greys and persistent rumors of armed conflict set the mood for the four o'clock appearance of fifteen of the men charged with riot. For safety, the hearing was conducted at the hotel with a guard of men with bayonets fixed.[5] The prosecution immediately called for a postponement. The defense wanted to proceed; they acknowledged the role of the mayor and the city council in ordering the destruction of the press and offered to post bail. After further discussion, Justice Robert F. Smith bound the case over for a Saturday hearing. He asked a rather high bond of five hundred dollars for each defendant, but friends of the accused offered their property as security to help meet the requirement. Most of the freed councilmen left the county seat soon afterward for Nauvoo.[6]

After supper that evening, Joseph and Hyrum Smith were served an arrest warrant on the charge of treason. The mittimus from Justice Robert Smith claimed that the pair had appeared for trial but that it had been postponed when Francis M. Higbee and others failed to appear as witnesses. In fact, the hearing earlier in the day had concluded without consideration of the charge. Clearly, the order was issued on false grounds. The Prophet's attorneys sought Ford's advice. Though sympathetic, the governor could see no way an executive could interfere in the judicial process. Let the legal process take its course, he counseled. Ford expressed willingness, if asked, to post a guard at the jail. John Taylor likewise asked Ford to intervene but received the same response. Apparently, Justice Robert Smith also consulted the governor, who advised him to call out the Carthage Greys to execute the arrest order. Because the justice served as captain of the militia, he thus ordered compliance to his own judicial ruling. He posted a guard of twenty men at the hotel door under Captain James Dunn. Meantime, Justice Smith assured the Prophet's attorneys that he had issued the mittimus only to create a reason for placing the Smiths under protective custody in the jail.[7]

It wasn't long before Dunn and his guard escorted Joseph and Hyrum from Hamilton's hotel to the jail. A few friends and counsel accompanied them. Stephen Markham and Dan Jones joined the procession. Markham carried a large hickory cane that he had nicknamed "the rascal-beater." Jones had his own smaller black hickory club. The two used the sticks against a few drunken men who broke through the ranks. Jailer George W. Stigall put his prisoners upstairs in the iron-barred cell reserved for criminals. Later, he moved them downstairs into the less-secure debtor's room. It was furnished with a bench, some blankets, and a "night bucket." After some "pleasant conversation about 'the secret of godliness,'" the ten men scattered themselves around the floor and slept until six o'clock the next morning.[8]

As dawn broke on the twenty-sixth, the jailer provided breakfast for the men and relocated them to his own upstairs bedroom, furnished with a bed, mattresses for children in the family, a writing table and chairs, a chest, and perhaps a wardrobe. Curtains hung at the windows, which were open for ventilation. Joseph Smith was anxious about legal developments at Carthage. He suggested that his attorneys, H. T. Reid of Fort Madison and James W. Woods of Burlington, seek a change of venue to Quincy.[9] Meanwhile, he sent a messenger to Knoxville to ask Judge Jesse B. Thomas of the circuit court to hear a request for a writ of habeas corpus. Thomas had given friendly but informal advice during the *Expositor* and perjury hearings. This time, Thomas declined for lack of jurisdiction in the treason charge.[10] Even though Smith trusted his legal counsel, he seemed nervous about their ability to handle all aspects of the case. His opponents had engaged five men to present their position. Joseph had only two attorneys from a single legal partnership. The Prophet sent for Latter-day Saint attorney Almon W. Babbitt, who had helped at the perjury hearing in May, but Babbitt had already hired on to help the opposition. Even so, threatened with his life by residents of Carthage, Babbitt hurried off to Macedonia. Friends of the Prophet were likewise harassed out of town during that day and the next.[11]

Besides his legal advisers, Joseph's other security lay with Governor Thomas Ford. The governor remained at Carthage to oversee a solution to the crisis through the law. After several failed attempts by the Prophet

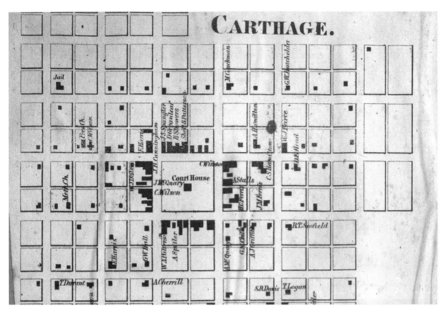

Carthage businesses, as shown in this 1859 map, clustered around Court House Square, with the Hancock County jail at the northwest edge of the business district.

to gain an interview, the two finally met in the jailer's upstairs bedroom at mid-morning. During a forty-five minute conversation, Joseph Smith defended the legality of the city council's actions against the *Expositor* and his issuance of martial law. A preventive measure, Smith said, could not be considered treason against the state if its intent was self-defense. Ford seemed to agree that the Saints had acted according to their best judgment. He reaffirmed his opinion that the destruction of the press was wrong. The Prophet recalled the long months of imprisonment that the Missouri judges had imposed on him without fair trial and without the benefit of witnesses. He did not want to repeat that experience. In response, the legalistic-minded Ford defended constitutional process and once again pledged protection. If his McDonough troops marched with him to Nauvoo on Thursday, the governor said, he would probably take the prisoners along to ensure their safety. The conversation ended shortly after ten with Smith's offer to pay for the loss of the press. He did not want the owners to suffer financial loss, he said, but neither did he want a libelous paper published in Nauvoo.[12]

The prisoners spent the rest of the morning biding their time, an outward calm belying inner tension. The Prophet's scribe, Willard Richards, kept busy taking dictation. John Taylor sang to entertain the men. Joseph Smith recalled a dream about the fall of William and Wilson Law and another dream about trying to save a steamboat in a storm. The men interacted with the guards posted from Captain Dunn's McDonough troops to protect them from harm and to prevent their escape. Some of the guards became so convinced of the prisoners' innocence that they were relieved of duty. Frank Worrell supervised the new guards posted from the Carthage Greys.[13]

During the afternoon, attorneys for the two sides jockeyed for control over the charge of treason. Counsel for the prisoners resisted a call for a hearing, but at half past three the issue was resolved. Justice Robert Smith sent Constable David Bettisworth back to the jail with a company of the Greys to serve as escort. Even with this guard, the prisoners feared the consequences of a march to the courthouse, so the Greys formed a hollow square for protection. The Prophet surprised the gathering crowd by locking arms with one of the bystanders for safety en route to the four o'clock hearing.[14]

At the courthouse, defense attorneys H. T. Reid and James W. Woods sought for an examination on the charges as soon as witnesses could be brought from Nauvoo, which would require adjournment for at least a day. The justice set the next phase of the hearing for noon on the twenty-seventh and remanded the prisoners to the county jail. Joseph and Hyrum were now legally incarcerated. The jailer confined them in the iron cage until a note from Ford half an hour later invited Stigall to return them to the more comfortable bedroom.[15]

The prisoners did not hear anything more about the governor's planned march to Nauvoo until around eight that night. At that time, Woods and Reid brought word that Ford and his advisers had decided he should take all but fifty or sixty of the assembled militia with him the following morning. The prisoners would remain behind, but the governor promised to handpick a guard for the jail. Justice Robert Smith had postponed Thursday's trial until Saturday, the twenty-ninth. After the attorneys left, the prisoners and their five companions prepared for the night. John Taylor led them in prayer. Hyrum Smith turned to the Book of Mormon for consolation. More confident than his brother of their eventual release, he selected accounts telling of the release from prison of other servants of God. This discussion piqued the interest of the guards at the door, so Joseph explained early events of the Restoration.

It was late when the men retired. Joseph and Hyrum were given the only bed in the room. Taylor, John S. Fullmer, Stephen Markham, and Dan Jones lay side by side on mattresses on the wood floor. A gunshot nearby prompted Joseph to find a spot on the floor between Jones and Fullmer. Fullmer remembered the quiet conversation between them. "I would to God that I could preach to the Saints in Nauvoo once more," he remembered Joseph saying. Fullmer tried to cheer the Prophet. Richards kept writing until his last candle burned out and left the room dark. Then he took the place on the bed vacated by the Prophet. The room quieted again. Joseph whispered a question to Jones, "Are you afraid to die?" Jones, like Fullmer, tried to disabuse Joseph of his foreboding. According to Jones, around midnight would-be assassins crept up the stairway but lost their courage when Joseph Smith shouted through the door and invited them in his "prophet's voice" to carry out their mission of death.[16]

The Murders at Carthage

Reports early on Thursday, June 27, did nothing to reassure Joseph Smith that the legal process would continue uninterrupted. In a letter to Emma dictated that morning, he encouraged the Saints to remain calm and to follow Ford's directions when the governor spoke to them. "There is no danger of any extermination order," he told Emma. "Should there be a mutiny among the troops (which we do not anticipate, excitement is abating) a part will remain loyal and stand for the defense of the state and our rights." If attacked, he said, it would be his duty to defend himself, but he anticipated "the last extreme" would not arrive. Taking up the pen himself, Joseph added a postscript: "Dear Emma," he wrote,

> I am very much resigned to my lot, knowing I am justified, and have done the best that could be done. Give my love to the children and all my friends . . . ; and as for treason, I know that I have not committed any, and they cannot prove anything of the kind, so you need not have any fears that anything can happen to us on that account.[17]

The penalty for treason was death by hanging.

Joseph had not forgotten the reports of previous days—threats that his life would end not with a rope around his neck but with bullet wounds in his flesh. Shortly before dictating his message to Emma, he had heard Dan Jones's reaffirmation of a plot against his life. Jones, venturing out of the jail to investigate the disturbance during the night, met Frank Worrell, head of the guard at the jail. According to Jones, Worrell had gloated, "'I can prophesy better than Old Joe, for neither he nor his brother, nor anyone who will remain with them will see the sun set today.'" Jones reported the conversation first to the Prophet and next, at his direction, to the governor. Ford discounted the threats as idle harassment. Jones then challenged Ford to place a friendlier guard. The prisoners are master Masons, Jones said, "'and as such I demand of you protection of their lives.'" Ford, too, had affiliated with the Masons and knew very well his fraternal obligation to protect a fellow member but persisted in his opinion. When the guards prevented Jones from reentering the jail, he lingered out of sight to watch developments.[18]

Those most active in the Carthage anti-Mormon effort, like the leaders of the movement in Warsaw, sought support from neighbors and friends. They organized a mass meeting at Carthage on June 27. The topic: how to prevent Joseph Smith from being elected president of the United States. If he failed in 1844, some had said, he would certainly succeed four years later, because his widely circulated *Views on Government* had attracted much favorable attention. A cooperative effort by Missouri and Illinois to kill him, they surmised, would be tolerated and go unpunished. The meeting claimed delegates from every state except three. It resembled in minor ways a political convention, a sampling of national opinion. More important, acting as a popular court, it passed judgment against two men considered enemies to the peace of the local community.[19]

To accompany Ford to Nauvoo, upwards of fourteen hundred troops had assembled in Carthage and another three hundred near the "shanties" of an abandoned speculator's town in the Warsaw-Green Plains area. The smaller group was led by Colonel Levi Williams, a farmer from Green Plains. The group planned to meet the governor at Golden's Point, six miles southeast of Nauvoo.[20] Among the troops congregating in Carthage from Schuyler County were a few Latter-day Saints who had answered the governor's call out of duty. Recognizing the awkwardness of the situation, their leaders somewhat sarcastically put the men first in the ranks. The

Latter-day Saint soldiers kept together with a few trusted neighbors and experienced only occasional harassment from their fellow militiamen.[21]

The governor's plans shifted during the morning. After consulting with militia officers, he decided against leading a military escort to Nauvoo. The governor had learned that some of these troops wanted to destroy the city. Hoping to prevent civil war, Ford disbanded both the forces gathered at Carthage and the Warsaw militia heading for Golden's Point. The Warsaw troops, anxious to sack Nauvoo, were disappointed with the dismissal. Thomas Sharp rallied about eighty of them to form a group of regulators. Accepting as their mission the assassination of Joseph Smith, they headed for Carthage.[22]

Meantime, news had reached the prisoners that Ford had cancelled his trip to Nauvoo. A short time later, word reached them that Governor Ford intended to go to Nauvoo but without the militia. Joseph dictated a postscript to his letter to Emma:

> P.S.—20 minutes to 10.—I just learn that the Governor is about to disband his troops, all but a guard to protect us and the peace, and come himself to Nauvoo and deliver a speech to the people. This is right as I suppose.[23]

Ford encouraged the dismissed militiamen in both groups to return to their homes and farms. Most of them left before noon, but a few in Carthage waited until the governor departed for Nauvoo and then joined the Warsaw posse to carry out the murderous decision sanctioned by the mass meeting. Ford posted a watch from McDonough County half a mile out on the Carthage-Warsaw road. The county jail sat on the outskirts of Carthage in that direction.[24] Ford ordered the Carthage Greys camped on the public square to continue a guard at the jail. The Carthage Riflemen, a militia company, also remained on alert. By mid-morning, the governor and Captain Dunn's Union Dragoons were headed west toward Nauvoo in a light rain. The long ride left Ford uneasy. He sent a messenger back to Captain Robert Smith, reminding the guards of his expectations for the prisoners' safety.[25]

Joseph Smith was sending out his own messenger. He dispatched Dan Jones to Quincy seeking yet another attorney, O. H. Browning, for Saturday's hearing. As he left the jail, Jones was threatened by men who feared Joseph was inviting the Nauvoo Legion to storm the jail and

Joseph Smith   *Hyrum Smith*

Latter-day Saint artists have memorialized the lives of Joseph and Hyrum Smith in numerous paired renderings. These steel engravings published by Frederick Piercy in 1855 reflect the influences of Sutcliffe Maudsley's watercolor profiles of Joseph and an unknown artist's Kirtland-era oil portrait of Hyrum.

rescue him. Jones rode off and joined Ford's convoy, barely missing the Warsaw regulators, who were waiting behind a ridge on the prairie for the governor's departure.[26]

The arrival of the governor at Nauvoo attracted a crowd. Residents gathered quickly near the Mansion House to hear Ford speak. He repeated what he had told Joseph Smith, that the destruction of the *Expositor* had been an unwise action and that the heavily armed Nauvoo Legion posed a threat to the peace of the region—thus the need to disarm it. Prejudice was real, he acknowledged, but the Saints could do much to disabuse public opinion. "You ought to be praying Saints, not military Saints," he said. The governor warned against any physical harm to the *Expositor*'s owners. Ford accepted dinner but turned down an invitation to spend the night at the Mansion House. His party left Nauvoo around 6:30 P.M., followed shortly afterward by Captain Singleton's police supplement. The governor's entourage marched at full width up Main Street with a show of military flourish. From the Mansion House to Lyon's Drug, near the Masonic Hall, the troops demonstrated their passes, guards, cuts, and thrusts to impress the residents. Those who heard the speech and saw the military show of Ford's well-disciplined troops reacted with indignation over the governor's criticism of Joseph Smith for imposing martial law.[27]

Just before the governor's departure for Nauvoo, Cyrus Wheelock had challenged Ford in a meeting at Hamilton's inn. "'These men [the prisoners] . . . are safe as regards the law,'" Wheelock told him, "'but they are not safe from the hands of traitors, and midnight assassins who thirst for their blood.'" The governor admitted that he felt himself caught in a dilemma. Nevertheless, he trusted the militia's agreement to sustain his pledge of safety and a fair trial. Disappointed by the conversation, Wheelock slipped a revolver into a side pocket of his raincoat and, with an entry pass signed by the governor, entered the jail without being searched. Upstairs, he quietly slipped the gun into Joseph Smith's pocket. The Prophet pulled it out, examined it, and kept it. Joseph handed to Hyrum a single-barrel pistol given to him earlier by John S. Fullmer and asked Wheelock to secure additional pistols for use in defending the jail.[28]

The prisoners and their friends busied themselves with preparations for the trial and for their own self-defense in the event of an armed attack. Richards wrote out a list of witnesses for the trial, which Joseph and Hyrum audited. Joseph instructed Wheelock to carry the list to Nauvoo and to ensure that the Saints observed Ford's counsel to remain calm. The men sent greetings to their families. Leaving the jail with Wheelock was John S. Fullmer, dispatched to help in locating witnesses for Saturday's hearing. Chief counsel James W. Woods left with them. In a parting assessment of the situation of the prisoners, Joseph reaffirmed his trust in an eventual era of peace for the Saints.[29] Wheelock remembered the conversation:

> Said Joseph, "Our lives have already become jeopardized by revealing the wicked and bloodthirsty purposes of our enemies; and for the future we must cease to do so. All we have said about them is truth, but it is not always wise to relate all the truth. Even Jesus, the Son of God, had to refrain from doing so, and had to restrain His feelings many times for the safety of Himself and His followers, and had to conceal the righteous purposes of His heart in relation to many things pertaining to His Father's kingdom. . . . So it is with the Church of Jesus Christ of Latter-day Saints; we have the revelation of Jesus, and the knowledge within us is sufficient to organize a

righteous government upon the earth, and to give universal peace to all mankind, if they would receive it, but we lack the physical strength . . . to defend our principles, and we have of necessity to be afflicted, persecuted and smitten, and to bear it patiently until Jacob is of age, then he will take care of himself."[30]

Joseph was in a reflective mood, as he had been six years earlier during his long confinement at Liberty. He related a dream of the previous night and applied it to his current situation. In the dream, he had defended his neglected farm outside Kirtland against a company of angry men who then ordered him to leave it, which he did. Apparently, for Joseph the farm represented the church. His departure from the farm represented his death, not a selfish abandonment of the religious mission for which he and Hyrum were about to give their lives. The two prophesied of the church's eventual worldwide triumph.[31]

Shortly after one o'clock that afternoon, Stigall announced dinner. Taylor and Markham joined the jailer and his family in the kitchen below. The Smiths and Richards ate in the upper room. Richards complained of illness, and Markham, who had a pass from the governor, left for medicine. The Greys blocked his return, hoisted him onto his horse, and forced him out of town at bayonet point. This act escalated their confidence. The prisoners upstairs noticed an increase in boasting. Just before a changing of the guard at four, John Taylor honored Hyrum Smith's request to sing a folk-hymn. Recently introduced in Nauvoo, "The Stranger and His Friend" tells of a man who offers food, water, clothing, and medical assistance to a stranger. Upon last of all finding the stranger illegally jailed, the friend discovers that the recipient of his good will is the Savior in disguise. The sixth stanza directly reflected the melancholy mood at Carthage:

> *In pris'n I saw him next, condemned*
> *To meet a traitor's doom at morn;*
> . . . .
> *My friendship's utmost zeal to try,*
> *He asked, if I for him would die;*
> *The flesh was weak, my blood ran chill,*
> *But the free spirit cried, "I will!"*

A bit later, again by Hyrum's request, Taylor sang the ballad a second time. Hyrum then read extracts from Josephus.[32]

A Memorable and Unjustifiable Assassination. *In this nineteenth-century engraving, the Carthage Greys arrive on the scene (right) as the militia begins its retreat from the jail. The artist accurately portrayed the Carthage Jail and outbuildings but uses an erroneous report that Joseph Smith was shot while leaning against the well after he fell from the window.*

A guard of six or eight men kept watch in three-hour shifts at the sandstone prison. Joseph struck up a conversation with some of them, once again defending his innocence against the charges of his opponents. At five o'clock, Stigall returned to the jail from an excursion and reported Markham's expulsion from Carthage. At the jailer's urging, his wards agreed to move to a safer location, in the iron cell, after supper. The quiet of the jail was about to be challenged.[33]

That afternoon, just beyond the northwest limits of Carthage, a group of vigilantes from the disbanded Warsaw militia had assembled with others privy to their plans. About two hundred in number, they acted not as militiamen but as independent citizens seeking to settle the Mormon question outside the law. Many of them had walked the muddy road from Warsaw behind an old wagon carrying a barrel of whiskey. Unlike some others, they had not been thwarted by a washed-out bridge that forced a half-mile detour. Others were stragglers from the dismissed militia companies or Nauvoo dissenters.[34]

The mob intended to accomplish the objectives urged upon them by

Thomas Sharp's newspaper editorials of the past weeks, the boasted threats of Joseph Jackson and other Mormon apostates, and the Carthage mass meeting. Representing Nauvoo's external and internal opponents as chief spokesmen were Jackson and Sharp. Captain Mark Aldrich, Sharp's colleague on the Warsaw correspondence committee,[35] plotted military logistics. With the governor away in Nauvoo, with posted guards from the Carthage Greys willing to cooperate, and with two targeted Latter-day Saint leaders resting in the jailer's upstairs bedroom, the opportunity for action had arrived.[36]

The men masked their identities by darkening their faces with a deep brown or black coloring.[37] They listened to the strategy of their self-appointed leaders. Then they moved quietly in single file through the woods and toward town, "shielding themselves from view by skulking along a rail fence." Two youths posted atop the courthouse with a telescope first spotted what they thought might be a militia unit from Nauvoo. They passed the word to the Carthage Greys and the Carthage Riflemen, who were camped on the square about seven hundred yards from the jail. Officers organized the men into formation and marched them double-time toward the jail. Before the militia could get there, the vigilantes circled around and approached from the north, split ranks, surrounded the building, subdued the cooperative guards, and entered the jail, their firearms ready for the attack.[38]

In a letter written a few days later, one of the arriving Greys summarized the event as he understood it:

> When the mob came up in front of the Jail our guard challenged them. The mob demanded the prisoners. They were told that if they did not retire the guard would fire on them. The mob raised a shout and commenced jumping over the low fence in front of the Jail when our guard fired on them. The guard were immediately overpowered and the Mob rushed into the Jail and did their work. The Guard were not hurt except some bruises. . . . The mob all had their faces blacked. When we were marching to the Jail about 150 yards from the jail we saw Jo[seph Smith] come to the window and turn back and in about a second or two afterwards he came to the window and tumbled out. He was shot several times and a bayonet run through him after he fell. From all the information I can get the mob were about 250 strong, the forces left to guard the prisoners about 60 or 65 strong.[39]

THE BLOOD ☞ THE MARTYRS ⚜ THE SEED ☞ THE CHURC

Hyrum Smith fell first in the June 27 attack on the occupants of the jailer's upstairs bedroom. The Prophet stands at left behind John Taylor, who attempts to divert the rifles, while Willard Richards waits behind the door. Artist C. C. A. Christensen depicted Joseph Smith in white to symbolize his calling. The caption reflects sentiments in Nauvoo at the time.

William Daniels, who accompanied the Warsaw vigilantes, agreed that Joseph was shot after he was on the ground. (More reliable evidence suggests otherwise.) A distorted version of his testimony published by Lyman Littlefield says that a young man approached the body with a bowie knife, intending to sever the Prophet's head, and that a bright flash of light stunned the man. Littlefield's exaggerations quickly entered popular discourse. Daniels maintained at the trial of the accused murderers that he had seen a flash like lighting but that the young man held only a flute.[40]

Other nearby witnesses reported seeing one of the regulators turn Joseph Smith's body, lean it up against the curb of the well, and announce, "Well, boys, he's dead!" The men then scattered toward the woods. One of the young watchmen, William R. Hamilton, son of the innkeeper, passed his hand over the Prophet's forehead, raised an arm, and confirmed that indeed Joseph Smith was dead. Hamilton looked inside the jail and saw Hyrum's body on the floor in a pool of blood, plaster dislodged from the ceiling onto his face. As he left, young Hamilton heard but ignored noises in the cell room; he ran to the inn to inform his parents of the murders.[41]

Willard Richards and John Taylor, who were inside the jail, provided another perspective on the murders.[42] The prisoners had first heard shouting, next a demand for surrender, and then the discharge of three or four firearms. The guards had fired wads over the head of the rushing attackers to cover their collusion.[43] Richards, the only man in the room still wearing his coat on that warm afternoon, parted the curtain at the south window. From this vantage point, fifteen or twenty feet above the ground, he could see that the mob had entered the lot and were surrounding the building. Pushing aside the guards, a number of the vigilantes entered the jail. At the top of the stairs and to the right, the hardwood door to the prisoners' quarters had been slammed shut, but the latch would not hold, despite prior efforts to repair it.[44] Now, only the weight of the six-foot-plus frame of Joseph Smith and his companions restrained the determined mob. Joseph, in shirtsleeves, had retrieved the six-shooter from his coat. Hyrum held the single-shot pistol. Taylor had Markham's large hickory cane in one hand, while Richards reached for Taylor's cane.[45]

From the bottom of the stairway, the attackers sent a volley of musket balls upward against the door of the prison chamber straight ahead of them. Apparently, they did not know that the iron cages inside were empty. Then, as the men advanced up the stairs to the landing, one of them fired at the keyhole of the sleeping-room door. The ball startled the prisoners as it passed between them. Hyrum pressed against the door with his left shoulder, his head bent. Almost instantly, a second ball punched through the door panel. Hyrum received the ball just left of his nose. The ball exited through his throat and grazed his breast. Blood soaked his vest and shirt. Knowing his wound was fatal, he stumbled across the room and, turning toward the door, fell backwards to the floor, exclaiming, "I am a dead man!"[46]

Joseph moved toward his fallen brother with a brief exclamation of sorrow. Then he returned to a position of safety against the wall and discharged his six-shooter into the entry through a now-open door. Shots fired from the hallway hit Hyrum's body or peppered the floor around it. One ball punctured his right thigh; another entered his left leg just below the knee. Other shots hit the ceiling of the room above his head.

Joseph reached around the door casing and discharged his six-shooter. Three or four of the barrels misfired. He wounded some of the attackers but now had no remaining firepower. Taylor, close behind the

Prophet, had been using Markham's "rascal-beater" to knock against the muskets and bayonets thrusting into the room. Richards waited behind Taylor, beyond striking distance. Without any way to shoot back, and certain death threatening from the landing, Taylor suddenly dashed toward the east window, intending to jump. A ball from the landing behind him struck Taylor in the left thigh, grazed the bone, and pushed within half an inch of the other side. He collapsed on the wide sill, denting the back of his vest pocket watch. The force shattered the glass cover of the timepiece against his ribs and pushed the internal gear pins against the enamel face, popping out a small segment later mistakenly identified as a bullet hole.[47]

Tumbling into the room, Taylor sprawled momentarily on the floor. As he crawled toward the nearby bed, one ball hit his left forearm, lodging in the wrist, and another struck the bone just below his left knee. Richards had moved to the door behind the Prophet to parry the thrusting muskets with his cane, but the volleys continued to target Taylor. Several shots from the landing hit around the wounded Taylor; one ball tore the flesh from his left hip and splattered blood on the wall and floor.

Some of the mob outside the doorway reached their guns around the corner, shooting left-handedly toward the two men in the corner behind the door. The Prophet and his clerk were armed with only a spent six-shooter and the walking cane. Further efforts at defense seemed futile. Dropping his pistol on the floor by the doorway, Joseph Smith ran across the room. Straddling the sill of the east window and with one leg dangling outside, Joseph reached out and lifted his hands in the Masonic signal of distress. Willard Richards heard the Prophet's last words, "O Lord, my God!"[48] A ball from the door pierced Smith's right hip and exited through the lower body. A shot from outside entered his right chest and exited below the shoulder blade; another hit under the heart. A fourth shot may have hit the right collarbone.[49] Joseph fell to the ground, landing on his left side. He died within moments, while trying to sit up against the well.[50]

Richards was now the lone unscathed prisoner, a nick on his left earlobe the only wound. The men on the stairs and landing withdrew when someone outside shouted that Joseph had leaped from the window. The immediate threat to his own life abated, Richards peered momentarily out the window at the lifeless body of Joseph Smith. He saw dozens of men surrounding the body and others approaching from the entrance they had just vacated. Richards expected them to return, seeking him. He ran out of the room, ignoring for the moment Taylor's plea, "Take me along." Discovering the doors to the cells in the prison room unbarred, he returned to Taylor and dragged him into the dungeon. Laying him on the straw-covered floor, Richards covered his friend with a straw tick and stood behind the closed door, awaiting his fate. He heard footsteps on the stairs. They entered the sleeping room and then returned down the stairway.[51] From behind the door, Richards heard shouts that ended the attack: "The Mormons are coming!" The cry scattered the assemblage.[52] The regulators fled into the woods from which they had emerged minutes earlier.

Taylor's smashed patent lever watch would in later years become a revered symbol of both the tragedy of the murders of Joseph and Hyrum Smith and the miracle of the nonfatal wounding of an apostle who would, thirty-three years later, head the church. The watch had stopped at the instant of its impact against the sill: 5 o'clock, 16 minutes, and 26 seconds.[53]

Aftermath of the Tragedy

Governor Ford first learned of the murders when he and his entourage were about three miles outside Nauvoo on the way back to Carthage. There he intercepted the westward-bound constable David Bettisworth and George D. Grant, a Latter-day Saint who lived just east of Carthage. Ford and his military advisers feared an armed uprising among the Saints. They convinced the two men to accompany them back to Carthage, where they intended to secure all public documents and evacuate the inhabitants. They left Grant at his home; he waited until they were out of sight and then headed again for Nauvoo on horseback. In Carthage, meantime, Willard Richards received help from the innkeeper in moving John Taylor and the bodies of the two martyrs to the Hamilton Hotel. At the first opportunity, Richards penned a short message to be sent to Nauvoo. He addressed it to Governor Ford, General Dunham, Colonel Markham, and Emma Smith:

> CARTHAGE JAIL, 8:05 o'clock, P.M., June 27th, 1844.
>
> Joseph and Hyrum are dead. Taylor wounded, not very badly. I am well. Our guard was forced, as we believe, by a band of Missourians from 100 to 200. The job was done in an instant, and the party fled

towards Nauvoo instantly. This is as I believe it. The citizens here are afraid of the Mormons attacking them. I promise them no!

Taylor cosigned the note to reassure his wife, Leonora, that his wounds were not life-threatening. Richards added a postscript informing readers that Carthage citizens had promised protection against further injury. The jailer obtained the help of Dr. Thomas L. Barnes and others to dress John Taylor's wounds and conduct a coroner's inquest.[54] About this time, Samuel H. Smith, who had journeyed from his brother William's inn at Plymouth, joined Richards and Taylor.[55]

Around midnight, Ford arrived at the county seat with his party, followed within the hour by Singleton's troops. At Ford's urging, the three Latter-day Saints signed another communication for the Saints, this one addressed to Emma Smith and Major General Dunham. The Mansion House was assumed to be the official point for dispersing news. In this 159-word letter, Richards, its author, repeated the messages of the earlier, shorter communication, not knowing which would be delivered first. "Joseph and Hyrum are dead," he affirmed. "We will prepare to move the bodies as soon as possible. . . . Mr. Taylor's wounds are dressed and not serious. I am sound." He said that the governor had promised a full inquiry and had ordered troops to help defend Nauvoo from a possible attack from Missouri mobbers. (Richards still assumed that the murderers were from Missouri, as earlier rumors had indicated.) Once again, Richards noted that he had promised Carthage citizens that the Saints would not wreak vengeance. "Be still, be patient," he counseled. Ford appended his own short postscript, advising that in the event of an anti-Mormon military assault on Nauvoo, "Defend yourselves until protection can be furnished [if] necessary," he wrote.[56]

While the governor's aides helped wash the bodies of the two murder victims,[57] Ford met with citizens gathered at the public square. It was an hour after midnight. He encouraged the people to leave town; many had already fled, leaving windows open and doors ajar. He worried that residents of Nauvoo would burn Carthage. Ford's words heightened anxiety and hurried the dispersal of all but a handful of the remaining citizens. The governor and his escort joined the exodus in a hasty departure southward. Eighteen miles down the muddy road and several hours later, they reached Augusta, where they deposited county records out of reach of the expected attack from Nauvoo. Ford took breakfast and continued on to Columbus and then to Quincy.[58]

Richards had entrusted his first announcement of the murders to Dr. Barnes, who asked two relatives from the Carthage militia to deliver it.[59] Fearing for their own safety if they bore the bad news to Nauvoo, the pair sought out Latter-day Saint farmer Arza Adams north of Carthage. With Benjamin Leyland as guide, Adams headed for Nauvoo around midnight by way of a back route. A dozen men had congregated at the Mansion House, having already heard early reports. News came from boys tending cows several miles out from Nauvoo on the La Harpe Road. Three men in a carriage headed for Appanoose had passed them in a hurry late Thursday evening, slowing only to shout, "Dig a grave for Joe and Hy Smith, for they are dead." The boys identified the driver as Dr. Robert Foster and the man who shouted as one of the Law brothers.[60] When Adams delivered Willard Richards's note just after sunrise, the concerns of Nauvoo's residents became a sudden reality. The Prophet and Patriarch were dead! Word spread rapidly from house to house. "It was a solemn time," Adams noted. "Many a rosy cheek was wet with tears, both men and women." The impossible news brought a solemn grief to the city, punctuated only here and there with a call for vengeance.[61]

Word of the assassinations spread quickly to Latter-day Saints in out-lying settlements. A resident at Macedonia remembered, "When the awful tidings reached us the people wept aloud. One could hear the sobs and crying from every quarter." The reaction was similar elsewhere. The Saints received the word with sorrow, pored over newspaper accounts when they came, and wrote to far-flung relatives with

> the *sad* and dreadful intelligence. . . . They had voluntarily given themselves up to trial upon the Governor['s request] with the people giving their words of honor that they *should* be protected from all violence (but they are dead). They died Martyrs in a religious persecution.[62]

At Carthage, the bodies had been prepared for transport in rough oak boxes, each loaded into its own wagon and covered with brush against the sun. A pair of white horses pulled Joseph's wagon. Governor Ford had ordered a guard, and General Deming provided eight soldiers. Willard Richards took responsibility for the arrangements. Innkeeper Artois

Hamilton drove his wagon, while the victims' brother Samuel H. Smith drove the other. The wagons covered the twenty miles between the two towns slowly. Around three o'clock an organized group from Nauvoo met the cortege a mile east of the temple on Mulholland Street. Under the direction of the city marshal, a procession accompanied the bodies to the Mansion House. The city council led the solemn train, accompanied by Joseph Smith's militia staff, Major General Jonathan Dunham and his staff, acting Brigadier General Hosea Stout and his staff, other commanders and officers of the Legion, the martial band, and a crowd estimated at several thousand. The people hungered for an explanation and for direction. Filling the streets near the Mansion House, they listened to Willard Richards, William W. Phelps, the attorneys Woods and Reid, and Stephen Markham—all of whom had witnessed firsthand the legal efforts or the murders at Carthage. The men spoke from atop the framed building where just ten days earlier the Prophet had lifted his sword to commit the Nauvoo Legion to a vow of self-defense.[63]

In his remarks, Richards emphasized his pledge to Ford that the Saints would conduct themselves peacefully. According to Wandle Mace, "He pled for them to be quiet, with the earnestness of a hungry man begging for bread, to trust in the law for redress, and when that failed, to call upon God to avenge us of our wrongs." Richards urged, "Brethren, think, *think,* and *think* again before you act." The politically astute apostle then called for a vote of support. The congregated Saints spoke with one voice in sustaining his proposition for peace and then dispersed with the announcement of a viewing of the bodies the following morning.[64]

As evening closed in upon Nauvoo, neighbors talked among themselves of the dramatic event at Carthage. An uneasiness pervaded the city. Rumors circulated that the dissenters had targeted nine other men for death.[65] Some "expected the mob would come into the city that night to kill the rest of the Saints," Sarah Leavitt remembered.

> There was orders for every man to arm himself and prepare to defend the city. The moon shone uncommonly bright, as we could see quite a distance. . . . They had guards out in every direction; they had a drum that could be heard a number of miles.[66]

With the doors of the Mansion House closed behind them, Emma's friend William Marks, president of the Nauvoo stake, supervised as

English immigrant George Cannon made molds of the faces of Joseph and Hyrum Smith and cast plaster masks to preserve the likenesses of the Prophet and the Patriarch.

William Huntington Sr. and his son Dimick washed the bodies and stopped the bullet wounds with cotton soaked in camphor. The blood-stained clothing was set aside for Zina Jacobs to wash.[67] George Cannon carefully took impressions from the faces from which to make death masks.[68] The attendants dressed each body in all-white clothing: shirt and pants, stockings, neckerchief, and shroud. Then, they stood aside while the family viewed the bodies, laid out side by side in their coffins set upon tables in the dining room.[69] "Such a house of mourning as was that I never before beheld," Almira Mack Covey noted.

> There was the aged Mother, the wives, the children, the brother and sisters, the more distant relatives. . . . a dry eye I did not behold. . . . It was enough to rend the heart of a stone to behold two Prophets of the Lord laid prostrate by those who were once their friends.

During the moonlit evening, close friends likewise viewed the remains and comforted the bereaved family.[70]

For the public viewing, the bodies were placed in coffins lined with white cambric. A square of glass mounted in a lid attached with brass hinges to the coffins served as a window through which the faces of the dead Prophet and Patriarch could be seen. Their bodies were covered with black velvet held taut with brass nails. The coffins were placed in outer boxes in the main floor parlor.[71] The rough oak boxes used to transport the bodies from Carthage were set aside, later to be cut up and fashioned into memorial canes for close friends.[72]

From eight on Saturday morning until five that afternoon, a procession of thousands passed in at the west front door to view their martyred Prophet and Patriarch and moved out again through a door on the north. They came from Nauvoo and from surrounding settlements, from Quincy, Burlington, and elsewhere. "Every heart is filled with sorrow, and the very streets of Nauvoo seem to mourn," Vilate Kimball wrote to her missionary husband in Boston. "Where it will end the Lord only knows." In Nauvoo, work stopped on the temple, and shopkeepers latched their doors. At Carthage, Justice Robert F. Smith quietly disregarded the trial he had scheduled for that day to consider charges of treason.[73]

The viewing concluded, thousands assembled at the preaching ground below the temple, where William W. Phelps pronounced the funeral sermon. He mourned the deaths of two good men in a failure of justice. He lamented the loss of freedom "to the popular will of mobocracy in this boasted . . . realm of liberty" but welcomed the future day of heavenly retribution. With these words, Phelps touched themes familiar to the Saints, including those brought forward in their appeals for redress for lost properties in Missouri. Phelps defended the character of the maligned prophet, extolled his accomplishments, and assured his listeners that the onward course of the church would continue but not without challenge. Phelps later reconstructed his message:

> Governor Ford said, when Moses rose up in Egypt with a *new religion,* against what the priests were then practicing, there was a mighty stir among the people, and all Israel had to leave; and so when Jesus came among the Jews with a *new religion,* they crucified him, and can the Mormons hope for anything less from our "higher order of society" in these "free" United States? Can Mr. Smith . . . hope to pass the scrutiny of public opinion without encountering the same destiny that has attended all *new religions?* . . . "the trial must come."[74]

At the Mansion House, meanwhile, the coffins were removed from the outer boxes and locked in a northeast bedroom. A bag of sand in each end of the outer boxes gave them sufficient weight to convince onlookers that the bodies were inside. These precautions were taken in response to reports that plotters had threatened to take the bodies.[75] With the box lids nailed shut, William Huntington and a few assistants drove the outer boxes in a horse-drawn hearse to the graveyard, past the preaching grounds where Phelps was speaking. The boxes were lowered into graves with the usual ceremonies. Around midnight, ten men—one of them leading the way with a musket—moved the coffins containing the bodies out of the Mansion House and across Water Street to a secret burial place in the basement of the unfinished Nauvoo House. Rain helped obscure the hiding place. "After the brethren were buried," one of the Prophet's plural wives recorded, "we had an awful thunder storm and lightning, so the mob did not come as they intended."[76] The bodies remained hidden until fall, when Emma had them reburied in a small outbuilding toward the river from the Homestead. This final resting place remained a closely held secret. "We supposed they were buried," one resident of Nauvoo wrote in 1845, "but I know not where. The sepulchre [near the temple] was prepared for them but as yet they are not interred in there."[77]

The grief of the Smith family over the murders of Joseph and Hyrum expanded with the deaths of two additional family members. The Prophet's younger brother Samuel, suffering from what he described to his mother as "a dreadful distress in my side ever since I was chased by the mob," died of bilious fever at the end of July. The following spring William Smith's wife, Caroline, died of a lingering case of dropsy, "brought on by her exposures in Missouri," Lucy Smith concluded, "so that she was what might be termed an indirect martyr to the cause of Christ, which makes the sum of martyrs in our family no less than six in number." Mother Smith reflected, "I had reared six sons to manhood, and of them all, one only [William] remained."[78]

Newspapers around the United States reported the assassinations at Carthage by copying reports from Quincy, St. Louis, or points east. Early reports were confused, but eventually more accurate information became available.[79] The papers responded to news of the death of Joseph Smith and his brother with editorial dismay. Just as Nauvoo's citizens had bemoaned the loss of liberty, editors in major cities denounced the vigilante action as a threat to American principles. "The spirit of lawlessness and violence . . . must be put down—must be subdued, or we may bid farewell to freedom of opinion and of speech," the New Bedford (Massachussetts) *Morning Register* declared.[80]

Many newspapers agreed with Latter-day Saints that the murders at Carthage were a disgrace not just to Illinois but to the entire nation. Violent actions of this sort had been reported in many other places in the country. Riots had resulted too frequently when law-abiding citizens took the law into their own hands to halt what they termed uncontrollable individuals or movements. Editors bemoaned this trend of spreading law-lessness even more than the singular event in Hancock County. They expressed no liking for Joseph Smith or the Latter-day Saints and some-times judged the Prophet worthy of the punishment even while they deplored the way he died. For them, the incident at Carthage merely fur-nished yet another sorry witness of the nation's turn to violence.[81]

While editors may have agreed that the judgment was justified, they reminded readers that "trial and conviction should [have] preceded sentence and execution."[82] Both Governor Ford and Thomas Sharp acknowledged the popularity of this sentiment. "Most well informed persons condemn in the most unqualified manner the mode in which the Smiths were put to death," Ford wrote, "but nine out of every ten . . . [express] their pleasure that they are dead."[83]

Within Illinois, some papers justified the mob's actions as the last resort when the law failed to bring Joseph Smith to justice through the courts. But many of the editors agreed with their colleagues throughout the nation that the vigilante action brought shame upon Illinois. Nauvoo's associate editor William W. Phelps immortalized the idea in his poem, "Praise to the Man," and John Taylor affirmed that the innocent blood shed at Carthage had both stained "the banner of liberty" and offered "a witness to the truth of the everlasting gospel that all the world cannot impeach."[84]

Only in Hancock County, among those most openly opposed to Joseph Smith as a civil, military, and religious leader, did the press and some people celebrate his death. At Warsaw, citizens cheered and threw their hats into the air. Two Latter-day Saint families in the town moved away because of harassment. Fearing retribution from Nauvoo, some resi-dents of Warsaw who had participated in the mob crossed the river into Missouri.[85] Thomas Sharp, whose *Warsaw Signal* had invited the murders, defended the people's right to take the law into their own hands. Sharp's first report claimed that the Smiths had been killed by the guards when Nauvoo's militia rushed the jail in attempt to free the prisoners.[86] Within weeks, Sharp was claiming that public opinion was shifting in favor of his anti-Mormon stance, and he published letters of support. Joining him in justifying the murders was George T. M. Davis, editor of the *Alton Telegraph Review* and mayor of the community just north of St. Louis.[87] Some individuals who had been convinced by the anti-Mormon press that corruption flourished and illegal political power prevailed in Nauvoo concluded, "So you see there is an end to two of perhaps the worst men that has ever lived on the land."[88] One of the vigilantes inscribed on his powder horn: "Warsaw Regulators / The end of the Poly[g]amist Joseph Smith kilt at Carthage June 27, 1844."[89]

In contrast, Church newspapers mourned the deaths of Joseph and Hyrum with black-line editions. The papers echoed their own twin themes—grief over the loss of the two church leaders and dismay at the actions of the perpetrators. Latter-day Saints in Nauvoo laid these actions at the feet of the state of Illinois. These ideas were repeated in news reports, editorials, tributes, a funeral sermon, personal letters, and in a lengthy poem by Eliza R. Snow, published on the final page of the *Times and Seasons*. Her eulogy began:

> *Ye heav'ns attend! Let all the earth give ear!*
> *Let Gods and seraphs, men and angels hear—*
> *The worlds on high—the universe shall know*
> *What awful scenes are acted here below!*
> *Had nature's self a heart, her heart would bleed;*
> *For never, since the Son of God was slain*
> *Has blood so noble,[90] flow'd from human vein*
> *As that which now, on God for vengeance calls*
> *From "freedom's ground"—from Carthage prison walls!*
> *Oh! Illinois! thy soil has drank the blood*
> *Of Prophets martyr'd for the truth of God.*
> *Once lov'd America! what can atone*
> *For the pure blood of innocence, thou'st sown?*
> *Were all thy streams in teary torrents shed*
> *To mourn the fate of those illustrious dead;*
> *How vain the tribute, for the noblest worth*
> *That grac'd thy surface, O degraded Earth!*[91]

This was the first of nine poetic tributes to the martyrs published in the two Nauvoo papers over the next year. Of varying literary quality, they expressed the grief of the Saints and memorialized, especially, the murdered prophet. Those most remembered in later years were a poem by W. W. Phelps, "Praise to the Man," and two by John Taylor, "The Seer" and "O Give Me Back My Prophet Dear."[92]

With the help of William W. Phelps, Nauvoo's *Times and Seasons* remade half of its June 15 issue and put a July 1 date on it. The paper was already delayed because of the disruptions of that week and editor John Taylor's absence in Carthage. The black-line edition was headlined "Awful assassination of JOSEPH AND HYRUM SMITH!—The pledged faith of the State of Illinois stained with innocent blood by a Mob!" Willard Richards wrote the lead article, a recital of the events at Carthage down through the public meeting at Nauvoo on the sorrowful afternoon of June 28. Richards's concluding refrain—like the sentiments in Eliza Snow's poem—would be echoed in numerous retellings in letters sent from Nauvoo to relatives and friends elsewhere. "Thus perishes the hope of law," he wrote.

> Thus vanishes the plighted faith of the state; thus the blood of innocence stains the constituted authorities of the United States, and thus have two among the most noble martyrs since the slaughter of Abel, sealed the truth of their divine mission, *by being shot by a Mob for their religion!*[93]

The church paper published statements by the attorneys H. T. Reid and James W. Woods and an editorial offering consolation and calling for faithfulness to the gospel and patience as unresolved problems of justice and church leadership were worked out. The editorial was written by W. W. Phelps and cosigned by Willard Richards and John Taylor. Also in the special issue was Governor Ford's statement to the people of Illinois, which included his plans for investigating the murders and steps he had taken to calm the immediate concerns in Carthage and Nauvoo. Ford felt no regret at the military precautions he had taken to prevent "the recent disgraceful affair at Carthage." He had placed a disarmed Nauvoo Legion under state control and had received the pledge of militias assembled at Carthage to protect the Smiths.[94]

Around the ninth of July, Latter-day Saints living outside Illinois first heard of the murders, often from local newspapers. The first inclination of the Saints was to distrust these reports. "I was not willing to believe it, for it was too much to bear," Heber C. Kimball wrote from the East. Yet, the Saints steeled themselves for the inevitable confirmation.[95] They waited for arrival of the Nauvoo newspapers or reliable messengers bearing "the mournful but authenticated intelligence." When the papers and letters arrived after another week or so, the Saints picked up immediately on the double message. As Louisa Follet put it, "A great man has fallen to stain with blood the free born rights of this great republic."[96]

Ford took immediate steps after the murders to secure the peace in Hancock and surrounding counties. His dismissal of the militias assembled at Carthage had been his way of preventing a mutiny of the troops if he led them, as previously promised, to Nauvoo. When he reached Quincy, Ford ordered the commanders of militia in ten nearby counties to enlist volunteers and outfit themselves with arms and supplies sufficient for a twelve-day campaign.[97] The force would stand ready if needed to oppose either the Saints or their enemies. He hoped to prevent one citizens' army attacking another. "I think present circumstances warrant the precaution of having competent force at my disposal in readiness to march at a moment's warning," he wrote. Ford dispatched Colonel Hart Fellows and Captain Abraham Jonas to Nauvoo and then to Warsaw to gather information on the mood of the people in those two opposition camps. Responding to a common fear, he charged the men to watch for people from Missouri and Iowa who might be gathering to join in an unprovoked attack on Nauvoo.[98]

At Nauvoo, Ford's delegates addressed a public meeting on the afternoon of July 1 at the stand east of the temple. They won a hearty "amen" from the crowd in support of the governor's efforts. Earlier in the day, the Nauvoo city council passed a series of five resolutions pledging to sustain the law and to denounce any tendency to seek private revenge on the assassins. The council urged Ford to disarm all other militias in the state as a further step toward peace. The councilmen pledged to restrain Nauvoo's citizens and to support Ford's efforts to ensure a lawful settlement of outstanding issues. "We are happy to say," the church paper reported, "that all appears to be PEACE at NAUVOO."[99]

It was an anxious peace at best. Uneasiness over the possibility of a violent response from Nauvoo on the one hand or the attempted extermination of the Latter-day Saints on the other continued for weeks. Most residents who had fled from Carthage and nearby farms returned gradually to their homes, some only after being reassured by their Latter-day Saint neighbors that retribution was not planned.[100] In some parts of the county, old citizens moved away, intending never to return.[101] Some believed that a reward had been offered in Nauvoo for the destruction of the *Warsaw Signal* and the murder of its editor.[102] A riverboat captain approaching Nauvoo loaded a howitzer, uncertain of what to expect.[103] Ford bemoaned the Saints' having established the Nauvoo Legion as such a strong defensive force. It created suspicion, he said, and prompted opponents to rally their own forces.[104]

The Latter-day Saints were likewise fearful; they expected further persecution. After what had happened at Carthage, they believed the bold assertions of certain antagonists. From Iowa, a law-and-order resident reported, "The mob say they [will] drive the Mormons from that state [Illinois] and burn Nauvoo to ashes."[105] Northeast of Nauvoo, a Latter-day Saint farmer recalled, "Our minds were in a constant tension expecting the mob to come and destroy all our labor."[106] At Columbus and in some other towns, old residents forcibly disarmed the few Saints living among them. The action seemed to ease tensions. Leading citizens at Columbus soon accepted the improbability "that a few 'Mormons' was agoing to overrun the state of Illinois . . . while the 'Mormons' themselves were scattered with their families throughout the entire State."[107]

At Warsaw and Quincy, Thomas Sharp rallied support for his claims that the Saints were mustering to attack Warsaw.[108] According to reports received in Nauvoo, the Warsaw militia was drilling and demanding expulsion of the Latter-day Saints at Lima. Not willing to depend on any local militia in western Illinois to ensure the peace, Ford asked Colonel S. W. Kearny to station some of the federal troops under his command in St. Louis temporarily in Hancock County. Kearney ignored the request.[109] On July 25, Ford challenged Illinois vigilantes to cease military activities and to learn to live in peace. Thomas Sharp denied charges of Warsaw military action as fabrications devised in Nauvoo. He claimed that theft and militarism existed at Nauvoo and urged the governor to ferret them out. The verbal sparring between the editor and the governor continued throughout the fall and winter. Sharp continued to depict Ford as a patsy of church leaders and said that the Saints themselves had been humbugged by the distorted rumors originated by others. Ford did his best to remain neutral. His goals were to ensure justice in the trial of the accused murderers and prevent further civil strife.[110]

Meanwhile, as instructed by the governor, the men of Nauvoo forgot their own offensive wishes and prepared instead to defend the city against threatened attack. Ford commended the Saints for their restraint. It was "much better than the opposite party," he noted.[111] The spirit of moderation in Nauvoo prompted George Alley to write on July 27, "We hope for the best, and prepare for the worst, not meaning to be the aggressors, nor the vanquished, but by the help of an omnipotent arm to retain our rights." Though frustrated by the failure of legal redress, two weeks later Alley echoed the opinion of the majority at Nauvoo when he wrote, "Justice will not always sleep; . . . we Mormons are perfectly willing to let the matter remain with . . . the great Jehovah. And let the guilty feed on the remorse of conscience."[112]

ATTEMPTS AT JUSTICE

The immediate aftermath of the tragedy at Carthage left unresolved two questions that the assassinations had precipitated. The first, a need to identify a new prophet and a new patriarch to continue the work of the Restoration, was a matter to be determined by the Latter-day Saints. They did so by placing Brigham Young and the Quorum of the Twelve at the helm in a special conference early in August. Taking longer was the second question, that of civil justice for those charged with the destruction of the *Expositor* and those involved in the killings at Carthage. Nauvoo's leaders had trusted in the judicial system to resolve the dispute between city officials and the owners of the destroyed newspaper. Now that the owners of the newspaper and political opponents of Nauvoo had taken the law into their own hands to carry out two murders, would the law bring them to justice? Would the murderers be hailed as popular heroes for their actions in ridding society of a threat to the peace of Hancock County? Or would a trial identify them as criminals guilty of taking innocent lives? These conflicting views of the Smiths' deaths would gain a hearing at Carthage nearly a year after the event.

In the *Warsaw Signal,* Thomas Sharp, one of the accused murderers, ridiculed Governor Ford for mishandling the situation in Carthage and for ignoring threats against the life of Joseph Smith. Sharp's effort to prove

SATURDAY, SEPTEMBER 13, 1845.

M A R T Y R S
OF THE
Latter Day Saints.

The following are the names of a few of the MAR-TYRS, who, for the testimony of Jesus, have been in-humanly murdered in the states of Missouri and Illinois.
Mr. Barber, *Martyred, Nov. 4th,* 1833, *in Jackson Co. Missouri.*

The following Saints were MARTYRED in Cald-well County, Missouri, October, 30th, 1838.

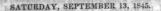

Thomas McBride	**Warren Smith,**
Levi Merrick	**Sardius Smith,**
William Merrick,	**George Richards**
Elias Benner,	**Mr. Napier,**
Josiah Fuller,	**Mr. Harmar,**
Benj. Lewis,	**Mr. Cox,**
Alex. Campbell,	**Mr. Abbot,**

Mr. York.

About the same time and in the same county the fol-lowing persons were MARTYRED, namely:

David W. Patten,
One of the Twelve Apostles.

Gideon Carter, **Mr. Obanion,**

Mr. Carey,

Martyred in Carthage JAIL, in the County of Han-cock, and State of Illinois on the **27th** *day of June,* 1844.

Joseph Smith, the Seer,
Hyrum Smith, the Patriarch.

Two of the noblest martyrs whose blood has stained the earth for ages.

The murderers of the foregoing persons, though the most of them are well known, are yet running at large, boast-ing of their horrid deeds.

Is there justice in heaven?
If so, let this nation fear!

More than a year after the assassinations at Carthage, editor Parley P. Pratt published this roster of Latter-day Saints "who, for the testimony of Jesus, have been inhumanly murdered in the states of Missouri and Illinois." The pistols were in the possession of Joseph Smith (top) and Hyrum Smith (bottom) during the vigilante attack.

Ford's "utter inadequacy to the occasion" was intended not so much to criticize him for the murders as to foster mistrust of the Democratic governor and thereby undercut support for legal action against the murderers. Ford understood that prejudice existed in Illinois against the Saints and that his actions had been misunderstood by some on all sides.[113] Between February and April 1845, anti-Mormon papers in Warsaw and Alton published a series of six letters signed "Hancock" that were probably written by Thomas Sharp. The letters criticized Ford's December 1844 explanation to the legislature of the Hancock County troubles. They raised familiar anti-Mormon issues—the practice of plural marriage, sanctioned stealing from non-Mormons, and military alliances with Indians. "Hancock" said that Parley P. Pratt's call for political unity in the *New York Prophet* early in 1845 was evidence that political Mormonism sought to destroy the freedom of others and dominate the government of the United States through a living constitution of twelve men. The critic argued that Governor Ford's unwillingness to believe any of these assertions had weakened his ability to recognize the enormity of the Mormon threat in Illinois and thus biased him in favor of the Latter-day Saints.[114]

Ford's Whig opponents applauded these arguments and joined in criticizing the governor. Latter-day Saint spokesmen chided Ford for the failure of military protection and justice at Carthage. Editor John Taylor was particularly frustrated with the failure of legal process "in a land of boasted liberty," and he doubted that a fair jury could be assembled anywhere in Hancock County.[115]

Those accused of planning and participating in the murders were men of varying motives and backgrounds. Whether giving voice to political rhetoric or religious dissention, all agreed that Joseph Smith's death would benefit the broader community. Men of prominence, accomplishment, and ability had joined both opposition camps—the anti-Mormon political party and the reformed church. They ignored legal remedies and appealed to a higher law—popular sovereignty.[116] No doubt some acted as opportunists, but motives cannot be discerned with accuracy in every instance, and much of their explanation appeared after the fact as justification and defense. Many others in western Illinois denounced the substitution of violence for the civil process no matter what the reason.

As Governor Ford orchestrated preparations for the arrest and trial of the Carthage assassins, various individuals compiled lists naming

participants in the murders. The two survivors of the attack, Willard
Richards and John Taylor, recognized some of those who fired on them
from the landing in the jail and named others. Richards's tally of sixteen
participants and several supporters included the Laws, the Fosters, the
Higbees, and Jackson.[117] William M. Daniels, a witness outside the jail,
identified ten others, most of them residents of Warsaw.[118] Sheriff Jacob
Backenstos listed all twenty-eight permanent members of the Carthage
Greys as parties to the massacre. He said that a militia company twice that
size from Green Plains and three companies of sixty each from Warsaw
joined in the conspiracy. The sheriff identified as active participants sixty
men from Warsaw, Green Plains, Quincy, Carthage, Augusta, St. Mary's,
Fountain Green, and Pontoosuc, and a few unnamed individuals who left
the area after the murders. According to Backenstos, the accused included
seven lawyers, seven farmers, four merchants, three tavern keepers, three
doctors, two "land sharks," six with "no business," and one (Major
Calvin A. Warren) "a damned villain."[119] Governor Ford believed that justice would best be served by charging only the leaders of the vigilantes.
His counsel eventually prevailed.[120]

As newly elected county officials took steps to organize a grand jury
in early September 1844, both sides in the issue watched for extralegal retribution. Supporters of the regulators feared vengeance from Nauvoo's
militia. Latter-day Saints alerted Governor Ford when they heard that the
Warsaw militia was planning a multicounty drill, or "Grand Military
Encampment," in late September. According to a Carthage resident who
wanted no part of it, "The people talk of a wolf hunt. They say that [thou-
sands] . . . will meet at Warsaw and pass through the timbers and prairies
in this county forming a circle, and at last all meet at the Temple at
Nauvoo. You may judge what the object is. The Mormons are fearful of
the event, and no wonder." The organizers denied such reports, claiming
that only three hundred troops would assemble for a routine drill.[121]

Despite criticism from his Whig detractors, Ford ignored the Warsaw
disclaimer and assembled his own private force to end the harassment. He
also needed help in arresting the accused murderers. He requested 2,500
volunteers from nine counties. Only a fraction of that number
responded.[122] The governor placed a prominent Whig, Brigadier General
John J. Hardin, in charge of his volunteers and in late September followed
them to Nauvoo. Two groups from Quincy swelled the militia to about

470 men. The Warsaw organizers cancelled their encampment. Some accused assassins fled across the river to Churchville, Missouri.[123]

At Nauvoo, the governor's militia camped on a vacant lot on the flats while he met with local officials. Ford presented Brigham Young with a commission as lieutenant general of the Nauvoo Legion and Charles C. Rich as major general. The following day, the Legion marched in review to acquaint Hardin with their numbers and their skills. Thinly armed and inexperienced, they made a poor showing. Hardin tested the mettle of the state troops by giving a false alarm. In the ensuing confusion, a volunteer cadet from Springfield was accidentally wounded. The governor and his troops left that afternoon for Warsaw, camping for the night in the woods three miles downriver from Nauvoo.[124]

With the possibility of a "wolf hunt" resolved, Ford concentrated on arresting the individuals accused of killing Joseph and Hyrum Smith. On September 22, he sent an agent to Nauvoo, Warsaw, and other points to gather evidence for the trial. Information from eyewitnesses and others was used to issue writs against Levi Williams, Thomas C. Sharp, William Law, Robert D. Foster, Charles A. Foster, Joseph H. Jackson, and the guards on duty at the jail, including their commander, Franklin A. Worrell. Learning that the men he sought had fled, Ford planned a secret midnight expedition into Missouri to capture them. But one of the militia officers in on the planning, E. D. Baker, a prominent Whig attorney, quietly made the trip himself during the day on September 30 to bargain with the fugitives. Upset by the private negotiations, Ford was nevertheless obligated to accept the compromise agreed to by Williams, Sharp, and Jackson. The trio agreed to appear before Judge Jesse B. Thomas Jr. at Quincy. The state promised a reasonable bail and a trial postponed until May 1845. After further negotiations with Judge Thomas, the defendants waived their right to a preliminary hearing and executed a bond of two thousand dollars to secure their appearance in court. Whig papers scorned the governor for his foolish "treaty" with the fugitives. In fact, he had done his best under difficult conditions to vindicate the state for his broken promises at Carthage and to bring the accused to trial.[125]

As the trial date approached, detractors once again raised questions about Latter-day Saint intentions. A commentary in the *Nauvoo Neighbor* created the opportunity. The writer, presumably editor John Taylor, challenged as illegal the repeal of the city charter. Noting that governments grant artificial rights, he argued that individuals also enjoy natural rights independent of earthly governments. "Every man is above the law and can act as he pleases if he does not interfere with his neighbor's right," he wrote. "This is clearly taught in the great foundation of all law, the ten commandments. Human law, the artificial contrivance of intellect, is not binding upon any honest man. . . . Laws are for transgressors." The *State Register* in Springfield took this statement to mean the Saints were justifying lawlessness. The newspaper raised concerns that the Saints would overrun Carthage during the circuit court session to force a conviction of the accused murderers of Joseph Smith.[126]

To quiet these misunderstandings, Brigham Young convened his political advisers, the Council of Fifty. The assemblage encouraged moderation but put Nauvoo's militia on alert and authorized letters of explanation to the governor and Hancock County's United States congressman. The council issued a public statement distancing the church from the *Neighbor's* editorial and pledged a patient waiting for justice. The *Neighbor* published the council's reassurance that the Saints were a law-abiding people. It also printed a letter from "Americus" that echoed the position of the Fifty. Though the residents of Nauvoo had no wish to resist the law, the letter said, they would be ready to oppose any conspiracy against the Saints. If the Saints were to adopt a political motto, the *Neighbor* editorialized, "*let it be a dove bearing a fruitful olive bough,* as a token of peace on earth."[127] These efforts to explain Latter-day Saint intentions reassured many, but a negative public attitude toward them prevailed.

In late May, Brigham Young informed Parley P. Pratt, "The trial of the murderers is now in progress, but there is every reason to suppose they will be acquitted." This widely held expectation among the Saints was exactly the conclusion reached by a jury of the circuit court in Carthage.[128] Those actually brought to trial for the murder of Joseph Smith included six prominent leaders of the vigilantes: Thomas Sharp, Colonel Levi Williams, land agent Mark Aldrich, state senator Jacob C. Davis, and Warsaw militia captain William N. Grover. After more than a week of testimony, the jury accepted the defense argument that no one individual could be held responsible for deaths accomplished to satisfy the will of the people. The prosecutors failed to appear for a separate June 24 trial for those accused in the murder of Hyrum Smith.[129]

Many of the Latter-day Saints expected the trial of Joseph Smith's

In May 1845, a circuit court jury meeting in the brick courthouse at Carthage acquitted five accused murderers of Joseph Smith. Five months later, another jury released the policemen charged with the destruction of the Expositor *press. This courthouse, Hancock County's second, was built in 1839 and razed in 1906.*

accused assassins to set off another round of harassment. They were pleased that things remained peaceful, even if, as one man put it, "the court has turned out to be a perfect mob court. . . . after advancing all the testimony necessary to convict men, the jury brought in . . . [a] verdict not guilty."[130]

Those who were charged with the deaths of Joseph and Hyrum Smith and judged by their peers not guilty of murder resumed their lives. Nauvoo's political opponents continued their anti-Mormon efforts until the Saints left Illinois. Then, despite legends to the contrary, they lived out their lives as respected citizens with successful careers in their communities. Likewise, many of the seceders from the church found other ways to make contributions to society and to other religious efforts.[131]

The trial of the accused murderers attracted much more attention in

Hancock County than the eventual hearings on riot charges against the city council and police. The Nauvoo municipal officers charged with inciting riot had been released by Daniel H. Wells in the justice's court at Nauvoo on June 17, 1844, and again by Robert F. Smith, a justice in Carthage, on June 25. The defendants posted a bond after Smith remanded the case to the next session of the Hancock County circuit court.[132] In October, the Nauvoo city council paid $725 to compensate the *Expositor* owners for the destruction of the press.[133]

The Nauvoo policemen believed to have been most prominently involved in destroying the *Expositor* press stood trial in Carthage on October 23, 1845. Security was high for the trial. Dozens of former Nauvoo Legion soldiers camped around the town to prevent violence against the defendants and witnesses. Brigham Young arrived with a guard of sixteen well-armed and mounted horsemen. Other witnesses likewise retained bodyguards. This was "a much more prudent and sensible way of securing safety than fighting," a visiting land agent quipped. Sheriff Jacob Backenstos doubted that the court of Judge Purple would give a fair hearing. The judge instructed the jury to find the defendants guilty if it could be shown that they had participated in the suppression. But when the key witness could not distinguish between pairs of policemen with the same surname, the jury dismissed the case with a verdict of not guilty. A correspondent for the *Warsaw Signal* complained that Mormons, many of them from Nauvoo, made up most of the jury.[134]

If the trial of the murderers of Joseph and Hyrum Smith had looked like a miscarriage of justice to the Saints, so to opponents of the church this trial likewise seemed a farce. Both sides now had evidence sufficient to themselves that for their own grievances, at least, justice could not be obtained in Hancock County.

CHAPTER 15

"Who Shall Lead the Church?"

We all felt as though the powers of darkness had overcome, and that the Lord had forsaken His People. Our Prophet and Patriarch were gone! Who now is to lead the Saints? In fact we mourned "as one mourneth for his only son." Yet after all the anguish of our hearts and deep mourning of our souls a spirit seemed to whisper "All is well. . . ." So we felt to trust in God.

—WARREN FOOTE, 1844

Most Latter-day Saints had not anticipated the need to adjust so suddenly to a leader other than Joseph Smith. Not yet thirty-nine when he died, physically robust and vital, the Prophet had inspired and attracted people with revelations and teachings for fifteen years. But now he was dead, as was his brother, who might have stood in his place. Hyrum Smith, forty-four when he died with his brother at Carthage, had been patriarch to the church for nearly four years and assistant president almost as long. In the latter office, Hyrum held two powers essential to the office of president. First, he had been appointed a prophet, seer, and revelator. In this calling, he acted in concert with the Prophet and other members of the First Presidency in announcing revelation to the whole church. Hyrum also shared with his brother the authority to administer in the ordinances that would be offered to the Saints in the Nauvoo Temple. "If Hyrum had lived," Brigham Young noted, "he would not have stood between Joseph and the Twelve but he would have stood for Joseph.

Did Joseph ordain any man to take his place? He did. Who was it? It was Hyrum, but Hyrum fell a martyr before Joseph did."[1]

With the Prophet and the Patriarch gone, important vacancies in the church needed to be filled. The office of president set expectations not easily met, for Joseph Smith had been not only president but prophet, honored by the Lord's call "to come forth in the fulness of times to take part in laying the foundations of the great latter-day work." "You cannot fill the office of a prophet, seer and revelator," Brigham Young told the Saints. "God must do this."[2] As for Hyrum's calling as assistant president, a new president could select another if he wished. The office of patriarch to the church, on the other hand, had been designated for patrilineal descent and was given to William Smith in 1845.[3]

Some outside observers believed that without Joseph Smith The Church of Jesus Christ of Latter-day Saints would not last. The editor of the *New York Herald* declared on July 8, "The death of the modern Mahomet will seal the fate of Mormonism. They cannot get another Joe Smith. The holy city must tumble into ruins, and the 'latter day saints' have indeed come to the latter day." Although some echoed this pessimism, other journalists saw different possibilities. Even the *Herald* editor amended his first opinion. The murders might actually strengthen the church, he suggested. The Prophet and the Patriarch would "be regarded as martyrs to their faith." The latter proved to be the more accurate assessment. That same day, Willard Richards and John Taylor used a popular phrase to summarize their feelings about the effect of the death of the Prophet and the Patriarch: "'The blood of the martyrs is the seed of the Church.'"[4]

Preparing for Succession

Reflecting on what Joseph Smith had said to them, many of his close associates at Nauvoo realized that their young leader had anticipated his own death. Even the Lord's promise in 1843 that Joseph would see the Second Coming if he lived to age eighty-five implied no promise that the Prophet would live until 1890.[5] Rather, for a number of years, the Prophet had talked of a foreshortened life under a specific timetable. When faced with vicious challenges from apostates at Kirtland in 1838, he told a council of priesthood leaders, "'I shall see you again, let what will happen, for I have a promise of life five years, and they cannot kill me until that time is expired.'" That fall, in Far West, Missouri, when Joseph and Hyrum were carried off in a wagon to prison, their mother felt inspired that her sons would not be harmed: "'And, in less than four years, Joseph shall speak before the judges and great men of the land . . . and in five years from this time he will have power over all his enemies.'" The Prophet reported a confirmation from the Lord while in the jail at Liberty that his life would not be shortened prematurely by his enemies. After the martyrdom, Lucy Smith concluded that God's promise of protection had expired. "I then thought upon the promise which I had received in Missouri, that in five years Joseph should have power over all his enemies. The time had elapsed and the promise was fulfilled." Furthermore, her dying husband's last blessing upon their prophet-son in September 1840 had promised, "'You shall even live to finish your work.'"[6]

Many Latter-day Saints embraced the idea that Joseph Smith had fulfilled his mission, that the Prophet and the Patriarch had died at Carthage for a greater purpose. Indirectly, this affirmation helped church members believe that the Lord would provide a new leader. "Perhaps it is all right," William Appleby reflected upon hearing of the murders. "It was necessary for them to seal their Mission with their own blood. . . . But if they have killed the Prophet and Patriarch, they cannot kill Mormonism or the Church. Its course is onward."[7]

Those who accepted Joseph Smith as a divine spokesman—as translator, revelator, seer, and prophet—saw his gifts as singular. They knew also that other leaders had been sustained as prophets, seers, and revelators. Worthy elders taught by the Spirit, and members shared in gifts of the Spirit, including the gift of revelation. The Saints could exercise the gift for themselves and for others within their circle of responsibility. Yet only a designated leader could speak in the name of the Lord for the entire church.[8] The question in 1844 was who had been chosen of God to lead the church, to hold the keys to all the spiritual gifts and ordinances.

Within Latter-day Saint congregations, certain related principles governed the appointment of church officers at all levels. Two of them were summarized in the Articles of Faith in 1842, stating "that a man must be called of God, by prophecy" and that he must receive an outward conferral of power "by the laying on of hands by those who are in authority." Between the inspired nomination and the authoritative ordination, a third condition had to be met. According to an 1830 revelation on church government, the candidate's name must be presented to church members for their concurrence.[9]

In the process of creating a church organization, Joseph Smith identified two callings with the additional qualification of lineage. The presiding bishop could receive the office either as a literal descendant of Aaron or as a high priest in the Melchizedek Priesthood. Nauvoo's bishops were drawn from the high priests quorum. The same revelation said that the office of patriarch to the church "was confirmed to be handed down from father to son." Patriarchs to the church were to be designated by revelation and ordained by the apostles. Hyrum Smith had succeeded to the office of patriarch in September 1840 after his father's death and was officially ordained the following January. Both offices for which lineage was a factor required that candidates be worthy and that they be appointed and ordained by those in authority and with the common consent of the members.[10] Neither presiding bishops nor church patriarchs were given responsibility or authority that would prepare them to succeed to the office of president of the church.[11]

Over the years, under the directives given him by revelation in 1831, Joseph Smith had designated replacements for his own position. The office or person he named changed as the ecclesiastical organization unfolded or as circumstances changed. Each new designation generally superseded an older action. Sometimes it added other possibilities to a hierarchical line of succession. In hindsight, we can see a clear pattern emerging with each new instruction or action. In Nauvoo, additional authority associated with the temple changed the requirements for serving as president of the church. Before his death, the Prophet prepared Hyrum Smith and the faithful members of the Twelve as successors. He gave them keys and authority needed to function in the office of president, which were to be activated through established procedures only upon his removal or death.[12]

After Joseph Smith's martyrdom, the Twelve, who had been given the priesthood keys necessary to govern the church, accepted the responsibility now placed upon them. The latent keys which Brigham Young held as president of the Quorum of the Twelve Apostles became active. President Young explained the situation to a conference in Nauvoo in August. The Saints accepted his proposition, and with the personal spiritual witness that many of them received, they sustained the Twelve as the governing body of the church, with Brigham Young as its head. This action set in place principles of succession that would guide future transitions.[13]

Not everyone knew of the counsel, ordinances, and conferral of authority that the Twelve had received from Joseph Smith. Some who stepped forward as alternate claimants drew upon earlier provisions or found their own ways to appeal to followers. Only James J. Strang professed new revelation in an appeal to direct, divine authority. William Smith asserted a right through lineage for the Prophet's eldest son, Joseph III.[14] Sidney Rigdon and a few others turned to the Doctrine and Covenants, where they sought specific counsel on succession. In these modern scriptures, they found reminders as well that all authorized callings come by revelation, congregational acceptance, and ordination. Many would-be leaders accepted the right of the Twelve to lead but opposed their desire to sustain and continue the Prophet's new revelations and practices of the Nauvoo era.[15]

Discussion of a successor for Joseph Smith had first appeared during the last months of 1830 in response to two concerns. Certain church members in Kirtland were offering revelations in competition with Joseph Smith. Concurrently, Oliver Cowdery and Sidney Rigdon wondered if they might not have roles to play in guiding the new church. Revelations in April had designated Oliver Cowdery as second elder. With the Prophet, he held the apostleship and responsibilities over the whole church, including missionary duties for the world, which would later be given to the Quorum of the Twelve Apostles.[16]

Three revelations established the Prophet's exclusive right to speak to the entire church in the Lord's name. In the first, the Lord told Oliver Cowdery that only Joseph Smith could receive commandments and revelations for this church, "for he receiveth them even as Moses." Cowdery was given the role of an Aaron, called to teach the Prophet's words to the people.[17] The concept of a prophet and his spokesman, here applied to Joseph Smith as first elder and Oliver Cowdery as second elder, later defined the relationship between Joseph Smith as president and his counselors in the First Presidency.

A second revelation, addressed to Sidney Rigdon, a former Campbellite preacher, called Rigdon as a scribe and informed him that the Lord had prepared him for a greater work yet to come. As for Joseph Smith's calling as presiding elder, the Lord said, "I have given unto him the keys of the mystery of those things which have been sealed, . . . if he abide in me, and if not, another will I plant in his stead. Wherefore, watch over him that his faith fail not."[18] This revelation assured the Saints that the Lord would not leave them without a leader.

In February 1831, the third revelation reaffirmed Joseph Smith's appointment as the sole revelator to the church and gave him power to identify his own successor. It said, "None else shall be appointed unto this gift [revelation for the church] except it be through him [Joseph]; for if it be taken from him he shall not have power except to appoint another in his stead." That mandate to confer essential authorities on others was restated in an 1833 revelation reminding the Prophet that "through you shall the oracles be given to another, yea even unto the church."[19] With this direction from the Lord, the Prophet made certain that the keys of the kingdom reserved only for the president were shared with others to ensure continuity after he was gone. Two years later, the Lord affirmed that the Prophet's calling as the head of the final dispensation had implications beyond mortality: "The keys of this kingdom shall never be taken from you, while thou art in the world, neither in the world to come."[20]

With the organization of the First Presidency early in 1832, Oliver Cowdery, who was living at the time in Missouri, ceased temporarily to function in his office. Sidney Rigdon and Jesse Gause were called as counselors, but Gause became disaffected and was replaced by Frederick G. Williams. A revelation in March 1833 made the new counselors "equal with [the President] in holding the keys of this last kingdom."[21] Despite this shared authority, Joseph Smith remained first among the "three Presiding High Priests" who formed "a quorum of the Presidency of the Church." All bore the title president, but the Prophet ranked first in the presidency, just as he had been first elder in the earlier paired-leadership council. The 1835 revelation said, "The duty of the President of the office of the High Priesthood is to preside over the whole church, and to be like unto Moses—behold, here is wisdom; yea, to be a seer, a revelator, a translator, and a prophet, having all the gifts of God which he bestows upon the head of the church."[22] This revelation implied a continuation of the role of the counselors as Aaronlike spokesmen for the prophet but gave the counselors a latent authority to act in the president's absence when the two of them agreed as one.

After a visit to Missouri, where he organized a high council, Joseph

Smith returned to Ohio and in early December 1834 expanded the First Presidency by calling three members of the Kirtland high council to the presiding quorum. For a time, all five counselors were referred to as assistant presidents. Oliver Cowdery, again available to serve, resumed service as an assistant president and by virtue of his previous ordination was given priority over counselors Rigdon and Williams. They were designated second and third assistant presidents. The next day, the Prophet called Hyrum Smith and Joseph Smith Sr. as the fourth and fifth assistants in the council of the First Presidency. The duties of an assistant president, Oliver Cowdery noted at the time, were "to assist in presiding over the whole Church, and to officiate in the absence of the President, according to his rank and appointment, . . . also to act as 'Spokesman.'"[23]

The arrangements for succession from 1830 to 1834 emphasized the role of the second elder, later known as the assistant president. Through this special calling, Oliver Cowdery and later Hyrum Smith held the latent keys needed to act following the death of the president. But with the creation of the high councils in 1834, the Lord introduced another concept of succession that would relate to the Council of the Twelve Apostles when they were organized a year later as a unique traveling high council.

Joseph Smith presided over the headquarters high council organized in February at Kirtland. He did so "according to the dignity of his office [as President of the church]." This standing council served as the court of appeals for temporary councils of high priests organized to deal with difficulties outside the seat of church government or other organized stakes.[24] In July, the Prophet organized a second standing high council, this one in Clay County, Missouri. Some presumed that this council in the land of Zion would have precedence over the council in Kirtland, a stake to Zion. On the contrary, when David Whitmer was called as president of the Missouri high council, he was sustained "as President, head and leader in Zion (in the absence of br. Joseph Smith jr.)." The ordination authorized Whitmer to preside in Missouri but retained for Joseph Smith the right of presidency if he were to locate at the Center Place. The Prophet explained in 1838 that Whitmer had been ordained "to be a leader, or a prophet to this Church, which (ordination) was on conditions that he (J. Smith jr) did not live to God himself." Although this explanation suggested that the president of the high council in Zion might succeed Joseph

Joseph Smith Jr.   *Hyrum Smith*

The positions of church president and patriarch, left vacant by the assassinations of Joseph and Hyrum Smith, were filled in August 1844 and May 1845. Hyrum's calling as assistant president was left vacant.

Smith, Whitmer apostatized and thus disqualified himself. He was excommunicated in 1838.[25]

Oliver Cowdery's service in the First Presidency also ended with his excommunication the same year. The ranking assistant president had been alienated from the Prophet because of such issues as consecration and plural marriage. Cowdery's disaffection resulted first in a reassignment. In 1837, he was appointed as an assistant counselor, a ranking below the first and second counselors. His excommunication the following year removed him, along with Whitmer, from the list of available successors.[26]

The two channels of succession set in place during the first years of the church were fully operative at the time of Joseph Smith's death. Both Hyrum Smith, as assistant president, and Brigham Young, as president of the Quorum of the Twelve Apostles, held the latent keys of presidency. The Lord reassured the Prophet at Liberty Jail in 1839 that he would live to finish his work. Perhaps because of this comfort, Joseph did not again become actively concerned over presidential succession until 1841. In that year, he began in earnest to prepare both the assistant president and the president of the Twelve as possible successors.

The first step was to fill the office of assistant president. After

January 24, 1841, the Prophet's brother Hyrum exercised the authority previously held by Oliver Cowdery as assistant president, including the apostleship. At the same time, Hyrum received his formal ordination to succeed his father in the office of patriarch to the Church. For the previous three and one-half years, he had served as assistant counselor and then as second counselor to Joseph. According to the authorizing revelation, Hyrum became "a prophet, and a seer, and a revelator unto my church, as well as my servant Joseph; that he may act in concert also with my servant Joseph; and that he shall receive counsel from my servant Joseph."[27]

This appointment, like that given earlier to Oliver Cowdery, gave Hyrum Smith administrative precedence over the counselors in the First Presidency and established his right to stand for his brother as president. The revelation also gave to Hyrum authority not held by Cowdery, which was the right to receive revelation for the church. At the same time, however, the first and second counselors were appointed prophets, seers, and revelators to share with Joseph Smith the right "to receive the oracles for the whole church." Rigdon was ordained to that calling in June 1841. Although the counselors clearly shared in the administrative and revelatory authority, none of this preempted Joseph Smith's priority as revelator to the church and as the only one who could exercise all priesthood keys.[28]

In a comment more than two years later, the Prophet may have been suggesting to the church that Hyrum was the one the Lord had prepared as his successor. As assistant president, Hyrum Smith already carried a great share of the administrative load of the First Presidency. His calling as a prophet, seer, and revelator suggested a greater role as teacher. Those and other implications came from a sermon delivered on Sunday afternoon, July 16, 1843. Joseph Smith announced "that Hyrum held the office of prophet to the church by birthright and he was going to have a reformation and the saints must regard Hyrum for he has authority."[29]

This statement raised two questions. First, was the prophetic office a right of lineage? The only publicly acknowledged birthright calling held by Hyrum at the time was that of patriarch to the church.[30] If Joseph Smith meant to suggest a similar right to the prophetic office, no record survives of further explanation. The question of patrilineal inheritance disappeared until after the martyrdom.

The second question got people talking. Was Joseph Smith intending to resign his own office as prophet in favor of his brother? After a week of puzzlement on the part of the Saints, the Prophet commented briefly in a speech on July 23. First, he noted that the spirit of prophecy was shared by many in the church. Several in the presiding councils had been sustained as prophets, seers, and revelators (including his brother Hyrum). They, too, could teach the Saints by the spirit of revelation. In both talks, the Prophet's comments suggest that he was looking to the eternities. He spoke of the covenant of eternal marriage and of priesthood government in the kingdom of God. He was clearly preparing the church to receive the temple ordinances. It may be that he also anticipated the time when he would move on to a mission beyond the veil. A few months earlier, he had administered endowments and sealings to selected couples. To provide for a succession of authority, he had conferred upon Hyrum and members of the Twelve—in latent form—the keys of administering the ordinances.[31]

Hyrum was prepared to function if that responsibility fell to him. Qualified as well was the president of a high council with responsibilities over the whole church and a commission as special witnesses of the Lord Jesus Christ. Joseph Smith had organized the Quorum of the Twelve Apostles in 1835. Known as the "twelve traveling councilors" or "Traveling Presiding High Council," this group differed in two ways from the high councils previously created. Geographically, they operated outside the designated gathering places known as stakes; ecclesiastically, they were called to be the church's Twelve Apostles. It was their duty to open the nations to the preaching of the gospel, "to build up the church, and regulate all the affairs of the same in all nations." At first, "all nations" meant those areas outside organized stakes, that is, where there was no standing high council. Except for being authorized to ordain patriarchs in all large branches of the church, the Twelve at that time held no authority over the stakes.[32]

An important priesthood revelation in 1835 established what became a line of succession through the hierarchical relationships it defined for the various quorums and councils. In their priesthood office, the quorum of the First Presidency as the Presidency of the High Priesthood held the "right to officiate in all the offices in the church," in both the Melchizedek and the Aaronic Priesthood. The president of the High Priesthood presided over the entire church.[33] The Twelve Apostles served "under the direction of the Presidency of the Church" and the Seventy acted "under the direction of the Twelve." The revelation gave the traveling council (the Twelve) a position above that of the standing high councils in Zion and her stakes. Joseph

Smith confirmed this in January 1836 when the question was raised by the Twelve. "Their authority . . . is next to the present Presidency," he said, "and . . . the Twelve are not subject to any other than the first Presidency."[34]

During the Nauvoo years, Joseph Smith expanded the administrative role of the Twelve as a presiding council in two ways. First, in 1841, he increased their authority within the stakes. Restricted for a time from traveling as apostolic witnesses in the world, the Twelve became, as it were, associates of the First Presidency in regulating the affairs of the whole church but with specific assignments within the gathered stakes. The Twelve accepted responsibilities in the headquarters stake that previously had been reserved to the First Presidency and to the stake president and his council.[35]

The second enlargement involved an expansion of the priesthood role of the Twelve. The Prophet gave them "the keys of the kingdom" in a sense beyond the apostolic and revelatory powers they already held. In Kirtland, the "keys of the kingdom" had reference to apostolic authority, "the Twelve being sent out, holding the keys, to open the door by the proclamation of the gospel of Jesus Christ."[36] In a priesthood sense, at Kirtland the president, the associate president, and the Twelve held apostolic keys. At Nauvoo, all of them eventually shared, in addition, the Melchizedek Priesthood keys of administering the sealing ordinances, including those of proxy baptism, endowment, and eternal marriage.

Joseph Smith gave to the Twelve (and some others) the endowment so that they could preserve the knowledge after his own death or removal. To the Twelve in March 1844, he entrusted the keys to authorize the administration of those ordinances to others. To Brigham Young, he gave the keys of the sealing power. Joseph and his assistant president Hyrum Smith held all of those keys as well, but counselors Sidney Rigdon and William Law did not.[37] "I don't know what it is," Joseph told the Twelve,

> but the Lord bids me to hasten and give you your endowment before the temple is finished. . . . Now if they kill me you have got all the keys, and all the ordinances and you can confer them upon others . . . ; and now says he on your shoulders will the responsibility of leading this people rest, for the Lord is going to let me rest a while.[38]

When the question of succession arose three months later, the Twelve knew that they had received ecclesiastical and priesthood priority over the counselors in the First Presidency and over all other church priesthoods and offices except those held by the president and assistant president. Because they understood the nature of this authority, which included the power to act in the office of the First Presidency and to reorganize that body, the Twelve stepped forward to lead the church in 1844. Along with the issue of revelator to the church, it was the issue of the keys of priesthood authority reposing with the Twelve that mattered. And the most important for the continuity of the expanded doctrine and practices introduced in Nauvoo were the keys associated with the promised blessings of the temple.[39]

Appointing a Successor

At the time of Joseph Smith's death, most of the Twelve were on a preaching and campaigning mission in the East. On June 27, only John Taylor and Willard Richards, both at Carthage, were nearby. Within two weeks, Parley P. Pratt had joined them in Nauvoo.[40] Other apostles would soon arrive to resolve pressing questions about succession.

Even though Sidney Rigdon still held the position of first counselor at the time of the martyrdom, he had moved his family to his native Pittsburgh to reestablish residence as the vice-presidential candidate on Joseph Smith's union ticket. During much of the Nauvoo period, illness, diffidence to duty, and the Prophet's growing distrust of him had limited Rigdon's ability to serve. The Prophet's able spokesman had been a reluctant resident of Nauvoo, anxious since 1841 to seek a place of refuge away from the appointed stake, even though enjoined by the Prophet not to do so. Rigdon had declared his unwillingness to follow the Prophet's revelations if they inconvenienced him personally. At the October 1843 conference, the Prophet attempted to release Rigdon and move Amasa Lyman into the spot, but with behind-the-scenes support from Hyrum Smith and William Marks, an impassioned plea from Rigdon won the congregation's sympathy and sustaining vote.[41]

William Law, second counselor in the First Presidency since 1841, had been excommunicated for rebellion on April 18, 1844, and not replaced. Amasa Lyman had served as an additional counselor in the First Presidency since about February 1843, when Orson Pratt was reinstated into the Quorum of the Twelve Apostles. In August 1844, the Twelve welcomed Lyman back into the quorum. The Prophet's uncle John Smith had served as an assistant counselor beginning in 1837. He was not reappointed after the martyrdom but remained a stake president in Macedonia.[42]

The president of the stake high council at Nauvoo, William Marks, was seated with the First Presidency at the April 1844 conference in the place of William Law, who was excommunicated two weeks later. Whether this signaled the possibility that Marks would replace Law is not certain, because no action was taken at the conference nor later. During the early months of 1838, there had been indications of future leadership roles for the former member of the Kirtland high council, and he became stake president in Nauvoo the following year. It is certain that in 1844 the Prophet did not see Marks as a successor.[43]

After the martyrdom, Marks did step forward with the first proposal to fill one aspect of the void in leadership. On Friday afternoon, July 12, he invited the presidents of the priesthood quorums in Nauvoo to appoint a trustee under civil law to manage church financial affairs. No organization could be without such a legal officer for long, and Emma Smith was anxious to resolve her personal finances. Willard Richards of the Twelve and Bishop Newel K. Whitney pressed for more time. At the Sunday preaching meeting, Richards proposed that the need could wait until other members of the Twelve returned. His schedule prevailed.[44]

Some wanted to invite the Council of Fifty to reorganize the church. Willard Richards, George A. Smith, and John Taylor conferred at Taylor's home and then told proponents George Miller and Alexander Badlam that the secular general council existed to seek redress of grievances and "to devise means to find and locate in some place where we could live in peace; and that the organization of the church belonged to the priesthood alone." Only a day earlier Richards had revealed his position that the Twelve held the authority to act in the office of president. He signed the licenses of two newly ordained elders: "Twelve Apostles, President."[45]

While available church leaders discussed the process for filling the offices of president and patriarch, some members and their neighbors wondered aloud about the possible candidates. James Blakesley, a member living in Rock Island County, Illinois, summarized the speculation:

> The church is left without an earthly head, unless the promise of the Lord shall be fulfilled, which saith, that if he removed Joseph, he would appoint another in his stead. But as this has not yet been done, what is the church to do? Now sir, if I have been correctly informed, some of the members of the church at Nauvoo, want Stephen

Markham for their head, and others Sidney Rigdon, and others President Marks, and others Little Joseph, and others B. Young, and some others P. P. Pratt, and if they can all have their choice, we shall soon have a multiplicity of churchs of Latter Day Saints.[46]

Sidney Rigdon heard the news of the martyrdom in Pittsburgh. He headed immediately for Nauvoo. Members of the Twelve assembled in Boston had written him, urging Elder Rigdon to participate in a joint consideration of the leadership question.[47] Rigdon arrived on Saturday, August 3, ahead of the group returning from Boston. He agreed to meet the following morning with those of the Twelve already in Nauvoo but failed to keep the appointment. At the regular ten o'clock Sunday preaching meeting at the grove, Rigdon offered a suggestion similar to that of William Marks—selection of a guardian (a president and trustee) to "build the church up to Joseph." Rigdon offered himself as that guardian. He cited neither precedent nor his position in the First Presidency to justify his claims but turned instead to scripture and modern revelation. Ancient prophets had foretold the present situation, he said. In addition, Rigdon claimed a personal revelation calling for "a guardian through whom Joseph will speak to the people . . . as a god to this dispensation, . . . as Moses was to the children of Israel."[48]

The ambitious orator described impending judgments, including a destructive global warfare in which he would personally lead a militant church to a triumphant victory over the nations of Babylon. He boasted "that he expected to walk into the palace of Queen Victoria and lead her out by the nose."[49] Parley Pratt later said of this message: "Elder Rigdon . . . said nothing about building the Temple, the city, feeding the poor, etc. We heard a great deal about the Mount of Olives—Brook Kedron—Queen Victoria—great battles, etc. . . . . We want to build up Nauvoo, never mind Gog and Magog."[50]

Rigdon had served as first counselor since March 1833 and was familiar with the original shared authority given the counselors in the 1833 revelation. He may not have understood that the Twelve had received additional sealing keys and authorities. They had received all temple ordinances; Rigdon had received only a partial endowment. Learning of the special conference proposed by Willard Richards, Rigdon asked Marks, as stake president, to convene a conference for August 6. Instead, at the

Sidney Rigdon   *William Smith*

Sidney Rigdon, of the First Presidency, and William Smith, of the Twelve, disagreed with the direction that Brigham Young and the Twelve were taking the church. Both men affiliated with others who rejected Joseph Smith's Nauvoo teachings that the Twelve supported.

Sunday afternoon preaching service on August 4, Marks set the date for Thursday, August 8. When high councilor Thomas Grover requested even more time for delegates to examine Rigdon's new revelation, Marks resisted. Rigdon was anxious to learn if the Saints at Nauvoo would accept his offer, Marks said; if not, Rigdon expected to find thousands of members in other branches who would receive him as their guardian.[51]

Talk in Nauvoo after Rigdon's impassioned plea included concern over his sense of urgency. Charles C. Rich, a counselor to Marks, worried that if the church did not wait for the rest of the Twelve to return, Rigdon might take unfair advantage of the situation and confuse the Saints into a premature decision. On Monday after dinner, Rigdon met with four members of the Twelve. Joining them were Amasa Lyman, who had arrived in Nauvoo July 31, and Bishop Newel K. Whitney. It was election day in Hancock County. Rigdon argued that without an acting head of the church to give counsel, the Saints would scatter their votes for the legislative and county candidates. The assembled council disagreed. A citizens' meeting at the grove the previous Friday had reached a consensus upon candidates friendly to the Saints.[52]

During the evening of Tuesday, August 6, the steamer *St. Croix* from Galena docked near the upper stone house at Nauvoo. Aboard were Elders Brigham Young, Heber C. Kimball, Orson Pratt, and Wilford Woodruff. They were delighted to be reunited with their families, yet to Woodruff "a deep gloom seemed to rest over the city of Nauvoo." Their arrival brought to eight the number of the Quorum of the Twelve in Nauvoo. Still absent on missions were Elders Orson Hyde, William Smith, John E. Page, and Lyman Wight. "The Brethern ware over joyed to see us come home," Brigham Young observed, "for they ware like Children with out a Father, and they felt so, you may be sure." The following morning, the Twelve met for a joyous reunion at the home of John Taylor, still recovering from his wounds.[53]

That same afternoon at four, Nauvoo's high council and all the high priests in the city joined the Twelve and Sidney Rigdon at the Seventies Hall. Rigdon explained the revelation he had received at Pittsburgh on the day of the martyrdom. It was a continuation of a vision published in the Doctrine and Covenants, he said, presumably the 1832 vision of the three heavenly glories that Rigdon shared with Joseph Smith. What the Lord wanted now, Rigdon said, was for Joseph's longtime spokesman to govern the church, receive revelations, and continue the Prophet's work.[54] Minutes of the meeting captured Rigdon's explanation:

> Joseph sustains the same relationship to this church as he has always done. No man can be the successor of Joseph. The kingdom is to be built up to Jesus Christ through Joseph; there must be revelation still. The martyred Prophet is still the head of this church; every quorum should stand as you stood in your washings and consecrations. I have been consecrated a spokesman to Joseph, and I was commanded to speak for him. The church is not disorganized though our head is gone.

Rigdon acknowledged that some would reject his revelation: "The people can please themselves whether they accept me or not."[55]

For the assembled church leaders, much of Rigdon's explanation rang true to the revelations and to their own feelings about Joseph Smith's unique role. The Twelve would soon declare to the church their intention

433

to build up the kingdom upon the foundation that the prophet Joseph has laid, who still holds the keys of this last dispensation, and will hold them to all eternity, as a king and priest unto the most high God. . . .

Let no man presume for a moment that his place will be filled by another; for *remember he stands in his own place,* and always will; and the Twelve Apostles of this dispensation stand in their own place and always will, both in time and in eternity, to minister, preside, and regulate the affairs of the whole church.[56]

Reflecting on his experience overseeing the work of the church in the British Isles, Brigham Young said, "I would like, were it my privilege, to take my valise and travel and preach till we had a people gathered who would be true . . . ; yet, whatever duty God places upon me, in his strength I intend to fulfill it." Not wanting to be presumptuous in what he saw as his duty as president of the Twelve nor as forthright as Rigdon in asserting a revelatory right to lead, Young demurred: "I do not care who leads the church, even though it were Ann Lee; but one thing I must know, and that is what God says about it. I have the keys and the means of obtaining the mind of God on the subject." He called for a special conference so that the people might consider the question.[57]

Young expressed one other concern during the leadership meeting. Joseph and Hyrum had been killed through the combined efforts of internal apostates and outside political opponents. Would those same murderers seek to kill the Twelve or other leaders? The senior apostle was ready to give his life, if necessary.[58] With that possibility in mind, he wanted to ensure the continuity of certain keys and authorities held only by the First Presidency and Twelve:

We shall ordain others and give the fulness of the priesthood, so that if we are killed the fulness of the priesthood may remain. Joseph conferred upon our heads all the keys and powers belonging to the Apostleship which he himself held before he was taken away, and no man or set of men can get between Joseph and the Twelve in this world or in the world to come. How often has Joseph said to the Twelve, "I have laid the foundation and you must build thereon, for upon your shoulders the kingdom rests."[59]

Rigdon had challenged the Twelve to take the place assigned to them when they received their washings and consecrations in the Kirtland Temple. But when Brigham Young spoke of the fulness of the priesthood, he meant the keys introduced in Nauvoo, including the keys of administering the covenants of the endowment and eternal marriage. Rigdon did not hold them. The Twelve felt the entire burden of responsibility on their shoulders to carry forth the kingdom as they and few others understood it.[60]

The meeting requested by Rigdon began at ten o'clock on Thursday, August 8, before a large crowd. Standing in a wagon about two rods in front of the preaching stand to get out of the wind, Rigdon expounded his proposal. He wanted a guardian appointed who would carry the titles of president and trustee. An experienced preacher, Rigdon occupied an hour and a half in unfolding his position. When Rigdon concluded, Brigham Young announced a special church conference at two o'clock. The congregation gathered again, with the quorums organized for a solemn assembly. Except for the convalescing John Taylor and those absent from Nauvoo, the members of the Twelve sat on the stand beside their quorum president.

Brigham Young spoke for his quorum, urging the congregation against the selection of a single leader. "You cannot fill the office of a prophet, seer and revelator: God must do this," he said. Even if a prophet were chosen, he added, only the Twelve had the authority to ordain him. The senior apostle felt impressed that the people would be happier with what he called a shepherd than with a guardian or president or leader. Rigdon's authority, he said, had ended with the death of the Prophet. Choosing him as the head would divide the church. "I will ask," he said,

> who has stood next to Joseph and Hyrum? I have, and I will stand next to him. We have a head, and that head is the Apostleship. . . . Brother Rigdon was at his side—not above. No man has a right to counsel the Twelve but Joseph Smith. Think of these things. You cannot appoint a prophet; but if you let the Twelve remain and act in their place, the keys of the kingdom are with them and they can manage the affairs of the church and direct all things aright.

Young suggested that the vacancy in the office of patriarch to the Church ought to be filled by a member of Joseph Smith's family and that the duties of trustee-in-trust should be given back to the bishops, who had responsibility for temporal affairs. Joseph Smith took that over, he added, only because the bishops failed in their duty.[61]

Brigham Young next invited Amasa Lyman to share his feelings about his unfulfilled appointment as a counselor to the First Presidency. Lyman acknowledged that he had no claim to precedence over the Twelve. The people's salvation depended upon union, he said, but they must unite for the right—behind the Twelve. Rigdon was given another opportunity to express himself, but he deferred to his old friend William W. Phelps. Phelps encouraged the congregation "to submit with deference to the authorities of the church." "If you want to do right," he concluded, "uphold the Twelve. . . . Do your duty and you will be endowed. I will sustain the Twelve as long as I have breath."[62]

It was soon time for the vote to be called. Brigham Young summarized the issues. Agreeing with Rigdon on procedure, he emphasized that each member should vote his or her independent mind and support only the propositions they could fully sustain with their actions in the days to come. Young proposed that Sidney Rigdon be sustained as a leader, guide, or spokesman. Rigdon interrupted the motion. He wished the other question taken first, namely, "Does the church want, and is it their only desire to sustain the Twelve as the First Presidency of this people?" Rather than polling each quorum one by one—the practice in a Latter-day Saint assembly of this type—Young chose instead to offer the motion to the entire congregation—quorums and unordained members alike. Would they sustain the Twelve? The congregation showed overwhelming support.[63]

Brigham Young's long discussion of succession options had touched the hearts of the assembled crowd. The president of the Quorum of the Twelve "gave the saints his views of what the Lord wanted," a summary of his talk noted. "Here are the 'Twelve,' appointed by the finger of God, who hold the keys of the priesthood, and the authority to set in order and regulate the church in all the world." It was as if the Prophet Joseph Smith himself was counseling them. In his autobiography, William C. Staines recalled the spiritual witness that had motivated the swell of support:

> Brigham Young said: "I will tell you who your leaders or guardians will be—the Twelve—I at their head." This was with the voice like the voice of the Prophet Joseph. I thought it was he, and so did thousands who heard it. This was very satisfactory to the people, and a vote was taken to sustain the Twelve in their office, which with a few dissenting voices, was passed.

Joseph Hovey recalled, "There were a few who were for Sidney Rigdon."[64]

Among men of influence besides Rigdon harboring questions about the conference decision were two apostles, Lyman Wight and William Smith, the Prophet's only surviving brother. Both had issues broader than the question of governance. William Marks, president of the stake at Nauvoo, also harbored misgivings. None of these men challenged the authority of the Twelve. Rather, they disagreed with the direction Brigham Young was leading the church. Discussions about Rigdon and other claimants to the Prophet's mantle caused some who were not well acquainted with the circumstances to speculate that the issue had not been resolved within the church. For some, it had not; but for most of the Saints, the answer had been made clear. Orson Hyde saw Rigdon's appeal as an attempt "to ensnare the people and allure their minds by his flowery eloquence; but the plan was defeated. The voice of the people was in favor of sustaining the Twelve to be their leaders."[65]

With the question of the priority of the Twelve over a counselor in the First Presidency resolved, the conference considered three other appointments. The standing of William Marks as Nauvoo stake president was deferred until the October conference because it was less urgent. The congregation authorized the Twelve to appoint a general patriarch from the Smith family. And those present voted to support Sidney Rigdon "in the place he occupies." The Saints also agreed to free the Twelve to travel again by shifting financial responsibilities to the bishops. Further, they pledged to support the Prophet's program for the church by completing the temple through a tithing of their time and money. This task, said Brigham Young, was the main responsibility of the Saints for that time. He concluded with a call to action, "Now let men stand to their posts and be faithful."[66]

Support and Discontent

The members who voted their own minds in support of the Twelve meant it. They accepted the Twelve's dual responsibilities in their own office and that of the First Presidency as an appropriate solution to a common concern. "There are others to fill their place," Edward Hunter said of Joseph's and Hyrum's deaths. Zilpha Williams informed her father in Pennsylvania, "Instead of two we have twelve to lead us, and the more they [the mob] destroy the stronger we are."[67] Some of the Saints drew a parallel with the pattern of apostolic succession found in the New Testament.[68] In the minds and hearts of these believers, the modern apostles did not usurp the unique position of the first prophet of the Restoration, nor was the church left without a head.

Many of those in attendance received a personal witness that Brigham Young had appropriately replaced Joseph Smith. For them, the very appearance, actions, and voice of Young were those of the dead Prophet. It was, paradoxically, the kind of experience anticipated by Sidney Rigdon, who promised that Joseph Smith would speak through him to the Saints in the same way God had spoken through Moses. But Rigdon was not to become the Mormon Moses. Henry and Catharine Brooke informed a friend in Pennsylvania:

> The loss of Br. Joseph and Hyrum has been greatly felt but we have the twelve apostles to preside in their stead. Br. Brigham Young is president of the twelve and stands as prophet, seer, and revelator to the Church. He is an excellent man, and favours Br. Joseph, both in person, and manner of speaking, more than any person ever you saw looks like another.[69]

Soon after the August 8 meeting, Howard Egan shared his witness in a letter to Jesse C. Little in New Hampshire. In December, Little repeated the comments to Brigham Young: "He said if a man had been blinded he would hardly have known if it were not Joseph." Dozens of Saints received this special witness at the August conference. Typical is John Harper's remembrance that "when Bro. Brigham arose on the stand I received a testimony for myself; he appeared to me as if it was Bro. Joseph and it was Joseph's voice and there the mantle of Joseph fell on Brigham."[70]

The new church leader felt the same spirit that touched so many of the Saints. While those gathered before him in the open preaching ground below the temple saw Brother Brigham transformed before their eyes, he experienced his own sacred confirmation. His diary for August 8 says,

> This day is long to be remembered by me. It is the first time I have met with the Church at Nauvoo since Bro. Joseph and Hyrum were killed—and the occasion on which the church was called was some-what painful to me. Br. Rigdon had come from Pittsburg to see the Brethren and find out if they would sustain him as the leader of the Saints. I perceived a spirit to hurry business, . . . right or wrong, and this grieved my heart. Now Joseph is gone. It seemed as though many wanted to draw off a party and be leaders, but this cannot be.

Joseph Smith   *Brigham Young, 1841*

The transition from one leader to another moved smoothly on the windy afternoon of August 8, 1844, when a congregation filled with the Spirit unitedly raised their hands in support of Brigham Young after witnessing a transformation of the senior apostle that made him look and sound like the deceased Prophet.

The church must be one or they are not the Lord's. . . . In this time of sorrow my heart was filled with compassion. After Br. Rigdon had made a long speech to the saints (I should think 5 thousand), I arose and spoke to the people, my heart was swollen with compassion toward them and by the power of the Holy Ghost, even the spirit of the prophets I was enabled to comfort the hearts of the Saints. . . . I laid before them the order of the church and the power of the Priesthood. After a long and laborous talk of about two hours in the open air with the wind blowing, the Church was of one heart and one mind. They wanted the Twelve to lead the church as Brother Joseph had done in his day.[71]

Throughout the period of transition in leadership, the Saints could not forget their beloved first president. Brigham Young shared with his daughter Vilate in Massachusetts another reflection on the week's events, "I have ben in Councel all most all the time sence I arived here but this much I can say, the spirit of Joseph is here, though we cannot enjoy their [Joseph's and Hyrum's] persons."[72]

Between the August and October conferences, the Twelve met church needs in Nauvoo and elsewhere. They issued general letters of instruction to the Saints and made administrative appointments in scattered branches. Of special significance was the Twelve's decision to involve the high priests in an expansion of settlement options and the seventies in an enlarged missionary labor. Both ventures implemented the intentions of the martyred Prophet and helped strengthen the church after the temporary disruptions of dissent and assassination.[73]

The creation of new quorums of the seventy set the stage for an expansion of the missionary work that was so close to the hearts of the Twelve. Brigham Young's older brother, Joseph, had served since 1837 as the senior president of the seventy. He and six other men made up the First Seven Presidents. These men acted as general presidents over all other seventies quorums. They counseled regularly with the senior president of each quorum, who in turn taught the other six men who made up that quorum presidency. Quorum leaders in turn urged their members to sustain the Twelve. This show of support, they said, was a necessary component of the desired unity of the church.[74]

A further influence in building harmony within the church was the conference held every six months in Nauvoo. Because the Prophet said that a general conference could not be held until completion of the temple, the semiannual assemblies since October 1841 had been called special conferences. They convened only for specified business. The special conferences in October 1844 and April 1845 continued the unifying spirit of August's solemn assembly. At the October meeting, church leaders presented a full slate of Nauvoo priesthood officers for approval or disapproval. They replaced the few disaffected leaders with men loyal to Joseph Smith and the Twelve. And they reemphasized the need to remain in Nauvoo to complete the temple. At the special April conference, members once again reconfirmed the Twelve in their own office and as the First Presidency over the whole church, with Brigham Young at the head. The Saints then endorsed the labors of Joseph and Hyrum Smith as prophets, seers, and revelators—proposals directly challenging the contentions of the dissenters.[75]

In a proclamation issued for the Saints in the British Isles, Parley P. Pratt spoke of the sealing powers received from Joseph Smith. Brigham Young served as president of the church because of his position as president of the Twelve and because he alone held the keys of the sealing power. Pratt recalled the event of early 1844:

> [Joseph Smith] proceeded to confer on Elder Young, the President of the Twelve, the keys of the sealing power, as conferred in the last days by the spirit and power of Elijah, in order to seal the hearts of the fathers to the children, and the hearts of the children to the fathers, lest the whole earth should be smitten with a curse.[76]

A key objective of the October conference of 1844 was to fill voids in the organization created by apostasy. The loyal Saints demonstrated a spirit of solidarity by manifesting their support to the newly chosen officers. Because the Twelve as a body served as the First Presidency, there was no need to replace counselors Sidney Rigdon and William Law. Amasa Lyman was retained "in his lot" as an apostle and counselor to the Twelve.[77] William Marks was rejected as stake president because of his support of Rigdon. He was replaced by the Prophet's uncle John Smith of Macedonia, who moved to Nauvoo. Smith retained Marks's only remaining counselor, Charles C. Rich (the other counselor, Austin Cowles, had been dropped in May for joining the seceders and was not replaced). The high council received two new members to replace a deceased councilor and another who had supported the seceders.[78]

In connection with the assignments given to the high priests to build up stakes, the Twelve reaffirmed that Lyman Wight and George Miller were free to take the Wisconsin pine company—but no one else—to Texas. Even so, Brigham Young chided Wight for proceeding with plans to colonize in Texas and James Emmett for disregarding counsel in his movements across Iowa toward Council Bluffs. The Saints could not get their endowments in the wilderness, Young cautioned, to correct rumors about Wight's mission. "North and South America is Zion and as soon as the Temple is done and you get your endowments you can go and build up stakes, but do not be in haste, wait until the Lord says go." The Saints appreciated Young's frank clarifications. William Huntington Sr. was even more direct: "The purging out of the Lawites, Lymanites, Emettites and the Rigdonites relieves the church of a great burden."[79]

Many of those who rejected the Twelve's right to guide the church through new revelation had already spurned the Nauvoo revelations of Joseph Smith. In conference addresses and epistles and through adjustments in church policy, Brigham Young helped the Saints understand his role as revelator to the church. An important opening statement came in the address in October. Young said, "It is the right of an individual to get revelations to guide himself. It is the right of the head of a family to get revelations to guide and govern his family. It is the right of an elder when he has built up a church to get revelations to guide and lead that people until he leads them and delivers them up to his superiors." Interlaced with this explanation, Young identified the president of the Twelve as chief revelator: "If you don't know whose right it is to give revelations, I will tell you. It is I."[80]

Another central tenet of the opponents was that no one could replace Joseph Smith. The Twelve did not disagree. A mid-August epistle affirmed that while "Joseph . . . still holds the keys of this last dispensation . . . the Twelve Apostles of this dispensation stand in their own place . . . to minister, preside and regulate the affairs of the whole church."[81] The Twelve wished to implement Joseph Smith's measures, not usurp his role in life and throughout the eternities as head of the last dispensation.[82] In early August, the Saints had acknowledged the Twelve as "presidents of the whole church when Joseph was not; and now he has stepped behind the vail, he is not here, and the Twelve are the presidents of the whole church." The Twelve believed that Hyrum had been ordained to be his brother's successor, but Hyrum had died before his brother, so authority resided with the Twelve. "There never has a man stood between Joseph and the Twelve, and unless we apostatize there never will," Young explained. "If Hyrum had lived he would not have stood between Joseph and the Twelve but he would have stood for Joseph."[83]

Not only had the Twelve stood next in line to the president and his associate president, Young noted in his October address, but the prophets and the apostles derived their authority from a common base—the apostleship. Paraphrasing Paul's instructions to the Corinthians, Young said, "The Bible says God hath set in the church, first apostles, then comes prophets, afterwards, because the keys and power of the apostleship are greater than that of the prophets."[84] Joseph Smith had been an apostle first, he declared, and a prophet by derivation from his apostolic keys. With this explanation, Young established not only the basis for an apostolic interregnum in 1844 but a precedent for the future.[85]

Young found it necessary on several occasions to counter a lingering

This presidential-style portrait was painted in July 1845 in the Seventies Hall at Nauvoo. President Young's hand rests on the Book of the Law of the Lord, next to the Bible and the Book of Mormon. The historical and classical works on the bookshelves reflect holdings of the seventies library.

apostate claim that sullied the reputation of Joseph Smith. Many of the dissenters claimed that the Prophet had fallen from grace and that, in keeping with the provisions revealed in the Doctrine and Covenants, the Lord had appointed them as new leaders. The distinction between competing claims to leadership centered increasingly on this point. "Time will tell who are the friends of Joseph Smith," Young said in early September. "We have no new commandments, but beseech the brethren to honor and obey the old ones."[86] During the October conference, Young explained this position:

> Every spirit that confesses that Joseph Smith is a prophet, that he lived and died a prophet and that the Book of Mormon is true, is of God, and every spirit that does not is of anti-christ.
>
> It is the test of our fellowship to believe and confess that Joseph lived and died a prophet of God in good standing; and I don't want any one to fellowship the Twelve who says that Joseph is fallen.[87]

This emphasis placed foremost the understanding that a Latter-day Saint best expressed his or her conviction of the truth of the Restoration by declaring a personal witness that "the Book of Mormon is true" and that Joseph Smith "was and is" God's prophet. With this declaration, the Saints set themselves apart from the dissenters. During the October conference, the Twelve won unanimous support for their proposal to carry out Joseph Smith's plans for the church.[88]

Other speakers reinforced the message of a continuity of leadership through the Twelve. John Taylor countered those who wanted the Saints to abandon the concept of a gathered community at Nauvoo. It was the Lord's program revealed through Joseph Smith, he said, that "'those who had made a covenant with God by sacrifice'" would gather together to be instructed.[89] Taylor's speech echoed proclamations issued by the Twelve in August and October reaffirming Nauvoo's role as the designated gathering place. The epistles corrected contrary claims made continually through the year by Rigdon, Law, and other dissidents who opposed the temple project in the place of gathering.[90]

The fall and spring conferences of 1844–45 helped build support for the Twelve among the Saints in and beyond Nauvoo. Consistently and tellingly, the Saints placed their confidence in their religious convictions and their sustained leaders, the Twelve. "Though our Prophet is dead I have confidence in the work of God and so has Mother," an English Saint wrote to relatives in Nauvoo.[91] Journalist and orator William W. Phelps joined in the chorus of support. "I know the Twelve, and they know me," he wrote in a published exchange of letters with his friend William Smith. Phelps characterized his associates with biblical titles that would become as well known as the men themselves:

> Their names are Brigham Young, the lion of the Lord; Heber C. Kimball, the herald of grace; Parley P. Pratt, the archer of paradise; Orson Hyde, the olive branch of Israel; Willard Richards, the keeper of the rolls; John Taylor, the champion of right; William Smith, the patriarchal Jacob staff; Wilford Woodruff, the banner of the gospel; George A. Smith, the entablature of truth; Orson Pratt, the gauge of philosophy; John E. Page, the sun dial; and Lyman Wight, the wild ram of the mountain. And they are good men; the best the Lord can find; they do the will of God, and the saints know it.

Phelps had one last word for his friend "Sidney Rigdon and his clique of dissatisfied beings": He was like the seed cast by the wayside in stony places. In Far West and Nauvoo, Phelps, who had himself temporarily apostatized at Far West, concluded that such men as George M. Hinkle, John C. Bennett, Wilson Law, and Sidney Rigdon—men who had once believed that "Mormonism is ETERNAL TRUTH, and God Almighty is the author of it!"—had turned away for one reason—to seek popularity in the world. In contrast, said Phelps, the Twelve sought not their own aggrandizement but only to support a higher cause. With his biblical characterizations, Phelps succeeded in identifying Brigham Young and other members of the Quorum of the Twelve with friendly epithets that would outlive them all.[92]

Anti-Mormons hoped that Joseph Smith's death would lead to a sudden scattering of the Saints, but it did not happen. One resident reported an increased exodus during the fall months of 1844. An estimated two hundred people a week, he said, were heading downriver on steamboats or in loaded wagons after selling their property at low prices.[93] Some of these exiles were people who followed Sidney Rigdon when he left in mid-September for Pittsburgh. Along with a few disaffected Saints, much of the traffic toward St. Louis would have been the usual departures of missionaries and of men seeking work for the winter. Saints fearful that vigilantes would sack Nauvoo may have left for personal safety. Heading in the other direction was Lyman Wight, returning to Wisconsin to prepare for a move to Texas.[94] Despite the reported outbound traffic, the population of Nauvoo actually grew during the year following the murders at Carthage.

During the August 1844 conference and in private deliberations, Brigham Young gave Sidney Rigdon every opportunity to remain in full fellowship. In a gesture of friendship, the senior apostle invited the fifty-one-year old Rigdon to step forward and receive a vote of confidence from the church only minutes after the same congregation had sustained the Twelve as the church's new leaders. "We are of one mind with him and he with us," Young said, inviting the congregation to uphold the former counselor "by the prayer of faith." Rigdon accepted the courtesy, apparently without comment. If a reconciliation had been intended by the action, it did not take. Many of the Twelve knew Rigdon too well. His erratic show of support over the years and his militancy had left them skeptical. The Twelve did not expect the former counselor to remain a true friend for long. Nor did others. Jedediah M. Grant believed that he knew "the mind of our beloved and martyred Prophet on that point. I cannot be deceived," he confided to Newel K. Whitney, "I know what he [Joseph] thought of the Twelve and also what he thought of Elder Rigdon. Did all know this they would say with me that the Twelve stand in their proper place."[95]

Rigdon preached one last sermon in Nauvoo on Sunday, September 1. It was a complicated, animated, and somewhat confused oration outlining millennial events through the final winding-up scene. "I will say it—in my opinion—was an enthusiastic discourse," William Huntington observed. Rigdon feigned support for the temple and the gathering to Nauvoo and claimed to be united with the Twelve, but the words Brigham Young heard did not jibe with what he knew of Rigdon's recent actions. Rigdon "was not with us in spirit," Young concluded, "but I took him at his word . . . until it [could] be proved."[96]

The Twelve learned two days later that Rigdon had met privately with a few supporters on Monday evening and established his own leadership group. His immediate supporters included Samuel James (of La Harpe), Dr. Samuel Bennett, Joseph H. Newton, John A. Forgeus, and Leonard Soby (of the high council).[97] In two separate meetings with members of the Twelve on Tuesday, Rigdon admitted under lengthy questioning the outlines of his administrative plans and new revelations. According to John Taylor, Rigdon "has been holding secret meetings; he has ordained men illegally, and contrary to the order of the priesthood . . . to the offices of prophets, priests and kings; whereas he does not hold that office himself." Furthermore, Brigham Young noted, Rigdon had convinced his council that "the man of sin spoken of in the revelations [2 Thessalonians 2:3], is the Twelve."[98] Rigdon claimed an authority higher than the Twelve and said that the revelation he received before he left Pittsburgh had given him "the keys of conquest, *the keys of David*," authorizing him to lead the Lord's troops into bloody battle.[99] When a committee of three apostles demanded his license, Rigdon threatened to publish what he knew of the Council of Fifty, other leadership councils, and the practice of plural marriage.[100]

The Twelve felt obliged to act. They called Rigdon in for a hearing on September 8 before First Bishop Newel K. Whitney and a council of

To protect against forgery and to certify documents as official, the Twelve authorized this seal in January 1845. Brigham Young and John Taylor specified the design, with George A. Smith and Orson Hyde assisting. Artist William Major drew the pattern for the engraver, who created the stamp.

twelve high priests (the high council of Nauvoo). At the advice of his friends, Rigdon ignored the invitation, but, in response to a general announcement in the *Nauvoo Neighbor*, a large congregation gathered that morning when the council convened on the meeting ground in the grove below the temple.[101]

The evidence presented by the knowledgeable witnesses confirmed a long-standing distrust of Rigdon's grounding in the church and its doctrines. While expressing personal feelings of friendship toward Rigdon, they refused to shirk their duty "when it touches the salvation of the people."[102] Those who had known Rigdon from before he joined the Latter-day Saints and those who had followed his eleven-year career as a spokesman for the Prophet were united in their censure. They found him unreliable in doctrine, a constant absentee from council meetings, uninterested in bearing his share of the burdens of leadership, and the subject of frequent reprimands from the Prophet.[103] A gifted man, Rigdon was known for his independent mind and self-centeredness. He had resigned from the Nauvoo city council in November 1841 because of chronic ill health; in his religious calling as counselor to Joseph Smith, the effect of "the violence of sickness" had "kept [him] in silence" since the Missouri exile. Newel K. Whitney said of Rigdon's mood swings, "He was always either in the bottom of the cellar or up in the garret window. At . . . Kirtland he was more sanguine than he is now."[104]

Of direct relevance to the trial were Rigdon's recent actions. He had admitted to members of the Twelve his claim to an authority higher than the Twelve, his efforts to divide the church, his unauthorized ordinations, and his untested revelations.[105] Rather than participate in government by council—the pattern established by the Prophet—Rigdon had met secretly with supporters. Parley Pratt reminded the high council that church leaders must be "chosen and upheld by the faith and prayer of the church, and then they must walk according to the revelations, or there is no power in their appointment."[106]

During the trial, the Twelve recalled Joseph Smith's 1843 attempt to shake Rigdon off as a counselor. Only Hyrum's compassionate pleadings had prevented Rigdon's release then.[107] Now, William Marks alone stood forth in defense. He was hesitant to vindicate the absent Rigdon in view of the weight of evidence against him. Nonetheless, more personally sympathetic to Rigdon than he let on, Marks offered several points in the former first counselor's favor. First, an investigating committee had cleared Rigdon of the charges raised at the 1843 conference. Marks had heard both Joseph and Emma Smith say since then "that all things were right between them" and Rigdon. Marks confirmed that Rigdon had not known that revelations were now to be cleared through what Marks called the "first quorum" (a group of endowed leaders). Marks admitted that he disagreed with the decision of the August conference. He believed that a quorum of the First Presidency was always necessary, that Rigdon had not transgressed, and that the quorum should be filled up. Citing the Doctrine and Covenants, Marks said his only objective was to discover the truth. He had stood with Joseph Smith when Rigdon was ordained a prophet, seer, and revelator in 1841. That ordination, Marks believed, had given Rigdon the keys and authority of the kingdom equally with the Prophet.[108]

Brigham Young answered Marks's concerns. Because of Hyrum Smith's pleadings, Young said, not all the evidence against Rigdon had been presented at the 1843 conference. Rigdon had left Missouri, saying that "he never would follow Brother Joseph's revelations any more, contrary to his own convenience. He said Jesus Christ was a fool to him in sufferings; was this not enough to cut him off?" Rigdon had pleaded with

Joseph to release him from the inconveniences of life in Nauvoo and allow him to return to Kirtland. Because of Hyrum's pleadings that "'he will yet straighten out,'" Joseph had ordained Rigdon a prophet, seer, and revelator. "But did he help Brother Joseph after this? No." Even after reluctantly moving his family near to Joseph's, Rigdon seldom attended the Prophet's councils. In response to Rigdon's claim of having equal authority with the Prophet, Young observed, "As to a person not knowing more than the written word, let me tell you that there are keys that the written word never spoke of, nor never will." Brigham testified that "Elder Rigdon's revelations . . . are from the Devil. . . . If you make Sidney Rigdon your president and leader, you will soon have John C. Bennett here, with the Laws and Fosters and all the murderous clan. Elder Rigdon . . . is liable to be deceived, and has already been deceived."[109]

With the testimony aired, Bishop Whitney pondered a decision. The bishop had known Rigdon in Kirtland before Rigdon's conversion. He accepted the testimony of the Twelve; he had heard Joseph Smith rebuke Rigdon many times in Kirtland for his revelations. Whitney believed that Rigdon was not deceived but "that he is dishonest . . . an evil designing man" who opposed Joseph's plans for building the temple. By unanimous decision, the ecclesiastical court supported Whitney's decision for excommunication. The assembled congregation concurred, with about ten dissenting votes. When asked, William Marks publicly concurred in the actions; a few months later he quelled lingering doubts by publishing his acceptance of the Twelve.[110]

Rigdon met with his followers on the evening of September 9 and left Nauvoo the next day, taking a few converts with him.[111] Latter-day Saints generally rejected Rigdon's right to govern alone. "The first Presidency being dead all but one, it was no longer a quorum," Isaac Haight declared.[112] Furthermore, the Saints did not trust Rigdon. A member in Montebello wrote, "Rigdon don't stand very high in the estimation of the people here. We all know here that Sidney is not fit to be [the] leader of God's people. We all know that he is a wolf and would destroy the sheep."[113] A Nauvoo couple reported, "Sidney Rigdon after Joseph's death, got so high, that he transgressed and has been cut off from the Church. He took some few with him and went back to Pittsburgh. He made some disturbance in the Church, but not much."[114]

Away from Nauvoo, Rigdon pursued his independent course. William

McClellin tried to get Rigdon and William Law to collaborate on reorganizing the church that winter, but the three men differed over too many points of doctrine. Law had rejected Joseph Smith as prophet and soon turned his back on all institutionalized religion.[115] Rigdon organized a church of Christ in Pittsburgh and promoted it through the *Latter Day Saints' Messenger and Advocate.* Among his new followers were Dr. Josiah Ells and James Blakesley, who became members of Rigdon's quorum of apostles. Rigdon also organized a quorum of seventy-three. He continued to claim authority by virtue of his calling in the First Presidency, arguing that Joseph Smith had lost his keys of authority and had been rejected as a prophet by God.[116]

In discussions at Nauvoo, Rigdon had claimed a fresh revelation calling him to lead the church, received on the day of Joseph Smith's death. Back in Pittsburgh, Rigdon unveiled a second revelation, purportedly given through Joseph Smith to the First Presidency on April 7, 1841, a day after John C. Bennett had been appointed an assistant counselor to the First Presidency. It supported Rigdon's proposition at the August conference that after Joseph's death the First Presidency should be dissolved and Rigdon become the Prophet's successor. A note on the revelation directed Bennett to hold the document until needed and then deliver it to a church agent. Bennett had visited Nauvoo in September 1844, a few days before Rigdon left for Pittsburgh. The unsubstantiated document had little effect in Nauvoo, where it was generally believed that Bennett was the author of the revelation.[117]

Another prominent leader discontented over ecclesiastical developments in Nauvoo was Lyman Wight, one of those most anxious to realize Joseph Smith's dream of an expanded Zion. Even though the Twelve gave Wight the freedom to make his own decision in the matter, they clearly preferred and eventually required that all such expansionist efforts await completion of the temple. It was Wight's belief that the commission he had received from the Prophet in late 1843 was irrevocable. Desirous of creating a stake of Zion with his Wisconsin pineries company, Native Americans from that area and from Texas, and the Southern Saints, Wight left for Texas with his followers. The next spring, the Twelve invited the group back to Nauvoo, but the independent "Wild Ram of the Mountains" persisted in his separatist stance. Wight's differences with the Twelve were not just geographical. Beginning in the late 1840s, he held

David Hyrum Smith, the last child of Joseph and Emma Smith, was born five months after his father's death. This daguerreotype of mother and son was probably made by Lucian R. Foster early in 1846.

to the belief "that Joseph Smith appointed those of his own posterity to be his successor."[118]

The hesitant testimony William Marks had given on behalf of Sidney Rigdon concealed his own feelings of uncertainty about the new leaders. He had supported Rigdon's efforts to resolve the leadership question independent of the Twelve. Marks knew about plural marriage and disagreed with the practice. As the Twelve moved forward with Joseph Smith's proposals for the church, Marks distanced himself from the new church leaders: Brigham Young and the Twelve.

Not long after Joseph and Hyrum were killed, Marks had discussed the question of succession with Emma Smith, who seemed to favor the stake president as her husband's successor. James Monroe, the schoolteacher of the Smith children, said he "obtained several new and interesting ideas concerning the organization and government of the Church" in conversations with Emma. Apparently, she believed that the stake president was "the next office in the Kingdom immediately below the First President," just as the vice-president of the United States, and not a cabinet officer, succeeded the president. "It is not the Twelve," Monroe learned from Emma, "because they have authority only among the branches in the world, and their peculiar province is to spread the gospel among the nations of the earth." This outdated view ignored the expanded authority given to the Twelve at Nauvoo.[119]

William Smith contended that the right to lead belonged to the Smith family in the same way the office of patriarch did. Even though he sustained his quorum's authority, Smith preferred authority by lineage. That claim eventually led to a coalescing of supporters around the Prophet's eldest surviving son, Joseph Smith III. Meantime, William Smith sought appointment to an office more easily obtained, that of patriarch.

At the August conference, Brigham Young had acknowledged the Smith family's right to the office of patriarch to the church. Young's first impression favored Samuel, had he lived, but with that option gone the Prophet's only surviving brother, William, or a son, or Uncle John Smith were possible candidates. The Twelve, he said wanted to "wait until they know who is the man."[120]

On May 24, 1845, William Smith became the third patriarch to the Church when the Twelve ordained him to the office left vacant for nearly a year. He had returned to Nauvoo after spending two or three years organizing and presiding over the branches in the Eastern United States in his calling as an apostle. He took up residence in William Marks's former home, and as soon as he was installed to the office held by his father and brother before him, he immediately began giving patriarchal blessings in Nauvoo and elsewhere.[121]

At the time of William Smith's appointment, William W. Phelps created a misunderstanding about the patriarch's role. In an editorial comment in the *Times and Seasons*, Phelps referred to the office as "Patriarch over the whole church," which some took to mean that Smith presided in an office above that of the Twelve.[122] Editor John Taylor issued a correction. The revelations clearly designated the church's president as the presiding officer. The 1841 revelation about the Nauvoo Temple, Taylor said, had named the patriarch first among the officers sustained only "in regard to seniority not in regard to authority in priesthood, for it immediately follows, 'I give unto you my servant Joseph to be a *presiding elder* over *all* my church.'"[123] For a decade, Taylor said, the Twelve had been ordaining evangelical ministers (patriarchs) in all large branches of the church abroad. It was not intended that the senior church patriarch serve scattered members, Taylor noted. Local patriarchs blessed members in their own areas. William Smith, he said, "is not the only Patriarch, but would act as a senior Patriarch, holding the keys of that priesthood; and his labors would be more especially connected with the church in *Zion*." "A Patriarch to the church is appointed to bless those who are orphans, or have no father in the church to bless them." Taylor placed the blame for the misunderstanding upon assistant editor Phelps and absolved Joseph Smith of "any such ideas" as those being raised.[124]

Even as he was being given the patriarchal office, William was challenging Brigham Young's authority. Smith believed that the Twelve must act in concert as a quorum of the whole and that Brigham was "merely President by courtesy." The quorum had in fact been sustained as the First Presidency of the church, but only one man held the right to preside and direct the work. Something more was at stake. James Monroe heard William Smith privately accusing the Twelve of wanting to profit personally from publishing church works. He also objected to reports about him in the *New York Messenger*. Monroe said of Smith, "His words seems to portend a rupture between him and the Twelve."[125]

The October conference in 1845 rejected William Smith in his apostolic and patriarchal offices for aspiring "to uproot and undermine the legal Presidency of the church, that he may occupy the place himself."[126] Excommunication followed two weeks later during a general conference of the seventies in the temple.[127] Evidence included two letters written by Smith from Galena threatening Brigham Young and a pamphlet against the Twelve published in St. Louis.[128] The church would not have another patriarch until 1849, when John Smith, the Prophet's uncle, was ordained by the Twelve to exercise the sacred calling.

William Smith headed for St. Louis, where he promoted the idea "that young Joseph is the only legal successor" to his father. Several members accepted the claim and were disfellowshipped by the branch there, among them the branch president. According to Almon Babbitt, Smith preached on a riverboat heading toward Nauvoo but failed to sway converts with his wonderful disclosures.[129] A few weeks later, Smith was supporting the claims of James J. Strang in Wisconsin and urged others in the Eastern states to support this new prophet.[130] But after a year or so, the erstwhile patriarch was in Kentucky promoting his own revelation appointing himself as prophet, seer, revelator, and translator until the Prophet's eldest surviving son, Joseph III, reached his majority.[131]

A few other Saints promoted the right of Joseph Smith III to the presidency. Twelve years old at the time of his father's death, young Joseph's claim centered on several supposed blessings that designated him as his father's heir in the office, subject to his preparation and the acceptance of the people.[132] Among the youth's advocates was his uncle William Smith. As early as the fall of 1845, William was contending "that young Joseph is the only legal successor to the presidency of this church." He was supported in this claim by George J. Adams, who served "as Little Joseph's spokesman" and who was helping to establish a reform church.[133] After the Saints left Nauvoo, others stepped forward as witnesses of Joseph III's right to his father's office, but in 1844, the youth lacked the maturity and priesthood qualifications to be considered a viable candidate.[134]

The Twelve advised members to avoid open speculation and to "*be patient* a little, till the proper time comes, and we will tell you all. 'Great wheels move slow.'" The August conference had accepted the Twelve as the presiding authorities, they said, "and when any alteration in the presidency shall be required, seasonable notice will be given."[135] The Twelve had other concerns about advocating a leadership role for Joseph III, including fears that those who had killed the Prophet would visit the same vengeance on any others who held or who might be given presiding authority, including young Joseph.[136] For the youth to receive a leadership position in the church, said one of the Twelve, "it will be at a proper time when he who holds the keys of the Presidency shall be moved by the spirit of God to make the proposition," and it will need the sustaining vote of the church. "If he ever come into power at all, he will come boldly in at the front door."[137] For two decades, the Twelve kept the door open for Joseph III and David Hyrum, but the Prophet's sons chose other paths.[138]

Church members had one option for a new leader different from all the others. They had known Sidney Rigdon, William Marks, and William Smith for years in positions of trust. Succession claims of these men stemmed from ordinations to positions of ecclesiastical authority. Of these three, only Rigdon claimed divine sanction. His Pittsburgh revelations were singular attempts to act upon a deeply felt Mormon belief in continuing revelation. But upstaging all these familiar Latter-day Saint leaders was James J. Strang, a newcomer to the scene, whose claim to both

Joseph Smith III, about 1846   *James J. Strang, about 1855*

For some, the Prophet's eldest son, Joseph, seen here in his mid-teens, seemed an appropriate candidate for a future place in church councils, but he chose another path. James J. Strang asserted a claim to lead the church in 1846 and attracted a small following. Dissatisfied followers killed the Wisconsin "prophet" ten years later.

revelatory and appointive authority mimicked most closely the leadership style of the church's first prophet. In his dramatic bid for Joseph Smith's office, Strang claimed revelations and translated an ancient record from metal plates, even offering them for inspection. He linked his authority to the Prophet's and created an organization imitating that in Nauvoo. His associates cited the revelations of 1830 that emphasized Joseph Smith's right to appoint a successor through revelation. Similarly, they pointed to early revelations identifying the Twelve as a traveling council without general administrative duties. In addition, Strang himself claimed that at the moment of Joseph Smith's death, an angel of the Lord appeared to Strang and ordained him the successor.[139]

James Strang had appeared in Nauvoo a few months before the martyrdom, a skeptical investigator. A lawyer from northwestern New York State, Strang and his wife moved to Wisconsin Territory in 1843. In

Illinois as a consultant on the Illinois Canal project, he found time to visit the much-publicized "Holy City." His baptism in the temple font in Nauvoo, allegedly performed by the Prophet himself in February 1844, gave Strang entrance into the church. The thirty-one-year-old convert was ordained an elder, and then he headed home with a supposed assignment from the Prophet to select a Great Lakes gathering place for a portion of the Saints.[140] When Strang heard of Joseph Smith's death, he quickly magnified his original calling. He claimed in an early issue of his religious newspaper, the *Voree Herald,* that the Prophet had designated him in a blessing as his personal successor.[141]

As further proof, Strang published a letter purportedly dictated by Joseph Smith identifying Strang as the Prophet's successor and designating a new place of refuge on the White River plain in Wisconsin Territory. The letter was dated June 18, 1844, but it carried a black postmark instead of the red ink used in Nauvoo. The letter demonstrated the extent to which Strang had tuned in on ideas important to the church. It told of a supposed revelation to the Prophet about his own impending death and Strang's call. It named the new gathering place "Voree, meaning, garden of peace."[142] Although laced with scriptural phrases familiar to Latter-day Saints, it did not ring true to many in its intended audience. A missionary who obtained a copy for Brigham Young declared, "The letter carried upon its face the marks of a base forgery, being written throughout in printed characters. . . . But above all the contents of the thing, was altogether bombastic unlike the work of God."[143]

To strengthen his claim, Strang issued his own revelations. One of them established a law of tithing; another directed him to buried plates. Strang took four friends to a designated place under an oak tree in September 1845, where they dug in "undisturbed" earth (the plates had been slipped into place through a horizontal tunnel). The men found three brass plates covered with unfamiliar characters. Strang's translation yielded a chieftain's account of the final destruction of his people. By the end of 1845, Strang was ready to challenge the Twelve in Nauvoo.[144]

Strang's claims to revelation and new scripture were a closer imitation of the original prophet's story than any of the early claimants to Joseph Smith's office offered. As one newspaper report put it, "A fresh plate-digger, translator, and prophet has arisen in the West. . . . Whether this will resolve itself into Mormonism, or become the basis of a new sect, is a matter of speculation. In either case it will find adherents."[145]

The early followers of James Strang included some who were skeptical of the leadership claims and teachings of the Twelve. Among them were William Smith, who served as Strang's patriarch; John E. Page of the Twelve, excommunicated in March 1846 for preaching Strangism at the temple in Nauvoo and an ardent advocate of restoring the church to its pre-Nauvoo framework;[146] John C. Bennett, whose influence eventually led Strang to introduce a version of the temple endowment and its doctrines that Bennett had previously rejected;[147] and Aaron Smith, a Latter-day Saint friend in Wisconsin.[148] With Emma Smith's support, William Marks had sat out the transition, but by 1845, he had bcome an affiliate of the Wisconsin "prophet."

Some of the Saints in Nauvoo and the Eastern branches were likewise lured away by Strang's revelatory approach and his interest in establishing a single head for the church.[149] Others listened to the perplexing pitch of Strang's missionaries with disdain.[150] Those who knew of the private teachings of plural marriage in Nauvoo found that Strang initially opposed the new doctrine. Strang also accepted the anti-Mormon claim that Nauvoo was a den of counterfeiters and thieves. When the westward migration from Nauvoo was announced, he opposed it. If the Saints follow the apostles to California, he told one reporter, "they will never reach there, but their bones will bleach on the plains."[151]

Thomas Sharp exaggerated reality with the claim that Strang was "making considerable inroads into the church at Nauvoo" and elsewhere. Some were misled by Strang's claims, but the Twelve were not concerned with this sifting. A Latter-day Saint in Philadelphia said that the branch "excommunicated the unruly Elders and lay Members that werc advocating Strangism, etc., from the Church, having expelled between fifty and sixty within a short time."[152] Other branches lost fewer members but felt some effects of Strang's appeal. From George Alley's perspective in Nauvoo, those leaving to follow Strang were part of a purging and purifying of the church. "They are the ones who have brought persecution on us by their evil deeds; so let them go. We are glad to get rid of all such."[153]

Confident in their own divine appointment, the Twelve had nothing but skeptical disbelief for the imitator of genuine revelation. They were concerned that others might be misled, however. Discussions between

Strang's supporters in Nauvoo and church leaders gave the Twelve and others an opportunity to speak out. They saw a copy of Strang's purported revelation as early as August 25, 1844, and pronounced it false. In Warsaw, Thomas Sharp rejoiced in prospects that the factionalism would lead to the destruction of the power of the Twelve.[154] But for Brigham Young and his colleagues, Strang was a nuisance with little meaningful influence.

Within the quorums of the priesthood in Nauvoo, Strang's early claims were challenged in two ways. First, in priesthood gatherings, quorum leaders invited individual expressions of support for the Twelve. Second, the quorums cleansed their membership of the few who became Strang's sympathizers. One quorum of seventy, for instance, dropped three members in February and March 1846 for joining the Strangites.[155] Another dismissed one of its presidents for a litany of spiritual infractions—"with getting drunk, denying the faith, and preaching Strangite doctrine."[156] Brigham Young and Orson Pratt spoke to an assembly on the second floor of the temple on Sunday, February 1, 1846, at which a Strang advocate was invited to present the Wisconsin prophet's message. Young made no comment "but simply ask[ed] the People if they had heard the voice of the Good Shepherd in what had been advanced, when No!! resounded all over the house." The presenter was cut off from the church along with Strang and his associate Aaron Smith.[157]

When Strang's followers cited scriptural precedents, defenders of the Twelve turned as well to the word of God. From the Doctrine and Covenants and the book of Abraham, they demonstrated the need for priesthood keys to govern a dispensation properly.[158] Their rejoinders emphasized Joseph Smith's right to appoint a successor[159] and the need for the officers to be accepted by common consent. Strang had been rejected through excommunication.[160] Defenders of the Twelve noted the primacy of apostolic authority.[161] They pointed out that the revelations required the president to be a high priest, whereas Strang had been an elder before his excommunication.[162] Defenders appealed as well to church history. They noted that Joseph Smith had given the keys of the kingdom to the Twelve. As prophets, seers, and revelators they would guide the church through revelation.[163] More importantly, Nauvoo writers observed that the Twelve possessed knowledge of the temple ordinances and the authority to administer them to others. Strang, they said, claimed a pale imitation of the endowment that he "revealed" only after John C. Bennett and William Smith informed him of its central role in the restored gospel.[164]

As preparations to remove the Saints from Nauvoo proceeded, interest in Strang gradually subsided. Orson Hyde, the last of the Twelve in Nauvoo, preached vigorously against Strang. In March 1846, Hyde published his own warning against following leaders who were "strangers" to the voice of the Lord's Spirit.[165] Others of the Twelve encouraged members to ignore Strang and other claimants to Joseph Smith's mantle. Likening the apostasy of schismatics to the plagues that God allowed to beset Job as a refining fire and ultimate blessing, John Taylor advised:

> Persecution is for our good, and if we have hard things to endure let us round up our shoulders and bear them in the name of the Lord, and not murmur. . . . Do not find fault if we have a few apostates among us here, for they are mean, damnable, and pitiable characters. . . . Do not find fault with them, but let them do their own business, and pursue their own course, and if they come across you, cuff their ears and send them over the river; but not too many at a time, lest by cutting off too many branches, you spoil the growth of the seed. It is necessary we should have such things to meet with that we may be made perfect through suffering.[166]

The Nauvoo schismatics would continue their efforts to gather up followers for many years to come. For most of the Saints, the question of a new leader for the church had been resolved. It would be Brigham Young and the Twelve. Andrew Moore, senior president in the fifth quorum of the seventy, summarized the matter for his quorum in February 1846. He spoke for all of those satisfied with how the authority to lead had been transferred to the Twelve:

> Suffice it to say Brigham Young and his counsel are the Leaders of this Church, placed there by Joseph Smith himself previous to his death, when he called them together and gave them the necessary qualifycatuns to accomplish the same, as he said upon you (the Twelve) rests the responsibility of the Church. Upon you I roll the burden, therefore round up your shoulder and bear it. There is something ahead but it matters not; now it is safe in spite of the Devil, and whether they kill me or not it makes no difference; the work will roll on in spite of Earth and Hell.[167]

PART IV

REMOVAL: NEW PLACES AND NEW PEOPLES

As regards the temporal prospects of our church, it has been various since its beginning, the wheel of fortune, in its revolution, sometimes carries us up and sometimes down; at present we are down. . . . We have to leave this place as soon as possible, say in the spring. Our religion is not tolerated in this day any more than Christ's was in his. Suffice it to say that we can not live in peace here in consequence of mob violence, and the inefficiency of the government, State and General. We must, therefore, and will remove from this place in the Spring to some place westward, and so remote that we surely [will] not be trodden underfoot all the day long and not receive an adequate protection from the laws of the land. We are going west of the Mountains; but how such a body of people can accomplish this is best known to the Great God. We will have to go with such preparations as each can make for themselves, and whatever property either in houses or land that can not be disposed of, will be entirely sacrificed.

—FROM A LETTER BY JOHN S. FULLMER, NOVEMBER 4, 1845

CHAPTER 16

The Peaceful Interlude

All is union and peace at Nauvoo, and the temple is rising rapidly as a token that God has not forsaken his church and people.

—JOHN TAYLOR, NOVEMBER 15, 1844

Though the papers report a total repeal of the Nauvoo Charter by a large majority in both houses, we remain undisturbed, and city affairs go on as usual. . . . The saints are more engaged than ever to finish the Temple. . . . The different quorums are becoming perfected in their several organizations, by which means the elders are learning their duty. Union, love and peace were never more universal among the saints at Nauvoo, than at the present time.

—BRIGHAM YOUNG, FEBRUARY 11, 1845

With the question of church leadership resolved for most Latter-day Saints and the voice of opposition muted, the Quorum of the Twelve focused on furthering projects launched by the Prophet Joseph Smith. During the eighteen months between the martyrdom and the removal from Nauvoo, the Saints worked hard to complete the temple on the bluff. Construction elsewhere in Nauvoo picked up again to provide for public needs and to supply homes and jobs for immigrating converts. Another economic effort engaged men, women, and children in home industries. The Twelve anticipated new stakes in the United States and early in their administration expanded the missionary force to accomplish that goal. The quorums that trained these messengers of peace urged their members to prepare themselves and their wives for the sacred experience of temple ceremonies. In addition, church leaders defined stricter personal standards to create harmony in the community of the Saints.

All of this had a real effect on the people of greater Nauvoo, and within a few months of Joseph Smith's death, Latter-day Saints felt a greater unity than ever before. Without lessening their vigilance, the Saints turned inward. Political, economic, social, and religious programs emphasized shared spiritual objectives. In June 1845, Brigham Young observed, "The most perfect union, peace and good feeling has invariably prevailed in our midst and still continues. It seems like a foretaste of celestial enjoyment and Millennial glory."[1]

Meanwhile, the old citizens outside the City Beautiful discussed the political implications of postmartyrdom Nauvoo. With the city's high-profile prophet-mayor-lieutenant general dead, his political opponents assessed their victory. They had wanted him out of power so that their own political influence could increase. They wanted elections decided in old ways, along traditional party lines, not by what they perceived as prophet-led block voting. And they still worried about the military might of Nauvoo's city militia. Initially, the heated rhetoric of the anti-Mormon press quieted. For the next year, the antagonism of local newspapers melted into silent celebration over Joseph Smith's demise. Yet lobbyists did not abandon their effort to end Nauvoo's political might. They recognized that the Saints had not given up their quest for community. The *Nauvoo Neighbor* carried a reminder of that goal on its masthead: "Our Motto.— The Saints' Singularity—is Unity, Liberty, Charity." When the legislature in Springfield assessed the Mormon question in its winter 1844–45 session, debate centered on Nauvoo's liberal charter. As representatives of the people of Illinois, legislators had created a powerful city and its now-mistrusted militia. The people's spokesmen decided that together they could strip Nauvoo of her clout.

REPEAL OF THE CITY CHARTER

The Latter-day Saints heard varying opinions on how to deal with political tensions. Governor Ford advised citizens of Nauvoo to dodge the political fray by sitting out the 1844 election. This, he hoped, would maintain the fragile peace in Hancock County. His Whig opponents applauded the counsel, because it gave them an opportunity to regain lost political posts. But some in Ford's own Democratic party visited Nauvoo and encouraged participation.[2] This pleased Latter-day Saints in Hancock County, who refused to give up their franchise, except in the 1844 presidential election. With their preferred candidate for president dead, they sat by and watched the Democrats' dark-horse candidate James K. Polk win a narrow national election victory over Whig Henry Clay.

In county elections, Nauvoo voters reached consensus at public caucuses held in the grove prior to the August 5 polling. They endorsed candidates on the Old Citizens Law and Order Ticket, people who decried the violence at Carthage. This nonpartisan ticket garnered all but five votes in Nauvoo and defeated most anti-Mormon candidates by a margin of one thousand votes. The Saints returned George Coulson, one of their own, to the three-member Hancock County commission and named as coroner Daniel H. Wells, a resident of Nauvoo, a non-Mormon, and a close friend of Joseph Smith. Another friend of the Latter-day Saints, Minor Deming, won the influential post of sheriff. Deming had been Ford's military commander at Carthage at the time of the murders; like others on the Law and Order ballot, he sought justice in the courts for the perpetrators. Latter-day Saint votes also sent church member Almon W. Babbitt and the friendly old citizen Jacob B. Backenstos to the state assembly. For the congressional seat representing the sixth district, the Saints endorsed Democrat Joseph P. Hoge, who carried the county by 76 percent.[3] All of these victories demonstrated Nauvoo's electoral strength.

The local elections roused supporters of the Anti-Mormon Party. Ten of them, including Thomas Sharp and William N. Grover of Warsaw, signed a proclamation addressed to the governor:

> It is impossible that the two communities can long live together. They can *never* assimilate. We repeat our firm conviction that one or the other *must* leave. The old citizens are now virtually disfranchised—they have no guaranty of protection from the law. The Mormons control our elections and the administration of our courts. *They* have nothing to fear from the law. . . . As long, sir, as Mormons possess means of shielding themselves and oppressing us, it can hardly be expected that we should live together in peace and amity.[4]

For the more moderate residents, removal of a body of American citizens from their homes and lands seemed an extreme proposal. But opponents did win wide support for a short-range goal. When the state legislature met for its 1844–45 session, the time for repeal of Nauvoo's city charter was right. Democrats controlled the Senate 26 to 15 and the House 67 to 33. Yet, debate and voting on repeal created odd alliances that crossed party lines, including a melding of interests between southern Democrats and Whigs. In a special message on the issue, Ford urged repeal only of the obnoxious parts of the Nauvoo charter. Some in his party agreed, but most wanted to strip Nauvoo of the entire charter.[5] Even though the anti-Mormon sentiment was strong among Whigs, many of them opposed the repeal movement and sided with Ford. These delegates accepted the Latter-day Saint argument that repeal was an illegal breach of contract.[6]

In the House, newly elected Hancock County legislators Almon W. Babbitt and Jacob Backenstos spoke on behalf of the charter. Babbitt carried written instructions from Nauvoo's mayor, Orson Spencer, imploring him to do his duty as a "watchman of Israel." Spencer argued that because the original charter had been issued in perpetuity and contained no provision for repeal, any ex post facto law attempting repeal would be illegal.[7] Babbitt made two speeches before the House Committee on Banks and Corporations. Among other things, he charged the political opposition with a long list of crimes against Latter-day Saints.[8] Babbitt became discouraged over prospects for saving the charter when legislators began grilling him about reports of counterfeiting in Nauvoo, the "spiritual wife" doctrine, and whether he believed Joseph Smith's revelations. When Backenstos spoke to the committee, he "pleaded like an apostle for the rights of his constituents."[9]

As the debate continued, many Democrats supported the bills introduced in the Senate and House in December for total repeal of the city charter. Others, mostly Whigs, took a contrary stance, offering compromise amendments. They proposed to weaken Nauvoo's independence by placing the Nauvoo Legion more clearly under the governor and by limiting the powers of the municipal court. As support for repeal solidified, some tried to eliminate the charters of the Nauvoo House and the Nauvoo Agricultural and Manufacturing Association. At the same time, efforts failed to repeal the city charters of Chicago, Alton, Springfield, and Quincy.[10]

A Scott County legislator argued that the charter was necessary to the peaceful governance of Nauvoo but could be amended to eliminate the city's excessive powers. State senator Jacob C. Davis of Hancock County argued that no tweaking of the charter would prevent abuse of power. Without repeal, he argued, the Latter-day Saints would continue to act as "a sovereignty within a sovereignty." Support swelled as one senator after another endorsed the call for repeal. The legislature, Davis said, could take away what it had given.[11] The Senate passed the repeal bill on December 19 on a vote of 25 to 14.[12] The House dropped its own bill and on January 24, 1845, voted 75 to 31 to approve the Senate bill stripping Nauvoo of its governing authority. The *Nauvoo Neighbor* reported that every negative vote was a Democrat. According to Babbitt, southern Illinois Democrats and Whigs joined forces to accomplish the repeal.[13] Spokesmen for the church position had done their best, but, in the words of Illinois attorney general Josiah Lamborn, "the tide of popular passion and frenzy was too strong to be resisted."[14]

Even before the final vote was taken, officials in Nauvoo set about to correct one widely held misconception about the Latter-day Saints. Governor Ford, in his opening message to the legislature, had tried to counter reports of illegal activities in Nauvoo: "I have investigated the charge of promiscuous stealing," he said, "and find it to be greatly exaggerated."[15] Nauvoo's leaders launched their own counteroffensive to the rumored illegalities in Nauvoo. They feared that reports of theft rings might prejudice the trial of the accused murderers of Joseph and Hyrum Smith. On the first Sunday of January, Brigham Young exhorted a large congregation "to rise up *en masse,* and put down the thieving, swearing, gambling, bogus-making, retailing spirituous liquors, bad houses, and all abominations practiced in our midst by our enemies, who . . . publish that these things were practiced by us." He "severely rebuked the civil authorities of the city . . . and censured parents" for their failure to maintain law and order in the city. Over the next few weeks, Young led a two-pronged effort to change public opinion and enhance police action. Working with the Twelve, he invited two dozen men from the seventies and forty-seven from the high priests quorum to accept a two-month mission to nearby counties on both sides of the river to correct misrepresentations about the church. The delegates left on their public relations assignment at the end of January. "We will undeceive . . . the honest in heart," Young promised.[16]

Meantime, in response to Young's chastisement, the city council passed resolutions to counter the negative image created by "foes within and foes without." The council denied that any criminals had been harbored and blamed Whig anti-Mormon newspapers for the false perception. The council resolved to bolster the city police by as many as five hundred part-time officers and to enjoin citizens to be more vigilant. An independent investigation by a Hancock County deputy sheriff concluded that a theft ring operating thirty miles inland was funneling contraband through six agents in Nauvoo to a holding depot ten miles inside Iowa. None of them were Latter-day Saints. Mayor Orson Spencer called a public meeting to endorse the city council's actions. Perhaps he recognized that repeal of the Nauvoo charter had, in effect, made it impossible for the council to take any legal action. The citizens authorized fifty delegates to visit surrounding counties, probably the same men already called as missionaries by the Twelve.[17]

With the charter invalidated and the Nauvoo city council and municipal courts unable to function, a seven-member committee appointed by church and city officials wrote to leading jurists and politicians seeking advice on the legality of the repeal. The committee asked Daniel Webster, Stephen A. Douglas, John Quincy Adams, Andrew Jackson, John Wentworth, and four others to direct them to the proper court of appeal. Leaders in Nauvoo seriously considered asking the United States Supreme Court to review the action.[18] With a substitute bill introduced in the House by Babbitt languishing in committee, the city was left with few options. Sympathetic attorney general Lamborn advised patience:

> All you have to do is to be quiet, submissive to the laws and circumspect in your conduct . . . and my word for it, there will be a mighty reaction in the public sentiment, which will ultimately overthrow all your enemies. The sober second thought of the people will always be right.[19]

News of Backenstos's letter confirming repeal circulated quickly in Nauvoo when it was received on January 29. Not all were ready to "be quiet . . . and circumspect" in voicing concern, as Lamborn had advised. The Saints had wanted to trust constituted government. Now it had voided the city's charter. Newspaper editors added insult to injury by making fun of the name of the city. They claimed it was a distortion of the Hebrew. Church newspapers in Nauvoo and Liverpool jumped to the defense of the name with quotations from a Hebrew Bible and a Hebrew-English dictionary.[20] Many took the actions of the legislature in stride. "They have taken away our charter," twenty-three-year-old Calvin Reed informed a friend, "but the chimneys to our houses stand straight and upwards and the smoke goes out at the top as usual."[21]

Following counsel, members in outlying branches pledged a renewed demonstration of pacifism. A church conference at St. Louis viewed the charter's repeal "with mingled emotions of grief and surprise." A resolution of support declared, "[If] the chartered rights of Nauvoo . . . were granted wrong: they were taken wrong; but be strong, the day will come when you can triumph."[22] The triumph of "Mormonism" was Thomas Sharp's greatest fear. At the news of repeal, he sarcastically proposed a new charter be written to keep the Latter-day Saints from abusing its powers.[23]

When official news of the repeal reached Nauvoo, the city was on the eve of a municipal election. The candidates had been selected on January 8 in a caucus made up of the Twelve, high councilor, and city officers. The Twelve had declined to accept elected office. To do so, they felt, might subject them to physical harm by opponents of Nauvoo. Residents approved the slate at a public nominating meeting convened on January 14 at the outdoor preaching stand where Sunday meetings were held. The city council met in emergency session on January 30 and decided to proceed with the voting, just in case Governor Ford vetoed the repeal bill. At the election at the Concert Hall on February 3, about eight hundred fifty voters approved the nominees without a dissenting vote. Hosea Stout, one of the election judges, declared that he had never before seen such union and peace at an election in Nauvoo. The election proved futile, however. Nauvoo's municipal charter had been eliminated, leaving the city without legal government.[24]

Following the repeal, the Twelve worried most about police protection. For two years, Hosea Stout's city police, with backup from the Nauvoo Legion, had kept the peace. Two months after the martyrdom, Brigham Young had replaced Joseph Smith as lieutenant general by election of the court-martial and subsequent appointment by Governor Ford.[25] John C. Bennett's position as major general already had been filled

Brigham Young　　　　　　　　　　　　*Hosea Stout*

Providing police and military protection for Nauvoo after repeal of the city charter required creativity. The city's police captain, Hosea Stout, was relieved of his duties by Brigham Young during a transitional period and then reinstated after Young accepted Governor Ford's suggestion to incorporate Nauvoo under a town government.

by Charles C. Rich. But with the repeal of the charter, the Nauvoo Legion ceased to exist as a legal entity, as did the city police force.

On March 14, 1845, the "old police" met at the Masonic Hall to effect a reorganization as "new police" under Stephen Markham. When the "old" police chief, Hosea Stout, arrived, reorganization into companies of ten with a captain over each had begun. Then someone challenged the action, perhaps pointing out that without a charter, a new police organization would be illegal. After discussion, it was concluded that a legal entity did exist under which Nauvoo could enjoy police protection. It was the church. According to Stout, "It was concluded to organize the whole community of Saints in this County into Quorums of 12 deacons and have a Bishop at their head and they could thus administer in the lesser offices of the Church and preserve order without a charter."[26]

The matter of military service, required of all able-bodied men between ages eighteen and forty-five, also concerned Nauvoo's leaders. Should they now join other militia units in Hancock County to fulfill their obligations? An ecclesiastical answer was found for that question as well. Because state law exempted ordained ministers from military duty, none of the county's Latter-day Saint priesthood holders would need to serve.[27]

In his Sunday sermon on March 16, Brigham Young gave the plan of ecclesiastical government a name. Nauvoo would be reorganized as the "City of Joseph." It would not be a legal organization under state law, he said, but rather an interim government operating under the bishops, who would keep order in the streets and care for the poor. The Council of Fifty considered the matter the next Saturday. Two days later, the Twelve and others met in the Concert Hall, where church leaders ordained bishops for each neighborhood and instructed them to set apart adult deacons within their wards.[28] These quorums of twelve deacons patrolled the streets in rotation day and night and served as bodyguards for church leaders under the direction of their bishop. Young told the new policemen the next afternoon that he was thinking about incorporating a town under state law. The legal town limit of one square mile within the old city would include the temple, Nauvoo House, and other public property. It would allow the appointment of a police force.[29] Meantime, provisional police operated under the suggested name—The City of Joseph. The April conference approved Young's motion to adopt the name "henceforth and forever."[30]

Despite the sound of permanence that the Twelve gave the arrangement, they were working quietly for a solution under state law. They had sought advice from Illinois officials, and Governor Ford responded in an April 8 letter repeating what Young's close advisors had already told him. A town corporation could not be larger than one mile square. Ford suggested a series of adjoining towns to cover the whole territory of the city of Nauvoo. These units, he said, could cooperate voluntarily to ensure compatible laws. Ford believed the Saints might win back the city charter in the next legislature. Meanwhile, diminished in power, a town government would be "somewhat better than none," Ford said.[31]

As for the future of the Nauvoo Legion, Ford proposed to make Nauvoo's troops part of the state militia, as were other local military groups. The militia would be under direct orders of the governor as commander-in-chief, whereas originally both governor and mayor could command. Ford intended to disarm the Carthage and Warsaw militias in response to reports that they were stockpiling weapons. "Whether they intend it as a mere bravado, to keep up agitation and excitement, until

Efforts to build an arsenal for the Nauvoo Legion continued during the fall of 1844, but after the city lost its charter, the stone building was adapted for use as a school.

after the trials [of the murderers of the Smiths, expected at the May 1845 court]; or whether there is to be a general move and renewal of the designs of last summer and fall I am not aware." Ford was willing to leave with the Mormon leaders the initiative should a crisis develop:

> In case a mob should be raised against you it will be your privilege and one of your highest duties to society and yourselves to resist it. But you know your condition as a people. You know the prejudices which exist; and the disposition of the public mind to believe evil of you. You will therefore have to be cautious. Do nothing which will allow your opponents to say that you have begun a war. Place them clearly in the wrong and keep them so.[32]

The governor's sympathetic counsel offered the only practical resolution to Nauvoo's need for basic civil government—maintenance of a peaceful society through simple regulations, police protection, and a judicial system under a town government. Brigham Young shared Ford's letter with the high priests and then discussed it at length with the Council of Fifty. Together they decided against multiplying town governments. Rather than seven (some speculated it would take twelve) separate but adjoining towns, they chose instead to replace the short-lived City of Joseph with a single Town of Nauvoo.

Organized the next day, on April 16, 1845, the new town consisted of only the most central part of the former city.[33] The five trustees appointed under the law—Alpheus Cutler, Orson Spencer, Charles C. Rich, Theodore Turley, and David Fullmer—were all members of the Council of Fifty. Three of them were among those who had won office in the February election. Spencer had been elected mayor, Rich an alderman, and Fullmer a councilor. The trustees then appointed Hosea Stout as the town's police captain, named the former policemen to serve with him, and designated assessors, tax collectors, and other officers.[34] The new functionaries set about meeting day-to-day needs without fanfare.

The issue of Nauvoo's municipal power had been resolved, and the system worked because of a consensus within the community. John Taylor observed:

> There never was so great union in the city before; with a few exceptions the whole population are saints, and are governed as easy as a "gentle hand would lead an elephant by a hair." The "exceptions" are mainly men who hang on "to keep taverns, stores, or groceries," contrary to the expressed wishes of the majority of the citizens.[35]

Because a town could not have its own militia, church leaders allowed the deacons (or new police) to continue as a church emergency defense force. Major General Charles C. Rich shed his military title for a new one: "President of all the Organized Quorums of the Church of Jesus Christ of Latter-day Saints in Hancock County." Brigham Young instructed President Rich to hold his quorums in readiness to act against mob threats in Nauvoo or in any of the outlying settlements. This thinly veiled militia organization was consistent with the governor's prescription to prepare for self-defense and to do so cautiously.[36]

Official church commentary encouraged a mood of optimism during the spring of 1845. Heber C. Kimball invited more immigration and construction. "Some think we shall be driven from Nauvoo; but we are going to stay in Nauvoo and we shall build it up. . . . The Legislature has repealed our city charter; but it cannot repeal Mormonism, neither can it take away our city." The Saints were reassured that law and order prevailed within Nauvoo and that threats from without were unlikely. The *Times and Seasons* editorialized that the Saints "were more willing to receive and listen to counsel" than ever before. "The high council have only had one [disciplinary] case in about seven weeks. Our magistrats have nothing to do. We have little or no use for charter or law. . . . Whenever a dispute or difficulty arises, a word from the proper source puts all to right, and no resort to law." A committee of the Council of Fifty agreed: "Great peace and union prevail among all the saints," they wrote to Lyman Wight. "All the saints feel spirited and determined to carry out the measures of our martyred Prophet. There is no prospect of any mob at present, and all things bid fair for peace and prosperity."[37]

To Brigham Young, president of the Twelve, the peace prevailing in Nauvoo signified that Zion—even a peace like that of the Millennium—had arrived. He counseled in April 1845:

> Learn to suffer wrong rather than do wrong, and by so doing we will outstrip all our enemies and conquer the evil one, for know ye not that here is Zion? know ye not that the millennium has commenced? We have had Zion upon the earth this fourteen years. Peace reigns among this people which is Zion. Union and true charity dwells with this people: this is the most orderly and peaceable people upon the face of the whole earth. Well, this is Zion, and it is increasing and spreading wider and wider, and this principle of Zion, which is peace, will stretch all over the earth; that is the millennium.[38]

FURTHERING THE PROPHET'S OBJECTIVES

The assassinations at Carthage and the repeal of Nauvoo's municipal, military, and educational charter gave the Quorum of the Twelve opportunities to make adjustments in the way the church and the city of Nauvoo were organized. They did so with one purpose—to accomplish the Prophet's objectives. During the year of peace that began in August 1844, leaders and residents of Nauvoo focused on completing Joseph Smith's most important project—the temple. In Brigham Young's spiritual searchings, he felt affirmed that this was the right thing to do. "I inquired of the Lord whether we should stay here and finish the temple," he noted in his diary. "The answer was we should."[39]

To accomplish the task, the Twelve repeated the Prophet's invitation to gather. Needed were temple construction workers but of greater need were investors in Nauvoo's economy as a support for the temple project. Open letters from the Twelve frankly acknowledged the economic necessity undergirding the call to move to Nauvoo. In his first epistle on August 15, 1844, Brigham Young encouraged capitalists to invest in industry, manufacture, and agriculture to provide employment for those desiring to gather. The temple, he said, would be completed by the tithing system already in place, a tithe of time or income, but both depended upon men of means to establish industry and cultivate farms. "Unless this is done," Young said, "it is impossible for the gathering to progress, because those who have no other dependence cannot live together without industry and employment."[40] The Twelve ratified this appeal in an October 1 epistle, in which they gave first priority to the temple "as a great and glorious public work" of great spiritual significance. They designated as their second priority the gathering "as a work of salvation, to be accomplished in wisdom and prudence" so that employment and economic support would be available in Nauvoo and surrounding areas. A third concern of the new leaders was the moral base of Nauvoo. They urged a retrenchment from what they judged a slackening of standards in the City of Righteousness.[41]

Within days after the burial of the martyrs, the Saints returned to work on the temple and pushed it forward at a rapid pace.[42] By October 1, 1844, the limestone walls were ready to receive the arches of the second-story windows. Seven of the sun stone capitals were in place and the others were being readied. Inside, timbers were being framed and raised. By the following May, the Twelve had expended more than three thousand dollars on framing timbers alone.[43]

Church leaders issued an urgent appeal for workers and for tithes and other free-will offerings. The plea revealed just how much both men and supporting resources were needed: "Let the saints now send in their young men who are strong to labor, together with money, provisions, clothing, tools, teams, and every necessary means, such as they know they will want when they arrive, for the purpose of forwarding this work," the Twelve wrote. The public relations missionaries sent out in January to correct misconceptions about thievery in Nauvoo carried this message as well, and many of them were authorized to collect tithing for the temple.[44]

The appeal to complete the temple caught on. Church members packed up and moved to Nauvoo, contributed time and means toward construction, and prepared themselves for the promised blessings. Many young volunteers moved to Nauvoo for summer work after the crops were planted. "The work of the Temple goes on as fast as possible," John Taylor editorialized in April 1845, "and, in fact, the anxiety is so great to labor upon this great house of the Lord, that the committee frequently have to set men at other work."[45] Thirteen months after the Prophet's death, a reporter for the *New York Sun* captured the mood converging on the Lord's House. "The building of the Mormon Temple under all the

A central focus for the Saints after Joseph Smith's death was completion of the temple. Artist Nathan Fish Moore, who visited Nauvoo from New York City in 1845, made the drawing from which J. W. Orr made this engraving.

troubles by which those people have been surrounded," he wrote, "seems to be carried on with a religious enthusiasm which . . . controls all the movements toward its completion." By August 1845, a St. Louis visitor found the walls of the temple nearly finished and a stone wall, intended to rise twelve to fifteen feet, well under way around the perimeter of the temple lot.[46]

With the placement of the final trumpet stones atop the sun stones on March 27, 1845, the work of the stonemasons on the Nauvoo Temple was nearly complete. This accomplishment turned the attention of the Twelve to the other project enjoined by the January 1841 revelation. As work on the temple continued at a heightened pace despite cold spring weather, deliberations in various councils centered on the neglected Nauvoo House. The Saints at April's special conference were reminded that God had sanctioned the project when Orson Pratt read the 1841 revelation and an extract from the Book of the Law of the Lord (Joseph Smith's official diary). The congregation unanimously accepted a motion to "fulfill the revelation, by completing the Nauvoo House, as soon as possible." Young sought and received pledges from those willing to buy shares of stock in the Nauvoo House.[47]

Later that month, crews began hauling bricks from Nauvoo's kilns to the riverfront site to lay on the stone basement walls. A portion of the temple lumber from Wisconsin arriving regularly at Nauvoo on rafts went

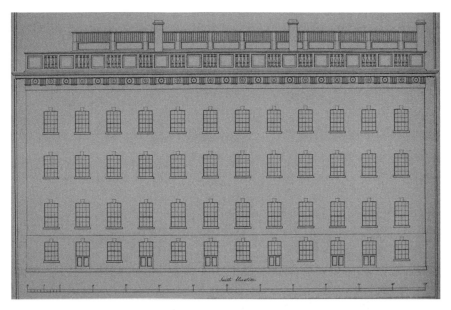

The Nauvoo House shared importance with the Nauvoo Temple in the January 1841 revelation. As work on the hotel was given renewed attention in 1845, architect William Weeks prepared detailed drawings, including this south elevation, the side facing the river.

to the Nauvoo House.[48] Brigham Young's energy kept things moving. In mid-August, Young climbed upon the stone basement walls of the Nauvoo House with Heber Kimball, who dedicated it to the Lord. The outline defined an L-shaped foundation, 120 feet in its longest dimension and 80 feet wide. Workmen started laying brick. Young called for more bricklayers at a priesthood meeting the next Sunday. Fifty responded, and the project moved forward.[49] In early September, citizens rallied to support a bee, held as a benefit for Nauvoo's hotel, "next in magnificence to the temple."[50]

On August 17, Brigham Young had an experience that caused him to pause and reflect on the crash course he had been pursuing on the hotel project. In a dream just before awakening, he later informed aides, "I saw Brother Joseph Smith, and as I was going about my business, he said, 'Brother Brigham, don't be in a hurry,' which was repeated the second and third times with a degree of sharpness."[51] The new head of the church pondered this advice before translating it into a redirection of effort. Events soon convinced the Twelve that the peaceful interlude in Hancock County was ending. They shifted attention once again toward completion

Many public buildings in Nauvoo were funded by selling shares in the venture. This certificate of shares for the Seventies Hall was issued in 1844 when work was beginning on the meeting hall.

of the House of the Lord. Nauvoo's grand hotel at the river's edge would be abandoned after the stone sills for the second-floor windows had been placed atop the brick walls.

Meanwhile, other public buildings went forward on their own schedules. One of the first was an arsenal or armory to store the powder, ammunition, and public armaments of the Nauvoo Legion. It had been contemplated for more than a year when on September 16, 1844, Lieutenant General Brigham Young dedicated a site near the temple "to the God of the armies of Israel" and broke ground for the cellar. After a slow start in construction work, the stone walls were completed the following June and roof timbers installed in mid-July.[52] This project had been launched even though Governor Ford had collected the state arms in June 1844. At the end of the year, Lieutenant General Young and Major General Charles C. Rich had encouraged Nauvoo's militiamen to return any state arms still in their keeping. Members of the Nauvoo Legion rearmed themselves privately and stored their own arms. Some of the arms and ammunition came from Saints in St. Louis. Local gunmaker William Kay drilled out a six-pounder cannon to prepare it for service. Three other cannon were secured as well. Because the armory was no longer needed for public arms, it was completed for use as a school instead.[53]

Another major building completed after Joseph Smith's death was the Seventies Hall. Begun early in 1844, construction had experienced delays occasioned by a windstorm but moved forward rapidly during the late summer and fall. By December 20, it was ready for use. Dedication ceremonies began on the twenty-sixth with a sermon and dedicatory prayer by Brigham Young. For eight days the services continued, with the families of each of fifteen quorums attending, two quorums per session. The Nauvoo Choir of Singers and a brass band furnished music at each gathering. John Kay premiered a new song composed for the occasion by John Taylor and dedicated to Brigham Young: "The Seer, Joseph the Seer." Participants were feted with fruits, nuts, and desserts. "Well might it be said," a reporter concluded, "that the saints enjoyed a feast of fat things."[54] High above the entrance, a stone inscription read in simple italic letters, "*Priesthood.*" Just above the entrance door, another entablature anticipated future buildings: "Seventies Hall No. 1."[55]

In the second block north of the temple, the Music Association dedicated a hall measuring 30 feet by 50 feet in March 1845. This single-story brick building had arched ceilings, a platform at one end, and a curved sounding board for the choir and other musicians. The high council, women's groups, the Nauvoo Lyceum, and others used the Music Hall (also known as the Concert Hall).[56] In remarks at one of the first concerts, Heber C. Kimball applauded the musicians for the variety of music offered to suit different tastes.[57]

In early June 1845, the Twelve decided to buy canvas for a tent to serve as a tabernacle for large preaching meetings at the west entrance of the temple. Some described it as an "outer court" to the temple. Joseph Smith had initiated the project. The elliptical tabernacle, to run north and south, was expected to seat as many as ten thousand people in seats rising "one above another in the form of an amphitheatre."[58] Orson Hyde headed east to raise funds for four thousand yards of canvas and appropriate fixtures, estimated to cost between one thousand and two thousand dollars. Howard Egan secured hemp for cords in St. Louis. The Twelve encouraged the Saints to contribute by tithing, donation, in-kind contribution, or even loans redeemable in land at Nauvoo. Hyde collected fourteen hundred dollars and paid out two-thirds of it for the canvas. According to one who heard Hyde's report of the cash raised, "He had got it not by loans from the rich, who held on to their money, but by begging and some voluntary donations."[59] Orson Pratt said the collection effort so drained the Saints' resources that tithing donations lagged for a time. By September 10, Hyde had raised the needed funds; a week later he shipped the canvas from New York to the bishops in Nauvoo.[60]

Not long after Hyde left for the East, a crew moved the preaching stand and benches from the public square east of the temple to a newly cleared area immediately west of the temple—the designated site for the tabernacle. Regular Sunday preaching meetings thereafter assembled in that place. By the time the canvas arrived in mid-October, the church did not need a conference tent in Nauvoo. Hyde loaded the canvas into wagons in 1846 and headed west with it.[61]

SUSTAINING THE POOR THROUGH HOME INDUSTRY

As the Twelve moved forward in their expanded role, they implemented Joseph Smith's desire to free the First Presidency from detailed involvement in temporal affairs. The Prophet had begun a transformation in 1841 by giving the Twelve increased responsibilities at home, yet his role as trustee-in-trust kept him absorbed. The Twelve gave the trusteeship to senior bishops Newel K. Whitney and George Miller, along with much day-to-day conduct of church business. Brigham Young accepted Joseph Smith's proprietorship of the steamboat *Maid of Iowa* on behalf of the church and secured the ferry license from the city in January 1845. He then immediately directed the bishops to sell the boat.[62]

All of these actions freed the Twelve to focus on ecclesiastical duties. Even so, they did not neglect Nauvoo's economy. They were anxious that all of Nauvoo's business interests serve the broader good—that they contribute directly to the furtherance of church programs and principles. For example, when apostate land developers lured immigrants away from church building lots, Brigham Young circulated a handbill to prospective buyers in Nauvoo. Young promised competitive prices on church lots and urged immigrants to consult with the trustees or their agents before buying. "It is your duty," he said.[63] Similarly, when a few Nauvoo merchants offended church standards by selling liquor contrary to city law, the Twelve privately encouraged priesthood quorums to boycott three storekeepers identified as "enemies to this people."[64]

An observer in Carthage complained that emigration from Hancock County since the murders of Joseph and Hyrum had depressed property values by two-thirds. Money was scarce, he said, and business could be conducted only through trade. These were largely symptoms of a lingering economic depression in America that had hit Illinois especially hard. The disruptive events of the summer of 1844 had added to the effects felt locally. After Joseph Smith's death, construction work slowed temporarily in Nauvoo, and some workmen joined the exodus of nervous Saints and other citizens. "A great many buildings partly finished were left on account of the mobs as a great many [people] left the city," Dwight Webster observed in December. Webster's diligent effort to find work as a carpenter in Nauvoo had failed. The conference in April 1845 offered some relief when the Saints voted to drop all old debts against the church, including "the debts of Kirtland, and Missouri, and the debts that are said to be accrued in consequence of purchasing the Galland tract in Iowa Territory."[65]

Despite the lingering depression, church leaders had for years hoped that industry and manufacturing would flourish in Nauvoo along with agriculture and a surging growth in population. The Twelve recognized that they could not pump substantial resources into construction of the temple without a sound economic base. At the time of the Prophet's death, the city was nearing eleven thousand residents, the point at which St. Louis had been eight years before. The Missouri metropolis and its suburbs had doubled in population in the next four years and did so again by 1845.[66] Its economy was burgeoning. Why not the same for Nauvoo?

In August 1844, the Twelve launched an effort to involve the entire Latter-day Saint community in home industry and to focus all economic energies toward church purposes.[67] They drew on ideas promoted before Joseph Smith's death (and carried those same ideas with them when they moved west eighteen months later). Brigham Young stated the objectives in an October 1844 epistle from the Twelve:

> Not only must farms be cultivated, houses built, and mills [erected] to grind the corn, but there must be something produced by industry, to send off to market in exchange for cash, and for such other articles as we need. This must be produced, not by singing, or praying, or going to meeting, or visiting, or friendly greetings, or conversation, BUT, BY THE UNITED INDUSTRY, SKILL, AND ECONOMY OF THE WHOLE PEOPLE. Men, women, and children must be well, and constantly employed. In order the more effectually to do this, we must turn our attention to the erection of work-shops for the manufacture of every useful article; and wares thus manufactured must find a market, not in Nauvoo alone but in all the wide country, and in cities and towns abroad.[68]

Advocates of industry felt assured that the natural resources for increased home production could be readily obtained. For example, Brigham Young lauded the abundance of raw materials—wool, flax, hemp, and cotton—that would feed British-style textile factories. Church trustees agreed to accept these raw materials as tithing and use them in fueling manufacturing industries in Nauvoo.[69] In this context, the Twelve and others taught the importance of work. "Time is property, and labor is capital" became a common phrase encouraging unemployed tradesmen to organize themselves into small manufacturing shops. "Labor is the manufacturer of wealth," a *Nauvoo Neighbor* editorial said. "It was ordained of God, as the medium to be used by man to obtain his living."[70]

Economic development fit well into Latter-day Saint religious belief. The consistent goal of Joseph Smith's economic policy had been to eliminate poverty. During the last year the Saints were headquartered in Nauvoo, the Twelve encouraged them to sustain themselves and the poor through home industry. If they would purchase the raw materials and then "employ their friends and themselves at home, instead of sending away all our cash for manufactured goods," the Twelve said, "we can soon produce millions of wealth, and the poor will have no cause of complaint."[71] As new industries created jobs and goods for local purchase, cash would remain in Nauvoo and tithing would increase for use in building the temple and for other church needs. In New Hampshire, Jesse C. Little caught the spirit of this emphasis and kept six to eight hands busy in a private manufacturing business. Little expected to build twenty-five sleighs during the winter of 1844–45 before turning to carriages, he informed Brigham Young. "I think the Saints ought to prepare themselves to help themselves and others. By so doing," he wrote, "it would relieve the poor by giving them labour."[72]

Another religious reason for economic development was to prepare for uncertain times ahead. At the end of time, when nations crumbled, many surmised that the kingdom of the Saints would be left to its own resources. "Come on then, all ye ends of the earth," Brigham Young said to converts abroad, "take hold together, and with a long, strong, steady and united exertion, let us build up a strong hold of industry and wealth." Orson Spencer urged tradesmen to use money and labor "'to build us all up as one—to secure us a home, a resting place from the impending storm that is gathering to burst over the world.'"[73] The concept of home industry found its greatest advocate in John Taylor. He published articles and editorials in the *Nauvoo Neighbor* and in October 1844 launched a series of weekly trades meetings for Nauvoo's mechanics (tradesmen). Through these town meetings, he hoped to create an economy in which Latter-day Saints could buy goods made in Nauvoo by local workers using locally produced raw materials. He told one of the gatherings, "'We can manufacture every thing that is necessary for us to use or wear, by uniting our industry and means; for labor is wealth and power if we will only carry it out.'"[74]

By common consent, Taylor chaired the Tuesday night gatherings and headed a general trades committee with Orson Spencer and Phineas Richards as his assistants. The general committee helped skilled craftsmen in Nauvoo organize. These committees reported their progress at gatherings known generally as the Trades Meeting but also as the Trades Association, Mechanics Association, or Trades Institute.[75]

The general trades council sponsored nothing directly but taught the principles by which it expected tradesmen to organize. Some worried about competition with imported goods or noncompetitive prices. Taylor reassured workers that small local companies would not create unfair monopolies in the market.[76] The trades committees found that local products could be sold for less than imported items. Edward Hunter cast the effort in patriotic terms—likening it to John Hancock's efforts to expel British manufactures from the American colonies.[77]

During its first four months, Taylor intentionally resisted organizing his general committee or the trades meetings themselves into any kind of formal body. Neither would he accept any authority over the trades subcommittees. His intention was to encourage the various committees to devise ways and means to organize separate companies for each trade. These companies would "manufacture articles and export them, instead of importing every thing we needed, impoverishing the city and mechanics."[78] Nor would Taylor commit church funds to any project. He insisted that they be private companies; the church in Nauvoo would avoid the pattern of united orders tried earlier in Kirtland and Independence.[79]

During October, the trades meetings helped organize many of Nauvoo's trades "to produce all the dry goods, hardware, cutlery, crockery, or any other commodity, that a community needs for comfort or convenience." Various speakers encouraged shops to make pottery, farm utensils, firearms, and leather goods. The city could use a paper mill, a chair factory, a stove factory, and, eventually, a pork-packing house, they said.[80] Organized into craftsmen's planning committees were weavers, shoemakers, carpenters, iron molders, blacksmiths, cutlers, coach and carriage makers, lace weavers, jewelers, tailors, cabinetmakers, hatmakers, and others—all encouraged to form their own businesses. "We are determined to make all our own materials that we can," Heber C. Kimball insisted.[81]

The iron molders, weavers, and carriage makers moved forward aggressively by forming three independent businesses. Hiram Kimball's iron foundry had closed earlier that year for lack of iron and coal but had produced plows selling for seven dollars, three dollars less than imports. In the spirit of home industry, two entrepreneurs put the iron foundry back in production. "By industry we live; By commerce we thrive," an advertisement in the *Neighbor* announced.[82]

The weavers committee identified ten workers ready to make shirting, sheeting, satinette, ladies shawls, and gingham. They needed only looms, wool, cotton, and cotton yarn. In mid-November, the committee reported twelve looms finished, spindles under construction, and cotton ordered. A supporter had donated a carding machine. Local farmers had agreed to raise sheep.[83]

The weavers were excited by an offer from a Mr. Livingston of Peterboro, New Hampshire, who offered to finance a cloth factory in Nauvoo.[84] A committee investigated.[85] They found local investors willing to provide twelve hundred dollars, less than half the amount needed for a three-story stone building. To meet their June completion deadline, sponsors invited subscriptions for twenty-five dollars each. If a joint-stock arrangement didn't work, they would seek direct capitalization.[86] Phineas Richards of the general committee estimated huge profits from the cotton factory. The weavers projected that they could produce cloth for wearing apparel at 75 cents per yard. They expected to launch the business by December with five or six looms.[87]

Carriage makers needed their own factory but wondered if they could share a building with the weavers.[88] They told the Trades Meeting that vehicles made in Nauvoo could compete successfully with imports. Carriages could be built for six hundred dollars per dozen and sold for sixty dollars each. The profit for common elliptic wagons would be even greater; for an investment of sixty dollars per wagon, workers could sell them for one hundred dollars and clear forty dollars.[89] Without waiting for a new building, the committee found a temporary workplace and on

COMMISSION STORE FOR HOME MANUFACTURE.

THE subscriber having opened a commission store on Mulholland street, about fifteen rods south east of the Temple, will receive and sell on commission, any article that can be made or manufactured in this city, comprising of Boots and Shoes of all kinds, Hats, Bonnets, Stockings, Socks, Gloves, Cabinet-ware, Chairs, Hoes, Pitch forks; finally, any thing that you can make or have on hand that will be useful in this vicinity, that you wish to sell; if you feel disposed to leave it with me I will sell it to the best advantage, for your benefit.

I will receive in exchange for the above articles, Pork, Beef, Butter, Cheese, Fowls, Eggs, Wheat, Corn, Buck-wheat, Flour, Meal, Potatoes, Beans, Wool, Hides, and finally any thing that will make food or clothing.

Please give me a call as I will intend to sell cheaper than the cheapest.

ABEL LAMB.

Nauvoo, Feb. 26, 1845—43tf

SEE HERE.

20 TON of hay, wanted immediately at the Nauvoo coach and carriage manufacturing association, for which good pay will be given.

Nauvoo, March 25-48-3m

NAUVOO MANUFACTURING ASSOCIATION.

Manufactured, by the Nauvoo Coach and Carriage Manufacturing Association, on Water street, in the city of Nauvoo, opposite Gen. Joseph Smiths' store, the following articles, to wit:—Coaches, Omnibuses, Chariotees, Chaises, Cabs, Barouches, Buggies and Buggy Wagons, Hearses, Sportsmens' Trotting Wagons, two and one Horse Lumber Wagons, Ox and Horse Carts, Ploughs, Scythe Sneaths, Pitch Forks, Rakes, Carding and Thrashing Machines, Horse Powers, Railroad Cars, and many other articles too numerous to mention, sold as cheap as can be purchased in any eastern market. All orders must be post paid, and addressed to GEO. W. HARRIS, Esq., Pres't. of the Association.

The Nauvoo Coach and Carriage Manufacturing Association was one of the first to organize and begin production under the emphasis given home industry. Commission stores, such as the one opened by Abel Lamb (left), charged a small commission for selling products made by Nauvoo craftsmen.

December 18 organized the Nauvoo Coach and Carriage Manufacturing Association.[90] Following John Taylor's advice, they created an organization independent of the Nauvoo Agricultural and Manufacturing Association. By early January 1845, they were ready to begin making vehicles.[91]

The informal Trades Association existed apart from the Nauvoo Agricultural and Manufacturing Association (NA&MA), which had been organized in 1841 under state charter. Many of the new trades groups hoped to organize their manufacturing businesses under the authority of the NA&MA charter. The Nauvoo city charter had yet to be repealed, but it was facing serious threats. After much discussion, on December 31, the Trades Meeting resolved "that instead of commencing business under any charter of Illinois, we will unite our efforts in all manufacturing and mechanical labors in common co-partnerships, or private form, according to law."[92]

This action failed to satisfy proponents of a dam to provide water power for industries and a harbor for Nauvoo. These men believed that the only entity with legal standing was the state-chartered Nauvoo Agricultural and Manufacturing Association. The Twelve supported the affiliation, even though legislative repeal of the association's charter seemed likely.[93] Because as many as a third of the founders of the NA&MA had left the church or had died, the organization lacked direction. John Taylor advised the remaining officers to reorganize and fill the vacancies. Before the men could respond, one of the group's council members, Theodore Turley, suggested instead a merger with the Trades Association, which he thought had been formally organized.[94]

This gave John Taylor the opportunity he needed. Because Turley offered no plan for merging the two groups, Taylor proposed a meeting to develop "an organization, something like the priesthood." First, the assembled tradesmen voted to repeal the charter of the Nauvoo Agricultural and Manufacturing Association. Only they, and not the state legislature, had the authority to do so, Taylor said. With the NA&MA disabled, Taylor proposed the creation of a trades union. It would have a presidency of three and a council of twelve men. The council would govern as a body known as the Living Constitution. There would be no formal charter or written bylaws. Separate associations and companies formed by tradesmen would be subject to the council. The concept of a living constitution had been used in the creation of another special group, the civic-oriented Council of Fifty. These groups echoed the governing principles of priesthood councils and the Relief Society. Taylor and Amasa Lyman were appointed to select the twelve men.[95]

Those associated with the old Agricultural and Manufacturing Association did not wait for the new Trades Council. They set about to replace the NA&MA with a private joint-stock corporation. On January 31, 1845, at a gathering in the Seventies Hall, they formed the Mercantile and Mechanical Association and elected twelve trustees. Its stated purpose was to foster home industry and forestall the importation of goods by merchants and the resulting drain of money from Nauvoo.[96] When organizers met four days later at the Masonic Hall to draft bylaws, John D. Lee, a member of the Council of Fifty, advised them "that the order of the Association differed from the arrangements then [in the] making by the Twelve in some points."[97]

The arrangements being made by the Twelve may have been considered that afternoon by the Council of Fifty. The meeting of the Fifty at the Seventies Hall that day, February 4, was its first since Joseph Smith's death. Brigham Young assembled the group to reorganize it, likely in response to the repeal of the city charter. During its short history, the Council of Fifty had dealt only with political issues and would continue that focus.[98] Now, the Twelve saw a need for a separate council to manage economic issues. John Taylor was absent from the meeting of the Fifty, but it was the proposal he had made the previous week that the Twelve implemented. At that time or within days, they appointed a new twelve-member board "to organize the temporal affairs of the church." According to William Huntington, "twelve men were chosen called the living constitution. These twelve chose three of the twelve apostles, viz John Taylor, George A. Smith, and Amasa Lyman to preside over the temporal affairs of all the church."[99]

The dozen members of the Living Constitution for economic affairs, or Trades Council, were appointed by the Twelve.[100] They were men of proven practical judgment: Samuel Bent, Alpheus Cutler, Phineas Richards, Edward Hunter, Daniel Spencer, John Benbow, Theodore Turley, Orson Spencer, David Fullmer, Charles C. Rich, William Weeks, and Joseph W. Coolidge.[101] Five already served on the Council of Fifty; three others would be admitted on March 1.[102] Seven had won municipal office in the February election but had been denied the right to serve because of repeal of the city charter.[103] Five had seen service on stake high councils.[104] Orson Spencer and Phineas Richards had served since October as John Taylor's counselors in the Trades Meeting council. The three apostles, all members of the Council of Fifty, served as presidents over the trades panel, with a relationship much like that of a stake presidency over its high council. Acting without charter or bylaws, this coordinating council for Nauvoo's economic affairs would operate under ecclesiastical authority as an executive, legislative, and judicial body.

The following Friday, February 7, the Trades Council met for the first time to plan a strategy. They decided to continue the informal Tuesday night trades meetings to promote home industry through a town meeting format. Four days later, the presidency of the Trades Council met with other members of the Twelve and drafted a significant document that became part of the incorporation papers of every trades company formed thereafter in Nauvoo.[105]

The stated purpose of the model constitution was to promote peace, to support the poor by employing them, and to eliminate any need to go to law to settle business problems. By adopting the guidelines, the board of directors of a participating company agreed to be "subject in all things to the counsel, advice, and directions of the body called the 'Living Constitution.'" Company directors would be appointed by this council with the advice and consent of association members. The board could appoint its own officers as long as the Living Constitution did not object. The company board pledged its loyalty to the Trades Council and agreed to be subject to council review and arbitration of its business. Company directors waived their right to sue in a court of law. They agreed to submit all grievances to the Living Constitution for arbitration, retaining the right to appeal only to the council's presidency.[106]

These actions of the Twelve in creating the Trades Council were presented and ratified on Monday, February 17, at a public meeting in the grove. At the gathering, the new presidency over Nauvoo's temporal affairs were introduced. They explained the religious nature of their economic stewardship. In an indirect reflection of the principles of consecration, they "urged the necessity of becoming one in feeling and in action in temporal things as well as spiritual."[107]

With the superstructure and guidelines in place, the trades groups proceeded. The Mercantile and Mechanical Association had been waiting for counsel since its first organizing meeting on January 31.[108] On February 18, the group learned from John Taylor and Theodore Turley "the true nature of organizing Associations of this kind." After agreeing to the governing principles outlined by the Living Constitution, the association elected Daniel Carns as president. Two days later, they adopted a constitution that included word-for-word the guidelines provided by the Living Constitution. On February 24, they began selling stock.[109]

Other groups soon followed suit to move forward the effort in Nauvoo to employ skilled craftsmen in productive private enterprises. In six meetings during the last week of February, a committee from the Living Constitution met with several gatherings of unorganized tradesmen to propose plans for creating cooperative manufacturing associations.[110] Between then and late April, at least three new companies were organized under the close supervision of the Trades Council. Among the new associations was one incorporating blacksmiths, whitesmiths, and

TO THE PUBLIC.

WE the Bricklayers, Stonelayers, and Plasterers of the city of Nauvoo, having formed ourselves into an Association for the purpose of our carrying on our business in all its branches; such as brick and stone laying, plastering, hard finish, cornice, together with all kinds of stucco work, cementing, rough casting houses, cistern building, &c., &c., would say we are now prepared to contract for jobs of any magnitude, and having all the facilities for carrying on the business to any extent, either to furnish or not to furnish materials, and accomplish all jobs with despatch, which we will warrant to be done in the best manner. Would recommend to any individual wishing work done in our line of business to apply to the President of the Association, (two blocks south of the Hay scales,) who is empowered to contract for all jobs at prices to suit the times.

JACOB FOUTZ, President.
C. R. DANA, Councillor.
H. HOAGLAND, Councillor.
ENOCH REESE, Secretary.
JAS. TOWNSEND, Treasurer.
April 2nd, 1845—48tf

COOPERS ASSOCIATION.

THE Coopers of the city of Nauvoo, wish to inform the public, that they have entered into an organization, for the purpose of carrying on the business of Coopering in all its various branches, and that we are now prepared to contract for jobs of any magnitude; and inasmuch as we have some of the best of workmen, we hope to merit the support and confidence of Merchants and others, who may favor us with a call.

Any person wishing for work done in our line of business, will please apply to the Superintendant of the Association on Hyrum Street, between Partridge and Hyde Streets; who is empowered to contract for all jobs at prices to suit the times.

We would also inform the public that we want immediately, ONE HUNDRED THOUSAND STAVES, for which we will pay the highest Western prices. Persons wishing to furnish us with good Staves can apply to the Superintendant as above.

Individual property of members of said Association will be exempt from liability for debts contracted by said Association

WM. EARL, President.
HENRY B HUFFMAN, } Counsellors
CYRUS WINGATE,   }
HUGH LYTLE, Superintendant.
H. B. HUFFMAN, Treasurer.
HENRY STANDAGE, Secretary.
May 18, 1845—3—3m

The brickmasons and coopers were among the trades organized cooperatively as private businesses under a model constitution. That constitution pledged the creation of new jobs as one way of eliminating poverty.

gunsmiths.[111] In December, five shoemakers had formed the Nauvoo Boot and Shoe Establishment on Mulholland Street next to Amos Davis's store and offered wholesale and retail goods.[112] A broader, competing enterprise appeared in April as the Tanners and Shoemakers Association. This group organized the Nauvoo Tannery and appealed for calfskins and hides to supply its operation. Harnessmakers soon joined the association. By April, the group operated a boot and shoe shop on Young Street, a saddle and harness shop near the Arsenal, and a tannery at Hibbard and Rich Streets.[113] The Association of Bricklayers, Stonelayers, and Plasterers sought work by advertising a detailed list of skills for hire. To accommodate its eleven members and the buying public, the Tailors' Association maintained two shops, one on Main Street and another on Mulholland.[114]

Many businesses, both new and old, existed outside the rules of the Living Constitution and the Trades Meeting movement because they were

NAUVOO TANNERY.

NOTICE—The Tanners and Shoemakers association, will pay in goods or Boots and Shoes, from four to five cents for calf-skins, and from three to four cents for hides, delivered at their tannery, situate on Hibbard and Rich streets, near Colton's brick yard, or at the Queens city store; we will also tan on shares. We also want a large quantity of White and Black Oak bark and Sumach, for which we will pay the highest Nauvoo prices.

G. W. ROSECRANS,

April 1-48-3m   Superintendent.

NOTICE TO THE LADIES.

There will be a meeting of the female association for the manufacturing of straw bonnets, hats, and straw trimmings at the Concert Hall on Saturday 31st inst. at 10 o'clock, A. M. The ladies in the branches abroad wishing to form a similar association are requested to be represented by their delegates.

NANCY H. ROCKWOOD, Prest.

Esther Huse, Secretary.

THE NAUVOO LEATHER, HARNESS, BOOT, AND SHOE MANUFACTORY.

The Tanners, Shoemakers, and Harnessmakers of Nauvoo, the City of Joseph:

HAVING associated themselves together under the above name and title, are prepared to enter extensively into all the above branches, and as the Association is composed of some of the best practical workmen, from the Eastern Cities and from Europe, who have had long experience in large Establishments; they are prepared to do work in their line, as neat, permanent, and fashionable, and also as reasonable as it can be done in any of the Western cities

Having purchased an extensive Tannery, they are prepared to tan any amount of hides and skins, and to suit the convenience of farmers they will tan on shares.

We are also prepared to make saddles, harness, boots and shoes, of every description, and on the shortest notice. We hope to merit the support and confidence of the Merchants and dealers in hides and leather, and wish to purchase all the hides &c., as we believe in home manufacture and also all the leather, so that our Mechanics may be employed in preference to those who have no interest in the prosperity of our city.

Boot, Shoe Saddle and Harness Shop, on Mulholland Street, in a building formerly occupied by Brim, as a saddle and shoe shop, three blocks east of the Temple. Samuel Mulliner, Superintendent.

The Tannery on Hibbard and Rich Street, near Colton's Brick Yard. George W. Rosecrans, Superintendent.

April, 23, 1845—51-3m.

Those who tanned leather and those who fashioned it into saddles, harnesses, boots, and shoes joined forces in a common association. They advertised for calfskins (top left) and explained their businesses to Nauvoo buyers (right). Lending their support to the home industry movement, women organized to make straw bonnets, hats, and trimmings (bottom left).

owned by individuals. These single proprietorships joined in the spirit of home manufacture by offering locally made products to residents.[115] The emphasis on home industry did not keep the import merchants from selling goods made elsewhere. When A. A. Lathrop opened his Key Stone Store on Mulholland Street, he appealed to Latter-day Saint buyers with the explanation, "Being a Mormon, he goes on the principle: our interest; our cause, and Nauvoo for ever."[116]

Many of the trades associations sold directly to the public from their shops. Others sought retail outlets. In December, the weavers urged the Trades Meeting to create a commission store where they could place their cloth for sale.[117] Three months later, the Living Constitution directed Samuel Gulley to establish just such an outlet. He did so as an affiliate of the newly organized Mercantile and Mechanical Association. Gulley quickly began to attract locally produced goods.[118] In late February, Abel Lamb sensed a growing need and opened a second, independent commission store on Mulholland Street.[119]

All of the new manufacturing companies operated in an economy based largely upon the exchange of goods. They recognized that the supply of cash was limited. For instance, when the Tailors' Association of Nauvoo advertised their prices, they agreed to "work for wheat."[120] As the new companies multiplied, church leaders encouraged residents to purchase the goods being produced, including pottery and rifles. The *Nauvoo Neighbor* advised buyers to let their imported shoes "go to Buncombe; the laborer is worthy of his *bread and meat,* and every good man will see that they have it."[121]

Women and children were likewise engaged in home industries. At a meeting of Aaronic Priesthood members in January 1845, Bishop Newel K. Whitney recommended that ward bishops establish "the manufacturing of palm leaf and straw hats, willow baskets and other business that children are capable of learning, that they may be raised to industrious habits." Two merchants had recently exhibited examples of willow baskets and worsted girting made in Nauvoo. It was evidence that local manufacturing had begun.[122] In March, Charles C. Rich and Hosea Stout organized the women at Evans Ward, about six miles south of Nauvoo, as "an Association according to their several occupations for the purpose of promoting the cause of home industry and manufacturing the necessary articles for their own use without being dependent on the stores for all that we need." The proposition received unanimous support. Three women from each occupation were appointed to supervise the business for their group.[123] Within weeks, the women of Nauvoo organized a Straw Manufactory to produce straw bonnets and hats. In the spirit of home industry, President Nancy H. Rockwood said, "The association agree to wear home manufacture, and to supply the place of ribbons by decorating their bonnets with straw trimmings." This pledge supported Heber C. Kimball's earnest call for "manufacturing our own materials and making our clothes."[124]

An important part of Nauvoo's effort to industrialize was the proposal to create a wing dam in the Mississippi to furnish better water power for factories and to improve access to the city's wharfs. Riverboats during the summer and fall depended upon portage service around the Des Moines Rapids, an expensive and risky detour. This series of five rapids along the eleven-mile stretch between Keokuk and Montrose consisted of miniature ridges of rock stretching across the river, invisible under the smooth, swift-flowing but unbroken sheet of water. The river stretched forty-five hundred feet between banks but had a mean depth of only two and one-half feet. Nauvoo's boosters proposed a dam that would bury the rapids under deeper water. A diversion dam on the Nauvoo side of the river would leave open the deeper steamboat channel on the Iowa side and create both a huge harbor and a head of water sufficient to power numerous mills.[125]

Promoters downstream from Nauvoo likewise recognized the benefits of tempering the effect of the rapids. In 1841, they attempted to build a wing dam at Montebello, midway between Warsaw and Nauvoo, but when high water washed out their beginnings, they abandoned the project. Two years later, a newcomer to Hancock County encouraged Eastern entrepreneurs to develop the water power at Warsaw, Nauvoo's chief economic competitor. The river fell twenty-five feet in twelve miles above Warsaw, and six feet in the last half mile of the rapids. He claimed that if it were harnessed, the river could supply power "for forty Lowells or one hundred Rochesters."[126]

Promoters in Nauvoo first considered the idea of a diversion dam in January 1841. Mayor John C. Bennett proposed a wing dam north of Nauvoo and a canal down Main Street, but it was judged impractical for the new city to attempt. In December 1843, with Nauvoo's population topping eight thousand, the city council authorized Mayor Joseph Smith to build a dam "from the lower line of the city [westward] to the island opposite Montrose, and from thence to the sand-bar above in the Mississippi."[127] The design promised "one of the best harbors on the Mississippi river . . . [and] the best mill privileges in the western country." Under contract with the mayor, Robert Campbell drew ten sets of construction plans based on findings by city surveyor Alanson Ripley and delivered them the following April.[128]

The greatest challenge to the project was the lack of funds. Joseph Smith estimated costs at a quarter of a million dollars. Because it was English immigrants who most needed jobs, the Twelve invited their agent in Liverpool to seek capitalists with seven thousand dollars to invest in the dam and a cotton or woolen factory, but the disruptions of politics and assassinations soon delayed the project.[129]

Nauvoo promoters who in December 1844 revived the proposal to build a dam faced their own hurdles. They needed government permission, an institutional sponsor or corporate organization, and sufficient funding. Because the dam would intrude into a major river, the committee appealed to Congress for a federal permit, but that request died in a congressional committee in February. Without waiting, they moved ahead under the authorization of local authorities.[130] The first hurdle was to gain rights from two previous grantees. The city council in April 1842 had given Newel Knight exclusive rights to build a wing dam to protect his water-powered gristmill from low water. The rights granted in December 1843 to "Joseph Smith and his successors for the term of perpetual succession" had been extensive and apparently ignored Knight's permit.[131] Upon the advice of John Taylor, promoters brought Knight into their committee as a partner, and the city council repealed Joseph Smith's charter.[132]

Sponsors of the dam had first presented their ideas to the Trades Meeting in early December, along with the plans designed for Joseph Smith. They believed the dam could create a head of water to power as many as ten mills. The Trades Meeting agreed to guide the project and appointed committees to fund and build it.[133] Sponsors planned to build fifty-three stone piers, connect them with timbers, and build a timber road atop them. The dam would extend eighty rods, or one-quarter mile, from the riverbank to the lower end of an island in the river. By mid-February, 1845, the committee had secured forty rods of riverfront property along the entire length of Davison Hibbard's farm.[134]

As promoters prepared to incorporate, Taylor invited them to consult with the Twelve, the temple committee, surveyors, and church trustee Newel K. Whitney.[135] Church trustees proposed that ownership of the dam be vested in them and leased to the Nauvoo Agricultural and Manufacturing Association for a 10 percent share of the income. The rest of the profit would go to association shareholders.[136]

Alanson Ripley was assigned to sell the project to investors. Between each of the fifty-three piers was space for a flume to propel a waterwheel for machinery. The piers could be built for $7,500, Ripley said, with the

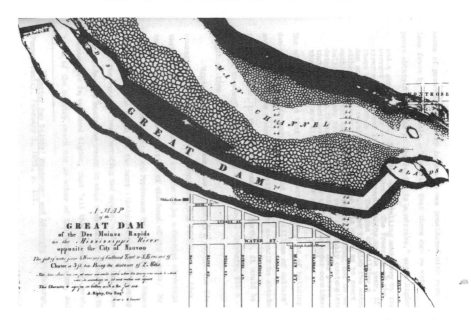

Promoters of Nauvoo's industrial potential first conceived of a canal running from north to south along Main Street. When the underlying sandstone shelf proved that idea impracticable, they decided to build a wing dam to harness the water power for industrial machines and to create a better harbor.

flumes and bridge costing another $7,500. Three hundred shares at $50 each would fund the project. Operating costs would be significantly less than a local steam engine. Ripley estimated eventual profits at more than $175 per year for each shareholder. He expected to see a cotton mill, two gristmills, a sawmill, a paper mill, and a carding machine. Sponsors proposed to church leaders that "citizens be invited to subscribe twelve thousand days work, which it was estimated would put a sufficient dam in the Mississippi to propel machinery."[137]

During the last week of February 1845, investors organized the Nauvoo Water Power Company with stock at fifty dollars a share. Company president John E. Page represented his twelve-member board in dedicating a site for the dam while a hundred citizens of Nauvoo looked on. Brigham Young said a few words and then organized workers as teams to quarry limestone.[138] A site one mile below Nauvoo soon yielded stone. A crew headed upriver to the Wisconsin pinery for lumber for the piers.[139] The project attracted the attention of the whole community, and the promoters encouraged a spirit of industry:

Like bees in a hive,
By labor we live,
By union we thrive,
By friendship we give.[140]

Despite this energetic beginning, in another two weeks the arrival of spring prompted a postponement of the project "till next winter." Workmen were needed on the Nauvoo Temple. More than one hundred workmen and thirty ox teams shifted their efforts from the riverbanks to the bluffs above Nauvoo. Officers in the power company agreed to the arrangement. Beginning in April, they offered riverfront lots for sale at bargain prices.[141] Construction of a dam would await another time and another location—closer to Warsaw.[142]

During its last full year, Mormon Nauvoo also experienced an important agricultural boom. As if anticipating the need the Saints would have for foodstuffs in 1846, the Twelve encouraged a massive gardening project. One objective of the April conference in 1845 was to "cultivate the earth both in the city and out."[143] In their own lots, the Saints enjoyed an abundant harvest of fruits and vegetables.[144] In addition, a community effort in what was called the Big Field east of Nauvoo expanded production significantly. By midsummer 1845, Brigham Young reported expectations for the fall harvest:

> Nauvoo, or, more properly, the "City of Joseph," looks like a paradise. All the lots and land, which have heretofore been vacant and unoccupied, were enclosed in the spring, and planted with grain and vegetables, which makes it look more like a garden of gardens than a city; and the season has been so favorable, the prospect is, there will be enough raised within the limits of the corporation to supply the inhabitants with corn, potatoes, and other vegetables. Hundreds of acres of prairie land have also been enclosed, and are now under good cultivation, blooming with corn, wheat, potatoes, and other necessaries of life.[145]

A NEW SOCIETY OF SAINTS

During his lifetime, Joseph Smith defined by revelation the basic shape of church organization and set it into place. Because the Prophet's energies were focused on translating and teaching, he delegated much responsibility to his colleagues in the presiding quorums—the First Presidency, the stake high councils, and the Twelve. In August 1844, administrative matters took on a new importance. First, the Twelve appointed bishops Newel K. Whitney and George Miller to serve as trustees of the church to give themselves time to focus on spiritual matters. Next, they assigned Wilford Woodruff to move his family to England and preside over the church members in the British Isles and Europe. Then, applying to the church in North America what they had learned in England, the Twelve further defined geographical administration. Brigham Young, Heber C. Kimball, and Willard Richards divided North America into districts and appointed a high priest over each. This trio of apostles managed both the general business of the church and also American affairs as a presidency over the continent. The Twelve entrusted to Parley P. Pratt the branches in the Eastern states and the regulation of church immigration through New York. Reuben McBride was given the presidency over all church affairs "in Kirtland—both spiritually and temporally."[146]

The Twelve wanted to regulate more closely the American branches. In the past, the district presidents convened quarterly and annual conferences to hear reports from the branches and to regulate ordinations. Now, they would be asked to bring greater order to the spiritual lives of individuals—members and missionaries alike. The Twelve concluded:

> This will save the trouble and confusion of the running to and fro of elders, detect false doctrine and false teachers, and make every elder abroad accountable to the conference in which he may happen to labor. Bishops also will be appointed in the larger branches, to attend to the management of the temporal funds, such as tithings and funds for the poor, according to the revelations of God and to be judges in Israel.[147]

Accountability was the key. Without a formal organization, the elders might be found "running to and fro," preaching all manner of doctrine, collecting funds for various church needs with or without specific authority, and reporting to no one their labors of preaching and raising up branches of the church. To the Twelve had been given responsibility for bearing off the kingdom in all the world, and they would do so in an orderly manner, just as they had done in Great Britain. The pattern of districts and conferences already existing in America would be reemphasized. The Twelve saw this system of governance as preparing the way for new stakes of Zion and an eventual millennial government.[148]

At the October conference in 1844, the Twelve used the boundaries of United States congressional districts to define eighty-five ecclesiastical districts. During and soon after the conference, the Twelve ordained forty new high priests. Then, from the expanded quorum, they assigned eighty-five men, whom they had selected two months earlier, to preside over members in these districts. In this dramatic organizational effort, the Twelve instructed the new leaders to move their families to their assigned areas, to raise up stakes, and to oversee the work of local branches. The district presidents were invited to visit Nauvoo when the temple was finished, receive their endowments, and then return to their homes and preside in full priesthood authority in their region.[149]

Brigham Young spoke openly of this comprehensive expansion plan for establishing the kingdom of God on the earth. Each worthy high priest would govern a portion of that peaceful kingdom as endowed leaders spread out over the continent. "Nauvoo will not hold all the people that will come into the kingdom," Brigham Young said.[150] Just four months earlier, Joseph Smith had challenged the church to establish just such regional gathering places in all of the Americas.[151] By accepting their assignments, the group of new high priests demonstrated loyalty to Joseph and to the Twelve, who held "the keys of the priesthood [to] go and build up the kingdom in all the world."[152]

Because unanimity in doctrine and practice was one of their concerns, the Twelve deliberated further about publications sponsored by and for the church. A New Year's Day message in 1845 conveyed their "great anxiety for the unity and prosperity of the whole church" with an endorsement of the *Times and Seasons,* the religious and historical biweekly publication, and the *Nauvoo Neighbor,* a general news weekly. All church members should subscribe and should encourage others to read these papers, they said. Such an effort would spread "correct principles, sanctioned by the highest authorities in the church, and . . . win the good feelings of the community, while the affections, and zeal of the brethren, are harmonized, by the same doctrines, the same rules, and the same laudable purposes."[153] The Twelve certainly did not mean to exclude from support the *Millennial Star,* published under General Authority supervision at Liverpool to serve members in Great Britain. Brigham Young had already endorsed Orson Pratt's *Prophetic Almanac.*[154]

Parley P. Pratt, who was presiding in the Eastern states, advised the Twelve that the New York paper, the *Prophet,* was dying for lack of subscriptions. "The churches [in New York] are few in number," he wrote. "We decrease while you increase." Brigham Young advised editor Pratt and publisher Sam Brannan not to subsidize the *Prophet* with tithing funds. Survival would depend on subscription income, he said. The owners would need to justify the venture on business reasons alone. Pratt renamed the paper *The New York Messenger* in May 1845, and Brannan continued it for another six months.[155]

The Twelve expanded the work of preaching the restored gospel by increasing the number of quorums of the seventy. In June 1844, this missionary force involved only one quorum of seventy members. Shortly before the fall conference, the Twelve and senior seventies president Joseph Young selected seven presidents for each of ten new quorums. Sixty-three of these came from the first quorum.[156] By the close of the conference, the Twelve had filled eleven quorums completely and a twelfth partially. The presidents of the seventies ordained more than four hundred men during the conference week alone, selecting men under age thirty-five from the elders and Aaronic Priesthood. That expansion was just the beginning. Thirty-five groups were functioning by January 1846.

With this action, Brigham Young and the Twelve implemented the priesthood revelation of 1835 in new ways. To the initial quorum of seventy, with its seven presidents, they looked toward the revelatory commission calling for "other seventy, until seven times seventy, if the labor in the vineyard of necessity requires it." Each quorum had its own presidency of seven members, and the presidencies of the first nine quorums retained membership in the First Quorum. The presidents of all seventies quorums living in Nauvoo met regularly to receive instruction from the seven senior presidents, who took counsel from the Twelve. "The seventies will have to be subject to their presidents and council," Brigham Young said in his announcement of the orderly management system for the missionary quorums.[157]

The Twelve expected to involve themselves in missionary labors once again, regulating the church in the East and overseeing the traveling elders. Instead, church members in Nauvoo prevailed upon them to remain at home. Because of this, the Twelve dispatched the seventy.[158] Said Young:

> We do not want any man to go to preaching until he is sent. If an

elder wants to go to preaching, let him go into the seventies. You are all apostles to the nations, to carry the gospel; and when we send you to build up the kingdom, we will give you the keys, and power and authority. If the people will let us alone we will convert the world, and if they persecute us we will do it the quicker. I would ex[h]ort all who go from this place to do right and be an honor to the cause. Inasmuch as you will go forth and do right you shall have more of the spirit than you have heretofore.[159]

Once again Young insisted on order within the kingdom. The missionaries would go when sent, would go with proper authority, and would go worthily so that they could carry the spirit of God in their hearts. Quorum leaders echoed the theme. "If it is necessary in framing a large building that the carpenters should meet with the master workman to receive orders and instructions," one president observed, "so it is necessary for the members of this quorum to meet with their presidents." This was the way of the priesthood—to "be governed in all things by those at our head."[160]

Order and unity were closely associated principles for governing the church and for personal relationships. The frequent mention of unity in public preaching reinforced aspirations for attaining the spiritual and millennial objective of harmony in human relationships. In November, Brigham Young spoke for two hours on the topic, giving it a central place in the faith of the Saints.[161] Many church members could not remember having ever experienced such a spirit of unity within the church. Perhaps the apostasies surrounding the martyrdom had removed the most vocal dissidents. In quorum meetings, men regularly pledged fealty to their quorum presidents and to the Twelve. Seventies presidents often "requested the Brethren to arise and tell their feelings as regards the present organisation of the Church."[162] Leaders strengthened the feeling of common interests by encouraging "a spirit of love and union one toward another," by forgiving the repentant, and by excommunicating men unwilling to meet church standards of morality, sobriety, or loyalty.[163] George A. Smith reminded the seventies at the dedication of their hall that a unity of heart and mind would make earthlings like the angels. "Perfect union and harmony exist among them," he said. "Hence their concert of action, and consequently their influence and power with God; and upon the same principle . . . we could make a heaven wherever in the dispensation of providence we might be placed."[164]

Because the calling of the seventies was missionary service, the quorums encouraged their members to prepare to leave their families on proselytizing missions. In seeking brethren to fill four vacancies in the fifth quorum, the senior president stated "that he wanted men that was ready and willing to go at any time or any call without any excuse and would magnify their calling."[165]

The seventies were urged to study the scriptures and to hone their preaching skills in preparation for missionary service. When the presidents had no counsel of their own to share, they invited quorum members to take turns speaking. To share the opportunity to speak more widely, one group limited each participant to five minutes, which the clerk timed.[166] Most of the quorums structured the experience less formally, merely going around the room and giving each member an opportunity. The Fifth Quorum organized a separate lecturing school that met weekly for three hours on Tuesday evenings. Speakers were given twenty minutes each to expound on a designated gospel topic.[167] These subjects typically included the principles the seventies expected to teach as missionaries: faith, repentance, baptism, the gift of the Holy Ghost, the resurrection, prophecy, the Book of Mormon, priesthood, and the gathering of Israel.[168]

It was to provide a preparatory school where the prospective missionaries could stand before quorum members and practice preaching from the pulpit that the Seventies Hall was pushed to completion in December 1844. The hall served other purposes as well, but its primary function was for training missionaries. For regular meetings, the quorums most often met in other halls or in schoolrooms and homes. During good weather, they gathered at the meeting ground.[169] The high priests were impressed by the accomplishment of the seventies and approved plans in January 1845 for their own hall, a single-story structure almost as large as the main floor assembly room in the temple. Brigham Young immediately discouraged the project and won support for an alternate effort: "I proposed to the quorum to finish off the upper story of the Temple in which they could receive their washings and anointings and endowments instead of undertaking a building from the commencement."[170]

Priesthood quorums in Nauvoo were expected to qualify quorum members to attend the temple. The presidents of quorums certified the worthiness of quorum members to receive temple endowments.[171] The plan was for quorums to receive the ordinances as a quorum, with their wives. Nauvoo's seventies took seriously their spiritual preparations to enter the temple. In their weekly quorum meetings, they learned about the criteria for entering the House of the Lord. Sometimes the counsel was of a practical nature ("to improve all the land we could, that we might have grain enough for our own use"), sometimes procedural ("to keep our wives at home when we transact church business"); often it was spiritual ("the necessity of preparing themselves to receive their endowments").[172]

A common theme was unity—the need for a uniformity of thought and action. In the months following the August 1844 conference, quorum members regularly voiced to each other their willingness to sustain their new leaders. By backing the Twelve, they were evidencing a lack of sympathy for Sidney Rigdon, James J. Strang, and other claimants to power. They shared feelings of distrust about Strang and his writings; some had investigated and rejected Strang's claims; others found no attraction in even considering the option. In this spirit, one brother "referred to Strangism as being too low to stoop to, and it was unnecessary to say anything about it."[173]

A more important objective of the quiet campaign for unity pointed toward a spiritual harmony to prepare themselves for the temple ordinances. "Let us cultivate a spirit of love and union one toward another and inasmuch as any of the brethren have had feelings against [another] brother . . . let them die and be forever forgotten," President Jacob Gates advised the fourth quorum.[174]

The seventies quorums met as frequently as possible to strengthen a sense of brotherhood. They appointed teachers to visit in the homes of quorum members and encourage them in their duties.[175] One quorum sponsored a band concert.[176] During the harvest season, another group picked grapes and juiced them for a quorum social. The activity was held at the home of a quorum leader, with band music, sermons, singing, and refreshments, including fresh juice and apples.[177]

Seventies presidents helped quorum members prepare for the temple by reminding them of gospel standards. President Harrison Burgess told the second quorum, "We have been councilled this day to put watch over ourselves, and endeavour to become a righteous people: ceasing all our lightness, evil ways, and habits, that we may have the favor of God and

Brigham Young was admired and trusted for his caring attitude towards the people he led. His role as leader is acknowledged on the name-plate attached to this letter opener: "Pres. Brigham Young 1845." This handsome item with its bone handle may have been made by a Nauvoo craftsman as a gift.

have peace this winter . . . to labor in building a Temple."[178] Quorum presidents instructed their members on the need for "virtue, chastity and strict honesty, also the disadvantage of profane swearing and finally every evil practice." The seventies were counseled to stay away from grogshops, to pray in their families, and in other ways to "keep a straitforward course."[179] Amasa Lyman advised one group, "It is of much more consequence to attend to such principles as will save us, and not pry so much at the things which are certainly out of place."[180] To be worthy of temple blessings, the seventies learned, they must hallow their lives in patterns of Christian purity and uprightness.

This preparation made sense to the quorum members in the context of what they understood about the purpose of the temple ordinances and about their missionary assignment. The Lord had commanded the Saints to build a temple, Lyman reminded one group of seventies and their wives, so he could "confer power upon them, and they become the ministers of life and salvation to others." As missionaries, the men would go forth, preach, raise up stakes, and govern those stakes through revelation that would enable them "to act independent in the sphere of your office in the world." The temple experience would help them to "understand principles of life and salvation and . . . know just what to do" when they presided over large groups of members.[181]

Even as the Twelve revitalized the priesthood quorums, the Female Relief Society of Nauvoo was in decline. The women of the church's only auxiliary had helped the poor in Nauvoo through a constant effort. They had preached against immorality through the voice of their president, Emma Smith. After Joseph Smith's death, the poor still needed help, but the Relief Society ceased to exist after the widowing of its president. Others accepted responsibility for the poor and for encouraging moral living.

By definition, the poor included men without work and women and children without husbands and fathers. Epistles from church leaders emphasized the need to create industrial jobs to reduce poverty caused by unemployment. A prosperous Nauvoo, they taught, would have "no poor except the widow, the orphan, or the infirm, and these could be abundantly provided for."[182] For more than two years, the Relief Society had helped the bishops care for the poor. With the women's group no longer meeting, the task fell solely on the priesthood leaders. Help for the needy came in part from the Thursday Fast Meeting. Brigham Young advised the Saints to deliver to their bishops the food they would otherwise have eaten. Don't forget "a few little comforts for them," he counseled, "among them a little ginger." This delicacy comforted the aged, who could make ginger tea. It interested the young, who enjoyed candied ginger as a sweet treat. In branches outside Nauvoo, presiding elders saw to the needs of the poor and the sick. At St. Louis, for instance, the city was divided into districts so that priests and teachers could more effectively care for needy church members.[183]

As president of the Relief Society, Emma Smith had discouraged participation in plural marriage. Those closest to her during the months after the Prophet's death heard her resist the leadership of the Twelve because of their willingness to carry on Joseph's doctrine and sponsor further plural marriages. To some, Emma claimed that Joseph Smith had taught only that these marriages were for eternity and did not mean that a man would live with his plural wife and have children by her.[184]

With this difference in interpretation dividing Emma and the Twelve, it was not surprising that the Twelve took over the Relief Society's special assignment to encourage virtue. The apostles broadened the discourse. "We must not only be industrious and honest, in providing abundantly for our temporal wants" and in caring for the poor, Young wrote on behalf of the Twelve in an October 1844 epistle. "But we must abstain from all intemperance, immorality and vice of whatever name or nature; we must set an example of virtue, modesty, temperance, continency, cleanliness, and charity. And be careful not to mingle in the vain amusements and sins of the world."[185]

This time of new beginnings in church leadership saw a reversal of the trend to mingle in public amusements. The Saints also heard admonitions to strengthen adherence to the Word of Wisdom. In social life, the Twelve had decided, the Saints who had gathered out of Babylon needed to leave behind some of the pleasures of the world, especially balls and dances, immodest theatricals, and magic shows. Young said that dances had been tolerated "for the sake of peace and good will. But it is not now a time for dancing or frolics but a time of mourning, and of humiliation and prayer." This retrenchment discouraged "all amusements in which saints and sinners are mingled." Such gatherings, he said, tended to corrupt the religious society of the Latter-day Saints and should be avoided. Young also urged the suppression of grogshops, gambling houses, and other houses or proceedings of disorder.[186]

What was allowed? The epistle endorsed "amusements which are at once both innocent, instructive, and entertaining. . . . Such for instance, as musical concerts, philosophical and astronomical exhibitions." These would be sufficient, Young said, along with regular religious meetings, "to exercise all our powers of enjoyment."[187]

The *Times and Seasons* hinted at two other things seen by many as inappropriate for a Latter-day Saint. Both notions reflected a rural society's distrust of certain professions. Both reinforced attitudes common among Nauvoo's people. An editorial titled "The Saints Make Nauvoo" said that good Christians should not take their grievances against one another to court and that they should depend upon the priesthood rather than doctors when ill. Nauvoo's two lawyers found little work among the Saints, the editor noted, and only one doctor kept busy "in his profession, and that is surgery." Attorney Almon W. Babbitt, a regular advertiser in the *Nauvoo Neighbor* who rented an upstairs office in the Red Brick Store, penned a friendly reply. Popular novels had created the negative view of lawyers, Babbitt said. Most lawyers were honest, and legal help was a necessity in a nation of laws. Lawyers may not be needed, he predicted, "in the kingdom of God, where men will be governed by His spirit and endure all patiently for sake of salvation."[188]

Whether dealing with benevolence, virtue, amusements, or the law and medicine, counsel from church leaders on such matters during the interlude between the martyrdom and the removal helped create a positive social atmosphere among members willing to listen to them. The Saints felt united and at peace. John Taylor summarized those feelings in a typically upbeat editorial: "Upon the whole, the union, perseverance, and love which pervades the bosoms of the saints, actually astonishes the world, and causes peace to reign in our midst; for which blessing we praise our Father in heaven."[189]

But during the relaxed months of the peaceful interlude, the Saints in Hancock County did not slacken their vigilance. Mosiah L. Hancock remembered his own last year in Nauvoo as a member of a junior militia. Known as the Sons of Helaman, the group drilled with real guns under the direction of a Brother Bailey, their captain. Hancock, eleven years old, served as a second lieutenant in the group, also known as the Prophet's Guard. Parley P. Pratt described the Sons of Helaman during a Nauvoo Legion parade for the governor in the fall of 1844 as a group of boys in full uniform, bringing up the rear with their banner sporting the motto "Our Fathers Will Protect Us." One of the boys, William Bryan Pace, remembered carrying wooden guns. All boys over age eight enrolled, he recalled. They were dressed in white pants, a blouse or sailor shirt, and a palm hat. And these, he said, were the boys who carried whittling knives and scabbards and went around Nauvoo whistling and whittling on sticks to warn ne'er-do-wells out of town.[190] They did not attack these people but wanted to let them know they were being watched. The roving guards jokingly referred to their targets—suspicious non-Mormon visitors and even some disaffiliated Mormon leaders or former Nauvoo residents—as "black ducks."[191]

Some references from the times mention "full grown boys" as members of the whittling crews. At the April conference in 1845, a group of nearly twenty young men approached a visiting Warsaw newspaper reporter, former state assemblyman Dr. John F. Charles, and under instructions from police chief Hosea Stout "invited him to leave." "He pretended to be our friend," Stout noted, "but in reality he was a secret enemy lurking in our midst." According to Charles, the boys carried bowie knives, dirks, and whittling sticks. They whistled in concert and cried out "Carthage" and "Warsaw" to hurry the journalist's departure. When Charles complained, Brigham Young provided sanctuary via an escort to the Mansion House.[192]

Without the protection of normal police operations under a city charter, the Sons of Helaman offered the citizens of Nauvoo informal, nonviolent protection against thieves, counterfeiters, and other undersirable characters. The objective, said the *Nauvoo Neighbor*, was to rid the community of disreputable persons "so every man minds his own business." Some citizens looked at the activity with a smile. "It is true the boys get a little saucy now and then," Dwight Webster admitted, "but if a complaint is made about the boys the answer is our charter is gone now, 'We know your cause is just but we can do nothing for you.'" The *Neighbor* good-naturedly defended the action as a replacement for "the writ of 'habeas corpus,' or even the display of the old Nauvoo Legion; it might be termed a precept of *Habeas Roustus*." "They did not molest them in any way," Wandle Mace remembered, "not even by talking to them but simply follow them, whittling and whistling as they went."[193]

Apparently the whittlers did their job too well. Men in Warsaw imitated a similar action against a Mormon trader in that city in late May. Church leaders halted Nauvoo's whittling in June. The menace from intruders had not been corrected, according to Heber C. Kimball. "When we sleep let us sleep with one leg out of bed, and one eye open," he told a Sunday congregation. "Let us beware of those fellows, that do not like us very well. At this time a few of them do not like to dwell in our midst; they are afraid of the boys. Well, we will have no more whittling at present; let the boys go to school and attend to their own business."[194]

For many others besides Elder Kimball, the reign of peace and unity in Nauvoo during the year following the murders at Carthage seemed tenuous. The steady efforts of the whittling and whistling boys reminded the Saints of past troubles and of ever present enemies. The residents of Nauvoo lost their prized charter not long after bidding a sorrowful farewell to "two of the greatest and best men who ever graced our planet."[195] The ghost of past glories failed to satisfy. Yes, the church was orderly and work pushed forward on the temple, a monument to Joseph Smith's religious mission. But the exoneration in 1845 of the murderers of the Prophet and the Patriarch seemed to many Latter-day Saints to be another in an unending series of injustices that would await resolution only in the Lord's time.[196] Nor at that time of civil confusion could they forget Brother Joseph's comments on government's failure to protect their civil rights.[197] For many, the Prophet's death and the repeal of the Nauvoo

charter wrenched their hope that America would someday honor constitutional rights for the Saints.[198]

In this vein, Eliza R. Snow offered a poetic recital of the sufferings
witnessed over many years by her mother-in-law, Lucy Mack Smith:

The standard of our country, she has seen
Rising in glorious majesty, and wave
Its fam'd unrival'd banner gracefully,
Till other hands than those that rear'd it, sapp'd
Its broad foundation, and its ensign marr'd—
Tott'ring and tremulous it now appears
Ready to fall and in its fall to make
The most tremendous crash the civil world
Has ever known![199]

Zion's poetess captured the feelings of many of her fellow Saints that
in the death of Joseph Smith, America had lost its last chance to be
redeemed by the elders carrying the restored gospel. Perhaps the millennial end to all governments was nigh.[200] The peaceful interlude in the City
of Peace allowed precious little time to finish the temple. The Saints would
save themselves and await God's judgment on the nations. "The continued abuses, persecutions, murders, and robberies practiced upon us, . . . in
a (Christian) republic, and land of liberty," John Taylor said, "have
brought us to the solemn conclusion that our exit from the United States
is the only alternative by which we can enjoy our share of the elements
which our heavenly Father created free for all." Other Latter-day Saints
agreed with Taylor that it was better to leave, "suffering wrong rather than
do wrong."[201] With Eliza Snow Smith, they were psychologically and spiritually prepared to turn their backs on the nation that had denied them
refuge and flee into the wilderness.

CHAPTER 17

A Solution to the Mormon Question

The Lord once said he would make Kirtland a stronghold for a time; and he has done it. He said in Missouri he would sustain the saints for a time; and he did it. And when we came here, the Lord said, that if the people of the state of Illinois would maintain us in our rights they would be blessed; if not we might find it to our advantage to leave them.

—AMASA M. LYMAN, OCTOBER 7, 1845

The repeal of Nauvoo's city charter in January 1845 marked the beginning of the end for Nauvoo as a Latter-day Saint stronghold. Governor Ford's initial supposition that a year of peaceful coexistence would heal old wounds and allow rechartering was a hopeful but unrealistic assumption. The governor modified his position in an April letter to Latter-day Saint leaders. Along with issues of governance, Brigham Young had asked Ford for his thoughts on what had come to be known as the Great Western Measure, a plan calling for the establishment of a homeland for the Saints in an area unoccupied by anyone else. Ford liked the idea. Joseph Smith had confided in him during the early summer of 1844 just such a plan, Ford said. (And some others knew that the Prophet had considered the Rocky Mountains as a personal refuge just before his murder.) The governor suggested that if Congress would not grant land in some unsettled territory within the United States, the Saints could establish an independent government in Mexican California. This would require secrecy, Ford intimated, because if the United States government

knew about the movement of a large body of people into a foreign territory, it would be obligated to halt the "invasion." "But," he noted, "if
you once cross the line of the United States territories you would be in
no danger of being interfered with." Ford's confidential suggestion
revealed his own pessimism about any reconciliation between the secular and religious communities of Hancock County. The governor reduced
the issue to its core:

> Your religion is new and it surprises the people as any great novelty
> in religion generally does. They cannot rise above the prejudices
> excited by such novelty. However truly and sincerely your own
> people may believe in it, the impression on the public mind every-
> where is that your leading men are impostors and rogues and that
> the others are dupes and fools. This impression in the minds of the
> great mass is sufficient to warrant them in considering and treating
> you as enemies and outcasts. . . . If you can get off by yourselves you
> may enjoy peace; but surrounded by such neighbors I confess that I
> do not foresee the time when you will be permitted to enjoy quiet.[1]

Because Ford saw no other way to resolve the Mormon question, he
wrote to President James K. Polk with a suggestion. Ford believed that if
Polk ordered a military force to block the departure of the Saints, Brigham
Young would order an immediate evacuation. Polk rejected the proposal as
inappropriate no matter how unacceptable the new religion was to the
people of Illinois.

THE GREAT WESTERN MEASURE

Even though many friends suggested wholesale removal to a new place
of refuge, Joseph Smith had intended to retain Nauvoo for at least some of
the Saints while establishing other gathering places in a Zion that was to
include all of America. He had charged the Council of Fifty with investigating potential settlement places outside the United States—in the independent Republic of Texas, in Mexican upper California, and in the
British and American regions of the Oregon country. In addition, the
Prophet hoped to organize new stakes in major cities of the United States.
Joseph Smith's successors were obligated by revelation to complete the
temple first and administer its ordinances to others. This held them to
Nauvoo, despite a growing pessimism that government officials would or

could protect their rights. In late January 1845, Brigham Young confided in his journal, "I inquired of the Lord whether we should stay here and finish the temple. The answer was we should."[2]

One of Joseph Smith's last revelations was his April 1844 announcement authorizing new stakes in the United States. The Twelve set out to implement this plan. Two weeks after the October 1844 conference, Brigham Young, Heber C. Kimball, and Parley P. Pratt left Nauvoo unbeknownst to most of the Saints to organize one of those stakes. Located at Ottawa, southwest of Chicago, they named it Norway because of the area's large number of Norwegian Latter-day Saints. When he returned, Young announced to a seventies' meeting, "We have created another place which will be a stake and a place of gathering in a short time, and there will be a great many more Stakes; but this place [Nauvoo] will be the Head place for the people to come to, and receive their endowments."[3]

The Latter-day Saints made two attempts to protect their Hancock County enclave. Both only further antagonized their opponents. During the winter of 1844–45, they canvassed the northern towns for signatures on petitions supporting a relocation of the county seat from Carthage to Nauvoo. Anti-Mormons saw this move as evidence that the Saints wanted to control county government. The matter died when the legislature failed to act on the petition.[4] Soon after the Nauvoo charter was repealed, Brigham Young invited the Saints in the Eastern United States to sell their property, move to Nauvoo, and contribute money to the church to buy out the anti-Mormons in Hancock County. Orson Spencer sounded out state officials in Springfield, but they rejected this idea and "strenuously urged the necessity that the saints should cease to gather in one place."[5]

As these efforts illustrate, in early 1845 the Twelve had no immediate plans to abandon Nauvoo. They sought to retain it as a temple city, as Joseph Smith had intended. At the same time, the Twelve resolved to send out an exploring expedition to prepare the way for an expansion of Latter-day Saint settlements toward the Pacific. If needed long-term, a new western gathering place could provide refuge for the Twelve against legal and physical harassment—and for any other Latter-day Saints needing a place of safety. That need became more evident with the repeal of the city charter. Despite the resolve of the Twelve to carry out the design of their martyred leader, developments during 1845 forced adjustments.

At the April 1845 conference, Brigham Young halted missionary work in the United States. This action in effect postponed Joseph Smith's hope of establishing stakes in major cities. At the same time, the decision emphasized the need to complete the plans at home. "By martyring the Prophet and Patriarch, the Gentiles have rejected the gospel," Young said. "We have travelled and preached to them enough. If they want salvation, let them come to us. . . . Let the elders stay at home and finish the Temple and get their endowment; and also finish the Nauvoo House."[6]

Besides efforts within Illinois, Church leaders consulted political leaders elsewhere for advice. A letter drafted by John Taylor went out from Nauvoo in late April and early May 1845 to President James K. Polk and the governors of every state except Missouri and Illinois. The missive invited legislators to provide a political asylum for the Latter-day Saints. Church leaders were willing to accept an appropriate site within one of the states, in United States territories, or even "at some place remote therefrom."[7] The governors typically understood the remote option to be the politically attractive region of Oregon. None of them offered asylum in his own state, and many ignored the petition. A few submitted it for legislative review. The Connecticut legislature referred the message to a committee on foreign relations. Letters from several of the governors and from citizens in Massachusetts and New York recommended California. One Bostonian suggested the Bay of San Francisco.[8] Arkansas governor Thomas S. Drew endorsed a move to the Oregon Territory but suggested other options—Mexican California, north Texas, or Nebraska Territory—for, he said, with the expansionist mood in the country, "the way is now open to the Pacific without . . . hindrance." Drew further recommended that Brigham Young accept Abraham's advice to Lot—counsel that led their herdsmen to avoid strife by settling on separate lands.[9]

All of this counsel supporting a wholesale relocation of the Saints in the West affirmed to the Twelve the necessity of that action. For two years, they had actively discussed the Prophet's plans with him and had pledged to fulfill all of them, including the Great Western Measure. Even as they invited governors to offer places for refuge in the United States, they quietly planned for "some place remote therefrom." They considered possible destinations and routes, transportation needs, and questions of future governance.

On New Year's Day 1845, Hiram Kimball hosted six members of the Twelve and their wives for an afternoon and evening of eating and visiting.

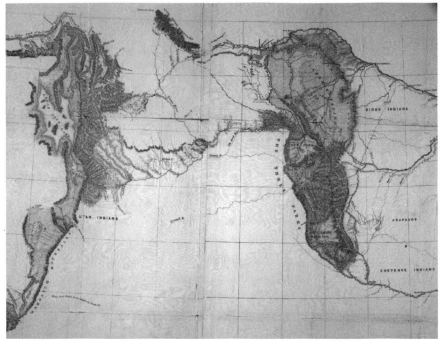

A Refuge in the Rockies. *Brigham Young and the Twelve studied the map from John C. Frémont's report of his 1842–44 expeditions to the Rockies, Oregon, and northern California. They paid special attention to the area (detail, above) from the Valley of the Great Salt Lake eastward to "The Three Parks" in what became Colorado.*

Among other topics, they discussed the propriety of establishing settlements for the Saints in uninhabited parts of the continent. A week later, the Twelve further considered sending an exploring company to the Mexican province of upper California.[10]

For years, church leaders had talked and read about the western and southwestern territories outside United States borders. Of special interest were the travels of government explorer John C. Frémont. Illinois senator Stephen A. Douglas had promised to mail to Nauvoo a copy of Frémont's latest report and new map of the West and apparently did so. Frémont's 1842 exploring expedition took him as far as the Wind River Mountains in modern Wyoming. His second expedition in 1843–44 along the Oregon Trail to the Pacific offered information of even greater value to the Twelve. The trip included a westbound reconnaissance around the north end of the Great Salt Lake and an eastbound excursion from southern California as far north as Utah Lake. The United States House of

Representatives sponsored a combined publication of the two documents in March 1845.[11]

Reports about the contested regions of Texas, California, and Oregon appeared regularly in the public press, including the newspapers read by Latter-day Saints. During 1843 and 1844, the *Nauvoo Neighbor* published more than a dozen articles on the West, giving highlights of Frémont's Wind River expedition, excerpts from the *Emigrants' Guide to Oregon and California* by Lansford W. Hastings, and a report of the California explorations of Charles Wilkes.[12] The pace increased during 1845, with additional reports from these three travelers, plus information on Colonel Stephen W. Kearny's trek to South Pass and general articles on the West. Extracts from Frémont's 1843–44 expedition published as early as January 1845 emphasized the Salt Lake region. Hastings shared his *Guide* with Sam Brannan during a promotional tour in New York, which led the *New York Messenger* to publish extensive extracts from it during the summer.[13]

The seriousness of the intentions of the Twelve in January 1845 is revealed by their attention to detail. After puzzling over how to transport a large expedition to California, they decided to recruit teams from branches of the church in and around Illinois. They wondered how they would organize a new state government once they found an uninhabited place of refuge. Through a notice in church publications, they invited missionaries to ask church members in the United States to help secure "the latest 'Revised Statutes' of each State and Territory" and to forward them to Nauvoo.[14]

To supplement the maps and travel reports available to them, the Twelve revived Joseph Smith's plan to seek firsthand information on the West. Brigham Young reorganized the Council of Fifty on February 4 for that purpose. Those who had left the church and the three men who were not Latter-day Saints were dropped from membership. Others were named in their place. As president of this special task group, Young renewed Joseph Smith's year-old assignment to organize an exploring expedition. During March and April, Young convened the council in a dozen working meetings to discuss the western mission, church construction projects, and city government.[15]

Initially, the Twelve considered asking Lewis Dana, an Oneida Indian convert, to lead a party of six men "to the west and especially to Texas." On the first of March, the Council of Fifty decided the party should include eight men to be sent westward toward the Pacific Ocean "to seek out a location and a home where the Saints can dwell in peace and health and where they can erect the ensign and standard of liberty." Along the way, they were to "proceed from tribe to tribe, to unite the Lamanites." Among the intended contacts was the Indian Council at Council Bluffs. The option of continuing on to the Pacific—on the route outlined by Orson Hyde a year earlier—was left to the best judgment of the men. The expedition planned to leave after the April conference.[16]

Few details are known of this private but successful mission. Dana left Nauvoo on April 24 accompanied by four other men on what had been called the Oregon Mission, the Western Mission, or a mission to the Indians. One of the explorers, Jonathan Dunham, died on July 28, two weeks' journey west of Nauvoo. His companions turned back sometime before the end of summer, having accomplished the primary focus of their mission. They had gained permission to establish settlements from relocated Indians living in the middle Missouri River region. Furthermore, they had found the Indians willing "to lend us any assistance they could or to go west with us to explore the country."[17]

To forestall government opposition, the Twelve kept confidential the precise regions being considered for new settlements. The Council of Fifty acknowledged the possibility of a settlement among the Native Americans of the middle Missouri River Valley, but by mid-March 1845, they were looking beyond the Rockies for a central gathering place. Church leaders had narrowed their options for what they would soon be calling a temporary way station. This main settlement would be a temple city in the northeastern portion of upper California. Immigrant agents and a few others would live in ports on the Pacific Coast. On April 11, John Taylor summarized this consensus in verses written and revised during a meeting of the Council of Fifty. The song identified upper California as a "land of life and liberty" for the Saints and their Native American friends, a place for the next temple, and a place of gathering.[18]

Persons close to the Twelve soon became aware of these discussions. In March, while Hosea Stout stood night guard at Brigham Young's house, the two men talked about plans for settling the Saints between the headwaters of the Arkansas and the headwaters of the Colorado of the West. On maps of the time, this area might have included the secluded valleys of the Central Rockies extending northward from modern Leadville, Colorado, or the region extending westward toward the Great Salt Lake.[19] On the eve of the departure of Dana's exploring party, James Monroe overheard the Twelve and others singing John Taylor's new song, whose words, "Upper California! O! that's the land for me," convinced Monroe "that it is the intention to go to that country when we remove from here."[20] It was clear to Nauvoo's leaders and to a few residents that the Saints would soon have another option beyond the temporary stronghold at Nauvoo—a new gathering place in the unsettled portions of Mexican upper California.

While centrally directed settlement plans were evolving during the year 1845, two others privy to leadership discussions moved ahead on their own. Apostle Lyman Wight wanted to establish the stake that the Prophet Joseph Smith had approved for Texas. But in April 1845, Brigham Young and others of the Twelve counseled delay in implementing this dispersionary mission until more important matters could be accomplished. While acknowledging that "all the saints feel spirited and determined to carry out the measures of our martyred Prophet," the Twelve saw no need to leave Nauvoo during a period of peace and prosperity. They counseled Wight to delay his westward journey. "If you go westward before you have received your endowments in the Temple," they said, "you will not prosper." Courier Samuel Bent carried the written counsel to the Wisconsin lumber camps and read it to Wight's entire company. Bent then privately explained to Wight the "proceedings and future calculations" of the Twelve.[21]

James Emmett, one of those who had volunteered in February 1844 to explore the mountain lands of Oregon and California, had already launched his western mission. Emmett remembered the vivid imagery of Joseph Smith's talk about preaching to the Indians and governing them as inspired priesthood leaders. A restless Kentuckian sometimes more ambitious than wise, Emmett had had enough of the Gentile society that had killed his beloved leader. He longed to see the children of Jacob restored to their promised birthright. Heber C. Kimball and George A. Smith labored in vain with Emmett in the fall of 1844 to convince him to halt his plans to launch a Lamanite mission settlement.[22]

Emmett set out to settle among the Sioux Indians of Nebraska in September 1844. He convinced around one hundred men, women, and children to follow him into the wilderness. Before Christmas, word reached Nauvoo of charges of stealing among the party. The Twelve sent John L. Butler to resolve the differences and remain among them. Because Emmett had earlier tried to recruit Butler, the messenger's help was accepted. Emmett's action to convert the Indians and take temple ordinances to them further displeased the Twelve. In late February 1845, they sent other delegates to dissuade Emmett or at least to turn back his followers. Amasa Lyman and Orson Spencer found the company at Fort Vermillion, 150 miles west of the Iowa River settlements and thirty miles beyond the mouth of the Big Sioux River. They were living on sparse rations, heavily armed, and ruled by Emmett with an iron hand. Most of Emmett's followers had consecrated their families and properties to his strict control under the belief that he was acting under the direction of the Twelve.[23] Even so, Lyman and Spencer expected that the followers would soon abandon the project, having been "honestly and sincerely deceived by [Emmett's] vain pretenses and misrepresentations."[24]

Brigham Young had no time for Emmett. "Living poor, being in the wilderness, etc., is nothing to me when I am called to endure it," he told a Sunday congregation in Nauvoo, "but people who run headlong into misery and bring upon themselves suffering, do not arrive at anything but darkness and despair. . . . We told James Emmett, if he went, he would get into trouble: this congregation can be led by a thread. Religion is one thing and fanaticism is another."[25]

When Emmett returned to Nauvoo in early August 1845, he pledged to abide counsel. Accompanied by advisers Henry G. Sherwood and John S. Fullmer as camp leaders, he returned to the campsite, a 325-mile trip on horseback across unsettled country to Council Bluffs and then upriver. The men arrived after a month's travel from Nauvoo. "Emmett's camp contained about one hundred souls and were in a better condition than we expected to find them," Fullmer later reported. "They were tolerably well provided with provisions but somewhat destitute of clothing."[26]

After hearing the message sent by the Twelve, most of Emmett's group were rebaptized in the river as a sign of commitment to the Twelve's counsel. The settlers were instructed to build cabins for protection during the winter. In the spring, they should either remain there or "proceed west [with others from Nauvoo] to some place then unknown."[27] After appointing Emmett as camp president, Fullmer and Sherwood returned to Nauvoo. The following spring, Emmett's chief assistant, John L. Butler, led Emmett's camp toward a rendezvous on the Missouri River with the westward-moving Nauvoo Saints.[28]

The Twelve opposed Emmett's unauthorized Indian mission in Nebraska Territory and the timing of Wight's proposed north Texas colony but moved ahead with their own plans for exploring and settling areas outside the organized states. The Council of Fifty had been adjourned sine die on May 10 when Brigham Young learned that the confidential talk of California was being spread outside the council.[29] During the summer, only the Twelve considered the matter, but word circulated privately among some residents of Nauvoo, and public comments raised other speculations. The *Neighbor* praised California and published two stanzas of Taylor's song. Orson Spencer informed Governor Ford in late May that within eighteen months "very many of our people would colonize distant parts." During a June 1 sermon at the stand, Heber C. Kimball signaled his willingness to abandon Nauvoo. Anxious to live in a place without a whittling brigade and "where a man will not be shook to pieces with the ague," he said, "I am bound to stay while they [the Twelve] stay, and when they go, I go." When the temple is finished, he added, "I am satisfied; I do not care if I go into the wilderness the next day. . . . Ten years will not more than pass away, before we will be . . . in a land of peace, where we can worship God without molestation. Let us go to work and build this house." Kimball was anxious that the missionaries not serve, as the Twelve had done, "for ten or twelve years, without an endowment; but we want when you go to the nations of the earth, you may have that blessing." When Thomas Sharp saw the song "Hurrah for California" in the *New York Messenger,* he concluded with satisfaction that the Saints were planning to leave Hancock County.[30]

Comments such as those by Kimball and Sharp served only to raise the level of concern in Nauvoo. The Twelve urged patience. Amasa Lyman told a group of seventies and their wives at an August feast meeting, "When we are called to go to California, we shall know how large to make our camp and so in all things. We shall know what to do just as fast as we want it. . . . So there is no need of being in a hurry." The immediate objective remained completion of the temple.[31]

In early September, Orson Spencer and Charles Shumway reported on their mission to Dana's exploring camp. Among other things, they reported that Cherokee Indians along the upper Missouri River would welcome

Latter-day Saint settlers among them and were willing to travel west with the Saints to explore the territory.[32] The missionaries' findings plus their visit to Emmett's camp and much research in published reports furnished helpful information about the route between Nauvoo and Council Bluffs. During his return trip from Emmett's camp, Fullmer heard rumors from other travelers "that the apostates are trying to get up an influence with the president of the United States to prevent the saints emigrating west-ward, and that they have written to the president informing him of the resolutions of the General Council [Council of Fifty] to move westward, and representing the Council guilty of treason."[33] This intimation could only have meant that word was spreading concerning the Twelve's deci-sion to settle in the Mexican territory of upper California. In that secluded place of refuge, they could establish a government operating under divine guidance. It would have a militia for self-defense. Civil officers would be sustained in public conferences and be subject to the counsel of the First Presidency. Both this system of government and its location raised con-cern among outside observers.[34]

Around this same time, the Twelve refined plans for the western expe-dition sketched out earlier in the year. On August 28, the Twelve decided to send three thousand armed men and their families to upper California in the spring of 1846 to establish a settlement in the neighborhood of Utah Lake. A few days later, the plan was changed. The apostles con-cluded "that they should go with the company to select a location and plant the standard" but travel without their families.[35] They sent specific information in private letters addressed to mission presidents outside the United States. They informed Wilford Woodruff, who presided in England, of their intent to establish immigration depots on the Pacific Coast within a year. More specifically, through Addison Pratt in Tahiti, they invited converts from the Pacific islands to immigrate to the Columbia River or to a planned settlement near the Gulf of Monterey or San Francisco, where agents would direct them to the larger Latter-day Saint settlements. "The [main] settlement will probably be in the neighborhood of Lake Tampanagos [Great Salt Lake] as that is represented as a most delightful district and no settlement near there," they wrote. Meanwhile, Parley P. Pratt informed his friend Isaac Rogers that the intent was to "maintain and build up Nauvoo, and settle other *places* too." The immigrant party would "stop near the Rocky Mountains about 800 miles nearer than the coast . . . and there make a stand until we are able to enlarge and to extend to the coast."[36]

Not until these plans were fully developed did the Twelve reconvene the Council of Fifty. On September 9, their first meeting in four months, the council accepted the assignment to organize the pioneer expedition. Brigham Young personally selected men from the council. They were allowed to recruit their own companies. Through this effort, many in Nauvoo learned of the Twelve's plans. The expedition was expected to scout out appropriate routes, locate viable settlement sites, and plant crops to establish a food supply for families and livestock. The Council of Fifty reduced the advance party by half and picked five men to find out what it would take to outfit fifteen hundred men for the trip.[37]

Citizens of Hancock County were unaware of these plans to establish other gathering places. Frustrated by the continued growth of the Latter-day Saints and their increased effort to complete the temple, they concluded that the Mormons were there to stay. On September 10, vigilantes began burning buildings and destroying crops in outlying settlements. Plans for the western mission swung into high gear. Discussions quickly shifted from considering a pioneer company followed by a selective, staged migration to planning for a total evacuation of the church from the region in the late spring of 1846. Brigham Young invited the harassed settlers to move to Nauvoo. "At a future day our course will be plain," he told leaders of Morley's Settlement. "Be calm and patient till all things are ready." Within a week, Young issued a printed declaration challenging Warsaw vigilante leader Levi Williams to halt the house burnings and allow the Saints to depart peacefully in the spring.[38]

As talk circulated in Nauvoo of a California destination for the Saints, local newspapers reinforced the idea. The *Neighbor* copied reports praising the climate and soil of California and anticipating that region's annexation to the United States as a territory.[39] The Nauvoo weekly acknowledged that friends were encouraging the Saints to migrate beyond the Rocky Mountains to upper California. Rumors of a third Frémont expedition prompted the *Neighbor* to observe: "We hope he will do something to hasten the *great western measure*." The writer concluded with two stanzas from the new migration song:

> *The upper California,*
> *O that's the place to be;*

It lies between the mountains,
And the great Pacific sea.

With a climate pure as Naples,
And budding liberty,
O clear away the rubbish,
And let us there be free.[40]

In mid-June, the *Warsaw Signal* had reported that a bloodless revolution of the settlers had established a free Republic of California.[41] The report was premature, but within a year Americans in California would declare their independence, and President Polk would use a military skirmish along the contested west Texas border to justify a declaration of war against Mexico. By then, exiles from Nauvoo would be on their way toward a territory soon to become part of the United States and a new homeland for the Saints.

ISSUES AND IMAGES

The centrifugal forces working on Nauvoo came from many quarters. Some were friendly invitations encouraging resettlement; others were hostile propaganda messages seeking to consolidate support for expulsion. The Saints had friends in Illinois who concurred in the growing consensus for removal. Though pained by the public diatribes against Nauvoo, these tolerant old citizens saw no end to the debate as long as Nauvoo remained an important Latter-day Saint gathering place. They concluded that the tension between the opposing groups could not be resolved. Even neutral Illinois residents had accepted many of the charges laid by the church's enemies and believed them to be real. Public opinion favored the opposition call for removal.

One friend of the Saints, William P. Richards, an attorney in Macomb, Illinois, urged Nauvoo's leaders to petition Congress for a land grant twenty-four miles square in the Wisconsin pineries or some other unorganized territory. The self-governing "Mormon Reserve" he suggested resembled the Indian reservations being established for displaced Native Americans, who, like the Saints, had been "removed" from their habitations. It echoed as well the image of the religious republics of Roger Williams and William Penn. Bishop George Miller told Richards that to meet Mormon needs the enclave should measure two hundred miles on each side in the region just west of the state of Missouri or enclose about eighty miles square in Wisconsin, Texas, or Oregon.[42]

Those most ardently promoting removal enlisted allies from both political parties to create the impression of a widely supported, nonpartisan campaign. The leaders of the movement collected information from former Latter-day Saints working against the success of the church at Nauvoo.[43] Feeding the anti-Mormon frenzy was the journalistic burr under Mormonism's saddle, Warsaw editor Thomas C. Sharp. During 1845, he continued his familiar litany of complaints over alleged Latter-day Saint theft and dupery and revisited control of county politics. Somewhat facetiously, Sharp supported the Twelve's willingness to seek an asylum away from Nauvoo. He wished them "a prosperous journey" and hoped that "the land where they settle may flow with milk and honey and be fanned by heaven's choicest breezes, so that they may never have any desire to return to their present Zion."[44]

The Twelve responded directly to Sharp's usually sarcastic and always focused attacks. They spoke through the Nauvoo press and sent emissaries into surrounding counties to disabuse their fellow citizens of the hostile journalistic claims.[45]

The *Warsaw Signal* was not alone in its biased reporting. In April 1845, the *New York Tribune* published a lengthy report mixing factual information with the familiar charges of fanaticism, despotism, and militarism in Nauvoo.[46] Closer to home and under the influence of prominent anti-Mormons, the *Quincy Whig* adopted a more critical editorial stance and began reporting "anti-social behavior" on grounds that the Latter-day Saints had misused their charter.[47]

Among Nauvoo's political friends was the Hancock County sheriff, Miner R. Deming. A leader of the Carthage militia, Deming had denounced the violence of June 1844 and thus lost the support of both his troops and many fellow citizens.[48] Nauvoo's leaders respected Deming for his evenhandedness. He won their support for reelection in August 1845. When Deming died unexpectedly of congestive fever in early September, Jacob Backenstos succeeded him as sheriff. The task of defending law-abiding citizens against vigilantes was left to Backenstos, another law-and-order friend of Nauvoo.[49]

Many of the opposition arguments distorted the religious beliefs of the Saints. Other attacks misconstrued their disappointment with

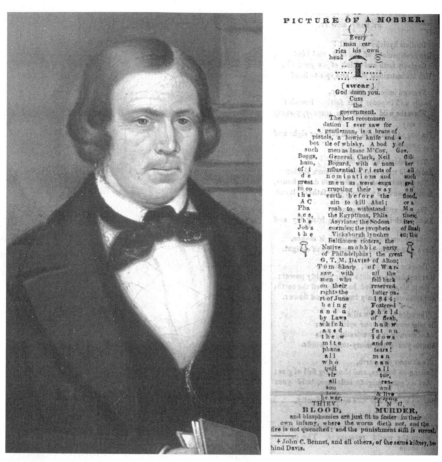

Confident in his role as peacemaker, Brigham Young governed with a steady hand after Joseph Smith's death and during the renewal of vigilante action a year later. The "Picture of a Mobber," a caricature created for the Nauvoo Neighbor, *defines Nauvoo's opponents as swearing, thieving murderers.*

government officials unwilling to help them gain compensation for property lost in Missouri. Some anti-Mormon journalists argued that Latter-day Saint doctrine was inconsistent with a republican form of government. The "spirit, designs, and tendency of Mormonism," one writer noted, includes a belief in a government of God, total obedience to leaders, political union, temporal union, and a millennial triumph— all threats to democratic diversity.[50]

One intriguing religious topic for the press was that of plural marriage. Very few Latter-day Saints participated in this form of marriage, nor was the doctrine taught publicly. The Twelve honored Joseph Smith's counsel that it was not yet the time nor the place to involve the entire church nor to acknowledge the private sealings. Those who knew of the marriage practice and many who did not offered denials or explanations. Paradoxically, many non-Mormons accepted newspaper reports that the Saints practiced "spiritual wifery," while some church members who did not understand the difference between the revealed doctrine and its profane counterfeit understandably believed the reports to be untrue.[51]

Much of the information disclosing the practice of plural marriage in Nauvoo originated in the East with Sidney Rigdon and his followers.[52] His missionaries in New York City urged the Saints to accept Rigdon as a purifier of the church. Joseph Smith, they said, had introduced abominations into the church under the influence of the Twelve.[53] Parley P. Pratt publicly pronounced these charges false. His rebuttal of the "spiritual wifery" counterfeit left open the possibility of an authorized plurality of wives.[54]

Apostle William Smith was one of those involved in encouraging unauthorized plural marriages in the East. After returning to Nauvoo at the request of the president of his quorum, he delivered in August 1845 what one contemporary termed "a singular discourse." Claiming that plural marriage was taught and practiced privately in Nauvoo and that he was not ashamed of it, Smith invited the Twelve to make the whole matter public. The Twelve rejected the proposal. With few exceptions, Nauvoo's church leaders in 1845 did not repudiate the talk of plural marriage. They mostly stood aside while others spoke out. But this time, John Taylor stepped forward and rebutted Smith's presentation, causing, according to a contemporary report, "considerable feelings" in Smith.[55]

Behind William Smith's pronouncement lay a deeper issue, a claim that he held independent authority to exercise the sealing power. Brigham Young had already responded in writing to the church patriarch's assertion. "Joseph said that the sealing power is always vested in one man," Young explained, "and that there never was, nor never would be but one man on the earth at a time to hold the keys of the sealing power in the church, that all sealings must be performed by the man holding the keys, or by his dictation, and that man is the president of the Church."[56]

Thomas Sharp published William Smith's taunting message on spiritual marriage as a front-page "Proclamation" in his *Warsaw Signal*[57] and printed other discussions of the subject that were copied by newspapers elsewhere. Even after the Twelve agreed to leave Nauvoo, Sharp used this issue to reinforce a negative view of the church. He continued to press the matter well after the Saints had departed for the West.[58]

Besides drumming the private practice of plural marriage to cast Latter-day Saint morals in a false light, detractors of Nauvoo added indictments of lawlessness. Anti-Mormon editors jumped at every chance to keep alive these notions transplanted from Missouri. The most noticeable effect on public opinion came from claims of counterfeiting. The issue had been actively raised against Joseph Smith two years before his death. Anti-Mormon spokesman Thomas Sharp voiced concern over bogus money in Nauvoo in his Warsaw newspaper again in 1845. These claims had some basis in fact. Alexander Neibaur learned that two apostates were involved in a counterfeiting group in Nauvoo.[59] Another distributor in the city was spreading paper notes throughout the Mississippi Valley. These actions led to false charges against Brigham Young and others on counterfeiting charges. Several of the Twelve resolved the matter in a discussion with the marshal who delivered the writ.[60]

In October 1845, a farmer in Iowa asserted that the Twelve were producing counterfeit money at his farm. His claims led to attempts to arrest church leaders, but Governor Ford refused to cooperate with these interstate charges, calling the issue a federal matter. Then in December 1845, a grand jury at Springfield indicted several of the Twelve and others in the Nauvoo area for "counterfeiting Mexican dollars and American half dollars, and dimes." According to newspaper reports, "the Mormons had three presses for counterfeiting the coin named" and turned out a high quality coin of base metal covered by a thin exterior layer of pure silver. Once again, Ford disclaimed jurisdiction. The Twelve issued a circular denying the charges. When federal marshals appeared in Nauvoo with arrest warrants, church leaders went into hiding. The memory of the events in Carthage was still too fresh for the Twelve to trust fully in the process of law. Continuance of unfounded legal charges and the threat of sending federal troops influenced the Twelve's decision to leave Nauvoo ahead of schedule.[61]

Outsiders erroneously believed that ecclesiastical control of civilian life was so complete that nothing could happen in Nauvoo unless the church allowed or encouraged it. Some western Illinois friends of the church and opponents of anti-Mormon harassment who were otherwise neutral understood that this was not true. They defended Thomas Ford's refusal to cooperate in the arrest of Nauvoo leaders on counterfeiting charges. Newspapers in St. Louis and Peoria predicted that after the Saints were gone, counterfeit money would continue to appear in the region. "In the name of Peace," the *Saint Louis Organ* proposed, "let them go, and end this disgraceful turmoil and strife."[62] When counterfeiting continued after the exodus, some of Nauvoo's neighbors were finally convinced of the innocence of the Latter-day Saint people generally.[63] Until then, the accusations of the *Warsaw Signal* and the existence of some counterfeiting in the city tainted public opinion against the Saints.

THE RESURGENCE OF MOBOCRACY

While church leaders dodged legal attacks and endured media disinformation, church members living in settlements away from Nauvoo felt the brunt of a resurgence of vigilante action. The attacks began first at Morley's Settlement, along the southwestern boundary of Hancock County, on Wednesday evening, September 10, 1845. A messenger carried the news to Brigham Young. "We are in trouble and no hopes of it being any better," Solomon Hancock and Alanson Ripley wrote. "The mob is upon us. They have burned six buildings already and still carrying it on. . . . They are in number about two hundred. They shoot at every brother they see." The vigilantes continued their torching at nearby Lima, across the boundary in Adams County.[64] After four days, the men led by Levi Williams had burned more than forty buildings belonging to Latter-day Saints. Within a week's time, all of Morley's Settlement had been destroyed. The self-appointed regulators then moved ten miles northeast to Bear Creek Settlement. Meanwhile, in the far northern edge of the county, marauders began driving out the Saints from Camp Creek and La Harpe Settlements.[65]

Over several weeks, bands of old settlers led by the Warsaw regulator Colonel Levi Williams torched two hundred homes and farm buildings, plus mills and grain stacks. The house burners intended to force the Saints into Nauvoo and then call upon "help from abroad" to expel them from Illinois.[66] Forced from their homes by the marauders, one family after another watched their log homes and farm buildings burn. The Saints

Carthage Convention

from Morley's Settlement and the Carthage area began to seek refuge in Nauvoo.[67]

The Twelve encouraged this response. They advised Morley branch president Solomon Hancock to move women, children, and grain to Nauvoo. The men would remain as watchmen to record in detail "all the movements of the enemy and friends, what houses are burned, by whom, at what hour, who were present, and who saw them do it." On the day after the burnings began, the Twelve sent messengers to Morley and Lima and further afield to Ottawa, Illinois, and to Michigan Territory. The advice was the same: The brethren should sell land and homes for live-stock, wagons, provisions, and other such movable goods (needed for the as yet unannounced migration). The farmers should negotiate permission to harvest their crops and transport them to Nauvoo, along with their stored grain and their families.[68]

In response to a plea from Solomon Hancock, a call went out in Nauvoo for men with teams to help in the evacuation. Within hours, men with 134 teams headed south to haul families and grain to Nauvoo. The shuttling continued as needed over the next two months. At Nauvoo, the refugees found shelter in private homes and public halls. Residents took in friends as well as strangers. The seventies who had been using the Music Hall shifted their meetings to homes to free the building for "some of our brethren who have been driven here by our enemies."[69]

"The Mormons were allowed to remove all their furniture," the *Signal* reported a week after the evacuation began, "and most of them have already taken all their movables to Nauvoo. A determined spirit exists among the Anti-Mormons, and they have resolved to accomplish their object of driving the thieving [settlers], and destroying their houses, or die in the attempt." The anti-Mormons had organized for a war of extermi-nation. One group calling itself the "Fire and Sword" party burned the buildings and drove off the occupants. A separate division acted as spies and guards.[70]

The leaders of Nauvoo may have believed initially that by withdraw-ing settlers permanently from the outlying areas and by sending them across the Mississippi, peace could be restored. This hope of resolving localized antagonisms by meeting specific demands of a few individuals quickly faded. The threat of a mass expulsion or war of extermination prompted Young to propose a broader solution to end the house burnings.

A council of church leaders on September 13 agreed to his proposition that all the Saints leave Hancock County in the spring. Young informed Sheriff Jacob C. Backenstos of the plan.[71]

Brigham Young had already invited the help of government officials. On September 11, he asked the new sheriff to suppress the extralegal invasion and to seek Governor Ford's help in protecting private property. "The Sheriff is not a Mormon but is a friend to equal rights," Young said of Backenstos.[72] The sheriff proved his loyalty to law and order by organizing an effort at self-defense. He informed Young in a letter on September 13, "My policy is to quell the mob peaceably if I can, and forcibly if *we* must." When no one in Warsaw would join a citizens' posse to stop the house burnings, the sheriff deputized the Saints of the Highland branch southeast of Warsaw. Then he asked Brigham Young's help in assembling a Nauvoo defense force of two thousand men. Young, who wished to avoid the appearance of a religious war, urged greater efforts to enlist old citizens for the resistance force. Backenstos reluctantly disbanded the Mormon volunteers he had enlisted at Bear Creek. Doing so, he told Young, will "give every [thing] into the hands of the enemies and expose the property and lives of the Peaceable Citizens. This may be good policy but I think different." Backenstos issued a general proclamation on the thirteenth, inviting all law-abiding citizens to join his posse. As he expected, few responded. The next day, as a precaution, Young ordered Charles C. Rich to hold in readiness the organized quorums (the deacons, or ad hoc militia, of the City of Joseph). On September 15, Young invited the second cohort of the first regiment of the disbanded Nauvoo Legion to ready themselves under their former officers to serve, if invited, as a sheriff's posse.[73] Young recognized that he lacked authority to reorganize the Nauvoo Legion as an independent force under its own officers. This action, he realized, "would be nothing more nor less than the alarm gun for an open and bloody war." Even so, he gave Backenstos advice on operations in the field and guided the deployment of Nauvoo's volunteers. Young's defensive-only stance reflected a policy of passive waiting.[74]

The marauders justified their attacks as the will of the people. As they had done earlier with Deming, they showed their dislike for Backenstos's attempt to defend the property rights of Latter-day Saints by threatening him verbally and physically. On September 15, vigilantes drove Backenstos from his house in Carthage. The sheriff fled to Warsaw, where

Among those who left their homes and farms when vigilantes started burning them was the family of Charles B. Hancock Sr. This 1880s painting shows the Hancock homestead near Lima. The family left in October 1845 after a neighbor's house was torched. The Hancock home was not burned.

he found attitudes no better. Several anti-Mormons confronted him on the night of the sixteenth while he was driving his buggy on the plains toward Carthage. Fearing for his life, the sheriff turned toward Nauvoo. He overtook two horsemen likewise headed toward Nauvoo and made them deputies. When one of the pursuing horsemen raised his gun, newly deputized Orrin Porter Rockwell fired. Rockwell's shot struck the man in his chest. The mortally wounded victim was Frank A. Worrell, who had been supervisor of the guard on the day of the murders at Carthage.

That evening, George Miller and a hundred Nauvoo cavalrymen from the first cohort of the old Nauvoo Legion escorted the sheriff to Carthage to bring his family to safety in Nauvoo. They were met with gunfire, which quickly subsided. The sheriff set up guards at the courthouse in Carthage to protect government officials but found most of them had already fled.[75] Rockwell and Backenstos were later indicted for murder in Worrell's death and were acquitted on grounds of self-defense.[76]

Meantime, the shooting of Frank Worrell inflamed the feelings of old citizens throughout the area. To calm the tension, a quickly organized

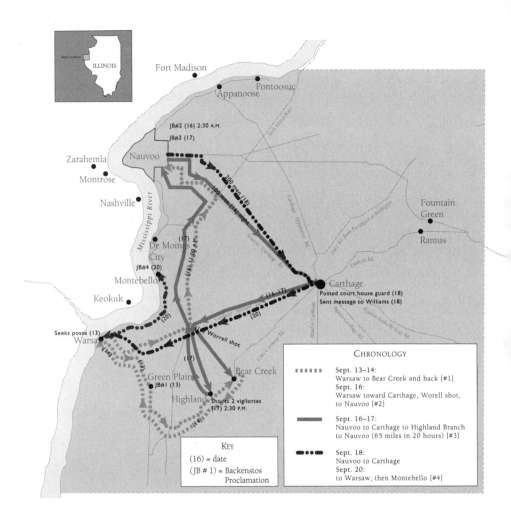

Negotiating Peace: Sheriff Jacob Backenstos, September 10–20, 1845

The following text appears within the map image:

ILLINOIS

Fort Madison
Pontoosuc
Appanoose
Zarahemla
Montrose
Nauvoo
JB#2 (16) 2:30 A.M.
JB#3 (17)
Nashville
Fountain Green
Ramus
De Moines City
JB#4 (20)
Montebello
Keokuk
Carthage
Posted court house guard (18)
Sent message to Williams (18)
Seeks posse (13)
Warsaw
Worrell shot
Bear Creek
Green Plains
JB#1 (13)
Highland Shoots 2 vigilantes (17) 2:30 P.M.
Mississippi River

200 men (18)
100 men (18)
(17) (17) 1:00 A.M.
(16) 11:00 P.M.
(16–17)
(20)
(20)
(14)
(17)

KEY
(16) = date
(JB # 1) = Backenstos Proclamation

CHRONOLOGY

Sept. 13–14:
Warsaw to Bear Creek and back [#1]

Sept. 16:
Warsaw toward Carthage, Worell shot, to Nauvoo [#2]

Sept. 16–17:
Nauvoo to Carthage to Highland Branch to Nauvoo (65 miles in 20 hours) [#3]

Sept. 18:
Nauvoo to Carthage

Sept. 20:
to Warsaw, then Montebello [#4]

citizens committee composed of Brigham Young and ten prominent men called for a truce in the hostilities. On the sixteenth, they issued a *Proclamation: To Col. Levi Williams, and Mob Party*. This document announced the council's decision made three days earlier to abandon Nauvoo. It informed vigilante leader Levi Williams of Green Plains "that if the mob would cease their destructive operations," the Saints would "leave the country in the spring."[77]

While Young sought peace, Thomas Sharp issued an immediate call to arms. "[Worrell's] death has kindled and will kindle a flame that cannot be quenched until every Mormon has left the vicinity," Sharp wrote. "REVENGE, REVENGE, Fellow Citizens is now the word. . . . Blood will and must flow if necessary to rid the county of the cursed authors of our troubles." The newspaper's former owner Thomas Gregg was displeased with the reaction. Concerned that no anti-Mormons were responding to Young's message, Gregg offered to help "bring about a reconciliation." In a letter to Brigham Young, Gregg said that if it were known more widely that the Saints were willing to leave Illinois, "there are men of influence enough among the disaffected portion of the population in this and the surrounding counties who can and will put a full stop to all violence." That solution would very soon be implemented.[78]

The house burnings continued, and the flame of vengeance broadened. Backenstos authorized the besieged Latter-day Saints to defend themselves against the house burners with force, if necessary. Brigham Young issued a supporting epistle quoting the sheriff's counsel and sent copies to three northeastern Hancock County Mormon settlements and two south of Nauvoo. If directly threatened by mobbers, Young advised, the Saints could, if needed, follow the sheriff's orders and "give them the cold lead."[79]

Because the Jack-Mormon friends of law and order were unwilling to respond to the sheriff's plea for help, Backenstos was left with the Nauvoo volunteers under General George Miller to challenge the anti-Mormon torchmen. The goal was to preserve life. The sheriff deputized eight of the men with authority to arrest Levi Williams and others accused by witnesses of burning houses.[80]

On September 16, Backenstos led his Nauvoo posse south from Carthage to Knowlton Settlement in Bear Creek precinct and on toward the Highland branch, where they "found the mob burning houses. We gave chase," a Latter-day Saint volunteer reported, "killing and wounding three men, then returned home." Another Nauvoo resident said he "went with eight well armed and mounted men under command of Colonel Markham to Bear Creek to arrest the house burning men but they all fled into Missouri."[81] Backenstos and Miller reported two house burners killed during their forced march of sixty-five miles over twenty hours on September 16 and 17. Efforts to locate and prosecute the perpetrators continued for at least several weeks.[82]

The sheriff and Nauvoo general George Miller decided to continue their campaign by attacking a reported eight hundred infantrymen below Warsaw. On September 18, Backenstos sent a message to Brigham Young asking for six hundred men and two cannon. Half the men would secure and hold Warsaw; the others would march downriver to cut off retreat. "We now intend to attack the stronghold and fortifications," he wrote. Young had just received a delegate from Warsaw who said Williams and six associates were willing to accept the Latter-day Saints' offer to leave Illinois, but the Warsaw committee wanted all references to a "mob party" and accusations of house burning deleted from the *Proclamation: To Col. Levi Williams.* The council at Nauvoo was unwilling to grant these concessions. Instead, they withdrew their offer to leave.[83]

With Williams seeking peace and quiet prevailing in the field, Young held the upper hand. "Everything indicates that the hottest of the mobbing is over," he concluded.[84] He denied the field general's request for reinforcements. He advised Miller and Backenstos to secure Carthage and let the regulators flee. They should post guards on the prairie, protect private property, and avoid a massacre. If the posse needed cannon, they could capture some in Warsaw. He instructed Miller to return to Nauvoo with any horsemen not needed for reconnaissance. "I am the Counsel or General in the field and I am going to direct the affair," Young said. Backenstos accepted Young's directives. His field council dropped the Warsaw campaign but requested reinforcements and one cannon to support a foray to Warsaw, where Backenstos intended to arrest any vigilantes who could be found. The sheriff received two hundred armed Nauvoo soldiers with wagons. When Backenstos reached Warsaw, he discovered that many of the house burners had fled temporarily to Missouri and Iowa.[85]

Overall, the efforts of the sheriff and his deputies began to turn the tide of public opinion against the marauders.[86] In response, the *Warsaw*

Signal published extras accusing the Latter-day Saints of being the aggressors.[87] Even with the quieted situation, watchmen patrolled Nauvoo and stood as sentinels along the river and on the prairie behind the city to protect against surprise invasion or sharpshooters' attacks.[88] These precautions taken in self-defense sometimes interrupted the journeys of innocent travelers, who were interrogated and then allowed to continue. The *Signal* complained of these protective measures and claimed that the sheriff's posse was driving off livestock and plundering homes and farms, or allowing marauding bands to wreak havoc on innocent farmers. Early in the confrontation, Brigham Young had warned his men against such actions. They should harvest their own crops from this last season in Hancock County, he said. Young instructed Major General Charles C. Rich to investigate allegations of theft and correct any problems.[89]

The anti-Mormon claims caused many neutral observers in Hancock County to conclude that the Saints had now undertaken to fight fire with fire. Some Latter-day Saint farmers acknowledged that while moving their own cattle and belongings from outlying settlements to Nauvoo, herders sometimes unintentionally gathered up livestock not their own. After advertising for three days to seek legal owners, they butchered the cattle in Nauvoo. The *Signal* scoffed at that explanation and dismissed Latter-day Saint reports that non-Mormon marauders were fueling the propaganda against the Nauvoo community by setting their own homes and outbuildings on fire.[90]

Governor Thomas Ford responded immediately to the confrontation in Hancock County. Recognizing Backenstos's weakening ability to maintain the peace because of strong anti-Mormon antagonism toward him, Ford sent about three hundred men from other counties under General John J. Hardin to do the job.[91] Men from this independent force replaced the sheriff's forty Nauvoo guards at Carthage on September 28. They called this post Camp Carthage. Hardin tried to prevent additional plundering in the latent civil war by outlawing the assembly of groups of more than four men.[92] The general's difficult task was to mediate between the two sides, forestall a military confrontation, and facilitate the Latter-day Saints' departure. To assist Hardin, Ford assembled an impressive advisory committee: Major William B. Warren, a Whig clerk of the Illinois Supreme Court; and two Democrats, attorney general James A. McDougal and

United States congressman Stephen A. Douglas, a former justice of the Illinois Supreme Court.

Brigham Young honored his promise to Governor Ford to sit out the fall election. He issued new orders counseling his people against retaliation and prohibiting even self-defense.[93] When the house burning started, plans for the western expedition had not yet been announced to the church. "Let the sheriff of Hancock county attend to the mob," he had told the Morley settlers, "and let us see whether he and the Jack-Mormons, so-called, the friends of law and order, will calmly sit down and watch the funeral processions of Illinois liberty. . . . At a future day our course will be plain. Be calm and patient till all things are ready."[94] It was important to Young that the Latter-day Saints not be the aggressors. Their only defense would be as victims. The better the evidence against the marauders, the easier the recovery of losses and the easier to win support from a broader American public.

On the afternoon of September 24, the Twelve and about thirty other men traveled to Carthage, where several of the party answered new charges of treason. The court dismissed the allegations when the signer of the affidavits could not explain what had been written by others. Those behind the writs were Thomas Sharp, Levi Williams, Chauncey Higbee, and Francis Higbee. For many of the Nauvoo party, among them John Taylor and Willard Richards, it would be the last opportunity to visit the jail where Joseph and Hyrum had died. They viewed the bloodstained floor and the shot-up walls and then headed along the dusty road into the setting sun. The Twelve had no desire for martyrdom. Their responsibility, even if it meant abandoning Nauvoo, was life, not death. All year, their preparations for expanding the kingdom had readied them to respond to the need to leave Illinois. President Young promised the Saints "a winter of peace in Nauvoo."[95]

At Quincy, meanwhile, the community that had extended charitable help to the Saints when they fled from Missouri nearly seven years earlier stepped in to broker a truce. Brigham Young had dispatched Hiram Kimball to Quincy on September 19 with printed proclamations from the Nauvoo citizens' committee and Sheriff Backenstos. Kimball returned the next day with a favorable report.[96] In a meeting at the Adams County courthouse, prominent Quincy residents condoned the actions of neither side. They were not justifying the house burnings, Quincy merchant

Joseph L. Heywood, a Latter-day Saint, explained to Brigham Young. The old settlers wanted to disclaim any responsibility for the actions of the vigilantes. Yet one speaker after another shared hostile feelings toward the Saints. "The most [hateful] set of speeches I ever heard, entirely mobocratic," Heywood reported.[97]

Intrigued that in the *Proclamation: To Col. Levi Williams* the Latter-day Saints had offered to leave Nauvoo, the meeting under its Whig chairman, Archibald Williams, proposed urging citizens of the counties surrounding Hancock to consider the offer. The resolution suggested a halt in the conflict to allow a peaceful departure—if that was the real intent of the Mormons. Otherwise, they should "break up their present organization as a distinct community and amalgamate with the general population of the State." A committee of seven headed to Nauvoo to discern Brigham Young's intentions firsthand.[98]

The Quincy delegates were waiting for the Twelve upon their return from Carthage at sunset on the twenty-fourth. After lengthy deliberations that involved the exchange of written proposals,[99] the Twelve issued a printed pledge affirming that the Saints would leave Hancock County as soon as grass was growing on the prairies. The statement urged an end to vexatious lawsuits and proposed that a joint committee coordinate property sales to help fund the relocation. Only the temple would not be sold, but it would be available for rent. The Nauvoo proclamation alluded to the expulsion from Missouri and pleaded for the right to worship freely. "It is very evident," William Clayton noted in his diary, "that the time is come for this people to separate themselves from all gentile governments and go to a place where they can erect the standard and live according to the law of God."[100]

A Quincy meeting on September 26 rejected the Twelve's proposal for a joint real estate committee and a cooperative exchange of Latter-day Saint property for cash, livestock, and travel supplies. The old citizens did not want to link the sale of property with removal. In contrast to their charitable offers seven years earlier, they offered only to collect contributions for Nauvoo's poor and widows. The Quincy delegates agreed that lawsuits and vigilante actions should end to allow a peaceful removal. They asked Governor Ford to dispatch troops to prevent theft and preserve the peace. Insisting that the Saints had brought their troubles upon themselves, the convention declared that the difficulties of Hancock

County could be resolved only through a mass exodus of the gathered community from Illinois.[101]

As a result of active lobbying from Quincy and careful organization, citizens' groups in surrounding counties met during the last ten days of September and passed resolutions following the pattern set in Quincy. In all, conventions in nine Illinois counties gave Nauvoo's opponents enough support to force a resolution of the Mormon question in favor of the Anti-Mormon Party. Each caucus named delegates to a convention called by the Quincy Committee for October 1 in Carthage. From across the Mississippi, a meeting at Churchville, Missouri, added its own perspective. These citizens criticized Governor Ford's handling of the issue. Wishing to add extermination as another option, they urged him "to take Lilburne W. Boggs as a pattern for his action in relation to the Mormons."[102]

THE AGREEMENT TO EVACUATE

Negotiations soon moved to a higher level. On September 30, General Hardin arrived in Nauvoo with his state militia and the governor's negotiating committee. The Council of Fifty was in session at the Seventies Hall, reporting progress in organizing emigrant companies for the spring exodus. It was noon when General Charles C. Rich brought word of General Hardin's arrival. The troops, Rich said, were waiting on the public square northeast of the temple. One member of Hardin's negotiating committee, Judge Stephen A. Douglas, was with Sheriff Backenstos at John Taylor's house on Main Street. The council adjourned immediately, and the Twelve walked the one block up Parley Street to Taylor's brick home.[103]

Douglas and Backenstos delivered a simple message. First, residents east across the Illinois River toward Springfield believed false reports that it was the Latter-day Saints who were torching the buildings. The *Warsaw Signal* had published sworn affidavits to that effect, and prejudices would not allow any other interpretation. Second, Hardin wished to meet with community leaders. Young and five of the Twelve proceeded to a consultation on the hill.[104] Hardin read his orders from the governor: Keep the peace in Hancock County. As a first step, Hardin gained Young's approval to search the city for the bodies of two men last seen in Nauvoo and supposed murdered. The troops searched the temple, Masonic Hall, Nauvoo House, and Mansion House stables in vain. At the stables, they found blood in the straw and resisted an explanation that a horse had been bled, preferring instead to stab their swords into the straw seeking evidence of dead men. Not finding any, the troops set up Camp Mississippi south of Nauvoo, after the two sides agreed to meet in council the following morning at John Taylor's home.[105]

Hardin's negotiating committee represented the governor but also served as liaison between the Latter-day Saints and the convention assembling at Carthage. Representatives came from Adams, Brown, Henderson, McDonough, Pike, Schuyler, Warren, Marquette, and Knox counties. Hancock, the seat of the problem, was excluded. Sponsored by the committee organized in Quincy a week earlier, the Carthage gathering was guided by three Adams County representatives—Isaac N. Morris as chair, William H. Benneson as secretary, and O. H. Browning as a dominant figure in the deliberations.[106]

With the governor's troops camped on Nauvoo's southern border, the Twelve and Bishop Whitney assembled for prayer and discussion at Willard Richards's home. "We asked the Lord to frustrate the designs of our enemies," Heber Kimball noted in his diary. Later in the evening, at John Taylor's, a council drafted another proposition to the state of Illinois declaring the church's intent to leave Nauvoo and inviting area citizens to purchase the Saints' property. The council considered the proposed Carthage meeting "impolitic" and asked Hardin to prevent it, if possible, or to move it to a site outside Hancock County.[107]

At the joint council meeting held at Nauvoo during the morning and afternoon of October 1, the governor's representatives joined in a friendly and informal discussion.[108] Young reiterated plans to leave Nauvoo and resettle in the West, probably, he said, at Vancouver Island (a ruse to keep confidential the actual plan to stop short of Oregon). The governor's committee endorsed the offer. When the Nauvoo leaders asked for help in selling or renting property, Hardin proposed that the church appoint trustees-in-trust to sell the property; they could continue sales after the people departed.[109]

The two sides exchanged written documents summarizing their discussions. The church memorandum, dated October 1 and signed by Brigham Young, included a copy of the printed proposal made to the Quincy Committee on September 24. Young noted that the church had "commenced making arrangements to remove from this county previous to the recent disturbances—that we now have four companies organized of one hundred families each, and six more companies now organizing of the same number." These companies, he said, included all church leaders and totaled from five thousand to six thousand people willing to leave in the spring whether or not they had sold their property. The remaining Saints would need to sell their property to raise the means necessary for removal. "If all these testimonies are not sufficient to satisfy any people that we are in earnest," he wrote, "we will soon give them a sign that cannot be mistaken, *we will leave them!*"[110]

While Hardin remained in his camp south of Nauvoo, members of his committee carried Young's proposals to Camp Carthage for presentation to the nine-county conference. Convention managers first made certain that the delegates heard reports of alleged Mormon depredations against old citizens (mostly accusations of theft). Then the body approved a proposal calling upon the Saints to leave the state as promised. This and six other resolutions consolidated but softened the demands of the county conventions. The Carthage Convention pledged itself not to interfere with the removal but advised the counties to hold volunteer militias in readiness. Delegates asked for an end to further arrests so that the old citizens could return to their homes. They endorsed the proposal to station the governor's military force in Hancock County. In firm words, the convention rejected the Latter-day Saint explanation of events. "We do not believe them to be a persecuted people," the declaration said. Because delegates believed that Nauvoo's leaders exercised autocratic control, they held the entire Latter-day Saint community responsible for individual offenses against the old citizens. If any of the Saints engaged in theft or destruction of property, the convention declared, the old citizens would activate volunteer militias and "march to Hancock, to put a final and summary end to such outrages."[111]

On October 3, the day following the convention, the governor's negotiating committee wrote to the Twelve from Camp Carthage even as Hardin's regiment was pulling up stakes at Camp Mississippi. The committee had not yet read the Carthage document but had learned of its contents. "We are convinced that affairs have reached such a crisis, that it has become impossible for your church to remain in this country," the committee wrote. "Should you not [leave], we are satisfied, however much we may deprecate violence and bloodshed, that violent measures will be resorted to, to compel your removal." Ford's committee said that public evidence of preparations to leave would convince Nauvoo's enemies to allow the Saints "to depart peaceably next spring for your destination, west of the Rocky Mountains." Both sides would need to exercise restraint to avoid outbreak of civil war, the committee concluded.[112]

Their mission of negotiation completed, Hardin's group published the official correspondence in a broadside. In a cover letter echoing Brigham Young's pledge, the governor's committee reassured residents of western Illinois that the Saints had pledged themselves

> by word and in writing, to remove from the state. . . . The history of their church has shown that wherever the leaders go the members will follow. This is a part of their religious duties. When, therefore, this colony will have started for a home west of the Rocky Mountains, it will be the best possible evidence that all design removing, and will remove.

The committee urged the anti-Mormons not to force a winter departure. Pleading with the house burners to halt and labeling the actions criminal and disgraceful, the committee argued that the negotiated agreement, though not ideal from either viewpoint, was "practicable and probable." The governor's committee had accomplished its mission. The Latter-day Saints would be leaving. The negotiators concluded: "Order and quiet are again restored."[113]

The committee reported to Ford that protection of property required a citizenry willing to abide by the law, a condition that these experienced public servants judged improbable. The marauders marched to a higher law, the negotiators wrote, and could not be controlled by the state. If the Latter-day Saints wished a place of peace, they would have to find it outside Illinois. Across the Mississippi, in Lee County, Iowa, a nonpartisan citizens' meeting echoed the Illinois resolutions and called for the removal of the Latter-day Saints living there as well.[114]

On Saturday, October 4, Brigham Young convened the Council of Fifty at the Seventies Hall to further study the correspondence from Hardin's committee, a letter from Governor Ford,[115] and the resolutions adopted at the Carthage convention. After reviewing the materials, the council agreed to proceed with the details of their preparations for removal. At Young's suggestion, the council decided to halt publication of

Nauvoo at its peak was a community of more than eleven thousand people living mostly in white-washed log homes, plus many frame and brick houses. This accurate model at the Nauvoo Visitors' Center was created using land and tax records.

the *Nauvoo Neighbor* and the *Times and Seasons*. The *Neighbor* had achieved only limited success in its attempt to communicate the church view in secular things to a broader reading audience. "Now let them alone," John Taylor agreed in a general conference talk a few days later, "and mind our own business, and let them print what they have a mind to. . . . The world doesn't wish any news from us, and we don't wish to urge it upon them."[116]

In another action, the Council of Fifty appointed Parley P. Pratt, Orson Spencer, and William W. Phelps to preserve published reports on recent events and to write a pointed indictment of United States treatment of the Saints. Drafted by Spencer, the October 23 letter emphasized the feelings of those Nauvoo residents who were most offended by state actions. In doing so it likened Ford to Missouri Governor Lilburn W. Boggs and argued for removal of the troops from Nauvoo.[117]

Ford drafted an immediate rebuff to what he saw as an intemperate and unfounded charge. First, Ford said that he had posted troops in Nauvoo to protect the Saints and prevent civil war. Sheriff Backenstos had secured a tenuous peace in Carthage, he added, but the delegates at Carthage had agreed to "drive [the Saints] away before they get stronger and more capable of resistance." Second, the governor was convinced that a band of thieves—not necessarily Latter-day Saints—was operating out of Nauvoo "as is the case in all other cities of ten or twelve thousand inhabitants." In addition, he said, some of those burnt out by the mob may have been taking property from their enemies as indemnification. Ford acknowledged the impossibility of pleasing the radical elements of either side through his legal moderation. "In the course of my official duties . . . I have been called to do both of you some good and some harm. The harm is always remembered: the good is either not understood or is forgotten. I do not expect any gratitude or applause from either party."[118]

Ford's concern that the lawlessness would continue was proven valid with several incidents during the last three months of the year. The most inflammatory were headlined in late November in the *Nauvoo Neighbor's* only extra after it ceased publication. "Murder and Arson," the heading shouted. "Edmund Durfee Shot—Two Houses Burned." Durfee, a fifty-seven-year-old New Englander who had joined the church in Ohio in 1831, had moved his family into Nauvoo after his house at Morley's Settlement had been burned, the first house attacked in the September mob actions. He and others had returned to the area to remove "a last load of grain." Around midnight, on Saturday, November 15, a small group of marauders set fire to a straw stack outside Solomon Hancock's barn. Hancock, Durfee, and others grabbed rakes to disperse the fire away from the barn. Hidden from view, the vigilantes fired six shots at the men and killed Durfee with a single shot to the chest, just above the heart.[119]

Two days earlier, again around midnight, an estimated thirty men appeared at the house of Samuel Hicks near Camp Creek and woke him with demands that he deliver William Rice to them. The marauders, claiming to be members of the governor's troops from Carthage, said they had a writ for Rice's arrest. When Hicks said Rice was not at the house, a few of the mob hauled Hicks off, dressed only in his nightshirt. His wife and child were sick with ague and remained behind. The remaining marauders instructed two men staying in the home to remove the family's belongings. Before these men could complete the job, however, the mob set fire to the stairs of the home. Hicks was returned to his family and harassed before the attackers left. The home was destroyed. The house burners later found Rice and burned his house as well.[120]

The *Neighbor's* report of the two events cautioned the Saints against retaliation for the unprovoked attacks and encouraged them to hasten preparations for the spring departure. "When we have settled on the other side of America," the editor wrote, "you will know of a truth that we were friends and not enemies to life, law, and liberty! That we were good men, engaged in a good cause, and will receive the meed of praise we deserve for universal benevolence, and everlasting friendship to goodness."[121]

Major Warren's handling of the two cases won the accolades of Latter-day Saints. Sheriff J. B. Backenstos thought the major had turned Jack-Mormon, so energetic were his efforts to apprehend and try the guilty parties. Warren and Mason Brayman succeeded in taking to Carthage three men charged with Durfee's murder and others with the burning of the two houses. One of them Warren had chased into Missouri and hauled back at gunpoint without the formalities of an extradition writ. Witnesses from Nauvoo traveled to Carthage for the court hearing but were not heard. The magistrate discharged the men without examination.[122]

IMPLEMENTING REMOVAL

The mob attacks of September 1845 and subsequent negotiations made necessary the immediate implementation of a general removal from Nauvoo. A massive exodus seemed the only option for preserving a large headquarters city. "The mob seem determined to drive us to our duty in gathering [to Nauvoo]," Brigham Young told Sheriff Backenstos in mid-September, "and then drive us to carry the fulness of the gospel from among them and carry it to Israel. We are all well."[123] News of the negotiated decision spread through the state, even as Latter-day Saints were gathering in Nauvoo for an October conference. Many of the Saints already knew that the Carthage Convention had accepted the offer of the Twelve to launch a migration westward from Nauvoo the following spring. By the time of Brigham Young's September 26 speech to the Camp Creek emigrants, team captains of the emigrating companies were actively recruiting for the California expedition.[124]

The Prophet Joseph Smith had declared in October 1841 that no general conferences would convene until they could be held in the completed Nauvoo Temple. Four years later, the temple was finally entirely enclosed, and, although technically not finished, it was judged by the Twelve ready for a conference. The roof was on, the windows were in, and seats provided for a meeting. On Sunday, October 5, 1845, Brigham Young offered a dedicatory prayer before a main-floor audience of thousands. The general conference, Nauvoo's last, opened on Monday for three days of business and instruction. One concern dominated the meeting—explaining and preparing for the evacuation of Nauvoo. Removal was the theme for the three principal speakers and for much of the business of the assembly.[125]

Monday morning was consumed with the presentation of general church officers, one by one. The conference accepted the Twelve as "Presidents of the whole church" and then sustained Brigham Young as president of the Quorum of the Twelve Apostles. All of the existing members of the Quorum of the Twelve Apostles were given unanimous support except two. William Smith was dropped as an apostle and patriarch for aspiring "to uproot and undermine the legal Presidency of the Church, that he may occupy the place himself." An absent Lyman Wight was objected to for ignoring the Twelve's counsel and leading away a group needed to help build the temple. He was retained pending further investigation of "conduct calculated to destroy . . . [and] divide the church."[126]

The Monday afternoon session settled into preaching. Parley P. Pratt introduced the major theme of the remaining sessions. In a moving address that justified the abandonment of a hard-won homeland on visionary and prophetic grounds, he said:

> We know that the great work of God must all the while be on the increase and grow greater. The people must enlarge in numbers and extend their borders; they cannot always live in one city, nor in one county. . . . The Lord designs to lead us to a wider field of action, where there will be more room for the saints to grow and increase, and where there will be no one to say we crowd them, and where we can enjoy the pure principles of liberty and equal rights.

Recognizing that the congregation would have concerns about leaving their homes and farms or businesses in Nauvoo, Pratt encouraged them to leave the city as "a monument to those who may visit the place of our industry, diligence and virtue." But, he said, despite the appearance of prosperity, a great deal had been squandered in vexatious lawsuits, mobocracy, and oppression. In a new country, "where the air, the water, soil and timber is equally free to every settler without money or without price, the climate healthy," and mobocracy absent, "we can become vastly more wealthy, have better possessions and improvements, and build a larger and better Temple in five years from this time than we now possess." Pratt illustrated his optimistic image of an expanded field with an agricultural metaphor:

> One small nursery may produce thousands of fruit trees, while they are small. But as they expand towards maturity, they must needs be transplanted, in order to have room to grow and produce the natural fruits. It is so with us. We want a country where we have room to expand.[127]

Expansion was on apostle George A. Smith's mind, too, as were the prospects of a new land where the natural resources belonged to God himself as the sole proprietor. Smith reminded the Saints that in leaving Missouri they had covenanted to help the poor leave too. At his request, the congregation approved a similar cooperative effort for evacuating Nauvoo. Brigham Young, who had sponsored the covenant at Far West in 1839, prophesied that with God's blessings on the people, church resources would allow everyone to move who wanted to go. The following day, four bishops accepted donations for the poor, a timely reminder of the need to sustain one another in temporal needs.[128]

During a conference session the next day, Heber C. Kimball introduced the image of a modern Israel fleeing Egypt. "I am glad the time of our exodus is come; I have looked for it for years," he said. Then, addressing the question of funding the migration, Kimball rejected what he called a common stock business religion preached by some, and advocated "Apostolic religion; i.e., you will sell all, and come and lay it down at the Apostles' feet. . . . Every man will be a steward over his house and property; and if he is an unfaithful steward, his stewardship will be given to another." On another frequently asked question, Kimball (and the others) defined the place of destination only in general terms:

> We want to take you to a land, where a white man's foot never trod, nor a lion's whelps, nor the devil's; and there we can enjoy it, with no one to molest and make us afraid; and we will bid all the nations welcome, whether Pagans, Catholics, or Protestants. We are not accounted as white people, and we don't want to live among them. I had rather live with the buffalo in the wilderness; and I mean to go if the Lord will let me, and spare my life.[129]

Amasa Lyman echoed Parley Pratt's image of a transplanted society.

The concept promised continuity in the face of disruption and adjustment. Lyman commended the Saints for their decision to follow the Twelve to a prophesied destiny. "The course of this people is unalterably fixed," he said.

> The people are becoming one, and their interests one. . . . And we calculate to go the same people we are now; preserving the same principles which have caused us to grow and expand as we have done. This people have grown until there is not room for them to grow, and now they need transplanting, where they can have more room: and however much the people may seem disposed to not go, the sails are set, the wind is fair, and we are bound to weather the point, whether we will or no; for we are not at the helm.[130]

At the conclusion of the conference, the Twelve issued a circular to inform the Saints living in the United States but away from Nauvoo of the decision to abandon the City of Peace because of "a crisis of extraordinary and thrilling interest."[131] This important church statement set the decision to leave the United States first in broad eschatological terms and then stated immediate reasons. It included both testimony and practical counsel. "The exodus of the Nation of the only true Israel from these U.S. to a far distant region of the West, where bigotry, intolerance and insatiable oppression will have lost its power over them, forms a new epoch, not only in the history of the church, but of this nation," the circular declared. "If the authorities of this church cannot abide in peace within the pale of this nation, neither can those who implicitly hearken to their wholesome counsel. A word to the wise is sufficient. . . . Two cannot walk together except they be agreed. Jacob must be expatriated while Esau held dominion."

The immediate reasons for the decision, the circular noted, were the murders of the Prophet and his brother, the Patriarch, and the more recent burning of the houses of scores of Latter-day Saint families in western Illinois. "It is our design to remove all the Saints as early next spring as the first appearance of thrifty vegetation," it said. In the meantime, work would continue on the Lord's House, with an anticipated dedication by the next general conference. Before then, temple ordinances would be given to the faithful. To facilitate this effort, the Saints outside Nauvoo

It seemed a bold move to abandon Nauvoo after long years of hard work in establishing the city and building a majestic temple. The Twelve saw the necessity of doing so to appease the anti-Mormons. Most of the Saints sustained their decision.

were invited to settle their affairs, dispose of their property, procure wagons and teams for the westward journey, and move their families to Nauvoo.

> Wake up, wake up dear brethren, we exhort you, from the Mississippi to the Atlantic, and from Canada to Florida, to the present glorious emergency in which the God of heaven has placed you, to prove your faith by your works, preparatory to a rich endowment in the Temple of the Lord, and the obtaining of promises and deliverances, and glories for yourselves and your children and your dead.

This grand call to action concluded with two afterthoughts. The first postscript advised that all new wagons be built on a five-foot track to make travel easier during winter months. In the second addition, a hint of destination was included: "There are said to be many good locations for settlements on the Pacific," it reads, "especially at Vancouver's Island near [actually 150 miles north of] the mouth of [the] Columbia." The public declaration of a haven in a politically acceptable region, rather than the real target in the valleys of the central Rocky Mountains, satisfied at once both the politicians' need for a safe Mormon escape and the Saints' curiosity. More important, it protected the true destination from pre-emption by opponents. Mention of the Oregon country anticipated an intended later expansion to the Pacific Coast.[132] A similar indirection two weeks later ("our future location will embrace California, Oregon, or Vancouver's Island") suggested only the certainty of a location on America's far western frontier.[133]

The press in Nauvoo, under the editorship of John Taylor, reported the church's agreement to leave western Illinois and eastern Iowa in both political and religious terms. The *Nauvoo Neighbor* bemoaned the failure of government to "protect its own citizens from the violence of corrupt men." In response, the Saints would follow the path the Savior had laid out. "We will suffer wrong rather than do wrong," the editor declared. "We could fight our way clear, but wisdom says let the wicked slay the wicked. The gospel whispers peace." He concluded, "We owe the United States nothing: we go out by force as exiles from freedom."[134] A two-column recital of persecutions in the *Times and Seasons* concluded with a prescient summation. The "Christian" nation of America would be left "*alone in her glory*," Taylor wrote, while Mormon Israel withdrew to a place of refuge. "The wilderness shall blossom as the rose, and Babylon fall like a millstone cast into the sea."[135]

In New York, Parley P. Pratt's *Messenger* reacted to first reports of a planned exodus as rumor. When copies of newspapers from Nauvoo verified the seriousness of events in the West, the *Messenger* encouraged Eastern Saints not to postpone migration to Nauvoo. The paper reprinted vivid news of the house burnings and explanations of the decision to abandon Nauvoo for a new gathering place in the West.[136]

In western Illinois, newspaper editors split along familiar lines. Opponents of Nauvoo's political influence celebrated the decision and threatened an aggressive implementation.[137] More neutral bystanders simply reported the news or puzzled over why Illinois citizens had violated the protected rights of others.[138] The *Springfield State Register* applauded the governor's actions and supported the cease-fire as a way to end hostilities on both sides and allow the Saints to prepare for removal.[139] On the other hand, after summarizing the troubles of the past summer and fall, the *Peoria American* sided carefully with the anti-Mormons.[140]

This range of ideas found its way into newspapers elsewhere in the United States. In St. Louis, editors generally reported developments in

Hancock County during the fall of 1845 with an attempt at fairness. The *St. Louis Organ,* for example, charged the opponents of the Mormons with intentionally misusing and provoking them. Any misdeeds committed by the Saints, the editor said, "will be lost in the recollection of the great barbarism of their persecutors." The *New York Sun* editorialized, "We could not believe that, in a government of laws, any sect, no matter what their faith might be, would ever have been driven out of the land *vi et armis.*" In Washington, D.C., the *National Intelligencer* copied balanced accounts from the St. Louis newspapers verbatim, issuing reports of the Quincy negotiating committee, Brigham Young's agreement to leave Illinois, and the church's general conference announcement.[141]

Despite its balanced news columns, the *St. Louis New Era* soon turned its editorial support toward the isolationist arguments of the anti-Mormons. Calling the church "an ecclesiastical oligarchy, exercising a despotic control over a large body of fanatics," the paper said, "The principles of the Mormons will always engender hostilities between them and the American people amongst whom they reside."[142] When early reports circulated that the Saints might leave Nauvoo, some editors expressed disbelief. "The Mormons will never leave Nauvoo—no, never!" one paper exclaimed. "They would relinquish life as soon as they would voluntarily, en masse, leave—their glorious habitation, which to them is the gate of heaven."[143]

In Great Britain, editors of the *Millennial Star* encouraged migration and justified the decision to leave Nauvoo. "The place became too small for us to dwell in—the church required to be sifted—the celestial laws to be put in force, and the foundation of Zion laid according to that pattern," David C. Kimball explained. Added Thomas Ward: "Houses and land, what are they? We can build more."[144]

For the Saints in the British Isles, the evacuation of Nauvoo may have seemed distant. Yet abandonment of the Zion they had planned to join affected them immediately. Many postponed their migration. Others hastened departure in order to receive their endowments in Nauvoo and join in the removal. Counsel from regional president Wilford Woodruff to the Saints was to prepare to join in the mass movement. In mid-January 1846, Woodruff sent his wife and two children to Nauvoo by way of New Orleans with a company of about forty Saints. A week later, he took a packet ship to New York so that he could visit relatives in New England

and arrangements move his parents with him to Nauvoo, where he arrived on April 13.[145]

Orson Pratt counseled members in his area of presidency in the Eastern states to move immediately to Nauvoo in order to be ready for the spring removal. Pratt offered no sympathy to the rich. He expected they might complain about losing money on the emergency sale of their property. "The Lord requires a sacrifice," he reminded those who had ignored earlier invitations to join in the gathering. Pratt advised the poor not to depend upon help in Nauvoo. Rather, they should purchase horses and wagons in the East or choose a cheaper route by sea. As encouraged by Brigham Young in September,[146] Pratt appointed Samuel Brannan to enlist a company to go by way of Cape Horn in January. If a sufficient number were interested, Pratt said, Brannan could charter an entire ship—or several ships—to the west coast. Sensing that some of the Saints would be reluctant to go, the departing apostle stressed the urgency of getting out of the United States. He wrote in his message of departure:

> It is with the greatest of joy that I forsake this republic; and all the saints have abundant reasons to rejoice that they are counted worthy to be cast out as exiles from this wicked nation. . . . If we die in the dens and caves of the Rocky Mountains, we shall die where freedom reigns triumphantly. Liberty in a solitary place, and in a desert, is far more preferable than martyrdom in these pious states.[147]

Church members in all parts of the United States and Great Britain talked among themselves and sought counsel from their leaders concerning the Great Western Measure. They wanted to know where the Saints would gather, when the migration from Nauvoo would begin, what the route would be, what was needed in the way of teams and supplies, how many would be going, and how long the journey would take. Certain information could not be shared, and other details were yet unknown. Church leaders shared what they could.[148]

For many Latter-day Saints, the pressing question was not where destiny would next lead them but how their close community might be affected. The anti-Mormons had encouraged the Saints to "break up their present organization as a distinct community and amalgamate with the general population."[149] In their meetings, Nauvoo's priesthood quorums considered the effect of the pending move on their continuing fellowship.

They expected to be scattered by the migration and by missionary assignments, "not knowing when we should meet again."[150] But those who supported the Twelve shared a sense that the decision to leave Nauvoo and, indeed, the entire United States behind them was right. The central idea in their conversations was not the place of relocation as much as the quality of life as a united people in that new location. They desired to find a new refuge of peace, freed from the harassments that had prompted the decision to leave. They looked forward "to a land where the Standard of Liberty might be hoisted and we might worship God and there would be none to molest or make afraid."[151] They wished to be free from the constraints on their desire to become a gathered people. In a letter to an unbelieving uncle in mid-November, John S. Fullmer explained the meaning of the mass migration:

> We are preparing ourselves to go as exiles from the state as we came into it. We cannot remain here in peace any longer. This is demonstrated to a certainty; and the spirit bids us flee into the wilderness . . . and although we will be broken up here, we will not be broken up as a people. The Lord is on our side, notwithstanding he suffers us to be persecuted and to endure great tribulation, *for the Kingdom is with us.*[152]

CHAPTER 18

Leaving Nauvoo

As life is sweet we have chosen banishment rather than death. . . . To stay [in Nauvoo], is death by "fire and sword," to go into banishment unprepared, is death by starvation.

—THE TWELVE TO GOVERNOR JAMES CLARK OF IOWA TERRITORY,
FEBRUARY 28, 1846

Our Pioneers are instructed to proceed west until they find a good place to make a crop, in some good valley in the neighborhood of the Rocky Mountains, where they will infringe upon no one, and not be likely to be infringed upon. Here we will make a resting place, until we can determine a place for a permanent location.

—NAUVOO HIGH COUNCIL, CIRCULAR TO THE CHURCH,
JANUARY 20, 1846

The task of preparing for removal from Nauvoo was an extraordinary effort. As the body in charge of all arrangements, the Quorum of the Twelve intended to equip and transplant an entire people. Besides more than ten thousand residents of the City of Nauvoo, the plan included several thousand others in the surrounding countryside and, eventually, every Latter-day Saint in the United States and Europe who would join in the journey. Arrangements extended beyond wagons and supplies to include a honing of religious motivations. To accomplish their objective, church

551

leaders at the October conference championed removal in scriptural terms. They unfolded a funding plan and a management philosophy.

One of the first matters addressed publicly was the question of how to finance the removal. The Twelve expected each head of household to marshal the resources needed to outfit and transport his or her own family. "Every man was to go to work and stew his pumpkins to the amount of 20 [bushels] and parch corn to the amount of ten bushels for flour could not be obtained," Joseph Hovey recalled.[1] Anyone lacking sufficient means would receive help through contributions from other members given to the church for distribution. This method emphasized self-reliant effort and echoed in spirit and intent the law of consecration.

Heber C. Kimball recognized the difficulty some Nauvoo Saints might have with what he termed the "apostolic religion," a voluntary sharing of resources managed by the Twelve. The Nauvoo emigration plan addressed one sensitive issue by allowing owners to retain all control over property. Under this proposal, the Saints would sell their houses and farms and volunteer to share their surplus. "It has taken a good scourging for fifteen years to bring us to this," Kimball observed. "There may be individuals who will look at their pretty houses and gardens and say, 'it is hard to leave them'; but I tell you, when we start, you will put on your knapsacks, and follow after us." John S. Fullmer echoed Kimball's counsel when he informed an uncle of the plan to dispose of their property and move west: "If we can't sell it we will leave it if we have to walk off with a bundle on our backs."[2]

The image of knapsack-carrying disciples following their leaders accurately reflected the religious ideal of Zion—a people brought to an equality of opportunity because the rich had consecrated their surplus to the church to help evacuate the poor. Brigham Young advised one man who sought clarification "that those who went must expect to go on the Apostles' doctrines and no man say aught that he has is his own, but all things are the Lord's: and we his stewards, and every man receive his stewardship."[3]

At the October conference, Amasa Lyman used a metaphor of seafaring to illustrate the notion of following spiritual leaders. From a secular perspective, it was a personal decision to select a place to live. For committed Latter-day Saints, it was the prerogative of prophets to designate a proper dwelling place. Lyman's image—of the ship of state ready to sail under fair winds with God at the helm—reminded the people that their choice was one of faith. They could whine and stay behind, Lyman said, or they could climb aboard and sail with the Saints. Some who had complained about losses in Missouri didn't feel like sacrificing their newly won resources in Hancock County. To them, Lyman suggested only that they had yet to experience real suffering. "They have to get rich, and be made poor, about twenty times over, before they will come straight," he said. "When the rich are rich; and the poor are rich; then there will be nobody rich and nobody poor; for all will be on a level." Sacrifice and obedience had refined the people, he said. Through persecution and suffering, they would "come up out of the fire as gold seven times tried."[4]

Church leaders sympathized with those who lacked the means to outfit themselves for yet another migration. Just seven years earlier a committee of removal endorsed by members of the Twelve had helped the poor get out of Missouri. It would be so in 1846 under the direction of Brigham Young and the Twelve.[5] Widows with limited means qualified for help. Some others received less sympathy. Brigham Young chided one delegation of thirty-eight men who felt ignored in their poverty brought on by the forced expulsion from Jackson County. The president apparently knew them too well. He reprimanded these men for their earlier slothfulness, their failure to magnify church callings, and their unwillingness to accept preaching missions. He would help the worthy poor, he said, but not those unwilling to help themselves and the kingdom.[6]

For many, the highlight of the final day of the conference was Lucy Mack Smith's lengthy address at the Wednesday morning session. Speaking at her own request, she discussed three topics. First, she advised parents on their duties in rearing their children in love and kindness. With the help of Martha Coray, the mother of the Prophet had recently completed her autobiography. This had turned her thoughts to children and to her own family. In the second portion of her talk, Lucy Smith reflected on the life of her prophet-son and recited her family's "hardships, trials, privations, persecutions, sufferings, etc.; some parts of which melted those who heard her to tears."[7] Then Mother Smith endorsed the decision to abandon Nauvoo. "If [it] so be the rest of my children go with you (and would to God they may all go)," she said, "they will not go without me; and if I go, I want my bones brought back in case I die away, and deposited with my husband and children." The Prophet's mother had

Lucy Mack Smith, the Prophet's mother, preserved the story of her family's religious searchings and persecutions and her son Joseph's role as Prophet of the Restoration. She often talked of these experiences and in 1845 dictated her memoirs. She supported the Twelve and wanted to go west with them.

previously told Brigham Young she would not accompany the church west. He had not pressed her on the question. Her public sanction of the migration buoyed him, and he promised to honor her request. "We are determined also," he concluded, "to use every means in our power to do all that Joseph told us."[8]

In the area of spiritual preparation, church leaders felt a strong obligation to provide members with promised temple blessings. For fifteen years, in Missouri and Illinois, the Saints had endured a testing time to prepare them to live a celestial law. For five of those years they had labored with various levels of enthusiasm to build the temple. The promise of a special endowment of godly power urged them on. It was a potential for which the Saints had been willing to work and wait.[9] The doors to the temple's upper level opened on Wednesday, December 10, 1845. On that date and for nearly two months following, a succession of members passed through the large front entrances and climbed two stories to the endowment rooms to receive their blessings. The long-awaited endowment prepared the Saints for their errand into the wilderness.[10]

As the temple experience ended and Latter-day Saints launched their trek west, they revived an Old Testament reference that had been applied at Independence and Nauvoo in a symbolic way. Now, looking beyond the Missouri River, Isaiah's "top of the mountains" could be understood more literally in geographic terms. Brigham Young had promised a new temple in the Rocky Mountains to replace the one being left behind at Nauvoo. In his closing editorial in the *Times and Seasons,* John Taylor proclaimed that the migrations of the Latter-day Saints were evidence of "the handy work of God":

> Certainly it is a strange work and a wonder! Well might the prophet Isaiah exclaim: "And it shall come to pass in the last days, that the mountain of the Lord's house shall be established in the top of the mountains, and shall be exalted above the hills; and all nations shall flow unto it. And many people shall go and say, Come ye, and let us go up to the mountain of the LORD, to the house of the God of Jacob; and he will teach us of his ways, and we will walk in his paths: for out of Zion shall go forth the law, and the word of the LORD from Jerusalem."
>
> Although we have to flee from the presence of *freemen,* or *civilized society,* mark the act; watch till the end of the matter, and then judge whether God had a hand in it or not. The power of Israel was lost, by disobedience and scattering; and his power will be regained by obedience and gathering. Stand fast in the faith, brethren, *the work of the Father hath commenced among all nations to restore Israel to mercy* . . . and the kingdoms of the world must pass out of your way like the chaff of the summer threshing floor.[11]

The most enduring of the religious metaphors adopted by those leaving Nauvoo was one that evoked ancient Israel's journey through the wilderness to their promised land. The Latter-day Saints saw themselves as a modern covenant people. "We shall leave here May next, for a place where the God of Israel is the sole proprietor and he can give it to whom he pleases," George Alley informed relatives in Massachusetts. "A place where the foot of a white man never trod, nor the pestilence never came. . . . We shall go as the Israelites, by the shadow of the tabernacle of the Lord."[12]

Preparations for the Migration

The wholesale removal of the gathered Saints from Hancock and Lee counties did not proceed without planning. From the very beginning, careful organization marked the effort to implement Joseph Smith's Great Western Measure. On September 9—ironically, the day before the house burnings began—Brigham Young began choosing leaders for the first company. Those selected became captains under Young and immediately set about filling up their groups. After the attacks began in Hancock County late in the month, the Twelve decided that together with their families, friends, and neighbors, they would all join the growing initial emigrant company.[13]

As word spread, company leaders were inundated with requests for inclusion. By the time of the October conference, inquiries from members and pressures from the marauders made it necessary to include the entire Mormon population but on a staggered departure schedule. Heber Kimball reassured the conference, "We calculate you are all going in the first company, both old and young, rich and poor; for there will be but one company." The first company had been expanded to avoid partiality. "We have a common interest, for the welfare of this whole people."[14]

The grand, unified migrating company that came to be known eventually as the Camp of Israel consisted of numerous manageably sized smaller groups, or emigrant companies, of about one hundred families each.[15] By the middle of October, captains had been appointed for twenty-five companies. Potentially, this number could accommodate more than twelve thousand people. The Quorum of the Twelve headed the first company, followed by fifteen companies with captains chosen from the Council of Fifty. They were listed in the same order as their names appeared in the Fifty's roster, by descending age. Of the nine captains not of the Twelve or Fifty, seven were assigned to organize companies in specific locations away from Nauvoo. In popular discourse, many of these numbered companies took on the name of their leader.[16]

Emigrating Company No. 1 set the pattern for organizing the migrants with a hierarchy of officers resembling a militia. Like the plan given by revelation for Zion's Camp in 1834, the Twelve divided their company into fifties and tens with a captain over each. Later they paired the fifties as hundreds, with captains over them. Young single men received a special invitation to join the company to help with the hard work of pioneering.[17] Twice during November, captains of the various emigrating companies met for counsel from Brigham Young and the

Twelve, a practice that continued at regular intervals during the drawn-out migration of 1846.[18]

The potential size of the Camp of Israel greatly increased the organizational task. Latter-day Saints in Nauvoo and nearby settlements numbered an estimated seventeen thousand. With all American and European members invited, the long-term migratory potential doubled. But not everyone accepted the invitation to join in the 1846 removal. Some delayed temporarily, and others never did join modern Israel's journey into the wilderness. In early October, Brigham Young told Stephen A. Douglas and his negotiating committee that about one thousand Nauvoo families (or between five thousand and six thousand Saints) would leave in the spring. This accounting left half the city's residents for later departure dates. By late November 1845, the captains of the emigrant companies reported that they had organized 3,285 families. If these groups averaged five persons per family, the captains had included 16,425 people, or virtually all the Latter-day Saints in the upper Mississippi River Valley.[19]

The intent was for an all-male lead group to pioneer a route and establish farms. After three weeks of study, Parley P. Pratt's outfitting committee reported a plan typical of those found in travel guidebooks of the time.[20] The list identified supplies that would support five men per wagon traveling all the way to the Pacific Coast. Each cluster of five was called a "family." Assuming the men had bedding and cooking utensils of their own, a complete outfit would cost about $250 for the group and weigh nineteen hundred pounds. The final draft of the committee's recommendation was ready on the Saturday before general conference.[21]

By this time, the Twelve had concluded that all of the Saints willing to go would be heading west. The supply list created for a thousand male pioneers was adjusted to accommodate women and children in traditional family groups of five. It was published in the *Nauvoo Neighbor* at the end of October. Broadening the immediate plan to include an entire people did not eliminate the need for the path markers. In late December, Orson Pratt took astronomical calculations of Nauvoo while his brother Parley worked out a schedule of travel from Nauvoo to the Great Salt Lake Valley for a pioneer company of one thousand men.[22]

Each emigrant company of one hundred families was responsible to identify and buy or build its own wagons for freight and transportation. Company leaders found wheelwrights, carpenters, and cabinetmakers to serve as foremen over less-experienced workers. While some men prepared timber for the wagon parts, others fashioned the metal parts. "The timber is cut and brought into the city green; hub, spoke, and felloe timber boiled in salt and water, and other parts kiln dried," according to a report in Brigham Young's history:

> Shops are established at the Nauvoo House, Masonic Hall, and Arsenal; nearly every shop in town is employed in making wagons. Teams are sent to all parts of the county to purchase iron; blacksmiths are at work night and day and all hands are busily engaged getting ready for our departure westward as soon as possible.[23]

When the supply of material for wagon covers in Nauvoo ran out, the Saints visited merchants in nearby towns and exhausted their stock of unbleached domestic. As for other materials, one migrant noted, "All the fences for miles around were searched for oak rails that would do to work into wagon timber. Iron was scarce. There was little or none to be had in Nauvoo and many wagons were made with wooden tires." Cash was scarce, too. Emigrants paid for their wagons in a typical medium of exchange—trade. For example, blacksmith Alfred Lambson accepted wood, cash, store orders, flour, books, and pork for doing the ironwork on wagons, making buckets, fashioning irons for a carriage, and shoeing horses.[24]

By the end of November, company captains reported 1,508 wagons ready to leave and another 1,892 under construction. This number, 3,400 in all, would provide an average of one wagon for each family counted among the twenty-five organized companies. That left another 115 wagons for other needs. But six months later, at the camps along the Missouri River, Brigham Young and his assistants concluded that only 1,000 wagons and about 775 teams were fit for the rugged overland journey beyond Winter Quarters. This was about half the wagons at or approaching the camps. In the spirit of the Twelve's cooperative management plan, Young decided to use the good wagons and their teams to shuttle immigrants across the plains and prairie in shifts. The trustees in Nauvoo stopped advertising for oxen. They passed along Young's advice encouraging the Saints to gather "cash, flour, meal, wheat, corn, dry goods and groceries, and be ready to load up when our teams return for them."[25]

Along with outfitting themselves for their journey, the Saints had to dispose of homes, lands, and unneeded belongings. Selling out was sometimes as great a challenge as fitting out. During the evacuations of the Morley and Hancock Settlements a Latter-day Saint committee in southern Hancock County tried a cooperative approach. They offered to sell property at reasonably low prices to the old settlers in exchange for livestock, wagons, and store goods. The Saints reserved the rights to the crops. But the Carthage settlement left the sale of Mormon property entirely to market forces. At the October conference, church leaders appointed a seven-member committee for Nauvoo and smaller committees for eight other nearby settlements to act as agents. In Iowa, the responsibility was left with individual landowners.[26]

The sale of Latter-day Saint property was disappointingly slow at first. Even so, much of the deeded and improved property of Nauvoo and surrounding settlements did eventually sell. "New citizens," as they came to be known, saw the opportunity as a bonanza. They bought good land and good houses at low prices in a buyer's market. Census taker Thomas H. Owen estimated in late 1845 that the Latter-day Saints had put twenty thousand acres under cultivation in the Nauvoo area and another ten thousand acres elsewhere in the county. He considered this land a bargain, with good titles and available to buy at about the value of a year's rent. All of it, he reported, "can be paid for in trade, such as cattle, oxen over three and under five years old, mules, sheep, wagons, and some good horses. Work oxen are very much wanted." He added, "They also have a great deal of other property to dispose of, such as cooking stoves, cupboard ware, household furniture, etc., for which the same kind of pay will be taken; and I suppose that cash will not be refused."[27]

By mid-November, church members in southern Hancock County and in the Fountain Green area had sold most of their property. Farms near Warsaw were selling at from five dollars to eight dollars an acre, considered a fair price by local buyers. Sales were slower at La Harpe, in the northeastern corner of the county and nearer Nauvoo. Farmers in these areas were asking twenty dollars to thirty dollars per acre, possibly because of higher initial purchase prices or more extensive cultivation.[28]

The proceeds realized from individual sales varied from one situation to another. "We have to make a great sacrifice in order to get away," Sally Randall informed her family in June 1846. "The most of the Saints are selling out although at a very low price. . . . We are going with a yoke of

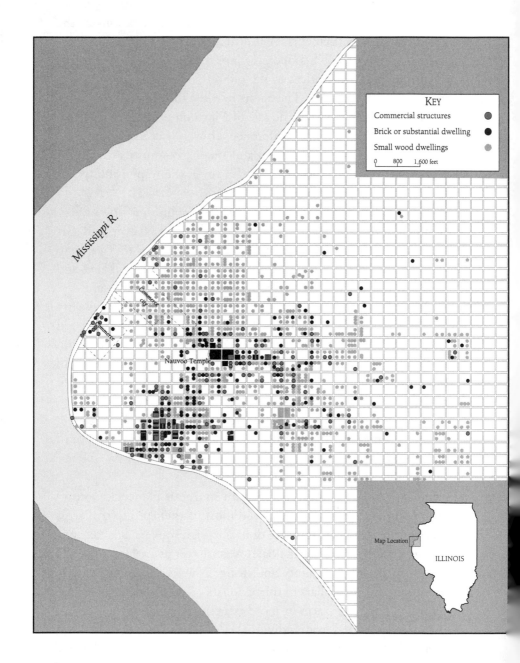

A City for Sale

oxen and a mule. We have cows to drive." Englishman Robert Pixton sold his half-acre town lot and small brick house in May for two cows, a rifle, and a few other things. When Mary Ann Pratt (Parley's wife) left Nauvoo after the final expulsion in September 1846, she took one last look at the stove, the furniture, and the pictures on the wall of their home, visited the burial place of loved ones, and left without selling any of it. John D. Lee refused an offer of eight hundred dollars for his large house on Carlin Street. "I locked it up, selling only one stove out of it, for which I received eight yards of cloth," he recalled. A group of Canadian Saints passing through Nauvoo in early April found many houses "standing empty and unsold." One of them recalled, "We could have [had] brick, frame, or log or stone houses in which were some of the furnishings, chairs and bedsteads, etc. The Saints had been driven away and what they could not readily sell they had to leave." It would be a buyer's market, John S. Fullmer told a prospective buyer in November: "Our city will . . . fall into the hands of our enemies, both by purchase and by plunder, and by sacrifice. It is a place of too much importance to be left unoccupied." Once the Saints had departed, he anticipated, property values would rise. "No one will lose by buying now."[29]

Church property was offered for sale through designated agents. In November 1845, the Twelve sent Almon Babbitt to investigate the possibility of selling the Nauvoo Temple to the Catholic church. The Catholic bishop in St. Louis agreed to seek the support of the head of the Illinois Diocese in Chicago. The plan was to send circulars to bishops in every state to encourage Catholic migration to Nauvoo. In December, Brigham Young and his council considered other inquiries and answered questions from land agents who talked of buying the entire town on speculation. Church officials offered Philadelphia land agents a 50 percent discount if they would purchase all or part of the city or any of the surrounding farms for ready cash. "We should much rather wholesale than retail it," Brigham Young informed the agent.[30] Hopes for a blanket sale died, leaving the task to piecemeal transactions.

As news of the pending mass exodus spread, offers of help arrived from various sources. The Twelve remained skeptical of most of them, including proposals from Oliver Cowdery encouraging an exploring expedition into northern California and one from James Arlington Bennet of New York to lead a revived Nauvoo military force in defense of Nauvoo.[31]

Another offer arrived in a late October letter from Palmyra, Missouri, signed only "Backwoodsman." The writer had learned from newspaper reports that the Saints were headed for California. Backwoodsman claimed to represent a partnership planning an independent, representative nation—the United States of the West—incorporating all of Oregon, upper California, and peninsular lower California. His party would occupy coastal California, with the Bay of San Francisco as their chief port. The Saints could have the eastern region as a self-governing state, with a port at the mouth of the Colorado River.[32] He noted, "Experience ought to have taught you by this time that it is impossible for you to exist as a community collected together in a city in the midst of another community, governed by other laws, than those you esteem paramount to all laws. You cannot be tolerated long in that manner of living, anywhere."[33] These sentiments were those of many Missouri citizens in 1838 and of the Illinois anti-Mormons in the 1840s.

On October 29 in their regular meeting, the Twelve read and discussed the proposal along with information on routes west.[34] Their later actions reveal the Twelve's decision to implement their own plan to remain loyal to the United States. They skirted any entangling alliance with the Missouri Backwoodsman and his friends but concluded that they should avoid moving in on old settlers in coastal California and Oregon.

The original proposal for the Territory of Deseret and the subsequent Provisional State of Deseret established in 1849 resembled in size and boundaries Backwoodsman's proposed independent commonwealth in eastern California. The Latter-day Saints would get themselves west, and they wished to govern themselves there as an American state without any interference from those whose motives they did not fully trust. They would remain a people apart in a new land of refuge.

BEGINNINGS OF THE EXODUS

Brigham Young's epistle to the Saints in October 1845 announced that the migration would begin "as early next spring as the first appearance of thrifty vegetation." The intent was to leave after a final dedication of the temple and the April general conference. Even then Young knew that attempts at arrest might force an earlier departure for at least the leading men and their families.[35]

A hint of this threat came in mid-September, shortly after marauders

began burning houses on the plains. One of the vigilantes swore out complaints of treason against six members of the Twelve and one other Latter-
day Saint. The charges listed military preparations of the Nauvoo Legion,
political involvements of the Council of Fifty, and a supposed plan for an
alliance with the Indians. The accused offered to meet with a constable
from Carthage at the Masonic Hall. But the officer wanted to meet at
A. G. Fellow's house on the prairie four miles from Carthage, a rendezvous
point used in June 1844 for Joseph Smith's party.[36] With the implications
of the last deadly trip to Carthage embedded in their memories, the men
ignored the invitation. Heber Kimball understood the intent of the legal
papers. "I positively know men . . . who with uplifted hands, swore they
would take President Brigham Young's life and my own," he told the
October conference. Kimball's associates remained on alert. When they
did appear before a judge in Carthage on the twenty-fourth of September,
the charges were dismissed as unwarranted.[37]

The Twelve could not be certain that any government officer would
protect their civil rights. Every rumor reaffirmed their conviction that the
enemies of the church would persist until the new leaders were dead or
the whole people expelled. These unsettling rumors, plus specific incidents
during the next several weeks, only increased the jitteriness of the cautious
leaders. In October, they heard reports that General Hardin had pledged
to use his troops and three hundred anti-Mormon volunteers to "unroof
every house in Nauvoo" until he had arrested Porter Rockwell and others
believed implicated in the shooting of former Missouri governor Lilburn
Boggs.[38] John S. Fullmer had heard that apostates were encouraging federal officials to prevent the move west. Migration to Mexican California,
they argued, would ally the Saints with a foreign power, an act of treason
against the United States.[39]

That same month, the Twelve had a verbal confrontation with Major
Warren over the posting of twenty or so Mormon watchmen on Nauvoo's
outer perimeter to guard against invasion. When Warren threatened to
place the county under martial law, the Council of Fifty asked Governor
Ford to withdraw his troops. "Some of the house-burners are actually in
the *posse* of state troops and are prowling round in Nauvoo every few
days," the council declared. Ford spent three hours listening to Nauvoo
delegates and then convinced them that his troops were necessary to
maintain an uneasy truce until the spring departure. The delegates left

By the time the exodus from Nauvoo began early in 1846, the temple dominated the city's landscape and symbolized its purposes and accomplishments. The gathered Saints had received their temple blessings, and they departed with the promise that other temples would be built in the West.

with a promise from Ford. After the Saints' voluntary departure, George Miller reported, the governor would bring the house burners and murderers "to justice and hang every devil of them."[40]

During the last months of the year, the Twelve were threatened a number of times with arrest. A marshal from Iowa made two attempts to serve writs sworn out in Iowa charging the Twelve with creating counterfeit money at the Iowa home of Dr. Abiather Williams. Iowa's Half-breed Tract had a reputation as "a sanctuary for coiners, horse thieves, and other outlaws," but the apostles were not culpable.[41]

On December 23, federal officials, reportedly escorted from Springfield by state troops, attempted to deliver warrants on counterfeiting charges issued there by the grand jury of a United States circuit court.[42] The officials asked permission to search the temple for Brigham Young and Amasa Lyman. In a diversionary tactic, coachman George D. Grant left the temple and pulled Young's carriage up to the door. Then William Miller, dressed in Brigham Young's cap and Heber C. Kimball's cloak, descended the stairs in company with several women, nodded to the marshal, and entered the carriage. The officers served Miller with a writ charging Brigham Young with counterfeiting. Miller objected and denied guilt. He was allowed to meet privately at the Mansion House with an attorney who joined in with the ruse, as did others who gathered around. The marshal hauled his captive and the attorney on a two-hour ride to Carthage. The charade on the marshal was discovered soon after they arrived. Several witnesses, including Sheriff Backenstos, verified that the man in custody was not Brigham Young. Miller later told friends in Nauvoo that he was kept awake that night by the guffaws of his attorney. Ever after it was remembered as the "Bogus Brigham" incident. Thomas Sharp agreed that the "Mormon hoax" was the best joke of the season.[43]

On the evening of December 30, temple officiators ended their work earlier than usual. Relieved from the tension of the previous days, they sought to lift their spirits and express their feelings about removal. Peter Hanson, working in the temple on a Danish translation of the Book of Mormon, picked up his fiddle. Elisha Averett joined in on his flute. They played "several lively airs, among the rest some very good lively dancing tunes. This was too much for the gravity of Brother Joseph Young, who indulged in [dancing] a hornpipe, and was soon joined by several others, and before the dance was over several French fours were indulged in." Brigham Young opened the first, and others soon joined in. "The spirit of dancing increased," William Clayton's diary notes, "until the whole floor was covered with dancers." Dancing and singing continued for an hour. Erastus Snow sang "Upper California." Elizabeth Ann Whitney sang a hymn in tongues. Her husband, Bishop Newel K. Whitney, interpreted it as a message about building the temple, meeting in it for the present festivities, and then departing into Indian country to begin converting Native Americans and gathering scattered Israel. Other similar musical evenings occurred in the temple until Brigham Young halted the practice on January 9. Apparently by then the mood was shifting from spiritual uplift to a festive mood unsuited to the sacred space.[44]

The fragile truce in Hancock County faced other challenges that added to the apprehension during the last months of 1845. In early November, fifty-seven-year-old Joshua Smith was arrested in Nauvoo merely for carrying a knife. Held in Carthage, he became violently ill after eating food provided by the militia. The sudden death of the church member was attributed to poisoning. A postmortem by three doctors confirmed the diagnosis. Nauvoo residents immediately labeled the death a murder and feared it would not be the last.[45]

Almost from the beginning, government officials who were asked for an opinion warned against Mexican California as a place of resettlement for the Saints. Most had suggested the contested Oregon country or other American territories. Even though church leaders had privately decided to settle in upper California, they allowed the public to believe the destination might be Oregon or Vancouver's Island. Only by keeping their plans confidential could they achieve them. But a few who knew of the upper California destination shared the secret. Apparently, it was a matter of discussion as far afield as Washington, D.C. Within Nauvoo's inner circle, a few believed that William Smith and other disaffected Saints were behind the effort to prevent removal by revealing plans for California.[46]

In mid-December 1845, Brigham Young received a letter from Samuel Brannan. This New York publisher had visited with the United States secretary of war and other cabinet members. Brannan reported that these men objected to the departure of an armed band of men from the United States either to California or Oregon. Nor, said Brannan, were they inclined to let the Saints remain in the United States. It sounded to Brannan like another effort at extermination. Young shared the news in the temple with the Twelve and the bishops. A response to Brannan sought to defuse the issue. In addition, letters written on December 17 sought help from several prominent state and national leaders, among them congressmen Stephen A. Douglas and John Wentworth and United States secretary of war William L. Marcy. Nauvoo's leaders asked their support in getting government contracts to build blockhouses or carry the mail along the Oregon Trail.[47]

Soon afterward, the Twelve stepped up their study of recently published reports of western regions and routes. Several of the quorum, meeting in the council room in the temple, read together from John C. Frémont's report of his visit to the Wind River Mountains in 1842 and to California and Oregon in 1843 to1844. Frémont's circuit through California had taken him through the Bear River Valley to the north end of the Great Salt Lake. These parts of the report and the carefully drafted maps of the Platte River route held special interest for the Twelve. They remembered Joseph Smith's inspired foretelling of a place of peace in the Rocky Mountains. Now the planners needed specifics as they prepared their trek to a new promised land.[48] Four United States maps were hung on the council room walls as references.[49]

Another text sampled by the apostles was the 1845 *Emigrants' Guide to Oregon and California* published by Lansford Hastings. The guide prepared by this avid promoter of emigration described a time-saving cutoff west from Fort Bridger to the Great Salt Lake and on to California. Church leaders must have seen other published reports of western travelers and explorers. They knew of the expeditions of Charles Wilkes and B. L. E. Bonneville, but reports of these trips had little of value to offer. Still other publications would have merely fed the interest of the Mormon planners.[50]

From firsthand witnesses and from newspaper articles monitored over many preceding months, the Twelve were reassured in their decision. Publicly they would say only that what they called the next "resting place" for the Saints would be somewhere "in some good valley in the neighborhood of the Rocky Mountains." The Nauvoo high council used those words in its mid-January circular.[51] Privately, church leaders had focused on the Great Salt Lake Valley. The January statement would not have jeopardized the Twelve's desire to be the first permanent American settlers in that region. For others who wondered where "some good valley" might be found, the options were legion. The Rocky Mountains extended all the way from the northern portions of the contested regions of Oregon territory into the northeastern regions of upper California. The range continued southward under other names to the boundary between Texas and New Mexico.

Church members who were not part of the presiding councils did wonder about just where they were headed. Their letters to friends and relatives reflected an understandable uncertainty. Many correspondents echoed the descriptions given in the October conference. They simply told their friends that they were headed to an unknown destination in the wilderness.[52] Some Latter-day Saints suspected they would land somewhere in Mexican California. One Nauvoo writer who knew of the San Francisco Bay destination of New York Mormons on the chartered ship *Brooklyn* informed relatives, "I go to seek a happy home on the coast of the Pacific Ocean."[53] Most would-be emigrants lacked the specific information available to such insiders as Parley P. Pratt, who told a friend in September that the destination would be eight hundred miles inland from the Pacific Coast. Pratt knew that the targeted destination lay somewhere between Utah Lake and the Bear River Valley.[54]

At the beginning of 1846, the Twelve focused on administering the endowment to as many worthy Saints as possible before leaving Nauvoo. That work had begun a month earlier, but many yet desired their temple blessings. They were not disappointed. For some, the spirit they felt in the House of the Lord was reminiscent of the apostolic day of Pentecost. Jacob Gates, who assisted in administering the endowments, noted in his journal: "The Ninth of January I stayed all Night in the Temple of the Lord. The Spirit of God seems to fill the House and cause every heart to rejoice with a joy unknown to the World of mankind . . . insomuch that the Brethren shouted for joy."[55]

From early January until the final company left the temple on February 7, endowment groups received the ordinances six days a week, with sessions underway some days from early morning until late at night. More than one hundred Saints were endowed on a typical day, two hundred or more on peak days, and more than five hundred made covenants with the Lord on each of the final two days.[56]

One of those who had waited patiently for the blessings of the temple was James Jones, an emigrant from England who had buried his wife at sea in the Caribbean. After settling in Nauvoo near British friends, he lost two sons from malaria contracted while they were working in St. Louis to support the family. A married son, Henry, had remained in England. Henry had joined the church but then left it. Father and son kept in touch across the miles. As James was preparing to leave Nauvoo with his daughter, he once more responded to the queries of his skeptical son and shared his feelings about the blessings of the restored gospel. "Once more, you have heard that there was to be a Temple built," he wrote,

> and that the pattern was given to one who has sealed his testimony with his own blood. . . . In the midst of mobs and persecution that house is built. The Lord has accepted the same at our hands. It is consecrated and in that house I myself with thousands more have received our washings, anointings, and endowments. . . . Now this one thing is worth all and more than all the sorrows and afflictions I have had to pass through.[57]

As the ordinance work continued, so did negotiations toward selling the temple and preparations for the migration. Behind it all was the worry that legal actions might lead to the arrest, incarceration, and murder of Brigham Young, who was anxious to get on his way.[58]

A few days into the new year, a troubling message reached Nauvoo. Writing from Springfield to Sheriff Backenstos, Governor Ford said that he had learned of plans in Washington to halt the evacuation of Nauvoo. President Polk, he said, might "order up a regiment or two of the regular army," supported by the state militia. Ford said he thought it "very likely that the government at Washington will interfere to prevent the Mormons from going west of the Rocky Mountains." Ford later admitted that this letter and his other efforts to convince Nauvoo's leaders that federal intervention was certain were part of an intentional ploy. The governor had encouraged Polk to activate the soldiers, hoping that news of the order would precipitate an early and certain departure of the Twelve. Polk refused to cooperate, but the artifice, Ford acknowledged, "had its intended effect."[59]

The governor's message solidified a feeling that the pioneer company should leave Nauvoo ahead of the spring schedule. Facing possible arrest with the help of United States troops, the Twelve reflected on an earlier arrest on false charges. "Our danger," Brigham Young noted, "consists only in being held still by the authorities while mobs massacre us as Governor Ford held Joseph and Hyrum Smith while they were butchered." Planning for an early departure began on Sunday, January 11, when the Twelve met with the Council of Fifty for the first time in four months. The Fifty assembled in the temple council room in their capacity as the heads of emigrant companies. The captains of fifties and tens had reported that only 140 horses and 70 wagons were ready to go. Presumably everyone else had been waiting until spring drew closer. Acting upon the false premise that federal intervention would prevent the planned spring departure and wishing to avoid arrest, the council vowed on January 18 to use all their resources to help one another get away from Nauvoo early.[60]

It was probably around this time that Brigham Young received an answer to a question that the Twelve had not resolved through much study, discussion, and prayer over the previous year. Joseph Smith had talked often of a refuge in the Rocky Mountains. The Twelve had concluded as early as the spring of 1845 that the Lord had prepared a place of peace somewhere in the northern reaches of the Mexican province of upper California. Sometime between March and August, they had narrowed their focus to the region between the Bear River Valley on the north and Utah Lake on the south. But President Young desired more specific information. During January 1846, while in the temple administering endowments to the Saints, he would find time to retreat to his office. In a spirit of fasting and prayer, he sought the Lord's will. During one of these contemplative moments, he saw a vision in which Joseph Smith showed him the precise place of settlement for the Saints. According to John D. Lee, Brigham Young told the captains in one of their January planning meetings "that the saying of the Prophets would never be verified unless the House of the Lord should be reared in the Tops of the Mountains and the proud banner of liberty wave over the valley." Young also noted, "I know where the spot is." George A. Smith said later that the Prophet Joseph Smith had pointed out a mountaintop with an ensign flying above it and said, "Build under the point where the colors fall and you will prosper and have peace."[61]

The decision to move up the departure of church leaders prompted the Nauvoo high council to issue a public circular. The January 20 notice filled at least three purposes: to deny charges of counterfeiting, murder, robbery, and treason made against the church; to reaffirm the Saints' intent to leave as agreed upon; and to offer the sale of Latter-day Saint property at bargain prices.[62] Although the Saints were not guilty of the recurring charges of counterfeiting, Brigham Young admitted privately to priesthood leaders that bogus land office coins were being minted in Nauvoo "by wagonloads." The makers, he said, blamed the Latter-day Saints to cover their own crime and to get revenge on Nauvoo officials who had refused to approve the business. To allay concerns that the Saints might inhabit a foreign territory, the high council adopted the popular American position of Manifest Destiny. The council defended America's right to occupy Oregon and pledged to help prevent foreign dominion there. Despite the wrongs committed against the church, the circular noted, "still we are Americans."[63]

The circular reminded readers that both sides had pledged to file no more lawsuits. "In good faith have we labored to fulfil this engagement. Governor Ford has also done his duty to further our wishes in this respect." The circular announced that an advance "company of pioneers, consisting mostly of young, hardy men, with some families," would go first, sometime in March, "to put in a spring crop, build houses," and prepare the way for those who would leave later in the spring. "These are destined to be furnished with an ample outfit; taking with them a printing press, farming utensils of all kinds, with mill irons and bolting cloths, seeds of all kinds, grain, etc."[64]

A few days after the release of the high council circular, Brigham Young informed priesthood leaders of plans and problems. Arrest attempts had made it necessary for the Twelve to be part of the pioneer company. To protect church property in the area, he said, "We shall drop all political operations and church government, and by so doing we may preserve our public buildings from the torch."[65]

Young opened the general migration to interested, law-abiding peoples of all faiths. "I look upon every man that is a true republican as bone of my bone and flesh of my flesh," he said. At the same time, he counseled church leaders to avoid pressuring lukewarm Saints to join the trek. All emigrants must be willing to support the Twelve. Two men in particular were making inroads with their appeal for followers. "If any wish to follow Sidney Rigdon or J. J. Strang I say let them go; we will cut them off from the church, and let them take their own course for salvation."[66]

Young acknowledged that some Latter-day Saints might die for their religion. He felt concern over the safety of the Twelve. In Iowa, there was talk of harrassment. According to one report, men in Keokuk dressed in Indian garb had participated in a mock war dance and then met "to concoct schemes to take the Twelve, when they cross the Mississippi or soon after."[67]

Of more immediate concern were ongoing legal problems, combined with new information to support rumors of planned federal intervention. Men seen prowling in Nauvoo were thought by the Saints to be state troops seeking the arrest of church leaders. In the East, Amos Kendall, late postmaster general in the Polk administration, told Sam Brannan that the government intended to disarm the migrating Saints on the pretext that they were planning to join another nation. Young received additional details of this report two days before leaving Nauvoo.[68]

With tensions high on both sides, Governor Ford feared a breakdown of civil control and the outbreak of armed conflict. His actions and those of his military officers were being misunderstood on both sides. Efforts to curb violence until the Saints could depart, he said, often "pleased neither

Phebe Woodruff packed this portrait into a trunk when she left Liverpool for Nauvoo. Painted early in 1846, it shows Phebe holding Joseph, the first son born after she and Wilford were sealed. Joseph died in Winter Quarters less than a year later.

the Mormons nor the anti-Mormons."[69] In this light, it was not surprising that Sheriff Backenstos returned from a visit with Ford convinced that the Illinois chief executive had turned against the Saints. An attorney in Springfield informed Brigham Young that the governor had sided with General Hardin's proposal to declare martial law in Hancock County, suspend civil offices, and halt the collection of taxes. In fact, Ford was doing all he could to speed the departure of the Saints. Meanwhile, he had agreed, tax collection should be deferred, if only to prevent misuse of the funds in a time of civil disruption. But he argued strongly against the imposition of martial law over a civilian population. It was an unconstitutional action, he said, except in an extreme national emergency. To do so would deny constitutionally protected freedoms and would be the first step toward anarchy and then despotism.[70]

The climate of uncertainty in Hancock County only reinforced the need to reconsider plans for a spring departure. On February 2, the Twelve, trustees, and members of the first company met to refine the schedule. "We agreed," according to Brigham Young's history, "that it was imperatively necessary to start as soon as possible." He alerted the captains of hundreds and fifties to procure boats for transporting wagons and teams across the Mississippi and to have supplies ready for loading with four hours' notice. "Our enemies have resolved to intercept us whenever we start," Young told a hastily assembled meeting with the captains later that day. "I should like to push on as far as possible before they are aware of our movements."[71]

Besides a surge of activity in physical preparations, talk that the Twelve would be leaving soon created a surge on the temple that day. Hundreds had not been endowed. Young told an assembly at the temple of the urgency of his departure. "We should build more Temples," he said, "and have further opportunities to receive the blessings of the Lord, as soon as the saints were prepared to receive them." He was ready to get his wagons and start for the West. He walked away, but the crowd failed to disperse. They had sacrificed for the temple and wanted the blessings. "Looking upon the multitude and knowing their anxiety, as they were thirsting and hungering for the word," Young noted, "we continued at work diligently in the House of the Lord." An additional 295 people received endowments that day. While the president loaded his wagons, the ordinance work continued until Saturday, February 7, with around eleven hundred endowed on the final two days.[72]

On Sunday morning, the day after completing the ordinance work, the Twelve met in Brigham Young's room in the southeast corner of the temple, knelt around the altar, and dedicated the entire, almost finished building to God. "We asked his blessing upon our intended move to the west," Brigham's clerk recorded. "Also asked him to enable us some day to finish the Temple, and dedicate it to him, and we would leave it in his hands to do as he pleased; and to preserve the building as a monument to Joseph Smith." Then they left the temple. At a meeting in the grove later in the day, Brigham Young announced that the pioneer company would cross the river that week.[73]

In one of his last actions before leaving Nauvoo, Brigham Young asked Major Warren to communicate his thanks to Governor Ford for refusing to cooperate with those who wanted to arrest church leaders on groundless warrants. Warren informed the governor that Young believed "that it was your action alone which permitted him and the Mormons to leave the country."[74]

The selective departure from Nauvoo soon swelled into a surge of wagons, teams, livestock, and people ferrying across the cold Mississippi. On Wednesday, February 4, an advance party of scouts led by Charles Shumway left Nauvoo with fifteen wagons. They set up camp at a place they called "the west side of Jordan" and prepared to help others ferry across the river.[75] On Friday, the sixth, Bishop George Miller, with his family and their six wagons, became the first of the authorities to cross into Iowa. Two days after that, Nauvoo's stake president, John Smith, and his clerk, Albert Carrington, took their families over. On Monday, February 9, George A. Smith sent his family across, as did some other church leaders. The Mississippi at Nauvoo, nearly nine-tenths of a mile across, soon became a busy river road serving a steady stream of refugees.[76]

Overloaded skiffs and unskilled helmsmen added confusion to the ferrying. When one of the skiffs started sinking, a flatboat came to the rescue and got the passengers aboard, then someone squirted tobacco juice into the eye of one of Thomas Grover's oxen that were attached to a wagon on the flatboat. The beast lunged into the river, taking with it the other ox and Grover's wagon. The accident tore the sideboards off the flatboat. The vessel began to fill with water. The men headed the floundering craft toward the Nauvoo shore, but it sank short of its destination. A few of the frantic passengers climbed atop the wagon, still visible above the water. "Some were on feather beds, sticks of wood, lumber, or any thing they could get hold of," a witness reported. After a time, an empty boat, skiffs, and sailboats rescued the cold and wet people. Two oxen drowned, but the wagon was later pulled out of the river with most of its baggage—wet but otherwise undamaged. To prevent similar problems, police chief Hosea Stout marshaled his men to operate many of the flatboats, skiffs, and "some old lighters" [barges]. Working from dawn until way into the night each day, they kept as many as six ferries running.[77]

The excitement of a sinking skiff added to the confusion of a day already busy with departing emigrants and punctuated by a fire in the temple. When someone noticed flames on the temple roof at 3:30 that afternoon, residents working or living close by rushed to the building. From his home on the flats, Brigham Young saw the blaze but felt powerless. "If it is the will of the Lord that the Temple be burned, instead of being defiled by the Gentiles," he told his family, "Amen to it." Ordinance work had ceased in the temple, and its only long-term use was as an asset to rent or sell. At the temple site, Willard Richards organized a bucket brigade. Lines of men and women passed water-filled buckets into the building and up the stairs to the attic and roof. The fire had started from an overheated stovepipe drying clothing in an upper room. It burned for half an hour, feeding on the wood shingles in a ten-foot to sixteen-foot circle surrounding the stovepipe. By the time Young arrived, the fire was out. Men on the deck roof shouted a triumphant "Hosannah!" to him. As the crowd dispersed, state troops arrived to investigate, but temple door-keepers kept them out. That night, a large number of Saints gathered in the temple and celebrated the victory "with music and rejoicing" until two o'clock the next morning. The temple was safe now for whatever future uses could be made of it.[78]

On February 10, the Twelve appointed Joseph Young, senior president of the seventy, to preside as long as members remained in the area. This concluded the formal business of organizing Nauvoo for the departure of the Twelve. On the fourteenth, Parley P. Pratt crossed the Mississippi with his six emigrant wagons, three-seated carriages, and a one-horse wagon pulled by the family's favorite steed, Old Dick. The small wagon carried cooked provisions ready for use. The next day, a Sunday, Brigham Young left his unsold house and turned his teams down Parley Street to the ferry landing. Thomas Sharp reported this procession as thirteen wagons. Joined by George A. Smith and the Willard Richards family, the party crossed the river and made its way to Sugar Creek. This temporary camp in Ambrosia township, nine miles from the Mississippi River, in Lee County, Iowa, was well supplied with timber for fires and with a good water supply. Throughout 1846, Sugar Creek served as a temporary stopping place for the westward-bound Latter-day Saints.[79]

John Taylor celebrated "the great move of the Saints out of the United States" in an editorial in the next-to-last issue of Nauvoo's church newspaper. "About two thousand are ready and crossing the Mississippi to pioneer the way, and make arrangements for summer crops at some point between this and the 'Pacific,'" he announced in the February 1 issue. Then he pleaded, "*Let us go—let us go.*"[80]

The spirit of removal had already captured the hearts and minds of Nauvoo's Latter-day Saints. But many of their non-Mormon kinfolk elsewhere opposed the decision. Letters written to Nauvoo invited the departing relatives to return to their ancestral homes in the East. "I think it a wild goose chase to cross the rocky mountains," a friend in Pennsylvania told Edward Hunter. A relative of Joseph Heywood wrote, "The romance of traveling 2000 miles in an ox waggon is pleasant enough when contemplated by a quiet fire-side, but the tedious reality will present a different picture."[81] Many writers imagined their Nauvoo relations heading off to a grave in the wilderness or into a country where there would be no further communication.[82]

Such comments typically left the Nauvoo emigrant unconvinced. These Saints wanted to stay with the church and had been convinced of the need to leave Illinois. A folk song making the rounds in Nauvoo captured their feelings. It began:

> *Early next spring we'll leave Nauvoo*
> *And on our journey we'll pursue.*
> *We'll go and bid the mob farewell*
> *And let them go to heaven or hell.*

> Chorus:
> *So on our way to California*
> *In the spring we'll take our journey:*
> *Far above the Arkansas' fountain*
> *We'll pass between the Rocky Mountain.*[83]

When anti-Mormons in Warsaw learned that the general departure had not waited for spring, they worried that Iowa's winter weather might discourage other Latter-day Saints. Any Mormons who stayed behind would frustrate the anti-Mormon agenda.[84] Even the scheduled pioneers seemed stalled. The first members of Emigrating Company No. 1 to leave Nauvoo waited at Sugar Creek nearly two weeks for the camp to gather. Not until Brigham Young arrived did things get organized. On February 17, "acting the part of a father to everybody," he issued the first of many instructions to the men of the Camp of Israel. Standing in his wagon to counsel those who had encircled the vehicle, he said, "We will have no laws we cannot keep, but we will have order in the camp. If any want to live in peace when we have left this [place], they must toe the mark." Young enlisted all the emigrants at Sugar Creek to join the pioneer camp, whether originally designated to do so or not. After making organizational assignments, Young returned to his tent and reorganized his own division of four companies of ten.[85] The company decided to wait for the tabernacle canvas,[86] the artillery,[87] and certain public property before moving on.

Organizational matters occupied much of the attention of the Twelve over the next two weeks until the Camp of Israel moved out of Sugar Creek and headed west. During this time, Brigham Young set more rules for the pioneer company and clarified its purposes, procured supplies needed for the journey, and revised the schedule of travel. Some exiles had left Nauvoo before readying themselves for the trip or before their scheduled departure. Young made sure everyone at the temporary camp was assigned to an organized emigrating company. With a kindly frankness that won immediate support, he praised the men for their devotion and urged upon them improvement.[88]

During this time, President Young resolved for a larger group a question concerning the destination of the Saints. In mid-February, he called a formal council meeting with seven members of the Twelve in a quiet spot half a mile east of the Sugar Creek camp. The subject was information in letters from Samuel Brannan that Young had brought from Nauvoo. The letters described one product of an effort Young had launched two months earlier to enlist federal help with the migration by seeking federal contracts along the Oregon Trail. President James K. Polk had already suggested to Congress the need for such contracts. But Polk found the Mormon options politically difficult to endorse.[89]

The Twelve hoped for federal help but were prepared to accomplish the removal on their own. Since mid-November, Sam Brannan had been organizing an emigrant company in New York. He expected to benefit from the proposed contract. But, growing impatient when the effort stalled, the Eastern Saints chartered their own ship, the *Brooklyn,* and sailed in February. Still optimistic about some eventual government business to aid the Saints, these emigrants no longer expected to see a federal "highway cast up for the deliverance of God's people."[90] Finding others interested, William I. Appleby began recruiting for a second shipload of Saints to sail from New York in May, but he dropped the project for a lack of means. In November, after he had visited with church leaders at the Missouri River, Jesse C. Little renewed the effort to move the Eastern Saints westward. Brigham Young had proposed an overland route and promised to shuttle the poor partway. Little shared Young's counsel in a circular, explaining that to conserve the strength of oxen for the trek to

A group of more than 230 New York area farmers and craftsmen made history in 1846 when they sailed around the tip of South America to San Francisco aboard the square-rigged Brooklyn. *The twenty-four-thousand-mile trip was the longest passage by any Mormon emigrant company. Orson Pratt directed Sam Brannan to organize the 177-day voyage.*

the mountains, the emigrants would charter steamships at St. Louis for the last leg of the journey to Council Bluffs. He expected as many as two thousand emigrants to make the journey.[91]

As the Camp of Israel moved westward across Iowa, a more acceptable assistance offer arrived from Washington. Events in the West were moving rapidly. During the last months of 1845, Polk had been attempting to resolve a long-standing financial claim against Mexico by purchasing New Mexico and upper California. Then, on December 29, Congress admitted Texas as the twenty-eighth state with a western boundary at the Rio Grande. Mexico challenged the line. Following a military clash within the disputed territory in late April, Polk declared war on Mexico. The United States government now found additional American settlers for California desirable.

The war presented a new way for the Latter-day Saints to secure government help in their forced removal. Young had asked Jesse C. Little, presiding officer over the Saints remaining in the East, to represent the church in Washington. With Thomas L. Kane advising him, Little offered to send one thousand Latter-day Saints from the Eastern states to California as settlers and a thousand men from camps scattered across Iowa for service in the American army. In a letter to Polk, Little included a hint that was intended to force Polk's hand. An absence of federal help, he said, might "compel us to be foreigners." Polk had given the shipping contract to others. Because he felt uncomfortable with an independent thousand-member Mormon militia and needed no more volunteers for the popular war anyway, Polk ordered General Stephen W. Kearny at Fort Leavenworth to organize a body half that size as a battalion in the United States Army of the West. Thus came about Kane's mission west with a message to Kearny authorizing the call of the Mormon Battalion.[92]

The Latter-day Saint contingent included 541 soldiers and more than one hundred others, among them wives enlisted as laundresses. This participation demonstrated Latter-day Saint loyalty to the nation and got the battalion across the country at government expense. The men's pay helped their families and others in the emigration.[93] Even though some of the soldiers saw Polk's recruitment offer negatively, the opportunity seemed to the Twelve an appropriate federal response to the request for assistance. At very least, it was a partial redress for the wrongs of earlier years.[94]

The original intent was to get the pioneer company as far as the Missouri River by April. That would allow a thrust across the Rockies in time to plant summer crops. By late February, with six inches of snow on the ground and storms delaying departure from the Sugar Creek Encampment, the Twelve decided to seek permission from Iowa governor James Clark to raise crops on the public land of the territory or to rent established farms. Their letter appealed to the governor's sympathy. Thousands were leaving "their peaceful homes and firesides, their property and farms, and their dearest constitutional rights—to wander in the barren plains, and sterile mountains of western wilds" rather than face extermination, the letter explained. With the governor's permission, the Saints established large farms at places that they named Garden Grove and Mount Pisgah.[95]

A roll call on February 18 counted about five hundred people and between three hundred and four hundred wagons in the encampment, most of the people organized into tens, fifties, and hundreds.[96] That evening, after setting up the wagon shuttle for emigrants, Brigham Young and Heber Kimball returned to Nauvoo for three days to conduct additional church business. They felt comfortable in making the trip because word had just arrived "stating that there were no hostile intentions on the part of the U.S. Government toward Mormon immigrants." The reassuring news had reached the City of Joseph through two channels—from state officials in Springfield and directly from an Illinois congressman. "The subject of the Mormons immigrating in armed bodies had been presented to the President," the letter said. "He deemed it of sufficient importance to call together his Cabinet and the conclusion was that if they stopped our immigrants they might with the same propensity stop all, and they decided none should be stopped on account of their religion."[97]

While in Nauvoo, the two apostles called a meeting in the temple to counsel anxious members. The new truss floor had just been completed in the first-floor room. The weight of the crowd caused a cracking sound as the floor settled on the truss girders underneath. The sound so frightened the congregation that some men overreacted and broke window sashes and glass in several windows in their attempt to flee the building. "Men plunged out like mad cats upon the frozen ground and stones below," Norton Jacob reported. One man broke an arm and bruised his face; another suffered a fractured leg. Failing in his efforts to calm the crowd, President Young dismissed the meeting and reassembled it in a foot of snow at the grove, where he and Orson Hyde spoke on apostasy and James J. Strang.[98]

After returning to Sugar Creek, Brigham Young met with the Twelve and captains of hundreds to resume preparations for moving the camp toward its westward destination. The men selected a route leading up the divide between the Des Moines and the Missouri Rivers. They dispatched Stephen Markham's pioneer company along the designated route to plot the course, to bridge sloughs and streams, and to select prairie sites for summer cropland in central Iowa.[99]

The emigrant companies of the Sugar Creek Encampment left in stages beginning that day. As spring broke on the mellow soil of Iowa Territory, the westward heading wagons slogged toward their immediate destination on the Missouri. For a few weeks, the roads were nearly impassable, but soon the soils dried and the way became more easily trod. Brigham Young established a second temporary camp about fifty-five miles west of Nauvoo at Richardson's Point, where his party rested for twelve rainy days in March. From this site, he wrote to his brother Joseph at Nauvoo, expressing his relief at being away from the threats of false arrest. "I am so free from bondage at this time," he wrote, "that Nauvoo looks like a prison to me. It looks pleasant ahead, but dark to look back."[100]

At Garden Grove, 150 miles from Nauvoo, Brigham Young issued one of his declarations of intent that helped define the march from Nauvoo to a new place of peace in the western wilderness. Under rainy skies on a Sunday morning, and before a congregation of three hundred, he rallied his people:

> He that falters or makes a misstep, can never regain that what he loses. Some have started with us and have turned back, and perhaps more will, but I hope better things of you my brethren. We have set out to find a land and a resting place, where we can serve the Lord in peace. We will leave some here because they cannot go farther at present. They can stay here for a season and recruit, and by and by pack up and come on, while we go a little farther and lengthen out the cords and build a few more stakes, and continue on until we can gather all the saints, and plant them in a place where we can build the house of the Lord in the tops of the mountains.

Orson Pratt endorsed this message. It had been exactly eight years to the day, he said, since the Twelve had departed from the foundation of the House of the Lord in Far West, Missouri, for their mission in the British Isles. Even before that time, he said, Joseph Smith had contemplated sending a company of young men on a pioneering expedition to find a location west of the Rocky Mountains, which, when proven with crops, would become a gathering place for families.[101]

During the trek to Garden Grove, William Clayton received welcome news from Nauvoo. His youngest wife, Diantha, who had remained behind with her parents, had given birth to a son. Clayton had experienced the cold rains of early April and had felt discouragement firsthand. He remembered Brigham Young's acknowledgment that some might die while establishing a new place of refuge. Now, celebrating the good news from Nauvoo, Clayton rewrote the words to an old English tune he'd sung for years, "All Is Well." His new trail song encouraged the migrating Saints not to fear the toil and labor of the hard journey. If they would but gird up their loins for the effort, he wrote, God would protect them. The journey into the wilderness would bring its rewards:

> *We'll find the place which God for us prepared,*
> *Far away in the West,*
> *Where none shall come to hurt or make afraid;*
> *There the Saints will be blessed.*
> *We'll make the air with music ring,*
> *Shout praises to our God and King;*
> *Above the rest this chorus swell—*
> *All is well! all is well!*[102]

Young's group, with Clayton along as the president's scribe, reached the Missouri River in mid-June. There, on Pottawatomie Indian lands west of the river, they established a resting place called Winter Quarters. Because of the lateness of the season, the planned pioneer thrust across the Rockies was postponed until the spring of 1847. Meanwhile, the men built a ferry and concentrated on the arduous task of getting the emigrant families, their wagons and teams, and the cannons of the Nauvoo Legion across the river. The size of the first season's migration would eventually make necessary other way stations on both sides of the Missouri River.

The new settlements in the middle Missouri River Valley blossomed with the constant flow of exiles from Nauvoo, where the task continued of transplanting a people. At least two thousand left Nauvoo during the initial winter departure in 1846 and perhaps as many more from settlements in the surrounding countryside.[103] Initially, the moderate winter weather had made ferrying the standard way for these Saints to cross the Mississippi River into Iowa. Then, cold winds from the Northwest dropped the temperatures. On February 19, a snowstorm pelted Nauvoo and the temporary camp across the river. Over the next two days, ice floes in the Mississippi began to catch along the banks of the river. Even though these chunks of ice made crossing the river dangerous, a few people attempted it, among them Brigham Young, Heber C. Kimball, and John Taylor in a heavily loaded skiff. Temperatures dropped as the storm passed. Another storm swept in from the Northwest on February 24, bringing with it severe cold. That night, temperatures dropped to twelve degrees below zero under clear skies, not unusual in Nauvoo for this time of year. Above Montrose, the Mississippi River was frozen over. The

The families with their ox-drawn wagons who left Nauvoo in late February 1846 benefited from an ice-clogged river. Later, departing Saints relied on skiffs and ferries to cross the Mississippi.

following morning, Charles C. Rich arrived at the Sugar Creek camp from Nauvoo. He had walked across the river. For several days, daytime temperatures measured on Orson Pratt's thermometer did not rise above eighteen degrees Fahrenheit.[104]

The cold weather now facilitated the migration. The ice bridge allowed foot-traffic and loaded wagons to cross the frozen Mississippi. This was a common occurrence most winters, sometimes as early as November, but more often in the early months of the year.[105] At Warsaw, the Mississippi had remained frozen during the previous winter from late November until the end of January.[106] The frozen crust on the river at Nauvoo compensated for time lost to the Saints by the running ice. Nelson Whipple found at least one-third of the surface covered with uneven "ice-blocks that had stopped in the strong current and frozen together." Crossing on foot, he said, "we wound our way from one to another until we reached the other shore." A few days later, he recrossed the mile-wide stretch again, this time in Judson Stoddard's sleigh.[107]

As the time arrived for the planned spring departure, thousands more from Nauvoo and beyond were on the road behind the Camp of Israel. Many of the men who had left with the first groups returned, with or without permission, to get their wives and children after the main camp reached Richardson's Point. Willard Richards set up a post office in his

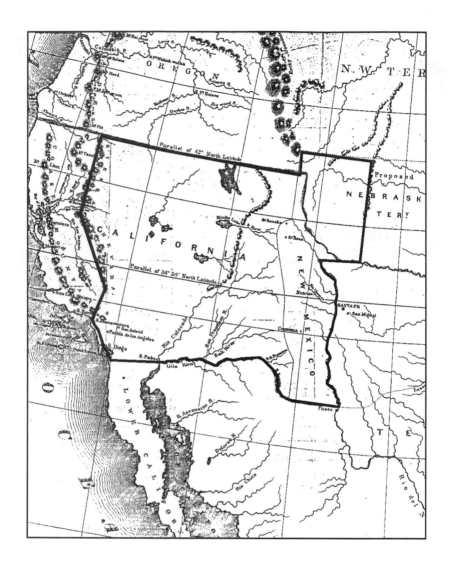

Proposed Territory of Deseret

tent to receive and dispatch the mail carried back and forth between the camp and the Saints at Nauvoo.[108] The early winter departure and the more general, planned mass movement in the spring soon left Nauvoo a city with a small remnant of Latter-day Saints unable then to leave but anxiously preparing themselves for the trek beyond the Rockies.

Those who left Nauvoo during the spring and summer of 1846 found themselves—as had many of the February exiles—ill-prepared for the experience. Overburdened with household goods, bedding, crockery ware, and other such things, and lacking sufficient food for themselves and their animals, they soon spread out from the emigrant road to exchange excess baggage "for corn, oats, and other provisions." Some found work along the way. They plowed fields, split rails, built houses, and contracted for any other work they could get in exchange for supplies.[109]

Brigham Young put a positive twist on the forced exile. Recognizing its necessity, he told the emigrant companies during a sermon in mid-April 1846 that he was satisfied that the decision would prove to be salvation to the Latter-day Saints as a people. Still dismayed with a few who justified stealing from settlers along the way in retribution for thefts from the emigrants, he chastised those guilty but praised the others. It was a difficult experience at best, he acknowledged. "I did not think there had ever been a body of people since the days of Enoch placed under the same unpleasant circumstances that this people have been, where there was so little grumbling; and I was satisfied that the Lord was pleased with the majority of the 'Camp of Israel.'"[110]

In a later reflection on the departure, Young's historian summarized the abandonment of Nauvoo with an entry inserted at the end of the February 1846 chronology:

Our homes, gardens, orchards, farms, streets, bridges, mills, public halls, magnificent Temple, and other public improvements we leave as a monument of our patriotism, industry, economy, uprightness of purpose and integrity of heart; and as a living testimony of the false-hood and wickedness of those who charge us with disloyalty to the Constitution of our country, idleness and dishonesty.[111]

As the directness of this recital demonstrates, the Latter-day Saints left Nauvoo bearing the burden they had brought to Illinois from Missouri. In a country that guaranteed the right of religious freedom, they had been denied not only the right to build a gathered community but the opportunity to enjoy the fruits of their temporal accomplishments. The Missouri experience had been repeated with some variation in Illinois.

The generation that lived through that era would never forget it. When challenged by an arriving federal army in their mountain retreat a decade later, they would recall the experience. The words of a new hymn composed at that time by Charles W. Penrose linked the experiences of the three gathering places. It anticipated that the exiled Saints and their children to the third and fourth generation would "remember the wrongs of Missouri; [and] forget not the fate of Nauvoo."[112] For the Latter-day Saints, the spiritual and the temporal were one. Having pursued their goals wherever they lived with vigor and self-confidence, the Saints would accept their role as a persecuted and exiled people of promise.

Brigham Young led the well-remembered 1847 pioneer trek to the Great Salt Lake Valley and then returned to Winter Quarters one last time. After a month spent discussing the need to reorganize the First Presidency and resolving concerns, the Quorum of the Twelve met in Orson Hyde's home near Miller's Hollow, and on Sunday, December 5, 1847, the apostles reorganized the First Presidency. Elder Hyde nominated Young, who then selected Heber C. Kimball and Willard Richards as his counselors. The following day, the council talked of plans for building a temple in Great Salt Lake City. On December 27, church members sustained the new First Presidency during a conference in the log tabernacle at Miller's Hollow (renamed Kanesville six months later in honor of Colonel Thomas L. Kane). At the same meeting, the Prophet's uncle John Smith was sustained as patriarch to the church.[113]

The apostolic interregnum that began with Joseph Smith's death had now ended. Church headquarters—moved four times in sixteen years—now raised an ensign in the tops of the mountains, while the Latter-day Saints enjoyed a refuge from the storm of political controversy. Brigham Young never again traveled east of the Rockies. When he left Winter Quarters on May 26, 1848, to return to the new Great Salt Lake City that he had founded in the valleys of the mountains, a new period in Latter-day Saint history was already underway.[114]

CHAPTER 19

Transition and Expulsion

Why is it that we have been at all this outlay and expense [to purchase lands and build houses and the temple], and then are called to leave it? . . . The people of God always were required to make sacrifices, and if we have a sacrifice to make, [I am] in favor of its being something worthy of the people of God. We do not want to leave a desolate place, to be a reproach to us but something that will be a monument of our industry and virtue.

—PARLEY P. PRATT, OCTOBER 6, 1845

It is with much satisfaction that I am able to state, that the people called Mormon have removed from the state. The great body of them removed voluntarily; but, a small remnant were barbarously expelled with force, and in a manner which reflects but little credit on the state and its institutions.

—GOVERNOR THOMAS FORD TO THE ILLINOIS LEGISLATURE,
DECEMBER 7, 1846

Throughout 1846, Nauvoo was in a time of transition. The management of church affairs, the makeup of the city, and the community's relationship with the old citizens of Hancock and surrounding counties was in constant flux. After the Twelve and other general and stake officers left for the West, Nauvoo was reduced from its ecclesiastical status as the headquarters stake of Zion to a small branch. The local president, Joseph

Young, looked after the rapidly shrinking group of Latter-day Saints. He acted alone, with neither counselors nor a high council. In March, the Twelve invited Orson Hyde to remain in Nauvoo to oversee completion of the temple in their absence. He dealt with general issues and public affairs, while Joseph Young acted as presiding elder over the branch.[1]

When bishops Newel K. Whitney and George Miller left in February, their responsibilities for financial and temporal affairs were assumed by five special trustees. At the time of their public appointment on January 24, 1846, Almon W. Babbitt, Joseph L. Heywood, and John S. Fullmer were charged with preparing the Nauvoo Temple for dedication. In addition, the Twelve asked them to find buyers for unsold church and private property. Two other trustees, Henry W. Miller and John M. Bernhisel, accepted the task of completing the Nauvoo House. With Brigham Young's concurrence, William Weeks transferred his duties as supervising architect of the two buildings to Truman O. Angell and delivered the plans and designs to him.[2]

The trustees felt considerable pressure to sell the property. They found less support for the construction projects in a city being evacuated. With so much attention on preparing to leave, volunteers were hard to find, but the trustees kept work going on the temple with hired laborers. Some of the men believed the projects were continued "so as to employ the brethren until they can sell their property and prepare to move." It was actually more than this. The Saints wanted to fulfill the 1841 revelation and avoid its warning: If they failed to complete the temple, the Lord would withhold promised blessings.[3]

For most, finishing the Nauvoo House seemed much the less important of the two projects, despite the revealed mandate of 1841. The Twelve had postponed the project in September 1845 and given the temple priority. Finding no interest in reviving it, hotel trustees Miller and Bernhisel joined the migration. An Ohio investor had offered to buy the unfinished building, but Emma Smith held title to the lot. Brigham Young asked the temple trustees to manage the property and resolve Emma Smith's claims. "The stockholders are scattered and cannot be consulted," Young said. But Emma sold the property to a buyer from Quincy.[4]

On Thursday evening, April 30, 1846, a small invited group met in the House of the Lord. Joseph Young led them in a prayer of dedication to mark the essential completion of the temple. Wilford Woodruff, who had recently returned from England, participated in these private services, along with Orson Hyde and about seventeen others, all clothed in white temple robes. Young, senior president of the seventy, dedicated the completed temple "and all that pertained thereto to the Lord, as an offering to Him as an evidence of the willingness of His people to fulfill His commandments, and build His holy house, even at the risk of their lives, and the sacrifice of all their labor and earthly goods." Hyde told a congregation the next Sunday that during the prayer, "while the earth was wrapped in the mantle of darkness, . . . the glory of the Lord shone throughout the room in matchless splendor." The elders rejoiced that the Saints had proven wrong the prophecies of Sidney Rigdon that the temple would not be finished and the threats of vigilantes that the building would not be dedicated. Hyde recalled the "oppression, robbery, burning, bloodshed, and murder" suffered over the preceding five years. He said the Saints "as it were, had to work with the trowel in one hand and the sword in the other." "At the close of the dedication," Woodruff noted, "we raised our voices in the united shout of Hosanna to God and the Lamb which entered the heavens to the joy and consolation of our hearts."[5]

The public attended services the following day in the main floor assembly room, each individual paying an admission fee of one dollar to help the trustees meet the payroll for construction workers. Music was provided by a choir with instrumental accompaniment. After Orson Hyde offered a public prayer of dedication, Almon Babbitt spoke for ninety minutes on the inspired design of the Nauvoo Temple and of a temple even more glorious to be built in the tops of the mountains. Babbitt reminded the Saints that to enjoy God's promised blessings, they must strictly observe their gospel covenants. Hyde began a speech on the nature of man that he concluded the following Sunday, observing "that man existed before the foundation of the world, and his chief end was to become even as God."[6]

Some of those who had left Nauvoo and were still camped along the Mississippi in Iowa returned for this special occasion. How many is not known. One who did was Elvira Stevens, a fourteen-year-old orphan under the care of relatives. She crossed the river to experience the spiritual power of the dedicatory services and then returned twice more just to feel the Spirit within the House of the Lord. She explained, "The heavenly power was so great, I then crossed and recrossed to be benefited

The Nauvoo Temple attracted several photographers and artists before the devastating fire of 1848. This image was made around 1847 and is attributed to Louis Rice Chaffin, a Latter-day Saint who lived in the Nauvoo area. In 1852, Chaffin opened a daguerreotypist shop in Kanesville, Iowa, a way station for those heading to Utah.

by it, as young as I was." Elvira was yet to receive the temple ordinances, but for Wilford Woodruff the saving power he had experienced was the crucial thing for which to be grateful. "The Saints had laboured faithfully and finished the temple," he wrote, "and were now received as a church with our dead. This is glory enough for building the temple, and thousands of the Saints have received their endowment in it. And the light will not go out."[7]

The temple's dedication closed another chapter in Nauvoo's religious life. After more than five years, the Saints had met their commitment to build a dwelling place for the Lord. The administration of temple ordinances had been suspended in February, but the building served other religious purposes. The remaining Saints enjoyed the Lord's house as a place of learning and a place of prayer. At preaching meetings held in the main floor hall at least monthly during 1846, the Saints heard from resident church authorities. In addition, a small group met every morning and evening during the summer in prayer meetings.[8]

SELLING OUT AND MOVING ON

Although completing the temple had great symbolic significance to the Saints, most of them had already participated in ordinances administered in rooms dedicated for that purpose. Of more immediate concern to those still preparing to head west was the sale of their homes and farms. Many of these people had no other way to buy a wagon and team and the provisions needed for the trek.

The selling that had begun with the October 1845 removal agreement continued under the direction of the trustees for nearly three years, longer than they had expected. They assisted resident Latter-day Saints in finding buyers and represented those who had left without selling. They were specifically charged with helping the poor buy outfits.[9] The trustees offered several public buildings for sale in Nauvoo, including the Masonic Hall, Concert Hall, and Arsenal. They also advertised themselves as agents for two hundred houses and lots and twenty thousand acres of farmland within eight miles of the city.[10]

Many potential buyers recognized the bargain prices being asked for rich prairie land already fenced and plowed. In 1846 and 1847, the agents sold more than two hundred parcels of land at prices ranging from one hundred to one thousand dollars. Much of the land was bartered for goods. The handsome brick houses in Nauvoo offered similar opportunities for buyers. At the high end were the sale of Heber Kimball's home for thirty-five yoke of oxen (worth at least $1,000) and Joseph Young's house for $650 cash. The trustees realized from 15 percent to 40 percent of the normal value of the Saints' property and eventually sold practically all of

KIRTLAND TEMPLE,
For Sale.

THE Church of Jesus Christ of Latter-
day Saints having come to a determina-
tion to sell all the church property, offer
for sale the TEMPLE situated in Kirtland,
Lake county, Ohio.
This splendid edifice will be sold on ad-
vantageous terms. For further information
concerning it, address the undersigned
Trustees of the Church.
ALMON W. BABBITT,
JOSEPH L. HEYWOOD,
JOHN S. FULLMER.
Nauvoo, May 20, 1846-8tf

TEMPLE FOR SALE.

THE undersigned Trustees of the Latter Day Saints
propose to sell the Temple on very low terms, if
an early application is made. The Temple is admira-
bly designed for Literary or Religious purposes.
Address the undersigned Trustees,
ALMON W. BABBITT,
JOSEPH L. HEYWOOD,
JOHN S. FULLMER.
Nauvoo, May 15, 1846.—7tf.

Brigham Young asked the trustees who were appointed to liquidate church and private holdings in Nauvoo to lease or sell the Nauvoo Temple and to sell the temple in Kirtland. These notices appeared in the Hancock Eagle *at Nauvoo in May 1846.*

the developed lots and land.[11] They felt pressure from all sides in every negotiation. From time to time, unhappy clients circulated complaints of maltreatment or malpractice, but, John Fullmer noted, "We do all that God gives us wisdom and ability to do." To protect the title to church-owned lots, Almon Babbitt attended a public auction in May 1847 and bid against local residents to prevent them from getting the land for back property taxes.[12]

Prospects for sales dwindled after the second year. The trustees had helped all leave who would go, said Fullmer, and "we alone are left to tell the tale." Brigham Young invited the agents "to leave all 'to the owls and the bats' and repair to headquarters without unnecessary delay, as best [they] could." Fullmer and Heywood transferred their agency to others and departed with their families in May 1848. They were replaced ten weeks later by two local citizens as agents and a third man as secretary. Babbitt, who had replaced Bernhisel in July 1846, stayed on for a time to help the new agents negotiate sales.[13]

In the weeks prior to the dedication of the temple, the trustees had continued to seek a suitable renter for the sacred building. In April, a well-to-do New Orleans Catholic offered to buy it and other Nauvoo property for two hundred thousand dollars. Brigham Young was by then camped at Garden Grove, three-and-one-half days' journey west of Nauvoo. Orson Hyde wrote for counsel, because the Twelve and a church conference had authorized the trustees only to rent the temple. Hyde suggested that both the Nauvoo and the Kirtland Temples be sold, with the proceeds going to help Nauvoo's poor emigrate westward. At an Iowa council meeting in April, church leaders agreed after some discussion that the temples were of no use if members could not live in the two abandoned gathering places. They concluded that the buildings would be better protected from vandalism in private hands. If the Saints were ever able to redeem their private dwellings, certainly "they could redeem the Temple also." The decision was sustained in subsequent meetings in Iowa and in Nauvoo. The Twelve later set two hundred thousand dollars as a minimum sale price for the temple, one-quarter of its estimated cost.[14]

At a gathering in early May in Garden Grove, Brigham Young reminded the Saints that the revelations allowed flexibility in designating places for temple cities. The church had shifted its focus from Missouri to Nauvoo and now would abandon that city and Kirtland for a new place of refuge beyond the Rocky Mountains. "Joseph Smith said that where the keys of the Kingdom were, there would be the place to gather," Young taught. "Wherever the Twelve and Council are, there will the keys be, and the place of Gathering." Temples would be built in gathering places, whether in the City of Zion or her stakes.[15]

Meanwhile, the trustees aggressively pursued the purchase offer for the Nauvoo Temple. Babbitt and Heywood journeyed to St. Louis in late June to meet with the agent of a wealthy New Orleans investor but accomplished nothing. A year later, an offer of seventy-five thousand dollars from the Catholic church for the temple and other Nauvoo property failed because of a reported defect in the title. Soon after that disappointment, trustee John S. Fullmer informed a relative, "The Temple is still unsold, and I do not know but the God of Heaven intends to have it so remain as a standing monument of our sacrifice, and as a witness against this nation. Sold or unsold, I should think it such as we shall not be able at best to get one dollar in twenty of what it cost." In November 1848, Babbitt deeded the temple to David T. and Esther M. LeBaron, his brother-in-law and sister-in-law, for a listed value of five thousand dollars. Perhaps this action was taken simply to clear the title, because the LeBarons then gave Babbitt power of attorney to continue seeking a buyer for the property.[16]

Meanwhile, in the *Hancock Eagle* in late April 1846, the trustees advertised the Kirtland Temple for sale. Completed just ten years earlier, it was no longer needed by a church in exile. The trustees suggested its suitability for a school, perhaps aware that a Kirtland minister was already teaching a school there. Dissident Latter-day Saints in control of the building were allowing other religious, educational, and civic groups to use it. But no one offered to buy the temple, and after a few years it fell into disrepair.[17]

The return to "normalcy" in Hancock County removed Nauvoo from prominence as a center of political influence. County residents prided themselves on their achievement in expelling the Latter-day Saints. The future seemed certain to offer more typical relationships in business, religion, and politics. New owners took over some of the shops of Nauvoo. Ministers arrived to serve the community's religious needs. New citizens moved into the empty houses. In all, the transition progressed rather quietly. Even though Mormon political influence ended when church leaders left, the most strident of the Anti-Mormon Party saw in the few remaining Saints the potential for a new challenge.

Discontinuance of the two Latter-day Saint newspapers created an immediate business and political opportunity in Nauvoo. Brigham Young was barely out of Nauvoo when William E. Matlack announced plans on February 23, 1846, to publish a replacement for the weekly *Nauvoo Neighbor*. It issued from the same printing shop, using the *Times and Seasons* presses and type.[18] In launching his venture with the *Hancock Eagle*, Matlack summarized the transformation in civil, ecclesiastical, and domestic affairs just beginning in the dwindling city of the Saints:

> Nauvoo and its immediate suburbs, until recently, contained over 15,000 inhabitants—the greater part of whom were known as "Mormons"—of these, some two or three thousand have already left together with an equal number from the country. A majority of those remaining, will, in due season depart upon their pilgrimage towards the setting sun. The high council is dissolved, and the church organization has been entirely broken up to be reestablished, we opine, in some distant region whose waters flow into the Pacific Ocean. The Twelve with their thousands of followers have abandoned their Temple and their city; with them, goes all that the enemies of Mormonism regard as inimical to the genius of our institutions and the well being of the community at large.[19]

It was indeed the beginning of a transition that would introduce what

Matlack called a "new order of things" in Nauvoo. Friends of the Saints who had benefited from the boomtown atmosphere noted the difference as Nauvoo's population began to leave in earnest. In mid-March, with removal entering its busiest stage, merchants Hiram and Phineas Kimball informed Brigham Young, "Business is very dull and Nauvoo appears to be almost forsaken and looks as desolate as a sheep pasture." Three months later, economic vibrancy was even further deteriorated. The trustees worried about their ability to find buyers for the remaining properties. "Nauvoo is becoming anything but desirable," John S. Fullmer reported.[20] The view that Nauvoo had contributed in a positive way to the economic life of its region was widely held. More than a decade after Nauvoo was evacuated, a land dealer forty miles upriver, in Henderson County, observed, "Since *Mormons* have left our midst *business is falling away.* . . . The Mormon people . . . had business sense, and in a few years, Nauvoo will be no more. I believe if Joseph Smith were still living we would all be richer."[21]

For some Hancock County residents, the "pilgrimage towards the setting sun" described by Matlack's prospectus did not happen fast enough. If the editor's estimate is correct, no more than one-fourth of the county's Latter-day Saints left during the first month of the exodus. Remaining for later migration were between nine thousand and eleven thousand people. Most of these residents abandoned their homes between March and the end of May 1846. Some who left during the spring months headed not west across Iowa but into neighboring regions to find work. A few had decided not to follow the Twelve west nor to remain in Nauvoo. Citizens of Warsaw noted three or four Mormon wagons from Nauvoo passing through their community headed south in early April. The migrants were escorted by two of Major William B. Warren's soldiers, allegedly for protection.[22]

When Governor Ford established the Hancock Guard—essentially the Quincy Riflemen—to keep the peace, he had expected the force to disband after the April conference. Major Warren maintained headquarters at the county seat and detachments there and in Warsaw.[23] But the Saints' departure took longer than expected, and Ford extended the guard's duty. The public dedication of the temple on May 1 coincided with Ford's anticipated deadline. Dedication signaled a formal end to Latter-day Saint activities in Nauvoo. But the event itself and the presence still of a thousand or more Latter-day Saint residents raised questions among anti-Mormons about intent. Committees in surrounding counties, anxious to enforce removal, set a new June 1 deadline for a complete Mormon withdrawal.[24] A committee in Quincy warned Nauvoo's newest citizens against encouraging the Saints to stay on. The committee threatened Mormons in Adams and Hancock counties with forced expulsion and extermination if they did not leave voluntarily.[25]

Major Warren cautioned the public through the Nauvoo and Warsaw newspapers that no one needed to tell the Saints to be gone. The governor, he said, fully expected them to honor the agreement forged by the October 1845 Carthage Convention. "The removal of the *entire Mormon population*," Warren said, "has been looked forward to, as an event that could alone restore peace and quiet to this portion of our State, and for the peace of the inhabitants and the honor of the State, public expectation must be gratified."[26]

Warren's guard had dropped from its original one hundred riflemen in 1845 to fifty during the winter, and only ten men remained during the spring. Because of the Quincy threat, they stayed on at Ford's request for another two weeks—and then until the end of the month—to assure the opposition party that the Saints really planned to leave.[27] In mid-May, Warren moved his men to Nauvoo, where they helped at the ferry. About the time Warren arrived, the *Hancock Eagle* was reporting that twelve thousand exiles were on the way west. A month later, the *Warsaw Signal* observed that three thousand to five thousand people remained in Nauvoo but that as many as half of them had no intention of leaving freely. To satisfy those outsiders who distrusted published figures, Warren issued his own weekly reports during May from his headquarters at the Mansion House. He estimated that 1,350 people left during the second week of May and 1,617 the following week. He based his count on his men's report that thirty-two teams had ferried across the Mississippi at Nauvoo each day and forty-five per day at Fort Madison.[28]

Despite this heavy traffic, at month's end the church trustees still were advertising for a thousand yoke of cattle to help in the westward trek. The Twelve had asked for twenty-four teams of oxen for a pioneer company and needed others for ill-equipped Saints waiting in eastern Iowa. Some were made available to the poor, anxious but unable to leave Nauvoo. Other Saints without means wrote to relatives seeking funds for steamboat fare to St. Louis or money for provisions and teams necessary for a trek into the wilderness.[29]

The steady spring migration accomplished its objective. In mid-July, the *Hancock Eagle* analyzed reports from across Iowa and reaffirmed its earlier estimate that at least twelve thousand Saints with thirty-seven hundred teams were somewhere between the Mississippi River and the Council Bluffs region. With the onset of summer, the paper estimated, only a few hundred Saints remained in Nauvoo and no more than eight hundred in all of Illinois. With that in mind, Ford rejected appeals from Nauvoo's new citizens for a further extension of Warren's assignment. He begrudged the cost of maintaining a token force too small to defend a dwindling city. On the first of June, Warren discharged his ten military guardians.[30]

As the Hancock riflemen left Nauvoo, Thomas Sharp commended Warren and his men for the impartial attitude toward the contending parties. Both sides had expected to find an ally in the Quincy Riflemen, Sharp said, but neither party found the troops biased in their favor. Brigham Young agreed that Warren had remained fair to both sides as he enforced the peace.[31] Warren issued his own reminder to the anti-Mormon minority who still argued for a military action against the Saints. To do so, he said, would violate an order issued when he took charge the previous fall. The order prohibited more than four armed men from assembling together unless they were state troops.[32]

Despite this warning, armed vigilantes once again took the law into their own hands and began to enforce the evacuation agreement. Small posses harassed Latter-day Saint families living on scattered farms in Hancock and surrounding counties. They demanded immediate removal. Vigilantes stripped several men, tied them to a fence, and whipped their bare backs with ox goads to draw blood. State officials denounced the beatings.[33] Threatened with their lives, Mormon families loaded up their belongings and headed for Nauvoo.

The stated intent of the dwindling Latter-day Saint population should have allayed concerns. By late summer, according to a private estimate by church agents, 750 adults who wanted to leave remained in Nauvoo. Another 250 adults waited in nearby gathering places and 200 more in St. Louis. If children were added, the total would be at least 2,400. Nearly all of the Saints in Nauvoo lacked the means to leave, the

NOTICE.

THE undersigned wish to purchase one thousand Yoke o Cattle, from four to eight years old for the removal of the Church of Jesus Christ of Latter Day Saints. A ready market will be found here for all the working Cattle and Mules that may be brought in.

BABBITT, HEYWOOD & FULMER,
Trustees.

Nauvoo, April 10, 1846.   no. 2—tf.

FOR SALE.

THE "Masonic Hall," located on Main Street, four stories high, with one half acre of ground. Well adapted for a Seminary, &c.

BABBITT, HEYWOOD & FULLMER.
April 10, 1846—2-tf

FOR SALE.

A large public building, one square north of the Temple, built by the Musical Association of this city ; known as "Concert Hall."

BABBITT, HEYWOOD & FULLMER
April 10, 1846—2-tf

FOR SALE.

THE large new Stone Building, three stories high, one square west of the Temple ; known as the Arsenal.

BABBITT, HEYWOOD & FULLMER.
April 10, 1846—2-tf

FOR SALE.

THE large Brick buildings on the corner of Main and Kimball streets, built by James Ivins. Said buildings are new and built in the most substantial style, and will be sold low for cash.

BABBITT, HEYWOOD & FULLMFR.
April 10, 1846—2-tf

For Sale.

THE new and large brick dwelling, with a barn and one acre of land; situated on the corner of Partridge and Johnson Streets.

BABBITT, HEYWOOD & FULLMER.
April 10, 1846—2-tf

For Sale.

THE new and well built brick dwelling, built the last season by Jno. D. Lee, on Hyde Street, one block east of Main.

BABBITT, HEYWOOD & FULLMER.
April 10, 1846.—2-tf

Brewery For Sale.

A BRICK building, adapted to the Brewery business near the Mansion House on Water street.

ALMON W. BABBITT.
April 10, 1846—2-tf

For Sale.

A LARGE two story building with half an acre of land, on which is a number of bearing fruit trees; known as the Coolidge House.

ALMON W. BABBITT.
April 10, 1846—2 tf

Store for Sale.

THE LARGE Store and dwelling house, known as the New York Store; one block south of the Temple.

BABBITT, HEYWOOD & FULLMER.
April 10, 1846—2-tf

Nauvoo's finest brick and stone houses and buildings were advertised in the city's new weekly paper, the Hancock Eagle, *during the spring and summer of 1846. Many of them sold but at discounted prices.*

agents discovered. The others had resources for everything except teams. By definition, all of these Saints intended to head west "as soon as a way can be opened to go."[34]

There were some, however, who resisted Brigham Young's counsel to head toward the Rockies in 1846. A few of these had sided with the seceders and ignored the call to leave. Still others intended to remain another winter before joining their fellow exiles on the trail. At the April conference in Nauvoo and consistently after that, Orson Hyde encouraged the remnants to get across the river and find work in Iowa until they could outfit themselves for the journey. Hyde confided to Brigham Young that an angel had warned him in a dream: "This people cannot stay here." To do so, Hyde said, would provoke an attack.[35]

Brigham Young had agreed to the October 1845 terms and supported the total evacuation of Nauvoo. Only the trustees and their families were authorized to remain behind. In July, Young urged departure for another reason. Enlistment of five hundred men and boys in the United States Army left the Saints in western Iowa short of herders and teamsters. Young encouraged the Nauvoo trustees to "call upon all the old men, the young men and boys, big enough to drive cattle," and send them to help move the Saints to a winter camp in Indian Territory west of the Missouri. The unloaded wagons could then return to Nauvoo for the families of these men. "Buy no more teams," he counseled, "for we have as many in the church as can be taken care of at present." Some volunteers were raised during a meeting in the Nauvoo Temple on July 20, but few able men were available to respond.[36] At the Missouri River, summer haying kept the men busy and delayed the return of empty wagons to Nauvoo. In late August, Young suggested that the trustees sell Nauvoo property and hire teams to transport the poor of Nauvoo to a point on the Missouri as close as possible to Council Bluffs.[37] He also asked families along the Missouri to send their spare oxen east to bring wagons waiting in Nauvoo. Four men with teams left on September 14 to help "remove all who want to come." "Nauvoo and the adjacent country must be cleared," Young said. He donated three yoke of his cattle as an example to others. He encouraged Iowa Saints busy with the haying to go with teams and wagons later, find work away, and shuttle the remaining families west in the spring.[38]

One night in June, someone slipped into the *Hancock Eagle* print shop and produced a handbill urging the citizens of Nauvoo to take arms against the remaining Mormons. The paper's editor discovered the subterfuge, pied the type, and destroyed the bills. Upset with the call to arms, a group of new citizens met at the Mansion House and issued a broadside denouncing the perpetrators. Fifty distraught residents, including Lewis C. Bidamon (who later married Emma Smith), signed a second circular cautioning citizens of surrounding counties to cease their militant expulsion plans. The new citizens wanted the anti-Mormon faction to know that they trusted the Saints to honor the agreement to leave.[39]

A congressional election in August heightened the political concerns of Nauvoo's opponents. The city cast 850 votes and helped elect the

Democratic candidate. Many new citizens had not been resident long enough to vote in the district, causing the Whigs and members of the Anti-Mormon Party to conclude, "Most of these votes must have either been Mormon votes or illegal votes." Some speculated wrongly that the vote was in return for Polk's favor in sponsoring the Mormon Battalion, a financial benefit to the Latter-day Saints.[40]

Despite the reassurances of the new citizens, impatient opponents of the Mormons once again turned to forceful action. Even as the teamsters were leaving from the Missouri River camps on September 14 to remove the poor Saints, an armed attack on Nauvoo was underway. The anti-Mormons had revived their plan of the previous summer—to drive the Saints into Nauvoo like sheep and then herd them across the river onto Iowa's grasslands.

THE BATTLE OF NAUVOO

The organized effort at expulsion from Illinois began when a group calling itself the Convention of Hancock County Old Citizens met at Carthage in early June to plan an Independence Day observance. The delegates concluded that the county could not celebrate its freedom as long as any Latter-day Saints remained. They decided to postpone the holiday festivities in a show of patriotic sacrifice and resort to force. Thomas Sharp trumpeted the decision in a headline: "War Declared in Hancock." As if to justify a military solution, the editor defined remaining Mormons as lazy, dishonest people seeking "an opportunity to pilfer and rob their neighbors."[41] In late June, acting under the authority of the Quincy anti-Mormon coordinating committee in neighboring Adams County, several hundred armed volunteers led by Levi Williams of Warsaw marched toward Nauvoo to demand an immediate surrender and evacuation.

The departure of Major Warren's force at the end of May had left Nauvoo with no military defenses. Governor Ford believed that the on-going departure of the Saints had eliminated the prospect of armed conflict. Left without state protection, the remaining Saints and their new neighbors decided to arm themselves for self-defense. Stephen Markham, newly arrived from the Missouri River camps, and Sheriff Jacob Backenstos organized a ragtag Nauvoo militia. But the invading posse stopped short of Nauvoo. They had not expected the new citizens to join in a military resistance. In addition, reports of Markham's return included rumors that he had been escorted by armed legionnaires. From a camp at Golden's Point, six miles south of Nauvoo, the vigilantes considered their options and dispersed to their homes. The Warsaw commanders then quarantined Nauvoo, prohibiting the Saints from leaving except to ferry to Iowa.[42]

Nauvoo's jubilant citizens ridiculed the failed invasion with doggerel verse making fun of "Old Williams and his plund'ring crew" of drunken mobbers. A second broadside published the words of a newly written folksong that scorned the fleeing mobbers and celebrated the efforts of the "noble brave boys of Nauvoo."[43] Feelings remained high. The uneasy truce led to a series of individual harassments during the summer. Ignoring the illegal quarantine, certain Nauvoo residents hired out as harvesters in the grain fields of the Amos Davis farm east of Nauvoo. Non-Mormon farm families during the first week of July accused three of these workmen of loitering and annoying mischief.[44]

Word of these incidents spread among others who were stung by the taunting doggerel and unhappy with the continuing Latter-day Saint presence. On Saturday morning, July 11, while harvesting wheat at the Davis farm, eight workmen from Nauvoo, two of them new citizens, found themselves surrounded by nearly eighty armed regulators under the command of Major John McAuley, a red-haired Irish immigrant from Appanoose. The farmhands were disarmed and marched to the nearby Rice home. Two by two, they were forced to kneel in a ditch and receive twenty lashes across their shoulders with hickory goads. The regulators kept four of the Mormon pistols and two long guns and smashed another four guns on a stump before ordering the workers back to Nauvoo in their wagons. The incident set off a serious round of charges and counter-charges. One of the harvesters from Nauvoo carried with him the handgun "of peculiar construction" that Sheriff Backenstos and his posse had taken at Green Plains during the 1845 house burnings. Under orders to "claim the gun if he should ever see it," McAuley confiscated the unusual firearm as stolen property.[45]

Returning to Nauvoo, the harvesters swore out a warrant against McAuley and his men. The charge included theft of the gun and the beatings. William Pickett, one of Nauvoo's new citizens, headed a posse of Latter-day Saints and a few newcomers to deliver the warrant. Riding through the night, they found and arrested McAuley and James W. Brattle and repossessed the gun before daylight Sunday. Over the next few days,

Pickett's men arrested fifteen other anti-Mormons, including former Latter-day Saint Francis M. Higbee, in connection with a lynching charge at the Davis field and hauled all of their prisoners to Nauvoo.[46]

"Things are hot here," deputy sheriff H. G. Ferris reported from Carthage on July 14. The regulators had vowed to destroy the whole city of Nauvoo, Ferris wrote, including the property of any new residents who defended Mormon rights. "The mobbers have sent messengers to every part of the country to raise a force," he said. "No efforts will be spared and no lies will fail to be manufactured to accomplish the object." In Nauvoo, the *Hancock Eagle* charged the Anti-Mormon Party with raising a ruckus to win votes in the August election.[47] The regulators placed the blame for the skirmishes on the Latter-day Saints. The Nauvoo workers, they claimed, had harvested only a few acres in a day and had spent most of their time threatening other settlers. The anti-Mormons denied that anyone had been beaten severely—each man received *only* twenty lashes. Their spokesman Thomas Sharp reiterated his declaration of war against the remaining Latter-day Saints.[48]

The Pontoosuc Regulators soon held their own prisoners in the "Mormon War." Four residents heading toward McQueen's mill in Henderson County to get wheat ground for the journey west were captured and kept at and near Pontoosuc "as hostages for the safety and release" of McAuley and the others. A fifth hostage was already in custody. A forty-man Nauvoo posse headed by William Anderson confronted the regulators and hunted for the hostages in vain. For nearly two weeks, the Mormon captives were shifted from place to place under cover of darkness to avoid detection. They were deprived of proper rest and nourishment and were transported as far away as McDonough County. "The excitement is spreading to other parts of the county," anti-Mormon editor Sharp intoned, "and if any serious collisions should take place, the whole country will become involved. The fact is, there is no peace for Hancock while a Mormon remains in it!"[49]

Now both sides bartered for the release of prisoners, each demanding that the other move first. The stalemate ended when the officer holding the anti-Mormons at a hotel in Nauvoo surrendered them under a writ of habeas corpus issued at Quincy on Tuesday, July 21. The prisoners left Nauvoo two days later by boat for Quincy. As might be expected, Judge Purple acquitted them of whipping the Mormon farm workers. On

REPORT OF THE TROOPS.
NAUVOO, MAY 22, 1846.

MR. MATLACK:—Sir, The undersigned desire, through the medium of your paper, to make the following report for the past week:

The Mormons still continue to leave the city in large numbers. The ferry at this place averages about thirty-two teams per day—and at Fort Madison, forty-five.

Thus it will be seen that five hundred and thirty-nine teams have left during the week which average about three persons to each, making in all one thousand six hundred and seventeen souls.

WM. B. WARREN, Maj.
JAMES D. MORGAN, Capt.
B. M. PRENTICE, 1st Lt.
W. Y. HENRY, 2 Lt.

F. HALL & CO.

CONTINUE to sell Goods at the Key Stone Store, Mulholland street, cheaper than any other Store in the country.— Our stock of DRY GOODS is the best assorted of any to be found.

Also, a complete assortment of
Variety Goods,
at the lowest prices. We keep constantly on hand, a complete assortment of Groceries, and sell them at the lowest prices.

Call and examine our stock and prices for yourselves.
F. HALL & CO.·
may 8, 1846-6:tf

To convince the anti-Mormons that the Saints were leaving Nauvoo, Major William B. Warren issued weekly reports on the progress of removal. Many vacated buildings were purchased and new businesses were started during this time. A few merchants, among them F. Hall & Co., continued in business during the transition.

Saturday, the anti-Mormons moved their five hostages to Warsaw and then across the river to Keokuk, where they released them.[50]

As the hostage crisis was being resolved, another event heightened tensions. The McDonough County sheriff visited Nauvoo on July 21 with writs charging William Pickett and three of his assistants with invading the county as an armed hostile force. Pickett's group had camped near McComb while looking for the captives from Nauvoo. After initially resisting, Pickett's men went with the sheriff to McComb, accompanied by their own guard, and posted bail. En route back to Nauvoo, Pickett swore that he would never again submit to arrest.[51]

These incidents left Hancock County citizens of all persuasions on alert. Wheat and corn fields ripened in the hot, dusty weather of August, but many farmers ignored the harvest, distracted by the political turmoil and fearful of violence against them by the marauding raiders.[52] Thomas Sharp's declaration of war awaited only an opportunity to justify shooting. If the Mormons left in Nauvoo ignored the vigilante injunction and left the city again, Sharp threatened, county citizens would "take to the bushes and pick the Saints off." Curiously, the Carthage Convention, organized in the fall of 1845 to negotiate the removal of the Saints, disbanded in July 1846 in the midst of this war of words. The Saints had promised the committee they would be gone by the summer. That time had arrived, and with most of the region's Latter-day Saints on their way west, the nine-county body decided it had no right to continue to function. Without the stabilizing influence of the peacekeepers, the more strident voices once again prevailed.[53]

The question of the peculiarly built gun captured at Green Plains had not yet been resolved. The captured firearm remained in Mormon hands in Nauvoo. To resolve this issue, John Carlin, a special constable of Hancock County (who, some claimed, had been illegally appointed), arrived in Nauvoo on August 7 with writs against William Pickett and two others who had taken the gun from McAuley. True to his pledge, Pickett refused to leave Nauvoo. He arranged for bodyguards and threatened to shoot anyone who attempted to arrest him. The others agreed to answer the charges in Green Plains, where both were eventually bound over for court appearances.[54]

In response to this standoff, on August 17 Carlin issued the *Proclamation to the Citizens of Hancock County* seeking volunteers to help him recover the gun. "Obedience [to the law] must be enforced at all hazards," Carlin wrote, "or its benefits will be at an end." The recruits were told to meet at Carthage on the twenty-fourth. Be prepared to "meet determined resistance," Carlin warned. There would be no "parlaying of committees." State officials would soon discern that Carlin had motives other than simply arresting Pickett.[55]

The *Hancock Eagle* responded with an extra, denouncing the militant tactics of the regulators. "The new citizens are as anxious for the removal of the Mormons as the worst anti can be," the editor wrote, "but they will not see cruelty practised upon the helpless families" of the city's remaining Latter-day Saints.[56]

Constable Carlin's appeal for help prompted Pickett to turn himself in. He traveled to Green Plains with four or five companions but found that Justice Banks had placed the arrest papers in the hands of an attorney in McDonough County. Pickett located the attorney, who had given the writs to an officer in Carthage. Separated from his companions, Pickett went alone to Warsaw, where he confronted the editor of the *Warsaw Signal*, Thomas Sharp, over the legality of the warrant. Avoiding

Carthage, Pickett then returned to Nauvoo without realizing his original objective.[57]

In Carthage, a volunteer militia that included some members of the Carthage Greys stood ready to push the remaining Latter-day Saints out of Nauvoo. Carlin had given command to Captain James W. Singleton of Brown County and J. B. Chittenden of Adams County. A Nauvoo spokesman asked Governor Thomas Ford for help. The governor had lost his more reliable officers, including General John J. Hardin and Major W. B. Warren, to recruitments in mid-July for the Mexican War. Nauvoo's friend Jacob B. Backenstos had also accepted a position in the army. These three, all Whigs, had been reasonably effective in restraining the Whiggish anti-Mormons and had earned the cautious trust of the Saints. On August 24, Ford sent another Whig to Hancock County. Major James R. Parker of the 32d Regiment of the Illinois State Militia and ten militiamen from Fulton County arrived in Carthage with the full authority of the state. The Hancock County vigilantes did not know Parker and assumed he was a Democrat. Because of his frank and fair handling of the issues, Parker was immediately discredited by the Whig newspapers, lessening his effectiveness in curbing Nauvoo's lawless opponents.[58]

Parker's assignment from the Democratic governor was to prevent an attack against Nauvoo and to prevent lynchings during the trials of Pickett's friends. In a circular on August 25 and a proclamation three days later, Parker put the anti-Mormons on notice by denying that the Mormons were the aggressors. He ordered Singleton and Chittenden to disperse their opposition forces. The Latter-day Saints are leaving as fast as they can, Parker declared. "I am informed by the Trustees of the Mormon Church, that if they could have peace, and sell their property, that every Mormon would be away before snow flies." His small body of Illinois volunteers was sufficient, he said, to keep the peace.[59]

In an exchange of letters with Parker, Constable John Carlin rejected the captain's authority. If Parker interfered with the regulators' efforts to disperse the Saints, Carlin said, he would treat Parker's government forces as if they were a mob. Carlin backed his threat with an assertion that he had six hundred men at Carthage and another four hundred at La Harpe. Parker responded in kind. The Carthage forces were the mob, he told Carlin. Yet, Parker wished to avoid bloodshed. In secret communications with Singleton, Parker pleaded for a peaceful solution. Singleton and

Chittenden agreed to let the Mormons leave in peace if they departed within sixty days. But Carlin and the Carthage posse rejected this agreement. Consequently, Singleton and Chittenden resigned their posts; Colonel Thomas S. Brockman, a former Brown County commissioner, took command of the Carthage militia. The posse now followed a man of action. Governor Ford described "Old Tom" Brockman, a Campbellite preacher, as large and awkward, an unschooled, self-serving man willing to use position for personal gain. At the same time, Major Benjamin Clifford of Quincy, who owned land and a store in Nauvoo, replaced Parker as head of the state forces in Nauvoo.[60]

With Ford's blessing, Clifford organized Nauvoo's able Latter-day Saints and new citizens into a militia, with Daniel H. Wells and William L. Cutler as aides and four other men as captains of fifty. The volunteers of the "New Organization" paraded and practiced to hone their skills. "We had no cannon," William Hickman remembered, "but cut into a steamboat's shaft, plugged it up, fixed it up on wagon wheels, [and] hammered out balls of pig lead, which was plenty." The makeshift cannon had the same firepower as a regular six-pounder but was not as accurate.[61]

As tensions grew, Governor Ford attempted to learn from reliable sources the real situation in Hancock County and to defuse it if possible. The governor sent his trusted attorney general pro tem, Mason Brayman, to investigate the situation. About the same time, Ford commissioned Mayor John M. Wood of Quincy to negotiate a truce. Soon after receiving his assignment on August 31, Brayman visited the posse camped east of Carthage, then still under Singleton's command. Brayman estimated the force at six hundred men, equipped with five six-pounders requisitioned from neighboring counties and a good supply of small arms. He left Carthage convinced that the fifty or sixty writs in Singleton's possession had been sworn for one purpose only, to give the forces the color of legal authority and hide their real intentions to expel the remaining Latter-day Saints. Brayman reached Nauvoo on September 8. He was told that the city had marshalled nearly six hundred well-armed soldiers, a figure he correctly dismissed as inflated. He found the militia ill-equipped, with only a remnant of the Nauvoo Legion's once formidable cache of small arms and six pieces of artillery, four of them newly made of steamboat shafts. A supply of muskets ordered by a Nauvoo merchant had been seized at Keokuk and diverted to the anti-Mormon camp.[62]

With considerable effort, Brayman concluded that only six hundred to eight hundred Latter-day Saints still lived in Nauvoo, around two hundred of them adult males. Opponents had pegged the figure at more than three thousand. The remnants of the once thriving city signaled no threat, Brayman observed. The departing Saints had hauled away all that would fit in their wagons

> without making proper provision for those who remained. Consequently there was much destitution among them; much sickness and distress. I traversed the city, and visited in company with a practicing physician many of the sick, and almost invariably found them destitute, to a painful extent, of the comforts of life. Much sickness and many deaths, I am persuaded, resulted from want of sufficient and proper food, particularly among the women and children, whose husbands or parents were dead or had left them. Everything in and about their habitations wore an appearance of decay and wretchedness. The gardens were thrown open, fences removed for fuel—the supply of furniture and ordinary household comforts meagre indeed. Wagons were standing before the doors of many dwellings, and great numbers were in process of construction, indicating preparations for removal. Many, I was told, had been for months in this condition, with their wagons, goods, and families prepared to leave—only awaiting the sale of their little homestead for enough to purchase a yoke of oxen to convey them away.[63]

Many of the stranded residents complained to Brayman that their ability to sell their property had been frustrated by the ongoing harassment of lawless mobs. Others, Brayman was convinced, had no intention of selling. This and one other condition concerned the old citizens. Nauvoo residents were fleeing the city, but would they stay away? "Hundreds of poor and destitute families were encamped in tents, in huts, and covered wagons on the opposite side of the river," Brayman told the governor, "and it was feared the approach of winter would drive them back to the city, reduced to pauperism and theft for subsistence." Among those who had just crossed the river was Mary Fielding Smith, Hyrum's widow. With the help of her sister, Mercy, this faithful Missouri exile would oversee the westward trek of eight children and several elderly adults. The Saints remaining in Nauvoo faced similar challenges of inadequate means or skills. Meanwhile, unable to raise a posse, Quincy mayor

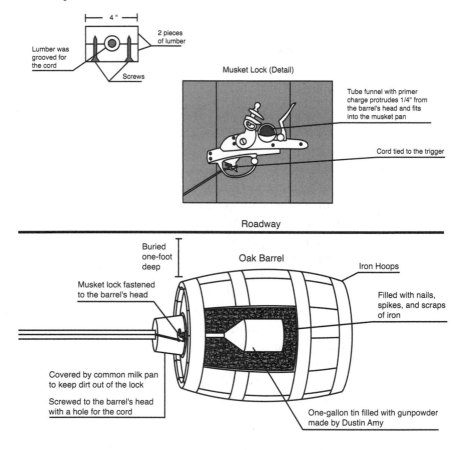

Ignition Column Cross Section

4"

Lumber was grooved for the cord

2 pieces of lumber

Screws

Musket Lock (Detail)

Tube funnel with primer charge protrudes 1/4" from the barrel's head and fits into the musket pan

Cord tied to the trigger

Roadway

Buried one-foot deep

Oak Barrel

Iron Hoops

Musket lock fastened to the barrel's head

Filled with nails, spikes, and scraps of iron

Covered by common milk pan to keep dirt out of the lock

Screwed to the barrel's head with a hole for the cord

One-gallon tin filled with gunpowder made by Dustin Amy

Preparations for the September 1846 attack on Nauvoo included the construction of four powder magazines that were buried at key defense points in and around Nauvoo. This drawing is based on a detailed description by Wandle Mace.

Wood reached Nauvoo two days after Brayman, with a dozen or so companions hoping to find a peaceful solution to the problem. Two attempts to convince the Carthage force they should disband failed.[64]

The citizens' armies of both sides readied themselves for a battle that would end the straggling Mormon occupation of Nauvoo. Some residents of outlying farms hurried into Nauvoo to join in the common defense. Others fled from the city for safety.[65] Egged on by the anti-Mormon press in Quincy and Warsaw, Nauvoo's opponents took the offensive.[66] On Thursday afternoon, September 10, Thomas Brockman left his new camp

five miles west of Carthage. He marched his anti-Mormon force composed of several hundred men toward Nauvoo. Militia banners and
United States flags led the way.[67] In Nauvoo, the temple bell sounded the
alarm. Clifford and his men hid themselves in a cornfield east of the city
on Parley Street. They intended an ambush but were spotted. The two
sides exchanged fire briefly. At nightfall, Brockman's men set up camp just
beyond Joseph Smith's farm near Jeremiah Woodbury's.[68]

To defend the city, Major Clifford decided to post his forces ten
blocks due east of the temple near Winchester Street, between Knight and
Mulholland Streets. He set up headquarters at a Dr. Bailey's home on
Knight Street. Working all night, the volunteers erected a breastworks. At
strategic points around the perimeter, they planted three shrapnel-laden
land mines assembled in the basement of the temple. A fourth powder keg
was buried near the entrance to the temple.[69] Next morning, the women
of Nauvoo furnished food and warm drinks as a breakfast for the workmen and baked bread to help sustain the soldiers for the expected battle.
Some of the women clustered with their children in a home near the
temple, a place they deemed safer than most because of guards posted
nearby.[70] Armed and ready by seven that morning, the army of Saints and
new citizens—composed of around two hundred men and boys drawn
from a city of about fifteen hundred residents—waited for another attack
by the invading force.[71]

On Friday morning, from their camp outside the city, Brockman's regulators and their support wagons headed east and circled around to the
new La Harpe Road, an extension of Young Street. This caught the
Nauvoo defenders off guard. They had dispatched William Anderson with
a company of thirty sharpshooters to engage Brockman at the Parley Street
entrance to the city. When spies notified the sharpshooters, they took off
running northwesterly to get ahead of the invading regulators. Halting in
a ravine, the men decided to break into two groups. Anderson's half called
themselves the Spartan Band. Alexander McCrae was elected to head the
remaining men. Around noon, Anderson's men spotted Brockman's
artillery moving toward Nauvoo. Anderson planned a pincer attack to separate the Carthage cannon from the three-hundred man posse following
behind, but he and his Spartan Band were discovered while waiting in a
cornfield. The two forces exchanged fire from a distance of fifty yards, the
Spartans with their repeating rifles, the invaders with cannon. One of

DEFENCE OF NAUVOO SEPTEMBER 1846.

The defenders against the assault on Nauvoo were outnumbered and not as well equipped as their attackers, but they fought valiantly to preserve their rights. After three Latter-day Saints were killed in the battle, they agreed to abandon the city immediately.

Anderson's men suffered a foot injury. Anderson retreated slowly, trying to draw Brockman's men over one of the buried mines. The Carthage posse would not follow. The two forces exchanged fire once again after Anderson's men had taken shelter in a cluster of log homes. This time, more than one hundred of the posse tried to take the log homes without realizing Anderson's men were inside. Reinforced with one of the steamboat-shaft cannons and using lead cannonballs, Anderson quickly scattered the posse, noting that a number of the opposition fell with wounds. Brockman's men withdrew to Law's Field for the night. The Spartan Band waited in the woods a short distance north of the camp until after dark. Their superiors decided against a night attack on the camp, but the Nauvoo forces remained on alert until well after midnight.[72]

Sporadic firing and brief encounters between the two forces continued through the following day. Sometime before noon on Saturday, September 12, the invaders sent in a white flag and demanded an unconditional surrender. The Nauvoo defenders refused. The anti-Mormon forces readied another attack. A crowd of onlookers numbering nearly as many as the invading force itself gathered from the surrounding countryside and Iowa to watch the battle. The tower of the temple offered a distant overview of the battlefield. Mayor Wood of Quincy and sentinels for the defenders watched from that vantage point.[73] Some residents did not wait for the confrontation but scattered to safety. Emma Smith boarded the riverboat *Uncle Toby*, whose captain was one of the few willing to defy the anti-Mormon warning to avoid the port. With her five children and housekeeper, Emma headed upriver to join relatives and Mormon dissenters, among them William Marks, at Fulton, Illinois.[74] Lucy Mack Smith moved with relatives to Knoxville, Illinois, for the winter and returned the following spring.

About one o'clock that afternoon, with dozens of banners waving, the posse marched in a solid column to engage the city's defenders. The five hundred troops of the ambitious Brockman barraged the Winchester Street barricades with cannon and musket shots. Clifford's defending forces clustered behind the barricades, but Brockman, a clever tactician, again surprised them by swinging southward to get around the breastworks. The Nauvoo soldiers followed on the posse's right flank. Clifford's men fired with their makeshift cannons and from nearby buildings with rifles. Outnumbered by the advancing anti-Mormons, they were being pushed house by house toward the city.[75]

William Anderson's picket company had been posted in the timber north of Brockman's camp, where they saw little action. When the invaders headed south, Daniel H. Wells sent the Spartan Band to get ahead of the advancing posse. Moving single file, their standard pattern, the Nauvoo soldiers crouched and scurried along the flanks of the posse to a point almost a mile away. Quickly Anderson's men filled the space between a brick house and nearby log barn with large corn shocks leaned against a fence to form a breastworks. When the invading army got within one hundred fifty yards, the Nauvoo force opened fire with their rifles. The posse returned fire but then broke and scattered. Encouraged by their officers, the anti-Mormons regrouped and made a second assault. Boldly setting aside caution, Anderson and a few others moved beyond the protection of the buildings, jumped a fence, and faced the advancing forces. Killed in this futile defense were Anderson himself—struck by a cannonball—his fifteen-year-old son, August, and David Norris. Three or four defenders suffered wounds. Another half dozen were injured in other encounters.[76] The invaders admitted to ten or twelve wounded but refused to indicate the number killed in the three-day attack on Nauvoo. Governor Ford said the posse lost one man. Anderson's Spartan Band had fired three hundred shots through their repeating rifles. "It appears," Ford told the House of Representatives in December, "the remarkable fact of so few being killed and wounded on either side, can only be accounted for by supposing great unskillfulness in the use of the arms, and by the very safe distance which the parties kept from each other."[77]

While Anderson's Spartan Band was trying to stop the advancing troops, other Nauvoo units harassed the invaders on the right. Nauvoo's respected justice of the peace Daniel H. Wells led one spirited counterattack. Rallying Captain Andrew L. Lamoreaux's company into action, Wells persuaded the men to engage in battle just as many of them were preparing to retreat. With that example, the units of Hiram Gates and William L. Cutler soon followed Wells's encouraging call.[78] Many of the men fought one-on-one against the invaders in a military engagement typical of the time.

After a battle lasting two hours, the attackers ran short of powder and cannonballs and withdrew. Fresh munitions had failed to arrive from Quincy. Brockman estimated that his men had captured two hundred houses—fewer than a tenth of the city's total. On the other side, Anderson's leaderless men had used up all of their ammunition as well and were about to make their own retreat. The defensive lines had held in a stalemate. "I had been anxious from a boy to be in a battle," William Hickman recalled, "but I assure you this fight took a great deal of starch out of me. . . . We saw our forces weakening, and knew eventually we should have to surrender; so we sent a flag of truce with a committee to settle in some way the existing war."[79]

The defenders of Nauvoo presumed that the waving of the white flag had ended the war, but sporadic skirmishes continued for two days. On Sunday, workers in a cornfield near Daniel H. Wells's home found members of the Carthage militia hiding there and exchanged shots. Fearing a renewed attack, work details set about building new defensive batteries Monday morning for self-protection until a peace treaty could be drafted.

As it had done a year earlier, a citizens' committee from Quincy interceded to forge terms of surrender. Mayor Wood's group had left Nauvoo on Sunday, September 13, after the decisive battle. A new committee, without the mayor and his more neutral colleagues, arrived in Nauvoo two days later. Discussions began that day and continued into the next, with negotiators "riding out and in to the mob . . . in a buggy and carrying a (white) flag of truce."[80] Negotiators on both sides signed the "Articles of Accommodation, Treaty and Agreement" on Wednesday, September 16, to end the fighting.

At a meeting in the temple early the next morning, residents learned the terms of the agreement: The City of Nauvoo would surrender and be occupied by Colonel Brockman's forces. Ten men from the Quincy Committee and the occupation forces had pledged to protect all citizens and property from violence. They would treat the sick and helpless humanely. The Latter-day Saints in Nauvoo would surrender the city and leave the state or otherwise disperse "as soon as they [could] cross the river." (Residents understood this to mean within ten days.) All Nauvoo citizens would turn in their arms, and the Quincy Committee would return the guns to the Saints after they had crossed the Mississippi. Five men with their families, including the church trustees, would be allowed to remain in Nauvoo to dispose of property, assisted by five more as clerks. The church trustees surrendered the key to the temple to the negotiating committee. With the peace in place, Nauvoo's military leaders dismissed their volunteer armies to prepare for evacuating the city. The Carthage militia entered Nauvoo that afternoon.[81]

The Latter-day Saints recognized the urgency of the situation. All who could do so left immediately. Thomas Bullock felt lucky to find a buyer willing to pay one hundred dollars for his house and lot, only to find the deal threatened by an interfering neighbor. "Many a house and lot were exchanged for a horse or a yoke of oxen," one observer noted. "Sometimes a cow drew the wagon on which the family's all was loaded, while the family itself trudged along beside it on foot."[82] Even though the Saints left quickly, and despite promises not to molest residents, the occupying forces harassed many who were frustrated by their own lack of preparations for the forced evacuation. The militia seized fleeing citizens at random and threw them into the river, shouting obscenities at some in mock baptisms. They held courts-martial for others, condemned them to die, and then expelled them from the city. The soldiers searched for arms in wagons and homes, burst open trunks and chests, and tore up floors. "The mob kept up one continual stream thro' the Temple," Bullock noted, "and up to the top of the tower, ringing the bell, shouting and halloing. Some enquired 'who is the keeper of the Lord's House now.' . . . A mob preacher ascended to the top of the tower and standing outside proclaimed with a loud voice,

The emotion created by the expulsion of several hundred poor Latter-day Saints is captured in this stylized 1851 drawing. It is the only known view of the rear of the Nauvoo Temple and also shows the wall under construction around the Temple Block.

'Peace, Peace, Peace to all the inhabitants of the earth, now the Mormons are driven.'"[83]

Besides the forced removal of Latter-day Saints, often given only an hour or two to depart, Brockman ordered the expulsion of the new citizens who had joined with them in defending Nauvoo and others who sympathized with the church. Abram Van Tuyl, who had leased the Mansion House from Emma Smith, furnished many of the names. The commander placed a detachment at the temple with orders to prevent the Saints and their Jack-Mormon sympathizers from returning. His men stationed a cannon on planks a few yards in front of the stairs. Governor Ford's emissary, Mason Brayman, discovered the harassment of new citizens when he arrived in Nauvoo on September 18. He was aghast. He could not believe that such a gross violation of the Quincy Committee agreement would be undertaken but learned from Brockman that such was in fact his intention. "This order," Brayman reported to Ford,

> was rigorously enforced throughout the day, with many circumstances of the utmost cruelty and injustice. Bands of armed men traversed the city, entering the houses of citizens, robbing them of arms,

throwing their household goods out of doors, insulting them, and threatening their lives. Many were seized, and marched to the camp, and after a military examination set across the river for the crime of sympathizing with the Mormons, or the still more heinous offense of fighting in defense of the city under the command of officers commissioned by you and instructed to make that defense. It is, indeed, painfully true that many citizens of this state have been driven from it by an armed force, because impelled by our encouragement and a sense of duty, they have bravely defended their homes . . . from the assaults of a force assembled for unlawful purposes.

Brayman estimated that upwards of half of Nauvoo's new citizens had been forced from their homes.[84] Some of them stayed away for several months. Only ten or fifteen Mormon families remained in the city. Following the initial takeover of the surrendered city and forcible expulsion of the Saints and their sympathizers, Brockman dismissed all but about one hundred of his forces.[85]

Evacuation of the Latter-day Saint remnant and most of their friends from Nauvoo following the siege created a memory not soon forgotten by former residents of the city. The evacuation the previous winter by church leaders had been largely of their own planning, even though under threat of arrest, and without military intervention. The steady spring removal had happened as groups of families prepared themselves and left. In contrast, the September Battle of Nauvoo precipitated a river crossing by those least prepared to endure it. A correspondent from the *Burlington Hawkeye* reported the situation during a visit to Nauvoo on September 19: "On either shore of the Mississippi may be seen a long line of tents, wagons, cattle, etc., with numberless wretched specimens of humanity. Since the armistice or 'treaty' the Mormons are crossing in almost breathless haste. Three or four 'flats' are running constantly, both day and night." The newsman found a small detachment of soldiers bivouacked at the Mansion House and others at the temple. "Some lay sleeping on their 'arms,' and others lay rolled up in their blankets," he wrote. "On every hand lay scattered about in beautiful confusion muskets, swords, cannon-balls, and terrible missiles of death. Verily, thought I, how are the *holy* places desecrated!" The city seemed desolate. "Not a human being was seen. Houses appeared suddenly deserted as though the inmates had precipitously fled from a pestilence or the burning of a volcano. . . . It appeared as if the vengeance of the Almighty rested upon this doomed city."[86]

The violation of their civil rights caused by the military occupation left the citizens of Nauvoo vulnerable to looting, vandalism, and other problems. Those rushing to leave sold what they could for pennies on the dollar. Few of the firearms turned in for "temporary" custody during the occupation were returned to their owners; some refugees received a substitute gun of inferior quality. Vandals cut holes in the temple floors, disfigured the stone oxen in the basement, and chiseled names in the wood. Stealing from abandoned homes and shops was commonplace. Only Amos Davis's store remained open for business. One exile returned to Nauvoo on the twenty-first for some belongings: "I *felt* indeed I was an outcast and a stranger there."[87]

Across the Mississippi, the refugees gathered in a temporary campsite to consolidate their resources and organize for the march across Iowa. In all, about three hundred Latter-day Saints and some new citizens crowded into makeshift tents on the river bottoms near Montrose, where they endured cold autumn rains and chills and fever. On the twenty-eighth, Fanny Wardle gave birth to a baby boy, who died the same afternoon. Dubbed the "poor camp" by their friends farther west, the exiled Saints helped one another with the basic needs of life. Mitigating their hunger was a willingness to share the limited resources of the united camp. Newel K. Whitney procured flour at Bonaparte and counseled on future options. He decided that fifty wagons would be ample to remove the camp to better quarters. Some of the exiles had scattered to Burlington, St. Louis, and other places of refuge.[88]

The Twelve learned of the situation on September 24. They directed those camped at Council Point, east of the Missouri, to assemble an immediate shipment of teams, wagons, tents, and provisions. Church leaders had already dispatched a small relief company on the fourteenth to bring the poor out of Nauvoo as a routine matter. That company completed the three-hundred-mile trip to the Mississippi on October 7 and removed 157 people in twenty-eight wagons. The Council Point express teams reached the poor camp several days later to rescue the remaining exiles and transport them west.[89]

Brigham Young took news of the forced expulsion in stride. He told a Sunday meeting in Winter Quarters that the Saints on the Missouri had suffered as well as those in Nauvoo. All were destitute together. The Lord would allow the suffering to continue, he said, until "the Saints are chastened enough. . . . I have never believed the Lord would suffer a general massacre of this people by a mob. If ten thousand men were to come against us, and no other way was open for our deliverance, the earth would swallow them up." He sent word to the Nauvoo trustees to sell the temple and other church property for the best price available. Proceeds would help the poor. With few drivers to spare and a scarcity of grain in the Missouri River camps, he could do little more.[90]

Meanwhile, Nauvoo trustee Joseph L. Heywood hurried to St. Louis to solicit help. Newspapers there had condemned the vigilante actions. Mayor Peter G. Camden appealed for donations, and several St. Louis merchants agreed to accept food, clothing, tents, and other provisions for shipment upriver.[91]

Almon Babbitt and William Pickett traveled to Winter Quarters early in October to confer there with Brigham Young. Babbitt reported that the trustees had paid off sixty thousand dollars in church debts but still held obligations for another twenty-five thousand dollars. They hoped to sell all of the church property and raise five times that amount. The surplus would help in the migration. Young encouraged Babbitt to liquidate the property in Nauvoo and Kirtland quickly.[92]

On the morning of October 9, as the poor camp prepared to move west, flocks of migrating quail settled onto the river bottoms for forty miles along the Mississippi. Grateful for the supplement to a spare diet, the exiled Saints caught the small birds with their hands and gave thanks to the Lord for welcome fresh meat. Thomas Bullock, whose suffering family was among those benefited, called the arrival of the quail

> a direct manifestation of the mercy and goodness of God, in a miracle being performed in the Camp. . . . Men who were not in the Church marvelled at the sight. The brethren and sisters praised God and glorified his name, that what was showered down upon the children of Israel in the wilderness is manifested unto us in our persecution. . . . Every man, woman and child had quails to eat for their dinner.

That same day, the trustees arrived from Nauvoo with clothing, shoes, molasses, salt, and salt pork. Lifted in spirits, the company started off on their trek west, "amid the songs of quails and blackbirds."[93]

Among the friends Mormon leaders had found in the East was a twenty-four-year-old Pennsylvania attorney, Thomas L. Kane. Schooled in Paris and Philadelphia, Kane hailed from a respected family active in civic and military life. Kane's father, John K. Kane, was a prominent Philadelphia judge. Thomas Kane himself had aspirations to political office. After learning of the migratory plans of the Saints from Jesse C. Little in May 1846, he sought a letter of introduction in Washington to allow him to journey to California with the Twelve.

Thomas Kane went west in 1846 on a mission from President Polk to deliver to General Stephen W. Kearny the president's authorization to enlist five hundred Latter-day Saint soldiers in the march on Mexico. The Pennsylvanian traveled to Fort Leavenworth by way of the Mississippi River and stopped off at Nauvoo for a brief visit to the near-vacant city. He arrived in late September. Most of the Saints had left by then. Those evacuated after the Battle of Nauvoo had just departed, along with a number of new citizens, creating the impression that the city's entire population had vanished in a day. When he returned to Philadelphia, Kane spoke to a public meeting called by his father to organize a charitable fundraising effort to aid the exiled Saints. Four years later, Kane's interest in pleading the Mormon cause in Washington led him to remember his 1846 visit again when he spoke before the Pennsylvania Historical Society about his misunderstood friends.[94]

Thomas Kane's memorable 1850 description of an empty Nauvoo created a lasting image of the Desolate City, similar in angle of vision to that of the Burlington reporter. Church leaders preferred a portrait of a deserted Nauvoo that emphasized accomplishment rather than abandonment. The Nauvoo of future memory, Parley P. Pratt had told the October 1845 conference, would be "something that will be a monument of our industry and virtue. Our houses, our farms, this Temple and all we leave will be a monument to those who may visit the place of our industry, diligence and virtue." The sacrifice of a developed city, he said, was worth the price paid by the Saints. Inside the temple, above the pulpit of the High Priesthood, an inscription paralleling Pratt's sentiments read, "The Lord has beheld our Sacrifice, come after us."[95] Kane saw the inscription and acknowledged the monumental accomplishments of the industrious people of Nauvoo. For his Eastern audiences, however, Kane went beyond the honorific in an attempt to win a nation's sympathy for the injustices against the Latter-day Saints.[96]

Because of low water, Kane had left his riverboat at Keokuk. Traveling overland by carriage through the Half Breed Tract in Iowa, he was not impressed by the ill-kept places of the settlers there. In contrast, while still opposite Nauvoo, Kane spotted the Mormon city, "a landscape in delightful contrast" to the scenes just witnessed. Brockman's forces still occupied Nauvoo. Kane described the scene in prose crafted to win the sympathy of his listeners for the unfairness of the forced evacuation. "The unmistakable marks of industry, enterprise, and educated wealth, everywhere, made the scene one of singular and most striking beauty," he wrote. Noting that he found the city deserted, Kane explained,

> I went into empty workshops, ropewalks, and smithies. The spinner's wheel was idle; the carpenter had gone from his workbench and shavings. . . . The blacksmith's shop was cold; but his coal heap, and ladling pool, and crooked water horn were all there, as if he had just gone off for a holiday. No work people anywhere looked to know my errand . . .—no one called out to me from any opened window, or dog sprang forward to bark an alarm. I could have supposed the people hidden in the houses, but the doors were unfastened, and when at last I timidly entered them, I found ashes dead upon the hearths, and had to tread a tiptoe, as if walking down the aisle of a country church to avoid rousing irreverent echoes from the naked floors.

In two sections of the city, Kane founds signs to explain the sudden evacuation. At the site of the battle in the southeastern portions of the city, he noted the effects of cannon shots on battered walls and foundations. At the temple, armed men were barracked amidst their arms and heavy ordnance. "They told me the story of the Dead City," Kane concluded, and how the battle a few days before had forced the remaining residents out of their homes. Kane visited the temple with militiamen and then resumed his journey westward. Along the route to Winter Quarters, he encountered the struggling poor camp and passed through Miller's Hollow, which the Saints would later rename Kanesville in his honor.[97]

Brayman's report of the Battle of Nauvoo and an appeal from the displaced new residents of Nauvoo brought yet another visitor to the empty city. Governor Ford arrived on October 28 with about two hundred fifty troops for a personal investigation. He set up camp within the Temple Block against the north wall. On November 7, the governor was visited by twelve "Ladies of Nauvoo," wives of anti-Mormons living in the area who considered Ford a Jack-Mormon. To show their disapproval of his fair-minded treatment of the Latter-day Saints and their friends, they presented him with a black petticoat (some said two—one a black one, the other fringed with red). His troops objected to the insult in a hastily called indignation meeting. A formal statement denouncing the event and praising Ford's courage appeared in a broadside signed by nineteen officers.[98] In response to the women's affront, another group of Nauvoo women visited the governor, each representing one of the twenty-nine states of the Union. These delegates were new citizens (Thomas Sharp called them "Jacks"). They presented Ford with an American flag. A handbill reporting this event quoted Ford as saying "no event of his life ever gave him more sincere pleasure."[99]

Satisfied that nothing more could be done, the governor posted a small guard of about eighteen men to maintain order. After a stay of some two weeks, he traveled to Quincy and on to Springfield. Residents would not see another Illinois governor in Nauvoo for sixty years.[100] The state forces remained until just after newly elected governor Augustus C. French took office in December.[101] The exiled non-Mormon citizens returned to their homes gradually during the fall and winter of 1846–47. With the tensions resolved, Thomas Sharp echoed the appeal of the new governor to residents of the Nauvoo region to avoid further trouble and to demonstrate to people elsewhere in Illinois that the Anti-Mormon Party believed in law and order.[102]

On his final day in office, Ford expressed satisfaction to the state general assembly that "the people called Mormons have removed from the State," most of them voluntarily. The mass migration had been inevitable, he acknowledged, but he regretted that the state of Illinois had been discredited by the forced expulsion of a small remnant. Despite his efforts, Ford confessed, he had failed to resolve the dilemma short of removal.[103]

With the Latter-day Saints gone, a new state administration and the people of Illinois could reflect on the experience of Mormon Nauvoo and move on to other challenges. In one of his last official acts as governor,

Ford issued a routine proclamation setting aside Thursday, December 17, as a statewide day of thanksgiving and prayer to God for his bounteous blessings during the year just past.[104] The returning new citizens at Nauvoo joined in the observance. The Battle of Nauvoo had served as a final event in the transition effectively ending the Mormon years in Nauvoo—and concluding the Nauvoo period in Latter-day Saint history. The forced expulsion of a relatively few innocent people, unpleasant for thoughtful citizens on both sides of the issue, allowed a new order of peace to prevail in the city.

CHAPTER 20

"The New Order of Things"

Our object in commencing the publication [of the Hancock Eagle *in Nauvoo] at this juncture is to anticipate the new order of things which will inevitably result from the changes now taking place in the civil, ecclesiastical, and domestic policy of this large city and the country adjacent.*

—PROSPECTUS FOR *HANCOCK EAGLE,* FEBRUARY 23, 1846

[The Mormon] society, like all others, in its organization and progress developed a history, and it is those developments, only, which constitute its history. From 1830 to 1840 those developments created an unbroken chain of history. In 1840 it culminated and its history tended in a different direction and found its level in the order of things which now exist in Utah. If the world ever gets that history it must, according to the laws of historiography, divide itself into those two divisions, for each one had its own peculiarities and its own results.

—SIDNEY RIGDON, JULY 9, 1858

The departure of the Latter-day Saints from Illinois in 1846 allowed Nauvoo to become a community like others in the surrounding countryside. It fulfilled the desire of anti-Mormon politicians for a city under a new order of civil, domestic, and ecclesiastical policy. Residents acted independently within existing political parties, as private entrepreneurs, and with diverse religious affiliations. They were typical Americans.

Meanwhile, the Saints who had tried to create a religious community in Nauvoo moved on. They remembered Nauvoo and what they had learned during those pleasant if troubled days. Many of them recalled Joseph Smith's earliest teachings and treasured what they termed "original Mormonism." Others embraced the changes implemented in Nauvoo as a further unfolding of revealed religion. Some had come late to the church; others had found it early. But more important than the length of their membership was what individual Saints heard and applied of the Prophet's teachings. Thus, while the Nauvoo years did indeed forever change the nature of Mormonism, believers responded differently to the changes. Mormonism meant one thing to the Saints who gathered in the Intermountain West and something else again to those who chose to remain behind in the Midwest. Church members in both places acknowledged the significance of the Prophet Joseph Smith's contributions in Nauvoo, but they viewed many of his accomplishments and messages with contrasting levels of acceptance.[1]

From every perspective, the events of the Nauvoo years made a significant difference in the subsequent history of the Latter-day Saints. As Sidney Rigdon noted in 1858 and as Brigham Young and others recognized during their last months in Nauvoo, the final years of Joseph Smith's life and the months immediately following his death marked a watershed in church doctrine, practices, and governance. The Reorganized Church of Jesus Christ of Latter Day Saints, with Joseph Smith III as its first president, in 1860 adopted the pre-Nauvoo patterns as its model of the Restoration. For the Reorganization in general, Nauvoo held dark memories because of the theological developments of those years. Many of its members rejected the temple doctrines and practices, including eternal and plural marriage and, eventually, proxy baptisms. It was the influence of man, not of God, they concluded, that had introduced those things. Savoring their independence in political, economic, and social aspects of life, they wished to severely limit ecclesiastical involvement in those arenas as well.[2]

In contrast, The Church of Jesus Christ of Latter-day Saints, with Brigham Young and the Twelve at the helm, headed in what Sidney Rigdon termed a "different direction." That direction was defined through the doctrines unfolded and expanded during the Nauvoo years by the Prophet Joseph Smith. Brigham Young and the Twelve pledged to the Saints that they would continue the Prophet's revealed program, including the revelations and ordinances of the Nauvoo years. The church that headed across the Rocky Mountains did so as a religious community—a distinctive, covenant people—centered in the doctrines and practices surrounding the House of the Lord, which were for them a recognition of the ultimate Source of eternal peace.[3]

For Brigham Young, the prophetic contributions of Joseph Smith that culminated at Nauvoo could best be preserved in a new and isolated gathering place. Relocation, a necessity anticipated by revelation through Joseph Smith, offered a fresh beginning under new leaders to accomplish a divinely established plan. It was in this context, four months before leaving Nauvoo, that Young said, "The exodus of the Nation of the only true Israel from these United States to a far distant region of the West . . . forms a new epoch . . . in the history of the church."[4] A new prophet and a new gathering place defined the changes. Transplanted from Nauvoo unaltered were the established religious beliefs and practices given to the church through the Prophet Joseph Smith. The members of the Quorum of the Twelve commissioned by the Prophet and given the keys to carry forward that spiritual agenda would nurture the church in the western refuge.

NAUVOO UNDER THE NEW ORDER

While the Saints of the exodus and the dissidents of the dispersion carried forward their separate understandings of what their years in the City of Peace would mean for the future, life in Nauvoo continued for other peoples. The city had grown from its small beginnings in 1839 as a result of an active real estate business, which gained its momentum from Joseph Smith's call to the Latter-day Saints to gather to a temple city. Over a busy six seasons, the Saints built an estimated two thousand homes in the city and another five hundred in what they called the suburbs. Half were small log or frame homes. According to a St. Louis newspaper reporter, the rest were about evenly divided between brick and frame houses. "Most of [these] are good buildings," he wrote, "and some are elegant and handsomely finished residences, such as would adorn any city." By late September 1846, he guessed, only two hundred of Nauvoo's houses had occupants.[5] In this buyer's market, the ten thousand departing residents and their agents offered properties at a significant discount of around 50 percent of market value. Most of it sold for much less than that, some of it to speculators expecting soon to resell at a profit. Some undeveloped lots reverted to the original patent holders.

For anyone willing to relocate to Nauvoo, the developed properties provided a head start in frontier village living. The first people to take advantage of the opportunity were those calling themselves new citizens. They arrived from nearby areas during the selling spree of 1845 and 1846. They tended to be moderates politically—law-and-order citizens who sympathized with the plight of the Latter-day Saints. The anti-Mormon community called them "Jacks" and expelled many of them in September 1846 along with lingering Saints. The anti-Mormons did not want anyone living in Nauvoo who would encourage the Saints to stay or invite them back. Even so, most of the tolerant new citizens returned to occupy the property they had purchased. For many years afterward, the Anti-Mormon Party kept a vigilant watch on Nauvoo to prevent it from again becoming a major gathering place for the Saints.[6]

Yet there were Latter-day Saints who returned, including members of the Smith family. Emma Smith returned to Nauvoo with her children in February 1847 from their temporary home in Fulton City, Illinois. She took possession of the Mansion House from a dishonest lessee and remained custodian of several city lots and the family farm. On Joseph Smith's birthday, December 23, 1847, Emma dressed in a plum-colored satin dress for her wedding to Lewis C. Bidamon. A tall and charming forty-five-year-old merchant in Nauvoo, Bidamon was a widower with two daughters. Emma had known Lewis and his brother John for several years through business dealings. During the year of transition, the Bidamon brothers had been law-and-order new citizens in Nauvoo. The marriage between the Prophet's widow and the new citizen from Canton, Illinois, was "the all absorbing topic of conversation" in Nauvoo. But residents soon allowed the Bidamons to become ordinary citizens. Meanwhile, the Prophet's mother, Lucy Mack Smith, had sought refuge with her daughter Lucy Milliken seventy miles north of Nauvoo. In 1851, she moved in with the Bidamons in Nauvoo. Crippled by arthritis, Mother Smith remained at Nauvoo until her death in May 1856.[7]

The initial effort to make something of the abandoned Mormon

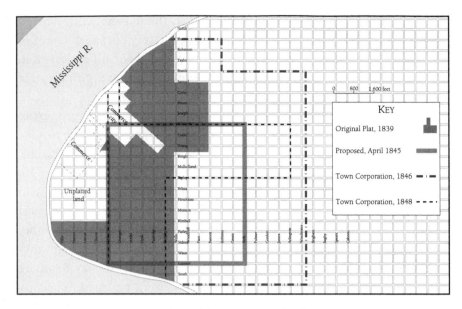

Nauvoo Town Limits, 1845–48

capital lacked the religious motivations and magnetism found in the City of the Prophet. Consequently, the community took on the characteristics of a small midwestern town. Its population hovered just over one thousand. Of necessity, the new order in Nauvoo required a scaling down of public life. New citizens purchased vacant public buildings and put them to new uses. For example, the Seventies Hall served for a time for public meetings, but after a few years became a storage shed for corn.[8] Parley P. Pratt's store became St. Patrick's Church to serve a congregation established in 1847 by a missionary priest.[9] Other public activities continued in a fashion typical of small-town America. Residents advertised for teachers to establish schools, and someone revived a lyceum to further adult education.[10] A town council governed Nauvoo within boundaries redefined optimistically in 1846 and reduced to a more modest size two years later to fit the realities of the new community.[11]

Private enterprise likewise served a diminished Nauvoo population. Merchants, millers, craftsmen, and others replaced those who had left. The commercial district on Mulholland Street east of the temple remained active; most of the stores and shops on lower Main Street were left empty. The most prominent of several merchants on the hill was Amos Davis. He had found early success in Commerce before the Saints arrived, made friends and enjoyed prosperity in Mormon Nauvoo, and then adapted to the needs of another group of customers in the new Nauvoo. "We have more goods and traders than business," a resident opined in 1848. "Money is scarce and business dull. We hope it will be better after harvest. The Post Office is moved to Davis' Store and the business seems coming on to the Hill."[12]

Even with this expected consolidation and normative economic development, Nauvoo retained some of the old tensions. By expelling the Saints, the anti-Mormons had neutralized the political influence of the Latter-day Saint voters who acted in unison. But local newspaper editors wielded a significant influence in county politics, and that influence continued. The editorial voice during the first months of the transition was William E. Matlack. Through the *Hancock Eagle,* he spoke hopefully of a "new order of things" in all aspects of life. A student of medicine at Princeton College and of Greek philosophy in Europe, Matlack promised to be religiously neutral and to support the Democrat Party and Nauvoo's general welfare. Despite this intent, the paper was criticized by anti-Mormons as too friendly to Latter-day Saints. The thirty-four-year-old editor had only a few months to articulate a new civic order in Nauvoo. His death in late July 1846 meant an early end to the *Eagle.*[13]

After the Battle of Nauvoo, the *Eagle* was replaced by the *Nauvoo New Citizen.* Even with most Latter-day Saints gone, control of the newspaper's editorial voice remained an issue. Within weeks, John M. Bernhisel informed Brigham Young that "the mobocrats" were behind the paper, with Iowa promoter Isaac Galland (Thomas Sharp's brother-in-law, who had helped establish the Saints in Commerce and Montrose) the intended editor. In fact, a Mr. Slocum maintained an editorial stance tolerant of both new and old citizens but with a clear bias against Latter-day Saints.[14] A year later, another change in ownership created the *Hancock Patriot.* This time Thomas Gregg criticized the paper for a pro-Mormon position that he said had continued from the *Neighbor* through the *Eagle* and the *New Citizen.*[15] The politicized editorial climate was finally neutralized in January 1851 when a new group of immigrants who lacked experience in the Nauvoo of Joseph Smith's time bought the *Patriot.* The Icarians, a communal group with roots in France, published the *Popular Tribune* to

The Icarians who remade Nauvoo into their own religious community used stones from the temple to build the school at left. It was used later as a Catholic school and in the 1960s as an information center by Nauvoo Restoration Incorporated. At right is the Icarian communal dining room.

serve their own interests—reforming society through a social and economic system of equality.[16]

This second wave of immigrants chose Nauvoo for many of the same reasons that had attracted the new citizens. Vacant homes and abandoned farms were selling at bargain prices. Etienne Cabet, the group's leader, was seeking a place to build a utopian community under a democratic form of government and with no private ownership of property.[17] An advance group from France in 1848 had failed in a first attempt along the Red River in Texas. While waiting in New Orleans for Cabet's arrival from France, the delegates heard about Nauvoo. Three of them visited the city and returned to New Orleans in February 1849 with glowing reports. Almost immediately, Cabet personally led nearly three hundred followers to Nauvoo to build factories, farms, and schools. They purchased abandoned houses for back taxes, rented eight hundred acres of farmland in Illinois, and later bought three thousand acres near Corning, Iowa.[18]

Among the sites purchased by the Icarians was the Nauvoo Temple Block and its burned-out temple. Just a year after the Latter-day Saint trustees left Nauvoo, a fire destroyed the internal wooden structure of the building. When first spotted about three o'clock on the morning of

October 9, 1848, fire was burning in the spire. Before firefighters could respond, the flames had spread to the roof timbers. The fire lit the streets of Nauvoo for nearly a mile in all directions, and the sound of falling timbers could be heard across the river. The stones cracked from the intense heat and remained hot to the touch for a day. "It was a sight of mournful sublimity," the *Hancock Patriot* reported. Who, the editor asked, would destroy such an elegant and celebrated work of art?[19]

Because first suspicions pointed to arson, local citizens raised a reward, but no arrests were made. Lewis C. Bidamon later told visitors from Utah that Joseph Agnew of Dallas City, Illinois, had been paid five hundred dollars to torch the temple. County residents who feared that the Saints would return if the temple remained intact had raised the funds. Agnew allegedly made a deathbed confession to a friend in 1870 implicating Thomas Sharp and John McAuley as coconspirators. Agnew said that he had been trapped in the burning building and was seriously injured when he threw himself into the flames and rolled to safety.[20]

The Icarians acquired the temple in March 1849 for the minimum established by the trustees, two thousand dollars. Before they could realize their plans to restore the gutted structure as a meeting hall, dining hall, and school, a second disaster hit. On the afternoon of June 27, 1850, a fierce windstorm toppled two walls of the temple and left a third unstable. Seven masons laying new foundations for interior supports in the basement narrowly escaped injury when the north wall slammed into the cavity. To save their investment, the Icarians salvaged the shaped temple stones for use in a communal dining hall, a boarding school, and other buildings.[21]

Not everyone welcomed the Icarians to Nauvoo. For some residents of Illinois, Cabet's effort to build a self-contained community seemed too much like that of the Latter-day Saints. The legislature rejected the Icarians' request for a city charter in February 1851. The memory of Mormon Nauvoo was too fresh.[22] A cholera epidemic among the new immigrants raised fears in Nauvoo that the Icarians had brought it with them from New Orleans. Actually, the epidemic affected communities up and down the Mississippi. A Latter-day Saint visiting St. Louis reported, "It was the Asiatic cholera. They would be taken first with the cramps in the stomach and vomiting, then they would begin to look a dark black color in the face, then their limbs would cramp up, and in a short time they would be dead." The Icarians buried their dead secretly to keep confidential the number of deaths.[23]

These temporary setbacks did not deter the Icarians from pursuing their dream. Residents and visitors alike complimented them on their orderly, industrious, virtuous approach to life. At Nauvoo, they operated a sawmill, a large flour mill, a brewery, a distillery, two weekly newspapers (one in French), and a communal vegetable garden and orchard. They exported local products to St. Louis. They preached against smoking, dressed uniformly and simply, ate in a common dining hall, emphasized education, and resolved community issues through deliberation and arbitration.[24]

It was internal dissension that thwarted Cabet's hope for a utopian community. Strife over leadership roles and the definition of economic equality prompted some followers to leave Nauvoo, but replacements kept coming from France. In 1855, Cabet announced plans to abandon Nauvoo. A third of the group in Nauvoo helped Cabet establish a colony in Cheltenham near St. Louis and elected him president for life. He died a month later of a stroke. The Cheltenham colony continued for a decade before collapsing. Other followers established communes on the group's lands in Iowa; still others moved to California. The scattered groups disbanded or died off in the late 1880s and 1890s. A few Icarians remained to continue their communal efforts in Nauvoo and died there.[25]

Besides the new citizens and the Icarians, Nauvoo attracted immigrants who had been drawn to the fertile lands of Illinois from Germany, Switzerland, England, Ireland, and Scotland. Arriving at the same time as the Icarians in the late 1840s and 1850s, these settlers came as individual families. German immigrants received direct encouragement to settle in Nauvoo from the United States and Foreign Emigration Homestead Association in Philadelphia. This group, whose motto read "Every Man a Freeholder!" promoted the city with a *Map of Nauvoo* created in 1848 by A. Cherill. It carried a title section in two languages.[26]

The Germans came in numbers sufficient to create a distinct identity for Nauvoo's economic and cultural life that lasted until World War I. By 1866, the city was dotted with two hundred fifty vineyards. Temple limestone lined many local wine cellars. As the Icarians withdrew, religion took a Germanic turn. For many years, the city's Catholic, Lutheran, Presbyterian, and Methodist churches offered services in the German language.

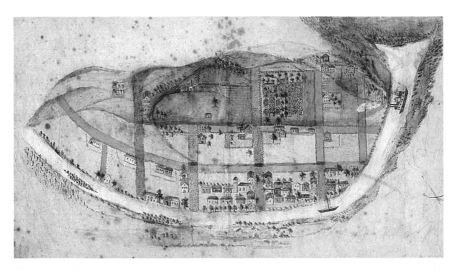

German settler Joseph Rheinberger created this watercolor drawing of Nauvoo in 1851. At the top left are ruins of the Nauvoo Temple and the Amos Davis store. Toward the right is the enclosed Rheinberger estate with home and vineyard. The four oblongs below the home may represent wine cellars. The Nauvoo Historical Society Museum now occupies the home.

The maturing of an English-speaking second generation eliminated this need. Nauvoo's German and English Presbyterian churches merged in 1890, with other denominations adjusting later on. The growth of German nationalism in Europe caused German-Americans in Nauvoo to minimize identification with their ancestral homeland, and a distinguishable Germanic Nauvoo faded further from view.

During the Icarian and German stages of Nauvoo's development, the new citizens coexisted with these and other cultural groups. As Germanic distinctiveness faded in the early twentieth century, Nauvoo's small-town identity reflected a gradual blending of various peoples and cultures. The new order that emerged after World War I became more typical of the rural Midwest. But residents of Nauvoo did not forget their past and eventually came to celebrate the best part of the several Nauvoos—those defined in turn by Joseph Smith, the New Citizens, Etienne Cabet, German immigrants, and the forces of American assimilation.

GATHERING THE REMNANTS

While Nauvoo was adjusting to new peoples and new ways of public life, Latter-day Saints faced again the question of the necessity of congregating as a people in a centralized location. The majority, who followed the Quorum of the Twelve to an isolated refuge beyond the Rocky Mountains, accepted this and other foundational doctrines. Besides their willingness to move to a new place of refuge, the westering Saints were set apart from the schismatic groups because they accepted the principles and practices centered on the ordinances of the House of the Lord and other doctrines taught by Joseph Smith. These the Prophet had implemented in Kirtland and Nauvoo.

The restoration of the "ancient order of things" as preached in the 1830s had emphasized three related points: the apostasy from the truth of Christ's pure religion after the death of his apostles, the failure of Christian reformers to remedy this falling away,[27] and the restoration of priesthood authority and the spiritual gifts of the New Testament Saints, including revelation and the visitations of angels. These last points encompassed acceptance of a new witness of Christ's ancient ministry, the Book of Mormon.[28] Early missionaries also focused on the new order of righteousness anticipated during the Millennium.[29] The schismatics of the dispersion from Nauvoo held to at least some of these early statements of Latter-day Saint doctrine.

But the Saints most in tune with Joseph Smith's teachings recognized that the ancient order of things included more than the doctrines and practices that had been restored during the first years of Joseph Smith's ministry. The early phase of the Restoration, including the heavenly visits in the Kirtland Temple, combined with the doctrines taught in Nauvoo to yield a fulness of the gospel, a joining of truths from all dispensations. This unfolding of doctrines, line upon line, included the keys to administer the exalting priesthood ordinances—not just baptism for the living but also for the dead and the temple covenants of the endowment and eternal marriage. These doctrines and ordinances, unique to The Church of Jesus Christ of Latter-day Saints, pointed worthy Saints toward the hallowed glories of exaltation.[30] This was the distinctive inheritance preserved in their wilderness refuge in the West.

Those who were ignorant of the doctrines unfolded in Kirtland and Nauvoo or who rejected them shunned the call to move west and sought fellowship apart from the gathered Saints. Some of these people dismissed the need for a centralized location. As others had done in 1839, they blamed the gathering for the violence and confrontation that had happened and would have no part of it. Once again, to gather or to scatter, temporally and spiritually, was a choice many had to make. Doctrinally, they remained anchored in the Book of Mormon and certain of the canonized revelations of the 1844 Doctrine and Covenants. Some of them rejected as the products of a fallen prophet the temple doctrines and practices introduced in Nauvoo. Others held to some of these essentials of the unfolding Restoration but without a full understanding or the authority to administer temple ordinances. A few, out of ignorance or apostasy, denied that such things existed in the church before the Twelve took charge. Most of these ungathered Saints remained behind in the Midwest. The others left Utah to rejoin scattered branches in Iowa, Illinois, Indiana, Michigan, Ohio, and eastern Canada.

Over a period of years, new dissident groups emerged. Most of them continued or redefined the religious core they had known before Nauvoo. Some leaders built a new church from ideas garnered from their experiences with the restored Church of Christ of the Kirtland years. Others underscored specific aspects of the faith to satisfy themselves and their followers. Through this process, the Prophet's spiritual inheritance was divided among many children of the Nauvoo experience. Eventually, some of the dispersed Saints in the Midwest coalesced around a movement that became the Reorganization, headed by Joseph Smith III. The Saints who followed the Twelve remained in numbers the majority and in doctrines and programs the heirs to the unabridged restoration of all things.

Some of those who abandoned their homes in Nauvoo in 1846 reversed the gathering and returned to relatives in the United States or Canada or elsewhere.[31] Each decision reflected individual needs and concerns. At the time of the western exodus, an estimated three hundred branches of the church existed in the United States and Canada and in the British Isles. These were the destinations for those seeking a home among the ungathered Saints. Many exiles from Nauvoo simply stopped at convenient places up and down the Mississippi River or in towns a convenient distance inland. This dispersion, like a similar scattering during the expulsion from Missouri, was a practical necessity at the time. As explained in an epistle from the Twelve at Winter Quarters, "The Saints were obligated to scatter to the north, south, east, and west, wherever they could find shelter and procure employment."[32]

One of the closest magnets was St. Louis. A large number of Latter-day

Saint men from the Hancock County area had worked in that booming commercial center during the years of Nauvoo's own rapid expansion. In 1846, some of them transported their families downriver. St. Louis became a place for the Nauvoo exiles to gather as well as a port of call for British immigrants. At a branch conference in January 1847, the elders reported 1,478 members in the city, an increase of more than one thousand in three years. Brigham Young encouraged able men in St. Louis to leave their families temporarily to help with the work in the Missouri River camps. Some of them accepted the invitation. Others fitted out wagons and, with their families, joined in the migration across the Rockies.[33]

When the Twelve returned to Winter Quarters after designating a place of settlement in the Great Salt Lake Valley, they launched an effort to reverse the scattering of the Saints. According to the Twelve, never before in the history of the church had so many members been scattered over such a broad area and become so isolated from normal communications channels. On December 23, 1847, Brigham Young signed an important epistle inviting the Saints to gather to a new Zion beyond the Rockies to help "build a house to the name of the God of Jacob, a place of peace, a city of rest, a habitation for the oppressed." The letter from the Twelve served as both a news sheet and a plan of action. It brought members up to date on the activities of the apostles, their travels, the pioneer journey, and the recruitment of the Mormon Battalion eighteen months earlier. The message addressed both economic and cultural needs. Continuing the emphasis from Nauvoo, it encouraged the rich to help the poor and to establish factories to create jobs. It reminded the Saints of the need to provide books and a museum for the education of the rising generation. Most important, it reemphasized the need to congregate in the West to accomplish the church's mission of salvation—to preach the gospel and to administer temple ordinances. "Should any ask, Where is Zion? tell them in America," the epistle instructed the elders; "and if any ask, What is Zion? tell them the pure in heart."[34]

The Twelve sent special missionaries across North America and to the British Isles to encourage the Saints to gather. The elders delivered copies of the epistle and sought funds to help transport the belongings of the Twelve to the Salt Lake Valley. Three members of the Twelve led out in the financial aspect of this mission: Orson Hyde and Ezra T. Benson were assigned to gather funds in the Eastern states, and Amasa Lyman, in the Southern states. A fourth apostle, Orson Pratt, was sent on a mission to England to preach, preside, and encourage the gathering. Meanwhile, the Twelve instructed Orson Spencer, presiding in England, to route emigrating Saints via New Orleans and St. Louis to Council Bluffs. A first group of eight missionary couriers left Winter Quarters on December 26 to seek those lost in the dispersal from Nauvoo. The men traveled together as far as St. Louis, where they had printed the *General Epistle from the Council of the Twelve Apostles,* then they fanned out along assigned routes.[35]

One of the missionaries, John Scott, visited towns along the Mississippi River northward to Galena. At every stop, he found a few Saints, some of them organized as a branch under a presiding elder. When appropriate, Scott would call a meeting to explain his mission. He would summarize or read the account from the eight-page *General Epistle* of the Twelve. Then he would rehearse the financial needs of poor members and church leaders. He encouraged the Saints to move soon to the Missouri River staging grounds in preparation for the spring 1848 migration to Great Salt Lake City. The response at Nashville, Iowa, was typical: "I found some of them very desirous to go with the church but they were generally very destitute of means. There are some that are rich and able to go but are not willing." A few declined because of poor health or their affiliation with James J. Strang or with others actively canvassing for support.[36]

Former Nauvoo city marshall Jonathan C. Wright crossed a frozen Mississippi from Iowa in mid-January 1848 on a similar mission to gather up the Saints in western Illinois. He visited with Emma Smith Bidamon and the church trustees in Nauvoo and later sailed downriver to St. Louis before launching his mission northward along an inland route to Springfield and beyond. In her conversation with Wright, Emma said she distrusted the Saints who had gone west, or Brighamites, as she labeled them. Among other things, she disliked their unwillingness to admit their covert practice of plural marriage. Reaffirming her belief that the church had been established by revelation, she told Wright that one of Joseph's revelations had warned of the church's destruction if it did not complete the temple. Emma wrongly believed the Saints had left an unfinished temple in Nauvoo. She declined Wright's invitation, saying that "she could go to Heaven without going to the Mountains."[37]

Other Illinois Saints visited by Wright who were unwilling to move west gave reasons as disparate as poverty and prosperity, poor health, and religious disagreements. Some remained puzzled over plural marriage, which they knew only through John C. Bennett's distorted exposé of the "spiritual wife doctrine." One man struggled to understand why William Smith, George Miller, and Lyman Wight had separated themselves from the church.[38] The Saints sometimes were merely uninformed about doctrinal developments in Nauvoo:

> I visited some persons who had been in the church and still were in but they said they believed Mormonism as it used to be preached, but as it is preached nowadays they did not know anything about it. I gave them such instructions as I had for them. They seemed to rejoice in it and said it appeared something like old times and they wished they was in the camp.[39]

For others, the comfort of the status quo interfered. A member in St. Clair County was reluctant to leave his prosperous four-hundred-acre farm and orchard. Besides, the man said, with so many schismatics claiming the right to lead, he would "wait awhile and see who was right." At Alton, Wright "found the Saints very cold, many of them, and not much of the Spirit of the Gospel, but a good deal of the spirit of the world." Wright cautioned those he contacted that their salvation depended upon their going to a temple city in the West and advised against procrastination.[40] On his visit to St. Louis, Wright similarly had "found many warm hearts in the city but a great many of the Saints . . . becoming much attached to the good things of this world. . . . They are more in favor of a City than a Wilderness life," he wrote, "yet there are many who are desirous to come with the Saints west and will do so."[41]

One of those anxious but unable to gather with the Saints was Sarah J. Potts. A convert with six children and two orphans under her care, she and her unbaptized husband could not afford to migrate. A government clerk for years with the Engineer Service in North Carolina, he had barely supported his family and faced a layoff because of reduced funding of public works. In April 1847, Sarah informed a church trustee in Nauvoo,

> It is very painful to me to think that my children should be brought up in Babylon, deprived of the privileges of the Church, perhaps never to hear the Gospel in its fulness, surrounded with so many

temptations and follies, but I must try and point out to them the straight and narrow path, and leave the result to God, in whom I put my trust.[42]

The missionaries who were sent out to gather the Saints were continuing a process begun in 1830. Congregating in designated gathering places remained for the Saints a test of faith, an outward manifestation of an inward conversion. It was a choice each convert had to make, time and again during the first decades, a choice influenced both by desire and by ability to act. "Come All Ye Saints," a migration song popular in the late 1840s, captured both the sacred promise of gathering and the premise that individual members were making their own decisions. They could heed the call to the wilderness refuge—with its promised temple blessings—or follow other options. The song concluded:

> *Who are these ye are leading forth*
> *Upon these lonely wilds?*
> *Yea, they're prophets, priests, and kings*
> *Who all have been exiled*
> *Together with their little ones*
> *And wives in sorrow moving,*
> *Have left their homes for better ones.*
> *This is a day of choosing.*[43]

The most significant religious factors keeping Latter-day Saints from moving west were concerns about teachings and practices. Scattered members often lacked a clear understanding of the doctrines and ordinances revealed to Joseph Smith. They heard contrasting claims and didn't know how to resolve their confusion. They knew of the temple but lacked the converting spirit that came to those who heard the Prophet explain the doctrines in Nauvoo. Those who wondered about what should be taught or who should lead the church listened for a convincing voice. One Iowa Saint confided to a relative in Vermont,

> We feel like a sheep without a shepherd. . . . Many of the church are wholly giving up the ship entirely and others are very restless not knowing the right way and want to find it. So it is with us. Strang has given some good revelations if they were true, but time will soon tell the story.[44]

Time did eventually resolve the question for the wondering Saints. Most found satisfaction for their spiritual yearnings through The Church of Jesus Christ of Latter-day Saints in the West. Others felt satisfied by the selection of doctrines and practices embraced by the Reorganized Church of Jesus Christ of Latter Day Saints in the Midwest. Some converts returned to their Protestant roots. Others were satisfied, at least for a time, with options proposed by various dissident groups.[45]

THOSE WHO DID NOT GO WEST

Of the schismatics, James J. Strang was the most outspoken early claimant to the Prophet's mantle. For a decade after Nauvoo was abandoned, he continued the proselytizing effort that he had launched immediately after the murder of Joseph Smith. In the spring of 1846, the thirty-three-year-old Strang published a notice in the *Warsaw Signal* inviting the Saints still in Hancock County to join him in Voree (later named Burlington), Wisconsin. The *Signal's* anti-Mormon editor, Thomas Sharp, optimistically predicted that Strang would attract as many disciples as Brigham Young. The number who actually accepted Strang as leader fluctuated continually. Estimates of those in various scattered branches ranged as high as two thousand overall. In 1847, Strang created a center on Beaver Island in northern Lake Michigan. The number of his followers who congregated there peaked seven years later at just above five hundred.[46]

The claims of the Wisconsin prophet appealed to some prominent Latter-day Saints who had been casualties of the transition after the assassination. They wanted to be "Mormon" without plural marriage or late Nauvoo doctrines. Acting largely upon the advice of some of these former leaders, Strang offered revelations and some practices imitating those of Joseph Smith. Strang established an Order of Enoch at Voree, Wisconsin, in 1848, with all property held in his name. He published a code of conduct and outlined a system of church government in *The Book of the Law of the Lord.*[47] Among his earliest supporters were John C. Bennett, George J. Adams, William Smith, John E. Page, and the former president of the Nauvoo stake, William Marks. Smith became the patriarch in Strang's organization. Bennett worked behind the scenes, and the others served as counselors or apostles. Bennett helped create a secret monarchical organization called the Order of Illuminati, with Strang as imperial primate. The body was governed by a grand council and noblemen.[48] At one time or another, Strang claimed as associates men who had first affiliated with Sidney Rigdon, among them Benjamin Winchester, Martin Harris, Warren Post, Lucian R. Foster, Jason W. Briggs, and Zenos H. Gurley Sr.[49] Many of these men later became leaders in other groups of Midwestern Mormons, including the Reorganization. Martin Harris rejoined the Latter-day Saints later in life and died in Utah.

Those who joined Strang on Beaver Island when he moved there from Voree soon faced new challenges. In 1850, Strang had himself crowned King James in an elaborate ceremony choreographed by George Adams. Then Strang further alienated many followers by taking a plural wife.[50] In the mid-1850s, he faced numerous lawsuits, including federal charges of counterfeiting, trespassing on United States lands, obstruction of the mail, and treason. Two disgruntled followers stalked Strang and in June 1856 boldly shot him. He died three weeks later at age forty-three, having maintained a following for twelve years. Even though he did not appoint a successor, a token organization continued through the twentieth century with several hundred members living in four states.[51]

Other less controversial leaders attempted to serve the scattered Saints during the late 1840s and 1850s. Some created formal organizations. Others offered casual counsel. Among these earnest shepherds were Lyman Wight, Alpheus Cutler, James C. Brewster, Austin W. Cowles, William E. McLellin, and John E. Page. Each of these men emphasized certain aspects of Latter-day Saint beliefs or practices. Most of them opposed teachings related to the temple. They shared an earnest desire to protect the church from dissolution. Even though they had not challenged the authority of the Twelve in 1844, all of them eventually rejected Brigham Young's right to lead the Saints.

Lyman Wight and Alpheus Cutler disagreed with the Twelve over the timing of carrying the restored gospel to Native Americans and living the law of consecration. Anxious to fulfill the assignments given to them by Joseph Smith, they abandoned their loyalty to the newly sustained authorities and struck out on their own. Wight failed to convince Wisconsin Indians to accompany his pineries group to Texas, nor did he find converts among displaced tribes south of the Red River. In late 1845, with about one hundred fifty Wisconsin Saints, Wight set up a settlement in the area of Austin, Texas. Two years later, the community moved west a

Dispersion: Northeast and Midwest

short distance and founded Zodiac along the Pedernales River near Fredricksburg. After the Twelve excommunicated Wight in December 1848 for his unwillingness to accept their counsel, he became president of his own Church of Jesus Christ of Latter Day Saints. Wight continued the doctrines and practices of the church in Nauvoo. His followers administered temple ordinances in the upper level of a large storehouse built to house their consecrated donations, and they accepted plural marriage. With some others, Wight soon came to believe that Joseph Smith III was the Prophet's rightful heir. In 1851, floods forced yet another relocation; two years later, the colony moved to Bandera, Texas. Wight died there suddenly in March 1858 at age sixty-three, leaving his followers to seek other affiliations.[52]

Cutler, a faithful convert from the Kirtland years, worked as a stonemason on the temples in Kirtland and Nauvoo. He followed Brigham Young across Iowa and established an encampment at Cutler's Park. Cutler was a member of the Council of Fifty and had served on the high council in Nauvoo. Like Lyman Wight and others, he had accepted from Joseph

Smith a special mission to the Indians and had helped lead the Wisconsin pine country expedition in 1841. Cutler and his wife, Lois, had received their temple endowments and sealing, and Cutler took plural wives in 1846. With Brigham Young's blessing, Cutler and about two hundred followers offered agricultural education and the gospel to the Delaware and Oneida Indians in Kansas Territory.[53]

Over the succeeding years, Cutler's actions alienated him from Orson Hyde and the Kanesville high council. They branded his message as "Lamanism" because of its single-minded concentration on preaching to the Lamanites, or Indians. The preaching mission was not aberrant, but other matters put Cutler into apostasy, including his creation of the True Church of Jesus Christ in 1850.[54] Cutler was excommunicated in 1851 for his unwillingness to take counsel. The Cutlerites formed a colony in Iowa in 1852 at a place they called Manti. Cutler claimed special authority from Joseph Smith to reorganize the church after the Prophet's death. In doctrine, the Cutlerites held to the ideal of a communal economic order and an eventual return to Jackson County, Missouri. By the late 1850s, Cutler's following included more than five hundred members in three branches in southwestern Iowa. Despite Cutler's death in 1864, at age eighty, his True Church of Jesus Christ carried out a planned move to Clitherall, Minnesota. Only part of the Clitherall congregation accepted the establishment in 1902 of a headquarters in Independence, Missouri. Eventually, only the Missouri congregation survived, a group reduced to fewer than three dozen by 1990. In the upper level of its meeting place, the surviving church administers some ordinances reminiscent of those given in Nauvoo but not temple marriages or sealings.[55]

Two other schismatic leaders found direction through revelation and doctrine. James C. Brewster imitated the early Joseph Smith, while Austin Cowles challenged the Prophet's Nauvoo teachings. Like James Strang, Brewster attracted followers when he issued revelations and translations of ancient books. Brewster had been claiming revelations for the church since 1836, at age ten. During the mid-1840s, Brewster issued "abridgements" of seven lost books of Esdras. The publications were filled with apocalyptic forecasts and challenged Joseph Smith's authority. In 1848, Brewster organized a Church of Christ at Springfield. Soon he had branches in Ohio and Iowa made up largely of former Strangites. For four years, Brewster's Kirtland colleagues published a periodical, *The Olive*

Branch. Meanwhile, the twenty-four-year-old Brewster took a band of pioneers to New Mexico on a mission to native peoples. Dissension led to an early dissolution of the group, and Brewster returned to Illinois, where in 1867 he joined Sidney Rigdon's church.[56]

While Brewster pursued the prophetic strains of Latter-day Saint beliefs, Austin Cowles reacted against developments in Nauvoo. A merchant and active Freemason, Cowles had served as a counselor in the stake presidency in Nauvoo. Disturbed by the institution of plural marriage, political involvements by church leaders, and the ordinances of the endowment, Cowles joined William Law's reformed church. When the group's members fled Nauvoo after the martyrdom, Cowles affiliated with Brewster for a time and then formed his own short-lived group in Kirtland.[57]

Another group with a Kirtland geographical and doctrinal base appeared in March 1847, when a six-member committee began publishing *The Ensign of Liberty* for about forty followers. William E. McLellin, one of the original apostles, whom Joseph Smith later described as having "more learning than sense," served as chairman and editor. McLellin had withdrawn from the church in 1836 but held to his belief in the Book of Mormon and his hopes for the establishment of Zion. Over the next decade, McLellin joined briefly first with George Hinkle, then with William Law, and next with Sidney Rigdon. After flirting with the Strangites, he and a few former Strang affiliates in Kirtland tried to reestablish the church on what they called its "old foundations." McClellin argued that Joseph Smith had lost his prophetic mantle when he manifested a militant spirit in leading Zion's Camp to Missouri in 1834 and succumbing to a spirit of speculation surrounding the Kirtland bank. The Kirtland group accepted David Whitmer as the Prophet's successor on the basis of his 1834 ordination as president of the Clay County high council with jurisdiction over the church in Missouri. On a visit to Richmond, Missouri, McClellin convinced Whitmer to head the new Church of Christ. Participating in this reorganization were Oliver Cowdery, Martin Harris, and Book of Mormon witnesses Hiram Page, Jacob Whitmer, and John Whitmer, all of them dropouts from the main body of the church in the mid-1830s. Leaving the new leaders in Missouri, McClellin returned to Kirtland to build up the church there. Through the *Ensign,* he challenged Brigham Young's leadership and

"Twelveite Latter Day Saintism." Besides their succession claims, McClellin's group believed that the original church had strayed when it added "Latter Day Saints" to its name. In less than two years, Whitmer's presidency in Missouri was denouncing McLellin's organizational efforts. A letter written by Hiram Page on behalf of Whitmer rejected the offices of high priest and seer and denounced the doctrine of the gathering. That ended McClellin's credibility. As his followers went their separate ways, McClellin resumed his practice of Thompsonian medicine. Though approached by others, he never again affiliated with any religious group.[58]

Another early apostle, John E. Page, a member of the Twelve from 1838 until his excommunication in 1846, turned first to Strang. Dissatisfied, he became an independent counselor in the early 1850s to those perplexed over competing claims to succeed the Prophet. His supporters included William Marks and William W. Blair, both of whom became leaders in the Reorganization. In 1863, Page joined Granville Hedrick, who was assembling disaffected followers of James J. Strang and William Smith and who later established the remnant Church of Christ on part of the Independence temple lot. Page died four years later at age sixty-eight, still not satisfied that he had found Joseph Smith's true successor.[59]

Many of those perplexed about issues of doctrine and succession found satisfaction in a form of Mormonism advocated by the Reorganized Church of Jesus Christ of Latter Day Saints. The Reorganization coalesced during the 1850s around individuals drawn together from various groups searching for answers in the postmartyrdom church. Individuals who had stayed aloof from other would-be leaders were among the early affiliates, along with most of Lyman Wight's followers, many Cutlerites and Strangites, and some from various other dissident groups and isolated branches. The emergence of what was first known as the New Organization was nurtured most effectively by Jason W. Briggs and Zenos H. Gurley Sr. They were two among many people seeking to preserve what they termed an "original Mormonism" reflecting aspects of the pre-Nauvoo church. Both affiliated first with James Strang but lost faith in him when he began to imitate the political and religious developments of Nauvoo. As did so many dissidents, these men rejected the final revealed teachings and practices of the Prophet. By 1851, they were working together to prepare a remnant to receive Joseph Smith III as their leader.[60]

Briggs, a native of upstate New York, was a Latter-day Saint convert of 1841. He served as presiding elder in Beloit, Wisconsin. In 1846, he and the entire branch switched their loyalties to James Strang. Briggs promoted Strang until 1850 and then spent a year with William Smith at Covington, Kentucky. Briggs rejected Strang's autocratic style but was attracted to William Smith's teachings on lineal descent. Briggs disagreed with both leaders when they introduced plural marriage. In November 1851, back on his Wisconsin farm, the thirty-year-old Briggs eventually concluded that a lineal descendant of Joseph Smith would ultimately be called by the Lord as "one mighty and strong" to preside over the high priesthood. In the meantime, Briggs decided that it was his mission to preserve this notion and to contend against the leadership of Brigham Young and the practice of plural marriage. He convinced most members of the Beloit branch to reject Strang and join him in preparing a people to accept the leadership of Joseph Smith III.[61]

Gurley followed a similar path to the New Organization. A Presbyterian leader in Bridgewater, New York, he joined the Methodist church and became a schoolteacher in Leeds, Ontario, Canada, where Latter-day Saint missionary James Blakesley baptized him in 1838. He moved to Far West, Missouri; then, as a seventy, he helped establish the church at La Harpe, Illinois. Attracted by the claims of James J. Strang, Gurley became a Strangite missionary in Canada and Wisconsin, where he became president of Strang's Yellow Stone branch in Wisconsin in 1850. A year later, the fifty-year-old seeker rejected Strang. He had decided that the right person to lead the church was Joseph Smith III, then a nineteen-year-old farmer in Nauvoo. By the spring of 1852, most members of the Yellow Stone branch had likewise rejected Strang and accepted Gurley as their spiritual leader.[62]

The two branches led by Briggs and Gurley met for a series of semi-annual conferences near Beloit beginning in June 1852. Gurley believed that an interim organization was necessary to formalize their shared beliefs. The conferences passed resolutions defining ecclesiastical matters and doctrine. Delegates agreed that the only legitimate heir to the authority of Joseph Smith Jr. would be a direct descendant. The New Organization disavowed any association with plural marriage and encouraged an active missionary effort. At the April conference in 1853, held at

Zarahemla, Wisconsin, a formal organization emerged with Jason W. Briggs as temporary president.[63]

It would be seven years before Joseph Smith III stepped forward as a leader of the New Organization. Meanwhile, missionaries from the New Organization established followings among scattered Saints in northern Illinois and across southern Iowa. In Iowa in 1859, they baptized a hundred members and organized six branches. At the spring conference that year, in Amboy, Illinois, former Nauvoo stake president William Marks joined the church and helped established the *True Latter Day Saints' Herald.*[64]

By 1855, Joseph Smith III had decided what he did not want to do. "The Mormons of Salt Lake are not the Mormons of my Father's faith," he informed a friend. "They teach doctrines which . . . my Father never taught or believed." His mother, Emma, had taken a similar position, ignoring or denying the role plural marriage had played in her life. The Prophet's associates in Utah knew the truth, for they had received personally from Joseph Smith the doctrines and ordinances that his family in Illinois had rejected.[65] Emma feared that harassments like those suffered by her deceased husband might beset any son who took an active role in church leadership. Yet she was not averse to the opinions of William Smith and William Marks that Joseph III might yet lead the scattered church. On this point, Emma's eldest son kept his own counsel. Over a period of several years, he pondered his options—whether to spend his life in secular pursuits or accept the invitation to guide a religious remnant looking for a leader.[66]

In October 1856, Joseph III and Emmeline Griswold of Nauvoo were married by a Presbyterian minister. Not a Latter-day Saint, Emmeline agreed to allow her husband to pursue an ecclesiastical path if he chose to do so. The following month, he was visited by George A. Smith and Erastus Snow, apostles from Utah. He rejected their invitation to move west, citing his disagreement with plural marriage. Nor was he ready yet to join the New Organization. He had been kept informed of the actions and publications of the interim conferences but ignored a letter from the New Organization in 1856 inviting him to fill the "vacant seat" of his father. For a time, Smith cared for the family farm outside Nauvoo. He had worked as a laborer and had tried his hand at merchandising with his stepfather, Lewis Bidamon. Later, he read law and served in Nauvoo as a

Lewis C. Bidamon, a hard-working, sociable storekeeper, became surrogate father to Emma Smith's sons in December 1847. Seated next to Bidamon in this photograph from about 1860 are Frederick and Joseph III. Standing are David Hyrum (left) and Alexander.

justice of the peace. Supporting a family was a difficult task in that economically depressed region. In late 1859, he decided against a secular vocation. Early the next year, he informed William Marks of his availability for religious service. With his mother, the twenty-eight-year-old Joseph attended the April conference at Amboy, Lee County, Illinois. He was accepted by unanimous vote of the conference, and then William Marks, Zenos Gurley Sr., Samuel Powers, and William W. Blair ordained him president of the high priesthood.[67]

This action allowed the Reorganized Church of Jesus Christ of Latter Day Saints, as it came to be known in the 1860s, to fulfill the needs of those uncomfortable with the structures and teachings of the church as they stood in 1844. (The Reorganization continued the traditional use of separate words for "Latter Day Saints" in its name; the British hyphenated usage "Latter-day Saints" prevailed in Salt Lake City.) The Midwestern church offered a familiar priesthood pattern, spiritual gifts, a hope for a communal Zion, and a promise of personal salvation. It had the quiet, steadying leadership of Joseph Smith III to guide it through the nineteenth century and into the twentieth.[68]

Through an active missionary program, focused on Latter-day Saints who had not yet moved to Utah, the church gradually expanded its beginning membership of five hundred followers. First, it contacted the scattered Midwestern Saints. Next, it reached out to Saints in Utah and England. Most of Lyman Wight's followers, who shared William Smith's emphasis on lineal succession, joined the Reorganization. Attempts to recruit the Cutlerites met with some success.[69] The largely unsuccessful effort in Utah included challenges against polygamy and the authority of Brigham Young. As many as two-thirds of those recruited there moved east, leaving fewer than a thousand members of the Reorganization in Utah by the end of the century.[70] Contacts made in England beginning in 1863 led to the creation of five congregations there, but many of these people migrated to America. Missionaries sailed to Tahiti, Australia, and Scandinavia in the 1870s and continental Europe in the 1880s. After twenty years, the church counted fifteen thousand members. By 1914, the year of Joseph III's death, membership had grown to more than seventy-one thousand; in contrast, more than six times that number were then affiliated with The Church of Jesus Christ of Latter-day Saints.[71]

During the first decade of his service, Joseph III filled the presiding quorums. Among those interested in serving was William Smith. Joseph III offered his uncle church membership but not appointment as an apostle or patriarch. William died in 1894, at age eighty-two, without obtaining the office he desired. Three years later Alexander Hale Smith, the next oldest surviving son of Joseph and Emma Smith, was called as patriarch.[72]

An essential step for the Reorganization was to clarify its beliefs. The new church stood by its commitment to the three standard books of scripture from the early days of the Restoration. Emma Smith Bidamon preserved the Prophet's "New Translation" of the Bible as family property and allowed the church to publish it in 1867. Acceptance of the Book of Mormon and the 1844 edition of the Doctrine and Covenants further identified the Reorganization as believing in the early translations and revelations of Joseph Smith. A grandson of David Whitmer donated the printer's copy of the Book of Mormon manuscript in 1903, providing another historical link with the past. The Reorganization eventually

Joseph Smith III   *Joseph F. Smith*

Joseph Smith III, son of the Prophet, and Joseph F. Smith, son of the Patriarch, both remembered the Nauvoo years but from differing perspectives. Both served in leadership positions in their respective churches from the 1860s until their deaths in the 1910s. Each is shown here near his twenty-first birthday.

rejected the book of Abraham, first published in Nauvoo, as an uninspired document. They expanded the Doctrine and Covenants with revelations from Joseph Smith III.[73]

Most of the divergent groups had spoken out against plural marriage, temple ordinances, and associated doctrines. With strong support within the church, Joseph Smith III made it a central endeavor of his administration to denounce plural marriage. For nearly twenty years, church agents actively encouraged the federal government to outlaw the practice and to curb Latter-day Saint political influence. Joseph III visited Utah several times, and he and his cousin Joseph F. Smith conducted a lifelong correspondence over this and other issues.[74]

Some members of the Reorganization accepted the doctrines of the nature of God taught in the King Follett sermon and in the book of Abraham. To accommodate this diversity of opinion, church leaders defined the belief as optional. As advocates died, the Nauvoo teachings faded. They were dismissed as heretical by an 1878 conference and replaced with a more orthodox Christian doctrine of the Trinity. During this same time, belief in the divinity of temple ordinances such as baptism for the dead and sealings diminished. Officially, the church allowed personal interpretation on proxy baptisms. By 1886, the practice was deemphasized as not binding by revelation. From a practical perspective, believing members lacked a place in which to implement these temple practices. Utah observers pointed out their lack of authority to do so anyway.[75]

To resolve differing positions on the question of gathering, Joseph III set a clear direction within months of his ordination. Members would remain "separated for the present," he said, to avoid the problems that gathering had caused in Missouri and Illinois. The establishment of Zion in Jackson County was not as urgent as many believed, he said, for the Millennium only seemed close through the "prophetic eye." He advised the Saints to avoid places of wickedness. They should seek out a tranquil place of peace and quiet—an encouragement to settle in the rural towns and farms of the Midwest. "Our land is wide, and full of pleasant places wanting good men for citizens," he said.[76] Smith's counsel was not uniformly accepted, and some followers began the movement back to Jackson County in 1867. A branch was organized there six years later, and a small brick church erected in 1884. A much larger stone building, seating fifteen hundred, was completed in 1892. A stake of the Reorganization was organized in Independence in 1901 and two more in 1916.[77]

Joseph III moved from Nauvoo in 1866 to make his home northeast across the state in Plano, Illinois, where the *Saints' Herald* was being published. He relocated to Lamoni, Iowa, in 1881 to support a communal experiment known as the United Order of Enoch, a joint stock company launched more than a decade earlier. In 1895, Graceland College opened its doors in Lamoni as a church-sponsored institution of higher education. In 1921, the Reorganization established its headquarters in Independence, Missouri. Within a few years, construction began of a building known as the Auditorium, which would serve as an assembly hall and office building. It was a daunting undertaking for a church of around 125,000 members. Financial problems, the Depression, and World War II delayed completion until the 1950s, but parts of the building were used earlier. The church completed a temple nearby in 1993. Not intended for ordinances like those performed in Latter-day Saint temples, it was designated instead as a house of learning, prayer, and contemplation and a place to promote the church's mission of world peace in families, congregations, communities, and nations. The Kirtland Temple, purchased by a member of the Reorganized church and later deeded to the church, became a historic site and meeting place. Title to the first temple of the Restoration was clarified in an 1880 court case denying the donor's claim to ownership.[78]

Joseph III was succeeded in office in May 1915 by his eldest living son, Frederick M. Smith, who had been serving as a counselor in the First Presidency. The office of president continued in the Smith line until 1996, when it passed to W. Grant McMurray, a counselor in the First Presidency who was not a descendant of Joseph Smith.[79]

By that time, many other traditional practices and doctrines of the Reorganization had been altered. The church in the twentieth century became even less like its sister church headquartered in Salt Lake City and more like contemporary Protestantism.[80] After more than a century of attempting to distinguish itself from its Utah relative, the Reorganized church inaugurated its own new order of things. Beginning in the late 1960s, its theological position shifted significantly toward compatibility with mainline Protestant churches. Authority was decentralized to allow more diversity within the organization. W. Paul Jones, an outside consultant whose advice had influenced that shift, cautioned that without a change in direction, "there will be an increasing liberal dilution until the RLDS Church simply becomes one more Protestant denomination."[81]

These trends and the ordination of women to priesthood office in 1984 created an internal schism. As the New Organization itself had done in the 1850s, a reactionary faction formed independent branches in an attempt to preserve the old order. The conservative leaders of this schism drew away around twenty thousand supporters. The remaining congregations, meantime, encouraged the participation of women in local ministries. The church basked in a broadening ecumenical spirit and moved forward its temple emphasis as a symbol of its mission of peace. At its biennial conference in April 2000, the Reorganization emphasized its differences with its roots by adopting a new name. One year later, it became the Community of Christ.[82]

The Reorganization's interest in distancing itself from the Utah-based Latter-day Saints led it ultimately to a new, Protestant definition of itself. As it moved toward internal pluralism and external ecumenism, the new identity of the Reorganized church became a pale imitation of its beginnings. In contrast, The Church of Jesus Christ of Latter-day Saints has carefully shepherded its core, unique doctrines, whose common thread lies in their relationship to the House of the Lord.[83]

During a symposium in 1989 celebrating the sesquicentennial of the founding of Nauvoo, a presentation on the doctrinal contribution of those years summarized the teachings of the Prophet Joseph Smith that began unfolding in the earliest years of the church and reached their full development in Nauvoo:

> [These] include some of Mormonism's most central doctrines and practices: celestial marriage, the familial relationship of God the Father and of his Son Jesus Christ to humanity, the character of God, the materiality of spirit, a more comprehensive understanding of the keys of the priesthood, premortal existence, the plurality of gods, ordinances for the dead, and the endowment. These precepts represent Joseph Smith's key Nauvoo teachings, the list of which reads like a summary of the most distinctive aspects of Latter-day Saint religion.[84]

Although dissidents and apostates rejected or drifted away from these central doctrines and practices, the church that had been transplanted to a new gathering place in the West nurtured them. The memory of Nauvoo that carries the greatest meaning for Latter-day Saints today is centered in these doctrines and their application. The geographical and spiritual center of Nauvoo during the 1840s was the temple. Nauvoo will be remembered in the future because of the House of the Lord and what it represents—a place where "the peaceable things of the kingdom" are taught and where God's covenant people receive sacred ordinances that point them along the path toward eternal life.[85]

CHAPTER 21

Remembering Nauvoo

[Nauvoo] reveals a piece of work so fine in character and of such signif-
icance and magnitude as to reflect great credit upon the people who did
it and upon the state where it took place. The example which those
people gave to the world of self-reliance, of faith in a just and beneficent
Creator, of power to do, to do without, to endure, to conquer . . . must be
preserved and passed on to coming generations.

—BRYANT S. HINCKLEY, AUGUST 1938

While the churches of the dispersion moved forward in time to meet the
changing needs of the world in which they lived, the Nauvoo they left
behind was not forgotten. Eventually, the two major churches that grew
out of the removal of the Saints from Nauvoo established congregations
in the City of Peace. In the twentieth century, these ecclesiastical steps paralleled the historic restoration of selected buildings in Old Nauvoo. At the
same time, the process continued of preserving the memory of the
Nauvoo experience by telling its stories and writing about the past.

The Reorganized church first attempted to reestablish a religious
Latter Day Saint presence in Nauvoo, in large part because of the Smith
family's long association with the city. Joseph Smith III, after accepting
appointment as the new church's first president in 1860, stayed in
Nauvoo. He remained active in civic affairs and served as branch president for six years. The presence of an organized group did not go unnoticed in Hancock County. Resolutions signed by a few area citizens in

1864 opposed the small congregation. But, according to the *Carthage Republican*, most residents viewed the Saints "as quiet, orderly, and industrious citizens, . . . who are generally esteemed and respected by their immediate neighbors."[1]

The Nauvoo branch of the Reorganization retained its strength until after the Smith family moved to a new headquarters across the state in Plano, Illinois, in 1866. Then, after a decade of declining participation in the Nauvoo area, the church discontinued worship services there. Nauvoo residents not only missed the Latter Day Saints as neighbors but noticed especially the loss of their economic contribution. Four hundred residents petitioned the Reorganization to reestablish its headquarters in Nauvoo. Only the Saints could make Nauvoo prosper, the local editor said. "Our citizens for many years have made no attempt to do it." A church site selection committee instead decided in 1881 to move the headquarters to Lamoni, Iowa, 210 miles west of Nauvoo.[2]

Because leaders of the Reorganized church had adopted a policy that allowed members to choose where they lived, rather than gathering to a particular location, some did choose Nauvoo. In 1920, the church purchased a vacant schoolhouse and organized a branch for the twenty-one members living in the area. Growth was slow, and membership in the Nauvoo region did not reach one hundred until the early 1980s. In 1988, the branch built a red brick church to serve these modern Latter Day Saints.[3]

Meanwhile, for Latter-day Saints in early Utah, Nauvoo eventually became a place of interest to visit. Many nineteenth-century missionaries passed through Nauvoo and reported on the situation in the city that they and their parents had abandoned. The creation of a local church organization depended more upon the conversion of local residents than move-ins from the West. Missionary efforts, begun in the 1860s, found few investigators. With time, prejudices diminished somewhat. During the early decades of the twentieth century, a scattering of members appeared. The first Latter-day Saint branch, created in 1956, served the members and the missionary guides called as temporary residents to serve visitors at restored historic sites. The first convert from among permanent Nauvoo residents was baptized in 1961. The branch moved from one existing building to another to serve a slowly growing congregation within a radius of twenty-five miles. The first meetinghouse built specifically for Latter-day Saint use, at the corner of Durphy and Hibbard Streets, was dedicated in 1969. A replica of the Nauvoo Temple bell was hung in its steeple. When a ward was organized a decade later to serve one hundred members, Walter H. Pierce, Nauvoo's first Latter-day Saint mayor since the 1840s, was called as bishop.[4]

That same year, the Nauvoo Ward and several branches in nearby communities qualified for organization as a stake. Creation of the Nauvoo stake attracted media attention because of its timing to reflect a landmark in church growth. On February 18, 1979, the one thousandth stake in the church was organized to serve the Nauvoo area. It included members affiliated with six wards and two branches in Canton, Galesburg, Kewanee, Macomb, Nauvoo, and Quincy, Illinois; Burlington, Iowa; and Hannibal, Missouri.[5]

Today's Latter-day Saints in Hancock County have much in common with the Saints who built Nauvoo in the 1840s. In other ways, they differ. Twenty-first century Mormons live and vote like their neighbors, privately and without ecclesiastical direction. No longer are local elections a contest between candidates virtually ensured of election by a Mormon majority and opponents standing on an Anti-Mormon Party platform. Still, in exercising their franchise, the Saints preserve the core principle of the political advice found in revelations given through Joseph Smith. That counsel applauded constitutional law and encouraged the election of individuals who would respect the property and religious rights of their constituents.[6]

The principles behind the law of consecration find place among today's Latter-day Saint congregations through applications that would seem familiar to Nauvoo's first Mormons. Now, as then, tithing supports overall church programs, including construction of meetinghouses and temples and administrative expenses. Local fast offerings by members and food and clothing from bishops' storehouses sustain the poor while they regain financial self-reliance. Educational opportunities, some of them sponsored by the church, have created a more prosperous people. Gone are the universal consecrations of property, cooperative enterprises, church-sponsored trades unions, and other economic programs that allowed Mormonism's first generation to curtail poverty. But though these specific applications no longer serve the needs of today's Latter-day Saints, the principle of consecrating one's means to further the Lord's work and assist the needy remains part of their religious life.[7]

Along with political and economic adjustments, the church also made social changes at the end of the nineteenth century while retaining the core doctrinal basis of earlier practices. Latter-day Saints in Nauvoo still answer questions about plural marriage, even though a revelation to President Wilford Woodruff ended its practice in 1890. His famous Manifesto, while preserving the central premise of the revelation on eternal marriage, halted the controversial aspects of that revelation, which Joseph Smith had committed to writing in Nauvoo. Today's Latter-day Saints place a significant focus on temple marriages and strive to establish eternal families.[8]

The expectation of many during the Nauvoo era that Christ's millennial rule was soon to begin softened with succeeding generations.[9] Church members now focus more on preparing their lives for the ultimate triumph of the King of Righteousness. They turn to the Savior as the center of their life, as their advocate before the Father. While continuing to build the church and kingdom of God through service to others, they seek guidance from scripture, living prophets, and personal revelation in their quest for eternal life. Placing Jesus Christ at the center of that quest, they strive to remember His ultimate sacrifice by keeping covenants made in His name and by serving others.[10]

For most of the twentieth century, temple ordinances were available to Latter-day Saints in Nauvoo only by traveling to the Intermountain West or, in the late 1970s, to Washington, D.C. An expansion of temple building in the 1990s brought that opportunity as close as Chicago and St. Louis. Nauvoo's historic temple site remained a grass-covered excavation, identified with memorial plaques and a model of the 1840s House of the Lord.[11] Demographics showed little prospect of justifying another temple in Nauvoo. Then President Gordon B. Hinckley surprised the church in April 1999 by announcing that the historic temple would be rebuilt. Church members in Nauvoo received the word in a live satellite broadcast of the general conference. Initial gasps of amazement quickly turned to hugs and tears.[12]

Constructed over the next three years of a limestone exterior on the original plot and patterned after the original design, the reconstructed Nauvoo Temple would look as it did when the Saints departed from the

The Nauvoo Temple dominated the landscape in this view from the river in 1846 and does so again, with the reconstructed spiritual center of Latter-day Saint life once again offering sacred ordinances to those who enter its doors.

City of Joseph. After a century and a half, it would once again become the physical and geographical focus of the community and a spiritual beacon for Latter-day Saints. An upright angel now stands atop the steeple, heralding as it had done in 1846 the restoration of the gospel of Jesus Christ. A bronze replica of the temple bell and four clocks are positioned on the tower beneath it. Inside, Latter-day Saints receive the sacred ordinances first introduced to the church in Nauvoo. These are administered in simply adorned rooms that reflect the fine craftsmanship of the past. As contractors and volunteers moved the House of the Lord toward completion, formal dedication was set for June 27, 2002, the anniversary of the deaths of Joseph and Hyrum Smith.[13]

In an international church, the Latter-day Saint congregation in Nauvoo differs little from thousands of others worldwide. Yet, despite Nauvoo's typicality in ecclesiastical terms, as a historic site, the area ranks high among the destinations of the modern Saint's vacation trip along the Mormon Trail from Vermont to Salt Lake City. The accomplishments of the first generation of Latter-day Saints, through their sacrifices during the Nauvoo years, became a monument to their faith, as the departing pioneers hoped it would.

Latter-day Saints are no longer enjoined to gather to any single geographical location. Stakes in numerous locations around the world provide a place for spiritual refuge from Babylon's evil. In December 1845, John S. Fullmer explained what would be needed to make that work. He told a relative who was resisting the call to gather in the Rocky Mountains:

> As to serving God as well in the South as here, [it] may become true some day, but is not true now, nor will it ever be unless some one will receive authority and power through the priesthood to organize a church there and rear a Temple, such as is done here, in which the ordinances pertaining to the order of salvation can be attended to as here.

The tithes of a twelve-million-member organization now fund temples in many regions. These same offerings provide for meetinghouses and other needs. As it was in the original Nauvoo, members are still reminded of the blessings to the church and to themselves that come through tithing their income. And they strive for unity within their wards and branches under a common set of beliefs.[14]

Nauvoo's restored historic buildings and the resurrected historic temple attract visitors to the city today. They make the trip to learn about the patterns of life for Nauvoo's first residents and the challenges endured by those early Saints. Old Nauvoo has become a popular vacation spot, especially for members of The Church of Jesus Christ of Latter-day Saints, whose current definition as a people depends so critically upon what happened in the city. For the people who look to Salt Lake City for prophetic direction, the Church of Jesus Christ is anchored not just in the doctrinal moorings of the past but in its past. As one historian so cogently put it, "Mormonism is history, not philosophy."[15]

An interest in honoring the early settlers and remembering Old Nauvoo grew steadily for Utah-based Latter-day Saints during the first half of the twentieth century. The first efforts, during the 1930s and 40s, involved the erection of a monument, the purchase of properties associated with the church or its people, and the celebration of centennials. The monument, commemorating the founding of the Relief Society, was installed at the suggestion of George Albert Smith, head of the Utah Pioneer Trails and Landmarks Association, in 1933. Wilford Wood, a Bountiful, Utah, furrier, who purchased a number of church historic sites,

Early visitors to Nauvoo often sought out the homes of Joseph and Emma Smith. Standing in front of the Mansion House in 1907 are Latter-day Saint missionaries and others gathered for a conference.

often with his own money, acquired the first parcel of the Nauvoo Temple Block in 1937 and later bought the James Ivins *Times and Seasons* complex. Wood urged the First Presidency to enlist volunteers to tell Nauvoo's story to visitors. Another advocate of Nauvoo as a tourist site was Lane K. Newberry, a Chicago artist with Mormon roots. For seven years during the 1930s Newberry visited Nauvoo and painted historic scenes. He lived in the area for a time and actively promoted the idea of a memorial on the Temple Block and restoration of surviving buildings on the bottomlands within the bounds of a state park. He won the support of Bryant S. Hinckley, president of the Northern States Mission, and of President Heber J. Grant. Together, they sponsored a celebration of Nauvoo's founding in 1939. A number of factors prevented development of the site at that time, including World War II. After the war ended, the Sons of the Utah Pioneers celebrated the centennial of Brigham Young's arrival in Utah by reenacting the exodus from Nauvoo to Salt Lake City with a caravan of automobiles decorated to look like covered wagons.[16]

It was J. LeRoy Kimball, a Salt Lake physician, whose interest in his own ancestral home ultimately secured a place on tourist maps for Nauvoo. His first step was the purchase in 1954 of the home of his great-grandfather, Heber C. Kimball. Interest by others in this family vacation home expanded into a dream of recreating a memorial to Old Nauvoo. In 1962, President David O. McKay organized Nauvoo Restoration Incorporated to buy and restore other buildings under the direction of the First Presidency. Dr. Kimball was named president. The National Park Service designated the city a Registered National Historic Landmark for its value in commemorating the nation's history. By the mid-1990s, the nonprofit corporation managed a thousand acres of the old city, and Latter-day Saint missionaries fostered understanding and appreciation of sixteen restored homes and shops by offering information about their histories. Among the sites opened to visitors were the houses of Brigham Young, John Taylor, and Wilford Woodruff, plus the shops of a gunsmith, baker, blacksmith, shoemaker, druggist, and tinsmith. Other restorations came later, and replica homes were built in 2001 as apartments for seasonal temple ordinance workers. At Carthage, the old county jail, purchased by Joseph F. Smith in 1903, became a memorial to Joseph and Hyrum Smith, with its own visitors' center.[17]

The holdings of Nauvoo Restoration Incorporated did not include the Smith family properties. The Reorganized church purchased the Mansion House in 1909. An offer to sell the building to the Utah church was rejected by President Joseph F. Smith. A caretaker-guide for the home was appointed in 1918. As negative attitudes towards Nauvoo and the "Brighamites" waned and as funding became available in the 1970s, the church now known as the Community of Christ launched its own professional preservation program on a forty-four-acre parcel at Nauvoo's southern border. By the late 1990s, trained guides were graciously hosting visitors at the rebuilt Red Brick Store and the restored Homestead and Mansion House of Joseph and Emma Smith. In addition, the Nauvoo House was furnished as a hostelry. Maintenance and operation of these sites fell to an adjunct entity known as the Restoration Trail Foundation. One project on their property involved a cooperative effort involving members of both churches. Descendants of the Joseph and Hyrum Smith families jointly raised funds to beautify the family burying ground behind the Homestead. In 1991, they erected new grave markers for Joseph, Emma, and Hyrum Smith.[18]

Today, the two churches welcome guests at separate visitors' centers. The Church of Jesus Christ of Latter-day Saints opened its Nauvoo Visitors' Center in 1971 toward the north end of the peninsula. In 1980, the Community of Christ completed the Joseph Smith Historic Center at Nauvoo's south extremity. A memorial garden established in 1978 at the Latter-day Saint Visitors' Center celebrates the organization of the Relief Society at Nauvoo and honors the role of women. The garden features thirteen life-size bronze statues by sculptors Florence P. Hansen and Dennis Smith. A musical pageant, *City of Joseph,* launched two years earlier, celebrates the triumphs of historic Nauvoo. Films and exhibits at the two centers provide consistent historical data, nuanced to fit the distinctive religious traditions and interpretive views of the host organizations. Even though the two groups see the Nauvoo years from different perspectives, they maintain a cordial relationship and have exchanged property and information about historic Nauvoo.[19]

In addition to the restored buildings at Nauvoo and Carthage, the Utah-based Latter-day Saints have actively celebrated their Nauvoo heritage through reminiscences, histories, and the arts. The effort began as the "Old Nauvooers"—those who had lived through the Nauvoo years—shared their vivid recollections in Sunday gatherings in the Salt Lake Valley. They spoke feelingly about their beloved Prophet and his death, and they relived the defense of the embattled Nauvoo. Others recorded these treasured memories of important events. Retrospective diaries, reminiscences, and verbal recountings of key events helped preserve the memory of Nauvoo. These efforts—together with visual, literary, and musical celebrations—helped descendants of the Nauvoo Saints to understand what happened during those critical years in the early 1840s and what the events mean today. These efforts have ensured that Nauvoo will be remembered.[20]

Descendants of the Old Nauvooers have not forgotten Nauvoo, but they have tried valiantly in recent years to reevaluate their feelings about the troubles of both Missouri and Illinois. In the spirit of the counsel given in Joseph Smith's letters from the jail at Liberty, Missouri, they have tried to forgive the people of that early time and leave ultimate judgment to God.[21] The phrase in Charles Penrose's hymn that enjoined early Latter-day Saints to remember the wrongs of those years has been altered. Since 1985, the Saints have sung, "Remember the *trials* of Missouri; / Forget not the *courage* of Nauvoo."[22] Through the efforts of church leaders in Salt Lake City and Independence, historic sites restorations and public relations efforts have emphasized the need for healing. As a symbol of this process, in June 1976 Missouri governor Christopher S. Bond rescinded the 1838 extermination order of Governor Lilburn W. Boggs. In 1989, officials of The Church of Jesus Christ of Latter-day Saints presented a plaque of friendship to the mayor of Quincy on the anniversary of the city's reception of the Mormon refugees from Missouri. In the same spirit, the Carthage Jail and an expanded visitors' center, refurbished in 1989, draw attention away from the injustices of the deaths of Joseph and Hyrum Smith. Instead, visitors are given a message of tolerance and reconciliation. Sesquicentennial monuments and statuary on a plaza outside the jail honor the role of the Prophet and his loyal brother in launching a new religion on the American frontier.[23]

As it once was for its original inhabitants, Nauvoo today has become again a place of inner peace and spiritual promise. Friendly interactions between the Community of Christ and The Church of Jesus Christ of Latter-day Saints and among Saints and local residents encourage congenial relationships. Tourism reinforces a sense of harmony, and visitors contribute to the local economy. In addition, the tradition of being a part of small-town America has continued from the days of the 1846 removal. The new citizens who arrived in Nauvoo immediately after the Latter-day Saint exodus easily made the town a place of peace because of its isolation from the turmoil of the larger world. Its small-town lifestyle has defined community relationships over the last century and a half.

One of those who found solace in Nauvoo was Ferdinand F. Bent. A resident of western Illinois during the Mormon period, Bent took advantage of the property bargains in the abandoned city. In late 1857, he informed Eastern relatives that he expected to spend the rest of his life in Nauvoo. "It is immaterial what part of the world we live or die in," he wrote. "If the Lord is with us we shall live and die happy." He explained further:

> I lived near Nauvoo before the Mormons came here. I was here frequently to market when the Mormons were at the height of their power and grandeur. I was acquainted with the celebrated Joe Smith. . . . He is now dead but alas the Mormons have been driven away . . . and Nauvoo is going to destruction rapidly.[24]

Despite Bent's negative assessment of the declining city, he wrote lyrically of the beauties of western Illinois. In four stanzas of verse, he celebrated the region as a land of beauty filled with green meadows, rich fields, wild animals, and sweet flowers. Bent's poem is reminiscent of the sentiments that Levi Hancock evoked in song on the rolling prairies of Missouri in 1838 to celebrate his search for peace and plenty among the Latter-day Saints.[25] Even with the people of promise gone from Nauvoo, the city retained for the new citizens a vestige of its role as a place of peace. Bent concluded his poem with that affirmation:

> *Here from the cares and the vexations of life—*
> *Riot, contention, bustle, and strife—*
> *Here the husbandman reaps almost without sowing,*
> *In this land of milk and honey flowing.*
> *Here is peace and plenty, gladness and joy,*
> *Pure earthly happiness without any alloy.*[26]

When Mary Fielding Smith left Missouri in 1839 in search of a new place of refuge, like Bent, she found peace by placing her relationship with God ahead of the many challenges that faced her people and her family. Her husband, Hyrum Smith, remained behind for several months in a cold jail in Liberty. Mary moved a few belongings and their infant son, Joseph F., to Illinois to await a reunion with her husband. Uprooted from her place of peace in upper Missouri, she was not weakened in her deep religious persuasions. Mary informed a missionary brother in their British homeland that no matter where she lived, she would find eternal rest in the kingdom of God through her faith in the restored gospel of the Lord Jesus Christ.[27]

In 1846, Mary Smith again left a Latter-day Saint gathering place with a displaced people—again without her husband—to seek a new place of refuge. Once more, her faith carried her forward with the Saints. This time the widowed mother of a future church president drove her own ox team to the new gathering place in the West, no doubt rejoicing in the goodness of God as she had in the 1840 letter to her brother Joseph:

> You will . . . have heard of our being driven, as a people, from the state [of Missouri], and from our homes. . . . I had to be removed more than 200 miles, chiefly on my bed. I suffered much on my journey; but . . . my health is now as good as ever it was. . . . We are

now living in Commerce, on the bank of the great Mississippi river. The situation is very pleasant; you would be much pleased to see it. How long we may be permitted to enjoy it I know not; but the Lord knows best what is best for us. I feel but little concerned about where I am, if I can but keep my mind staid upon God; for, you know in this there is perfect peace. . . . I have a hope that our brothers and sisters will also embrace the fulness of the Gospel, and come into the new and everlasting covenant. . . . I do not feel the least discouraged: no, though my sister [Mercy Fielding Thompson] and I are here together in a strange land, we have been enabled to rejoice, in the midst of our privations and persecutions, that we were counted worthy to suffer these things, so that we may, with the ancient saints who suffered in like manner inherit the same glorious reward. If it had not been for this hope, I should have sunk before this; but, blessed be the God and Rock of my salvation, here I am, and am perfectly satisfied and happy, having not the smallest desire to go one step backward.[28]

The Saints who followed the Twelve into the wilderness moved forward. They left behind their homes, farms, and businesses and the temple they had sacrificed to build. But they did not abandon their faith nor their sense of mission. Within days of his arrival, Brigham Young launched construction of a temple in Salt Lake City, the first of four he authorized during his thirty years as church president. These and later temples provided succeeding generations of Latter-day Saints with opportunities to receive exalting ordinances for themselves and for their deceased ancestors. Church leaders continued and expanded the divine mandate to carry the gospel to the people of all nations. They established a cornerstone stake in the Salt Lake Valley and other stakes in regional gathering places in the Rocky Mountain refuge and eventually in many other locations where the Saints could be nurtured in their faith.[29]

In its new place of refuge, the church that had been restored through the Prophet Joseph Smith endured new challenges and flourished. Under the guidance of men sustained as prophets, seers, and revelators, the Church of Jesus Christ continued its steady rise "out of obscurity." The objectives behind that expanding presence had been defined by the Lord in 1831: revelation would guide His latter-day work, the fulness of the gospel would be preached to all people, faith in His atoning sacrifice would increase, and His everlasting covenant would be established in preparation for His return to earth in glory. The inheritance received by Latter-day Saints from the Nauvoo period includes all that had been revealed and all that had been accomplished up to that time in the on-going process of establishing the Lord's church and kingdom on the earth for the last time "in these last days."[30]

Abbreviations

The following abbreviations for publications, repositories, and collections have been used throughout the Notes and the Sources.

PUBLICATIONS

BYU Studies	*Brigham Young University Studies.* Brigham Young University, Provo, Utah. Quarterly, 1959–.
CHC	B. H. Roberts, *A Comprehensive History of The Church of Jesus Christ of Latter-day Saints, Century One.* 6 vols. Salt Lake City: Deseret News Press, 1930.
Dialogue	*Dialogue: A Journal of Mormon Thought.* Dialogue Foundation. Quarterly, 1966–.
D&C	Doctrine and Covenants of The Church of Jesus Christ of Latter-day Saints. Salt Lake City: The Church of Jesus Christ of Latter-day Saints, 1981. First published in 1835.
Ensign	*The Ensign of The Church of Jesus Christ of Latter-day Saints.* Salt Lake City, 1971–.
HC	Joseph Smith, *History of The Church of Jesus Christ of Latter-day Saints.* 7 vols. Salt Lake City: Deseret News, 1902–12, 1932.
JD	*Journal of Discourses.* 26 vols. London: Latter-day Saints' Book Depot, 1855–86.
MS	*Latter-Day Saints' Millennial Star* (Manchester and Liverpool, 1841–46).
Neighbor	*Nauvoo Neighbor* (Nauvoo, Illinois, 1843–44), continues *The Wasp.*
Signal	*Warsaw Signal* (Warsaw, Illinois, 1840–53).
T&S	*Times and Seasons* (Commerce and Nauvoo, Illinois, 1839–46).
Wasp	*The Wasp* (Nauvoo, Illinois, 1842–43), renamed *Nauvoo Neighbor.*

REPOSITORIES AND COLLECTIONS

BYU Library	Mormon and Western Americana Collection, L. Tom Perry Special Collections of the Harold B. Lee Library, Brigham Young University, Provo, Utah.

Church Archives   Church Archives, The Church of Jesus Christ of Latter-day Saints, Salt Lake City, Utah.

Church History   Church History Library, The Church of Jesus Christ of Latter-day Saints, Library   Salt Lake City, Utah.

Coe Collection   The William Robertson Coe Collection of Western Americana, Beinecke Library, Yale University, New Haven, Connecticut, microfilm copy, Church Archives.

DUP Museum   International Society of the Daughters of Utah Pioneers, Pioneer Memorial Museum, Salt Lake City, Utah.

Lyon Collection   T. Edgar Lyon Collection, on loan to the author, for eventual deposit at the Church Archives. The collection includes articles, papers, and notes on people, places, and historical and restoration topics assembled while Lyon was historian for Nauvoo Restoration Incorporated. Much of the material is duplicated in the NRI Archives, because Lyon and Rowena Miller, NRI executive secretary, cross-filed their research material.

NRI Archives   Nauvoo Restoration Incorporated Collection, Land and Records Office, Nauvoo, Illinois.

Community of   Library and Archives, Community of Christ (formerly Reorganized Church Christ Archives   of Jesus Christ of Latter Day Saints), Independence, Missouri.

University of Utah   Special Collections, Marriott Library, University of Utah, Salt Lake City, Utah.

USHS Library   Utah History Information Center, Utah State Historical Society, Salt Lake City, Utah.

Notes

Abbreviated references to books, articles, theses, and other such sources have been used in Notes. Full citations can be found in Sources. Original manuscript sources and most articles in early Latter-day Saint periodicals with identified authors are cited in full in Notes and are therefore not included in Sources. Generally, we have used published versions of manuscript or early published sources from scholarly editions of letters, diaries, or documents. These works are cited by author rather than editor. When an original manuscript, early published source, or scholarly transcription that we consulted is also found in Joseph Smith's *History of the Church,* a parenthetical citation to this documentary collection immediately follows the citation to the original source, for example: Smith, *Words,* 11 (*HC* 3:390–91). As a convenience for readers interested in using more readily available published works, we have used this pattern of double citation for other published documentary sources when we consulted the original.

Frontispiece: Joseph Smith, June 24, 1844, as remembered by Dan Jones in a letter to Thomas Bullock, January 20, 1855, Church Archives (*HC* 5:554).

PREFACE

Epigraph: Bushman, "Historians and Mormon Nauvoo," 61.

1. Sidney Rigdon to William H. Paynes, July 9, 1858, Sidney Rigdon Collection, Church Archives.
2. The historical works consulted are credited in Notes and Sources. Spitz's presidential address to the American Society of Church History, "History: Sacred and Secular," has been especially helpful in clarifying interpretive options. Informative works on the writing of religious history include Gager, *Kingdom and Community,* and Eliade, *The Quest.* For a recent discussion on this topic, see Shipps, *Sojourner in the Promised Land,* 170–92. Useful essays about writing Mormon history are Bushman, "Historians and Mormon Nauvoo" and "Faithful History"; Flanders, "Some Reflections on the New Mormon History"; Godfrey, "The Nauvoo Neighborhood"; Gaustad, "Historical Theology and Theological History"; Arrington, "Clothe These Bones"; and Underwood, "Re-visioning Mormon History" and "Mormon History: A Dialogue." For bibliographies, prepared at approximately ten-year intervals, see Poll, "Nauvoo

and the New Mormon History" (1978); Leonard, "Recent Writing on Mormon Nauvoo" (1988); and Hallwas and Launius, *Kingdom on the Mississippi Revisited* (1996), 251–67.

3. Bushman, "Historians and Mormon Nauvoo," 60.

4. Bushman's excellent assessment of the historical literature of Nauvoo inspired this approach. His invitation to "recapture the life of the spirit" in histories of Nauvoo is found in "Historians and Mormon Nauvoo," 60–61.

5. For more on his life, see the biography written by his son T. Edgar (Ted) Lyon Jr., *T. Edgar Lyon: A Teacher in Zion* (Provo: BYU Studies, 2002).

6. We met twice in July and once early in August 1978; Ed died on September 20. Two weeks later, Hermana invited me to pick up the research materials from her husband's basement study. They will be deposited with other papers in the T. Edgar Lyon Collection at the Church Archives (notes on discussion with Ed Lyon, July 28, 31, August 7, 1978; memo on loan of Nauvoo research materials, October 3, 1978, both in author's files).

7. Sidney Rigdon to William H. Paynes, July 9, 1858, Rigdon Collection, Church Archives.

8. See Lyon, "Recollections of 'Old Nauvooers': Memories from Oral History," and Leonard, "Truman Leonard," 243–45.

9. Tuchman, "Telling All," 176.

10. Gaustad, "Historical Theology and Theological History," 107.

11. See Ellsworth, "Utah History," 367.

12. In a review of Miller and Miller, *Nauvoo,* Touchet agreed: "We do not yet have a study of Nauvoo which is complete—and we may never—but it should be attempted," 412).

13. Pliny, *Encyclopaedia of Natural and Artificial Rarities.*

PART I. ESTABLISHING NAUVOO: A PLACE OF PEACE

Epigraph: John S. Fullmer to John Price, February 15, 1841, John S. Fullmer Letterbook, Church Archives.

CHAPTER 1. JOSEPH SMITH'S PLAN FOR ZION

Epigraph: D&C 45:64–67.

1. Joseph Smith to the Elders of the Church of Latter-day Saints, September 1, 1835, *Messenger and Advocate* 1 (September 1835): 179–80 (*HC* 2:253–54); D&C 38:18–20, 24, 25, 41; 52:42; 53:7; 54:8; 57:1–2; 58:6.

2. Pratt, *Voice of Warning,* in *T&S* 1 (April 1840): 89–90; and see *T&S* (June 1840): 125; cf. Joseph Smith, editorial, *T&S* 3 (July 15, 1842): 856–57; Taylor, *Government of God,* 86–90, 101, 103–5.

3. For an overview and list of readings on persecution, see *Encyclopedia of Latter-day Saint History,* s.v. "Persecution," by Glen M. Leonard. For doctrinal insights, see D&C 109:67, 48; the Liberty Jail letters discussed below; and McConkie, *Mormon Doctrine,* 569–71.

4. John Gager's proposal that early Christianity can best be understood through the sacred world-view of its adherents and the people who created this perspective applies as well to the Restored Church (*Kingdom and Community,* 9–11). In 1922, Ephraim Ericksen expressed a similar view concerning the Latter-day Saints, with the additional insight that "it is the ideals and sentiments resulting from experiences themselves which reveal the true life of a people. . . . They develop out of the social intercourse which takes place in connection with the larger economic, social, and religious problems of the community" (*Mormon Group Life,* 8).

5. D&C 57:2–3; 82:13–14; see 96:1.
6. Dummelow, *Bible Commentary,* 24; Isaiah 1:26; Hebrews 7:2.
7. Matthew 13:43; Philippians 2:15.
8. Reps, *Making of Urban America,* 466–72.
9. For background on American local government, see Meinig, *Shaping of America,* 1:235–39. Discussions of Mormon city planning include the economic perspective in Arrington, Fox, and May, *Building the City of God,* 1–40, and a comparison with Puritan patterns in Cooper, *Promises Made to the Fathers,* 78–79. Bushman has addressed Mormon city planning in "New Jerusalem, U.S.A.," *Making Space for the Mormons,* and in unpublished lectures. Another look at the Mormon Zion as a New Jerusalem is Olsen, "The Mormon Ideology of Place" and "Joseph Smith's Concept of the City of Zion."
10. Backman, *Heavens Resound,* 1–19.
11. Marvin Hill demonstrates that the concept of a Zion society in all of its aspects was defined by Joseph Smith and his followers even before the Church of Christ was organized in 1830 (*Quest for Refuge,* 14, 30, 35–36).
12. Seven of the blocks contained sixteen acres each. Three of these were designated for public buildings; the other four were divided into thirty-two half-acre residential lots. The hand-drawn map is reproduced from the original in Church Archives in Brown, Cannon, and Jackson, *Historical Atlas of Mormonism,* s.v. "The City of Zion Plat," by Richard H. Jackson, 44–45.
13. There is no explanation why the instructions anticipated fifteen thousand to twenty thousand inhabitants (*HC* 1:358).
14. *HC* 1:357–59, with the temple for the First Presidency described on 359–62.
15. *HC* 1:358.
16. The prophecy was published as D&C 118.
17. Editorial, *T&S* 3 (May 2, 1842): 776.
18. "Proclamation," in *T&S* 2 (January 15, 1841): 274.
19. D&C 97:21; Moses 7:18.
20. *T&S* 2 (January 15, 1841): 273–74; D&C 134; Gager, *Kingdom and Community,* 11–12.
21. *T&S* 2 (January 15, 1841): 276.
22. The story of Zion's Camp is told in Backman, *Heavens Resound,* 175–200.
23. D&C 105:2–6.
24. *HC* 3:16–18.
25. This idea is explored at length in Winn, *Exiles in a Land of Liberty;* see, especially, 106–28.
26. Tithing appeared in Restoration scriptures as early as 1831 (D&C 64: 23–24). In 1832, the biblical injunction to tithe was met through the law of consecration (D&C 85:3). A revelation in 1833 mentions tithing as the prescribed way to build the temple in Jackson County (D&C 97:10–12); presumably this building was also to be accomplished through consecration and stewardship.
27. D&C 119:4; see also vv. 1–5.
28. D&C 42:70–73; 119:1–2.
29. For a more detailed history of the imprisonment, see Jessee, " 'Walls, Grates, and Screeking Iron Doors.' "
30. For financial problems in Kirtland, see Hill, Rooker, and Wimmer, "The Kirtland Economy Revisited," 391–472, or the summary in Allen and Leonard, *Story of the Latter-day Saints,* 117–25.
31. Johnson, *Mormon Redress Petitions,* xxxiv. The causes of Mormon-Gentile conflict have been

widely discussed and will be explored in later chapters in this volume. For helpful insights, see Ericksen, *Mormon Group Life*, 18–25, 30; Winn, *Exiles in a Land of Liberty*, 63–65, 85–88, 94–98, 103–4; Baugh, "Call to Arms"; and Allen and Leonard, *Story of the Latter-day Saints*, 710, 713–14.

32. Smith, *Personal Writings*, 416 (*HC* 3:226–27); see Acts 14:22; 2 Corinthians 4:17; 1 Peter 1:11; D&C 58:3; 63:66.

33. *HC* 3:188–89, 228; Smith, *Personal Writings*, 416–17.

34. Smith, *Personal Writings*, 422 (*HC* 3:232).

35. Smith, *Personal Writings*, 415–21 (*HC* 3:226–31).

36. Smith, *Personal Writings*, 420–21 (*HC* 3:178–81, 231–32).

37. Alma 34:40.

38. Smith, *Personal Writings*, 415–16 (*HC* 3:226–27).

39. Smith, *Personal Writings*, 422 (*HC* 3:233).

40. *CHC* 1:523, 526; cf. Arrington, "Church Leaders in Liberty Jail," 24.

41. The extracts have been part of the D&C (sections 121–23) since 1876. The complete epistle, dated March 20, 1830, was first published in *T&S* 1 (May and July 1840): 99–104, 131–34; later in *HC* 3:289–305 and in Smith, *Personal Writings*, 430–46; and most recently in *BYU Studies* 39, no. 3 (2000): 124–45. It was dictated by Joseph Smith in response to letters from his wife, Emma, his brothers Don Carlos and William, and Bishop Edward Partridge (see Smith, *Personal Writings*, 429–30, and *HC* 3:272–74). Joseph instructed Emma to share the letter with his parents, preserve it for his history, and forward a copy to Bishop Partridge for church members (Smith, *Personal Writings*, 448–49).

42. D&C 109:38–59 seeks to resolve the competing demands of righteous judgment on the wicked and the greater hope of saving their souls through repentance.

43. D&C 121:5, 7; cf. a similar promise in 2 Nephi 2:1–4.

44. D&C 122:7, 9; see also vv. 1–9.

45. D&C 123:1–3, 15; see also vv. 4–17.

46. D&C 121:11, 17–21.

47. D&C 121:36–37, 39–43, 45.

CHAPTER 2. FINDING A PLACE OF PEACE

Epigraph: T&S 1 (November 1839): 12. The epistle was written by the Twelve in July, just before they left for England.

1. Smith, *Personal Writings*, 428, 442; cf. *HC* 3:286, 301.

2. D&C 37:1–4; 38:17–33; 42:61–67.

3. D&C 97:10–21 (August 1833).

4. D&C 57:1–5.

5. D&C 45:66–67; see vv. 63–65, 68–71.

6. D&C 57:1–3; Moses 7:18–21.

7. D&C 59:23; see also entire section and headnote.

8. D&C 48.

9. D&C 51:16–17; Backman, *Heavens Resound*, chapters 6, 9.

10. D&C 64:21–22.

11. City of Zion Plat, Church Archives (*HC* 1:358); D&C 42:66–67; 68:26; 82:13–15.

12. D&C 58:44–48.

13. D&C 96, headnote. The term *Shinehah* appears in the headnote in editions of the D&C before 1981 (*HC* 1:352).

14. D&C 52:42.

15. Almira Mack Covey to Harriet Mack Hatch Whittemore, June 9, 1835, Church Archives.

16. Ibid.

17. *Messenger and Advocate* 2 (August 1836): 354, punctuation standardized (*HC* 2:450).

18. *Encyclopedia of Mormonism*, s.v. "Missouri," by Clark V. Johnson, and "Missouri Conflict," by Max H. Parkin; Allen and Leonard, *Story of the Latter-day Saints*, 61–67, 92–103, 113–14.

19. *CHC* 1:425; and note 32, below.

20. Levi Hancock, "Life of Levi W. Hancock," 1849, 150–52, Hancock Collection, Church Archives. A second, longer version of the song, titled "My Peaceful Home, 1837," appears in Hancock's "Book of Poems" in the same collection.

21. Averett, Autobiography, typescript, 4, BYU Library. For other letters promoting Missouri as a place of settlement, see Anderson, "Jackson County in Early Mormon Descriptions," 270–93.

22. *Encyclopedia of Mormonism*, s.v. "Far West, Missouri," by Larry C. Porter, and "Adam-ondi-Ahman," by Lamar C. Berrett; Smith, *Papers*, 2:243–48 (*HC* 3:34–38); 2:324 (*HC* 3:382); Smith, *Words*, 9 (*HC* 3:388); D&C 116.

23. Scriptory Book of Joseph Smith, July 27, 1838, Church Archives; Matthew 5:13; Baugh, "Call to Arms," 33–36; *CHC* 1:437–39.

24. *IIC* 3.9, 41–42; *CHC* 1:440–44; Baugh, "Call to Arms," 38–39, 172–73.

25. Sidney Rigdon, *Oration delivered . . . on the 4th of July, 1838; Elder's Journal* (Far West), August 1838, 54, spelling standardized.

26. Albert P. Rockwood to parent, October 29, 1838, Coe Collection. In this letter, Rockwood is quoting from his own diary (published in Jessee and Whittaker, eds., "Last Months of Mormonism in Missouri").

27. *HC* 3:182–87. Missouri governor Christopher S. Bond rescinded the extermination order on June 25, 1976, and issued a formal apology "for the undue suffering which was caused by this 1838 order" (*Deseret News*, June 25, 1976).

28. See Baugh, "Call to Arms," 149–50; *HC* 3:150, 188–95; Pratt, *Autobiography*, 186–87; and Knight to William Cooper, February 8, 1838 [1839], typescript, Church Archives (orig. at DUP Museum). For another contemporary description of the Far West confrontation, see Josiah Butterfield, Quincy, Illinois, to John Elden, Buxton, Maine, June 17, 1839, Church Archives.

29. *HC* 3:190–91; Emma Smith to Joseph Smith, November 4, 1838, in Smith, *Personal Writings*, 400–401, spelling and punctuation standardized.

30. *HC* 3:209, 212, 215, 245, 264.

31. Varying interpretations of Mormon Danite activities in Missouri can be found in Allen and Leonard, *Story of the Latter-day Saints*, 130–32; Gentry, "Danite Band of 1838," 421–50; Jessee and Whittaker, "Last Months of Mormonism in Missouri," 18–35. For an analysis of how historians have viewed Joseph Smith's role, see Baugh, "Call to Arms," 40–43.

32. David W. Rogers, Statement, February 1, 1839, Church Archives; Wandle Mace, Autobiography, 32–34, Church Archives; *HC* 3:265–66. About twenty-five participants in the Battle of Crooked River left Far West on November 1, as did another forty-five who were warned by Hyrum Smith to leave.

33. McCandless, *History of Missouri*, 2:108, suggested the Caldwell County figure. Early estimates of twelve thousand to fourteen thousand exiles noted in *T&S* 1 (November 1839): 2, and 5 (January 15, 1844): 404, seem too large given Nauvoo's subsequent development. Parkin

found fewer than a thousand Saints in Jackson County in 1833, half of them children ("History of the Latter-day Saints in Clay County," 29–33). LeSeuer's analysis of Missouri voting and census records led to his estimate of ten thousand Mormons before the exodus. We concluded that eight thousand is a more accurate total. LeSeuer reports between three thousand and four thousand Saints in Missouri when Joseph Smith arrived in Far West. During 1838, many but not all of the four thousand members in Ohio migrated west. LeSeuer estimates five thousand Ohio immigrants (*Mormon War,* 16, 26, 29, 35–36, 155). Latter-day Saints still in Far West in early 1839 estimated that ten thousand had been expelled from Missouri (Elias Smith to Ira Smith, March 11, 1839, Church Archives; Heber C. Kimball to Joseph Fielding, March 12, 1839, Church Archives, spelling standardized).

34. Albert P. Rockwood to family, January 1839, 38, Coe Collection.

35. Zodak Knapp Judd, Autobiography, 10, University of Utah.

36. Vinson Knight to William Cooper, February 8, 1838 [1839], typescript, Church Archives (orig. at DUP Museum); *T&S* 1 (September 1840): 165; *HC* 3:323; Wandle Mace, Autobiography, 30, Church Archives.

37. Sarah Pea Rich, Autobiography, 45–48, Church Archives; and Wandle Mace, Autobiography, 31–32, Church Archives.

38. George Washington Bean, Autobiography, 1897, 23–24, Church Archives, describes several family-owned houses and cabins near Mendon, Illinois, filled with "those homeless exiles."

39. Jesse W. Johnstun, Reminiscences, 15–18, Church Archives.

40. Rhoda Richards, Journal, June 21, 1839, Church Archives; Jenson, *LDS Biographical Encyclopedia,* 4:378.

41. Wandle Mace, Autobiography, 30, Church Archives.

42. Sarah Pea Rich, Autobiography, 49, Church Archives; Ira Ames, Journal, 13–14, NRI Collection; "Journal History," February 18, 1920; Jacob Gates, Journal, 1839, Church Archives.

43. Kimball, "Saints and St. Louis," 494; Zodak Knapp Judd, Autobiography, 10, University of Utah.

44. *HC* 3:209, 241, 260; "Journal History," June 13, 1839. Brigham Young may have felt that Partridge was neglecting his duty to the poor in Missouri (*HC* 3:247; Arrington, *Brigham Young,* 70; but compare Collette, "In Search of Zion," 122–24). Pressures from Missouri vigilantes forced Young to leave as well in mid-February (*HC* 3:261).

45. Far West Committee, Minutes, January 26, 29, February 1, 1839, Church Archives (*HC* 3:249–51, 254–55).

46. Far West Committee, Minutes, January 29, 1839, Church Archives (*HC* 3:250–54). The list of 218 signers in the "covenant to stand by and assist one another" is a partial roster. The reference to Brigham Young's securing of subscribers is found only in *HC* 3:254.

47. Far West Committee, Minutes, March 8, 1839, Church Archives (*HC* 3:274–75); Conference, Minutes, Quincy, Illinois, March 17, 1839, *T&S* 1 (November 1839): 15 (*HC* 3:283); John P. Greene's letter of appointment, May 6, 1839, Joseph Smith Letter Book 1838–43, 45, Church Archives (*HC* 3:347–48).

48. Far West Committee, Minutes, March 8, February 14, March 17, April 5, April 11, 1839, Church Archives (*HC* 3:274–75, 261–63, 284, 308, 315); meeting of church members at Quincy, Minutes, March 9, 1839, copy in Joseph Smith Letter Book, 1838–43, 48–49, Church Archives (*HC* 3:275–76, incorrectly titled "Minutes of the Adjourned Meeting of the Democratic Association of Quincy); Elias Smith to Ira Smith, March 11, 1839, Church Archives.

49. Far West Committee, Minutes, February 1, 1839 (*HC* 3:254–55); Missouri River route: Quincy Committee to Far West Committee, March 29, 1839, Church Archives; Theodore Turley, Memoranda (ca. 1845), Joseph Smith History documents, Church Archives (*HC* 3:323).

50. *HC* 3:256, 261–62 (entries for February 6, 7, 14, 15, 1839); Albert P. Rockwood to family, January 1839, 38, Coe Collection; Lucy Mack Smith, *History,* 293–97.

51. *HC* 3:322–23, 340 (April 18, 26, 1839).

52. Far West Committee, Minutes, April 6, 14, 1839, Church Archives (*HC* 3:308, 319); Turley Memoranda (*HC* 3:340).

53. Alexander McRae to *Deseret News,* November 2, 1854 (*HC* 3:257–58n); *HC* 3:264; Joseph Smith to the Church and Edward Partridge, March 20, 1839, in Smith, *Personal Writings,* 432–33; and Jessee, "'Walls, Grates, and Screeking Iron Doors,'" 29–31.

54. Joseph Smith, Missouri Journal, September 4, 1838, in Smith, *Papers,* 2:282–83 (*HC* 3:69); Joseph Smith to the Honorable Legislature of Missouri, January 24, 1839, copy in Joseph Smith Letter Book, 1838–43, 66–67, Church Archives (*HC* 3:248).

55. Turner Committee Report to the Missouri Legislature, December 18, 1838, *HC* 3:235–38, 246, 255–56 (from *Document Containing the Correspondence, Orders, &c., in Relation to the Disturbances with the Mormons, . . . begun November 12, 1838, . . .* [Fayette, Missouri, 1841]); David H. Redfield, Report, 1839, Church Archives (*HC* 3:238–40).

56. *HC* 3:256n; 4:299.

57. Joseph Smith to the Honorable Legislature of Missouri, January 24, 1839, *HC* 3:247–49.

58. Alanson Ripley, Statement (1845), Joseph Smith History documents, Church Archives (*HC* 3:264–65); Alanson Ripley, Joseph Smith, et al., to the Honorable Judge Tompkins, Joseph Smith Letter Book, 1838–43, 21–24, Church Archives (*HC* 3:277–82); Far West Committee, Minutes, January 18, 1839, Church Archives (*HC* 3:285); Theodore Turley, Memoranda (1845), Joseph Smith History documents, Church Archives (*HC* 3:288–89, 306).

59. For a sampling of that opinion, see Pratt, *Autobiography,* 281–85.

60. *HC* 3:289, 306–15.

61. *HC* 3:316, 317, 319–21; Affidavit of Hyrum Smith, July 1, 1843, *T&S* 4 (July 1, 1843): 255–56 (*HC* 3:421–22); David W. Rogers, Statement, February 1, 1839, Church Archives.

62. *HC* 3:334–35; Parley P. Pratt to Judge Austin A. King, May 13, 1839, in Pratt, *Autobiography,* 230–32; *HC* 3:360, 363–64, 368, 382, 399–402.

63. See Winn, *Exiles in a Land of Liberty,* 85–105, 129–51, for an expanded treatment of this idea.

64. For a sampling of discussions of this point, see Hallwas, "Mormon Nauvoo from a Non-Mormon Perspective"; Hallwas and Launius, *Cultures in Conflict,* especially 29–108; Shipps, *Sojourner in the Promised Land,* chapters 4, 15; and Daynes, "Mormons and Abortion Politics," 12–13.

65. *T&S* 1 (November 1839): 12. An extract from the epistle is quoted in the epigraph at the beginning of this chapter.

66. For expressions on Missouri persecutions, see Joseph Smith to the Church, March 21, 1839, in Smith, *Personal Writings,* 431; and an 1857 hymn text by Charles W. Penrose, "Up, Awake, Ye Defenders of Zion," *Hymns* (1948), no. 37.

CHAPTER 3. A BEAUTIFUL PLACE OF REST

Epigraph: Joseph Smith and others, Liberty Jail, Clay County, Missouri, March 20, 1839, to the

Church at Quincy and elsewhere, and to Bishop Partridge, in Smith, *Personal Writings,* 442, spelling and punctuation standardized.

1. Edward Partridge to Joseph Smith, March 5, 1839, copy in Joseph Smith Letter Book, 1838–43, 3–4, Church Archives (*HC* 3:272–73); Isaac Galland to David W. Rogers, February 26, 1839, copy in Joseph Smith Letter Book, 1838–43, 1–3 (*HC* 3:265–66). Galland's letter to Israel Barlow apparently has not survived.

2. D&C 101:22.

3. Joseph Smith to the Church, March 20–21, 1839, in Smith, *Personal Writings,* 435, 442.

4. Smith, *Personal Writings,* 439.

5. Smith, *Personal Writings,* 435, 440.

6. Joseph Smith to Isaac Galland, March 22, 1839, in Smith, *Personal Writings,* 462.

7. Zarahemla was a Book of Mormon city founded by the people of Mulek, the son of Zedekiah, the last king of Judah, after they were led by the Lord to the Americas around 587 B.C. to escape the Babylonian exile (Omni 1:14–19).

8. Quincy had grown rapidly since being incorporated in 1834 with six hundred residents (Carlson, *Illinois Military Tract,* 66).

9. Meetings of the Democratic Association, Quincy, February 25, 1839, in *HC* 3:263–64; February 27 and 28, 1839, in *HC* 3:267–71; and in *Quincy Whig,* March 2, 1839, as found in Pratt, *Autobiography,* 283–84. In a letter to the weekly *Quincy Argus,* John Taylor warned Quincy citizens against impostors pretending to be Latter-day Saints who were fraudulently accepting charitable help (Minutes of a council meeting, Quincy, Illinois, April 24, 1839, General Church Minutes Collection, Church Archives [*HC* 3:335]; John Taylor to the Editor of the *Argus,* May 1, 1839, copy in Joseph Smith Letter Book, 1838–43, 139–40, Church Archives [*HC* 3:341–42]).

10. Minutes of meetings of the Democratic Association, February 27, 28, 1839, in *HC* 3:267–71 and *Quincy Whig,* March 2, 1839, as found in Pratt, *Autobiography,* 283–84; Minutes of the Church Committee, Quincy, March 9, 1839, copy in Joseph Smith Letter Book, 1838–43, 48–49 (*HC* 3:275); letters of recommendation to John P. Greene and Sidney Rigdon from Quincy citizens, May 8, 1839, copies in Joseph Smith Letter Book, 41–42, 44 (*HC* 3:348–49). Greene raised $50 in a New York meeting when a mechanic gave $5 and challenged nine others to match his contribution (Pratt, *Autobiography,* 289–90, quoting "Meeting in Behalf of the Mormons," in New York *Commercial Advertiser*).

11. Hill, *Quest for Refuge,* 107.

12. Robert B. Thompson to First Presidency, May 13, 1839, copy in Joseph Smith Letter Book, 1838–43, 7–11, Church Archives (*HC* 3:351–52); First Presidency to *Quincy Whig,* May 17, 1839, copy in Joseph Smith Letter Book, 14–15 (*HC* 3:354–55); First Presidency to Robert B. Thompson, May 25, 1839, copy in Joseph Smith Letter Book, 11 (*HC* 3:363–64); Joseph Smith to Lyman Wight, May 27, 1839, copy in Joseph Smith Letter Book, 13–14 (*HC* 3:366–67).

13. Joseph Smith to Lyman Wight, May 27, 1839, in Joseph Smith Letter Book, 1838–43, 13–14, Church Archives (*HC* 3:367). Also see Smith's comments on tolerance and compassion in his letters to Emma Smith, April 4, 1839, and to W. W. Phelps, July 22, 1840, in Smith, *Personal Writings,* 465, 509–10.

14. Atwater, *Remarks Made on a Tour,* 60–61; Petersen, "Pike's Mississippi Expedition," 176–77.

15. Pike, *An Account of Expeditions,* 9; Kelly, "Mysterious D. Julien," 85–88.

16. Other forts were Fort Armstrong, 1816 (Rock Island, Illinois), and Fort Snelling, 1819, at St. Anthony Falls (now Minneapolis).

17. Carlson, *Illinois Military Tract*, 1–5, 49–57; Pooley, *Settlement of Illinois*, 397.

18. Pease, *Frontier State*, 2:154–56.

19. Keokuk remained in the area, received a copy of the Book of Mormon from Joseph Smith, and visited the Prophet in August 1841 with other Sauk and Fox Indians (*HC* 4:401–2, according to Christy Best, Church Archives, is possibly an elaboration by George A. Smith from memory, an expansion of his journal entry: "went over to Nauvoo and heard a conversation with the Sacks chiefs[.] a very interesting time").

20. Pease, *Frontier State*, 2:152–72; McKasick, "Fort Des Moines (1834–1837)."

21. T. Edgar Lyon traced the tradition that the transaction took place under an oak tree on present Parley Street to an 1890 written report publicized in the *Nauvoo Independent* as early as 1893. After lightning killed the tree about 1969, a count of annual rings dated the tree to about 1860, long after the captain's death. The Sauk and Fox had relinquished title in earlier treaties, but White may have wanted to formalize his purchase and discourage Indian visits to the farm and village.

22. Miller and Miller, *Nauvoo*, 235–36; Gregg, *Hancock County*, 217. When water backed up by the 1913 Keokuk Dam threatened the house, Elmer Buckert, a Nauvoo carpenter and cabinetmaker, purchased it for its salvage value (notes, Lyon draft, Lyon Collection).

23. Gregg, *Hancock County*, 214, 229.

24. Lyon, "Account Books of the Amos Davis Store," 242–43; no records survive in the post office department to explain the name's origin.

25. Adams, *Illinois Place Names*, s.v. "Carthage"; *Illinois: Guide and Gazetteer*, 108; Gregg, *Hancock County*, 687, 238–39.

26. Pooley, *Settlement of Illinois*, 400.

27. Hancock County Deed Records, "Index to Town Lots [Venus]," 403, Hancock County Court House, Carthage. Current county records contain no plat for Venus. In 1966, T. Edgar Lyon found this index in the basement of the courthouse and identified it as the forerunner of the present "Index to Town Lots" in the county clerk's office. Several of the thirteen lots listed on page 403 designate the property as being in Venus. The word *VACATED* had been written across the page and all thirteen lots transferred with identical block and lot numbers to the new "Index" for Commerce. This suggests that Commerce was platted over Venus on the same grid. These same property owners appear in Commerce when it was recorded in 1834.

28. Hancock County Records, Plat Book I, 10, Hancock County Court House, Carthage. The United States Postmaster General's office has no record of an application for the name change. Mary Ann Cutler was appointed October 11, 1834 (letter from General Service Administration, National Archives and Records Service, May 1964, NRI Archives).

29. Jenson, *LDS Biographical Encyclopedia*, 2:372–73; Gregg, *Portrait and Biographical Record*, 353; and Hiram Kimball files, NRI Archives.

30. Jenson, *LDS Biographical Encyclopedia*, 1:62–66; family group sheet for Charles and Jerusha Robison, Family History Library.

31. Gregg, *Hancock County*, 950; notes on various interviews with descendants, deed records, and newspaper accounts, in Lyon Collection; and Lyon, "Account Books of the Amos Davis Store at Commerce, Illinois," 241–43.

32. Cook, "Isaac Galland, Mormon Benefactor," 261–65; David Martin, Galland portrait noted in *Ft. Madison Democrat*, August 13, 1976, as cited in *Martin Mormon Miscellaneous* 2 (March 1977): 4; Miller and Miller, *Nauvoo*, 239–41; letter from General Services Administration, National Archives and Records Service, May 1964.

33. Hancock County Records, Plat Book I, 26–27, Hancock County Courthouse, Carthage, Illinois.

34. The most exhaustive study of the Commerce City-Hotchkiss syndicate land deals, from 1836 through the 1850s, was made by the late Rowena J. Miller, for many years executive secretary of Nauvoo Restoration Inc. Her private papers containing this study are not presently available.

35. Wandle Mace, Autobiography, 33, Church Archives; *HC* 3:265.

36. David W. Rogers, Statement, February 1, 1839, Church Archives; Wandle Mace, Autobiography, 33, Church Archives. Barlow and Rogers may have included a broader area than do the sources noting ten available dwellings in the Commerce area (Miller and Miller, *Nauvoo,* 21; *HC* 3:375).

37. Conference of the Church, Quincy, Illinois, Minutes, February 1839, in Far West Committee Minutes, Church Archives (*HC* 3:260).

38. Albert P. Rockwood to Family, containing diary entries for January 10–30, 1839, Rockwood Letterbook, 38, Coe Collection.

39. Conference at Quincy, February 1839, in Far West Committee, Minutes, Church Archives (*HC* 3:260); D&C 105:1–10.

40. Conference at Quincy, February 1839, in Far West Committee, Minutes, Church Archives (*HC* 3:260–61).

41. Smith, *Personal Writings,* 439.

42. Isaac Galland to D. W. Rogers, February 26, 1839, copy in Joseph Smith Letter Book, 1838–43, 1–3, Church Archives (*HC* 3:266–267); Joseph Smith to Isaac Galland, March 22, 1839, in Smith, *Personal Writings,* 454–62.

43. Flanders, *Nauvoo,* 35–36; Miller and Miller, *Nauvoo,* 27, says Smith pledged $18,000 for the Galland parcel.

44. *HC* 3:349; Smith, "Missouri Journal, 1838," April 27, 1838, and "Illinois Journal, 1839," June 10–14, 1839, in Smith, *Papers,* 2:233, 321; "History (1839 Draft)" and "History, 1839," Smith, *Papers,* 1:230–31, 265, 267.

45. Alanson Ripley, Statement [1845], in Joseph Smith History documents, Church Archives (*T&S* 1 [December 1839]: 24; *HC* 3:342, 378); *T&S* 2 (October 15, 1841): 568; Miller and Miller, *Nauvoo,* 20, 51; Flanders, *Nauvoo,* 41–42.

46. Miller and Miller, *Nauvoo,* 29; Flanders, *Nauvoo,* 42; Manuscript History, vol. C-1, August 18, 1839, Church Archives, an elaboration from Smith, "Illinois Journal, 1839," August 18, 1839, in Smith, *Papers,* 2:330 (*HC* 4:7).

47. Zucker, "Joseph Smith as a Student of Hebrew," 48, located the verb *nauvoo* in Seixas, *Manual Hebrew Grammar for the Use of Beginners* (1834 edition), 111.

48. *T&S* 2 (January 15, 1841): 273–74. One resident found an application for Nauvoo in the words of the Psalmist, "Beautiful for situation, the joy of the whole earth, is mount Zion" (Psalm 48:2). See Edson Whipple to Brethren and Friends in Philadelphia, December 17, 1842, Edson Whipple Record Books, Church Archives.

49. From a commentary by David H. Garner, January 18, 1979, copy in Lyon Collection. Consider also the messianic reference in Isaiah 52:7.

50. John C. Bennett to friends, August 15, 1840, copy in Joseph Smith Letter Book, 1838–43, 171–72, Church Archives (*HC* 4:179); letter from General Services Administration, National Archives and Records Service, May 1964, NRI Archives; *Western World,* May 27, 1840. The *Times and Seasons* changed its masthead in the May 1840 issue, when it reported the change in

the name of the post office (*T&S* 1: 106). Both names were in parallel use before that time (see, for example, *T&S* 1: 48, 77, and 91).

51. Statement concerning the survey marker by James W. Brattle, Hancock County Surveyor, August 30, 1830, Hancock County Recorders Office; Enders, *Platting the City Beautiful,* 409–10.

52. First Presidency (Joseph Smith, Sidney Rigdon, and Hyrum Smith), "Proclamation," *T&S* 2 (January 15, 1841): 276.

CHAPTER 4. GATHERING THE SAINTS

Epigraph: Revelation to Joseph Smith, November 3, 1831, in D&C 133: 9, 14, 17; Newel K. Whitney to George Miller, February 15, 1845, Whitney Collection, BYU Library.

1. The doctrinal groundwork was introduced in D&C 10 (summer 1828); unfolded in D&C 29; 33–35; 37–39; 42–43; 45; 49; and capped with the preface and appendix to the D&C, sections 1 and 133.

2. One of the most reasoned discourses on the gathering appeared over four issues of the *Times and Seasons,* probably written by its editor, John Taylor. See *T&S* 5 (January 15, February 1, February 15, March 1, 1844): 407–10, 423–27, 441–42, 456–57.

3. D&C 63:37. For examples of Joseph Smith's views on the gathering, see *HC* 1:313, 315; 2:357–58; 4:610; 5:423–27.

4. Smith, *Words,* 25 n. 9, 60.

5. The classification of Christian congregations as other-worldly (establishing a sanctuary and engaging in evangelistic labors) as opposed to helping people live in this world (through social activist and civic engagement) is found in Roozen, McKinnery, and Carroll, *Varieties of Religious Presence,* 32–36, 160–75, and is applied by Wind, *Places of Worship,* 34–35.

6. Smith, *Words,* 11 (*HC* 3:390–91). This instruction echoes an 1831 revelation (D&C 45:63–71).

7. "Epistle of the Twelve," *MS* 1 (April 1841): 310; reprinted in *T&S* 3 (September 1, 1842): 895.

8. Along with other parts of scripture, Moroni quoted Isaiah 11 verbatim (Joseph Smith–History 1:36–41). The "remnant" is mentioned in 1 Nephi 10:14; 2 Nephi 25:17; 29:14; 30:3; 3 Nephi 5:23; and Ether 13:7. Enoch's Zion is spoken of in Moses 7:62.

9. References to a chosen people include Exodus 6:7; Deuteronomy 4:20; 7:6; Isaiah 51:7; Ezekiel 34:30; Daniel 7:14; Matthew 1:21; Luke 1:17; Acts 15:14; 2 Corinthians 6:16; 1 Peter 2:10; 1 Nephi 21:22; Alma 31:18; D&C 42:9; 109:59.

10. Remnant peoples are identified in D&C 19:27; 45:24, 43; 52:2; and in D&C 109:65; 113:10, they are invited to return. For Joseph Smith's uses of scriptural references, see the subject index to Smith, *Scriptural Teachings,* s.v. "Enoch," "Gathering of Israel," "Gentiles," "Israel," "Jews," and "Saints." For biblical classifications, see Shipps, *Mormonism,* 37–39, 81–85.

11. Examples abound in the autobiographies and diaries in the Church Archives, BYU Library, and Daughters of Utah Pioneers collections and publications. The content summaries in Bitton, *Guide to Mormon Diaries,* easily illustrate the point. Only missionary accounts occupy more space in typical records of the Nauvoo years.

12. D&C 59:23.

13. D&C 37:3; 38:32; *CHC* 1:312. The Plat of the City of Zion is reproduced in Brown, Cannon,

and Jackson, *Historical Atlas of Mormonism*, s.v. "The City of Zion Plat," by Richard H. Jackson, 45, from the original in the Church Archives.

14. D&C 58:7; 101:20–21.

15. D&C 105:34.

16. Joseph Smith et al., To the Church of Latterday Saints at Quincy, March 20, 1839, in Smith, *Personal Writings*, 442; and see Conference at Quincy, Illinois, March 17, 1839, in *T&S* 1 (November 1839): 15 (*HC* 3:283).

17. Smith, *Words*, 11 (*HC* 3:390).

18. *T&S* 2 (April 15, 1841): 385–87 (*HC* 4:337–40).

19. General Conference, Minutes, April 8, 1844, in *HC* 6:318–19, an amalgamation of four reports (see Smith, *Words*, 362–64).

20. Parley P. Pratt, "Present Condition and Prospects of the American Indians, or Lamanites," *MS* 2 (July 1841): 41–42; William Smith, "Evidences of the Book of Mormon," *Messenger and Advocate* 3 (January 1837): 434; Articles of Faith 10.

21. William W. Phelps, "The Far West," *Evening and Morning Star* 1 (October 1832); Parley P. Pratt, "Present Condition and Prospects of the American Indians, or Lamanites," *MS* 2 (July 1841): 41–42.

22. *T&S* 1 (April 1840): 94.

23. Flanders, "Dream and Nightmare," 144–45.

24. Kimball, "Nauvoo West," 132–38; Elias Smith to Jesse Smith, August 31, 1841, NRI Archives.

25. Whitney, "Aaronic Priesthood," 604–5; Kimball, "Nauvoo West," 132. The Adams County, Illinois, stakes were headquartered in Lima, Quincy, Mt. Hope, and Freedom. Other Illinois stakes were headquartered in Geneva, Morgan County; Springfield, Sangamon County; and Pleasant Vale (now New Canton), Pike County, Illinois. The congregations in Philadelphia and New York City each became "more perfectly organized as a branch" under Hyrum Smith's supervision in mid-April. The presiding elders (an administrative title) in these branches were ordained to the office of high priest, an office in the Melchizedek Priesthood reserved for those who preside over larger congregations (*T&S* 2 [May 15, 1841]: 412–13, and [August 2, 1841]: 499).

26. Gregg, *Hancock County*, 819–20; *Warsaw Western World*, April 1, 1841.

27. *T&S* 2 (November 15, 1840): 222–23.

28. Johnson, *Mormon Redress Petitions*, xviii; *T&S* 1 (February 1840): 64.

29. Kimball, "The Saints and St. Louis," 493–503; Lyman Wight and Heber C. Kimball to Joseph Smith, June 19, 1844, Joseph Smith Papers, Church Archives (*HC* 7: 136); Fielding, "Nauvoo Journal," ed. Ehat, 140.

30. The missionary story is told in Arrington, *Brigham Young*, chapter 6; Kimball, *Heber C. Kimball*, chapters 4 and 7; and in Allen, Esplin, and Whittaker, *Men with a Mission*.

31. Joseph Smith to the Twelve, December 15, 1840, in Smith, *Personal Writings*, 517.

32. *HC* 2:492.

33. For example, see Heber C. Kimball, letter, August 5, 1841, in *T&S* 2 (October 1, 1841): 557–58; and Wilford Woodruff to Heber C. Kimball and George A. Smith, September 12, 1840, in Emily Smith Stewart Collection, fd. 3, NRI Archives.

34. Brigham Young to Joseph Young, October 16, 1840, spelling standardized, quoted in Allen, Esplin, and Whittaker, *Men with a Mission*, 232, 403.

35. William Clayton to Edward Martin, November 29, 1840, in Carter, *Heart Throbs of the West*, 5:374.

36. *MS* 2 (February 1842): 154–55.

37. In his study of the motivations for the British gathering through 1870, Taylor found the evidence inconclusive on this point; he looked at religious and economic factors as well as the influence of church assistance and interpersonal contagion ("Why Did British Mormons Emigrate?" 251–52, 269).

38. *MS* 3 (April 1843): 195; reprinted in *T&S* 4 (October 1, 1843): 350–51.

39. Millen Attwood, Reminiscences and Diary, May 21 and 23, 1841, Church Archives; Alfred Cordon, Reminiscences, 3:174–75, Church Archives.

40. Quoted in *T&S* 4 (October 1, 1843): 350–51.

41. Allen, Esplin, and Whittaker, *Men with a Mission,* 134–37.

42. Allen, "'We Had a Very Hard Voyage,'" 339, 341.

43. *T&S* 4 (February 15, 1843): 98–99.

44. *MS* 2 (October 1841): 88–89.

45. Criticism and responses in *T&S* 5 (February 1, 1844): 429; *Signal,* May 19, 1841; and *T&S* 2 (June 1, 1841): 431–33; Rowley in *T&S* 5 (February 1, 1844): 429.

46. Minutes of their April meetings sent to Nauvoo brought enthusiastic support from Joseph Smith (Allen, Esplin, and Whittaker, *Men with a Mission,* 134–35).

47. Allen, Esplin, and Whittaker, *Men with a Mission,* 181; Cannon, "'Gathering' of the British Mormons to Western America," 56–59; Sonne, *Saints on the Seas,* 91.

48. *T&S* 3 (September 1, 1842): 896.

49. *T&S* 4 (April 15, 1843): 163, punctuation standardized.

50. Sonne, *Saints on the Seas,* 148–49. Taylor, in *Expectations Westward,* 144, placed the total British migration at fifty-five thousand through 1890, and the total European migration at more than eighty-eight thousand. Pratt to Editor, April 1, 1843, *T&S* 4 (April 1, 1843): 149.

51. Sonne, *Saints on the Seas,* 92–93, 148–49, 169; *T&S* 5 (February 1, 1844): 430.

52. "Autobiography of Robert Crookston, Sr.," 4; copy in NRI Archives.

53. *MS* 2 (October 1841): 94; *Hymns* (1985), no. 85.

54. *T&S* 1 (October 1840): 178–79 (*HC* 4:185–86).

55. D&C 124:2, 25–27.

56. *T&S* 3 (October 1, 1842): 936–37. As editor at this time, Joseph Smith was possibly the author of the article.

57. *T&S* 2 (January 15, 1841): 276.

58. *T&S* 2 (June 1, 1841): 434.

59. "Epistle of the Twelve," August 26, 1841, in *T&S* 2 (September 1, 1841): 520–21. An incomplete manuscript draft in the handwriting of Willard Richards is in Brigham Young Papers, Church Archives.

60. *HC* 4:467, 477, 491.

61. *Signal,* May 19, 1841. This first volley in a rapidly increasing war of words in Hancock County brought an immediate response from Nauvoo (see *T&S* 2 [June 1, 1841]: 431–32). The exchange centered on the candidacy of George Coulson of La Harpe, a former county commissioner who had joined the Latter-day Saints and was seeking election as a county school commissioner.

62. By the end of June, anti-Mormons had organized their own political faction at Warsaw to counter what they saw as a Mormon-dominated convention at Carthage (*Signal,* June 9, 23, 1841).

63. *MS* 1 (November 1840): 191; Journal History, July 5 and 24, 1842; Jenson, "New York," Manuscript History, July 29, 1840, and May 9, 1843, Church Archives; *T&S* 1 (October 1840): 179.

64. Charles Dickens called the Ohio River the "canal" in his *American Notes* (1842), a report on a trip through America. D&C 61:23–24, which prohibited travel on the Missouri and Mississippi rivers, allowed travel on the "canal" between Jackson County, Missouri, and Kirtland, Ohio, in August 1831 (see *HC* 1:206).

65. For excellent maps of these and other migration routes, see Buisseret, *Historic Illinois from the Air,* 51, 57–59, 72, and 85.

66. Examples of such reports will be found in a forthcoming collection of letters from the Nauvoo period edited by Glen M. Leonard.

67. That standard was established in D&C 64:33–35; 68:25–35; 105:5.

68. *T&S* 3 (October 1, 1842): 937.

69. *T&S* 2 (January 15, 1841): 276–77 and (June 15, 1841): 440.

70. See Dwight Webster and Eunice W. Webster to Wilford Woodruff, May 4, 1845, Church Archives; remarks of Amasa Lyman in Seventies, Records, Fourth Quorum, Minutes, August 23, 1845, Church Archives.

71. D&C 64:21–22.

72. The story of the principal exodus from Kirtland is told in Backman, *Heavens Resound,* 342–67, and is outlined in *Kirtland Elders' Quorum Record,* 62 n. 1. Population figures are from Backman, "Warning from Kirtland," 26, 29–30; see Backman, *Heavens Resound,* 361.

73. D&C 117; see Joseph Smith to Kirtland Presidency, March 29, 1838, in Smith, *Personal Writings,* 396–97 (*HC* 3:12).

74. Backman, "Warning from Kirtland," 26–30.

75. *T&S* 1 (December 1839): 29.

76. *T&S* 1 (October 1840): 185–86; 2 (June 1, 1841): 434.

77. D&C 124:82–85; *T&S* 3 (November 1, 1841): 588. The proposed title of the periodical referred to a major Kirtland revelation of that name dealing with the search for truth, temple procedures, and the Second Coming (D&C 88). Austin Cowles used a similar title, *The Olive Branch; or, Herald of Peace and Truth to All Saints,* for his schismatic newspaper launched in August 1848.

78. *T&S* 2 (October 15, 1841): 577; 3 (November 1, 1841): 589. The reprimand appeared in the newspaper along with a full report of the conference held at Kirtland.

79. Joseph Smith, Illinois Journal, 1841–1842, December 15, 1841, in Smith, *Papers,* 2:339–40 (*HC* 4:476).

80. *T&S* 4 (December 15, 1842): 37–38.

81. See Jenson, "New York," Manuscript History, entries for 1839–46, Church Archives.

82. Based on listings compiled in *Nauvoo Journal* 2 (October 1990): 115–37; 3 (January, April, July 1991): 5–21, 40–52, 71–88.

83. Bennett, "'Plucking Not Planting,'" 22–30.

CHAPTER 5. NAUVOO'S MAGNA CHARTA

Epigraph: First Presidency (Joseph Smith, Sidney Rigdon, and Hyrum Smith), "Proclamation," *T&S* 2 (January 15, 1841): 273 (*HC* 4:267–68).

1. Thomas Ford to Brigham Young, April 8, 1845, in *HC* 7:396–97.

2. See Joseph Smith, "The Government of God," *T&S* 3 (July 15, 1842): 857, col. 2. For more on this religious worldview, see Esplin, "The Emergence of Brigham Young," chapter 1.

3. D&C 102.

4. The business of the Far West high council and its predecessor in Clay County can be followed in Cannon and Cook, *Far West Record*.

5. Minutes of conference at Commerce, Illinois, October 5–7, 1839, copy in Joseph Smith Letter Book, 1838–43, 164–67, Church Archives (*HC* 4:12); Marks's appointment, general conference, Quincy, Illinois, May 6, 1839, in General Church Minutes Collection, Church Archives (*HC* 3: 347); prior service: *HC* 2:124, 366, 511, 523; 3:14, 155, 225; and Cannon and Cook, *Far West Record*, biographical appendix, s.v. William Marks.

6. For examples of council regulations, see Nauvoo High Council, Minutes, October 20, 1839, in *HC* 4:16–17; *T&S* 1 (June 1840): 127.

7. Churchwide actions can be noted in Nauvoo High Council, Minutes, April 12, 19, July 17, 1840, in *HC* 4:114, 120, 161; credentials, July 22, 1840, in *HC* 4:164.

8. For the doctrinal basis of councils, see D&C 96:2–3; 102:1–2, 8–9; 107:27–32, 36–37, 78–81; 120:1; for examples of application, *MS* 1 (February 1841): 264; 3 (April 1843): 198; 4 (December 1843): 131; *T&S* 2 (February 15, 1842): 697; 4 (September 15, 1843): 334.

9. Powell, *Puritan Village*, 5; and see Gross, *The Minutemen and Their World*, 1–12.

10. D&C 102; 107:36–37; Nauvoo High Council, Minutes, July 11, 1840, in *HC* 4:154.

11. Nauvoo High Council, Minutes, October 20, 1839; March 15, 1840, in *HC* 4:16–17, 95.

12. Nauvoo High Council, Minutes, October 20, 1839; July 3, 1840, in *HC* 4:16–17, 144–45; General Conference, Minutes, April 7, 1840, *HC* 4:106; Memorial of Joseph Smith Jun. to the High Council, June 18, 1840, in *HC* 4:136–37; Proceedings of the High Council on the Foregoing Memorial, June 20, 1840, in *HC* 4:138.

13. Nauvoo High Council, Minutes, October 20, December 1, 30, 1839; March 16, 1840, in *HC* 4:16–18, 39, 49, 96; Kimball, "Wall to Defend Zion," 491–92.

14. Nauvoo High Council, Minutes, October 20, December 29, 1839, in *HC* 4:16–17, 49.

15. Nauvoo High Council, Minutes, October 20, December 15, 1839; January 8, 19, June 20, July 3, 1840, in *HC* 4:18, 46, 75, 76, 144.

16. Nauvoo, High Council, Minutes, April 12, 1840 (agents), December 1, 7, 1839 (Kirtland), in *HC* 4:114, 39, 44–45; First Presidency and Nauvoo High Council, "To the Saints scattered abroad, in the region westward from Kirtland, Ohio," *T&S* 1 (December 1839): 29.

17. Nauvoo High Council, Minutes, February 23, 1840, in *HC* 4:88.

18. Nauvoo High Council, Minutes, September 5, December 13, 20, 1840, in *HC* 4:187–88, 239, 250; General Conference, Minutes, April 6, 1840, *T&S* 1 (April 1840): 92.

19. Nauvoo, High Council, Minutes, October 20, December 1, 1839, in *HC* 4:16, 39.

20. Election results, council organized, *T&S* 2 (February 1, 1841): 309 and (February 15, 1841): 319; trustee authorized and registered, Minutes of a Special Conference, January 30, 1841, in *HC* 4:286–88.

21. Transfer of duties approved, Special Conference, Minutes, August 16, 1841, General Church Minutes Collection, Church Archives; also in *T&S* 2 (September 1, 1841): 521–22 (*HC* 4:402–3); duties relinquished, High Council Resolution, September 22, 1841, in *HC* 4:417.

22. "The High Council of the Church of Jesus Christ, to the Saints of Nauvoo," *T&S* 3 (February 15, 1842): 699–700.

23. Iowa High Council, Minutes, March 6, 1840, in *HC* 4:93; joint meeting of the Nauvoo and Iowa high councils, held in Nauvoo, August 17, 1840, in *HC* 4:180.

24. General Conference, October 5, 1839, *HC* 4:12; Iowa High Council, in *HC* 4:16; "Journal History," August 9, 1841.

25. Kimball, "Nauvoo West," 137–41; Olsen, "Cosmic Urban Symbolism," 82–83; Mosiah 1:18; Alma 5:2; 3 Nephi 3:22–23.

26. "Manuscript History of the Church in Iowa," December 6–7, 1839; January 4, February 7, 1840; Church Archives (*HC* 4:42, 54, 80).

27. "Manuscript History of the Church in Iowa," December 6, 1839; March 6, 1840 (*HC* 4:42, 93–94); Bates, "Uncle John Smith," 83.

28. D&C 63:26. For revelations supporting constitutional government, see D&C 98:5–6; 101:77, 80; 109:54. Subjection to civil law is defined in D&C 42:79, 84–86; 58:21–22; 98:4–7. In Articles of Faith 11 and 12, Joseph Smith summarized Latter-day Saint views on religious freedom and civic duty.

29. D&C 134:4–5; Perry, *Puritanism and Democracy,* 356–57. Also see Perry's discussion of the separation of church and state in Puritan belief (321–62).

30. General Conference, Minutes, October 3–5, 1840, in General Church Minutes Collection, Church Archives (also in *T&S* 1 [October 1840]: 185–87 and *HC* 4:204–5).

31. John C. Bennett to Joseph Smith and Sidney Rigdon, July 25, 27, 30, and August 15, 1840; and Joseph Smith to Bennett, August 8, 1840, in *HC* 4:168–70, 172, 177–79.

32. Smith, *Saintly Scoundrel,* 54–57; Bennett to Smith and Rigdon, July 25, 27, 1840, in *HC* 4:168–70.

33. Bennett to Smith and Rigdon, July 27, 1840; Smith to Bennett, August 8, 1840, in *HC* 4:169–70, 177–78.

34. General Conference, Minutes, October 4, 1840, *T&S* 1 (October 1840): 186–87 *(HC* 4:205–6); Smith, *Saintly Scoundrel,* 58; Flanders, *Nauvoo,* 96.

35. Currey, *Chicago,* 1:221–23; Kimball, "Study of the Nauvoo Charter," 33.

36. Kimball, "Wall to Defend Zion," 491–97; Tillson, *History of the City of Quincy,* 67–68; Kimball, "Study of the Nauvoo Charter," 34.

37. Charter, secs. 4–11, in *HC* 4:240–42; "Officers of the City of Nauvoo," *T&S* 3 (December 15, 1841): 638; Kimball, "Nauvoo Charter," 71–73.

38. Charter, sec. 2, in *HC* 4:240; Kimball, "Study of the Nauvoo Charter," 44. See chapter 6 of this volume for a discussion of the development and extension of the plat.

39. Charter, sec. 13, in *HC* 4:242; Kimball, "Nauvoo Charter," 73.

40. Charter, secs. 16–19, in *HC* 4:242–43.

41. Kimball, "Nauvoo Charter," 73–74.

42. Charter, sec. 17, in *HC* 4:243; Kimball, "Nauvoo Charter," 74–75.

43. Kimball, "Nauvoo Charter," 77; First Presidency, "Proclamation," January 15, 1841, *T&S* 2 (January 15, 1841): 273.

44. Charter, secs. 24–25, in *HC* 4:243–44; Kimball, "Nauvoo Charter," 76–77.

45. Kimball, "Nauvoo Charter," 76–77.

46. Kimball, "Nauvoo Charter," 77–78; Flanders, *Nauvoo,* 96–98.

47. General Conference, Minutes, October 4, 1840, General Church Minutes Collection, Church Archives (*T&S* 1 [October 1840]: 186); Ford, *History of Illinois* (1995 ed.), 182. Bennett's comments were omitted when the minutes from *Times and Seasons* were published in the *Millennial Star* (nor are they in *HC* 4:206).

48. Kimball, "Wall to Defend Zion," 492–93; Flanders, *Nauvoo,* 96; *HC* 4:389.

49. *Sangamo Journal,* December 15, 1840; Illinois, Twelfth General Assembly, 1840, Senate Journal, 45, cited in *Wasp,* June 18, 1842; *HC* 4:479n. Also see Kimball, "Wall to Defend Zion," 492–93; Flanders, *Nauvoo,* 96–97.

50. Illinois, Twelfth General Assembly, 1840, House Journal, 100, cited in *Wasp,* June 18, 1842; Gregg, *Hancock County,* 145; Kimball, "Wall to Defend Zion," 493–94.

51. Joab, General in Israel [John C. Bennett] to Editors of the *Times and Seasons,* December 16, 1840, in *T&S* 2 (January 1, 1841): 266–67; compare Gregg, *Hancock County,* 448–49.

52. *T&S* 2 (January 1, 1841): 267.

53. *T&S* 2 (January 1, 1841): 266–67; editorial, 264.

54. First Presidency, "Proclamation," *T&S* 2 (January 15, 1841): 273–74, 277; Don Carlos Smith, editor, "Proclamation," *T&S* 2 (January 15, 1841): 281.

55. Lucy Mack Smith, *History,* 307.

56. *Warsaw Western World,* January 13, 1841; *Sangamo Journal* article, reprinted in *Wasp,* June 18, 1842.

57. First Presidency, "Proclamation," *T&S* 2 (January 15, 1841): 274.

58. Nauvoo Charter, sec. 11, in *T&S* 2 (January 15, 1841): 282.

59. *T&S* 2 (January 1, 1841): 264; (January 15, 1841): 287. At least two candidates, Don Carlos Smith and Vinson Knight (both later elected as councilors), joined the slate after its publication on January 15.

60. *T&S* 2 (February 1, 1841): 309; D&C 98:4–10. Elected as aldermen were William Marks, Samuel H. Smith, Daniel H. Wells (not a Mormon), and Newel K. Whitney; not elected were Elias Higbee, Isaac Higbee, and Alexander Stanley [number of votes uncertain]. Voters chose as councilors Joseph Smith, Hyrum Smith, Sidney Rigdon, Charles C. Rich, John T. Barnett (not a Mormon), Wilson Law, Don Carlos Smith, John P. Greene, and Vinson Knight; voters rejected Arthur Morrison [number of votes uncertain], Robert D. Foster, William Huntington, Titus Billings, Noah Packard, Hiram Kimball (not a Mormon), James Robinson, Stephen Winchester, Stephen Markham, David Dort, and W. G. Wilson.

61. "Officers," *T&S* 3 (January 1, 1842): 646; and list of officers, 638.

62. Nauvoo City Council, Minutes, 1841–44, in *HC* vols. 3–6; Quinn, "Evolution of the Presiding Quorums," 29; high councilors in July 1840, in *HC* 4:164.

63. "Officers," *T&S* 3 (January 1, 1842): 646; list of regents, 631.

64. *Wasp,* July 2, 1842.

65. *Wasp,* June 4, July 16, 23, October 1, 1842; March 1, 1843.

66. *Western World,* January 6, 1841. Ordinances regulating liquor, entertainments, and morals are discussed in later chapters.

67. City Council, Minutes, August 23, 1842; Ordinances of September 26, 1842, in *Wasp,* October 1, 1842.

68. Godfrey, "Crime and Punishment in Mormon Nauvoo," 195–222; Givens, *In Old Nauvoo,* 101–11.

69. *T&S* 3 (December 1, 1841): 615–18. Also see Godfrey, "Crime and Punishment in Mormon Nauvoo," 205–6.

70. *Wasp,* May 21, June 4, July 9, 1842; *HC* 5:3–5. The sham cavalry battle, organized by John C. Bennett, led to rumors outside Nauvoo that Joseph Smith had actually been killed (*Wasp,* June 4, 1842, quoting newspapers in St. Louis and Charleston, Missouri).

71. Nauvoo Charter, sec. 13; *Wasp,* February 8, 1843; Isaac Haight, Journal, 11, entries for December 1843 and Spring 1844, University of Utah.

72. Stout, *Diary,* 1:9, 16–17, 30–31, entries for November 11, 1844; January 18, 25, April 1, 1845.

73. *T&S* 2 (May 15, 1841): 416, emphasis in original; Eliza R. Snow, "The Nauvoo Legion," *T&S* 2 (July 1, 1841): 467.

74. *Wasp,* June 18, 1842, responding to a critique by Francis in the *Sangamo Journal.*

75. *T&S* 2 (April 15, 1841): 380–83; (May 15, 1841): 418; *HC* 4:326–27; Smith, *Papers,* 2:381, entry for May 7, 1842.

76. *Wasp,* June 11, 1842.

77. Nauvoo Charter, sec. 25, in *HC* 4:244; *Wasp,* June 18, 1842, responding to a critique by S. Francis in the *Sangamo Journal.*

78. Congress voted 28–20 to table the Mexican War bill (*Signal,* January 30, 1847). Lucy Mack Smith noted the Missouri exemption in her *History,* 260, 54–58.

79. *Wasp,* June 18, 1842.

80. John C. Bennett, "To the Militia of Illinois," May 8, 1841, in *T&S* 2 (May 15, 1841): 419. The rifles issued to western states were most often Springfield flintlocks, leftovers from the War of 1812. The most prominent of these muskets was the military model 1795. Two contract models were used in lesser numbers, models 1798 and 1808. A .69 caliber musket now in private possession, a U.S. model 1816 flintlock made at the National Armory at Harper's Ferry in 1841 and stamped with the name "Nauvoo Legion," challenges this assumption. However, the 1816 muskets were obsolete and overproduced, and thus were freely shared with state militia units (memos from David Packard to Glen Leonard, July 12, 17, 2001, in author's possession).

81. Alton *Telegraph,* July 23, 1842, in Miller and Miller, *Nauvoo,* 100; *HC* 5:201.

82. "General Return of the Second Cohort or Brigade of the Nauvoo Legion of the Illinois Militia for the Year 1843," Special Collections, Southern Utah University, Cedar City, Utah; see Saunders, "Officers and Arms," 143–46, 149.

83. *Signal,* July 31, 1844. See Ford's address to the General Assembly, December 23, 1844, in *Signal,* January 8 and 15, 1845.

84. *Signal,* July 31, 1844.

85. John M. Bernhisel to Joseph Smith, March 8, 1843, Newel K. Whitney Collection, BYU Library; John Bills, advertisement, *T&S* 2 (June 15, 1841): 454.

86. *T&S* 2 (April 15, 1841): 381; *T&S* 3 (May 16, 1842): 790; Woodruff, *Journals,* 2:173–75, May 7, 1842.

87. Nauvoo Charter, sec. 25, *T&S* 2 (January 15, 1841): 284; *T&S* 2 (February 15, 1841): 320; Kimball, "Study of the Nauvoo Charter," 41–44.

88. Joseph Smith and John C. Bennett, "Nauvoo Legion, General Orders," May 4, 1841, in *T&S* 2 (May 15, 1841): 417–18.

89. *HC* 4:326; *T&S* 2 (April 15, 1841): 380–83; (May 15, 1841): 381; Stephen A. Douglas to John C. Bennett, May 3, 1841, in (May 15, 1841): 417–18.

90. *T&S* 2 (May 15, 1841): 417–18; mandatory law, reported in Pardoe, *Lorin Farr,* 64; criticism, in *Wasp,* October 29, 1842.

91. *T&S* 3 (January 1 1842): 654; "General Return of the Second Cohort," 1843, Southern Utah University.

92. *Daily Evening Gazette* (St. Louis), June 20, 1844; Saunders, "Officers and Arms," 142–43; Miller and Miller, *Nauvoo,* 118–19. With twelve thousand residents in 1845, half of them under eighteen, and half of all adults women, the potential in the city would be three thousand legionnaires. Eight thousand Saints outside Nauvoo would supply at most another two thousand men.

93. Drills of June 18, 19, 27, 1844, in Hale, *Bishop J. H. Hale,* 89–91.

94. *Wasp,* June 11, 1842.

95. *T&S* 3 (January 1, 1842): 654; 2 (May 15, 1841): 418; 3 (March 15, 1842): 733.

96. *T&S* 4 (June 15, 1843): 234, quoting *Salem (Mass.) Advertiser and Argus.*

97. *Wasp,* May 14, 1842; John S. Fullmer to Uncle James Rucker, March 7, 1841, Church Archives.

98. Vilate Kimball to Heber C. Kimball, October 11, 1840, Church Archives.

PART II. LIFE IN NAUVOO: A PEOPLE OF PROMISE

Epigraph: Moses 7:18–20; Parley P. Pratt, "Mirror for the Saints to Look In to See Themselves," *T&S* 5 (September 2, 1844): 631.

CHAPTER 6. THE PROMISE OF PROSPERITY

Epigraph: Orson Hyde, in *T&S* 4 (February 1, 1843): 90; Lewis, *Valley of the Mississippi,* 257.

1. Editorial, *T&S* 2 (April 1, 1841): 368, punctuation standardized.

2. Heber C. Kimball to Parley P. Pratt, July 15, 1841, in *MS* 2 (September 1841): 77–78.

3. *T&S* 3 (November 15, 1841): 605.

4. *T&S* 4 (February 1, 1843): 90.

5. E.g., Deuteronomy 29:9, 25–28; Psalm 122:6–7; 4 Nephi 1:13.

6. "An Epistle of the Twelve," October 12, 1841, *T&S* 2 (October 15, 1841): 567.

7. 3 Nephi 6:15.

8. David White Rogers, Report, typescript, Church Archives.

9. Isaac Galland to D. W. Rogers, February 26, 1839, Joseph Smith Letter Book, Church Archives; Wandle Mace, Autobiography, 38, Church Archives; *T&S* 1 (June 1840): 124 (cf. *HC* 3:375).

10. Robinson, *The Return* 2 (May 1890): 257; "Autobiography of Robert Crookston, Sr." (copy in NRI Archives), 4; see also Esshom, *Pioneers and Prominent Men of Utah,* 820; Whitney, *Life of Heber C. Kimball,* 257–58, 261.

11. Mortensen and Mulder, *Among the Mormons,* 116; *T&S* 4 (May 15, 1843): 198.

12. Editorial, *MS* 3 (August 1842): 67.

13. See Journal of Charles C. Rich, entry for March 1845, Church Archives; Alfred B. Lambson, Account Book, Spring 1844, 7, Church Archives.

14. Turley's cabin was between Water and Sidney Streets, on the northeast corner of Lot 4 of Block 147. See *HC* 3:375; 4:10; Theodore Turley, "Reminiscences and Journal, 1839–1840 July," entry for September 21, 1839, Church Archives.

15. Whitney, *Life of Heber C. Kimball,* 260–61. The Kimballs remained in the small but comfortable log home until Heber built a larger one on another lot in 1841. The second log home, with three rooms on the lower floor and one upstairs, was replaced in October 1845 with the two-story brick home that still stands today (Holzapfel and Cottle, *Old Mormon Nauvoo,* 83).

16. Job Taylor Smith, "Father Bundy's All-Wood Wagon," 169–74. For another example, see Marsden, "Journal and Diary of William Marsden," 147–48.

17. *T&S* 1 (June 1840): 124; bond for deed, August 10, 1841, Hancock County, recorded July 28, 1842, Book M-1, 260, spelling and punctuation standardized. The home was built by contractor Reuben Hedlock for James Whiteside.

18. Winchester to Erastus Snow, November 12, 1841, in *T&S* 3 (November 15, 1841): 605; John Taylor, editorial, *T&S* 5 (January 1, 1844): 392. Ebenezer Robinson confirmed this report in *T&S* 5 (January 15, 1844): 413.

19. *T&S* 5 (March 15, 1844): 472; Henry Kearns to Leonard Pickel, December 7, 1842, Coe

Collection, microfilm at Church Archives; John N. Harper, Autobiography, 8, Church Archives; Greenlagh, *Narrative of James Greenlagh,* 6.

20. *T&S* 5 (January 1, 1844): 393.

21. *T&S* 2 (October 15, 1841): 568.

22. For additional information, see Holzapfel and Cottle, *Old Mormon Nauvoo,* 119–20. Ebenezer Robinson (*The Return* 3 [January 1891]: 3) says he was the owner.

23. Nauvoo High Council, Minutes, May 3, 1840, typescript, 32, Church Archives. The committee was Henry G. Sherwood, Charles C. Rich, and Dimick Huntington.

24. George and Ellen Douglas to her parents, June 2, 1842, in Ellen W. [Douglas] Parker, Letters, Church Archives.

25. *T&S* 4 (April 15, 1843): 164; Richman, "Nauvoo and the Prophet," 136.

26. Proverbs 30:7–9.

27. Rohrer and Douglas, *Agrarian Transition in America,* 25–28; Hill, "Quest for Refuge," 5–14.

28. William Mosley to Father, February 18, 1844, Church Archives.

29. *T&S* 5 (January 1, 1844): 393.

30. Calvin Reed to Plimpton Simonds, July 1845, Church Archives; M. H., "Memorandum," 4, Church Archives; Drusilla Hendricks, Reminiscences, 22–24, Church Archives.

31. Lorant, *The Presidency,* 222.

32. John Needham to James Needham, July 7, 1843, in *MS* 4 (October 1843): 87–90. The other buyer was Joseph Fielding.

33. William Mosley to Father, February 18, 1844, Church Archives.

34. The Big Field is described in George Alley to Joseph Alley III, July 4, 1843, Church Archives; Buckingham, *Illinois As Lincoln Knew It,* 167.

35. Carlson, *Illinois Military Tract,* 30; Pooley, *Settlement of Illinois,* 544–45; William Mosley to Father, February 18, 1844, Church Archives. John Deere, a Vermont blacksmith who had settled at Grand Detour, Illinois, sold four hundred of his new, self-scouring steel plows between 1837 and 1843. His invention changed the possibilities for farming the rich prairies, but its effect apparently did not reach Nauvoo (Burns, "Le Grand Detour," 6–8).

36. Givens, *In Old Nauvoo,* 57–59; *Prairie Farmer* 8 (April 1848): 113; Joseph Fielding, November 1841, in "Fences," Lyon Collection; *Western World,* November 25, 1840; *Prairie Farmer* 8 (June 1848): 199, (August 1848): 250, (October 1848): 302; *Illinois State Register,* November 11, 1848, February 10, 1849.

37. For an excellent recent community study, see Rugh, "Conflict in the Countryside: the Mormon Settlement at Macedonia, Illinois," 149–74.

38. See the simple barns and granaries illustrated incidentally in Jensen and Oman, *C. C. A. Christensen,* figures 60, 75, 97.

39. Henry Kearns to Leonard Pickel, December 7, 1842, Coe Collection; Jonah R. Ball to Harvey Howard, January 15, 1843, Church Archives; George and Ellen Douglas to her parents, June 2, 1842, in Ellen W. [Douglas] Parker Letters, Church Archives; William Clayton to Edward Martin, November 29, 1840, Church Archives.

40. *T&S* 4 (October 15, 1843): 356; Pooley, *Settlement of Illinois,* 547.

41. Newel K. Whitney to Samuel F. Whitney, August 26, 1843, Whitney Collection, BYU Library; George Alley to Joseph Alley III, July 5, 1845, Church Archives; Pooley, *Settlement of Illinois,* 550.

42. Mary Ann Stearns Winters, Autobiography, 11, Church Archives.

43. Irene H. Pomeroy to Ashbel G. Hascall, July 6 and 12, 1845, Missouri Historical Society, copy in Church Archives, spelling standardized.

44. George Alley to Joseph Alley III, July 4, 1843, and April 15, 1844, Church Archives.

45. George and Ellen Douglas to her parents, June 2, 1842, in Ellen W. [Douglas] Parker, Letters, Church Archives.

46. *T&S* 2 (December 1, 1840): 238–39; (January 1, 1841): 267–69.

47. *Neighbor,* September 11, 1844; *Missouri Republican* (St. Louis), March 1, 1841.

48. *MS* 6 (1845): 124.

49. *HC* 4:16; 5:421.

50. Staines, "Reminiscences," 198.

51. Franklin D. Richards split oak and maple slabs for his picket fence (*Contributor* [1884]); "Articles of Agreement between Emma Smith and Jonathan Streeper," July 22, 1845, to fence block 92, in "Fences," Lyon Collection.

52. Mosiah L. Hancock, Autobiography, 27, Church Archives; Temple Committee Ledger C, April 12, 21, May 15, 1845, in "Fences," Lyon Collection.

CHAPTER 7. ECONOMIC EXPECTATIONS

Epigraph: "Editorial Address," *T&S* 5 (January 1, 1844): 392–93.

1. D&C 42:32; see also 42:33; 48:6; 51:3; 82:17.

2. In addition to explanations in chapter 1 in this volume, see the standard interpretation in Clark, "United Order and Law of Consecration," 21–28.

3. Clark, "United Order and Law of Consecration," 21–28; D&C 97:11–12; 119:1–7.

4. Acts 2:44–45; 4:31–32; 3 Nephi 26:19–20; 4 Nephi 1:2–4.

5. Allen Stout to Hosea Stout, September 13, 1843, Hosea Stout papers, file 8, USHS.

6. Backman, *Heavens Resound,* 15, 63–81.

7. Smith, *Words,* 248, 250, 310 n. 3 (lectures on September 13–14, 24, 1843); 1 Timothy 5:8; D&C 75:28.

8. Smith, *Words,* 248; Heber C. Kimball, Journal no. 94, manuscript, April 1838, 116–17, Church Archives.

9. Smith, *Words,* 114. See also *HC* 4:601, where "pronounced a curse on" is replaced with "reproved."

10. Cook, "William Law, Nauvoo Dissenter," 48–49, 53–54.

11. Lucy Mack Smith, *History,* 32, 37; Joseph Smith to Edward Hunter, January 5, 1842, in Smith, *Personal Writings,* 542–43 (*HC* 4:491).

12. Joseph Smith to Edward Hunter, December 21, 1841, in *HC* 4:482; Hunter to Smith, February 10 [1842], BYU Library; and Smith to Hunter, March 9, 1842, in *HC* 4:548–49. The February letter makes clear this was Hunter's own money, not collections from the Saints as suggested in Launius and McKiernan, *Joseph Smith Junior's Red Brick Store,* 16.

13. Joseph Smith Daybooks, July 5–12, 14–16 [1842], Manuscript, Iowa Masonic Library, Cedar Rapids, microfilm, Church Archives.

14. Launius and McKiernan, *Joseph Smith Junior's Red Brick Store,* 11–14, 17–18; *HC* 4:491; Smith, *Words,* 257; Joseph Smith Daybooks, entries for June 1842, microfilm, Church Archives; *Neighbor,* December 20, 1843.

15. Gregg, *Hancock County,* 950; Leonora Taylor, Montrose, Iowa Territory, to John Taylor, Liverpool, April 12, 1840, in *MS* 1 (July 1840): 63; Lyon, "Account Books of the Amos Davis Store," 241–43; information from Hancock County tax records compiled by Rowena Miller, NRI Archives; and *Signal,* July 16, 1845.

16. *T&S* 5 (January 1, 1844): 392.

17. Launius and McKiernan, *Joseph Smith Junior's Red Brick Store*, 33–35.

18. Erastus Snow, Journal, winter of 1843–44, typescript, 3:14, Church Archives; *Wasp*, June 25, 1842.

19. *T&S* 5 (January 1, 1844): 392.

20. *Wasp*, April 30, 1842; January 24, 1844.

21. *T&S* 3 (March 15, 1842): 732–33.

22. Ordinance of February 15, 1841, in *T&S* 2 (February 15, 1841): 321; noted in *Western World*, February 24, 1841.

23. *T&S* 3 (April 15, 1842): 765–66; *Warsaw Message*, January 10, 1844; Flanders, *Nauvoo*, 245–47.

24. Petersen, "Steamboating on the Upper Mississippi," 55–63.

25. Hess, *My Farmington, 1847–1976*, 177–78; *HC* 4:204, 233; Cook, "'More Virtuous Man Never Existed,'" 402–3. Henry Miller was named president of the Freedom stake at Payson, Illinois, in October 1840; George Miller became a bishop and military leader in Nauvoo; both continued to play an important economic role in Nauvoo.

26. Oaks and Bentley, "Joseph Smith and Legal Process," 738–45, 752–65, 769–71, 777–79.

27. Most steamboats operating on the Mississippi at this time were side-wheelers. The *Maid of Iowa* is so described by files in the National Archives (Sonne, *Ships, Saints, and Mariners*, 134) and in reminiscences (Ivins, *Pen Pictures of Early Western Days*, 12). A sketch in the Church Archives by an unknown artist showing it as a stern-wheel paddle steamboat is questionable (Sonne, *Ships, Saints, and Mariners*, 134). For the ship's full story, see Enders, "*Maid of Iowa*."

28. Jenson, *LDS Biographical Encyclopedia*, 3:658–59; *Wasp*, April 12, 1843.

29. *HC* 5:386, 416–18, 421; 7:351; Sonne, *Ships, Saints, and Mariners*, 134–35; *Neighbor*, June 7, 1843; *Warsaw Message*, May 24, 1843; Joseph Smith Daybooks, 1842–44, entries for April–September 1843, Manuscript, Iowa Masonic Library, Cedar Rapids, microfilm, Church Archives.

30. Alexander Daugherty, Memoirs, *Nauvoo Rustler*, September 26, 1916, quoted in Ida Blum, "Mississippi River Boats," *Nauvoo Independent*, October 25, 1972, 10.

31. *HC* 4:16; Rowley, "Nauvoo, A River Town," 260–61.

32. *Neighbor*, May 22, 1844; Ida Blum, "The Ferry Landing," *Nauvoo Independent*, September 27, 1972.

33. City ordinances, June 1 and 10, 1843, in *Neighbor*, June 7 and 14, 1843; *Western World*, April 21 [24], 1841.

34. *T&S* 5 (January 1, 1844): 392. The attempt to build the dam is noted in chapter 16 of this volume.

35. *Nauvoo Independent*, November 3, 1882.

36. *Western World*, January 13, 1841; Enders, "The Des Moines Rapids," 70–85; Doyle, *Jacksonville*, 79, 82; *New Citizen*, December 12, 1846.

37. Smith, *Words*, 257.

38. Orson Hyde, *T&S* 4 (February 1, 1843): 90; see also *Neighbor*, May 3, 1843, for an endorsement of fruit and vegetable gardening and a proposal for employing British weavers in a Nauvoo silk industry.

39. Smith, *Words*, 257; *T&S* 5 (January 1, 1844): 393; 5 (November 1, 1844): 695.

40. "An Epistle of the Twelve," Manchester, April 15, 1841, in *MS* 1 (April 1841): 310–11 (quoted as reprinted in *T&S* 3 [September 1, 1842]: 895–96).

41. Cordon, Reminiscences and Journals, April-May 1843, 3:169–73, Church Archives; Bolton,

Reminiscences and Journals, 1844–45, 4–5, Church Archives; Taggart to brothers, September 6, 1843, Albert Taggart Correspondence, Church Archives, spelling standardized.

42. Irene Pomeroy to Ursula B. Hascall, September 1845, Missouri Historical Society, microfilm at Church Archives; John Bourne, Reminiscences, 12–13, Church Archives; Dwight Webster to Aphek Woodruff, December 1, 1844, Church Archives; Ellen Douglas to parents, June 2, 1842, Church Archives; *Narrative of James Greenlagh* (Liverpool, 1842), 6; M. H. Harris, "Memorandum," 2–6, Church Archives; George Taggart to brothers Samuel, Henry, and Albert, September 6 and 10, 1843, Church Archives.

43. The situation of the comfortable Saints is reflected in many of the quotations used in chapter 7.

44. D&C 124: 74–82, 111.

45. *HC* 4:311.

46. *T&S* 2 (March 15, 1841): 355–56; *HC* 4:303–4. The charter named as the first trustees the first twenty names on the membership list, with five of that number to be elected to conduct the business.

47. *Signal,* June 16, 1841.

48. *T&S* 3 (December 15, 1841): 630.

49. *T&S* 3 (January 15, 1842): 663–64; Joseph Smith to Edward Hunter, in *HC* 4:491–92; Edward Hunter to Joseph Smith, February 10 [1842], BYU Library; William Law to Edward Hunter, March 9, 1842, Church Archives; *St. Louis Daily Evening Gazette,* June 17, 1844; *Wasp,* June 11, 1842.

50. *T&S* 3 (October 1, 1842): 937; *Wasp,* June 11, 25, 1842; October 8, 29, 1842; City Council, Minutes, April 9, 1842; Arrington, *From Quaker to Latter-day Saint,* 140; Henry Kearns to Leonard Pickel, December 7, 1842, Coe Collection.

51. *T&S* 3 (October 1, 1842): 937, citing D&C 42:40.

52. *T&S* 3 (January 15, 1842): 664; cf. Joseph Smith to Edward Hunter, December 21, 1841, in *HC* 4:482; and see comments of British immigrants in Flanders, *Nauvoo,* 146–48.

53. For examples, see John N. Harper, Autobiography, 8, Church Archives; John L. Butler, Autobiography, 37, Church Archives; Staines, "Reminiscences" (February 1891): 122, and (April 1891): 207.

54. Smith, *Words,* 124–25, from Wilford Woodruff's Journal. This emphasis on the poor was not included in the report in *HC* 5:34–35, 44. The meetings were held on June 18, 21, and 26.

55. Smith, *Papers,* 2:390–94 (*HC* 5:25, 44–46). The return of Woolley's goods is reported in Jenson, *Biographical Encyclopedia* 1:632; Arrington, *From Quaker to Latter-day Saint,* 86–87.

56. *Wasp,* July 16, 1842; *Neighbor,* May 17, June 21, 1843; *HC* 5:436–38; Flanders, *Nauvoo,* 149–50.

57. Flanders, *Nauvoo,* 153–55; Pease, *Frontier State,* 348–49.

58. Ellen Douglas to parents, April 14, 1844, in Ellen W. [Douglas] Parker, Letters, Church Archives.

59. William Clayton to Edward Martin, November 29, 1840, Church Archives; Ellen Douglas to parents, June 2, 1842, Church Archives; David Jenkins to Leonard Pickel, September 28 [1841], Coe Collection; Henry Kearns to Leonard Pickel, December 7, 1842, Coe Collection.

60. Horace Roberts, family history sheets, copy in NRI Archives; *Wasp,* July 16, 1842.

61. *Neighbor,* May 7–August 27, 1845; see also Kimball, *Diaries,* February 6, 1845.

62. *Neighbor,* August 27, 1845, February 7, 1844; *Compendium of 1840 U.S. Census for Illinois,* 307.

63. George Riser, Life Sketch, 6, University of Utah.

64. Henry Kearns to Leonard Pickel, December 7, 1842, Coe Collection.

65. Mary Field Garner, Autobiography, 2, Church Archives.

66. *Wasp,* June 4, 1842.

67. *HC* 5:45; Arrington, *From Quaker to Latter-day Saint,* 88; Lewis Barney, Autobiography, 21, Church Archives.

68. Stout, *Diary,* 1:32, April 2, 1845, reports a personal loan from the trustee-in-trust; an 1841 printed form for short-term loans payable to the Temple Committee is at BYU Library.

69. Recorded August 29, 1844, in Hancock County, Bonds and Mortgages, Book 1, 521.

70. *Wasp,* November 12, 1842.

71. The payment pattern is evident in the records of merchants Amos Davis (University of Utah) and Joseph Smith (Iowa Masonic Library), blacksmith Alfred Lambson (Church Archives), and tailor William McIntire (BYU Library).

72. *T&S* 2 (May 1, 1841): 406.

73. Givens, *In Old Nauvoo,* 68–69; *HC* 4:549; *Signal,* March 2, 1842.

74. *HC* 4:549, punctuation standardized; Smith was answering Hunter's letter of February 10, Edward Hunter Collection, BYU Library.

75. *Signal,* February 16, 1842; March 6, 1844; Ford's report of December 7, 1846, cited in *New Citizen,* December 12, 1967.

76. Kimball advertisement, *Wasp,* March 22, 1843; Alvin C. Graves advertisement, *T&S* 2 (April 15, 1841): 406; Lambson, Account Book, entries for 1844–1845, 5–7, Church Archives.

77. *Wasp,* July 16, 1842; *St. Louis Directory* (1845), 200.

78. Cook, "Isaac Galland—Mormon Benefactor," 277–78; *Galland's Map of Iowa* (1840).

79. Flanders, *Nauvoo,* 128–30, 136 n. 42; Cook, "Isaac Galland—Mormon Benefactor," 278–79; *HC* 4:391–92, 435–36, 519.

80. Joseph Smith to Tuttle, October 9, 1841, in *HC* 4:430–32; *Signal,* September 22, 1841.

81. Cook, "Isaac Galland—Mormon Benefactor," 279–83, 282 n. 98; *T&S* 3 (January 15, 1842): 667; Flanders, *Nauvoo,* 132–36.

82. *T&S* 2 (October 15, 1841): 568; Flanders, *Nauvoo,* 135–37. The Hotchkiss purchase is detailed in chapter 3 of this volume.

83. Sermon of April 13, 1843, in Joseph Smith, *Words,* 192, spelling and punctuation standardized.

84. For a thorough account of the drawn-out negotiations with Hotchkiss, see Flanders, *Nauvoo,* 128–36, 171–75.

85. Gregg, *Hancock County,* 77.

86. Firmage and Mangrum, *Zion in the Courts,* 120–21; *HC* 4:594–95.

87. Warren's firm handled bankruptcy cases for Joseph Smith, Hyrum Smith, Samuel H. Smith, Sidney Rigdon, Vinson Knight, Reynolds Cahoon, Elias Higbee, John P. Green, Henry G. Sherwood, Amos Davis, Windsor P. Lyon, and others.

88. Oaks and Bentley, "Joseph Smith and Legal Process," 743–44, 752–59, 763–65, 773–79; *Wasp,* April 16, May 7, 14, 1842; *HC* 4:600; Firmage and Mangrum, *Zion in the Courts,* 122–24.

89. Helen S. Soby to her father, October 3, 1841, Church Archives; Mary Ann Fullmer to Elizabeth C. Price, September 24, 1842, John S. Fullmer Letterbook, 168, Church Archives; John S. Fullmer to George D. Fullmer, July 8, 1842, John S. Fullmer Letterbook, 164, Church Archives.

90. *HC* 4:594–95, 600.

91. *T&S* 2 (October 14, 1841): 569 (see also 579, col. 1); Smith to Hunter, November 24, 1841, Edward Hunter Collection, BYU Library, spelling and punctuation standardized.

92. Pratt, "Mirror for the Saints," *T&S* 5 (September 2, 1844): 629–31.

93. Editorial, *T&S* 5 (October, 15, 1844): 679.

94. Newel K. Whitney to Samuel K. Whitney, January 30, 1844, Newel K. Whitney Collection, BYU Library.

95. *T&S* 4 (January 2, 1843): 58–59.

CHAPTER 8. NEIGHBORS IN NAUVOO

Epigraph: John Bennion, Nauvoo, to his parents in Liverpool, February 16, 1844, Church Archives, spelling and punctuation standardized.

1. See Psalm 133:1; Acts 4:32; Philippians 1:27; Moses 7:18; 18–21; 2 Nephi 1:21; D&C 132:8; 38:27.

2. *T&S* 2 (January 15, 1841): 276–77, spelling standardized; cf. John Bennion to parents, February 16, 1844, Church Archives.

3. William Mosley to his father, February 18, 1844, Church Archives, spelling standardized.

4. Based on the author's computation of plats on Cherill, *Map of Nauvoo,* 1846, and, when not shown there, on Gustavus Hills, *Map of the City of Nauvoo,* 1842.

5. "Conference Minutes," August 16, 1841, *T&S* 2 (September 1, 1841): 520–22 (*HC* 4:402–3); *MS* 20 (August 28, 1858): 549; see also *HC* 5:272–73. The high council formally relinquished its involvement in land sales on September 22, 1841 (*HC* 4:417).

6. For a map of the four wards, see page 176 in this chapter.

7. This arrangement was set by city ordinance after the first election (*T&S* 2 [March 1, 1841]: 337).

8. Hartley, "Nauvoo Stake . . . and the Church's First Wards," 61–62.

9. *T&S* 1 (December 1839): 390–31 (*HC* 4:12).

10. George Miller's bishopric was defined in January 1841 when he was called to the Nauvoo House committee (D&C 124:20–22).

11. *HC* 4:517; 5:119–20, 199; Clayton, "History of Nauvoo Temple," Church Archives, 6. For maps of ward boundaries, see Cannon, *Nauvoo Panorama,* 24.

12. *HC* 4:312; *T&S* 2 (September 1, 1841): 521.

13. Marryat, *Narrative,* 325.

14. United States Census; 1842 Nauvoo church census. The teachers reports were First Ward, 758; Second, 924; Third, 955; and Fourth, 927. The church census contrasts with less reliable estimates of from ten thousand to fifteen thousand residents in *New York Herald,* January 19, 1842 (quoted in *MS* 2 [March 1842]: 166) and in "Nauvoo," *T&S* 3 (October 1, 1842): 936.

15. *Signal,* April 22, 1846, quoting *Quincy Whig,* estimating the Springfield population in 1841.

16. Carlson, *Illinois Military Tract,* 66–67; Smith, "Frontier Nauvoo," 17–18; Illinois Census, 1845; *T&S* 6 (November 15, 1845): 1031.

17. Carlson, *Illinois Military Tract,* 79–80.

18. *T&S* 4 (April 15, 1843): 165. Pratt's comments were immediately echoed by other citizens of Nauvoo (Jonah R. Ball to Harvey Howard, May 19, 1843, Church Archives).

19. The total population ratio was 111 to 100 (*Warsaw Western World,* December 19, 1840).

20. Smith, "Frontier Nauvoo," 18–19; Nauvoo census, 1842.

21. Resolutions of the Anti-Mormon Party, June 28, 1841, in Hallwas and Launius, *Cultures in Conflict*, 82.
22. Millen Attwood, Diary, May 23, 1841, Church Archives.
23. These preliminary estimates (and others in later paragraphs) are based on an analysis of birthplaces of 5,727 adults listed in the Nauvoo Temple Endowment Register, typescript, Family History Library, Salt Lake City. Nearly 30 percent of the names in the list give no place of birth. It is not known how well the remaining 70 percent reflects an accurate cross-section of Nauvoo adults, but see note 32 to chapter 8 of this volume for a comment on British-born residents.
24. Heber C. Kimball to Parley Pratt, July 15, 1841, in *MS* 2 (September 1841): 77–78.
25. Hunter, *Edward Hunter*, 56–59, 69–70; James Rodeback to Edward Hunter, November 21, 1841, Hunter Collection, BYU Library.
26. Henry Kearns to Leonard Pickel, December 1, 1842, Coe Collection.
27. Analysis of Nauvoo Temple Endowment Register, LDS Church Family History Library, Salt Lake City, Utah.
28. Joel Hills Johnson, Autobiography, Church Archives; "Early Branches," *Nauvoo Journal* 3 (January 1991): 46–49.
29. John Harris Henderson, Reminiscences, 1909, 7, Church Archives.
30. Bringhurst, "Elijah Abel," 23–26; Wolfinger, "Test of Faith," 129–30.
31. *HC* 6:210; 5:217.
32. Based on the author's analysis of the Nauvoo Temple Endowment Register, Family History Library, and Jensen, "Transplanted to Zion," 81–84. In comparison, the 1850 census for Utah Territory reported 1,857 British-born residents of all ages, or 16.7 percent of the total. Ten years later, the Utah count was 10,197 British citizens, or 25.3 percent (Leonard, "History of Farmington, Utah," 33, 35).
33. Smith, "Frontier Nauvoo," 17; see also the discussion of agriculture in chapter 6 of this volume.
34. James Jones to Henry Jones, October 19, 1845, and May 19, 1846, Church Archives.
35. James Jones to Henry Jones, June 10, 1844, Church Archives, spelling standardized.
36. James Jones to Henry Jones, October 19, 1845, Church Archives.
37. Smith, "Father Bundy and the All-Wood Wagon," 169–74. These families stayed together at Mt. Pisgah, Iowa, in 1846. Members of the Cox, Harris, Roberts, Pixton, Slater, and Daniel Browett families joined the Mormon Battalion together.
38. The offer at Chili came from Elisha Worrell, who had platted the town in 1835; its population ten years later was only 125 (Worrell to [Joseph Smith?], March 26, 1841, Whitney Collection, BYU Library; *Warsaw Western World*, March 10, 1841.)
39. *Signal*, July 21 and August 4, 1841.
40. The Warren story is told in *HC* 4:403, 412, 471–72; and Brigham Young, Diary, August 19, 1841, in *MS* 26 (February 6, 1864): 87. See also Hamilton, "Money-Diggersville," 49–58; and Fielding, "Journal," 140–41.
41. Clayton, *Journal*, 201; Allen, *Trials of Discipleship*, 52–53, 58.
42. Lucy Mack Smith, *History*, 303, 307, 319.
43. Examples of such gathered families in greater Nauvoo include the Allred, Benbow, Bird, Call, Chase, Clark, Haven, Higbee, Hill, Holbrook, Huntington, Johnson, Jolley, Knight, Law, Lyon, Mendenhall, Miller, Moon, Perkins, Pitt, Pratt, Richards, Robison, Woodruff, and Woolley families.

44. The following discussion of the content of personal letters is based on a reading of five hundred letters in collections at the Church Archives, BYU Library, and University of Utah Library.
45. See Ellen Douglas to parents, June 2, 1842, Church Archives; Almira Mack Covey to Harriet Mack H. Whittemore, June 9, 1835, Covey Correspondence, Church Archives.
46. For example, see Mary Heywood Shumway to Joseph L. Heywood, March 22, 1841, Joseph L. Heywood Letters, Church Archives.
47. Smith, *Words,* 234; Smith, *Papers,* 2:438–39.
48. Smith, *Papers,* 2:415–16, 438–41; quotation at 416–17.
49. Smith, *Papers,* 2:416. Willard Richards served as a trusted clerk to Joseph Smith. George A. Smith, John Taylor, and Wilford Woodruff, when not serving missions, played key trusted roles in Nauvoo. Orson Pratt's friendship with Rigdon tainted his standing, and his problems over plural marriage in 1842 excluded him from the innermost circle of friends. Parley Pratt, absent on assignment in England, Orson Hyde, and Lyman Wight played less central but faithful roles.
50. General Conference Minutes, April 7, 1841, *T&S* 2 (April 15, 1841): 386–87 (*HC* 4:339–41).
51. *HC* 5:529.
52. Smith, *Papers,* 2:416.
53. Flanders, *Nauvoo,* 176; Givens, *In Old Nauvoo,* 158–64; Hill, *Joseph Smith,* 373.
54. *T&S* 5 (March 1, 1844): 459–60; Charlotte Haven, February 24, 1843, in Mulder and Mortensen, *Among the Mormons,* 121; Givens, *In Old Nauvoo,* 159–60; "Record Book of Effie Adelia Phippin Knight," entry for March 1837, Church Archives; Winters, "Autobiography of Mary Ann Stearns Winters," 2, Church Archives.
55. Ebenezer Robinson, *The Return,* 2 (June 1890): 287; Halford, "Nauvoo—the City Beautiful," 136.
56. Willard Richards to Brigham Young, July 18, 1843, Brigham Young Papers, Church Archives (*HC* 5:511–12); *HC* 6:346, 350, 361–63; *Neighbor,* May 1, 1844; *Signal,* May 15, 1844; *T&S* 5 (October 1, 1844): 669.
57. Ordinance of July 5, 1842, in *Wasp,* July 16, 1842.
58. Givens, *In Old Nauvoo,* 176–77; Whitney, "The Nauvoo Brass Band," 134–36; *Wasp,* June 11, 1842.
59. Miller and Miller, *Nauvoo,* 128; Stout, *Diary,* 1:33–34, April 7–9, 1845; *Grand Concert . . . April 7, 8, and 9, 1845,* broadside, BYU Library.
60. *T&S* 3 (January 15, 1842): 664; Nauvoo Music Association, capital stock, January 1845, examples in Church Archives and BYU Library; James Monroe, Tutorial Diary, 125, 133, entries of May 16, 30, 1845, Coe Collection; Miller and Miller, *Nauvoo,* 128.
61. D&C 90:15; 93:53; James Arlington Bennet, *T&S* 4 (December 1, 1842): 31.
62. Dr. H. Tate, in *T&S* 4 (December 15, 1842): 46–47; D&C 88:118.
63. *T&S* 3 (December 15, 1841): 630–31, 646; *HC* 4:293.
64. An 1835 Illinois law legitimized a college at Jacksonville (existing since 1829) and authorized new ones at Lebanon, Galesburg, and Alton. See Weil, "Movement to Establish Lebanon Seminary," 384–406.
65. Musical lyceum: *T&S* 3 (January 15, 1842): 666; faculty: 3 (December 15, 1841): 631; (January 1, 1842): 646.
66. *T&S* 2 (January 15, 1841): 274.
67. *Neighbor,* August 20, 1845.
68. *T&S* 3 (February 15, 1842): 700; certificates of matriculation, 1841, Samuel Miles Collection, Church Archives; *T&S* 3 (January 15, 1842): 666; *Wasp,* October 1, 1842.

69. Givens, *In Old Nauvoo,* 237–38.

70. Givens, *In Old Nauvoo,* 239–46; *T&S* 3 (December 15, 1841): 631–32, and (January 1, 1842): 646.

71. *T&S* 4 (September 1, 1843): 306.

72. Givens, *In Old Nauvoo,* 240; *Wasp,* August 20, 1842; Monroe, Tutorial Diary, 112–13, 117, Coe Collection; Howard Coray, Autobiographical Sketches, no. 2, 15–16, Church Archives.

73. Robinson advertised the Eclectic series in *T&S* 2 (August 16, 1841): 518; the new list and Robinson's agreement appear in *T&S* 3 (January 1, 1842): 652. By ignoring this chronology, Givens (*In Old Nauvoo,* 248) erroneously places the Eclectic readers on the authorized list.

74. *Wasp,* April 26, 1843; *Neighbor,* August 30, 1843.

75. William Patterson McIntire, Notebook, containing minutes of the Nauvoo Lyceum, January 8, 1840-April 6, 1841, Church Archives; Wandle Mace, Autobiography, 69–70, 85, Church Archives.

76. Givens, *In Old Nauvoo,* 169–72.

77. *Neighbor,* January 24, February 28, 1844; *HC* 6:180; Godfrey, "Note on the Nauvoo Library," 386–89; Givens, *In Old Nauvoo,* 259–60.

78. *Neighbor,* November 25, 1844; January 1, 1845; *Signal,* January 22, 1845.

79. "Description of Stock, Nauvoo Seventies Library and Institute Association," Church Archives, typescript in Lyon Collection.

80. Caswall, *City of the Mormons,* 56–57; Moore, *Trip from New York . . . in 1845,* 44–45; Adams, "Charles Francis Adams Visits the Mormons in 1844," 285; LaFayette Knight to James H. and Sharon Fellows, December 21, 1843, Church Archives.

81. *T&S* 4 (May 15, 1843): 201–2; *HC* 5:404, 406; Leonard, "Antiquities, Curiosities, and Latter-day Saint Museums," 291–319; Givens, *In Old Nauvoo,* 260.

82. *T&S* 5 (January 1, 1845): 762.

CHAPTER 9. A PEOPLE OF FAITH AND DESTINY

Epigraph: George Alley to Joseph Alley III, April 13, 1843, Church Archives; Joseph Smith, "Nauvoo," *T&S* 3 (October 1, 1842): 936.

1. The sense among Latter-day Saints that they were living in a new gospel dispensation whose history would be sacred is reflected in Bushman's observation that "Mormonism was history, not philosophy" (Bushman, *Joseph Smith and the Beginnings of Mormonism,* 187–88).

2. *HC* 4:380–81, citing the *Joliet Courier,* June 22, 1841.

3. Samuel A. Prior, "A Visit to Nauvoo," *T&S* 4 (May 15, 1843): 197–98.

4. Prior, "A Visit to Nauvoo," *T&S* 4 (May 15, 1843): 197; *T&S* 4 (March 15, 1843): 143.

5. Prior, "A Visit to Nauvoo," *T&S* 4 (May 15, 1843): 197.

6. *T&S* 4 (May 1, 1843): 181, emphasis in original; *HC* 5:328–29.

7. See *HC* 4:204, 362. The process called an "election" in Nauvoo is today called a "sustaining."

8. *T&S* 2 (April 15, 1841): 388.

9. Smith, *Papers,* 2:488.

10. Haven, "Girl's Letters from Nauvoo," 231. If the sacrament of the Lord's Supper was administered in homes, it was with the understanding that both preaching meetings and the sacrament service would eventually take place in the main floor assembly room of the Lord's House (D&C 95:16–17; *HC* 6:299). It was in early Utah that bishops became presiding officers in wards.

11. Compare Holifield, "Peace, Conflict, and Ritual in Puritan Congregations," 555–57.

12. Lucy Mack Smith, *History,* 190; Porter, "'The Field Is White,'" 76–79.

13. D&C 24:1, 5–9.

14. For other insights, see Bushman, "Joseph Smith in the Current Age," 35–38.

15. See Jonah R. Ball to Howard Harvey, May 19, 1843, Church Archives.

16. George W. Taggart to Henry Taggart, September 6–10, 1843, Albert Taggart Correspondence, Church Archives; George W. Alley to Joseph Alley III, July 4, 1843, Church Archives.

17. They did so in the spirit of Micah 3:8, 11.

18. *T&S* 5 (January 1, 1844): 392. A song in the *Neighbor,* February 5, 1845, identified apostles, prophets, and the gathering as three distinct elements of Mormonism, along with a different God and a different heaven from those of the sectarians.

19. Smith, *Words,* 156, January 22, 1843.

20. *T&S* 3 (September 15, 1842): 919.

21. *T&S* 4 (January 2, 1843): 56–57; see also D&C 20:26; 68:2–4; 121:26.

22. *T&S* 6 (July 1, 1845): 955, reporting an April 6 sermon.

23. E. H. Davis, New Haven, Connecticut, September 9, 1843, to Leonard Pickel, Bart, Pennsylvania, Church Archives, spelling standardized. For a similar reaction to preaching by Hyrum Smith and Brigham Young, see Clarissa Chase, Nauvoo, to Charles Marsh, Sparta, N.Y., undated (1840–44), Church Archives.

24. D&C 68:4; Seventy, Third Quorum, Minutes, December 23, 1845, Church Archives; D&C 68:1–8.

25. Joseph Smith to Brother Carter, Kirtland, April 13, 1833, in *HC* 1: 338–39 (manuscript copy in Joseph Smith Letter Book, 1829–1835, 29–32, Church Archives). The principle was revealed in D&C 28 and 43. For a discussion, see Crawley, "Passage of Mormon Primitivism," 29.

26. See Smith, *Words,* for a comprehensive compilation of the Prophet's Nauvoo sermons. The most prominent diarist was Wilford Woodruff, who considered it a priority to keep a complete record of the sermons, lives, and official acts of church leaders (Woodruff, *Diaries,* 175–76, 191–93, 303). So confident was he of his transcriptions that he said, "I warn the future historians to give credence to my history; for my testimony is true and the truth of its record will be manifest in the world to come" (*JD* 19 [1878]:229).

27. *T&S* 2 (September 1, 1841): 520.

28. Smith, *Words,* 156, 161.

29. D&C 88:118; Wilford Woodruff's journal report of the sermon, in Joseph Smith, *Words,* 318, spelling and punctuation standardized; D&C 93:36.

30. Lucy Mack Smith, *History,* 82, 90; D&C 128:19–21.

31. D&C 45:60–61; see also 42:56–58, 61; 93:53. The prophecies and visions of Enoch are published in Moses 6–7, in the Pearl of Great Price.

32. Matthews, *"A Plainer Translation,"* 12–13, 26–29, 37–39, 42–48, 52, 65, 96.

33. Critics in the 1830s used these answers to theological controversies as evidence of Joseph Smith's authorship of the Book of Mormon (see Bushman, *Joseph Smith and the Beginnings of Mormonism,* 125–26). For an excellent summary of doctrines taught in the Book of Mormon, see D&C 20:7–12, 17–36.

34. *Encyclopedia of Mormonism,* s.v. "Book of Mormon Editions (1830–1981)," by Royal Skousen; Flake, *Mormon Bibliography,* items 597, 599. Skousen corrects Flake's earlier assumption that Robinson and Smith printed the 1840 edition in Nauvoo (as may be inferred from *T&S* 1 [October 1840]: 186). Robinson contracted for both stereotyping and printing in Ohio (*T&S* 1 [July 1840]: 139, 144).

35. *T&S* 1 (July 1840): 144; 1 (November 1, 1840): 208.

36. *T&S* 3 (June 15, 1842): 822; 3 (August 15, 1842): 894.

37. Allen, Esplin, and Whittaker, *Men with a Mission,* 246–52.

38. Doctrine and Covenants of the Church of the Latter Day Saints: Carefully Selected from the Revelations of God, compiled by Joseph Smith Junior, Oliver Cowdery, Sidney Rigdon, and Frederick G. Williams, Presiding Elders of the Church and Proprietors (Kirtland: Printed by F. G. Williams & Co. for the Proprietors, 1835).

39. Flake, *Mormon Bibliography,* items 2861, 2862, 2863, 2864.

40. *Encyclopedia of Mormonism,* s.v. "Translation and Publication of the Book of Abraham," by H. Donl Peterson; "Facsimiles from the Book of Abraham," by Michael D. Rhodes, 135–37. For another explanation—that Joseph Smith translated a papyrus document that has been lost—see Nibley, *Message of the Joseph Smith Papyri,* 1–3. For Joseph Smith's comments on translating the Book of Mormon, see his letter to John Wentworth, *T&S* 3 (March 1, 1842): 707 (*HC* 4:537) (cf. a letter to N. E. Seaton, January 4, 1833, *HC* 1:315; D&C 1:29; 20:8). For his comment on the papyrus, see *HC* 2:236.

41. *Encyclopedia of Mormonism,* s.v. "Facsimiles from the Book of Abraham," by Michael D. Rhodes.

42. Years after Joseph Smith's death, clear parallels came to light in such pseudepigraphic texts as the *Apocalypse of Abraham.*

43. *Encyclopedia of Mormonism,* s.v. "Contents of the Book of Abraham," by Stephen E. Thompson; "Studies about the Book of Abraham," by Michael D. Rhodes, 137–38; *T&S* 4 (February 1, 1843): 95; *HC* 2:236. For a detailed study, see Peterson, *Story of the Book of Abraham.*

44. Explanation for Facsimile No. 2 from the book of Abraham; see also Nibley, *Message of the Joseph Smith Papyri,* esp. xii-xiii, 14.

45. Reported first in the *Quincy Whig,* summarized in *T&S* 4 (May 1, 1843): 185–87, with comment by editor John Taylor, and then reprinted in *Neighbor,* June 24, 1843, with etchings of the plates (*HC* 5:372–79).

46. The Prophet's journal kept by Willard Richards (May 1–9, 1843, Church Archives) does not mention the plates. A report that the plates described a descendant of an Egyptian Pharoah was inserted in the *History of the Church* (5:372) from William Clayton's personal diary and is thus less reliable than a direct dictation (Clayton, *Journals,* 100, entry of May 1, 1843; Allen, *Trials of Discipleship,* 117). Parley P. Pratt informed a friend that the plates contained "the genealogy of one of the ancient Jaredites back to Ham the son of Noah" (Pratt to John Van Cott, May 7, 1843, Church Archives).

47. *T&S* 4 (May 1, 1843): 185–87; Haven, "Girl's Letters from Nauvoo," 630; Wilbur Fugate to James T. Cobb, April 8, 1879, cited in Kimball, "Kinderhook Plates," 72. Also see W. P. Harris to W. C. Flagg, April 25, 1855, in *Journal of the Illinois Historical Society* 5 (July 1912): 271–73.

48. For a summary of various physical tests, see Kimball, "Kinderhook Plates," 68–70.

49. This interpretation is from Kimball, "Kinderhook Plates," 66–74.

50. The book of Moses and a translation of Matthew 24 date to the Kirtland period. The first pages of Joseph Smith's history were written in 1838 in Missouri. The book of Abraham and the Articles of Faith were completed during the Nauvoo years. All of these were compiled later into the Pearl of Great Price.

51. From an extended essay signed "Junior," *T&S* 4 (October 15, 1843): 362.

52. Kirtland High Council, Minutes, August 19, 1835 (*HC* 2:252); Joseph Smith, conversation with Mr. Butterfield (*HC* 5:215).

53. Doctrine and Covenants (1835), iii-iv; Underwood, "Apocalyptic Adversaries," 55; Crawley, "The Passage of Mormon Primitivism," 26–27; Whittaker, "'Articles of Faith' in Early Mormon Literature and Thought," 77–78, 82, 87 n. 43.

54. Doctrine and Covenants of the Church of the Latter Day Saints (1835), i, iii-iv.

55. Cannon and Cook, *Far West Record*, 1; Woodford, "Historical Development of the Doctrine and Covenants," 292–93.

56. "Address," *Latter-day Saints' Messenger and Advocate* 1 (October 1834), 2 (reprinted in *HC* 2:167–68n).

57. *Encyclopedia of Mormonism*, s.v. "Lectures on Faith," by Larry E. Dahl. The lectures were dropped from the Utah scripture in 1921 because they were not revelations (McConkie, *New Witness for the Articles of Faith*, 72; Dahl and Tate, eds., *Lectures on Faith in Historical Perspective*, 16–19). For comments on the shift away from an anticreedal stance, see Crawley, "Joseph Smith and A Book of Commandments," 18–32.

58. Whittaker, "'Articles of Faith' in Early Mormon Literature and Thought," 68–69; John Young, in John Hayward, *The Religious Creeds and Statistics* (Boston, 1836), 139–40.

59. Allen, Esplin, and Whittaker, *Men with a Mission*, 259–64. Pratt especially influenced Orson Hyde, *Ein Ruf aus der Wuste* (*A Cry from the Wilderness*), published in Frankfurt in August 1842.

60. Pratt, Report of March 19, 1843, in *T&S* 4 (April 15, 1843): 162; Allen, Esplin, and Whittaker, *Men with a Mission*, 244–45, 252–59, 264–65, 310–12.

61. Whittaker, "'Articles of Faith' in Early Mormon Literature and Thought," 69–70; *T&S* 4 (December 1, 1842): 28. Winchester's 256-page book was called *Synopsis of the Holy Scriptures and Concordance* (Philadelphia: Author, 1842).

62. *T&S* 3 (March 15, 1842): 706–10; Whittaker, "'Articles of Faith' in Early Mormon Literature and Thought," 63; *HC* 4:535–41.

63. Whittaker, "'Articles of Faith' in Early Mormon Literature and Thought," 78–82. The Articles of Faith appeared in 1851 in Franklin D. Richards's British compilation, *The Pearl of Great Price*, which was accepted as scripture by the church in 1880. The Articles of Faith were specifically accepted as scripture in October 1890.

64. *HC* 5:215.

65. See chapter 10 of this volume.

66. Quotation from the preface to the 1835 hymnal; Hicks, *Mormonism and Music*, 3–6, 9–10; cf. Holifield, "Peace, Conflict and Ritual in Puritan Congregations," 555.

67. D&C 25:11 12; Hicks, *Mormonism and Music*, 10–14, 20–22.

68. *T&S* 1 (December 1839): 31 (*HC* 4:14); Hicks, *Mormonism and Music*, 23–29.

69. *T&S* 1 (June 1840): 120–22; Hicks, *Mormonism and Music*, 26–28, 31; and see Flake, *Mormon Bibliography*, 130.

70. Allen, Esplin, and Whittaker, *Men with a Mission*, 254–55.

71. The initial delay is noted in *T&S* 1 (November 1839): 16. For a later apology, see *T&S* 4 (April 1, 1843): 153–54. Editors skipped the November 1, 1842, and the September 1 through October 15, 1845, issues.

72. "Brigham Young's History," *MS* 24 (February 22, 1862): 119.

73. For example, see reports and the editorial in *T&S* 4 (April 1, 1843): 149–53. The *Times and Seasons* announced at the outset that it intended to dwell on the gathering and the anticipated Millennium (*T&S* 1 [November 1839]: 1).

74. Two other religious papers—*The Gospel Reflector,* published by Benjamin Winchester at Philadelphia for six months in early 1841, and the *Gospel Light,* issued by John E. Page at Pittsburgh in three issues between June 1843 and May 1844—had less effect (see *T&S* 2 [July 1, 1841]: 463; Flake, *Mormon Bibliography,* 275).

75. Lucy Mack Smith, *History,* 151, 154, and 43; Joseph Smith–History 1:14 (*HC* 1:4–5).

76. Warren Foote, Autobiography, 67, March 12, 1843, Church Archives.

77. Kimball is quoted in Alexander Neibaur to George A. Smith and Heber C. Kimball, September 21, 1840, George A. Smith Collection, Church Archives, cited in Allen, Esplin, and Whittaker, *Men with a Mission,* 196. Compare Joseph Smith's editorial comment, "The advancement of the cause of God and the building up of Zion is as much one man's business as another. The only difference is that one is called to fulfil one duty and another another duty" (*T&S* 3 [May 2, 1841]: 776).

78. *T&S* 2 (September 15, 1841): 548.

79. *HC* 4:312.

80. D&C 20:46–59; Lucy Mack Smith, *History,* 195.

81. High Priests, Minutes, December 12, 1844, Church Archives.

82. Jill Derr, "'Strength in Our Union,'" in Beecher and Anderson, *Sisters in Spirit,* 155–58.

83. For a full story of the organization, see Derr, Cannon, and Beecher, *Women of Covenant,* 25–38.

84. Derr, Cannon, and Beecher, *Women of Covenant,* 39–43; Oaks, "Relief Society and the Church," 36.

85. George and Ellen Douglas to her parents, June 2, 1842, in Ellen W. Parker, Letters, Church Archives.

86. Smith, *Words,* March 17, 1842, 104–5; Ellen W. Douglas to parents, June 2, 1842, in Ellen W. Parker, Letters, Church Archives.

87. Ellen W. Douglas to parents, April 14, 1844 (Relief Society), and June 2, 1841, and February 1, 1843 (housing), in Ellen W. Parker, Letters, Church Archives.

88. D&C 25:3, 7.

89. Minutes of the Female Relief Society of Nauvoo, April 28, 1842, in Joseph Smith, *Words,* 116–18; Derr, Cannon, and Beecher, *Women of Covenant,* 43–50; Oaks, "The Relief Society and the Church," 35–36. President Boyd K. Packer said that when Joseph Smith turned the key, he turned it for all women, not just those present that day (Packer, "The Relief Society," *Ensign* 28 [May 1998]: 72).

90. Ordinance of May 14, 1842, in *Wasp,* same date.

91. *T&S* 4 (April 1, 1843): 154–57 (*HC* 5:320–23).

92. Mary Ann Stearns Winters, Autobiography, 13, Church Archives; for the revival, see the editorial, "The Youth," *T&S* 6 (March 1, 1845): 830.

93. D&C 68:25–28; see also 68:31; 93:40.

94. *T&S* 6 (March 1, 1845): 830.

95. Jessee, "Writing of Joseph Smith's History," 439–40, 464–69, 472; *HC* 3:375–77.

96. Jessee, "Reliability of Joseph Smith's History," 23–26, 34–39.

97. *T&S* 2 (November 1, 1840): 204, punctuation standardized. This comment introduces a reprinting of Oliver Cowdery's 1834 letters on church history.

98. Joseph Smith–History 1:22; *HC* 1:7.

99. *T&S* 5 (January 15, 1844): 413; *T&S* 6 (May 1, 1845): 887.

100. See personal diaries of Saints who lived in Nauvoo for examples of such experiences; Joel 2:28; Acts 2:17–18.

101. The conference minutes for April 6, 1845, identified the date after a pattern found in the Old Testament and the Book of Mormon, as "being the first day of the sixteenth year" (*T&S* 6 [April 15, 1845]: 869).

102. *T&S* 3 (May 2, 1842): 776.

103. See Joseph Smith to Emma Smith, August 16, 1842, in Smith, *Personal Writings*, 555, in which he expressed the desire to "pour upon the world the truth," and Smith, Journal, 1843, kept by Willard Richards, May 19, 1843, Church Archives.

104. Howard Coray, Autobiography, Sketches no. 2, Church Archives, reports Lucy's invitation to Howard and Martha Coray. Earlier recitations are reported in Wandle Mace, Autobiography, 43–44, Church Archives; *HC* 7:375 (meeting at the home of Bishop Hales, February 23, 1845); and in Relief Society, Minute Book, March 30, 1842. The manuscript was published as *Biographical Sketches of Joseph Smith the Prophet, and His Progenitors for Many Generations* (Liverpool, 1853).

105. Caswall quickly expanded the eighty-seven-page report threefold and published it as *The Prophet of the Nineteenth Century; or, The Rise, Progress, and Present State of the Mormons, or Latter-day Saints* (London, 1843).

106. These observations, and the paragraphs which follow, reflect an examination of a hundred diaries of the Nauvoo era in the collections of the Church Archives, BYU Library, and DUP Museum. Synopses can be read in Bitton, *Guide to Mormon Diaries*.

107. *MS* 10 (October 1840): 159–61; D&C 20:81–83; 21:1; 47:1–3; 69:2–3; 85:1; see also 1 Nephi 1:1; 19:1; Alma 37:2.

CHAPTER 10. THE HOUSE OF THE LORD

Epigraph: Phebe Chase, Nauvoo, to her mother, April 5 [1844], Charles Marsh Correspondence, Church Archives; James Jones, near Nauvoo, to Henry Jones (his son, in England), June 10, 1844, Church Archives, spelling standardized.

1. *T&S* 2 (April 15, 1841): 375 (*HC* 4:327).

2. *T&S* 2 (April 15, 1841): 376 (*HC* 4:328); Norton Jacob, Reminiscences, April 6, 1841.

3. *T&S* 2 (April 15, 1841): 377 (*HC* 4:331).

4. D&C 95:16–17; Hyrum Smith, General Conference, April 6, 1844; *T&S* 5 (August 1, 1844): 596–97 (*HC* 6:299).

5. Flanders, *Nauvoo*, 125–26; *HC* 4:205; Clayton, "History of Nauvoo Temple," Church Archives, 3–4.

6. Smith, *Revelations*, 246.

7. D&C 124:49, 2.

8. Joseph Smith to Oliver Cowdery, August 11, 1834, Kirtland High Council, Minutes, in *HC* 2:239, with reference to D&C 105:2–6, 9–13, 18, 33 (June 22, 1834). He gave similar counsel to Missouri's church leaders: "The first elders are to receive their endowment in Kirtland before the redemption of Zion" (Joseph Smith to Lyman Wight and others, August 16, 1834, in Smith, *Personal Writings*, 348 [*HC* 1:144]).

9. Joseph Smith's June 11, 1843, sermon suggests his continuing interest in the gathering as a vehicle for building the temple; see *HC* 5:423–27 and Smith, *Words*, 209–16.

10. D&C 124:25–26, 28–36.

11. D&C 124:28, 40–41, 39.

12. D&C 109:10, 35–37, 16.

13. D&C 13; Ezekiel 43:18–27.

14. D&C 38:32; 88:139–41; 95:8; 124:39; Kirtland ordinances: Joseph Smith, Diary, 1835–1836, November 12, 1835, January 21–22, February 6, 1836, in Smith, *Personal Writings*, 110–11, 174–78, 185–87 (*HC* 2:308, 379–83, 390–93).

15. Useful studies for the discussion that follows are Lyon, "Doctrinal Development," and Porter and Backman, "Doctrine and the Temple in Nauvoo."

16. *Elders' Journal* 1 (July 1838): 43, an expansion of the 1836 revelation now published as D&C 137.

17. Only Simon Baker's reminiscent account of the sermon survives, in "Journal History," August 15, 1840; it is quoted in Smith, *Words*, 49. The Prophet mentioned the sermon in an October 19, 1840, letter to the Twelve in Great Britain (*HC* 4:231).

18. Smith, *Words*, 37–38, 70–71, 77, 131, 210–13, 318, 333, 363–65, 368–72; *T&S* 6 (July 1, 1845): 954; *HC* 4:424–25.

19. The letters are in D&C 127 and 128. See William Taylor, "Joseph Smith the Prophet," 547; D&C 127:10.

20. D&C 128:15–18; Hebrews 11:40; Malachi 4:5–6.

21. D&C 128:12–13; 1 Corinthians 15:29.

22. 1 Kings 7:23–26.

23. 1 Peter 3:18–21; 4:6; 1 Corinthians 15:29.

24. He issued the corrective in a remark made to the Relief Society August 31, 1842 (Smith, *Words*, 131), and followed up with written instructions the next day (D&C 127).

25. James C. Snow, Record Book, Lima Branch, October 29, November 7, 14, 1840, 384–85, Church Archives; D&C 128:3; see also 127:6; 128:2–4.

26. D&C 128:9–10; Matthew 16:18–19; cf. Parley P. Pratt to John Van Cott, May 7, 1843, Church Archives.

27. Revelation 20:12; D&C 127:7–9; 128:5–8, 24. For context, see *Encyclopedia of Mormonism*, s.v. "Book of Life," by J. Lewis Taylor.

28. Joseph Smith, Epistle to the Twelve, October 19, 1840 (*HC* 4:231).

29. See Thomas Bullock's report of a May 12, 1844, sermon, in Smith, *Words*, 368 (*HC* 6:365–66). The lack of knowledge for properly judging the intent of the dead was one reason given for eliminating this requirement (*Words*, 98 n. 23, 404 n. 30). According to one account of the sermon of October 3, 1841, Smith excluded only murderers from the proxy ordinance (Warren Foote, Autobiography, 57, Church Archives).

30. For comments on the restriction, see Vilate Kimball to Heber C. Kimball, October 11, 1840, Church Archives. Ehat and Cook see a parallel with the permission required from the Prophet for plural marriages (Smith, *Words*, 404 n. 30; D&C 132:7, 19).

31. Israel Barlow encouraged the policy (Sixth Quorum of Seventy, Minutes, January 9, 1845, Church Archives), as did Brigham Young at the April conference (*T&S* 6 [July 1, 1845]: 953–54). Young was concerned that after a woman had been baptized and confirmed for a deceased male ancestor, she might then ask to be ordained to a priesthood office on his behalf. This could not be allowed, Young noted, since the woman could not receive for someone else an authority she did not herself hold.

32. Vilate Kimball to Heber C. Kimball, October 11, 1840, Church Archives; D&C 76.

33. Smith, *Words*, 340–62, amalgamated in *T&S* 5 (August 15, 1844): 612–17 (*HC* 6:302–17). For additional information, see Cannon, "The King Follett Discourse"; Hale, "The Doctrinal Impact"; and Larson, "The King Follett Discourse."

34. For a comprehensive overview of temple-related Nauvoo doctrines, see Porter and Backman,

"Doctrine and the Temple in Nauvoo," 41–54. See also *T&S* 6 (May 1 and June 1, 1845): 891–92, 917–18, a rare article on premortal life.

35. The 1832 vision is recorded in D&C 76. The 1842 teaching is from a source identified only as *Exchange Paper,* reprinted with the added comment in *T&S* 3 (September 15, 1842): 926. See also Parley P. Pratt, "The True God," *MS* 2 (April 1842): 184.

36. D&C 130:22; Lucy Mack Smith, *History,* 161.

37. Lectures on Faith, 5:2; McConkie, *Mormon Doctrine,* 319–20 (citing 1 Corinthians 15:44–45 and D&C 88:27).

38. Smith, *Teachings,* 345; Genesis 1:26–27; see also the commentary of John Greenhow, in *T&S* 5 (February 1, 1844): 428.

39. Smith, *Teachings,* 391–92; editorial, "The Living God," *T&S* 6 (February 15, 1845): 808.

40. *T&S* 6 (February 15, 1845): 809.

41. *HC* 6:184–85; cf. Smith, *Words,* 318–19.

42. Arrington, "William Weeks," 337–59; Clayton, "History of Nauvoo Temple," 4, Church Archives.

43. *HC* 6:197 (February 5, 1844).

44. The dimensions of the Nauvoo Temple gave it 11,264 gross square feet on the main floor compared with 4,661 square feet for Kirtland (79 feet by 59 feet and 50 feet high with a tower reaching 110 feet). The St. Louis cathedral, dedicated in 1834, measured 136 feet by 84 feet (11,424 square feet), with walls 50 feet high topped by a tower of more than 100 feet. The St. Louis courthouse was 183 feet by 64 feet (11,712 square feet) and about 50 feet high. The St. Louis theater was 160 feet by 73 feet (11,680 square feet). The Springfield state house was 123 feet by 89 feet (11,027 square feet) and 59 feet high, plus a 54-foot cupola. The first temple completed in Utah, in St. George, echoed Nauvoo's size more closely than did later Utah temples: 56,062 total square feet, 142 feet by 96 feet (13,632 square feet) and 80 feet high, with a vane reaching 175 feet. Sizes from Lyon subject note file, under "S," Lyon Collection; *Deseret News 1993–1994 Church Almanac,* 318, 323, 331–32; and Bigamon, "Old State House."

45. For a thorough description of the building, see Kimball, "The Nauvoo Temple," 974–82. Comparisons with the Jerusalem temple can be made from information in Jewish Theological Seminary Library, *Towards the Eternal Center,* 62–64.

46. Buckingham, *Illinois as Lincoln Knew It,* 171; Powell, "Temple for Sale," 130. William W. Phelps identified the east pews as being for the First Presidency (Moses' seat in Solomon's temple), Melchizedek presidency, presidency of the high priesthood, and presidency of the elders (*T&S* 5 [January 1, 1845]: 759). Similar inscriptions were used in Kirtland (see Peterson, "The Kirtland Temple," 400–409).

47. Abraham 3:1–19; D&C 84:32; 88:119; Nibley, *Message of the Joseph Smith Papyri,* 79–80. Note also the poem by W. W. Phelps, "The Temple of God at Nauvoo," *T&S* 3 (June 15, 1842): 830, which concludes, "And new things are opening, now, under the sun:/And knowledge on knowledge will burst to our view,/From Seers in the Temple of God at Nauvoo."

48. Numbers 24:17; Revelation 22:16; D&C 133:49. Some writers find a link between the death's heads and winged-soul effigies on New England gravestones (Andrew, *Early Temples of the Mormons,* 82, cited in Holzapfel and Cottle, *Old Mormon Nauvoo,* 231 n. 57). The evidence in Welch, *Gravestones of Early Long Island, 1680–1810,* 3, 13–18, 33–69, does not support this supposition.

49. "The Placing of the Last Capital on the Temple," Minutes, December 6, 1844, *HC* 7:323.

50. Parley P. Pratt, "The Morning Breaks," in *Hymns* (1985), no. 1.

51. Joseph Smith to Edward Hunter, December 21, 1841 (*HC* 4:481–82); Miller and Miller, *Nauvoo*, 108–9.

52. Rowley, "Wisconsin Pineries," 121, 125; Willard Richards to Brigham Young, July 18–19, 1843, entry for July 18; *HC* 5:512.

53. Allen Stout to Hosea Stout, September 10, 1843, in supplement to Hosea Stout Diary, typescript, 59, BYU Library; Rowley, "Wisconsin Pineries," 121–22, 140.

54. Rowley, "Wisconsin Pineries," 139; Miller to Newel K. Whitney, April 28, 1845, Whitney Collection, BYU Library; Brigham Young to Wilford Woodruff, June 27, 1845, in *MS* 6 (September 1, 1845): 91–92 (*HC* 7:430–31). Russell's invoices for around 200,000 board feet, May 1845 through February 1846, are found in the Whitney Collection, BYU Library.

55. Donations from Radcliffe branch, England, September 9 to January (no years given); James H. Adams, Andover, Ohio, to Joseph Smith, November 16, 1842; and other donation lists, in Whitney Collection, BYU Library.

56. Lucy Mack Smith, *History*, 231; Derr, Cannon, and Beecher, *Women of Covenant*, 26.

57. Mary Smith and M. R. Thompson to the Sisters in England, Nauvoo, December 25, 1843, *MS* 5 (June 1844): 15 (*HC* 6:142–43); *MS* 5 (November 1844): 85–86; 6 (August 15, 1845): 75; Clayton, "History of Nauvoo Temple," 43–44, Church Archives.

58. Smith, *Papers*, 2:335; Clayton, "History of Nauvoo Temple," 14, 16–18, 30–31, 35, Church Archives. A number of trustees' documents are preserved in the Whitney Collection, BYU Library.

59. *HC* 5:329–32.

60. Circular of the Twelve and Trustees in Trust, *T&S* Extra (January 22, 1845), Church History Library (cf. *HC* 7:369); and two letters authorizing Benjamin Clapp to serve as an agent, one dated October 18, 1844, and the other undated, Whitney Collection, BYU Library.

61. Alfred Cordon, Reminiscences, 135 (June 26, 1842), Church Archives.

62. List of donations by branch, June 1841, Whitney Collection, BYU Library.

63. Examples of early 1844 notes to the print shop are in Whitney Collection, BYU Library.

64. Carpenters' certificates, signed by William F. Cahoon, August 5, 1845, BYU Library.

65. William Huntington, Diary, 15 (retrospective account for 1844), Church Archives; Willard Richards, advertisement in *Wasp*, June 25, 1842; General Conference, Minutes, General Church Minutes Collection, Church Archives, April 7, 1843 (*HC* 5:338).

66. "Memorandum of Bonds and Deeds," undated, in Whitney Collection, BYU Library; list of donations from branches, June 1841, in Whitney Collection, BYU Library.

67. Epistle of the Twelve Apostles, Nauvoo, December 13, 1841, *T&S* 3 (December 15, 1841): 626 (*HC* 4:473); Joseph Smith to the Brethren in Nauvoo City, February 21, 1842, *HC* 4:517; Clayton, "History of Nauvoo Temple," 6, Church Archives.

68. Temple recorder Willard Richards appealed for payment of these notes in an advertisement in the *Wasp*, June 25, 1842.

69. "List of Names" of individuals invited to "board the bearer who desires to work on the Temple," certificate signed by A. Cutler, R. Cahoon, and E. Higbee, undated, Whitney Collection, BYU Library; Epistle of the Twelve, to the brethren scattered abroad on the Continent of America, Nauvoo, October 12, 1841, *T&S* 2 (October 15, 1841): 567 (*HC* 4:434).

70. Clayton, "History of Nauvoo Temple," 91–100, Church Archives.

71. For chronologies, see Miller and Miller, *Nauvoo*, 117; Kimball, "The Nauvoo Temple," 982 n. 2; and Clayton, "History of Nauvoo Temple," Church Archives.

72. Dedication of Baptismal Font, November 8, 1841, *HC* 4:446.

73. Clayton, "History of Nauvoo Temple," 22–23, Church Archives.
74. *Wasp,* July 9, 1842; Meeting in the Temple, October 30, 1842, Smith, *Papers,* 2:490 (*HC* 5:182); General Conference, Minutes, April 6, 1843, *T&S* 4 (May 1, 1843): 180 (*HC* 4:327); Clayton, "History of Nauvoo Temple," 24–32, Church Archives.
75. Clayton, "History of Nauvoo Temple," 40, Church Archives; Conference of the Twelve, Boston, September 9, 1843, *HC* 6:13–14; Special Conference, Nauvoo, Minutes, October 8, 1843, *T&S* 4 (September 15, 1843): 331 (*HC* 6:49–50).
76. *T&S* 5 (January 1, 1844): 392; Clayton, "History of Nauvoo Temple," 45, 53–54, 56–57, Church Archives; *HC* 5:284. Woodworth was replaced as architect of the Nauvoo House by William Weeks in 1845.
77. Placing the Last Capital, Minutes, December 6, 1844, *HC* 7:323; William Huntington, Diary, 27, University of Utah; Clayton, "History of Nauvoo Temple," 59–63, Church Archives.
78. Clayton, "History of Nauvoo Temple," 55, 64–66, Church Archives.
79. Laying of the Capstone, May 24, 1845, *HC* 7:417–18; Clayton, "History of Nauvoo Temple," 67–68, 70–77, Church Archives; William Huntington, Diary, 30–32, University of Utah; comment on the capstone, Wilford Woodruff to Aphek and Azubah Woodruff, July 22, 1845, Church Archives; quotation on singing and shouting, Irene Hascall Pomeroy to Ashbel G. Hascall, July 12, 1845, Missouri Historical Society; Joseph G. Hovey, Reminiscences, August 23, 1845, Church Archives; and Norton Jacob, Reminiscences, Church Archives.
80. George P. Dykes to George Miller, July 5, 11, 1845, Whitney Collection, BYU Library; Reuben Miller to William Clayton, July 29, 1845, USHS; Clayton, *Journals,* 180, August 31, 1845 (the date the glass arrived in Nauvoo).
81. Dedication by Brigham Young, October 5, 1845, *T&S* 6 (November 1, 1845): 1017–18 (*HC* 7:456–57).
82. *T&S* 6 (January 15, 1845): 779; Meeting of High Priests Quorum, January 26, 1845, Minutes, *HC* 7:364; Brown, "The Sacred Departments," 365–66.
83. Isaac C. Haight, Journal, September 15, 1845, typescript, 15, University of Utah.
84. Norton Jacob, Reminiscences and Journal, November 3, 8, 17, 26, 1845, 23–24, Church Archives.
85. Wilford Woodruff to Aphek and Azubah Woodruff, July 22, 1845, Church Archives; "Amount of Labor done on Temple pr Tinners Association," Whitney Collection, BYU Library; gold foil, on "Invoice of Goods by Amos Davis, November 2, 17, [18]45," Whitney Collection; *HC* 7:577; Perrigrine Sessions, Journal, January 30, 1846, Church Archives.
86. Seventies Quorums, Records, Second Quorum, November 23, 30, December 7, 28, 1845; January 4, 1846; Fifth Quorum, December 16, 1845; January 3, 15, 1846; and Fourteenth Quorum, September 14, 1845, January 4, 1846, Church Archives; Badger, "Sketch of the Life of Susan Hammond Ashby Noble," 2, Church Archives.
87. Epistle of the Twelve, January 14, 1845, *T&S* 6 (January 15, 1845): 779–80 (*HC* 7:358). This same epistle anticipated use of the anterooms above the main floor assembly room for the administration of the endowment.
88. Brown, "Sacred Departments for Temple Work," 370–73; Clayton, *Journals,* 204–6; Kimball, "The Nauvoo Temple," 978–80. The maps were studied by the Twelve as they sought a new western gathering place (Clayton, *Journals,* 244–45 (*HC* 7:558).
89. Smith, *Words,* 98 n. 23; William Huntington, Diary, 15, University of Utah; and the following letters in Church Archives: Vinson Knight to Rizpah Knight, February 14, 1842; Mary Heywood Shumway to Joseph Heywood, March 22, 1847, Joseph L. Heywood Letters; John Sweat to Samuel Akers, April 16, 1843; George Alley to Joseph Alley III, July 5, 1845; Jonah

R. Ball to Harvey Howard, May 19, 1843; and Phebe Chase to her mother, April 5 [1844], Charles Marsh Correspondence.

90. Vilate Kimball to Heber C. Kimball, October 11, 1840, Church Archives, spelling standardized.

91. Lucy Mack Smith, *History,* 308.

92. William I. Appleby, Autobiography, 71–72, Church Archives; General Conference, Minutes, October 3, 1841, *T&S* 2 (October 15, 1841): 578 (*HC* 4:426); Warren Foote, Autobiography, 57, Church Archives.

93. For receipts authorizing use of the font, see Anson Call, Receipts, November 12, 1845, Church Archives; and handwritten document, signed by William Clayton, recorder, January 16, 1846, William Rowley Collection, University of Utah.

94. "Our City, and the Present Aspect of Affairs," *T&S* 5 (March 15, 1844): 471–72 (*HC* 6:266).

95. D&C 124:28–41.

96. Promised endowment: Council of High Priests, Minutes, June 23, 1834, in Cannon and Cook, *Far West Record,* 68–69 (*HC* 2:112–13); Joseph Smith, Diary, 1835–1836, November 3, 1835, in Smith, *Personal Writings,* 72 (*HC* 2:301); Kirtland ordinances: Smith, Diary, November 12, 1835, January 21–22, February 6, 1836, in Smith, *Personal Writings,* 80–82, 145–49, 156–57 (*HC* 2:308–9, 379–83, 390–93); promise of additional blessings, D&C 110:9 (April 3, 1836).

97. Preparations: Joseph Smith Diary, 1835–1836, November 3, 12, 1835, in Smith, *Personal Writings,* 101, 110–11 (*HC* 2:300, 309–10); promises: Joseph Smith, General Charge to the Twelve, Kirtland, February 21, 1835, *HC* 2:197; Brigham Young, dedicatory prayer, Seventies Hall, December 26, 1844, *T&S* 6 (February 1, 1845): 794–95 (*HC* 7:332–33).

98. First Quorum of Elders, Minutes, Kirtland, February 6, 1836, *Kirtland Elders' Quorum Record,* 6–7; Lucy Mack Smith, *History,* 224. In Kirtland, the Prophet limited the ordinance of washing of feet to priesthood holders, probably in reference to its administration by Christ to the Twelve ("Prophet's Remarks to the Twelve," November 12, 1835, in Smith, *Personal Writings,* 109–11 [*HC* 2:308–9]).

99. Joseph C. Kingsbury, Autobiography, January 13, 1836, University of Utah.

100. Backman, *Heavens Resound,* 289–92.

101. Joseph Smith, Ohio Journal, 1835–1836, October 5, November 12, 1835, in Smith, *Papers,* 2:47–48, 75–77, spelling and punctuation standardized (*HC* 2:287, 308–9).

102. Joseph Smith, Diary, 1835–1836, November 12, 1835, in Smith, *Personal Writings,* 111 (*HC* 2:309); Joseph Smith, General Charge to the Twelve, Kirtland, February 21, 1835, *HC* 2:197; D&C 95; 110:7–10; 105:9–13.

103. "A Facsimile from the Book of Abraham, No. 2," *T&S* 3 (March 15, 1842): facing 720, fig. 8; McConkie, *Mormon Doctrine,* 779.

104. *Encyclopedia of Mormonism,* s.v. "Studies about the Book of Abraham," by Michael D. Rhodes; and see Abraham, Facsimile no. 2, fig. 8.

105. D&C 124:41; see also vv. 39–40. At the conference on October 5, 1840, the Prophet explained the restoration of ordinances held by successive dispensations beginning with Adam; see Smith, *Words,* 38–44 (*HC* 4:207–12); Smith, *Teachings,* 166–73).

106. Talmage, *House of the Lord,* 84, 99–101; Nibley, *Message of the Joseph Smith Papyri,* xiii.

107. The nine were Patriarch Hyrum Smith; William Law, second counselor in the First Presidency; President Brigham Young and Elders Heber C. Kimball and Willard Richards of the Twelve; bishops Newel K. Whitney and George Miller; stake president William Marks; and Springfield branch president James Adams.

108. *HC* 5:1–2, an expanded version of Joseph Smith, Illinois Journal, 1841–42, May 4, 1842, in

Smith, *Papers,* 2:380. The expansion probably uses information supplied by Brigham Young or Willard Richards.

109. Joseph Smith, Journal, 1843, May 26, 1843, kept by Willard Richards, Church Archives (*HC* 5:409 adds "gave them their endowments," but that had happened the previous May); Watson, *Manuscript History of Brigham Young, 1801–1844,* 120–21.

110. Joseph Smith, Journal, 1843, May 26, 28, 29, 1843, kept by Willard Richards, Church Archives (*HC* 5:412–13). Others sealed at this time were James and Harriet Adams, Hyrum and Mary Smith, Brigham and Mary Ann Young, and Willard and Jenetta Richards.

111. Esplin, "Joseph, Brigham and the Twelve," 315, 319–20, with quotation from undated Certificate of the Twelve, written fall 1844 or winter 1845, Brigham Young Papers, Church Archives; cf. remarks of Orson Hyde, Sidney Rigdon trial, *T&S* 5 (September 15, 1844): 651, col. 1.

112. Esplin, "Joseph, Brigham and the Twelve," 314–15; D&C 110:12–16; Smith, *Words,* 244–47 and notes at 303–7.

113. Woodruff, *Journals,* August 6, 1843 (*HC* 5:527); Joseph Smith, *Words,* 244–47 and notes at 303–7.

114. Elias Adams to George Adams, July 25, 1845, Church Archives, spelling standardized.

115. *Encyclopedia of Mormonism,* s.v. "Endowment," by Alma P. Burton; *HC* 7:556; Lee, *Diaries,* December 28, 1845, Church Archives. Most of the reported 5,670 ordinances administered were endowments (*HC* 7:xxv).

116. Clayton, *Journals,* 203–4, 207–9, 215–17.

117. Norton Jacob, Reminiscences and Journal, 24, Church Archives; Wandle Mace, Autobiography, 128, Church Archives; Seventies Quorums, Records, Second Quorum, November 30, December 14, 1845; Fifth Quorum, November 18 and [25], December 30, 1845; January 20, February 3, 1846; Lee, *Diaries,* December 19, 1845, Church Archives. Attendance by quorum was not required after December 26, 1845 (*HC* 7:552–53, but see 566).

118. Deseret News, *1976 Church Almanac,* G-34.

119. Clayton, *Journals,* 257–58 (*HC* 7:566); *Encyclopedia of Mormonism,* s.v. "Eternal Marriage," by James T. Duke. A few marriages before the completion of the altar on January 7 had the couples standing for the ceremony (Clayton, *Journals,* 245–47.)

120. Clayton, *Journals,* 245–46; Deseret News, *1976 Church Almanac,* G-34.

121. Marriage of Newel Knight and Lydia Goldthwaite, Joseph Smith, Ohio Journal, 1835–36, November 24, 1835, in Smith, *Papers,* 2:89 (*HC* 2:320); D&C 101:2 (1835 ed.). Section 101 in the 1835 edition was replaced by section 132 in the 1876 Salt Lake City edition.

122. Marriage of Newel Knight and Lydia Goldthwaite, November 24, 1835, and of J. F. Boynton and Miss Lowell, January 20, 1836, Joseph Smith, Ohio Journal, 1835–36, in Smith, *Papers,* 2:89, 153–54 (*HC* 2:320, 377).

123. D&C 42:56; and see Matthews, *Plainer Translation,* 64–65, 261–66; D&C 35:17–20; 45:60–62.

124. Matthews, "*Plainer Translation,*" 264–65; "Marriage of Newel Knight," November 24 1835, in *HC* 2:320; and see Genesis 2:22–25; Moses 3:22–25.

125. D&C 110:12–14 (and see Genesis 17:2–17; Malachi 4:6); Bible Dictionary, in Holy Bible (1979 LDS edition), s.v. "Abraham, Covenant of"; McConkie, *New Witness,* 322, 503–5, 508–9. Elijah's power had been promised to a young Joseph Smith by the resurrected Nephite prophet Moroni in 1823 (D&C 2). As assistant president, Cowdery—and, later, Hyrum Smith—held all the keys, but only the Prophet could exercise them (D&C 124:94–96; 132:7).

126. D&C 131:1–4; 132:15–19, 30.

127. See Matthew 16:19; D&C 132:7; and compare Helaman 10:5–10; McConkie, *New Witness*, 319–23.

128. D&C 132:45–46; *MS* 5 (March 1845): 151; Esplin, "Joseph, Brigham and the Twelve," 319–20.

129. Irving, "The Law of Adoption," 295–313; Wilford Woodruff's April 1894 sermon can be found in *MS* 56 (May 28, 1894): 335–39, and Woodruff, *Discourses*, 154–57. Examples of the adoptions at Nauvoo are noted in David Candland, Journal, January 25, 29, 1846, Church Archives; and Joseph C. Kingsbury, Autobiography, January 26, 1846, University of Utah.

130. Watson, *Manuscript History of Brigham Young, 1846–47*, 26–28 (*HC* 7:579–80).

131. Watson, *Manuscript History of Brigham Young, 1846–47*, 147–48.

132. McConkie, *Mormon Doctrine*, 368; and see Psalm 118:25; Matthew 21:9, 15.

PART III. CHALLENGES TO THE CITY BEAUTIFUL

Epigraph: John Taylor, discourse, July 6, 1845, in *T&S* 6 (January 20, 1846): 1100–1101.

CHAPTER 11. PATRIOTS AND PROPHETS

Epigraph: T&S 5 (July 15, 1844): 578 (*HC* 6:294).

1. Van Deusen, *Jacksonian Era*, xi–xii, 26, 47–51; "The Whig Party," *Providence Journal*, June 19, 1845.

2. For a helpful assessment, see Hallwas, "Mormon Nauvoo from a Non-Mormon Perspective."

3. D&C 101:77–80; cf. D&C 109:54.

4. D&C 98:8–10.

5. In later decades, the term *Jack-Mormon* referred to marginal Latter-day Saints rather than friends of the church.

6. Mosiah 23:8; 29:13, 16, 35–36; Articles of Faith 12.

7. D&C 134; quotation at 9.

8. Moses 7:53. For Latter-day Saints, the Indians are a people of promise whose potential is prophesied in the Book of Mormon (2 Nephi 30:3–6; see also D&C 49:24; *T&S* 3 [August 15, 1842]: 891; 6 [March 1, 1845]: 829–30).

9. Conference address, April 5, 1844; *T&S* 5 (July 15, 1844): 578 (*HC* 6:293).

10. Phelps, *T&S* 5 (January 1, 1845): 758; Eliza R. Snow to Esquire Streator, Caldwell County, Missouri, February 22, 1839, published as "Eliza R. Snow Letter from Missouri," 545–46.

11. D&C 124:2–11; *T&S* 3 (November 15, 1841): 593–96. This *Times and Seasons* reprinting of Pratt's *Letter* was one of several.

12. *T&S* 5 (May 1, 1844): 524 (*HC* 6:292).

13. Snow, "Columbia—My Country," *Quincy Whig*, reprinted in *T&S* 2 (December 1, 1840): 240; compare her "Ode for the Fourth Day of July," in *T&S* 2 (May 1841): 16.

14. Greene, "The Gathering of Zion," *Wasp*, June 25, 1842.

15. Thirteen petitions dated 1845 survive in the Church Archives, evidence, perhaps, of plans for another appeal; Johnson, "Missouri Redress Petitions," 34.

16. According to Lucy Mack Smith (*History*, 305), while still jailed at Liberty, the Prophet concluded to seek redress for the wrongs of Missouri through legal channels outside the state.

17. *Wasp*, April 23, 1842; Staines, "Reminiscences," 198.

18. *Sangamon Journal* (Springfield), December 22, 1840.

19. *HC* 4:19–21; Smith and Higbee to Hyrum Smith, December 5, 1839, in *HC* 4:40; John S. Fullmer to George Fullmer, February 4, 1841, 105–6, Church Archives. The Prophet had been appointed chief delegate by a split vote of the high council (Nauvoo High Council, Minutes, October 20, 1839, Church Archives).

20. Joseph Smith to Emma Smith, from Springfield, Illinois, November 9, 1839, Community of Christ Archives, copy at Church Archives (Smith, *Personal Writings*, 485).

21. *HC* 4:74. For a key to the location of 823 known petitions, see Johnson, "Missouri Redress Petitions," 32–33, and Richards, "Missouri Persecutions," 120–24.

22. The submitted publications were Pratt's *History of the Late Persecution Inflicted by the State of Missouri upon the Mormons* (Detroit: Dawson and Bates, 1839), Greene's *Facts Relative to the Expulsion of the Mormons or Latter-Day Saints from the State of Missouri under the "Exterminating Order"* (Cincinnati: R. P. Brooks, 1839), and the Assembly's *Document Containing the Correspondence, Orders, &C. in Relation to the Disturbances with the Mormons.* . . . (Fayette, Mo.: Missouri General Assembly, 1841).

23. Lyman Cowdery to Governor Thomas Reynolds, February 20, 1841, Church Archives.

24. Heber C. Kimball, Wilmington, Delaware, to Vilate Kimball, June 12, 1844, Kimball Family Correspondence, Church Archives.

25. *HC* 6:88, 124, 286; Johnson, *Mormon Redress Petitions*, 563; Richards, "Missouri Persecutions," 524. The summary is based on known surviving petitions, compiled by Johnson, "Missouri Redress Petitions," 32–33.

26. The petitions are quoted in Richards, "Missouri Persecutions," 528–30.

27. Conference address, April 1844, in *T&S* 5 (July 15, 1844): 578, echoing a similar statement by Taylor in *T&S* 4 (October 1, 1843): 343–44 (*HC* 6:39–40). See also the "Political Motto" signed by Joseph Smith, Brigham Young, and others in Far West in March 1838, defending the Constitution and denouncing "tyrants, mobs, aristocracy, anarchy, and toryism" (*HC* 3:9).

28. *T&S* 1 (April 1840): 93–94 (*HC* 4:108). These decisions were consistent with an 1833 revelation concerning appeals for redress of the wrongs committed against the Saints in Missouri (D&C 101:86–89).

29. The extradition attempts are discussed in an editorial in *T&S* 5 (February 1, 1844): 442.

30. Joseph Smith, Sidney Rigdon, and Elias Higbee, to the Senate and House of Representatives, January 27, 1840, in Johnson, *Mormon Redress Petitions*, 116 (*HC* 4:35–36); *T&S* 1 (September 1840): 169–70 (*HC* 4:198–99); Firmage and Mangrum, *Zion in the Courts*, 93–94.

31. *T&S* 2 (June 15, 1841): 447–49 (*HC* 4:364–71); Firmage and Mangrum, *Zion in the Courts*, 94.

32. McLaws, "Attempted Assassination," 50–56; Schindler, *Orrin Porter Rockwell*, 72–77.

33. Edward Partridge made this comment in 1839.

34. *Whig*, May 21, 1842; Joseph Smith to Mr. Bartlett (*Whig* editor), May 22, 1842, in *Whig*, June 4, 1842 (*HC* 5:15); Thomas Carlin, Quincy, Illinois, to Joseph Smith, June 30, 1842, in Smith, *Papers*, 2:422–23 (*HC* 5:49–51).

35. *Wasp*, May 28, 1842; Joseph Smith, Illinois Journal, 1841–1842, May 15, 1842, in Smith, *Papers*, 2:383 and n. 4 (*HC* 5:9). Schindler suggests that "Vortex" was possibly the paper's editor, William Smith (*Rockwell*, 76 n. 10), but Roberts denies this possibility (*HC* 5:xxii).

36. Thomas Carlin to Joseph Smith, June 30, 1842, in Smith, *Papers*, 2:421–23 (*HC* 5:50).

37. Schindler, *Rockwell*, 76–80; Flanders, *Nauvoo*, 229–30.

38. *Wasp*, July 27, 1842, quoting *Sangamo Journal.*

39. Ordinance of July 5, 1842, in *Wasp,* July 16, 1842; Firmage and Mangrum, *Zion in the Courts,* 95–96.

40. Emma Smith to Thomas Carlin, August 16, 27, 1842, in Smith, *Papers,* 2:433–37, 452–55; Thomas Carlin, Quincy, Illinois, to Emma Smith, August 24, September 7, 1842, in Smith, *Papers,* 2:450–52, 476–78 (*HC* 5:153–54), quotation in Smith, *Papers,* 2:477; Firmage and Mangrum, *Zion in the Courts,* 96.

41. "Ordinance regulating the mode of proceeding in cases of habeas corpus before the municipal court," August 8, 1842, in *HC* 5:87–88. Besides its timing, another indication that the ordinance was special legislation to deal with Joseph Smith's needs was the section providing for a replacement for the chief justice (Joseph Smith) when he was unable to officiate (Sec. 3).

42. *HC* 5:xxii–xxvii; Affidavit of Lilburn W. Boggs, July 20, 1842, in Smith, *Papers,* 2:499–500 (*HC* 5:67); arrest, August 8, 1842, Smith, *Papers,* 2:402 (*HC* 5:86); *HC* 5:87–88; reflection on Rockwell, Book of the Law of the Lord, in Smith, *Papers,* 2:439 (*HC* 5:125).

43. Smith, *Papers,* 2:403–13 (*HC* 5:89–97); visits, Smith, *Papers,* 2:418, 488 (*HC* 5:117–18, 172, 180); Joseph Smith to Emma Smith, August 16, 1842, in Smith, *Papers,* 2:430 (*HC* 5:104).

44. Justin Butterfield to Sidney Rigdon, October 20, 1842, in *T&S* 4 (December 15, 1842): 33–36 (also in *Wasp,* December 16, 1842; *HC* 5:173–79); additional details, *HC* 5:215–45.

45. Schindler, *Rockwell,* 81–88; *HC* 5:252–53; Snow, "Jubilee Song," *T&S* 4 (February 1, 1843): 96; Law and Richards, "The Mormon Jubilee," *Wasp,* January 14, 1843.

46. *HC* 5:250–52.

47. "Missouri vs Joseph Smith," *T&S* 4 (July 1, 1843): 242–43, with the warrants at 245–46; Joseph Smith, address, June 30, 1843, in Smith, *Words,* 219–21; *HC* 5:431, 440–43.

48. *T&S* 4 (July 1, 1843): 243; *HC* 5:443–48; *Chicago Democrat,* June 26, 1843, in *HC* 5:448–49; *Warsaw Message,* September 20, 1843.

49. *T&S* 4 (July 1, 1843): 243–45; dismissal, *T&S* 4 (August 1, 1843): 278; *HC* 5:449–56, 458–97.

50. Joseph Smith, speech, June 30, 1843, in *HC* 5:467–68, an amalgamation from Wilford Woodruff's Journal and Joseph Smith's Diary kept by Willard Richards, in Smith, *Words,* 217–18, 222–23.

51. *HC* 5:466, based on Joseph Smith, Diary, June 30, 1843, in Smith, *Words,* 222.

52. Wilford Woodruff Journal, June 30, 1843, in Smith, *Words,* 217, punctuation and capitalization standardized (*HC* 5:466).

53. *HC* 5:466, an expansion of Joseph Smith, Diary, kept by Willard Richards, in Smith, *Words,* 222.

54. Hill, *Joseph Smith,* 330; Firmage and Mangrum, *Zion in the Courts,* 104–5.

55. *Chicago Democrat,* June 26, 1843, in *HC* 5:449; editorial, *Neighbor,* July 12, 1843 (*HC* 5:507).

56. *Neighbor,* reprinted in *Warsaw Message,* January 10, 1843 (*HC* 6:105–6); city charter, *HC* 4:242–43.

57. *HC* 6:124; *Wasp,* July 16, 1842.

58. *HC* 6:212.

59. *HC* 6:416, 418–23; Gregg, *Hancock County,* 301.

60. *Warsaw Message,* September 13, 20, 27, 1843.

61. *Signal,* February 14, 1844; *T&S* 5 (February 15, 1844): 443–44.

62. *Signal,* February 14, 1844; *T&S* 5 (February 15, 1844): 443.

63. *HC* 6:134–42; Schindler, *Rockwell,* 84, 88–97, 103–9.

64. Nauvoo City Council Minutes, December 21, 1843; "Memorial of the City Council to Congress," containing "An Ordinance for the protection of the people styled the Church of

Jesus Christ of Latter-day Saints, residing on the western borders of the State of Illinois," copy in the handwriting of Thomas Bullock, Church Archives (*HC* 6:125–32).

65. *HC* 6:125–32.

66. *HC* 6:132 note; *Signal,* February 14, 21, 1844.

67. Of the many political studies of the Nauvoo period, we have followed Flanders, *Nauvoo,* 211–41, for the basic outline, with helpful insights from Hampshire, *Mormonism in Conflict,* and others noted below.

68. Flanders, *Nauvoo,* 212–15.

69. Pease, *Frontier State,* 362.

70. Constitution of the United States, Amendment I; D&C 134:9; First Presidency, "Declaration," *T&S* 2 (January 15, 1841): 277; law enacted March 1, 1841, Nauvoo City Council, Minutes, 13 (*HC* 4:306).

71. *Signal,* February 28, 1844.

72. *T&S* 5 (February 15, 1844): 442; Patterson, Reminiscences, manuscript, 31, typescript, 102–3, USHS Library.

73. Marryat, *Narrative,* 324–25, 327–28, 347.

74. Flanders, *Nauvoo,* 217–23; *HC* 4:108–9, 99; A. H. Mathews (writing from Carthage) to William Woodbridge, August 3, 1841, Church Archives; Pease, *Frontier State,* 344–45.

75. Flanders, *Nauvoo,* 221–23.

76. *T&S* 2 (May 15, 1841): 414 (*HC* 4:356–58).

77. *T&S* 3 (January 1, 1841): 651 (*HC* 4:479–80).

78. Joseph Smith supported the United States Constitution, other forms of government, and democracy in civil life (*T&S* 1 [November 1839]: 6–7; D&C 109:54; Article of Faith 12). At the same time, he headed a theocracy—the church and kingdom of God—and anticipated the day when a perfect theocracy would govern all people on the earth during the Millennium under the King of kings (Smith, *Teachings,* 252, 322; D&C 65:2–6; 105:32; Smith, "Government of God," *T&S* 3 [July 15, 1842]: 857).

79. *Peoria Register and Northwestern Gazetteer,* January 21, 1842, and *Quincy Whig,* January 22, 1842, both quoted in Flanders, *Nauvoo,* 226–27.

80. Joseph Duncan to G. T. M. David, June 14, 1842, Church Archives; *Wasp,* July 2, 1842.

81. *Metro-East Journal* (East St. Louis), May 21, 1968.

82. Flanders, *Nauvoo,* 228–31; *New York Herald,* March 3, 1843.

83. *Wasp,* April 23, June 4, 1842.

84. John F. Charles, the Mormon convention's senate candidate, may have suspected Joseph Smith's hand in Rigdon's decision; the Prophet tried later to convince Charles "that I did not deal in politics" (*HC* 6:133).

85. *Wasp,* June 11, 1842.

86. Shipps, "Mormons in Politics," 103.

87. Flanders, *Nauvoo,* 231–33; Joseph Smith to editor of the *Wasp,* January 23, 1843, in *HC* 5:259.

88. Joseph Smith, speech, July 4, 1843, in Smith, *Words,* 228 (*HC* 5:490); additional information, Flanders, *Nauvoo,* 233–39.

89. Taylor explained the motto in his inaugural editorial, *Neighbor,* May 3, 1843, noting that the paper would "not interfere with the rights of others, either politically or religiously. We shall advocate the cause of the innocent and oppressed, uphold the cause of right, sustain the principles of Republicanism, and fly to the succor of the helpless and forlorn."

90. Joseph Smith, speech, August 6, 1832, in Smith, *Words,* 236–37 (*HC* 5:527).

91. Ford, *History of Illinois,* 319. Sharp noted the move toward expulsion in a comment reprinted in the *Neighbor,* April 16, 1844.
92. Flanders, *Nauvoo,* 240–41.

CHAPTER 12. A RENEWED SEARCH FOR REFUGE

Epigraph: James Arlington Bennet, *New York Herald,* October 16, 1841 (*HC* 5:171); Joseph Smith, sermon, reported in Woodruff, *Journals,* 2:358, March 7, 1844 (Smith, *Words,* 326; compare February 8, *Words,* 320).

1. Reported at a conference in Kirtland, Ohio, October 28, 1842, *T&S* 4 (December 15, 1842): 39. The woman is not named.
2. Smith, *Words,* 323–24, spelling standardized (*HC* 6:237).
3. This sermon is a commentary on the parable of the olive trees in D&C 101:43–62.
4. Jessee, "Joseph Smith's 19 July 1840 Discourse," 392–93, spelling standardized (also in Smith, *Words,* 415–16). Because the date written across the top of this document appears to be a later annotation, Ehat and Cook have suggested 1843 as a more appropriate time for the discourse (Smith, *Words,* 418 n. 1).
5. *Signal,* August 28, 1844, reprinted from the *St. Louis New Era.*
6. Founded by D. N. White to support construction of a Warsaw-to-Carthage railroad in early 1840, the newspaper was first called the *Western World.* It was Hancock County's only newspaper when the Saints arrived (*Western World,* September 30, November 4, 11, 1840). During 1843 Thomas Gregg edited the paper as the *Warsaw Message.*
7. *Western World,* November 11, 1840; *Signal,* May 19, 1841.
8. *Signal,* July 21, October 20, 1841; July 9, 1842.
9. Godfrey, "Non-Mormon Views of the Martyrdom," 12–13, 13 n. 8.
10. *Western World,* January 20, 1841; echoed in *Signal,* May 19, 1841.
11. For examples, see *Warsaw Message,* February 7, 1844; *Signal,* March 27, May 22, 1844.
12. *Signal,* February 28, 1844.
13. Hallwas, *Thomas Gregg,* 45.
14. *Signal,* August 21, 1844. Other uses of *Jack-Mormon* are found in *Signal,* August 18, 1844, and November 12, 1845. Marshal Hamilton notes that Sharp has been incorrectly credited with coining the term *Jack-Mormon* and its supposed predecessor *Jack-Mason.* The attribution appeared in the *Illinois State Register* and was reprinted in *Neighbor,* November 18, 1844 (Hamilton, "From Assassination to Expulsion," 236).
15. When the *Signal* said that Mormons and non-Mormons could not live together in Hancock County, for instance, the *Philadelphia Inquirer* reprinted the article and asked "Why not?" Then *Pitt's Spirit of the Age* suggested that the St. Louis press answer the question. The *St. Louis New Era* took up the challenge, and its answer was reprinted in the *Signal.*
16. *T&S* 4 (October 15, 1843): 357.
17. Printed in *Wasp,* December 17, 24, 1842, with commentary.
18. *Wasp,* January 14, February 1, 8, March 1 and 15, 1843; *Illinois State Register,* March 31, 1843; Shipps, "Mormons in Politics," 110–16.
19. *Illinois State Register,* February 10, 1843.
20. *Signal,* February 21, 1844.
21. Reports of increased theft in nine Mormon settlement areas were published in the *Signal*

between December 1844 and March 1845. Quotation from Thomas Holt (first letter, 1844), Church Archives.

22. Quoted in *HC* 4:464n. This activity was concentrated in Ogle, Winnebago, Lee, and DeKalb Counties.

23. Ford, *History of Illinois,* 229–30; Miller and Miller, *Nauvoo,* 58–59; *HC* 4:454, 460–66.

24. *T&S* 4 (May 1, 1843): 183–84 (*HC* 5:332–33). The wicked Book of Mormon leader Gadianton used his band of thieves and murderers to gain political power and threaten the rule of righteous judges (Helaman 2:13–14).

25. Summarized from city council minutes by Miller and Miller, *Nauvoo,* 56–63.

26. *Wasp,* March 8, 1843; *HC* 5:297; 6:212.

27. Givens, *In Old Nauvoo,* 72; *Signal,* April 25, 1844.

28. *Signal,* June 12, 1844.

29. *Signal,* June 5, 1844; T&S 4 (May 1, 1844): 183 (*HC* 5:333); *HC* 5:297; George Alley to Joseph Alley III, April 13, 1843, Church Archives.

30. *T&S* 5 (June 1, 1844): 548–49.

31. Davis, "Some Themes of Counter-Subversion," 205–24; Hogan, *Joseph Smith's Embracement of Freemasonry,* 2; Allen, "Nauvoo's Masonic Hall," 42–43.

32. Hogan, *Joseph Smith's Embracement of Freemasonry,* 3–4, 19; Godfrey, "Joseph Smith and the Masons," 80–81.

33. Godfrey, "Joseph Smith and the Masons," 81–82, 85; *Ontario Phoenix,* March 2, 1831, copy at Church History Library. Joseph Smith's friendship with George Harris and Lucinda P. Morgan Harris is noted in Hogan, "Cryptic Cable Tow," 12, 18–21. On supposed elements of anti-Masonry in the Book of Mormon, see Bushman, *Joseph Smith and the Beginnings of Mormonism,* 128–31.

34. *HC* 4:20; Heber C. Kimball predicted Adams's imminent baptism after meeting him in Springfield (Kimball to Vilate Kimball, October 24, 1839, Church Archives). An undated document in the Community of Christ Archives suggests a December 1835 baptism date, which Mervin B. Hogan accepts, but 1839 or 1840 seems more likely (W. Wallace Smith to Mervin B. Hogan, September 22, 1969, copy in Lyon Collection; Hogan, "Mormonism and Freemasonry," 311). Hogan, an active freemason in twentieth-century Utah, was an avid Latter-day Saint researcher and publisher of original documents on the history of the Masonic lodges of the Nauvoo period.

35. Hogan, "Mormonism and Freemasonry," 309–12; Godfrey, "Joseph Smith and the Masons," 82–83; *HC* 4:20, 271; 6:51. The judge's son, Lucien, remained a friend to the Saints (*HC* 7:545).

36. *HC* 4:271, 293; 5:1–2; 6:51–52.

37. *HC* 5:406, 413. Adams purchased the boat with 1,760 acres of land north and south of Nauvoo and donated half the land's value when he sold it to the church (Trustees' Ledger Book, Church Archives).

38. Gregg, *Hancock County,* 299; *T&S* 4 (August 1, 1843): 287; *HC* 5:527, 537.

39. Rejection was based on Thomas Sharp's report of rumors of Bennett's immorality in Ohio (*Signal,* May 19, 1841). Nauvoo Masons learned from Abraham Jonas in May 1842 that Bennett had been expelled from his Ohio lodge, an unfounded claim. The Columbus Lodge took an elitist approach; its 1839 dispensation stated that "there ought to be but few Masons" (cited in Hogan, "Abraham Jonas," 5).

40. Marcombe, "Masonry and Mormonism," 448; Hogan, "Mormonism and Freemasonry," 281–82, citing H. G. Sherwood Statement, reporting an October 8, 1843, hearing before the

Grand Lodge of Illinois, Church Archives; "Copy of Dispensation," Church Archives, reprinted in Hogan, *Founding Minutes,* 3.

41. Smith, *Personal Writings,* 444 (*HC* 3:303); Doyle, *Social Order of a Frontier Community,* 178–82.

42. Hogan, *Masonic Pilgrimage,* 2, 31–33; Hogan, "What of Mormonism and Freemasonry?" 9–11; Jonas, address, 1859, quoted in Hogan, "Abraham Jonas," 21; see also 19–20; Jonas, *Masonic Address* (1843), 1–3.

43. Jonas, *Masonic Address,* 1–5.

44. D&C 124:41; Smith, *Words,* 42, October 5, 1840.

45. Johnson, *My Life's Review,* 96; *Encyclopedia of Mormonism,* s.v. "Freemasonry and the Temple," by Kenneth W. Godfrey.

46. *Encyclopedia of Mormonism,* s.v. "Freemasonry and the Temple," by Kenneth W. Godfrey; Melvin J. Ballard, sermon on Masonry, January 28, 1932, Church Archives; "The Prophet's Connection with Masonry," reproducing a letter from B. H. Roberts to a stake president in Idaho [name deleted in transcription], March 11, 1921, multilith, Lyon Collection. For other respondents to the question in the years since Nauvoo, see Godfrey's bibliographies in *Encyclopedia of Mormonism,* 528, 529.

47. Bennett mentioned parallels in his *History of the Saints.* Kimball to Parley P. Pratt, June 17, 1842, Church Archives (spelling standardized), quoted in Kimball, "Heber C. Kimball and Family," 458; Fielding, "Nauvoo Journal," 145, 147. See also Esplin, "Joseph Smith's Mission and Timetable," 305.

48. Allen, "Nauvoo's Masonic Hall," 43; Hogan, *Joseph Smith's Embracement of Freemasonry,* 4–10, 19–20; Doyle, *Social Order of a Frontier Community,* 184–86.

49. Warren Foote, Autobiography and Journals, 55 (August 3, 1841), Church Archives, spelling standardized. Foote's father was converted in 1834; Warren was baptized in 1842.

50. Waller, "Some Half-Forgotten Towns in Illinois," 67.

51. T. Edgar Lyon to Lowell L. Bennion, May 28, 1969, copy in Masonry file, Lyon Collection. The county can be seen on H. S. Tanner's *A New Map of Illinois* (1841), copy in Church History Library.

52. Hogan, *Mormonism and Freemasonry,* 314–15; Goodwin, *Mormonism and Masonry* (1934), 18–19.

53. Abiff (pseud.), "Mormonism and Masonry in Illinois," 19; Hogan, *Founding Minutes,* 3–4, 8; Lyon, "Free Masonry at Nauvoo," 76–77. Except for Orson Hyde and the Pratt brothers, all members of the Twelve became Freemasons by May 1842; Orson Pratt petitioned but was not initiated (Hogan, *Founding Minutes,* 8, 10–11, 14–17, 22–27, 29).

54. Hogan, *Founding Minutes,* 11–14; Abraham Jonas, letter of authorization, March 15, 1842, in "Letters on Freemasonry in Nauvoo, 1842," Church Archives; Smith, *Papers,* 2:370; Hogan, "Abraham Jonas," 11, 14–17.

55. Jonas report, *T&S* 3 (April 1, 1842): 749–50 (*HC* 4:565–66).

56. Joseph Smith to Abraham Jonas, March 25, 1843, Whitney Collection, BYU Library.

57. Hogan, *Founding Minutes,* 14–18; "Grand Lodge of Illinois Membership," table, in Hogan, "Nauvoo Lodge at Work," typescript, Lyon Collection.

58. Bilderback, "Masonry and Mormonism," 65; Marcombe, "Masonry and Mormonism," 454. Hogan maintains that Nye lacked the political motivation found in Jonas and Helm ("Rise and Fall of Nauvoo Lodge," 17–18).

59. *HC* 5:85; Hogan, *Mormon Masonry in Illinois,* 29–30; Marcombe, "Masonry and

Mormonism," 453; Hogan, "Utah's Memorial," 203. For Joseph Smith's comments on Nye, see *HC* 5:370–71.

60. *Wasp,* April 30, 1842; Allen, "Nauvoo's Masonic Hall," 44–45.

61. Marcombe, "Masonry and Mormonism," 448–51; Goodwin, *Mormonism and Masonry,* 28–29; Marcombe, "Freemasonry at Nauvoo," 416–19; Hogan, "Rise and Fall of Nauvoo Lodge," 18–19.

62. *HC* 5:12, 22, 73–75; Joseph King to Dr. M. Helm, May 17, 1842, and Willard Richards to Abraham Jonas, June 17, 1842, both in "Letters on Freemasonry in Nauvoo, 1842," Church Archives; Hogan, "Rise and Fall of Nauvoo Lodge," 5. Miller confirmed Bennett's adulterous activities in Ohio during an 1841 investigation, but the Prophet did not disclose the information until Bennett had repeatedly ignored opportunities to reform (*T&S* 3 [July 1, 1842]: 839, 842).

63. *T&S* 3 (July 1, 1842): 842–43 (*HC* 5:32); Nauvoo Lodge Statement on John C. Bennett, "Copied from the Minutes of Nauvoo Lodge, U.D., Thursday, July 7, 1842," in "Letters on Freemasonry in Nauvoo," Church Archives; *Sangamo Journal,* July 8, 15, and 22, 1842.

64. Marcombe, "Masonry and Mormonism," 452–53; George Miller to Abraham Jonas, September 29, 1842, in "Letters on Freemasonry," Church Archives. Helm, Statement, in "Letters on Freemasonry," Church Archives; Goodwin, *Mormonism and Masonry,* 29–31.

65. Marcombe, "Masonry and Mormonism," 453–54, 523–24; Goodwin, *Mormonism and Masonry,* 32–34.

66. Hogan, *Mormon Masonry in Illinois,* 45–46; Hogan, "Mormonism and Freemasonry," 281; Hogan, "Rise and Fall of Nauvoo Lodge," 23. Alexander Dunlap of Jacksonville replaced Helm as grand master and Levi Lusk of Rushville became deputy grand master. The Prophet's *History* (5:370) characterizes Nye as bossy and as "a hypocritical Presbyterian preacher." Nye started an opposition lodge on the hill.

67. Marcombe, "Masonry and Mormonism," 525–26, 529–30; Goodwin, *Mormonism and Masonry,* 35–37; Bilderback, "Masonry and Mormonism in Nauvoo," 69–70; Godfrey, "Joseph Smith and the Masons," 90. Brigham Young apparently did not affiliate meaningfully with Masonry in New York but petitioned for membership in Nauvoo and became a master Mason in April 1842 (Hogan, *Founding Minutes,* 8, 10, 14–15).

68. For further detail on matters considered in the balance of this section, see Flanders, *Nauvoo,* 278–305; Esplin, "'A Place Prepared.'"

69. The revelations noted are D&C 124:2, 60, 131; 101:21.

70. Walker, "Seeking the 'Remnant,'" 1–14, 21, 31; Esplin, "'A Place Prepared,'" 87–88; D&C 49:24–25; 54:8; 57:1–6. Jeffersonians typically excluded the Pacific Coast from their expansionist aims (Merk, *Manifest Destiny and Mission,* 8).

71. Walker, "Seeking the 'Remnant,'" 20–25.

72. See *Wasp,* May through September 1842 (e.g., August 13, September 21, 1842), and February 15, 22, March 3, 29, 1843; and the *Neighbor,* from 1843 onward. The *Signal* likewise carried such notices. Under Thomas Gregg's editorship, the Whig-oriented *Warsaw Message* opposed acquiring California and annexing Texas (January 11, 1843).

73. *Wasp,* January 7, 1842; *T&S* 2 (May 15, 1841): 419.

74. Esplin, "'A Place Prepared,'" 90–91; Walker, "Seeking the 'Remnant,'" 24–25.

75. Oliver Olney letter, July 20, 1842, Coe Collection; *HC* 4:552, March 17, 1842; Esplin, "'A Place Prepared,'" 91–93.

76. "Extracts from Journal of Elder Jonathan Dunham," *HC* 5:541–49 (from vol. 3 of Dunham's diaries, Church Archives); Walker, "Seeking the 'Remnant,'" 28–29.

77. Those participating in this special council are named in Clayton, *Journal,* 126, March 11, 1844 (*HC* 6:220–61).

78. Joseph Smith, Journal, 1843–44, kept by Willard Richards, February 20, 1844, Church Archives, spelling standardized (*HC* 6:222); Woodruff, *Journals,* 350–51, February 20, 21, 23, 1844.

79. *HC* 6:224; Wilford Woodruff, Diary, February 25, 1844, Church Archives. The initial volunteers were Jonathan Dunham, Phineas H. Young, David D. Yearsley, and David Fullmer. Added on February 23 were George D. Watt, Samuel Bent, Joseph A. Kelting, David Fullmer, James Emmett, Daniel Spencer, Samuel Rolfe, Daniel Avery, and Samuel W. Richards. Seth Palmer, Amos Fielding, Charles Shumway, John S. Fullmer, Ira S. Miles, Almon L. Fullmer, and Hosea Stout enlisted soon afterward. Alphonzo Young was nominated but chose not to participate.

80. *HC* 6:244, 255–61; cf. 7:213. On February 20, church leaders discussed Lyman Wight's proposal to preach to the Wisconsin Indians. Two men who had left Wisconsin January 1 brought the question to Nauvoo. Wilford Woodruff said, "Joseph thought it wisdom not to do it," but the Prophet let Wight make his own decision (Woodruff, Diary, February 20, 1844, Church Archives; *HC* 6:222). The proposal of settlement in Texas, contained in letters written February 15, arrived in Nauvoo with George Miller on March 8 and was reviewed two days later.

81. Clayton, *Journals,* 153–54, January 1, 1845; Joseph Smith, Journal, 1844, kept by Willard Richards, March 10, 11, 1844 (*HC* 6:260–61).

82. See D&C 65:5–6; Daniel 2:34–35, 44–45; Shipps, *Mormonism,* 126–27; Hill, *Quest for Refuge,* 125–26; D&C 58:21–22; 65. The overall purposes of the Council of Fifty are noted in Clayton, *Journals,* 153–54, January 1, 1845. For comments by church leaders on the government of the Kingdom of God, see *HC* 7:381–82; Young, *Discourses,* 354–57; Taylor, *Gospel Kingdom,* 205–20; Woodruff, *Discourses,* 193–98; McConkie, *Mormon Doctrine,* 415–18; and Smith, *Doctrines of Salvation,* 1:229–46. Also instructive is Ehat, "'It Seems Like Heaven Began on Earth,'" 253–79.

83. *T&S* 3 (July 15, 1842): 857. Also see restatements by John Taylor, "Religion and Politics," *T&S* 5 (March 15, 1844): 470–71; and by Sidney Rigdon, in April conference, *T&S* 5 (May 1, 1844): 523.

84. Hill, *Quest for Refuge,* 139–40.

85. *Louisville Journal,* reprinted in *Signal,* April 10, 1844; Thomas Ford to Brigham Young, April 8, 1845, Brigham Young Papers, Church Archives.

86. Hansen, *Quest for Empire,* 82–89; Lyman Wight, George Miller, et al., to the First Presidency and Quorum of the Twelve, February 15, 1844, Church Archives (*HC* 6:255–57), and same authors to Joseph Smith, February 15, 1844, Church Archives (*HC* 6:257–60); Woodworth mission, Joseph Smith, Journal, 1844, kept by Willard Richards, March 14, May 2–3, 1844, Church Archives (*HC* 6:264, 351, 356); Fielding, "Nauvoo Journal," 148.

87. Joseph Smith's prophecy, in Orson Pratt to George A. Smith, January 21, 1841, Orson Pratt file, Church Archives, quoted and discussed in Hill, "Quest for Refuge," 19–20. Similar statements are found in Jessee, "Joseph Smith's 19 July 1840 Discourse," 392–94; Smith, *Words,* 199, 279 n. 1, May 6, 1843; and 415–18, 418 n. 1, July 19, 1840.

88. *HC* 7:213; 6:87–88. Willard Richards and William W. Phelps drafted the memorial and Brigham Young chaired the meeting.

89. *HC* 6:80, 83, 88–95; Smith, *Words,* 218, 221, 225, speech of June 30, 1843 (*HC* 5:468). Mentioned in the Prophet's *History* are letters of Parley P. Pratt to New York (*HC* 6:99), Sidney

Rigdon to Pennsylvania (*HC* 6:191–92), and Phinehas Richards to Massachusetts (*HC* 6:193). Noah Packard's petition to Massachusetts is in *T&S* 5 (May 1, 1844): 514–19.

90. Benjamin Andrews to Maine, November 29, 1843 (*T&S* 5 [January 15, 1844]: 403–5; *HC* 6:178).

91. Reply of Green Mountain Boys, February 15, 1844, addressed "to the editor of the *Warsaw Message* or *Signal*," Coe Collection.

92. The Avery story is documented in *HC* 6:99–104, 108–15, 119–23, 133, 142, 145–48.

93. *Neighbor*, Extra, December 9, 1843; also in *Neighbor*, December 13, 1843 (*HC* 6:101–2, 105–6).

94. "An Ordinance," *HC* 6:130–32.

95. "The Weather," *T&S* 5 (March 1, 1844): 458; "Friendly Hint," *T&S* 5 (March 15, 1844): 473–74 (*HC* 6:247). William W. Phelps drafted the petition for Joseph's signature.

96. Esplin, "'A Place Prepared,'" 100; *HC* 6:270, 274–77, 281–83.

97. Orson Hyde to Joseph Smith, April 25, 1844, Joseph Smith Papers, Church Archives (*HC* 6:371). This is the first of two letters on the subject; the second was written the next day, April 26.

98. Orson Hyde to Joseph Smith, April 25, 1844, Joseph Smith Papers, Church Archives (*HC* 6:371).

99. Orson Hyde to Joseph Smith, April 26, 1844, Joseph Smith Papers, Church Archives (*HC* 6:373).

100. Orson Hyde to Joseph Smith, April 25, 1844, Joseph Smith Papers, Church Archives (*HC* 6:372).

101. Orson Hyde to Joseph Smith, April 26, 1844, Joseph Smith Papers, Church Archives (*HC* 6:374).

102. *HC* 6:282–83n, citing *Congressional Globe* 13:624; *HC* 6:370.

103. A similar Mormon offer to protect westering migrants by building blockhouses and forts along western trails in 1846 led to the creation of the Mormon Battalion to help secure upper California for the United States—and potentially for the Latter-day Saints.

104. *HC* 6:318–19 (not in *T&S*), an amalgamation from the diaries of William Clayton, Wilford Woodruff, Thomas Bullock, and Joseph Smith (as kept by Willard Richards). These diaries make clear that the combined rendering "the whole of America is Zion itself from north to south" meant both the north and south portions of what in that time was considered a single American continent (Smith, *Words*, 362–65 [April 8, 1844]).

105. *HC* 6:319.

106. *HC* 6:321–23; Woodruff, *Journals*, 390. A dictionary defines *economy* as "the method of the divine administration of the world, especially as it affects a particular nation or time; dispensation" (*World Book Encyclopedia Dictionary*, q.v. "economy," meaning 6).

107. *HC* 6:318.

108. *T&S* 4 (October 1, 1843): 343; 5 (February 1, 1844): 427; and 5 (February 15, 1844): 439–41; *HC* 6:188. Supportive editorials appear in *T&S* 5 (March 1, 15, 1844): 455, 470–71.

109. Hyrum Smith, address, April 9, 1844, *HC* 6:323.

110. *T&S* 5 (January 1, 1844): 393–96.

111. *T&S* 5 (June 1, 1844): 544 (*HC* 6:376).

112. *HC* 6:188 (January 29, 1844), referring to *HC* 5:393 (May 18, 1843).

113. *T&S* 5 (January 1, 1844): 395–96.

114. D&C 134:2, 7, 11.

115. D&C 101:76–78, 85–89.

116. *T&S* 5 (March 1, 1844): 456.

117. U.S. Constitution, Article IV, Sec. 4; "Public Meeting," *T&S* 5 (February 15, 1844): 441.

118. See also the discussion in Wood, "Prophet and the Presidency," 176–77, 180–85. *Views* quotes

from every inaugural address from Washington to Harrison, except for Van Buren, who was cited as the cause of the republic's decline. Tyler was called a president of perplexity.

119. *T&S* 5 (May 15, 1844): 528–33. The platform was published as a tract at Nauvoo in March and reprinted several times during the next two months, in Nauvoo and elsewhere (see Flake, *Mormon Bibliography,* 625–26). Besides the full text in *T&S,* cited above, *Views* is reprinted in Roberts, *Rise and Fall of Nauvoo,* 389–403, and (with minor editing and without some foreign language quotations) in *HC* 6:197–209. Useful commentaries are Poll, "Joseph Smith and the Presidency," and Hickman, "Political Legacy of Joseph Smith."

120. *T&S* 3 (July 1, 1842): 843.

121. *T&S* 3 (March 1, 1842): 722–23; (June 1, 1842): 808; Joseph Smith, Journal, 1842, kept by Willard Richards, December 30, 1842, Church Archives; "General Smith's Views on the Government," *T&S* 5 (May 15, 1844): 532.

122. Willard Richards to James Arlington Bennet, March 4, 1844, *HC* 6:231; Mosiah 29:26. Also, on reluctance, see Smith, *Words,* 325–26 (*HC* 6:243).

123. *HC* 5:286, expanded from Smith, *Words,* 166–67. See also his May 6, 1843, comments in Smith, *Words,* 199 (*HC* 5:384).

124. Woodruff, *Journal,* 2:349, February 8, 1844 (Smith, *Words,* 320; *HC* 6:210); commentary, *HC* 6:211 (from the *Neighbor*).

125. Garr, "Joseph Smith: Candidate," 164; Willard Richards to James Arlington Bennet, March 4, 1844, in *HC* 6:231; Joseph Smith to Henry Clay, May 13, 1844, *T&S* 5 (June 1, 1844): 547.

126. Richards to James Arlington Bennet, March 4, 1844, in *HC* 6:231.

127. *HC* 6:268–70; *T&S* 5 (April 15, 1844): 507.

128. Joseph Smith, Journal, 1843–44, kept by Willard Richards, January 29, 1843, Church Archives, spelling standardized; *HC* 6:188.

129. *T&S* 5 (April 15, 1844): 504–7 (*HC* 6:325, 334–40); *Neighbor,* April 24, 1844. Special emphasis was placed on New York (47 delegates), Ohio (41), Illinois (36), Tennessee (24), and Indiana (23). The delegates planned the national convention for Baltimore on July 13; the Twelve moved it to the nation's capital.

130. Robertson, "Campaign and the Kingdom," 149–50, 152–54, 158–65; Jacob E. Terry, Journal, May 29, June 24, 1844, Church Archives.

131. Minutes, state convention, *HC* 6:386–97; vice presidency, *HC* 6:231–22, 244, 248, 356.

132. Heber C. Kimball to Helen M. Kimball (his daughter), June 9, 1844, Kimball family correspondence, Church Archives, spelling standardized.

133. Sermon, April 9, 1844, *HC* 6:322.

134. Joseph Smith to Henry Clay, May 13, 1844, *T&S* 5 (June 1, 1844): 547–48.

CHAPTER 13. FOES WITHIN: THE CHURCH OF THE SECEDERS

Epigraph: "A Proclamation to the Saints Scattered Abroad," *T&S* 2 (January 15, 1841): 276–77 (*HC* 4:272–73).

1. See Joseph Smith, "The Temple," *T&S* 3 (May 2, 1842): 776 (*HC* 4:609). For this idea in scripture, see John 17:11; Romans 12:5; Galatians 3:28; 3 Nephi 26:19; 4 Nephi 1:3, 25; Moses 7:18; D&C 38:27; 42:30; 78:5.

2. "Proclamation to the Saints," *T&S* 2 (January 15, 1841): 277 (*HC* 4:273). The epigraph for

this chapter precedes this advice. The sentiment is expressed also in Eliza R. Snow's poem "Think Not, When You Gather to Zion" (*Hymns,* 1948, no. 21).

3. Smith, *Words,* 7; D&C 121:41–45.

4. Smith, *Words,* 347, 361.

5. See Flanders, *Nauvoo,* 242–43, 277, and all of chapter 9.

6. Jacob 2:23, 30; see also vv. 24–29.

7. Biblical references include Genesis 25:6; 26:5; Exodus 21:1, 7–11; Matthew 22:23–33; 1 Corinthians 11:11. Eternal marriage is defined in D&C 132:4–7, 15–20. The Prophet explained the answer he received concerning Matthew 22:30 during a Nauvoo city council meeting in June 1844. The minutes say: "He received for answer, 'Man in this life must marry in view of eternity, otherwise they must remain as angels, or be single in heaven.'"

8. B. H. Roberts, "Introduction to Volume V," *HC* 5:xxix-xxxii; D&C 132:1–3, 34–39 and cross-references to the Old Testament from these verses.

9. On the 1831 revelation, see D&C 132 heading; Orson Pratt, *MS* 40 (December 16, 1878): 787–88; Joseph Bates Noble, *MS* 45 (July 16, 1883): 454; W. W. Phelps to Brigham Young, August 12, 1861, Brigham Young Papers, Church Archives; Bachman, "Study of . . . Plural Marriage," 56, 68–70; and Bachman, "New Light on an Old Hypothesis," 21–26. See also the discussion on marriage in chapter 10 of this volume.

10. Orson Pratt, discourse, October 7, 1869, *JD* 13 (1871): 193; and Bachman, "Study of . . . Plural Marriage," 56–57. In 1889, using data supplied by church spokesmen, Hubert Howe Bancroft offered as "the orthodox and authorized explanation" of the origins of plural marriage facts similar to those outlined above (Bancroft, *History of Utah,* 161–62).

11. Mosiah Hancock, "Autobiography," Church Archives, 61–63; Cannon and Cook, *Far West Record,* 167–68; Compton, "Fannie Alger Smith Custer," 175–76, 188–90; Bachman, "Study of . . . Plural Marriage," 81–82.

12. Jenson, "Plural Marriage," 233; Anderson and Faulring, "The Prophet Joseph Smith," 75. That possible second plural wife is Lucinda Pendleton Morgan Harris, the widow of anti-Masonic campaigner William Morgan.

13. Bachman, "Study of . . . Plural Marriage," 78; Compton, "Fanny Alger Smith Custer," 199–202; Joseph F. Smith, discourse, July 7, 1878, *JD* 20 (1880): 29; Cannon and Cook, *Far West Record,* 167–68 and 171 n. 18.

14. Compton, "Fanny Alger Smith Custer," 181 and 181 n. 23. The "Article on Marriage" (*HC* 2:246–47) appeared in the D&C as section 101 between 1835 and 1876 and was removed when section 132 was added.

15. "Plural Marriage," *MS* 45 (July 16, 1883): 454; Snow, *Biography of Lorenzo Snow,* 69–70; Bachman, "Study of . . . Plural Marriage," 74–75; Mary Elizabeth Lightner, "Remarks," April 14, 1905, typescript, BYU Library.

16. Lightner, "Remarks," April 14, 1905, BYU Library. Most reminiscent accounts suggest that the angel commanded Joseph Smith to enter the practice himself. Some imply that he was to involve others in order to establish the doctrine and practice within the church. See Joseph F. Smith, discourse, July 7, 1878, *JD* 20 (1880): 28–29; Zina D. H. Smith, remarks, December 23, 1894, in *Collected Discourses* 5 (1896–1898): 31–32.

17. Joseph Bates Noble, "Plural Marriage," *MS* 45 (July 16, 1883): 454. Andrew Jenson identified twenty-seven wives; Bachman, thirty one; and Anderson and Faulring, twenty-nine (Jenson, "Plural Marriage," 219; Bachman, "Study of . . . Plural Marriage," 111–15; Anderson and Faulring, "The Prophet Joseph Smith," 72).

18. Mary Elizabeth Lightner, "Remarks," April 14, 1905, typescript, BYU Library. A Statement

of Lucy Meserve Smith, May 18, 1892, in Emily Smith Stewart Papers, University of Utah, says Emma served as midwife for the birth of a child of a plural wife of Joseph Smith. Other claims are summarized in Bachman, "Study of . . . Plural Marriage," 136–42; and Anderson and Faulring, "The Prophet Joseph Smith," 83.

19. Brigham Young, discourse, July 14, 1855, *JD* 3 (1856): 266.

20. For preliminary lists of the wives and marriage dates of known Nauvoo plural marriages, see Smith, "Nauvoo Roots of Mormon Polygamy," 37–72.

21. Wilford Woodruff's manifesto ending new plural marriages is dated September 24, 1890. It was accepted by a general conference two weeks later and is published in the Doctrine and Covenants as Official Declaration 1.

22. Examples can be found in Holzapfel and Holzapfel, *Women of Nauvoo,* 97–101; and Bachman, "Study of . . . Plural Marriage," 144–56. See also *JD* 20 (1880): 28–29.

23. D&C 110:1–15; 132:4; Wilford Woodruff, in Smith, *Words,* 200, and compare 81; D&C 128:21.

24. D&C 131:1–4; 132:19.

25. Smith, *Words,* 216, June 24, 1843; 232–33, July 16, 1843, afternoon sermon. For reactions, see Wilford Woodruff to parents, July 25, 1845, Church Archives; and James Jones to Henry Jones, June 10, 1844, Church Archives.

26. Clayton, *Journals,* 110, July 12, 1843; *HC* 5:500–501; D&C 132:37, 51–66.

27. Clayton, *Journals,* 110, July 12–13, 1843; Bachman, "Study of . . . Plural Marriage," 59–61.

28. D&C 132:52, 62; see also vv. 53–54, 61, and 63–65.

29. Helen M. Whitney, *Plural Marriage as Taught by the Prophet Joseph,* 11–12; Joseph L. Robinson, Journal, typescript, 12–13, Church Archives; George A. Smith, sermon, March 18, 1855, *JD* 2 (1855): 217–19; Bachman, "Study of . . . Plural Marriage," 203–4. Whitney cites an 1841 sermon; Smith places it in 1843. Robinson's account parallels Smith's in details. These reminiscent accounts may be referencing the Prophet's sermons of May 16, 1841 (Smith, *Words,* 72–74) and July 16, 1843 (Smith, *Words,* 232).

30. Orson Pratt, discourse, October 7, 1869, *JD* 13 (1871): 194; Hill, *Joseph Smith,* 348–49, 352–54; Bachman, "Study of . . . Plural Marriage," 157–67.

31. Cook, *William Law,* 23–25; Roberts, *Succession in the Presidency,* 122–25.

32. These numbers are from a comprehensive but tentative study by Smith, "Nauvoo Roots of Mormon Polygamy," 13–16, 37–72. We have reduced Smith's listing of forty-three marriages for Joseph Smith to reflect recent research by Todd Compton, Richard Anderson, and Scott Faulring. For Kimball and Young, we have used Kimball, *Heber C. Kimball,* 307–16; Kimball, "Heber C. Kimball and Family," 460–61, 479; and Arrington, *Brigham Young,* 420–21.

33. Whitney, *Life of Heber C. Kimball,* 439–40; John Taylor, *Deseret Evening News,* December 9, 1879; Bachman, "Study of . . . Plural Marriage," 124–26, 134–35; Widtsoe, *Joseph Smith,* 240; Hill, "Secular or Sectarian History?" 95. The latest evaluation confirms that Joseph Smith was sealed to eight women who continued to live with an existing husband (Anderson and Faulring, "The Prophet Joseph Smith," 81–82).

34. Smith, "Nauvoo Roots of Mormon Polygamy," 2 n. 4.

35. *T&S* 3 (April 15, 1842): 763.

36. *HC* 5:12; *T&S* 3 (June 15 and July 1, 1842): 830, 839–42. Joseph Smith replaced Bennett as mayor on May 19. Wilson Law became the major general of the Legion in August by a small majority over Lyman Wight.

37. Bachman, "Study of . . . Plural Marriage," 248–52; *Wasp,* September 24, December 3, 1842.

38. Pratt to John Van Cott, May 7, 1843, Church Archives. For similar reactions, see Mary Ann

Fullmer to Elizabeth C. Price, September 24, 1842, John S. Fullmer Letterbook, 169–71, Church Archives; and Newel K. Whitney to Samuel F. Whitney, October 5, 1842, Whitney Collection, BYU Library.

39. *T&S* 3 (July 1, 1842): 839–40; *Wasp,* June 25, July 27, 1842; *HC* 5:35–36.

40. *T&S* 3 (July 1, 1842): 840–41; *HC* 5:37–38.

41. *HC* 5:38–39, 42–44; Smith, *Words,* 126–27.

42. *HC* 5:40; *Wasp,* May 21, 1842; Wandle Mace, Autobiography, 98–99, Church Archives.

43. *T&S* 3 (July 1, 1842): 842; *Wasp,* June 25, 1842; D&C 124:16–17.

44. *Wasp,* July 27, 1842, quoting *Sangamo Journal.* Bennett's role in the Boggs case is outlined in chapter 11 of this volume.

45. England, *Orson Pratt,* 77–86; *Wasp,* Extra, July 27, 1842; Orson Pratt, *MS* 40 (December 16, 1878): 788. For other instances of adultery influenced by Bennett, see affidavits in *Neighbor,* May 29, 1844.

46. E. Malin to Edward Hunter, September 14, 1842, Edward Hunter Collection, BYU Library.

47. *Wasp,* September 24, 1842; reproduced in Pratt, *Journals,* 182–83.

48. *T&S* 4 (December 1, 1842): 28, from *Baltimore Clipper;* Freeman Nickerson to Albert Nickerson, November 4, 1842, Church Archives.

49. *T&S* 3 (September 1, 1842): 909, citing D&C 101 (1835).

50. Udney Hay Jacob, *An Extract. From a Manuscript Entitled The Peace Maker; or The Doctrines of the Millennium. . . .* (Nauvoo, Ill.: J. Smith, Printer, 1842); *T&S* 4 (December 1, 1842): 32. For additional information, see Foster's speculative exploration of the purposes and authorship of the pamphlet, "A Little-Known Defense of Polygamy," 23–34; Godfrey, "New Look at the Alleged Little Known Discourse," 49–53.

51. Jenson, "Plural Marriage," 225–27; Bachman, "Study of . . . Plural Marriage," 262–63.

52. Robinson to Joseph Smith III, December 29, 1873, in *The Return* 1 (December 1889): 174–75.

53. *HC* 6:81. The accused was William Henry Harrison Sagers (*HC* 2:35, 185; 3:38; 4:413, 429; 6:333).

54. John S. Fullmer to George D. Fullmer, July 8, 1842, John S. Fullmer Letterbook, 164, Church Archives.

55. *T&S* 4 (March 15, 1843): 143.

56. The revelation on eternal marriage clearly distinguished between adultery and the righteous union of a couple (see D&C 132: 41–44, 48, 59–63).

57. *Signal,* February 7, 1844 (noted in *HC* 6:210, which credits Wilson Law as author); reprinted in a shortened version in the *Burlington Hawkeye.* A second poem appeared in the *Signal* on April 25, 1844.

58. *T&S* 5 (February 1, 1844): 423 and (March 15, 1844): 474; D&C 131:2.

59. *T&S* 5 (April 1, 1844): 490.

60. Madsen, *In Their Own Words,* 17, 202.

61. Cook, *William Law,* 5–6.

62. Lucy Mack Smith, *History,* 240–43; CES, *Church History in the Fulness of Times,* 173–78; Brigham Young and Willard Richards to Reuben Hedlock, May 3, 1844, *HC* 6:354. Like Young, Fielding noted that some "revolted from the Church, saying that Joseph was fallen, the same as all the apostates have said," and then listed Warren Parrish, Oliver Cowdery, Martin Harris, and Isaac Russell as examples. (Fielding, "Nauvoo Journal," 146).

63. Cook, *William Law,* 11–22.

64. Cook, *William Law,* 21–29, 46–48, 52–53; *HC* 6:408–11, 427.

65. *T&S* 5 (April 15, 1844): 511.
66. *HC* 6:356–57.
67. *HC* 4:287, 296.
68. *T&S* 5 (May 15, 1844): 543; *HC* 7:57–58.
69. Lucy Mack Smith, *History,* 321; *HC* 6:272, 435–36.
70. *Signal,* June 1, 1844; *HC* 5:400. Jackson also claimed to be a Catholic priest (*HC* 5:394).
71. *HC* 6:278–80; Lucy Mack Smith, *History,* 320–22; Cummings, "Conspiracy of Nauvoo," 251–60; Dennison L. Harris, Statement, Church Archives.
72. *Signal,* April 24, 1844; *HC* 6:240–41, 332–33.
73. *HC* 6:344–46, 348, 350, 355.
74. *HC* 6:346–47, 354. The church is named in Charles A. Foster to editor, *St. Louis Daily Evening Gazette,* June 12, 1844.
75. *Signal,* May 15, 1844; *Expositor,* June 7, 1844, Resolution No. 10; Godfrey, "Non-Mormon Views of the Martyrdom," 13.
76. *HC* 4:273.
77. *Neighbor,* June 12, 1845; Smith, *Words,* 367, May 12, 1844 (*HC* 6:364).
78. *Signal,* June 12, 1844; *T&S* 5 (May 15, 1844): 535.
79. *Signal,* May 15, 1844; P. P. Pratt to Joseph Smith and Orson Spencer, May 3, 1844, reporting the charges circulated in Richmond, Massachussetts, by Augustine Spencer, in *HC* 6:354–55.
80. H. H. Bliss to Franklin Bliss, July 8, 1844, Indiana University, in Shipps, "A Little Known Account," 390.
81. *HC* 6:357–61.
82. Cook, *William Law,* 52–53.
83. *HC* 6:405, 412–15; *Signal,* May 29, 1844.
84. Huntress, "Governor Thomas Ford and the Murderers of Joseph Smith," 47; Oaks, "Suppression of the *Nauvoo Expositor,*" 891–97.
85. *HC* 6:357, 363; Waller, "Some Half-Forgotten Towns in Illinois," 67; *Signal,* May 22, 1844; Cook, *William Law,* 55.
86. *Expositor,* Resolution No. 10; *Signal* announcement, quoted in *New York Daily Tribune,* June 5, 1844. Almon Babbitt argued in January 1845 that "the press in Nauvoo was established for political purposes by the Whigs" (*Neighbor,* March 5, 1845 [*CHC* 2:485]).
87. Oaks, "Suppression of the *Nauvoo Expositor,*" 868–73; *Expositor,* June 7, 1844.
88. *HC* 6:473–79; Nathan C. Cheney to Charles Beebe, June 28, 1844, Church Archives.
89. *HC* 6:430, 432. The proceedings were reported in Nauvoo, City Council, Minutes, June 8 and 10, 1844, Church Archives, and published in *Neighbor,* June 19, 1844 (*HC* 6:432–49).
90. Synopsis of city council proceedings, *HC* 6:435, 441–42. The Prophet's words here echo his teaching of the principle of eternal marriage covenants on July 16, 1843 (Smith, *Words,* 232).
91. *HC* 6:435–42.
92. *HC* 6:433–34, 443–49, 470, 484–85, 534; Joseph Smith to Thomas Ford, June 22, 1844, in *HC* 6:539.
93. Firmage and Mangrum, *Zion in the Courts,* 109, 111.
94. *HC* 1:374, 390–91; Schindler, *Orrin Porter Rockwell,* 124; Oaks, "Suppression of the *Nauvoo Expositor,*" 874. Prior to this final attack, three of Lovejoy's presses had been destroyed between 1835 and 1837. In March 1846, a former Ohio legislator sledge-hammered the press of the *Eaton Democrat* and tossed the cases into the street, an event duly noted in Nauvoo (*Hancock Eagle,* April 10, 1846).

95. *Signal,* June 12, 1844; quoted in *Daily Evening Gazette* (St. Louis), July 12, 1844; Rigdon to Ford, June 14, 1844, *HC* 6:470.

96. *HC* 6:453–61, 487–91, 494; Vilate Kimball to Heber C. Kimball, June 9, 1844, addendum of June 11, in Esplin, "Life in Nauvoo," 234.

97. *HC* 6:495; *Daily Evening Gazette* (St. Louis), June 12, 1844.

98. *HC* 6:496, reprinting editorial in *Neighbor,* Extra, of June 17.

99. "Retributive Justice," *Neighbor,* June 12, 1844 (*HC* 6:460).

100. Jacob Gates, Journals, following entry for May 16, 1844, Church Archives.

101. *Signal,* June 12, 1844; *HC* 6:451–52, 462–63, 480–81, 492, 502–3; *CHC* 7:123.

102. Matthias Cowley remembered his father's expulsion from Warsaw (Reminiscences [1856], Church Archives); James Robbins to Leanna Robbins, June 16, 1844, Church Archives, punctuation and capitalization standardized.

103. *Signal,* June 12, 1844; *HC* 6:462–66, 481; Sarah D. Gregg to Thomas Gregg, June 14, 1844, Illinois State Historical Society, copy at Church Archives; mayor's proclamation, June 11, 1844, in *HC* 6:449.

104. Sidney Rigdon to Thomas Ford, June 14, 1842, Rigdon Collection, Church Archives; *HC* 6:479–86, 492–93; 7:13–18; Anson Call, Statement, 1848, re June 15, 1844, journal entry, Church Archives.

105. *HC* 6:514–15; Robert Crookston, Autobiography, 8, Church Archives.

106. Martial law, *HC* 6:497; H. H. Bliss to Franklin Bliss, July 8, 1844, Indiana University, in Shipps, "A Little Known Account," 392, spelling standardized.

107. George Laub, Reminiscences, 48–51, Church Archives.

108. Schindler, *Orrin Porter Rockwell,* 126; *HC* 6:497, citing *Signal,* Extra, June 17.

109. *HC* 6:499–500; cf. George Laub, Reminiscences, 48–51, Church Archives; Joseph G. Hovey, 9–10, Church Archives; and Smith, *Words,* 383–84. The quoted material from the *History of the Church,* including Hovey's, is based on oral reminiscences compiled in Utah.

110. *HC* 6:505, 524; Taylor, Reminiscences of Martyrdom Time, Church Archives; St. Louis report, reprinted in *Signal,* June 22, 1844.

111. *Daily Evening Gazette* (St. Louis), June 17, 1844; Vilate Kimball to Heber C. Kimball, June 9, 1944, addendum of June 24, in Esplin, "Life in Nauvoo," 235; *Neighbor,* June 19, 1844.

112. *Signal,* June 12, 1844; *HC* 6:452.

113. *HC* 6:519, 486–87, 494, 532. Hyrum's letter was dated June 17. Vilate Kimball recorded the indecision about sending the letters to the Twelve (Vilate Kimball to Heber C. Kimball, June 9, 1844, addendum of June 24, published in Esplin, "Life in Nauvoo," 236).

114. *HC* 6:507, 517–18, 528, 532. For typical comments on the weather and bridges, see Vilate Kimball to Heber C. Kimball, June 9, 1844, in Esplin, "Life in Nauvoo, June 1844," 234.

115. *HC* 6:471, 479, 487, 497, 502–3, 507, 517–18.

116. Godfrey, "Non-Mormon Views of the Martyrdom," 14.

117. *HC* 6:521–22. Bernhisel and Taylor left on Friday, June 21; Lucien Woodworth followed the next day with additional documents and a longer letter of explanation from the Prophet (*HC* 6:525–27). It was at this point that Smith assigned Thomas Bullock to set up an office in the Masonic Hall and collect affidavits documenting reported threats against Nauvoo (*HC* 6:494).

118. *HC* 6:526.

119. Thomas Ford to Mayor and City Council, June 22, 1844, in *Signal,* June 29, 1844 (*HC* 6:533–37). Judge Jesse B. Thomas had earlier advised the Prophet to resolve the *Expositor* issue before a court outside Nauvoo (*HC* 6:479). A legal analysis in 1965 supported the city council's

decisions as consistent with the law except in destroying the printing press (Oaks, "Suppression of the *Nauvoo Expositor*," 877–97).

120. Vilate Kimball to Heber C. Kimball, June 9, 1844, addendum of June 24, in Esplin, "Life in Nauvoo, June 1844," 235.

121. Allen, *Trials of Discipleship*, 139; *HC* 6:545–47.

122. Unsigned editorial comment, "Pacific Innuendo," in *T&S* 5 (February 15, 1844): 442–43.

123. Taylor, *John Taylor Papers*, 1:77; *HC* 6:540. We have used the interpretation in the *Taylor Papers* (except for its timing) rather than the account in Cannon, *Life of John Taylor*, 125, as cited in *HC* 6:545n.

124. *HC* 6:538–41.

125. *HC* 6:540–41.

126. *HC* 6:540–41.

127. *HC* 6:547–48.

128. Allen, *Trials of Discipleship*, 139; Smith, Diary, June 22, 1844.

129. *HC* 6:548.

130. Joseph Smith to Emma Smith, June 23, 1844, in Smith, *Personal Writings*, 616, spelling standardized.

131. *HC* 6:548–50; Fielding, "Nauvoo Journal of Joseph Fielding," ed. Ehat, 150; Vilate Kimball to Heber C. Kimball, June 9, 1844, addendum of June 24, in Esplin, "Life in Nauvoo," 235.

132. Taylor, *John Taylor Papers*, 1:78; *HC* 6:550–52.

133. Vilate Kimball to Heber C. Kimball, June 9, 1844, addendum of June 24, Church Archives, in Esplin, "Life in Nauvoo, June 1844," 235.

134. *HC* 6:551–54.

135. Those charged with riot for destroying the *Nauvoo Expositor* press (*HC* 6:453) were Joseph Smith, Hyrum Smith, Samuel Bennett, John Taylor, William W. Phelps, John P. Greene, Stephen C. Perry, Dimick B. Huntington, Jonathan Dunham, Stephen Markham, William W. Edwards, Jonathan Holmes, Jesse P. Harmon, John Lytle, Joseph W. Coolidge, Harvey D. [David Harvey (*HC* 6:554)] Redfield, Orrin P. Rockwell, and Levi Richards.

136. Reported in Dan Jones to Thomas Bullock, January 20, 1855, in Jones, "The Martyrdom," 96 (*HC* 6:554). In his 1847 Welsh pamphlet, Jones remembered these words as "'Oh, city, once the most blessed, but now the most pitiful in sadness. This is the kindest and most godly people and most beloved by Heaven of all the world. Oh, if only they knew what awaits them'" (Jones, "The Martyrdom," 86). Robert Crookston said that "Joseph's horse was a pacer and the other three [ridden by Hyrum Smith, John Taylor, and Willard Richards] were trotters. He rode his horse in a kingly manner" (Crookston, Autobiography, 8, Church Archives).

137. *HC* 6:554–59; 7:14–16; Jones, "The Martyrdom," 96–97.

138. *HC* 6:555–58. The number of arms surrendered is discussed in Thomas Ford, address to General Assembly, December 23, 1844, found in *Signal*, January 8 and 15, 1845.

139. Personal arms were stored in a warehouse at Smith's request (Oliver B. Huntington Diary, typescript, 1:45, USHS Library).

140. *HC* 6:555, 558; Joseph G. Hovey, Reminiscences, 10, Church Archives; Fielding, "Nauvoo Journal," 151.

141. *HC* 6:557–60; 7:18; Stephen C. Perry, Statement, 6–8, Church Archives.

142. *HC* 6:559–60, 563; 7:20.

CHAPTER 14. "JOSEPH AND HYRUM ARE DEAD"

Epigraph: T&S 5 (July 1, 1844): 575.

1. Godfrey, "Non-Mormon Views of the Martyrdom," 14; *HC* 6:561–62.

2. Jones, "The Martyrdom," 97–98; *HC* 6:566, 569.

3. *HC* 6:563–64; witness Cyrus Wheelock to George A. Smith, December 29, 1854, Church Archives; confirmed by Stephen C. Perry, Statement (ca. 1888), 9–10, Church Archives.

4. *HC* 6:564–65; William Clayton to Joseph Smith, June 26, 1844, in *HC* 6:598–99; *Signal,* January 22, 1845.

5. Dan Jones's testimony placed the hearing at the hotel (Jones, "The Martyrdom," 87), and Stephen C. Perry remembered the guards (Statement [ca. 1888], 11, Church Archives).

6. *HC* 6:567–69.

7. *HC* 6:569–73. The Prophet's attorneys asked Ford to bring in a military guard from outside Hancock County.

8. *HC* 6:573–74; Jones, "The Martyrdom," 88, 98; Godfrey, "Return to Carthage," 10. Those with Joseph and Hyrum at this time included Stephen Markham, Dan Jones, Willard Richards, John Taylor, John P. Greene, John S. Fullmer, Lorenzo D. Wasson, and Dr. [Wall] Southwick.

9. *HC* 6:575; Godfrey, "Non-Mormon Views of the Martyrdom," 16.

10. Thomas had advised the Prophet to take the *Expositor* case to a non-Latter-day Saint, meaning the justice who had issued the writ, but Smith used Squire Wells. Anson Call carried Smith's letter to Judge Thomas and conveyed the rejection note to Emma Smith (*HC* 6:413, 479, 590–91; 7:92; Call, Statement, 1848, regarding June 15, 1844, journal entry, Church Archives).

11. *HC* 6:600, 596, 598; Robert Crookston, Autobiography, 10, Church Archives; Isaac Haight, Journal, 13, University of Utah. The five representing the *Expositor* owners were Chauncey L. Higbee, O. C. Skinner, Thomas Sharp, Sylvester Emmons, and Thomas Morrison. Along with Babbitt, Skinner and his colleague William A. Richardson had helped Smith in May; both joined the defense in the murder case, along with Calvin A. Warren and O. H. Browning (*HC* 6:513; 7:50).

12. *HC* 6:563, 569, 575–86; Huntress, "Governor Thomas Ford," 48–49.

13. *HC* 6:592–93, 602; Godfrey, "Remembering the Deaths," 311–13; Jones, "The Martyrdom," 89, 99.

14. *HC* 6:593–95. Dan Jones says it was Stigall [Steigle] who insisted that Joseph Smith lock arms with the mob member for protection (Jones, "The Martyrdom," 88).

15. *HC* 6:595–98.

16. *HC* 6:599–601; Jones, "The Martyrdom," 89, 101; Jessee, "Return to Carthage," 14.

17. Smith, *Personal Writings,* 629–30; *HC* 6:605, 616.

18. Jones, "The Martyrdom," 102–3.

19. Stephen Markham to Wilford Woodruff, June 20, 1856, Church Archives; *Signal,* January 15, 1845; *HC* 6:605–6; cf. Littlefield, *Martyrs,* 72–73; Jessee, "Return to Carthage," 14.

20. *Signal,* January 15, 1845; *HC* 6:606.

21. Solomon Wixom, Diary and Reminiscences, 12, Church Archives.

22. *HC* 7:140–41; Littlefield, *Martyrs,* 75–76, ostensibly quoting William Daniels; Huntress, "Governor Thomas Ford," 51–52.

23. Smith, *Personal Writings,* 629–30; *HC* 6:605, 610–11.

24. *HC* 6:606–7; Isaac Haight, Journal, 13, University of Utah; Godfrey, "Non-Mormon Views of the Martyrdom," 15–16.

25. *HC* 6:606, 616; Samuel O. Williams to John A. Pricket, July 10, 1844, Chicago Historical Society, copy in Church Archives.

26. *HC* 6:613–14; Jones, "The Martyrdom," 90–91, 103–4; Smith to Browning, June 27, 1844, Community of Christ Archives, copy, Church Archives.

27. *HC* 6:623–24; cf. Jones, "The Martyrdom," 104–5.

28. Cyrus Wheelock to George A. Smith, December 29, 1854, Church Archives. John S. Fullmer said he smuggled the single-shot pistol into the jail in his boot on June 26 (Fullmer to George A. Smith, November 27, 1854, Church Archives). In 1855, Dan Jones said that he had provided Joseph with "one little bulldog" during a visit on June 25 and that Wheelock smuggled the revolver into the jail in his boot (Jones, "The Martyrdom," 97, 98–99). We have ignored the reminiscence of Jones as being less reliable. See also Jessee, "Return to Carthage," 7–9, 14.

29. *HC* 6:607–8.

30. *HC* 6:608–9.

31. *HC* 6:609–10.

32. Hicks, "'Strains Which Will Not Soon Be Allowed to Die,'" 393–400; *HC* 7:101; 6:614–15. According to Hicks, the tradition that Joseph requested the hymn (*HC* 7:615) reflects popular belief in the 1850s, when this part of the *History of the Church* was being compiled. The hymn later became known by its opening line, "A Poor Wayfaring Man of Grief" (*Hymns,* 1985, no. 29).

33. *HC* 6:614–16; 7:101.

34. "Life of Henry Day," Church Archives.

35. *HC* 6:8; 7:143.

36. Godfrey, "Non-Mormon Views of the Martyrdom," 15–16.

37. John L. Butler, Autobiography (1859), 46, Church Archives; D&C 135:1. Littlefield described it as "wet powder" (*Martyrs,* 77). Although most sources agree on the "blackened" faces, some contemporary writers report the use of black, red, and yellow paint in imitation of Indian face painting ("Journal and Letters of Rhoda Richards," June 27, 1844, Richards Family Collection, Church Archives; Albert Brown to Amos L. Underwood, November 11, 1844, Church Archives; and John Gooch, compiler (for Freeman Nickerson), *Death of the Prophets.* In 1894, M. B. Darnell described the paint as "a sort of brown color" or "a kind of Indian color" ("Tragedy at Carthage," 3).

38. Driggs, "Visits to Carthage," 320–21; Samuel O. Williams to John A. Pricket, July 10, 1844, Chicago Historical Society, copy in Church Archives.

39. Samuel O. Williams to John A. Pricket, July 10, 1844, Chicago Historical Society, copy in Church Archives. Apparently, one young guard was not in on the conspiracy and resisted the attack (Godfrey, "Non-Mormon Views of the Martyrdom," 16).

40. Daniels, *Correct Account of the Murder;* also in Littlefield, *Martyrs,* 80–81; Oaks and Hill, *Carthage Conspiracy,* 89–90, 164–68; Jessee, "Return to Carthage," 5, 14–18. For individual responses to Daniels's claims, see Albert Brown to Amos L. Underwood, November 11, 1844, Church Archives, and Edson Whipple to E. Whipple, November 29, 1844, Church Archives.

41. Interview with Driggs, "Visits to Carthage," 321–22; Oaks and Hill, *Carthage Conspiracy,* 21.

42. Except as noted, the story which follows is based on Richards's account, "Two Minutes in Jail," *T&S* 5 (August 1, 1844): 598–99; from other information in *HC* 6:617–21, 627; and John Taylor's account in *HC* 7:102–6.

43. Richards and many other Latter-day Saints believed guards had fired into the air as a warning

shot to the mob (see Isaac Haight, Journal, 13, University of Utah). Others cite the use of blanks (Driggs, "Visits to Carthage," 321), or both (Thomas L. Barnes [non-LDS] to Miranda Haskett, November 1, 1897, in "Carthage Jail Physician Testifies," 51; George Laub, Reminiscences, 52, Church Archives).

44. Dan Jones and Stephen Markham had hewed at the edge of the warped door for half a day on Wednesday with their penknives trying to get the latch to hold (Jones, "The Martyrdom," 98–99; *HC* 6:592).

45. The two pistols and Markham's cane are preserved at the Museum of Church History and Art. In 1855, Dan Jones said that on June 25 he left behind the switch—a black hickory club—used by Taylor (Jones, "The Martyrdom," 97).

46. A study by Joseph L. Lyon and David W. Lyon helped us sort through contradictory information to reach this interpretation ("Observations on the Physical Evidence at the Carthage Jail," unpublished article in author's possession). Later inspection of Hyrum's body showed that a ball had entered the right side of his back, passed through the body, and smashed against his vest pocket watch. Richards and Taylor believed this ball entered the window and struck the Patriarch about the time he was hit from the front. It is possible that a shot from some distance away could have hit him as described. The Lyons offer another plausible option, a shot fired through the doorway as Hyrum turned away after receiving the face wound.

47. Neal and Gayle Ord have gathered evidence suggesting this interpretation ("Artifacts of the Martyrdom," unpublished manuscript in author's possession).

48. The distress signal is reported in *T&S* 5 (July 15, 1844): 585 and D&C 135:1. It is discussed in Lambert, "Mormonism and Masonry: A Private Notebook," 100–117, Church Archives. Thomas Sharp's report was as follows: "Joe Smith raised the window, exclaimed 'O, my God' and threw himself out. He fell heavily on the ground and was soon dispatched" (*Signal,* June 29, 1844 [issued three days late]). See also Godfrey, "Non-Mormon Views of the Martyrdom," 16–17.

49. While reports tend to agree on four shots (some causing both entry and exit wounds), they differ in where the balls struck Joseph Smith and whether he was hit before or after falling to the ground. With minor adjustment and interpretation, we have followed information from those who prepared the bodies for burial (*HC* 6:627) after comparing the initial report of Willard Richards (*HC* 6:618 and 620) and a draft letter from Richards to Brigham Young, June 30, 1844, Richards Papers, Church Archives (also in Oaks and Hill, *Carthage Conspiracy,* 21). This last source is the only one that mentions the collarbone. There is no credence to Littlefield's distortion of William Daniels's report that all of the shots were fired execution-style on orders of Colonel Williams after Joseph was propped against the well (Littlefield, *Martyrs,* 79–81). See also the testimony of Thomas Dixon, cited in Jessee, "Return to Carthage," 17 n. 30.

50. Hamilton confirmed that shots from both inside and outside struck Joseph in the window (Driggs, "Visits to Carthage," 321). He and others said no shots or wounds were inflicted after the Prophet hit the ground (Oaks and Hill, *Carthage Conspiracy,* 21; M. B. Darnell, in *Deseret Weekly News,* March 17, 1894, reprinted in *Liahona* 8 [June 22, 1910]: 3–4). Darnell remembered that a young man struck Joseph with his bayonet or rifle butt. John Taylor was influenced by those who thought that both Hyrum and Joseph were shot again after they died (D&C 135:1). Some believed that Joseph jumped from the window unharmed, was stunned by the fall, and was propped up against the well and then shot (see Williams to Pricket, July 10, 1844; Isaac Haight, Journal, 13, University of Utah); this opinion was popularized in the Daniels account (Littlefield, *Martyrs,* 79–81).

51. Richards believed members of the mob had returned; he may have heard William Hamilton, whose visit is described.

52. Oaks and Hill, *Carthage Conspiracy*, 21.

53. John Taylor's watch, the hands now missing, is preserved at the Museum of Church History and Art.

54. *HC* 6:621–24. Years later, Barnes remembered finding the bodies in the jail before the midnight hour mentioned by Richards. Barnes said that Hyrum was upstairs and Joseph stretched out in the hall at the foot of the stairs, where he had been moved. Barnes claimed to have prompted Richards to write the first note to Nauvoo (Thomas L. Barnes to Miranda Haskett, November 1, 1897, in "Carthage Jail Physician Testifies," *Pioneer*, 51–53).

55. John Taylor's account (1856), *HC* 7:110–11.

56. *HC* 6:624–25.

57. Godfrey, "Non-Mormon Views of the Martyrdom," 19 n. 4 and 20 n. 39.

58. *HC* 6:624–26; Lewis Barney, Autobiography, 23, Church Archives; Samuel O. Williams to John A. Pricket, July 10, 1844, Chicago Historical Society, copy in Church Archives; Godfrey, "Non-Mormon Views of the Martyrdom," 18.

59. Barnes to Haskett, November 6, 1897, in "Carthage Jail Physician Testifies," 53; and *HC* 6:622 (but see the names in *HC* 7:142).

60. Joseph Millett Sr., "The first news of the Prophet's death to reach Nauvoo," March 13, 1898, Abraham Owen Woodruff Collection, BYU Library.

61. Arza Adams, Diary and Reminiscences, Church Archives, spelling standardized; *HC* 6:622.

62. Robert Crookston, of Macedonia, Autobiography, 10, Church Archives; Joseph E. Johnson to Benjamin Willson (written from Macedonia), July 3, 1844, Church Archives.

63. The use of white horses to pull the wagon and the location of the speech were noted in the diary of Zina Diantha Huntington Jacobs (Smith), in Beecher, "'All Things Move in Order in the City,'" 299, 293.

64. Wandle Mace, Autobiography (ca. 1890), 110, Church Archives, spelling standardized; Richards's comments, in William M. Allred, Reminiscences (1885), 10, Church Archives; *HC* 6:225–26.

65. Vilate Kimball to Heber C. Kimball, June 30, 1844, Church Archives, and published in Esplin, "Life in Nauvoo," 238; Sally Randall to friends, July 1, 1844, Church Archives, and published in Godfrey, Godfrey, and Derr, *Women's Voices*, 142.

66. "History of Sarah Studevant Leavitt (1875)," 23, University of Utah.

67. Zina Diantha Huntington Jacobs (Smith), Diary, June 28, 1844, Church Archives, published in Beecher, "'All Things Move in Order in the City,'" 293. Hyrum's clothing was preserved by the family; its current caretaker is Eldred G. Smith.

68. Cannon, *George Cannon, the Immigrant*, 131. The original castings, from the Wilford C. Wood collection, are now at the Museum of Church History and Art.

69. *HC* 6:627; Jones, "The Martyrdom," 108.

70. Almira Mack Covey to Harriet Mack Hatch Whittemore, July 18, 1844, Church Archives; Sarah M. Kimball to Sarepta Heywood, [late June 1844], Joseph L. Heywood Letters, Church Archives.

71. *HC* 6:627.

72. Barnett, "Canes of the Martyrdom," 205–11. The Dimick Huntington cane and one given to Sidney Rigdon are preserved at the Museum of Church History and Art. Others who owned canes made from the coffins were Wilford Woodruff, Heber C. Kimball, Willard Richards,

Newel Knight, and possibly Brigham Young. James Bird made two additional canes from wood left over from construction of the burial coffins.

73. Vilate Kimball to Heber C. Kimball, June 30, 1844, Church Archives, in Esplin, "Life in Nauvoo," 238, spelling standardized; Jones, "The Martyrdom," 108; *HC* 6:626–29.

74. Van Wagoner and Walker, "The Joseph/Hyrum Funeral Sermon," 9–18. The quoted portion (15) was recorded by Phelps in 1855 from memory and may reflect some ideas current at that time.

75. Jones, "The Martyrdom," 94.

76. *HC* 6:628; Zina Diantha Huntington Jacobs (Smith), Diary, June 29, 1844, Church Archives, in Beecher, "'All Things Move in Order in the City,'" 293, spelling standardized.

77. Joseph G. Hovey, Reminiscences, 11, Church Archives; Barnett, "Canes of the Martyrdom," 205–6, 209–10. The exact site was confirmed in a 1928 archaeological excavation (Bernauer, "Still 'Side by Side,'" 17–33).

78. Lucy Mack Smith, *History,* 325–27; *HC* 6:213, 215–22. In addition to the three sons who died in 1844 and William's wife, Caroline Grant, Lucy may have counted among the six family martyrs her husband, Joseph Sr., and their son Alvin.

79. As one example, confused reports appeared in the *New York Herald,* July 8, 1844 (copying *Quincy Herald,* June 28, and *Cincinnati Gazette,* July 3), with additional information on July 10 (from the *Quincy Whig,* Extra, June 28, and *St. Louis New Era,* June 29), and a report from Nauvoo on July 12 (from *Neighbor,* June 30).

80. *Morning Register,* July 10, 1844, in Ellsworth, "Mobocracy and the Rule of Law," 81.

81. Grimsted, "Rioting in Its Jacksonian Setting," 362; Ellsworth, "Mobocracy and the Rule of Law," 72–82; editorial, *New York Herald,* July 12, 1844.

82. *Albany Evening Journal,* July 9, 1844, cited in Ellsworth, "Mobocracy and the Rule of Law," 80.

83. Ford to W. W. Phelps, July 22, 1844, in *MS* 25 (February 14, 1863): 103–5, 119–21 (*HC* 7:203–8; *CHC* 2:302–7). Sharp's comments are in *Signal,* July 24, 1844.

84. Ellsworth, "Mobocracy and the Rule of Law," 79–81; *Hymns,* 1985, no. 27; D&C 135:7. John Taylor's statement (now D&C 135) was appended to the first European edition (Liverpool, 1845). In a gesture of reconciliation, editors altered Phelps's phrase in the 1927 and later editions of the Latter-day Saint hymnbook to read "Long shall his blood, which was shed by assassins, plead unto heaven" instead of " . . . stain Illinois" (Davidson, *Our Latter-day Hymns,* 56).

85. Matthias Cowley, Reminiscences (1856), 2–3, Church Archives; Jones, "The Martyrdom," 107.

86. The *Signal,* Extra, also claimed that Carthage had been burned and Ford killed (Jones, "The Martyrdom," 92, 105). The *Signal* of June 29 (issued three days late) had a correct account.

87. *Signal,* July 24 and 31 and September 25, 1844; Godfrey, "Non-Mormon Views of the Martyrdom," 12. Davis compiled his articles in a pamphlet published at St. Louis in August 1844.

88. James Robbins to Alexander Robbins, June 30, 1844, Church Archives.

89. Don Oscarson purchased the powder horn from an Illinois antiques dealer and later donated it to the Museum of Church History and Art.

90. This phrase echoes Marc Antony's reference to Julius Caesar as "the most noble blood" in Shakespeare's *Julius Caesar.*

91. *T&S* 5 (July 1, 1844): 575.

92. The poems are listed and discussed in Bitton, "The Martyrdom of Joseph Smith," 30, 34–37. Phelps's was published August 1, 1844, and Taylor's on January 1 and August 1, 1845.

93. See Bitton, "The Martyrdom of Joseph Smith," 35–37, for a discussion of the ideas of blood and sacrifice in the early poems.

94. *T&S* 5 (July 1, 1844): 562–68. For a defense of the idea that Joseph Smith may be called a religious martyr, see Bachman, "Joseph Smith, a True Martyr."

95. Kimball, *Diaries,* 73, entry for July 9, 1844, spelling standardized; Wilford Woodruff, *Journals,* July 17, 1844.

96. Louisa Follett, Diary, July 21, 1844, Church Archives, spelling standardized. Follett copied extracts from Eliza Snow's poem into her diary. Additional responses can be found in Bitton, "The Martyrdom of Joseph Smith," 33–34.

97. Invited were men from Adams, Marquette, Pike, Brown, Schuyler, Morgan, Scott, Cass, Fulton, and McDonough Counties. Ford also called up the regiments of a General Stapp's brigade (location unknown) and the Sangamon County militia.

98. *T&S* 5 (July 1, 1844): 564–65.

99. *T&S* 5 (July 1, 1844): 564–67.

100. Arza Adams, Diary and Reminiscences, June 29, 1844, Church Archives.

101. Thomas Holt (first letter, 1844), Church Archives.

102. Godfrey, "Non-Mormon Views of the Martyrdom," 13; *HC* 6:463–66.

103. H. H. Cooper, Reminiscences, *Deseret Evening News,* September 2, 1905.

104. Ford to Phelps, July 22, 1844, in *CHC* 2:204.

105. S. Holbrook to S. D. Cowles, July 1, 1844, Church Archives.

106. Ira Ames, Autobiography and Journal (1858), June 28, 1844, Church Archives. Similar reports are found in Nathan C. Cheney to Charles Beebe, June 28, 1844, Church Archives; and in Vilate Kimball to Heber C. Kimball, June 30, 1844, Church Archives.

107. Warren Foote, Autobiography and Journals, 73 (June 30, 1844), Church Archives.

108. Jones, "The Martyrdom," 92–93.

109. Ford to Phelps, July 22, 1844, in *CHC* 2:305–6.

110. *Signal,* July 31, 1844; Ford to Phelps, July 22, 1844, in *CHC* 2:302–5.

111. "History of Sarah Studevant Leavitt," 23, University of Utah; Ford to Phelps, July 22, 1844, in *CHC* 2:302.

112. George Alley to Joseph Alley III, July 27 and August 11, 1844, Church Archives. Similar sentiments are in Warren Foote, Autobiography and Journals, July 7, 1844, 73, Church Archives.

113. *Signal,* January 15, 1845; Ford to Phelps, July 22, 1844, in *CHC* 2:302–3.

114. The series appeared in the *Alton Telegraph* and was reprinted in the *Signal,* February 26, March 12 and 26, April 9 and 16, 1845; Pratt's article in the *Prophet,* February 15, 1845, "Great Secret Revealed," was cited in Hancock's last letter.

115. Hill and Oaks, *Carthage Conspiracy,* 32–33; Taylor, Remarks, Church Archives (an edited version appears in *CHC* 2:528–29).

116. Oaks and Hill, *Carthage Conspiracy,* 210–14.

117. *HC* 7:146. In 1845, William Clayton compiled a list of twenty apostates, most of them implicated in plotting or participating in the killings at Carthage ("History of the Nauvoo Temple," 46, Church Archives).

118. *HC* 7:163.

119. *HC* 7:142–45. Among those on Backenstos's list were *Signal* editor Thomas C. Sharp, *Quincy Whig* editor Sylvester M. Bartlett, Colonel Levi Williams, Mark Aldrich, attorneys Onias C. Skinner and Calvin A. Warren, coroner Thomas L. Barnes, Captain James E. Dunn, and Major W. B. Warren.

120. Ford to Phelps, July 22, 1844, in *CHC* 2:307.

121. *Signal,* September 25, 1844; Oaks and Hill, *Carthage Conspiracy,* 34–37; B. Powell to Wilson C. Sanders, October 6, 1844, Church Archives. The quoted passage is from B. A. Gallop, September 17, 1844, Church Archives, spelling standardized.

122. Apparently Ford received no volunteers from Rushville or from McDonough County but did receive support from fifty Green County men.

123. *Signal,* October 2, 9, 1844; Oaks and Hill, *Carthage Conspiracy,* 37–39; *HC* 7:274, 277. The troops arrived on September 24, and Ford three days later.

124. Oaks and Hill, *Carthage Conspiracy,* 34–42; *Signal,* October 2, 1844; *HC* 7:276–78.

125. *HC* 7:274; Thomas Ford, Agreement, September 30, 1844, Chicago Historical Society, copy at Church Archives; Oaks and Hill, *Carthage Conspiracy,* 38–42.

126. *Neighbor,* April 23 and May 7, 1845.

127. *Neighbor,* May 7, 1845; *HC* 7:406–7.

128. Brigham Young to Parley P. Pratt, May 26, 1845, Church Archives; Albert Brown to Amos L. Underwood, November 11, 1844, Church Archives.

129. *HC* 7:420–23. For a thorough account of the complicated trial, see Oaks and Hill, *Carthage Conspiracy.* See also Allen, *Trials of Discipleship,* 157–58.

130. William Huntington, Diary, May 26, 1845, 32, University of Utah, spelling standardized.

131. For a discussion of some of the inaccurate depictions of the later lives of the opponents, see Oaks and Hill, *Carthage Conspiracy,* 217–21; and Poulsen, "Fate and the Persecutors of Joseph Smith." The later religious involvements of some dissenters are noted in chapter 20 of this volume.

132. *HC* 6:488, 567–68.

133. Leonard Soby received a note for $100 and Charles Ivins notes for $513.75, $30, and $81.25, figures reached by independent appraisers (Nauvoo, City Council, Minutes, October 12, 1844, 220, Church Archives).

134. *HC* 7:483–85; *Signal,* November 12, 1845; Oaks and Hill, *Carthage Conspiracy,* 201; James M. Sharpe (land agent), Journal, October 23, 1844, Coe Collection, spelling standardized. The *Signal* incorrectly reported the trial as that of city councilmen who had ordered the abatement.

CHAPTER 15. "WHO SHALL LEAD THE CHURCH?"

Epigraph: Warren Foote, Autobiography, entry for June 28, 1844, Church Archives. The entry is retrospective and may reflect thoughts after this date.

1. D&C 124:91–96; *T&S* 5 (October 15, 1844): 683.

2. D&C 138:53; cf. 21:1–2; 27:13; Brigham Young, special meeting, August 8, 1844, *HC* 7:233.

3. The 1835 priesthood revelation authorized the Twelve to select "evangelical ministers" for the stakes through revelation. Office by lineal descent was interpreted to apply only to the general church patriarch (see D&C 107:39–40).

4. *New York Herald,* July 8, 10, 1844; Richards and Taylor to Reuben Hedlock, July 9, 1844, in *HC* 7:174. The saying expands upon Revelation 17:6.

5. D&C 130:15; Smith, *Words,* 179–81.

6. Lucy Mack Smith, *History,* 248, 291, 310, 325; D&C 122:9.

7. William I. Appleby, Autobiography (1848, incorporating entries from his diary), 114, Church Archives.

8. D&C 20:2–6; 28:1–7; 43:2–7; 46:8–29; *HC* 7:285–86.

9. Articles of Faith 5; D&C 20:60, 65. Verse 65 was added to the revelation later as a clarification. See also D&C 42:11; 102:3, 9; 107:22.

10. D&C 107:76, 39–40. That Hyrum's role in the church included a factor of lineage was intimated as early as April 1830 (D&C 23:3).

11. D&C 107:13–15, 63–68.

12. D&C 43:2–7. For additional information, see Esplin, "Joseph, Brigham and the Twelve," 301–41.

13. Helpful articles describing this process are *Encyclopedia of Mormonism*, s.v. "Succession in the Presidency," by Martin B. Hickman; and "Joseph, Brigham, and the Twelve," by Ronald K. Esplin.

14. Jan Shipps pointed out to me Weber's thesis identifying three ways through which claims to succession usually come: lineage, office, or charisma.

15. For example, see D&C 20:63–67; 28:12–13; 107:22. It was not until the end of the century that a distinction began to be made between "ordination" to priesthood office and "setting apart" to an administrative position (McConkie, *Mormon Doctrine*, 549). During the Nauvoo years, *ordain* was the common term for both procedures.

16. D&C 20:2–3; 21:1–5, 10–12.

17. D&C 28:1–7.

18. D&C 35:3–4, 17–20.

19. D&C 43:2–7; 90:4.

20. D&C 90:1–3.

21. D&C 81:1–2; headnote to 90 and v. 6; Smith, *Papers*, 1:21.

22. D&C 107:22, 91–92.

23. Smith, *Papers*, 1:20–21.

24. D&C 102:3, 9–11, 24–29.

25. Cannon and Cook, *Far West Record*, 71–73, 151, July 7, 1834; March 15, 1838. This evidence does not support Quinn's view that Whitmer was ordained secretly, setting a precedent for secret ordinations (Quinn, "Mormon Succession Crisis," 193–94). Both the Kirtland and the Clay County councils received the approval of a general council of high priests, and Whitmer was ordained in a conference of priesthood officers and members (Cannon and Cook, *Far West Record*, July 3, 7, 1834).

26. For a general discussion of the early options for succession in the presidency, see Durham and Heath, *Succession in the Church*, 1–12.

27. *T&S* 2 (February 1, 1841): 310 and (June 1, 1841): 428; also in D&C 124:94–95; see v. 124.

28. *T&S* 2 (June 1, 1841): 428–29 (D&C 124:94, 125–26; 132:7). Rigdon's ordination, *T&S* 2 (June 1, 1841): 431.

29. Clayton, *Journals*, 110, July 16, 1843; cf. *HC* 5:510; see also D&C 23:3.

30. D&C 124:91–93.

31. Smith, *Words*, 232, 234, 294 note 15; Smith, *Teachings*, 318; D&C 124:94–95.

32. D&C 107:23, 33, 35, 39.

33. D&C 107:8–9, 91.

34. D&C 107:8–9, 23, 33–34, 63–68; *HC* 2:373–74. The phrase which follows next, "and where I am not, there is no First Presidency over the Twelve," was added by compilers in 1852.

35. D&C 107:33, 58.

36. D&C 27:13; 107:35.

37. Esplin, "Joseph, Brigham, and the Twelve," 312–15, 19–20; *T&S* 5 (September 15, 1844): 651; Parley P. Pratt, "Proclamation," January 1, 1845, in *MS* 5 (March 1845): 151.

38. *T&S* 5 (September 15, 1844): 651. The words are those of Orson Hyde, speaking at the trial of Sidney Rigdon, September 4, 1844, recalling Joseph Smith's words. The same message is contained in Pratt, "Proclamation," *MS* 5 (March 1845): 151.

39. See Esplin, "Joseph, Brigham, and the Twelve," 319–20.

40. Pratt arrived before July 11 (*HC* 7:183).

41. D&C 124:103–9; *T&S* 5 (October 1, 1844): 666–67; *HC* 6:47–49.

42. Law's removal, *T&S* 5 (April 15, 1844): 511 (cf. *HC* 6:341); Lyman's 1843 calling, *T&S* 5 (October 1, 1844): 664 col. 2; meeting of the Twelve, August 12, 1844, *HC* 7:248; conference, October 7, 1844, *T&S* 5 (November 1, 1844): 692; see also *HC* 7:295 n.

43. *T&S* 5 (May 1, 1844): 522 (*HC* 6:287); *HC* 3:12; D&C 117:1–10. Marks was among the first endowed in 1842 and had been sealed to his wife in 1843 (see chapter 10 of this volume).

44. *HC* 7:183–84.

45. *HC* 7:212–13.

46. James Blakesley to Jacob Scott, August 16, 1844 (written before he received word of the action of the August 8 meeting), quoted in Smith, "Succession in the Presidency," 3–4.

47. *T&S* 5 (September 15, 1844): 649.

48. William Huntington, Diary, 19, August 4, 1844, University of Utah.

49. *HC* 7:223–27. According to one account, Parley P. Pratt intervened when Rigdon attempted to press for a vote on his proposal (Lewis Barney, Reminiscences [ca. 1888], 13, Church Archives).

50. *HC* 7:298; cf. *T&S* 5 (September 15, 1844): 652.

51. *HC* 7:238, 225; Heber C. Kimball, in *T&S* 5 (October 1, 1844): 663.

52. *HC* 7:223, 225–27; *T&S* 5 (September 15, 1844): 652. For more on the election, see chapter 16 of this volume.

53. Brigham Young to Vilate Young, August 11, 1844; *HC* 7:228–29.

54. *HC* 7:229; D&C 76:7–8; 100:9–11.

55. Quoted in *HC* 7:229.

56. *T&S* 5 (August 15, 1844): 618–20.

57. Young initially suggested Tuesday, August 13, for the meeting (*MS* 25:216), but at the conclusion of Rigdon's August 8 meeting, Young convened the special conference for that afternoon. B. H. Roberts unnecessarily speculates that the date in the *Millennial Star* was misprinted (*HC* 7:230 n).

58. Lewis Barney, Reminiscences (ca. 1888), 16, Church Archives.

59. *HC* 7:230.

60. Just before Rigdon's departure for Pittsburgh, William W. Phelps had invited Rigdon to meet with those who had been endowed, but Rigdon did not receive all available ordinances (Testimony of Heber C. Kimball, *T&S* 5 [October 1, 1844]: 663).

61. *HC* 7:232–36.

62. *HC* 7:236–39.

63. *HC* 7:234, 239–40.

64. *T&S* 5 (September 2, 1844): 638; Staines, quoted in *HC* 6:236n; Hovey, Reminiscences, 12, Church Archives.

65. *T&S* 5 (September 15, 1845): 650.

66. *HC* 7:234, 239–42.

67. Edward Hunter to his sister, July 16 [1844], Hunter Collection, BYU Library; Zilpha Williams to Samuel Cilley, July 13, 1845, Church Archives.

68. Calvin Reed to Plimpton Simonds, July 1845, Church Archives.

69. Henry and Catharine Brooke to Leonard Pickell, November 15, 1844, Yale University, copy at Church Archives.

70. Jesse C. Little to Brigham Young, December 30, 1844, Brigham Young Papers, Church Archives; John N. Harper, Autobiography (ca. 1861), 10, Church Archives. The experience is discussed by Harper, "The Mantle of Joseph." Jorgensen et al, "Mantle of the Prophet Joseph," chronicles numerous individual accounts.

71. Brigham Young, Diary, 1837–1845, August 8, 1844, Brigham Young Papers, Church Archives, spelling standardized.

72. Brigham Young to Vilate Young, August 11, 1844, Church Archives.

73. The expansion of these quorums is discussed in detail in chapter 16 of this volume.

74. See additional discussion of this point in chapter 16 of this volume.

75. *HC* 4:426; *T&S* 6 (April 15, 1845): 869–70.

76. Pratt, "Proclamation," *MS* 5 (March 1845): 151.

77. On August 12, 1844, the Twelve had admitted Lyman as a member of the quorum (*HC* 7:248), but that would have brought the membership to thirteen. At the October conference, Brigham Young explained that Lyman was "one of the Twelve, just in the same relationship as he sustained to the First Presidency. He is one in our midst and a counselor with us" (*HC* 7:295 and note). The following April, Lyman was "continued as one of the Twelve," as were the other apostles. Meantime, Lyman Wight was neither sustained nor specifically dropped from the quorum but allowed to "remain for the present" with the hope that he would in the future "hearken to counsel" (*T&S* 6 [April 15, 1845]: 870).

78. On Cowles, see *HC* 6:347, 398. See the list of those sustained in *T&S* 5 (November 1, 1844): 692 (*HC* 7:296).

79. *HC* 7:258 and see 269–70; William Huntington, Diary, 22, November 1844, University of Utah. Orson Hyde added other names to the list of schismatics: "The church [in Boston] is nearly free from the effects of Rigdonism, and nearly free from a worse malady, Adamsism and Ballism [George J. Adams and Joseph Ball]" (Orson Hyde to Bishop Whitney, Newel K. Whitney Collection, BYU Library).

80. *T&S* 5 (October 15, 1844): 682–83 (*HC* 7:285, 288). Young further explained his role as revelator at the April conference (*T&S* 6 [July 1, 1845] 953–54).

81. *T&S* 5 (August 15, 1844): 618.

82. James Monroe believed that Joseph Smith would reclaim the office of president at the Second Coming (Diary, April 24, 1845, Coe Collection).

83. Young's talk is reported in *T&S* 5 (October 15, 1844): 682–84 (*HC* 7:284–88).

84. *T&S* 5 (October 15, 1844): 288 (*HC* 7:288); 1 Corinthians 12:28; see D&C 112:30–32 for a comment on the keys shared by the First Presidency and Twelve, spelling standardized.

85. See D&C 20:1–4, 38; 21:1; cf. 27:8–13. Young's address is in *T&S* 5 (October 15, 1844): 684, and in *HC* 7:288.

86. *T&S* 5 (September 2, 1844): 638.

87. *T&S* 5 (November 1, 1844): 683, and *HC* 7:287–88.

88. *T&S* 5 (November 1, 1844): 691–92.

89. *T&S* 5 (October 15, 1844): 684.

90. *T&S* 5 (August 15, 1844): 619; (October 1, 1844): 668–69 (*HC* 7:250–51, 280–81).

91. John Melling, Anne Carr, and John Carr to Edward Martin, August 29, 1844, Edward Martin Correspondence, Church Archives.

92. *T&S* 5 (January 1, 1845): 761.

93. *Signal,* September 18, 1844, and earlier issues.

94. William Huntington, Diary, 21, University of Utah.

95. *HC* 5:242; Grant to Whitney, October 11, 1844, Whitney Collection, BYU Library, spelling standardized.

96. *HC* 7:266; William Huntington, Diary, 21, September 1, 1844, University of Utah; testimony of Young at Rigdon trial, *T&S* 5 (September 15, 1844): 648, corroborated by Parley Pratt, *T&S* 5 (September 15, 1844): 652.

97. James was disfellowshipped and the others excommunicated with Rigdon in September 1844 (*T&S* 5 [October 15, 1844]: 687). Bennett and Soby had been ordained prophets, priests, and kings by Rigdon.

98. Testimony of Taylor and Young at Rigdon trial, *T&S* 5 (October 1, 1844): 661, 664; and see Heber Kimball's comments, *T&S* 5 (October 1, 1844): 663.

99. Testimony of Amasa Lyman, *T&S* 5 (September 15, 1844): 655.

100. Testimony of Young, Hyde, and Pratt at Rigdon trial, *T&S* 5 (September 15, 1844): 648, 650, 652–53, and (October 1, 1844): 661.

101. Requirements for the council are defined in D&C 107:82–84. Complete minutes were published in *T&S* 5 (September 15, October 1, 15, 1844): 647–55, 660–67, 685–87. A short extract appears in *HC* 7:268–69, reproducing verbatim a manuscript in the Rigdon Collection, Church Archives. Jedediah M. Grant published the minutes in his *Collection of Facts, Relative to the Course Taken by Elder Sidney Rigdon. . . .* (Philadelphia, 1844).

102. Brigham Young, *T&S* 5 (September 15, 1844): 648; see similar ideas echoed by Parley P. Pratt (*T&S* 5 [September 15, 1844]: 651) and John Taylor, (*T&S* 5 [October 1, 1844]: 661).

103. *T&S* 5 (October 1, 1844): 660–64, (October 15, 1844): 686–87; D&C 124:103–10.

104. Rigdon to Mayor John C. Bennett, November 1, 1841, Rigdon Collection, Church Archives; *HC* 6:288; Whitney testimony, *T&S* 5 (October 15, 1844): 686–87.

105. Testimony of Orson Hyde, *T&S* 5 (September 15, 1844): 649–50. Hyde said, "It is known to some who are present that there is a quorum organized where revelation can be tested. Brother Joseph said, let no revelation go to the people until it has been tested here." Hyde refers to the endowment council. In later years, a council of the First Presidency and the Twelve would sustain a revelation before presenting it to the church (see D&C 138: heading; Official Declaration–2, introduction).

106. Testimony of Heber C. Kimball, *T&S* 5 (October 1, 1844): 663; testimony Parley P. Pratt, *T&S* 5 (September 15, 1844): 653–54.

107. Testimony of Heber C. Kimball, *T&S* 5 (October 1, 1844): 663–64.

108. *T&S* 5 (October 1, 1844): 665–66.

109. Testimony of Young, *T&S* 5 (October 1, 1844): 666–67; see Heber C. Kimball to Parley P. Pratt, June 17, 1842, Pratt Papers, Church Archives, for a similar sentiment. The revelation mentioned was D&C 124:103–10.

110. *T&S* 5 (October 15, 1844): 686–87; (December 15, 1844): 742.

111. Beecher, "Nauvoo Diary of Zina Diantha Huntington Jacobs," 295; Abram Hatch, Autobiography (1897), 3, 4, 6–7, Church Archives.

112. Isaac C. Haight, Journal, 15, University of Utah.

113. Elias Adams to George Adams, July 25, 1845, Church Archives.

114. Henry and Catharine Brooke to Leonard Pickell, November 15, 1844, Coe Collection, spelling standardized.

115. Cook, *William Law,* 28–33, 28 n. 91.

116. For an extended explanation of this point and a brash critique of Rigdon's claims, see "The

Apostles and Apostates," an article by "An Old Man of Israel," in *T&S* 5 (November 15, 1844): 711–16.

117. *Signal,* May 14, 1845; *Prophet,* May 10, 1845; *T&S* 5 (September 15 1844): 654–55.

118. *Gospel Herald* (Strangite), August 31, 1848; quotation from Lyman Wight, Diary, December 8, 1850; see also Lyman Wight, Diary, December 23, 1850, cited in Smith, "Succession in the Presidency," 4–7.

119. Monroe, Tutorial Diary, 105, April 24, 1845, Coe Collection. Monroe said further, "Mr. Rigdon is not the proper successor of President Smith, being only his councelor, but Elder Marks should be the individual as he was not only his councillor at the time of his death, but also President of the High Council. And according to the ordination pronounced upon him by Br Joseph he is the individual contemplated by him for his successor. The Twelve . . . were aware of these facts but acted differently" (105–6). It is not clear whether Monroe believed that Marks received the supposed ordination as stake president in October 1839 or some later time.

120. *HC* 7:234, 241–42.

121. *T&S* 6 (May 15, 1845): 904–5; James Monroe, Tutorial Diary, 132, May 28–29, 1845, Coe Collection.

122. *T&S* 6 (May 15, 1845): 905.

123. *T&S* 6 (June 1, 1845): 921, quoting from D&C 124:125, with emphasis added by Taylor; see also 107:8–9; 124:124.

124. *T&S* 6 (June 1, 1845): 920–22; see also D&C 107:39.

125. James Monroe, Tutorial Diary, 131–32, May 27, 29, 1845, Coe Collection; *New York Messenger,* September 20, 1845, 92, an editorial attributed to one of the Pratts (Monroe suggests Parley; but O. Pratt, *Journals,* 281, says Orson). Young's right to regulate the Quorum of the Twelve was challenged by others as well but was resolved finally at Winter Quarters in late 1847 (see Pratt, "Parley P. Pratt in Winter Quarters").

126. Parley P. Pratt, October 6, 1845, *T&S* 6 (November 1, 1845): 1008 (*HC* 7:459–60); William I. Appleby, Autobiography (1848), 137–38, October 30, 1845, Church Archives.

127. Willard Richards dates excommunication to a week after conference, or Wednesday, October 12 (*T&S* 6 [November 1, 1845]: 1019), but other sources confirm the Wednesday, October 19, date (Clayton, *Journals,* 187; *HC* 7:483). Heber C. Kimball's entries, kept by Thomas Bullock, indirectly confirm the action (Kimball, Diary No. 91, October 12, 19, 1845, Church Archives).

128. Norton Jacob, Reminiscences and Journal, 21, October 19, 1845, Church Archives. The pamphlet is mentioned in *HC* 7:483 and also by Jacob (Reminiscences and Journal), William Clayton (*Journals,* 187), and Willard Richards (*T&S* 6 [November 1, 1845]: 1019), but no copies are extant. It was reprinted in full in *Signal,* October 29, 1845.

129. *MS* 7 (May 1, 1846): 134–35; Kimball, "Saints and St. Louis," 503–4; Almon W. Babbitt to Brigham Young, November 4, 1845, Brigham Young Papers, Church Archives.

130. Smith, *Minutes of a Conference . . .* (Nauvoo, January 6, 1846).

131. *A Revelation Given to William Smith in 1847 on the Apostasy of the Church . . .* (Philadelphia, 1848); Smith, *William Smith, Patriarch and Prophet of the Most High God* (Ottawa, Ill.: 1847).

132. Smith, "Succession in the Presidency," 5–6, 9–11. See also *Saints Herald,* November 6, 1834; Launius, *Joseph Smith III,* 7–8, 15–16, 32–33.

133. James Kay of St. Louis to *MS,* November 22, 1845; *MS* 7 (May 1, 1846): 134–35; *New York Messenger,* September 20, 1845, in O. Pratt, *Journals,* 281–82.

134. See additional discussion of Joseph Smith III's claim in chapter 20 of this volume.

135. *T&S* 5 (September 2, 1844): 632.

136. Heber Kimball, in *T&S* 5 (October 1, 1844): 664; William Smith, in *Signal*, October 29, 1845.

137. Editorial, *New York Messenger*, September 20, 1845, in O. Pratt, *Journals*, 281–82.

138. For more on the Twelve's view of Joseph III, see Esplin, "Joseph, Brigham, and the Twelve," 333–41.

139. Hazen Aldrich to Samuel Akers and Joshua Small, July 12, 1846, Church Archives, citing D&C 43:1–2; 35:18; 28:2–7; 106:4–8; 102:11; 107:33; Van Noord, *King of Beaver Island*, 4. Aldrich was the first appointed to the presidency of the seventy in 1835.

140. Van Noord, *King of Beaver Island*, 4–6, 31–32.

141. *Signal*, February 6, August 18, 1846.

142. Joseph Smith to "My Dear Son," June 18, 1844, in Strang, Gospel Tract No. 4, *The Diamond*, 3–6.

143. Norton Jacob, Reminiscences and Journal, August 1844, Church Archives, spelling standardized. Jacob's companion was Moses Smith, a Burlington settler who had married a sister of Strang's wife and moved to Nauvoo (Van Noord, *King of Beaver Island*, 9).

144. Van Noord, *King of Beaver Island*, 33–38.

145. *National Intelligencer*, October 25, 1845, quoting the *True Sun*.

146. Jacob Gates, Journals, March 1, 8, 1846, Church Archives; Warren Post, Diaries, June 20, 1847, Church Archives.

147. William I. Appleby, Autobiography (1848), 150, November 1, 1846, Church Archives.

148. Van Noord, *King of Beaver Island*, 6–11; Norton Jacob, Reminiscences and Journal, August 1844, February 1, 1846, Church Archives.

149. For an example, see Jacob Gibson, Reminiscences (1849), Church Archives, who decided to try the doctrine in 1846 but "was not satisfied and I thought the Bell was cract."

150. Samuel Taggart, Petersborough, N. H., to Albert Taggart, April 11, 1845, Albert Taggart Correspondence, Church Archives.

151. *Daily Democrat* (Rochester), quoted in *Signal*, August 18, 1846.

152. *Signal*, December 31, 1845; William I. Appleby, Autobiography (1848), 150, November 1, 1846, Church Archives.

153. George Alley to Joseph Alley III, April 5, 1846, Church Archives.

154. Norton Jacob, Reminiscences and Journal, August 24, 1844, Church Archives; *Signal*, January 7, 28, 1846.

155. Minutes, Sixth Quorum of Seventy, 6–7, Church Archives.

156. Fifth Quorum, February 10, 3, 1845, Church Archives.

157. Norton Jacob, Reminiscences and Journal, 29, February, 1, 1846; *HC* 7:578. The presenter was Moses Smith, Norton Jacob's missionary companion during the 1844 presidential campaign and brother of Aaron Smith.

158. The references in the following notes have been translated from 1835 D&C sections and verses to the current citations. They are cited in Elias Adams to George Adams (his brother), February 18, 1847, Church Archives (George had joined Strang's movement), and/or in Reuben Miller, *James J. Strang, Weighed in the Balance of Truth and Found Wanting* (September 1846), copy at BYU Library (Miller spent three months with Strang before returning to the church in Nauvoo).

159. See D&C 43:1–2; 90:3–5; 107:91–92; 28:2–7.

160. See D&C 20:67; 107:22, 82–83; 64:37–39.

161. See D&C 27:12–14; 107:23–24.

162. See D&C 107:22, 65–66.

163. Elias Adams to George Adams, February 18, 1847, Church Archives.

164. Miller, *James J. Strang* (1846), 3–4, 6–8, 12–13, 20. Miller, a short-time affiliate of Strang, centered his argument in this point. Strang outlined his succession claims in *The Diamond* (1848).

165. Orson Hyde, *He That Hath Ears to Hear* (Nauvoo, March 14, 1846), copy at BYU Library; also quoted in Joseph C. Kingsbury, Autobiography, 25–26, March 15, 1846, University of Utah.

166. *T&S* 6 (January 20, 1846): 1101–2.

167. Seventies Quorums, Records, Fifth Quorum, Minutes, February 17, 1846, Truman Leonard, clerk, Church Archives, spelling standardized.

PART IV. REMOVAL: NEW PLACES AND NEW PEOPLES

Epigraph: John S. Fullmer to John Price, November 4, 1845, John S. Fullmer Letterbook, Church Archives.

CHAPTER 16. THE PEACEFUL INTERLUDE

Epigraph: Unsigned editorial, *T&S* 5 (November 15, 1844): 711; see also Phebe Foster to John Taylor, January 13, 1845, who echoes, "I am happy to learn that all is union and peace at Nauvoo, and that evidences present themselves to show that God has not forsaken his church and people" (*T&S* 6 [March 1, 1845]: 821). Brigham Young to Wilford Woodruff, February 11, 1845, in *HC* 7:373; cf. *HC* 7:394.

1. Brigham Young to Wilford Woodruff, June 27, 1845, Brigham Young Papers, Church Archives (extracts, *MS* 6 [September 1, 1845]: 91; *HC* 7:430).

2. Ford, *History,* 254–55 (*HC* 7:44–45).

3. Oaks and Hill, *Carthage Conspiracy,* 33–35, with election returns at 43 n. 28; *HC* 7:223, 225–27; *T&S* 5 (September 15, 1844): 652.

4. *Signal,* Extra, August 7, 1844.

5. Legislative message, *Neighbor,* February 19, 1845; Jacob Backenstos to Brigham Young, January 25, 1845, Brigham Young Papers, Church Archives; *CHC* 2:488–90.

6. Kimball, "Study of the Nauvoo Charter," 109–10.

7. *Signal,* January 29, 1845; *HC* 7:325.

8. *Neighbor,* March 12, 1845 (*CHC* 2:486–88).

9. Babbitt to Elias Smith, *HC* 7:363.

10. *Signal,* December 25, 1844.

11. *Signal,* January 8, 1845.

12. *Signal,* January 1, 1845; Kimball, "Study of the Nauvoo Charter," 106–7.

13. *Neighbor,* January 29, 1845; Babbitt to Brigham Young, January 23, 25, 1845, Brigham Young Papers, Church Archives; Gregg, *Hancock County,* 336.

14. Lamborn to Brigham Young, January 28, 1845, *HC* 7:370.

15. *Neighbor,* January 1, 1845.

16. *HC* 7:350–52, 360, 365, 372; Taylor, "Nauvoo Journal," 22–26. Taylor lists the seventies and high priests by name. Church trustees certified forty-six of the high priests as tithing agents (*T&S* 6 [January 15, 1845]: 780).

17. *T&S* 6 (January 15, 1845): 773–76, 780 (*HC* 7:354–56, 361). The city did not publish its list, so no comparison can be made with Taylor's list of high priests and seventies.

18. *HC* 7:368–69; Stout, *Diary,* 1:17–18, January 30, 1845; Brigham Young and others to Daniel Webster, February 1, 1845, Illinois State Historical Society Papers; form letter, in Taylor, "Nauvoo Journal," 37–38.

19. Lamborn to Young, *HC* 7:370–71.

20. *Neighbor,* January 29, 1845; *MS* 2 (May 1841): 5; Isaiah 52:7. The Hebrew word transliterated as *nauvoo* (NAVU) is an inflected form with the literal meaning "they are beautiful." The *Millennial Star* article cites Frey's *Hebrew and English Dictionary* (London: George Wightman, 1839).

21. Calvin Reed to Plimpton Simonds, July 1845, Church Archives.

22. St. Louis conference, February 10, 1845, *T&S* 6 (February 15, 1845): 806.

23. *Signal,* January 29, February 26, 1845. Nauvoo remained a town until the state issued a city charter on April 10, 1899 (Clayton, *Illinois Fact Book,* 69).

24. Stout, *Diary,* 1:14–16, 19–20; *HC* 7:368–70; election judges, *Neighbor,* January 15, 1845; response to criticism, *Neighbor,* March 19, 1845. Orson Spencer, president pro tem of the city council after the death of Joseph Smith, was named mayor. Aldermen were Daniel Spencer, Newel K. Whitney, George W. Harris, and Charles C. Rich. City councilors elected were David Fullmer, John Pack, George Miller, William W. Phelps, Jonathan C. Wright, Samuel Bent, Phineas Richards, James Sloan, and Edward Hunter.

25. *HC* 7:265, August 31, 1844.

26. Stout, *Diary,* 1:27.

27. Stout, *Diary,* 1:27.

28. *HC* 7:386–88; Samuel Rogers, Diary, March 24, 1845, BYU Library. Young's intended March 17 organizing meeting for the deacons was delayed one week for an unstated reason (*HC* 7:381).

29. Stout, *Diary,* 1:29.

30. *HC* 7:386–88, 394.

31. *HC* 7:389, 396–97.

32. *HC* 7:396–97. Ford detailed his advice on the Legion in a letter to Hancock County legislator Almon Babbitt (not in *HC*).

33. The proposed boundary extended from Joseph Smith's properties on the south to Hibbard Street and from the unplatted Munson lands inland as far as Rich Street (*Neighbor,* April 2, 1845). The Cherill map of 1846 describes a much larger Town Corporation, suggesting that the original proposal was rejected. See map on page 626 of this volume.

34. *HC* 7:370; see also 396, 399–400; Stout, *Diary,* 1:35.

35. *T&S* 6 (April 1, 1845): 856.

36. Ford to Young, April 8, 1845, Brigham Young Papers, Church Archives (*HC* 7:397; see also 399–400); and Brigham Young to Charles C. Rich, September 14, 1845, Brigham Young Papers, Church Archives (*HC* 7:444).

37. Kimball, in *Neighbor,* April 7, 1845; *T&S* 6 (April 15, 1845): 871 (*HC* 7:394); letter to Wight, *HC* 7:400.

38. *T&S* 6 (July 1, 1845): 956, reporting an April 6 talk.

39. Brigham Young, Journal, January 24, 1845, Church Archives, spelling standardized.

40. *T&S* 5 (August 15, 1844): 619.

41. *T&S* 5 (October 1, 1844): 668–69.

42. Brigham Young to Vilate Young, August 11, 1844, Church Archives.

43. Brigham Young to Parley P. Pratt, May 26, 1845, Church Archives.

44. *T&S* 5 (October 1, 1844): 668; Taylor, "Nauvoo Journal," 22–26.

45. *Neighbor,* April 7, 1845; editorial, *T&S* 6 (April 1, 1845): 856.

46. *New York Sun,* in *HC* 7:434; *St. Louis Gazette,* quoted in *Neighbor,* August 20, 1845.

47. *HC* 7:393; D&C 124:22–24.

48. *HC* 7:400, 407; John Kenny Richards, Notebook, May 13, 1845, Church Archives.

49. *HC* 7:435–36.

50. Jacob Gates, Journals, September 8, 1845, Church Archives; LaFayette Knight to James H. Fellows and wife, December 21, 1843, Church Archives.

51. *HC* 7:435.

52. *HC* 5:422, 430; 7:270–71; William Huntington, "Life," 19, June 8, 1845, BYU Library; Stout, *Diary,* 1:10, 53, November 15, 1844, July 17, 1845.

53. *Neighbor,* January 9, 1845; *HC* 7:274, 417; Brigham Young to Parley P. Pratt, May 26, 1845, Church Archives.

54. *T&S* 6 (February 1, 1845): 794–99. These published minutes by John D. Lee lack details and report only the sessions on December 26, 27, and 30.

55. Journal of Peter M. Wentz, April 21, 1854, typescript, BYU Library.

56. *HC* 7:363–64; *Neighbor,* February 26, 1845; Charles C. Rich, Journal, March 2, 8, 1845, Church Archives.

57. *Neighbor,* April 7, 1845.

58. Kimball, *Diaries,* 120–21, June 6, 18, 1845. Irene Hascall Pomeroy reported, "Elder Hyde has gone to purchase canvass for the outer court or tabernacle [to] spread in front of the temple for meetings" (Pomeroy to Ashbel G. Hascall, July 6, 12, 1845, Church Archives). Orson Pratt to Reuben Hedlock, August 20, 1845, *New York Messenger,* August 30, 1845 (also in O. Pratt, *Journals,* 259–60, and in Watson, "Nauvoo Tabernacle," 420).

59. *HC* 7:426–27, 431, 483; Watson, "Nauvoo Tabernacle," 417–18; Norton Jacob, Reminiscences and Journal, 21, October 19, 1845, Church Archives. Jacob reported that Hyde had collected eighteen hundred dollars, or six hundred dollars more than he had planned.

60. Orson Pratt to Brigham Young, September 4, 1845, BYU Library; Orson Hyde to Newel K. Whitney, August 24, 1845, Whitney Collection, BYU Library; *HC* 7:509; *New York Messenger,* September 20, 1845.

61. *HC* 7:431–32; Watson, "Nauvoo Tabernacle," 416–21.

62. *HC* 7:351; *Neighbor,* January 15, 1845; Sonne, *Ships, Saints, and Mariners,* 134–35.

63. Brigham Young, *A Few Words to Emigrants and to All Who Wish to Purchase Property in Nauvoo and Its Vicinity,* broadside, November 12, 1844, Church History Library.

64. Charles C. Rich, Journal, 30, December 19, 1844, Church Archives; Seventies, Second Quorum, February 26, 1845; Fifth Quorum, February 27, 1845. After discussing the proposal, these quorums unanimously supported it.

65. B. A. Gallop, September 17, 1844, Church Archives; Dwight Webster to Aphek Woodruff, December 1, 1844, Church Archives; *T&S* 6 (April 15, 1845): 870.

66. Keemble, *St. Louis Directory for 1840–41,* 6; Taylor and Crooks, *Sketch Book of St. Louis.*

67. *T&S* 5 (August 15, 1844): 619.

68. Epistle of the Twelve, *T&S* 5 (October 1, 1844): 668–69.

69. *T&S* 5 (October 1, 1844): 669; Taylor, "Nauvoo Journal," 33, November 19, 1844.

70. Comments from "An Observer on Men and Things," *Neighbor,* December 4, 1844; editorial, *Neighbor,* October 16, 1844.

71. *T&S* 5 (October 1, 1844): 669. Robert Sutton has challenged traditional assumptions that urban growth is governed by economic factors in a study of three Illinois towns: Quincy,

Nauvoo, and Oquawka. He found the most important factors to be sociological, ideological, and cultural developments ("Illinois River Towns," 21–31).

72. Jesse C. Little to Brigham Young, December 30, 1844, Brigham Young Papers, Church Archives.

73. *T&S* 5 (October 1, 1844): 669; Spencer, comments, November 12 trades meeting, *Neighbor,* November 13, 1844.

74. *Neighbor,* November 13, 1844.

75. *Neighbor,* October 2, 9, 1844; Taylor, "Nauvoo Journal," 32, October 9, 1844.

76. Trades Meeting, October 15, 1844, in Taylor, "Nauvoo Journal," 32.

77. Trades Meetings, October 15, November 19, 26, 1844, in *Neighbor,* October 16, November 27, December 18, 1844.

78. Taylor, "Nauvoo Journal," 31–32, 35, October 12, 13, 14, 1844; January 14, 28, 1845.

79. Trades Meeting, November 19, 1884, *Neighbor,* November 27, 1844; meeting, January 28, Taylor, "Nauvoo Journal," 35.

80. Trades Meeting, October 9, November 19, 26, 1844; Taylor, "Nauvoo Journal," 32–33, and *Neighbor,* December 18, 1844.

81. Trades Meeting, October 15, 1844, Taylor, "Nauvoo Journal," 32; Heber Kimball, April 1845 conference, in Joseph G. Hovey, Reminiscences, Church Archives.

82. Trades Meeting, October 15, November 26, 1844, *Neighbor,* October 16, December 18, 1844; advertisement, *Neighbor,* December 25, 1844.

83. Trades Meeting, October 15, November 19, 1844, *Neighbor,* October 16, November 27, 1844.

84. Trades Meeting, November 12, 1844, *Neighbor,* November 13, 1844, and Taylor, "Nauvoo Journal," 32.

85. Trades Meeting, December 2, 1844, *Neighbor,* January 9, 1845, identifies the committee as D. M. Repsher and Edward Hunter; Taylor, "Nauvoo Journal," 32, November 12, 1844, lists Repsher, Lucius N. Scovil, and a Mr. Adams.

86. Taylor, "Nauvoo Journal," 33; Trades Meeting, November 19, December 2, 1844, *Neighbor,* November 27, 1844; January 9, 1845. The factory was to be eighty feet long and sixty feet wide and to cost more than twenty-five hundred dollars.

87. Trades Meeting, November 26, December 2, 1844, *Neighbor,* December 18, 1844, January 9, 1845.

88. Trades Meeting, November 26, 1844, *Neighbor,* December 18, 1844.

89. Trades Meeting, November 19, 1844, *Neighbor,* November 27, 1845.

90. Trades Meeting, December 2, 1844, *Neighbor,* January 9, 1845; advertisement, *Neighbor,* January 22, 1845.

91. Trades Meeting, January 7, 28, 1845, *Neighbor,* January 9, February 5, 1845.

92. Trades Meeting, December 31, 1844, *Neighbor,* January 1, 1845.

93. Meeting of the Twelve, trustees, Nauvoo Temple committee, surveyors, and a committee of the NA&MA, January 10, 1845, *Neighbor,* February 5, 1845, (mentioned in *HC* 7:351).

94. Trades Meeting, January 14, 1845, *Neighbor,* January 19, 1845; meeting, January 28, Taylor, "Nauvoo Journal," 35.

95. Trades Meeting, January 28, *Neighbor,* February 5, 1845, and Taylor, "Nauvoo Journal, 35–36.

96. Minutes, Mercantile and Mechanical Association, January 31, 1845, Church Archives; Stout, *Diary,* 1:18–19, January 30–31, 1845; *HC* 7:369. Listed as trustees were Samuel Bent, Daniel Carn, Shadrach Roundy, John D. Lee, Lucius N. Scovil, Joseph Wortham [Worthen], Joseph Horn[e], Hosea Stout, Edward Hunter, Gustavius Williams, Charles C. Rich, and Charles A. Davis. Bent chaired the planning meeting.

97. Quoted from Stout, *Diary,* 1:19, February 4, 1845; also reported in Minutes, Mercantile and Mechanical Association, February 4, 1845, Church Archives.

98. Clayton, *Journals,* 157–65, February 4, March 1, 4, 11, 18, 22, 25, April 11, 15, May 6, 1845; also see Ehat, "'It Seems like Heaven Began on Earth,'" 268–69. In its spring meetings, the Council of Fifty considered such things as western exploration and settlement, city government, the church printing business, and vigilante actions.

99. All quotations from William Huntington, Diary, 26, February 17, 1845, University of Utah. That the Twelve appointed the new council is clear from Stout, *Diary,* 1:19, February 7, 1845.

100. Stout, *Diary,* 1:19, February 7, 1845.

101. Sample constitution for trades companies, Church Archives (MS 4282); Minutes, Mercantile and Mechanical Association, February 20, 1845, Church Archives.

102. Daniel Spencer, Turley, and Fullmer were added to the Council of Fifty on March 1, 1845. The four not identified as members of the Fifty were Phinehas Richards, Edward Hunter, John Benbow, and William Weeks (Quinn, "Council of Fifty and Its Members," 193–97).

103. Orson Spencer, as mayor; Daniel Spencer (a former mayor) and Charles C. Rich as aldermen; and David Fullmer, Samuel Bent, Phineas Richards, and Edward Hunter as city councilors.

104. High councilors included Samuel Bent (Zion and Nauvoo), Alpheus Cutler (Nauvoo), Phineas Richards (Kirtland), David Fullmer (Nauvoo), and Charles C. Rich (Nauvoo, and a counselor in the stake presidency). Daniel Spencer would become a member of the Salt Lake High Council. Edward Hunter was bishop of the Nauvoo Fifth Ward.

105. Taylor, "Nauvoo Journal," 39, February 7, 11, 1845; *HC* 7:371–72; Kimball, *Diaries,* 96, February 11, 1845.

106. A copy of the model in the handwriting of Lucian R. Foster is preserved in the Church Archives under the supplied title "[Form of model constitution for trades associations]" (ms 4282). To see how it was adopted by a trades group, see Minutes, Mercantile and Mechanical Association, February 20, 1845, Church Archives. Both documents list by name the presidency and also the members of the board or council known as the Living Constitution.

107. William Huntington, Diary, 26, February 17, 1845, University of Utah; Taylor, "Nauvoo Journal," 39, February 17, 1845.

108. Samuel Bent, Charles C. Rich, and Hosea Stout received some preliminary counsel at a February 7 meeting of the Living Constitution (Stout, *Diary,* 1:19, February 7, 1845).

109. Minutes, Mercantile and Mechanical Association, February 18, 20, 24, 1845, Church Archives; Stout, *Diary,* 1:19, 21–25, February 18, 19, 20, 24, 28, March 3–4, 1845; William Huntington, Diary, 26, February 23, 1845, University of Utah. Samuel Bent, Charles C. Rich, and Edward Hunter were replaced by Erastus Snow, Levi Hancock, and James Mendenhall on the association's board of control.

110. Notice in *Neighbor,* February 19, 1845. Invited groups included smiths, leather workers, construction workers, cabinetmakers and chair makers, weavers and spinners, and laborers.

111. Advertisement, *Neighbor,* March 12, 1845.

112. *Neighbor,* January 1, 1845.

113. Advertisements, *Neighbor,* January 1, April 2, 23, 1845.

114. Advertisements, *Neighbor,* April 2, 1845.

115. Among the companies that may have fit this definition are J. Grocott's earthenware manufactory (*Neighbor,* January 1, 1845), Alexander Neibaur's Nauvoo Match Manufactory (*Neighbor,* January 22, 1845), and the Rope Manufactory opened by Egan and Sanders (*Neighbor,* February 19, 1845).

116. Advertisement, *Neighbor,* March 19, 1845.

117. Trades Meeting, December 2, 1844, *Neighbor,* January 9, 1845.
118. *Neighbor,* March 12, 1845; Stout, *Diary,* 1:26, March 10–12, 1845; Minutes, Mercantile and Mechanical Association, February 14, March 11, 1845; Mendenhall advertisement, *Neighbor,* January 1, 1845.
119. *Neighbor,* February 26, 1845.
120. *Neighbor,* July 30 through August 27, 1845. Many of the advertisements include such notices.
121. *Neighbor,* April 30, May 7, 1845.
122. Whitney, *HC* 7:351; Trades Meeting, December 31, 1844, *Neighbor,* January 1, 1845.
123. Stout, *Diary,* 1:27, March 13, 1845.
124. *Neighbor,* April 16, 1845.
125. *T&S* 5 (January 1, 1844): 392–93.
126. *Warsaw Message,* January 14, 1843.
127. Bennett proposal, Enders, "Dam for Nauvoo," 247–48; *HC* 6:80, 106; Flanders, *Nauvoo,* 151–52; quotation, from Brigham Young and Willard Richards to Reuben Hedlock, May 3, 1844, Church Archives (*HC* 6:353).
128. John Taylor, *T&S* 5 (January 1, 1844): 392–93; invoice, Campbell to Joseph Smith, April 24, 1844, Whitney Collection, BYU Library. The plans, $2.40 each, were delivered to A. Fielding and William Clayton.
129. D. M. Repsher estimate, *Neighbor,* January 9, 1845; Brigham Young and Willard Richards to Reuben Hedlock, May 3, 1844, *HC* 6:353.
130. *Neighbor,* February 5, 1845; Enders, "Dam for Nauvoo," 251–52.
131. City Council, Minutes, April 9, 1842; *HC* 6:106; *T&S* 5 (January 1, 1844): 392.
132. Trades Meeting, January 7, 1845, Taylor, "Nauvoo Journal," 33.
133. Trades Meeting, December 2, 31, 1844, *Neighbor,* January 1, 9, 1845; meeting, January 14, 1845, Taylor, "Nauvoo Journal," 33, and *Neighbor,* January 15, 1845.
134. Trades Meeting, January 28, 1845, Taylor, "Nauvoo Journal," 35–36; *Neighbor,* February 5, 12, 1845; Enders, "Dam for Nauvoo," 252; *Neighbor,* April 16, 1845.
135. Trades Meeting, January 7, 1845, Taylor, "Nauvoo Journal," 33; *HC* 7:351.
136. Trades Meeting, January 14, 28, 1845, *Neighbor,* January 15, February 5, 1845.
137. *Neighbor,* February 12, 1845; *HC* 7:372, February 11, 1845.
138. According to William Huntington, a riverside meeting was held on the 25th, an organizing meeting on the 26th, and the dedication on the 27th (Huntington, Diary, February 25, 1845, University of Utah); Samuel Rogers, Diary, February 26–27, 1845, BYU Library; *Neighbor,* March 5, 1845 (*HC* 7:377).
139. *Neighbor,* March 5, 12, 1845; Stout, *Diary,* 1:26.
140. *Neighbor,* March 5, 1845.
141. *HC* 7:383, 385–87; Samuel Rogers, Diary, March 17, 1845, BYU Library; *Neighbor,* April 16, July 16, 1845.
142. A lock and dam built at Keokuk in 1910–12 accomplished the same purpose, backing up the Mississippi River to Nauvoo and lifting the river's surface above the smooth-flowing Des Moines Rapids (*Nauvoo Independent,* December 9, 21, 24, 1910; October 25, 1911).
143. From a conference planning meeting, Kimball, *Diary,* 101, April 2, 1845. Also see talks on home industry by Kimball and Young on the second day of the conference (*HC* 7:393; *Neighbor,* April 16, 1845).
144. See Dwight and Eunice W. Webster to Wilford Woodruff, May 4, 1845, Church Archives.
145. Brigham Young to Wilford Woodruff, June 27, 1845, Brigham Young Papers, Church Archives (excerpted in *MS* 6 [September 1, 1845]: 91–92 and *HC* 7:431).

146. *HC* 7:247, 249, 317–18, 326.

147. *HC* 7:252.

148. *HC* 7:303, 305–6.

149. *HC* 7:249, 251–52, 305–6.

150. *HC* 7:258–599, 239.

151. *HC* 6:318–22 and chapter 12 of this volume.

152. Brigham Young, *HC* 7:235; cf. D&C 112:30–32.

153. *HC* 7:347.

154. *HC* 7:299 (October 1844). Young called it the *Mormon Almanac.*

155. *HC* 7:425, 445, 509.

156. *HC* 7:274, 279.

157. D&C 107:96; *T&S* 5 (November 1, 1844): 695–96 (*HC* 7:307–8).

158. Brigham Young to Vilate Young, August 11, 28, 1844, Church Archives; Edson Whipple to Bro. Chamberlin, ca. November 29, 1844, Whipple Record Books, Church Archives.

159. *T&S* 5 (November 1, 1844): 696 (*HC* 7:307–8, October 8, 1844).

160. Second Quorum, Minutes, quoting Edson Barney, June 1, and Lewis Robbins, November 16, 1845, Church Archives.

161. Beecher, "Nauvoo Diary of Zina Diantha Huntington Jacobs," 297; *HC* 7:315.

162. Seventies, Records, Fifth Quorum, Minutes, December 18, 1844, Church Archives; also see invited testimonies on January 9, June 15, and December 14, 1845.

163. For expressions of unity, see Fourth Quorum, Minutes, January 22, February 26, and May 18, 1845. For examples of discipline, see Second Quorum, Minutes, February 26, April 9, 1845; Fifth Quorum, Minutes, February 3, 10, 1846; and Ninth Quorum, Minutes, February 15, 1846.

164. Fourth Quorum, Minutes, December 26, 1844.

165. Ibid., November 13, December 25, 1844; Fifth Quorum, Minutes, June 15, 1845.

166. Second Quorum, Minutes, February 5, 19, 26, 1845; Third Quorum, Minutes, January 8, 1845.

167. Fifth Quorum, Minutes, January 21, February 20, March 4, 1845.

168. Sample topics from the Ninth Quorum, Minutes, December 12, 25, 1844; January 25, February 7, 14, March 4, 7, 14, April 1, 1845; and the Fourteenth Quorum, Minutes, February 24, 1845; January 25, 1846.

169. The Second Quorum, for example, considered the Music Hall (Concert Hall) its regular meeting place during 1845, but members sometimes met in the Seventies Hall, Council Hall (Court Hall), in Joseph Smith's store, Masonic Hall, and private homes. The Fourth Quorum met almost exclusively in homes or in schoolrooms.

170. *HC* 7:364. The proposed dimensions were 80'W x 120'L x 33'H, compared with 88'W x 128'L x 65'H for the temple.

171. Fifth Quorum, Minutes, February 27, 1845.

172. All quotations reflect counsel received from Brigham Young and shared with the Second Quorum by one of their presidents (Minutes, March 14, 1845).

173. Second Quorum, Minutes, December 14, 1845; February 1, March 15, 1846.

174. Fourth Quorum, Minutes, February 26, 1845; Gates, Fourth Quorum, Minutes, May 18, 1845.

175. Second Quorum, Minutes, June 1, July 27, August 3, 1845.

176. Second Quorum, Minutes, February 5, 12, March 14, 1845.

177. Second Quorum, Minutes, September 7, 14, 27, 1845.

178. Second Quorum, Minutes, September 27, February 5, 1845.

179. Fourth Quorum, Minutes, December 11, 1844; Fifth Quorum, Minutes, February 24, 1846; Second Quorum, Minutes, February 26, September 14, June 22, 1845.

180. Fourth Quorum, Minutes, August 23, 1845.

181. Fourth Quorum, August 23, 1845. When this expectation was fulfilled late in the twentieth century, the seventy presided as general authorities over areas of the world comprising multiple stakes.

182. *HC* 7:281 (Epistle of the Twelve, October 1, 1844).

183. *MS* 6 (November 1, 1845):124; *T&S* 5 (November 1, 1844): 702.

184. James Monroe, Tutorial Diary, April and May, 1845, Coe Collection; Lucy Meserve Smith, Statement, May 18, 1892, Emily Smith Stewart Collection, University of Utah.

185. *T&S* 5 (October 1, 1844): 669.

186. *T&S* 5 (October 1, 1844): 669.

187. *T&S* 5 (October 1, 1844): 669.

188. *T&S* 6 (April 1, 1845): 856; *Neighbor*, April 23, 1845.

189. *T&S* 6 (April 1, 1845): 856.

190. Mosiah Hancock, Autobiography, 25, Church Archives; Pratt to cousins, September 28, 1844, typescript, courtesy James L. Kimball Jr.; William Byram Pace, "Life Story," typescript, 2, Church Archives.

191. Stout, *Diary*, April 27, 1845, tells of the harassment of Old Father [Austin E.] Cowles, one of Law's followers. Mosiah L. Hancock, Autobiography, 26–27, Church Archives, mentions the "black ducks."

192. James Pace, Autobiographical Sketch (ca. 1861), 4, Church Archives; *Signal*, April 9, 1845; Stout, *Diary*, 1:33.

193. *CHC* 2:527; *Neighbor*, May 7, 1845; Dwight and Eunice W. Webster to Wilford Woodruff, May 4, 1845, Church Archives; *Neighbor*, cited in *Signal*, April 23, 1845; Wandle Mace, Autobiography, typescript, 186–87, BYU Library.

194. *Signal*, June 4, 1845; *T&S* 6 (August 1, 1845): 988.

195. Parley P. Pratt, "Proclamation," *MS* 5 (March 1845): 150.

196. See "To the Saints Abroad," *T&S* 5 (July 15, 1844): 587; Parley P. Pratt, "Cry of the Martyrs," *T&S* 5 (September 2, 1844): 639.

197. Smith, *Words*, 320 (*HC* 6:210); see also "Who Shall Be Our Next President?" *T&S* 5 (February 15, 1844): 439–40.

198. For examples, see "An Epistle of the Twelve," *T&S* 5 (August 15, 1844): 619–20; Brigham Young, Circular, *T&S* 6 (November 1, 1845): 1018–19 (*HC* 7:478–80); "Mobocracy," *T&S* 6 (November 15, 1845): 1031.

199. *T&S* 6 (May 15, 1845): 911. Eliza Snow's mournful lamentation over Missouri's loss of honor is an earlier reflection of failed justice ("Missouri," *T&S* 5 [February 1, 1844]: 431).

200. A number of published comments in 1844–45 warned the Saints about pending judgments on the nations. Examples include "Calamity," *T&S* 6 (May 15, 1845): 910–11; and "The Times and the Report," *T&S* 6 (June 1, 1845): 925–26. Joseph Smith's call to gather to the refuge of Zion and his prediction "that not many years shall pass away, before the United States shall present such a scene of *bloodshed* as has not a parallel in the history of our nation" (*HC* 1:315) appeared as part of the serialized "History of Joseph Smith" in *T&S* 5 (November 2, 1844): 707.

201. "Great Persecution . . . in Illinois," *T&S* 6 (November 1, 1845): 1017, spelling standardized.

CHAPTER 17. A SOLUTION TO THE MORMON QUESTION

Epigraph: Amasa M. Lyman, conference talk, October 7, 1845, *T&S* 6 (November 1, 1845): 1013 (*HC* 7:469).

1. Ford to Young, April 8, 1845, Brigham Young Papers, Church Archives (*HC* 7:397–98); Young to Ford, March 31, 1845, Brigham Young Papers, Church Archives (*HC* 7:389); Clayton, *Journals,* 163, April 15, 1845. Thomas Sharp held similar views: "It is impossible that the two communities can long live together. They can *never* assimilate. We repeat our firm conviction that one or the other *must* leave" (*Signal,* Extra, August 7, 1844).

2. Brigham Young, Journal, January 24, 1845, cited in Arrington, *Brigham Young,* 119, spelling standardized.

3. Seventies, Records, Fourth Quorum, Minutes, October 30, 1844, LDS Archives.

4. *Signal,* June 25, 1845; James H. Glines, "Autobiography," 42, Church Archives.

5. *Neighbor,* February 19, 1845; *HC* 7:423.

6. *Neighbor,* April 6, 1845; also see William Huntington, Diary, 29–30, University of Utah.

7. The letter to Polk is in *HC* 7:402–4; an extract from the letter prepared for governors in *CHC* 2:522–23, with others in Church Archives (see, e.g., Brigham Young to Hugh J. Anderson, governor of Maine, April 25, 1845, photocopy, original in Maine State Archives). Discussions about sending the letters began a month earlier (Clayton, *Journals,* 159–60, March 11, 1845; Ehat, "'It Seems like Heaven Began on Earth,'" 270). The letter to Polk is dated May 10 and signed by Young and the trustees Newel K. Whitney and George Miller (Polk Papers, Box 86, Library of Congress, microfilm at Church Archives, but a different date and signatures are in *HC* 7:402–4).

8. *Signal,* June 4, 25, 1845, published reactions copied from newspapers in Kentucky and Connecticut; a comment from Boston is in *HC* 7:510.

9. *CHC* 2:525–26; *HC* 7:419; Genesis 13:5–18.

10. *HC* 7:348–50.

11. *Signal,* April 23, 1845, summarized Frémont's trip from June 1843 through the party's return to the mouth of the Kansas River on July 31, 1844.

12. See *Neighbor,* October 25, 1843 (Frémont), April 10 (Hastings), and July 10, 1844 (Wilkes); Christian, "Mormon Foreknowledge," 409–10.

13. *Neighbor,* January 29, March 19, September 10, 17, 24 (Frémont), February 19 (Wilkes), July 23 (Kearny), and August 13, 1845 (Hastings); *Messenger,* July 12 through September 6, 1845 (Hastings).

14. *HC* 7:350; *T&S* 6 (February 1, 1845): 791, where the *Prophet* is invited to copy the notice.

15. Clayton, *Journals,* 157, February 4, March 1, 1845. Reports of council discussions in Clayton, *Journals,* 158–65, are brought together in Ehat, "'It Seems Like Heaven Began on Earth,'" 268–72.

16. Clayton, *Journals,* 158–59, 163, March 1, April 15, 1845, and cf. *HC* 7:374, 379; William Huntington, Diary, 28, March 23, 1845, University of Utah.

17. Clayton, *Journals,* 163, 180–81, April 15, September 1, 9, 1845; *HC* 7:434, 437. The number of men assigned to the party continued in flux until the group departed (see Clayton, *Journals,* 162–63, April 11, 15, 1845; *HC* 7:401, 434, 437).

18. Clayton, *Journals,* 163, April 15, 17, 1845; Parley P. Pratt to Isaac Rogers, September 6, 1845, Church Archives. The text of "The Upper California" from *Sacred Hymns* (Liverpool, 1851) is included in Ehat, "'It Seems Like Heaven Began on Earth,'" 280. For variations collected by

folklorists, see Cheney, *Mormon Songs,* 68–69. A variant version of the second stanza is quoted below.

19. Stout, *Diary,* 1:28, March 19, 1845; *HC* 7:387. The Leadville region appeared in nineteenth-century maps as an open country extending from the Front Range of the Rockies west of Denver to the Uinta Mountains of eastern Utah; explorers had not yet filled in the mesas and plateaus of western Colorado.

20. Monroe, Tutorial Diary, 104–5, April 23, 1845, Coe Collection.

21. Clayton, *Journals,* 163, April 17, 1845; *HC* 7:400–401; Flanders, *Nauvoo,* 294–95.

22. *HC* 6:224; 2:482; 4:352; 7:269–70. Sidney Rigdon erroneously reported that Emmett had actually left Nauvoo secretly in the fall of 1844 under instructions from the Twelve to explore a Red River site in Texas (Rigdon's claim in the *Messenger and Advocate* was picked up by the *Quincy Whig* and copied in the *Signal,* May 28, 1845).

23. John L. Butler, Autobiography (1859), 47–49, Church Archives; *HC* 6:149; 7:383–84.

24. Letter from joint council, February 27, 1845, in *HC* 7:378. Emmett's inhumane treatment of camp members is detailed in William D. Kartchner, Autobiography, BYU Library (microfilm at Church Archives).

25. *HC* 7:385.

26. Clayton, *Journals,* 176–77, August 7, 1845; *HC* 7:434–35, 495. For difficulties between Butler and Emmett, see John L. Butler, Autobiography (1859), 50–51, Church Archives. The mileage given in Fullmer's report, 625 miles (*HC* 7:495), does not fit the description given of the route.

27. Clayton, *Journals,* 177, August 12, 1845; Butler, Autobiography, 52–53, Church Archives.

28. *HC* 7:494, 497–98, 513; Butler, Autobiography, 52–53, Church Archives.

29. Clayton, *Journals,* 165, May 10, 1845; cf. *HC* 7:498, August 13, 1845.

30. *Neighbor,* May 5, 1845; Spencer's report, in *HC* 7:424; Kimball, in *T&S* 6 (August 1, 1845): 987–88; *Signal,* July 30 1845. The poem appeared in *New York Messenger,* July 12, 1845, with authorship credited to "A Saint."

31. Seventies, Records, Fourth Quorum, August 23, 1845, Church Archives.

32. Clayton, *Journals,* 181, September 9, 1845.

33. *HC* 7:494, 498; also reported in Clayton, *Journals,* 190, October 29, 1845, where William Smith is named as the writer of the letter.

34. The plan is spelled out in Brigham Young to James Arlington Bennet, October 17, 1845, Brigham Young Papers, Church Archives.

35. Clayton, *Journals,* 180, August 28, 31, 1845; Taylor, "Nauvoo Journal," 86, August 28, 1845.

36. Young to Woodruff, August 21, 1845, in *MS* 6 (October 1, 1845): 124; Council of the Twelve to Addison Pratt, August 28, 1845, Brigham Young Papers, Church Archives; Parley P. Pratt to Isaac Rogers, September 6, 1845, Church Archives.

37. Clayton, *Journals,* 180–81, September 9, 1845 (*HC* 7:439–40).

38. *HC* 7:439–41 (September 12, 1845); Clayton, *Journals,* 183, September 16, 1845; *Proclamation: To Col. Levi Williams, and Mob Party,* September 16, 1845.

39. *Neighbor,* April 30, 1845.

40. *Neighbor,* May 7, 1845. Note that the second stanza differs from the version collected by Cheney, *Mormon Songs.*

41. *Signal,* June 18, 1845, copying a *New York Sun* report.

42. *Neighbor,* February 26, 1845 (*HC* 7:367–68). Thomas Sharp headlined the proposal: "A Bright Idea" (*Signal,* February 10, 1845; also see March 5 issue). For a comment on the use of the euphemism of "removal" in both Indian and Latter-day Saint displacement, see Smith, "Frontier Nauvoo," 17.

43. "To the Democrats of the State of Illinois," in *Signal,* May 14, 1845; Clayton, *Journals,* 182, September 14, 1845.

44. *Signal,* September 17, May 14, June 25, 1845.

45. For a personal response, see Calvin Reed to Plimpton Simonds, July 1845, Church Archives.

46. From the reprint in *Signal,* May 28, 1845.

47. Reprinted in *Signal,* February 26, 1845.

48. *HC* 7:22, 27, 31, from Ford's *History of Illinois,* and *HC* 7:84 from John Taylor's "The Martyrdom of Joseph Smith."

49. Backenstos to Young, September 10, 1845, Brigham Young Papers, Church Archives; Young to Backenstos, July 31, 1845, Brigham Young Papers, Church Archives; *HC* 7:432, 439–40; Backenstos to Young, September 10, 1845, Brigham Young Papers, Church Archives.

50. *Signal,* May 14, 1845.

51. One anonymous Latter-day Saint writer offered this explanation: "The law of the land and the rules of the church do not allow one man to have more than one wife alive at once, but if any man's wife die, he has a right to marry another, and to be sealed to both for eternity; to the living and the dead! There is no law of God or man against it! This is all the spiritual wife system that ever was tolerated in the church, and they [the apostates] know it" (*T&S* 5 [November 15, 1844]: 715).

52. *Signal,* January 29, 1845.

53. *Signal,* November 27, 1844. These arguments became popular with those who opposed Brigham Young's leadership (see Howard, *Church through the Years,* 1:293). Also see William A. Moore to Brigham Young and Heber C. Kimball, September 25, 1844, Brigham Young Papers, Church Archives, for similar comments made in Chester County, Pennsylvania; and *Signal,* February 3, 1845, for comments from Portland, Maine.

54. *New York Messenger,* May 1845.

55. William Huntington, "Life," 22, Church Archives; *Signal,* September 3, 1845; Stout, *Diary,* 1:57–58; Bates, "William Smith," 19. The sermon was delivered August 17, 1845. A denial that plural marriage was practiced in the church appears in *T&S* 6 (May 1, 1845): 894.

56. Smith, "Patriarchal Crisis of 1845," 33–34; Clayton, *Journals,* 166, May 23, 1845; Brigham Young to William Smith, August 10, 1845, Brigham Young Papers, Church Archives.

57. *Signal,* October 29, 1845. Smith also circulated his statement as a pamphlet published in St. Louis.

58. *Signal,* November 26, December 24, 1845; March 4, 1846.

59. *Signal,* January 8, 22, 1845; Neibaur, Diary, June 3, 1845, Church Archives.

60. Stout, *Diary,* 1:34, April 13, 1845; *HC* 7:396, 398.

61. *HC* 7:491–92; Godfrey, "Crime and Punishment in Mormon Nauvoo," 218; Ford to Backenstos, October 29, 1845, Illinois State Historical Society, microfilm, Church Archives; see additional discussion in chapters 18 and 19 of this volume.

62. *St. Louis Organ,* January 9, 1846, and *Peoria Register,* no date, quoted in *T&S* 6 (February 1, 1846): 1114–15.

63. George Edmunds, October 4, 1904, to Reverend Ashley Bartlett, Church Archives; interview with A. A. Cooper, *Deseret Evening News,* September 2, 1905, 26.

64. Solomon Hancock and Alanson Ripley to Brigham Young, September 11, 1845, Brigham Young Papers, Church Archives; Hancock to Young, September 12, 1845, Brigham Young Papers, Church Archives; *Neighbor,* September 10, 1845; *Neighbor,* Extra, September 12, 1845, which includes a list of houses destroyed. Hancock furnished more details for Young in another letter on September 13, Brigham Young Papers, Church Archives.

65. *HC* 7:439–40, 444; *Signal,* September 17, 1845. Quincy citizens criticized militant reactions on both sides and adopted the view that Latter-day Saint expansion led to the crisis (Resolutions of September 23 meeting, in *Quincy Whig,* October 1, 1845).

66. *HC* 7:441–42, 445. Governor Ford's final report to state legislators charged the Anti-Mormon Party with burning 150 to 175 houses, cabins, and hotels (*Signal,* December 19, 1846).

67. Jacob Gates, Diary, September 13, 1845, Church Archives; James H. Glines, Diary, September 12, 1845, Church Archives. Lewis Barney reported the offer of protection for giving up his faith (Autobiography, 23, Church Archives).

68. *HC* 7:440–43; William Clayton, *Journals,* 181, September 11, 1845.

69. *HC* 7:441; Seventies Quorums, Records, Second Quorum, Minutes, September 27, 1845, Church Archives.

70. *Signal,* September 17, 1845; *American Penny Magazine* (New York City), October 11, 1845, quoting *St. Louis Republican,* September 17, 1845.

71. Young to Solomon Hancock, September 11, 1845, Brigham Young Papers, Church Archives; Young to Backenstos, September 13, 1845, in Journal History, same date. The intention to expel or exterminate the Saints was reported from Warsaw in the *St. Louis Republican,* September 17, 1845, and repeated in *American Penny Magazine* (New York City), October 11, 1845.

72. Young to Backenstos, September 11, 1845, Brigham Young Papers, Church Archives (paraphrased in *HC* 7:439–40); Young to Sam Brannan, September 15, 1845.

73. Backenstos to Young, September 13, 1845, Brigham Young Papers, Church Archives; *HC* 7:443–45; Backenstos, "Proclamation 1," September 13, 1845, in *Signal,* October 15, 1845; Backenstos to Young, September 15, 1845, Brigham Young Papers, Church Archives.

74. Young to James Arlington Bennet, October 17, 1845, Brigham Young Papers, Church Archives; Seventies, Records, Third Quorum, September 14, 1845, Church Archives.

75. J. B. Backenstos, Proclamation 3, September 17, 1845, in *Signal,* October 15, 1845; Samuel Rogers, Diary, September 16, 1845, BYU Library; Clayton, *Journals,* 183, September 16–17, 1845; Stout, *Diary,* 1:64, 66, September 16–17, 1845; *HC* 7:445–46; Schindler, *Orrin Porter Rockwell,* 144–46; *MS* 6 (November 1, 1845): 154–55.

76. Ford to Backenstos, September 24, October 29, 1845, and Backenstos to Almeron Wheat, November 17, 1845, Illinois State Historical Society, microfilm, Church Archives; *HC* 7:541; Schindler, *Orrin Porter Rockwell,* 154–55. Backenstos stood trial before the circuit court at Peoria. Rockwell was tried in Galena in July 1846.

77. *Proclamation: To Col. Levi Williams, and Mob Party,* September 16, 1845. The quotations are from a paraphrase in Clayton, *Journals,* 183, September 16, 1845.

78. *Signal,* September 17, 1845.

79. Backenstos, Proclamation 2, September 16, 1845, in *Signal,* October 15, 1846; Epistle to Ramus, in Journal History, September 16, 1845.

80. Stout, *Diary,* 1:65, September 17, 1845; Clayton, *Journals,* 183, September 19, 1845 (authorization of self-defense); Journal History, September 17–18, 1845.

81. Samuel Rogers, Diary, September 17, 1845, BYU Library; Isaac Haight, Diary, September 17, 1845, University of Utah.

82. Backenstos, Proclamation 3, in *Signal,* October 15, 1845 (Hallwas and Launius, *Cultures in Conflict,* 281–83); Stout, *Diary,* 1:66, September 17, 1845; *MS* 6 (November 1, 1845): 154–55.

83. Backenstos to Young, September 18, 1845, Brigham Young Papers, Church Archives; Journal

History, September 18, 1845; Solomon Hancock to Brigham Young, Carthage, November 18, 1845, Brigham Young Papers, Church Archives.

84. Young to Howard Egan, September 19, 1845, Brigham Young Papers, Church Archives.

85. Journal History, September 18–19, 1845; Backenstos to Young, September 19, 1845, 2:00 P.M., Brigham Young Papers, Church Archives; Young to George Miller, September 19, 1845, 3:00 P.M., and same day at 11:00 P.M., Brigham Young Papers, Church Archives, spelling standardized; Stout, *Diary,* 1:67–68, September 19–20, 1845; Kimball, *Diaries,* 135, September 20, 1845; John D. Lee, Journal, 58, September 20, 1845, Church Archives.

86. Stout, *Diary,* 1:68, September 19, 1845.

87. *Signal,* Extra, September 24, 1845, and second Extra issued at 10:00 P.M. that same night. Governor Ford repeated this claim in his report to the House of Representatives in December 1846 (see *Signal,* December 19, 1846).

88. Stout, *Diary,* 1:65–66, 72–73, September 17, 24–25, 1845; Young to Howard Egan, September 21, 1845, Brigham Young Papers, Church Archives; Egan to Young, September 20, 1845, Brigham Young Papers, Church Archives.

89. *Signal,* Extras, September 24 and 27, 1845; Journal History, September 19, 1845; Stout, *Diary,* 1:67, 81, September 19, October 7–8, 1845.

90. *Signal,* Extra, September 27, 1845.

91. *Signal,* second Extra of September 24, 1846. This Extra reported the force assembled at Augusta as 800 men. Information reaching the Twelve numbered the militia at 250 men (Kimball, *Diaries,* 136, September 27, 1845) and then at 320 men (Stout, *Diary,* 1:76, September 28, 1845). Other sources reported 200 men (Stout, *Diary,* 1:74, September 27, 1845; *Signal,* October 15, 1845).

92. *Whig,* October 1, 1845; Kimball, *Diaries,* 137, September 28, 1845.

93. Stout, *Diary,* 1:73–74, 81, September 26–27, October 8, 1845.

94. Letter to Solomon Hancock, September 12, 1845, in *HC* 7:440–41.

95. Clayton, *Journals,* 182, September 14, 1845; *HC* 7:444; Stout, *Diary,* 1:72, September 24, 1845; Kimball, *Diaries,* 136, September 24, 1845.

96. Journal History, September 19–20, 1845.

97. Joseph L. Heywood to Brigham Young, September 23, 1845, Brigham Young Papers, Church Archives, spelling standardized.

98. Resolutions of September 23, 1845, in *Quincy Whig,* October 1, 1845. The *Signal* Extra, September 24, 1845, said the committee was "to go to Nauvoo and invite the Mormons to leave."

99. Proposals and responses from the Quincy committee include Henry Asbury et al. to Brigham Young and others, September 24, 25, 1845, Brigham Young Papers, Church Archives.

100. Kimball, *Diaries,* 136, September 24, 1845; Brigham Young to the Quincy Committee, September 24, 1845, in *Quincy Whig,* October 1, 1845 (Hallwas and Launius, *Cultures in Conflict,* 302–4). The decision to retain the temple was noted in a handwritten cover letter dated September 25 (retained copy, Brigham Young Papers, Church Archives); Clayton, *Journals,* 183, September 24, 1845.

101. Quincy Resolutions, adopted September 26, 1845, published in *Signal,* Extra, September 30, 1845 (*HC* 7:451–53, from *Quincy Whig,* October 1, 1845).

102. *Signal,* second Extra, September 24, 1845; Extra, September 27, 1845; Extra, September 30, 1845; *Whig,* October 1, 1845.

103. *HC* 7:447–48; Stout, *Diary,* September 30, 1845, 1:77.

104. *Signal,* Extra, September 24, and Extra, September 27, 1845; *HC* 7:447. Young's companions were Heber C. Kimball, Willard Richards, John Taylor, George A. Smith, and Amasa Lyman.

105. Stout, *Diary,* 1:78, 78 n. 39, 81, September 30, October 8, 1845; *HC* 7:448.

106. See *HC* 7:449, where the term Quincy Committee is used incorrectly to identify the governor's committee; and compare *Signal,* October 22, 1845. The list of convention officers published in the *Signal* includes vice presidents William Ross (Pike Co.), James McCallen (Warren Co.), and John Kirk (McDonough Co.). Pike and Knox Counties were not originally committed to the conference (Ford to Backenstos, September 24, 1845, Illinois State Historical Society Papers, microfilm, Church Archives).

107. Kimball, *Diaries,* 137, September 30, 1845, spelling standardized; Young to Hardin, September 30, 1845, Brigham Young Papers, Church Archives.

108. Kimball, *Diaries,* 137–38, September 31 [October 1], 1845, notes that Colonel W. B. Warren joined the party and notes a reconvening of the council after a noon meal.

109. *HC* 7:447–49.

110. Hardin, Douglas, Warren, and McDougal to the First President and Council, October 1, 1845; and Young to Hardin, Douglas, Warren, and McDougal, October 1, 1845, in *To the Anti-Mormon Citizens of Hancock and the Surrounding Counties,* broadside, issued about October 4, 1845 (printed at the *Signal* job press); also in *National Intelligencer* (Washington, D.C.), October 18, 1845, quoting the *St. Louis Republican.* The committee letter, but not the church reply, is in *HC* 7:449–50.

111. *Signal,* October 22, 1845. Proceedings of the convention's second day, including the resolutions, also appear in Hallwas and Launius, *Cultures in Conflict,* 304–9.

112. Hardin, Warren, Douglas, and McDougal to The First President and High Council, Carthage, October 3, 1845, in *To the Anti-Mormon Citizens* (*HC* 7:450–51, where it is erroneously dated October 2). Young apparently received the document from Camp Mississippi, south of Nauvoo, after Hardin added his signature (*HC* 7:450).

113. Hardin, Douglas, Warren, and McDougal, cover letter, October 4, 1845, in *To the Anti-Mormon Citizens.* The broadside contained the committee's two letters to church leaders and Brigham Young's response, together with a cover letter addressed to the Anti-Mormon Citizens of the nine-county area.

114. *Notice: There Will Be a Meeting Held of the American Citizens of Lee County,* broadside, October 3, 1845, Church History Library; *Lee County Anti-Mormon Meeting,* held in Fort Madison, Iowa, October 16, 1845, broadside of Minutes, inserted in the Church History Library microfilm of the *Signal,* after the issue of October 15, 1845.

115. Presumably Ford to Backenstos, September 24, 1845, Illinois State Historical Society Papers, microfilm, Church Archives.

116. *HC* 7:453–55, quotation at 473. The *Neighbor* ceased regular publication after the October 29 issue. With the approval of the conference, the *Times and Seasons* skipped its four September and October numbers but resumed with a November 1 conference issue and continued bimonthly papers until its final number, dated February 15, 1846.

117. *HC* 7:454, 502–5.

118. *HC* 7:505–8. Young had ordered General Charles C. Rich to investigate and put a stop to any confirmed cattle theft (Stout, *Diary,* 1:81, October 7–8, 1845).

119. *HC* 7:145 n., 523–25, 527–32. Ford's emissary, Mason Brayman, reported the incident [to the governor?] on November 16, 1845 (see Hallwas and Launius, *Cultures in Conflict,* 295–96).

120. *HC* 7:530, 532; Mason Brayman to [Thomas Ford?], November 16, 1845, in Hallwas and Launius, *Cultures in Conflict,* 295–96.

121. *Neighbor,* Extra, November 19, 1845, in *HC* 7:529.

122. *HC* 7:527–32.

123. Young to Backenstos, September 15, 1845, in *HC* 7:445.

124. Jacob Gates, Journals, September 26, 30, 1845, Church Archives.

125. Smith, October 3, 1841, *HC* 4:426; general conference, October 5–8, 1845, *HC* 7:456–77; *T&S* (November 1, 1845): 1017–18.

126. *HC* 7:457–63, 483.

127. *HC* 7:463–64.

128. *HC* 7:464–65, 469; Clayton, *Journals,* 184–85, October 6, 1845.

129. *HC* 7:466–67.

130. *HC* 7:468–69.

131. *Circular to the Whole Church of Jesus Christ of Latter Day Saints,* broadside [Nauvoo: 1845], copy at Church Historical Library (also in *T&S* 6 [November 1, 1845]: 1018; and *HC* 7:478). Although signed by Young as president of the Twelve and echoing his ideas, the circular was drafted by others, perhaps his associate Willard Richards, who cosigned as clerk, or Parley P. Pratt or William W. Phelps.

132. *T&S* 6 (November 1, 1845): 1018–19; *HC* 7:478–80.

133. *T&S* 6 (November 15, 1845): 1031.

134. *Neighbor,* October 29, 1845.

135. *T&S* 6 (November 1, 1845): 1017 (*HC* 7:511–12). John Taylor edited both Nauvoo newspapers.

136. *New York Messenger,* October 4, 1845.

137. *Signal,* November 19, 1845; see also "Note of Preparation," *Signal,* December 17, 1845, copying *T&S* 6 (November 15, 1845): 1031.

138. Among those reporting the decision as straight news was the *St. Louis Republican* (copied by the *National Intelligencer* [Washington, D.C.], October 30, 1845). The *Quincy Whig* (October 1, 1845) responded to the *Herald* and *New Era* by denying political intent in its anti-Mormonism.

139. Reprinted in *Signal,* December 31, 1845.

140. Reprinted in *Signal,* November 12, 1845.

141. *St. Louis Organ,* January 1, 1845, in *T&S* 6 (February 1, 1846): 114–15; *New York Sun,* copied in *Washington Union,* then in *T&S* 6 (December 1, 1845): 1052; *National Intelligencer,* October 7, 9, 16, 18, 30, 1845.

142. Reprinted in *National Intelligencer,* October 18, 1845.

143. Unidentified clipping, undated, McKensie-Lindsey Collection, Ontario Archives, microfilm copy in NRI Collection.

144. *MS* 8 (July 15, 1846): 8–10.

145. *HC* 7:566–68, 573.

146. Young to Brannan, September 15, 1845, Brigham Young Papers, Church Archives (quoted in *HC* 7:445, but without the final phrase, "and we will meet you there").

147. "Farewell Message of Orson Pratt," New York, November 8, 1845, in *T&S* 6 (December 1, 1845): 1042 (*HC* 7:515).

148. See Young to E. L. Barnam of Chicago, December 26, 1845, retained copy, Brigham Young Papers, Box 12, Fd 2, Church Archives.

149. Resolution of Quincy public meeting, September 23, 1845, in *Quincy Whig,* October 1, 1845.

150. Seventies Quorums, Records, Fifth Quorum, Minutes, April 7, 1846.

151. Andrew Moore, Seventies Quorums, Records, Fifth Quorum, Minutes, December 9, 1845; D. D. Hunt, Seventies Quorums, Records, Fifth Quorum, Minutes, December 14, 1845.

152. John S. Fullmer to Uncle John, November 18, 1845, John S. Fullmer Letterbook, 241, Church Archives.

CHAPTER 18. LEAVING NAUVOO

Epigraph: The Twelve to Governor James Clark of Iowa Territory, February 28, 1846, *HC* 7:601 (*CHC* 3:44); Nauvoo High Council, Circular to the Church, *T&S* 6 (January 20, 1846): 1096 (*HC* 7:570).

1. Joseph G. Hovey, Reminiscences, Church Archives, 25, October 1845.

2. Conference talk, October 7, 1845, *T&S* 6 (November 1, 1845): 1011–12 (*HC* 7:466); John S. Fullmer to Uncle John Fullmer, November 18, 1845, John S. Fullmer Letterbook, 242, Church Archives.

3. Conversation with Andrew Perkins, September 13, 1845, *HC* 7:442.

4. Conference talk, October 7, 1845, *T&S* 6 (November 1, 1845): 1012–13 (*HC* 7:469).

5. *HC* 7:453; George A. Smith, October 6, and Heber C. Kimball, October 7, 1845, *T&S* 6 (November 1, 1845): 1011–12 (*HC* 7:464–65, 467); Missouri committee, *HC* 3:250–54.

6. *HC* 7:531. Also see October conference remarks by Parley P. Pratt and Heber C. Kimball, *T&S* 6 (November 1, 1845): 1011 (*HC* 7:464, 466).

7. *HC* 7:470–71.

8. *HC* 7:471–72. The original transcript of Lucy's talk has been published in Walker, "Lucy Mack Smith Speaks," 276–84.

9. McConkie, *Mormon Doctrine*, 226–28, 425–26; Brigham Young, "Circular," *T&S* 6 (November 1, 1845): 1018 (*HC* 7:479–80).

10. See, especially, *HC* 7:541–43, 567; see also chapter 10 of this volume.

11. *T&S* 6 (February 15, 1846): 1128. The quotation is from Isaiah 2:2–3.

12. George Alley to Joseph Alley III, October 9, 1845, Church Archives, spelling standardized.

13. Clayton, *Journals,* 180–84, September 9, 11, 30, 1845; (cf. *HC* 7:440, 442); *HC* 7:447.

14. *T&S* 6 (November 1, 1845): 1012 (*HC* 7:467).

15. D&C 136:1–3. Samuel Rogers noted the call of seven companies of one hundred families each at conference (Rogers, Diary, 64, October 8, 1845, BYU Library).

16. The captains are listed in *HC* 7:481–82 and members of the Fifty in Ehat, "'It Seems Like Heaven Began on Earth,'" 267–68, April 18, 1844, February 4, 1845.

17. D&C 103:30; *HC* 7:483, 513–14, 469–70. The Zion's Camp organizational plan was reaffirmed in the "Word and Will of the Lord," a January 1847 revelation for the emigrant companies of the Camp of Israel (D&C 136:3).

18. Ehat, "'It Seems Like Heaven Began on Earth,'" 276–77; *HC* 7:519, 532; Norton Jacob, Reminiscences and Journal, 26, January 19, 1846, Church Archives.

19. *Neighbor,* October 1, 1845; *HC* 7:532; John S. Fullmer to James Rucker, July 24, 1846, John S. Fullmer Letterbook, 266, Church Archives.

20. Pratt's "Requirements of Each Family of Five" was reported on September 30 (*HC* 7:447) and inserted in the *History of the Church* with the entry for October 4, 1845 (*HC* 7:454–55).

21. Meetings of the General Council, September 30, October 4, 1845, *HC* 7:447, 454–55 (identified by their more common name, Council of Fifty, in Clayton, *Journals,* 183–84). The list

was created "from calculation and from the best works on the subject" (*HC* 7:454). For comparison, see a typical outfit for four people compiled from a dozen guidebooks of the 1840s in Faragher, *Women and Men on the Overland Trail,* 192.

22. *Neighbor,* October 29, 1845 (*CHC* 2:539–40); *HC* 7:554, 557.

23. *HC* 7:535–36.

24. *Signal,* December 3, 1845; Zodak Knapp Judd, Autobiography, 16, University of Utah; Alfred B. Lambson, Account Book, December 1845-January 1846, Church Archives.

25. *HC* 7:532; *Hancock Eagle,* April 10, 1846; Mt. Pisgah Journal, July 7, 1846, Church Archives; Young to Babbitt, Heywood, and Fullmer, July 7, 1846; Watson, *Manuscript History of Brigham Young,* 224–25.

26. *HC* 7:441–42, 474. Agents were named in Nauvoo, La Harpe, Macedonia, Camp Creek, Bear Creek, Knowlton's Settlement, Highland Branch, Montebello, and Yelrome.

27. *HC* 7:536; *Signal,* December 31, 1845. Brigham Young used Owens's estimate of thirty thousand acres of improved farmland in his report to the governor's negotiating committee (*Neighbor,* October 1, 1845).

28. *Signal,* November 19, 1845.

29. Sally Randall to Parents and Brothers and Sisters, June 1, 1846, typescript, Church Archives; Robert Pixton, Autobiography, copy in NRI Collection; Mary Ann Pratt story, in Elizabeth B. Winters, ed., "Stearns-Winters Book of Remembrance," Part II, 17–18, copy in NRI Collection; Lee, *Mormonism Unveiled,* 175; Canadian Saints, in "Robert Gardner, Utah Pioneer," multilithed memoirs, 1934, 13–14, copy in NRI Collection; John S. Fullmer to C. C. Trubue, November 8, 1845, John S. Fullmer Letterbook, 238, Church Archives.

30. Almon W. Babbitt to Brigham Young, November 4, 1845, Brigham Young Papers, Church Archives; Brigham Young to H. H. Duncan, December 21, 1845, Brigham Young Papers; *HC* 7:538.

31. Oliver Cowdery to Brigham Young, October 7, 1846, Brigham Young Papers, Church Archives; Young to Bennet, October 17, 1845, Brigham Young Papers; for more on Bennet, see *HC* 7:482–83, 488, 528.

32. *HC* 7:499–501.

33. *HC* 7:499.

34. *HC* 7:499, 501–2; Clayton, *Journals,* 190, October 29, 1845.

35. "Epistle," October 8, 1845, in *T&S* 6 (November 1, 1845): 1018 (*HC* 7:479).

36. Clayton, *Journals,* 182, September 14, 1845 (*HC* 7:444). The writs named Brigham Young, Heber C. Kimball, Willard Richards, John E. Page, William Smith, and George A. Smith, all members of the Twelve, and Daniel Garn.

37. *HC* 7:467, 470. The visit to Carthage is described in chapter 17 of this volume.

38. Clayton, *Journals,* 185, 190, October 10–11, 29, 31, 1845 (*HC* 7:481–82).

39. Clayton, *Journals,* October 29, 31, 1845 (*HC* 7:498).

40. *HC* 7:487–93; Stout, *Diary,* 1:86–87, October 25, 1845.

41. *HC* 7:491–94, 533–35. The quotation is from Kane, *The Mormons,* 1.

42. *Signal,* January 7, 1846. The counterfeiting charges are discussed in chapter 17 of this volume.

43. *HC* 7:549–51; *Signal,* December 31, 1845.

44. Quotations from Clayton, *Journals,* 244–45, December 30, 1845; see also 250–51, January 2, 1846; and *HC* 7:554, 557–58, 564–66.

45. *HC* 7:514.

46. For rumors of Smith's involvement, see Clayton, *Journals,* 190, October 29, 31, 1845. Governor Ford admitted his involvement after removal was accomplished.

47. Clayton, *Journals,* 195, December 11, 1845 (*HC* 7:544); *HC* 7:547; Young to Wentworth, December 17, 1845, in *Signal,* January 31, 1846; and Young to Marcy, December 17, 1845, Church Archives.

48. *HC* 7:548, 556, 558. The famous Rocky Mountain prophecy, delivered at Montrose, Iowa, in August 1842, is reported in *HC* 5:85–86; Anson Call's statement is in a note on page 85.

49. Clayton, *Journals,* 206, December 11, 1845. Stanley B. Kimball explores as possibilities the popular map by Major S. H. Long (1823), and maps by Frémont (1843 and 1845), Wilkes (Oregon, 1845), and Bonneville (1837); in January 1846, Brigham Young ordered a copy of S. A. Mitchell's 1846 map (Kimball, *Latter-day Saints' Emigrants' Guide,* 25–30). On April 4, 1847, at Council Bluffs, "T. Bullock made a sketch of Cap. Frémont's topographical map of road to Oregon for the use of the Pioneers" (Watson, *Manuscript History of Brigham Young,* 545). See also *CHC* 3:161–62 and a reproduction of Frémont's Platte River map with the 1847 pioneer route superimposed on it (*CHC* 3: facing 168). Clayton collected other hand-drawn maps from Lansford Hastings and Miles Goodyear during the 1847 pioneer trek (Korns and Morgan, *West from Fort Bridger,* 245–48).

50. *HC* 7:555, 558; Kimball, *Latter-day Saints' Emigrants' Guide,* 20–25. Other reports appeared in *Signal,* December 2, 1845, and in publications of the Charles Wilkes and B. L. E. Bonneville expeditions.

51. *T&S* 6 (January 15 [20], 1846): 1096.

52. See, e.g., Maria Dewey to Ashbel Dewey, October 11, 1845, USHS Library; Sally Randall to her family, June 1, 1846, Church Archives; and Betsey Heydon to her children, August 17, 1846, Church Archives.

53. Azubah and Aphek Woodruff to Wilford Woodruff, November 28, 1845, Church Archives; Joel Sands to "Dear Brother," January 2, 1846, Church Archives.

54. Pratt to Isaac Rogers, September 6, 1845, Church Archives.

55. *HC* 7:579; Jacob Gates, Journals, January 9, 16, 1846, Church Archives, spelling standardized.

56. Watson, *Manuscript History of Brigham Young,* 2–28 (*HC* 7:561–80).

57. James Jones to Henry Jones, May 19, 1846, Henry Jones Correspondence, Church Archives, spelling standardized.

58. *HC* 7:562, a paraphrase of Clayton, *Journals,* 251–52, January 2, 1846.

59. Ford, *History of Illinois,* 291, 303 (*HC* 7:563–74); Polk, *Diary of James K. Polk,* 205–6.

60. *HC* 7:564, 567, 569, 576; Clayton, *Journals,* 196–97, January 11, 18, 23, 1846; Stout, *Diary,* 1:104–5, January 11, 13, 1846.

61. John D. Lee, Journal, 77, 79, January 11, 13, 1846, Church Archives, spelling standardized; George A. Smith, discourse, June 20, 1869, *JD* 13 (1871): 85–86; Esplin, "'A Place Prepared,'" 101, 110–11.

62. *Circular of the High Council,* broadside, Nauvoo, January 20, 1846. The circular also is found in *T&S* 6 (January 15 [dated internally January 20], 1846): 1096–97, and in *HC* 7:570–72. It was noted in *Signal,* January 28, 1846.

63. *Circular of the High Council* (*HC* 7:570–72); *HC* 7:574.

64. *Circular of the High Council* (*HC* 7:570–71). The second quotation in the epigraph of this chapter immediately follows the last sentence quoted here.

65. *HC* 7:573, 576. Joseph L. Heywood had counseled Young in mid-January that the Twelve's departure would help the Saints (Bennett, *Mormons at the Missouri,* 23–24). Compare the

dating in *HC* with Clayton, *Journals,* 196–97, January 23, 1846; and Stout, *Diary,* 1:108–9, January 24, 1846.

66. *HC* 7:574; Clayton, *Journals,* 196, January 23, 1846.

67. Brigham Young, Comments, general priesthood meeting, January 24 [23?], 1846, *HC* 7:573–75; Alphonzo Young to Heber C. Kimball, January 1846, *HC* 7:572.

68. *HC* 7:577; Samuel Brannan to Brigham Young, January 12, 1846, Brigham Young Papers, Church Archives.

69. Ford, *History of Illinois,* 290.

70. *HC* 7:577; Ford, *History of Illinois,* 302–3, 307–8.

71. *HC* 7:578; Stout, *Diary,* 1:111, February 2, 1846.

72. Stout, *Diary,* 1:111–13, February 2–7, 1846; Watson, *Manuscript History of Brigham Young,* 26–27, February 3, 1846 (*HC* 7:579).

73. Watson, *Manuscript History of Brigham Young,* 28, February 8, 1846 (*HC* 7:580–81).

74. Warren to Ford, February 12, 1846, in *Public Ledger,* March 6, 1846, reprinted from the *Illinois State Register.*

75. John D. Lee, Journal (1846), 1, Church Archives.

76. Journal History, March 27, 1846; *HC* 7:580–81. To settle an argument, two men with a fifty-foot tape measured the distance at its widest point when the river froze early in 1877. They found it 4,595 feet from shore to shore (*Nauvoo Independent,* April 20, 1877).

77. *HC* 7:582, 599; the witness, Stout, *Diary,* 1:113–14, February 9, 1846; six ferries, Major Warren to Governor Ford, February 12, 1846, *Public Ledger,* March 6, 1846.

78. *HC* 7:581; Stout, *Diary,* 1:114, February 9, 1846; Major Warren to Governor Ford, February 12, 1846, reported in *Public Ledger,* March 6, 1846; Jacob Gates, Journals, February 9, 1846. The *HC* says the west stovepipe, while Stout mentions the center pipe.

79. *HC* 7:584–85; Pratt departure in Elizabeth B. Winters, ed., *Stearns-Winters Book of Remembrance,* Part II, 14–15, photocopy in NRI file; *Signal,* March 18, 1846. The trustees sold Young's house at auction in July to John C. Bidamon for six hundred dollars, only one hundred dollars more than Young had paid for the lot alone five years earlier ("Brigham Young's Home," NRI Archives).

80. *T&S* 6 (February 1, 1846): 1114.

81. William L. Cochman to Edward Hunter, January 13, 1846, Edward Hunter Collection, BYU Library; Edward B. Talcott, note added to letter from Mary Talcott to Joseph L. Heywood, December 9, 21, 1845, Heywood Correspondence, Church Archives.

82. For examples, see S. B. Heywood to Joseph L. Heywood, December 7, 1845, Heywood Correspondence, Church Archives; William Jackman to Levi Jackman, February 16, 1846, Church Archives.

83. *Signal,* February 18, 1846.

84. *Signal,* February 11, 1846.

85. *HC* 7:585–86, 599; Stout, *Diary,* 1:124, February 17, 1846; John D. Lee, Journal, 2–4, February 17, 1846, Church Archives.

86. William Smith claimed that the tabernacle canvas had been secretly intended for use as wagon covers (*Signal,* October 29, 1845). At least before mid-February 1846, as this report indicates, it had not been appropriated for that purpose. By late February, the Saints had secured other cloth specifically for tent-ends and wagon covers (*HC* 7:591, 597; John D. Lee, Journal, 4–6, February 18, 1846, Church Archives).

87. The cannon arrived on February 28 under the command of Colonel John Scott (*HC* 7:592, 602).

88. See, e.g., *HC* 7:591–92, 602; and Stout, *Diary,* 1:125, 127, 129, February 21, 25, March 3, 1846.

89. *HC* 7:587; *Circular of the High Council,* January 20, 1846 (*HC* 7:570–71); Young to John Wentworth, December 17, 1845, in *Signal,* January 31, 1846; and Young to William L. Marcy, December 17, 1845, Church Archives.

90. *New York Messenger,* quoted in *T&S* 6 (January 15 [20], 1846): 1103. See Hansen, "Voyage of the *Brooklyn,*" 47–72, for a thorough treatment, passenger list, and bibliography.

91. William I. Appleby, Autobiography (1848), 147–48, Church Archives; Jesse C. Little, *Circular: Epistle to the Church . . . in the Eastern States,* November 12, 1846, broadside.

92. *HC* 7:611–12. For details on the calling of the Mormon Battalion, see Bennett, *Mormons at the Missouri,* 51–63.

93. *HC* 7:611–12.

94. Reminiscent of the reactions toward Governor Thomas Ford in his management of Hancock County issues, the response to President Polk's call for military volunteers was appreciation from church leaders and denigration from many lay members.

95. *HC* 7:599, 601; *Signal,* February 18, 1846. The first quotation in the epigraph to this chapter is from this letter.

96. *HC* 7:592, 602; *Signal,* February 18, 1846; Stout, *Diary,* 1:124–25, February 18, 1846.

97. *HC* 7:592; Joseph L. Heywood, February 14, 1846, to Brigham Young, Brigham Young Papers, Church Archives, spelling standardized. Heywood's sources were a letter from Congressman Joseph Hoge and Jacob Backenstos, who had just returned from a Democratic convention at Springfield. The quotations are Heywood's paraphrase of Backenstos's report.

98. *HC* 7:594; see also 592–95; Norton Jacob, Reminiscences and Journal, 31, February 22, 1846, Church Archives.

99. *HC* 7:595; see also 596–99.

100. *HC* 7:598, 604–7; Brigham Young to Joseph Young, March 9, 1846, in Watson, *Manuscript History of Brigham Young,* 75.

101. Watson, *Manuscript History of Brigham Young,* 140, 142, April 26, 1846.

102. *Hymns,* 1948, no. 13.

103. *HC* 7:596.

104. Watson, *Manuscript History of Brigham Young,* 42–50 (*HC* 7:591–602).

105. See *T&S* 2 (December 15, 1840): 249; 4 (February 1, 1843): 91; 4 (April 1, 1843): 153–54; 5 (February 1, 1844): 427; 5 (March 1, 1844): 458; *HC* 5:194, 327, 339, 345.

106. *Signal,* December 3, 31, 1845; January 14, February 4, 25, March 4, 1846.

107. Nelson W. Whipple, Journal, February 1846, Church Archives, extracted in N. W. Whipple, "Journal of a Pioneer," *Instructor* 81 (1946): 575–76.

108. *HC* 7:610.

109. *HC* 7:605–6.

110. *HC* 7:608.

111. *HC* 7:603, and compare with 7:580, February 8, 1846, where, prior to leaving Nauvoo, Young dedicated the temple as a monument to Joseph Smith. William I. Appleby preached on persecution in Philadelphia on December 18, 1845, and made a similar reference to the temple as "a monument of the industry of the Saints" (Appleby, Autobiography, 142, Church Archives).

112. *Hymns,* 1948, no. 37.

113. *HC* 7:621, 624. Two other general conferences sustained the First Presidency, one on August 14, 1848, at Manchester, England, representing nearly eighteen thousand members, and

another on October 8, 1848, in Salt Lake City, with five thousand members present (*HC* 7:623n, 628).

114. *HC* 7:625.

CHAPTER 19. TRANSITION AND EXPULSION

Epigraph: Parley P. Pratt, general conference address, October 6, 1845, *T&S* 6 (November 1, 1845): 1010; Governor Thomas Ford to Illinois Legislature, December 7, 1846, *Signal,* December 5, 1846 [published after date], and in *Nauvoo New Citizen,* December 12, 1846.

1. Watson, *Manuscript History of Brigham Young,* 72–73.

2. *HC* 7:576, 247, 580, 601; William Weeks to Truman O. Angell, February 13, 1846, with postscript by Brigham Young, Church Archives. Bishop Miller left February 6, and Bishop Whitney, February 28.

3. Norton Jacob, Reminiscences and Journal, 27, January 24, 1846, Church Archives; D&C 124:45–55.

4. Brigham Young to John M. Bernhisel, June 22, 1846, and Bernhisel to Young, June 10, August 3, Brigham Young Papers, Church Archives; Newel and Avery, *Mormon Enigma,* 233–34.

5. Summary of dedicatory prayer, in Watson, *Manuscript History of Brigham Young,* 147–48, April 30, 1846; Woodruff, *Journals,* 3:41, April 30, 1846, capitalization standardized; Hyde on "the glory of the Lord," James Allen Scott, Diaries, May 3, 1846, Church Archives; John S. Fullmer, notes on Hyde's comments, April 30, 1846, John S. Fullmer Letterbook, 253, Church Archives. Curtis E. Bolton recalled that in 1846 "the temple was Illuminated from cellar to vane supernaturally one evening this summer" (Reminiscences and Journal, 5, Church Archives).

6. Woodruff, *Journals,* 3:42, May 1, 1846; James Allen Scott, Diaries, May 3, 1846, Church Archives.

7. Madsen, *In Their Own Words,* 23, spelling standardized; Woodruff, *Journals,* 3:46–47, May 3, 1846, spelling standardized.

8. Watson, *Manuscript History of Brigham Young,* 158, 180, 192, 289.

9. John S. Fullmer to James Fullmer, April 21, 1846, John S. Fullmer Letterbook, Church Archives.

10. On April 10, the trustees subscribed for thirteen separate advertisements offering buildings and land for sale (*Hancock Eagle,* May 8, 1846); comments on the farms, W. W. Cole to James Winans, November 26, 1846, Church Archives.

11. Rowena Miller extracted this information from the Hancock County Deed Records, Books Q, R, S, and T; see also Lyon, "History Highlights," 70.

12. John S. Fullmer to George D. Fullmer, May 30, 1847, John S. Fullmer Letterbook, Church Archives.

13. John S. and Mary Ann Fullmer to Uncles James, William, and Benjamin Fullmer and Samuel Rucker, November 30, 1847, John S. Fullmer Letterbook, Church Archives. The August 1 appointment of David Cowen and John Snider as agents and A. A. Timmons as secretary, recorded August 8, and notice of election, recorded November 13, 1848 (Hancock County, Mortgages, 3:144, 188, Courthouse, Carthage, Illinois).

14. Orson Hyde to Brigham Young, April 5, 14, 1846, and John Taylor to Orson Hyde, April 27, 1846, paraphrased in Watson, *Manuscript History of Brigham Young,* 143–47; Brigham Young to Almon Babbitt, Joseph L. Heywood, and John S. Fullmer, August 25, 1846, Brigham Young

Papers, Church Archives; James Allen Scott, Diaries, May 3, 1846, Church Archives; John S. Fullmer to H. H. Blackwell, April 24, 1846, John S. Fullmer Letterbook, Church Archives; Clayton, *Journals*, 272, April 26, 1846.

15. Sermon, May 3, 1846, Watson, *Manuscript History of Brigham Young,*149–50.

16. John S. Fullmer to Brigham Young, June 26, 1846, Brigham Young Papers, Church Archives; and Almon W. Babbitt, John L. Heywood, and John S. Fullmer to Young, July 15, 1846, Brigham Young Papers, Church Archives; *Daily Missouri Republican,* June 16, July 28, 1847; John S. Fullmer to George Fullmer, September 2, 1847, John S. Fullmer Letterbooks, Church Archives; Abstract of Record of Title, Lot 1, Block 20, Wells Addition, Nauvoo, Church Archives; Cannon, *Nauvoo Panorama,* 52.

17. *Hancock Eagle,* May 29, 1846; Backman, *Heavens Resound,* 371–72.

18. *Hancock Eagle,* April 3, 1846. The Twelve wanted all printing and stereotyping equipment shipped west, but this was not done (Brigham Young to Almon W. Babbitt, Joseph L. Heywood and John S. Fullmer, September 27, 1846, Brigham Young Papers, Church Archives).

19. Prospectus of the *Hancock Eagle,* February 23, 1846, Church Library (*HC* 7:596).

20. Hiram Kimball and Phineas Kimball to Brigham Young, March 19, 1846, Brigham Young Papers, Church Archives; and John S. Fullmer to Brigham Young, June 26, 1846, Brigham Young Papers, Church Archives.

21. Mr. Harris, of Harris and Waters Co., of Oquawka, Illinois, to Reed and Co., of St. Louis, July 18, 1859, Church Archives.

22. *Signal,* March 15, April 8, 1846. On the protection claim, Thomas Sharp says that Jackson Redding and Orrin P. Rockwell had returned to Nauvoo to "frighten certain obnoxious persons out of Nauvoo" and that the two had told him "they were after some *scalps*" (*Signal,* March 25, 1846).

23. *Signal,* June 3, 1846.

24. *Signal,* April 15, 1846, reports April 4 meetings at McQueen's Mill in Henderson County that ratified an earlier McDonough County resolution setting a June 1 ultimatum.

25. *Quincy Whig,* April 29, 1844; Conyers, *Hancock Mob,* 26–28.

26. *Signal,* April 22, 1846, carries its own short notice from Warren and reprints a longer one from the *Hancock Eagle* of the previous week.

27. *Signal,* May 6, 1846.

28. Gregg, *Hancock County,* 346–47, citing published reports in the *Signal,* n.d., and *Quincy Whig,* May 20, 1846.

29. *Hancock Eagle,* May 2, 1846; Brigham Young to Almon W. Babbitt, Joseph L. Heywood, and John S. Fullmer, May 12, 1846, Brigham Young Papers, Church Archives; and George Alley to Joseph Alley III, May 12, 1846, Church Archives.

30. *Hancock Eagle,* July 10, 1846; A. W. Babbitt, J. L. Heywood, and J. S. Fullmer, to Brigham Young, August 31, 1846, enclosure, "Number of Adults in Nauvoo," Church Archives; Ford, *History of Illinois,* 411; *Signal,* June 3, 1846.

31. *Signal,* June 3, 1846; Watson, *Manuscript History of Brigham Young,* 163.

32. Proclamation, May 11, 1846, *Quincy Whig,* May 20, 1846 (*CHC* 3:4).

33. Warren report, May 11, 1846, *Quincy Whig,* May 20, 1846.

34. John S. Fullmer to George D. Fullmer, July 16, 1846, John S. Fullmer Letterbook, Church Archives; see also *Hancock Eagle,* July 17, 1846.

35. Orson Hyde to Brigham Young, May 16, 1846, written on the back of Hyde's broadside *He that hath ears to hear . . .* (issued March 14, 1846), Church Archives. Hyde personally delivered

the letter to Young in Winter Quarters and discussed it with the Twelve (Watson, *Manuscript History of Brigham Young*, 187–88, June 18, 1846).

36. Brigham Young to Almon Babbitt, Joseph L. Heywood, and John S. Fullmer, July 7, 15, 1846, Brigham Young Papers, Church Archives; Watson, *Manuscript History of Brigham Young*, 224–25, 267, 329.

37. Brigham Young to Almon Babbitt, Joseph L. Heywood, and John S. Fullmer, August 25, 1846, Brigham Young Papers, Church Archives.

38. Meeting of September 8, 1846, reported in Watson, *Manuscript History of Brigham Young*, 375; see also 377–78, 382, 385.

39. J. Todd, chairman, *Public Meeting of the New Citizens of Nauvoo*, broadside, [June 1846]; *Committee in Behalf of the New Citizens*, broadside, June 1846, signed by fifty citizens.

40. *St. Louis Daily New Era*, August 17, 21, 1846.

41. *Signal*, June 10, 1846.

42. John S. Fullmer to Brigham Young, June 26, 1846, Brigham Young Papers, Church Archives; Conyers, *Hancock Mob*, 8–9, 37, 42 (*CHC* 3:5–6).

43. *New Citizen Doggerel; Being an Account of the Wonderful Escape of Some "Respectable Old Citizens" from Golden's Point, June 14, 1846*, broadside (Warsaw: Printed at the *Signal* office, 1846); *The Boys of Nauvoo*, broadside (Nauvoo: 1846).

44. *Signal*, Extra, July 16, 1846. The trouble may have started in the Rice wheat field, one-quarter mile from the Lofton place.

45. *CHC* 3:6; *Hancock Eagle*, Extra, July 13, 1846; *Signal*, August 11, 1846; John S. Fullmer to George D. Fullmer, July 16, 1846, John S. Fullmer Letterbook, Church Archives.

46. *Hancock Eagle*, Extra, July 13, 1846; *Signal*, July 14, 16, 1846; *Citizens of Nauvoo! Once More to Arms in Defense of Your Persons and Property!*, broadside, Nauvoo, July 11, 1846; Almon Babbitt, Joseph L. Heywood, and John S. Fullmer to Brigham Young, July 15, 1846, Brigham Young Papers, Church Archives. The *Eagle* says Clifford led the law-and-order delegation.

47. H. G. Ferris to G. Edmunds, Jr., July 14, 1846, Watson, *Manuscript History of Brigham Young*, 240–41.

48. *Signal*, July 16, 1845; *Nauvoo New Citizen*, December 12, 1846. The regulators' report was signed by J. H. Sherman, J. W. Brattle (one of those arrested for the Davis farm beatings), Joseph Sibley, and Abram Van Tuyl (lessee of the Mansion House and accused by Emma Smith in 1847 of stealing furniture and drapes).

49. Watson, *Manuscript History of Brigham Young*, 233, 267, 277–85, 329; Curtis E. Bolton, Reminiscences, 6, Church Archives; *Signal*, Extra, July 16, 1846; Richard Ballantyne, Sketch of 1846 Kidnapping, Church Archives. The Nauvoo captives were Phineas H. Young, his son Brigham H. Young, Richard Ballantyne, James Standing, and the previously captured James Herring.

50. *Signal*, July 28, 1846; Curtis E. Bolton, Reminiscences, 6, Church Archives.

51. *Signal*, July 28, and Extra of July 29, 1846.

52. Wesley Williams to John W. Williams, August 1, 1846, Church Archives.

53. *Signal*, August 4, 1846 [issued the 5th]; *Hancock Eagle*, July 17, 24, 1846.

54. *Hancock Eagle*, Extra, August 18, 1846; *Signal*, August 18, 1846. McAuley, Brattle, Levi Williams, and a Mr. Douglass initiated the writs.

55. *Signal*, August 18, 1846; M. Brayman to Thomas Ford, September 22, *Signal*, October 20, 1846.

56. *Hancock Eagle*, Extra, August 18, 1846.

57. *Signal*, August 25, 1846.

58. *CHC* 3:8; Ford, *History of Illinois,* 416. Backenstos served in Mexico and then went to Oregon, where he accidentally drowned in a lake (Jacob B. Backenstos to Joseph McCubbin, June 26, 1846, with note added by copyist J. C. McCubbin, in 1933, Church Archives).

59. *CHC* 3:8; Parker, *Circular: To the Citizens of Adams and Adjacent Counties in This State,* August 25, 1846 (reprinted as "Proclamation. No. 1," in *Hancock Eagle,* August 28, 1846); Parker, *Proclamation* [No. 2], August 28, 1846 (Watson, *Manuscript History of Brigham Young,* 355–56, and Conyer, *Hancock Mob,* 48–49); Parker, *Circular: To the Citizens of Adams and Adjacent Counties in This State,* broadside, September 5, 1846.

60. Parker, *Proclamation,* August 28, 1846; Parker, *To the Public,* broadside, September 3, 1846; Conyer, *Hancock County Mob,* 53–54; *CHC* 3:8–11, 11 n. 17; Ford, *History of Illinois,* 417–18; *Signal,* August 25, 1846.

61. Curtis E. Bolton, Reminiscences, 6, Church Archives. The captains were Andrew H. Lamoureaux, Hiram Gates, Alexander McCrea, and Bolton. Hickman report, in Miller and Miller, *Nauvoo,* 201.

62. Brayman to Ford, September 22, 1846, *Signal,* October 20, 1846. A confrontation between Mormons who went to Keokuk to get the guns and five men en route to Keokuk from Fort Madison was reported in *Burlington Hawkeye,* September 10, 1846. The citizens of Nauvoo were "heavily armed with 'seven shooters'" (pistols probably made in Nauvoo).

63. Brayman to Ford, September 22, 1846, *Signal,* October 20, 1846; *Nauvoo New Citizen,* December 12, 1846.

64. M. Brayman to Thomas Ford, reported in *Signal,* October 20, 1846; Thomas Bullock to Willard Richards, September 10, 1846, Church Archives, reporting Mary Smith's departure; "Mary Fielding Smith," in Madsen, *In Their Own Words,* 97; Hiram Gates, letter, September 14, 1846, Church Archives.

65. The basic chronology and story that follows is drawn from Miller and Miller, *Nauvoo,* 199–202; the *Burlington Hawkeye,* September 13, 19, 1846; Curtis E. Bolton, Reminiscences, Church Archives; a 1965 analysis of the chronology and geography of the battle by Rowena Miller, NRI Archives; and other sources as cited. Governor Ford recounts the story in his *History of Illinois,* 293–300.

66. *Quincy Whig,* September 9, 1846, quoted in *St. Louis Weekly Reveille,* September 14, 1846, in Watson, *Manuscript History of Brigham Young,* 386–87.

67. Some in Nauvoo believed Brockman's invading force to be from a thousand to fifteen hundred soldiers and the occupying force as high as two thousand, with five hundred wagons. The initial posse of around seven hundred received some reinforcements after the first forays (Thomas Bullock to Willard Richards, September 10, 1846, Church Archives; Thomas Bullock Journal, September 17, 1846, Church Archives; Mary Field Garner, Autobiography, 5, Church Archives; W. W. Cole to James Winans, November 26, 1846, Church Archives; George Alley to Joseph Alley III, January 26, 1847, Church Archives; and John A. Woolf to Phebe Woolf, February 19, 1847, Church Archives; and Jonathan O. Duke, History, 3, BYU Library).

68. Curtis E. Bolton, Reminiscences, 7, Church Archives.

69. Miller and Miller, *Nauvoo,* 200; Robert Lang Campbell, Diary, 39, BYU Library; Wandle Mace described in detail how he made four makeshift cannons out of two steamboat shafts and four powder magazines for use as land mines (Autobiography, 139, Church Archives). Thomas Ford said of the kegs, "This kind of contrivance was called by the Mormons a 'hell's half acre'" (*History of Illinois,* 299).

70. Mary Ann Stearns Winters, Autobiography, 16, Church Archives.

71. Philo Johnson put the city's population at 1,500 (Reminiscence, 1894, Church Archives).

Major James R. Parker gave up trying to get an accurate count (Parker, *To the Public,* September 3, 1846). The church trustees reported 750 destitute adults waiting to go west (A. W. Babbitt, J. L. Heywood, and J. S. Fullmer to Brigham Young, August 31, 1846, enclosure, "Number of Adults in Nauvoo . . . ," Brigham Young Papers, Church Archives). Residents informed M. Brayman that the Nauvoo forces were as high as 500 or 600 men, with another 300 in reserve in Iowa (Brayman to Ford, September 22, 1846, *Signal,* October 20 1846.) Mary Field Garner remembered it as 400 defenders against 2,000 in the mob (Autobiography, Church Archives). In contrast, John A. Woolf reported about 100 adult Mormon males in Nauvoo (Woolf to Phebe Woolf, February 1, 1847, Church Archives). Similarly, Wandle Mace reported "one hundred men against one thousand in the mob" (Autobiography, 141, Church Archives). George Alley was probably closest in his estimate of about 170 Mormons plus around 100 new citizens facing against a mob of about 1,000 (Alley to Joseph Alley III, January 26, 1847, Church Archives). A similar estimate was 250 soldiers in a city of 1,000 (James Whitehead to Brigham Young, August 18, 1846, Brigham Young Papers, Church Archives). W. W. Cole put the ratio at 78 armed Nauvoo defenders against 1,200 attackers (Cole to James Winans, November 26, 1846, Church Archives). The number actually on the field varied from day to day as men came and went.

72. Curtis E. Bolton, Reminiscences, 7–8, Church Archives; Robert Lang Campbell, Diary, 39, BYU Library. Bolton, one of Anderson's Spartan Band, heard that the posse lost nine dead and thirteen wounded in the Friday noon engagement and "many others" later in the day. Official sources later denied the report (Governor Ford, reported in *Signal,* December 19, 1846).

73. Ford places the onlookers at nearly seven hundred and Brockman's forces at eight hundred (*History of Illinois,* 424). Mary Ann Stearns Winters, Autobiography, 16, Church Archives, reports sentinels; George Alley to Joseph Alley III, January 26, 1847, Church Archives, mentions Quincy's mayor.

74. Launius, *Joseph Smith III,* 45; Newel and Avery, *Mormon Enigma,* 236–37.

75. *Burlington Hawkeye,* September 17, 1846 (Miller and Miller, *Nauvoo,* 200–201).

76. Curtis E. Bolton, Reminiscences, 8–9, Church Archives; William Hickman, in Miller and Miller, *Nauvoo,* 201. Hickman said Anderson was hit in the first of the two assaults; Bolton said it happened in the second attack.

77. *Signal,* December 19, 1846. Mormon sources commonly reported an exaggerated one hundred deaths in the mob (George Alley to Joseph Alley III, January 26, 1847, Church Archives; Warren Post, Diaries, Church Archives; John A. Woolf to Phebe Woolf, February 19, 1847 [reporting 150 dead], Church Archives; and Jonathan O. Duke History, 3, BYU Library).

78. *CHC* 3:14–15 and 15 n. 25.

79. Regulators' committee, *Nauvoo New Citizen,* December 12, 1846; battle report and Hickman quotation, Miller and Miller, *Nauvoo,* 201–2.

80. Robert Lang Campbell, Diary, 40, BYU Library.

81. Agreement, original draft, Chicago Historical Society (Miller and Miller, *Nauvoo,* 202; *CHC* 3:15–16); Wandle Mace, Autobiography, 143, Church Archives.

82. Thomas Bullock to Willard Richards, September 10, 1846, Church Archives; Marsh, "When the Mormons Dwelt among Us," 406. The *St. Louis Daily Missouri Republican,* October 2, 1846, reported lots valued at two hundred to three hundred dollars selling for a cow or a horse.

83. Thomas Bullock to Franklin D. Richards, *MS* 10 (January 15, 1848): 29 (Miller and Miller, *Nauvoo,* 203; *CHC* 3:19 n. 30); Bullock, Journal, September 18, 22, 24–26, 30, 1846, Church

Archives. Also reporting mock baptisms were Wandle Mace, Autobiography, 145, Church Archives; and Robert Lang Campbell, Diary, September 27, 1846, 44, BYU Library.

84. Robert Lang Campbell, Diary, September 21, 1846, 42, BYU Library; Brayman report, September 18, 1846, *CHC* 3:17–18, punctuation standardized; Ford supported this view in his report to the legislature in December.

85. *Hancock Eagle,* Extra, October 5, 1846 (Watson, *Manuscript History of Brigham Young,* 406).

86. Miller and Miller, *Nauvoo,* 204–5.

87. *Hancock Eagle,* Extra, October 5, 1846 (excerpted in Watson, *Manuscript History of Brigham Young,* 406–7); Robert Lang Campbell, Diary, September 21, 1846, 42, BYU Library.

88. Watson, *Manuscript History of Brigham Young,* 407–8; Thomas Bullock, Journal, September 23, 27–28, 1846, Church Archives.

89. Watson, *Manuscript History of Brigham Young,* 385, 409; Thomas Bullock, Journal, October 7, 1846, Church Archives.

90. Brigham Young to Almon Babbitt, Joseph L. Heywood, and John S. Fullmer, September 27, 1846, Brigham Young Papers, Church Archives; Watson, *Manuscript History of Brigham Young,* 395–99.

91. Watson, *Manuscript History of Brigham Young,* 386–87, 403, 405–6.

92. Watson, *Manuscript History of Brigham Young,* 407, 409.

93. Watson, *Manuscript History of Brigham Young,* 410–11; Bullock, Journal, October 9, 1846, Church Archives; Bennett, "Eastward to Eden," 107. Some quail were present as early as October 2: "Abundance of quail are shot by the Brethren and a good many wild ducks; some fine large fishes are caught here by our tent which weigh 14 lbs" (Robert Lang Campbell, Diary, October 2, 1846, 45, BYU Library).

94. Kane, *The Mormons; Meeting for the Relief of the Mormons,* broadside (Philadelphia, 1846).

95. *T&S* 6 (November 1, 1845): 1010; William I. Appleby, Autobiography, November 1, 1848, Church Archives.

96. Wilford Woodruff's last wish for Nauvoo similarly was that the Lord would "preserve it as a monument of the sacrifice of his Saints" (Woodruff, *Journals,* 3:49, May 22, 1846).

97. Kane, *The Mormons,* 1–12 (Miller and Miller, *Nauvoo,* 206–8).

98. *Insult to the Governor!* broadside, November 7, 1846, BYU Library (also, *Signal,* after November 7 issue, microfilm, Church Library; reprinted, *Signal,* November 14, 1846).

99. *Signal,* November 21, 1846.

100. Such was the claim when Governor Charles S. Dennen visited the newspaper office in 1906 (*Independent,* September 8, 1906).

101. *Signal,* December 12, 19, 1846; Augustus C. French, *To the Citizens of Hancock,* broadside, December 12, 1846.

102. *Signal,* December 19, 1846; Miller and Miller, *Nauvoo,* 208.

103. *Signal,* December 5, 1846 [published after date]; also in *Nauvoo New Citizen,* December 12, 1846.

104. *Nauvoo New Citizen,* December 12, 1846.

CHAPTER 20. "THE NEW ORDER OF THINGS"

Epigraph: Prospectus of the *Hancock Eagle,* February 23, 1846; Sidney Rigdon to William H. Paynes, July 9, 1858, Rigdon Collection, Church Archives.

1. Good introductory overviews are Esplin, "Significance of Nauvoo for Latter-day Saints"; and Howard, "Nauvoo Heritage of the Reorganized Church."

2. Sidney Rigdon to William H. Paynes, July 9, 1858, Rigdon Collection, Church Archives; Esplin, "Joseph, Brigham, and the Twelve," 326–31; Howard, *The Church through the Years,* 1:275–76, 284–85, 289–96, 298–99.

3. Sidney Rigdon to William H. Paynes, July 9, 1858, Rigdon Collection, Church Archives. Chapter 16 of this volume examines ways in which the Twelve carried forward the Prophet's "measures." See also Porter and Backman, "Doctrine and the Temple," 41–42, for a comment on possible early origins of doctrines expanded or first implemented fully in Nauvoo.

4. Circular to the church in the United States, October 1845, *T&S* 6 (November 1, 1845): 1018, abbreviations expanded.

5. *St. Louis Daily Missouri Republican,* October 2, 1846.

6. For example, the *Illinois Journal* (Springfield), September 8, 1848, reported two meetings held in Nauvoo "for the purpose of making arrangements to drive the remaining Mormons out of Hancock County."

7. Watson, *Manuscript History of Brigham Young, 1846–47,* 324; Newel and Avery, *Mormon Enigma,* 234–37, 242–50, 265; Sarah M. Kimball to Marinda Hyde, January 2, 1848, Church Archives.

8. *Hancock Eagle,* July 3, 1845; Peter M. Wentz, Journal, April 21, 1854, BYU Library.

9. Blum, "Church Bell's Role," 655.

10. *Hancock Eagle,* May 29, 1846; *New Citizen,* December 5, 1846.

11. See the map on page 626, where information compiled by Nauvoo Restoration Inc. on these and earlier boundaries is platted.

12. E. D. Fish to Amos M. Musser, June 12, 1848, Church Archives.

13. *Hancock Eagle,* April 3, July 31, 1846. The *Signal,* February 11, 1846, identified Illinois attorney general Josiah Lamborn, Hancock sheriff Jacob Backenstos, and Mormon trustee Almon Babbitt as sponsors of the paper.

14. John M. Bernhisel to Brigham Young, November 26, 1847, Church Archives; *Nauvoo New Citizen,* December 5, 1846 (the first issue).

15. *Signal,* November 15, 1847.

16. Prospectus for *Popular Tribune,* undated; *Popular Tribune: A Journal of Social Reorganization,* January 16, 1851.

17. For an overview of the origins and ultimate failure of Cabet's system, see Sutton, *Les Icariens.*

18. Grant, *Icarian Communist in Nauvoo,* notes on 14–18, 21; Shaw, *Icaria,* 48, 52; Vallet, *Communism,* 1, 10.

19. Arrington, "Destruction of the Mormon Temple," 418–19; *Boston Semi-Weekly Advertiser,* October 28, 1848, reprinting an article from the *New York Tribune* reported from Nauvoo on October 11, 1848. The fire is incorrectly dated as November 19 in *HC* 7:617n through a misreading of the *Hancock Patriot,* November 19, 1848, and Young's "Manuscript History" (see Harwell, *Manuscript History of Brigham Young,* 134–35, November 19, 1848).

20. Arrington, "Destruction of the Mormon Temple," 19–25. George H. Rudisill reported Agnew's confession in the *Fort Madison Democrat,* January 1877, clipping in Church History Library. Rudisill's article was reprinted as "The Destruction of the Nauvoo Temple" in *Autumn Leaves.*

21. Hancock County, Deed Records, 5:408, April 2, 1849; Vallet, *Communism,* 6, 8–10; Blum, *Nauvoo,* 23–24.

22. *Popular Tribune,* February 15, 1851.

23. Emil J. Baxter, "Nauvoo History," *Nauvoo Independent*, November 14, 1923; James Moyle, Reminiscences (written 1886, based on St. Louis trip diary, 1854), Church Archives.

24. Grant, *Icarian Communist in Nauvoo*, notes on 18, 20, 27; Cannon, *Nauvoo Panorama*, 55–56; Vallet, *Communism*, 5, 10–11.

25. Vallet, *Communism*, 7–8, 10, 13–30; Grant, *Icarian Communist in Nauvoo*, 10, and notes on 36–37, 40; Cannon, *Nauvoo Panorama*, 56–57.

26. Cherill, *Map of Nauvoo*, copy in Nauvoo Historical Society Museum. The German caption was deleted from the amended copy printed by Nauvoo Restoration Inc. in 1963 (*Deseret News*, September 21, 1963, *Church News* section, 4).

27. For example, see Editor, "Signs of the Times," *The Evening and the Morning Star* 1 (October 1832): 38; "Faith of the Church of Christ in These Last Days. No. III," *The Evening and the Morning Star* 2 (April 1834): 153; "Foreign News," *T&S* 2 (December 15, 1840): 251–52; "Dialogue between a Saint and an Enquirer after Truth," *MS* 2 (December 1841): 132.

28. Elias Higbee and Parley P. Pratt, Washington, D.C., February 9, 1840, "Friends and Fellow-Citizens," *T&S* 1 (March 1840): 69; "Try the Spirits," *MS* 3 (July 1842): 38–39.

29. One example is "Millennium. No. I," *The Evening and the Morning Star* 2 (December 1833): 117, spelling standardized.

30. "Try the Spirits," *MS* 3 (July 1842): 38–39; "Baptism for the Dead," *MS* 3 (August 1842): 57; "The Gathering," *T&S* 5 (January 15, 1844): 409–10. The temple ordinances are discussed in chapter 10 of this volume. On the ancient order of the priesthood, see D&C 76:57; 107:40–42; 131:2.

31. Card et al, *Mormon Presence*, xvi, 2.

32. *General Epistle from the Council of the Twelve Apostles . . .* , written at Winter Quarters, December 23, 1847, signed by Brigham Young on behalf of the Twelve [St. Louis, January 1848; reprinted at Liverpool, 1848], 2; Flake, *Mormon Bibliography*, entry 1507.

33. Kimball, "Saints and St. Louis," 506–7.

34. *General Epistle*, 1–7.

35. *HC* 7:622, 624; John Scott, Journal, December 26, 1847 to March 9, 1848, transcribed by Louie S. Neville Clements, August 1955, Church Archives.

36. John Scott, Journal, 1848, passim, Church Archives; *General Epistle*, 1–4, 6.

37. Jonathan C. Wright, Journal, 6, January 13, 1848, Church Archives. The revealed warning is in D&C 124:31–38, 44–55.

38. Wright, Journal, 37–42, February 21–25, 1848.

39. Wright, Journal, 37–38, February 21, 1848.

40. Wright, Journal, 16–17, 40, February 1, 7, 24, 1848.

41. Wright, Journal, 10, January 21, 1848.

42. Sarah J. Potts to Joseph L. Heywood, April 13, 1847, Heywood Correspondence, Church Archives.

43. Copy in William Patterson McIntire, Daybook, BYU Library.

44. Blair, "Reorganized Church," 208–10; Jonas Putnam to Abel Putnam, May 23, 1847, Church Archives. For groups not discussed here, see the summary treatments in Shields, *Divergent Paths of the Restoration*.

45. No demographic study has yet tackled the question of where all of the Nauvoo-era Saints finally landed and when. Census records and ecclesiastical head counts do not agree. Church tallies mix in new converts along with old migrants. As an example of the problem, the Utah territorial census for 1850 counted 11,130 residents, while church records (reported in the *Deseret News 1999–2000 Church Almanac*, 550) show 18,756 members in the Salt Lake stake

and 33,083 members elsewhere in the world, including large numbers in the Midwest and in the camps along the Missouri River. An 1845 Illinois state census found 11,057 residents in Nauvoo, not all of them Mormon, and 22,559 people in Hancock County (perhaps 17,000 of them Latter-day Saint). Compare this to a church count of 17,020 members in the Nauvoo stake and 13,312 members elsewhere. To answer the specific question, it would be necessary to track individuals, a daunting task at best.

46. *Signal,* March 18, May 13, 1846; Van Noord, *King of Beaver Island,* 245.

47. Van Noord, *King of Beaver Island,* 76–78, 97, 127.

48. *Signal,* December 5, 1846; January 23, July 30, 1847; Nauvoo *New Citizen,* December 12, 1846; Van Noord, *King of Beaver Island,* 45, 49.

49. Cummings, "L. D. Hickey," 50–75; Strang's *Star of the East* 1 (November 1846): 21–24.

50. Van Noord, *King of Beaver Island,* 100–101; *History of the Reorganized Church,* 3:53–61.

51. Van Noord, *King of Beaver Island,* 133–37, 248–50, 263–65.

52. Shields, *Divergent Paths of the Restoration,* 46–48; Bitton, "Mormons in Texas," 5–26; Howard, *The Church through the Years,* 1:318.

53. Bennett, "Lamanism, Lymanism, and Cornfields," 49–50; Jorgensen, "The Old Fox," 158–65.

54. Bennett, "Lamanism, Lymanism, and Cornfields," 50–52; Jorgensen, "The Old Fox," 165–70.

55. Young, "Minnesota Mormons," 117–30; Shields, *Divergent Paths of the Restoration,* 60–61; Jorgensen, "The Old Fox," 170–72; *History of the Reorganized Church,* 3:77–78.

56. Vogel, "James Colin Brewster," 120–34; *History of the Reorganized Church,* 3:62–73; *HC* 2:520, 525; 5:214–15, 215n; Shields, *Divergent Paths of the Restoration,* 55–56.

57. *HC* 4:323; 6:347, 398; *History of the Reorganized Church,* 3:72–74; Jenson, *LDS Biographical Encyclopedia,* 4:183.

58. Porter, "Odyssey of William Earl McLellin," 291–92, 311–12, 321–23, 329–47; *Ensign of Liberty* 1 (May 1848): 89.

59. *History of the Reorganized Church,* 3:53–61; Shields, *Divergent Paths of the Restoration,* 39–40, 76–77.

60. Blair, "Moderate Mormonism," 208–10; Howard, *The Church through the Years,* 1:328–32, 337–40.

61. Howard, *The Church through the Years,* 1:331–36.

62. Howard, *The Church through the Years,* 1:337–39.

63. Howard, *The Church through the Years,* 1:341–47.

64. Howard, *The Church through the Years,* 1:347–52.

65. Joseph Smith III to Emma Knight, May 24, 1855, Community of Christ Archives, quoted in Howard, *The Church through the Years,* 1:360; Newel and Avery, *Mormon Enigma,* 272, 292, 301–3; Woodruff, *Discourses,* 148.

66. Newel and Avery, *Mormon Enigma,* 269; Howard, *The Church through the Years,* 1:362–64.

67. Edwards, *Our Legacy of Faith,* 131–32; Howard, *The Church through the Years,* 1:362, 365–75; Newell and Avery, *Mormon Enigma,* 271–73.

68. Blair, "Moderate Mormonism," 210.

69. Edwards, *Our Legacy of Faith,* 117–18; Young, "Minnesota Mormons," 130–37.

70. Embry, "Josephites . . . in Utah," 57–64.

71. Edwards, *Our Legacy of Faith,* 137, 146–48, 177, 202. The church in Utah reported 454,718 members as of December 31, 1914.

72. Edwards, "William B. Smith," 150–53.

73. Matthews, *"A Plainer Translation,"* 100–104; Edwards, *Our Legacy of Faith,* 151, 161–62, 304.

74. Edwards, *Our Legacy of Faith,* 162–67; Launius, "Politicking against Polygamy," 35–44; Newell, "Cousins in Conflict," 3–16.

75. Edwards, *Our Legacy of Faith,* 144–45, 160–62, 167–68.

76. Howard, *The Church through the Years,* 1:352; *Saints' Herald,* November 1860, quoted in Howard, *The Church through the Years,* 1:376–77.

77. Edwards, *Our Legacy of Faith,* 303–5, 168.

78. Edwards, *Our Legacy of Faith,* 142, 152, 173–76, 188–89, 217–18, 282–83, 304–5; Doctrine and Covenants (1984 RLDS ed.) 156:5; Romig, "Temple Lot Suit," 3–15.

79. Launius, *Joseph Smith III,* 346–50, 54–55.

80. For a thoughtful comparison of the two churches, see Alder and Edwards, "Common Beginnings, Divergent Beliefs," 18–28.

81. Edwards, *Our Legacy of Faith,* 260–61, 264–66, 274; Launius, "Coming of Age?" 39–46, 49–54; Howard, "Evolving RLDS Identity," 3–10; Jones, "Theological Re-Symbolization," 3–15, with quotation at 9.

82. *Encyclopedia of Mormonism,* s.v. "Reorganized Church of Jesus Christ of Latter Day Saints (RLDS Church)," by Richard P. Howard; *Deseret News,* April 5, 2001.

83. For examples of addresses on this theme by General Authorities, see Boyd K. Packer, *Ensign* 15 (November 1985): 80–83; and M. Russell Ballard, *Ensign* 20 (July 1998): 62–68.

84. Porter and Backman, "Doctrine and the Temple in Nauvoo," 41.

85. D&C 36:2, 42:61; 132:19–25.

CHAPTER 21. REMEMBERING NAUVOO

Epigraph: Hinckley, "The Nauvoo Memorial," 459.

1. Howard, "Nauvoo Heritage of the Reorganized Church," 43–44; "The Last of the Mormon Temple," *Carthage Republican,* February 2, 1865, 3.

2. *Nauvoo Independent,* December 21, 1877; January 4, 11, 25, 1878.

3. *Nauvoo Independent,* February 11, 1920; Cannon, *Nauvoo Panorama,* 62–63.

4. Cannon, *Nauvoo Panorama,* 84–86.

5. *Deseret News,* February 24, 1979, *Church News* section, 3, 9–10.

6. D&C 134:1–12; 98:5–6, 10.

7. For recent teachings on these principles, see *Ensign* 31 (May 2001): 51–53, 62, 73–75; (November 2001): 33–35.

8. D&C, Official Declaration 1, October 6, 1890; *The Family: A Proclamation to the World,* in *Ensign* 25 (November 1995): 102; *Ensign* 31 (May 2001): 6–9; *Ensign* 31 (November 2001): 69–71.

9. *Encyclopedia of Mormonism,* s.v. "Millenarianism," by Grant Underwood.

10. Recent general conference sermons on the centrality of Jesus Christ include those by Elders Marlin K. Jensen and Neal A. Maxwell, *Ensign* 31 (May 2001): 9–11, 59–61; and President James E. Faust, *Ensign* 31 (November 2001): 18–20.

11. The temple site was purchased for the church by Wilford C. Wood in February 1937 (Marba C. Josephson, "Church Acquires Nauvoo Temple Site," *Improvement Era,* 40 [April 1937]: 226–27).

12. Steve Fidel, "Nauvoo Temple to Rise Again," and Jason Swensen, "News Brings Cheers in Nauvoo," *Deseret News,* April 5, 1999, A-1, A-6.

13. Steve Fidel, "Nauvoo Temple to Rise Again," and Jason Swensen, "News Brings Cheers in

Nauvoo," *Deseret News,* April 5, 1999, A-1, A-6; "Open House, Dedication Dates Announced for Nauvoo Temple," *Deseret News,* September 15, 2001, *Church News* section, 2.

14. John S. Fullmer to Elizabeth Fullmer Cook, December 27, 1845, Church Archives; Jeffrey R. Holland, *Ensign* 31 (November 2001): 33–35.

15. Bushman, *Joseph Smith and the Beginnings of Mormonism,* 388.

16. Cannon, *Nauvoo Panorama,* 69–79; "Nauvoo in the World of Art," *Deseret News,* September 28, 1935, "Church Section," 1; Hinckley, "Nauvoo Memorial," 458–61, 511.

17. Henry A. Smith, "Steps Taken to Restore Historic Nauvoo," *Deseret News,* June 30, 1962, *Church News* section, 3, 14; Lyon, "Current Restoration of Nauvoo," 19–20; Cannon, *Nauvoo Panorama,* 77–84.

18. Howard, "Nauvoo Heritage of the Reorganized Church," 49–50; *Nauvoo,* brochure (n.p.: Joseph Smith Historic Center, Reorganized Church of Jesus Christ of Latter Day Saints, n.d.); Edwards, *Our Legacy of Faith,* 269; *Deseret News,* October 14, 1990.

19. *Deseret News,* July 8, 1978, *Church News* section, 3; "Two New Pageants Added to Annual Events," *Ensign* 6 (July 1976): 79; Cannon, *Nauvoo Panorama,* 87; *Saints Herald* 126 (December 1, 1979): 4.

20. Leonard, "Remembering Nauvoo," 30–35; Lyon, "Recollections of 'Old Nauvooers.'"

21. Joseph Smith, March 1839, in *HC* 3:302–3 and D&C 123.

22. "Up, Awake, Ye Defenders of Zion," *Hymns,* 1985, no. 248, italics added.

23. *Deseret News,* July 3, 1976, *Church News* section, 7; "Illinois City Still Friendly to Church," *Deseret News,* February 18, 1989, *Church News* section, 3, 5; "Renovated Carthage Jail Dedicated," *Ensign* 19 (September 1989): 74–75.

24. Ferdinand F. Bent to Isaac Bent, December 1, 1857, Church Archives.

25. See verses from Hancock's song beginning on page 25 of this volume.

26. Ferdinand F. Bent to Isaac Bent, December 1, 1857, Church Archives.

27. *MS* 1 (June 1840): 40–41.

28. *MS* 1 (June 1840): 40–41.

29. For an overview of these accomplishments, see Allen and Leonard, *Story of the Latter-day Saints,* beginning with chapter 7.

30. D&C 1:30, 18, 20–23, 4.

Sources

Abiff, Hiram Jr. [pseud.]. "Mormonism and Masonry in Illinois." *Masonic Voice Review,* August 1908–June 1909. Copy in Lyon Collection.

Adams, James N., compiler. *Illinois Places Names.* Edited by William E. Keller. Springfield: Illinois State Historical Society, 1968.

Adams, Henry, Jr., ed. "Charles Francis Adams Visits the Mormons in 1844." *Massachusetts Historical Society Proceedings* 68 (1952): 267–300.

Alder, Douglas D., and Paul M. Edwards. "Common Beginnings, Divergent Beliefs." *Dialogue* 11 (Spring 1978): 18–28.

Alexander, Thomas G. *Things in Heaven and Earth: The Life and Times of Wilford Woodruff, a Mormon Prophet.* Salt Lake City: Signature Books, 1991.

Allen, James B. "Nauvoo's Masonic Hall." *John Whitmer Historical Association Journal* 10 (1990): 39–49.

———. "One Man's Nauvoo: William Clayton's Experience in Mormon Illinois." *Journal of Mormon History* 6 (1979): 37–59.

———. *Trials of Discipleship: The Story of William Clayton, a Mormon.* Urbana: University of Illinois Press, 1987.

———. "'We Had a Very Hard Voyage for the Season': John Moon's Account of the First Emigrant Company of British Saints." *BYU Studies* 17 (Spring 1977): 330–41.

Allen, James B., and Glen M. Leonard. *The Story of the Latter-day Saints.* 2d ed. Salt Lake City: Deseret Book, 1992.

Allen, James B., and Malcom R. Thorp. "The Mission of the Twelve to England, 1840–41: Mormon Apostles and the Working Classes." *BYU Studies* 15 (Summer 1975): 499–526.

Allen, James B., Ronald K. Esplin, and David J. Whittaker. *Men with a Mission: The Quorum of the Twelve Apostles in the British Isles, 1837–1841.* Salt Lake City: Deseret Book, 1992.

Allman, John Lee. "Policing in Mormon Nauvoo." *Illinois Historical Journal* 89 (Summer 1996): 85–98.

Anderson, Richard Lloyd. "Jackson County in Early Mormon Descriptions." *Missouri Historical Review* 65 (April 1971): 270–93.

Anderson, Richard L., and Scott H. Faulring. "The Prophet Joseph Smith and His Plural Wives." *FARMS Review of Books* 10, no. 1 (1998): 67–104.

Arrington, Joseph Earl. "Destruction of the Mormon Temple at Nauvoo." *Journal of the Illinois State Historical Society* 40 (December 1947): 414–25.

———. "William Weeks, Architect of the Nauvoo Temple." *BYU Studies* 19 (Spring 1979): 337–59.

Arrington, Leonard J. *Brigham Young: American Moses.* New York: Alfred A. Knopf, 1985.

———. "Church Leaders in Liberty Jail." *BYU Studies* 13 (Autumn 1972): 20–26.

———. "Clothe These Bones: The Reconciliation of Faith and History." Unpublished typescript, 1978. In author's files.

———. *From Quaker to Latter-day Saint: Bishop Edwin D. Woolley.* Salt Lake City: Deseret Book, 1976.

Arrington, Leonard J., and Davis Bitton. *The Mormon Experience: A History of the Latter-day Saints.* New York: Alfred A. Knopf, 1979.

Arrington, Leonard J., Feramorz Y. Fox, and Dean L. May. *Building the City of God: Community and Cooperation among the Mormons.* Salt Lake City: Deseret Book, 1976.

Atwater, Caleb. *Remarks Made on a Tour to Prairie de Chien, thence to Washington City.* Columbus, Ohio: Jenkins and Glover, 1831.

Bachman, Danel W. "A Study of the Mormon Practice of Plural Marriage before the Death of Joseph Smith." M.A. thesis, Purdue University, 1975.

———. "Joseph Smith, a True Martyr." In *Joseph Smith: The Prophet, the Man,* edited by Susan Easton Black and Charles D. Tate Jr., 317–32. Provo, Utah: Brigham Young University, Religious Studies Center, 1993.

———. "New Light on an Old Hypothesis: The Ohio Origins of the Revelation on Eternal Marriage." *Journal of Mormon History* 5 (1978): 19–32.

———. "Prologue to the Study of Joseph Smith's Marital Theology." *FARMS Review of Books* 10, no. 1 (1998): 105–37.

Backman, Milton V., Jr. *American Religions and the Rise of Mormonism.* Salt Lake City: Deseret Book, 1970.

———. *The Heavens Resound: A History of the Latter-day Saints in Ohio, 1830–1838.* Salt Lake City: Deseret Book, 1983.

———. "'The Keys Are Right Here.'" In *Lion of the Lord: Essays on the Life and Service of Brigham Young,* edited by Susan Easton Black and Larry C. Porter, 107–27. Salt Lake City: Deseret Book, 1995.

———. "A Warning from Kirtland." *Ensign* 19 (April 1989): 26–30.

Bancroft, Hubert Howe. *History of Utah.* 1890. Photo reprint, Las Vegas: Nevada Publications, 1982.

[Barnes, Thomas L.] "Carthage Jail Physician Testifies." *The Pioneer (Sons of Utah Pioneers).* Spring 1954, 47–53.

Barnett, Steven G. "The Canes of the Martyrdom." *BYU Studies* 21 (Spring 1981): 205–11.

Bates, Irene R. "Uncle John Smith, 1781–1854: Patriarchal Bridge." *Dialogue* 20 (Fall 1987): 79–89.

———. "William Smith, 1811–93, Problematic Patriarch," *Dialogue* 16 (Summer 1983): 11–23.

Baugh, Alexander L. "A Call to Arms: The 1838 Mormon Defense of Northern Missouri." Ph.D. diss., Brigham Young University, 1996.

Beecher, Dale. "The Office of Bishop." *Dialogue* 15 (Winter 1982): 103–15.

Beecher, Maureen Ursenbach. "'All Things Move in Order in the City': The Nauvoo Diary of Zina Diantha Huntington Jacobs." *BYU Studies* (Spring 1979): 285–320.

Beecher, Maureen Ursenbach, and Lavina Fielding Anderson. *Sisters in Spirit: Mormon Women in Historical and Cultural Perspective.* Urbana: University of Illinois Press, 1987.

Bennett, Richard E. "'Dadda, I Wish We Were Out of This Country': The Nauvoo Poor Camps in Iowa, Fall 1846." In *The Iowa Mormon Trail: Legacy of Faith and Courage,* edited by Susan Easton Black and William G. Hartley, 155–169. Orem, Utah: Helix Publishing, 1997.

———. "Eastward to Eden: The Nauvoo Rescue Missions." *Dialogue* 19 (Winter 1986): 100–108.

———. "Lamanism, Lymanism, and Cornfields." *Journal of Mormon History* 13 (1986–87): 44–59.

———. *Mormons at the Missouri, 1846–1852: "And Should We Die . . ."* Norman: University of Oklahoma Press, 1987.

———. "'Plucking Not Planting': Mormonism in Eastern Canada 1830–1850." In *The Mormon*

Presence in Canada, edited by Brigham Y. Card et al., 22–30. Edmonton, Alberta: University of Alberta Press, 1990; Logan, Utah: Utah State University Press, 1990.

Bernauer, Barbara Hands. "Still 'Side by Side': The Final Burial of Joseph and Hyrum Smith." *John Whitmer Historical Association Journal* 11 (1991): 17–33.

Bigamon, Charles C. "The Old State House." Unidentified source, 1968. Copy in Lyon Collection.

Bilderback, James C. "Masonry and Mormonism, Nauvoo, Illinois, 1841–1847." M.A. thesis, State University of Iowa, 1937.

Bitton, Davis. "Early Nauvooans: A People of 'Culture and Refinement.'" Paper delivered at Nauvoo Sesquicentennial Symposium, Brigham Young University, September 21, 1989. Copy in possession of author.

———. *Guide to Mormon Diaries and Autobiographies.* Provo, Utah: Brigham Young University Press, 1977.

———. "In Memoriam: T. Edgar Lyon (1903–1978)." *Dialogue* 11 (Winter 1978): 11–12.

———. "The Martyrdom of Joseph Smith in Early Mormon Writings." *John Whitmer Historical Association Journal.* 3 (1983): 29–39.

———. *The Martrydom Remembered: Reactions to the Assassination of the Prophet Joseph Smith.* Salt Lake City: Aspen Books, 1994.

———. "Mormons in Texas: The Ill-Fated Lyman Wight Colony, 1844–1858." *Arizona and the West* 11 (Spring 1969): 5–26.

———. "The Waning of Mormon Kirtland." *BYU Studies* 12 (Summer 1972): 455–64.

Bitton, Davis, and Maureen Ursenbach Beecher, eds. *New Views of Mormon History: Essays in Honor of Leonard J. Arrington.* Salt Lake City: University of Utah Press, 1987.

Blair, Alma R. "Reorganized Church of Jesus Christ of Latter Day Saints: Moderate Mormonism." In *The Restoration Movement: Essays in Mormon History,* edited by F. Mark McKiernan, Alma R. Blair, and Paul M. Edwards. Lawrence, Kans.: Coronado Press, 1973.

Blum, Ida. "Church Bell's Role." In *History of Hancock County,* edited by Robert Cochran et al. Carthage: Hancock County Board of Supervisors, 1968.

———. *Nauvoo: Gateway to the West.* Carthage, Ill.: Author, 1974.

The Book of Mormon. Translated by Joseph Smith Jr. 1830. Salt Lake City: The Church of Jesus Christ of Latter-day Saints, 1980.

Bringhurst, Newell G. "Elijah Abel and the Changing Status of Blacks within Mormonism." *Dialogue* 12 (Summer 1979): 22–36.

Brown, Lisle "G." "The Sacred Departments for Temple Work in Nauvoo: The Assembly Room and the Council Chamber." *BYU Studies* 19 (Spring 1979): 361–74.

Brown, S. Kent, Brian Q. Cannon, and Richard H. Jackson, eds. *Historical Atlas of Mormonism.* New York: Simon & Schuster, 1994. S.v. "The City of Zion Plat," by Richard H. Jackson, and various maps as cited in Credits for Maps and Illustrations, this volume, 789.

Buckingham, J. H. *Illinois As Lincoln Knew It: A Boston Reporter's Record of a Trip in 1847.* In *Papers in Illinois History and Transactions for the Year 1937.* Springfield, Ill.: Illinois State Historical Society, 1938.

Buisseret, David. *Historic Illinois from the Air.* Illustrations and cartography by Tom Willcockson. Chicago: University of Chicago Press, 1990.

Burns, Robert Taylor. "Le Grand Detour." *Outdoor Illinois,* 8 [December 1968]: 6–8.

Bush, Lester E., Jr. "Mormonism's Negro Doctrine: An Historical Overview." *Dialogue* 8 (Spring 1973): 11–68.

Bushman, Richard L. "Faithful History." *Dialogue* 4 (Winter 1969): 11–25.

———. "The Historians and Mormon Nauvoo." *Dialogue* 5 (Spring 1970): 51–61.

———. *Joseph Smith and the Beginnings of Mormonism.* Urbana: University of Illinois Press, 1984.

———. "Joseph Smith in the Current Age." In *Joseph Smith: The Prophet, the Man,* edited by Susan Easton Black and Charles D. Tate Jr., 38–48. Provo, Utah: Brigham Young University, Religious Studies Center, 1993.

———. *Making Space for the Mormons: Ideas of Sacred Geography in Joseph Smith's America.* Vol. 2

of Leonard J. Arrington Mormon History Lecture Series. Logan, Utah: Utah State University Press, 1997.

———. "New Jerusalem, U.S.A.: The Early Development of the Latter-day Saint Zion Concept on the American Frontier." Honor's thesis, Harvard University, 1955.

Campbell, Isaac R. "Recollections of the Early Settlement of Lee County [Iowa]." *Annals of Iowa* (July 1867): 884–85.

Cannon, Donald Q. "The King Follett Discourse: Joseph Smith's Greatest Sermon in Historical Perspective." *BYU Studies* 18 (Winter 1978): 179–82.

———. "Mormon Satellite Settlements in Hancock County, Illinois, and Lee County, Iowa." In *The Iowa Mormon Trail: Legacy of Faith and Courage*, edited by Susan Easton Black and William G. Hartley, 21–34. Orem, Utah: Helix Publishing, 1997.

Cannon, Donald Q. and Lyndon W. Cook, eds. *Far West Record: Minutes of The Church of Jesus Christ of Latter-day Saints, 1830–1844.* Salt Lake City: Deseret Book, 1983.

Cannon, H. Hamblin, ed. "Bankruptcy Proceedings against Joseph Smith in Illinois." *Pacific Historical Review* 14 (June 1945): 425–33.

———. "The 'Gathering' of British Mormons to Western America: A Study of Religious Migration." Ph.D. diss., American University, 1950.

Cannon, Janath. *Nauvoo Panorama: Views of Nauvoo Before, During and After Its Rise, Fall, and Restoration.* [Salt Lake City:] Nauvoo Restoration Inc., 1991.

Cannon, John Q. *George Cannon, the Immigrant.* Salt Lake City: Deseret News Press, 1927.

Card, Brigham Y., Herbert C. Northcott, John E. Foster, Howard Palmer, and George K. Jarvis, eds. *The Mormon Presence in Canada.* Logan: Utah State University Press, 1990.

Carlson, Theodore L. *The Illinois Military Tract: A Study of Land Occupation, Utilization, and Tenure.* Urbana: University of Illinois Press, 1951.

Carter, Kate B., ed. *Heart Throbs of the West.* Vol. 5. Salt Lake City: Daughters of the Utah Pioneers, 1944.

Caswall, Henry. *The City of the Mormons; or, Three Days at Nauvoo in 1842.* London: J. G. F. & J. Rivington, 1842.

Cheney, Thomas E., ed. *Mormon Songs from the Rocky Mountains: A Compilation of Mormon Folksong.* Austin, Texas: University of Texas Press, 1968.

Cherill, A. *A Map of Nauvoo, with All the Additions and the Towns of Commerce and Commerce City. Compiled from the Records of Hancock County.* Philadelphia: S. Bechtold Jr., 1846.

Christian, Lewis Clark. "A Study of Mormon Knowledge of the American Far West Prior to the Exodus (1830-February 1846)." M.A. thesis, Brigham Young University, 1972.

———. "Mormon Foreknowledge of the West." *BYU Studies* 21 (Fall 1981): 403–15.

Clark, J. Reuben, Jr. "The United Order and Law of Consecration as Set Out in the Revelations of the Lord." In *The One Mighty and Strong . . . [and three other articles]*, 15–40. Articles reprinted from the Church News section of the *Deseret News.* [Salt Lake City] N.p., n.d.

Clayton, John. *Illinois Fact Book and Historical Almanac, 1673–1968.* Carbondale: Southern Illinois University Press, 1970.

Clayton, William. *An Intimate Chronicle: The Journals of William Clayton.* Edited by George D. Smith. 1991. 2d ed. Salt Lake City: Signature Books in association with Smith Research Associates, 1995. Cited as Clayton, *Journals.*

———. *Manchester Mormons: The Journal of William Clayton, 1840 to 1842.* Edited by James B. Allen and Thomas G. Alexander. Salt Lake City: Peregrine Smith, 1974.

Coates, Lawrence G. "Refugees Meet: The Mormons and Indians in Iowa." *BYU Studies* 21 (Fall 1981): 491–514.

Collected Discourses. Compiled by Brian H. Stuy. 5 vols. to date. Woodland Hills, Utah: B.H.S. Publishing, 1987–92.

Collette, D. Brent. "In Search of Zion: A Description of Early Mormon Millennial Utopianism as Revealed Through the Life of Edward Partridge." Master's thesis, Brigham Young University, 1977.

Compton, Todd. *In Sacred Loneliness: The Plural Wives of Joseph Smith.* Salt Lake City: Signature Books, 1997.

———. "Fanny Alger Smith Custer: Mormonism's First Plural Wife?" *Journal of Mormon History* 22 (Spring 1996): 174–207.

Conyers, Josiah B. *A Brief History of the Leading Causes of the Hancock Mob, in the Year 1846.* St. Louis: Cathart & Prescott, 1846.

Cook, Lyndon W. "Isaac Galland, Mormon Benefactor." *BYU Studies* 19 (Spring 1979): 261–84.

———. "'A More Virtuous Man Never Existed on the Footstool of the Great Jehovah': George Miller on Joseph Smith." *BYU Studies* 19 (Spring 1979): 402–7.

———. "William Law, Nauvoo Dissenter." *BYU Studies* 22 (Winter 1982): 47–72.

Cooper, Rex E. *Promises Made to the Fathers: Mormon Covenant Organization.* Salt Lake City: University of Utah Press, 1990.

Cornwall, Marie. "The Paradox of Organization." *Sunstone* 14 (October 1990): 44–47.

Crawley, Peter. "Joseph Smith and a Book of Commandments." *Princeton University Library Chronicle* 42 (Autumn 1980): 18–32.

———. "Parley P. Pratt: Father of Mormon Pamphleteering." *Dialogue* 15 (Autumn 1982): 13–26.

———. "The Passage of Mormon Primitivism." *Dialogue* 13 (Winter 1980): 26–37.

Cummings, John. "L. D. Hickey: The Last of the Apostles." *Michigan History* 50 (March 1966): 50–75.

Cummings, Horace H. "Conspiracy of Nauvoo." *Contributor* 5 (April 1884): 251–56.

Currey, J. Seymour. *Chicago: Its History and Its Builders, a Century of Marvelous Growth.* 5 vols. Chicago: S. J. Clarke Publishing, 1912.

Dahl, Larry E., and Charles D. Tate Jr., eds. *The Lectures on Faith in Historical Perspective.* Provo: Religious Studies Center, Brigham Young University, 1990.

Daniels, William M. [pseud.] *Correct Account of the Murder of Generals Joseph and Hyrum Smith at Carthage, on the 27th Day of June, 1844.* Nauvoo: John Taylor, 1845. Written by Lyman O. Littlefield.

Darnell, M. B. "The Tragedy at Carthage." Article from unidentified periodical, 1894.

Davidson, Karen Lynn. *Our Latter-day Hymns: The Stories and the Messages.* Salt Lake City: Deseret Book, 1988.

Davis, David Brion. "Some Themes of Counter-Subversion: An Analysis of Anti-Masonic, Anti-Catholic, and Anti-Mormon Literature." *Mississippi Valley Historical Review* 47 (September 1970): 205–24.

Daynes, Byron W., and Raymond Tatalovich. "Mormons and Abortion Politics in the United States." *International Review of History and Political Science* 23 (May 1986): 1–13.

Daynes, Kathryn M. "Family Ties: Belief and Practice in Nauvoo." *John Whitmer Historical Association Journal* 8 (1988): 63–75.

De Pillis, Mario S. "The Persistence of Mormon Community into the 1990s." *Sunstone* 15 (October 1991): 28–49.

———. "The Quest for Religious Authority and the Rise of Mormonism." *Dialogue* 1 (Spring 1966): 68–88.

Derr, Jill Mulvay, Janath R. Cannon, and Maureen Ursenbach Beecher. *Women of Covenant: The Story of Relief Society.* Salt Lake City: Deseret Book, 1992.

Deseret News. Salt Lake City, 1850–.

Deseret News. *1976 Church Almanac.* Salt Lake City: Deseret News, 1976.

———. *1989–1990 Church Almanac.* Salt Lake City: Deseret News, 1988.

The Doctrine and Covenants of The Church of Jesus Christ of Latter-day Saints. 1835. Salt Lake City: The Church of Jesus Christ of Latter-day Saints, 1980.

Doyle, Don Harrison. *The Social Order of a Frontier Community: Jacksonville, Illinois, 1825–70.* Urbana: University of Illinois Press, 1978.

Driggs, Howard R. "Visits to Carthage." *Juvenile Instructor* 46 (June 1911): 319–24.

Dummelow, J. R. *The One-Volume Bible Commentary.* New York: Macmillan, 1973.

Durham, Reed C., Jr., and Steven H. Heath. *Succession in the Church.* Salt Lake City: Bookcraft, 1970.

Easton, Susan W. "Suffering and Death on the Plains of Iowa." *BYU Studies* 21 (Fall 1981): 431–39.

Edwards, Paul M. *Our Legacy of Faith: A Brief History of the Reorganized Church of Jesus Christ of Latter Day Saints.* Independence: Herald House, 1991.

———. "William B. Smith: A Wart on the Ecclesiastical Tree." In *Differing Visions: Dissenters in Mormon History,* edited by Roger B. Launius and Linda Thatcher, 140–54. Urbana: University of Illinois Press, 1994.

Ehat, Andrew F. "'It Seems Like Heaven Began on Earth': Joseph Smith and the Constitution of the Kingdom of God." *BYU Studies* 20 (Spring 1980): 253–79.

Elders' Journal of the Church of Latter-Day Saints. Kirtland, Ohio, and Far West, Missouri, 1837–38.

Eliade, Mircea. *The Quest: History and Meaning in Religion.* Chicago: University of Chicago Press, 1969.

———. *The Sacred and the Profane: The Nature of Religion.* Translated by Willard R. Trask. New York and London: Harcourt Brace Jovanovich, 1959.

Ellsworth, Paul D. "Mobocracy and the Rule of Law: American Press Reactions to the Murder of Joseph Smith." *BYU Studies* 20 (Fall 1979): 71–82.

Ellsworth, S. George. "Utah History: Retrospect and Prospect." *Utah Historical Quarterly* 40 (Fall 1972): 342–67.

Embry, Jessie L. "Josephites at the Tops of the Mountains: RLDS Congregations in Utah." *John Whitmer Historical Association Journal* 16 (1996): 57–64.

Encyclopedia of Latter-day Saint History. Edited by Arnold K. Garr, Donald Q. Cannon, and Richard O. Cowan. Salt Lake City: Deseret Book, 2000.

Encyclopedia of Mormonism: The History, Scripture, Doctrine, and Procedure of the Church of Jesus Christ of Latter-day Saints. Edited by Daniel H. Ludlow. 4 vols. New York: Macmillan, 1992.

Enders, Donald L. "A Dam for Nauvoo: An Attempt to Industrialize the City." *BYU Studies* 18 (Winter 1978): 246–54.

———. "The Des Moines Rapids: A History of Its Adverse Effects on Mississippi River Traffic and Its Use as a Source of Water Power to 1860." Master's thesis, Brigham Young University, 1973.

———. "Platting the City Beautiful: A Historical and Archaeological Glimpse of Nauvoo Streets." *BYU Studies* 19 (Spring 1979): 409–15.

———. "Spokes on the Wheel: Early Latter-day Saint Settlements in Hancock County, Illinois." *Ensign* 16 (February 1986): 62–68.

———. "The Steamboat *Maid of Iowa:* Mormon Mistress of the Mississippi." *BYU Studies* 9 (Spring 1979): 321–35.

England, Breck. *The Life and Thought of Orson Pratt.* Salt Lake City: University of Utah Press, 1985.

Ensign. The Church of Jesus Christ of Latter-day Saints, 1971–.

Ericksen, Ephraim E. *The Psychological and Ethical Aspects of Mormon Group Life.* Chicago: University of Chicago Press [1922].

Esplin, Ronald K. "The Emergence of Brigham Young and the Twelve to Mormon Leadership, 1831–1841." Ph.d. diss., Brigham Young University, 1981.

———. "Joseph, Brigham, and the Twelve: A Succession of Continuity." *BYU Studies* 21 (Summer 1981): 301–41.

———. "Joseph Smith's Mission and Timetable: 'God Will Protect Me until My Work Is Done.'" In *The Prophet Joseph Smith: Essays on the Life and Mission of Joseph Smith,* edited by Larry C. Porter and Susan Easton Black, 280–319. Salt Lake City: Deseret Book, 1998.

———. "Life in Nauvoo, June 1844: Vilate Kimball's Martyrdom Letters." *BYU Studies* 19, no. 2. (1979): 231–40.

———. "'A Place Prepared': Joseph, Brigham, and the Quest for Promised Refuge in the West." *Journal of Mormon History* 9 (1982): 85–111.

———. "The Significance of Nauvoo for Latter-day Saints." *Journal of Mormon History* 16 (1990): 71–86.

Esshom, Frank E. *Pioneers and Prominent Men of Utah.* 2 vols. Salt Lake City: Utah Pioneers Book Publishing, 1913.

The Evening and the Morning Star. Independence, Missouri, 1832–33, and Kirtland, Ohio, 1834–35.

Faragher, John Mack. *Women and Men on the Overland Trail.* New Haven: Yale University Press, 1979.

Fielding, Joseph. "'They Might Have Known That He Was Not a Fallen Prophet'—The Nauvoo Journal of Joseph Fielding." Transcribed and edited by Andrew F. Ehat. *BYU Studies* 19 (Winter 1979): 133–66.

Firmage, Edwin Brown, and Richard Collin Mangrum. *Zion in the Courts: A Legal History of the Church of Jesus Christ of Latter-day Saints, 1830–1900.* Urbana: University of Illinois Press, 1988.

Flake, Chad J., ed. *A Mormon Bibliography, 1830–1930: Books, Pamphlets, Periodicals, and Broadsides Relating to the First Century of Mormonism.* Introduction by Dale L. Morgan. Salt Lake City: University of Utah Press, 1978.

Flanders, Robert Bruce. "Dream and Nightmare: Nauvoo Revisited." In *The Restoration Movement: Essays in Mormon History,* edited by Mark F. McKiernan, Alma R. Blair, and Paul M. Edwards. Lawrence, Kans.: Coronado Press, 1973.

———. "The Kingdom of God in Illinois: Politics in Utopia." *Dialogue* 5 (Spring 1970): 26–36.

———. *Nauvoo: Kingdom on the Mississippi.* Urbana: University of Illinois Press, 1965.

———. "Some Reflections on the New Mormon History." *Dialogue* 9 (Spring 1974): 34–41.

———. "To Transform History: Early Mormon Culture and the Concept of Time and Space." *Church History* 40 (March 1971): 108–17.

Ford, Thomas. *A History of Illinois: From Its Commencement as a State in 1818 to 1847.* Chicago: S. C. Griggs, 1854. Annotation and introduction by Rodney O. Davis. Urbana: University of Illinois Press, 1995.

———. *Message of the Governor of the State of Illinois in Relation to the Disturbances in Hancock County, December 21, 1844.* Springfield: Walters & Weber, Public Printers, 1844. Copy at Church History Library.

Foster, Lawrence. "A Little-Known Defense of Polygamy from the Mormon Press in 1842." *Dialogue* 9 (Winter 1974): 21–34.

———. *Religion and Sexuality: Three American Communal Experiments of the Nineteenth Century.* New York: Oxford University Press, 1981.

Gager, John G. *Kingdom and Community: The Social World of Early Christianity.* Englewood Cliffs, N. J.: Prentice-Hall, 1975.

Galland's Map of Iowa. Engraved by J. C. Darby. Akron, Ohio: Isaac Galland, 1840. Available at Church History Library.

Gardner, Hamilton. "The Nauvoo Legion, 1840–1845: A Unique Military Organization." *Journal of the Illinois State Historical Society* 54 (Summer 1961): 181–97.

Garr, Arnold K. "Joseph Smith: Candidate for President of the United States." In *Regional Studies in Latter-day Saint Church History: Illinois,* edited by H. Dean Garrett. Provo: Brigham Young University, Department of Church History and Doctrine, 1995.

Gaustad, Edwin S. "Historical Theology and Theological History: Mormon Possibilities." *Journal of Mormon History* 11 (1984): 78–97.

Gayler, George R. "Governor Ford and the Death of Joseph and Hyrum Smith." *Journal of the Illinois State Historical Society* 50 (Winter 1957): 391–411.

———. "The Mormons and Politics in Illinois: 1839–1844." *Journal of the Illinois State Historical Society* 49 (Spring 1956): 48–66.

Gentry, Leland H. "The Danite Band of 1838." *BYU Studies* 14 (Summer 1974): 421–50.

Gibson, H. W. "Frontier Arms of the Mormons." *Utah Historical Quarterly* 42 (Winter 1974): 4–26.

Givens, George W. *In Old Nauvoo: Everyday Life in the City of Joseph.* Salt Lake City: Deseret Book, 1990.

Godfrey, Kenneth W. "Crime and Punishment in Mormon Nauvoo, 1839–1846." *BYU Studies* 32 (Winter and Spring 1992): 195–227.

———. "Joseph Smith and the Masons." *Journal of the Illinois State Historical Society* 64 (Spring 1971): 79–90.

———. "The Nauvoo Neighborhood: A Little Philadelphia or a Unique City Set Upon a Hill?" *Journal of Mormon History* 11 (1984): 78–97.

———. "A New Look at the Alleged Little Known Discourse by Joseph Smith." *BYU Studies* 9 (Autumn 1968): 49–53.

———. "Non-Mormon Views of the Martyrdom: A Look at Some Early Published Accounts." *John Whitmer Historical Association Journal* 7 (1987): 12–20.

———. "A Note on the Nauvoo Library and Literary Institute," *BYU Studies* 14 (Spring 1974): 386–89.

———. "Remembering the Deaths of Joseph and Hyrum Smith." In *Joseph Smith: The Prophet, the Man*, edited by Susan Easton Black and Charles D. Tate Jr. Provo: Religious Studies Center, Brigham Young University, 1993.

———. "Return to Carthage." Unpublished paper given at Mormon History Association Annual Meeting, Quincy, Ill., May 1989. Copy in author's files.

———. "The Road to Carthage Led West." *BYU Studies* 8 (Winter 1968): 204–15.

Godfrey, Kenneth W., Audrey M. Godfrey, and Jill Mulvay Derr. *Women's Voices: An Untold History of the Latter-day Saints.* Salt Lake City: Deseret Book, 1982.

Gooch, John, comp. *Death of the Prophets Joseph and Hyrum Smith.* Boston: J. Gooch, 1844. Compiled for Freeman Nickerson.

Goodwin, S. H. *Mormonism and Masonry: A Utah Point of View.* Salt Lake City: Grand Lodge F. & A. M. of Utah, 1925, 1934.

Grand Concert . . . April 7, 8, & 9, 1845. Poster. Nauvoo, 1845. Copy at Church History Library.

Grandstaff, Mark R., and Milton V. Backman, Jr. "The Social Origins of the Kirtland Mormons." *BYU Studies* 30 (Spring 1990): 47–66.

Grant, H. Roger, ed. *An Icarian Communist in Nauvoo: Commentary by Emile Vallet.* Springfield, Ill.: Illinois State Historical Society, 1971.

Greenlagh, James. *A Narrative of James Greeenlagh, Cotton Spinner, Egerton, Bolton-le-Moors.* Liverpool: Richard Scragg, Printer, 1842.

Gregg, Thomas. *History of Hancock County, Illinois.* Chicago: Charles C. Chapman, 1880.

———. *Portrait and Biographical Record of Hancock County.* Chicago: Lake City Publishing, 1890.

Grimsted, David. "Rioting in Its Jacksonian Setting." *American Historical Review* 77 (April 1972): 361–97.

Gross, Robert A. *The Minutemen and Their World.* New York: Hill and Wang, 1976.

Hale, Heber Q. *Bishop Jonathan H. Hale of Nauvoo: His Life and Ministry.* Salt Lake City: n.p., 1938.

Hale, Van. "The Doctrinal Impact of the King Follett Discourse." *BYU Studies* 18 (Winter 1978): 209–25.

———. "The King Follett Discourse: A Newly Amalgamated Text." *BYU Studies* 18 (Winter 1978): 193–208.

Halford, Reta Latimer. "Nauvoo—The City Beautiful." Master's thesis, University of Utah, 1945.

Hallwas, John E. "Mormon Nauvoo from a Non-Mormon Perspective." *Journal of Mormon History* 16 (1990); 53–69.

———. *Thomas Gregg: Early Illinois Journalist and Author.* Macomb, Ill.: Western Illinois University, 1983.

Hallwas, John E., and Roger D. Launius. *Cultures in Conflict: A Documentary History of the Mormon War in Illinois.* Logan, Utah: Utah State University Press, 1995.

Hamilton, Marshall. "From Assassination to Expulsion: Two Years of Distrust, Hostility, and Violence." *BYU Studies* 32 (Winter/Spring 1992): 229–48.

———. "'Money-Diggersville'—The Brief, Turbulent History of the Mormon Town of Warren." *John Whitmer Historical Association Journal* 9 (1989): 49–58.

Hampshire, Annette P. *Mormonism in Conflict: The Nauvoo Years.* Vol. 11 of *Studies in Religion and Society.* New York: Edwin Mellen Press, 1985.

———. "Thomas Sharp and Anti-Mormon Sentiment in Illinois." *Journal of the Illinois State Historical Society* 72 (May 1979): 82–100.

———. "The Triumph of Mobocracy in Hancock County, 1844–1846." *Western Illinois Regional Studies* 5 (Spring 1892): 17–37.

Hansen, Klaus J. "The Metamorphosis of the Kingdom of God: Toward a Reinterpretation of Mormon History." *Dialogue* 1 (Autumn 1966): 63–83.

———. *Mormonism and the American Experience.* Chicago: University of Chicago Press, 1981.

———. "The Political Kingdom as a Cause for Mormon-Gentile Conflict." *BYU Studies* 2 (Spring-Summer 1960): 241–60.

———. *Quest for Empire: The Political Kingdom of God and the Council of Fifty in Mormon History.* East Lansing, Mich.: Michigan State University Press, 1967; Lincoln: University of Nebraska Press, Bison Books, 1974.

Hansen, Lorin K. "Voyage of the *Brooklyn*," *Dialogue* 21 (Autumn 1988): 47–72.

Hareven, Tamara K. *Family and Kin in Urban Communities, 1700–1930.* New York: New Viewpoints, 1978.

Harper, Reid L. "The Mantle of Joseph: Creation of a Mormon Miracle." *Journal of Mormon History* 22 (Fall 1996): 35–71.

Hartley, William G. "Joseph Smith and Nauvoo's Youth." *Ensign* 9 (September 1979): 26–29.

———. *My Best for the Kingdom: History and Autobiography of John Lowe Butler, a Mormon Frontiersman.* Salt Lake City: Aspen Books, 1993.

———. "Nauvoo Stake, Priesthood Quorums, and the Church's First Wards." *BYU Studies* 32 (Winter-Spring 1992): 57–80.

———. "Spring Exodus from Nauvoo: Act Two in the 1846 Mormon Evacuation Drama." In *The Iowa Mormon Trail: Legacy of Faith and Courage,* edited by Susan Easton Black and William G. Hartley, 61–83. Orem, Utah: Helix Publishing, 1997.

Harwell, William S. *Manuscript History of Brigham Young, 1847–1850.* Salt Lake City: Collier's Publishing, 1997.

Haven, Charlotte. "A Girl's Letters from Nauvoo." *Overland Monthly* 16 (December 1890): 616–138.

Hayward, John. *The Religious Creeds and Statistics of Every Christian Denomination in the United States and British Provinces.* Boston: John Hayward, 1836.

Hess, Margaret Steed. *My Farmington, 1847–1976.* Farmington, Utah: Helen Mar Miller Camp, Daughters of Utah Pioneers, 1976.

Hickman, Marvin B. "The Political Legacy of Joseph Smith." *Dialogue* 3 (Autumn 1968): 22–27.

Hicks, Michael. *Mormonism and Music: A History.* Urbana: University of Illinois Press, 1989.

———. "'Strains Which Will Not Soon Be Allowed to Die . . .': 'The Stranger' and Carthage Jail." *BYU Studies* 23 (Fall 1983): 389–400.

Hill, Donna. *Joseph Smith: The First Mormon.* Garden City, N.Y.: Doubleday, 1977.

Hill, Marvin S. "Mormon Religion in Nauvoo: Some Reflections." *Utah Historical Quarterly* 44 (Spring 1976): 170–80.

———. "Quest for Refuge: An Hypothesis As to the Social Origins and Nature of the Mormon Political Kingdom." *Journal of Mormon History* 2 (1975): 3–20.

———. *Quest for Refuge: The Mormon Flight from American Pluralism.* Salt Lake City: Signature Books, 1989.

———. "Secular or Sectarian History?": A Critique of *No Man Knows My History.*" *Church History* 43 (March 1974): 78–96.

Hill, Marvin S., C. Keith Rooker, and Larry T. Wimmer. "The Kirtland Economy Revisited: A Market Critique of Sectarian Economics." *BYU Studies* 17 (Summer 1977): 391–472.

Hills, Gustavus. *Map of the City of Nauvoo.* Drawn 1842. New York: J. Childs, Lithographer, 1844. Reprint, Nauvoo: Nauvoo Restoration Inc., 1971.

Hinckley, Bryant S. "The Nauvoo Memorial," *Improvement Era* 41 (August 1938): 458–61, 511.

History of the Reorganized Church of Jesus Christ of Latter Day Saints. Compiled and edited by Heman C. Smith et al. 8 vols. Independence, Mo.: Herald Publishing House, 1967–76.

Hogan, Mervin B. "Abraham Jonas, First Grand Master of Illinois." Photocopy of typescript, n.d. Lyon Collection.

———. "The Cryptic Cable Tow between Mormonism and Freemasonry." Paper presented before the Arizona Research Lodge No. 1, F. & A. M., Phoenix, Arizona, February 24, 1970. Photocopy of typescript. Lyon Collection.

———. *The Founding Minutes of Nauvoo Lodge.* Des Moines, Iowa: Research Lodge Number 2, A. F. &. A. M. [February 1971].

———. *Freemasonry and Civil Confrontation on the Illinois Frontier.* Salt Lake City: Author, 1981.

———. *Joseph Smith's Embracement of Freemasonry.* Salt Lake City: Author, 1988.

———. *Masonic Pilgrimage.* Salt Lake City: Author, 1984.

———. "Mormonism and Freemasonry: The Illinois Episode." In *Little Masonic Library: Book II.* Richmond, Va.: Macoy Publishing & Masonic Supply, 1977.

———. *Mormon Masonry in Illinois: Review by a "Grand Master."* Salt Lake City: Published by the Author, 1984.

———. "Nauvoo Lodge at Work." Photocopy of typescript, ca. January 1970. Lyon Collection.

———. "The Rise and Fall of Nauvoo Lodge." Photocopy of typescript, [1970]. Lyon Collection.

———. "Utah's Memorial to Freemasonry." *The Royal Arch Mason* 2 (Fall 1974): 199–204.

———. "What of Mormonism and Freemasonry?" Photocopy of typescript. Salt Lake City: Research Lodge of Utah, F. &. A. M., August 15, 1975. Lyon Collection.

Holifield, E. Brocks. "Peace, Conflict, and Ritual in Puritan Congregations." *Journal of Interdisciplinary History* 23 (Winter 1993): 553–70.

Holmes and Arnold's Map of Hancock County, Illinois. Lithography and printed by Charles Shober. Chicago: Holmes and Arnold, 1859.

Holzapfel, Richard N., and T. Jeffery Cottle. *Old Mormon Kirtland and Missouri: Historic Photographs and Guide.* Santa Ana, Calif.: Fieldbrook Productions, 1991.

———. *Old Mormon Nauvoo and Southeastern Iowa: Historic Photographs and Guide.* Santa Ana, Calif.: Fieldbrook Productions, 1991.

———. *Old Mormon Palmyra and New England: Historic Photographs and Guide.* Santa Ana, Calif.: Fieldbrook Productions, 1991.

Holzapfel, Richard Neitzel, and Jeni Broberg Holzapfel. *Women of Nauvoo.* Salt Lake City: Bookcraft, 1992.

Howard, Richard P. *The Church through the Years.* 2 vols. Independence, Mo.: Herald House, 1992–93.

———. "The Evolving RLDS Identity." *John Whitmer Historical Association Journal* 14 (1994): 2–10.

———. "The Nauvoo Heritage of the Reorganized Church." *Journal of Mormon History* 16 (1990): 41–52.

Hunter, William E. *Edward Hunter: Faithful Steward.* Salt Lake City: Lithographed by Publishers Press, ca. 1970.

Huntress, Keith. "Governor Thomas Ford and the Murderers of Joseph Smith." *Dialogue* 4 (Summer 1969): 41–52.

Hymns. Salt Lake City: The Church of Jesus Christ of Latter-day Saints, 1948.

Hymns of The Church of Jesus Christ of Latter-day Saints. Salt Lake City: The Church of Jesus Christ of Latter-day Saints, 1985.

Illinois: Guide and Gazetteer. Prepared for the Illinois Sesquicentennial Commission. Chicago: Rand McNally, 1969.

Improvement Era. The Church of Jesus Christ of Latter-day Saints, 1897–1970.

Instructor. The Church of Jesus Christ of Latter-day Saints, 1866–1970.

Irving, Gordon. "The Law of Adoption: One Phase of the Development of the Mormon Concept of Salvation, 1830–1900." *BYU Studies* 14 (Spring 1974): 291–314.

———. "The Mormons and the Bible in the 1830s." *BYU Studies* 13 (Summer 1973): 473–88.

Ivins, Virginia Wilcox. *Pen Pictures of Early Western Days*. Keokuk, Iowa: Author, 1908.

Jackson, Richard H. "The Mormon Village: Genesis and Antecedants of the City of Zion Plan." *BYU Studies* 17 (Winter 1977): 223–40.

Jeffress, MeLinda Evans. "Mapping Historic Nauvoo." *BYU Studies* 32 (Winter-Spring 1992): 269–75.

Jensen, Richard L. "Transplanted to Zion: The Impact of British Latter-day Saint Immigration upon Nauvoo." *BYU Studies* 31 (Winter 1991): 77–87.

Jensen, Richard L., and Richard G. Oman. *C. C. A. Christensen, 1831–1912: Mormon Immigrant Artist*. Salt Lake City: The Church of Jesus Christ of Latter-day Saints, 1984.

Jenson, Andrew. *Latter-day Saint Biographical Encyclopedia*. 4 vols. Salt Lake City: Andrew Jenson History Co. and Andrew Jenson Memorial Association, 1901–1936; Salt Lake City: Western Epics, 1971.

———. "Plural Marriage." *Historical Record* 6 (July 1887): 219–34.

Jessee, Dean C. "Joseph Smith's 19 July 1840 Discourse." Historian's Corner. *BYU Studies* 19 (Spring 1979): 390–94.

———. "The Reliability of Joseph Smith's History." *Journal of Mormon History* 3 (1976): 23–46.

———. "Return to Carthage: Writing the History of Joseph Smith's Martyrdom." *Journal of Mormon History* 8 (1981): 3–19.

———. "'Walls, Grates, and Screeking Iron Doors': The Prison Experience of Mormon Leaders in Missouri, 1838–1839." In *New Views of Mormon History*, edited by Davis Bitton and Maureen Ursenbach Beecher. Salt Lake City: University of Utah Press, 1987.

———. "The Writing of Joseph Smith's History." *BYU Studies* 11 (Summer 1971): 439–73.

Jessee, Dean C., and David J. Whittaker, eds. "The Last Months of Mormonism in Missouri: The Albert Perry Rockwood Journal." *BYU Studies* 28 (Winter 1988): 1–41.

The Jewish Theological Seminary Library. *Towards the Eternal Center: Israel, Jerusalem and the Temple: An Exhibition*. New York: The Library of The Jewish Theological Seminary of America, 1996.

Johnson, Benjamin F. *My Life's Review*. Kansas City, Mo.: Zion's Printing and Publishing, 1947.

Johnson, Clark V. "The Missouri Redress Petitions: A Reappraisal of Mormon Persecutions in Missouri." *BYU Studies* 26 (Spring 1986): 31–44.

———, ed. *Mormon Redress Petitions: Documents of the 1833–1838 Missouri Conflict*. Provo, Utah: Religious Studies Center, Brigham Young University, 1992.

Jolley, Jerry C. "The Sting of the *Wasp*: Early Nauvoo Newspaper, April 1842 to April 1843." *BYU Studies* 22 (Fall 1982): 487–96.

Jonas, Abraham. *Masonic Address*. N.p., n.d. Copy in Lyon Collection.

Jones, Dan. "The Martyrdom of Joseph Smith and His Brother Hyrum." Translated by Ronald D. Dennis. *BYU Studies* 24 (Winter 1984): 78–109.

Jones, W. Paul. "Theological Re-Symbolization of the RLDS Tradition: The Call to a Stage beyond Demythologizing." *John Whitmer Historical Association Journal* 16 (1996): 3–15.

Jorgensen, Danny L. "The Old Fox: Alpheus Cutler, Priestly Keys to the Kingdom, and the Early Church of Jesus Christ." In *Differing Visions: Dissenters in Mormon History*, edited by Roger D. Launius and Linda Thatcher. Urbana: University of Illinois Press, 1994.

Jorgensen, Lynne Watkins, and *BYU Studies* staff. "The Mantle of the Prophet Joseph Passes to Brother Brigham: A Collective Spiritual Witness." *BYU Studies* 36 (1996–97): 125–204.

Journal History of The Church of Jesus Christ of Latter-day Saints. Multivolume compilation. Church History Library, Family and Church History Department of The Church of Jesus Christ of Latter-day Saints.

Kane, Thomas L. *The Mormons: A Discourse Delivered before the Historical Society of Pennsylvania; March 26, 1850*. Philadelphia: King and Baird, 1850.

Keemble, Charles. *St. Louis Directory for 1840–1841*. St. Louis: Charles Keemble, 1840.

Kelly, Charles. "The Mysterious D. Julien." *Utah Historical Quarterly* 6 (July 1933): 85–88.

Kimball, Heber C. *On the Potter's Wheel: The Diaries of Heber C. Kimball*. Edited by Stanley B. Kimball. Salt Lake City: Signature, 1987.

Kimball, James L., Jr. "The Nauvoo Charter: A Reinterpretation." *Journal of the Illinois State Historical Society* 64 (Spring 1971): 66–78.

———. "A Study of the Nauvoo Charter, 1840–1845." M.A. thesis, University of Iowa, 1966.

———. "A Wall to Defend Zion: The Nauvoo Charter." *BYU Studies* 15 (Summer 1975): 491–97.

Kimball, Stanley B. "Also Starring Brigham Young." *Ensign* 5 (October 1975): 51–52.

———. "Heber C. Kimball and Family: The Nauvoo Years." *BYU Studies* 14 (Summer 1975): 447–79.

———. *Heber C. Kimball: Mormon Patriarch and Pioneer*. Urbana: University of Illinois Press, 1981.

———. "Kinderhook Plates Brought to Joseph Smith Appear to be a Nineteenth-Century Hoax." *Ensign* 11 (August 1981): 66–74.

———. "The Mormons in Illinois, 1838–1846: A Special Introduction." [Theme issue] *Journal of the Illinois State Historical Society* 64 (Spring 1971): 4–21.

———. "The Nauvoo Temple." *Improvement Era* 66 (November 1963): 974–84.

———. "Nauvoo West: The Mormons of the Iowa Shore." *BYU Studies* 18 (Winter 1978): 132–42.

———. "The Saints and St. Louis, 1831–1857: An Oasis of Tolerance and Security." *BYU Studies* 13 (Summer 1973); 489–519.

———, ed. *The Latter-day Saints' Emigrants' Guide*, by William Clayton. 1848; Gerald, Mo.: Patrice Press, 1983.

The Kirtland Elders' Quorum Record, 1836–1841. Edited by Lyndon W. Cook and Milton V. Backman Jr. Orem, Utah: Grandin Book, 1985.

Korns, Roderick, and Dale Morgan, eds. *West from Fort Bridger: The Pioneering of Immigrant Trails across Utah, 1846–1850*. Revised by Will Bagley and Harold Schindler. Logan: Utah State University Press, 1994.

Lanman, Charles. "Nauvoo in 1846." *Improvement Era* 18 (January 1915): 191–94. Extracted from Lanman's *A Summer in the Wilderness* (1847).

Larson, Stan. "The King Follett Discourse: A Newly Amalgamated Text." *BYU Studies* 18 (Winter 1978): 193–208.

Latter-Day Saints' Messenger and Advocate. Kirtland, Ohio, 1834–37.

Launius, Roger D. "The American Home Missionary Society Collection and Mormonism." Historians Corner. *BYU Studies* 23 (Spring 1983: 201–10.

———. "Coming of Age? The Reorganized Church of Jesus Christ of Latter Day Saints in the 1960s." *Dialogue* 28 (Summer 1995): 31–57.

———. "Joseph Smith III and the Mormon Succession Crisis, 1844–1846." *Western Illinois Regional Studies* 6 (Spring 1983): 5–22.

———. *Joseph Smith III: Pragmatic Prophet*. Urbana: University of Illinois Press, 1988.

———. "Politicking against Polygamy: Joseph Smith III, the Reorganized Church, and the Politics of the Antipolygamy Crusade, 1860–1880." *John Whitmer Historical Association Journal* 7 (1987): 35–44.

Launius, Roger D., and John E. Hallwas. *Kingdom on the Mississippi Revisited: Nauvoo in Mormon History*. Urbana: University of Illinois Press, 1996.

Launius, Roger D., and F. Mark McKiernan. *Joseph Smith Junior's Red Brick Store*. Western Illinois Monograph Series, No. 5. Macomb, Ill.: Western Illinois University, 1985.

LeBaron, E. Dale. *Benjamin Franklin Johnson: Friend to the Prophet*. Provo, Utah: Grandin Book, 1997.

Lee, John D. *A Mormon Chronicle: The Diaries of John D. Lee, 1848–1876*. Edited by Juanita Brooks. San Marino, Calif.: Huntington Library; Los Angeles: Anderson, Ritchie & Simon,1955.

———. *Mormonism Unveiled; or, The Life and Confessions of . . . John D. Lee.* St. Louis: Byran, Brand & Co., 1877.

Leonard, Glen M. "Antiquities, Curiosities, and Latter-day Saint Museums." In *The Disciple as Witness,* edited by Stephen D. Ricks, Donald W. Parry, and Andrew H. Hedges. Provo: Foundation for Ancient Research and Mormon Studies, 2000.

———. "Early Saints and the Millennium." *Ensign* 9 (August 1979): 42–47.

———. "A History of Farmington, Utah, to 1890." M.A. thesis, University of Utah, 1966.

———. "Picturing the Nauvoo Legion." *BYU Studies* 35, no. 2 (1995): 95–135.

———. "Recent Writing on Mormon Nauvoo." *Western Illinois Regional Studies* 11 (Fall 1988): 69–93.

———. "Remembering Nauvoo: Historiographical Considerations." *Journal of Mormon History* 16 (1990): 25–39.

———. "Truman Leonard: Pioneer Mormon Farmer." *Utah Historical Quarterly* 44 (Summer 1976): 240–60.

Leonard, Glen M., and T. Edgar Lyon. "The Nauvoo Years." *Ensign* 9 (September 1979): 10–15.

Lewis, Henry. *The Valley of the Mississippi Illustrated.* Edited by Bertha L. Heilbron. Translated from the German by H. Hermina Poatigieter. St. Paul: Minnesota Historical Society, 1967. Originally published as *Das Illustrirte Mississippithal.* Leipzig, 1854.

LeSueur, Stephen C. *The 1838 Mormon War in Missouri.* Columbia: University of Missouri Press, 1987.

Littlefield, Lyman O. *The Martyrs.* Salt Lake City: Juvenile Instructor, 1882.

Lorant, Stevan. *The Presidency.* New York: Macmillan, 1951.

Louder, Dean R. "A Distributional and Spatial Analysis of the Mormon Church, 1850–1870." Ph.D. diss., University of Washington, 1972.

Lundwall, N. B., comp. *The Fate of the Persecutors of the Prophet Joseph Smith.* Salt Lake City: Bookcraft, 1952.

Lyon, T. Edgar. "The Account Books of the Amos Davis Store at Commerce, Illinois." *BYU Studies* 19 (Winter 1979): 241–43.

———. "The Current Restoration of Nauvoo." *Dialogue* 5 (Spring 1970): 13–25.

———. "The Development of Church Organization and Doctrine at Nauvoo, 1839–1846." Talk given at Salt Lake Institute of Religion, March 1, 1968. In *L.D.S. Student Forum.* Salt Lake City: LDS Student Association, 1968.

———. "Doctrinal Development of the Church during the Nauvoo Sojourn, 1839–1846." *BYU Studies* 15 (Summer 1975): 435–46.

———. "Free Masonry at Nauvoo." Copy in Lyon Collection.

———. "History Highlights." In *CES Church History Symposium, 1977.* Salt Lake City: The Church of Jesus Christ of Latter-day Saints, 1977.

———. "Nauvoo and the Council of the Twelve." In *The Restoration Movement: Essays in Mormon History,* edited by F. Mark McKiernan, Alma R. Blair, and Paul M. Edwards, 167–205. Lawrence, Kans.: Coronado Press, 1973.

———. "Recollections of 'Old Nauvooers': Memories from Oral History." *BYU Studies* 18 (Winter 1978): 143–50.

Madsen, Carol Cornwall. "Faith and Community: Women of Nauvoo." In *Joseph Smith: The Prophet, the Man,* edited by Susan Easton Black and Charles D. Tate Jr. Provo, Utah: Religious Studies Center, Brigham Young University, 1993.

———. *In Their Own Words: Women and the Story of Nauvoo.* Salt Lake City: Deseret Book, 1994.

Marryat, Frederick. *Narrative of the Travels and Adventures of Monsieur Violet in California, Sonora, and Western Texas.* Leipzig: Bernhard Tauchnitz, 1843.

Marsden, William. "Journal and Diary of William Marsden." In *Heart Throbs of the West,* edited by Kate B. Carter, 12:147–48. Salt Lake City: Daughters of the Utah Pioneers, 1951.

Marsh, Eudocia Baldwin. "When the Mormons Dwelt among Us." *Bellman,* April 8, 1916. Also available as "Mormons in Hancock County: A Reminiscence." Edited by Douglas L. Wilson and Rodney O. Davis. *Journal of the Illinois State Historical Society* 654 (Spring 1971): 22–65.

Matthews, Robert J. "Doctrinal Development during the Kirtland Era." *BYU Studies* 11 (Summer 1971): 400–20.

———. *"A Plainer Translation": Joseph Smith's Translation of the Bible, a History and Commentary.* Provo, Utah: Brigham Young University Pres, 1975.

Maxwell, Neal A. *"But for a Small Moment": Light from Liberty Jail.* Salt Lake City: Bookcraft, 1986.

McCandless, Perry. *A History of Missouri, 1820–1860.* Columbia: University of Missouri Press, 1972.

McConkie, Bruce R. *Mormon Doctrine.* 2d ed. Salt Lake City: Bookcraft, 1966.

———. *A New Witness for the Articles of Faith.* Salt Lake City: Deseret Book, 1995.

McKasick, Marshall. "Fort Des Moines (1834–1838): An Archaeological Test." *Annals of Iowa* 42 (Winter 1975).

McKiernan, F. Mark, Alma R. Blair, and Paul M. Edwards, eds. *The Restoration Movement: Essays in Mormon History.* Lawrence, Kans.: Coronado Press, 1973.

McKiernan, F. Mark, and Roger D. Launius, eds. *An Early Latter-day Saint History: The Book of John Whitmer.* Independence, Mo.: Herald House, 1980.

McLaws, Monte B. "The Attempted Assassination of Missouri's Ex-Governor Lilburn W. Boggs." *Missouri Historical Review* 60 (October 1965): 50–62.

Meinig, D. W. "The Mormon Culture Region: Strategies and Patterns in the Geography of the American West, 1847–1964." *Annals of the Association of American Geographers* 55 (June 1965): 191–220.

———. *The Shaping of America: A Geographical Perspective on 500 Years of History.* 3 vols to date. New Haven: Yale University Press, 1986–.

Merk, Frederick. *Manifest Destiny and Mission in American History: A Reinterpretation.* New York: Alfred A. Knopf, 1963.

Messenger. New York, 1845. Successor to the *Prophet* (New York, 1844–45).

Miller, David E., and Miller, Della S. *Nauvoo: The City of Joseph.* Salt Lake City: Peregrine Smith, 1974.

Miller, Reuben. *James J. Strang, Weighed in the Balance of Truth, and Found Wanting.* Burlington, Wisconsin Territory: [Author], September 1846.

Moody, Thurmon D. "Nauvoo's Whistling and Whittling Brigade." *BYU Studies* 15 (Summer 1975): 480–90.

Moore, Nathaniel Fish. *A Trip from New York to the Falls of St. Anthony in 1845.* Chicago: University of Chicago Press, 1946.

Morcombe, Joseph E. "Freemasonry at Nauvoo." Introduction by Heman Smith. *Journal of History* 10 (July 1917): 368–69, (October 1917); 408–39.

———. "Masonry and Mormonism: A Record and Study of Events in Illinois and Iowa Transpiring between the Years 1840 and 1846–No. 1." *The New Age: Illustrated Monthly* 11 (May 1905) 445–54.

Mulder, William. "Nauvoo Observed." *BYU Studies* 32 (Winter-Spring 1992): 95–118.

Mulder, William, and A. Russell Mortensen. *Among the Mormons: Historic Accounts by Contemporary Observers.* 1958. Reprint, Lincoln: University of Nebraska Press, Bison Books, 1973.

Nauvoo, Ill. Charters: The City Charter: Laws, Ordinances, and Acts of the City Council of the City of Nauvoo. And Also the Ordinances of the Nauvoo Legion. Nauvoo: Nauvoo City Council, 1842.

Nauvoo Legion. *Rank Roll of the Nauvoo Legion.* [Nauvoo: Nauvoo Legion, 1842.] Copy at Chicago Historical Society.

Nauvoo Neighbor. Nauvoo, Illinois, 1843–45. Continued as *The Wasp.*

Newell, Linda King. "Cousins in Conflict: Joseph Smith III and Joseph F. Smith." *John Whitmer Historical Association Journal* 9 (1989): 3–16.

Newell, Linda King, and Valeen Tippetts Avery. *Mormon Enigma: Emma Hale Smith, Prophet's Wife, "Elect Lady," Polygamy's Foe, 1804–1879.* Garden City, N.Y.: Doubleday, 1984.

Nibley, Hugh. *Message of the Joseph Smith Papyri: An Egyptian Endowment.* Salt Lake City: Deseret Book, 1975.

———. *Mormonism and Early Christianity.* Edited by Todd M. Compton and Stephen D. Ricks. Salt Lake City: Deseret Book, and Provo: Foundation for Ancient Research and Mormon Studies, 1987.

Oaks, Dallin H. "The Relief Society and the Church." *Ensign* 22 (May 1992): 34–37.

———. "The Suppression of the *Nauvoo Expositor.*" *Utah Law Review* 9 (Winter 1965): 862–903.

Oaks, Dallin H., and Joseph I. Bentley, "Joseph Smith and Legal Process: In the Wake of the Steamboat *Nauvoo.*" *BYU Studies* 19 (Winter 1979): 167–99.

Oaks, Dallin H., and Marvin S. Hill. *Carthage Conspiracy: The Trial of the Accused Assassins of Joseph Smith.* Urbana: University of Illinois Press, 1975.

Olsen, Steven L. "Cosmic Urban Symbolism in the Book of Mormon." *BYU Studies* 23 (Winter 1983): 79–92.

———. "Joseph Smith's Concept of the City of Zion." In *Joseph Smith: The Prophet, the Man,* edited by Susan Easton Black and Charles D. Tate Jr. Provo, Utah: Religious Studies Center, Brigham Young University, 1993.

———. "The Mormon Ideology of Place: Cosmic Symbolism of the City of Zion, 1830–1846." Ph.D. diss., University of Chicago, 1985.

Pardoe, T. Earl. *Lorin Farr, Pioneer.* Provo, Utah: Brigham Young University, 1953.

Parkin, Max H. "History of the Latter-day Saints in Clay County, Missouri, 1833–1837." M.A. thesis, Brigham Young University, 1976.

Pearson, Carol Lynn. "'Nine Children Were Born': A Historical Problem from the Sugar Creek Episode." *BYU Studies* 21 (Fall 1981): 441–44.

Pease, Theodore Calvin. *The Frontier State, 1818–1848.* Vol. 2 of *The Centennial History of Illinois.* Chicago: A. C. McClurg, 1918.

Perkins, Keith W. "De Witt—Prelude to Expulsion." In *Regional Studies in Latter-day Saint Church History: Missouri.* Ed. A. K. Garr and C. V. Johnson, 262–63, 276. Provo, Utah: Brigham Young University, Department of Church History and Doctrine, 1994.

Perry, Ralph Barton. *Puritanism and Democracy.* New York: Vanguard Press, 1944; New York: Harper & Row, Torchbooks, 1964.

Peterson, H. Donl. *The Story of the Book of Abraham.* Salt Lake City: Deseret Book, 1995.

Peterson, Lauritz G. "The Kirtland Temple." *BYU Studies* 12 (Summer 1972): 400–9.

Petersen, William J. "Pike's Mississippi Expedition," *Palimpsest* 3 (May 1955): 171–204.

———. *Steamboating on the Upper Mississippi.* Iowa City, Iowa: State Historical Society of Iowa, 1968.

Piercy, Frederick Hawkins. *Route from Liverpool to Great Salt Lake Valley.* Edited by James Linforth. 1855. Reprint, edited by Fawn M. Brodie. Cambridge, Mass.: Belnap Press of Harvard University Press, 1962.

Pike, Zebulon M. *An Account of Expeditions to the Sources of the Mississippi and through the Western Parts of Louisiana.* Philadelphia: C. and A. Conrad, 1819.

Polk, James K. *The Diary of James K. Polk during His Presidency, 1845 to 1849.* Ed. Milo Milton Quaife. 4 vols. Chicago: A. C. McClurg, 1910.

Poll, Richard. "Joseph Smith and the Presidency, 1844." *Dialogue* 3 (Autumn 1968): 17–21.

———. "Nauvoo and the New Mormon History: A Bibliographical Survey." *Journal of Mormon History* 5 (1978): 105–23.

Pooley, William Vipond. *The Settlement of Illinois from 1830 to 1850. University of Wisconsin Bulletin,* no. 220; History Series, vol. 1, no. 4. Madison, Wis.: University of Wisconsin, 1908.

Porter, Larry C. "Christmas with the Prophet Joseph." *Ensign* 8 (December 1978): 8–11.

———. "'The Field Is White Already to Harvest': Earliest Missionary Labors and the Book of Mormon." In *The Prophet Joseph: Essays on the Life and Mission of Joseph Smith,* edited by Larry C. Porter and Susan Easton Black, 73–89. Salt Lake City: Deseret Book, 1988.

———. "The Odyssey of William Earl McLellin: Man of Diversity, 1806–83." In William E.

McLellin. *The Journals of William E. McLellin, 1831–1836,* edited by Jan Shipps and John W. Welch, 290–378. Provo: Brigham Young University, *BYU Studies;* Urbana and Chicago: University of Illinois Press, 1994.

Porter, Larry C., and Milton C. Backman, Jr. "Doctrine and the Temple in Nauvoo." *BYU Studies* 32 (Winter-Spring 1992): 41–57.

Porter, Larry C., and Susan Easton Black, eds. *The Prophet Joseph: Essays on the Life and Mission of Joseph Smith.* Salt Lake City: Deseret Book, 1988.

Portrait and Biographical Record of Hancock, McDonough, and Henderson Counties. Chicago: Lake City Publishing, 1894.

Poulsen, Richard C. "Fate and the Persecutors of Joseph Smith: Transmutations of an American Myth." *Dialogue* 11 (Winter 1978): 63–70.

Powell, Sumner Chilton. *Puritan Village: The Formation of a New England Town.* Middletown, Conn.: Wesleyan University Press, 1963.

Powell, William. *"Temple for Sale."* [N.p.]: William Powell, 1969. Includes facsimile extracts of William A. Gallup, Diary, 1847–48.

Pratt, Orson. *The Orson Pratt Journals.* Compiled by Elden J. Watson. Salt Lake City: Elden Jay Watson, 1975.

Pratt, Parley P. *Autobiography of Parley P. Pratt.* 1873. Edited by Parley P. Pratt [Jr.]. 3d ed. Salt Lake City: Deseret Book, 1938.

———. *The Voice of Warning and Instruction to All People.* New York: Printed by W. Sandford, 1837.

Pratt, Stephen F., "Parley P. Pratt in Winter Quarters and the Trail West." *BYU Studies* 24 (Summer 1984): 373–88.

The Prophet. New York, 1844–45. Renamed *Messenger* (New York, 1845).

Quincy, Ill., Citizens. *Public Meeting of the Citizens of Quincy! . . . February 28, 1839.* [Quincy: n.p., 1839.] Copy at Chicago Historical Society.

Quincy Argus. Quincy, Illinois, 1838–41. Renamed *Quincy Herald.*

Quincy Herald. Quincy, Illinois, 1841–1909. Continuing the *Quincy Argus.*

Quincy Whig. Quincy, Illinois, 1837–57.

Quinn, Michael. "The Council of Fifty and Its Members, 1844 to 1945." *BYU Studies* 20 (Winter 1980): 163–97.

———. "The Evolution of the Presiding Quorums of the L.D.S. Church." *Journal of Mormon History* 1 (1975): 21–38.

———. "The Mormon Succession Crisis of 1844." *BYU Studies* 16 (Winter 1976): 187–233.

Rees, Thomas. "Nauvoo, Illinois, under Mormon and Icarian Occupation." *Journal of the Illinois State Historical Society* 21 (April 1928-January 1929): 506–24.

Reps, John W. *The Making of Urban America: A History of City Planning in the United States.* Princeton: Princeton University Press, 1965.

Reynolds, John C. History of the M. W. Grand Lodge of Illinois, Ancient, Free, and Accepted Masons. Springfield, Ill.: H. G. Reynolds, 1869.

Richards, Franklin D. "A Tour of Historic Scenes." *Contributor* 7 (May 1886): 296–304.

Richards, Paul C. "Missouri Persecutions: Petitions for Redress." *BYU Studies* 13 (Summer 1973): 520–24.

Richman, Irving B. "Nauvoo and the Prophet," in *John Brown among the Quakers and Other Sketches,* 123–89. Des Moines, Iowa: Historical Department of Iowa, 1894.

Rigdon, Sidney. *Oration Delivered by Mr. S. Rigdon on the 4th of July, 1838, at Far West, Caldwell Co., Missouri.* Far West: Printed at the Journal Office, 1838.

Roberts, B. H. *A Comprehensive History of the Church of Jesus Christ of Latter-day Saints, Century One.* 6 vols. Salt Lake City: The Church of Jesus Christ of Latter-day Saints, 1930.

———. *The Rise and Fall of Nauvoo.* Salt Lake City: Deseret News, 1900.

———. *Succession in the Presidency of The Church of Jesus Christ of Latter-day Saints.* 1894. 2d ed. Salt Lake City: G. Q. Cannon and Sons, 1900.

Robertson, Margaret C. "The Campaign and the Kingdom: The Activities of the Electioneers in Joseph Smith's Presidential Campaign." *BYU Studies* 39, no. 3 (2000): 147–80.

Rohrer, Wayne C., and Louis H. Douglas. *The Agrarian Transition in America: Dualism and Change.* Indianapolis and New York: Bobbs-Merrill, 1969.

Romig, Ronald E. "The Temple Lot Suit after 100 Years." *John Whitmer Historical Association Journal* 12 (1992): 3–15.

Roozen, David A., William McKinnery, and Jackson W. Carroll. *Varieties of Religious Presence: Mission in Public Life.* New York: The Pilgrim Press, 1984.

Rowley, Dennis. "The Mormon Experience in the Wisconsin Pineries, 1841–1845." *BYU Studies* 32 (Winter-Spring 1992): 119–48.

———. "Nauvoo: A River Town." *BYU Studies* 18 (Winter 1978): 255–72.

Rudisill, George H. "The Destruction of the Nauvoo Temple." *Autumn Leaves,* November-December 1905, 549–52. From the *Fort Madison Democrat,* 1877.

Rugh, Susan Sessions. "Conflict in the Countryside: The Mormon Settlement at Macedonia, Illinois." *BYU Studies* 32 (Winter-Spring 1992): 149–74.

Saunders, Richard L. "Officers and Arms: The 1843 General Return of the Nauvoo Legion's Second Cohort." *BYU Studies* 35, no. 2 (1995): 138–51.

Schindler, Harold. *Orrin Porter Rockwell: Man of God, Son of Thunder.* 1966. 2d ed. Salt Lake City: University of Utah Press, 1983.

Searle, Howard C. "Willard Richards as Historian." *BYU Studies* 31 (Spring 1991): 41–62.

Seixas, James. *A Manual Hebrew Grammar for the Use of Beginners.* 2d ed. Andover: Gould and Newman, 1834.

Shaw, Albert. *Icaria: A Chapter in the History of Communism.* New York: Putnam, 1884.

Shields, Steven L. *Divergent Paths of the Restoration: A History of the Latter-day Saint Movement.* Provo, Utah: David C. Martin, 1975. 4th ed. Los Angeles: Restoration Research, 1990.

Shipps, Jan. "A Little Known Account of the Murders of Joseph and Hyrum Smith." *BYU Studies* 14 (Spring 1974): 389–92.

———. *Mormonism: The Story of a New Religious Tradition.* Urbana and Chicago: University of Illinois Press, 1985.

———. "The Mormons in Politics: The First Hundred Years." Ph.D. diss., University of Colorado, 1965.

———. *Sojourner in the Promised Land: Forty Years among the Mormons.* Urbana and Chicago: University of Illinois Press, 2000.

Smith, Andrew F. *Saintly Scoundrel: The Life and Times of Dr. John Cook Bennett.* Urbana: University of Illinois Press, 1997.

Smith, E. Gary. "The Patriarchal Crisis of 1845." *Dialogue* 16 (Summer 1983): 24–35.

Smith, George. "Nauvoo Roots of Mormon Polygamy, 1841–46: A Preliminary Demographic Report." *Dialogue* 27 (Spring 1994): 1–72.

Smith, Heman C. "Succession in the Presidency." *Journal of History* 2 (January 1909): 3–14.

Smith, James E. "Frontier Nauvoo: Building a Picture from Statistics." *Ensign* 9 (September 1979): 16–19.

Smith, Job Taylor. "Father Bundy's All-Wood Wagon." *Improvement Era* 11 (January 1908): 169–74.

Smith, Joseph. *Autobiographical and Historical Writings.* Edited by Dean C. Jessee. Vol. 1 of *The Papers of Joseph Smith.* Salt Lake City: Deseret Book, 1989.

———. *History of The Church of Jesus Christ of Latter-day Saints.* Edited by B. H. Roberts. 2d ed., rev. 7 vols. Salt Lake City: The Church of Jesus Christ of Latter-day Saints, 1932–51.

———. *Journal, 1832–1842.* Edited by Dean C. Jessee. Vol. 2 of *The Papers of Joseph Smith.* Salt Lake City: Deseret Book, 1992.

———. *The Personal Writings of Joseph Smith.* Compiled and edited by Dean C. Jessee. 2d ed. Salt Lake City: Deseret Book, 2002.

———. *The Revelations of the Prophet Joseph Smith: A Historical and Biographical Commentary of the*

Doctrine and Covenants. Edited by Lyndon W. Cook. Provo, Utah: Seventies Mission Bookstore, 1981.

———. *The Scriptural Teachings of the Prophet Joseph Smith.* Selected by Joseph Fielding Smith. Edited by Richard C. Galbraith. Salt Lake City: Deseret Book 1993.

———. *The Words of Joseph Smith: The Contemporary Accounts of the Nauvoo Discourses of the Prophet Joseph Smith.* Edited by Andrew F. Ehat and Lyndon W. Cook. Provo, Utah: Brigham Young University, Religious Studies Center, 1980.

Smith, Joseph Fielding. *Doctrines of Salvation.* 3 vols. Compiled by Bruce R. McConkie. Salt Lake City: Bookcraft, 1954–56.

Smith, Lucy Mack. *History of Joseph Smith.* 1853. Rev. ed., edited by George A. Smith and Elias Smith, 1901. New ed. with Notes and Comments by Preston Nibley. Salt Lake City: Bookcraft, 1958.

Smith, Paul Thomas. "A Historical Study of the Nauvoo, Illinois, Public School System, 1841–1845." M.E. Field Study, Brigham Young University, 1969.

Snider, Cecil L. "Development of Attitudes in Sectarian Conflict: A Study of Mormonism in Illinois in Contemporary Newspaper Sources." Master's thesis, State University of Iowa, 1933.

Snow, Eliza R. *Biography and Family Record of Lorenzo Snow.* Salt Lake City: Deseret News, 1884.

———. "Eliza R. Snow's Nauvoo Journal." Edited by Maureen Ursenbach. *BYU Studies* 15 (Summer 1975): 391–416.

———. "Eliza R. Snow Letter from Missouri" (Letter to Esquire Streator, Caldwell County, Missouri, February 22, 1839). *BYU Studies* 13 (Summer 1973): 545–46.

Sonne, Conway B. *Saints on the Seas: A Maritime History of Mormon Migration, 1830–1890.* Salt Lake City: University of Utah Press, 1983.

———. *Ships, Saints, and Mariners: A Maritime Encyclopedia of Mormon Migration, 1830–1890.* Salt Lake City: University of Utah Press, 1987.

Sorenson, Parry D. "Nauvoo Times and Seasons." *Journal of the Illinois State Historical Society* 55 (Summer 1962): 117–35.

Spitz, Lewis W. "History: Sacred and Secular." *Church History* 47 (March 1978): 11–22.

Staines, William C. "Reminiscences of William C. Staines." *Contributor* 12 (February-October 1891), 8-part series.

Stenhouse, T. B. H. *The Rocky Mountain Saints.* New York: D. Appleton and Company, 1873.

Stout, Hosea. *On the Mormon Frontier: The Diary of Hosea Stout, 1844–1861.* Edited by Juanita Brooks. 2 vols. Salt Lake City: University of Utah Press and Utah State Historical Society, 1964.

Sutton, Robert P. "Illinois River Towns: Economic Unity or Melting Pots?" *Western Illinois Regional Studies* 13 (Fall 1990): 21–31.

———. *Les Icariens: The Utopian Dream in Europe and America.* Urbana: University of Illinois Press, 1994.

Sweeney, John, Jr. "A History of the Nauvoo Legion in Illinois." Master's thesis, Brigham Young University, 1974.

Talmage, James E. *The House of the Lord: A Study of Sacred Sanctuaries Ancient and Modern.* 1912. Rev. ed. Salt Lake City: Deseret Book, 1976.

Taylor, Jacob N., and O. M. Crooks. *Sketch Book of Saint Louis.* St. Louis: G. Knapp and Co., 1858.

Taylor, John. *The Gospel Kingdom: Selections from the Writings and Discourses of John Taylor.* Edited by G. Homer Durham. Salt Lake City: Bookcraft, 1964.

———. *The Government of God.* Liverpool: S. W. Richards, 1852.

———. "The John Taylor Nauvoo Journal." Ed. Dean C. Jessee. *BYU Studies* 23 (Summer 1983): 1–103.

———. *The John Taylor Papers: Records of the Last Utah Pioneer.* Ed. Samuel Taylor and Raymond Taylor. 2 vols. Redwood City, Calif.: Taylor Trust, 1984–85.

Taylor, Philip A. M. *Expectations Westward: The Mormons and the Emigration of Their British Converts in the Nineteenth Century.* Edinburgh and London: Oliver & Boyd, 1965.

————. "Why Did British Mormons Emigrate?" *Utah Historical Quarterly* 12 (July 1954): 249–70.

Taylor, William. "Joseph Smith the Prophet." *Young Woman's Journal* 17 (December 1906): 547.

Tillson, John. *History of the City of Quincy, Illinois.* Revised and edited by William H. Collins. Chicago: S. J. Clarke, 1905.

Tuchman, Barbara W. "Telling All." *Wilson Quarterly* 3 (Summer 1979): 176.

Underwood, Grant. "Apocalyptic Adversaries: Mormonism Meets Millerism." *John Whitmer Historical Association Journal* 7 (1987): 53–61.

————. "Book of Mormon Usage in Early LDS Theology." *Dialogue* 17 (Autumn 1984): 35–74.

————. "Millenarianism and the Early Mormon Mind." *Journal of Mormon History* 9 (1982): 41–51.

————. "Mormon History: A Dialogue with Jan Shipps, Richard Bushman, and Leonard Arrington." *Century 2: A Brigham Young Univeristy Student Journal* 4 (Spring/Summer 1980): 27–39.

————. "Re-visioning Mormon History." *Pacific Historical Review* 55 (August 1986): 403–26.

Vallet, Emile. *Communism: History of the Experiment at Nauvoo of the Icarian Settlement.* Nauvoo: Author, 1917.

Van Noord, Roger. *King of Beaver Island: The Life and Assassination of James Jesse Strang.* Urbana: University of Illinois Press, 1988.

Van Wagoner, Richard, and Steven C. Walker. "The Joseph/Hyrum Smith Funeral Sermon." *BYU Studies* 23 (Winter 1983): 3–18.

Vogel, Dan. "James Colin Brewster: The Boy Prophet Who Challenged Mormon Authority." In *Differing Visions: Dissenters in Mormon History,* edited by Roger D. Launius and Linda Thatcher. Urbana: University of Illinois Press, 1994.

Walgren, Kent. "James Adams: Early Springfield Mormon and Freemason." *Journal of the Illinois State Historical Society* 75 (Summer 1982): 121–36.

Walker, Ronald W. "Lucy Mack Smith Speaks to the Nauvoo Saints." *BYU Studies* 32 (Winter-Spring 1992): 276–84.

————. "Seeking the 'Remnant': The Native American during the Joseph Smith Period." *Journal of Mormon History* 19 (Spring 1992): 1–33.

Waller, Elbert. "Some Half-Forgotten Towns in Illinois." *Transactions of the Illinois State Historical Society.* Illinois State Historical Society, 1927.

Warsaw Message. late 1842-February 7, 1844. Edited by Thomas Gregg.

Warsaw Signal. May 1841[?]–late 1842, 1844–. Edited by Thomas Sharp.

Watson, Elden J., ed. *Manuscript History of Brigham Young, 1846–47.* Salt Lake City: Elden J. Watson, 1971.

————. "The Nauvoo Tabernacle." *BYU Studies* 19 (Spring 1979): 416–21.

————, comp. *The Orson Pratt Journals.* Salt Lake City: Elden J. Watson, 1975.

Weil, Oscar A. "The Movement to Establish Lebanon Seminary (McKendree College), 1833–1835." *Journal of the Illinois State Historical Society* 59 (Winter 1966): 384–406.

Welch, John W., and David J. Whittaker. "'We Believe . . . ': Development of the Articles of Faith." *Ensign* 9 (September 1979): 50–55.

Welch, Richard F. *Gravestones of Early Long Island, 1680–1810.* Syosset, N.Y.: Friends for Long Island's Heritage, 1983.

Western World. Warsaw, Illinois, 1840–early 1841[?]. Edited by D. N. White.

Whitney, Helen Mar. *Plural Marriage, as Taught by the Prophet Joseph.* Salt Lake City: Juvenile Instructor Office, 1882.

Whitney, Orson F. "Aaronic Priesthood." *Contributor* 6 (July-September 1885): 604–5.

————. "An Interesting Record (Nauvoo Brass Band Minutes, October 1845-April 1846)." *Contributor* 1 (June 1880): 195–98.

————. *Life of Heber C. Kimball.* 1888. Reprint, Salt Lake City: Stevens & Wallace, 1945.

————. "The Nauvoo Brass Band." *Contributor* 1 (March 1880): 134–37.

Whittaker, David J. "The 'Articles of Faith' in Early Mormon Literature and Thought." In *New*

Views of Mormon History, edited by Davis Bitton and Maureen Ursenbach Beecher. Salt Lake City: University of Utah Press, 1987.

———. "Early Mormon Pamphleteering." *Journal of Mormon History* 4 (1977): 35–49.

Widtsoe, John A. *Joseph Smith: Seeker After Truth, Prophet of God.* Salt Lake City: Deseret News, 1951.

Wind, James P. *Places of Worship: Exploring Their History.* Nashville: American Association for State and Local History, 1990.

Winn, Kenneth H. *Exiles in a Land of Liberty: Mormons in America, 1830–1846.* Chapel Hill: University of North Carolina Press, 1989.

Wolfinger, Henry J. "Jane Manning James: A Test of Faith." In *Worth Their Salt,* edited by Colleen Whitley, 13–30. Logan, Utah: Utah State University Press, 1996.

Wood, Timothy L. "The Prophet and the Presidency: Mormonism and Politics in Joseph Smith's 1844 Presidential Campaign." *Journal of the Illinois State Historical Society* 93, no. 2 (Summer 2000): 167–93.

Woodford, Robert J. "The Historical Development of the Doctrine and Covenants." Ph.D. diss., Brigham Young University, 1974.

Woodruff, Wilford. *Waiting for World's End: The Diaries of Wilford Woodruff.* Edited by Susan Staker. Salt Lake City: Signature, 1993.

———. *Discourses of Wilford Woodruff.* Edited by G. Homer Durham. Salt Lake City: Bookcraft, 1946.

———. *Wilford Woodruff's Journals.* Edited by Scott G. Kenney. 9 vols. Midvale, Utah: Signature Books, 1985.

World Book Encyclopedia Dictionary. Chicago: Field Enterprises, 1966.

Yorgason, Laurence M. "Preview on a Study of the Social and Geographical Origins of Early Mormon Converts, 1830–1845." *BYU Studies* 10 (Spring 1970): 279–82.

———. "Some Demographic Aspects of One Hundred Early Mormon Converts, 1830–1837." Master's thesis, Brigham Young University, 1974.

Young, Biloine W. "Minnesota Mormons: The Cutlerites." *Courage* 3 (Winter-Spring 1973): 117–37.

Young, Brigham. *Discourses of Brigham Young.* Edited by John A. Widtsoe. Salt Lake City: Deseret Book, 1925.

Zucker, Louis C. "Joseph Smith as a Student of Hebrew." *Dialogue* 3 (Summer 1968): 41–55.

Credits for Maps
and Illustrations

All images from the Museum of Church History and Art and the Church Archives, divisions of the Family and Church History Department of The Church of Jesus Christ of Latter-day Saints, are © Intellectual Reserve Incorporated and are used by permission.

DUST JACKET

Joseph Smith preaching from the stand east of the Nauvoo Temple during April general conference 1844 (detail), published by George Lloyd, about 1845. Courtesy Church Archives. The complete image appears on page 332 of this volume.

FRONTISPIECE

David Rogers, *Joseph Smith Jr.* (detail), oil on canvas, created September 16–20, 1842 (see *HC* 5:153, 164–65). Courtesy Community of Christ Archives, Independence, Missouri. View of Nauvoo Temple from the flats, January 1846 (detail), by Lucian R. Foster. Courtesy Illinois State Historical Society.

PART I. ESTABLISHING NAUVOO: A PLACE OF PEACE

Page xxiv: A. Cherill, *A Map of Nauvoo,* 1846; reprint, New York: Randolph Spears, 1971 (detail).

Page 1: "Corporation Seal of City of Nauvoo, 1840," copy in Nauvoo Restoration Inc. files of a carbonized impression of a seal on an "Order on City Treasurer" to pay James Sloan, June 7, 1843, Church Archives.

CHAPTER 1. JOSEPH SMITH'S PLAN FOR ZION

Page 7: Revised plat for the City of Zion (detail), ink on paper, drawn by Frederick G. Williams, 1833. Courtesy Church Archives.

Page 13: Kirtland Temple. Lithograph, from Henry Howe, *Historical Collections of Ohio* (Cincinnati, 1847). Courtesy Church Archives.

Page 15: Oliver Cowdery, by unknown artist/engraver, detail from "The Three Witnesses," *Contributor,* October 1883, frontispiece. Courtesy Church Archives. Daniel A. Weggeland, *Joseph*

Smith the Prophet, charcoal and ink on paper, about 1875. Courtesy Museum of Church History and Art.

CHAPTER 2. FINDING A PLACE OF PEACE

Page 23: Attributed to C. C. A. Christensen, *Mobbers Raiding Printing Property & Store at Independence, Mo., July 20, 1833,* conceived and commissioned by Charles B. Hancock, Panorama, about 1882. Photograph of mural. Courtesy Church Archives.

Page 24: Upper Missouri Settlements. Research by Glen M. Leonard. Cartography by Robert Spencer, BYU Press. Adapted from Brown, Cannon, and Jackson, *Historical Atlas of Mormonism,* maps 19, 23.

Page 29: *The Extermination of the Latter Day Saints from the State of Missouri in the Fall of 1838,* lithograph by H. R. Robinson (New York: Samuel Brannan, *The Prophet* Office, 1845). Courtesy Church Archives.

Page 32: In Search of Refuge, 1838–39. Research by Glen M. Leonard. Cartography by Robert Spencer, BYU Press. Sources: "Missouri-Illinois-Iowa Counties," in Johnson, *Mormon Redress Petitions,* xviii; "Likely Routes of LDS Exodus from Missouri, 1838–1839," in Hartley, *My Best for the Kingdom,* 88; Milton D. Rafferty, *Historical Atlas of Missouri* (Norman, Oklahoma: University of Oklahoma Press, 1982), map 42.

Page 37: B. H. Roberts, photographer, Liberty Jail, Clay Co., Missouri, 1885. Courtesy Church Archives.

CHAPTER 3. A BEAUTIFUL PLACE OF REST

Page 45: Henry Lewis, "Quincy, Ill.," lithograph of Quincy in 1848, in Lewis, *Valley of the Mississippi.* Courtesy Museum of Church History and Art.

Page 49: At the Head of the Rapids. J. T. Sprigg, *Map of the Half Breed Sauk and Fox Reservation, 1833* (detail), black ink on linen, 25 x 28 inches, RG 49, Old Map File, Iowa-1, National Archives. We first noticed this map in Enders, "The DeMoines Rapids." The complete map is reproduced in Kimball, "Nauvoo West," 133.

Page 50: Homesteaders and Speculators. Adapted by Glen M. Leonard. Cartography by Robert Spencer, BYU Press. Source: Rowena J. Miller, "Land Patents, 1830–35," researched and platted 1968, NRI Archives.

Page 51: Johann Schroeder, *View of Nauvoo* (detail), oil on metal, 1859. Courtesy Museum of Church History and Art.

Page 56: Church Purchases and Nauvoo Plat. Cartography by Robert Spencer, BYU Press. Adapted from "L.D.S. Land Purchases" and "Original Plat of Nauvoo," in Miller and Miller, *Nauvoo,* 28, 34.

Page 60: "Half Breed Land Co.," Montrose, Iowa, stock certificate, 5 shares, $100, sold to Vinson Knight, May 1839, by Isaac Galland. Courtesy Church Archives. Ripley quote, *T&S* 1 (December 1839): 24.

CHAPTER 4. GATHERING THE SAINTS

Page 65: [Danquart A. Weggeland], *Joseph Smith the Prophet,* steel engraving, published by photographer Charles W. Carter, Salt Lake City, about 1880. This image is based on a retouched photograph of an oil portrait done from life in 1842 by David Rogers. Lithographic copies were misunderstood by some to have been an actual photograph from life. Courtesy Museum of Church History and Art.

Page 69: Stakes in Iowa and Illinois. Research by T. Edgar Lyon and Glen M. Leonard. Cartography by Robert Spencer, BYU Press.

Page 75: Both portraits, painted around 1840, of unidentified women and by unknown artists are on display at Pioneer Memorial Museum, Salt Lake City. Courtesy International Society Daughters of Utah Pioneers.

Page 79: "Farewell at Liverpool Harbor," woodcut, based on a Frederick C. Piercy drawing, 1853, in Piercy, *Route from Liverpool* (1855), 23.

Page 84: Routes to Nauvoo. Research by Glen M. Leonard. Cartography by Robert Spencer, BYU Press. Adapted from Brown, Cannon, and Jackson, *Historical Atlas of Mormonism,* map 31; and Buisseret, *Historic Illinois from the Air,* cartography by Tom Willcockson, figs. 76 and 116.

CHAPTER 5. NAUVOO'S MAGNA CHARTA

Page 93: William Marks, photograph, undated. Courtesy Community of Christ Archives, Independence, Missouri. Unknown artist, *John Smith,* oil on canvas, about 1836. Gift of the children of Stephen G. and Louise Richards Covey: Irene Covey Gaddis, Helen Jean Covey Williams, Marilyn Covey Williams, Stephen Richards Covey, and John Mack Richards Covey. Courtesy Museum of Church History and Art.

Page 100: Towns and Cities in Nauvoo History. Additional research by Glen M. Leonard. Cartography by Robert Spencer, BYU Press. Adapted from Brown, Cannon, and Jackson, *Historical Atlas of Mormonism,* map 30.

Page 102: Surveyed Plats to 1842. Research by Glen M. Leonard. Cartography by Robert Spencer, BYU Press. Sources: Gustavus Hills, *Map of the City of Nauvoo* (drawn 1842), published in 1845; A. Cherill, *A Map of Nauvoo [1846];* Miller and Miller, *Nauvoo,* 37.

Page 106: "Nauvoo Legion," insets (detail) in "The Home of the Saints in Illinois" (Nauvoo city map), in Stenhouse, *Rocky Mountain Saints,* 121. Courtesy Church Archives.

Page 109: Metal ballot box, used in the Nauvoo Third Municipal Ward, date unknown. Courtesy Museum of Church History and Art.

Page 114: Sutcliffe Maudsley, *Lt. Gen. Joseph Smith,* lithographic imprint by Robert Campbell, about 1842. Privately owned. Photo courtesy Museum of Church History and Art. *Maj. Gen. John C. Bennett* (detail), engraving from Bennett's *History of the Saints; or, An Exposé of Joe Smith and Mormonism* (Boston: Leland & Whiting; New York: Bradbury, Soden & Co.; Cincinnati: E. S. Norris & Co., 1842). Courtesy Museum of Church History and Art.

Page 117: Nauvoo Brass Band Flag, made in Nauvoo and carried to Utah by the band's leader and trumpet player, William Pitt. Donated by Ida Pitts Lee. Courtesy International Society Daughters of Utah Pioneers.

PART II. LIFE IN NAUVOO: A PEOPLE OF PROMISE

Page 120: Henry Lewis, "View of Nauvoo" (detail), lithograph of Nauvoo in 1848, from Lewis, *Valley of the Mississippi Illustrated.* Courtesy Museum of Church History and Art.

Page 121: Seth Eastman, *Nauvoo* (detail), pencil sketch, 1846. Courtesy Museum of Church History and Art.

CHAPTER 6. THE PROMISE OF PROSPERITY

Page 126: Unknown artist, View of Nauvoo from across the Mississippi, oil on canvas, about 1848. A well-known engraving based on this painting was published in 1848 by Hermann J. Meyer. Courtesy Museum of Church History and Art.

Page 129: B. H. Roberts, photographer, Widow's Row, 1885. Courtesy Church Archives.

Page 134: Landowners and Developers. Cartography by Robert Spencer, BYU Press. Adapted from Rowena J. Miller, "Early Mormon Purchases, 1839ff," platted 1968, on Gustavus Hills, *Map of the City of Nauvoo* (drawn 1842), NRI Archives.

Page 138: Latter-day Saint Settlements and Farmland. Concept by Glen M. Leonard. Cartography by Robert Spencer, BYU Press. Sources: Lyndon W. Cook, "Lands Purchased from Isaac Galland by Mormon Land Agents in 1839," map in Cook, "Isaac Galland," 275; Rowena J. Miller, "Mormon Ownership 1846," platted on Hill, Ripley and Campbell, *Map of Hancock County* (1843), NRI Archives.

Page 140: Nauvoo Houses, April 1846, detail from Steven K. Rogers, "A Bird's Eye View of Old Nauvoo, The City Beautiful," unpublished pencil drawing, 1995. Courtesy the artist.

CHAPTER 7. ECONOMIC EXPECTATIONS

Page 144: Nauvoo House Association, stock certificate no. 3, February 6, 1841. Courtesy Church Archives.

Page 146: Commercial Districts of Nauvoo. Concept by Glen M. Leonard. Cartography by Robert Spencer, BYU Press. Data extracted from Rowena J. Miller, "Mormon Period, 1839–46," platted 1968, on Gustavus Hills, *Map of the City of Nauvoo* (drawn 1842), NRI Archives.

Page 150: *Maid of Iowa.* Drawing by John Fryant, for the Church Museum, 1991. Based on information in Sonne, *Ships, Saints, and Mariners,* 134–35. Courtesy Museum of Church History and Art.

Page 157: Waterfront Businesses. Johann Schroeder, "View of Nauvoo" (detail), from *Map of Hancock County, Illinois,* Charles Shober, lithographer (Chicago: Holmes and Arnold, 1859). Courtesy Church Archives.

Page 162: Hancock County. Cartography by Robert Spencer, BYU Press. Sources: Brown, Cannon, and Jackson, *Historical Atlas of Mormonism,* map 28; Hill, Ripley, and Campbell, *Map of Hancock County* (1843).

Page 163: Nauvoo City Scrip, $1.00, July 14, 1842, no. 431, signed "Joseph Smith," and January 1, 1842, no. 119, signed "John C. Bennett." Courtesy Church Archives.

Page 167: Nauvoo Shops, April 1846, detail from Steven K. Rogers, "A Bird's Eye View of Old Nauvoo, The City Beautiful," unpublished pencil drawing, 1995. Courtesy the artist.

CHAPTER 8. NEIGHBORS IN NAUVOO

Page 176: Occupied Lots, 1842. Cartography by Robert Spencer, BYU Press. Source: Henry May, "Nauvoo" (original map, after Gustavus Hills, *Map of the City of Nauvoo* [drawn 1842]), platted in 1989 from records of the 1842 Church census, NRI Archives.

Page 181: William W. Major, *Joseph Smith and His Friends,* oil on canvas, about 1845. Courtesy Museum of Church History and Art.

Page 185: The "English Countryside," near Nauvoo. Concept by Glen M. Leonard. Research by James L. Kimball Jr. Cartography by Robert Spencer, BYU Press. Sources: Hill, Ripley, and Campbell, *Map of Hancock County* (1843); Rowena J. Miller, research in Hancock County land records, NRI Archives.

Page 189: Unknown artist, *Joseph Smith and Hyrum Smith,* undated charcoal sketch. From the papers of Taylor Alstrom Woolley, a Salt Lake architect whose friends included early Utah artists. Donated by Richard W. Jackson. Courtesy Museum of Church History and Art.

Page 191: Playbill (reprint) advertising *Pizzaro, or the Death of Rolla,* at the Masonic Hall, Nauvoo, April 24, 1844. Courtesy Church Archives.

Page 193: Nauvoo Music Association stock certificate, $2.50, June 5, 1843, no. 47, signed "Stephen H. Goddard" and "William F. Cahoon," trustees. Courtesy Church Archives.

Page 195: Ellen S. Pratt Report Card, handwritten original, 1844, preserved in the Addison Pratt Bible. Donated by Othello P. Pearce. Courtesy Church Archives.

Page 198: Sutcliffe Maudsley, *Lucy Mack Smith,* ink and watercolor on paper, about 1845. Courtesy Museum of Church History and Art.

CHAPTER 9. A PEOPLE OF FAITH AND DESTINY

Page 203: Public Places in Nauvoo. Concept and research by Glen M. Leonard. Cartography by Robert Spencer, BYU Press. Source: Research by Rowena Miller, NRI Archives.

Page 207: "Joseph Smith Preaching in the Wilderness," *Harper's New Monthly Magazine,* April 1853. Courtesy Church Archives. In some republications of this illustration Brigham Young's name is substituted.

Page 211: Unknown maker, "Joseph Smith's Office," oil on tin, about 1842. Donated by Roy W. Simmons and Elizabeth E. Simmons. Courtesy Museum of Church History and Art.

Page 215: William W. Major, *Joseph Smith and His Friends* (detail), oil on canvas, about 1845. Courtesy Museum of Church History and Art. The full image appears on page 181 of this volume.

Page 217: *Millennial Star,* masthead, July 1841. Courtesy Church Archives.

Page 223: Sutcliffe Maudsley, *Emma Hale Smith,* ink and watercolor on paper, about 1842. Donated by the Silver Foundation. Courtesy Museum of Church History and Art. Joseph Smith's matching portrait appears on page 337 of this volume.

Page 229: History of the Church, Book A-1, p. 1, manuscript, in the handwriting of James Mulholland. Courtesy Church Archives. Quotation, from Joseph Smith, *Papers,* 1:267.

CHAPTER 10. THE HOUSE OF THE LORD

Page 236: Nauvoo Temple, lithograph, from Gustavus Hills, *Map of the City of Nauvoo* (1842), published 1844, based on William Weeks, ink on paper rendering, 1842, not extant. Courtesy Museum of Church History and Art. James McCord, Nauvoo Temple, elevation drawing, September 1842, Church Architectural Collection. Courtesy Church Archives.

Page 239: William Weeks, Nauvoo Temple, front elevation, original drawings, about 1842–43, Church Architectural Collection. Courtesy Church Archives.

Page 243: Kirtland Temple, photograph of lower auditorium, Melchizedek Priesthood pulpits. Courtesy Museum of Church History and Art.

Page 247: Penny collection box. Used in Nauvoo and carried to Utah by Mary Fielding Smith. Courtesy Museum of Church History and Art.

Page 250: Nauvoo Temple with font, woodcut, *Graham's Magazine,* April 1849, based on John Rawson Smith panorama, 1848. Courtesy Museum of Church History and Art.

Page 253: William Weeks, design for angel weather vane, ink on paper, about 1842–43, Church Architectural Collection. Courtesy Church Archives.

Page 259: B. H. Roberts, photographer, Joseph Smith General Store (also known as the Red Brick Store, located at Water Street near Granger Street), 1885. Courtesy Church Archives.

Page 263: Nauvoo Temple sun stone and trumpet stone, original owned by State of Illinois, displayed in Nauvoo. Courtesy Museum of Church History and Art.

PART III. CHALLENGES TO THE CITY BEAUTIFUL: FAILED PROMISES OF PEACE

Page 266: Robert Campbell, *General Joseph Smith Addressing the Nauvoo Legion* (detail), water-color and ink on paper, 1845. Courtesy Museum of Church History and Art. For the complete image, see page 371 of this volume.

Page 267: "For President, Gen. Joseph Smith," *T&S* 5 (June 1, 1844): 552.

CHAPTER 11. PATRIOTS AND PROPHETS

Page 273: J. Childs, lithographer, "Lt. Gen. Joseph Smith, Nauvoo Legion" (detail), after Sutcliffe Maudsley, ink and watercolor on paper, 1842; published on Gustavus Hills, *Map of the City of Nauvoo* (New York, 1844). Courtesy Museum of Church History and Art. Red wax seal, impressed on a letter from James Arlington Bennet to Joseph Smith, October 24, 1843. The design was cut into a carnelian stone by Thomas Brown, New York City. Courtesy Church Archives.

Page 278: John McGahey, lithographer, *Joseph Smith, the Prophet. . . . Addressing the Chiefs and Braves of several tribes of Indians in the City of Nauvoo, . . . June 1843,* from unidentified book, about 1870. Courtesy Museum of Church History and Art.

Page 283: "Lt. Gen. Joseph Smith," in Stenhouse, *Rocky Mountain Saints,* 32. Courtesy Museum of Church History and Art.

Page 290: Patterns of Conflict. Concept and research by Glen M. Leonard. Cartography by Robert Spencer, BYU Press. Sources: Rowena J. Miller, "Mormon Ownership 1846," platted on Hill, Ripley and Campbell, *Map of Hancock County* (1843), NRI Archives. Lowell C. "Ben" Bennion provided the geographical terms and arranged for Suzan Logwood to create an initial draft of this map.

Page 293: Joseph Smith, woodcut, *The Prophet* (New York), January 4, 1845. Thomas C. Sharp, woodcut, *The Prophet,* April 19, 1845. Both courtesy Church Archives.

CHAPTER 12. A RENEWED SEARCH FOR REFUGE

Page 306: Thomas Sharp, photograph, undated. Courtesy Archives and Special Collections, Western Illinois University Library, Macomb. Governor Thomas Ford by unknown artist, drawing, undated. Courtesy Church Archives.

Page 310: Nauvoo Legion Musket. Photos by David Packard. Courtesy private owner, photographer, and Museum of Church History and Art.

Page 317: Henry Lewis, "Warsaw, Illinois," lithograph of Warsaw in 1848, in Lewis, *Valley of the Mississippi,* plate 50. Courtesy Church Archives.

Page 319: William Weeks, Nauvoo Masonic Hall, rendering, ink on paper, Church Architectural Collection. Courtesy Church Archives.

Page 322: "A Place of Our Own": Options for Relocation. Research and design by Glen M. Leonard. Cartography by Robert Spencer, BYU Press. Base map adapted from Alan Wexler, *Atlas of Westward Expansion,* maps by Molly Braun (New York: Facts on File, 1995), maps 4.14, 5.2, 5.8, 5.12.

Page 332: "All of North and South America Is Zion": Joseph Smith Addressing the April Conference, 1844. Colored lithograph, issued by George Lloyd, about 1845, in private possession. Photograph courtesy Church Archives.

Page 337: Sutcliffe Maudsley, *Lt. Gen. Joseph Smith,* ink and watercolor on paper, 1842. Courtesy Museum of Church History and Art.

CHAPTER 13. FOES WITHIN: THE CHURCH OF THE SECEDERS

Page 346: Unknown artist, "Joe Smith of Nauvoo, July 1842," pencil on paper. Courtesy New-York Historical Society Collections. Sutcliffe Maudsley, *Eliza Patridge Smith Lyman,* ink and watercolor on paper, about 1843. Courtesy International Society Daughters of Utah Pioneers.

Page 359: Unknown artist, "La Colonie de Nauvoo," etching, from an unidentified periodical in France, about 1848. The scene represents Nauvoo when the French Icarians arrived there. Courtesy Museum of Church History and Art.

Page 363: *Prospectus of the Nauvoo Expositor,* broadside, May 10, 1844, copy at Church History Library. Courtesy Church Archives.

Page 365: George Edward Anderson, *Nauvoo Expositor Building,* photograph, May 1907, Anderson Collection, #14363h. Courtesy L. Tom Perry Special Collections, Harold B. Lee Library, Brigham Young University.

Page 371: Robert Campbell, *General Joseph Smith Addressing the Nauvoo Legion,* ink and watercolor on paper, 1845. Courtesy Museum of Church History and Art. Philo Dibble commissioned this drawing and then hired William Major and others to enlarge it as a mural.

CHAPTER 14. "JOSEPH AND HYRUM ARE DEAD"

Page 382: Charles Shober, lithographer, "Carthage Hotel by C. S. Hamilton," in *Holmes and Arnold's Map of Hancock County* (1859), [45], copy at Church History Library. Courtesy Church Archives.

Page 385: Carthage. Charles Shober, lithographer, "Carthage Business District" (detail), in *Holmes and Arnold's Map of Hancock County* (1859), [43], copy at Church History Library. Courtesy Church Archives.

Page 390: Frederick Piercy, "Joseph Smith" and "Hyrum Smith," *Route from Liverpool* (1855), plate XIV. Courtesy Church Archives.

Page 393: "A Memorable and Unjustifiable Assassination," by Held Engraving, n.d., from an unidentified book (adapted from an 1845 woodcut in Daniels, *A Correct Account of the Murder*). Courtesy Museum of Church History and Art.

Page 395: C. C. A. Christensen, *Interior of Carthage Jail,* Mormon Panorama, no. 14, tempera on canvas, about 1880. Courtesy Brigham Young University Museum of Art. All rights reserved. For more on the maxim "The Blood of the Martyrs Is the Seed of the Church," see Bitton, *The Martyrdom Remembered,* 114; and *MS* 14 (July 3, 1852): 299.

Page 402: Death masks of Joseph Smith and Hyrum Smith, original plaster castings at Museum of Church History and Art, made by George Cannon (1794–1844), June 28, 1844. Courtesy Ephraim Hatch (Joseph) and Museum of Church History and Art (Hyrum).

Page 411: Parley P. Pratt, "Martyrs of the Latter Day Saints," *New York Messenger,* September 13, 1845. Courtesy Church Archives. Pistols held by Joseph Smith (top) and Hyrum Smith (bottom), at Carthage Jail. Photographed by David Packard. Courtesy Museum of Church History and Art.

Page 416: Charles Shober, lithographer, "Court House at Carthage," in *Holmes and Arnold's Map of Hancock County* (1859), [43], copy at Church History Library. Courtesy Church Archives.

CHAPTER 15. "WHO SHALL LEAD THE CHURCH?"

Page 425: Attributed to William W. Major, after Sutcliffe Maudsley, *Joseph Smith* and *Hyrum Smith,* oil on canvas, about 1850. Courtesy Museum of Church History and Art.

Page 432: Sidney Rigdon, engraving by Charles Hall, 1880s. William Smith, photograph, n.d. Both courtesy Church Archives.

Page 439: Alvin Gittins, *Joseph Smith, the Prophet* (detail), oil on canvas, 1959. Courtesy Museum of Church History and Art. Unknown artist, *Brigham Young,* oil on canvas, New York or Pennsylvania, June 1841 (the painting has not survived); copy photograph, Widtsoe Family Collection, used by permission, Utah State Historical Society, all rights reserved.

Page 443: Selah Van Sickle, *Brigham Young,* oil on canvas, painted in the Nauvoo Seventies Hall, July 1845. Courtesy International Society Daughters of Utah Pioneers.

Page 447: Seal of the Twelve, imprinted on a document in the Church Archives. Photograph courtesy Dean C. Jessee. For the seal's use on certificates of agency, see *New York Messenger,* July 5, 1845.

Page 451: Attributed to Lucian R. Foster, Emma Smith and David Hyrum Smith, daguerreotype, about 1846. Courtesy Community of Christ Archives, Independence, Missouri.

Page 455: Attributed to Lucian R. Foster, Joseph Smith III, about 1846. Courtesy Community of Christ Archives, Independence, Missouri. Unknown photographer, James J. Strang, about 1855. Courtesy Church Archives.

PART IV. REMOVAL: NEW PLACES AND NEW PEOPLES

Page 460: C. C. A. Christensen, *Defense of Nauvoo in September 1846* (detail), oil on canvas, 1886. Used by permission of owner, Joy Cannon Barton. Photograph courtesy Museum of Church History and Art. The full image appears on page 610 of this volume.

Page 461: "For Sale," advertisement in *Hancock Eagle* (Nauvoo), May 22, 1846, microfilm, Church History Library. Courtesy Church Archives.

CHAPTER 16. THE PEACEFUL INTERLUDE

Page 470: W. H. Gibbs, engraver, *Brigham Young,* steel engraving, based on a sketch by Frederick Piercy. Published in Piercy, *Route from Liverpool* (1855), plate XXXIV. Courtesy Church Archives. Attributed to Robert Campbell, *Hosea Stout,* lithographic print, after drawing by Sutcliffe Maudsley, about 1846; original, Reed A. Stout. Photograph used by permission, Utah State Historical Society, all rights reserved.

Page 472: Capital stock certificate of the Arsenal of the Nauvoo Legion Association, no. 161, $5.00, issued to Daniel H. Wells, October 8, 1844. Courtesy Church Archives.

Page 476: Nathan Fish Moore, *The Temple at Nauvoo,* steel engraving, in Moore, *A Trip from New York,* 1845. Courtesy Museum of Church History and Art.

Page 477: William Weeks, "The Nauvoo House," south elevation, ink on paper, 1845, Church Architectural Collection. Courtesy Church Archives.

Page 478: Seventies Hall Certificate of Shares, Share no. 40, May 9, 1844. Courtesy Church Archives.

Page 485: Marketing advertisements: "Commission Store for Home Manufacture," "See Here. 20 ton of hay, wanted immediately at the Nauvoo coach and carriage manufacturing association," and "Nauvoo Manufacturing Association," *Nauvoo Neighbor,* May 28, 1845, Church Library. Courtesy Church Archives.

Page 489: Tradesmen's advertisements: "To the Public: We the Bricklayers, Stonelayers, and Plasterers . . ." and "Coopers Association," *Nauvoo Neighbor,* May 28, 1845, Church Library. Courtesy Church Archives.

Page 490: Home manufacturer's advertisements: "Nauvoo Tannery," "Notice to the Ladies," and "The Nauvoo Leather, Harness, Boot, and Shoe Manufactory," *Nauvoo Neighbor,* May 28, 1845, Church Library. Courtesy Church Archives.

Page 494: *A Map of the Great Dam of the Des Moines Rapids on the Mississippi River opposite the City of Nauvoo,* Alanson Ripley, city engineer; drawn by Robert Campbell, ink on paper, 1845, National Archives. Drawn to our attention by Donald L. Enders, "The DeMoines Rapids," fig. 11.

Page 502: Letter opener, steel and bone, with brass name plate engraved "Pres. Brigham Young 1845." Donated by Afton L. Smith. Courtesy Museum of Church History and Art.

CHAPTER 17. A SOLUTION TO THE "MORMON QUESTION"

Page 512: A Refuge in the Rockies. Detail from *Map of an Exploring Expedition to the Rocky Mountains in the Year 1842 and to Oregon & North California in the Years 1843–44,* by Brevet Capt. J. C. Frémont (Baltimore, Md.: E. Weber & Co., lithographers, for the Corps of Topographical Engineers, 1845). Courtesy Church Archives.

Page 522: William W. Major, *Brigham Young and Mary Ann Angel Young and Family* (detail), oil on canvas, 1845–51. Courtesy Museum of Church History and Art. "A Picture of a Mobber," caricature set in type, *Nauvoo Neighbor,* August 24, 1844. Courtesy Church Archives.

Page 526: Carthage Convention. Research and design by Glen M. Leonard. Cartography by Robert Spencer, BYU Press. Sources: Military Tract, on John Melish, *Map of Illinois,* 1818; *Times and Seasons* agents, *T&S* 1 (February 1840): 64.

Page 529: Attributed to C. C. A. Christensen, *Attack by Mobbers on the Hancock Homestead. Hancock Co., Ill.,* mural from the Charles B. Hancock Sr. panorama, about 1882, not extant. Photograph in Church Archives. Courtesy Museum of Church History and Art.

Page 530: Negotiating Peace: Sheriff Jacob Backenstos, September 1845. Research by Glen M. Leonard. Cartography by Robert Spencer, BYU Press. Base maps: Brown, Cannon, and Jackson, *Historical Atlas of Mormonism,* map 28; Hill, Ripley, and Campbell, *Map of Hancock County* (1843).

Page 540: Nauvoo City Model, displayed in Nauvoo Visitors' Center, based on information compiled by Rowena Miller for Nauvoo Restoration Inc., Lands and Records Office, Nauvoo. Photograph courtesy Museum of Church History and Art.

Page 546: Henry Lewis, "View of Nauvoo," lithograph of Nauvoo in 1848, in Lewis, *Valley of the Mississippi.* Courtesy Museum of Church History and Art

CHAPTER 18. LEAVING NAUVOO

Page 554: W. H. Gibbs, engraver, *Lucy Mack Smith,* steel engraving, after drawing by Frederick Piercy, 1853, in Piercy, *Route from Liverpool* (1855), plate XIII. Courtesy Church Archives.

Page 560: A City for Sale. Research by Rowena J. Miller, "Mormon Period, 1839–46," platted in 1968 on Gustavus Hills, *Map of the City of Nauvoo* (drawn 1842), NRI Archives. Cartography by Robert Spencer, BYU Press.

Page 564: Lucian R. Foster, Nauvoo, daguerreotype, early 1846, Charles R. Carter Collection. Courtesy Church Archives. This view looks northeasterly from Parley Street across the Joseph Coolidge yard toward the temple. For identification of buildings, see Holzapfel and Cottle, *Old Mormon Nauvoo,* 225.

Page 572: Thomas Ward, *Phebe Carter Woodruff and Son Joseph,* oil on canvas, Liverpool, January 1846. Gift of Robert Needham Sears. Courtesy Museum of Church History and Art.

Page 578: Arnold Friberg, *The Ship Brooklyn,* oil on canvas, 1951. Created for the *Improvement Era* 54 (April 1951): cover. Courtesy Museum of Church History and Art.

Page 583: C. C. A. Christensen, *Crossing the Mississippi, Feb. 1846,* oil on canvas, undated.

Used by permission of owners Mr. and Mrs. Morgan Dyreng. Photograph courtesy Museum of Church History and Art.

Page 584: Proposed Territory of Deseret. Research by Glen M. Leonard. Cartography by Deseret Book staff. Historical base map: E. Gilman, *House Executive Document* 1, 30th Congress, 2d Session, 1848–49, between pages 48–49.

CHAPTER 19. TRANSITION AND EXPULSION

Page 590: Attributed to Louis Rice Chaffin, Nauvoo Temple, daguerreotype, about 1847. Courtesy Daughters of Utah Pioneers, Cedar City, Utah, used by permission. Photograph courtesy Church Archives.

Page 592: "Kirtland Temple, For Sale" and "[Nauvoo] Temple for Sale," advertisements, *Hancock Eagle* (Nauvoo), May 22, 1846, copy at Church History Library. Courtesy Church Archives.

Page 598: Houses and buildings for sale, advertisements, *Hancock Eagle* (Nauvoo), May 22, 1846 (one column presented here as two), copy at Church History Library. Courtesy Church Archives.

Page 603: "Report of the Troops" and "F. Hall & Co." notice and advertisement, *Hancock Eagle* (Nauvoo), May 22, 1846, copy at Church History Library. Courtesy Church Archives.

Page 608: Powder Magazine, September 1846. Research and design by Glen M. Leonard. Additional research and drawing by Corbin Frost. Source: Wandle Mace, Autobiography (about 1890), 139–41, Church Archives.

Page 610: C. C. A. Christensen, *Defense of Nauvoo in September 1846,* oil on canvas, 1886. Used by permission of owner, Joy Cannon Barton. Photograph courtesy Museum of Church History and Art.

Page 614: G. W. Fasel, "Expulsion from Nauvoo," lithograph, 1851. Courtesy Museum of Church History and Art.

CHAPTER 20. "THE NEW ORDER OF THINGS"

Page 626: Nauvoo Town Limits, 1845–48. Research by Glen M. Leonard. Cartography by Robert Spencer, BYU Press. Sources: Rowena J. Miller, "Plats, 1839–48," platted in 1968 on Gustavus Hills, *Map of the City of Nauvoo* (drawn 1842), NRI Archives; proposed 1845 boundary, *Neighbor*, April 2, 1845.

Page 628: *Etablissement provisoire à Nauvoo (ancien couvent des Mormons, dans l'Illinois, Etats-Unis) de la colonie Icarienne arrivée le 15 mars 1849* [Temporary Settlement at Nauvoo (former convent of the Mormons in Illinois, United States) of the Icarian colony, which arrived March 15, 1849], pen, ink, and watercolor on paper, 1850s. Courtesy Print Collection, Miriam and Ira D. Wallach Division of Art, Prints and Photographs, The New York Public Library, Astor, Lenox and Tilden Foundations.

Page 631: Joseph Rheinberger, View of Nauvoo, watercolor on paper, 1851, Joseph Rheinberger Papers, Vault MSS 454. Gift of Marie Masberg. Courtesy L. Tom Perry Special Collections, Harold B. Lee Library, Brigham Young University. Information on the home, Holzapfel and Cottle, *Old Mormon Nauvoo,* 101.

Page 640: Dispersion: Northeast and Midwest. Cartography by Robert Spencer, BYU Press. Adapted from Brown, Cannon, and Jackson, *Historical Atlas of Mormonism,* map 33.

Page 646: Lewis Bidamon and the sons of Joseph and Emma Smith, photograph, about 1860. Seated (left to right) are Lewis Crum Bidamon (1806–91), Frederick Granger Williams Smith

(1836–63), and Joseph Smith III (1832–1914). Standing (left to right) David Hyrum Smith (1844–1904) and Alexander Hale Smith (1838–1909). Courtesy Community of Christ Archives, Independence, Missouri.

Page 648: W. H. Gibbs, engraver, *Joseph Smith III* (1832–1914), steel engraving, after drawing by Fredrick Piercy, 1853, in Piercy, *Route from Liverpool* (1855), plate XI. Courtesy Church Archives. Unknown photographer, Joseph F. Smith (1838–1918), photograph, about 1860. Courtesy Church Archives.

CHAPTER 21. REMEMBERING NAUVOO

Page 656: "Nauvoo," woodcut, from J. W. Gunnison, *The Mormons, or Latter-day Saints* (Philadelphia, 1860), frontispiece. Courtesy Church Archives.

Page 658: George Edward Anderson, "Missionaries and Their Friends at the Mansion House," photograph, 1907. Courtesy Church Archives.

Index

Pages on which photos or maps appear are designated in italic type.

Aaronic Priesthood, 17, 178; and duties of fathers, 222; keys pertaining to the, 260; rights of First Presidency in, 427
Abbot, Lewis, 277
Abel, Elijah, 184
Abraham, book of, 210–12, 258
Accountability, 496
Adam and Eve, 259
Adam-ondi-Ahman, 9, 26, 46, 87
Adams, Arza, 400
Adams, George J., 454, 638–39
Adams, James, 314, 319
Adams, John Quincy, 44, 468
Adams County, 70, 179, 316–17
Adoption, law of, 264
Adultery, 347
Agnew, Joseph, 629
Aldrich, Mark, 297, 394, 415
Alger, Fannie, 344–45
Algonquin Indians, 46
Alley, George, 135, 200, 205; and hope for the best, 410; on Strang's followers, 457; on migration of Saints, 555
Alton, Illinois, 101
Alton Telegraph Review, 406
Ambrosia branch, 96
America, 63, 76
American Common School Society, 196
American Far West, 323
American principles, vigilante action perceived as acting on, 404–5
American Revolution, 89
American Sunday School Union, 227
"Americus," 415
Ancient York Masons, 318
Anderson, August, 611
Anderson, William, 602, 609–10, 611
Angell, Truman O., 588
Antibigamy laws, 349
Anti-Mormon(s), 39–40, 44, 291, 360; correspondence committees, 289; accusations of Saints fusing church and state, 292, 510; delegates attend convention, 295; press, 305; Carthage, 388; issues, 412; hope for scattering Saints, 445; rhetoric, 464; and elections, 465; journalists, 522; organize war of extermination, 527; and Saints' exodus from Iowa, 576; question intent of remaining Saints, 595–96, 599; attack, 600; Whigs, 605
Anti-Mormonism: Wight denounces Democratic, 294; Duncan makes, issue of campaign, 296
Anti-Mormon Party, 293, 304, 306, 412, 536; challenges remaining Saints, 594; and elections, 600, 654; charged with

raising a ruckus, 602; watches Nauvoo, 625

Apostasy, 26–27; in Missouri, 14; and dissension, 17; and priesthood authority, 18; in Kirtland, 87; Joseph Smith predicts, 303; creates vacancies in Twelve, 441; of schismatics, 459

Apostates: hostility of, 342–43; actions of, 356–60; at Hamilton's Inn, 379

Apostleship, 442

Appleby, William I., 420, 577

Armory, 478

Arms, call to, 368

Army of the West, 332

Arrington, Leonard J., xix

Arsenal, *203*, 478

"Articles and Covenants," 214

"Articles of Accommodation, Treaty and Agreement, 613

Articles of faith, principal, 214

Articles of Faith, the, 216, 420

Assassination attempt on Boggs, 278–79

Assembly, solemn, 435

Assistant president, 425–26

Association of Bricklayers, Stonelayers, and Plasterers, 489

Asylum, political, for LDS, 511

Atchison, David R., 27, 37

Atonement, Christ's, 259

Attwood, Millen, 76

Auditorium, the, 649

Authority: church and state, 91–92, 103–4; marriage and, 344; shared, 423

Avard, Sampson, 15, 17, 351

Averett, Elisha, 565

Averett, George W., 26

Avery, Daniel, 329

Avery, Philander, 329

Babbitt, Almon, 88, 183, 384, 453; as assemblyman, 465–66; on lawyers, 504; to investigate sale of temple, 561; appointment of, 588; speaks at temple dedication, 589; bids on property in Nauvoo, 592; travels to St. Louis, 593; travels to Winter Quarters, 617

Babylon, spiritual, 62

Backenstos, Jacob B., 190, 297, 413; on Judge Purple, 417; as assemblyman, 465–66; letter of, confirms repeal of charter, 468; as sheriff, 521, 528; driven from his home, 528–29; negotiates peace, *530;* sends message to Young, 532; proclamation of, to Quincy citizens, 534; and Hardin, 536; on Major Warren, 542; visits with Ford, 572; organizes Nauvoo militia, 600

Backwoodsman, 562

Badlam, Alexander, 430

Baker, E. D., 414

Baldwin, Caleb, 30, 38–39

Baltimore, Maryland, 73

Banking, 161

Banks, failure of, 54

Baptism, 63; converts and, 90; for the dead, 216, 237; proxy, 238

Barlow, Israel, 34, 41, 54–55

Barnes, Thomas L., 399, 400

Barnett, John T., 109, 110

Barstow, George, 216

Battle of Nauvoo, 615, 627

Beaman, Louisa, 345

Bear Creek Settlement, 525

Beaver Island, 638

Bellevue, Illinois, 73

Benbow, Jane, 78, 185–86

Benbow, John, 78, 185–86, 487

Benbow, William, 185–86

Benneson, William H., 537

Bennet, James Arlington, 189, 273, 301, 340; invited to gather volunteers for Nauvoo's defense, 371; offers to defend Nauvoo, 561

Bennett, James Gordon, 189

Bennett, John C., *114,* 186, 189, 348, 636; and incorporation of Nauvoo, 98, 99, 101; and Invincible Dragoons, 104; lobbies key leaders, 105; reports in *Times and Seasons,* 106; organizes public meetings, 108; and Nauvoo Legion, 112; moves to Nauvoo, 119; promotes tomatoes, 139; appoints Joseph Smith to head temperance committee, 148; accuses Joseph Smith of fraud, 168;

named university chancellor, 193; recommends school texts, 196; behaves immorally, 226; and rumored conspiracy, 280; religious exposé of, 292; claims friendship with Moore, 296; Masonic experience of, 314, 316; pleads for forgiveness, 320; public disclosures of, 321; antislavery views of, 337; fall of, 342; excommunication of, 350; publishes *History of the Saints,* 350; teaches doctrine of promiscuity, 350–51; Joseph Smith on, 353–55; Phelps on, 445; and Rigdon, 449–50; and Strang, 457, 638; and diversion dam, 492

Bennett, Samuel, 161, 446

Bennett, Selina, 161

Bennion, John, 173

Benson, Ezra T., 634

Bent, Ferdinand F., 661–62

Bent, Samuel, 487, 515

Bernhisel, John M., 338, 372, 588, 627

Bettisworth, David, 381, 386, 398

Bible, the, 208–9; Joseph Smith studies, 263–64; Emma Smith retains "New Translation" of, 647

Bidamon, Emma Smith, 635

Bidamon, John, 625

Bidamon, Lewis C., 599, 625, 629, 645; as surrogate father to Smith sons, *646*

Bills, John, 115

Bird, Charles, 35

Bishop, 202, 421

"Black ducks," 505

Black Hawk, 47; Purchase, 47; War, 54

Blacklegs, 309

Blackstone, Sir William, 364, 367

Blair, William W., 643, 646

Blakesley, James, 358, 359, 361, 430, 450, 644

Bliss, H. H., 369

Bloomfield, Missouri, 34

Bodley Lodge, 314, 317–18

Bogart, Samuel, 28, 30

Boggs, Lilburn: issues extermination order, 28; and the "Mormon war," 38; condemnation of, 72; assassination attempt against, 278–79, 320; and

Bennett, 351–52; Foster accuses Joseph Smith of attempting to kill, 359; offered as pattern, 536; Hardin plans arrest of Saints accused of shooting, 563; extermination order of, rescinded, 661

"Bogus Brigham" incident, 564–65

Bolton, Curtis and Rebecca, 154

Bond, Christopher S., 661

Bonneville, B. L. E., 567

Book of Commandments, 210

Book of Mormon, the: translation of, 63, 211; as witness, 201, 632; as keystone, 209; publication of, 210; corrections to, 213; plates of, packed up, 376

Book of the Law of the Lord, The, 188, 190, 638

Books, dead to be judged out of, 239

Boone, Daniel, 22

Boston, Massachusetts, 73

Boston Bee, 354

Boundaries, reconfiguration of ecclesiastical, 177–78

Bowman, William, 39

Brannan, Sam, *29,* 498, 513, 549; writes to Young, 566; on government intervention, 571; organizes emigrant company in New York, 577

Brattle, James W., 601

Brayman, Mason, 542, 606–7, 614–15

Brewster, James C., 639, 641, 642

Briggs, Jason W., 639, 643–44

Brighamites, 635

British: countryside, *185;* Isles, Saints in, 548

British North America, 89, 185–87

Brockman, Thomas S., 606, 608–10, 615

Brooke, Henry and Catharine, 438

Brooklyn, the, 577

Browning, O. H., 278, 295, 389, 537

Brunson, Seymour, 238

Bullock, Thomas, 613, 617

Bundy, George and Mary, 186

Burgess, Harrison, 501–2

Burlington Hawkeye, 615–16

Bushman, Richard, xvii–xviii

Butler, John L., 516–17

Butterfield, Justin, 282

Caber, Etienne, 628

Cahoon, Reynolds, 245–46, 373, 375–76

Caldwell County Saints, 16, 25, 36

Calhoun, John C., 276, 335

California: colony considered in Mexican Upper, 324, 508–9, 518; revolution in, 520; Saints to settle in Upper, 566, 578

Callings, qualification of lineage in, 421

Camden, Peter G., 617

Campbell, Alexander, 64–65, 98–99

Campbell, Isaac, 48

Campbell, Robert, 492

Campbellites, 7

Camp Carthage, 533, 538

Camp Creek, 525

Camp Mississippi, 537, 538

Camp of Israel, 556, 576–77

Canada, missionary work in, 89

Cannon, George, 402

Canon, need for open, 208

Cape Horn, 549

Carlin, John, 604, 605

Carlin, Thomas, 113, 156, 277–78, 281; immigrant vote and, 289; supports Saints, 294

Carns, Daniel, 488

Carthage, Illinois, 34, 92; Joseph Smith arraigned on riot charge at, 381; map of, 385; incarceration at jail in, 385–86; anti-Mormon effort at, 388; bodies of Joseph and Hyrum prepared for transport, 400

Carthage Convention, 538, 542, 596, 604; map, 526

Carthage Greys, 378, 386, 393, 394; Ford orders, to guard jail, 389; listed as parties to massacre, 413; county seat moved from, 510

Carthage Jail, 661; incarceration at, 385–86; guards convinced of prisoners' innocence, 386; Taylor sings at, 386, 392; Joseph writes Emma from, 387–88; memorial at, 659; Joseph F. Smith purchases, 659

Carthage Republican, 653

Carthage Riflemen, 389, 394

Cass, Lewis, 335

Caswall, Rev. Henry, 231

Catholic church, 561

Caton, John D., 283

Center Place, 321

Chaffin, Louis Rice, 590

Chandler, Michael H., 210–11

Charles, John F., 83, 106, 297, 505

Charter, Nauvoo, 91, 92, 305, 464–67

Chase, Phebe, 233

Cherill, A., 630

Chicago, Illinois, 101

Chicago Democrat, 216, 285

Chicago Historical Society, 213

Children, 491

Chittenden, J. B., 605

Cholera, 629–30

Christensen, C. C. A., 395

Church of Christ, 228, 633, 641, 642

Church of Jesus Christ of Latter-day Saints, The: as cause of watershed, xvii; history of, xix; members of, and Zion, 3; purchases property, 58; mission of, 63–64; organizational structure of, 68; and needs of the poor, 127–28; regulate commercial ferries, 151; newspapers of, print black-line editions, 406; collapse of, after martyrdom, 419; revelation of government of, 420–21; expansionist policy of, 497; property of, offered for sale, 561; protection of property of, 571; direction of, 623–24; doctrines and ordinances unique to, 632; satisfaction through, 638; membership of, 647; reestablished in Nauvoo, 653–54; opens Nauvoo Visitors' Center, 660; officials of, present plaque to mayor of Quincy, 661; relations of, with Community of Christ, 661; rise of, out of obscurity, 663

Church of Jesus Christ of Latter Day Saints, 640. See also Reorganized Church of Jesus Christ of Latter Day Saints.

Church-state issue, 292–93

Circuit court, 103

Citizens, new, 612–15

Citizenship, right of implied, 289, 291

City council of Nauvoo, 108–12, 329

City-founding, Mormon, 10

City of God, 132
City of Joseph, 471, 580
City of Joseph, 660
City of Nauvoo, 101
City of the Mormons, 231
Clark, James, 551, 579
Clay, Henry, 335, 465
Clay County, 22
Clayton, Diantha, 581
Clayton, William, 75, 78, 187, 190; as
    record-keeper, 207; keeps journal for
    Prophet, 248; records revelation on
    marriage, 347; protects records of
    Council of Fifty, 375; notes it is time for
    exodus of Saints, 535; writes in diary,
    565; writes song on learning of birth of
    son, 581–82
Cleveland, John, 36
Cleveland, Sarah M., 36, 224
Clifford, Benjamin, 606
Clitherall, Minnesota, 641
Coffins, 403–4
Collection of Sacred Hymns, 216
Columbus Lodge, 314
"Come All Ye Saints," 637
Commerce, Illinois, 31, 51, 92; as gathering
    place, 42, 69; Saints purchase property
    in, 57; renamed Nauvoo, 58–59; Joseph
    Smith on, 93; and ferry to Montrose, 95;
    stake at, 96–97
Community: covenants and, 6–7; sense of,
    190–92; religious, 201; building of, 204
Community of Christ, xviii, 650; launches
    preservation program, 659; completes
    Joseph Smith Historic Center, 660;
    relations of, with The Church of Jesus
    Christ of Latter-day Saints, 661. *See also*
    Reorganized Church of Jesus Christ of
    Latter Day Saints
Compensation, Saints seek, 275
Concert Hall, 192
Conferences, 202–4; quarterly, 68; special,
    440; general, in Nauvoo Temple,
    542–43
Congress, Saints' petitions to, 275
Consecration, 11,12, 55, 142, 639, 654–55
Conspirators, 358

Constitution, U.S., 270, 277, 334, 335
Conversion, 63
Converts, 182, 292, 202–4
Cook County, Iowa, 179
Coolidge, Joseph W., 487
Coray, Martha Jane Knowlton, 303, 553
Cordon, Alfred, 76, 154
Coulson, George, 465
Council, standing, 424
Council Bluffs, 599
Council of Fifty, 326, 329, 332, 415; and
    reorganization, 430, 487, 513; and
    trustees, 472–73; write to Lyman Wight,
    473–74; to organize pioneer expedition,
    519; in session in Seventies Hall, 536;
    Brigham Young convenes, 539;
    appointments of, 540; captains chosen
    from, 556; ask Governor Ford to
    withdraw troops, 563
Council of the Kingdom, 326
Councils, disciplinary, 221–22
Counterfeiting, 311–12, 524, 564, 570
Court, municipal, 103
Courthouse Square, *385*
Covenants, 5; community and, 6–7; temple,
    63–64, 259; priesthood-centered
    marriage, 264; keys of, 435; keeping,
    655
"Covenants and Commandments," 214
Covey, Almira Mack, 22, 402
Cowdery, Oliver *15,* 188; trial of fellowship
    of, 11–12; excommunication of, 12,
    425; as dissenter, 27; on foundational
    principles, 214; record-keeping of, 228;
    revelation to, 237–38, 257; denied
    permission to take plural wife, 344–45;
    role of Aaron, 422; ceases to function in
    office, 423; resumes service, 424;
    encourages exploring expedition, 561;
    and the Church of Christ, 642
Cowles, Austin A., 359, 441, 639; on plural
    marriage, 363–64; challenges Prophet's
    teachings, 641; joins Law's church, 642
Crime in Nauvoo, 110
Crooked Creek, 71, 183
Crooked River, 28, 30
Crookston, Robert, 80

Crops, 137

Currency, political debate regarding, 311–12

Cutler, Alpheus, 245, 246, 472, 487, 639–40; and "Lamanism," 641; creates "True Church of Jesus Christ," 641

Cutler, George Y., 48

Cutler, Lois, 640

Cutler, William, 606, 612

Cutlerites, 641

Cutler's Grove, *203*

Cutler's Park, 640

Cut Nose Village, 47

Dam, 491–94; map of Great, *494*

Dana, Lewis, 513–14

Dancing, 190

Daniels, William, 395, 413

Danites, 15, 17, 28, 359

Daviess County, 25, 38

Davis, Amos, 53, 58, 126, 626–27; as first merchant in Nauvoo, 145; moves onto bluff, 147; Prophet befriends, 189; store of, remains open, 616

Davis, Daniel C., 151

Davis, Elvira Hibbard, 53, 206

Davis, George T. M., 406

Davis, Jacob C., 415, 467

Dead, proxy baptism for the, 238

Debt, imprisonment for, abolished, 168

"Declaration of Belief," 271, 335

"Declaration of Independence," 27

Delaware Indians, 641

Deming, Miner R., 382, 400, 465, 521

Democratic Party, 269

Democrats: Jacksonian, 44; rivalry of, and Whigs, 291; and anti-Mormon rhetoric, 291–92, 294; many Nauvoo residents vote for, 295; and Mormons, 297, 299–300; side with Whigs to defeat repeal of charters, 307

Deseret, proposed territory of, *584*

Des Moines, 149

Des Moines Rapids, 46

DeWitt, fighting at, 27

Disfellowshipment, 95, 97

Disobedience, 11

Dissension, 17

Doctors, 504

Doctrine and Covenants, 210, 213, 376

Dodge, A. R., 105

Doniphan, Alexander W., 29, 37, 287

Douglas, Ellen, 130, 139, 158–59, 225

Douglas, George, 130

Douglas, Stephen A., 116–17, 190, 278, 289; as state supreme court justice, 291; supports Nauvoo charter, 294; courts Saints' vote, 295; encourages Saints to emigrate, 331; Saints seek advice of, 468; and Frémont's report, 512; appointed to advisory committee, 533–34; as member of negotiating committee, 536; told numbers of departing Saints, 557; Saints seek assistance from, 566

Drew, Thomas, S., 511

Drinking, social, 148

Duncan, Joseph, 296

Dunham, Jonathan, 111, 324, 325, 398–99; accompanies cortege of Joseph and Hyrum, 401; death of, 514

Dunn, James, 377, 383–84, 389

Dunn, Loren C., xix

Durfee, Edmund, 541

Duzett, Edward P., *117*

Dykes, George P., 253

Eagle Lodge, 319

Economy, 155

Education, 192–97, 654

Egan, Howard, 438, 479

Eggleston, Samuel, 140

Elders' Journal, 27, 218

Elections, 204, 269, 294, 464–65

Ells, Hannah, 282

Ells, Josiah, 450

Emigrants' Guide to Oregon and California, 567

Emigrating Company No. 1, 556, 576

Emigration, 63

Emmett, James, 142, 441, 515

Employment, 129

Endowment(s), 237; of power, 237–38; in Nauvoo Temple, 254, 256–57; Prophet expands meaning of the, 257–58; first, given in Joseph Smith's store, *259;* and Freemasonry, 315; given to the Twelve, 428; keys of covenant of, 435; Saints promised, 554; Twelve focus on administering, 568

England, 74

Ensign of Liberty, The, 642

Esdras, 641

Evans Ward, 491

Ewing, William, 46

Excommunication, 18

Expansionists, 323, 544

Expositor. See Nauvoo Expositor

Expulsion, 276

Extermination order, 28, 661

Extradition, 282, 285, 292

"Extra Ordinance for the Extra Case of Joseph Smith and Others," 286

Ezekiel, 237

Factory, cotton, 484

Fairfield Institute, 104

Faith: Lectures on, 214; statement on, 271

Families, 180, 187

Family, as center for religious activity, 220; eternal nature of, 262, 655

Far West: and Zion city pattern, 9; Saints settle in, 25; Joseph Smith settles in, 26; and "Mormon war," 27; Missouri militia approaches, 31; petition delivered to Saints in, 36; as headquarters, 65–66; stake, 87; high council in, 93; Temple, 95

Fast offerings, 654

Father: responsibilities, of, 220–21; in heaven, 241

Fellows, A. G., 563

Fellows, Hart, 408

Fellowship, loss of, 177

Female Relief Society of Nauvoo, 222–23; living constitution of the, 223; responsibilities of the, 224; ceases to meet, 226; decline of, 502–3; special assignment of, 503–4

Ferris, H. G., 602

Fielding, Joseph, 72–73, 316, 378, 662–63

Finances, 95, 437, 552

Finch, John, 142–43

"Fire and Sword" Party, 527

First Presidency: families of, 36; and gathering, 66, 81, 305; and proclamation on Nauvoo, 81–82; warnings from, 86; on Nauvoo charter, 91; oversees high council, 95; thanks legislature, 107; and doctrinal consistency, 213; and Nauvoo Temple site, 235; and proxy baptism, 238; direct consecrations to church trustees, 248; counsels patience, 341–42; organization of, 423; expansion of, 424; rights of, 427; reorganization of, 586; and building restoration, 659

"Fishing River" revelation, 11, 55

Flatboat, sinking of, 574

Follet, Louisa, 408

Foote, Warren, 418

Ford, Thomas, 105, 164, 281–82, 286–87, *306;* rebukes candidates for Congress, 285; as state supreme court justice, 291; as replacement candidate, 297; on Mormons and politics, 300; on repeal of Nauvoo charter, 307; Prophet informs, of plan to relocate Saints, 327; appeal made to, 329; Sidney Rigdon reports to, 366; fears outbreak of civil war, 369, 571–72; denounces destruction of *Expositor,* 372–73; Joseph Smith's security with, 384–85; learns of murders, 398–99; flees Carthage for Quincy, 399–400; orders guard to accompany bodies, 400; on the murders, 405; statement to the crowd, 407; dismisses army at Carthage, 408; prepares to arrest assassins, 412–13; plans to charge only leaders, 413; and reports of illegal activities, 467; on reconciliation, 509; sends troops to maintain peace, 533; likened to Governor Boggs, 540; and plans to halt evacuation of Nauvoo, 569; Brigham Young sends thanks to, 573; on removal of Mormons from Illinois, 587; appealed to for help, 605; issues proclamation, 620–21

Fordham, Elijah, 96, 250

Forgeus, John A., 446
Forgiveness, 660
Fort Des Moines, 46–47, 54, 70
Fort Edwards, 46, 48–49, *317*
Foster, Charles A., 359, 366; plans to kill
    Joseph Smith, 379; named as assassin,
    413; writ issued against, 414
Foster, Lucian R., *451, 639*
Foster, Robert D., 342, 353, 358–59, 370;
    accuses Joseph Smith, 359, 361; ·
    testimony offered against character of,
    364; plans to kill Joseph Smith, 379;
    announces deaths of Joseph and Hyrum,
    400; named as assassin, 413; writ issued
    against, 414
Fountain Green, Illinois, 34, 559
Fourteenth Amendment, 336
Fox Tribe, 46
Freedom, 270–71, 585–86
Freeholder, 630
Freemasonry, 302, 313, 315, 318–19
Frémont, John C., 330, *512,* 512–13, 566
Friendship, 188
Frontier, 22
Fullmer, David, 472–73, 487
Fullmer, John S., 1, 118–19, 168, 461; lies
    on mattress on floor of jail, 387; gives
    gun to Prophet, 391; accompanies
    Emmett, 516; on mass migration, 550;
    appointment of, 588; on sale of property
    in Nauvoo, 592, 593; on business in
    Nauvoo, 595; on spiritual refuge, 657
Fullmer, Mary Ann, 168

Galena, Illinois, 101
Galland, Isaac, 41, 53–55, 57, 99; joins
    Church, 110; property of, 125–26, 165;
    directs railway project, 152; as agent for
    the church, 166; Prophet befriends, 189
Gamblers, 309
Garden Grove, 579
Gates, Hiram, 612
Gates, Jacob, 501, 568
Gathering, 21, 25, 55; missionaries and, 61,
    62–63, 87, 132; out of the world, 63;
    geography of the, 64–65; refinement of
    policy of, 83; excommunication and

preaching the spirit of, 85; to Kirtland,
    88; Joseph Smith's expectations of, 242;
    perceived as political threat, 305;
    Nauvoo as place of, 444, 475; new place
    of, 624; principle of, 657
Gause, Jesse, 423
General Council, the, 326
*General Epistle from the Council of the Twelve
    Apostles,* 635
Gentiles, 272
Gillet, John, 53, *57,* 166
Glory, celestial, 259
Goddard, Stephen, 227
Godhead, 197, 213–14, 241, 343
Gods, corporeal, 241
Golden's Point, 601
Gospel, effort to codify the, 215
Government (s): theocratic seat of, 67; lines
    between church and state, 91–92;
    Nauvoo and civil, 98, 108–12;
    declaration on, 98, 291; Saints' beliefs
    in, and politics, 269; grass-roots
    participation in, 269; theocratic, 270; to
    protect citizens' rights, 271, 301; Saints'
    believe in imminent end of secular,
    271–72; revelation on church, 420–21;
    Saints' support of constituted, 468–69
Graceland College, 649
Grand Council, 326
Grand Military Encampment, 413
Granger, Oliver, *23, 87*
Grant, George D., 398
Grant, Heber J., 658
Grant, Jedediah M., 446
Great Britain, 74, 75–78, 215
Great Lakes, 89
Great Salt Lake City, temple in, 586
Great Salt Lake Valley, *512,* 567, 586
Great Western Measure, 323, 324–25, 508,
    549, 556
Greene, John P., 54, 365
Greenhow, John, 77
"Green Mountain Boys," 328
Gregg, Thomas, 627
Grover, Thomas, 354, 432, 574
Grover, William N., 415, 465
Guards at Carthage Jail, 386

Gulley, Samuel, 490–91
Gurley, Zenos H., Sr., 639, 643–44, 646

Habeas corpus, writ of, 280, 281, 285, 384
Haight, Isaac C., 85, 449
Half-Breed Tract, 42, 48, 53, 58, 564, 619
Hamilton, Artois, 400–401
Hamilton, William R., 395
Hamilton Hotel, *382,* 384, 378–79, 398
Hancock, John, 483
"Hancock," 412
Hancock, Levi, 25–26, 131, 344, 662;
    composes "Song of Freedom," 27
Hancock, Mosiah L., 505
Hancock, Solomon, 525, 527, 541
Hancock County, 48, 71; circuit court, 103;
    committee, 286; jail, *385;* celebrates
    martyrdom, 405; Saints agree to leave,
    528; settlement, 559; fragile truce in,
    565–66
Hancock Eagle, 593–94, 596–97, 627;
    handbill printed at, printshop, 599;
    charges Anti-Mormon Party, 602;
    denounces militant tactics, 604;
    prospectus for, 622
Hancock Guard, 595, 597
Hancock Patriot, 627, 629
Hansen, Florence P., 660
Hanson, Peter, 565
Hardin, John J., 413, 533, 536, 605;
    pledges to "unroof" Nauvoo, 563;
    proposes martial law, 572
Harper, John, 298, 438
Harris, George W., 314, 363–64
Harris, Martin, 314, 639, 642
Harrison, William Henry, 294, 296
Hastings, Lansford W., 513, 567
Haun's Mill Massacre, 28
Haven, Charlotte, 127
Haven, Jesse, 33
Haws, Peter, 149, 246
Healing, need for, 661
Hedlock, Reuben, 31
Hedrick, Granville, 643
Helm, Meredith, 319–20
Henderson, John H., 183
Heywood, Joseph L., 535, 576;

appointment of, 588; journeys to St.
    Louis, 593, 617
Hibbard, Davison, *51,* 53, 110, 126, 156,
    493
Hickman, William, 606, 612
Hicks, John A., 379
Higbee, Chauncey L., 342, 379, 413, 534
Higbee, Elias, 43; in Quincy, 54–55; travels
    to Commerce, 55; as friend of Prophet,
    190; on temple building committee,
    245; records temple contributions, 247;
    seeks compensation, 275–76
Higbee, Francis M., 342, 359, 361, 366;
    plans to kill Joseph Smith, 379; fails to
    appear for trial, 383; named as assassin,
    413; files charges against Mormons, 534;
    arrest of, 602
High councils, 68; dual role of, 92–95; in
    Far West, Missouri, 93; regulations of,
    94; appoints delegates to seek redress,
    95; judicial function of, 95; city council
    replaces, 108–9
Highland Branch, 531–32
Hills, Gustavus, 109, 192, *236*
Hinckle, George M., 445; conspiracy of,
    28–29; Phelps on, 445; McClellin joins
    with, 642
Hinckley, Bryant S., 652, 658
Hinckley, Gordon B., 655
History: personal, 231–32; church, 228,
    230
"History of Joseph Smith," 228–29
Hodge, A. C., 378
Hoge, Joseph P., 285, 299, 465
Holladay, Benjamin, 149–50
Holladay, William, 149–50
Holy City, Zion as the, 6
Holy Ghost, 90, 206
Homestead, Joseph Smith's, restored, 659
Homesteaders, *50,* 133
"Hospes," 312–13
Hotchkiss, Horace R., 53–54, 166, 167–68
House Committee on Counties, 308
House of the Lord, 235, 237
Houston, Sam, 327
Hovey, Joseph, 436, 552
Hubbard, Charles, 182

Hunter, Edward, 156, 158, 164, 169, 487; on successors to Joseph and Hyrum, 437; on home industry, 483; letter to, 575–76

Huntington, Dimick, 111, 190, 402

Huntington, William, 35, 404, 446

Huntington, William, Sr., 402, 441, 487

Husband, responsibilities of, 220–21

Hyde, Orson, 123, 327; on Nauvoo's greatest need, 153; German tract written by, 216; pronounces dedicatory prayer, 265; presents memorial in Washington, 276, 330–31; absence of, 433; the Olive Branch, 444; preaches against Strang, 459; to raise funds, 479; route outlined by, 514; speaks in grove, 580; Twelve meet in home of, 586; participates in temple dedication, 589; writes regarding sale of temple, 592–93; encourages Saints to leave Nauvoo, 598–99; sent to gather funds, 634; Cutler alienated from, 641

Hymns, 216–17, 218

Icarians, 627, 628

Illinois: welcome in, 43–45; Military Tract in, 47; stakes in, 69; tension resurfaces in western, 302; Volunteers, 605

Immigrants, 47; dissatisfied, 77–78; employment opportunities for, 154; human resources in British, 157, 492–93; Prophet warns potential, 174; encouraged to buy church land, 175; vote of the, 289; Nauvoo attracts German, 630–31

Increase, eternal, 347, 356

Independence, Missouri, 3, 5, 8, 20

Indian Removal Act, 46

Indians, 23, 207; Algonquin, 46; City of Zion and, 67; proselyting missions to, 323, 514, 516, 517, 640; Cherokee, 517–18; Deleware, 641; Oneida, 641. See also Native Americans

Industrialization, 140

Industry, Nauvoo and, 129, 481–86

Inheritance, patrilineal, 426

Interesting Account of Several Remarkable Visions, An, 214

Introduction, letter of, 222

Invincible Dragoons, 99, 104, 112

Iowa, 55, 69, 70

Iowa Democrat, 338

Iowa Twins, 151

Isolationism, 274

Israel, 61

Israelites, modern, 63–64

Ivins, Charles, 342, 359

Ivins, James, 197, 658

Jack-Mormons, 271, 291, 306, 620; refuse to help Backenstos, 531; expelled from Nauvoo, 625

Jackson, Andrew, 44, 269, 336, 468

Jackson, Joseph H., 358, 361–62, 364, 376; plans to kill Joseph Smith, 379; boasts, 394; named as assassin, 413; writ issued against, 414

Jackson County, 65

Jacob, Norton, 580

Jacob, Udney Hay, 353

Jacobs, Zina, 402

James, Isaac, 184

James, Jane Manning, 184

James, Samuel, 446

Jefferson, Thomas, 6, 131

Jennings, William O., 28

Jerusalem, 5, 6

Jesus Christ: preparation for returning, 62; hope of salvation through, 266; return of, to rule as King of kings, 271, 655

Johnson, Benjamin F., 315

Johnson, Joel H., 71, 183

Johnson, John., 198

Johnson, Lyman E., 27

Johnson, Richard M., 335

Johnstun, Jesse W., 33

Jonas, Abraham, 314–15, 316–18, 408

Jones, Dan, 150, 151, 377, 384; lies on mattress on floor of jail, 387; Joseph dispatches, to Quincy, 389

Jones, Henry, 568

Jones, James, 233, 568

Jones, John, 185

Jones, W. Paul, 650
Joseph, land of, 67
Joseph Smith Historic Center, 660
Judd, Zodak, 34
Judgment, ultimate, 660
Julien, Denis, 46, 48
Justice, 16–17, 381, 410

Kane, John K., 618
Kane, Thomas L., 578, 618–19
Kanesville, 586, 619
Kay, John, 185, 479
Kay, William, 478
Kearny, Stephen W., 47, 409, 513, 579, 618
Kendall, Amos, 571
Keokuk, 319
Keys, 239, 264, 421, 632
Key Stone Store, 490
Kimball, D. C., 548
Kimball, Ethan, 175
Kimball, Heber C., 19, 72, 83, 119, 143;
    on Missouri expulsion, 31; in Missouri,
    34–35; entreats state officials, 38;
    organizes conference in Preston,
    England, 74; on Nauvoo's growth, 124;
    in Commerce, 127; and house raising,
    128; the Prophet relies on, 189;
    education of, 193; on priesthood, 221;
    and Young People's Meetings, 226; letter
    from wife of, 256; Masonic experience
    of, 314, 316; visits nation's capital, 340;
    takes plural wife, 346; on the murders,
    408; as herald of grace, 444; invites
    immigration, 473; and Nauvoo House,
    477; and manufacturing, 484, 491;
    divides North America into districts,
    496; on whittling boys, 506; on
    abandoning Nauvoo, 517; records prayer
    at Taylor's home, 537; talks of modern
    Israel fleeing Egypt, 544; on first
    company to depart, 556; on intent of
    affidavits, 563; crosses Mississippi, 582;
    selected as counselor, 586; home of, sold,
    591; home of, purchased, 659
Kimball, Hiram, 52–53, 126, 182, 348–49;
    on Nauvoo city council, 109; land of,
    purchased, 128; and iron foundry, 156;

offers land for work, 164; Prophet
    befriends, 189; as political candidate,
    297; leaves for Iowa, 375–76; arrives on
    steamer, 433; iron foundry, 484; hosts
    gathering, 511–12; sent to Quincy, 534;
    returns to Nauvoo, 579–80; on business
    in Nauvoo, 595
Kimball, J. LeRoy, 658–59
Kimball, Phineas, 595
Kimball, Sarah Granger, 223
Kimball, Spencer W., xviii
Kimball, Vilate, 119, 240, 255–56, 349,
    367; on Governor Ford's response,
    372–73; writes of martyrdom, 403
Kinderhook plates, 212
King, Austin A., 30, 37, 38, 287
Kingdom of God, 326
King Follett discourse, 240–41, 363, 648
Kirtland, Ohio, 20–21, 73, 87, 88
Kirtland Camp, 182–83
Kirtland declaration, 292
Kirtland High Council, 257
Kirtland Temple, 13, 237; Nauvoo Temple
    resembles, 242–43; dedication, 257;
    advertised for sale, 593–94; and
    Reorganized church, 649–50
Klamet (Klamath) Valley, 332
Knight, Joseph, Sr., 188
Knight, Newel, 156, 493
Knight, Vinson, 29, 58, 60
Knight, Zenos, 110
Knowlton Settlement, 531

La Harpe, Illinois, 34, 251, 525, 559
"Lamanism," 641
Lamanites, 323, 515–16. See also Native
    Americans
Lamborn, Josiah, 467–68
Lambson, Alfred, 164–65, 558
Lamoreaux, Andrew L., 612
Late Persecutions, 214
Lathrop, A. A., 490
Latter-day Saints: Clay County citizens and
    the, 23; settlements of the, 26, 138;
    philosophy of education, 193; and belief
    in Bible, 213; self-definition, 219; family
    and institutional church, 221; as

covenant people, 260; offended by political stance of Ford, 297; vote of, becomes issue, 298–300; search for refuge, 301–2; public opposition to, 304; and self-government, 308; charges of lawlessness against, 309; economic influence of, 311; resolve to exterminate, 368; fear extermination, 409; congregation of, in Nauvoo, 656; and principle of gathering, 656–57; inheritance of, from Nauvoo, 664. *See also* Saints

Latter-day Saints Millennial Star, 217, 218

Law, Jane, 357–58, 363

Law, William, 108, 144–45, 441; named commissioner of NA&MA, 156; and steam flour mill, 156; as friend of Prophet, 190; appointed university registrar, 193; becomes foe of Prophet, 342; rejects plural marriage, 348, 354; and Nauvoo secessionist movement, 357–58; as leader of "Reformed Mormon Church," 359, 642; charges Joseph Smith with adultery, 361; on revelation on plural marriage, 363–64; plans to kill Joseph Smith, 379; named as assassin, 413; writ issued against, 414; and keys of sealing power, 428; excommunication of, 429; McClellin joins with, 642

Law, Wilson, 108, 114–15, 144–45, 376; and steam flour mill, 156; and land speculation, 177; pledges loyalty to Illinois, 282; becomes foe of the Prophet, 342; as member of "Reformed Mormon Church," 359; and *Expositor,* 364; plans to kill Joseph Smith, 379; named as assassin, 413; Phelps on, 445

Law-and-order citizens, 306, 465, 625

Lawlessness, Saints charged with, 309, 524

Lawyers, Saints' view of, 504

Leadership, transition in, 439

Learning, worldly, 205–6

Leavitt, Sarah, 401

Lectures on Faith, 214, 241

Lee, Ann, 434

Lee, John D., 486, 561, 570

Lee County, Iowa, 42, 82, 179

Leniency, 221–22

Leonard, Ortentia White, 262

Leonard, Truman, 262

Lewis, Henry, 123

Leyland, Benjamin, 400

Liberty Jail, 13–14, 16–18, 19, 39

Libraries, 197

Lightner, Mary, 345

Lincoln, Abraham, 106, 289, 294–95

Lineage, qualifications of, 421

Liquor, sale of, 148

Little, Jesse C., 438, 482, 577–79, 618

Little, Sidney H., 105–6, 294

Littlefield, Lyman, 395

Liverpool, England, 79–81

Lives, eternal, 241

Living Constitution, the, 326, 488, 490

Livingston, Mr., 484

Log Cabin Bill, 133

Lord, 206–7, 270–71, 420

Louisville Journal, 327

Lovejoy, Elijah, 366

Loyalty, 188

Lucas, Robert, 41

Lucas, Samuel D., 28, 30

Lumber, 246

Lyman, Amasa, 86, 429, 432, 486; Brigham Young invites, to speak, 435–36; retained as apostle, 441; to preside over temporal affairs, 487; advises seventies, 502; on leaving Illinois, 508; on call to go to California, 517; and a transplanted society, 544–45; on following spiritual leaders, 552–53; temple searched for, 564; sent to southern states, 635

Lyne, Thomas A., *191*

Lyon, C. W., 163–64

Lyon, T. Edgar, xix

Lyon's Drug, 390–91

Mace, Wandle, 34, 126, 197, *608;* oversees framing of Nauvoo Temple, 246; on Richards' speech, 401; on whittling and whistling boys, 506

Macedonia, 71, 136, 251

Magna Charta, 91

Maid of Iowa, 150, 190, 284, 373, 480

Manifest Destiny, 570

Manifesto, xvii, 655

Mansion House, 140, 190, *658;* schooling at, 196; Prophet hosts dinner at, 284; Rockwell refused entrance to, 287–88; Ford and party dine at, 390; is official point for dispersing news of the martyrdom, 399; bodies brought to, 401; Reorganized church purchases, 659; guides host visitors at restored, 659

Manufacturing, 141

Marauders, 562

Marcy, William L., 566

Maritime Provinces, 89

Markham, Stephen, 36, 283–84, 384; lies on mattress on floor of jail, 387; Richards writes to, 398–99; speaks on martyrdom, 401; as police chief, 470; pioneer company of, 580; organizes Nauvoo militia, 600

Marks, William, 87, *93,* 189, 357, 373, 611; chairs meeting, 54; named as stake president, 93–94, supports apostate Law, 354; supervises preparation of bodies for burial, 401–2; seeks appointment as trustee, 430–31; standing of, 437; rejection of, 441; defends Rigdon, 448–49, 451; as Strang affiliate, 457, 638; and Reorganization, 643; joins the New Organization, 644; Joseph III contacts, 645–46; ordains Joseph III, 646

Marquette County, 308, 317

Marriage: plural, 180, 343; Emma Smith denounces plural, 226; Joseph Smith administers ordinance of, 262; civil, 263; eternal, 264, 343; monogamy as only authorized practice, 345; Prophet explains blessings of eternal, 347, 427; celestial order of, 347; new and everlasting covenant of, 356; keys of covenant of, 435; focus on temple, 655. *See also* Plural marriage

Martin, Edward, 75

Martyrs, 419

Masonic Hall (Nauvoo), 118, 190, *203, 319,* 321

Masonry. *See* Freemasonry

Materials, 214–15, 245–46

Matlack, William E., 594–95, 627

Maudsley, Sutcliffe, 227

McAuley, John, 601–2

McBride, Reuben, 496

McClellin, William E., 98, 449–50, 639; challenges Brigham Young, 642; and "Latter Day Saints," 642–43; as editor for *The Ensign of Liberty,* 642; joins with apostates, 642

McCord, James, *236*

McCrae, Alexander, 609

McDonough County militia, 377, 382

McDougal, James A, 533–34

McFall, Hugh, 109

McKay, David O., 659

McMurray, W. Grant, 650

McRae, Alexander, 30, 38–39

Mechanics Association, 483

Melchizedek Priesthood, 17, 212; quorums, 221; keys pertaining to the, 260; rights of First Presidency in, 427; keys of the, 428

Memorials to martyrs, 660, 661

Mercantile and Mechanical Association, 486, 491

Mercy, justice and, 16–17

Mexico, declaration of war against, 520, 578

Michigan, branches in, 73

Michigan Glass Works, 253

Middle Missouri River Valley, 582

Migration, 75, 562

Militarism, threat of, 289

Military: organization in Nauvoo, 112; service, 470–71

Militia, 14, 471–72

Millennial Star, 76–77, 207, 497, 548

Millennium, 62–63, 197, 272

Miller, George, 62, 149, 190, 246, 430, 636; as temple trustee, 248; offers Prophet refuge, 281; Masonic experience of, 314; proposes migration to west Texas, 325; on Bennett, 351–52; and Texas colonization, 441; as church

trustee, 480, 496; escorts sheriff to
Carthage, 529; and Nauvoo volunteers,
531–32; on Ford's promise, 564; poses as
Young, 564–65; leaves Nauvoo, 588
Miller, Henry W., 148, 588
Miller's Hollow, 586, 619
Milliken, Lucy, 625
Missionaries: and gathering, 61, 85, 207–8,
637; in Great Britain, 74; needs of wives
of, 129–30; convert Southerners, 183;
and Lectures on Faith, 214; interference
of, with slaves, 271; campaign, 339;
expansion of work of, 440; public
relations, 467–68, 475; sent across
North America and to British Isles, 634;
in Nauvoo, 659
Missionary: hymns and work, 218;
expanding, force, 463–641; Seventy and,
499–500; Young halts, work, 510–11;
program of Reorganized church, 646–47
Missouri: exodus from, 19–20, 30, 33;
abandoned property in, 35, 302;
prisoners seek redress from supreme
court of, 37; general assembly of, 276;
calls for redress of wrongs suffered in,
367–68
Missourians, conspiracy with, 28–29
Mobocracy, resurgence of, 525
Moderation, spirit of, 410
Moffitt, Levi, 150
Money, paper, 164, 312
Money-Diggersville, 186
Monroe, James M., 196, 451–53, 515
Montrose, 47, 69–70, 96
Moon, Francis, 77
Moon, John, 77–78
Moore, Andrew, 176, 459
Moore, John, 296
Moore, Nathan Fish, 476
Morgan, William, 39, 313
Moriah Lodge, 314
Morley's Settlement, 525, 527, 559
Mormon: "war," 27–28, 38, 39; army, 116;
sympathizers, 271; reparation bill, 328;
solution to the, question, 508; Reserve,
520; volunteers disbanded, 528; Hoax,
565; Battalion, 579, 634; Trail, 656

Mormon Expositor, 73
Mormon-Indian settlement, 327
Mormonism: attempts to explain, 215–16;
fate of, 419; triumph of, 469; original,
623, 643
Mormon Trail, 656
"Mormon war," 27–28, 38, 39
Morris, Isaac N., 537
Mosely, William, 132, 135
Mother in heaven, 241
Mound, the, 185
Mount Pisgah, 579
Mount Zion, 5, 241
Mulholland, James, 58, 228, 229
Munson, Mr., 61
Murderers, trial of, of Joseph and Hyrum,
415–17
Museum, Nauvoo, 198
Music, 192; Hall, 192, 527; Association,
479
"My Peaceful Home, 1837," 25–26

Nashville, Iowa, 82, 96
National Park Service, 659
National Reform Party, 340
National Union Party, 335–36
Native Americans, 46, 47, 142; burial
mounds, 212; failure of U.S. to help,
272; Zion to be established among, 323;
friendship of Joseph Smith with, 324;
carrying restored gospel to, 639. See also
Indians
Nauvoo: legacy of Mormon, xviii, 664;
Joseph Smith's letter published in, 16;
period of history, 19; settlement of, 46;
map of, 56; Joseph Smith names
community, 58–59; home industry of,
60, 158; gathering to, 66, 76, 81–82,
143, 444; as hub, 69–70; stake, 81, 177;
as refuge, 82; map of routes to, 84;
Magna Charta, 91; and civil
government, 98; bill, 105; crime in, 110;
economics in, 124–25; agrarian lifestyle
in, 125; industry in, 129; and agrarian
ideal, 131; as religious sanctuary, 132;
sense of community in, 136, 190–92;
production of crops in, 137–38;

industrialization of, 140, 153, 158; commercial districts of, *146;* and joint-stock organization, 155–56; banking in, 161; council issues scrip, 163; voting strength of, 179; tension between, and neighbors, 180; and regional origins, 182–85; black residents of, 184; British immigrants in, 184–85; friendships in, 188; and education, 192, 195; theatrical performances and dance in, 190–92; museum, 198; "city of the prophet," 201–2; public places in, *203;* adopts seal, 275; as closest place to hear writs, 284; municipal court of, 286, 361; federal protection of, 288–89; as an armed camp, 289; as cornerstone to Zion, 321; Governor Ford arrives at, 390; anxious peace at, 408–9; policemen stand trial, 417; population of, expands, 445; Town of, 472; plans to abandon, 510, 517, 537; removal of Saints from, 541–42, 587; high council circular, 551; reduced to a small branch, 587; sale of property in, 591–92; attack on, 608–11; surrender of, 613; new order of, 624; town limits, *626;* key, teachings of Joseph Smith, 651; Utah LDS visit, 653; celebration of founding of, 658

Nauvoo, the, 149–50

Nauvoo Agricultural and Manufacturing Association (NA&MA), 156, 158, 485; and pottery, 159; attempt to eliminate charter of, 466, 486; and diversion dam, 493

Nauvoo Boot and Shoe Establishment, 489

Nauvoo Brass Band, *117,* 192

Nauvoo Carriage and Coach Making Association, 485

Nauvoo charter, 99, 101, 104–5, 110, 116–17; authority of, 284–86; Sidney Little and enactment, 294; repeal of, 307, 464–67, 508

Nauvoo Choir of Singers, 479

Nauvoo City: council regulates commerce, 148; attempts to protect moral values, 148–49; grants Joseph Smith certain exclusive rights, 151; proposed

ordinance granting powers to, 288; council supports ordinance, 310–11; a city of Righteousness, 475; officers of, charged with inciting riot, 417; for sale, *560*

Nauvoo Expositor, 362, 365, 374, 381

Nauvoo House, 81, 143, 165, 272; revelation on, 235–36; lumber for, 246; progress on building, 251–52; coffins secretly buried in basement of, 404; attempt to eliminate charter of, 466; motion to complete, 476–77; completing the, 588

Nauvoo Legion, the, 104, 109; organization of, 112–13; Bennett assumes control of, 114; uniforms for, 115–16; membership in, 116–17; drills and reviews of, 118; Band, 192; parade ground, *203;* at Nauvoo Temple cornerstone laying ceremony, 233–35; defensive purpose of, *283;* to meet Prophet at Monmouth, 284; U.S. forces to join with, in defending the Saints, 288; and defense of Nauvoo, 371; is disbanded, 374; is disarmed, 377; future of, 471

Nauvoo Library and Literary Institute, 197

Nauvoo Lodge, 318, 320

Nauvoo Lyceum, 197

Nauvoo Masonic Hall, 118, 190, *203, 319,* 321

Nauvoo Music: Association, 192; Hall, *203*

Nauvoo Neighbor, 212, 219, 285, 299; excerpts Frémont's expedition report, 330; challenges repeal of city charter, 414–15; announces hearing, 446–47; masthead of, 464; on repeal bill, 467; and home industry, 482–84; Twelve's endorsement of, 497; production of, halted, 539–40; publishes extra, 541; on government's failure to protect citizens, 547; publishes supply list, 557; celebrates Saints exodus, 575; replacement for, 594

Nauvoo Potters' Association, 159

Nauvoo Relief Society, *247*

Nauvoo Restoration Incorporated, xix, *628,* 659

Nauvoo Sunday School, 227

Nauvoo Tannery, 489

Nauvoo Temple, 67, 81, *203;* funds required for, 88; excavation begins for, 147; cornerstone laying for, 233–34; revelation on, 235–36; design for, *236,* 242–44; meaning of symbols of, 244–45; lumber for, 246–47; labor on the, 249–51; baptismal font, *250;* capstone, 252; furnishings for the, 254–55; and development of temple theology, 257; completion of, 261, 265, 440, 463, 500; revelation regarding, 272; proxy ordinance work to be done in, 333; laborers needed for, 495; dedication of, 542, 562, 573, 588–91; sale of, 561, 568–69, 592, 628; ordinance work in, 573; fire in, 574–75; dedication of, signals formal end to Saints' activity, 595–96; trustees surrender key to, 613; as spiritual center, 651; replica of bell of, 654; plans to rebuild, 655–56

Nauvoo Theater, 190–91

Nauvoo Tinners' Association, 254

Nauvoo University, 194

Nauvoo Visitors' Center, 660

Nauvoo Wasp, 148, 219, 279, 307; denounces lawbreakers, 308–9; publishes articles about California, 323

Nauvoo Water Power Company, 49

Neibaur, Alexander, 524

New Bedford (Mass.) *Morning Register,* 404–5

Newberry, Lane K., 658

New Jerusalem, 20, 42, 67

New Organization, 643–44

New Orleans, 79–80

Newspapers: accounts of martyrdom in, 404–5; publish anti-Mormon issues, 413. *See also* names of individual newspapers

New West, 323–24

New York City, 70, 85

New York Herald, 189

New York Messenger, 453, 498, 547

New York Prophet, 412

New York State, 89

New York Sun, 475–76

New York Tribune, 338, 521

New Zarahemla, 42

Noble, Joseph Bates, 345

Norris, David, 611

Notes on Virginia, 131

Nye, Jonathan, 319

Obedience, 553

Ohio, 87, 88–89

Old Burying Ground, *203*

Old Citizens Law and Order Ticket, 465

Old Nauvoo, 657, 659

"Old Nauvooers," 660

Olive Branch, The, 641

Olive Leaf, The, 88

Oneida Indians, 641

Opposition, 18

Order of Enoch, 638

Order of Illuminati, 638

Ordinances, 5, 81; temple, 235, 255, 591, 663; performance of religious, 239; proxy, restricted to Nauvoo Temple, 240, 333; marriage sealing, 260; initiatory, 262; of salvation, 326; priesthood, 632; availability of temple, 655

Oregon: and California Exploring Expedition, 325; possibility of sanctuary in, 331–32, 509; Mission, 514; federal contracts along trail to, 577

Owen, Thomas H., 298, 559

Pace, William Bryan, 505

Pacifism, 469

Page, Hiram, 642

Page, John E., 19, 109–10, 189, 348, 639; presents memorial in Washington, D.C., 276; and water company, 294; absence of, 433; as the sun dial, 444; as follower of Strang, 457, 638; and successor to Joseph Smith, 643

Panic of 1837, 44, 52, 54

Papyri, Egyptian, 258

Parades, 118

Parker, James R., 605

Partridge, Edward, 34, 41, 54–55

Patriarch, Church, 410, 419, 421, 426;

vacancy in office of, 435; Twelve
authorized to appoint general, 437
Patriotism, Latter-day Saint, 270
Patronage, control of, 289
Patten, David W., 28, 30
Peace: failed promises of, 267; negotiating, 530
Pearl of Great Price, 213
Penn, William, 520
Penrose, Charles W., 586, 660
Peoria American, 547
Perkins, Ute, 83, 183
Perkins, William J., 83
Persecution, religious, 4, 91, 553; in
Missouri, 14; 55, 230; threats of, to the
Saints, 409
Peterborough, New Hampshire, 73
Phelps, William W., 27, 67, 216–17; on
Christ's kingdom, 272; and
Freemasonry, 314; reads appeal to
"Green Mountain Boys," 328; drafts
position paper, 336; supports Prophet's
candidacy for U.S. presidency, 338;
"Article on Marriage," 345; reads call for
expulsion of the Saints, 370; asked to
prepare petitions, 375; speaks on
martyrdom, 401; pronounces funeral
sermon, 403; writes "Praise to the Man,"
405, 407; on sustaining the Twelve, 436,
444; characterizes Twelve with biblical
titles, 444; on role of patriarch, 452;
appointed by Council of Fifty, 540
Philadelphia, 70, 73
Pickaway Lodge, 320
Pickett, William, 601–2, 603–4, 617
Pike, Major Zebulon, 46
Pineries, 142
Pitt, William, *117,* 192
Pixton, Robert, 561
Pizarro, or the Death of Rolla, 191
Player, William N., 251
Pluralism, American religious, 292
Plural marriage, 343–47, 348–49, 360, 635;
public defense of, 352; Emma Smith
discourages participation in, 503;
journalists and, 522–23; apostates and,

644; Joseph III denounces, 648; Saints
questioned about, 655. *See also* Marriage
Police force, 469–70
Politics, 432–33; Saints' influence in, 45,
83, 91–92, 108; Saints' beliefs in
government and, 27, 269, 412
Polk, James K. 335, 465, 509; letter to, 511;
and declaration of war, 520, 578; and
plans to halt evacuation of Nauvoo, 569;
and need for contracts, 577; and the
Mormon Battalion, 579, 600
Pomeroy, Francis, 155
Pomeroy, Irene, 137, 155
Pontoosuc Regulators, 602
Poor, 170; needs of, 127–28; Joseph Smith
advises youth to care for, 226–27; camp,
616; bishop's storehouses sustain, 654
Pope, Judge Nathaniel, 282
Popular Tribune, 627–28
Post, Warren, 639
Pottawattomie Indians, 324, 582
Potts, Sarah J., 636–37
Poverty, 141
Powers, Samuel, 646
Pratt, Addison, *195,* 198–99, 518
Pratt, Ellen Sophronia, *195*
Pratt, Louisa Barnes, 195
Pratt, Mary Ann, 561
Pratt, Orson, 214, 216; publishes Smith
family history, 231; presents memorial in
Washington, 276; letter to, 282;
convention nominates, 297; quotes
Prophet on government, 328; and
plurality of wives, 344, 346–47; arrives
on steamer, 433; as gauge of philosophy,
444; on completing Nauvoo House,
476; on collection effort, 479; Brigham
Young endorses *Prophetic Almanac* of,
497; counsels Saints to move to Nauvoo,
549; takes astronomical calculations,
557; endorses Brigham Young's
declarations, 581; mission of, to
England, 635
Pratt, Parley P., 124, 182, 587; on church
and kingdom of God, 3–4, 121; arrest
of, 29; at Richmond Jail, 30, 36; and
gathering places, 67; on migration from

Great Britain, 77, 80; reorganizes
emigration agency, 79–80; and house
raising, 128; on Nauvoo, 130; on
principle of gathering, 169–70; returns
to Nauvoo, 180; writings of, 214–15;
launches *The Latter-day Saints Millennial
Star, 217;* hymns by, 218; publishes *A
Letter to the Queen of England,* 272–73;
meets with Illinois delegation, 330;
excommunication of, 352; publishes
roster of the dead, *411;* calls for political
unity, 412; and acquittal of murderers,
415; reinstatement of, 429; on building
up Nauvoo, 431; on sealing powers,
440–41; as the archer, 444; on choosing
church leaders, 448; to regulate
immigration, 496; on the *Prophet,*
497–98; on the Sons of Helaman, 505;
and spiritual wifery, 523; appointed by
Council of Fifty, 540; justifies
abandonment of Nauvoo, 543–44;
outfitting committee reports plan of,
557; works out schedule of travel, 557;
on destination of pioneers, 567–68;
crosses Mississippi, 575; on Nauvoo of
memory, 618; store, 626
Pratt, Sarah, 352
Pre-Emption Act, 133
Prejudice, 412
Presbyterian churches, 631
Press, partisan, 302; and negative images of
Saints, 312–13; freedom of the, 362
Preston, England, 74
Priesthood(s): Aaronic and Melchizedek, 17;
authority, 18; quorums organized,
66–67; affiliation with, quorum, 221;
Abraham's patriarchal priesthood, 261;
Brigham Young speaks on, 435;
presidency of organized quorums of,
473; ordination of women to, 650
Primary Mutual Improvement Association,
227–28
Prior, Rev. Samuel A., 127, 201–2
Prisoners, families of, 36
*Proclamation: To Col. Levi Williams, and
Mob Party,* 531, 535

*Proclamation to the Citizens of Hancock
County,* 604
Progression, plan for, 240
Prophecy, spirit of, 427
Prophet, living, 205; succession in office of,
410, 435
Prophet, the, 497–98
Prophetic Almanac, 497
Prosperity, promise of, 123
Protestant Sunday School, 227
Provisional State of Deseret, 562
Publications, 95, 497
Purple, Judge, 417, 602

Quail, miracle of, 617
Quashquema, 46, 48, 52, 59
Queen Victoria, 273–74
Quincy, Illinois, 30–31, 33, 179; residents
of, rescue Mormons, 33; Democratic
Association of, 43, 292; hospitality of,
72; charter of, 101; Committee, 536,
537–38, 613–14
Quincy Argus, 44
Quincy Grays, 43
Quincy Herald, The, 338
Quincy Riflemen, 595, 597
Quincy Whig, The, 44, 212, 296, 338, 521
Quorum of the Twelve Apostles: on
emigration, 63, 77–78; and business
regulation, 68; expanded responsibilities
of, 82, 95–96; and politics, 109–11; care
of wives of, 130; on entrepreneurship in
Nauvoo, 153–54; to act as land agents,
166, 175, 177; and theater, 191; on
gathering, 207–8; second mission of, in
Great Britain, 215; direct consecrations
to church trustees, 248; as
administrators of the kingdom, 260–61;
denounce thievery, 309; Prophet
prepares, to succeed him, *332,* 421; join
in campaign, 340; learn of doctrine of
plural marriage, 345–46; placed at the
helm, 410; sustained as governing body,
421–22; authorized to ordain patriarchs,
427; expansion of role of, 428; lead the
church, 429; members vote to support,
437, 440; divine appointment of,

457–58; focus of, 463; and missionary labors, 498; and California settlement, 518, 546; issue circular on abandonment of Nauvoo, 545–46; letter of, to Governor Clark, 551; head first company, 556; on loyalty to United States, 562; confrontation of, with Major Warren, 563; focus on administering the endowment, 568; arrest of, attempted, 571; hear of forced expulsion from Nauvoo, 616; pledge to continue Prophet's program, 624

Ramus (Macedonia), Illinois, 34, 82, 136; stake, 70, 82–83, 183; branch, 309
Randall, Sally, 559, 561
Redress, presidential campaign and, 327
Reed, Calvin, 469
"Reformed Mormon Church," 359, 360, 412
Refuge, 301, 663
Refugees, 40
Regents, 110
Registered National Historic Landmark, 659
Reid, H. T., 384, 386, 407
Relief Society, 224. See also Female Relief Society of Nauvoo
Religion: autonomy of, 98; as purpose for Nauvoo, 200; rejection of state-supported, 292; and politics, 339
Relocation, 41, 322, 624
Remnants, gathering the, 631–38
Reorganization, 633
Reorganized Church of Jesus Christ of Latter Day Saints, the, xviii, 623, 638, 643, 646; expands Doctrine and Covenants, 647; members of, accept King Follett sermon, 648; reestablishes presence in Nauvoo, 652–53
Repentance, 21, 74
Resettlement, 566
Restoration: story of the, 201, 228–29; doctrine of, in hymnal, 216–17; Trail Foundation, 659
Retaliation, Saints cautioned against, 541–42

Revelation: "Fishing River," 11, 55; continuing, 199, 454; Joseph Smith and direct, 205; contemporary, 208; on Nauvoo Temple, 272; gift of, 420; in competition with the Prophet, 422; right to, for the church, 426
Revelator, Brigham Young's role as, 442
Revolution, industrial, 125
Revolutionaries, Mormons as, 274
Reynolds, Joseph H., 282
Reynolds, Thomas, 277, 281, 286
Rheinberger, Joseph, 631
Rice, William, 541
Rich, Charles C., 114, 182; commissioned as major general, 414, 470; on Rigdon, 432; retained as counselor, 441; as trustee, 472–73; and Nauvoo Legion, 478; as member of Trades Council, 487; and home industry, 491; to hold ad hoc militia in readiness, 528; brings word of Hardin's arrival, 536; walks across Mississippi, 583
Richards, Levi, 31
Richards, Phineas, 483, 484, 487
Richards, Willard, 83, 186, 373, 395; as record-keeper, 207, 228; keeps journal for Prophet, 248; pledges loyalty to Illinois, 282; drafts memorial to Congress, 329–30; antislavery views of, 337; supports Prophet's candidacy for U.S. presidency, 338; takes plural wife, 346; invites Bennet to gather volunteers for defense of Nauvoo, 371; heads for Carthage, 377; takes dictation in Carthage Jail, 386; lists witnesses, 391; gives account of martyrdom, 395–98; moves Taylor and bodies of martyrs to Hamilton Hotel, 398; emphasizes pledge to governor, 401; writes on events at Carthage, 407; names assassins, 413; on effect of the martyrdom, 419; and reorganization, 430; proposes special conference, 431; as keeper of the rolls, 444; divides North America into districts, 496; visits Carthage, 534; Twelve and bishopric at home of, 537; organizes bucket brigade, 575; Brigham

Young, 575; sets up post office, 583, 585; selected as counselor, 586

Richards, William P., 520

Richardson's Point, 580, 583, 585

Richman, Irving, 130–31

Richmond Jail, 30, 39

Rigdon, Nancy, 361

Rigdon, Sidney, 189, *432,* 441; on Nauvoo, xviii; delivers "Salt Sermon," 26–27; issues "Declaration of Independence," 27; arrest of, 29; moved to Liberty Jail, 30; speech of, and extermination order, 30; release of, 36–37; studies law, 37; operates post office, *51;* in Quincy, 54–55; travels to Commerce, 55; purchases land, 57, 58; and Bennett, 98, 99, 101; lodging for, 126; endorses communitarian system, 142; named commissioner of NA&MA, 156; on politics, 158; dinner parties in home of, 190; education of, 193; at cornerstone laying for Nauvoo Temple, 233–34; on government, 274; drafts affidavit, 275; seeks compensation, 275–76; letter to, 282; as candidate for state senate, 297–98; applies for membership in Nauvoo Lodge, 318; raised to master Mason, 320; as vice-presidential candidate, 340; on overcoming prejudices, 341; rejects plural marriage, 348; talks with William Law, 361; seeks counsel on succession, 422; called as counselor, 423; and keys of sealing power, 428; offers to be guardian of church, 431; meets with the Twelve, 432–33; challenges Twelve, 434–35; conference votes to support, 437; not a Mormon Moses, 438; Phelps on, 445; fellowship of, 445–46; called in for hearing, 446; mood swings of, 447–48; leaves Nauvoo, 449; unveils second revelation, 450; lack of sympathy for, 501; and rumors of plural marriage, 523; followers of, 571; proven wrong, 589; on Mormon society, 622; McClellin joins with, 642

Rights, constitutional, 91–92, 340

Ripley, Alanson, 35, *60,* 492–94, 525

Riser, George, 159–60

Riser, John, 160

Rising Sun Lodge, 319, 320–21

Robbins, Lewis, 158

Robedeaux, Joseph, *49*

Roberts, B. H., 16

Roberts, Horace, 159

Robinson, Angeline, 354

Robinson, Ebenezer, 109, 196, 209–10, 218, 314, 354

Robinson, George W., 29, 59, 156

Rockies, Refuge in the, 512

Rockwell, Luana, 279

Rockwell, Orrin P., 188, 279–80, 370; seeks compensation, 275–76; Boggs charges, with shooting, 281; arrest of, 287; invited to accompany Prophet, 373, 375; mortally wounds Worrell, 529; Hardin pledges to arrest, 563

Rockwood, Albert, 15, 27–28, 55

Rockwood, Nancy H., 491

Rocky Mountains: Prophet considers refuge in, 302, 373, 508, 566–67, 569; Young promises temple in the, 555; as resting place of Saints, 567; refuge, 663

Rogers, David W., 35, 41, 54, 281

Rogers, Isaac, 518–19

Roosevelt, William H., 295

Rowley, William, 78

Russell, Samuel, 246

Sacrifice, 553

Saddle and Harness Shop, 489

St. Croix, 433

St. John's Day, 320

St. Louis, Missouri, 34, 52, 72, 101

St. Louis New Era, 548

Saint Louis Organ, 525, 548

St. Patrick's Church, 626

Saints: and conversion and baptism, 63–64; nurturing the, 67–74; emigration of British, 77–78; call to gather American, 81; British, and open prairie, 134–35; feel rejection, 277; new society of, 495–96; and self-defense, 528; resettlement of, 566; as Americans, 570;

lack means to leave place of gathering, 597–98; and exercising franchise, 654; Nauvoo heritage of, 664. *See also* Latter-day Saints

Saints' Herald. See True Latter Day Saints' Herald

Salt Lake Temple, 244–45, 663

"Salt Sermon," 26–27

Salvation, 5, 266, 326

Sanctuary, Nauvoo as religious, 132

Sangamo Journal, 107, 280

Sauk Tribe, 46

Schismatics, Nauvoo, 459

Schools, 194–95, 196

Scott, John, 635

Scovil, Lucius N., 314, 320–21

Scrip, 163, 312

Scripture, origins for, 212

Seceders, 341, 416

Secessionist movement, 357

Second Coming, 3, 270, 419

Second Congregational Church, 353

Second United States Bank, 52

"The Seer, Joseph the Seer," 479

Seixas, Joshua, 58, 211

Self-defense, 528, 534

Self-government, 308

Self-reliance, 654

Self-sufficiency, 137

Semple, James, 330

Senate, 467

Senate Judiciary Committee, 276, 296

Service, humanitarian, 224, 655

Sessions, Perrigrine, 254

Seventies: Library and Institute Association, 197; leave Music Hall, 527

Seventies Hall, *203,* 478–79, 626; completion of, 500

Seventy: Twelve have jurisdiction over, 427; new quorums of, 440; First Seven Presidents of, 440; sent as missionaries, 498–99

Sharp, Thomas, 107, *306,* 394; on Nauvoo Legion, 115; intimates governor has sided with the Mormons, 287; helps organize Anti-Mormon Party, 293; calls for independent candidate, 297; as anti-Mormon spokesperson, 304–5; maligns Joseph Smith, 304–6; criticizes Saints, 305–6; on Joseph Smith and bogus coins, 312; declares inevitability of extermination of Saints, 368; forms group of regulators, 389; on the murders and vigilante justice, 405–6; spars with governor, 409, 410–12; writ issued against, 414; charged with murder, 415; on Strang, 457, 638; and triumph of Mormonism, 469; and exodus of the Saints, 517; complains against Saints, 521; publishes "Proclamation," 523–24; voices concern over counterfeiting, 524; issues call to arms, 531; files charges against Mormons, 534; reports on Young's exodus, 575; commends troops on impartiality, 597; supports anti-Mormon aggression, 600; reiterates declaration of war, 602–3; Pickett confronts, 604; pleads for law and order, 620. *See also* Warsaw Signal

Sherwood, Henry G., 377, 516

Shumway, Charles, 574

Singleton, James W., 383, 605

Sinners, withdrawing fellowship from, 342

Slavery, 336–37

Slaves, missionaries and, 271

Smith, Aaron, 458

Smith, Alexander, *646, 647*

Smith, Alvin, 256

Smith, Caroline, 404

Smith, David Hyrum, *451, 454, 646*

Smith, Dennis, 660

Smith, Don Carlos, 34, 106–7; on construction in Nauvoo, 123–24; publishes Book of Mormon, 209–10; publishes newspaper, 218–19; on Nauvoo Temple cornerstone laying ceremony, 234

Smith, Elias, 35, 187, 276

Smith, Eliza Maria Partridge, *346,* 348

Smith, Eliza Partridge, *346*

Smith, Eliza Snow, 507

Smith, Emily Dow, *346,* 348

Smith, Emma Hale, 29–30, *93,* 187; finds refuge, 36; moves into White's farmhouse, 57; and Marks, 189, 358, 451, 457; schooling of children of, 196; collects hymns, 216–17; and Female Relief Society, *223*, 224; speaks in defense of virtue, 226; urges governor to review habeas corpus ordinance, 280; Lord's guidance for, 347; and plural marriage, 348, 503, 645; and the Laws, 358; receives news of martyrdom, 398–99; has bodies reburied, 404; seeks to settle finances, 430; and Rigdon, 448; returns to Nauvoo, 625; denies Salt Lake Mormons, 645; attends conference of Reorganized church, 646; retains "New Translation" of the Bible, 647; visitors see restored home of, 659; new grave marker for, 659

Smith, Emmeline Griswold, 645

Smith, Fannie Alger, 344–45

Smith, Frederic, *646*

Smith, Frederick M., 650

Smith, George A., 19, *191*, 430; as entablature of truth, 444; to preside over temporal affairs, 487; on the Seventy, 499–500; and expansion, 544; on vision of Young, 570; joins Young, 575; visits Joseph III, 645; suggests monument to Relief Society founding, 657

Smith, Hyrum, *395*, 662; moved to Liberty Jail, 30; grand jury indicts, 38–39; purchases property, 57; dissolves stake, 82–83; publishes article, 88; and law of consecration, 97; secures patterns for uniforms, 115–16; as partner, 149; given positions of trust, 188–89; endorses scripture concordance, 215; becomes temple overseer, 246; defends penny fund, 247; portrait of, in Nauvoo Temple, 255; administers endowment, 260; presides over city council, 281; endorses Democratic candidate Hoge, 299; denies sanctioning bands of robbers, 309; as Freemason, 313–14, 320; on overseas gathering, 333–34; on overcoming prejudices, 341; and doctrine of marriage, 347, 354, 356; on mysteries of God, 355–56; on attempt to

murder Joseph, 373; martyrdom of, 380, *395;* treason warrant against, 381; reads from Book of Mormon, 386–87; portrait of, *390;* requests Taylor sing in Carthage Jail, 392; prosecutors fail to appear for trial of murderers of, 415; authority of, 418, 426; as patriarch, 421; called as assistant, 424; holds office by birthright, 426; keys held by, 428; memorial to, 659; new grave marker for, 659

Smith, John, 34, *93;* as president of stake in Commerce, 96–97; denounces counterfeiters, 312; Masonic experience of, 314; as stake president in Macedonia, 429; replaces Marks, 441; as patriarch, 453, 586

Smith, Joseph, Jr., *15, 37, 65, 93, 114, 181, 439*

Arrests, imprisonment, and trials of
Incarcerated at Liberty Jail, 13–14, 30, 36; arrest of, 28–30; escapes execution, 29; grand jury indicts, 38–39; charges filed against, 361–62; officer arrests, 366–67; treason warrant against, 381

Business and financial affairs
Purchases land, 47, 57, 58, 133, 144; deeds transferred to, 83; on folly of common stock, 143; on Nauvoo as gathering place, 143–44; builds brick store, 145; closes business, 147; heads temperance committee, 148; as partner, 149; and Jones, 150; receives exclusive rights for ferry, 151; and Nauvoo's industrial development, 153; named commissioner of NA&MA, 156; encourages local manufacturing, 157; approaches businessmen for donations, 158; on safe money, 164; and land speculation, 166–67; declares bankruptcy, 168; files titles to real estate in Emma's name, 169

Church affairs
Plan of, for Zion, 3; concept of Zion, 4–6; and the cause of God, 9; on

Rigdon's speech, 27; and relocation of Saints, 41–42; and high council, 94–95; and British immigrants, 186; sustaining of, 203–4; and Bible study, 208–9; and Kinderhook plates, 212; account of first vision of, published, 214; organizes Female Relief Society of Nauvoo, 222–23; and youth organization, 226–27; sense of mission of, 230–31; at Nauvoo Temple cornerstone laying ceremony, 234–35; reprimands Wight, 294; denies secretly sanctioning bands of robbers, 309; concedes some Church members involved in crime, 309–10; on Council of Fifty, 326; appeals to the "Green Mountain Boys," 328; discloses new gathering places, 333

Correspondence
Writes to Caldwell County Saints, 16; letter of, published in *Times and Seasons,* 16; Liberty Jail letter of, 16–18; writes Edward Hunter, 156

Detractors
Attempts to discredit, 197; harassment of, 285

Martyrdom
Troops accept mission to assassinate, 389; trial of those accused of murdering, 415–17

Masonic affairs
On freemasonry, 315; applies for membership in Nauvoo Lodge, 318; raised to master Mason, 320; gives Masonic signal of distress, 397

Nauvoo Legion
As head of Nauvoo Legion, 112–15; on mission of Nauvoo Legion, *283*

Personal and family life
Leaves Kirtland, 26; studies law, 37; as God's living spokesman, 76; lodging for, 126–27; denounces Finch, 142; and pottery, 159; kinship with, 181; and friendship, 188–90; and dancing,

190–91; as speaker, 197; role of, in Nauvoo, 200–201; as prophet-teacher, 204–13; expectations of, 242; as trustee, 248; portrait of, 255; encourages Saints' claims, 275; seeks compensation, 275–76; attempted arrest of, 277; goes into hiding, 281; extradition of, to Missouri, 282, 292; befriends Adams, 314; seeks refuge in American Far West, 323; friendship of, with Native Americans, 324; calls for volunteers, 325; plural marriages of, 344–45; urges peace, 368–69; calls for defensive action, 370; agrees to travel to Carthage, 376–77; martyrdom of, 380; offers to pay for *Expositor* press, 385; profile of, *390;* succession of authority of, 418–20; promise to, of seeing Second Coming, 419; mission of, fulfilled, 420; as presiding elder, 422–23; as sole revelator, 423; unique role of, 433–34; and Rigdon, 448; appears in vision to Brigham Young, 570; and pioneering expedition, 581; legitimate heir to authority of, 644–45; memorial to, 659; visitors see restored home of, 659; new grave marker for, 659

Political and civil affairs
Organizes Zion's Camp, 10–11; and incorporation of Nauvoo, 98, 99, 101; as mayor, 109,111; influence of, on voters, 293, 295–96, 299; interaction of, with Van Buren, 294, 302, 327–28; withdraws from political involvement, 298; arrest of, reinvolves him politically, 298–99; explains political commitment, 299, 338; on government, 301; on constitutional guarantees, 302–3, 340; signs memorial to Congress, 329–30; and U.S. Army, 330; on being president, 334; on overcoming prejudices, 341; and diversion dam, 492–93

Revelations
On temple ordinances, xvii; at Kirtland, 237, 257; on Nauvoo Temple, 235–37, 242–43

Teachings of
On places of refuge, 41; and spiritual
Babylon, 62; and gathering, 63; on
stakes in Zion, 66; on Kirtland as limit,
73; and emigration, 78; on temple
ordinances, 81, 239; and Saints in
Kirtland, 87–88; and law of
consecration, 97; on City of Holiness,
121; and individual ownership, 142;
warns potential immigrants, 174;
encourages land purchase, 175; on
marriage between races, 184; on
education, 193; retells story of the
Restoration, 201; on gift of translation,
211; defines basic beliefs, 214, 216; on
commandment to build House of the
Lord, 236; on baptism for the dead, 238;
limits proxy ordinances to temple, 240,
256; and concept of universal salvation,
240; delivers King Follett discourse,
240–41; on the Godhead, 241; on
corporeal gods, 241; on Saints becoming
saviors on Mount Zion, 242; expands
meaning of endowment, 257–58, 261;
administers endowment, 260; endorses
U.S. Constitution, 270; on faith, 271;
on authority of the Twelve, 427–28;
doctrines taught by, 632; key Nauvoo
teachings of, 651

Writings of
Dictates personal history, 58; and Book
of the Law of the Lord, 188, 190; and
translation of the Bible, 209;
contributions to scripture, 213; as editor,
219; dictates history of Restoration, *229;*
from Liberty Jail, 342; and translation of
the Bible, 343; writes letter to Emma
from Carthage Jail, 387–88
Smith, Joseph, Sr., 36, 187; holds religious
family services, 220; called as assistant,
424
Smith, Joseph, III, 422, 452, *646, 648;*
right of, to presidency, 454, 640; as first
president of Reorganized church, 623,
633, 643–44; as leader of New
Organization, 644–45; attends

conference of Reorganized church, 646;
revelations to, C, 647; denounces plural
marriage, 648; on establishment of Zion,
649; remains in Nauvoo, 652
Smith, Joseph F., 344, *648;* corresponds
with Joseph III, 648; purchases Carthage
jail, 659
Smith, Joshua, 565–66
Smith, Lovina, 358
Smith, Lucy Mack, 36, 107, *198,* 208, *554;*
holds religious family services, 220;
compiles family history, 231; on
Caroline Smith, 404; on Joseph's
promise, 420; poem for, 507; sanctions
migration, 553–54; remains at Nauvoo,
625
Smith, Maria Lawrence, 361
Smith, Mary Fielding, *247,* 378, 607,
662–63
Smith, Mercy, 607
Smith, Robert F., 383–84, 386, 403, 417
Smith, Samuel H., 399, 401
Smith, William, 150, 187, 189, *432,* 636;
edits *Wasp,* 219; spars with Sharp, 297;
elected state representative, 298; on
Nauvoo charter, 307; and revelation on
plural marriage, 362–63; claims right to
be church patriarch, 419, 452; on
lineage right of Joseph III, 422, 454;
absence of, 433; issues held by, 437;
Phelps writes to, 444; challenges Young's
authority, 453; excommunication of,
453; and Strang, 457, 638; and
unauthorized plural marriages, 523;
dropped as an apostle, 543; reveals plans
of departing Saints, 566; and Briggs,
644; on Joseph III as leader, 645; and
Reorganized church, 647
Snow, Eliza R., 112, *191;* drafts
constitution, 223; as secretary of Relief
Society, 224; as leader of Relief Society,
226; on work of the Lord, 272;
celebrates patriotism, 274; dines at
Prophet's home, 282; marries the
Prophet, *346;* writes eulogy, 380–81,
406; writes poem about Lucy Mack
Smith, 507

Snow, Erastus, 645
Snow, Lorenzo, 345
Snyder, Adam W., 105, 296, 297
Soby, Helen, 168
Soby, Leonard, 446
Soldiers, LDS, 388–89
Solemn assembly, 435
"Song of Freedom," 27
Sons of Helaman, 505–6
Sons of the Utah Pioneers, 658
Spartan Band, 609, 611–12
Spaulding, Jacob, 246
Special Council, the, 326
Specie, 164
Speculators, 50
Spencer, Daniel, 487
Spencer, Orson, 171–72, 193; on Joseph
    Smith, 206; and Nauvoo charter, 466;
    calls public meeting, 468; as trustee,
    472–73; and industry, 482–83; as
    member of Trades Council, 487; talks to
    state officials, 510; on colonization of
    Saints, 517; appointed by Council of
    Fifty, 540; and emigrating Saints, 635
Spirit: witness of the, 206; receptivity to the,
    206–7
"Spiritual wifery," 350–51, 523. See also
    Plural marriage
Springfield, Illinois, 101
Springfield State Register, 307, 338, 415, 547
Staines, William C., 436
Stakes, 66, 82, 510
Standard works, 213
Stevens, Elvira, 589–90
Stigall, George W., 384, 386
Stoddard, Judson, 583
Storehouse, bishops,' 12, 654
Stout, Hosea, 401, 469, 470, 505;
    appointed police captain, 473; and home
    industry, 491; and resettling the Saints,
    514–15
Strang, James J., 422, 453, 638; claims of,
    454–56; followers of, 457, 571, 635,
    643; cut off from church, 458; lack of
    sympathy for, 501; has himself crowned,
    639; and Yellow Stone Branch, 644
Strangism, 457

Straw Manufactory, 491
Stuart, John T., 294–95
Succession: questions over, 380–81;
    preparation for, 419–2; principles of,
    422; channels of, 425; revelation
    establishes line of, 427; apostolic, 437
Successor, Joseph Smith to name his, 423
Suffering, 553
Sugar Creek Encampment, 576–77, 580
Sunday School, 227
Symbols, temple, 244–45

Tabernacle, 479
Taggart, George W., 154, 155, 205
Tailors' Association of Nauvoo, 491
Tanners and Shoemakers Association, 489
Taxation, 161
Taylor, John, 19, 29, 83, 395, 463; on
    church and kingdom of God, 3–4;
    criticizes lithograph, 29; family of,
    resides at Mace's, 34; on construction in
    Nauvoo, 125–29; on homesteading,
    133; on manufacturing, 141, 153; rebuts
    Finch, 143; on importing, 148; on labor,
    171; encourages missionaries to gather
    library materials, 199; on inspiration,
    205; issues Doctrine and Covenants,
    210; assists with newspaper, 219; on
    Sunday School for children, 227–28;
    historical mission of, 230; on godhood,
    241; on persecution, 267; on exiled
    Saints, 269, 277; on eternal kingdom,
    272; signs memorial, 276; praises
    governor, 287; on harmony of society,
    294; favors Democratic candidate Hoge,
    299; explains Expositor affair, 372; packs
    stereotype plates and heads for Upper
    Canada, 376; asks governor to intervene,
    383; sings in Carthage Jail, 386, 392;
    leads prisoners in prayer, 386; lies on
    mattress on floor of jail, 387; account of
    martyrdom, 395–99; on murders, 405;
    poems written by, 407; names assassins,
    413; on effect of the martyrdom, 419;
    on organization of the church, 430;
    members of the Twelve meet at home of,
    433; on gathering, 444; on Rigdon, 446;

on persecution, 459; on union of
Nauvoo, 473; on work of the temple,
475; advocates home industry, 482–83;
proposes Trades Union, 486; to preside
over temporal affairs, 487; on unity and
love, 505; on exodus from the United
States, 507; drafts letter to Polk, 511;
visits Carthage, 534; reports agreement
to leave Illinois and Iowa, 547; on
migration, 555; writes editorial on
exodus, 575; crosses Mississippi, 582;
visitors see Nauvoo house of, 659
Teachers, compensation for, 195–96
Teas, Joseph, 51
Telegraph, Alton, 115
Temperance, 148
Temple(s): the Prophet's revelations on, xvii;
doctrines, xviii; plans for, abandoned,
12–13; and ordinances, 81, 663; and
baptism for the dead, 237; endowments
to be received in, 237; architectural
symbolism in, 244; heavenly symbols in,
244–45; funding for, 246; provisions in
storeroom of, 248; construction of,
249–50; authority associated with, 421;
priority of completing, 437, 474–75;
members urged to prepare for
ceremonies in, 464, 546; blessings of
the, 554; to be built in gathering places,
593; expanded building of, 655
Tenney's Grove, 36
Terry, Jacob, 339–40
Texas: settlement proposal, 325, 327;
declares independence, 330; possibility
of sanctuary for Saints in, 332, 509
Theater, 191–92
Theft, allegations of, investigated, 533
Theodemocrat, Joseph Smith as a, 296
Thomas, Jesse B., 384, 414
Thompson, Mercy Fielding, 247
Thompson, Robert B., 99
Times and Seasons, 29, 86; Joseph Smith's
letter published in, 16; Hyrum Smith's
article in, 88; high council regulations
published in, 94; Bennett reports in,
106; editors of, offer defense, 109; on
military organization, 112; on housing
in Nauvoo, 126; reports conference
proceedings, 207; and Doctrine and
Covenants, 210; publishes book of
Abraham, 211, 258; and Kinderhook
plates, 212; defines religious community,
218; purchased by the church, 219;
suggests transformation of meaning of
temple ceremony, 258; publishes
governor's reply, 287; Robinson becomes
editor and publisher of, 314; publishes
news about American West, 323; solicits
letters endorsing Prophet's candidacy,
338–39; publishes Saints' beliefs on
marriage, 353; editorial in, 356; on
dissenters, 360; publishes eulogy by Eliza
R. Snow, 406; publishes black-line
edition, 407; Phelps writes editorial for,
452; Twelve's endorsement of, 497;
production of, halted, 539–40; John
Taylor writes on migration, 555;
complex, 658
Tithes, 160, 246–48, 657
Tithing: law of, 12, 97, 125, 142–43;
collection agents, 248; in kind, 248–49;
laborers on the temple, 250; payment of,
as requirement for receiving temple
ordinances, 256; missionaries authorized
to collect, 475; and church programs,
654
Tolerance, 199, 202
Tompkins, John, 210
Tories, 74–75
Tourism, 661
Townships, 92
Trades Association, 483, 485
Trades Council, 487–88
Trades Institute, 483
Trades Meetings, 483
Trades Union, 486
Traveling presiding high council, 427
Treason, 381, 387
True Church of Jesus Christ, the, 641
True Latter Day Saints' Herald, the, 645, 649
Trustee-in-trust, 435
Turley, Theodore, 38, 78, 128, 346; as
trustee, 472–73; suggests merger, 486
Turnham, Joel, 37

Tuttle, Smith, 53, 166
Twelfth General Assembly, 105
Twelve. *See* Quorum of the Twelve Apostles
Tyler, John, 329–30, 331–32, 335

Umpqua Valley, 331–32
United Order of Enoch, 649
United States: Saints in southern, 89–90;
    Saints to leave, 549–50; of the West,
    562; and Foreign Emigration
    Homestead Association, 630
U.S. Army: Joseph Smith and the, 330; of
    the West, 579; Saints enlist in, 599
U.S. Constitution, 270, 277, 334, 335
U.S. House of Representatives, 512–13
U.S. Supreme Court, 285, 468
Unity: political, 10; in faith, 174; spirit of,
    334, 440, 464, 499
University of the City of Nauvoo, 104, 193
Upper Mississippi River Valley, 46

Van Buren, Martin, 276, 335; Joseph
    Smith's interaction with, 294, 302,
    327–28
Vancouver Island, 537
Van Tuyl, Abram, 614
Venus, Illinois, 51, 59
Viewing, public, 402–3
Views on Government, 388
Vigilantes, 393, 519, 525; drive Backenstos
    from his home, 528–29; old settlers
    disclaim, 535; swear out complaints of
    treason, 563; enforce evacuation
    agreement, 597; disperse, 601
Virtue, 225–26
Voice of Warning, A, 4, 215
Voree Herald, 456
Vote, immigrant, 289

Walker, Cyrus, 283, 285, 295, 298–99
Ward, Thomas, 548
Wardle, Fanny, 616
Ware, W. G., 367
War of 1812, farmland sold to veterans of,
    46–47
Warrant, arrest, 277–79
Warren, Calvin A., 168, 413

Warren, Illinois, 2, 186
Warren, William B., 533, 542, 563, 573,
    605; soldiers of, escort migrants, 595;
    leaves Nauvoo undefended, 600; issues
    weekly reports, 603
Warrington, Benjamin, 109
Warsaw, Illinois, 46, 92, 99, 559
Warsaw Signal, 83, 107, 355, 366, 638;
    publishes governor's reply, 287; ridicules
    Joseph Smith, 304–5; on Mormons and
    crime, 308; predicts *Expositor* will lead to
    fall of Mormonism, 362; and
    martyrdom, 405–6; complains about
    jury, 417; on revolution in California,
    520; biased reporting of, 521;
    accusations of counterfeiting in, 525;
    publishes extras accusing Saints, 532–33;
    publishes affidavits blaming Saints for
    burnings, 536. *See also* Thomas Sharp
Washington, D.C., delegation to, 276
Wasp, Nauvoo, 148, 219, 279, 307;
    denounces lawbreakers, 308–9; publishes
    articles about California, 323
Wasson, Lorenzo D., 376
Wattle, 128
Webster, Daniel, 468
Webster, Dwight, 481, 506
Weeks, William, *236, 239,* 242–43; designs
    weathervane for temple, 253; and
    Masonic Hall, *319;* as member of Trades
    Council, 487; transfers duty to Angell,
    588
Wells, Daniel H., 53, 60, 126, 161, 367; on
    Nauvoo city council, 109; as regent,
    110; moves onto bluff, 147; Prophet
    befriends, 189; and Nauvoo Temple site,
    235; as political candidate, 297; releases
    Nauvoo officers, 417; as coroner, 465; as
    militia aide, 606; leads counterattack,
    612
Wells Addition, 147
Wentworth, John, 189, 216, 332; offers
    perspective on harassment of General
    Smith, 285; advice of, sought, 468;
    Saints seek assistance from, 566
Western Mission, 514
Wheelock, Cyrus, 379, 391–92

Whigs, 44, 74, 269; 289; rivalry of, and Democrats, 291; promise to repeal Nauvoo charter, 292; Saints committed to, 294; oppose immigrant vote, 295; side with Democrats to defeat repeal of charter, 307

Whipple, Nelson, 583

Whistling and whittling crew, 505–6

White, Alexander, 48, 51, 53

White, James, 48–49, *51,* 53, 126

White, Hugh, 48, 57, 58, 126–27, 144

White, James, *49*

White, William, 58

Whitmer, David, 27, 188, 424; excommunication of, 425; as successor to the Prophet, 642; denounces McClellin, 643; donates printer's copy of Book of Mormon, 647

Whitmer, Jacob, 642

Whitmer, John, 27, 188, 642

Whitney, Elizabeth Ann Smith, 224, 356, 565

Whitney, J. W., 43

Whitney, Luther, 48

Whitney, Newel K., *23,* 62, 188, 430; as bishop in Adam-ondi-Ahman, 87; on personal prosperity, 171; as temple trustee, 248; Masonic experience of, 314; and plural marriage, 356; family packs up, 376; meets with Rigdon, 432; Grant writes to, 446; and hearing for Rigdon, 446–47; on Rigdon, 447–48, 449; as church trustee, 480, 493, 496; interprets wife's hymn, 565; leaves Nauvoo, 588; aids refugees, 616

Widows, 129–30

Wight, Lyman, 89, 246, 348, 636, 639; arrest of, 29; moved to Liberty Jail, 30; publishes letters in *Quincy Whig,* 44–45; reprimanded by Joseph Smith, 294; proposes migration to west Texas, 325; absence of, 433; issues of, 437; and colonization of Texas, 441; as wild ram, 444; returns to Wisconsin, 445; expansionist efforts of, 450–51; committee writes to, 473–74; and stake in Texas, 515; retained pending

investigation, 543; excommunication of, 639–40; followers of, join Reorganized church, 643

Wightman, William, 71, 83

Wilkes, Charles, 513, 567

Williams, Abiather, 564

Williams, Archibald, 535

Williams, Frederick G., 357, 423

Williams, Levi, 388; writ issued against, 414; charged with murder, 415; leads mob in burnings, 525; proclamation issued to, 531; files charges against Mormons, 534; leads army to Nauvoo, 600

Williams, Roger, 520

Williams, Zilpha, 437

Wilson, Dunbar, 354

Wilson, Harmon T., 282–83

Winchester, Benjamin, 124, 197, 215, 353, 639

Winter Quarters, 558, 582, 586

Wisconsin, 327, 639

Witness(es): to proxy baptisms, 238–39; Three, to the Book of Mormon, 357; personal, of Brigham Young, 438

"Wolf hunt," 414

Women, 222, 491

Wood, John M., 606, 607–8, 612

Wood, Wilford, 657–58

Woodbury, Jeremiah, 609

Woodruff, Joseph, *572*

Woodruff, Phebe, *572*

Woodruff, Wilford, 19, 185–86, 325, 347; revelation of, xvii; as record-keeper, 207; issues European edition of Doctrine and Covenants, 210; and newspaper printing, 219–20; raises money, 254; receives revelation to stop performing adoptive sealings, 265; arrives on steamer, 433; as banner of gospel, 444; to preside over British Isles and Europe, 496; and immigration depots, 518; counsels Saints to migrate, 548; travels to Nauvoo, 548–49; participates in temple dedication, 588–90; ends practice of plural marriage, 655; visitors see Nauvoo house of, 659

Woods, James W., 377, 384, 386, 391, 407

Woodworth, Lucien, 251, 327

Wooley, Edwin D., 158

Worldliness, 90, 91

World War II, 658

Worrell, Frank, 386, 388, 414, 529

Wright, Jonathan C., 635

Yellow Stone Branch, 644

Young, Brigham, 19, 83, *191,* 346, 348–49, *439, 470*

Business and civic affairs
As land agent, 177; supervises newspaper printing purchase, 219; refuses to reconsider colonizing proposal, 327; counsels captains of emigrating companies, 556–57; decides on shuttle plan, 558; meets with land agents, 561; announces beginning of migration, 562

Church affairs
Leads Saints to Utah, xviii; on emigration, 75, 78–79; hires Eggleston, 140; calls for united action, 158; and publication of the Book of Mormon, 210; dedicates Nauvoo Temple baptismal font, 251; puts capstone on temple, 252–53; dedicates completed sections of temple, 253–54; performs sealings, 255; participates in temple sessions, 261–62; performs first temple marriage, 262; announces cessation of endowments and sealings, 265; and gathering, 333; supports Prophet's candidacy for U.S. presidency, 338; takes plural wife, 346; on claims of Nauvoo reformers, 357; is placed at helm of Church, 410; and Council of Fifty, 415, 487; keys held by, 421, 428; and priority of completing the temple, 437, 510; divides North America into districts, 496; and resettling Saints, 514–15; convenes Council of Fifty, 539; on stewardship, 552; opens migration to all faiths, 571; continues ordinance work, 573; and sale of temple, 592–93; on Warren's

enforcement of peace, 597; counsels Saints to head for Rockies, 598; supports total evacuation of Nauvoo, 599; learns of forced expulsion from Nauvoo, 616–17; invites Saints to gather, 634; and Salt Lake Temple, 663

Education of
Formal, 193; school opened in home of, 196; reorganizes Council of Fifty, 513

Masonic affairs
Urges Scovil to suspend Masonic activities in Nauvoo, 321

Martyrdom
On acquittal of murderers, 415; arrives at trial, 417

Personal and family life
The Prophet relies on, 189; is commissioned as lieutenant general, 414; arrives on steamer, 433; receives sacred confirmation, 438–39; Pratt speaks of, 440–41; as the lion of the Lord, 444; and Rigdon, 445–46, 448–49; as lieutenant general, 469; and City of Joseph, 471; and town of Nauvoo, 472; and Zion, 474; dream of, 477–78; dedicates site for armory, 478; studies route of Frémont, 512, 566; and Emmett, 516; receives news of attacks, 525; receives message from Backenstos, 532; prohibits self-defense, 534; reiterates plans to leave Nauvoo, 537; temple searched for, 564; charged with counterfeiting, 565; departure of, 569; has vision of Joseph Smith, 570; sends thanks to governor, 573; sets rules for encampment of Saints, 576–77; returns to Nauvoo, 579–80; speaks in grove, 580; establishes second temporary camp, 580–81; issues declarations of intent, 581; crosses Mississippi, 582; on forced exile, 585; Hyde nominates as president of church, 586; *Ensign of Liberty* challenges leadership of, 642–43; Briggs contends against, 644; centennial of

arrival of, celebrated, 658; visitors see Nauvoo house of, 659

Teachings of
On revealed knowledge, 206; on proxy baptism, 240; on Hyrum Smith, 418–19; on filling the office of prophet, 419; on continuity of keys and authorities, 434; on choosing prophet, 435; and succession, 436; explains role as revelator, 442; explains anti-Christ, 443; on Nauvoo, 463; on law and order in Nauvoo, 467; on home industry, 481; on fall harvest, 495; on missionaries, 498–99; on spirit of unity, 499; on evacuation, 509; on sealing power, 523; on helping the worthy, 553
Young, John, 214
Young, Joseph, 34, 565, 575, 580–81; looks after Saints in Nauvoo branch, 587–88; home of, sold, 591

Young, Vilate, 439
Young Gentlemen and Ladies Relief Society of Nauvoo, 226
Young People's Meetings, 226

Zarahemla, New, 42, 70, 82, 96–97
Zion: Joseph Smith's plan for, 3, 30; Jerusalem as, 5; Plat of the City of, *7*; pattern of city of, 8; people, 10, 173–74; American, 63; in Jackson County, 65; as North and South America, 67; gathering to, 74, 321; cornerstone stake of, 87; agrarian ideal and city of, 131; economic ideal of, 142; Enoch's, 209; becoming saviors on Mount, 240, 241; communities, 323; Young and, 474; abandonment of, 548; religious ideal of, 552
Zion's Camp, 11, 236, 328, 556–57
Zodiac, 639